Mun'im Sirry
The Qur'an with Cross-References

Mun'im Sirry

The Qur'an with Cross-References

Qur'an Translation by
Talal Itani

DE GRUYTER

ISBN 978-3-11-154385-7
e-ISBN (PDF) 978-3-11-078244-8
e-ISBN (EPUB) 978-3-11-078256-1

Library of Congress Control Number 2022939317

Bibliographic information published by the Deutsche Nationalbibliothek
The Deutsche Nationalbibliothek lists this publication in the Deutsche Nationalbibliografie; Detailed bibliographic data are available in the Internet at http://dnb.dnb.de.

© 2024 Walter de Gruyter GmbH, Berlin/Boston
This volume is text- and page-identical with the hardback published in 2022.
Cover image: Mert Guncuer/iStock/Getty Images Plus
Typesetting: Dörlemann-Satz GmbH & Co. KG, Lemförde

www.degruyter.com

Acknowledgments

This volume has its origins in a gathering of Qur'an scholars at the University of Notre Dame in 2012–2013. This academic project, known as "The Qur'an Seminar," was led by Gabriel Said Reynolds with the purpose of advancing scholarly understanding of the Qur'anic text. As the participants of the seminar were encouraged to address the Qur'an directly, this volume is the result of an endeavor to provide a much-needed tool to approach the text of the Qur'an on its own terms. My first gratitude goes to Gabriel Reynolds, my friend and colleague, at the Department of Theology, for his advice and encouragement, which helped bring this work to completion. I would also like to extend my gratitude to all participants in the Qur'an Seminar, particularly, Mehdi Azaiez, Tommaso Tesei, and Hamza Zafer, whose generous help has shaped the scope of this project. Mr. Talal Itani has been very supportive as he allowed me to use his Qur'an translation for this volume. *Shukran kathīran*!

Preparing this volume has been a long journey, almost ten years in the making. I couldn't have done it without support all along the way. I have been fortunate to be surrounded by a supportive community at the University of Notre Dame, both faculty and students. The theology faculty, especially the World Religions and World Church (WRWC) area, provided the amiable congeniality and intellectual space for me to work on this project. I should note my thanks to colleagues in the WRWC area as a token of my appreciation: Emmanuel Katongole, Paul Kollman, CSC, David Lantigua, Bradley Malkovsky, Francesca Murphy, Paulinus Odozor, CSC, R. Trent Pomplun, Gabriel Reynolds, and Todd Whitmore. They are not only great scholars, but also nice individuals. I am also grateful to my *ustādh*, Rashied Omar from the Kroc Institute, for his continuous support. The students in my "Qur'anic Exegesis" course likewise deserve a special thanks. One of the strongest motivators many of us have for writing books comes from teaching. Teaching Qur'anic exegesis and other Qur'an-related courses has convinced me of the deep need for a Qur'an with cross-references. I must single out Jacob Kildoo for helping me with various tasks as I worked on the Introduction.

I am indebted to my friends and family – without their help and emotional support this project would not have been possible. One unparalleled friend must be thanked for his unique contributions: Sukidi not only continuously encouraged me to finish this book (there were moments of low spirits due to the long process), but also offered insightful comments on my Introduction. Above and beyond the academic endeavor, I would like to express my special thanks to my wife, Nunung Nurhasanah, for her love, quiet encouragement, and patience. I have sometimes been too much preoccupied with this project. I dedicate this work to the beautiful souls of my dad, Achmad Sirry, and my mom, Samsumi. "O tranquil soul. Return to your Lord, pleased and accepted" (Q 89:27–28).

Table of Contents

Acknowledgments —— V

An Introduction to *The Qur'an with Cross-References* —— 1
User's Guides —— 35

Sūrah 1–114
    Sūrah 1: Al-Fātiḥah (The Opening) —— 39
    Sūrah 2: Al-Baqarah (The Cow) —— 39
    Sūrah 3: Āli 'Imrān (The Family of Amran) —— 80
    Sūrah 4: Al-Nisā' (Women) —— 105
    Sūrah 5: Al-Mā'idah (The Table) —— 130
    Sūrah 6: Al-An'ām (Livestock) —— 148
    Sūrah 7: Al-A'rāf (The Elevation) —— 169
    Sūrah 8: Al-Anfāl (The Spoils) —— 194
    Sūrah 9: Al-Tawbah (Repentance) —— 203
    Sūrah 10: Yūnus (Jonah) —— 221
    Sūrah 11: Hūd (Hūd) —— 234
    Sūrah 12: Yūsuf (Joseph) —— 248
    Sūrah 13: Al-Ra'd (Thunder) —— 260
    Sūrah 14: Ibrāhīm (Abraham) —— 266
    Sūrah 15: Al-Ḥijr (The Rock) —— 272
    Sūrah 16: Al-Naḥl (The Bee) —— 280
    Sūrah 17: Al-Isrā' (The Night Journey) —— 294
    Sūrah 18: Al-Kahf (The Cave) —— 306
    Sūrah 19: Maryam (Mary) —— 318
    Sūrah 20: Ṭā-Hā (Ṭā-Hā) —— 326
    Sūrah 21: Al-Anbiyā' (The Prophets) —— 338
    Sūrah 22: Al-Ḥajj (The Pilgrimage) —— 349
    Sūrah 23: Al-Mu'minūn (The Believers) —— 358
    Sūrah 24: Al-Nūr (The Light) —— 368
    Sūrah 25: Al-Furqān (The Criterion) —— 377
    Sūrah 26: Al-Shu'arā' (The Poets) —— 385
    Sūrah 27: Al-Naml (The Ant) —— 401
    Sūrah 28: Al-Qaṣaṣ (The Stories) —— 410
    Sūrah 29: Al-'Ankabūt (The Spider) —— 420
    Sūrah 30: Al-Rūm (The Romans) —— 428
    Sūrah 31: Luqmān (Luqmān) —— 435
    Sūrah 32: Al-Sajdah (Prostration) —— 439
    Sūrah 33: Al-Aḥzāb (The Confederates) —— 442

Sūrah 34: Saba' (Sheba) —— 451
Sūrah 35: Fāṭir (Originator) —— 458
Sūrah 36: Yā-Sīn (Yā-Sīn) —— 463
Sūrah 37: Al-Ṣaffāt (The Aligners) —— 470
Sūrah 38: Ṣād (Ṣād) —— 482
Sūrah 39: Al-Zumar (Throngs) —— 489
Sūrah 40: Ghāfir (Forgiver) —— 498
Sūrah 41: Fuṣṣilat (Detailed) —— 507
Sūrah 42: Al-Shūrā (Consultation) —— 513
Sūrah 43: Al-Zukhruf (Decorations) —— 520
Sūrah 44: Al-Dukhān (Smoke) —— 528
Sūrah 45: Al-Jāthiyah (Kneeling) —— 532
Sūrah 46: Al-Aḥqāf (The Dunes) —— 536
Sūrah 47: Muḥammad (Muhammad) —— 541
Sūrah 48: Al-Fatḥ (Victory) —— 545
Sūrah 49: Al-Hujurāt (The Chambers) —— 549
Sūrah 50: Qāf (Qāf) —— 552
Sūrah 51: Al-Dhāriyāt (The Spreaders) —— 555
Sūrah 52: Al-Ṭūr (The Mount) —— 559
Sūrah 53: Al-Najm (The Star) —— 563
Sūrah 54: Al-Qamar (The Moon) —— 568
Sūrah 55: Al-Raḥmān (The Compassionate) —— 572
Sūrah 56: Al-Wāqiʻah (The Inevitable) —— 577
Sūrah 57: Al-Ḥadīd (Iron) —— 583
Sūrah 58: Al-Mujādilah (The Argument) —— 588
Sūrah 59: Al-Ḥashr (The Mobilization) —— 591
Sūrah 60: Al-Mumtaḥanah (The Woman Tested) —— 595
Sūrah 61: Al-Ṣāf (Column) —— 597
Sūrah 62: Al-Jumuʻah (Friday) —— 599
Sūrah 63: Al-Munāfiqūn (The Hypocrites) —— 600
Sūrah 64: Al-Taghābun (Gathering) —— 602
Sūrah 65: Al-Ṭalāq (Divorce) —— 604
Sūrah 66: Al-Taḥrīm (Prohibition) —— 606
Sūrah 67: Al-Mulk (Sovereignty) —— 608
Sūrah 68: Al-Qalam (The Pen) —— 611
Sūrah 69: Al-Ḥāqqah (Reality) —— 614
Sūrah 70: Al-Maʻārij (Ways of Ascent) —— 618
Sūrah 71: Nūḥ (Noah) —— 621
Sūrah 72: Al-Jinn (The Jinn) —— 623
Sūrah 73: Al-Muzammil (The Enwrapped) —— 626
Sūrah 74: Al-Muddaththir (The Enrobed) —— 628
Sūrah 75: Al-Qiyāmah (Resurrection) —— 632

Sūrah 76: **Al-Insān** (Man) —— 634
Sūrah 77: **Al-Mursalāt** (Unleased) —— 637
Sūrah 78: **Al-Naba'** (The Event) —— 640
Sūrah 79: **Al-Nāzi'āt** (The Snatchers) —— 643
Sūrah 80: **'Abasa** (He Frowned) —— 646
Sūrah 81: **Al-Takwīr** (The Rolling) —— 649
Sūrah 82: **Al-Infiṭār** (The Shattering) —— 651
Sūrah 83: **Al-Muṭaffifīn** (The Defrauders) —— 652
Sūrah 84: **Al-Inshiqāq** (The Rupture) —— 655
Sūrah 85: **Al-Burūj** (The Constellation) —— 656
Sūrah 86: **Al-Ṭāriq** (The Night Visitor) —— 658
Sūrah 87: **Al-A'lā** (The Most High) —— 659
Sūrah 88: **Al-Ghāshiyah** (The Overwhelming) —— 661
Sūrah 89: **Al-Fajr** (The Dawn) —— 662
Sūrah 90: **Al-Balad** (The Land) —— 665
Sūrah 91: **Al-Shams** (The Sun) —— 666
Sūrah 92: **Al-Layl** (The Night) —— 667
Sūrah 93: **Al-Duḥā** (Morning Light) —— 669
Sūrah 94: **AL-Sharḥ** (The Soothing) —— 670
Sūrah 95: **Al-Tīn** (The Fig) —— 670
Sūrah 96: **Al-'Alaq** (Clot) —— 671
Sūrah 97: **Al-Qadr** (Degree) —— 672
Sūrah 98: **Al-Bayyinah** (Clear Evidence) —— 673
Sūrah 99: **Al-Zalzalah** (The Quake) —— 674
Sūrah 100: **Al-'Ādiyāt** (The Racers) —— 674
Sūrah 101: **Al-Qāri'ah** (The Shocker) —— 675
Sūrah 102: **Al-Takāthur** (Abundance) —— 676
Sūrah 103: **Al-'Aṣr** (Time) —— 677
Sūrah 104: **Al-Humazah** (The Backbiter) —— 677
Sūrah 105: **Al-Fīl** (The Elephant) —— 678
Sūrah 106: **Quraysh** (Quraysh) —— 678
Sūrah 107: **Al-Mā'ūn** (Assistance) —— 679
Sūrah 108: **Al-Kawthar** (Plenty) —— 680
Sūrah 109: **Al-Kāfirūn** (The Disbelievers) —— 680
Sūrah 110: **Al-Naṣr** (Victory) —— 681
Sūrah 111: **Al-Masad** (Thorns) —— 681
Sūrah 112: **Al-Ikhlāṣ** (Monotheism) —— 682
Sūrah 113: **Al-Falaq** (Daybreak) —— 682
Sūrah 114: **Al-Nās** (Mankind) —— 683

An Introduction to *The Qur'an with Cross-References*

Scholars have long maintained that scripture is its own interpreter and expositor.[1] It has been widely accepted that the Qur'an explains itself and that the best approach to understanding its verses is to compare them internally. The twentieth century Indian scholar Ḥamīd al-Dīn al-Farāhī (d. 1930) argues that the process of interpreting the Qur'an through the Qur'an is based on a simple principle: "The Qur'an mentions things in a variety of ways, sometimes brief and at other times in detail; what is left out in one place is mentioned in another."[2] The idea that the text is self-interpreting implies that the Qur'an is of paramount importance to its own interpretation. Thus, the best method of understanding the Qur'anic text is to let it speak for itself through cross-references in such a way that some parts are understood to shed light on others. As a result, a specific genre of Qur'anic exegesis (*tafsīr*), known as "tafsīr al-Qur'ān bi'l-Qur'ān" (TQbQ), has emerged as an alternative approach to the Islamic scripture, which combines the more traditional atomistic (verse-by-verse) type of interpretation with thematic cross-references. It is no exaggeration to say that TQbQ is a manifestation of the cross-referentiality of the Qur'an. Yet, the Qur'an in all of its printed editions has, to date, never been cross-referenced.[3] *The Qur'an with Cross-References* is therefore the first book of its kind, meant to provide a much-needed tool for approaching the text of the Qur'an on its own terms.

Cross-references are a study tool used to direct the reader to related content, which may define or explain the meaning of a given verse. Many ideas, themes, and stories are repeated frequently in many religious traditions' scriptures. By using cross-references, readers can follow the treatment of a specific theme throughout the Qur'anic corpus, and might consequently be led to a more holistic understanding than can be achieved by approaching the Qur'an as a collection of isolated verses. Indeed, modern Muslim scholars like Fazlur Rahman have criticized the atomistic approach that has dominated traditional exegetical works. For Rahman, this verse-by-verse interpretation has

---

[1] Muslim commentators of the Qur'an – both classical and modern – have emphasized the importance of understanding the Qur'an though the Qur'an or *tafsīr al-Qur'ān bi'l-Qur'ān*. Their views of the significance of this approach will be discussed in the first section of this Introduction.
[2] Ḥamīd al-Dīn al-Farāhī, *Rasā'il al-imām al-Farāhī fī 'ulūm al-Qur'ān*, ed. Badr al-Dīn al-Iṣlāḥī (Azamghar: Al-Dā'irah al-Ḥamīdiyyah, 1991), 242.
[3] By way of comparison, the Bible's cross-references have been a long-established tradition. The history of the Bible's cross-references in English can be traced back to the sixteenth century with the translation of the New Testament by William Tyndale in 1525 and the complete translation of the Bible by Miles Coverdale in 1535. In the "Preface" to his 1534 New Testament, Tyndale writes, "I have also in many places set light in the margin to understand the text by." See David Daniel (ed.), *Tyndale's New Testament* (New Heaven: Yale University Press, 1989), 3. For a brief discussion on the history of cross-references of the Bible, see Roger Tomes, "Scripture Its Own Commentator: A History of English Cross-Reference Bibles," *Expository Times* 119:10 (2008): 487–494. Today, most versions of the Bible are printed with cross-references.

resulted in "a general failure to understand the underlying unity of the Qur'an"[4] that provides a specific worldview or *Weltanschauung*. He goes on to argue that "the result of this 'atomistic' approach was that laws were often derived from verses that were not at all legal in intent."[5] Thus, he proposes a thematic approach, which aims at what he calls a "holistic understanding of the Qur'an." Building on Rahman's criticism, Amina Wadud contends that "despite consensus [among exegetes] that the interpretation of the Qur'an by the Qur'an itself (*tafsīr al-Qur'ān bi'l-Qur'ān*) is the number one tool [for Qur'anic interpretation], traditional Qur'anic exegesis is atomistic, applying meaning to one lexical item or passage at a time."[6] She concludes that "the atomistic approach that characterizes traditional exegesis does not sufficiently explain or exemplify the extent and impact of total Qur'anic coherence and perhaps never tried to nor made claim to such."[7]

While *The Qur'an with Cross-References* will certainly contribute to a more coherent understanding of the Qur'an, it would be wrong to suggest that the atomistic approach adopted by Muslim exegetes throughout the centuries is devoid of any use of cross-references. While it is true that most commentators treat the Qur'anic verses one after the other according to their order in the *muṣḥaf* (codex), in certain instances they might have gone beyond the specific verse or set of verses they are explaining and looked into other verses with related import. This approach has helped them to clarify and enrich the meaning of the verse(s) at hand. It should be admitted, however, that their use of cross-references is very limited. Wadud is correct in noting that "[o]ccasional references to other specific verses are inconsistent, unsystematic, and haphazard."[8] That is to say that, although Muslim commentators have recognized from quite early on that the Qur'an is the best interpreter of itself, TQbQ has not been implemented on a large scale. This fact is ultimately a testament to the value of the project undertaken in *The Qur'an with Cross-References*.

In what follows, I will highlight what has been said about TQbQ, its significance and scope, and how it has been practiced in the long history of the *tafsīr* tradition. Examples of TQbQ will be discussed, including some modern exegetical works devoted to this genre. In the final section, I address the development of thematic approaches among modern scholars of the Qur'an.

---

[4] Fazlur Rahman, *Islam and Modernity: Transformation of an Intellectual Tradition* (Chicago: University of Chicago Press, 1984), 2.
[5] Ibid., 2–3.
[6] Amina Wadud, "Qur'an, Gender, and Interpretive Possibilities," *Hawwa* 2:3 (2004), 327.
[7] Ibid., 331. Similarly, the Iraqi Shi'i scholar Muḥammad Bāqir Ṣadr highlights the negative impact of the atomistic interpretation in that Muslims tend to pick up certain passages from the scripture which seem to support their own views. According to him, this situation can be avoided if they take a step further by looking at the Qur'an as a whole. For a discussion on Ṣadr's view and other modernist Muslims in English, see Mohamed El-Tahir El-Mesawi, "The Methodology of *al-Tafsīr al-Mawḍū'ī*: A Comparative Analysis," *Intellectual Discourse* 13:1 (2005): 1–30.
[8] Wadud, "Qur'an, Gender, and Interpretive Possibilities," 327.

Tafsīr al-Qur'ān bi'l-Qur'ān and Cross-Referentiality

In his *Muqaddimah fī uṣūl al-tafsīr* (Prolegomena to the principles of interpretation), Ibn Taymiyyah (d. 728/1328) writes, "If one asks: 'What is the best method of interpretation?', the answer is that the most correct method is for the Qur'an to be explained using the Qur'an. For, what the Qur'an alludes to at one place is explained at the other, and what it says in brief on one occasion is elaborated upon at the other."[9] Ibn Taymiyyah goes on to say that the next source of interpretation is the prophetic tradition (*sunnah*), as the latter can likewise explain the Qur'an. If the Qur'an and sunnah do not offer any explanation, he argues that one must turn to the views of the Companions and then the Successors.[10] His disciple, Ibn Qayyim (d. 751/1350) affirms this principle, noting that *"Tafsīr al-Qur'ān bi'l-Qur'ān* is the most eloquent type of exegesis."[11] Elsewhere, Ibn Qayyim explains that this is the method followed by the Companions (*ṣaḥābah*), Successors (*tābi'ūn*) and the leading scholars after them (*a'immah ba'dahum*). "Interpreting the Qur'anic verses in light of each other," he writes, "is the most noble *tafsīr* that one should follow whenever and wherever is possible."[12]

This method of interpretation, as elucidated by Ibn Taymiyyah and Ibn Qayyim, sets the tone of later exegetical works. While neither Ibn Taymiyyah nor Ibn Qayyim have produced Qur'anic commentaries in the traditional sense, it was Ibn Kathīr (d. 774/1373), Ibn Taymiyyah's own student, who put this method into practice.[13] In the main part of his introduction to *Tafsīr al-Qur'ān al-'aẓīm (The Interpretation of the Great Qur'an)*, Ibn Kathīr incorporates his teacher's principle of interpretation without attributing it to him.[14] Even if he is not identified as the author, the reader of the Introduction will recognize that the text is from Ibn Taymiyyah. As Roy Curtis argues, it is possible that "Ibn Kathīr wanted this text to be a testament to his belief in the righteousness of his shaykh's movement and leadership; the insider, friend or

---

9 Taqī al-Dīn Aḥmad b. Taymiyyah, *al-Muqaddimah fī uṣūl al-tafsīr*, ed. 'Adnān Zurzūr (Kuwait: Dār al-Qur'ān al-karīm, 1972), 93.
10 Ibid.
11 Shams al-Dīn Abū 'Abd Allāh b. Qayyim, *al-Tibyān fī aqsām al-Qur'ān*, ed. 'Iṣṣām al-Ḥarastānī (Mu'assasat al-Risālah, 1995), 185.
12 Shams al-Dīn Abū 'Abd Allāh b. Qayyim, *Sharḥ Qaṣīdat Ibn Qayyim*, ed. Zuhayr al-Shāwīsh (Beirut: al-Maktab al-Islāmī, 1985), 2:306
13 This does not mean, however, that Ibn Kathīr's *tafsīr* must be seen as an extension of Ibn Taymiyyah's method. Younus Mirza argues that the kind of traditionalism that Ibn Taymiyyah and Ibn Kathīr advocated is different: The former "rationalized the transmitted materials and contended that reason and revelation were complimentary," the latter gave absolute authority to the transmitted materials and avoided speculation." See Younus Y. Mirza, "Was Ibn Kathīr the 'Spokesperson' for Ibn Taymiyya? Jonah as a Prophet of Obedience," *Journal of Qur'anic Studies* 16:1 (2014), 13.
14 Ismā'īl b. 'Umar b. Kathīr, *Tafsīr al-Qur'ān al-'aẓīm*, ed. Sāmī b. Muḥammad al-Salāmah (Riyadh: Dār Ṭayyibah, 1997), 1:7–15.

foe, cannot but realize that the *'aqīdah* 'religious perspective' of Ibn Kathīr and that of Ibn Taymiyyah were the same."[15] Or, perhaps he simply sought to apply the exegetical principle developed by his teacher—though this does not mean that both authors would reach the same interpretations or conclusions.[16]

At any rate, Ibn Taymiyyah's method of interpretation is widely accepted and cited by later scholars of the Qur'an. The two greatest scholars of *'ulūm al-Qur'ān* (sciences of the Qur'an), Badr al-Dīn al-Zarkashī (d. 794/1392), the author of *al-Burhān fī 'ulūm al-Qur'ān (The Elucidation of the Sciences of the Qur'an)*, and Jalāl al-Dīn al-Suyūṭī (d. 911/1505), the author of *al-Itqān fī 'ulūm al-Qur'ān (The Perfect Guide to the Sciences of the Qur'an)*, quote Ibn Taymiyyah in support of the idea that TQbQ is the most authentic method of interpreting the Qur'an.[17] Among modern authors, the *Shaykh al-Islām*'s statement is cited by Muḥsin 'Abd al-Majīd, Khālid 'Abd al-Raḥmān, and Fahd b. 'Abd al-Raḥmān al-Rūmī, all of whom have authored books with the title *Uṣūl al-tafsīr (Principles of Exegesis)*.[18]

Of course, Ibn Taymiyyah is not the first to develop the TQbQ method. Indeed, many scholars across the theological spectrum have subscribed to the same principle. The Muʿtazilī scholar Abū ʿAlī al-Fārisī (d. 377/987) is among the first to have articulated the importance of TQbQ, writing that "the whole Qur'an is like one sūrah. Thus, one thing is mentioned in one sūrah, and the answer can be found in another."[19] As an example, Fārisī refers to Q 15:6: "And they said, 'O you who received the message, you are insane'." For Fārisī, the answer to this accusation of Muhammad's insanity is given in Q 68:2: "By the grace of your Lord, you are not insane." The celebrated Muʿtazilī exegete Zamakhsharī (d. 538/1144) follows suit, saying that "the most relevant meaning is that which the Qur'an itself indicates."[20]

---

15 Roy Young Muhammad Mukhtar Curtis, *Authentic Interpretation of Classical Islamic Text: An Analysis of the Introduction of Ibn Kathīr's Tafsīr al-Qur'ān al-'Aẓīm* (The University of Michigan, 1989), 273.
16 After a close examination of Ibn Kathīr's and Ibn Taymiyyah's exegetical writings, Younus Mirza concludes, "Ibn Taymiyya's hermeneutic was to defend traditionalism from what he perceived as heretical ideologies, particular that of the dominant Ash'arism represented by Fakhr al-Dīn al-Rāzī. In contrast, Ibn Kathīr built off previous traditionalist exegetes, such as that of al-Ṭabarī and Ibn Abī Ḥātim al-Rāzī, and indirectly marginalized rational commentaries." See Younus Y. Mirza, *Ibn Kathīr (d. 774/1373): His Intellectual Circle, Major Works and Qur'anic Exegesis* (Georgetown University, 2012), 26.
17 Badr al-Dīn al-Zarkashī, *al-Burhān fī 'ulūm al-Qur'ān*, ed. Muḥammad Abū'l-Faḍl Ibrāhīm (Beirut: al-Maktabah al-'Aṣriyyah, 1972), 2:175; Jalāl al-Dīn al-Suyūṭī, *al-Itqān fī 'ulūm al-Qur'ān*, ed. Muḥammad Abū'l-Faḍl Ibrāhīm (Beirut: al-Maktabah al-'Aṣriyyah, 1987), 4:174.
18 Muḥsin 'Abd al-Ḥamīd, *Dirāsāt fī uṣūl tafsīr al-Qur'ān* (Morocco: Dār al-Thaqāfah, 1984); Khālid 'Abd al-Raḥmān al-'Akk, *Uṣūl al-tafsīr wa-qawā'iduhu* (Beirut: Dār al-Nafā'is, 1986); Fahd b. 'Abd al-Raḥmān al-Rūmī, *Buḥūth fī uṣūl al-tafsīr wa-manāhijuhu* (Riyadh: Maktabat al-Tawbah, 1994).
19 Cited by 'Abd Allāh b. Yūsuf b. Aḥmad b. Hishām al-Anṣārī, *Mughnī al-labīb 'an kutub al-aghārib*, ed. Māzin al-Mubārak and Muḥammad 'Alī Ḥamd Allāh (Beirut: Dār al-Fikr, 1985), 1:249.
20 Maḥmūd b. 'Umar al-Zamakhsharī, *al-Kashshāf 'an ḥaqā'iq al-tanzīl wa-'uyūn al-aqāwīl min wujūh al-ta'wīl*, ed. Khalīl Ma'mūn Shīḥā (Beirut: Dār al-Ma'rifah, 2009), 828.

Among Sunni exegetes, Fakhr al-Dīn al-Rāzī (d. 606/1210) often draws connections between one verse and another. For instance, when interpreting Q 10:26, "For those who have done good is goodness, and more. Neither gloom nor shame will come over their faces. These are the inhabitants of Paradise, abiding therein forever," he makes a connection with Q 55:60: "Is the reward of goodness anything but goodness?"[21] Rāzī's discussion of Q 10:26 reflects his recognition of the Qur'an's cross-referentiality. He begins by identifying some disagreements among exegetes on a number of issues. First, concerning the meaning of the phrase, "For those who have done good," he says that Ibn ʿAbbās is of the opinion that the phrase means "Those who said 'there is no god but God'," while the Muʿtazilī scholar Abū Bakr al-Aṣam (d. 200/816) refers to "Those have done good in everything they worshiped." Rāzī is inclined to agree with Aṣam. Second, on the meaning of goodness (*ḥusnā*), he agrees with Zamakhsharī, and then cites Q 55:60 as his scriptural attestation. Third, Rāzī spends a great deal of time discussing the controversy over the term "and more" (Q 10:26). For Rāzī, this verse ultimately deals with the kind of rewards that "those who have done good" would enjoy when they were brought into Paradise (*dār al-salām*, the abode of peace).

Let us consider more closely Rāzī's discussion of the second point. According to the verse, their good deed will be rewarded with goodness and more (*wa-ziyādah*). What is this "more"? Rāzī mentions two conflicting views. A group of scholars argue that the people of Paradise will see God, based on two types of argumentation: textual and rational. The textual prooftexts include prophetic tradition on the subject to the effect that "al-ḥusnā" (goodness) is meant "Paradise" and "more" is the vision of God (*ruʾyat Allāh*). As for the rational argument, it is evident that the word "al-ḥusnā" is singular with a definite article, which should be understood to refer to the aforementioned reward, namely, the abode of peace or Paradise. So, "those who have done good" on the earth would be given Paradise and everything in it. The phrase "and more" must, therefore, entail something other than what is in Paradise. As Rāzī puts it, "Everyone who follows this view agrees that 'and more' is the beatific vision."[22] To reinforce this view, he identifies a few other verses as cross-references. For instance, Q 75:22–23, "Faces on that Day will be radiant; Looking towards their Lord," points to the vision of God. Moreover, Q 76:20 describes the joys of Paradise, saying, "Wherever you look, you see bliss, and a vast kingdom," which suggests a *vision* of bliss and vast kingdom. Concerning this cross-referential procedure, Rāzī asserts that "Qur'anic verses explain each other" (*āyāt al-Qurʾān yufassir baʿḍuhā baʿḍ^{an}*),[23] a principle of exegesis that is central to his thought.

Another group of scholars, the Muʿtazilites, contends that this additional reward ("and more") should not be understood as the beatific vision. These scholars put forth

---

21 Fakhr al-Dīn al-Rāzī, *Mafātīḥ al-Ghayb* (Beirut: Dār al-Fikr, 1981), 17:81.
22 Ibid.
23 Ibid.

several arguments for this claim. Firstly, rational proofs indicate that the vision of God is not possible. Secondly, the additional reward must be of the same kind as the original "goodness." However, the beatific vision is not of the same kind of bliss. Thirdly, the Qur'anic narration of the vision of God calls for a figurative interpretation as it is unbefitting of the Divine. "Looking toward" in Q 75:23 implies "turning eyes to a certain direction," and this requires the object to be in that direction. Thus, this anthropomorphic expression should not be taken to mean literal "vision", but must rather refer to something else. For Abū 'Alī Muḥammad al-Jubbā'ī (d. 303/915), the Qur'anic phrase "goodness and more" is a reference to the well-deserved reward (*thawāb mustaḥaqq*) and any additional reward of bounty that God is willing to provide. Jubbā'ī cites not only a cross-reference (Q 35:30 "He will pay them their dues in full, and will increase them from His bounty. He is Forgiving and Appreciative"), but also the views of early authorities, such as 'Alī b. Abī Ṭālib (d. 40/661), Ibn 'Abbās (d. 68/688), Ḥasan Baṣrī (d. 110/728) and Mujāhid (d. 103/721), all of whom have explained "and more" in other ways besides the vision of God.[24]

For his part, Rāzī sides with the first view, refuting each of the Mu'tazilites' arguments point-by-point. He says, "Our group of scholars (*ashābunā*) have responded to these arguments."[25] The rational argument concerning the impossibility of seeing God, according to Rāzī, is weak and incoherent. He does not elaborate how it is so, other than saying that he has offered sufficient proofs against such a view in his book on *uṣūl* (principles). "If reason does not establish that 'seeing God' is not impossible, while sound reports confirm it," Rāzī writes, "then the matter must be understood in its literal meaning."[26] As is well known, the possibility of the vision of God is one of the defining doctrinal differences between the rival Ash'arite and Mu'tazilite schools of theology in the classical period. Rāzī elects to defend the Ash'arite position on this contested issue.[27] Interestingly, both sides marshalled philosophical arguments and scriptural prooftexts to their position.

Rāzī's insistence on the cross-referential procedure is based on his conviction that the Qur'an itself is self-referential. The Muslim scripture refers to itself as "a Scripture consistent and paired" or "kitāb[an] mutashābih[an]" (Q 39:23). For Rāzī, this is an indispensable characteristic of the Qur'an. He cites Ibn 'Abbās' interpretation of Q 39:23 that "some parts of the Qur'an resemble the other," and argues that such resemblance

---

24 'Alī: "Ghurfah min lu'lu'ah wāḥidah"; Ibn 'Abbās: 'Ashrah amthāliha'; Ḥasan: 'Ashrah amthāliha ilā sab'i mi'ah ḍu'f"; Mujāhid: Maghfirat Allāh wa-riḍwānuhu." See ibid., 17:82.
25 Ibid.
26 Ibid.
27 For more discussion, see Tariq Jaffer, *Rāzī: Master of Qur'anic Interpretation and Theological Reasoning* (New York: Oxford University Press, 2015); Yasin Ceylan, *Theology and Tafsīr in the Major Works of Fakhr al-Dīn al-Rāzī* (Kuala Lumpur: International Institute of Islamic Thought and Civilization, 1996); Mohd Farid Mohd Shahran, *Fakhr al-Dīn al-Rāzī on Divine Transcendence and Anthropomorphism: A Refutation against the Literalists* (Putrajaya: ISSI, 2017).

can be understood in the sense that "its verses and explanations strengthen and reinforce each other."[28] Many other Sunni exegetes follow the same procedure. Al-'Izz b. 'Abd al-Salām (d. 660/1262), the author of *Majāz al-Qur'ān (Allegory of the Qur'an)*, signals the importance of TQbQ, writing: "Deciding the meaning of the Qur'an in light of what appears in other parts of the Qur'an is preferable to any other decisions."[29]

In another vein, the Zaydī exegete Muḥammad b. Ibrāhīm b. 'Alī al-Murtaẓā (d. 840/1436), known as Ibn al-Wazīr, is reported to have said: "The best interpretation is the interpretation of the Qur'an with the Qur'an and then with hadith."[30] Some jurists like Shāṭibī (d. 790/1388) or linguists like Bāqūlī (d. 543/1148) also uphold this principle of interpretation. In his *al-Muwāfaqāt fī uṣūl al-sharī'ah (The Reconciliation of the Fundamentals of Islamic Law)*, Shāṭibī argues that

> Since the Qur'an is self-explaining, some parts of the Qur'an cannot be understood in their true sense unless through the other parts or other sūrahs. Explicit texts include various kinds of necessity (ḍarūriyyāt), some of which are connected with complementary (ḥājiyyāt). Thus, understanding some parts is contingent on the other. In this sense, the whole Qur'an is unity.[31]

This idea of interconnectedness and self-referentiality is also emphasized by Bāqūlī, who says that "it is always necessary for you to interpret the Qur'an in reference to its parts, whenever possible. It is also necessary to take up the interpretation of a specific verse in light of other verses that explain it."[32] All of the aforementioned views reflect the significant value that TQbQ has in the eyes of early Muslim authorities.

Some modern Muslim exegetes contend that scholars have long agreed upon TQbQ as the best method of interpretation. The Indian exegete Farāhī, for instance, argues that "the people of *ta'wīl* from the *salaf* (early) generations through *khalaf* (later) have agreed that the Qur'an interprets each other. Indeed, it is the most reliable explanation and the best interpretation."[33] In a similar vein, Muḥammad al-Amīn al-Shinqīṭī (d. 1972) refers to the consensus of scholars (*ijmā' al-ulamā'*) about the status of TQbQ as the most noble type of *tafsīr*.[34] While it is difficult to ascertain the existence of such

---

28 Rāzī, *Mafātīḥ al-ghayb*, 26:271.
29 Al-'Izz b. 'Abd al-Salām, *Majāz al-Qur'ān*, ed. Muḥammad Muṣṭafā al-Ḥajj (Tripoli: Manshūrāt Kulliyat al-Da'wah al-Islāmiyyah, 1980), 110.
30 See Muḥammad al-Shawkānī, *al-Badr al-ṭāli' bi-maḥāsin man ba'd al-qarn al-sābi'*, (Beirut: Dār al-Ma'rifah, 1980), 2:86; Khayr al-Dīn al-Zarkalī, *al-A'lām: Qāmūs al-tarājim li-ashhar al-rijāl wa'l-nisā' min al-'arab wa'l-musta'ribīn wa'l-mustshriqīn*, (Beirut: Dār al-'Ilm li'l-Malāyīn, 2002), 5:300.
31 Abū Isḥāq Ibrāhīm b. Mūsā al-Shāṭibī, *al-Muwāfaqāt fī uṣūl al-sharī'ah*, ed. Abū 'Ubayd Allāh Āl Sulaymān (Cairo: Dār Ibn 'Affān, 2006), 4:275.
32 'Alī b. Ḥusayn b. 'Alī al-Bāqūlī, *Kashf al-mushkilāt wa-īḍāḥ al-mu'ḍalāt*, ed. Muḥammad al-Dārī (Damascus: Majma' al-Lughah al-'Arabiyyah, 11995), 2:918.
33 Cited by Dr. Muḥammad Ajmal Ayyūb al-Iṣlāḥī, the editor of Farāhī's *Mufradāt al-Qur'ān: Naẓarāt jadīdah fī tafsīr alfāẓ Qur'āniyyah* (Beirut: Dār al-Gharb al-Islāmī, 2002), 29.
34 Muḥammad al-Amīn al-Shinqīṭī, *Aḍwā' al-bayān fī īḍāḥ al-Qur'ān bi'l-Qur'ān* (Jiddah: Dār 'Ālam al-Fawā'id, n.d.), 1:8.

a consensus,³⁵ scholars' agreement on its usefulness cannot be denied. Even those who do not specifically mention this mode of interpretation in their exegetical method usually employ it to a certain extent, as will be discussed in the next section.

Major Interest of Early Authorities

Proponents of TQbQ believe that their method is strongly encouraged by the Qur'an itself and has been practiced by the Prophet Muhammad. As their scriptural prooftexts, they refer to several passages from the Qur'an that enjoin contemplation and discernment of the scripture (Q 4:82; 23:68; 38:29; 47:24). In these verses, the Qur'an encourages "tadabbur" (reflection and contemplation) of its verses. And it is through deep thinking, discernment and consideration that one can identify connections between one verse and another or to find synthesis between verses that appear to be contradictory.³⁶ Another set of verses to which the command to "reflect" might apply are those in which the audience is told to refer a given matter to God and to seek judgement from Him and His messenger, especially, when disagreement occurs (Q 4:59; 42:10). For many scholars, referring to God and His messenger means to return to the Qur'an and hadith. Muḥammad Qajwī offers the following explanation: "Since God knows better than any others concerning the secret of this scripture and its meanings, and after Him His messenger, He teaches the Muslims to turn to the Qur'an and sunnah whenever they encounter any difficulty in revealing its meanings."³⁷

In addition, the Qur'an attributes the task of explaining to God: "Upon Us is its collection and its recitation. Then, when We have recited it, follow its recitation. Then upon Us is its explanation" (Q 75:17–19). The Andalusian scholar Ibn Ḥazm (d. 456/1064) marshals these verses to challenge those who might have opposed the principle of TQbQ. On this matter, he writes:

> If someone says that it is not allowed to interpret the Qur'an except by sunnah on the basis of Q 16:44 ("And We revealed to you the Reminder, that you may clarify to the people what was revealed to them"), I would say that nothing in the verse you just mentioned (Q 16:44) to support what you said. Rather, the verse includes a clear explanation and explicit statement that God revealed to him [Muhammad] the Reminder in order for him to explain to the people, and that explanation is through the divine speech (*kalām*). When the Prophet recited it, he explained it.

---

35 Sohaib Saeed Bhutta agrees with this assessment, saying that "This claim of consensus is, in my estimation, little more than an assertion based on the apparent lack of an opposing view." See Sohaib Saeed Bhutta, *Intraquranic Hermeneutics: Theories and Methods in Tafsīr of the Qur'ān through the Qur'ān* (Ph.D. dissertation, University of London, 2017), 48.
36 Dr. Muḥsin b. Ḥāmid al-Muṭayrī, *Tafsīr al-Qur'ān bi'l-Qur'ān: Ta'ṣīl wa-taqwīm*, (Riyadh: Dār al-Tadmuriyyah, 2011), 62; Dr. Muḥammad Qajwī, *Tafsīr al-Qur'ān bi'l-Qur'ān: Dirāsah tārīkhiyyah wa-naẓariyyah* (Riyadh: al-Rābiṭah al-Muḥammadiyyah li'l-'Ulamā', 2020), 31.
37 Qajwi, *Tafsīr al-Qur'ān bi'l-Qur'ān*, 31.

> Moreover, if the verse is too ambiguous in such a way that its meaning cannot be understood from its word (*lafdh*), God would clarify it through a revelation revealed to him, either recited (*matluw*) or unrecited revelation (*ghayr matluw*), as God says "When We have recited it, follow its recitation. Then upon Us is its explanation" (75:18–19). In this verse, God informs that the explanation of the Qur'an is upon Him. If it is upon Himself to explain, then the explanation must come from Him. Generally speaking, the revelation is either recited or unrecited, all of which come from God, as He says "God makes things clear for you" (4:176). When describing the Qur'an, He says "We have revealed to you the Book, as an explanation of all things" (16:89). Based on this verse, it is evident that the recited verse can serve as an explanation of other verses.[38]

This long quotation from Ibn Ḥazm makes it clear that TQbQ is justifiable on the basis of the Qur'an. His point is to show that the author of the Qur'an must know better than anyone else about the meaning of His words. The fact that Ibn Ḥazm offers scriptural reasons to support TQbQ suggests that his opponents might have also relied on Qur'anic passages as the basis for their position that only the Prophet can clarify the Qur'an. Despite their disagreement on the status of TQbQ, they nonetheless concur that sunnah can explain the Qur'an.

Proponents of TQbQ tend to mention a few specific examples to show that TQbQ has been practiced by Muhammad himself. While instances of his resort to this principle are not many, they are still significant testimonies to the value of TQbQ since the Prophet is to be seen as a role model. Among the most well-known examples is the one recorded in both Bukhārī's and Muslim's collections of hadith, according to which the Companion Ibn Masʿūd narrates that when Q 6:82 ('Those who believe and do not obscure their faith with *ẓulm* [wrongdoing] – those will have security, and they are guided') was revealed, several Companions became anxious. They came to the Prophet, saying "Who is among us that does not obscure his faith with any wrongdoing?" The Prophet responded: "No, it is not what you think! Don't you hear Luqmān's advice to his son in Q 31:13 ('Surely, idolatry is wrongdoing')?"[39] It thus appears that the Companions understood the word "ẓulm" in its general meaning, and the Prophet corrected their conception by arguing that "ẓulm" in Q 6:82 has a specific connotation, namely, associating God with others (*shirk*).

Another instance of prophetic TQbQ can be seen in the way that Muhammad clarifies Q 6:59, "With Him are the keys of the unseen; none knows them except He," with reference to Q 31:34, "With God rests the knowledge of the Hour. He sends down the rain, and He knows what the wombs contain. No soul knows what it will reap tomorrow, and no soul knows in what land it will die. God is All-Knowing, Well-Informed." Through this cross-referential interpretation, he argues that "the keys of the unseen"

---

38 Abū Muḥammad ʿAlī b. Ḥazm, *al-Iḥkām fī uṣūl al-aḥkām*, ed. Aḥmad Muḥammad Shākir (Cairo: Dār al-Ḥadīth, 1983), 1:79.
39 Muḥammad b. Ismāʿīl al-Bukhārī, *Ṣaḥīḥ al-Bukhārī* (*kitāb al-tafsīr*), number 4629 (Damascus: Dār Ibn Kathīr, 2002), 1139–1140; Abūʾl-Ḥusayn Muslim b. al-Ḥajjāj, *Ṣaḥīḥ Muslim* (*kitāb al-īmān*), number 124 (Riyadh: Bayt al-Afkār al-Dawliyyah, 1998), 75.

in 6:59 are five, as enumerated in 31:34, namely: (1) knowledge of the hour, (2) sending down of the rain, (3) what the wombs contain, (4) what soul will reap, and (5) in what land it will die.[40] In yet another example, the Prophet interprets a certain word with another in the same verse. It is reported by Nu'mān b. Bashīr that when the Prophet recited Q 40:60, "Your Lord has said, 'Pray to Me, and I will respond to you'," he explained that the command "pray to Me" means "worship Me" on the basis of the second part of the verse: "But those who are too proud to worship Me will enter Hell forcibly."[41]

Other examples are frequently cited by proponents of TQbQ—however, a closer look at these latter testimonies reveals that they fall under an altogether different category. For instance, Muḥammad Qajwī and Muḥsin al-Muṭayrī refer to an incident in which the Prophet said to Abū Sa'īd b. Mu'allā: "I will tell you the greatest sūrah in the Qur'an before I exit this mosque." When he was about to leave the mosque, Abū Sa'īd reminded him of his promise. Muhammad then said: "'Praise be to God, Lord of the Worlds' [Q 1:2] is the seven pairs [15:87] and the noble Qur'an that I was given."[42] This hadith does not present a case of TQbQ, but rather an instance of Muhammad simply explaining the Qur'an. The phrase "seven of the pair" (*sab' min al-mathānī*) in Q 15:87 ("We have given you seven of the pairs, and the Grand Qur'an") is here understood by the Prophet to refer to the first chapter of the Qur'an (*sūrat al-Fātiḥah*). In other words, this is an example of interpreting the Qur'an by sunnah, rather than Muhammad's interpretation of a verse in light of the other.

During the era of Companions and Successors, more examples of TQbQ can be found. In fact, reports about their use of TQbQ are abundantly recorded in later exegetical works, particularly by Ṭabarī (d. 310/923) Qurṭubī (d. 671/1273), Ibn Kathīr, and Suyūṭī. Abū Bakr (d. 13/634), the first caliph after Muhammad's death, is reported to have interpreted Q 9:119 "O you who believe! Be conscious of God, and be with the sincere," with reference to Q 59:8, "To the poor refugees who were driven out of their homes and their possessions, as they sought the favor of God and His approval, and came to the aid of God and His Messenger. These are the sincere."[43] Through comparison of the two verses, it becomes evident that Q 59:8 clarifies the identity of "the sincere" (*ṣiddīqūn*) with whom the believers are encouraged to associate (Q 9:119).

Ibn 'Abbās is reported to have frequently referred to other Qur'anic passages to clarify a certain verse at hand. For instance, the word "leader" (*imām*) in Q 17:71, "On the Day when We call every people with their leader," is understood by Ibn 'Abbās to

---

40 Bukhārī, *Ṣaḥīḥ al-Bukhārī* (*kitāb al-tafsīr*), number 4627.
41 Abū Dāwud al-Sijistānī, *Sunan Abī Dāwud* (*kitāb al-ṣalāt*), number 1479 (Damascus: Dār al-Risālah al-'Ālamiyyah, 2009), 2:603.
42 Bukhārī, *Ṣaḥīḥ al-Bukhārī* (*kitāb al-tafsīr*), number 4474. Cf, Qajwī, *Tafsīr al-Qur'ān bi'l-Qur'ān*, 44–45; Muṭayrī, *Tafsīr al-Qur'ān bi'l-Qur'ān*, 71.
43 Muḥammad b. Aḥmad al-Qurṭubī, *al-Jāmi' li-aḥkām al-Qur'ān*, ed. 'Abd Allāh b. 'Abd al-Muḥsin al-Turkī (Beirut: Mu'assasat al-Risālah, 2006), 10:421.

mean "documented or recorded deed." When one of the God-conscious (*muttaqūn*) is resurrected on the Day of Judgment, he will have his record in his right hand. When he reads it, he will be pleased. To support this view, Ibn 'Abbās refers to Q 15:79 "So We took revenge upon them. Both are clearly documented (*imām mubīn*)."[44] Similarly, 'Umar b. Khaṭṭāb (d. 23/644) interprets Q 81:7, "When the souls are paired," in light of 37:22, "Gather those who did wrong, and their mates, and what they used to worship,"[45] because both verses involve a pair working together consequently receiving the consequence of their work. In another case, 'Alī b. Alī Ṭālib interprets the word "saqf" (roof) in Q 52:5 as "sky" on the basis of 21:32, "And We made the sky a protected roof; yet they turn away from its wonders."[46]

Among the successive generations, this type of interpretation is expanded. Some exegetes are concerned to clarify the meaning of particular terms, such as *'ahd* (covenant, pledge) in Q 2:40 "fulfill your pledge to Me, and I will fulfill My pledge to you." For Ḥasan Baṣrī, Mujāhid and Qutādah (d. 117/735), this *'ahd* is connected to the pledge of the Children of Israel as elaborated in Q 2:63; 3:188 and 5:12.[47] Or, the word *ni'mah* (blessing) in the same verse (2:40: "O Children of Israel! Remember My blessings which I bestowed upon you") is spelt out in 2:20, "When Moses said to his people, 'O my people, remember God's blessings upon you, when He placed prophets among you, and made you kings, and gave you what He never gave any other people'."[48] 'Abd al-Raḥmān b. Zayd (d. 182/799) clarifies the intended reference of the term "nadhīr" (warner) in Q 35:37 "And the warner did come to you" as the Prophet, pointing to Q 53:56, "This is a warning, just like the first warnings."[49]

Other successors develop general principles on the basis of several verses that share the same basic axis (*miḥwar*). Sa'īd b. Jubayr (d. 95/714), for instance, argues that *'afw* has three dimensions. The first is the intention to give, as it is stated in Q 2:219: "And they ask you about what they should give: say, 'The surplus' (*'afw*)." The second is to go beyond the sin, based on Q 4:149, "If you let a good deed be shown, or conceal it, or pardon (*ta'fū*) an offense—God is Pardoning and Capable." The third dimension is doing good for people (Q 2:237 "unless they forego (*ya'fūna*) the right, or the one in whose hand is the marriage contract foregoes (*ya'fuwa*) it").[50] When interpreting the word "ashhād" (witnesses) in Q 40:51, 'Abd al-Raḥmān b. Zayd mentions four kinds of witnesses: Angels (50:21), Prophets (4:41), Muhammad's community (22:78), and

---

44 Muḥammad b. Jarīr al-Ṭabarī, *Jāmi' al-bayān fī ta'wīl āy al-Qur'ān*, ed. 'Abd Allāh b. 'Abd al-Muḥsin al-Turkī (Cairo: Dār Hijr, 2001), 15:7. A few other examples involving Ibn 'Abbās include Q 2:124 with 53:37, 9:112, 33:34, 23:1–9, and 70:34; 7:171 with 4:154; 6:57 with 12:3, 27:76, and 6:130; and 6:23 with 4:42.
45 Ibid., 24:145.
46 Ibn Kathīr, *Tafsīr al-Qur'ān al-'aẓīm*, 7:429.
47 Qurṭubī, *al-Jāmi' li-aḥkām al-Qur'ān*,2:8; Ibn Kathīr, *Tafsīr al-Qur'ān al-'aẓīm*, 1:84; Jalāl al-Dīn al-Suyūṭī, *al-Durr al-manthūr fī al-tafsīr bi'l-ma'thūr* (Beirut: Dār al-Fikr, 2011), 1:154.
48 Ibn Kathīr, *Tafsīr al-Qur'ān al-'aẓīm*, 1:83.
49 Ṭabarī, *Jāmi' al-bayān*, 19:387.
50 Suyūṭī, *al-Itqān*, 2:138.

bodily organs and skins (41:20).[51] Mujāhid contends that whenever the Qur'an used the word "khayr" (goodness) it is always connected to wealth, citing Q 100:8; 38:32; 24:33; 2:180.[52]

The most common uses of TQbQ among later exegetes are (1) to harmonize apparent contradictions (e. g. Q 77:36 vs 39:31; 88:6 vs 69:36), (2) to specify an instance of general wording (e. g. 3:90 with 4:18; 3:102 with 64:16), or (3) to identify which verse abrogates which (e. g. 2:240 with 2:232; 4:33 with 8:76). Some exegetes utilize the principle of TQbQ to support their preference of variant readings. Ṭabarī and Ibn Katīr, for instance, mention two different readings of Q 2:119 "You will not be questioned (*tus'al*) about the inmates of Hell." The reading of most readers is *lā tus'al* (you will be questioned), which suggests that Muhammad is not responsible regarding the people of Hell. Some Medinan readers, however, read it as *lā tas'al* (do not question or do not ask) on the basis of a report by Muḥammad b. Ka'b in which the Prophet says, "I wish I know what happened with my parent." According to this report, Q 2:119 was revealed in response to Muhammad's wish. Ṭabarī ultimately prefers the reading of the majority (*tus'al*) in light of the preceding and following verses, which talk about Jews and Christians. Ibn Kathīr follows Ṭabarī in this regard, reinforcing his preference of reading by providing a list of cross-references (Q 13:40; 88:21–22; 50:45) which show that the task of the Prophet as a warner (*nadhīr*) is merely to deliver the message, not to bear responsibility for the result of his preaching.[53] In other words, since Muhammad was sent as a deliverer of good news and a warner, whose task is only to deliver the message and to remind people, he will not be asked about the outcome of his mission. Ṭabarī adds Ibn Mas'ūd's reading *lan tus'al* (you will never be asked or questioned), of which he also approves.[54]

Between Tradition-Based and Reason-Based Exegesis

The above discussion has highlighted some of the ways in which cross-references have been used by Muslim exegetes of various generations. However, the application of cross-references is not confined to works of exegesis alone, but also occurs in a wide range of literature. In fact, various genres that fall under the category "'ulūm al-Qur'ān" (Qur'anic sciences) include some form of Qur'anic cross-references. Of these genres, the most prominent in the use of cross-references are books on "wujūh wa-naẓā'ir" (homonymy), "manāsabah" (correlation), "mushkilat al-Qur'ān" (difficulties of the Qur'an), and nāsikh wa-mansūkh" (abrogating and abrogated). The "wujūh wa-naẓā'ir" genre, sometimes called "ashbāh wa-naẓā'ir," mostly deals with

---

51 Qurṭubī, *al-Jāmi' li-aḥkām al-Qur'ān*, 18:369; Suyūṭī, *al-Durr al-manthūr*, 7:293.
52 Ṭabarī, *Jāmi' al-bayān*, 3:135.
53 Ṭabarī, *Jāmi' al-bayān*, 2:480–483; Ibn Kathīr, *Tafsīr*, 1:400–401.
54 Ṭabarī, *Jāmi' al-bayān*, 2:483.

the repetition of a word or phrase in different contexts with multiple connotations. Muqātil b. Sulaymān (d. 150/767) is one of the earliest, if not the earliest, authors whose book with this title is extant. For Muqātil, the word "maraḍ" (sickness), for instance, has four different meanings in the Qur'an: doubt (Q 2:10), immorality (Q 33:32), wound (Q 4:43), and sickness (Q 2:184).[55] Some authors known for their works in this genre include al-Ḥākim al-Tirmidhī (d. 320/910), Muḥammad b. Ḥasan al-Nuqqāsh (d. 351/962), ʿAbd al-Malik b. Muḥammad al-Thaʿālabī (d. 429/1038), Ḥusayn b. Muḥammad al-Dāmighānī (d. 478/1085), and Ibn Jawzī (d. 597/1201).[56]

The genre on textual relations (*munāsabah*) in the Qur'an is attractive to Muslims whose interest is to show the organic unity of their scripture. Unlike "wujūh wa-naẓāʾir", however, this genre seems to develop much later—as Salwa El-Awa writes, "the theoretical side of the issue of textual relations was only dealt with later when scholars like Zarkashī embarked on establishing the study of the essential tools of exegesis, *ʿulūm al-Qurʾān*, based on re-reading the works of exegetes."[57] While Biqāʿī (d. 885/1480)'s *al-Burhān fī munāsabāt al-Qurʾān (The Elucidation of Correlations of the Qurʾan)* represents the major work on this genre, it was Suyūṭī who heavily relied on cross-references to establish connections between one sūrah and another. In his *Tanāsuq al-durar fī tanāsub al-suwar (The Arrangement of Pearls on the Correlation of Chapters)*, Suyūṭī addresses textual relations between each chapter and the preceding one by showing how the latter acts as an expositor of the former. For instance, Q 2:3 refers generically to "what was revealed before you"; for Suyūṭī, the elaboration of this verse can be found in Q 3:3–4: "He sent down the Torah and the Gospel. Aforetime, as guidance for mankind."[58]

The other two genres, "mushkilāt" and "nāsikh wa-mansūkh," are concerned, respectively, with difficult issues due to the intricacies of the Qur'an and the apparent contradictions in the text. Since the Qur'an is not an easy text to understand, interest in the "mushkilāt" genre emerges early in the history of Qur'anic exegesis. I have already discussed some examples of how early generations of Muslims explained certain words that might not be immediately accessible to a general audience. Later scholars developed this enterprise further into a specific genre in the subfield of Qur'anic studies. It is remarkable how much has been written on this issue, including – to mention but few – Ibn Qutaybah's *Taʾwīl Mushkilāt al-Qurʾān (The Interpretation of Difficulties of the Qurʾan)*, Abū Muḥammad Makkī al-Qīsī's *Mushkilāt al-Qurʾān waʾl-tafsīr (Difficulties of the Qurʾan and Interpretation)*, Bayān al-Ḥaq al-Naysābūrī's *Waḍḥ*

---

55 Muqātil b. Sulaymān, *al-Wujūh waʾl-naẓāʾir fī al-Qurʾān al-ʿaẓīm*, ed. Ḥātim Muḥammad al-Ḍāmin (Riyadh: Maktabat al-Rushd, 2011), 30–31.
56 For discussion, see Qawjī, *Tafsīr al-Qurʾān biʾl-Qurʾān*, 96–105.
57 Salwa Muhamed Salem El-Awa, *Textual Relations in the Qurʾan* (Ph.D. Dissertation, University of London, 2002), 27.
58 Suyūṭī, *Tasāsuq al-durar fī tanāsub al-suwar*, ed. ʿAbd al-Qādir Aḥmad al-ʿAṭā (Beirut: Dār al-Kutub al-ʿIlmiyyah, 1986), 70–75.

al-burhān fī mushkilāt al-Qur'ān (Clear Exposition on the Difficulties of the Qur'an) and 'Izz al-Dīn 'Abd al-Salām's *al-Qawā'id fī mushkil al-Qur'ān (Essentials on the Difficulty of the Qur'an)*. Ibn Qutaybah draws on cross-references to clarify difficult words and verses. For instance, the word "tataqallab" in Q 24:37 is explained through Q 50:22.[59] Elsewhere, he offers a detailed explanation of the term "ummah" by putting together various relevant verses (Q 2:213; 6:38; 12:45; 11:8; 16:93, 120; 23:52; 43:22), concluding that this one word can mean different things in different contexts.[60] Bayān al-Ḥaqq elucidates the word "ghayb" (unseen) in Q 2:3 as something hidden from the senses and cannot be grasped except through reason, based on Q 12:52 and 50:33.[61] As for the *nāsikh wa-mansūkh* genre, it is obvious that contradictions can only be identified when two or more verses on the same issue are compared and analyzed. Major works on this genre include Qatādah b. Di'āmah's *al-Nāsikh wa'l-mansūkh*, al-Nuḥḥās's *al-Nāsikh wa'l-mansūkh*, Ibn Ḥazm's *al-Nāsikh wa'l-mansūkh fī al-Qur'ān*, Ibn Jawzī's *Nawāsikh al-Qur'ān*, to mention a few.

In light of these observations, it should be clear that the above genres might be understood as an extension of TQbQ—though, of course, each employs this technique in unique ways and for particular purposes. Likewise, in the *tafsīr* tradition, the use of cross-references is not monolithic. Some exegetes employ the principle of TQbQ to explain the Qur'anic vocabulary, while others use it to specify the general wording or generalize the specific one. Still others use TQbQ to explain the ambiguous words or identify the missing parts. Sometimes interpreters read a certain verse and then compare it with similar verses that can help to clarify any difficulties. In other words, cross-referencing is an indispensable tool that readers can use to unlock the meaning of verses and enrich one's understanding of the Qur'an. Furthermore, comparing two or more similar verses can sometimes bring new perspectives to light. For instance, when reading Q 4:42, "On that Day, those who disbelieved and disobeyed the Messenger will wish that the earth were leveled over them," Qurṭubī compares it with Q 78:40, "The faithless will say, 'O, I wish I were dust'." For Qurṭubī, the connection between these two verses makes sense because the unbelievers wished that "the earth [would be] leveled over them" on the Day of Judgement when they saw that the animals had become dust, since they knew that they would be put in Fire forever.[62]

Such intra-Qur'anic connections can be established in various ways. Sometimes it is self-evident from the text itself, as when the Qur'an asks, "Do you know what it is?" Concerning "al-qāri'ah" (the shocker), for instance, the Qur'an asks, "Do you know what *al-qāri'ah* is?" (Q 101:3)—then the following verses explain: "The Day

---

[59] 'Abd Allāh b. Muslim b. Qutaybah, *Ta'wīl Mushkilāt al-Qur'ān*, ed. al-Sayyid Aḥmad Ṣaqar (Cairo: Dār al-Turāth, 1973), 329.
[60] Ibid., 445–446.
[61] Bayān al-Ḥaqq al-Naysābūrī, *Waḍḥ al-burhān fī mushkilāt al-Qur'ān*, ed. Ṣafwān 'Adnān Dāwūdī (Beirut: al-Dār al-Shāmiyyah, 1990), 1:104.
[62] Qurṭubī, *al-Jāmi' li-aḥkām al-Qur'ān*, 6:328; see also Ibn Kathīr, *Tafsīr al-Qur'ān al-'aẓīm*, 2:307.

when the people will be like scattered moths. And the mountains will be like tufted wool" (101:4–5). Similarly, in Q 86 the text asks, "Do you know what al-ṭāriq is?" and then answers: "The Piercing Star" (86:2–3). Another example is the description of human being as "restless" (halūʿ) in Q 70:19, which is explained in the following verses "Touched by adversity, he is fretful. Touched by good, he is ungenerous" (70:20–21). Thus, when the Kūfan grammarian Abū'l-ʿAbbās Thaʿlab (d. 291/904) was asked about the meaning of halūʿ, his response was "God has already explained it!"[63]

In most cases, however, the connection is not so self-evident, or at least requires a close reading of other parts of the Qur'an. In these cases, the degree of interconnectedness might vary, with some connections being more obvious than others. For instance, the meaning of "Lord of the Worlds" (rabb al-ʿālamīn) in Q 1:2 can be explicated through a question raised by Pharaoh in Q 26:23–24, where he asks, "And what is the Lord of the Worlds?" To this, Moses replies, "The Lord of the heavens and the earth, and everything between them, if you are aware." In other words, the connection between these two passages is rather plain. In some cases, certain passages specify particular examples of what is alluded to in another passage, such as Q 2:158 and 22:36, which refer to "Ṣafā and Marwā" and "the animal offerings" as being among the "rites of God" (min shaʿāʾir Allāh)—a concept which is left unexplained in Q 22:32: "Whoever venerates the rites of God – it is from the piety of the hearts." On other occasions the connections between passages are not straightforward, though they can still add to our meaning of a Qur'anic verse we read. Therefore, establishing connections between one verse and another and even the whole enterprise of TQbQ are open to discussion and debate, since the proponents of this method can be accused of Qur'an sufficiency.

While some scholars regard TQbQ as a form of tradition-based exegesis (tafsīr bi'l-maʾthūr), the fact of the matter is that the process of selecting which verse sheds light on which involves interpretive reasoning (ijtihād) on the part of the reader. Each interpreter exerts serious intellectual effort to understand the meaning of a verse, and to identify which other verses might help to unveil its intended meaning. Thus, TQbQ is humane scholarship which requires rigorous study and rational reflection. It is of course true, as we already discussed, that some reports indicate that Muhammad explained the Qur'an through other parts of the Qur'an. However, this does not mean that TQbQ is necessarily a form of tradition-based exegesis. After all, there is no consensus among scholars that everything the Prophet did or said is part of his prophetic authority, nor on the question of whether or not Muhammad performed ijtihād. It is not impossible, after all, that his selection of one verse to clarify another was based on his own personal interpretation. Even if we accept the view that Muhammad's resort to TQbQ is divinely revealed and therefore cannot be challenged, there are nonethe-

---

[63] Qajwī, Tafsīr al-Qurʾān bi'l-Qurʾān, 76–77.

less only a handful examples of his *tafsīr* reported in the hadith collections. Al-Qāḍī Shams al-Dīn al-Khūyī, as cited by Zarkashī, says:

> The science of *tafsīr* is both complex and simple. Its complexity is evident from a number of issues, the most obvious of which is the fact that the intended meaning of the divine speech does not reach us through *samāʿ* ("revealed meaning"; lit. "listening") and there is no way to access it. In contrast to parables and poetry in which people can learn the intention of the speaker by listening to him or listen to whoever heard it from him. As for the Qurʾan, its interpretation cannot be precisely understood except by listening to the Prophet. However, that is impossible except on a tiny number of verses (*āyāt qalāʾil*). So the knowledge of the intended meaning is derived from signs (*amārāt*) and indications (*dalāʾil*). The underlying reason for this is that God wants his servants to think about His scripture, so He does not instruct His Prophet to reveal its intended meaning.[64]

It seems clear that the vast majority of exegetes heavily rely on intellectual reasoning in their interpretation of the Qurʾan through the Qurʾan. Interestingly however, scholars like Ibn Taymiyyah do not consider TQbQ to be a form of reason-based exegesis even if it involves turning to the deeper meaning from the literal one. On this issue, he writes: "There is no problem with [TQbQ] according to a group of the People of Sunnah, even if it is called 'taʾwīl' and turning away from the apparent meaning, as long as it is based on an indication from the Qurʾan and in conformity with sunnah and *salaf*, since such an endeavor belongs to *tafsīr al-Qurʾan biʾl-Qurʾan*, and not *tafsīr biʾl-raʾy* (reason-based exegesis)."[65] Ibn Taymiyyah's view tends to shape the scholarship of modern Muslims. Thus we find modern Muslim scholars such as Zarqānī (d. 1948), Dhahabī (d. 1977), Mannāʾ al-Qaṭṭān (d. 1999), and Abdullah Saeed categorize TQbQ under the heading "tradition-based exegesis."[66] Saeed writes, "Four different types of interpretation may be grouped under the heading of tradition-based *tafsīr*. These comprise (1) interpretation of the Qurʾan by the Qurʾan, (2) interpretation of the Qurʾan by the Prophet, (3) interpretation of the Qurʾan by the Companions of the Prophet, and (4) interpretation of the Qurʾan by the Successors."[67]

The inclusion of TQbQ in the category of tradition-based exegesis is problematic if it is assumed that the exegetes simply pick a verse or a set of verses to explain the other in the same way as they pass on the views of the Prophet or the Companions or the Successors. TQbQ involves scriptural reasoning and intellectual effort—after all, one can only decide how to fit Qurʾanic verses together after a close examination of

---

64 Zarkashī, *al-Burhān*, 1:16.
65 Ibn Taymiyyah, *Majmūʿ Fatāwā Ibn Taymiyyah*, ed. ʿAbd al-Raḥmān b. Muḥammad al-ʿĀṣimī (Medina: Majmaʿ al-Malik Fahd, 1995), 6:21.
66 Muḥammad ʿAbd al-ʿAẓīm al-Zarqānī, *Manāhil al-ʿirfān fī ʿulūm al-Qurʾān* (Beirut: Dār al-Kitab al-ʿArabī, 1995); Muḥammad Ḥusayn al-Dhahabī, *al-Tafsīr waʾl-mufassirūn* (Cairo: Maktabat Wahbah, n.d.); Mannāʾ al-Qaṭṭān, *Mabāḥith fī ʿulūm al-Qurʾān* (Cairo: Maktabat Wahbah, 2020); and Abdullah Saeed, *Interpreting the Qurʾan: Towards a Contemporary Approach* (London: Routledge, 2006).
67 Saeed, *Interpreting the Qurʾan*, 42.

their shared vocabulary or narratives, related linguistic structures, *raison d'être*, issues of specificity/generality, correlation, and so forth. This enterprise involves far more than simply reproducing transmitted materials. In the last resort, then, TQbQ is beset with *ijtihād* and subjective judgement. This is why exegetes may disagree on their methods of identifying which verses can be used to explain others.

To make this last point clear, let's examine two exegetes' differences in identifying cross-references. In his commentary, Ṭabarī suggests that the word *'asʿas* in Q 81:17 means "to turn back": "[I swear] by the night as it turns back." He supports his view by referring to the following verse "And by the morn as it breathes" (81:18). By cross-referencing these two verses, Ṭabarī concludes that the passage refers to the oath by the night as it departs and by the morning as it shows up (starts the day).[68] While Ibn Kathīr does not fully disagree with Ṭabarī, he contends that the word *'asʿas* is better understood as "to show up" (*aqbala*). This means that God takes oath by the night and its darkness when it comes/shows up and by the morning when and its brightness when it shines. This meaning, according to Ibn Kathīr, is explained by several verses, including Q 92:1, "By the night as it covers," 93:1, "And the night as it settles," and 6:96, "And He made the night for rest."[69] Thus, both Ṭabarī and Ibn Kathīr utilized interpretive reasoning and personal judgement not only in explicating the meaning of a verse with other verses, but also in their selection of cross-references.

Still, while TQbQ is dependent on discernment and *ijtihād*, it is equally problematic to associate it with reason-based exegesis for the simple reason that most exegetical works that are based on the principle of TQbQ rely heavily on the views of earlier authorities—such as Ṭabarī and Ibn Kathīr. As will be discussed in the following section, most modern exegetes who claim to follow the cross-referential procedure draw their materials from classical *tafsīr*s. Ultimately, the dichotomy between *tafsīr bi'l-ma'thūr* (tradition-based exegesis) and *tafsīr bi'l-ra'y* (reason-based exegesis) seems to be too simplistic of an analytical tool to explore the emerging form of TQbQ that has attracted modern Muslim scholars. Most of these scholars heavily rely on older materials, and their selection of these materials necessarily involves personal reasoning.[70]

---

68 Ṭabarī, *Jāmiʿ al-bayān*, 24:159–163.
69 Ibn Kathīr, *Tafsīr al-Qurʾān al-ʿaẓīm*, 14:269.
70 Walid Saleh argues that this *tafsīr bi'l-ma'thūr-tafsīr bi'l-ra'y* division is ideological aiming "at consolidating the mainstream Sunni interpretive tradition and undermining the non-Sunni approaches as well as deviant Sunni interpretations […]. Most of *the tafsīr bi'l-ma'thūr* is in reality a *tafsīr bi'l-ra'y*." See Walid Saleh, *The Formation of the Classical Tafsīr Tradition: The Commentary of al-Thaʿlabī (d. 427/1035)* (Leiden: Brill, 2004), 16.

Modern Endeavor and Its Controversy

While the usefulness of TQbQ was widely recognized by early exegetes, no one produced an exegetical work that could be exclusively identified as TQbQ until the modern period. The first *tafsīr* that follows the TQbQ method is the one composed by Muḥammad b. Ismāʿīl al-Amīr al-Ṣanʿānī (d. 1768), known as "Ibn al-Amīr," entitled *Mafātiḥ al-riḍwān fī tafsīr al-dhikr bi'l-āthār wa'l-Qur'ān (Keys to Paradise on the Interpretation of the Remembrance by the Transmitted Materials and the Qur'an)*.[71] Later publications on TQbQ appeared in the twentieth century, which marks the flourishing of this genre. I have come across several books which fall under the category "tafsīr al-Qur'ān bi'l-Qur'ān," some of which have stirred up controversy, which I will address shortly. In addition to Ibn al-Amīr's commentary, modern works of TQbQ include:

- *Tafsīr niẓām al-Qur'ān wa-ta'wīl al-furqān bi'l-furqān (The Interpretation of the Coherence of the Qur'an and the Ta'wīl of the Furqān by the Furqān)* by Ḥamīd al-Dīn al-Farāhī (d. 1930), published in 2008 in India (I wasn't able to find the publication date of the first edition). This one-volume book is comprised of 13 short chapters, and represents the application of his theory of "niẓām al-Qur'ān" (coherence of the Qur'an) which he developed in his other publications. In the Introduction, he writes, "I fully appreciate that the first thing to be resorted to in the task of interpreting the Qur'an is the Qur'an itself."[72]
- *Tafsīr al-Qur'ān bi-kalām al-Raḥmān (The Interpretation of the Qur'an by the Speech of the Merciful)* by Abū'l-Wafā' Thanā'ullāh al-Hindī al-Amritsarī (d. 1948), published in 1903 in India, most recently (in 2002) reprinted in one volume by Dār al-Salām in Riyadh. While most of his numerous books were in Urdu, this *tafsīr* was originally written in Arabic. In addition to his extensive use of cross-references, the author sometimes refers to prophetic traditions, including occasions of revelation. In his explication of the Qur'an, the author often addresses theological issues with the purpose of offering his corrections of what he considers "deviant groups."
- *Al-Hidāyah wa'l-ʿirfān fī tafsīr al-Qur'ān bi'l-Qur'ān (Guidance and Gnosis in the Interpretation of the Qur'an)* by Muḥammad Abū Zayd al-Damanhūrī, published in 1930 in Egypt. This three-volume work includes the Arabic Qur'an with commentaries on selected verses placed at the margins. While his comments are often brief, he includes useful cross-references of other parts of the Qur'an. The author is critical of the existing *tafsīr* literature, arguing that Muslim exegetes have devel-

---
[71] ʿAbd al-Raḥmān b. Sūqān al-Zahrānī edited a small portion of this book (from Q 26 to 311) in his M.A. thesis presented to the Islamic University of Medina in 1989, entitled *Mafātīḥ al-riḍwān fī tafsīr al-dhikr bi'l-āthār wa'l-Qur'ān min sūrat aal-Shuʿarā' ilā sūrat Luqmān* (M.A. Thesis, al-Jāmiʿah al-Islāmiyyah, Madīnah, 1410 H).
[72] ʿAbd al-Ḥamīd al-Farāhī, *Tafsīr niẓām al-Qur'ān wa-ta'wīl al-Furqān bi'l-Furqān* (Azamgarh: Dairah Hameedia Madrasatul Islam, 2008), 23.

oped their own categories (e. g., legal and theological) as principles with which they judged the Qur'an. This urges him to develop his own Qur'anist approach, principally relying on the text of revelation itself.

- *Aḍwā' al-bayān fī Īḍāḥ al-Qur'ān bi'l-Qur'ān (The Lights of Clarification on the Explanation of the Qur'an by the Qur'an)* by Muḥammad al-Amīn al-Shinqīṭī (d. 1972), published in 1967 in Egypt. This seven-volume book represents a verse-by-verse interpretation of the Qur'an, up through verse 22 of chapter 58 (*al-Mujādilah*). A rich source for understanding the Qur'an, this book includes cross-references and detailed discussions on select theological and legal issues, mostly through explorations of medieval exegetical works.
- *Al-Tafsīr al-Qur'ānī li'l-Qur'ān (The Qur'anic Interpretation of the Qur'an)* by 'Abd al-Karīm Maḥmūd al-Khatīb (d. 1985), published in 1967–1970 in Egypt. This five-volume book, although it is divided into sixteen parts covering the whole Qur'an, represents a novel approach to TQbQ in which the author expresses his personal experience with the text without reliance on the transmitted materials or the views of early authorities. At the beginning of each chapter, he provides basic information concerning the context of revelation (Meccan or Medinan), the number of verses, words, and letters as well as the various titles that have been given to the chapter. His primary concern is to convey his understanding of the verse at hand in light of other passages, and to find unity within each chapter.
- *Al-Furqān fī tafsīr al-Qur'ān bi'l-Qur'ān wa'l-sunnah (The Furqān on the Interpretation of the Qur'an by the Qur'an and Sunnah)* by Mohammad Sadeqi Tehrani, published in 1986 in Iran. This book consists of 30 volumes and, without a doubt, is the most comprehensive in its treatment of the Qur'an. As its title suggests, the author resorts to both the Qur'an and prophetic tradition, in addition to the views of various Shi'ite imāms. In the Introduction to his *tafsīr*, he argues that while the obedience to God, the Prophet, and the imāms is necessary, the Qur'an nonetheless remains "the solid base" (*qā'idah rāsinah*).[73] What makes this exegesis unique is that it brings together extensive cross-references—even between those verses whose connections may not be easily detected.
- *Al-Bayān bi'l-Qur'ān (Clarification by the Qur'an)* by Muṣṭafā Kamāl al-Mahdawī, published in 1990 in Libya. This two-volume book follows the Qur'anist approach by explaining the Qur'an in light of itself, without relying on any external sources. He draws on extensive verses of the Qur'an to support the idea that the Qur'an is its own interpreter. Like Abū Zayd, he is critical of traditional exegesis that does not go beyond the transmitted materials. Unlike other TQbQ, however, the author focuses on "selected Qur'anic laws (*aḥkām al-kitāb*) that we derive from

---

[73] Mohammad Sadeqi Tehrani, *al-Furqān fī tafsīr al-Qur'ān bi'l-Qur'ān wa'l-sunna* (Beirut: Dār al-Turāth al-'Islāmī, 1985), 17.

the Qur'an in light of its clear verses which interpret one another."[74] It is worth noting that this book includes a substantial introduction (78 pages!) in which the author makes a case for his method.

- *Tafsīr al-Fārūq: Tafsīr al-Qur'ān bi'l-Qur'ān (The Interpretation of Fārūq: Interpreting the Qur'an by the Qur'an)* by Maulana Muhammad al-Faruq, published in 2004 in Pakistan. This book is published in two versions: One with short commentaries on each verse, and the other without commentaries but simply a list of cross-references. He claims that his aim is to help students (*tullāb al-'ilm*) who desire to understand the Qur'an by putting together relevant passages in such a way that they can clarify the meaning of a given verse. Concerning his method, he says, "I was trying not to include any verse unless I found an exegete of the previous generation already considered it relevant for that verse."[75] This book is also available in Urdu.

- *Tafsīr al-Qur'ān bi'l-Qur'ān (The Interpretation of the Qur'an by the Qur'an)* by Ṭāhā Jābir al-'Alwānī (d. 2016), published in 2020 in the United States. This book represents a significant contribution to the field of TQbQ, despite the fact that it only covers 11 chapters. In addition to drawing on extensive cross-references in his interpretation of the Qur'an, the author discusses specific virtues which constitute the "central theme" (*'amūd*) of each chapter. He describes his method as "tadabbur" (deep reflection) which is clearly evident in his critical engagement with both the classical sources and the project of rethinking the Qur'an in the modern context.

- *Mafhūm-ul-Qur'ān* by Ghulam Ahmed Parwez (d. 1985), published in 1961 in Pakistan. This three-volume book is one of the few non-Arabic books on the subject that have been published. Originally written in Urdu, this book includes a long introduction (32 pages) in which Parwez explains the situation leading to the production of this work as well as his defense for advancing his Qur'anist approach. It's therefore hardly surprising that Parwez utilizes cross-references to a large extent. The English version of this book appears in 1987 under the title *Exposition of the Holy Qur'an*.

- *Der Koran: Kommentar und Konkordanz* by Rudi Paret (d. 1983), published in 1966 in Germany. This book offers a brief commentary on almost every verse of the Qur'an by providing extensive cross-references to compare the Qur'anic usage and concepts. Although Paret uses the word "Konkordanz," this book not only tracks the Qur'anic incidence of particular words, but also of similar phrases, grammatical forms, and related subject matter throughout the text. In addition to various cross-references, this work also includes alternate renderings and interpretations

---

[74] Muṣṭafā Kamāl al-Mahdawī, *al-Bayān bi'l-Qur'ān* (Benghazi: Dār al-Kutub al-Waṭaniyyah, 1990), 1:9.

[75] Maulana Muhammad al-Faruq, *Tafsīr al-Fārūq*. Both versions of this *tafsīr* are available online at http://www.tafseeralfarooq.com/ (accessed 4 April 2022).

of particular verses or passages, well as references to relevant scholarly studies, often with a short critical assessment.
- *The Qur'an as It Explains Itself* by Shabir Ahmed, first published in 2003 in the United States. This book includes the Arabic text of the Qur'an and Ahmed's translation with brief commentaries and cross-references. In the Introduction to the 6th edition (2016), Ahmed acknowledges that he has "purposely refrained from explaining the Qur'an through extrinsic sources such as Hadith and a very questionable History."[76] For Ahmed, explaining the Qur'an through non-Qur'anic sources, which were collected centuries later, "has only served to confound the Word of God with man-made traditions and it takes away the profound glory of the Divine Message."[77] Thus, he prefers to look at the Qur'an on its own terms and concepts because such a method "has helped me explain every verse from within the Qur'an itself."[78]

I have benefitted from the above books in preparing the present volume.[79]

To further illustrate the excitement of TQbQ in the modern exegesis of the Qur'an, the past few years have witnessed an unprecedented interest in the study of this genre, especially in Arabic. This is evident in the number of publications on the subject, including Ph.D. and M.A. theses. In 2011, Dr. Muḥsin b. Ḥāmid al-Muṭayrī published his study, entitled *Tafsīr al-Qur'ān bi'l-Qur'ān: Ta'ṣīl wa-taqwīn (The Interpretation of the Qur'an by the Qur'an: Authentication and Assessment)*, in which he examines parameters to be observed by anyone interested in practicing TQbQ.[80] The historical development of TQbQ has recently been studied by Dr. Muḥammad Qajwī in a monograph titled *Tafsīr al-Qur'ān bi'l-Qur'ān: Dirāsah tārīkhiyyah naẓariyyah (The Interpretation of the Qur'an by the Qur'an: Historical and Theoretical Studies)*.[81] Both books are based on their Ph.D. dissertations. A similar study on TQbQ is Dr. Aḥmad b. Muḥammad al-Barīdī's *Tafsīr al-Qur'ān bi'l-Qur'ān: Dirāsah ta'ṣīliyyah (The Interpretation of the Qur'an by the Qur'an: A Detailed Study)*.[82] These three publications mostly

---

[76] Shabir Ahmed, *The Qur'an as It Explains Itself* (Lighthouse, 2003), xii. The sixth edition is available at: http://drshabbir.com/library/qxp_vi_english.pdf (accessed 4 April 2022).
[77] Ibid.
[78] Ibid.
[79] There are other works of TQbQ that, unfortunately, I have not been able to acquire, including *Tafsīr al-kitāb bi'l-kitāb (The Interpretation of Scripture by Scripture)* by 'Abd al-Raḥmān b. 'Abd al-'Anbar al-Ṭahṭāwī and *Tafsīr al-Qur'ān min al-Qur'ān fī dā'irat al-'ilm wa'l-'aql wa'l-waqi' al-maḥsūs (The Interpretation of the Qur'an from the Qur'an within the Realms of Knowledge, Reason, and Tangible Reality)* by Aḥmad Fā'iq Rushd.
[80] Dr. Muḥsin b. Ḥāmid al-Muṭayrī, *Tafsīr al-Qur'ān bi'l-Qur'ān: Ta'ṣīl wa-taqwīn*.
[81] Dr. Muḥammad Qajwī, *Tafsīr al-Qur'ān bi'l-Qur'ān: Dirāsah tārīkhiyyah naẓariyyah*.
[82] Dr. Aḥmad b. Muḥammad al-Barīdī, *Tafsīr al-Qur'ān bi'l-Qur'ān: Dirāsah ta'ṣīliyyah*, published by the *Majallat ma'had al-imām al-Shāṭibī li'l-dirāsāt al-Islāmiyyah* 2 (2006).

share commonalities in their treatment of the subject and reflect a growing interest in the scholarly study of TQbQ.

Of the aforementioned TQbQ works, Shinqīṭī's *Aḍwā' al-bayān* has drawn a great deal of scholarly attention. A quick online search reveals that at least 9 Ph.D. dissertations and 14 M.A. theses on Shinqīṭī's *tafsīr* have been written at various universities throughout the Arab Middle East.[83] Most of these studies praise Shinqīṭī's *tafsīr* for its encyclopedic nature, as it brings together not only Qur'anic cross-references but also detailed, nuanced discussions on legal and theological issues. Despite its title, which seems to suggest a focus on interpreting the Qur'an by the Qur'an, Shinqīṭī heavily relies on transmitted materials, including both prophetic tradition and the traditions of the next two generations, as well as later exegetical works. On several occasions, he offers insightful discussions of certain legal issues by presenting different views among Muslim jurists (*ikhtilāf al-fuqahā'*) on the subject. In this way, he broadens the content of TQbQ through traditional sources and, at the same time, addresses various juridical issues. This sense of comprehensiveness seems to have attracted the interest of students. Therefore, studies on his *tafsīr* not only focus on his exegetical method, but also his use of sunnah and transmitted materials (*āthār*), or his legal preferences (*ittijāh fiqhī*). Ahmad Shāyif al-Damīnī, for instance, wrote his dissertation on the law of marriage and divorce in Shinqīṭī's *Aḍwā' al-bayān*.[84]

This vibrancy of TQbQ, however, is not without its own dynamics. While Shinqīṭī's *tafsīr* has been applauded for its fidelity to the tradition, a few others have caused backlash on account of their deviation from tradition-based exegesis. For instance, two major works of modern TQbQ have been accused of being rationalistic, materialistic and even atheistic, and hence inauthentic: Abū Zayd's *al-Hidāyah wa'l-'Irfān* and Muṣṭafā Kamāl al-Mahdawī's *al-Bayān bi'l-Qur'ān*. As mentioned earlier, Abū Zayd represents the Qur'anist approach *par excellence*. In his own words, "the Qur'an interprets itself as God tells it and does not need anything external to it."[85] As for the sunnah of the Prophet, he argues that "it is the practical implementation of the Qur'an, and thus the task of the Prophet is only to deliver the Qur'an and to guide people in living with it." In his interpretation of Q 24:63, "So let those who oppose his orders beware, lest an ordeal strikes them, or a painful punishment befalls them," Abū Zayd argues that the warning in this verse concerns objection to the Prophet's

---

[83] My online search reveals the following: 7 Ph.D. dissertations and 3 M.A. theses in Sudan; 1 Ph.D. dissertation and 3 M.A. Theses in Saudi Arabia; 1 Ph.D. dissertation and 1 M.A. Thesis in Tunisia; 2 M.A. Theses in Algeria, Iraq, and Jordan; 1 M.A. Thesis in Egypt.

[84] Aḥmad Shāyif al-Damīnī, *Fiqh al-nikāḥ wa'l-ṭalāq min kitāb Aḍwā' al-bayān li'l-Shaykh Muḥammad al-Amīn al-Shinqīṭhī: Dirāsah muqāranah* (Ph.D. dissertation, Omdurman Islamic University, Sudan, 2010).

[85] Muḥammad Abū Zayd al-Damanhūrī, *al-Hidāyah wa'l-'irfān fī tafsīr al-Qur'ān bi'l-Qur'ān* (Cairo: Maṭba'at Muṣṭafā al-Bābī al-Ḥalabī, 1930), jīm.

order. "There is nothing wrong with having differences with the Prophet's order," he says, "as long as it is based on reason and public interest."[86]

Abū Zayd calls for freedom of expression and argues that the Muslim understanding of the Qur'an should not be confined to the views of previous exegetes, because they are shaped by their own historical contexts. Since the context has changed, "restricting the Qur'an to their views is dangerous because that will make it irrelevant in every situation."[87] Therefore, different interpretations should be welcome. He challenges scholars of his time for their close-mindedness. "It is unfortunate," he says, "that when one of us develops an idea that contradicts their understanding, they assail us with curse and slander. That is the biggest cause of the Muslim decadence."[88] Abū Zayd seems to have anticipated what will happen with his TQbQ: his unorthodox renderings and interpretations of certain Qur'anic passages were condemned by conservative Muslims.

Both Muḥammad Ḥusayn al-Dhahabī and Fahd b. 'Abd al-Raḥmān al-Rūmī denounce Abū Zayd's *tafsīr* as an atheistic form of exegesis (*ilḥādī*).[89] They identify several problems with his interpretation of both legal and theological verses, such as the punishments for adultery (Q 24:2) and theft (5:38), polygamy (4:3), divorce (65:1), usury (2:278–280; 3:130), the Prophets' miracles (about Jesus in 3:39; 5:110; about Moses in 7:160; 26:63; about Abraham in 21:69; about Muhammad in 17:1), the existence of Angels, jinn and demons (e. g. 2:34; 27:17; 38:37) and the prophethood of Adam (e. g. 20:115, 121). According to Abū Zayd, Q 24:2 refers specifically to male and female adulterers whose adultery is well-known and habitual, and who have no interest in getting married. To reinforce his view, he refers to Q 5:5, 38; 4:25; and 17:32.[90] So also the punishment for theft (5:38) should only be applied to a thief who steals habitually—not someone who steals, say, once or twice. He also argues that the amputation of hands must be strictly a last resort, "when all other treatments have failed."[91] His rationalist approach also leads him to reject the existence of unseen creatures such as Angels, jinn and demons. In his booklet, *Mudhakkarat Abū Zayd fī qaḍiyyat Ādam*, he argues that there is no textual proof, either the Qur'an or reliable hadith, to suggest that belief in Adam's prophethood is core part of the Islamic faith. As he argues, the Qur'an refers to Adam's neglect and disobedience (20:115 and 121), a wrongdoing which makes him unqualified to be an infallible prophet.[92]

---

86 Ibid., 281.
87 Ibid., ḥā'.
88 Ibid., zāy.
89 Dhahabī, *al-Tafsīr wa'l-mufassirūn*, 2:390–400; Fahd b. 'Abd al-Raḥmān b. Sulaymān al-Rūmī, *Ittijāt al-tafsīr fī al-qarn al-rābi' 'ashar* (Beirut: Mu'assasat al-Risālah, 1997), 5:1076–1104.
90 Abū Zayd, *al-Hidāyah wa'l-'irfān*, 2:274.
91 Ibid., 1:88.
92 Abū Zayd, *Mudhakkarat Abū Zayd fī qaḍiyyat Ādam*, cited by Dr. 'Alī Jum'ah, "Bayn al-tajdīd wa'l-tabdīd: Muḥammad Abū Zayd al-Damanhūrī namūdhajan," *Majallat kulliyat al-dirāsāt al-Islāmiyyah* (2017), 257–298.

Soon after the publication of Abū Zayd's *al-Hidāyah wa'l-'irfān*, scholars of al-Azhar, including its shaykh Muḥammad Aḥmadī al-Zawāhirī, examined the book and issued a 75-page report strongly criticizing the *tafsīr* and urging the authorities to prohibit him from preaching in mosques or holding religious meetings.[93] Rashīd Riḍā (d. 1935) published four essays in his journal *al-Manār* condemning Abū Zaid's *tafsīr* and accusing him of apostasy.[94] He also sent his articles to popular daily *al-Ahrām* to reach a wider audience. As a consequence, a group of conservative 'ulama from Damanhur, the birthplace of Abū Zayd, took him to the court to have him declared an apostate and separated from his wife. The local court did declare Abū Zayd's apostasy, however, the Cairo court of appeals ruled in his favor. As Amy Ayalon notes, "After that no more was heard of Muḥammad Abū Zayd. He and his story sank into oblivion."[95]

Like Abū Zayd in Egypt in the 1930s, Mahdawī's *al-Bayān bi'l-Qur'ān* sparked a major controversy in Libya in the 1990s. Soon after the publication of his book, Mahdawī was under ferocious attack led by Libyan conservative Muslims and the press. They took him to court in the city of Benghazi. While the court of appeals acquitted him, it nonetheless prohibited the distribution or the reprinting of his book.[96] Mahdawī's approach is similar to that of Abū Zayd: he interprets the Qur'an without reliance on transmitted materials, including prophetic tradition. He rejects the commonly held idea that sunnah can explain the Qur'an. Since his book focuses on selected legal issues, it is understandable that his treatment of the subject is much more detailed than that of Abū Zayd. His discussion of punishments for adultery and theft, for instance, is quite elaborate. Like Abū Zayd, he does not distinguish whether the offender is married or non-married adult. On the basis of Q 24:2, the punishment for adultery is considered to be one hundred lashes, and this punishment should only be applied to those who repeatedly committed adultery, for the Qur'an describes "al-zānī" (*the* adulterer) with a definite article (al-), which suggests a known (and habitual) actor. That is also the case with stealing (Q 5:38). To support his contention, Mahdawī draws on Q 4:16, "If two men among you commit it, punish them both. But if they repent and reform, leave them alone. God is Redeemer, Full of Mercy," arguing that those who commit adultery under a specific situation are not properly described as adulterers with a definite article, and thus Q 24:2 is not applicable.[97]

Of course, without reliance on prophetic tradition, Islamic practice will take on a wholly different form—after all, it is primarily from sunnah that the details of Islamic

---

[93] Arthur Jeffery, "The suppressed Qur'an Commentary of Abu Zaid," *Der Islam* 20 (1932), 301–308. See also H.A.R. Gibb, *Modern Trends in Islam* (Chicago: Chicago University Press, 1947), 54.
[94] See *al-Manār*, June 1931: 673–97; July 1931: 753–70; October 1931: 33–48.
[95] Amy Aylon, *Egypt's Quest for Cultural Orientation* (Moshe Dayan Center for Middle Eastern and African Studies, Tel Aviv University, 1999), 5.
[96] Reports about lawsuits against Mahdawī can be found in 'Abd al-Karīm al-Dinā', *Muḥākamat al-Bayān bi'l-Qur'ān* (Libya: Dār al-Anīs li'l-Ṭibā'ah, 1998), 25–90.
[97] Mahdawī, *al-Bayān bi'l-Qur'ān*, 1:343–356.

law are derived. According to Mahdawī's reading of Q 30:17–18; 17:78–79 and 2:187, morning prayer is not obligatory and should be performed after sunrise, not before.[98] He also contends that there is no Qur'anic evidence to support the idea that menstruating women should not pray or fast, because Q 2:222 concerns the matter of physical purity, which can be achieved with a partial or full ablution.[99] Pilgrimage can be performed anytime during the four months mentioned in Q 2:197 and 9:2, namely, Shawwāl, Dhu'l-Qaʿdah, Dhu'l-Hijjah and Muḥarram.[100] Likewise, the rites of pilgrimage are limited to those mentioned in Q 22:29, 36–37; 2:1255, 158, 196, 198, and 200. On the basis of Q 22:29, he argues that there is no prescribed number of *ṭawāf* (circumambulating the Kaʿbah), as the term *wa'l-yaṭṭawwafū* means "circumambulate repeatedly around the ancient house."[101]

In addition, his interpretation of various legal terms contradicts the traditional understanding. For instance, Q 4:43, "Do not approach the prayer while you are intoxicated (*sukārā*)" is understood differently. The word *sukārā* is commonly rendered "drunk" or "intoxicated" due to drinking wine. For Mahdawī, Q 4:43 simply refers to those whose minds are unconscious on account of their preoccupation with worldly affairs.[102] In his discussion of Qur'anic verses dealing with wine and gambling (e. g. 5:90), he rejects the idea of abrogation. While the Qur'an itself uses the word *naskh* (2:106), his rejection of the classical principle of *naskh* seems to represent an extension of his method of TQbQ. In another vein, his views on "polygamy" (Q 4:3) and the "gentile/unlettered prophet" (7:157) seem to reflect the findings of recent scholarship. Indeed, some of his critics have accused him of being influenced by "claims of orientalists and missionaries and whoever follows their views – not knowingly – among our thinkers and exegetes aiming to humiliate the Qur'an. They say that the Prophet was not illiterate but able to read and write in order to maintain that the Qur'an is nothing but a summary of the teachings of the Gospel and the Torah which the Prophet received from Rabbis and monks."[103]

Mahdawī's unorthodox and unconventional views have made him the target of attacks by traditional ulama from the Arab Middle East. Sayyid b. Ḥusayn al-ʿAffānī strongly criticizes Mahdawī using the worst possible descriptions, including "dajjāl" (deceiver), "ḍāll" (deviant), "maʾfūn" (idiot), and so forth. In his book refuting what he calls the "rational school" (*madrasah ʿaqliyyah*), ʿAffānī groups Mahdawī's

---

98 Ibid., 1:108.
99 Mahdawī writes, "We do not find in the Book of God anything that allows a menstruating woman not to pray or fast." Ibid., 1:118.
100 Ibid., 1:87.
101 Ibid., 1:93.
102 Ibid., 1:114.
103 Ramaḍān al-Barkī, "Kitāb... wa-qaḍiyyah," *Majallah Lāʾ* 23 (1992). This article is included in ʿAbd al-Karīm al-Dīnāʾ, *Muḥākamat al-Bayān biʾl-Qurʾān*, 120. This book is a collection of articles and court documents surrounding the controversies of Mahdawī's book.

tafsīr among the rejecters of sunnah.[104] This tendency to regard those who deviate from mainstream, traditional exegesis as whimsical and capricious, using personal opinion as their guide, is likewise the cause of earlier controversies involving classical exegetes such as the Muʿtazilī Zamakhsharī, who expresses a sympathetic view towards TQbQ. Zamakhsharī has been condemned for interpreting certain Qurʾanic passages in a way that deviates from the mainstream traditionalist position. A good example of this is his interpretation of Q 6:82: "Those who believe and do not obscure their faith with *ẓulm* [wrongdoing] – those will have security, and they are guided." Unlike the vast majority of Sunni exegetes who follow the Prophet's understanding of *ẓulm* as *shirk* (polytheism) as we discussed earlier, he interprets the term as "disobedience" (*maʿṣiyyah*), arguing that "what prevents the interpretation of *ẓulm* as 'unbelief' is the word *lubs* ('obscure' or 'confuse')."[105] It is unlikely that Zamakhsharī was unaware of the Prophetic *tafsīr*, for most exegetes prior to him, such Ṭabarī (d. 310/923), Samarqandī (d. 375/985), Thaʿlabī (d. 427/1035), Māwardī (d. 450/1058), Wāḥidī (d. 450/1058), and Ṭūsī (d. 460/1067), cited this hadith.[106] Even those who do not explicitly mention it, such as Muqātil b. Sulaymān (d.150/767, interpreted *ẓulm* as *shirk*.[107] However, Zamakhsharī's interpretation is in line with the Muʿtazilite doctrine that a believer can commit sin/disobedience, but one cannot be a believer and sinner at the same time.

Abū Ḥayyān al-Andalusī (d.745/1344) notices the sectarian underpinnings of Zamakhsharī's interpretation, which aims to reinforce his personal beliefs and the doctrine of his sect. While it is also possible that Zamakhsharī does not consider the hadith authentic, Abū Ḥayyān nonetheless criticizes him, arguing that "the Prophet's interpretation must be accepted."[108] The contrast between Muʿtazilite and mainstream Sunni interpretations is highlighted by Rāzī, who problematizes the Muʿtazilite view on two grounds. Firstly, the meaning of *ẓulm* as *shirk* can be established by another verse (Q 31:13). In addition to cross-reference, Rāzī contends that the context of Q 6:82 buttresses the view of his groups (*aṣḥābunā*, our friends) since the preceding and

---

104 Dr. Sayyid b.Ḥusayn al-ʿAffānī, *Riyāḍ al-jannah fī al-radd ʿalā al-madrasah al-ʿaqliyyah wa-munkirī al-sunnah* (Cairo: Dār al-ʿAffānī, 2005), 58–68. See also idem, *Wā Muhammadahū: Inna shāʾniaka huwaʾl-abtar*, (Cairo: Dār al-ʿAffānī, 2006), 2:540–543.
105 Zamakhsharī, *al-Kashshāf*, 335.
106 Ṭabarī, *Jāmiʿ al-bayān*, 9:368; Abūʾl-Layth al-Samarqandī, *Baḥr al-ʿulūm*, ʿAlī Muḥammad al-Muʿawwaḍ et al. (Beirut: Dār al-kutub al-ʿilmiyyah, 1993), 1:498; Abū Isḥāq Aḥmad al-Thaʿlabī *al-Kashf waʾl-bayān*, ed. ʿAlī b. ʿĀshūr (Beirut: Dār iḥyāʾ al-Turāth al-ʿArabī, 2002), 4:166; Abūʾl-Ḥasan al-Māwardī, *al-Nukat waʾl-ʿuyūn*, ed. al-Sayyd b. ʿAbd al-Maqṣūd (Beirut: Dār al-Kutub al-ʿIlmiyyah, n.d.), 2:138; ʿAlī b. Aḥmad al-Wāḥidī, *al-Wasīṭ fī tafsīr al-Qurʾān al-Majīd*, ʿĀdil Aḥmad ʿAbd al-Mawjūd et al. (Beirut: Dār al-Kutub al-ʿIlmiyyah, 1994), 2:293; Muḥammad b. al-Ḥasan al-Ṭūsī, *al-Tibyān fī tafsīr al-Qurʾān*, ed. Aḥmad Ḥabīb Qusayr al-ʿĀmilī (Beirut: Dār Iḥyāʾ al-Turāth al-ʿArabī, n.d.), 4:190.
107 Muqātil b. Sulaymān, *Tafsīr Muqātil b. Sulaymān*, d. ʿAbd Allāh Maḥmūd Shaḥḥātah (Beirut: Muʾassasat al-Tārīkh al-ʿArabī, 2002), 1:573.
108 Abū Ḥayyān on 6:82.

following verses are concerned with negating God's partners or other deities, and nothing is mentioned about obedience. Rāzī writes, "thus, the word *ẓulm* here must be understood as *shirk*."¹⁰⁹ Secondly, Rāzī attempts to prove that a sinner remains a believer, arguing the divine threat (*waʿīd*)) against a sinner does not mean she/he will positively be punished—for God may punish or forgive her/him as He wishes.

Interestingly, Rāzī does not refer to Zamakhsharī by name, but rather addresses his criticism to Muʿtazilites broadly. The nineteenth century Yemeni scholar Muḥammad b. ʿAbd Allāh al-Shawkānī (d. 1839) expressed his astonishment at Zamakhshari's view, saying "It is weird that the author of *al-Kashshāf* refuses to interprets '*ẓulm*' as unbelief (*kufr*) because of the word *lubs* (obscure), while he knows that God has explained in that way."¹¹⁰ He continues arguing that reason cannot contradict the Divine's explanation. The modern Syrian exegete, Jamāl al-Dīn al-Qāsimī (d. 1914) cites Rāzī in his criticism of Zamakhsharī. He refers to Zamakhsharī's view as a hallucination (*hadhaya*) and accuses him of being captivated by Muʿtazilite doctrine. Qāsimī contends the Sunnis' view is based on a conclusive proof (*dalīl qaṭʿī*) which cannot be repudiated. Any attempt to reject this proof, Qāsimī claims, is a "great slander" (*buhtān aẓīm*). As he writes, "O my God, how strange are those people who compare the sound sunnah with the worthless reason, why are they not shamed from God and His messenger with their transgression? Where do their reasons take them? To the truth or to falsehood?"¹¹¹

The controversy over the rationalist or Qurʾanist impulse of certain TQbQ works is a significant part of this genre's dynamics. By simply emphasizing the significance of TQbQ, one risks being categorized as a Qurʾanist. The Iranian Mohammad Sadeqi Tehrani, for instance, has been charged with "Qurʾan sufficiency,"¹¹² despite the fact that he titled his work *Tafsīr al-Qurʾān biʾl-Qurʾān waʾl-sunnah*. However, TQbQ continues to flourish not only among scholars who developed the genre through their publications, as mentioned above, but also in the works of exegetes who follow the traditional paradigm. The Iranian Muḥammad Ḥusayn Ṭabāṭabāʾī (d. 1981), for instance, often claims to explore the meaning of a verse or a set of verses that can be established by other parts of the Qurʾan, even though he does not title his exegesis as a work of TQbQ. For Ṭabāṭabāʾī, letting the Qurʾan speak by itself is "the oldest inherited method in *tafsīr*."¹¹³

---

109 Rāzī, *Mafātīḥ al-ghayb*, 13:64.
110 Muḥammad b. ʿAbd Allāh al-Shawkānī, *Fatḥ al-qadīr al-jāmiʿ bayn fannay al-riwāyah waʾl-dirāyah min ʿilm al-tafsīr*, ed. Yūsuf al-Ghūsh (Beirut: Dār al-Fikr, 2007), 1:431.
111 Jamāl al-Dīn al-Qāsimī, *Maḥāsin al-taʾwīl*, ed. Muḥammad Bāsil ʿUyūn al-Sūd (Beirut: Dār al-Kutub al-ʿIlmiyyah, 2003), 4:415.
112 Seyed Ali Hosseini Dolatabad, Hossein Naseri Moghadam, and Ali Reza Abedi Sar Asiya, "Pillars, Proofs, and Requirements of the Quran-Sufficiency Theory, Along with Its Criticism," *International Journal of Humanities and Cultural Studies* 2 (2016:4), 2303–2319.
113 Muḥammad Ḥusayn Ṭabāṭabāʾī, *al-Mīzān fī tafsīr al-Qurʾān* (Beirut: Muʾassasat al-Aʿlā liʾl-Maṭbūʿāt, 1997), 1:17.

Thematic Approaches and Cross-References

In the final section of this Introduction, we will turn to the development of "thematic interpretation" (*tafsīr mawḍūʿī*) and its main characteristics. The TQbQ method, with its use of cross-references, naturally lends itself to systematic examinations of various subjects based on all relevant verses, and has thus given rise to this emerging subfield of Qur'anic interpretation. At the heart of thematic interpretation is the idea that a proper examination of Qur'anic cross-referentiality enables an exegete to discern what the Muslim scripture has to say about a certain topic or a set of topics. There is no question that thematic interpretation opens up new perspectives which the study of isolated, individual verses cannot offer—for, *tafsīr mawḍūʿī* involves closely examining the Qur'anic views on a specific topic, or the unifying theme of each chapter, or how a particular word or phrase is presented in the entire Qur'an. Therefore, thematic interpretation might be thought of as an extension of TQbQ with a specific focus on selected topics. Those who adopt this exegetical method examine various themes which the Qur'an presents in different chapters (*sūrahs*) by gathering all relevant verses and connecting different parts of the Qur'an to form a complete picture of a select theme. Like TQbQ, it is only in the twentieth century that exegetical works of this genre came to fruition, though its significance might have been alluded to by earlier exegetes.

Some scholars contend that *tafsīr mawḍūʿī* was first taught by Shaykh Aḥmad al-Kūmī as a separate course at Al-Azhar University in Egypt in the 1960s, which has since inspired several studies and publications.[114] The first dissertation on the subject was written by an Azhari student, Dr. Muḥammad Maḥmūd Hijāzī, entitled *al-Wiḥdah al-mawḍūʿiyyah fī al-Qurʾān al-karīm (The Unified Theme in the Noble Qur'an)*, published in 1970. In this book, Hijāzī outlines the exegetical procedure of thematic interpretation as follows: (1) collecting verses on one topic; (2) arranging them according to their occasions of revelation; (3) Examining their occurrence in the sūrah through an examination of their context; and (4) analyzing various themes in which those verses occur in order to understand the ultimate purpose, which is the unified theme in the Qur'an.[115] Other authors develop different procedures, depending on whether their unit of analysis is themes within the sūrah or the entire Qur'an.[116]

It should be noted, however, that Western scholars have likewise paid attention to thematic issues of the Qur'an from the early twentieth century onward. This work was

---

114 See Muṣṭafā Muslim, *Mabāḥith fī al-tafsīr al-mawḍūʿī* (Damascus: Dār al-Qalam, 2000), 17.
115 See Dr. Muḥammad Maḥmūd Hijāzī, *al-Wiḥdah al-mawḍūʿiyyah fī'l-Qurʾān al-karīm* (Cairo: Maṭbaʿat al-Madanī, 1970), 23–24.
116 For theoretical discussions on thematic interpretation, see ʿAbd al-Sattār Fatḥ Allāh Saʿīd, *al-Madkhal ilā al-tafsīr al-mawḍūʿī* (Cairo: Dār al-Nashr wa'l-Tawzīʿ, 1990); Ziyād al-Daghghāmīn, *Manhajiyyat al-baḥth fī al-tafsīr al-mawḍūʿī* (Amman: Dār al-Bashīr, 1995); Sāmir Riswānī, *Manhaj al-tafsīr al-mawḍūʿī* (Syria: Dār al-Multaqā, 2009).

perhaps facilitated by the availability of Qur'anic concordances, produced by nineteenth century scholars like Gustave Flügel (d. 1870) and Jules La Beaume (d. 1876).[117] Themes treated in these early twentieth-century publications include a variety of topics from Divine names to proper names, to Christians, Biblical narratives, to unseen creatures such as jinns, demons, and Angels.[118] Scholarly attention to major themes has expanded rapidly in recent years with the publication of various encyclopaedias and dictionaries of the Qur'an. The popularity of the "thematic content" approach to the Qur'an is also evident in the publication of handbooks of and/or companions to the Qur'an, which include discussions of certain themes and topics. *The Oxford Handbook of Qur'anic Studies*, for example, has a specific section (part v) on "Topics and Themes of the Qur'an."[119] Both *The Cambridge Companion to the Qur'an* and *The Blackwell Companion to the Qur'an* also address thematic contents of the Muslim scripture.

In Muslim scholarship, the Egyptian literary scholar Amīn al-Khūlī (d. 1966) is among the first to call for a thematic approach to the Qur'an. For Khūlī, thematic interpretation involves careful research of Qur'anic terms, phrases and sentences using literary tools, and paying attention to the culture and history of the text. According to Khūlī, interpreting the Qur'an verse-by-verse or chapter-by-chapter will not allow for deep understanding and correct knowledge of its meanings and objectives, except through a thorough examination of the entire Qur'an. The fact that the Qur'an is not thematic, he argues, "requires an exegete to interpret the Qur'an topic-by-topic by putting together all relevant verses on one topic with knowledge of their historical contexts, their coherence and interconnectedness, and by looking closely to explain and understand them. Such hermeneutical procedure is better guided to the meaning and more coherent in its definition."[120]

Some of Khūlī's students who applied this literary method have become famous for a variety of reasons. Ahmad Khalafallah, for instance, wrote a dissertation under Khūlī's supervision, entitled *al-Fann al-qaṣaṣī fī'l-Qur'ān al-karīm (Narrative Art in the*

---

[117] Gustave Flügel, *Nujūm al-Furqān fī aṭrāf al-Qur'ān: Concordantiae Corani Arabicae* (Leipzig: Bredtil, 1842); Jules La Beaume, *Le Koran analysé* (Maisonneuve, 1878).
[118] Maurice Gaudefroy-Demombynes, "Sur quelques noms d'Allah dans le Coran," Paris, Ecole Pratique des Hautes Etudes, Section des Sciences Religieuses, *Annuaire* (1929–30), 3–21; Josef Horovitz, "Jewish Proper Names and Derivatives in the Koran," *Hebrew Union College Annual* 2 (1925), 145–227; Anton Baumstark, "Jüdischer und christlicher Gebetstypus im Koran," *Der Islam* 16 (1927), 229–248; Samuel Sycz, *Ursprung und Wiedergabe der biblischen Eigennamen im Koran* (Frankfurt: J. Kaufmann, 1903); Karl Ahrens, "Christliches im Qoran. Eine Nachlese," *Wiener Zeitschrift für die Kunde des Morgenlandes* 37 (1930), 148–190; Heinrich Speyer, *Die Biblischen Erzählungen im Qoran* [1931], (Hildesheim and New York: Georg Olms Verlag, 1971); Paul Arno Eichler, *Die Dschinn, Teufel und Engel im Koran* (Ph.D. dissertation, University of Leipzig, 1928).
[119] Mustafa Shah and Muhammad Abdel Haleem, *The Oxford Handbook of Qur'anic Studies* (Oxford: Oxford University Press, 2020).
[120] Amīn al-Khūlī, *Manāhij al-tajdīd fī al-naḥw wa'l-balāghah wa'l-tafsīr wa'l-adab* (Cairo: Dār al-Ma'rifah, 1961), 306.

Noble Qur'an), faced backlash when information about his dissertation was leaked to the media, giving rise to a heated polemical debate questioning the authenticity of his Muslim identity. In his dissertation, presented to the Department of Arabic Language and Literature at Fu'ad al-Awwal University (now Cairo University) in 1947, Khalafallah argues that stories of the Qur'an do not present actual historical facts, an idea which was regarded by some Egyptian Muslims as blasphemy, amounting to apostasy. However, as Nasr Hamid Abu-Zayd correctly notes, "Khalafallah does not apply the thematic study by collecting together the fragments of the stories mentioned in different sūrahs; he considers every piece of narrative an independent story in itself."[121] With the exception of the story of Joseph (Q 12), most stories in the Qur'an are repeated in various places. The story of Moses, for example, occurs in Q 2, 4, 5, 7, 10, 18, 19, 20, 26, 28, 40, 43, 51, 79. A thematic analysis would violate the contextual dimension emphasized by Khalafallah, for each of the stories in which Moses is mentioned represents a narrative unit that should be studied on its own.[122]

During the same period of Khalafallah's controversy, Shukrī Muḥammad 'Ayyād wrote his M.A. thesis, entitled *Yawm al-dīn wa'l-ḥisāb fī'l-Qur'ān* (*The Day of Judgement in the Qur'an*), under Khūlī's supervision. Upon completing his program, 'Ayyād was under pressure from his university to choose "either to continue Qur'anic studies under the supervision of another professor or to continue studying with Amīn al-Khūlī, but to work on a discipline other than Qur'anic studies. 'Ayyād was, like most of Khūlī's students, so attached to his professor that he preferred the second option."[123] It took about thirty years for 'Ayyād to publish this work, on account of "academic difficulties caused by public misunderstanding and narrow-minded reaction that faced the literary approach to the Qur'an in the forties." As for Khalafallah, he obtained his Ph.D. degree two years later with another dissertation, entitled *Abū al-Faraj al-Aṣfahānī wa-kitāb al-Aghānī*.

It was Khūlī's student and wife Ā'ishah 'Abd al-Raḥmān (d. 1998), known as Bint al-Shaṭi', who put Khūlī's idea of thematic interpretation into practice. In the introduction to her *al-Tafsīr al-bayānī li'l-Qur'ān* (*Literary Interpretation of the Qur'an*), she writes:

> The basic method in this *tafsīr* – as I received it from my teacher [i.e. Amīn al-Khūlī] – is a thematic treatment (*tanāwul mawdū'ī*). This method is devoted to the study of a single subject matter in the Qur'an and it brings together all verses in the Qur'an which speak of the subject in order to understand the usual Qur'anic usages of the words and structures – after seeking their original linguistic sense. This method is different from that of Qur'an commentaries known as chapter-by-chapter method, in which a word or a verse is looked at in isolation from its specific textual context (*siyāq khāṣṣ*) which is signified by the general textual context (*siyāq 'ām*) of its overall

---

[121] Nasr Hamid Abu-Zayd, "The Dilemma of the Literary Approach to the Qur'an," *Alif* 23 (2003), 25.
[122] Ibid.
[123] Ibid.

Qur'anic usage. The chapter-by-chapter method is insufficient to understand the Qur'anic text, or to reveal its clear structures and unique rhetoric.[124]

Bint al-Shāṭi' insistence on the cross-referential procedure as a starting point of her rhetorical exegesis represents a form of thematic interpretation which brings together all relevant verses on particular themes. An exegete of this type chooses a theme or narrative, examines all verses that appear to address the same subject, identifies connections of the various verses and oftentimes also draws on external sources to enrich her/his perspective on the theme/story. This type of thematic interpretation is adopted by most exegetes of this genre, as it allows them to select any Qur'anic theme that relates to their intellectual interests. Scholars who champion this model include the Pakistani-born Fazlur Rahman in his *Major Themes of the Qur'an*, and the Indonesian exegete Quraish Shihab in his *Wawasan al-Qur'an: Tafsir Maudu'i atas Pelbagai Persoalan Umat (Horizon of the Qur'an: Thematic Interpretation on Various Problems Facing the Ummah)*.[125] While Rahman work's includes such themes as "man", "nature", prophethood and revelation", "eschatology", "satan and evil", and "religious diversity", Shihab discusses 32 topics from such common themes as "God", "Prophet", "human", "women", "death", "hereafter" to less common such as "food", "dress", "ethics", "society", "nationhood", "art", "science and technology", "politics", "economy", solidarity", and so forth. Notably, many of these themes address issues of distinctly modern concern.

Another type of thematic interpretation is the one developed by the Egyptian Muḥammad al-Ghazālī (d. 1996) in his widely read book, entitled *Naḥw tafsīr mawḍūʿī li-suwar al-Qurʾān (Towards a Thematic Interpretation of Qur'anic Chapters)*, first published in 1995 and reprinted almost every year since. As its title indicates, Ghazālī's *tafsīr* devotes much attention to the unity of theme (*waḥdat al-mawḍūʿ*) in each sūrah. The aim of his book, as he puts it, is to "treat the sūrah as a whole in order to reveal the hidden threads connecting the whole sūrah such that the first part becomes a prolegomena to its last part, and the last part confirms its first part."[126] Ghazālī presents the themes of each sūrah in sequential order. He typically embeds a single verse or group of verses within the discussion of each theme. If verses that support the theme occur later in the sūrah, they are also referenced. In line with Ghazālī, Muntansir Mir takes up the idea of sūrahs as unity as developed by the Pakistani exegete Amīn Aḥsan Iṣlāḥī (d. 1997). In his *Coherence in the Qur'an*, Mir identifies a central theme for each

---

124 Bint al-Shāṭi', *al-Tafsīr al-bayānī li'l-Qurʾān al-karīm* (Cairo: Dār l-Maʿārif, 1962), 1:10.
125 Muhammad Quraish Shihab, *Wawasan al-Qur'an: Tafsir Maudu'i atas Pelbagai Persoalan Umat* (Bandung: Mizan, 1997).
126 Muḥammad al-Ghazālī, *Naḥw tafsīr mawḍūʿī li-suwar al-Qurʾān* (Cairo: Dār l-Shurūq, 2000), 5.

sūrah and explores relationships between sūrahs and sūrah groupings, organizing them into pairs.[127]

The purpose of this model is to identify the thematic axis of each sūrah and establish the chapter's unity and coherence on the basis of this axis and related themes. Ghazālī often refers to prophetic tradition (hadith) as well as later Muslim traditions, and sometimes relates his discussion to contemporary issues facing the Muslim community. Perhaps the most extensive work that employs this kind of thematic approach is *al-Tafsīr al-mawḍūʿī li-suwar al-Qurʾān al-karīm (Thematic Interpretation of Chapters of the Noble Qurʾan)*, prepared by 31 scholars of the Qurʾan and *tafsīr* under the supervision of Muṣṭafā Muslim from the University of Sharjah, United Arab Emirates. Published in 2010, after 6 years of collaborative work, this *tafsīr* consists of 9 volumes, the 10th of which is dedicated to indexes of verses, hadiths and bibliography. Like that of Ghazālī, their treatment of subjects often involves identifying a number of thematic characteristics in each sūrah, including the central theme of the sūrah, the connection between the sūrah's name and its theme, and the sūrah's unity.[128]

The third type of the thematic approach focuses on Qurʾanic terms or vocabulary, such as particular words, figures and places. Those who follow this model first choose a particular word from the Qurʾan and then gather all verses in which the word and its derivatives occur and identify other words that may shed light on it. The purpose of this exegetical enterprise, like the previous one, is to arrive at a holistic understanding of the Qurʾanic worldview. It is possible that a Qurʾanic term can be developed into a theme, such as *"īmān"* (belief), *"jihād"*, *"ʿadl"* (justice), *"insān"* (human), and thus the distinction between this model and the previous ones cannot easily be drawn. As Toshihiko Isutzu has demonstrated, one word like *"īmān"* may semantically be connected to other words such as *"kufr"* (disbelief), *"shukr"* (gratitude), *"fāsiq"* (sinner), *"hidāyah"* (guidance) and so on.[129] Other scholars have published works that are narrowly focused on specific terms, which suggest that this model might be seen as a distinct area of thematic interpretation. A good example of this is *al-Muṣṭalaḥāt al-arbaʿah fī al-Qurʾān (Four terms in the Qurʾan)* by the Pakistani author Abuʾl-Aʿla al-Maududi (d. 1972). In this book, Maudūdī focuses on the words "ilāh" (God), "rabb" (Lord), "ʿibādah" (worship), and "dīn" (religion).[130] In his *Les grands themes du Coran*,

---

127 Mustansir Mir, *Coherence in the Qurʾan: A Study of Iṣlahi's Concept of Naẓm in Tabaddur-I Qurʾan* (Indianapolis: American Trust Publications, 1986).

128 Muṣṭafā Muslim et al., *al-Tafsīr al-mawḍūʿī li-suwar al-Qurʾān al-karīm* (UAE: University of Sharjah Press, 2010).

129 Toshihiko Isutzu, *Concept of Belief in Islamic Theology: A Semantic Analysis of Iman and Islam* (Tokyo: Kio Institute of Cultural and Linguistic Studies, 1965); Idem, *Ethico-Religious Concepts in the Qurʾan* (Montreal: McGill-Queen's University Press, 2002), 119–202. Wilfred Smith's discussion of the word "īmān" in the Qurʾan follows a similar approach. See Wilfred C. Smith, "Faith in the Qurʾan and Its Relation to Belief," in his *On Understanding Islam: Selected Studies* (The Hague: Mouton Publishers, 1981), 110–134.

130 Abuʾl-Aʿla al-Maududi, *al-Muṣṭalaḥāt al-arbaʿah fī al-Qurʾān* (Kuwait: Dār al-Qalam, 1955).

Jacques Jomier includes discussions of, among other things, Biblical figures, such as Adam, Abraham, and Jesus.[131] Recently, Muḥammad Amaḥzūn published his extensive study of Qur'anic terms, entitled *al-Muṣṭalaḥāt fī al-Qur'ān: al-Ma'ānī wa'l-dilālāt (Terms in the Qur'an: Meanings and Indications)* in six volumes.[132]

One of the earliest studies of Qur'anic terms in the Western academia is Arthur Jeffery's *The Foreign Vocabulary of the Qur'an*, first published in 1938. As the title suggests, this book elucidates 275 foreign words (not including proper nouns) found in the Qur'an.[133] Jeffery's use of external sources of a total of 56 languages (Hebrew, Aramaic, Syriac, Greek, Persian, Avestan, Pahlavi, Ethiopian, Armenian, South Arabic, Sanskrit, etc.) is remarkable. In his 1953 article "Some Minor Problems in the Qur'an," Franz Rosenthal focuses on three Qur'anic terms: *'an yadin*, *ṣamad*, and *rajīm*, each of which has been the subject of some discussions.[134] Both the *Encyclopaedia of the Qur'an* published in five volumes by Brill in 2001–2006 and *The Integrated Encyclopaedia of the Qur'an*, the first volume of which was published in 2013 (originally conceived as a seven-volume work) by the Center for Islamic Sciences, likewise contribute to scholarly discussion on Qur'anic terms and themes. A more modest example is *The Qur'an: An Encyclopaedia*, published in 2006 by Routledge. Also worthy of mention here is the appearance of Qur'anic dictionaries covering various terms and concepts, such as Mustansir Mir's *Dictionary of Qur'anic Terms and Concepts* and Mohammad Ali Amir-Moezzi's *Dizionario del Corano*.[135] Currently, Gabriel Said Reynolds is leading a research group to produce a dictionary of the Qur'an focused on Qur'anic characters and places, theological and anthropological terms, structure and rhetoric, as well as manuscripts and variant readings.

All of these efforts – both confessional and scholarly – reflect the vibrancy of Qur'anic studies today, as the field shifts towards textual studies meant to understand the scripture on its own terms. While the atomistic interpretation of the Qur'an that relies on the long-established *tafsīr* tradition is not impeded by the development of thematic interpretation and TQbQ, the emergence of the exegetical works discussed above suggests a deep interest in intra-Qur'anic textual operations, which has gained

---

[131] Jacques Jomier, *Les grands themes du Coran* (Paris: Le Centurion, 1978). The English version is titled *Great Themes of the Qur'an* (London: SCM Press, 1997).
[132] Muḥammad Amaḥzūn, *al-Muṣṭalaḥāt fī al-Qur'ān: al-Ma'ānī wa'l-dilālāt* (Beirut: Dār Ibn Kathīr, 2020).
[133] For a critical study on Jeffery's work, see Catherine Pennacchio, "Les emprunts lexicaux dans le Coran: Les problems de la liste d'Arthur Jeffery," *Le Bulletin du Centre de recherche français à Jérusalem* 22 (2011), 1–23.
[134] Franz Rosenthal, "Some Minor Problems in the Qur'an" in *The Joshua Starr Memorial Volume* (New York: 1953), 67–84; see also M.J. Kister, "An Yadin (Qur'an IX/29," *Arabica* 3 (1964), 272–278; Uri Rubin, "Al-Ṣamad and the High God: An Interpretation of sūra CXII," *Der Islam* 61 (1984), 197–217; Gabriel Said Reynolds, *The Qur'ān and Its Biblical Subtext* (London: Routledge, 2010), 54–64.
[135] Mustansir Mir, *Dictionary of Qur'anic Terms and Concepts* (New York: Garland Publishing Inc., 1987); Mohammad Ali Amir-Moezzi (ed.), *Dizionario del Corano* (Milan: Mondadori, 2007).

popularity in the age of specialization. Since the early twentieth century we have seen an unprecedented development not only in the compilation of TQbQ works but also modern approaches to thematic interpretation. My survey of modern Islamic hermeneutical works reveals the importance of the idea of Qur'anic cross-referentiality in recent scholarship, as well as the diversity of its impact. It is in light of these developments, I hope, that *The Qur'an with Cross-References* will further accelerate and diversify future research on the Qur'anic text.

User's Guide

What can *The Qur'an with Cross-References* (*QwCR*) do for the reader? This text provides, for almost every verse in the Qur'an, a selection of other passages which shed light upon, clarify, or explain the verse at hand. These cross-references are based on connections in meaning between words, phrases, themes, concepts, narratives, and characters. The *QwCR* is not based on connections between individual words without regard to whether there is any connection in meaning—rather, these cross-references relate to the meaning of the whole verse or passage. One word may occur several times in the Qur'an, but cross-references will be noted only where there is a connection in meaning between two verses or more. Since the purpose of *QwCR* is to bring to light those other parts of the Qur'an which can add to our understanding of a given verse, it is possible that one verse will include more than a single cross-reference, which is true in most cases. If two or more verses are connected in the sense that one sheds light on the other, the *QwCR* cross-references those Qur'anic verses. Thus, every related verse has been selected and organized into particular topics, which are printed on the margin in the same line of the corresponding verse. All efforts have been made to ensure that the cross-references are always directly applicable.

Since the *QwCR* uses a synchronic approach, the cross-references are arranged in the order of the verses as they occur in the Qur'an. In this way, we avoid the subjectivity of selecting particular passages which seem more connected to the referenced verse than other passages. For instance, Q 1:6; 2:142, 213; 4:68; and 10:25 are connected in meaning. Therefore, if you read 1:6, you will find the cross-references as follows: 2:142, 213; 10:25. If you read 2:142, the cross-references are 1:6; 2:213; 10:25; and so forth. In cases where the referenced verse contains more than one topic/issue, each topic and/or issue is cross-referenced using superscripted letters [a], [b], [c] in alphabetical order, following the referenced phrase in both the Arabic text and the reference list. This marker helps the reader to identify which reference refers to which part of the verse. The superscripted letters [pp] are used to show that a particular cross-reference has a parallel verse that says much the same thing or describes the same event. While the *QwCR* is not accompanied by any explanation or justification, the connection between a verse and its references is clear enough that the reader should able to understand the rationale behind each cross-reference on close examination.

Reading the Qur'an through cross-references can be confusing, but will nonetheless be rewarding for attentive readers. The most obvious advantage of studying and learning cross-references is that this exercise can point us to other passages in the Qur'an that will broaden our understanding. For instance, when reading Q 1:2 "Praise be to God, Lord of the Worlds," the reader may ask, what does the "Lord of the Worlds" mean? The *QwCR* lists Q 26:23–24 as a possible reference. Turning to the latter passage, we find this question answered by Moses, who responds to the inquiry of Pharaoh: "Pharaoh said, 'And what is the Lord of the Worlds?' He said, 'The Lord of the heavens and the earth, and everything between them, if you are aware'." When you read a certain verse, look at the cross-references on the margin. Read each verse one-by-one within its full context when necessary. The real fun begins when looking up cross-references' cross-references. For instance, when reading Q 1:4 "Master of the Day of Judgment," the *QwCR* directs readers to Q 82:17–19, in which verse 19 says: "The Day when no soul will avail another soul anything; and the decision on that Day is God's." This verse explains the previous two verses (17–18), which raise the question: "what will convey to you what the Day of Judgment is?" But one need not stop there—indeed, the *QwCR* likewise gives a list of cross-references for Q 82:19, namely, Q 3:145; 99:6–7; 101:4, which will further enrich one's perspective on the Day of Judgement.

This *QwCR* is ultimately an interpretive work. The decision to include and/or exclude cross-references involves personal reasoning which is a basic feature of any commentary. This is true even if the commentator makes the attempt to base himself or herself upon traditional materials written down in earlier centuries. Given the vastness of those materials, the commentator has to choose which ones to include and/or exclude, and the criteria of inclusion and exclusion can vary from one commentator to another. The selection of cross-references likewise involves various interpretive decisions. While the *QwCR* makes use of many works which purport to explicate the Qur'an through the Qur'an, in the end, it is the compiler who makes a reasonable decision to include and/or exclude certain cross-references. The primary set of criteria for inclusion/exclusion includes (1) similarities in message, (2) topically related-passages, (3) allusions to the same narratives, events and characters, and (4) parallelism in phrasing. It must be admitted, however, that the process of inclusion/exclusion is subjective. Of course, the selection is not *arbitrary* in the sense that it is guided by previous works on the subject—though, in the final analysis the selection is based on the compiler's personal judgment. Various works have been consulted to compare the *QwCR*'s selection of cross-references with those found in the works mentioned in the Introduction. Given the variety of literary properties in the Qur'an, the best method of selection involves a careful examination of each case, with an eye to connections in meaning between the referenced verse and its cross-references.

Since the compiler has exercised interpretive reasoning in the process of selecting cross-references, the reader should also play an active role in making meaningful connections between the various verses of the Qur'an dealing with the same topic. After all, reading topical cross-references like this one requires the reader to participate in the creation of meaning. This involves the reader's ability to *identify* similarities (and lack thereof) between the cross-references, *compare* them, *account* for a meaningful synthesis, and finally *evaluate* the chosen meaning in light of other possible interpretations. This four-fold reading strategy will help the reader to become conversant with the text. Conversant readers are discerning readers whose fundamental disposition is one of active engagement and sustained conversation with the Qur'anic text.

Sūrah 1–114

Sūrah 1: Al-Fātiḥah
سُورَةُ ٱلْفَاتِحَة (The Opening)

بِسْمِ اللَّهِ الرَّحْمَٰنِ الرَّحِيمِ ١

1
pp 27:30

1 In the name of God, the Gracious, the Merciful.

الْحَمْدُ لِلَّهِ^a رَبِّ الْعَالَمِينَ^b ٢

2
pp 6:45; 37:182; 39:75
^a 6:1; 18:1; 27:93; 35:1
^b 26:23–24

2 Praise be to God, Lord of the Worlds.

الرَّحْمَٰنِ الرَّحِيمِ ٣

3 The Most Gracious, the Most Merciful.

مَالِكِ يَوْمِ الدِّينِ ٤

4
82:17–19

4 Master of the Day of Judgment.

إِيَّاكَ نَعْبُدُ وَإِيَّاكَ نَسْتَعِينُ ٥

5 It is You we worship, and upon You we call for help.

اهْدِنَا الصِّرَاطَ الْمُسْتَقِيمَ ٦

6
2:142, 213; 4:68; 10:25

6 Guide us to the straight path.

صِرَاطَ الَّذِينَ أَنْعَمْتَ عَلَيْهِمْ غَيْرِ الْمَغْضُوبِ عَلَيْهِمْ وَلَا الضَّالِّينَ ٧

7
4:69; 19:58

7 The path of those You have blessed, not of those against whom there is anger, nor of those who are misguided.

Sūrah 2: Al-Baqarah
سُورَةُ ٱلْبَقَرَة (The Cow)

بِسْمِ اللَّهِ الرَّحْمَٰنِ الرَّحِيمِ

الم ١

1–5
31:1–5

1 Alif, Lām, Mīm.

ذَٰلِكَ الْكِتَابُ لَا رَيْبَ ۛ فِيهِ ۛ هُدًى لِلْمُتَّقِينَ ٢

2
32:2; 41:44

2 This is the Book in which there is no doubt, a guide for the righteous.

الَّذِينَ يُؤْمِنُونَ بِالْغَيْبِ وَيُقِيمُونَ الصَّلَاةَ وَمِمَّا رَزَقْنَاهُمْ يُنْفِقُونَ ٣

3
8:3; 13:22

3 Those who believe in the unseen, and perform the prayers, and give from what We have provided for them.

ومَا أُنْزِلَ مِن قَبْلِكَ وَبِالْآخِرَةِ هُمْ يُوقِنُونَ ٤

4 And those who believe in what was revealed to you, and in what was revealed before you, and are certain of the Hereafter.

4
2:136, 285; 3:84; 4:152

أُولَٰئِكَ عَلَىٰ هُدًى مِّن رَّبِّهِمْ ۖ وَأُولَٰئِكَ هُمُ الْمُفْلِحُونَ ٥

5 These are upon guidance from their Lord. These are the successful.

5
pp 31:5

إِنَّ الَّذِينَ كَفَرُوا سَوَاءٌ عَلَيْهِمْ أَأَنذَرْتَهُمْ أَمْ لَمْ تُنذِرْهُمْ لَا يُؤْمِنُونَ ٦

6 As for those who disbelieve—it is the same for them, whether you have warned them, or have not warned them—they do not believe.

6
26:136; 36:10

خَتَمَ اللَّهُ عَلَىٰ قُلُوبِهِمْ وَعَلَىٰ سَمْعِهِمْ ۖ وَعَلَىٰ أَبْصَارِهِمْ غِشَاوَةٌ ۖ وَلَهُمْ عَذَابٌ عَظِيمٌ ٧

7 God has set a seal on their hearts and on their hearing, and over their vision is a veil. They will have a severe torment.

7
16:108; 36:9; 45:23

وَمِنَ النَّاسِ مَن يَقُولُ آمَنَّا بِاللَّهِ وَبِالْيَوْمِ الْآخِرِ وَمَا هُم بِمُؤْمِنِينَ ٨

8 Among the people are those who say, "We believe in God and in the Last Day," but they are not believers.

8–9
4:142; 9:101

يُخَادِعُونَ اللَّهَ وَالَّذِينَ آمَنُوا وَمَا يَخْدَعُونَ إِلَّا أَنفُسَهُمْ وَمَا يَشْعُرُونَ ٩

9 They seek to deceive God and those who believe, but they deceive none but themselves, though they are not aware.

فِي قُلُوبِهِم مَّرَضٌ فَزَادَهُمُ اللَّهُ مَرَضًا ۖ وَلَهُمْ عَذَابٌ أَلِيمٌ بِمَا كَانُوا يَكْذِبُونَ ١٠

10 In their hearts is sickness, and God has increased their sickness. They will have a painful punishment because of their denial.

10
9:125; 47:29; 74:31

وَإِذَا قِيلَ لَهُمْ لَا تُفْسِدُوا فِي الْأَرْضِ قَالُوا إِنَّمَا نَحْنُ مُصْلِحُونَ ١١

11 And when it is said to them, "Do not make trouble on earth," they say, "We are only reformers."

أَلَا إِنَّهُمْ هُمُ الْمُفْسِدُونَ وَلَٰكِن لَّا يَشْعُرُونَ ١٢

12 In fact, they are the troublemakers, but they are not aware.

وَإِذَا قِيلَ لَهُمْ آمِنُوا كَمَا آمَنَ النَّاسُ قَالُوا أَنُؤْمِنُ كَمَا آمَنَ السُّفَهَاءُ ۗ أَلَا إِنَّهُمْ هُمُ السُّفَهَاءُ وَلَٰكِن لَّا يَعْلَمُونَ ١٣

13 And when it is said to them, "Believe as the people have believed," they say, "Shall we believe as the fools have believed?" In fact, it is they who are the fools, but they do not know.

وَإِذَا لَقُوا الَّذِينَ آمَنُوا قَالُوا آمَنَّا وَإِذَا خَلَوْا إِلَىٰ شَيَاطِينِهِمْ قَالُوا إِنَّا مَعَكُمْ إِنَّمَا نَحْنُ مُسْتَهْزِئُونَ ١٤

14 And when they come across those who believe, they say, "We believe"; but when they are alone with their devils, they say, "We are with you; we were only ridiculing."

14
2:76; 3:119

اللَّهُ يَسْتَهْزِئُ بِهِمْ وَيَمُدُّهُمْ فِي طُغْيَانِهِمْ يَعْمَهُونَ ١٥

15 It is God who ridicules them, and leaves them bewildered in their transgression.

Sūrah 2: Al-Baqarah

١٦ أُولَـٰئِكَ الَّذِينَ اشْتَرَوُا الضَّلَالَةَ بِالْهُدَىٰ فَمَا رَبِحَت تِّجَارَتُهُمْ وَمَا كَانُوا مُهْتَدِينَ

16 Those are they who have bartered error for guidance; but their trade does not profit them, and they are not guided.

16
2:175; 3:177; 4:44; 31:6

١٧ مَثَلُهُمْ كَمَثَلِ الَّذِي اسْتَوْقَدَ نَارًا فَلَمَّا أَضَاءَتْ مَا حَوْلَهُ ذَهَبَ اللَّهُ بِنُورِهِمْ وَتَرَكَهُمْ فِي ظُلُمَاتٍ لَّا يُبْصِرُونَ

17 Their likeness is that of a person who kindled a fire; when it illuminated all around him, God took away their light, and left them in darkness, unable to see.

١٨ صُمٌّ بُكْمٌ عُمْيٌ فَهُمْ لَا يَرْجِعُونَ

18 Deaf, dumb, blind. They will not return.

18
2:171; 6:39; 8:22; 44:26

١٩ أَوْ كَصَيِّبٍ مِّنَ السَّمَاءِ فِيهِ ظُلُمَاتٌ وَرَعْدٌ وَبَرْقٌ يَجْعَلُونَ أَصَابِعَهُمْ فِي آذَانِهِم مِّنَ الصَّوَاعِقِ حَذَرَ الْمَوْتِ ۚ وَاللَّهُ مُحِيطٌ بِالْكَافِرِينَ

19 Or like a cloudburst from the sky, in which is darkness, and thunder, and lightning. They press their fingers into their ears from the thunderbolts, in fear of death. But God surrounds the disbelievers.

19
13:13

٢٠ يَكَادُ الْبَرْقُ يَخْطَفُ أَبْصَارَهُمْ ۖ كُلَّمَا أَضَاءَ لَهُم مَّشَوْا فِيهِ وَإِذَا أَظْلَمَ عَلَيْهِمْ قَامُوا ۚ وَلَوْ شَاءَ اللَّهُ لَذَهَبَ بِسَمْعِهِمْ وَأَبْصَارِهِمْ ۚ إِنَّ اللَّهَ عَلَىٰ كُلِّ شَيْءٍ قَدِيرٌ

20 The lightning almost snatches their sight away. Whenever it illuminates for them, they walk in it; but when it grows dark over them, they stand still. Had God willed, He could have taken away their hearing and their sight. God is capable of everything.

20
13:19; 24:48–49

٢١ يَا أَيُّهَا النَّاسُ اعْبُدُوا رَبَّكُمُ الَّذِي خَلَقَكُمْ وَالَّذِينَ مِن قَبْلِكُمْ لَعَلَّكُمْ تَتَّقُونَ

21 O people! Worship your Lord who created you and those before you, that you may attain piety.

21
19:67; 21:104; 22:55; 30:27; 56:62

٢٢ الَّذِي جَعَلَ لَكُمُ الْأَرْضَ فِرَاشًا وَالسَّمَاءَ بِنَاءً وَأَنزَلَ مِنَ السَّمَاءِ مَاءً فَأَخْرَجَ بِهِ مِنَ الثَّمَرَاتِ رِزْقًا لَّكُمْ ۖ فَلَا تَجْعَلُوا لِلَّهِ أَندَادًا وَأَنتُمْ تَعْلَمُونَ

22 He who made the earth a habitat for you, and the sky a structure, and sends water down from the sky, and brings out fruits thereby, as a sustenance for you. Therefore, do not assign rivals to God while you know.

22
7:57; 51:47–48

٢٣ وَإِن كُنتُمْ فِي رَيْبٍ مِّمَّا نَزَّلْنَا عَلَىٰ عَبْدِنَا فَأْتُوا بِسُورَةٍ مِّن مِّثْلِهِ وَادْعُوا شُهَدَاءَكُم مِّن دُونِ اللَّهِ إِن كُنتُمْ صَادِقِينَ

23 And if you are in doubt about what We have revealed to Our servant, then produce a chapter like these, and call your witnesses apart from God, if you are truthful.

23
10:38; 11:13; 17:88

٢٤ فَإِن لَّمْ تَفْعَلُوا وَلَن تَفْعَلُوا فَاتَّقُوا النَّارَ الَّتِي وَقُودُهَا النَّاسُ وَالْحِجَارَةُ ۖ أُعِدَّتْ لِلْكَافِرِينَ

24 But if you do not—and you will not—then beware the Fire whose fuel is people and stones, prepared for the disbelievers.

24
21:98

٢٥ وَبَشِّرِ الَّذِينَ آمَنُوا وَعَمِلُوا الصَّالِحَاتِ أَنَّ لَهُمْ جَنَّاتٍ تَجْرِي مِن تَحْتِهَا الْأَنْهَارُ ۖ كُلَّمَا رُزِقُوا مِنْهَا مِن ثَمَرَةٍ رِّزْقًا ۙ قَالُوا هَٰذَا الَّذِي رُزِقْنَا مِن قَبْلُ ۖ وَأُتُوا بِهِ مُتَشَابِهًا ۖ وَلَهُمْ فِيهَا أَزْوَاجٌ مُّطَهَّرَةٌ ۖ وَهُمْ فِيهَا خَالِدُونَ

25 And give good news to those who believe and do righteous deeds; that they will have gardens beneath which rivers flow. Whenever they are provided with fruit therefrom as sustenance, they will say, "This is what we were provided with before," and they will be given the like of it. And they will have pure spouses therein, and they will abide therein forever.

25
3:15; 4:57; 37:48; 47:15; 55:56; 56:22–23

٢٦ إِنَّ اللَّهَ لَا يَسْتَحْيِي أَن يَضْرِبَ مَثَلًا مَّا بَعُوضَةً فَمَا فَوْقَهَا ۚ فَأَمَّا الَّذِينَ آمَنُوا فَيَعْلَمُونَ أَنَّهُ الْحَقُّ مِن رَّبِّهِمْ ۖ وَأَمَّا الَّذِينَ كَفَرُوا فَيَقُولُونَ مَاذَا أَرَادَ اللَّهُ بِهَٰذَا مَثَلًا ۘ يُضِلُّ بِهِ كَثِيرًا وَيَهْدِي بِهِ كَثِيرًا ۚ وَمَا يُضِلُّ بِهِ إِلَّا الْفَاسِقِينَ

26 God does not shy away from making an example of a gnat, or something above it. As for those who believe, they know that it is the Truth from their Lord. But as for those who disbelieve, they say, "What did God intend by this example?" He leads astray many thereby, and He guides many thereby; but He misleads thereby only the evildoers.

٢٧ الَّذِينَ يَنقُضُونَ عَهْدَ اللَّهِ مِن بَعْدِ مِيثَاقِهِ وَيَقْطَعُونَ مَا أَمَرَ اللَّهُ بِهِ أَن يُوصَلَ وَيُفْسِدُونَ فِي الْأَرْضِ ۚ أُولَٰئِكَ هُمُ الْخَاسِرُونَ

27 Those who violate God's covenant after its confirmation, and sever what God has commanded to be joined, and commit evil on earth. These are the losers.

27
2:87; 13:25; 22:47

٢٨ كَيْفَ تَكْفُرُونَ بِاللَّهِ وَكُنتُمْ أَمْوَاتًا فَأَحْيَاكُمْ ۖ ثُمَّ يُمِيتُكُمْ ثُمَّ يُحْيِيكُمْ ثُمَّ إِلَيْهِ تُرْجَعُونَ

28 How can you deny God, when you were dead and He gave you life, then He will put you to death, then He will bring you to life, then to Him you will be returned?

28
22:66; 26:81; 30:40; 45:26

٢٩ هُوَ الَّذِي خَلَقَ لَكُم مَّا فِي الْأَرْضِ جَمِيعًا ثُمَّ اسْتَوَىٰ إِلَى السَّمَاءِ فَسَوَّاهُنَّ سَبْعَ سَمَاوَاتٍ ۚ وَهُوَ بِكُلِّ شَيْءٍ عَلِيمٌ

29 It is He who created for you everything on earth, then turned to the heaven, and made them seven heavens. And He is aware of all things.

29
41:11–12

٣٠ وَإِذْ قَالَ رَبُّكَ لِلْمَلَائِكَةِ إِنِّي جَاعِلٌ فِي الْأَرْضِ خَلِيفَةً ۖ قَالُوا أَتَجْعَلُ فِيهَا مَن يُفْسِدُ فِيهَا وَيَسْفِكُ الدِّمَاءَ وَنَحْنُ نُسَبِّحُ بِحَمْدِكَ وَنُقَدِّسُ لَكَ ۖ قَالَ إِنِّي أَعْلَمُ مَا لَا تَعْلَمُونَ

30 When your Lord said to the angels, "I am placing a successor on earth." They said, "Will You place in it someone who will cause corruption in it and shed blood, while we declare Your praises and sanctify You?" He said, "I know what you do not know."

30
6:65; 27:27; 35:39

٣١ وَعَلَّمَ آدَمَ الْأَسْمَاءَ كُلَّهَا ثُمَّ عَرَضَهُمْ عَلَى الْمَلَائِكَةِ فَقَالَ أَنبِئُونِي بِأَسْمَاءِ هَٰؤُلَاءِ إِن كُنتُمْ صَادِقِينَ

31 And He taught Adam the names, all of them; then he presented them to the angels, and said, "Tell Me the names of these, if you are sincere."

٣٢ قَالُوا سُبْحَانَكَ لَا عِلْمَ لَنَا إِلَّا مَا عَلَّمْتَنَا ۖ إِنَّكَ أَنتَ الْعَلِيمُ الْحَكِيمُ

32 They said, "Glory be to You! We have no knowledge except what You have taught us. It is you who are the Knowledgeable, the Wise."

٣٣ قَالَ يَا آدَمُ أَنبِئْهُم بِأَسْمَائِهِمْ ۖ فَلَمَّا أَنبَأَهُم بِأَسْمَائِهِمْ قَالَ أَلَمْ أَقُل لَّكُمْ إِنِّي أَعْلَمُ غَيْبَ السَّمَاوَاتِ وَالْأَرْضِ وَأَعْلَمُ مَا تُبْدُونَ وَمَا كُنتُمْ تَكْتُمُونَ

33 He said, "O Adam, tell them their names." And when he told them their names, He said, "Did I not tell you that I know the secrets of the heavens and the earth, and that I know what you reveal and what you conceal?"

٣٤ وَإِذْ قُلْنَا لِلْمَلَائِكَةِ اسْجُدُوا لِآدَمَ فَسَجَدُوا إِلَّا إِبْلِيسَ أَبَىٰ وَاسْتَكْبَرَ وَكَانَ مِنَ الْكَافِرِينَ

34 And We said to the angels, "Bow down to Adam." They bowed down, except for Satan. He refused, was arrogant, and was one of the disbelievers.

34
7:12; 15:30–33; 17:61; 18:50; 29:28; 38:75; 71:72

٣٥ وَقُلْنَا يَا آدَمُ اسْكُنْ أَنتَ وَزَوْجُكَ الْجَنَّةَ وَكُلَا مِنْهَا رَغَدًا حَيْثُ شِئْتُمَا وَلَا تَقْرَبَا هَٰذِهِ الشَّجَرَةَ فَتَكُونَا مِنَ الظَّالِمِينَ

35 We said, "O Adam, inhabit the Garden, you and your spouse, and eat from it freely as you please, but do not approach this tree, lest you become wrongdoers."

35
7:19; 20: 116–119

٣٦ فَأَزَلَّهُمَا الشَّيْطَانُ عَنْهَا فَأَخْرَجَهُمَا مِمَّا كَانَا فِيهِ ۖ وَقُلْنَا اهْبِطُوا بَعْضُكُمْ لِبَعْضٍ عَدُوٌّ ۖ وَلَكُمْ فِي الْأَرْضِ مُسْتَقَرٌّ وَمَتَاعٌ إِلَىٰ حِينٍ

36 But Satan caused them to slip from it, and caused them to depart the state they were in. We said, "Go down, some of you enemies of one another. And you will have residence on earth, and enjoyment for a while."

36
7:27; 20:120

٣٧ فَتَلَقَّىٰ آدَمُ مِن رَّبِّهِ كَلِمَاتٍ فَتَابَ عَلَيْهِ ۚ إِنَّهُ هُوَ التَّوَّابُ الرَّحِيمُ

37 Then Adam received words from his Lord, so He relented towards him. He is the Relenting, the Merciful.

37
7:23, 35; 20:122

٣٨ قُلْنَا اهْبِطُوا مِنْهَا جَمِيعًا ۖ فَإِمَّا يَأْتِيَنَّكُم مِّنِّي هُدًى فَمَن تَبِعَ هُدَايَ فَلَا خَوْفٌ عَلَيْهِمْ وَلَا هُمْ يَحْزَنُونَ

38 We said, "Go down from it, all of you. Yet whenever guidance comes to you from Me, then whoever follows My guidance—they have nothing to fear, nor shall they grieve.

38
7:24; 20:123

٣٩ وَالَّذِينَ كَفَرُوا وَكَذَّبُوا بِآيَاتِنَا أُولَٰئِكَ أَصْحَابُ النَّارِ ۖ هُمْ فِيهَا خَالِدُونَ

39 But as for those who disbelieve and reject Our signs—these are the inmates of the Fire—wherein they will remain forever."

٤٠ يَا بَنِي إِسْرَائِيلَ اذْكُرُوا نِعْمَتِيَ الَّتِي أَنْعَمْتُ عَلَيْكُمْ[a] وَأَوْفُوا بِعَهْدِي أُوفِ بِعَهْدِكُمْ وَإِيَّايَ فَارْهَبُونِ[b]

40 O Children of Israel! Remember My blessings which I bestowed upon you, and fulfill your pledge to Me, and I will fulfill My pledge to you, and fear Me.

40
[a] 2:57; 5:20; 28:5–6
[b] 5:13, 20

٤١ وَآمِنُوا بِمَا أَنْزَلْتُ مُصَدِّقًا لِمَا مَعَكُمْ وَلَا تَكُونُوا أَوَّلَ كَافِرٍ بِهِ ۖ[a] وَلَا تَشْتَرُوا بِآيَاتِي ثَمَنًا قَلِيلًا وَإِيَّايَ فَاتَّقُونِ[b]

41 And believe in what I revealed, confirming what is with you; and do not be the first to deny it; and do not exchange My revelations for a small price; and be conscious of Me.

41
[a] 2: 91, 97; 5:48; 3:3; 35:31
[b] 2:79, 174; 3:77, 187, 9:9; 16:95

٤٢ وَلَا تَلْبِسُوا الْحَقَّ بِالْبَاطِلِ وَتَكْتُمُوا الْحَقَّ وَأَنْتُمْ تَعْلَمُونَ

42 And do not mix truth with falsehood, and do not conceal the truth while you know.

42
pp 3:71

٤٣ وَأَقِيمُوا الصَّلَاةَ وَآتُوا الزَّكَاةَ وَارْكَعُوا مَعَ الرَّاكِعِينَ

43 And attend to your prayers, and practice regular charity, and kneel with those who kneel.

٤٤ أَتَأْمُرُونَ النَّاسَ بِالْبِرِّ وَتَنْسَوْنَ أَنْفُسَكُمْ وَأَنْتُمْ تَتْلُونَ الْكِتَابَ ۚ أَفَلَا تَعْقِلُونَ

44 Do you command people to virtuous conduct, and forget yourselves, even though you read the Scripture? Do you not understand?

44
61:3

٤٥ وَاسْتَعِينُوا بِالصَّبْرِ وَالصَّلَاةِ ۚ وَإِنَّهَا لَكَبِيرَةٌ إِلَّا عَلَى الْخَاشِعِينَ

45 And seek help through patience and prayer. But it is difficult, except for the devout.

45
2:153

٤٦ الَّذِينَ يَظُنُّونَ أَنَّهُمْ مُلَاقُو رَبِّهِمْ وَأَنَّهُمْ إِلَيْهِ رَاجِعُونَ

46 Those who know that they will meet their Lord, and that to Him they will return.

46
2:249

٤٧ يَا بَنِي إِسْرَائِيلَ اذْكُرُوا نِعْمَتِيَ الَّتِي أَنْعَمْتُ عَلَيْكُمْ وَأَنِّي فَضَّلْتُكُمْ عَلَى الْعَالَمِينَ

47 O Children of Israel! Remember My favor which I bestowed upon you, and that I favored you over all nations.

47
pp 2:122

٤٨ وَاتَّقُوا يَوْمًا لَا تَجْزِي نَفْسٌ عَنْ نَفْسٍ شَيْئًا وَلَا يُقْبَلُ مِنْهَا شَفَاعَةٌ وَلَا يُؤْخَذُ مِنْهَا عَدْلٌ وَلَا هُمْ يُنْصَرُونَ

48 And beware of a Day when no soul will avail another in the least, nor will any intercession be accepted on its behalf, nor will any ransom be taken from it, nor will they be helped.

48
pp 2:123
2:281; 16:111

Sūrah 2: Al-Baqarah

٤٩ وَإِذْ نَجَّيْنَاكُمْ مِنْ آلِ فِرْعَوْنَ يَسُومُونَكُمْ سُوءَ الْعَذَابِ يُذَبِّحُونَ أَبْنَاءَكُمْ وَيَسْتَحْيُونَ نِسَاءَكُمْ ۚ وَفِي ذَٰلِكُمْ بَلَاءٌ مِنْ رَبِّكُمْ عَظِيمٌ

49 And recall that We delivered you from the people of Pharaoh. They inflicted on you terrible persecution, killing your sons and sparing your women. Therein was a tremendous trial from your Lord.

49
7:141, 167; 14:6

٥٠ وَإِذْ فَرَقْنَا بِكُمُ الْبَحْرَ فَأَنْجَيْنَاكُمْ وَأَغْرَقْنَا آلَ فِرْعَوْنَ وَأَنْتُمْ تَنْظُرُونَ

50 And recall that We parted the sea for you, so We saved you, and We drowned the people of Pharaoh as you looked on.

50
7:136–138; 8:54; 10:90; 17:103; 20:77; 26:60–66; 44:17–31

٥١ وَإِذْ وَاعَدْنَا مُوسَىٰ أَرْبَعِينَ لَيْلَةً ᵃ ثُمَّ اتَّخَذْتُمُ الْعِجْلَ ᵇ مِنْ بَعْدِهِ وَأَنْتُمْ ظَالِمُونَ

51 And recall that We appointed for Moses forty nights. Then you took to worshiping the calf after him, and you turned wicked.

51
ᵃ 7:142
ᵇ 2:54, 92; 4:153; 7:152; 20:85–98

٥٢ ثُمَّ عَفَوْنَا عَنْكُمْ مِنْ بَعْدِ ذَٰلِكَ لَعَلَّكُمْ تَشْكُرُونَ

52 Then We pardoned you after that, so that you might be grateful.

52
21:48

٥٣ وَإِذْ آتَيْنَا مُوسَى الْكِتَابَ وَالْفُرْقَانَ لَعَلَّكُمْ تَهْتَدُونَ

53 And recall that We gave Moses the Scripture and the Criterion, so that you may be guided.

53
21:48; 23:49

٥٤ وَإِذْ قَالَ مُوسَىٰ لِقَوْمِهِ يَا قَوْمِ إِنَّكُمْ ظَلَمْتُمْ أَنْفُسَكُمْ بِاتِّخَاذِكُمُ الْعِجْلَ فَتُوبُوا إِلَىٰ بَارِئِكُمْ فَاقْتُلُوا أَنْفُسَكُمْ ذَٰلِكُمْ خَيْرٌ لَكُمْ عِنْدَ بَارِئِكُمْ فَتَابَ عَلَيْكُمْ ۚ إِنَّهُ هُوَ التَّوَّابُ الرَّحِيمُ

54 And recall that Moses said to his people, "O my people, you have done wrong to yourselves by worshiping the calf. So repent to your Maker, and kill your egos. That would be better for you with your Maker." So He turned to you in repentance. He is the Accepter of Repentance, the Merciful.

54
2:51, 92; 4:153; 7:148, 152; 20:87–88; 87:88

٥٥ وَإِذْ قُلْتُمْ يَا مُوسَىٰ لَنْ نُؤْمِنَ لَكَ حَتَّىٰ نَرَى اللَّهَ جَهْرَةً فَأَخَذَتْكُمُ الصَّاعِقَةُ وَأَنْتُمْ تَنْظُرُونَ

55 And recall that you said, "O Moses, we will not believe in you unless we see God plainly." Thereupon the thunderbolt struck you, as you looked on.

55
4:153

٥٦ ثُمَّ بَعَثْنَاكُمْ مِنْ بَعْدِ مَوْتِكُمْ لَعَلَّكُمْ تَشْكُرُونَ

56 Then We revived you after your death, so that you may be appreciative.

٥٧ وَظَلَّلْنَا عَلَيْكُمُ الْغَمَامَ وَأَنْزَلْنَا عَلَيْكُمُ الْمَنَّ وَالسَّلْوَىٰ ۖ كُلُوا مِنْ طَيِّبَاتِ مَا رَزَقْنَاكُمْ ۖ وَمَا ظَلَمُونَا وَلَٰكِنْ كَانُوا أَنْفُسَهُمْ يَظْلِمُونَ

57 And We shaded you with clouds, and We sent down to you manna and quails: "Eat of the good things We have provided for you." They did not wrong Us, but they used to wrong their own souls.

٥٨ وَإِذْ قُلْنَا ادْخُلُوا هَٰذِهِ الْقَرْيَةَ فَكُلُوا مِنْهَا حَيْثُ شِئْتُمْ رَغَدًا وَادْخُلُوا الْبَابَ سُجَّدًا وَقُولُوا حِطَّةٌ نَغْفِرْ لَكُمْ خَطَايَاكُمْ ۚ وَسَنَزِيدُ الْمُحْسِنِينَ

58
7:161

58 And recall that We said, "Enter this town, and eat plentifully from it whatever you wish; but enter the gate humbly, and say, 'Pardon.' We will forgive your sins, and give increase to the virtuous."

٥٩ فَبَدَّلَ الَّذِينَ ظَلَمُوا قَوْلًا غَيْرَ الَّذِي قِيلَ لَهُمْ فَأَنْزَلْنَا عَلَى الَّذِينَ ظَلَمُوا رِجْزًا مِنَ السَّمَاءِ بِمَا كَانُوا يَفْسُقُونَ

59
pp 7:162

59 But the wrongdoers among them substituted words other than those given to them, so We sent down on the wrongdoers a plague from heaven, because of their wicked behavior.

٦٠ وَإِذِ اسْتَسْقَىٰ مُوسَىٰ لِقَوْمِهِ فَقُلْنَا اضْرِبْ بِعَصَاكَ الْحَجَرَ ۖ فَانْفَجَرَتْ مِنْهُ اثْنَتَا عَشْرَةَ عَيْنًا ۖ قَدْ عَلِمَ كُلُّ أُنَاسٍ مَشْرَبَهُمْ ۖ كُلُوا وَاشْرَبُوا مِنْ رِزْقِ اللَّهِ وَلَا تَعْثَوْا فِي الْأَرْضِ مُفْسِدِينَ

60
7:160, 168

60 And recall when Moses prayed for water for his people. We said, "Strike the rock with your staff." Thereupon twelve springs gushed out from it, and each tribe recognized its drinking-place. "Eat and drink from God's provision, and do not corrupt the earth with disobedience."

٦١ وَإِذْ قُلْتُمْ يَا مُوسَىٰ لَنْ نَصْبِرَ عَلَىٰ طَعَامٍ وَاحِدٍ فَادْعُ لَنَا رَبَّكَ يُخْرِجْ لَنَا مِمَّا تُنْبِتُ الْأَرْضُ مِنْ بَقْلِهَا وَقِثَّائِهَا وَفُومِهَا وَعَدَسِهَا وَبَصَلِهَا ۖ قَالَ أَتَسْتَبْدِلُونَ الَّذِي هُوَ أَدْنَىٰ بِالَّذِي هُوَ خَيْرٌ ۚ اهْبِطُوا مِصْرًا فَإِنَّ لَكُمْ مَا سَأَلْتُمْ ۗ وَضُرِبَتْ عَلَيْهِمُ الذِّلَّةُ وَالْمَسْكَنَةُ وَبَاءُوا بِغَضَبٍ مِنَ اللَّهِ ۗ ذَٰلِكَ بِأَنَّهُمْ كَانُوا يَكْفُرُونَ بِآيَاتِ اللَّهِ وَيَقْتُلُونَ النَّبِيِّينَ بِغَيْرِ الْحَقِّ ۗ ذَٰلِكَ بِمَا عَصَوْا وَكَانُوا يَعْتَدُونَ

61
2: 91, 3:21, 181; 4:155

61 And recall when you said, "O Moses, we cannot endure one kind of food, so call to your Lord to produce for us of what the earth grows: of its herbs, and its cucumbers, and its garlic, and its lentils, and its onions." He said, "Would you substitute worse for better? Go down to Egypt, where you will have what you asked for." They were struck with humiliation and poverty, and incurred wrath from God. That was because they rejected God's revelations and wrongfully killed the prophets. That was because they disobeyed and transgressed.

٦٢ إِنَّ الَّذِينَ آمَنُوا وَالَّذِينَ هَادُوا وَالنَّصَارَىٰ وَالصَّابِئِينَ[a] مَنْ آمَنَ بِاللَّهِ وَالْيَوْمِ الْآخِرِ وَعَمِلَ صَالِحًا فَلَهُمْ أَجْرُهُمْ عِنْدَ رَبِّهِمْ وَلَا خَوْفٌ عَلَيْهِمْ وَلَا هُمْ يَحْزَنُونَ[b]

62
pp 5:69
[a] 22:17
[b] 2:277

62 Those who believe, and those who are Jewish, and the Christians, and the Sabeans—any who believe in God and the Last Day, and act righteously—will have their reward with their Lord; they have nothing to fear, nor will they grieve.

٦٣ وَإِذْ أَخَذْنَا مِيثَاقَكُمْ وَرَفَعْنَا فَوْقَكُمُ الطُّورَ خُذُوا مَا آتَيْنَاكُمْ بِقُوَّةٍ وَاذْكُرُوا مَا فِيهِ لَعَلَّكُمْ تَتَّقُونَ

63
2:93; 7:171

63 And recall when We received a pledge from you, and raised the Mount above you: "Take what We have given you earnestly, and remember what is in it, that you may attain righteousness."

٦٤ ثُمَّ تَوَلَّيْتُم مِّنۢ بَعْدِ ذَٰلِكَ ۖ فَلَوْلَا فَضْلُ اللَّهِ عَلَيْكُمْ وَرَحْمَتُهُ لَكُنتُم مِّنَ الْخَاسِرِينَ

64 But after that you turned away. Were it not for God's grace and mercy towards you, you would have been among the losers.

٦٥ وَلَقَدْ عَلِمْتُمُ الَّذِينَ اعْتَدَوْا مِنكُمْ فِي السَّبْتِ فَقُلْنَا لَهُمْ كُونُوا قِرَدَةً خَاسِئِينَ

65 And you surely knew those of you who violated the Sabbath. We said to them, "Be despicable apes!"

65
7:163, 166

٦٦ فَجَعَلْنَاهَا نَكَالًا لِّمَا بَيْنَ يَدَيْهَا وَمَا خَلْفَهَا وَمَوْعِظَةً لِّلْمُتَّقِينَ

66 Thus We made it a deterrent for their generation, and for subsequent generations, and a lesson for the righteous.

٦٧ وَإِذْ قَالَ مُوسَىٰ لِقَوْمِهِ إِنَّ اللَّهَ يَأْمُرُكُمْ أَن تَذْبَحُوا بَقَرَةً ۖ قَالُوا أَتَتَّخِذُنَا هُزُوًا ۖ قَالَ أَعُوذُ بِاللَّهِ أَنْ أَكُونَ مِنَ الْجَاهِلِينَ

67 And recall when Moses said to his people, "God commands you to sacrifice a heifer." They said, "Do you make a mockery of us?" He said, "God forbid that I should be so ignorant."

٦٨ قَالُوا ادْعُ لَنَا رَبَّكَ يُبَيِّن لَّنَا مَا هِيَ ۚ قَالَ إِنَّهُ يَقُولُ إِنَّهَا بَقَرَةٌ لَّا فَارِضٌ وَلَا بِكْرٌ عَوَانٌ بَيْنَ ذَٰلِكَ ۖ فَافْعَلُوا مَا تُؤْمَرُونَ

68 They said, "Call upon your Lord to show us which one." He said, "He says she is a heifer, neither too old, nor too young, but in between. So do what you are commanded."

٦٩ قَالُوا ادْعُ لَنَا رَبَّكَ يُبَيِّن لَّنَا مَا لَوْنُهَا ۚ قَالَ إِنَّهُ يَقُولُ إِنَّهَا بَقَرَةٌ صَفْرَاءُ فَاقِعٌ لَّوْنُهَا تَسُرُّ النَّاظِرِينَ

69 They said, "Call upon your Lord to show us what her color is." He said, "He says she is a yellow heifer, bright in color, pleasing to the beholders."

٧٠ قَالُوا ادْعُ لَنَا رَبَّكَ يُبَيِّن لَّنَا مَا هِيَ إِنَّ الْبَقَرَ تَشَابَهَ عَلَيْنَا وَإِنَّا إِن شَاءَ اللَّهُ لَمُهْتَدُونَ

70 They said, "Call upon your Lord to show us which one; the heifers look alike to us; and God willing, we will be guided."

٧١ قَالَ إِنَّهُ يَقُولُ إِنَّهَا بَقَرَةٌ لَّا ذَلُولٌ تُثِيرُ الْأَرْضَ وَلَا تَسْقِي الْحَرْثَ مُسَلَّمَةٌ لَّا شِيَةَ فِيهَا ۚ قَالُوا الْآنَ جِئْتَ بِالْحَقِّ ۚ فَذَبَحُوهَا وَمَا كَادُوا يَفْعَلُونَ

71 He said, "He says she is a heifer, neither yoked to plow the earth, nor to irrigate the field; sound without blemish." They said, "Now you have brought the truth." So they slew her; though they almost did not.

٧٢ وَإِذْ قَتَلْتُمْ نَفْسًا فَادَّارَأْتُمْ فِيهَا ۖ وَاللَّهُ مُخْرِجٌ مَّا كُنتُمْ تَكْتُمُونَ

72 And recall when you killed a person, and disputed in the matter; but God was to expose what you were hiding.

٧٣ فَقُلْنَا اضْرِبُوهُ بِبَعْضِهَا ۚ كَذَٰلِكَ يُحْيِي اللَّهُ الْمَوْتَىٰ وَيُرِيكُمْ آيَاتِهِ لَعَلَّكُمْ تَعْقِلُونَ

73 We said, "Strike him with part of it." Thus God brings the dead to life; and He shows you His signs, that you may understand.

٧٤ ثُمَّ قَسَتْ قُلُوبُكُم مِّن بَعْدِ ذَٰلِكَ فَهِيَ كَالْحِجَارَةِ أَوْ أَشَدُّ قَسْوَةً ۚ وَإِنَّ مِنَ الْحِجَارَةِ لَمَا يَتَفَجَّرُ مِنْهُ الْأَنْهَارُ ۚ وَإِنَّ مِنْهَا لَمَا يَشَّقَّقُ فَيَخْرُجُ مِنْهُ الْمَاءُ ۚ وَإِنَّ مِنْهَا لَمَا يَهْبِطُ مِنْ خَشْيَةِ اللَّهِ ۗ وَمَا اللَّهُ بِغَافِلٍ عَمَّا تَعْمَلُونَ

74
5:13; 57:16

74 Then after that your hearts hardened. They were as rocks, or even harder. For there are some rocks from which rivers gush out, and others that splinter and water comes out from them, and others that sink in awe of God. God is not unaware of what you do.

٧٥ أَفَتَطْمَعُونَ أَن يُؤْمِنُوا لَكُمْ وَقَدْ كَانَ فَرِيقٌ مِّنْهُمْ يَسْمَعُونَ كَلَامَ اللَّهِ ثُمَّ يُحَرِّفُونَهُ مِن بَعْدِ مَا عَقَلُوهُ وَهُمْ يَعْلَمُونَ

75
4:46; 5:13, 41

75 Do you hope that they will believe in you, when some of them used to hear the Word of God, and then deliberately distort it, even after understanding it?

٧٦ وَإِذَا لَقُوا الَّذِينَ آمَنُوا قَالُوا آمَنَّا وَإِذَا خَلَا بَعْضُهُمْ إِلَىٰ بَعْضٍ قَالُوا أَتُحَدِّثُونَهُم بِمَا فَتَحَ اللَّهُ عَلَيْكُمْ لِيُحَاجُّوكُم بِهِ عِندَ رَبِّكُمْ ۚ أَفَلَا تَعْقِلُونَ

76
2:14; 3:119

76 And when they come across those who believe, they say, "We believe," but when they come together privately, they say, "Will you inform them of what God has disclosed to you, so that they might dispute with you concerning it before your Lord?" Do you not understand?

٧٧ أَوَلَا يَعْلَمُونَ أَنَّ اللَّهَ يَعْلَمُ مَا يُسِرُّونَ وَمَا يُعْلِنُونَ

77 Do they not know that God knows what they conceal and what they reveal?

٧٨ وَمِنْهُمْ أُمِّيُّونَ لَا يَعْلَمُونَ الْكِتَابَ إِلَّا أَمَانِيَّ وَإِنْ هُمْ إِلَّا يَظُنُّونَ

78
4:123

78 And among them are uneducated who know the Scripture only through hearsay, and they only speculate.

٧٩ فَوَيْلٌ لِّلَّذِينَ يَكْتُبُونَ الْكِتَابَ بِأَيْدِيهِمْ ثُمَّ يَقُولُونَ هَٰذَا مِنْ عِندِ اللَّهِ لِيَشْتَرُوا بِهِ ثَمَنًا قَلِيلًا ۖ فَوَيْلٌ لَّهُم مِّمَّا كَتَبَتْ أَيْدِيهِمْ وَوَيْلٌ لَّهُم مِّمَّا يَكْسِبُونَ

79
3:78; 4:46

79 So woe to those who write the Scripture with their own hands, and then say, "This is from God," that they may exchange it for a little price. Woe to them for what their hands have written, and woe to them for what they earn.

٨٠ وَقَالُوا لَن تَمَسَّنَا النَّارُ إِلَّا أَيَّامًا مَّعْدُودَةً ۚ قُلْ أَتَّخَذْتُمْ عِندَ اللَّهِ عَهْدًا فَلَن يُخْلِفَ اللَّهُ عَهْدَهُ ۖ أَمْ تَقُولُونَ عَلَى اللَّهِ مَا لَا تَعْلَمُونَ

80
3:24

80 And they say, "The Fire will not touch us except for a number of days." Say, "Have you received a promise from God—God never breaks His promise—or are you saying about God what you do not know?"

٨١ بَلَىٰ مَن كَسَبَ سَيِّئَةً وَأَحَاطَتْ بِهِ خَطِيئَتُهُ فَأُولَٰئِكَ أَصْحَابُ النَّارِ ۖ هُمْ فِيهَا خَالِدُونَ

81 Indeed, whoever commits misdeeds, and becomes besieged by his iniquities—these are the inmates of the Fire, wherein they will dwell forever.

٨٢ وَالَّذِينَ آمَنُوا وَعَمِلُوا الصَّالِحَاتِ أُولَٰئِكَ أَصْحَابُ الْجَنَّةِ ۖ هُمْ فِيهَا خَالِدُونَ

82 As for those who believe and do righteous deeds—these are the inhabitants of Paradise, wherein they will dwell forever.

٨٣ وَإِذْ أَخَذْنَا مِيثَاقَ بَنِي إِسْرَائِيلَ لَا تَعْبُدُونَ إِلَّا اللَّهَ وَبِالْوَالِدَيْنِ إِحْسَانًا وَذِي الْقُرْبَىٰ وَالْيَتَامَىٰ وَالْمَسَاكِينِ وَقُولُوا لِلنَّاسِ حُسْنًا وَأَقِيمُوا الصَّلَاةَ وَآتُوا الزَّكَاةَ ثُمَّ تَوَلَّيْتُمْ إِلَّا قَلِيلًا مِّنكُمْ وَأَنتُم مُّعْرِضُونَ

83
4:36; 17:23; 29:8

83 We made a covenant with the Children of Israel: "Worship none but God; and be good to parents, and relatives, and orphans, and the needy; and speak nicely to people; and pray regularly, and give alms." Then you turned away, except for a few of you, recanting.

٨٤ وَإِذْ أَخَذْنَا مِيثَاقَكُمْ لَا تَسْفِكُونَ دِمَاءَكُمْ وَلَا تُخْرِجُونَ أَنفُسَكُم مِّن دِيَارِكُمْ ثُمَّ أَقْرَرْتُمْ وَأَنتُمْ تَشْهَدُونَ

84
3:81

84 And We made a covenant with you: "You shall not shed the blood of your own, nor shall you evict your own from your homes." You agreed, and were all witnesses.

٨٥ ثُمَّ أَنتُمْ هَٰؤُلَاءِ تَقْتُلُونَ أَنفُسَكُمْ وَتُخْرِجُونَ فَرِيقًا مِّنكُم مِّن دِيَارِهِمْ تَظَاهَرُونَ عَلَيْهِم بِالْإِثْمِ وَالْعُدْوَانِ وَإِن يَأْتُوكُمْ أُسَارَىٰ تُفَادُوهُمْ وَهُوَ مُحَرَّمٌ عَلَيْكُمْ إِخْرَاجُهُمْ ۚ أَفَتُؤْمِنُونَ بِبَعْضِ الْكِتَابِ وَتَكْفُرُونَ بِبَعْضٍ ۚ فَمَا جَزَاءُ مَن يَفْعَلُ ذَٰلِكَ مِنكُمْ إِلَّا خِزْيٌ فِي الْحَيَاةِ الدُّنْيَا ۖ وَيَوْمَ الْقِيَامَةِ يُرَدُّونَ إِلَىٰ أَشَدِّ الْعَذَابِ ۗ وَمَا اللَّهُ بِغَافِلٍ عَمَّا تَعْمَلُونَ

85 But here you are, killing your own, and expelling a group of your own from their homes—conspiring against them in wrongdoing and hostility. And if they come to you as captives, you ransom them, although it was forbidden to you. Is it that you believe in part of the Scripture, and disbelieve in part? What is the reward for those among you who do that but humiliation in this life? And on the Day of Resurrection, they will be assigned to the most severe torment. God is not unaware of what you do.

٨٦ أُولَٰئِكَ الَّذِينَ اشْتَرَوُا الْحَيَاةَ الدُّنْيَا بِالْآخِرَةِ ۖ فَلَا يُخَفَّفُ عَنْهُمُ الْعَذَابُ وَلَا هُمْ يُنصَرُونَ

86 Those are they who bought the present life for the Hereafter, so the punishment will not be lightened for them, nor will they be helped.

٨٧ وَلَقَدْ آتَيْنَا مُوسَى الْكِتَابَ وَقَفَّيْنَا مِنْ بَعْدِهِ بِالرُّسُلِ ۖ وَآتَيْنَا عِيسَى ابْنَ مَرْيَمَ الْبَيِّنَاتِ وَأَيَّدْنَاهُ بِرُوحِ الْقُدُسِ ۗ أَفَكُلَّمَا جَاءَكُمْ رَسُولٌ بِمَا لَا تَهْوَىٰ أَنْفُسُكُمُ اسْتَكْبَرْتُمْ فَفَرِيقًا كَذَّبْتُمْ وَفَرِيقًا تَقْتُلُونَ

87 We gave Moses the Scripture, and sent a succession of messengers after him. And We gave Jesus son of Mary the clear proofs, and We supported him with the Holy Spirit. Is it that whenever a messenger comes to you with anything your souls do not desire, you grew arrogant, calling some impostors, and killing others?

87
2:253; 3:87; 5:110

٨٨ وَقَالُوا قُلُوبُنَا غُلْفٌ ۚ بَلْ لَعَنَهُمُ اللَّهُ بِكُفْرِهِمْ فَقَلِيلًا مَا يُؤْمِنُونَ

88 And they said, "Our hearts are sealed." Rather, God has cursed them for their ingratitude. They have little faith.

88
4:155

٨٩ وَلَمَّا جَاءَهُمْ كِتَابٌ مِنْ عِنْدِ اللَّهِ مُصَدِّقٌ لِمَا مَعَهُمْ وَكَانُوا مِنْ قَبْلُ يَسْتَفْتِحُونَ عَلَى الَّذِينَ كَفَرُوا فَلَمَّا جَاءَهُمْ مَا عَرَفُوا كَفَرُوا بِهِ ۚ فَلَعْنَةُ اللَّهِ عَلَى الْكَافِرِينَ

89 And when a scripture came to them from God, confirming what they have—although previously they were seeking victory against those who disbelieved—but when there came to them what they recognized, they disbelieved in it. So God's curse is upon the disbelievers.

٩٠ بِئْسَمَا اشْتَرَوْا بِهِ أَنْفُسَهُمْ أَنْ يَكْفُرُوا بِمَا أَنْزَلَ اللَّهُ بَغْيًا أَنْ يُنَزِّلَ اللَّهُ مِنْ فَضْلِهِ عَلَى مَنْ يَشَاءُ مِنْ عِبَادِهِ ۖ فَبَاءُوا بِغَضَبٍ عَلَىٰ غَضَبٍ ۚ وَلِلْكَافِرِينَ عَذَابٌ مُهِينٌ

90 Miserable is what they sold their souls for—rejecting what God has revealed, out of resentment that God would send down His grace upon whomever He chooses from among His servants. Thus they incurred wrath upon wrath. And there is a demeaning punishment for the disbelievers.

٩١ وَإِذَا قِيلَ لَهُمْ آمِنُوا بِمَا أَنْزَلَ اللَّهُ قَالُوا نُؤْمِنُ بِمَا أُنْزِلَ عَلَيْنَا وَيَكْفُرُونَ بِمَا وَرَاءَهُ وَهُوَ الْحَقُّ مُصَدِّقًا لِمَا مَعَهُمْ ۗ قُلْ فَلِمَ تَقْتُلُونَ أَنْبِيَاءَ اللَّهِ مِنْ قَبْلُ إِنْ كُنْتُمْ مُؤْمِنِينَ

91 And when it is said to them, "Believe in what God has revealed," they say, "We believe in what was revealed to us," and they reject anything beyond that, although it is the truth which confirms what they have. Say, "Why did you kill God's prophets before, if you were believers?"

91
2: 61, 3:21, 181; 4:155

٩٢ وَلَقَدْ جَاءَكُمْ مُوسَىٰ بِالْبَيِّنَاتِ ثُمَّ اتَّخَذْتُمُ الْعِجْلَ مِنْ بَعْدِهِ وَأَنْتُمْ ظَالِمُونَ

92 Moses came to you with clear proofs, yet you adopted the calf in his absence, and you were in the wrong.

92
2:51, 54; 4:153; 7:152

٩٣ وَإِذْ أَخَذْنَا مِيثَاقَكُمْ وَرَفَعْنَا فَوْقَكُمُ الطُّورَ خُذُوا مَا آتَيْنَاكُمْ بِقُوَّةٍ وَاسْمَعُوا ۖ قَالُوا سَمِعْنَا وَعَصَيْنَا وَأُشْرِبُوا فِي قُلُوبِهِمُ الْعِجْلَ بِكُفْرِهِمْ ۚ قُلْ بِئْسَمَا يَأْمُرُكُمْ بِهِ إِيمَانُكُمْ إِنْ كُنْتُمْ مُؤْمِنِينَ

93 And We made a covenant with you, and raised the Mount above you: "Take what We have given you firmly, and listen." They said, "We hear and disobey." And their hearts became filled with the love of the calf because of their disbelief. Say, "Wretched is what your faith commands you to do, if you are believers."

93
2:63; 7:171

Sūrah 2: Al-Baqarah

٩٤ قُلْ إِن كَانَتْ لَكُمُ ٱلدَّارُ ٱلْآخِرَةُ عِندَ ٱللَّهِ خَالِصَةً مِّن دُونِ ٱلنَّاسِ فَتَمَنَّوُا۟ ٱلْمَوْتَ إِن كُنتُمْ صَٰدِقِينَ

94 Say, "If the Final Home with God is yours alone, to the exclusion of all other people, then wish for death if you are sincere."

٩٥ وَلَن يَتَمَنَّوْهُ أَبَدًۢا بِمَا قَدَّمَتْ أَيْدِيهِمْ ۚ وَٱللَّهُ عَلِيمٌۢ بِٱلظَّٰلِمِينَ

95 But they will never wish for it, because of what their hands have forwarded. God is aware of the evildoers.

٩٦ وَلَتَجِدَنَّهُمْ أَحْرَصَ ٱلنَّاسِ عَلَىٰ حَيَوٰةٍ وَمِنَ ٱلَّذِينَ أَشْرَكُوا۟ ۚ يَوَدُّ أَحَدُهُمْ لَوْ يُعَمَّرُ أَلْفَ سَنَةٍ وَمَا هُوَ بِمُزَحْزِحِهِۦ مِنَ ٱلْعَذَابِ أَن يُعَمَّرَ ۗ وَٱللَّهُ بَصِيرٌۢ بِمَا يَعْمَلُونَ

96 You will find them, of all mankind, the most eager for life, even more than the polytheists. Every one of them wishes he could live a thousand years; but to be granted a long life will not nudge him from the punishment. God is Seeing of what they do.

٩٧ قُلْ مَن كَانَ عَدُوًّا لِّجِبْرِيلَ فَإِنَّهُۥ نَزَّلَهُۥ عَلَىٰ قَلْبِكَ بِإِذْنِ ٱللَّهِ مُصَدِّقًا لِّمَا بَيْنَ يَدَيْهِ وَهُدًى وَبُشْرَىٰ لِلْمُؤْمِنِينَ

97 Say, "Whoever is hostile to Gabriel—it is he who revealed it to your heart by God's leave, confirming what preceded it, and guidance and good news for the believers."

٩٨ مَن كَانَ عَدُوًّا لِّلَّهِ وَمَلَٰٓئِكَتِهِۦ وَرُسُلِهِۦ وَجِبْرِيلَ وَمِيكَىٰلَ فَإِنَّ ٱللَّهَ عَدُوٌّ لِّلْكَٰفِرِينَ

98 Whoever is hostile to God, and His angels, and His messengers, and Gabriel, and Michael—God is hostile to the faithless.

٩٩ وَلَقَدْ أَنزَلْنَآ إِلَيْكَ ءَايَٰتٍۭ بَيِّنَٰتٍ ۖ وَمَا يَكْفُرُ بِهَآ إِلَّا ٱلْفَٰسِقُونَ

99 We have revealed to you clear signs, and none rejects them except the sinners.

١٠٠ أَوَكُلَّمَا عَٰهَدُوا۟ عَهْدًا نَّبَذَهُۥ فَرِيقٌ مِّنْهُم ۚ بَلْ أَكْثَرُهُمْ لَا يُؤْمِنُونَ

100 Is it not that whenever they make a covenant, some of them toss it aside? In fact, most of them do not believe.

١٠١ وَلَمَّا جَآءَهُمْ رَسُولٌ مِّنْ عِندِ ٱللَّهِ مُصَدِّقٌ لِّمَا مَعَهُمْ نَبَذَ فَرِيقٌ مِّنَ ٱلَّذِينَ أُوتُوا۟ ٱلْكِتَٰبَ كِتَٰبَ ٱللَّهِ وَرَآءَ ظُهُورِهِمْ كَأَنَّهُمْ لَا يَعْلَمُونَ

101 And when there came to them a messenger from God, confirming what they had, a faction of those who were given the Book threw the Book of God behind their backs, as if they do not know.

١٠٢ وَٱتَّبَعُوا۟ مَا تَتْلُوا۟ ٱلشَّيَٰطِينُ عَلَىٰ مُلْكِ سُلَيْمَٰنَ ۖ وَمَا كَفَرَ سُلَيْمَٰنُ وَلَٰكِنَّ ٱلشَّيَٰطِينَ كَفَرُوا۟ يُعَلِّمُونَ ٱلنَّاسَ ٱلسِّحْرَ وَمَآ أُنزِلَ عَلَى ٱلْمَلَكَيْنِ بِبَابِلَ هَٰرُوتَ وَمَٰرُوتَ ۚ وَمَا يُعَلِّمَانِ مِنْ أَحَدٍ حَتَّىٰ يَقُولَآ إِنَّمَا نَحْنُ فِتْنَةٌ فَلَا تَكْفُرْ ۖ فَيَتَعَلَّمُونَ مِنْهُمَا مَا يُفَرِّقُونَ بِهِۦ بَيْنَ ٱلْمَرْءِ وَزَوْجِهِۦ ۚ وَمَا هُم بِضَآرِّينَ بِهِۦ مِنْ أَحَدٍ إِلَّا بِإِذْنِ ٱللَّهِ ۚ وَيَتَعَلَّمُونَ مَا يَضُرُّهُمْ وَلَا يَنفَعُهُمْ ۚ وَلَقَدْ عَلِمُوا۟ لَمَنِ ٱشْتَرَىٰهُ مَا لَهُۥ فِى ٱلْآخِرَةِ مِنْ خَلَٰقٍ ۚ وَلَبِئْسَ مَا شَرَوْا۟ بِهِۦٓ أَنفُسَهُمْ ۚ لَوْ كَانُوا۟ يَعْلَمُونَ

102 And they followed what the devils taught during the reign of Solomon. It was not Solomon who disbelieved, but it was the devils

94–95
62:6–7

97
3:3; 5:48; 35:31
16:102; 26:193–194

100
3:187; 8:56

who disbelieved. They taught the people witchcraft and what was revealed in Babylon to the two angels Harut and Marut. They did not teach anybody until they had said, "We are a test, so do not lose faith." But they learned from them the means to cause separation between man and his wife. But they cannot harm anyone except with God's permission. And they learned what would harm them and not benefit them. Yet they knew that whoever deals in it will have no share in the Hereafter. Miserable is what they sold their souls for, if they only knew.

١٠٣ وَلَوْ أَنَّهُمْ آمَنُوا وَاتَّقَوْا لَمَثُوبَةٌ مِنْ عِنْدِ اللَّهِ خَيْرٌ ۚ لَوْ كَانُوا يَعْلَمُونَ

103   3:110

103 Had they believed and been righteous, the reward from God would have been better, if they only knew.

١٠٤ يَا أَيُّهَا الَّذِينَ آمَنُوا لَا تَقُولُوا رَاعِنَا وَقُولُوا انْظُرْنَا وَاسْمَعُوا ۗ وَلِلْكَافِرِينَ عَذَابٌ أَلِيمٌ

104   4:46

104 O you who believe! Do not say ambiguous words, but say words of respect, and listen. The disbelievers will have a painful torment.

١٠٥ مَا يَوَدُّ الَّذِينَ كَفَرُوا مِنْ أَهْلِ الْكِتَابِ وَلَا الْمُشْرِكِينَ أَنْ يُنَزَّلَ عَلَيْكُمْ مِنْ خَيْرٍ مِنْ رَبِّكُمْ ۗ وَاللَّهُ يَخْتَصُّ بِرَحْمَتِهِ مَنْ يَشَاءُ ۚ وَاللَّهُ ذُو الْفَضْلِ الْعَظِيمِ

105   3:74

105 It is never the wish of the disbelievers from among the People of the Book, nor of the polytheists, that any good should be sent down to you from your Lord. But God chooses for His mercy whomever He wills. God is Possessor of Sublime Grace.

١٠٦ مَا نَنْسَخْ مِنْ آيَةٍ أَوْ نُنْسِهَا نَأْتِ بِخَيْرٍ مِنْهَا أَوْ مِثْلِهَا ۗ أَلَمْ تَعْلَمْ أَنَّ اللَّهَ عَلَىٰ كُلِّ شَيْءٍ قَدِيرٌ

106   13:39; 16:101; 17:86

106 We never nullify a verse, nor cause it to be forgotten, unless We bring one better than it, or similar to it. Do you not know that God is capable of all things?

١٠٧ أَلَمْ تَعْلَمْ أَنَّ اللَّهَ لَهُ مُلْكُ السَّمَاوَاتِ وَالْأَرْضِ ۗ وَمَا لَكُمْ مِنْ دُونِ اللَّهِ مِنْ وَلِيٍّ وَلَا نَصِيرٍ

107   7:158; 9:116

107 Do you not know that to God belongs the sovereignty of the heavens and the earth, and that apart from God you have no guardian or helper?

١٠٨ أَمْ تُرِيدُونَ أَنْ تَسْأَلُوا رَسُولَكُمْ كَمَا سُئِلَ مُوسَىٰ مِنْ قَبْلُ ۗ وَمَنْ يَتَبَدَّلِ الْكُفْرَ بِالْإِيمَانِ فَقَدْ ضَلَّ سَوَاءَ السَّبِيلِ

108   4:153

108 Or do you want to question your Messenger as Moses was questioned before? Whoever exchanges faith for disbelief has strayed from the right path.

١٠٩ وَدَّ كَثِيرٌ مِنْ أَهْلِ الْكِتَابِ لَوْ يَرُدُّونَكُمْ مِنْ بَعْدِ إِيمَانِكُمْ كُفَّارًا حَسَدًا مِنْ عِنْدِ أَنْفُسِهِمْ مِنْ بَعْدِ مَا تَبَيَّنَ لَهُمُ الْحَقُّ ۖ فَاعْفُوا وَاصْفَحُوا حَتَّىٰ يَأْتِيَ اللَّهُ بِأَمْرِهِ ۗ إِنَّ اللَّهَ عَلَىٰ كُلِّ شَيْءٍ قَدِيرٌ

109   3:69, 100, 149; 4:54, 113

109 Many of the People of the Book wish to turn you back into unbelievers after you have believed, out of envy on their part, after the Truth has become clear to them. But pardon and overlook, until God brings His command. God has power over all things.

١١٠ وَأَقِيمُوا الصَّلَاةَ وَآتُوا الزَّكَاةَ ۚ وَمَا تُقَدِّمُوا لِأَنفُسِكُم مِّنْ خَيْرٍ تَجِدُوهُ عِندَ اللَّهِ ۗ إِنَّ اللَّهَ بِمَا تَعْمَلُونَ بَصِيرٌ

110
73:20

110 And perform the prayer, and give alms. Whatever good you forward for yourselves, you will find it with God. God is Seeing of everything you do.

١١١ وَقَالُوا لَن يَدْخُلَ الْجَنَّةَ إِلَّا مَن كَانَ هُودًا أَوْ نَصَارَىٰ ۗ تِلْكَ أَمَانِيُّهُمْ ۗ قُلْ هَاتُوا بُرْهَانَكُمْ إِن كُنتُمْ صَادِقِينَ

111
2:120, 135, 145; 3:73; 5:18; 13:37

111 And they say, "None will enter Heaven unless he is a Jew or a Christian." These are their wishes. Say, "Produce your proof, if you are truthful."

١١٢ بَلَىٰ مَنْ أَسْلَمَ وَجْهَهُ لِلَّهِ وَهُوَ مُحْسِنٌ فَلَهُ أَجْرُهُ عِندَ رَبِّهِ وَلَا خَوْفٌ عَلَيْهِمْ وَلَا هُمْ يَحْزَنُونَ

112
4:125; 31:22

112 In fact, whoever submits himself to God, and is a doer of good, will have his reward with his Lord—they have nothing to fear, nor shall they grieve.

١١٣ وَقَالَتِ الْيَهُودُ لَيْسَتِ النَّصَارَىٰ عَلَىٰ شَيْءٍ وَقَالَتِ النَّصَارَىٰ لَيْسَتِ الْيَهُودُ عَلَىٰ شَيْءٍ وَهُمْ يَتْلُونَ الْكِتَابَ ۗ كَذَٰلِكَ قَالَ الَّذِينَ لَا يَعْلَمُونَ مِثْلَ قَوْلِهِمْ ۚ فَاللَّهُ يَحْكُمُ بَيْنَهُمْ يَوْمَ الْقِيَامَةِ فِيمَا كَانُوا فِيهِ يَخْتَلِفُونَ

113
22:69

113 The Jews say, "The Christians are not based on anything;" and the Christians say, "The Jews are not based on anything." Yet they both read the Scripture. Similarly, the ignorant said the same thing. God will judge between them on the Day of Resurrection regarding their differences.

١١٤ وَمَنْ أَظْلَمُ مِمَّن مَّنَعَ مَسَاجِدَ اللَّهِ أَن يُذْكَرَ فِيهَا اسْمُهُ وَسَعَىٰ فِي خَرَابِهَا ۚ أُولَٰئِكَ مَا كَانَ لَهُمْ أَن يَدْخُلُوهَا إِلَّا خَائِفِينَ ۚ لَهُمْ فِي الدُّنْيَا خِزْيٌ وَلَهُمْ فِي الْآخِرَةِ عَذَابٌ عَظِيمٌ

114
17:7; 48:25

114 Who is more unjust than him who forbids the remembrance of God's name in places of worship, and contributes to their ruin? These ought not to enter them except in fear. For them is disgrace in this world, and for them is a terrible punishment in the Hereafter.

١١٥ وَلِلَّهِ الْمَشْرِقُ وَالْمَغْرِبُ ۚ فَأَيْنَمَا تُوَلُّوا فَثَمَّ وَجْهُ اللَّهِ ۚ إِنَّ اللَّهَ وَاسِعٌ عَلِيمٌ

115
2:142, 177, 187

115 To God belong the East and the West. Whichever way you turn, there is God's presence. God is Omnipresent and Omniscient.

١١٦ وَقَالُوا اتَّخَذَ اللَّهُ وَلَدًا ۗ سُبْحَانَهُ ۖ بَل لَّهُ مَا فِي السَّمَاوَاتِ وَالْأَرْضِ ۖ كُلٌّ لَّهُ قَانِتُونَ

116
4:171; 6:100; 10:68; 17:40, 111; 19:35; 21:26; 23:91; 25:2

116 And they say, "God has begotten a son." Be He glorified. Rather, His is everything in the heavens and the earth; all are obedient to Him.

١١٧ بَدِيعُ السَّمَاوَاتِ وَالْأَرْضِ ۖ وَإِذَا قَضَىٰ أَمْرًا فَإِنَّمَا يَقُولُ لَهُ كُن فَيَكُونُ

117
3:59; 19:35; 36:82

117 Originator of the heavens and the earth. Whenever He decrees a thing, He says to it, "Be," and it becomes.

١١٨ وَقَالَ الَّذِينَ لَا يَعْلَمُونَ لَوْلَا يُكَلِّمُنَا اللَّهُ أَوْ تَأْتِينَا آيَةٌ ۗ كَذَٰلِكَ قَالَ الَّذِينَ مِن قَبْلِهِم مِّثْلَ قَوْلِهِمْ ۘ تَشَابَهَتْ قُلُوبُهُمْ ۗ قَدْ بَيَّنَّا الْآيَاتِ لِقَوْمٍ يُوقِنُونَ

118
20:133; 21:5; 6:37; 13:7; 29:50

118 Those who do not know say, "If only God would speak to us, or a sign would come to us." Thus said those who were before them. Their hearts are alike. We have made the signs clear for people who are certain.

١١٩ إِنَّا أَرْسَلْنَاكَ بِالْحَقِّ بَشِيرًا وَنَذِيرًا ۖ وَلَا تُسْأَلُ عَنْ أَصْحَابِ الْجَحِيمِ

119
13:40; 50:45; 88:21–22

119 We have sent you with the truth—bringing good news, and giving warnings. You will not be questioned about the inmates of Hell.

١٢٠ وَلَن تَرْضَىٰ عَنكَ الْيَهُودُ وَلَا النَّصَارَىٰ حَتَّىٰ تَتَّبِعَ مِلَّتَهُمْ ۗ قُلْ إِنَّ هُدَى اللَّهِ هُوَ الْهُدَىٰ ۗ وَلَئِنِ اتَّبَعْتَ أَهْوَاءَهُم بَعْدَ الَّذِي جَاءَكَ مِنَ الْعِلْمِ ۙ مَا لَكَ مِنَ اللَّهِ مِن وَلِيٍّ وَلَا نَصِيرٍ

120
2:111, 135, 145; 3:73; 5:18; 13:37

120 The Jews and the Christians will not approve of you, unless you follow their creed. Say, "God's guidance is the guidance." Should you follow their desires, after the knowledge that has come to you, you will have in God neither guardian nor helper.

١٢١ الَّذِينَ آتَيْنَاهُمُ الْكِتَابَ يَتْلُونَهُ حَقَّ تِلَاوَتِهِ أُولَٰئِكَ يُؤْمِنُونَ بِهِ ۗ وَمَن يَكْفُرْ بِهِ فَأُولَٰئِكَ هُمُ الْخَاسِرُونَ

121 Those to whom We have given the Scripture follow it, as it ought to be followed—these believe in it. But as for those who reject it—these are the losers.

١٢٢ يَا بَنِي إِسْرَائِيلَ اذْكُرُوا نِعْمَتِيَ الَّتِي أَنْعَمْتُ عَلَيْكُمْ وَأَنِّي فَضَّلْتُكُمْ عَلَى الْعَالَمِينَ

122
pp 2:47

122 O Children of Israel! Remember My blessing which I bestowed upon you, and that I have favored you over all people.

١٢٣ وَاتَّقُوا يَوْمًا لَا تَجْزِي نَفْسٌ عَن نَّفْسٍ شَيْئًا وَلَا يُقْبَلُ مِنْهَا عَدْلٌ وَلَا تَنفَعُهَا شَفَاعَةٌ وَلَا هُمْ يُنصَرُونَ

123
pp 2:48

123 And beware of a Day when no soul will avail another soul in any way, and no ransom will be accepted from it, and no intercession will benefit it, and they will not be helped.

١٢٤ وَإِذِ ابْتَلَىٰ إِبْرَاهِيمَ رَبُّهُ بِكَلِمَاتٍ فَأَتَمَّهُنَّ ۖ قَالَ إِنِّي جَاعِلُكَ لِلنَّاسِ إِمَامًا ۖ قَالَ وَمِن ذُرِّيَّتِي ۖ قَالَ لَا يَنَالُ عَهْدِي الظَّالِمِينَ

124
37:113; 53:37

124 And when his Lord tested Abraham with certain words, and he fulfilled them. He said, "I am making you a leader of humanity." He said, "And my descendants?" He said, "My pledge does not include the wrongdoers."

١٢٥ وَإِذْ جَعَلْنَا الْبَيْتَ مَثَابَةً لِلنَّاسِ وَأَمْنًا وَاتَّخِذُوا مِنْ مَقَامِ إِبْرَاهِيمَ مُصَلًّى ۖ وَعَهِدْنَا إِلَىٰ إِبْرَاهِيمَ وَإِسْمَاعِيلَ أَنْ طَهِّرَا بَيْتِيَ لِلطَّائِفِينَ وَالْعَاكِفِينَ وَالرُّكَّعِ السُّجُودِ

125
14:37, 40

125 And We made the House a focal point for the people, and a sanctuary. Use the shrine of Abraham as a place of prayer. And We commissioned Abraham and Ishmael, "Sanctify My House for those who circle around it, and those who seclude themselves in it, and those who kneel and prostrate."

١٢٦ وَإِذْ قَالَ إِبْرَاهِيمُ رَبِّ اجْعَلْ هَٰذَا بَلَدًا آمِنًا وَارْزُقْ أَهْلَهُ مِنَ الثَّمَرَاتِ مَنْ آمَنَ مِنْهُمْ بِاللَّهِ وَالْيَوْمِ الْآخِرِ ۖ قَالَ وَمَنْ كَفَرَ فَأُمَتِّعُهُ قَلِيلًا ثُمَّ أَضْطَرُّهُ إِلَىٰ عَذَابِ النَّارِ ۖ وَبِئْسَ الْمَصِيرُ

126
14:35; 28:57

126 When Abraham said, "O My Lord, make this a peaceful land, and provide its people with fruits—whoever of them believes in God and the Last Day." He said, "And whoever disbelieves, I will give him a little enjoyment, then I will consign him to the punishment of the Fire; how miserable the destiny!"

١٢٧ وَإِذْ يَرْفَعُ إِبْرَاهِيمُ الْقَوَاعِدَ مِنَ الْبَيْتِ وَإِسْمَاعِيلُ رَبَّنَا تَقَبَّلْ مِنَّا ۖ إِنَّكَ أَنْتَ السَّمِيعُ الْعَلِيمُ

127
3:96–97; 22:26; 62:2–3

127 As Abraham raises the foundations of the House, together with Ishmael, "Our Lord, accept it from us, You are the Hearer, the Knower.

١٢٨ رَبَّنَا وَاجْعَلْنَا مُسْلِمَيْنِ لَكَ وَمِنْ ذُرِّيَّتِنَا أُمَّةً مُسْلِمَةً لَكَ وَأَرِنَا مَنَاسِكَنَا وَتُبْ عَلَيْنَا ۖ إِنَّكَ أَنْتَ التَّوَّابُ الرَّحِيمُ

128 Our Lord, and make us submissive to You, and from our descendants a community submissive to You. And show us our rites, and accept our repentance. You are the Acceptor of Repentance, the Merciful.

١٢٩ رَبَّنَا وَابْعَثْ فِيهِمْ رَسُولًا مِنْهُمْ يَتْلُو عَلَيْهِمْ آيَاتِكَ وَيُعَلِّمُهُمُ الْكِتَابَ وَالْحِكْمَةَ وَيُزَكِّيهِمْ ۚ إِنَّكَ أَنْتَ الْعَزِيزُ الْحَكِيمُ

129
2:151; 3:164; 62:2

129 Our Lord, and raise up among them a messenger, of themselves, who will recite to them Your revelations, and teach them the Book and wisdom, and purify them. You are the Almighty, the Wise."

١٣٠ وَمَنْ يَرْغَبُ عَنْ مِلَّةِ إِبْرَاهِيمَ إِلَّا مَنْ سَفِهَ نَفْسَهُ ۚ وَلَقَدِ اصْطَفَيْنَاهُ فِي الدُّنْيَا ۖ وَإِنَّهُ فِي الْآخِرَةِ لَمِنَ الصَّالِحِينَ

130
6:161; 16:123

130 Who would forsake the religion of Abraham, except he who fools himself? We chose him in this world, and in the Hereafter he will be among the righteous.

١٣١ إِذْ قَالَ لَهُ رَبُّهُ أَسْلِمْ ۖ قَالَ أَسْلَمْتُ لِرَبِّ الْعَالَمِينَ

131 When his Lord said to him, "Submit!" He said, "I have submitted to the Lord of the Worlds."

١٣٢ وَوَصَّىٰ بِهَا إِبْرَاهِيمُ بَنِيهِ وَيَعْقُوبُ يَا بَنِيَّ إِنَّ اللَّهَ اصْطَفَىٰ لَكُمُ الدِّينَ فَلَا تَمُوتُنَّ إِلَّا وَأَنتُم مُّسْلِمُونَ

132 And Abraham exhorted his sons, and Jacob, "O my sons, God has chosen this religion for you, so do not die unless you have submitted."

١٣٣ أَمْ كُنتُمْ شُهَدَاءَ إِذْ حَضَرَ يَعْقُوبَ الْمَوْتُ إِذْ قَالَ لِبَنِيهِ مَا تَعْبُدُونَ مِن بَعْدِي قَالُوا نَعْبُدُ إِلَٰهَكَ وَإِلَٰهَ آبَائِكَ إِبْرَاهِيمَ وَإِسْمَاعِيلَ وَإِسْحَاقَ إِلَٰهًا وَاحِدًا وَنَحْنُ لَهُ مُسْلِمُونَ

133 Or were you witnesses when death approached Jacob, and he said to his sons, "What will you worship after Me?" They said, "We will worship your God, and the God of your fathers, Abraham, Ishmael, and Isaac; One God; and to Him we submit."

١٣٤ تِلْكَ أُمَّةٌ قَدْ خَلَتْ ۖ لَهَا مَا كَسَبَتْ وَلَكُم مَّا كَسَبْتُمْ ۖ وَلَا تُسْأَلُونَ عَمَّا كَانُوا يَعْمَلُونَ

134
2:141, 286

134 That was a community that has passed; for them is what they have earned, and for you is what you have earned; and you will not be questioned about what they used to do.

١٣٥ وَقَالُوا كُونُوا هُودًا أَوْ نَصَارَىٰ تَهْتَدُوا ۗ قُلْ بَلْ مِلَّةَ إِبْرَاهِيمَ حَنِيفًا ۖ وَمَا كَانَ مِنَ الْمُشْرِكِينَ

135
[a] 2:111, 3:67
[b] 2:130; 3:95; 6:161; 12:38; 16:123; 22:78

135 And they say, "Be Jews or Christians, and you will be guided." Say, "Rather, the religion of Abraham, the Monotheist; he was not an idolater."

١٣٦ قُولُوا آمَنَّا بِاللَّهِ وَمَا أُنزِلَ إِلَيْنَا وَمَا أُنزِلَ إِلَىٰ إِبْرَاهِيمَ وَإِسْمَاعِيلَ وَإِسْحَاقَ وَيَعْقُوبَ وَالْأَسْبَاطِ وَمَا أُوتِيَ مُوسَىٰ وَعِيسَىٰ وَمَا أُوتِيَ النَّبِيُّونَ مِن رَّبِّهِمْ لَا نُفَرِّقُ بَيْنَ أَحَدٍ مِّنْهُمْ وَنَحْنُ لَهُ مُسْلِمُونَ

136
2:285; 3:84; 4:152

136 Say, "We believe in God; and in what was revealed to us; and in what was revealed to Abraham, and Ishmael, and Isaac, and Jacob, and the Patriarchs; and in what was given to Moses and Jesus; and in what was given to the prophets—from their Lord. We make no distinction between any of them, and to Him we surrender."

١٣٧ فَإِنْ آمَنُوا بِمِثْلِ مَا آمَنتُم بِهِ فَقَدِ اهْتَدَوا ۖ وَّإِن تَوَلَّوْا فَإِنَّمَا هُمْ فِي شِقَاقٍ ۖ فَسَيَكْفِيكَهُمُ اللَّهُ ۚ وَهُوَ السَّمِيعُ الْعَلِيمُ

137
3:20

137 If they believe in the same as you have believed in, then they have been guided. But if they turn away, then they are in schism. God will protect you against them; for He is the Hearer, the Knower.

١٣٨ صِبْغَةَ اللَّهِ ۖ وَمَنْ أَحْسَنُ مِنَ اللَّهِ صِبْغَةً ۖ وَنَحْنُ لَهُ عَابِدُونَ

138 God's coloring. And who gives better coloring than God? "And we are devoted to Him."

١٣٩ قُلْ أَتُحَاجُّونَنَا فِي اللَّهِ وَهُوَ رَبُّنَا وَرَبُّكُمْ وَلَنَا أَعْمَالُنَا وَلَكُمْ أَعْمَالُكُمْ وَنَحْنُ لَهُ مُخْلِصُونَ

139 Say, "Do you argue with us about God, when He is our Lord and your Lord, and We have our works, and you have your works, and we are sincere to Him?"

139 29:46; 109:2–5

١٤٠ أَمْ تَقُولُونَ إِنَّ إِبْرَاهِيمَ وَإِسْمَاعِيلَ وَإِسْحَاقَ وَيَعْقُوبَ وَالْأَسْبَاطَ كَانُوا هُودًا أَوْ نَصَارَىٰ ۗ قُلْ أَأَنْتُمْ أَعْلَمُ أَمِ اللَّهُ ۗ وَمَنْ أَظْلَمُ مِمَّنْ كَتَمَ شَهَادَةً عِنْدَهُ مِنَ اللَّهِ ۗ وَمَا اللَّهُ بِغَافِلٍ عَمَّا تَعْمَلُونَ

140 Or do you say that Abraham, Ishmael, Isaac, Jacob, and the Patriarchs were Jews or Christians? Say, "Do you know better, or God?" And who does greater wrong than he who conceals a testimony he has from God? God is not unaware of what you do.

١٤١ تِلْكَ أُمَّةٌ قَدْ خَلَتْ ۖ لَهَا مَا كَسَبَتْ وَلَكُمْ مَا كَسَبْتُمْ ۖ وَلَا تُسْأَلُونَ عَمَّا كَانُوا يَعْمَلُونَ

141 That was a community that has passed. To them is what they have earned, and to you is what you have earned. And you will not be questioned about what they used to do.

141 2:134

١٤٢ سَيَقُولُ السُّفَهَاءُ مِنَ النَّاسِ مَا وَلَّاهُمْ عَنْ قِبْلَتِهِمُ الَّتِي كَانُوا عَلَيْهَا ۚ قُلْ لِلَّهِ الْمَشْرِقُ وَالْمَغْرِبُ ۚ يَهْدِي مَنْ يَشَاءُ إِلَىٰ صِرَاطٍ مُسْتَقِيمٍ

142 The ignorant among the people will say, "What has turned them away from the direction of prayer they once followed?" Say, "To God belong the East and the West. He guides whom He wills to a straight path."

142 1:6; 2:115, 117, 187, 213; 10:25

١٤٣ وَكَذَٰلِكَ جَعَلْنَاكُمْ أُمَّةً وَسَطًا لِتَكُونُوا شُهَدَاءَ عَلَى النَّاسِ وَيَكُونَ الرَّسُولُ عَلَيْكُمْ شَهِيدًا ۗ وَمَا جَعَلْنَا الْقِبْلَةَ الَّتِي كُنْتَ عَلَيْهَا إِلَّا لِنَعْلَمَ مَنْ يَتَّبِعُ الرَّسُولَ مِمَّنْ يَنْقَلِبُ عَلَىٰ عَقِبَيْهِ ۚ وَإِنْ كَانَتْ لَكَبِيرَةً إِلَّا عَلَى الَّذِينَ هَدَى اللَّهُ ۗ وَمَا كَانَ اللَّهُ لِيُضِيعَ إِيمَانَكُمْ ۚ إِنَّ اللَّهَ بِالنَّاسِ لَرَءُوفٌ رَحِيمٌ

143 Thus We made you a moderate community, that you may be witnesses to humanity, and that the Messenger may be a witness to you. We only established the direction of prayer, which you once followed, that We may distinguish those who follow the Messenger from those who turn on their heels. It is indeed difficult, except for those whom God has guided. But God would never let your faith go to waste. God is Kind towards the people, Merciful.

143 4:41–42; 22:78

١٤٤ قَدْ نَرَىٰ تَقَلُّبَ وَجْهِكَ فِي السَّمَاءِ ۖ فَلَنُوَلِّيَنَّكَ قِبْلَةً تَرْضَاهَا ۚ فَوَلِّ وَجْهَكَ شَطْرَ الْمَسْجِدِ الْحَرَامِ ۚ وَحَيْثُ مَا كُنْتُمْ فَوَلُّوا وُجُوهَكُمْ شَطْرَهُ ۗ وَإِنَّ الَّذِينَ أُوتُوا الْكِتَابَ لَيَعْلَمُونَ أَنَّهُ الْحَقُّ مِنْ رَبِّهِمْ ۗ وَمَا اللَّهُ بِغَافِلٍ عَمَّا يَعْمَلُونَ

144 We have seen your face turned towards the heaven. So We will turn you towards a direction that will satisfy you. So turn your face towards the Sacred Mosque. And wherever you may be, turn your faces towards it. Those who were given the Book know that it is the Truth from their Lord; and God is not unaware of what they do.

144 2:149–150

١٤٥ وَلَئِنْ أَتَيْتَ الَّذِينَ أُوتُوا الْكِتَابَ بِكُلِّ آيَةٍ مَا تَبِعُوا قِبْلَتَكَ ۚ وَمَا أَنْتَ بِتَابِعٍ قِبْلَتَهُمْ ۚ وَمَا بَعْضُهُمْ بِتَابِعٍ قِبْلَةَ بَعْضٍ ۚ وَلَئِنِ اتَّبَعْتَ أَهْوَاءَهُمْ مِنْ بَعْدِ مَا جَاءَكَ مِنَ الْعِلْمِ ۙ إِنَّكَ إِذًا لَمِنَ الظَّالِمِينَ

145
2:111, 135, 145; 3:73;
5:18; 13:37

145 Even if you were to bring to those who were given the Book every proof, they would not follow your direction, nor are you to follow their direction, nor do they follow the direction of one another. And if you were to follow their desires, after the knowledge that has come to you, you would be in that case one of the wrongdoers.

١٤٦ الَّذِينَ آتَيْنَاهُمُ الْكِتَابَ يَعْرِفُونَهُ كَمَا يَعْرِفُونَ أَبْنَاءَهُمْ ۖ وَإِنَّ فَرِيقًا مِنْهُمْ لَيَكْتُمُونَ الْحَقَّ وَهُمْ يَعْلَمُونَ

146
6:20, 114

146 Those to whom We have given the Book recognize it as they recognize their own children. But some of them conceal the truth while they know.

١٤٧ الْحَقُّ مِنْ رَبِّكَ ۖ فَلَا تَكُونَنَّ مِنَ الْمُمْتَرِينَ

147
pp 3:60

147 The truth is from your Lord, so do not be a skeptic.

١٤٨ وَلِكُلٍّ وِجْهَةٌ هُوَ مُوَلِّيهَا ۖ فَاسْتَبِقُوا الْخَيْرَاتِ ۚ أَيْنَ مَا تَكُونُوا يَأْتِ بِكُمُ اللَّهُ جَمِيعًا ۚ إِنَّ اللَّهَ عَلَىٰ كُلِّ شَيْءٍ قَدِيرٌ

148
5:48

148 To every community is a direction towards which it turns. Therefore, race towards goodness. Wherever you may be, God will bring you all together. God is capable of everything.

١٤٩ وَمِنْ حَيْثُ خَرَجْتَ فَوَلِّ وَجْهَكَ شَطْرَ الْمَسْجِدِ الْحَرَامِ ۖ وَإِنَّهُ لَلْحَقُّ مِنْ رَبِّكَ ۗ وَمَا اللَّهُ بِغَافِلٍ عَمَّا تَعْمَلُونَ

149–150
2:144

149 And wherever you come from, turn your face towards the Sacred Mosque. This is the truth from your Lord, and God is not heedless of what you do.

١٥٠ وَمِنْ حَيْثُ خَرَجْتَ فَوَلِّ وَجْهَكَ شَطْرَ الْمَسْجِدِ الْحَرَامِ ۚ وَحَيْثُ مَا كُنْتُمْ فَوَلُّوا وُجُوهَكُمْ شَطْرَهُ لِئَلَّا يَكُونَ لِلنَّاسِ عَلَيْكُمْ حُجَّةٌ إِلَّا الَّذِينَ ظَلَمُوا مِنْهُمْ فَلَا تَخْشَوْهُمْ وَاخْشَوْنِي وَلِأُتِمَّ نِعْمَتِي عَلَيْكُمْ وَلَعَلَّكُمْ تَهْتَدُونَ

150 And wherever you come from, turn your face towards the Sacred Mosque. And wherever you may be, turn your faces towards it. So that the people may not have any argument against you—except those who do wrong among them. So do not fear them, but fear Me, that I may complete My blessings upon you, and that you may be guided.

١٥١ كَمَا أَرْسَلْنَا فِيكُمْ رَسُولًا مِنْكُمْ يَتْلُو عَلَيْكُمْ آيَاتِنَا وَيُزَكِّيكُمْ وَيُعَلِّمُكُمُ الْكِتَابَ وَالْحِكْمَةَ وَيُعَلِّمُكُمْ مَا لَمْ تَكُونُوا تَعْلَمُونَ

151
2:129; 3:164; 62:2

151 Just as We sent to you a messenger from among you, who recites Our revelations to you, and purifies you, and teaches you the Book and wisdom, and teaches you what you did not know.

Sūrah 2: Al-Baqarah — 59

١٥٢ فَاذْكُرُونِي أَذْكُرْكُمْ وَاشْكُرُوا لِي وَلَا تَكْفُرُونِ

152 So remember Me, and I will remember you. And thank Me, and do not be ungrateful.

١٥٣ يَا أَيُّهَا الَّذِينَ آمَنُوا اسْتَعِينُوا بِالصَّبْرِ وَالصَّلَاةِ ۚ إِنَّ اللَّهَ مَعَ الصَّابِرِينَ

153 O you who believe! Seek help through patience and prayers. God is with the steadfast.

153
2:45

١٥٤ وَلَا تَقُولُوا لِمَنْ يُقْتَلُ فِي سَبِيلِ اللَّهِ أَمْوَاتٌ ۚ بَلْ أَحْيَاءٌ وَلَٰكِنْ لَا تَشْعُرُونَ

154 And do not say of those who are killed in the cause of God, "Dead." Rather, they are alive, but you do not perceive.

154
3:169

١٥٥ وَلَنَبْلُوَنَّكُمْ بِشَيْءٍ مِنَ الْخَوْفِ وَالْجُوعِ وَنَقْصٍ مِنَ الْأَمْوَالِ وَالْأَنْفُسِ وَالثَّمَرَاتِ ۗ وَبَشِّرِ الصَّابِرِينَ

155 We will certainly test you with some fear and hunger, and some loss of possessions and lives and crops. But give good news to the steadfast.

155
3:186

١٥٦ الَّذِينَ إِذَا أَصَابَتْهُمْ مُصِيبَةٌ قَالُوا إِنَّا لِلَّهِ وَإِنَّا إِلَيْهِ رَاجِعُونَ

156 Those who, when a calamity afflicts them, say, "To God we belong, and to Him we will return."

156
6:60, 164; 11:4; 39:7

١٥٧ أُولَٰئِكَ عَلَيْهِمْ صَلَوَاتٌ مِنْ رَبِّهِمْ وَرَحْمَةٌ ۖ وَأُولَٰئِكَ هُمُ الْمُهْتَدُونَ

157 Upon these are blessings and mercy from their Lord. These are the guided ones.

١٥٨ إِنَّ الصَّفَا وَالْمَرْوَةَ مِنْ شَعَائِرِ اللَّهِ ۖ فَمَنْ حَجَّ الْبَيْتَ أَوِ اعْتَمَرَ فَلَا جُنَاحَ عَلَيْهِ أَنْ يَطَّوَّفَ بِهِمَا ۚ وَمَنْ تَطَوَّعَ خَيْرًا فَإِنَّ اللَّهَ شَاكِرٌ عَلِيمٌ

158 Safa and Marwa are among the rites of God. Whoever makes the Pilgrimage to the House, or performs the Umrah, commits no error by circulating between them. Whoever volunteers good—God is Appreciative and Cognizant.

158
22:32

١٥٩ إِنَّ الَّذِينَ يَكْتُمُونَ مَا أَنْزَلْنَا مِنَ الْبَيِّنَاتِ وَالْهُدَىٰ مِنْ بَعْدِ مَا بَيَّنَّاهُ لِلنَّاسِ فِي الْكِتَابِ ۙ أُولَٰئِكَ يَلْعَنُهُمُ اللَّهُ وَيَلْعَنُهُمُ اللَّاعِنُونَ

159 Those who suppress the proofs and the guidance We have revealed, after We have clarified them to humanity in the Scripture—those—God curses them, and the cursers curse them.

159
2:174; 5:15; 6:91

١٦٠ إِلَّا الَّذِينَ تَابُوا وَأَصْلَحُوا وَبَيَّنُوا فَأُولَٰئِكَ أَتُوبُ عَلَيْهِمْ ۚ وَأَنَا التَّوَّابُ الرَّحِيمُ

160 Except those who repent, and reform, and proclaim. Those—I will accept their repentance. I am the Acceptor of Repentance, the Merciful.

160
3:89; 24:5

١٦١ إِنَّ الَّذِينَ كَفَرُوا وَمَاتُوا وَهُمْ كُفَّارٌ أُولَٰئِكَ عَلَيْهِمْ لَعْنَةُ اللَّهِ وَالْمَلَائِكَةِ وَالنَّاسِ أَجْمَعِينَ

161 3:87, 91; 4:18; 47:34

161 But as for those who reject faith, and die rejecting—those—upon them is the curse of God, and of the angels, and of all humanity.

١٦٢ خَالِدِينَ فِيهَا ۖ لَا يُخَفَّفُ عَنْهُمُ الْعَذَابُ وَلَا هُمْ يُنظَرُونَ

162 3:88

162 They will remain under it forever, and the torment will not be lightened for them, and they will not be reprieved.

١٦٣ وَإِلَٰهُكُمْ إِلَٰهٌ وَاحِدٌ ۖ لَّا إِلَٰهَ إِلَّا هُوَ الرَّحْمَٰنُ الرَّحِيمُ

163 Your God is one God. There is no god but He, the Benevolent, the Compassionate.

١٦٤ إِنَّ فِي خَلْقِ السَّمَاوَاتِ وَالْأَرْضِ وَاخْتِلَافِ اللَّيْلِ وَالنَّهَارِ وَالْفُلْكِ الَّتِي تَجْرِي فِي الْبَحْرِ بِمَا يَنفَعُ النَّاسَ وَمَا أَنزَلَ اللَّهُ مِنَ السَّمَاءِ مِن مَّاءٍ فَأَحْيَا بِهِ الْأَرْضَ بَعْدَ مَوْتِهَا وَبَثَّ فِيهَا مِن كُلِّ دَابَّةٍ وَتَصْرِيفِ الرِّيَاحِ وَالسَّحَابِ الْمُسَخَّرِ بَيْنَ السَّمَاءِ وَالْأَرْضِ لَآيَاتٍ لِّقَوْمٍ يَعْقِلُونَ

164 45:5; 3:190; 50:5-8; 67:3-5, 15

164 In the creation of the heavens and the earth; in the alternation of night and day; in the ships that sail the oceans for the benefit of mankind; in the water that God sends down from the sky, and revives the earth with it after it had died, and scatters in it all kinds of creatures; in the changing of the winds, and the clouds disposed between the sky and the earth; are signs for people who understand.

١٦٥ وَمِنَ النَّاسِ مَن يَتَّخِذُ مِن دُونِ اللَّهِ أَندَادًا يُحِبُّونَهُمْ كَحُبِّ اللَّهِ ۖ وَالَّذِينَ آمَنُوا أَشَدُّ حُبًّا لِّلَّهِ ۗ وَلَوْ يَرَى الَّذِينَ ظَلَمُوا إِذْ يَرَوْنَ الْعَذَابَ أَنَّ الْقُوَّةَ لِلَّهِ جَمِيعًا وَأَنَّ اللَّهَ شَدِيدُ الْعَذَابِ

165 14:30; 34:33; 39:8; 41:9

165 Yet among the people are those who take other than God as equals to Him. They love them as the love of God. But those who believe have greater love for God. If only the wrongdoers would realize, when they see the torment; that all power is God's, and that God is severe in punishment.

١٦٦ إِذْ تَبَرَّأَ الَّذِينَ اتُّبِعُوا مِنَ الَّذِينَ اتَّبَعُوا وَرَأَوُا الْعَذَابَ وَتَقَطَّعَتْ بِهِمُ الْأَسْبَابُ

166 6:94; 18:48; 19:80, 95

166 Those who were followed will then disown those who followed them, and they will see the retribution, and ties between them will be severed.

١٦٧ وَقَالَ الَّذِينَ اتَّبَعُوا لَوْ أَنَّ لَنَا كَرَّةً فَنَتَبَرَّأَ مِنْهُمْ كَمَا تَبَرَّءُوا مِنَّا ۗ كَذَٰلِكَ يُرِيهِمُ اللَّهُ أَعْمَالَهُمْ حَسَرَاتٍ عَلَيْهِمْ ۖ وَمَا هُم بِخَارِجِينَ مِنَ النَّارِ

167 26:102; 39:58

167 Those who followed will say, "If only we can have another chance, we will disown them, as they disowned us." Thus God will show them their deeds, as regrets to them, and they will not come out of the Fire.

١٦٨ يَا أَيُّهَا النَّاسُ كُلُوا مِمَّا فِي الْأَرْضِ حَلَالًا طَيِّبًا وَلَا تَتَّبِعُوا خُطُوَاتِ الشَّيْطَانِ ۚ إِنَّهُ لَكُمْ عَدُوٌّ مُّبِينٌ

168 2:208; 5:88; 6:142; 8:69; 24:21

168 O people! Eat of what is lawful and good on earth, and do not follow the footsteps of Satan. He is to you an open enemy.

١٦٩ إِنَّمَا يَأْمُرُكُم بِالسُّوءِ وَالْفَحْشَاءِ وَأَن تَقُولُوا عَلَى اللَّهِ مَا لَا تَعْلَمُونَ

169 2:268; 5:103; 10:59; 24:21

169 He commands you to do evil and vice, and to say about God what you do not know.

١٧٠ وَإِذَا قِيلَ لَهُمُ اتَّبِعُوا مَا أَنزَلَ اللَّهُ قَالُوا بَلْ نَتَّبِعُ مَا أَلْفَيْنَا عَلَيْهِ آبَاءَنَا ۗ أَوَلَوْ كَانَ آبَاؤُهُمْ لَا يَعْقِلُونَ شَيْئًا وَلَا يَهْتَدُونَ

170 5:104; 10:78; 31:21; 43:22–24

170 And when it is said to them, "Follow what God has revealed," they say, "We will follow what we found our ancestors following." Even if their ancestors understood nothing, and were not guided?

١٧١ وَمَثَلُ الَّذِينَ كَفَرُوا كَمَثَلِ الَّذِي يَنْعِقُ بِمَا لَا يَسْمَعُ إِلَّا دُعَاءً وَنِدَاءً ۚ صُمٌّ بُكْمٌ عُمْيٌ فَهُمْ لَا يَعْقِلُونَ

171 2:18; 6:39; 8:22

171 The parable of those who disbelieve is that of someone who calls upon someone who hears nothing except screaming and yelling. Deaf, dumb, and blind—they do not understand.

١٧٢ يَا أَيُّهَا الَّذِينَ آمَنُوا كُلُوا مِن طَيِّبَاتِ مَا رَزَقْنَاكُمْ وَاشْكُرُوا لِلَّهِ إِن كُنتُمْ إِيَّاهُ تَعْبُدُونَ

172 O you who believe! Eat of the good things We have provided for you, and give thanks to God, if it is Him that you serve.

١٧٣ إِنَّمَا حَرَّمَ عَلَيْكُمُ الْمَيْتَةَ وَالدَّمَ وَلَحْمَ الْخِنزِيرِ وَمَا أُهِلَّ بِهِ لِغَيْرِ اللَّهِ ۖ فَمَنِ اضْطُرَّ غَيْرَ بَاغٍ وَلَا عَادٍ فَلَا إِثْمَ عَلَيْهِ ۚ إِنَّ اللَّهَ غَفُورٌ رَحِيمٌ

173 5:3; 6:45; 16:115

173 He has forbidden you carrion, and blood, and the flesh of swine, and what was dedicated to other than God. But if anyone is compelled, without desiring or exceeding, he commits no sin. God is Forgiving and Merciful.

١٧٤ إِنَّ الَّذِينَ يَكْتُمُونَ مَا أَنزَلَ اللَّهُ مِنَ الْكِتَابِ وَيَشْتَرُونَ بِهِ ثَمَنًا قَلِيلًا ۙ أُولَٰئِكَ مَا يَأْكُلُونَ فِي بُطُونِهِمْ إِلَّا النَّارَ وَلَا يُكَلِّمُهُمُ اللَّهُ يَوْمَ الْقِيَامَةِ وَلَا يُزَكِّيهِمْ وَلَهُمْ عَذَابٌ أَلِيمٌ

174 2:159; 3:71; 5:15; 6:91

174 Those who conceal what God revealed in the Book, and exchange it for a small price—those swallow nothing but fire into their bellies. And God will not speak to them on the Day of Resurrection, nor will He purify them, and they will have a painful punishment.

١٧٥ أُولَٰئِكَ الَّذِينَ اشْتَرَوُا الضَّلَالَةَ بِالْهُدَىٰ وَالْعَذَابَ بِالْمَغْفِرَةِ ۚ فَمَا أَصْبَرَهُمْ عَلَى النَّارِ

175 2:16; 3:177; 31:6

175 It is they who exchange guidance for error, and forgiveness for punishment. But why do they insist on the Fire?

١٧٦ ذَٰلِكَ بِأَنَّ اللَّهَ نَزَّلَ الْكِتَابَ بِالْحَقِّ ۗ وَإِنَّ الَّذِينَ اخْتَلَفُوا فِي الْكِتَابِ لَفِي شِقَاقٍ بَعِيدٍ

176 That is because God has revealed the Book in truth; and those who differ about the Book are in deep discord.

١٧٧ لَيْسَ الْبِرَّ أَن تُوَلُّوا وُجُوهَكُمْ قِبَلَ الْمَشْرِقِ وَالْمَغْرِبِ وَلَٰكِنَّ الْبِرَّ مَنْ آمَنَ بِاللَّهِ وَالْيَوْمِ الْآخِرِ وَالْمَلَائِكَةِ وَالْكِتَابِ وَالنَّبِيِّينَ وَآتَى الْمَالَ عَلَىٰ حُبِّهِ ذَوِي الْقُرْبَىٰ وَالْيَتَامَىٰ وَالْمَسَاكِينَ وَابْنَ السَّبِيلِ وَالسَّائِلِينَ وَفِي الرِّقَابِ وَأَقَامَ الصَّلَاةَ وَآتَى الزَّكَاةَ وَالْمُوفُونَ بِعَهْدِهِمْ إِذَا عَاهَدُوا ۖ وَالصَّابِرِينَ فِي الْبَأْسَاءِ وَالضَّرَّاءِ وَحِينَ الْبَأْسِ ۗ أُولَٰئِكَ الَّذِينَ صَدَقُوا ۖ وَأُولَٰئِكَ هُمُ الْمُتَّقُونَ

177
2:115, 142, 187

177 Righteousness does not consist of turning your faces towards the East and the West. But righteous is he who believes in God, and the Last Day, and the angels, and the Scripture, and the prophets. Who gives money, though dear, to near relatives, and orphans, and the needy, and the homeless, and the beggars, and for the freeing of slaves; those who perform the prayers, and pay the obligatory charity, and fulfill their promise when they promise, and patiently persevere in the face of persecution, hardship, and in the time of conflict. These are the sincere; these are the pious.

١٧٨ يَا أَيُّهَا الَّذِينَ آمَنُوا كُتِبَ عَلَيْكُمُ الْقِصَاصُ فِي الْقَتْلَى ۖ الْحُرُّ بِالْحُرِّ وَالْعَبْدُ بِالْعَبْدِ وَالْأُنثَىٰ بِالْأُنثَىٰ ۚ فَمَنْ عُفِيَ لَهُ مِنْ أَخِيهِ شَيْءٌ فَاتِّبَاعٌ بِالْمَعْرُوفِ وَأَدَاءٌ إِلَيْهِ بِإِحْسَانٍ ۗ ذَٰلِكَ تَخْفِيفٌ مِّن رَّبِّكُمْ وَرَحْمَةٌ ۗ فَمَنِ اعْتَدَىٰ بَعْدَ ذَٰلِكَ فَلَهُ عَذَابٌ أَلِيمٌ

178 O you who believe! Retaliation for the murdered is ordained upon you: the free for the free, the slave for the slave, the female for the female. But if he is forgiven by his kin, then grant any reasonable demand, and pay with good will. This is a concession from your Lord, and a mercy. But whoever commits aggression after that, a painful torment awaits him.

١٧٩ وَلَكُمْ فِي الْقِصَاصِ حَيَاةٌ يَا أُولِي الْأَلْبَابِ لَعَلَّكُمْ تَتَّقُونَ

179 There is life for you in retaliation, O people of understanding, so that you may refrain.

١٨٠ كُتِبَ عَلَيْكُمْ إِذَا حَضَرَ أَحَدَكُمُ الْمَوْتُ إِن تَرَكَ خَيْرًا الْوَصِيَّةُ لِلْوَالِدَيْنِ وَالْأَقْرَبِينَ بِالْمَعْرُوفِ ۖ حَقًّا عَلَى الْمُتَّقِينَ

180–182
5:106–108

180 It is decreed for you: when death approaches one of you, and he leaves wealth, to make a testament in favor of the parents and the relatives, fairly and correctly—a duty upon the righteous.

١٨١ فَمَن بَدَّلَهُ بَعْدَمَا سَمِعَهُ فَإِنَّمَا إِثْمُهُ عَلَى الَّذِينَ يُبَدِّلُونَهُ ۚ إِنَّ اللَّهَ سَمِيعٌ عَلِيمٌ

181 But whoever changes it after he has heard it, the guilt is upon those who change it. God is All-Hearing, All-Knowing.

١٨٢ فَمَنْ خَافَ مِن مُّوصٍ جَنَفًا أَوْ إِثْمًا فَأَصْلَحَ بَيْنَهُمْ فَلَا إِثْمَ عَلَيْهِ ۚ إِنَّ اللَّهَ غَفُورٌ رَّحِيمٌ

182 Should someone suspect bias or injustice on the part of a testator, and then reconciles between them, he commits no sin. God is Forgiving and Merciful.

Sūrah 2: Al-Baqarah

١٨٣ يَا أَيُّهَا الَّذِينَ آمَنُوا كُتِبَ عَلَيْكُمُ الصِّيَامُ كَمَا كُتِبَ عَلَى الَّذِينَ مِنْ قَبْلِكُمْ لَعَلَّكُمْ تَتَّقُونَ

183 O you who believe! Fasting is prescribed for you, as it was prescribed for those before you, that you may become righteous.

183
2:185

١٨٤ أَيَّامًا مَعْدُودَاتٍ ۚ فَمَنْ كَانَ مِنْكُمْ مَرِيضًا أَوْ عَلَىٰ سَفَرٍ فَعِدَّةٌ مِنْ أَيَّامٍ أُخَرَ ۚ وَعَلَى الَّذِينَ يُطِيقُونَهُ فِدْيَةٌ طَعَامُ مِسْكِينٍ ۖ فَمَنْ تَطَوَّعَ خَيْرًا فَهُوَ خَيْرٌ لَهُ ۚ وَأَنْ تَصُومُوا خَيْرٌ لَكُمْ ۖ إِنْ كُنْتُمْ تَعْلَمُونَ

184 For a specified number of days. But whoever among you is sick, or on a journey, then a number of other days. For those who are able: a ransom of feeding a needy person. But whoever volunteers goodness, it is better for him. But to fast is best for you, if you only knew.

184

١٨٥ شَهْرُ رَمَضَانَ الَّذِي أُنْزِلَ فِيهِ الْقُرْآنُ هُدًى لِلنَّاسِ وَبَيِّنَاتٍ مِنَ الْهُدَىٰ وَالْفُرْقَانِ ۚ فَمَنْ شَهِدَ مِنْكُمُ الشَّهْرَ فَلْيَصُمْهُ ۖ وَمَنْ كَانَ مَرِيضًا أَوْ عَلَىٰ سَفَرٍ فَعِدَّةٌ مِنْ أَيَّامٍ أُخَرَ ۗ يُرِيدُ اللَّهُ بِكُمُ الْيُسْرَ وَلَا يُرِيدُ بِكُمُ الْعُسْرَ وَلِتُكْمِلُوا الْعِدَّةَ وَلِتُكَبِّرُوا اللَّهَ عَلَىٰ مَا هَدَاكُمْ وَلَعَلَّكُمْ تَشْكُرُونَ

185 Ramadan is the month in which the Qur'an was revealed. Guidance for humanity, and clear portents of guidance, and the Criterion. Whoever of you witnesses the month, shall fast it. But whoever is sick, or on a journey, then a number of other days. God desires ease for you, and does not desire hardship for you, that you may complete the number, and celebrate God for having guided you, so that you may be thankful.

185
44:3; 20:183; 97:1

١٨٦ وَإِذَا سَأَلَكَ عِبَادِي عَنِّي فَإِنِّي قَرِيبٌ ۖ أُجِيبُ دَعْوَةَ الدَّاعِ إِذَا دَعَانِ ۖ فَلْيَسْتَجِيبُوا لِي وَلْيُؤْمِنُوا بِي لَعَلَّهُمْ يَرْشُدُونَ

186 And when My servants ask you about Me, I Am near; I answer the call of the caller when he calls on Me. So let them answer Me, and have faith in Me, that they may be rightly guided.

186
6:41; 11:61; 27:62; 40:60

١٨٧ أُحِلَّ لَكُمْ لَيْلَةَ الصِّيَامِ الرَّفَثُ إِلَىٰ نِسَائِكُمْ ۚ هُنَّ لِبَاسٌ لَكُمْ وَأَنْتُمْ لِبَاسٌ لَهُنَّ ۗ عَلِمَ اللَّهُ أَنَّكُمْ كُنْتُمْ تَخْتَانُونَ أَنْفُسَكُمْ فَتَابَ عَلَيْكُمْ وَعَفَا عَنْكُمْ ۖ فَالْآنَ بَاشِرُوهُنَّ وَابْتَغُوا مَا كَتَبَ اللَّهُ لَكُمْ ۚ وَكُلُوا وَاشْرَبُوا حَتَّىٰ يَتَبَيَّنَ لَكُمُ الْخَيْطُ الْأَبْيَضُ مِنَ الْخَيْطِ الْأَسْوَدِ مِنَ الْفَجْرِ ۖ ثُمَّ أَتِمُّوا الصِّيَامَ إِلَى اللَّيْلِ ۚ وَلَا تُبَاشِرُوهُنَّ وَأَنْتُمْ عَاكِفُونَ فِي الْمَسَاجِدِ ۗ تِلْكَ حُدُودُ اللَّهِ فَلَا تَقْرَبُوهَا ۗ كَذَٰلِكَ يُبَيِّنُ اللَّهُ آيَاتِهِ لِلنَّاسِ لَعَلَّهُمْ يَتَّقُونَ

187 Permitted for you is intercourse with your wives on the night of the fast. They are a garment for you, and you are a garment for them. God knows that you used to betray yourselves, but He turned to you and pardoned you. So approach them now, and seek what God has ordained for you, and eat and drink until the white streak of dawn can be distinguished from the black streak. Then complete the fast until nightfall. But do not approach them while you are in retreat at the mosques. These are the limits of God, so do not come near them. God thus clarifies His revelations to the people, that they may attain piety.

187
2:115, 142, 177

١٨٨ وَلَا تَأْكُلُوا أَمْوَالَكُم بَيْنَكُم بِالْبَاطِلِ وَتُدْلُوا بِهَا إِلَى الْحُكَّامِ لِتَأْكُلُوا فَرِيقًا مِنْ أَمْوَالِ النَّاسِ بِالْإِثْمِ وَأَنتُمْ تَعْلَمُونَ

188 4:29, 161; 9:34

188 And do not consume one another's wealth by unjust means, nor offer it as bribes to the officials in order to consume part of other people's wealth illicitly, while you know.

١٨٩ يَسْأَلُونَكَ عَنِ الْأَهِلَّةِ ۖ قُلْ هِيَ مَوَاقِيتُ لِلنَّاسِ وَالْحَجِّ ۗ وَلَيْسَ الْبِرُّ بِأَن تَأْتُوا الْبُيُوتَ مِن ظُهُورِهَا وَلَٰكِنَّ الْبِرَّ مَنِ اتَّقَىٰ ۗ وَأْتُوا الْبُيُوتَ مِنْ أَبْوَابِهَا ۚ وَاتَّقُوا اللَّهَ لَعَلَّكُمْ تُفْلِحُونَ

189 They ask you about the crescents. Say, "They are timetables for people, and for the Hajj." It is not virtuous that you approach homes from their backs, but virtue is to be pious. So approach homes from their doors, and observe God, that you may succeed.

١٩٠ وَقَاتِلُوا فِي سَبِيلِ اللَّهِ الَّذِينَ يُقَاتِلُونَكُمْ وَلَا تَعْتَدُوا ۚ إِنَّ اللَّهَ لَا يُحِبُّ الْمُعْتَدِينَ

190 9:2, 36

190 And fight in the cause of God those who fight you, but do not commit aggression; God does not love the aggressors.

١٩١ وَاقْتُلُوهُمْ حَيْثُ ثَقِفْتُمُوهُمْ وَأَخْرِجُوهُم مِّنْ حَيْثُ أَخْرَجُوكُمْ ۚ وَالْفِتْنَةُ أَشَدُّ مِنَ الْقَتْلِ ۚ وَلَا تُقَاتِلُوهُمْ عِندَ الْمَسْجِدِ الْحَرَامِ حَتَّىٰ يُقَاتِلُوكُمْ فِيهِ ۖ فَإِن قَاتَلُوكُمْ فَاقْتُلُوهُمْ ۗ كَذَٰلِكَ جَزَاءُ الْكَافِرِينَ

191 4:89; 9:5; 22:40; 33:61

191 And kill them wherever you overtake them, and expel them from where they had expelled you. Oppression is more serious than murder. But do not fight them at the Sacred Mosque, unless they fight you there. If they fight you, then kill them. Such is the retribution of the disbelievers.

١٩٢ فَإِنِ انتَهَوْا فَإِنَّ اللَّهَ غَفُورٌ رَّحِيمٌ

192–193 8:38, 39

192 But if they cease, then God is Forgiving and Merciful.

١٩٣ وَقَاتِلُوهُمْ حَتَّىٰ لَا تَكُونَ فِتْنَةٌ وَيَكُونَ الدِّينُ لِلَّهِ ۖ فَإِنِ انتَهَوْا فَلَا عُدْوَانَ إِلَّا عَلَى الظَّالِمِينَ

193 And fight them until there is no oppression, and worship becomes devoted to God alone. But if they cease, then let there be no hostility except against the oppressors.

١٩٤ الشَّهْرُ الْحَرَامُ بِالشَّهْرِ الْحَرَامِ وَالْحُرُمَاتُ قِصَاصٌ ۚ فَمَنِ اعْتَدَىٰ عَلَيْكُمْ فَاعْتَدُوا عَلَيْهِ بِمِثْلِ مَا اعْتَدَىٰ عَلَيْكُمْ ۚ وَاتَّقُوا اللَّهَ وَاعْلَمُوا أَنَّ اللَّهَ مَعَ الْمُتَّقِينَ

194 The sacred month for the sacred month; and sacrilege calls for retaliation. Whoever commits aggression against you, retaliate against him in the same measure as he has committed against you. And be conscious of God, and know that God is with the righteous.

١٩٥ وَأَنفِقُوا فِي سَبِيلِ اللَّهِ وَلَا تُلْقُوا بِأَيْدِيكُمْ إِلَى التَّهْلُكَةِ ۛ وَأَحْسِنُوا ۛ إِنَّ اللَّهَ يُحِبُّ الْمُحْسِنِينَ

195 And spend in the cause of God, and do not throw yourselves with your own hands into ruin, and be charitable. God loves the charitable.

١٩٦ وَأَتِمُّوا الْحَجَّ وَالْعُمْرَةَ لِلَّهِ ۚ فَإِنْ أُحْصِرْتُمْ فَمَا اسْتَيْسَرَ مِنَ الْهَدْيِ ۖ وَلَا تَحْلِقُوا رُءُوسَكُمْ حَتَّىٰ يَبْلُغَ الْهَدْيُ مَحِلَّهُ ۚ فَمَن كَانَ مِنكُم مَّرِيضًا أَوْ بِهِ أَذًى مِّن رَّأْسِهِ فَفِدْيَةٌ مِّن صِيَامٍ أَوْ صَدَقَةٍ أَوْ نُسُكٍ ۚ فَإِذَا أَمِنتُمْ فَمَن تَمَتَّعَ بِالْعُمْرَةِ إِلَى الْحَجِّ فَمَا اسْتَيْسَرَ مِنَ الْهَدْيِ ۚ فَمَن لَّمْ يَجِدْ فَصِيَامُ ثَلَاثَةِ أَيَّامٍ فِي الْحَجِّ وَسَبْعَةٍ إِذَا رَجَعْتُمْ ۗ تِلْكَ عَشَرَةٌ كَامِلَةٌ ۗ ذَٰلِكَ لِمَن لَّمْ يَكُنْ أَهْلُهُ حَاضِرِي الْمَسْجِدِ الْحَرَامِ ۚ وَاتَّقُوا اللَّهَ وَاعْلَمُوا أَنَّ اللَّهَ شَدِيدُ الْعِقَابِ

196 48:27

196 And carry out the Hajj and the Umrah for God. But if you are prevented, then whatever is feasible of offerings. And do not shave your heads until the offering has reached its destination. Whoever of you is sick, or has an injury of the head, then redemption of fasting, or charity, or worship. When you are secure: whoever continues the Umrah until the Hajj, then whatever is feasible of offering. But if he lacks the means, then fasting for three days during the Hajj and seven when you have returned, making ten in all. This is for he whose household is not present at the Sacred Mosque. And remain conscious of God, and know that God is stern in retribution.

١٩٧ الْحَجُّ أَشْهُرٌ مَّعْلُومَاتٌ ۚ فَمَن فَرَضَ فِيهِنَّ الْحَجَّ فَلَا رَفَثَ وَلَا فُسُوقَ وَلَا جِدَالَ فِي الْحَجِّ ۗ وَمَا تَفْعَلُوا مِنْ خَيْرٍ يَعْلَمْهُ اللَّهُ ۗ وَتَزَوَّدُوا فَإِنَّ خَيْرَ الزَّادِ التَّقْوَىٰ ۚ وَاتَّقُونِ يَا أُولِي الْأَلْبَابِ

197 The Hajj is during specific months. Whoever decides to perform the Hajj—there shall be no sexual relations, nor misconduct, nor quarrelling during the Hajj. And whatever good you do, God knows it. And take provisions, but the best provision is righteousness. And be mindful of Me, O people of understanding.

١٩٨ لَيْسَ عَلَيْكُمْ جُنَاحٌ أَن تَبْتَغُوا فَضْلًا مِّن رَّبِّكُمْ ۚ فَإِذَا أَفَضْتُم مِّنْ عَرَفَاتٍ فَاذْكُرُوا اللَّهَ عِندَ الْمَشْعَرِ الْحَرَامِ ۖ وَاذْكُرُوهُ كَمَا هَدَاكُمْ وَإِن كُنتُم مِّن قَبْلِهِ لَمِنَ الضَّالِّينَ

198 4:135; 5:2, 8, 97; 22:32, 36

198 You commit no error by seeking bounty from your Lord. When you disperse from Arafat, remember God at the Sacred Landmark. And remember Him as He has guided you. Although, before that, you were of those astray.

١٩٩ ثُمَّ أَفِيضُوا مِنْ حَيْثُ أَفَاضَ النَّاسُ وَاسْتَغْفِرُوا اللَّهَ ۚ إِنَّ اللَّهَ غَفُورٌ رَّحِيمٌ

199 Then disperse from where the people disperse, and ask God for forgiveness. God is Most Forgiving, Most Merciful.

٢٠٠ فَإِذَا قَضَيْتُم مَّنَاسِكَكُمْ فَاذْكُرُوا اللَّهَ كَذِكْرِكُمْ آبَاءَكُمْ أَوْ أَشَدَّ ذِكْرًا ۗ فَمِنَ النَّاسِ مَن يَقُولُ رَبَّنَا آتِنَا فِي الدُّنْيَا وَمَا لَهُ فِي الْآخِرَةِ مِنْ خَلَاقٍ

200 When you have completed your rites, remember God as you remember your parents, or even more. Among the people is he who says, "Our Lord, give us in this world," yet he has no share in the Hereafter.

٢٠١ وَمِنْهُم مَّن يَقُولُ رَبَّنَا آتِنَا فِي الدُّنْيَا حَسَنَةً وَفِي الْآخِرَةِ حَسَنَةً وَقِنَا عَذَابَ النَّارِ

201 And among them is he who says, "Our Lord, give us goodness in this world, and goodness in the Hereafter, and protect us from the torment of the Fire."

201
7:156

٢٠٢ أُولَٰئِكَ لَهُمْ نَصِيبٌ مِّمَّا كَسَبُوا ۚ وَاللَّهُ سَرِيعُ الْحِسَابِ

202 These will have a share of what they have earned. God is swift in reckoning.

202
4:32, 34; 33:35

٢٠٣ وَاذْكُرُوا اللَّهَ فِي أَيَّامٍ مَّعْدُودَاتٍ ۚ فَمَن تَعَجَّلَ فِي يَوْمَيْنِ فَلَا إِثْمَ عَلَيْهِ وَمَن تَأَخَّرَ فَلَا إِثْمَ عَلَيْهِ ۚ لِمَنِ اتَّقَىٰ ۗ وَاتَّقُوا اللَّهَ وَاعْلَمُوا أَنَّكُمْ إِلَيْهِ تُحْشَرُونَ

203 And remember God during the designated days. But whoever hurries on in two days commits no wrong, and whoever stays on commits no wrong—provided he maintains righteousness. And obey God, and know that to Him you will be gathered.

203
22:28

٢٠٤ وَمِنَ النَّاسِ مَن يُعْجِبُكَ قَوْلُهُ فِي الْحَيَاةِ الدُّنْيَا وَيُشْهِدُ اللَّهَ عَلَىٰ مَا فِي قَلْبِهِ وَهُوَ أَلَدُّ الْخِصَامِ

204 Among the people is he whose speech about the worldly life impresses you, and he calls God to witness what is in his heart, while he is the most hostile of adversaries.

٢٠٥ وَإِذَا تَوَلَّىٰ سَعَىٰ فِي الْأَرْضِ لِيُفْسِدَ فِيهَا وَيُهْلِكَ الْحَرْثَ وَالنَّسْلَ ۗ وَاللَّهُ لَا يُحِبُّ الْفَسَادَ

205 When he gains power, he strives to spread corruption on earth, destroying properties and lives. God does not like corruption.

٢٠٦ وَإِذَا قِيلَ لَهُ اتَّقِ اللَّهَ أَخَذَتْهُ الْعِزَّةُ بِالْإِثْمِ ۚ فَحَسْبُهُ جَهَنَّمُ ۚ وَلَبِئْسَ الْمِهَادُ

206 And when he is told, "Beware of God," his pride leads him to more sin. Hell is enough for him—a dreadful abode.

٢٠٧ وَمِنَ النَّاسِ مَن يَشْرِي نَفْسَهُ ابْتِغَاءَ مَرْضَاتِ اللَّهِ ۗ وَاللَّهُ رَءُوفٌ بِالْعِبَادِ

207 And among the people is he who sells himself seeking God's approval. God is kind towards the servants.

٢٠٨ يَا أَيُّهَا الَّذِينَ آمَنُوا ادْخُلُوا فِي السِّلْمِ كَافَّةً وَلَا تَتَّبِعُوا خُطُوَاتِ الشَّيْطَانِ ۚ إِنَّهُ لَكُمْ عَدُوٌّ مُّبِينٌ

208 O you who believe! Enter into submission, wholeheartedly, and do not follow the footsteps of Satan; he is to you an outright enemy.

208
2:168; 5:88; 6:142; 8:69

٢٠٩ فَإِن زَلَلْتُم مِّن بَعْدِ مَا جَاءَتْكُمُ الْبَيِّنَاتُ فَاعْلَمُوا أَنَّ اللَّهَ عَزِيزٌ حَكِيمٌ

209 But if you slip after the proofs have come to you, know that God is Powerful and Wise.

٢١٠ هَلْ يَنظُرُونَ إِلَّا أَن يَأْتِيَهُمُ اللَّهُ فِي ظُلَلٍ مِّنَ الْغَمَامِ وَالْمَلَائِكَةُ وَقُضِيَ الْأَمْرُ ۚ وَإِلَى اللَّهِ تُرْجَعُ الْأُمُورُ

210 Are they waiting for God Himself to come to them in the shadows of the clouds, together with the angels, and thus the matter is settled? All things are returned to God.

210
6:158; 15:8; 16:33; 25:25

٢١١ سَلْ بَنِي إِسْرَائِيلَ كَمْ آتَيْنَاهُم مِّنْ آيَةٍ بَيِّنَةٍ ۗ وَمَن يُبَدِّلْ نِعْمَةَ اللَّهِ مِن بَعْدِ مَا جَاءَتْهُ فَإِنَّ اللَّهَ شَدِيدُ الْعِقَابِ

211
7:103; 17:101; 44:33

211 Ask the Children of Israel how many clear signs We have given them. Whoever alters the blessing of God after it has come to him—God is severe in retribution.

٢١٢ زُيِّنَ لِلَّذِينَ كَفَرُوا الْحَيَاةُ الدُّنْيَا وَيَسْخَرُونَ مِنَ الَّذِينَ آمَنُوا ۘ وَالَّذِينَ اتَّقَوْا فَوْقَهُمْ يَوْمَ الْقِيَامَةِ ۗ وَاللَّهُ يَرْزُقُ مَن يَشَاءُ بِغَيْرِ حِسَابٍ

212
83:34

212 Beautified is the life of this world for those who disbelieve, and they ridicule those who believe. But the righteous will be above them on the Day of Resurrection. God provides to whomever He wills without measure.

٢١٣ كَانَ النَّاسُ أُمَّةً وَاحِدَةً فَبَعَثَ اللَّهُ النَّبِيِّينَ مُبَشِّرِينَ وَمُنذِرِينَ وَأَنزَلَ مَعَهُمُ الْكِتَابَ بِالْحَقِّ لِيَحْكُمَ بَيْنَ النَّاسِ فِيمَا اخْتَلَفُوا فِيهِ ۚ وَمَا اخْتَلَفَ فِيهِ إِلَّا الَّذِينَ أُوتُوهُ مِن بَعْدِ مَا جَاءَتْهُمُ الْبَيِّنَاتُ بَغْيًا بَيْنَهُمْ ۖ فَهَدَى اللَّهُ الَّذِينَ آمَنُوا لِمَا اخْتَلَفُوا فِيهِ مِنَ الْحَقِّ بِإِذْنِهِ ۗ وَاللَّهُ يَهْدِي مَن يَشَاءُ إِلَىٰ صِرَاطٍ مُّسْتَقِيمٍ

213
1:6; 2:142; 10:19; 11:118

213 Humanity used to be one community; then God sent the prophets, bringing good news and giving warnings. And He sent down with them the Scripture, with the truth, to judge between people regarding their differences. But none differed over it except those who were given it—after the proofs had come to them—out of mutual envy between them. Then God guided those who believed to the truth they had disputed, in accordance with His will. God guides whom He wills to a straight path.

٢١٤ أَمْ حَسِبْتُمْ أَن تَدْخُلُوا الْجَنَّةَ وَلَمَّا يَأْتِكُم مَّثَلُ الَّذِينَ خَلَوْا مِن قَبْلِكُم ۖ مَّسَّتْهُمُ الْبَأْسَاءُ وَالضَّرَّاءُ وَزُلْزِلُوا حَتَّىٰ يَقُولَ الرَّسُولُ وَالَّذِينَ آمَنُوا مَعَهُ مَتَىٰ نَصْرُ اللَّهِ ۗ أَلَا إِنَّ نَصْرَ اللَّهِ قَرِيبٌ

214
3:142; 5:71; 7:95; 9:16; 10:21; 47:31

214 Or do you expect to enter Paradise before the example of those who came before you had reached you? Adversity and hardship had afflicted them, and they were so shaken up, that the Messenger and those who believed with him said, "When is God's victory?" Indeed, God's victory is near.

٢١٥ يَسْأَلُونَكَ مَاذَا يُنفِقُونَ ۖ قُلْ مَا أَنفَقْتُم مِّنْ خَيْرٍ فَلِلْوَالِدَيْنِ وَالْأَقْرَبِينَ وَالْيَتَامَىٰ وَالْمَسَاكِينِ وَابْنِ السَّبِيلِ ۗ وَمَا تَفْعَلُوا مِنْ خَيْرٍ فَإِنَّ اللَّهَ بِهِ عَلِيمٌ

215
4:8, 33

215 They ask you what they should give. Say, "Whatever charity you give is for the parents, and the relatives, and the orphans, and the poor, and the wayfarer. Whatever good you do, God is aware of it.

٢١٦ كُتِبَ عَلَيْكُمُ الْقِتَالُ وَهُوَ كُرْهٌ لَّكُمْ ۖ وَعَسَىٰ أَن تَكْرَهُوا شَيْئًا وَهُوَ خَيْرٌ لَّكُمْ ۖ وَعَسَىٰ أَن تُحِبُّوا شَيْئًا وَهُوَ شَرٌّ لَّكُمْ ۗ وَاللَّهُ يَعْلَمُ وَأَنتُمْ لَا تَعْلَمُونَ

216
2:246; 4:77; 42:20

216 Fighting is ordained for you, even though you dislike it. But it may be that you dislike something while it is good for you, and it may be that you like something while it is bad for you. God knows, and you do not know.

٢١٧ يَسْأَلُونَكَ عَنِ الشَّهْرِ الْحَرَامِ قِتَالٍ فِيهِ ۖ قُلْ قِتَالٌ فِيهِ كَبِيرٌ ۖ وَصَدٌّ عَن سَبِيلِ اللَّهِ وَكُفْرٌ بِهِ وَالْمَسْجِدِ الْحَرَامِ وَإِخْرَاجُ أَهْلِهِ مِنْهُ أَكْبَرُ عِندَ اللَّهِ ۚ وَالْفِتْنَةُ أَكْبَرُ مِنَ الْقَتْلِ ۗ وَلَا يَزَالُونَ يُقَاتِلُونَكُمْ حَتَّىٰ يَرُدُّوكُمْ عَن دِينِكُمْ إِنِ اسْتَطَاعُوا ۚ وَمَن يَرْتَدِدْ مِنكُمْ عَن دِينِهِ فَيَمُتْ وَهُوَ كَافِرٌ فَأُولَٰئِكَ حَبِطَتْ أَعْمَالُهُمْ فِي الدُّنْيَا وَالْآخِرَةِ ۖ وَأُولَٰئِكَ أَصْحَابُ النَّارِ ۖ هُمْ فِيهَا خَالِدُونَ

217 5:54; 9:69

217 They ask you about fighting during the Holy Month. Say, "Fighting during it is deplorable; but to bar others from God's path, and to disbelieve in Him, and to prevent access to the Holy Mosque, and to expel its people from it, are more deplorable with God. And persecution is more serious than killing. They will not cease to fight you until they turn you back from your religion, if they can. Whoever among you turns back from his religion, and dies a disbeliever—those are they whose works will come to nothing, in this life, and in the Hereafter. Those are the inmates of the Fire, abiding in it forever."

٢١٨ إِنَّ الَّذِينَ آمَنُوا وَالَّذِينَ هَاجَرُوا وَجَاهَدُوا فِي سَبِيلِ اللَّهِ أُولَٰئِكَ يَرْجُونَ رَحْمَتَ اللَّهِ ۚ وَاللَّهُ غَفُورٌ رَحِيمٌ

218 3:157; 9:20; 16:41; 22:58

218 Those who believed, and those who migrated and fought for the sake of God—those look forward to God's mercy. God is Forgiving and Merciful.

٢١٩ يَسْأَلُونَكَ عَنِ الْخَمْرِ وَالْمَيْسِرِ ۖ قُلْ فِيهِمَا إِثْمٌ كَبِيرٌ وَمَنَافِعُ لِلنَّاسِ وَإِثْمُهُمَا أَكْبَرُ مِن نَّفْعِهِمَا ۗ وَيَسْأَلُونَكَ مَاذَا يُنفِقُونَ قُلِ الْعَفْوَ ۗ كَذَٰلِكَ يُبَيِّنُ اللَّهُ لَكُمُ الْآيَاتِ لَعَلَّكُمْ تَتَفَكَّرُونَ

219 5:90–91; 16:36; 22:30; 39:17

219 They ask you about intoxicants and gambling. Say, "There is gross sin in them, and some benefits for people, but their sinfulness outweighs their benefit." And they ask you about what they should give: say, "The surplus." Thus God explains the revelations to you, so that you may think.

٢٢٠ فِي الدُّنْيَا وَالْآخِرَةِ ۗ وَيَسْأَلُونَكَ عَنِ الْيَتَامَىٰ ۖ قُلْ إِصْلَاحٌ لَّهُمْ خَيْرٌ ۖ وَإِن تُخَالِطُوهُمْ فَإِخْوَانُكُمْ ۚ وَاللَّهُ يَعْلَمُ الْمُفْسِدَ مِنَ الْمُصْلِحِ ۚ وَلَوْ شَاءَ اللَّهُ لَأَعْنَتَكُمْ ۚ إِنَّ اللَّهَ عَزِيزٌ حَكِيمٌ

220 About this world and the next. And they ask you about orphans. Say, "Improvement for them is best. And if you intermix with them, then they are your brethren." God knows the dishonest from the honest. Had God willed, He could have overburdened you. God is Mighty and Wise.

٢٢١ وَلَا تَنكِحُوا الْمُشْرِكَاتِ حَتَّىٰ يُؤْمِنَّ ۚ وَلَأَمَةٌ مُّؤْمِنَةٌ خَيْرٌ مِّن مُّشْرِكَةٍ وَلَوْ أَعْجَبَتْكُمْ ۗ وَلَا تُنكِحُوا الْمُشْرِكِينَ حَتَّىٰ يُؤْمِنُوا ۚ وَلَعَبْدٌ مُّؤْمِنٌ خَيْرٌ مِّن مُّشْرِكٍ وَلَوْ أَعْجَبَكُمْ ۗ أُولَٰئِكَ يَدْعُونَ إِلَى النَّارِ ۖ وَاللَّهُ يَدْعُو إِلَى الْجَنَّةِ وَالْمَغْفِرَةِ بِإِذْنِهِ ۖ وَيُبَيِّنُ آيَاتِهِ لِلنَّاسِ لَعَلَّهُمْ يَتَذَكَّرُونَ

221 28:41; 49:41

221 Do not marry idolatresses, unless they have believed. A believing maid is better than an idolatress, even if you like her. And do not marry idolaters, unless they have believed. A believing servant is better than an idolater, even if you like him. These call to the Fire, but God calls to the Garden and to forgiveness, by His leave. He makes clear His communications to the people, that they may be mindful.

٢٢٢ وَيَسْأَلُونَكَ عَنِ الْمَحِيضِۖ قُلْ هُوَ أَذًى فَاعْتَزِلُوا النِّسَاءَ فِي الْمَحِيضِۖ وَلَا تَقْرَبُوهُنَّ حَتَّىٰ يَطْهُرْنَۖ فَإِذَا تَطَهَّرْنَ فَأْتُوهُنَّ مِنْ حَيْثُ أَمَرَكُمُ اللَّهُۚ إِنَّ اللَّهَ يُحِبُّ التَّوَّابِينَ وَيُحِبُّ الْمُتَطَهِّرِينَ

222 And they ask you about menstruation: say, "It is harmful, so keep away from women during menstruation. And do not approach them until they have become pure. Once they have become pure, approach them in the way God has directed you." God loves the repentant, and He loves those who keep clean."

٢٢٣ نِسَاؤُكُمْ حَرْثٌ لَكُمْ فَأْتُوا حَرْثَكُمْ أَنَّىٰ شِئْتُمْۖ وَقَدِّمُوا لِأَنْفُسِكُمْۚ وَاتَّقُوا اللَّهَ وَاعْلَمُوا أَنَّكُمْ مُلَاقُوهُۗ وَبَشِّرِ الْمُؤْمِنِينَ

223 Your women are cultivation for you; so approach your cultivation whenever you like, and send ahead for yourselves. And fear God, and know that you will meet Him. And give good news to the believers.

٢٢٤ وَلَا تَجْعَلُوا اللَّهَ عُرْضَةً لِأَيْمَانِكُمْ أَنْ تَبَرُّوا وَتَتَّقُوا وَتُصْلِحُوا بَيْنَ النَّاسِۗ وَاللَّهُ سَمِيعٌ عَلِيمٌ

224 And do not allow your oaths in God's name to hinder you from virtue, and righteousness, and making peace between people. God is Listener and Knower.

٢٢٥ لَا يُؤَاخِذُكُمُ اللَّهُ بِاللَّغْوِ فِي أَيْمَانِكُمْ وَلَٰكِنْ يُؤَاخِذُكُمْ بِمَا كَسَبَتْ قُلُوبُكُمْۗ وَاللَّهُ غَفُورٌ حَلِيمٌ

225 God does not hold you responsible for your unintentional oaths, but He holds you responsible for your intentions. God is Forgiving and Forbearing.

225
3:79; 5:89; 29:27; 45:16

٢٢٦ لِلَّذِينَ يُؤْلُونَ مِنْ نِسَائِهِمْ تَرَبُّصُ أَرْبَعَةِ أَشْهُرٍۖ فَإِنْ فَاءُوا فَإِنَّ اللَّهَ غَفُورٌ رَحِيمٌ

226 Those who vow abstinence from their wives must wait for four months. But if they reconcile—God is Forgiving and Merciful.

٢٢٧ وَإِنْ عَزَمُوا الطَّلَاقَ فَإِنَّ اللَّهَ سَمِيعٌ عَلِيمٌ

227 And if they resolve to divorce—God is Hearing and Knowing.

٢٢٨ وَالْمُطَلَّقَاتُ يَتَرَبَّصْنَ بِأَنْفُسِهِنَّ ثَلَاثَةَ قُرُوءٍۚ ᵃ وَلَا يَحِلُّ لَهُنَّ أَنْ يَكْتُمْنَ مَا خَلَقَ اللَّهُ فِي أَرْحَامِهِنَّ إِنْ كُنَّ يُؤْمِنَّ بِاللَّهِ وَالْيَوْمِ الْآخِرِۚ وَبُعُولَتُهُنَّ أَحَقُّ بِرَدِّهِنَّ فِي ذَٰلِكَ إِنْ أَرَادُوا إِصْلَاحًاۚ وَلَهُنَّ مِثْلُ الَّذِي عَلَيْهِنَّ بِالْمَعْرُوفِۚ ᵇ وَلِلرِّجَالِ عَلَيْهِنَّ دَرَجَةٌۗ ᶜ وَاللَّهُ عَزِيزٌ حَكِيمٌ

228 Divorced women shall wait by themselves for three periods. And it is not lawful for them to conceal what God has created in their wombs, if they believe in God and the Last Day. Meanwhile, their husbands have the better right to take them back, if they desire reconciliation. And women have rights similar to their obligations, according to what is fair. But men have a degree over them. God is Mighty and Wise.

228
ᵃ 33:49; 65:4
ᵇ 4:34; 33:35; 65:4
ᶜ 4:34

٢٢٩ الطَّلَاقُ مَرَّتَانِ ۖ فَإِمْسَاكٌ بِمَعْرُوفٍ أَوْ تَسْرِيحٌ بِإِحْسَانٍ ۗ وَلَا يَحِلُّ لَكُمْ أَنْ تَأْخُذُوا مِمَّا آتَيْتُمُوهُنَّ شَيْئًا إِلَّا أَنْ يَخَافَا أَلَّا يُقِيمَا حُدُودَ اللَّهِ ۖ فَإِنْ خِفْتُمْ أَلَّا يُقِيمَا حُدُودَ اللَّهِ فَلَا جُنَاحَ عَلَيْهِمَا فِيمَا افْتَدَتْ بِهِ ۗ تِلْكَ حُدُودُ اللَّهِ فَلَا تَعْتَدُوهَا ۚ وَمَنْ يَتَعَدَّ حُدُودَ اللَّهِ فَأُولَٰئِكَ هُمُ الظَّالِمُونَ

229–231
4:4, 24; 65:1–7;
4:20–21

229 Divorce is allowed twice. Then, either honorable retention, or setting free kindly. It is not lawful for you to take back anything you have given them, unless they fear that they cannot maintain God's limits. If you fear that they cannot maintain God's limits, then there is no blame on them if she sacrifices something for her release. These are God's limits, so do not transgress them. Those who transgress God's limits are the unjust.

٢٣٠ فَإِنْ طَلَّقَهَا فَلَا تَحِلُّ لَهُ مِنْ بَعْدُ حَتَّىٰ تَنْكِحَ زَوْجًا غَيْرَهُ ۗ فَإِنْ طَلَّقَهَا فَلَا جُنَاحَ عَلَيْهِمَا أَنْ يَتَرَاجَعَا إِنْ ظَنَّا أَنْ يُقِيمَا حُدُودَ اللَّهِ ۗ وَتِلْكَ حُدُودُ اللَّهِ يُبَيِّنُهَا لِقَوْمٍ يَعْلَمُونَ

230 If he divorces her, she shall not be lawful for him again until she has married another husband. If the latter divorces her, then there is no blame on them for reuniting, provided they think they can maintain God's limits. These are God's limits; He makes them clear to people who know.

٢٣١ وَإِذَا طَلَّقْتُمُ النِّسَاءَ فَبَلَغْنَ أَجَلَهُنَّ فَأَمْسِكُوهُنَّ بِمَعْرُوفٍ أَوْ سَرِّحُوهُنَّ بِمَعْرُوفٍ ۚ وَلَا تُمْسِكُوهُنَّ ضِرَارًا لِتَعْتَدُوا ۚ وَمَنْ يَفْعَلْ ذَٰلِكَ فَقَدْ ظَلَمَ نَفْسَهُ ۚ وَلَا تَتَّخِذُوا آيَاتِ اللَّهِ هُزُوًا ۚ وَاذْكُرُوا نِعْمَتَ اللَّهِ عَلَيْكُمْ وَمَا أَنْزَلَ عَلَيْكُمْ مِنَ الْكِتَابِ وَالْحِكْمَةِ يَعِظُكُمْ بِهِ ۚ وَاتَّقُوا اللَّهَ وَاعْلَمُوا أَنَّ اللَّهَ بِكُلِّ شَيْءٍ عَلِيمٌ

231 When you divorce women, and they have reached their term, either retain them amicably, or release them amicably. But do not retain them to hurt them and commit aggression. Whoever does that has wronged himself. And do not take God's revelations for a joke. And remember God's favor to you, and that He revealed to you the Scripture and Wisdom to teach you. And fear God, and know that God is aware of everything.

٢٣٢ وَإِذَا طَلَّقْتُمُ النِّسَاءَ فَبَلَغْنَ أَجَلَهُنَّ فَلَا تَعْضُلُوهُنَّ أَنْ يَنْكِحْنَ أَزْوَاجَهُنَّ إِذَا تَرَاضَوْا بَيْنَهُمْ بِالْمَعْرُوفِ ۗ ذَٰلِكَ يُوعَظُ بِهِ مَنْ كَانَ مِنْكُمْ يُؤْمِنُ بِاللَّهِ وَالْيَوْمِ الْآخِرِ ۗ ذَٰلِكُمْ أَزْكَىٰ لَكُمْ وَأَطْهَرُ ۗ وَاللَّهُ يَعْلَمُ وَأَنْتُمْ لَا تَعْلَمُونَ

232 When you divorce women, and they have reached their term, do not prevent them from marrying their husbands, provided they agree on fair terms. Thereby is advised whoever among you believes in God and the Last Day. That is better and more decent for you. God knows, and you do not know.

٢٣٣ وَالْوَالِدَاتُ يُرْضِعْنَ أَوْلَادَهُنَّ حَوْلَيْنِ كَامِلَيْنِ ۖ لِمَنْ أَرَادَ أَن يُتِمَّ الرَّضَاعَةَ ۚ وَعَلَى الْمَوْلُودِ لَهُ رِزْقُهُنَّ وَكِسْوَتُهُنَّ بِالْمَعْرُوفِ ۚ لَا تُكَلَّفُ نَفْسٌ إِلَّا وُسْعَهَا ۚ لَا تُضَارَّ وَالِدَةٌ بِوَلَدِهَا وَلَا مَوْلُودٌ لَّهُ بِوَلَدِهِ ۚ وَعَلَى الْوَارِثِ مِثْلُ ذَٰلِكَ ۗ فَإِنْ أَرَادَا فِصَالًا عَن تَرَاضٍ مِّنْهُمَا وَتَشَاوُرٍ فَلَا جُنَاحَ عَلَيْهِمَا ۗ وَإِنْ أَرَدتُّمْ أَن تَسْتَرْضِعُوا أَوْلَادَكُمْ فَلَا جُنَاحَ عَلَيْكُمْ إِذَا سَلَّمْتُم مَّا آتَيْتُم بِالْمَعْرُوفِ ۗ وَاتَّقُوا اللَّهَ وَاعْلَمُوا أَنَّ اللَّهَ بِمَا تَعْمَلُونَ بَصِيرٌ

233
31:14; 46:15; 65:6

233 Mothers may nurse their infants for two whole years, for those who desire to complete the nursing-period. It is the duty of the father to provide for them and clothe them in a proper manner. No soul shall be burdened beyond its capacity. No mother shall be harmed on account of her child, and no father shall be harmed on account of his child. The same duty rests upon the heir. If the couple desire weaning, by mutual consent and consultation, they commit no error by doing so. You commit no error by hiring nursing-mothers, as long as you pay them fairly. And be wary of God, and know that God is Seeing of what you do.

٢٣٤ وَالَّذِينَ يُتَوَفَّوْنَ مِنكُمْ وَيَذَرُونَ أَزْوَاجًا يَتَرَبَّصْنَ بِأَنفُسِهِنَّ أَرْبَعَةَ أَشْهُرٍ وَعَشْرًا ۖ فَإِذَا بَلَغْنَ أَجَلَهُنَّ فَلَا جُنَاحَ عَلَيْكُمْ فِيمَا فَعَلْنَ فِي أَنفُسِهِنَّ بِالْمَعْرُوفِ ۗ وَاللَّهُ بِمَا تَعْمَلُونَ خَبِيرٌ

234
2:240; 65:4

234 As for those among you who die and leave widows behind, their widows shall wait by themselves for four months and ten days. When they have reached their term, there is no blame on you regarding what they might honorably do with themselves. God is fully acquainted with what you do.

٢٣٥ وَلَا جُنَاحَ عَلَيْكُمْ فِيمَا عَرَّضْتُم بِهِ مِنْ خِطْبَةِ النِّسَاءِ أَوْ أَكْنَنتُمْ فِي أَنفُسِكُمْ ۚ عَلِمَ اللَّهُ أَنَّكُمْ سَتَذْكُرُونَهُنَّ وَلَٰكِن لَّا تُوَاعِدُوهُنَّ سِرًّا إِلَّا أَن تَقُولُوا قَوْلًا مَّعْرُوفًا ۚ وَلَا تَعْزِمُوا عُقْدَةَ النِّكَاحِ حَتَّىٰ يَبْلُغَ الْكِتَابُ أَجَلَهُ ۚ وَاعْلَمُوا أَنَّ اللَّهَ يَعْلَمُ مَا فِي أَنفُسِكُمْ فَاحْذَرُوهُ ۚ وَاعْلَمُوا أَنَّ اللَّهَ غَفُورٌ حَلِيمٌ

235
2:87; 3:46; 5:100

235 You commit no error by announcing your engagement to women, or by keeping it to yourselves. God knows that you will be thinking about them. But do not meet them secretly, unless you have something proper to say. And do not confirm the marriage tie until the writing is fulfilled. And know that God knows what is in your souls, so beware of Him. And know that God is Forgiving and Forbearing.

٢٣٦ لَّا جُنَاحَ عَلَيْكُمْ إِن طَلَّقْتُمُ النِّسَاءَ مَا لَمْ تَمَسُّوهُنَّ أَوْ تَفْرِضُوا لَهُنَّ فَرِيضَةً ۚ وَمَتِّعُوهُنَّ عَلَى الْمُوسِعِ قَدَرُهُ وَعَلَى الْمُقْتِرِ قَدَرُهُ مَتَاعًا بِالْمَعْرُوفِ ۖ حَقًّا عَلَى الْمُحْسِنِينَ

236–237
33:49

236 You commit no error by divorcing women before having touched them, or before having set the dowry for them. And compensate them—the wealthy according to his means, and the poor according to his means—with a fair compensation, a duty upon the doers of good.

٢٣٧ وَإِنْ طَلَّقْتُمُوهُنَّ مِنْ قَبْلِ أَنْ تَمَسُّوهُنَّ وَقَدْ فَرَضْتُمْ لَهُنَّ فَرِيضَةً فَنِصْفُ مَا فَرَضْتُمْ إِلَّا أَنْ يَعْفُونَ أَوْ يَعْفُوَ الَّذِي بِيَدِهِ عُقْدَةُ النِّكَاحِ وَأَنْ تَعْفُوا أَقْرَبُ لِلتَّقْوَىٰ وَلَا تَنْسَوُا الْفَضْلَ بَيْنَكُمْ إِنَّ اللَّهَ بِمَا تَعْمَلُونَ بَصِيرٌ

237 If you divorce them before you have touched them, but after you had set the dowry for them, give them half of what you specified—unless they forego the right, or the one in whose hand is the marriage contract foregoes it. But to forego is nearer to piety. And do not forget generosity between one another. God is seeing of everything you do.

٢٣٨ حَافِظُوا عَلَى الصَّلَوَاتِ وَالصَّلَاةِ الْوُسْطَىٰ وَقُومُوا لِلَّهِ قَانِتِينَ

238 Guard your prayers, and the middle prayer, and stand before God in devotion.

٢٣٩ فَإِنْ خِفْتُمْ فَرِجَالًا أَوْ رُكْبَانًا فَإِذَا أَمِنْتُمْ فَاذْكُرُوا اللَّهَ كَمَا عَلَّمَكُمْ مَا لَمْ تَكُونُوا تَعْلَمُونَ

239 But if you are in fear, then on foot, or riding. And when you are safe, remember God, as He taught you what you did not know.

٢٤٠ وَالَّذِينَ يُتَوَفَّوْنَ مِنْكُمْ وَيَذَرُونَ أَزْوَاجًا وَصِيَّةً لِأَزْوَاجِهِمْ مَتَاعًا إِلَى الْحَوْلِ غَيْرَ إِخْرَاجٍ فَإِنْ خَرَجْنَ فَلَا جُنَاحَ عَلَيْكُمْ فِي مَا فَعَلْنَ فِي أَنْفُسِهِنَّ مِنْ مَعْرُوفٍ وَاللَّهُ عَزِيزٌ حَكِيمٌ

240
2:234

240 Those of you who die and leave wives behind—a will shall provide their wives with support for a year, provided they do not leave. If they leave, you are not to blame for what they do with themselves, provided it is reasonable. God is Mighty and Wise.

٢٤١ وَلِلْمُطَلَّقَاتِ مَتَاعٌ بِالْمَعْرُوفِ حَقًّا عَلَى الْمُتَّقِينَ

241 And divorced women shall be provided for, equitably—a duty upon the righteous.

٢٤٢ كَذَٰلِكَ يُبَيِّنُ اللَّهُ لَكُمْ آيَاتِهِ لَعَلَّكُمْ تَعْقِلُونَ

242 God thus explains His revelations to you, so that you may understand.

٢٤٣ أَلَمْ تَرَ إِلَى الَّذِينَ خَرَجُوا مِنْ دِيَارِهِمْ وَهُمْ أُلُوفٌ حَذَرَ الْمَوْتِ فَقَالَ لَهُمُ اللَّهُ مُوتُوا ثُمَّ أَحْيَاهُمْ إِنَّ اللَّهَ لَذُو فَضْلٍ عَلَى النَّاسِ وَلَٰكِنَّ أَكْثَرَ النَّاسِ لَا يَشْكُرُونَ

243
33:16

243 Have you not considered those who fled their homes, by the thousands, fearful of death? God said to them, "Die." Then He revived them. God is Gracious towards the people, but most people are not appreciative.

٢٤٤ وَقَاتِلُوا فِي سَبِيلِ اللَّهِ وَاعْلَمُوا أَنَّ اللَّهَ سَمِيعٌ عَلِيمٌ

244 Fight in the cause of God, and know that God is Hearing and Knowing.

٢٤٥ مَنْ ذَا الَّذِي يُقْرِضُ اللَّهَ قَرْضًا حَسَنًا فَيُضَاعِفَهُ لَهُ أَضْعَافًا كَثِيرَةً ۚ وَاللَّهُ يَقْبِضُ وَيَبْسُطُ وَإِلَيْهِ تُرْجَعُونَ

245 — 57:11; 64:17

245 Who is he who will offer God a generous loan, so He will multiply it for him manifold? God receives and amplifies, and to Him you will be returned.

٢٤٦ أَلَمْ تَرَ إِلَى الْمَلَإِ مِنْ بَنِي إِسْرَائِيلَ مِنْ بَعْدِ مُوسَىٰ إِذْ قَالُوا لِنَبِيٍّ لَهُمُ ابْعَثْ لَنَا مَلِكًا نُقَاتِلْ فِي سَبِيلِ اللَّهِ ۖ قَالَ هَلْ عَسَيْتُمْ إِنْ كُتِبَ عَلَيْكُمُ الْقِتَالُ أَلَّا تُقَاتِلُوا ۖ قَالُوا وَمَا لَنَا أَلَّا نُقَاتِلَ فِي سَبِيلِ اللَّهِ وَقَدْ أُخْرِجْنَا مِنْ دِيَارِنَا وَأَبْنَائِنَا ۖ فَلَمَّا كُتِبَ عَلَيْهِمُ الْقِتَالُ تَوَلَّوْا إِلَّا قَلِيلًا مِنْهُمْ ۗ وَاللَّهُ عَلِيمٌ بِالظَّالِمِينَ

246 — 2:216; 4:77; 42:20

246 Have you not considered the notables of the Children of Israel after Moses? When they said to a prophet of theirs, "Appoint a king for us, and we will fight in the cause of God." He said, "Is it possible that, if fighting was ordained for you, you would not fight?" They said, "Why would we not fight in the cause of God, when we were driven out of our homes, along with our children?" But when fighting was ordained for them, they turned away, except for a few of them. But God is aware of the wrongdoers.

٢٤٧ وَقَالَ لَهُمْ نَبِيُّهُمْ إِنَّ اللَّهَ قَدْ بَعَثَ لَكُمْ طَالُوتَ مَلِكًا ۚ قَالُوا أَنَّىٰ يَكُونُ لَهُ الْمُلْكُ عَلَيْنَا وَنَحْنُ أَحَقُّ بِالْمُلْكِ مِنْهُ وَلَمْ يُؤْتَ سَعَةً مِنَ الْمَالِ ۚ قَالَ إِنَّ اللَّهَ اصْطَفَاهُ عَلَيْكُمْ وَزَادَهُ بَسْطَةً فِي الْعِلْمِ وَالْجِسْمِ ۖ وَاللَّهُ يُؤْتِي مُلْكَهُ مَنْ يَشَاءُ ۚ وَاللَّهُ وَاسِعٌ عَلِيمٌ

247 Their prophet said to them, "God has appointed Saul to be your king." They said, "How can he have authority over us, when we are more worthy of authority than he, and he was not given plenty of wealth?" He said, "God has chosen him over you, and has increased him in knowledge and stature." God bestows His sovereignty upon whomever He wills. God is Embracing and Knowing.

٢٤٨ وَقَالَ لَهُمْ نَبِيُّهُمْ إِنَّ آيَةَ مُلْكِهِ أَنْ يَأْتِيَكُمُ التَّابُوتُ فِيهِ سَكِينَةٌ مِنْ رَبِّكُمْ وَبَقِيَّةٌ مِمَّا تَرَكَ آلُ مُوسَىٰ وَآلُ هَارُونَ تَحْمِلُهُ الْمَلَائِكَةُ ۚ إِنَّ فِي ذَٰلِكَ لَآيَةً لَكُمْ إِنْ كُنْتُمْ مُؤْمِنِينَ

248 And their prophet said to them, "The proof of his kingship is that the Ark will be restored to you, bringing tranquility from your Lord, and relics left by the family of Moses and the family of Aaron. It will be carried by the angels. In that is a sign for you, if you are believers."

٢٤٩ فَلَمَّا فَصَلَ طَالُوتُ بِالْجُنُودِ قَالَ إِنَّ اللَّهَ مُبْتَلِيكُمْ بِنَهَرٍ فَمَنْ شَرِبَ مِنْهُ فَلَيْسَ مِنِّي وَمَنْ لَمْ يَطْعَمْهُ فَإِنَّهُ مِنِّي إِلَّا مَنِ اغْتَرَفَ غُرْفَةً بِيَدِهِ ۚ فَشَرِبُوا مِنْهُ إِلَّا قَلِيلًا مِنْهُمْ ۚ فَلَمَّا جَاوَزَهُ هُوَ وَالَّذِينَ آمَنُوا مَعَهُ قَالُوا لَا طَاقَةَ لَنَا الْيَوْمَ بِجَالُوتَ وَجُنُودِهِ ۚ قَالَ الَّذِينَ يَظُنُّونَ أَنَّهُمْ مُلَاقُو اللَّهِ كَمْ مِنْ فِئَةٍ قَلِيلَةٍ غَلَبَتْ فِئَةً كَثِيرَةً بِإِذْنِ اللَّهِ ۗ وَاللَّهُ مَعَ الصَّابِرِينَ

249 — 2:46

249 When Saul set out with the troops, he said, "God will be testing you with a river. Whoever drinks from it does not belong with me. But whoever does not drink from it, does belong with me, except for whoever scoops up a little with his hand." But they drank from it, except for a few of them. Then, when he crossed it, he and those who

believed with him, they said, "We have no strength to face Goliath and his troops today." But those who knew that they would meet God said, "How many a small group has defeated a large group by God's will. God is with the steadfast."

٢٥٠ وَلَمَّا بَرَزُوا لِجَالُوتَ وَجُنُودِهِ قَالُوا رَبَّنَا أَفْرِغْ عَلَيْنَا صَبْرًا وَثَبِّتْ أَقْدَامَنَا وَانْصُرْنَا عَلَى الْقَوْمِ الْكَافِرِينَ

250 And when they confronted Goliath and his troops, they said, "Our Lord, pour down patience on us, and strengthen our foothold, and support us against the faithless people."

٢٥١ فَهَزَمُوهُمْ بِإِذْنِ اللَّهِ وَقَتَلَ دَاوُودُ جَالُوتَ وَآتَاهُ اللَّهُ الْمُلْكَ وَالْحِكْمَةَ وَعَلَّمَهُ مِمَّا يَشَاءُ ۗ وَلَوْلَا دَفْعُ اللَّهِ النَّاسَ بَعْضَهُمْ بِبَعْضٍ لَفَسَدَتِ الْأَرْضُ وَلَٰكِنَّ اللَّهَ ذُو فَضْلٍ عَلَى الْعَالَمِينَ

251 And they defeated them by God's leave, and David killed Goliath, and God gave him sovereignty and wisdom, and taught him as He willed. Were it not for God restraining the people, some by means of others, the earth would have gone to ruin. But God is gracious towards mankind.

٢٥٢ تِلْكَ آيَاتُ اللَّهِ نَتْلُوهَا عَلَيْكَ بِالْحَقِّ ۚ وَإِنَّكَ لَمِنَ الْمُرْسَلِينَ

252
3:108; 28:2; 45:6

252 These are God's revelations, which We recite to you in truth. You are one of the messengers.

٢٥٣ تِلْكَ الرُّسُلُ فَضَّلْنَا بَعْضَهُمْ عَلَىٰ بَعْضٍ ۘ مِنْهُمْ مَنْ كَلَّمَ اللَّهُ [a] وَرَفَعَ بَعْضَهُمْ دَرَجَاتٍ ۚ وَآتَيْنَا عِيسَى ابْنَ مَرْيَمَ الْبَيِّنَاتِ وَأَيَّدْنَاهُ بِرُوحِ الْقُدُسِ [b] وَلَوْ شَاءَ اللَّهُ مَا اقْتَتَلَ الَّذِينَ مِنْ بَعْدِهِمْ مِنْ بَعْدِ مَا جَاءَتْهُمُ الْبَيِّنَاتُ وَلَٰكِنِ اخْتَلَفُوا فَمِنْهُمْ مَنْ آمَنَ وَمِنْهُمْ مَنْ كَفَرَ ۚ وَلَوْ شَاءَ اللَّهُ مَا اقْتَتَلُوا وَلَٰكِنَّ اللَّهَ يَفْعَلُ مَا يُرِيدُ

253
[a] 4:164; 7:144
[b] 2:87

253 These messengers: We gave some advantage over others. To some of them God spoke directly, and some He raised in rank. We gave Jesus son of Mary the clear miracles, and We strengthened him with the Holy Spirit. Had God willed, those who succeeded them would not have fought one another, after the clear signs had come to them; but they disputed; some of them believed, and some of them disbelieved. Had God willed, they would not have fought one another; but God does whatever He desires.

٢٥٤ يَا أَيُّهَا الَّذِينَ آمَنُوا أَنْفِقُوا مِمَّا رَزَقْنَاكُمْ مِنْ قَبْلِ أَنْ يَأْتِيَ يَوْمٌ لَا بَيْعٌ فِيهِ وَلَا خُلَّةٌ وَلَا شَفَاعَةٌ ۗ وَالْكَافِرُونَ هُمُ الظَّالِمُونَ

254
14:31; 36:47; 63:10

254 O you who believe! Spend from what We have given you, before a Day comes in which there is neither trading, nor friendship, nor intercession. The disbelievers are the wrongdoers.

٢٥٥ اللَّهُ لَا إِلَٰهَ إِلَّا هُوَ الْحَيُّ الْقَيُّومُ ۚ لَا تَأْخُذُهُ سِنَةٌ وَلَا نَوْمٌ ۚ لَهُ مَا فِي السَّمَاوَاتِ وَمَا فِي الْأَرْضِ ۗ مَن ذَا الَّذِي يَشْفَعُ عِندَهُ إِلَّا بِإِذْنِهِ ۚ يَعْلَمُ مَا بَيْنَ أَيْدِيهِمْ وَمَا خَلْفَهُمْ ۖ وَلَا يُحِيطُونَ بِشَيْءٍ مِّنْ عِلْمِهِ إِلَّا بِمَا شَاءَ ۚ وَسِعَ كُرْسِيُّهُ السَّمَاوَاتِ وَالْأَرْضَ ۖ وَلَا يَئُودُهُ حِفْظُهُمَا ۚ وَهُوَ الْعَلِيُّ الْعَظِيمُ

255
3:2; 28:70; 59:22

255 God! There is no god except He, the Living, the Everlasting. Neither slumber overtakes Him, nor sleep. To Him belongs everything in the heavens and everything on earth. Who is he that can intercede with Him except with His permission? He knows what is before them, and what is behind them; and they cannot grasp any of His knowledge, except as He wills. His Throne extends over the heavens and the earth, and their preservation does not burden Him. He is the Most High, the Great.

٢٥٦ لَا إِكْرَاهَ فِي الدِّينِ ۖ قَد تَّبَيَّنَ الرُّشْدُ مِنَ الْغَيِّ ۚ فَمَن يَكْفُرْ بِالطَّاغُوتِ وَيُؤْمِن بِاللَّهِ فَقَدِ اسْتَمْسَكَ بِالْعُرْوَةِ الْوُثْقَىٰ لَا انفِصَامَ لَهَا ۗ وَاللَّهُ سَمِيعٌ عَلِيمٌ

256
109:6

256 There shall be no compulsion in religion; the right way has become distinct from the wrong way. Whoever renounces evil and believes in God has grasped the most trustworthy handle; which does not break. God is Hearing and Knowing.

٢٥٧ اللَّهُ وَلِيُّ الَّذِينَ آمَنُوا يُخْرِجُهُم مِّنَ الظُّلُمَاتِ إِلَى النُّورِ ۖ وَالَّذِينَ كَفَرُوا أَوْلِيَاؤُهُمُ الطَّاغُوتُ يُخْرِجُونَهُم مِّنَ النُّورِ إِلَى الظُّلُمَاتِ ۗ أُولَٰئِكَ أَصْحَابُ النَّارِ ۖ هُمْ فِيهَا خَالِدُونَ

257
4:119; 7:27, 30; 45:19

257 God is the Lord of those who believe; He brings them out of darkness and into light. As for those who disbelieve, their lords are the evil ones; they bring them out of light and into darkness—these are the inmates of the Fire, in which they will abide forever.

٢٥٨ أَلَمْ تَرَ إِلَى الَّذِي حَاجَّ إِبْرَاهِيمَ فِي رَبِّهِ أَنْ آتَاهُ اللَّهُ الْمُلْكَ إِذْ قَالَ إِبْرَاهِيمُ رَبِّيَ الَّذِي يُحْيِي وَيُمِيتُ قَالَ أَنَا أُحْيِي وَأُمِيتُ ۖ قَالَ إِبْرَاهِيمُ فَإِنَّ اللَّهَ يَأْتِي بِالشَّمْسِ مِنَ الْمَشْرِقِ فَأْتِ بِهَا مِنَ الْمَغْرِبِ فَبُهِتَ الَّذِي كَفَرَ ۗ وَاللَّهُ لَا يَهْدِي الْقَوْمَ الظَّالِمِينَ

258 Have you not considered him who argued with Abraham about his Lord, because God had given him sovereignty? Abraham said, "My Lord is He who gives life and causes death." He said, "I give life and cause death." Abraham said, "God brings the sun from the East, so bring it from the West," so the blasphemer was confounded. God does not guide the wrongdoing people.

٢٥٩ أَوْ كَالَّذِي مَرَّ عَلَىٰ قَرْيَةٍ وَهِيَ خَاوِيَةٌ عَلَىٰ عُرُوشِهَا قَالَ أَنَّىٰ يُحْيِي هَٰذِهِ اللَّهُ بَعْدَ مَوْتِهَا ۖ فَأَمَاتَهُ اللَّهُ مِائَةَ عَامٍ ثُمَّ بَعَثَهُ ۖ قَالَ كَمْ لَبِثْتَ ۖ قَالَ لَبِثْتُ يَوْمًا أَوْ بَعْضَ يَوْمٍ ۖ قَالَ بَل لَّبِثْتَ مِائَةَ عَامٍ فَانظُرْ إِلَىٰ طَعَامِكَ وَشَرَابِكَ لَمْ يَتَسَنَّهْ ۖ وَانظُرْ إِلَىٰ حِمَارِكَ وَلِنَجْعَلَكَ آيَةً لِّلنَّاسِ ۖ وَانظُرْ إِلَى الْعِظَامِ كَيْفَ نُنشِزُهَا ثُمَّ نَكْسُوهَا لَحْمًا ۚ فَلَمَّا تَبَيَّنَ لَهُ قَالَ أَعْلَمُ أَنَّ اللَّهَ عَلَىٰ كُلِّ شَيْءٍ قَدِيرٌ

259 Or like him who passed by a town collapsed on its foundations. He said, "How can God revive this after its demise?" Thereupon God caused him to die for a hundred years, and then resurrected him. He said, "For how long have you tarried?" He said, "I have tarried for a

day, or part of a day." He said, "No. You have tarried for a hundred years. Now look at your food and your drink—it has not spoiled—and look at your donkey. We will make you a wonder for mankind. And look at the bones, how We arrange them, and then clothe them with flesh." So when it became clear to him, he said, "I know that God has power over all things."

٢٦٠ وَإِذْ قَالَ إِبْرَاهِيمُ رَبِّ أَرِنِي كَيْفَ تُحْيِي الْمَوْتَىٰ ۖ قَالَ أَوَلَمْ تُؤْمِن ۖ قَالَ بَلَىٰ وَلَٰكِن لِّيَطْمَئِنَّ قَلْبِي ۖ قَالَ فَخُذْ أَرْبَعَةً مِّنَ الطَّيْرِ فَصُرْهُنَّ إِلَيْكَ ثُمَّ اجْعَلْ عَلَىٰ كُلِّ جَبَلٍ مِّنْهُنَّ جُزْءًا ثُمَّ ادْعُهُنَّ يَأْتِينَكَ سَعْيًا ۚ وَاعْلَمْ أَنَّ اللَّهَ عَزِيزٌ حَكِيمٌ

260 And when Abraham said, "My Lord, show me how You give life to the dead." He said, "Have you not believed?" He said, "Yes, but to put my heart at ease." He said, "Take four birds, and incline them to yourself, then place a part on each hill, then call to them; and they will come rushing to you. And know that God is Powerful and Wise."

٢٦١ مَّثَلُ الَّذِينَ يُنفِقُونَ أَمْوَالَهُمْ فِي سَبِيلِ اللَّهِ كَمَثَلِ حَبَّةٍ أَنبَتَتْ سَبْعَ سَنَابِلَ فِي كُلِّ سُنبُلَةٍ مِّائَةُ حَبَّةٍ ۗ وَاللَّهُ يُضَاعِفُ لِمَن يَشَاءُ ۚ وَاللَّهُ وَاسِعٌ عَلِيمٌ

261 The parable of those who spend their wealth in God's way is that of a grain that produces seven spikes; in each spike is a hundred grains. God multiplies for whom He wills. God is Bounteous and Knowing.

٢٦٢ الَّذِينَ يُنفِقُونَ أَمْوَالَهُمْ فِي سَبِيلِ اللَّهِ ثُمَّ لَا يُتْبِعُونَ مَا أَنفَقُوا مَنًّا وَلَا أَذًى ۙ لَّهُمْ أَجْرُهُمْ عِندَ رَبِّهِمْ وَلَا خَوْفٌ عَلَيْهِمْ وَلَا هُمْ يَحْزَنُونَ

262
2:264; 4:38

262 Those who spend their wealth in the way of God, and then do not follow up what they spent with reminders of their generosity or with insults, will have their reward with their Lord—they have nothing to fear, nor shall they grieve.

٢٦٣ قَوْلٌ مَّعْرُوفٌ وَمَغْفِرَةٌ خَيْرٌ مِّن صَدَقَةٍ يَتْبَعُهَا أَذًى ۗ وَاللَّهُ غَنِيٌّ حَلِيمٌ

263
47:21

263 Kind words and forgiveness are better than charity followed by insults. God is Rich and Clement.

٢٦٤ يَا أَيُّهَا الَّذِينَ آمَنُوا لَا تُبْطِلُوا صَدَقَاتِكُم بِالْمَنِّ وَالْأَذَىٰ كَالَّذِي يُنفِقُ مَالَهُ رِئَاءَ النَّاسِ وَلَا يُؤْمِنُ بِاللَّهِ وَالْيَوْمِ الْآخِرِ ۖ فَمَثَلُهُ كَمَثَلِ صَفْوَانٍ عَلَيْهِ تُرَابٌ فَأَصَابَهُ وَابِلٌ فَتَرَكَهُ صَلْدًا ۖ لَّا يَقْدِرُونَ عَلَىٰ شَيْءٍ مِّمَّا كَسَبُوا ۗ وَاللَّهُ لَا يَهْدِي الْقَوْمَ الْكَافِرِينَ

264
2:262; 4:38

264 O you who believe! Do not nullify your charitable deeds with reminders and hurtful words, like him who spends his wealth to be seen by the people, and does not believe in God and the Last Day. His likeness is that of a smooth rock covered with soil: a downpour strikes it, and leaves it bare—they gain nothing from their efforts. God does not guide the disbelieving people.

٢٦٥ وَمَثَلُ الَّذِينَ يُنفِقُونَ أَمْوَالَهُمُ ابْتِغَاءَ مَرْضَاتِ اللَّهِ وَتَثْبِيتًا مِنْ أَنفُسِهِمْ كَمَثَلِ جَنَّةٍ بِرَبْوَةٍ أَصَابَهَا وَابِلٌ فَآتَتْ أُكُلَهَا ضِعْفَيْنِ فَإِن لَّمْ يُصِبْهَا وَابِلٌ فَطَلٌّ ۗ وَاللَّهُ بِمَا تَعْمَلُونَ بَصِيرٌ

265 And the parable of those who spend their wealth seeking God's approval, and to strengthen their souls, is that of a garden on a hillside. If heavy rain falls on it, its produce is doubled; and if no heavy rain falls, then dew is enough. God is seeing of everything you do.

٢٦٦ أَيَوَدُّ أَحَدُكُمْ أَن تَكُونَ لَهُ جَنَّةٌ مِّن نَّخِيلٍ وَأَعْنَابٍ تَجْرِي مِن تَحْتِهَا الْأَنْهَارُ لَهُ فِيهَا مِن كُلِّ الثَّمَرَاتِ وَأَصَابَهُ الْكِبَرُ وَلَهُ ذُرِّيَّةٌ ضُعَفَاءُ فَأَصَابَهَا إِعْصَارٌ فِيهِ نَارٌ فَاحْتَرَقَتْ ۗ كَذَٰلِكَ يُبَيِّنُ اللَّهُ لَكُمُ الْآيَاتِ لَعَلَّكُمْ تَتَفَكَّرُونَ

266
3:117

266 Would anyone of you like to have a garden of palms and vines, under which rivers flow—with all kinds of fruit in it for him, and old age has stricken him, and he has weak children—then a tornado with fire batters it, and it burns down? Thus, God makes clear the signs for you, so that you may reflect.

٢٦٧ يَا أَيُّهَا الَّذِينَ آمَنُوا أَنفِقُوا مِن طَيِّبَاتِ مَا كَسَبْتُمْ وَمِمَّا أَخْرَجْنَا لَكُم مِّنَ الْأَرْضِ ۖ وَلَا تَيَمَّمُوا الْخَبِيثَ مِنْهُ تُنفِقُونَ وَلَسْتُم بِآخِذِيهِ إِلَّا أَن تُغْمِضُوا فِيهِ ۚ وَاعْلَمُوا أَنَّ اللَّهَ غَنِيٌّ حَمِيدٌ

267
3:92

267 O you who believe! Give of the good things you have earned, and from what We have produced for you from the earth. And do not pick the inferior things to give away, when you yourselves would not accept it except with eyes closed. And know that God is Sufficient and Praiseworthy.

٢٦٨ الشَّيْطَانُ يَعِدُكُمُ الْفَقْرَ وَيَأْمُرُكُم بِالْفَحْشَاءِ ۖ وَاللَّهُ يَعِدُكُم مَّغْفِرَةً مِّنْهُ وَفَضْلًا ۗ وَاللَّهُ وَاسِعٌ عَلِيمٌ

268
2:169; 4:49; 24:21

268 Satan promises you poverty, and urges you to immorality; but God promises you forgiveness from Himself, and grace. God is Embracing and Knowing.

٢٦٩ يُؤْتِي الْحِكْمَةَ مَن يَشَاءُ ۚ وَمَن يُؤْتَ الْحِكْمَةَ فَقَدْ أُوتِيَ خَيْرًا كَثِيرًا ۗ وَمَا يَذَّكَّرُ إِلَّا أُولُو الْأَلْبَابِ

269 He gives wisdom to whomever He wills. Whoever is given wisdom has been given much good. But none pays heed except those with insight.

٢٧٠ وَمَا أَنفَقْتُم مِّن نَّفَقَةٍ أَوْ نَذَرْتُم مِّن نَّذْرٍ فَإِنَّ اللَّهَ يَعْلَمُهُ ۗ وَمَا لِلظَّالِمِينَ مِنْ أَنصَارٍ

270
2:273; 3:92; 59:8

270 Whatever charity you give, or a pledge you fulfill, God knows it. The wrongdoers have no helpers.

٢٧١ إِن تُبْدُوا الصَّدَقَاتِ فَنِعِمَّا هِيَ ۖ وَإِن تُخْفُوهَا وَتُؤْتُوهَا الْفُقَرَاءَ فَهُوَ خَيْرٌ لَّكُمْ ۚ وَيُكَفِّرُ عَنكُم مِّن سَيِّئَاتِكُمْ ۗ وَاللَّهُ بِمَا تَعْمَلُونَ خَبِيرٌ

271 If you give charity openly, that is good. But if you keep it secret, and give it to the needy in private, that is better for you. It will atone for some of your misdeeds. God is cognizant of what you do.

٢٧٢ لَيْسَ عَلَيْكَ هُدَاهُمْ وَلَٰكِنَّ اللَّهَ يَهْدِي مَن يَشَاءُ ۗ وَمَا تُنفِقُوا مِنْ خَيْرٍ فَلِأَنفُسِكُمْ ۚ وَمَا تُنفِقُونَ إِلَّا ابْتِغَاءَ وَجْهِ اللَّهِ ۚ وَمَا تُنفِقُوا مِنْ خَيْرٍ يُوَفَّ إِلَيْكُمْ وَأَنتُمْ لَا تُظْلَمُونَ

272
28:56

272 Their guidance is not your responsibility, but God guides whom He wills. Any charity you give is for your own good. Any charity you give shall be for the sake of God. Any charity you give will be repaid to you in full, and you will not be wronged.

٢٧٣ لِلْفُقَرَاءِ الَّذِينَ أُحْصِرُوا فِي سَبِيلِ اللَّهِ لَا يَسْتَطِيعُونَ ضَرْبًا فِي الْأَرْضِ يَحْسَبُهُمُ الْجَاهِلُ أَغْنِيَاءَ مِنَ التَّعَفُّفِ تَعْرِفُهُم بِسِيمَاهُمْ لَا يَسْأَلُونَ النَّاسَ إِلْحَافًا ۗ وَمَا تُنفِقُوا مِنْ خَيْرٍ فَإِنَّ اللَّهَ بِهِ عَلِيمٌ

273
2:270; 3:93; 59:8

273 It is for the poor; those who are restrained in the way of God, and unable to travel in the land. The unaware would think them rich, due to their dignity. You will recognize them by their features. They do not ask from people insistently. Whatever charity you give, God is aware of it.

٢٧٤ الَّذِينَ يُنفِقُونَ أَمْوَالَهُم بِاللَّيْلِ وَالنَّهَارِ سِرًّا وَعَلَانِيَةً فَلَهُمْ أَجْرُهُمْ عِندَ رَبِّهِمْ وَلَا خَوْفٌ عَلَيْهِمْ وَلَا هُمْ يَحْزَنُونَ

274
13:22; 14:31; 16:75; 35:29

274 Those who spend their wealth by night and day, privately and publicly, will receive their reward from their Lord. They have nothing to fear, nor shall they grieve.

٢٧٥ الَّذِينَ يَأْكُلُونَ الرِّبَا لَا يَقُومُونَ إِلَّا كَمَا يَقُومُ الَّذِي يَتَخَبَّطُهُ الشَّيْطَانُ مِنَ الْمَسِّ ۚ ذَٰلِكَ بِأَنَّهُمْ قَالُوا إِنَّمَا الْبَيْعُ مِثْلُ الرِّبَا ۗ وَأَحَلَّ اللَّهُ الْبَيْعَ وَحَرَّمَ الرِّبَا ۚ فَمَن جَاءَهُ مَوْعِظَةٌ مِّن رَّبِّهِ فَانتَهَىٰ فَلَهُ مَا سَلَفَ وَأَمْرُهُ إِلَى اللَّهِ ۖ وَمَنْ عَادَ فَأُولَٰئِكَ أَصْحَابُ النَّارِ ۖ هُمْ فِيهَا خَالِدُونَ

275–276
3:130; 4:161; 30:39

275 Those who swallow usury will not rise, except as someone driven mad by Satan's touch. That is because they say, "Commerce is like usury." But God has permitted commerce, and has forbidden usury. Whoever, on receiving advice from his Lord, refrains, may keep his past earnings, and his case rests with God. But whoever resumes—these are the dwellers of the Fire, wherein they will abide forever.

٢٧٦ يَمْحَقُ اللَّهُ الرِّبَا وَيُرْبِي الصَّدَقَاتِ ۗ وَاللَّهُ لَا يُحِبُّ كُلَّ كَفَّارٍ أَثِيمٍ

276 God condemns usury, and He blesses charities. God does not love any sinful ingrate.

٢٧٧ إِنَّ الَّذِينَ آمَنُوا وَعَمِلُوا الصَّالِحَاتِ وَأَقَامُوا الصَّلَاةَ وَآتَوُا الزَّكَاةَ لَهُمْ أَجْرُهُمْ عِندَ رَبِّهِمْ وَلَا خَوْفٌ عَلَيْهِمْ وَلَا هُمْ يَحْزَنُونَ

277
2:62; 5:69

277 Those who believe, and do good deeds, and pray regularly, and give charity—they will have their reward with their Lord; they will have no fear, nor shall they grieve.

٢٧٨ يَا أَيُّهَا الَّذِينَ آمَنُوا اتَّقُوا اللَّهَ وَذَرُوا مَا بَقِيَ مِنَ الرِّبَا إِن كُنتُم مُّؤْمِنِينَ

278 O you who believe! Fear God, and forgo what remains of usury, if you are believers.

٢٧٩ فَإِن لَّمْ تَفْعَلُوا فَأْذَنُوا بِحَرْبٍ مِّنَ اللَّهِ وَرَسُولِهِ ۖ وَإِن تُبْتُمْ فَلَكُمْ رُءُوسُ أَمْوَالِكُمْ لَا تَظْلِمُونَ وَلَا تُظْلَمُونَ

279 If you do not, then take notice of a war by God and His Messenger. But if you repent, you may keep your capital, neither wronging, nor being wronged.

٢٨٠ وَإِن كَانَ ذُو عُسْرَةٍ فَنَظِرَةٌ إِلَىٰ مَيْسَرَةٍ ۚ وَأَن تَصَدَّقُوا خَيْرٌ لَّكُمْ ۖ إِن كُنتُمْ تَعْلَمُونَ

280 But if he is in hardship, then deferment until a time of ease. But to remit it as charity is better for you, if you only knew.

٢٨١ وَاتَّقُوا يَوْمًا تُرْجَعُونَ فِيهِ إِلَى اللَّهِ ۖ ثُمَّ تُوَفَّىٰ كُلُّ نَفْسٍ مَّا كَسَبَتْ وَهُمْ لَا يُظْلَمُونَ

281
2:48; 16:111

281 And guard yourselves against a Day when you will be returned to God; then each soul will be rewarded fully for what it has earned, and they will not be wronged.

٢٨٢ يَا أَيُّهَا الَّذِينَ آمَنُوا إِذَا تَدَايَنتُم بِدَيْنٍ إِلَىٰ أَجَلٍ مُّسَمًّى فَاكْتُبُوهُ ۚ وَلْيَكْتُب بَّيْنَكُمْ كَاتِبٌ بِالْعَدْلِ ۚ وَلَا يَأْبَ كَاتِبٌ أَن يَكْتُبَ كَمَا عَلَّمَهُ اللَّهُ ۚ فَلْيَكْتُبْ وَلْيُمْلِلِ الَّذِي عَلَيْهِ الْحَقُّ وَلْيَتَّقِ اللَّهَ رَبَّهُ وَلَا يَبْخَسْ مِنْهُ شَيْئًا ۚ فَإِن كَانَ الَّذِي عَلَيْهِ الْحَقُّ سَفِيهًا أَوْ ضَعِيفًا أَوْ لَا يَسْتَطِيعُ أَن يُمِلَّ هُوَ فَلْيُمْلِلْ وَلِيُّهُ بِالْعَدْلِ ۚ وَاسْتَشْهِدُوا شَهِيدَيْنِ مِن رِّجَالِكُمْ ۖ فَإِن لَّمْ يَكُونَا رَجُلَيْنِ فَرَجُلٌ وَامْرَأَتَانِ مِمَّن تَرْضَوْنَ مِنَ الشُّهَدَاءِ أَن تَضِلَّ إِحْدَاهُمَا فَتُذَكِّرَ إِحْدَاهُمَا الْأُخْرَىٰ ۚ وَلَا يَأْبَ الشُّهَدَاءُ إِذَا مَا دُعُوا ۚ وَلَا تَسْأَمُوا أَن تَكْتُبُوهُ صَغِيرًا أَوْ كَبِيرًا إِلَىٰ أَجَلِهِ ۚ ذَٰلِكُمْ أَقْسَطُ عِندَ اللَّهِ وَأَقْوَمُ لِلشَّهَادَةِ وَأَدْنَىٰ أَلَّا تَرْتَابُوا ۖ إِلَّا أَن تَكُونَ تِجَارَةً حَاضِرَةً تُدِيرُونَهَا بَيْنَكُمْ فَلَيْسَ عَلَيْكُمْ جُنَاحٌ أَلَّا تَكْتُبُوهَا ۗ وَأَشْهِدُوا إِذَا تَبَايَعْتُمْ ۚ وَلَا يُضَارَّ كَاتِبٌ وَلَا شَهِيدٌ ۚ وَإِن تَفْعَلُوا فَإِنَّهُ فُسُوقٌ بِكُمْ ۗ وَاتَّقُوا اللَّهَ ۖ وَيُعَلِّمُكُمُ اللَّهُ ۗ وَاللَّهُ بِكُلِّ شَيْءٍ عَلِيمٌ

282 O you who believe! When you incur debt among yourselves for a certain period of time, write it down. And have a scribe write in your presence, in all fairness. And let no scribe refuse to write, as God has taught him. So, let him write, and let the debtor dictate. And let him fear God, his Lord, and diminish nothing from it. But if the debtor is mentally deficient, or weak, or unable to dictate, then let his guardian dictate with honesty. And call to witness two men from among you. If two men are not available, then one man and two women whose testimony is acceptable to all—if one of them fails to remember, the other would remind her. Witnesses must not refuse when called upon. And do not think it too trivial to write down, whether small or large, including the time of repayment. That is more equitable with God, and stronger as evidence, and more likely to prevent doubt—except in the case of a spot transaction between you—then there is no blame on you if you do not write it down. And let there be witnesses whenever you conclude a contract, and let no harm be done to either scribe or witness. If you do that, it is corruption on your part. And fear God. God teaches you. God is aware of everything.

٢٨٣ وَإِنْ كُنْتُمْ عَلَىٰ سَفَرٍ وَلَمْ تَجِدُوا كَاتِبًا فَرِهَانٌ مَقْبُوضَةٌ ۖ فَإِنْ أَمِنَ بَعْضُكُمْ بَعْضًا فَلْيُؤَدِّ الَّذِي اؤْتُمِنَ أَمَانَتَهُ وَلْيَتَّقِ اللَّهَ رَبَّهُ ۗ وَلَا تَكْتُمُوا الشَّهَادَةَ ۚ وَمَنْ يَكْتُمْهَا فَإِنَّهُ آثِمٌ قَلْبُهُ ۗ وَاللَّهُ بِمَا تَعْمَلُونَ عَلِيمٌ

283 If you are on a journey, and cannot find a scribe, then a security deposit should be handed over. But if you trust one another, let the trustee fulfill his trust, and let him fear God, his Lord. And do not conceal testimony. Whoever conceals it is sinner at heart. God is aware of what you do.

٢٨٤ لِلَّهِ مَا فِي السَّمَاوَاتِ وَمَا فِي الْأَرْضِ ۗ وَإِنْ تُبْدُوا مَا فِي أَنْفُسِكُمْ أَوْ تُخْفُوهُ يُحَاسِبْكُمْ بِهِ اللَّهُ ۖ فَيَغْفِرُ لِمَنْ يَشَاءُ وَيُعَذِّبُ مَنْ يَشَاءُ ۗ وَاللَّهُ عَلَىٰ كُلِّ شَيْءٍ قَدِيرٌ

284
3:129; 5:40

284 To God belongs everything in the heavens and the earth. Whether you reveal what is within your selves, or conceal it, God will call you to account for it. He forgives whom He wills, and He punishes whom He wills. God is Able to do all things.

٢٨٥ آمَنَ الرَّسُولُ بِمَا أُنْزِلَ إِلَيْهِ مِنْ رَبِّهِ وَالْمُؤْمِنُونَ ۚ كُلٌّ آمَنَ بِاللَّهِ وَمَلَائِكَتِهِ وَكُتُبِهِ وَرُسُلِهِ لَا نُفَرِّقُ بَيْنَ أَحَدٍ مِنْ رُسُلِهِ ۚ وَقَالُوا سَمِعْنَا وَأَطَعْنَا ۖ غُفْرَانَكَ رَبَّنَا وَإِلَيْكَ الْمَصِيرُ

285
2:136; 3:84; 4:152

285 The Messenger has believed in what was revealed to him from his Lord, as did the believers. They all have believed in God, and His angels, and His scriptures, and His messengers: "We make no distinction between any of His messengers." And they say, "We hear and we obey. Your forgiveness, our Lord. To you is the destiny."

٢٨٦ لَا يُكَلِّفُ اللَّهُ نَفْسًا إِلَّا وُسْعَهَا ۚ لَهَا مَا كَسَبَتْ وَعَلَيْهَا مَا اكْتَسَبَتْ ۗ [a] رَبَّنَا لَا تُؤَاخِذْنَا إِنْ نَسِينَا أَوْ أَخْطَأْنَا ۚ رَبَّنَا وَلَا تَحْمِلْ عَلَيْنَا إِصْرًا كَمَا حَمَلْتَهُ عَلَى الَّذِينَ مِنْ قَبْلِنَا ۚ رَبَّنَا وَلَا تُحَمِّلْنَا مَا لَا طَاقَةَ لَنَا بِهِ ۖ وَاعْفُ عَنَّا وَاغْفِرْ لَنَا وَارْحَمْنَا ۚ [b] أَنْتَ مَوْلَانَا فَانْصُرْنَا عَلَى الْقَوْمِ الْكَافِرِينَ

286
[a] 6:152; 7:42; 23:62
[b] 2:134, 141

286 God does not burden any soul beyond its capacity. To its credit is what it earns, and against it is what it commits. "Our Lord, do not condemn us if we forget or make a mistake. Our Lord, do not burden us as You have burdened those before us. Our Lord, do not burden us with more than we have strength to bear; and pardon us, and forgive us, and have mercy on us. You are our Lord and Master, so help us against the disbelieving people."

Sūrah 3: Āli 'Imrān

سُورَةُ آلِ عِمْرَان (The Family of Amran)

بِسْمِ اللَّهِ الرَّحْمَٰنِ الرَّحِيمِ

١ الم

1 Alif, Lām, Mīm.

٢ اللَّهُ لَا إِلَهَ إِلَّا هُوَ الْحَيُّ الْقَيُّومُ

2 God, there is no god but He, the Living, the Eternal.

2
28:70; 59:22

٣ نَزَّلَ عَلَيْكَ الْكِتَابَ بِالْحَقِّ مُصَدِّقًا لِمَا بَيْنَ يَدَيْهِ وَأَنْزَلَ التَّوْرَاةَ وَالْإِنْجِيلَ

3 He sent down to you the Book with the Truth, confirming what came before it; and He sent down the Torah and the Gospel.

3
2:97; 5:48; 35:31

٤ مِنْ قَبْلُ هُدًى لِلنَّاسِ وَأَنْزَلَ الْفُرْقَانَ ۗ إِنَّ الَّذِينَ كَفَرُوا بِآيَاتِ اللَّهِ لَهُمْ عَذَابٌ شَدِيدٌ ۗ وَاللَّهُ عَزِيزٌ ذُو انْتِقَامٍ

4 Aforetime, as guidance for mankind; and He sent down the Criterion. Those who have rejected God's signs will have a severe punishment. God is Mighty, Able to take revenge.

4
21:48; 25:1

٥ إِنَّ اللَّهَ لَا يَخْفَىٰ عَلَيْهِ شَيْءٌ فِي الْأَرْضِ وَلَا فِي السَّمَاءِ

5 Nothing is hidden from God, on earth or in the heaven.

5
14:38

٦ هُوَ الَّذِي يُصَوِّرُكُمْ فِي الْأَرْحَامِ كَيْفَ يَشَاءُ ۚ لَا إِلَهَ إِلَّا هُوَ الْعَزِيزُ الْحَكِيمُ

6 It is He who forms you in the wombs as He wills. There is no god except He, the Almighty, the Wise.

6
7:11; 23:12–14; 40:64; 59:24; 64:3; 82:7

٧ هُوَ الَّذِي أَنْزَلَ عَلَيْكَ الْكِتَابَ مِنْهُ آيَاتٌ مُحْكَمَاتٌ هُنَّ أُمُّ الْكِتَابِ وَأُخَرُ مُتَشَابِهَاتٌ ۖ فَأَمَّا الَّذِينَ فِي قُلُوبِهِمْ زَيْغٌ فَيَتَّبِعُونَ مَا تَشَابَهَ مِنْهُ ابْتِغَاءَ الْفِتْنَةِ وَابْتِغَاءَ تَأْوِيلِهِ ۗ وَمَا يَعْلَمُ تَأْوِيلَهُ إِلَّا اللَّهُ ۗ وَالرَّاسِخُونَ فِي الْعِلْمِ يَقُولُونَ آمَنَّا بِهِ كُلٌّ مِنْ عِنْدِ رَبِّنَا ۗ وَمَا يَذَّكَّرُ إِلَّا أُولُو الْأَلْبَابِ

7 It is He who revealed to you the Book. Some of its verses are definitive; they are the foundation of the Book, and others are unspecific. As for those in whose hearts is deviation, they follow the unspecific part, seeking dissent, and seeking to derive an interpretation. But none knows its interpretation except God and those firmly rooted in knowledge say, "We believe in it; all is from our Lord." But none recollects except those with understanding.

7
11:1; 22:52; 39:23; 47:20

٨ رَبَّنَا لَا تُزِغْ قُلُوبَنَا بَعْدَ إِذْ هَدَيْتَنَا وَهَبْ لَنَا مِنْ لَدُنْكَ رَحْمَةً ۚ إِنَّكَ أَنْتَ الْوَهَّابُ

8 "Our Lord, do not cause our hearts to swerve after You have guided us, and bestow on us mercy from Your presence; You are the Giver."

٩ رَبَّنَا إِنَّكَ جَامِعُ النَّاسِ لِيَوْمٍ لَا رَيْبَ فِيهِ ۚ إِنَّ اللَّهَ لَا يُخْلِفُ الْمِيعَادَ

9 "Our Lord, You will gather the people for a Day in which there is no doubt." God will never break His promise.

9
4:87; 42:7; 45:26

١٠ إِنَّ الَّذِينَ كَفَرُوا لَنْ تُغْنِيَ عَنْهُمْ أَمْوَالُهُمْ وَلَا أَوْلَادُهُمْ مِنَ اللَّهِ شَيْئًا ۖ وَأُولَٰئِكَ هُمْ وَقُودُ النَّارِ

10 As for those who disbelieve, neither their wealth nor their children will avail them anything against God. These will be fuel for the Fire.

10
3:116; 8:28; 23:56; 26:88; 34:35; 58:17; 63:9; 64:15

11

١١ كَدَأْبِ آلِ فِرْعَوْنَ وَالَّذِينَ مِنْ قَبْلِهِمْ ۚ كَذَّبُوا بِآيَاتِنَا فَأَخَذَهُمُ اللَّهُ بِذُنُوبِهِمْ ۗ وَاللَّهُ شَدِيدُ الْعِقَابِ

11 Like the behavior of Pharaoh's people and those before them. They rejected Our signs, so God seized them for their sins. God is Strict in retribution.

pp 8:52

12

١٢ قُلْ لِلَّذِينَ كَفَرُوا سَتُغْلَبُونَ وَتُحْشَرُونَ إِلَىٰ جَهَنَّمَ ۚ وَبِئْسَ الْمِهَادُ

12 Say to those who disbelieve, "You will be defeated, and rounded up into Hell—an awful resting-place."

8:36

13

١٣ قَدْ كَانَ لَكُمْ آيَةٌ فِي فِئَتَيْنِ الْتَقَتَا ۖ فِئَةٌ تُقَاتِلُ فِي سَبِيلِ اللَّهِ وَأُخْرَىٰ كَافِرَةٌ يَرَوْنَهُمْ مِثْلَيْهِمْ رَأْيَ الْعَيْنِ ۚ وَاللَّهُ يُؤَيِّدُ بِنَصْرِهِ مَنْ يَشَاءُ ۗ إِنَّ فِي ذَٰلِكَ لَعِبْرَةً لِأُولِي الْأَبْصَارِ

13 There was a sign for you in the two parties that met. One party fighting in the way of God, and the other was disbelieving. They saw them with their own eyes twice their number. But God supports with His help whomever He wills. In that is a lesson for those with insight.

3:123; 8:44

14

١٤ زُيِّنَ لِلنَّاسِ حُبُّ الشَّهَوَاتِ مِنَ النِّسَاءِ وَالْبَنِينَ وَالْقَنَاطِيرِ الْمُقَنْطَرَةِ مِنَ الذَّهَبِ وَالْفِضَّةِ وَالْخَيْلِ الْمُسَوَّمَةِ وَالْأَنْعَامِ وَالْحَرْثِ ۗ ذَٰلِكَ مَتَاعُ الْحَيَاةِ الدُّنْيَا ۖ وَاللَّهُ عِنْدَهُ حُسْنُ الْمَآبِ

14 Adorned for the people is the love of desires, such as women, and children, and piles upon piles of gold and silver, and branded horses, and livestock, and fields. These are the conveniences of the worldly life, but with God lies the finest resort.

18:46

15

١٥ قُلْ أَؤُنَبِّئُكُمْ بِخَيْرٍ مِنْ ذَٰلِكُمْ ۚ لِلَّذِينَ اتَّقَوْا عِنْدَ رَبِّهِمْ جَنَّاتٌ تَجْرِي مِنْ تَحْتِهَا الْأَنْهَارُ خَالِدِينَ فِيهَا وَأَزْوَاجٌ مُطَهَّرَةٌ وَرِضْوَانٌ مِنَ اللَّهِ ۗ وَاللَّهُ بَصِيرٌ بِالْعِبَادِ

15 Say, "Shall I inform you of something better than that? For those who are righteous, with their Lord are Gardens beneath which rivers flow, where they will remain forever, and purified spouses, and acceptance from God." God is Observant of the servants.

2:25; 4:57

16

١٦ الَّذِينَ يَقُولُونَ رَبَّنَا إِنَّنَا آمَنَّا فَاغْفِرْ لَنَا ذُنُوبَنَا وَقِنَا عَذَابَ النَّارِ

16 Those who say, "Our Lord, we have believed, so forgive us our sins, and save us from the suffering of the Fire."

17

١٧ الصَّابِرِينَ وَالصَّادِقِينَ وَالْقَانِتِينَ وَالْمُنْفِقِينَ وَالْمُسْتَغْفِرِينَ بِالْأَسْحَارِ

17 The patient, and the truthful, and the reverent, and the charitable, and the seekers of forgiveness at dawn.

10:27; 33:17; 51:18; 70:22-35

18

١٨ شَهِدَ اللَّهُ أَنَّهُ لَا إِلَٰهَ إِلَّا هُوَ وَالْمَلَائِكَةُ وَأُولُو الْعِلْمِ قَائِمًا بِالْقِسْطِ ۚ لَا إِلَٰهَ إِلَّا هُوَ الْعَزِيزُ الْحَكِيمُ

18 God bears witness that there is no god but He, as do the angels, and those endowed with knowledge—upholding justice. There is no god but He, the Mighty, the Wise.

4:166; 5:8; 13:43; 16:43

١٩ إِنَّ الدِّينَ عِندَ اللَّهِ الْإِسْلَامُ ۗ وَمَا اخْتَلَفَ الَّذِينَ أُوتُوا الْكِتَابَ إِلَّا مِن بَعْدِ مَا جَاءَهُمُ الْعِلْمُ بَغْيًا بَيْنَهُمْ ۗ وَمَن يَكْفُرْ بِآيَاتِ اللَّهِ فَإِنَّ اللَّهَ سَرِيعُ الْحِسَابِ

19 [a] 3:85; 5:3 [b] 3:105

19 Religion with God is Islam. Those to whom the Scripture was given differed only after knowledge came to them, out of envy among themselves. Whoever rejects the signs of God—God is quick to take account.

٢٠ فَإِنْ حَاجُّوكَ فَقُلْ أَسْلَمْتُ وَجْهِيَ لِلَّهِ وَمَنِ اتَّبَعَنِ ۗ وَقُل لِّلَّذِينَ أُوتُوا الْكِتَابَ وَالْأُمِّيِّينَ أَأَسْلَمْتُمْ ۚ فَإِنْ أَسْلَمُوا فَقَدِ اهْتَدَوا ۖ وَّإِن تَوَلَّوْا فَإِنَّمَا عَلَيْكَ الْبَلَاغُ ۗ وَاللَّهُ بَصِيرٌ بِالْعِبَادِ

20 2:137

20 If they argue with you, say, "I have surrendered myself to God, and those who follow me." And say to those who were given the Scripture, and to the unlearned, "Have you surrendered?" If they have surrendered, then they are guided; but if they turn away, then your duty is to convey. God is Seeing of the servants.

٢١ إِنَّ الَّذِينَ يَكْفُرُونَ بِآيَاتِ اللَّهِ وَيَقْتُلُونَ النَّبِيِّينَ بِغَيْرِ حَقٍّ وَيَقْتُلُونَ الَّذِينَ يَأْمُرُونَ بِالْقِسْطِ مِنَ النَّاسِ فَبَشِّرْهُم بِعَذَابٍ أَلِيمٍ

21 2:61, 91; 3:181; 4:80, 155

21 As for those who defy God's revelations, and kill the prophets unjustly, and kill those who advocate justice among the people—promise them a painful retribution.

٢٢ أُولَٰئِكَ الَّذِينَ حَبِطَتْ أَعْمَالُهُمْ فِي الدُّنْيَا وَالْآخِرَةِ وَمَا لَهُم مِّن نَّاصِرِينَ

22 2:217; 9:69

22 They are those whose deeds will come to nothing, in this world and in the Hereafter; and they will have no saviors.

٢٣ أَلَمْ تَرَ إِلَى الَّذِينَ أُوتُوا نَصِيبًا مِّنَ الْكِتَابِ يُدْعَوْنَ إِلَىٰ كِتَابِ اللَّهِ لِيَحْكُمَ بَيْنَهُمْ ثُمَّ يَتَوَلَّىٰ فَرِيقٌ مِّنْهُمْ وَهُم مُّعْرِضُونَ

23 Have you not considered those who were given a share of the Scripture, as they were called to the Scripture of God to arbitrate between them; then some of them turned back, and declined?

٢٤ ذَٰلِكَ بِأَنَّهُمْ قَالُوا لَن تَمَسَّنَا النَّارُ إِلَّا أَيَّامًا مَّعْدُودَاتٍ ۖ وَغَرَّهُمْ فِي دِينِهِم مَّا كَانُوا يَفْتَرُونَ

24 2:80

24 That is because they said, "The Fire will not touch us except for a limited number of days." They have been misled in their religion by the lies they fabricated.

٢٥ فَكَيْفَ إِذَا جَمَعْنَاهُمْ لِيَوْمٍ لَّا رَيْبَ فِيهِ وَوُفِّيَتْ كُلُّ نَفْسٍ مَّا كَسَبَتْ وَهُمْ لَا يُظْلَمُونَ

25 2:79, 272, 281

25 How about when We gather them for a Day in which there is no doubt, and each soul will be paid in full for what it has earned, and they will not be wronged?

٢٦ قُلِ اللَّهُمَّ مَالِكَ الْمُلْكِ تُؤْتِي الْمُلْكَ مَن تَشَاءُ وَتَنزِعُ الْمُلْكَ مِمَّن تَشَاءُ وَتُعِزُّ مَن تَشَاءُ وَتُذِلُّ مَن تَشَاءُ ۖ بِيَدِكَ الْخَيْرُ ۖ إِنَّكَ عَلَىٰ كُلِّ شَيْءٍ قَدِيرٌ

26 2:247, 258; 35:13; 39:6; 64:1; 67:1

26 Say, "O God, Owner of Sovereignty. You grant sovereignty to whom You will, and You strip sovereignty from whom you will. You honor whom you will, and You humiliate whom you will. In Your hand is all goodness. You are Capable of all things."

٢٧ تُولِجُ اللَّيْلَ فِي النَّهَارِ وَتُولِجُ النَّهَارَ فِي اللَّيْلِ ۖ وَتُخْرِجُ الْحَيَّ مِنَ الْمَيِّتِ وَتُخْرِجُ الْمَيِّتَ مِنَ الْحَيِّ ۖ وَتَرْزُقُ مَن تَشَاءُ بِغَيْرِ حِسَابٍ

27 57:6

27 "You merge the night into the day, and You merge the day into the night; and you bring the living out of the dead, and You bring the dead out of the living; and You provide for whom you will without measure."

٢٨ لَّا يَتَّخِذِ الْمُؤْمِنُونَ الْكَافِرِينَ أَوْلِيَاءَ مِن دُونِ الْمُؤْمِنِينَ ۖ وَمَن يَفْعَلْ ذَٰلِكَ فَلَيْسَ مِنَ اللَّهِ فِي شَيْءٍ إِلَّا أَن تَتَّقُوا مِنْهُمْ تُقَاةً ۗ وَيُحَذِّرُكُمُ اللَّهُ نَفْسَهُ ۗ وَإِلَى اللَّهِ الْمَصِيرُ

28 4:89; 5:51, 55, 57

28 Believers are not to take disbelievers for friends instead of believers. Whoever does that has nothing to do with God, unless it is to protect your own selves against them. God warns you to beware of Him. To God is the destiny.

٢٩ قُلْ إِن تُخْفُوا مَا فِي صُدُورِكُمْ أَوْ تُبْدُوهُ يَعْلَمْهُ اللَّهُ ۗ وَيَعْلَمُ مَا فِي السَّمَاوَاتِ وَمَا فِي الْأَرْضِ ۗ وَاللَّهُ عَلَىٰ كُلِّ شَيْءٍ قَدِيرٌ

29 Say, "Whether you conceal what is in your hearts, or disclose it, God knows it." He knows everything in the heavens and the earth. God is Powerful over everything.

٣٠ يَوْمَ تَجِدُ كُلُّ نَفْسٍ مَّا عَمِلَتْ مِنْ خَيْرٍ مُّحْضَرًا وَمَا عَمِلَتْ مِن سُوءٍ تَوَدُّ لَوْ أَنَّ بَيْنَهَا وَبَيْنَهُ أَمَدًا بَعِيدًا ۗ وَيُحَذِّرُكُمُ اللَّهُ نَفْسَهُ ۗ وَاللَّهُ رَءُوفٌ بِالْعِبَادِ

30 18:49

30 On the Day when every soul finds all the good it has done presented. And as for the evil it has done, it will wish there were a great distance between them. God cautions you of Himself. God is Kind towards the servants.

٣١ قُلْ إِن كُنتُمْ تُحِبُّونَ اللَّهَ فَاتَّبِعُونِي يُحْبِبْكُمُ اللَّهُ وَيَغْفِرْ لَكُمْ ذُنُوبَكُمْ ۗ وَاللَّهُ غَفُورٌ رَّحِيمٌ

31–32 5:67, 92; 8:20; 24:54

31 Say, "If you love God, then follow me, and God will love you, and will forgive you your sins." God is Forgiving and Merciful.

٣٢ قُلْ أَطِيعُوا اللَّهَ وَالرَّسُولَ ۖ فَإِن تَوَلَّوْا فَإِنَّ اللَّهَ لَا يُحِبُّ الْكَافِرِينَ

32 Say, "Obey God and the Messenger." But if they turn away—God does not love the faithless.

٣٣ إِنَّ اللَّهَ اصْطَفَىٰ آدَمَ وَنُوحًا وَآلَ إِبْرَاهِيمَ وَآلَ عِمْرَانَ عَلَى الْعَالَمِينَ

33 16:121

33 God chose Adam, and Noah, and the family of Abraham, and the family of Imran, over all mankind.

٣٤ ذُرِّيَّةً بَعْضُهَا مِن بَعْضٍ ۗ وَاللَّهُ سَمِيعٌ عَلِيمٌ

34 Offspring one of the other. God is Hearer and Knower.

٣٥ إِذْ قَالَتِ امْرَأَتُ عِمْرَانَ رَبِّ إِنِّي نَذَرْتُ لَكَ مَا فِي بَطْنِي مُحَرَّرًا فَتَقَبَّلْ مِنِّي ۖ إِنَّكَ أَنتَ السَّمِيعُ الْعَلِيمُ

35 The wife of Imran said, "My Lord, I have vowed to You what is in my womb, dedicated, so accept from me; You are the Hearer and Knower."

٣٦ فَلَمَّا وَضَعَتْهَا قَالَتْ رَبِّ إِنِّي وَضَعْتُهَا أُنْثَىٰ وَاللَّهُ أَعْلَمُ بِمَا وَضَعَتْ وَلَيْسَ الذَّكَرُ كَالْأُنْثَىٰ ۖ وَإِنِّي سَمَّيْتُهَا مَرْيَمَ وَإِنِّي أُعِيذُهَا بِكَ وَذُرِّيَّتَهَا مِنَ الشَّيْطَانِ الرَّجِيمِ

36 And when she delivered her, she said, "My Lord, I have delivered a female," and God was well aware of what she has delivered, "and the male is not like the female, and I have named her Mary, and have commended her and her descendants to Your protection, from Satan the outcast."

٣٧ فَتَقَبَّلَهَا رَبُّهَا بِقَبُولٍ حَسَنٍ وَأَنْبَتَهَا نَبَاتًا حَسَنًا وَكَفَّلَهَا زَكَرِيَّا ۖ كُلَّمَا دَخَلَ عَلَيْهَا زَكَرِيَّا الْمِحْرَابَ وَجَدَ عِنْدَهَا رِزْقًا ۖ قَالَ يَا مَرْيَمُ أَنَّىٰ لَكِ هَٰذَا ۖ قَالَتْ هُوَ مِنْ عِنْدِ اللَّهِ ۖ إِنَّ اللَّهَ يَرْزُقُ مَنْ يَشَاءُ بِغَيْرِ حِسَابٍ

37 Her Lord accepted her with a gracious reception, and brought her a beautiful upbringing, and entrusted her to the care of Zechariah. Whenever Zechariah entered upon her in the sanctuary, he found her with provision. He said, "O Mary, where did you get this from?" She said, "It is from God; God provides to whom He wills without reckoning."

٣٨ هُنَالِكَ دَعَا زَكَرِيَّا رَبَّهُ ۖ قَالَ رَبِّ هَبْ لِي مِنْ لَدُنْكَ ذُرِّيَّةً طَيِّبَةً ۖ إِنَّكَ سَمِيعُ الدُّعَاءِ

38 Thereupon Zechariah prayed to his Lord; he said, "My Lord, bestow on me good offspring from Your presence; You are the Hearer of Prayers."

38
19:2–6; 21:8

٣٩ فَنَادَتْهُ الْمَلَائِكَةُ وَهُوَ قَائِمٌ يُصَلِّي فِي الْمِحْرَابِ أَنَّ اللَّهَ يُبَشِّرُكَ بِيَحْيَىٰ مُصَدِّقًا بِكَلِمَةٍ مِنَ اللَّهِ وَسَيِّدًا وَحَصُورًا وَنَبِيًّا مِنَ الصَّالِحِينَ

39 Then the angels called out to him, as he stood praying in the sanctuary: "God gives you good news of John; confirming a Word from God, and honorable, and moral, and a prophet; one of the upright."

39
19:7

٤٠ قَالَ رَبِّ أَنَّىٰ يَكُونُ لِي غُلَامٌ وَقَدْ بَلَغَنِيَ الْكِبَرُ وَامْرَأَتِي عَاقِرٌ ۖ قَالَ كَذَٰلِكَ اللَّهُ يَفْعَلُ مَا يَشَاءُ

40 He said, "My Lord, how will I have a son, when old age has overtaken me, and my wife is barren?" He said, "Even so, God does whatever He wills."

40
19:8

٤١ قَالَ رَبِّ اجْعَلْ لِي آيَةً ۖ قَالَ آيَتُكَ أَلَّا تُكَلِّمَ النَّاسَ ثَلَاثَةَ أَيَّامٍ إِلَّا رَمْزًا ۖ وَاذْكُرْ رَبَّكَ كَثِيرًا وَسَبِّحْ بِالْعَشِيِّ وَالْإِبْكَارِ

41 He said, "My Lord, give me a sign." He said, "Your sign is that you shall not speak to the people for three days, except by gestures. And remember your Lord much, and praise in the evening and the morning."

41
19:10

٤٢ وَإِذْ قَالَتِ الْمَلَائِكَةُ يَا مَرْيَمُ إِنَّ اللَّهَ اصْطَفَاكِ وَطَهَّرَكِ وَاصْطَفَاكِ عَلَىٰ نِسَاءِ الْعَالَمِينَ

42 The angels said, "O Mary, God has chosen you, and has purified you. He has chosen you over all the women of the world.

٤٣ يَا مَرْيَمُ اقْنُتِي لِرَبِّكِ وَاسْجُدِي وَارْكَعِي مَعَ الرَّاكِعِينَ

43 "O Mary, be devoted to your Lord, and bow down, and kneel with those who kneel."

٤٤ ذَٰلِكَ مِنْ أَنْبَاءِ الْغَيْبِ نُوحِيهِ إِلَيْكَ ۚ وَمَا كُنْتَ لَدَيْهِمْ إِذْ يُلْقُونَ أَقْلَامَهُمْ أَيُّهُمْ يَكْفُلُ مَرْيَمَ وَمَا كُنْتَ لَدَيْهِمْ إِذْ يَخْتَصِمُونَ

44 11:49; 12:102

44 These are accounts from the Unseen, which We reveal to you. You were not with them when they cast their lots as to which of them would take charge of Mary; nor were you with them as they quarreled.

٤٥ إِذْ قَالَتِ الْمَلَائِكَةُ يَا مَرْيَمُ إِنَّ اللَّهَ يُبَشِّرُكِ بِكَلِمَةٍ مِنْهُ اسْمُهُ الْمَسِيحُ عِيسَى ابْنُ مَرْيَمَ وَجِيهًا فِي الدُّنْيَا وَالْآخِرَةِ وَمِنَ الْمُقَرَّبِينَ

45 19:17–19

45 The Angels said, "O Mary, God gives you good news of a Word from Him. His name is the Messiah, Jesus, son of Mary, well-esteemed in this world and the next, and one of the nearest.

٤٦ وَيُكَلِّمُ النَّاسَ فِي الْمَهْدِ وَكَهْلًا وَمِنَ الصَّالِحِينَ

46 5:110

46 He will speak to the people from the crib, and in adulthood, and will be one of the righteous."

٤٧ قَالَتْ رَبِّ أَنَّىٰ يَكُونُ لِي وَلَدٌ وَلَمْ يَمْسَسْنِي بَشَرٌ ۖ ᵃ قَالَ كَذَٰلِكِ اللَّهُ يَخْلُقُ مَا يَشَاءُ ۚ ᵇ إِذَا قَضَىٰ أَمْرًا فَإِنَّمَا يَقُولُ لَهُ كُنْ فَيَكُونُ

47
ᵃ 19:20, 29, 33
ᵇ 28:68

47 She said, "My Lord, how can I have a child, when no man has touched me?" He said, "It will be so. God creates whatever He wills. To have anything done, He only says to it, 'Be,' and it is."

٤٨ وَيُعَلِّمُهُ الْكِتَابَ وَالْحِكْمَةَ وَالتَّوْرَاةَ وَالْإِنْجِيلَ

48 And He will teach him the Scripture and wisdom, and the Torah and the Gospel.

٤٩ وَرَسُولًا إِلَىٰ بَنِي إِسْرَائِيلَ أَنِّي قَدْ جِئْتُكُمْ بِآيَةٍ مِنْ رَبِّكُمْ ۖ أَنِّي أَخْلُقُ لَكُمْ مِنَ الطِّينِ كَهَيْئَةِ الطَّيْرِ فَأَنْفُخُ فِيهِ فَيَكُونُ طَيْرًا بِإِذْنِ اللَّهِ ۖ وَأُبْرِئُ الْأَكْمَهَ وَالْأَبْرَصَ وَأُحْيِي الْمَوْتَىٰ بِإِذْنِ اللَّهِ ۖ وَأُنَبِّئُكُمْ بِمَا تَأْكُلُونَ وَمَا تَدَّخِرُونَ فِي بُيُوتِكُمْ ۚ إِنَّ فِي ذَٰلِكَ لَآيَةً لَكُمْ إِنْ كُنْتُمْ مُؤْمِنِينَ

49 5:110

49 A messenger to the Children of Israel: "I have come to you with a sign from your Lord. I make for you out of clay the figure of a bird; then I breathe into it, and it becomes a bird by God's leave. And I heal the blind and the leprous, and I revive the dead, by God's leave. And I inform you concerning what you eat, and what you store in your homes. In that is a sign for you, if you are believers."

٥٠ وَمُصَدِّقًا لِمَا بَيْنَ يَدَيَّ مِنَ التَّوْرَاةِ وَلِأُحِلَّ لَكُمْ بَعْضَ الَّذِي حُرِّمَ عَلَيْكُمْ ۚ وَجِئْتُكُمْ بِآيَةٍ مِنْ رَبِّكُمْ فَاتَّقُوا اللَّهَ وَأَطِيعُونِ ᵇ

50
ᵃ 3:93; 5:46; 46:30; 61:6
ᵇ 4:160; 6:146; 43:63–64

50 "And verifying what lies before me of the Torah, and to make lawful for you some of what was forbidden to you. I have come to you with a sign from your Lord; so fear God, and obey me."

٥١ إِنَّ اللَّهَ رَبِّي وَرَبُّكُمْ فَاعْبُدُوهُ ۚ هَٰذَا صِرَاطٌ مُسْتَقِيمٌ

51 "God is my Lord and your Lord, so worship Him. That is a straight path."

٥٢ فَلَمَّا أَحَسَّ عِيسَىٰ مِنْهُمُ الْكُفْرَ قَالَ مَنْ أَنْصَارِي إِلَى اللَّهِ ۖ قَالَ الْحَوَارِيُّونَ نَحْنُ أَنْصَارُ اللَّهِ آمَنَّا بِاللَّهِ وَاشْهَدْ بِأَنَّا مُسْلِمُونَ

52
61:14

52 When Jesus sensed disbelief on their part, he said, "Who are my allies towards God?" The disciples said, "We are God's allies; we have believed in God, and bear witness that we submit."

٥٣ رَبَّنَا آمَنَّا بِمَا أَنْزَلْتَ وَاتَّبَعْنَا الرَّسُولَ فَاكْتُبْنَا مَعَ الشَّاهِدِينَ

53
5:83

53 "Our Lord, we have believed in what You have revealed, and we have followed the Messenger, so count us among the witnesses."

٥٤ وَمَكَرُوا وَمَكَرَ اللَّهُ ۖ وَاللَّهُ خَيْرُ الْمَاكِرِينَ

54 They planned, and God planned; but God is the Best of planners.

٥٥ إِذْ قَالَ اللَّهُ يَا عِيسَىٰ إِنِّي مُتَوَفِّيكَ وَرَافِعُكَ إِلَيَّ وَمُطَهِّرُكَ مِنَ الَّذِينَ كَفَرُوا وَجَاعِلُ الَّذِينَ اتَّبَعُوكَ فَوْقَ الَّذِينَ كَفَرُوا إِلَىٰ يَوْمِ الْقِيَامَةِ ۖ ثُمَّ إِلَيَّ مَرْجِعُكُمْ فَأَحْكُمُ بَيْنَكُمْ فِيمَا كُنْتُمْ فِيهِ تَخْتَلِفُونَ

55
4:157–158; 19:33

55 God said, "O Jesus, I am terminating your life, and raising you to Me, and clearing you of those who disbelieve. And I will make those who follow you superior to those who disbelieve, until the Day of Resurrection. Then to Me is your return; then I will judge between you regarding what you were disputing.

٥٦ فَأَمَّا الَّذِينَ كَفَرُوا فَأُعَذِّبُهُمْ عَذَابًا شَدِيدًا فِي الدُّنْيَا وَالْآخِرَةِ وَمَا لَهُمْ مِنْ نَاصِرِينَ

56 As for those who disbelieve, I will punish them with a severe punishment, in this world and the next, and they will have no helpers.

٥٧ وَأَمَّا الَّذِينَ آمَنُوا وَعَمِلُوا الصَّالِحَاتِ فَيُوَفِّيهِمْ أُجُورَهُمْ ۗ وَاللَّهُ لَا يُحِبُّ الظَّالِمِينَ

57 And as for those who believe and do good works, He will give them their rewards in full. God does not love the unjust."

٥٨ ذَٰلِكَ نَتْلُوهُ عَلَيْكَ مِنَ الْآيَاتِ وَالذِّكْرِ الْحَكِيمِ

58 This is what We recite to you of the Verses and the Wise Reminder.

٥٩ إِنَّ مَثَلَ عِيسَىٰ عِنْدَ اللَّهِ كَمَثَلِ آدَمَ ۖ خَلَقَهُ مِنْ تُرَابٍ ثُمَّ قَالَ لَهُ كُنْ فَيَكُونُ

59
2:117; 19:35; 36:82

59 The likeness of Jesus in God's sight is that of Adam: He created him from dust, then said to him, "Be," and he was.

٦٠ الْحَقُّ مِنْ رَبِّكَ فَلَا تَكُنْ مِنَ الْمُمْتَرِينَ

60
pp 2:147 6:114; 10:94

60 The truth is from your Lord, so do not be of those who doubt.

٦١ فَمَنْ حَاجَّكَ فِيهِ مِنْ بَعْدِ مَا جَاءَكَ مِنَ الْعِلْمِ فَقُلْ تَعَالَوْا نَدْعُ أَبْنَاءَنَا وَأَبْنَاءَكُمْ وَنِسَاءَنَا وَنِسَاءَكُمْ وَأَنْفُسَنَا وَأَنْفُسَكُمْ ثُمَّ نَبْتَهِلْ فَنَجْعَلْ لَعْنَتَ اللَّهِ عَلَى الْكَاذِبِينَ

61 And if anyone disputes with you about him, after the knowledge that has come to you, say, "Come, let us call our children and your children, and our women and your women, and ourselves and yourselves, and let us invoke God's curse on the liars."

٦٢ إِنَّ هَٰذَا لَهُوَ الْقَصَصُ الْحَقُّ ۚ وَمَا مِنْ إِلَٰهٍ إِلَّا اللَّهُ ۚ وَإِنَّ اللَّهَ لَهُوَ الْعَزِيزُ الْحَكِيمُ

62 This is the narrative of truth: there is no god but God. God is the Mighty, the Wise.

٦٣ فَإِنْ تَوَلَّوْا فَإِنَّ اللَّهَ عَلِيمٌ بِالْمُفْسِدِينَ

63 But if they turn away—God knows the corrupt.

٦٤ قُلْ يَا أَهْلَ الْكِتَابِ تَعَالَوْا إِلَىٰ كَلِمَةٍ سَوَاءٍ بَيْنَنَا وَبَيْنَكُمْ أَلَّا نَعْبُدَ إِلَّا اللَّهَ وَلَا نُشْرِكَ بِهِ شَيْئًا وَلَا يَتَّخِذَ بَعْضُنَا بَعْضًا أَرْبَابًا مِنْ دُونِ اللَّهِ ۚ فَإِنْ تَوَلَّوْا فَقُولُوا اشْهَدُوا بِأَنَّا مُسْلِمُونَ

64 3:80; 9:31

64 Say, "O People of the Book, come to terms common between us and you: that we worship none but God, and that we associate nothing with Him, and that none of us takes others as lords besides God." And if they turn away, say, "Bear witness that we have submitted."

٦٥ يَا أَهْلَ الْكِتَابِ لِمَ تُحَاجُّونَ فِي إِبْرَاهِيمَ وَمَا أُنْزِلَتِ التَّوْرَاةُ وَالْإِنْجِيلُ إِلَّا مِنْ بَعْدِهِ ۚ أَفَلَا تَعْقِلُونَ

65–66 2:140

65 O People of the Book! Why do you argue about Abraham, when the Torah and the Gospel were not revealed until after him? Will you not reason?

٦٦ هَا أَنْتُمْ هَٰؤُلَاءِ حَاجَجْتُمْ فِيمَا لَكُمْ بِهِ عِلْمٌ فَلِمَ تُحَاجُّونَ فِيمَا لَيْسَ لَكُمْ بِهِ عِلْمٌ ۚ وَاللَّهُ يَعْلَمُ وَأَنْتُمْ لَا تَعْلَمُونَ

66 Here you are—you argue about things you know, but why do you argue about things you do not know? God knows, and you do not know.

٦٧ مَا كَانَ إِبْرَاهِيمُ يَهُودِيًّا وَلَا نَصْرَانِيًّا وَلَٰكِنْ كَانَ حَنِيفًا مُسْلِمًا وَمَا كَانَ مِنَ الْمُشْرِكِينَ

67 2:135; 3:95; 4:125; 6:161; 16:23, 120

67 Abraham was neither a Jew nor a Christian, but he was a Monotheist, a Muslim. And he was not of the Polytheists.

٦٨ إِنَّ أَوْلَى النَّاسِ بِإِبْرَاهِيمَ لَلَّذِينَ اتَّبَعُوهُ وَهَٰذَا النَّبِيُّ وَالَّذِينَ آمَنُوا ۗ وَاللَّهُ وَلِيُّ الْمُؤْمِنِينَ

68 The people most deserving of Abraham are those who followed him, and this prophet, and those who believe. God is the Guardian of the believers.

٦٩ وَدَّتْ طَائِفَةٌ مِنْ أَهْلِ الْكِتَابِ لَوْ يُضِلُّونَكُمْ وَمَا يُضِلُّونَ إِلَّا أَنْفُسَهُمْ وَمَا يَشْعُرُونَ

69 2:109; 3:100, 149; 4:113

69 A party of the People of the Book would love to lead you astray, but they only lead themselves astray, and they do not realize it.

٧٠ يَا أَهْلَ الْكِتَابِ لِمَ تَكْفُرُونَ بِآيَاتِ اللَّهِ وَأَنْتُمْ تَشْهَدُونَ

70 O People of the Book! Why do you reject the revelations of God, even as you witness?

٧١ يَا أَهْلَ الْكِتَابِ لِمَ تَلْبِسُونَ الْحَقَّ بِالْبَاطِلِ وَتَكْتُمُونَ الْحَقَّ وَأَنْتُمْ تَعْلَمُونَ

71 O People of the Book! Why do you confound the truth with falsehood, and knowingly conceal the truth?

71
pp 2:42

٧٢ وَقَالَتْ طَائِفَةٌ مِنْ أَهْلِ الْكِتَابِ آمِنُوا بِالَّذِي أُنْزِلَ عَلَى الَّذِينَ آمَنُوا وَجْهَ النَّهَارِ وَاكْفُرُوا آخِرَهُ لَعَلَّهُمْ يَرْجِعُونَ

72 Some of the People of the Book say, "Believe in what was revealed to the believers at the beginning of the day, and reject it at its end, so that they may return."

72
2:14, 76; 3:119

٧٣ وَلَا تُؤْمِنُوا إِلَّا لِمَنْ تَبِعَ دِينَكُمْ قُلْ إِنَّ الْهُدَى هُدَى اللَّهِ أَنْ يُؤْتَى أَحَدٌ مِثْلَ مَا أُوتِيتُمْ أَوْ يُحَاجُّوكُمْ عِنْدَ رَبِّكُمْ ۗ قُلْ إِنَّ الْفَضْلَ بِيَدِ اللَّهِ يُؤْتِيهِ مَنْ يَشَاءُ ۗ وَاللَّهُ وَاسِعٌ عَلِيمٌ

73 And trust none except those who follow your religion." Say, "Guidance is God's guidance. If someone is given the like of what you were given, or they argue with you before your Lord, say, "All grace is in God's hand; He gives it to whomever He wills." God is Bounteous and Knowing.

73
2:111, 120, 135, 145; 5:18; 13:37

٧٤ يَخْتَصُّ بِرَحْمَتِهِ مَنْ يَشَاءُ ۗ وَاللَّهُ ذُو الْفَضْلِ الْعَظِيمِ

74 He specifies His mercy for whomever He wills. God is Possessor of Sublime Grace.

74
2:105

٧٥ وَمِنْ أَهْلِ الْكِتَابِ مَنْ إِنْ تَأْمَنْهُ بِقِنْطَارٍ يُؤَدِّهِ إِلَيْكَ وَمِنْهُمْ مَنْ إِنْ تَأْمَنْهُ بِدِينَارٍ لَا يُؤَدِّهِ إِلَيْكَ إِلَّا مَا دُمْتَ عَلَيْهِ قَائِمًا ۗ ذَٰلِكَ بِأَنَّهُمْ قَالُوا لَيْسَ عَلَيْنَا فِي الْأُمِّيِّينَ سَبِيلٌ وَيَقُولُونَ عَلَى اللَّهِ الْكَذِبَ وَهُمْ يَعْلَمُونَ

75 Among the People of the Book is he, who, if you entrust him with a heap of gold, he will give it back to you. And among them is he, who, if you entrust him with a single coin, he will not give it back to you, unless you keep after him. That is because they say, "We are under no obligation towards the gentiles." They tell lies about God, and they know it.

٧٦ بَلَىٰ مَنْ أَوْفَىٰ بِعَهْدِهِ وَاتَّقَىٰ فَإِنَّ اللَّهَ يُحِبُّ الْمُتَّقِينَ

76 Indeed, whoever fulfills his commitments and maintains piety— God loves the pious.

76
6:152; 13:20; 16:91; 48:10

٧٧ إِنَّ الَّذِينَ يَشْتَرُونَ بِعَهْدِ اللَّهِ وَأَيْمَانِهِمْ ثَمَنًا قَلِيلًا أُولَٰئِكَ لَا خَلَاقَ لَهُمْ فِي الْآخِرَةِ وَلَا يُكَلِّمُهُمُ اللَّهُ وَلَا يَنْظُرُ إِلَيْهِمْ يَوْمَ الْقِيَامَةِ وَلَا يُزَكِّيهِمْ وَلَهُمْ عَذَابٌ أَلِيمٌ

77 Those who exchange the covenant of God, and their vows, for a small price, will have no share in the Hereafter, and God will not speak to them, nor will He look at them on the Day of Resurrection, nor will He purify them. They will have a painful punishment.

77
2:79, 174; 3:187, 199; 16:95

	78
٧٨ وَإِنَّ مِنْهُمْ لَفَرِيقًا يَلْوُونَ أَلْسِنَتَهُم بِالْكِتَابِ لِتَحْسَبُوهُ مِنَ الْكِتَابِ وَمَا هُوَ مِنَ الْكِتَابِ وَيَقُولُونَ هُوَ مِنْ عِندِ اللَّهِ وَمَا هُوَ مِنْ عِندِ اللَّهِ وَيَقُولُونَ عَلَى اللَّهِ الْكَذِبَ وَهُمْ يَعْلَمُونَ	2:79; 4:46

78 And among them are those who twist the Scripture with their tongues, that you may think it from the Scripture, when it is not from the Scripture. And they say, "It is from God," when it is not from God. They tell lies and attribute them to God, knowingly.

	79
٧٩ مَا كَانَ لِبَشَرٍ أَن يُؤْتِيَهُ اللَّهُ الْكِتَابَ وَالْحُكْمَ وَالنُّبُوَّةَ ثُمَّ يَقُولَ لِلنَّاسِ كُونُوا عِبَادًا لِّي مِن دُونِ اللَّهِ وَلَٰكِن كُونُوا رَبَّانِيِّينَ بِمَا كُنتُمْ تُعَلِّمُونَ الْكِتَابَ وَبِمَا كُنتُمْ تَدْرُسُونَ	2:225; 5:89; 29:27; 45:16

79 No person to whom God has given the Scripture, and wisdom, and prophethood would ever say to the people, "Be my worshipers rather than God's." Rather, "Be people of the Lord, according to the Scripture you teach, and the teachings you learn."

	80
٨٠ وَلَا يَأْمُرَكُمْ أَن تَتَّخِذُوا الْمَلَائِكَةَ وَالنَّبِيِّينَ أَرْبَابًا ۗ أَيَأْمُرُكُم بِالْكُفْرِ بَعْدَ إِذْ أَنتُم مُّسْلِمُونَ	3:64; 9:31

80 Nor would he command you to take the angels and the prophets as lords. Would he command you to infidelity after you have submitted?

	81
٨١ وَإِذْ أَخَذَ اللَّهُ مِيثَاقَ النَّبِيِّينَ لَمَا آتَيْتُكُم مِّن كِتَابٍ وَحِكْمَةٍ ثُمَّ جَاءَكُمْ رَسُولٌ مُّصَدِّقٌ لِّمَا مَعَكُمْ لَتُؤْمِنُنَّ بِهِ وَلَتَنصُرُنَّهُ ۚ قَالَ أَأَقْرَرْتُمْ وَأَخَذْتُمْ عَلَىٰ ذَٰلِكُمْ إِصْرِي ۖ قَالُوا أَقْرَرْنَا ۚ قَالَ فَاشْهَدُوا وَأَنَا مَعَكُم مِّنَ الشَّاهِدِينَ	33:7

81 God received the covenant of the prophets, "Inasmuch as I have given you of scripture and wisdom; should a messenger come to you verifying what you have, you shall believe in him, and support him." He said, "Do you affirm My covenant and take it upon yourselves?" They said, "We affirm it." He said, "Then bear witness, and I am with you among the witnesses."

	82
٨٢ فَمَن تَوَلَّىٰ بَعْدَ ذَٰلِكَ فَأُولَٰئِكَ هُمُ الْفَاسِقُونَ	5:12; 24:55

82 Whoever turns away after that—these are the deceitful.

	83
٨٣ أَفَغَيْرَ دِينِ اللَّهِ يَبْغُونَ وَلَهُ أَسْلَمَ مَن فِي السَّمَاوَاتِ وَالْأَرْضِ طَوْعًا وَكَرْهًا وَإِلَيْهِ يُرْجَعُونَ	3:19, 85

83 Do they desire other than the religion of God, when to Him has submitted everything in the heavens and the earth, willingly or unwillingly, and to Him they will be returned?

	84
٨٤ قُلْ آمَنَّا بِاللَّهِ وَمَا أُنزِلَ عَلَيْنَا وَمَا أُنزِلَ عَلَىٰ إِبْرَاهِيمَ وَإِسْمَاعِيلَ وَإِسْحَاقَ وَيَعْقُوبَ وَالْأَسْبَاطِ وَمَا أُوتِيَ مُوسَىٰ وَعِيسَىٰ وَالنَّبِيُّونَ مِن رَّبِّهِمْ لَا نُفَرِّقُ بَيْنَ أَحَدٍ مِّنْهُمْ وَنَحْنُ لَهُ مُسْلِمُونَ	2:136, 285; 4:152

84 Say, "We believe in God, and in what was revealed to us; and in what was revealed to Abraham, and Ishmael, and Isaac, and Jacob, and the Patriarchs; and in what was given to Moses, and Jesus, and the prophets from their Lord. We make no distinction between any of them, and to Him we submit."

٨٥ وَمَنْ يَبْتَغِ غَيْرَ الْإِسْلَامِ دِينًا فَلَنْ يُقْبَلَ مِنْهُ وَهُوَ فِي الْآخِرَةِ مِنَ الْخَاسِرِينَ

85 3:19, 83

85 Whoever seeks other than Islam as a religion, it will not be accepted from him, and in the Hereafter he will be among the losers.

٨٦ كَيْفَ يَهْدِي اللَّهُ قَوْمًا كَفَرُوا بَعْدَ إِيمَانِهِمْ وَشَهِدُوا أَنَّ الرَّسُولَ حَقٌّ وَجَاءَهُمُ الْبَيِّنَاتُ ۚ وَاللَّهُ لَا يَهْدِي الْقَوْمَ الظَّالِمِينَ

86–87 2:161; 3:91; 47:34

86 How will God guide a people who disbelieved after having believed, and had witnessed that the Messenger is true, and the clear proofs had come to them? God does not guide the unjust people.

٨٧ أُولَٰئِكَ جَزَاؤُهُمْ أَنَّ عَلَيْهِمْ لَعْنَةَ اللَّهِ وَالْمَلَائِكَةِ وَالنَّاسِ أَجْمَعِينَ

87 Those—their penalty is that upon them falls the curse of God, and of the angels, and of all mankind.

٨٨ خَالِدِينَ فِيهَا لَا يُخَفَّفُ عَنْهُمُ الْعَذَابُ وَلَا هُمْ يُنْظَرُونَ

88 2:162

88 Remaining in it eternally, without their punishment being eased from them, and without being reprieved.

٨٩ إِلَّا الَّذِينَ تَابُوا مِنْ بَعْدِ ذَٰلِكَ وَأَصْلَحُوا فَإِنَّ اللَّهَ غَفُورٌ رَحِيمٌ

89 2:160; 24:5

89 Except those who repent afterwards, and reform; for God is Forgiving and Merciful.

٩٠ إِنَّ الَّذِينَ كَفَرُوا بَعْدَ إِيمَانِهِمْ ثُمَّ ازْدَادُوا كُفْرًا لَنْ تُقْبَلَ تَوْبَتُهُمْ وَأُولَٰئِكَ هُمُ الضَّالُّونَ

90 4:18, 90, 137

90 As for those who disbelieve after having believed, then plunge deeper into disbelief, their repentance will not be accepted; these are the lost.

٩١ إِنَّ الَّذِينَ كَفَرُوا وَمَاتُوا وَهُمْ كُفَّارٌ فَلَنْ يُقْبَلَ مِنْ أَحَدِهِمْ مِلْءُ الْأَرْضِ ذَهَبًا وَلَوِ افْتَدَىٰ بِهِ ۗ أُولَٰئِكَ لَهُمْ عَذَابٌ أَلِيمٌ وَمَا لَهُمْ مِنْ نَاصِرِينَ

91 3:87; 5:36; 57:15

91 As for those who disbelieve and die disbelievers, even the earth full of gold would not be accepted from any of them, were he to offer it for ransom. These will have a painful torment, and will have no saviors.

٩٢ لَنْ تَنَالُوا الْبِرَّ حَتَّىٰ تُنْفِقُوا مِمَّا تُحِبُّونَ ۚ وَمَا تُنْفِقُوا مِنْ شَيْءٍ فَإِنَّ اللَّهَ بِهِ عَلِيمٌ

92 2:177, 267

92 You will not attain virtuous conduct until you give of what you cherish. Whatever you give away, God is aware of it.

٩٣ كُلُّ الطَّعَامِ كَانَ حِلًّا لِبَنِي إِسْرَائِيلَ إِلَّا مَا حَرَّمَ إِسْرَائِيلُ عَلَىٰ نَفْسِهِ مِنْ قَبْلِ أَنْ تُنَزَّلَ التَّوْرَاةُ ۗ قُلْ فَأْتُوا بِالتَّوْرَاةِ فَاتْلُوهَا إِنْ كُنْتُمْ صَادِقِينَ

93 4:160; 6:146; 16:118; 19:7

93 All food was permissible to the Children of Israel, except what Israel forbade for himself before the Torah was revealed. Say, "Bring the Torah, and read it, if you are truthful."

٩٤ فَمَنِ افْتَرَىٰ عَلَى اللَّهِ الْكَذِبَ مِنْ بَعْدِ ذَٰلِكَ فَأُولَٰئِكَ هُمُ الظَّالِمُونَ

94 Whoever forges lies about God after that—these are the unjust.

٩٥ قُلْ صَدَقَ اللَّهُ ۗ فَاتَّبِعُوا مِلَّةَ إِبْرَاهِيمَ حَنِيفًا وَمَا كَانَ مِنَ الْمُشْرِكِينَ

95 Say, "God has spoken the truth, so follow the religion of Abraham the Monotheist; he was not a Pagan."

95
16:122

٩٦ إِنَّ أَوَّلَ بَيْتٍ وُضِعَ لِلنَّاسِ لَلَّذِي بِبَكَّةَ مُبَارَكًا وَهُدًى لِلْعَالَمِينَ

96 The first house established for mankind is the one at Bekka; blessed, and guidance for all people.

96–97
2:127; 22:26

٩٧ فِيهِ آيَاتٌ بَيِّنَاتٌ مَقَامُ إِبْرَاهِيمَ ۖ وَمَنْ دَخَلَهُ كَانَ آمِنًا ۗ وَلِلَّهِ عَلَى النَّاسِ حِجُّ الْبَيْتِ مَنِ اسْتَطَاعَ إِلَيْهِ سَبِيلًا ۚ وَمَنْ كَفَرَ فَإِنَّ اللَّهَ غَنِيٌّ عَنِ الْعَالَمِينَ

97 In it are evident signs; the Station of Abraham. Whoever enters it attains security. Pilgrimage to the House is a duty to God for all who can make the journey. But as for those who refuse—God is Independent of the worlds.

٩٨ قُلْ يَا أَهْلَ الْكِتَابِ لِمَ تَكْفُرُونَ بِآيَاتِ اللَّهِ وَاللَّهُ شَهِيدٌ عَلَىٰ مَا تَعْمَلُونَ

98 Say, "O People of the Scripture, why do you reject the Revelations of God, when God witnesses what you do?"

٩٩ قُلْ يَا أَهْلَ الْكِتَابِ لِمَ تَصُدُّونَ عَنْ سَبِيلِ اللَّهِ مَنْ آمَنَ تَبْغُونَهَا عِوَجًا وَأَنْتُمْ شُهَدَاءُ ۗ وَمَا اللَّهُ بِغَافِلٍ عَمَّا تَعْمَلُونَ

99 Say, "O People of the Scripture, why do you hinder from God's path those who believe, seeking to distort it, even though you are witnesses? God is not unaware of what you do."

99
7:45; 11:19

١٠٠ يَا أَيُّهَا الَّذِينَ آمَنُوا إِنْ تُطِيعُوا فَرِيقًا مِنَ الَّذِينَ أُوتُوا الْكِتَابَ يَرُدُّوكُمْ بَعْدَ إِيمَانِكُمْ كَافِرِينَ

100 O you who believe! If you obey a party of those who were given the Scripture, they will turn you, after your belief, into disbelievers.

100
2:109; 3:69, 149; 4:113

١٠١ وَكَيْفَ تَكْفُرُونَ وَأَنْتُمْ تُتْلَىٰ عَلَيْكُمْ آيَاتُ اللَّهِ وَفِيكُمْ رَسُولُهُ ۗ وَمَنْ يَعْتَصِمْ بِاللَّهِ فَقَدْ هُدِيَ إِلَىٰ صِرَاطٍ مُسْتَقِيمٍ

101 And how could you disbelieve, when God's revelations are being recited to you, and among you is His Messenger? Whoever cleaves to God has been guided to a straight path.

101
4:146, 175

١٠٢ يَا أَيُّهَا الَّذِينَ آمَنُوا اتَّقُوا اللَّهَ حَقَّ تُقَاتِهِ وَلَا تَمُوتُنَّ إِلَّا وَأَنْتُمْ مُسْلِمُونَ

102 O you who believe! Revere God with due reverence, and do not die except as Muslims.

١٠٣ وَاعْتَصِمُوا بِحَبْلِ اللَّهِ جَمِيعًا وَلَا تَفَرَّقُوا ۚ وَاذْكُرُوا نِعْمَتَ اللَّهِ عَلَيْكُمْ إِذْ كُنْتُمْ أَعْدَاءً فَأَلَّفَ بَيْنَ قُلُوبِكُمْ فَأَصْبَحْتُمْ بِنِعْمَتِهِ إِخْوَانًا وَكُنْتُمْ عَلَىٰ شَفَا حُفْرَةٍ مِنَ النَّارِ فَأَنْقَذَكُمْ مِنْهَا ۗ كَذَٰلِكَ يُبَيِّنُ اللَّهُ لَكُمْ آيَاتِهِ لَعَلَّكُمْ تَهْتَدُونَ

103
49:10

103 And hold fast to the rope of God, altogether, and do not become divided. And remember God's blessings upon you; how you were enemies, and He reconciled your hearts, and by His grace you became brethren. And you were on the brink of a pit of fire, and He saved you from it. God thus clarifies His revelations for you, so that you may be guided.

١٠٤ وَلْتَكُنْ مِنْكُمْ أُمَّةٌ يَدْعُونَ إِلَى الْخَيْرِ وَيَأْمُرُونَ بِالْمَعْرُوفِ وَيَنْهَوْنَ عَنِ الْمُنْكَرِ ۚ وَأُولَٰئِكَ هُمُ الْمُفْلِحُونَ

104
3:110, 114, 199; 7:157; 9:71

104 And let there be among you a community calling to virtue, and advocating righteousness, and deterring from evil. These are the successful.

١٠٥ وَلَا تَكُونُوا كَالَّذِينَ تَفَرَّقُوا وَاخْتَلَفُوا مِنْ بَعْدِ مَا جَاءَهُمُ الْبَيِّنَاتُ ۚ وَأُولَٰئِكَ لَهُمْ عَذَابٌ عَظِيمٌ

105
3:19; 6:159; 21:93; 42:13

105 And do not be like those who separated and disputed after the clear proofs came to them; for them is a great punishment.

١٠٦ يَوْمَ تَبْيَضُّ وُجُوهٌ وَتَسْوَدُّ وُجُوهٌ ۚ فَأَمَّا الَّذِينَ اسْوَدَّتْ وُجُوهُهُمْ أَكَفَرْتُمْ بَعْدَ إِيمَانِكُمْ فَذُوقُوا الْعَذَابَ بِمَا كُنْتُمْ تَكْفُرُونَ

106
10:27; 39:60; 80:40

106 On the Day when some faces will be whitened, and some faces will be blackened. As for those whose faces are blackened: "Did you disbelieve after your belief?" Then taste the punishment for having disbelieved.

١٠٧ وَأَمَّا الَّذِينَ ابْيَضَّتْ وُجُوهُهُمْ فَفِي رَحْمَةِ اللَّهِ هُمْ فِيهَا خَالِدُونَ

107 But as for those whose faces are whitened: they are in God's mercy, remaining in it forever.

١٠٨ تِلْكَ آيَاتُ اللَّهِ نَتْلُوهَا عَلَيْكَ بِالْحَقِّ ۗ وَمَا اللَّهُ يُرِيدُ ظُلْمًا لِلْعَالَمِينَ

108
2:252; 28:2; 45:6

108 These are the revelations of God. We recite them to you in truth. God desires no injustice for mankind.

١٠٩ وَلِلَّهِ مَا فِي السَّمَاوَاتِ وَمَا فِي الْأَرْضِ ۚ وَإِلَى اللَّهِ تُرْجَعُ الْأُمُورُ

109
42:53; 57:5

109 To God belongs everything in the heavens and everything on earth, and to God all events are referred.

١١٠ كُنْتُمْ خَيْرَ أُمَّةٍ أُخْرِجَتْ لِلنَّاسِ تَأْمُرُونَ بِالْمَعْرُوفِ وَتَنْهَوْنَ عَنِ الْمُنْكَرِ وَتُؤْمِنُونَ بِاللَّهِ ۗ وَلَوْ آمَنَ أَهْلُ الْكِتَابِ لَكَانَ خَيْرًا لَهُمْ ۚ مِنْهُمُ الْمُؤْمِنُونَ وَأَكْثَرُهُمُ الْفَاسِقُونَ

110
3:104, 114; 7:157; 9:71

110 You are the best community that ever emerged for humanity: you advocate what is moral, and forbid what is immoral, and believe in God. Had the People of the Scripture believed, it would have been better for them. Among them are the believers, but most of them are sinners.

١١١ لَنْ يَضُرُّوكُمْ إِلَّا أَذًى ۖ وَإِنْ يُقَاتِلُوكُمْ يُوَلُّوكُمُ الْأَدْبَارَ ثُمَّ لَا يُنْصَرُونَ

111 — 48:22; 59:12

111 They will do you no harm, beyond insulting you. And if they fight you, they will turn around and flee, then they will not be helped.

١١٢ ضُرِبَتْ عَلَيْهِمُ الذِّلَّةُ أَيْنَ مَا ثُقِفُوا إِلَّا بِحَبْلٍ مِنَ اللَّهِ وَحَبْلٍ مِنَ النَّاسِ وَبَاءُوا بِغَضَبٍ مِنَ اللَّهِ وَضُرِبَتْ عَلَيْهِمُ الْمَسْكَنَةُ ۚ ذَٰلِكَ بِأَنَّهُمْ كَانُوا يَكْفُرُونَ بِآيَاتِ اللَّهِ وَيَقْتُلُونَ الْأَنْبِيَاءَ بِغَيْرِ حَقٍّ ۚ ذَٰلِكَ بِمَا عَصَوْا وَكَانُوا يَعْتَدُونَ

112 — 2:61

112 They shall be humiliated wherever they are encountered, except through a rope from God, and a rope from the people; and they incurred wrath from God, and were stricken with misery. That is because they rejected God's revelations, and killed the prophets unjustly. That is because they rebelled and committed aggression.

١١٣ لَيْسُوا سَوَاءً ۗ مِنْ أَهْلِ الْكِتَابِ أُمَّةٌ قَائِمَةٌ يَتْلُونَ آيَاتِ اللَّهِ آنَاءَ اللَّيْلِ وَهُمْ يَسْجُدُونَ

113 — 2:121; 17:107, 109; 28:52–53

113 They are not alike. Among the People of the Scripture is a community that is upright; they recite God's revelations throughout the night, and they prostrate themselves.

١١٤ يُؤْمِنُونَ بِاللَّهِ وَالْيَوْمِ الْآخِرِ وَيَأْمُرُونَ بِالْمَعْرُوفِ وَيَنْهَوْنَ عَنِ الْمُنْكَرِ وَيُسَارِعُونَ فِي الْخَيْرَاتِ وَأُولَٰئِكَ مِنَ الصَّالِحِينَ

114 — 3:104, 110, 199; 7:157; 9:71

114 They believe in God and the Last Day, and advocate righteousness and forbid evil, and are quick to do good deeds. These are among the righteous.

١١٥ وَمَا يَفْعَلُوا مِنْ خَيْرٍ فَلَنْ يُكْفَرُوهُ ۗ وَاللَّهُ عَلِيمٌ بِالْمُتَّقِينَ

115 — 98:4

115 Whatever good they do, they will not be denied it. God knows the righteous.

١١٦ إِنَّ الَّذِينَ كَفَرُوا لَنْ تُغْنِيَ عَنْهُمْ أَمْوَالُهُمْ وَلَا أَوْلَادُهُمْ مِنَ اللَّهِ شَيْئًا ۖ وَأُولَٰئِكَ أَصْحَابُ النَّارِ ۚ هُمْ فِيهَا خَالِدُونَ

116 — 3:10; 8:28; 26:88; 58:17; 63:9; 64:15

116 As for those who disbelieve, neither their possessions nor their children will avail them anything against God. These are the inhabitants of the Fire, abiding therein forever.

١١٧ مَثَلُ مَا يُنْفِقُونَ فِي هَٰذِهِ الْحَيَاةِ الدُّنْيَا كَمَثَلِ رِيحٍ فِيهَا صِرٌّ أَصَابَتْ حَرْثَ قَوْمٍ ظَلَمُوا أَنْفُسَهُمْ فَأَهْلَكَتْهُ ۚ وَمَا ظَلَمَهُمُ اللَّهُ وَلَٰكِنْ أَنْفُسَهُمْ يَظْلِمُونَ

117 — 2:266

117 The parable of what they spend in this worldly life is that of a frosty wind that strikes the harvest of a people who have wronged their souls, and destroys it. God did not wrong them, but they wronged their own selves.

١١٨ يَا أَيُّهَا الَّذِينَ آمَنُوا لَا تَتَّخِذُوا بِطَانَةً مِنْ دُونِكُمْ لَا يَأْلُونَكُمْ خَبَالًا وَدُّوا مَا عَنِتُّمْ قَدْ بَدَتِ الْبَغْضَاءُ مِنْ أَفْوَاهِهِمْ وَمَا تُخْفِي صُدُورُهُمْ أَكْبَرُ ۚ قَدْ بَيَّنَّا لَكُمُ الْآيَاتِ ۖ إِنْ كُنْتُمْ تَعْقِلُونَ

118 O you who believe! Do not befriend outsiders who never cease to wish you harm. They love to see you suffer. Hatred has already appeared from their mouths, but what their hearts conceal is worse. We have made the messages clear for you, if you understand.

١١٩ هَا أَنْتُمْ أُولَاءِ تُحِبُّونَهُمْ وَلَا يُحِبُّونَكُمْ وَتُؤْمِنُونَ بِالْكِتَابِ كُلِّهِ وَإِذَا لَقُوكُمْ قَالُوا آمَنَّا وَإِذَا خَلَوْا عَضُّوا عَلَيْكُمُ الْأَنَامِلَ مِنَ الْغَيْظِ ۚ قُلْ مُوتُوا بِغَيْظِكُمْ ۗ إِنَّ اللَّهَ عَلِيمٌ بِذَاتِ الصُّدُورِ

119
2:14, 76; 3:119

119 There you are, you love them, but they do not love you, and you believe in the entire scripture. And when they meet you, they say, "We believe;" but when they are alone, they bite their fingers in rage at you. Say, "Die in your rage; God knows what is within the hearts."

١٢٠ إِنْ تَمْسَسْكُمْ حَسَنَةٌ تَسُؤْهُمْ وَإِنْ تُصِبْكُمْ سَيِّئَةٌ يَفْرَحُوا بِهَا ۖ وَإِنْ تَصْبِرُوا وَتَتَّقُوا لَا يَضُرُّكُمْ كَيْدُهُمْ شَيْئًا ۗ إِنَّ اللَّهَ بِمَا يَعْمَلُونَ مُحِيطٌ

120
9:50

120 If something good happens to you, it upsets them; but if something bad befalls you, they rejoice at it. But if you persevere and maintain righteousness, their schemes will not harm you at all. God comprehends what they do.

١٢١ وَإِذْ غَدَوْتَ مِنْ أَهْلِكَ تُبَوِّئُ الْمُؤْمِنِينَ مَقَاعِدَ لِلْقِتَالِ ۗ وَاللَّهُ سَمِيعٌ عَلِيمٌ

121 Remember when you left your home in the morning, to assign battle-positions for the believers. God is Hearing and Knowing.

١٢٢ إِذْ هَمَّتْ طَائِفَتَانِ مِنْكُمْ أَنْ تَفْشَلَا وَاللَّهُ وَلِيُّهُمَا ۗ وَعَلَى اللَّهِ فَلْيَتَوَكَّلِ الْمُؤْمِنُونَ

122
3:152; 4:59; 8:43

122 When two groups among you almost faltered, but God was their Protector. So in God let the believers put their trust.

١٢٣ وَلَقَدْ نَصَرَكُمُ اللَّهُ بِبَدْرٍ وَأَنْتُمْ أَذِلَّةٌ ۖ فَاتَّقُوا اللَّهَ لَعَلَّكُمْ تَشْكُرُونَ

123 God had given you victory at Badr, when you were weak. So fear God, that you may be thankful.

١٢٤ إِذْ تَقُولُ لِلْمُؤْمِنِينَ أَلَنْ يَكْفِيَكُمْ أَنْ يُمِدَّكُمْ رَبُّكُمْ بِثَلَاثَةِ آلَافٍ مِنَ الْمَلَائِكَةِ مُنْزَلِينَ

124
8:9

124 When you said to the believers, "Is it not enough for you that your Lord has reinforced you with three thousand angels, sent down?"

١٢٥ بَلَىٰ ۚ إِنْ تَصْبِرُوا وَتَتَّقُوا وَيَأْتُوكُمْ مِنْ فَوْرِهِمْ هَٰذَا يُمْدِدْكُمْ رَبُّكُمْ بِخَمْسَةِ آلَافٍ مِنَ الْمَلَائِكَةِ مُسَوِّمِينَ

125 It is; but if you persevere and remain cautious, and they attack you suddenly, your Lord will reinforce you with five thousand angels, well trained.

١٢٦ وَمَا جَعَلَهُ اللَّهُ إِلَّا بُشْرَىٰ لَكُمْ وَلِتَطْمَئِنَّ قُلُوبُكُمْ بِهِ ۗ وَمَا النَّصْرُ إِلَّا مِنْ عِنْدِ اللَّهِ الْعَزِيزِ الْحَكِيمِ

126
8:10

126 God made it but a message of hope for you, and to reassure your hearts thereby. Victory comes only from God the Almighty, the Wise.

١٢٧ لِيَقْطَعَ طَرَفًا مِنَ الَّذِينَ كَفَرُوا أَوْ يَكْبِتَهُمْ فَيَنْقَلِبُوا خَائِبِينَ

127 He thus cuts off a section of those who disbelieved, or subdues them, so they retreat disappointed.

١٢٨ لَيْسَ لَكَ مِنَ الْأَمْرِ شَيْءٌ أَوْ يَتُوبَ عَلَيْهِمْ أَوْ يُعَذِّبَهُمْ فَإِنَّهُمْ ظَالِمُونَ

128 It is no concern of yours whether He redeems them or punishes them. They are wrongdoers.

١٢٩ وَلِلَّهِ مَا فِي السَّمَاوَاتِ وَمَا فِي الْأَرْضِ ۚ يَغْفِرُ لِمَنْ يَشَاءُ وَيُعَذِّبُ مَنْ يَشَاءُ ۚ وَاللَّهُ غَفُورٌ رَحِيمٌ

129 To God belongs everything in the heavens and the earth. He forgives whom He wills, and He punishes whom He wills. God is Most Forgiving, Most Merciful.

129
2:284; 5:40

١٣٠ يَا أَيُّهَا الَّذِينَ آمَنُوا لَا تَأْكُلُوا الرِّبَا أَضْعَافًا مُضَاعَفَةً ۖ وَاتَّقُوا اللَّهَ لَعَلَّكُمْ تُفْلِحُونَ

130 O you who believe! Do not feed on usury, compounded over and over, and fear God, so that you may prosper.

130
2:275–276; 4:161; 30:39

١٣١ وَاتَّقُوا النَّارَ الَّتِي أُعِدَّتْ لِلْكَافِرِينَ

131 And guard yourselves against the Fire that is prepared for the disbelievers.

١٣٢ وَأَطِيعُوا اللَّهَ وَالرَّسُولَ لَعَلَّكُمْ تُرْحَمُونَ

132 And obey God and the Messenger, that you may obtain mercy.

١٣٣ وَسَارِعُوا إِلَىٰ مَغْفِرَةٍ مِنْ رَبِّكُمْ وَجَنَّةٍ عَرْضُهَا السَّمَاوَاتُ وَالْأَرْضُ أُعِدَّتْ لِلْمُتَّقِينَ

133 And race towards forgiveness from your Lord, and a Garden as wide as the heavens and the earth, prepared for the righteous.

133
57:21

١٣٤ الَّذِينَ يُنْفِقُونَ فِي السَّرَّاءِ وَالضَّرَّاءِ وَالْكَاظِمِينَ الْغَيْظَ وَالْعَافِينَ عَنِ النَّاسِ ۗ وَاللَّهُ يُحِبُّ الْمُحْسِنِينَ

134 Those who give in prosperity and adversity, and those who restrain anger, and those who forgive people. God loves the doers of good.

134
4:64, 100

١٣٥ وَالَّذِينَ إِذَا فَعَلُوا فَاحِشَةً أَوْ ظَلَمُوا أَنْفُسَهُمْ ذَكَرُوا اللَّهَ فَاسْتَغْفَرُوا لِذُنُوبِهِمْ وَمَنْ يَغْفِرُ الذُّنُوبَ إِلَّا اللَّهُ وَلَمْ يُصِرُّوا عَلَىٰ مَا فَعَلُوا وَهُمْ يَعْلَمُونَ

135 And those who, when they commit an indecency or wrong themselves, remember God and ask forgiveness for their sins—and who forgives sins except God? And they do not persist in their wrongdoing while they know.

135
4:64; 9:104; 73:20

١٣٦ أُولَٰئِكَ جَزَاؤُهُمْ مَغْفِرَةٌ مِنْ رَبِّهِمْ وَجَنَّاتٌ تَجْرِي مِنْ تَحْتِهَا الْأَنْهَارُ خَالِدِينَ فِيهَا ۚ وَنِعْمَ أَجْرُ الْعَامِلِينَ

136 Those—their reward is forgiveness from their Lord, and gardens beneath which rivers flow, abiding therein forever. How excellent is the reward of the workers.

١٣٧ قَدْ خَلَتْ مِن قَبْلِكُمْ سُنَنٌ فَسِيرُوا فِي الْأَرْضِ فَانظُرُوا كَيْفَ كَانَ عَاقِبَةُ الْمُكَذِّبِينَ

137 Many societies have passed away before you. So travel the earth and note the fate of the deniers.

137
15:13;

١٣٨ هَٰذَا بَيَانٌ لِّلنَّاسِ وَهُدًى وَمَوْعِظَةٌ لِّلْمُتَّقِينَ

138 This is a proclamation to humanity, and guidance, and advice for the righteous.

١٣٩ وَلَا تَهِنُوا وَلَا تَحْزَنُوا وَأَنتُمُ الْأَعْلَوْنَ إِن كُنتُم مُّؤْمِنِينَ

139 And do not waver, nor feel remorse. You are the superior ones, if you are believers.

139
4:104; 47:35

١٤٠ إِن يَمْسَسْكُمْ قَرْحٌ فَقَدْ مَسَّ الْقَوْمَ قَرْحٌ مِّثْلُهُ ۚ وَتِلْكَ الْأَيَّامُ نُدَاوِلُهَا بَيْنَ النَّاسِ وَلِيَعْلَمَ اللَّهُ الَّذِينَ آمَنُوا وَيَتَّخِذَ مِنكُمْ شُهَدَاءَ ۗ وَاللَّهُ لَا يُحِبُّ الظَّالِمِينَ

140 If a wound afflicts you, a similar wound has afflicted the others. Such days We alternate between the people, that God may know those who believe, and take martyrs from among you. God does not love the evildoers.

١٤١ وَلِيُمَحِّصَ اللَّهُ الَّذِينَ آمَنُوا وَيَمْحَقَ الْكَافِرِينَ

141 So that God may prove those who believe, and eliminate the disbelievers.

١٤٢ أَمْ حَسِبْتُمْ أَن تَدْخُلُوا الْجَنَّةَ وَلَمَّا يَعْلَمِ اللَّهُ الَّذِينَ جَاهَدُوا مِنكُمْ وَيَعْلَمَ الصَّابِرِينَ

142 Or do you expect to enter Paradise, before God has distinguished those among you who strive, and before He has distinguished the steadfast?

142
2:214; 5:71; 7:95; 9:16;
10:21; 47:31

١٤٣ وَلَقَدْ كُنتُمْ تَمَنَّوْنَ الْمَوْتَ مِن قَبْلِ أَن تَلْقَوْهُ فَقَدْ رَأَيْتُمُوهُ وَأَنتُمْ تَنظُرُونَ

143 You used to wish for death before you have faced it. Now you have seen it before your own eyes.

١٤٤ وَمَا مُحَمَّدٌ إِلَّا رَسُولٌ قَدْ خَلَتْ مِن قَبْلِهِ الرُّسُلُ ۚ أَفَإِن مَّاتَ أَوْ قُتِلَ انقَلَبْتُمْ عَلَىٰ أَعْقَابِكُمْ ۚ وَمَن يَنقَلِبْ عَلَىٰ عَقِبَيْهِ فَلَن يَضُرَّ اللَّهَ شَيْئًا ۗ وَسَيَجْزِي اللَّهُ الشَّاكِرِينَ

144 Muhammad is no more than a messenger. Messengers have passed on before him. If he dies or gets killed, will you turn on your heels? He who turns on his heels will not harm God in any way. And God will reward the appreciative.

144
5:75

١٤٥ وَمَا كَانَ لِنَفْسٍ أَن تَمُوتَ إِلَّا بِإِذْنِ اللَّهِ كِتَابًا مُّؤَجَّلًا ۗ وَمَن يُرِدْ ثَوَابَ الدُّنْيَا نُؤْتِهِ مِنْهَا وَمَن يُرِدْ ثَوَابَ الْآخِرَةِ نُؤْتِهِ مِنْهَا ۚ وَسَنَجْزِي الشَّاكِرِينَ

145 No soul can die except by God's leave, at a predetermined time. Whoever desires the reward of the world, We will give him some of it; and whoever desires the reward of the Hereafter, We will give him some of it; and We will reward the appreciative.

145
4:134; 11:15; 17:18

١٤٦ وَكَأَيِّنْ مِنْ نَبِيٍّ قَاتَلَ مَعَهُ رِبِّيُّونَ كَثِيرٌ فَمَا وَهَنُوا لِمَا أَصَابَهُمْ فِي سَبِيلِ اللَّهِ وَمَا ضَعُفُوا وَمَا اسْتَكَانُوا ۗ وَاللَّهُ يُحِبُّ الصَّابِرِينَ

146 How many a prophet fought alongside him numerous godly people? They did not waver for what afflicted them in the cause of God, nor did they weaken, nor did they give in. God loves those who endure.

١٤٧ وَمَا كَانَ قَوْلَهُمْ إِلَّا أَنْ قَالُوا رَبَّنَا اغْفِرْ لَنَا ذُنُوبَنَا وَإِسْرَافَنَا فِي أَمْرِنَا وَثَبِّتْ أَقْدَامَنَا وَانْصُرْنَا عَلَى الْقَوْمِ الْكَافِرِينَ

147 Their only words were, "Our Lord, forgive us our offences, and our excesses in our conduct, and strengthen our foothold, and help us against the disbelieving people."

١٤٨ فَآتَاهُمُ اللَّهُ ثَوَابَ الدُّنْيَا وَحُسْنَ ثَوَابِ الْآخِرَةِ ۗ وَاللَّهُ يُحِبُّ الْمُحْسِنِينَ

148 So God gave them the reward of this world, and the excellent reward of the Hereafter. God loves the doers of good.

١٤٩ يَا أَيُّهَا الَّذِينَ آمَنُوا إِنْ تُطِيعُوا الَّذِينَ كَفَرُوا يَرُدُّوكُمْ عَلَىٰ أَعْقَابِكُمْ فَتَنْقَلِبُوا خَاسِرِينَ

149
2:217; 3:69, 100, 150; 4:113

149 O you who believe! If you obey those who disbelieve, they will turn you back on your heels, and you end up losers.

١٥٠ بَلِ اللَّهُ مَوْلَاكُمْ ۖ وَهُوَ خَيْرُ النَّاصِرِينَ

150
8:40; 22:78

150 God is your Master, and He is the Best of Helpers.

١٥١ سَنُلْقِي فِي قُلُوبِ الَّذِينَ كَفَرُوا الرُّعْبَ بِمَا أَشْرَكُوا بِاللَّهِ مَا لَمْ يُنَزِّلْ بِهِ سُلْطَانًا ۖ وَمَأْوَاهُمُ النَّارُ ۚ وَبِئْسَ مَثْوَى الظَّالِمِينَ

151
8:12; 22:71; 33:26; 59:2

151 We will throw terror into the hearts of those who disbelieve, because they attribute to God partners for which He revealed no sanction. Their lodging is the Fire. Miserable is the lodging of the evildoers.

١٥٢ وَلَقَدْ صَدَقَكُمُ اللَّهُ وَعْدَهُ إِذْ تَحُسُّونَهُمْ بِإِذْنِهِ ۖ حَتَّىٰ إِذَا فَشِلْتُمْ وَتَنَازَعْتُمْ فِي الْأَمْرِ وَعَصَيْتُمْ مِنْ بَعْدِ مَا أَرَاكُمْ مَا تُحِبُّونَ ۚ مِنْكُمْ مَنْ يُرِيدُ الدُّنْيَا وَمِنْكُمْ مَنْ يُرِيدُ الْآخِرَةَ ۚ ثُمَّ صَرَفَكُمْ عَنْهُمْ لِيَبْتَلِيَكُمْ ۖ وَلَقَدْ عَفَا عَنْكُمْ ۗ وَاللَّهُ ذُو فَضْلٍ عَلَى الْمُؤْمِنِينَ

152
3:122; 4:59; 8:43, 46

152 God has fulfilled His promise to you, and you defeated them by His leave; until when you faltered, and disputed the command, and disobeyed after He had shown you what you like. Some of you want this world, and some of you want the next. Then He turned you away from them, to test you; but He pardoned you. God is Gracious towards the believers.

١٥٣ إِذْ تُصْعِدُونَ وَلَا تَلْوُونَ عَلَىٰ أَحَدٍ وَالرَّسُولُ يَدْعُوكُمْ فِي أُخْرَاكُمْ فَأَثَابَكُمْ غَمًّا بِغَمٍّ لِكَيْلَا تَحْزَنُوا عَلَىٰ مَا فَاتَكُمْ وَلَا مَا أَصَابَكُمْ ۗ وَاللَّهُ خَبِيرٌ بِمَا تَعْمَلُونَ

153
57:23

153 Remember when you fled, not caring for anyone, even though the Messenger was calling you from your rear. Then He repaid you with sorrow upon sorrow, so that you would not grieve over what you missed, or for what afflicted you. God is Informed of what you do.

١٥٤ ثُمَّ أَنزَلَ عَلَيْكُم مِّن بَعْدِ الْغَمِّ أَمَنَةً نُّعَاسًا يَغْشَىٰ طَائِفَةً مِّنكُمْ ۖ وَطَائِفَةٌ قَدْ أَهَمَّتْهُمْ أَنفُسُهُمْ يَظُنُّونَ بِاللَّهِ غَيْرَ الْحَقِّ ظَنَّ الْجَاهِلِيَّةِ ۖ يَقُولُونَ هَل لَّنَا مِنَ الْأَمْرِ مِن شَيْءٍ ۗ قُلْ إِنَّ الْأَمْرَ كُلَّهُ لِلَّهِ ۗ يُخْفُونَ فِي أَنفُسِهِم مَّا لَا يُبْدُونَ لَكَ ۖ يَقُولُونَ لَوْ كَانَ لَنَا مِنَ الْأَمْرِ شَيْءٌ مَّا قُتِلْنَا هَاهُنَا ۗ قُل لَّوْ كُنتُمْ فِي بُيُوتِكُمْ لَبَرَزَ الَّذِينَ كُتِبَ عَلَيْهِمُ الْقَتْلُ إِلَىٰ مَضَاجِعِهِمْ ۖ وَلِيَبْتَلِيَ اللَّهُ مَا فِي صُدُورِكُمْ وَلِيُمَحِّصَ مَا فِي قُلُوبِكُمْ ۗ وَاللَّهُ عَلِيمٌ بِذَاتِ الصُّدُورِ

154 Then after the setback, He sent down security upon you. Slumber overcame some of you, while others cared only for themselves, thinking of God thoughts that were untrue—thoughts of ignorance—saying, "Is anything up to us?" Say, "Everything is up to God." They conceal within themselves what they do not reveal to you. And they say, "If it was up to us, none of us would have been killed here." Say, "Even if you Had stayed in your homes, those destined to be killed would have marched into their death beds." God thus tests what is in your minds, and purifies what is in your hearts. God knows what the hearts contain. [8:11]

١٥٥ إِنَّ الَّذِينَ تَوَلَّوْا مِنكُمْ يَوْمَ الْتَقَى الْجَمْعَانِ إِنَّمَا اسْتَزَلَّهُمُ الشَّيْطَانُ بِبَعْضِ مَا كَسَبُوا ۖ وَلَقَدْ عَفَا اللَّهُ عَنْهُمْ ۗ إِنَّ اللَّهَ غَفُورٌ حَلِيمٌ

155 Those of you who turned back on the day when the two armies clashed—it was Satan who caused them to backslide, on account of some of what they have earned. But God has forgiven them. God is Forgiving and Prudent. [8:41]

١٥٦ يَا أَيُّهَا الَّذِينَ آمَنُوا لَا تَكُونُوا كَالَّذِينَ كَفَرُوا وَقَالُوا لِإِخْوَانِهِمْ إِذَا ضَرَبُوا فِي الْأَرْضِ أَوْ كَانُوا غُزًّى لَّوْ كَانُوا عِندَنَا مَا مَاتُوا وَمَا قُتِلُوا لِيَجْعَلَ اللَّهُ ذَٰلِكَ حَسْرَةً فِي قُلُوبِهِمْ ۗ وَاللَّهُ يُحْيِي وَيُمِيتُ ۗ وَاللَّهُ بِمَا تَعْمَلُونَ بَصِيرٌ

156 O you who believe! Do not be like those who disbelieved, and said of their brethren who marched in the land, or went on the offensive, "Had they stayed with us, they would not have died or been killed." So that God may make it a cause of regret in their hearts. God gives life and causes death. God is Seeing of what you do. [3:168; 44:8]

١٥٧ وَلَئِن قُتِلْتُمْ فِي سَبِيلِ اللَّهِ أَوْ مُتُّمْ لَمَغْفِرَةٌ مِّنَ اللَّهِ وَرَحْمَةٌ خَيْرٌ مِّمَّا يَجْمَعُونَ

157 If you are killed in the cause of God, or die—forgiveness and mercy from God are better than what they hoard. [2:218; 9:20; 22:58]

١٥٨ وَلَئِن مُّتُّمْ أَوْ قُتِلْتُمْ لَإِلَى اللَّهِ تُحْشَرُونَ

158 If you die, or are killed—to God you will be gathered up.

١٥٩ فَبِمَا رَحْمَةٍ مِّنَ اللَّهِ لِنتَ لَهُمْ ۖ وَلَوْ كُنتَ فَظًّا غَلِيظَ الْقَلْبِ لَانفَضُّوا مِنْ حَوْلِكَ ۖ فَاعْفُ عَنْهُمْ وَاسْتَغْفِرْ لَهُمْ وَشَاوِرْهُمْ فِي الْأَمْرِ ۖ فَإِذَا عَزَمْتَ فَتَوَكَّلْ عَلَى اللَّهِ ۚ إِنَّ اللَّهَ يُحِبُّ الْمُتَوَكِّلِينَ

159 It is by of grace from God that you were gentle with them. Had you been harsh, hardhearted, they would have dispersed from around you. So pardon them, and ask forgiveness for them, and consult them in the conduct of affairs. And when you make a decision, put your trust in God; God loves the trusting.

١٦٠ إِنْ يَنْصُرْكُمُ اللَّهُ فَلَا غَالِبَ لَكُمْ ۖ وَإِنْ يَخْذُلْكُمْ فَمَنْ ذَا الَّذِي يَنْصُرُكُمْ مِنْ بَعْدِهِ ۗ وَعَلَى اللَّهِ فَلْيَتَوَكَّلِ الْمُؤْمِنُونَ

160 If God supports you, there is none who can overcome you. But if He fails you, who is there to help you after Him? So in God let the believers put their trust.

١٦١ وَمَا كَانَ لِنَبِيٍّ أَنْ يَغُلَّ ۚ وَمَنْ يَغْلُلْ يَأْتِ بِمَا غَلَّ يَوْمَ الْقِيَامَةِ ۚ ثُمَّ تُوَفَّىٰ كُلُّ نَفْسٍ مَا كَسَبَتْ وَهُمْ لَا يُظْلَمُونَ

161 It is not for a prophet to act dishonestly. Whoever acts dishonestly will bring his dishonesty on the Day of Resurrection. Then every soul will be paid in full for what it has earned, and they will not be wronged.

١٦٢ أَفَمَنِ اتَّبَعَ رِضْوَانَ اللَّهِ كَمَنْ بَاءَ بِسَخَطٍ مِنَ اللَّهِ وَمَأْوَاهُ جَهَنَّمُ ۚ وَبِئْسَ الْمَصِيرُ

162
5:80; 9:109

162 Is someone who pursues God's approval the same as someone who incurs God's wrath and his refuge is Hell—the miserable destination?

١٦٣ هُمْ دَرَجَاتٌ عِنْدَ اللَّهِ ۗ وَاللَّهُ بَصِيرٌ بِمَا يَعْمَلُونَ

163 They have different ranks with God, and God is Seeing of what they do.

١٦٤ لَقَدْ مَنَّ اللَّهُ عَلَى الْمُؤْمِنِينَ إِذْ بَعَثَ فِيهِمْ رَسُولًا مِنْ أَنْفُسِهِمْ يَتْلُو عَلَيْهِمْ آيَاتِهِ وَيُزَكِّيهِمْ وَيُعَلِّمُهُمُ الْكِتَابَ وَالْحِكْمَةَ وَإِنْ كَانُوا مِنْ قَبْلُ لَفِي ضَلَالٍ مُبِينٍ

164
2:129, 151; 62:2

164 God has blessed the believers, as He raised up among them a messenger from among themselves, who recites to them His revelations, and purifies them, and teaches them the Scripture and wisdom; although before that they were in evident error.

١٦٥ أَوَلَمَّا أَصَابَتْكُمْ مُصِيبَةٌ قَدْ أَصَبْتُمْ مِثْلَيْهَا قُلْتُمْ أَنَّىٰ هَٰذَا ۖ قُلْ هُوَ مِنْ عِنْدِ أَنْفُسِكُمْ ۗ إِنَّ اللَّهَ عَلَىٰ كُلِّ شَيْءٍ قَدِيرٌ

165 And when a calamity befell you, even after you had inflicted twice as much, you said, "How is this?" Say, "It is from your own selves." God is Able to do all things.

١٦٦ وَمَا أَصَابَكُمْ يَوْمَ الْتَقَى الْجَمْعَانِ فَبِإِذْنِ اللَّهِ وَلِيَعْلَمَ الْمُؤْمِنِينَ

166 What befell you on the day the two armies clashed was with God's permission; that He may know the believers.

١٦٧ وَلِيَعْلَمَ الَّذِينَ نَافَقُوا ۚ وَقِيلَ لَهُمْ تَعَالَوْا قَاتِلُوا فِي سَبِيلِ اللَّهِ أَوِ ادْفَعُوا ۖ قَالُوا لَوْ نَعْلَمُ قِتَالًا لَاتَّبَعْنَاكُمْ ۗ هُمْ لِلْكُفْرِ يَوْمَئِذٍ أَقْرَبُ مِنْهُمْ لِلْإِيمَانِ ۚ يَقُولُونَ بِأَفْوَاهِهِمْ مَا لَيْسَ فِي قُلُوبِهِمْ ۗ وَاللَّهُ أَعْلَمُ بِمَا يَكْتُمُونَ

167
5:41; 48:11

167 And that He may know the hypocrites. And it was said to them, "Come, fight in the cause of God, or contribute." They said, "If we knew how to fight, we would have followed you." On that day they were closer to infidelity than they were to faith. They say with their mouths what is not in their hearts; but God knows what they hide.

١٦٨ الَّذِينَ قَالُوا لِإِخْوَانِهِمْ وَقَعَدُوا لَوْ أَطَاعُونَا مَا قُتِلُوا ۗ قُلْ فَادْرَءُوا عَنْ أَنْفُسِكُمُ الْمَوْتَ إِنْ كُنْتُمْ صَادِقِينَ

168   3:156

168 Those who said of their brethren, as they stayed behind, "Had they obeyed us, they would not have been killed." Say, "Then avert death from yourselves, if you are truthful."

١٦٩ وَلَا تَحْسَبَنَّ الَّذِينَ قُتِلُوا فِي سَبِيلِ اللَّهِ أَمْوَاتًا ۚ بَلْ أَحْيَاءٌ عِنْدَ رَبِّهِمْ يُرْزَقُونَ

169   2:154

169 Do not consider those killed in the cause of God as dead. In fact, they are alive, at their Lord, well provided for.

١٧٠ فَرِحِينَ بِمَا آتَاهُمُ اللَّهُ مِنْ فَضْلِهِ وَيَسْتَبْشِرُونَ بِالَّذِينَ لَمْ يَلْحَقُوا بِهِمْ مِنْ خَلْفِهِمْ أَلَّا خَوْفٌ عَلَيْهِمْ وَلَا هُمْ يَحْزَنُونَ

170 Delighting in what God has given them out of His grace, and happy for those who have not yet joined them; that they have nothing to fear, nor will they grieve.

١٧١ يَسْتَبْشِرُونَ بِنِعْمَةٍ مِنَ اللَّهِ وَفَضْلٍ وَأَنَّ اللَّهَ لَا يُضِيعُ أَجْرَ الْمُؤْمِنِينَ

171 They rejoice in grace from God, and bounty, and that God will not waste the reward of the faithful.

١٧٢ الَّذِينَ اسْتَجَابُوا لِلَّهِ وَالرَّسُولِ مِنْ بَعْدِ مَا أَصَابَهُمُ الْقَرْحُ ۚ لِلَّذِينَ أَحْسَنُوا مِنْهُمْ وَاتَّقَوْا أَجْرٌ عَظِيمٌ

172 Those who responded to God and the Messenger, despite the persecution they had suffered. For the virtuous and the pious among them is a great reward.

١٧٣ الَّذِينَ قَالَ لَهُمُ النَّاسُ إِنَّ النَّاسَ قَدْ جَمَعُوا لَكُمْ فَاخْشَوْهُمْ فَزَادَهُمْ إِيمَانًا وَقَالُوا حَسْبُنَا اللَّهُ وَنِعْمَ الْوَكِيلُ

173 Those to whom the people have said, "The people have mobilized against you, so fear them." But this only increased them in faith, and they said, "God is enough for us; He is the Excellent Protector."

١٧٤ فَانْقَلَبُوا بِنِعْمَةٍ مِنَ اللَّهِ وَفَضْلٍ لَمْ يَمْسَسْهُمْ سُوءٌ وَاتَّبَعُوا رِضْوَانَ اللَّهِ ۗ وَاللَّهُ ذُو فَضْلٍ عَظِيمٍ

174 So they came back with grace from God, and bounty, and no harm having touched them. They pursued what pleases God. God possesses immense grace.

١٧٥ إِنَّمَا ذَٰلِكُمُ الشَّيْطَانُ يُخَوِّفُ أَوْلِيَاءَهُ فَلَا تَخَافُوهُمْ وَخَافُونِ إِنْ كُنْتُمْ مُؤْمِنِينَ

175 That is only Satan frightening his partisans; so do not fear them, but fear Me, if you are believers.

١٧٦ وَلَا يَحْزُنْكَ الَّذِينَ يُسَارِعُونَ فِي الْكُفْرِ ۚ إِنَّهُمْ لَنْ يَضُرُّوا اللَّهَ شَيْئًا ۗ يُرِيدُ اللَّهُ أَلَّا يَجْعَلَ لَهُمْ حَظًّا فِي الْآخِرَةِ ۖ وَلَهُمْ عَذَابٌ عَظِيمٌ

176   5:41; 10:65

176 And do not be saddened by those who rush into disbelief. They will not harm God in the least. God desires to give them no share in the Hereafter. A terrible torment awaits them.

١٧٧ إِنَّ الَّذِينَ اشْتَرَوُا الْكُفْرَ بِالْإِيمَانِ لَن يَضُرُّوا اللَّهَ شَيْئًا وَلَهُمْ عَذَابٌ أَلِيمٌ

177
2:16, 175; 31:6

177 Those who exchange blasphemy for faith will not harm God in the least. A painful torment awaits them.

١٧٨ وَلَا يَحْسَبَنَّ الَّذِينَ كَفَرُوا أَنَّمَا نُمْلِي لَهُمْ خَيْرٌ لِّأَنفُسِهِمْ ۚ إِنَّمَا نُمْلِي لَهُمْ لِيَزْدَادُوا إِثْمًا ۚ وَلَهُمْ عَذَابٌ مُّهِينٌ

178
23:55–56

178 Those who disbelieve should not assume that We respite them for their own good. In fact, We only respite them so that they may increase in sinfulness. A humiliating torment awaits them.

١٧٩ مَّا كَانَ اللَّهُ لِيَذَرَ الْمُؤْمِنِينَ عَلَىٰ مَا أَنتُمْ عَلَيْهِ حَتَّىٰ يَمِيزَ الْخَبِيثَ مِنَ الطَّيِّبِ ۗ وَمَا كَانَ اللَّهُ لِيُطْلِعَكُمْ عَلَى الْغَيْبِ وَلَٰكِنَّ اللَّهَ يَجْتَبِي مِن رُّسُلِهِ مَن يَشَاءُ ۖ فَآمِنُوا بِاللَّهِ وَرُسُلِهِ ۚ وَإِن تُؤْمِنُوا وَتَتَّقُوا فَلَكُمْ أَجْرٌ عَظِيمٌ

179
42:13

179 God will not leave the believers as you are, without distinguishing the wicked from the sincere. Nor will God inform you of the future, but God elects from among His messengers whom He wills. So believe in God and His messengers. If you believe and practice piety, you will have a splendid reward.

١٨٠ وَلَا يَحْسَبَنَّ الَّذِينَ يَبْخَلُونَ بِمَا آتَاهُمُ اللَّهُ مِن فَضْلِهِ هُوَ خَيْرًا لَّهُم ۖ بَلْ هُوَ شَرٌّ لَّهُمْ ۖ سَيُطَوَّقُونَ مَا بَخِلُوا بِهِ يَوْمَ الْقِيَامَةِ ۗ وَلِلَّهِ مِيرَاثُ السَّمَاوَاتِ وَالْأَرْضِ ۗ وَاللَّهُ بِمَا تَعْمَلُونَ خَبِيرٌ

180
4:37; 9:75; 47:38; 57:24

180 Those who withhold what God has given them of his bounty should not assume that is good for them. In fact, it is bad for them. They will be encircled by their hoardings on the Day of Resurrection. To God belongs the inheritance of the heavens and the earth, and God is well acquainted with what you do.

١٨١ لَّقَدْ سَمِعَ اللَّهُ قَوْلَ الَّذِينَ قَالُوا إِنَّ اللَّهَ فَقِيرٌ وَنَحْنُ أَغْنِيَاءُ ۘ سَنَكْتُبُ مَا قَالُوا وَقَتْلَهُمُ الْأَنبِيَاءَ بِغَيْرِ حَقٍّ وَنَقُولُ ذُوقُوا عَذَابَ الْحَرِيقِ

181
2:61, 91; 3:21; 4:155

181 God has heard the statement of those who said, "God is poor, and we are rich." We will write down what they said, and their wrongful killing of the prophets; and We will say, "Taste the torment of the burning."

١٨٢ ذَٰلِكَ بِمَا قَدَّمَتْ أَيْدِيكُمْ وَأَنَّ اللَّهَ لَيْسَ بِظَلَّامٍ لِّلْعَبِيدِ

182
8:51; 22:10

182 "This is on account of what your hands have forwarded, and because God is not unjust towards the creatures."

١٨٣ الَّذِينَ قَالُوا إِنَّ اللَّهَ عَهِدَ إِلَيْنَا أَلَّا نُؤْمِنَ لِرَسُولٍ حَتَّىٰ يَأْتِيَنَا بِقُرْبَانٍ تَأْكُلُهُ النَّارُ ۗ قُلْ قَدْ جَاءَكُمْ رُسُلٌ مِّن قَبْلِي بِالْبَيِّنَاتِ وَبِالَّذِي قُلْتُمْ فَلِمَ قَتَلْتُمُوهُمْ إِن كُنتُمْ صَادِقِينَ

183 Those who said, "God has made a covenant with us, that we shall not believe in any messenger unless he brings us an offering to be consumed by fire." Say, "Messengers have come to you before me with proofs, and with what you asked for; so why did you assassinate them, if you are truthful?"

١٨٤ فَإِن كَذَّبُوكَ فَقَدْ كُذِّبَ رُسُلٌ مِّن قَبْلِكَ جَاءُوا بِالْبَيِّنَاتِ وَالزُّبُرِ وَالْكِتَابِ الْمُنِيرِ

184   16:44; 35:25

184 If they accuse you of lying, messengers before you were accused of lying. They came with the proofs, and the Psalms, and the Illuminating Scripture.

١٨٥ كُلُّ نَفْسٍ ذَائِقَةُ الْمَوْتِ ۗ وَإِنَّمَا تُوَفَّوْنَ أُجُورَكُمْ يَوْمَ الْقِيَامَةِ ۖ فَمَن زُحْزِحَ عَنِ النَّارِ وَأُدْخِلَ الْجَنَّةَ فَقَدْ فَازَ ۗ وَمَا الْحَيَاةُ الدُّنْيَا إِلَّا مَتَاعُ الْغُرُورِ

185   21:35; 29:57

185 Every soul will have a taste of death, and you will receive your recompense on the Day of Resurrection. Whoever is swayed from the Fire, and admitted to Paradise, has won. The life of this world is merely enjoyment of delusion.

١٨٦ لَتُبْلَوُنَّ فِي أَمْوَالِكُمْ وَأَنفُسِكُمْ وَلَتَسْمَعُنَّ مِنَ الَّذِينَ أُوتُوا الْكِتَابَ مِن قَبْلِكُمْ وَمِنَ الَّذِينَ أَشْرَكُوا أَذًى كَثِيرًا ۚ وَإِن تَصْبِرُوا وَتَتَّقُوا فَإِنَّ ذَٰلِكَ مِنْ عَزْمِ الْأُمُورِ

186   2:155

186 You will be tested through your possessions and your persons; and you will hear from those who received the Scripture before you, and from the idol worshipers, much abuse. But if you persevere and lead a righteous life—that indeed is a mark of great determination.

١٨٧ وَإِذْ أَخَذَ اللَّهُ مِيثَاقَ الَّذِينَ أُوتُوا الْكِتَابَ لَتُبَيِّنُنَّهُ لِلنَّاسِ وَلَا تَكْتُمُونَهُ فَنَبَذُوهُ وَرَاءَ ظُهُورِهِمْ وَاشْتَرَوْا بِهِ ثَمَنًا قَلِيلًا ۖ فَبِئْسَ مَا يَشْتَرُونَ

187   2:100; 8:56

187 God received a pledge from those who were given the Scripture: "You shall proclaim it to the people, and not conceal it." But they disregarded it behind their backs, and exchanged it for a small price. What a miserable exchange they made.

١٨٨ لَا تَحْسَبَنَّ الَّذِينَ يَفْرَحُونَ بِمَا أَتَوا وَيُحِبُّونَ أَن يُحْمَدُوا بِمَا لَمْ يَفْعَلُوا فَلَا تَحْسَبَنَّهُم بِمَفَازَةٍ مِّنَ الْعَذَابِ ۖ وَلَهُمْ عَذَابٌ أَلِيمٌ

188   2:162; 39:61

188 Do not think that those who rejoice in what they have done, and love to be praised for what they have not done—do not think they can evade the punishment. They will have a painful punishment.

١٨٩ وَلِلَّهِ مُلْكُ السَّمَاوَاتِ وَالْأَرْضِ ۗ وَاللَّهُ عَلَىٰ كُلِّ شَيْءٍ قَدِيرٌ

189

189 To God belongs the sovereignty of the heavens and the earth. God has power over all things.

١٩٠ إِنَّ فِي خَلْقِ السَّمَاوَاتِ وَالْأَرْضِ وَاخْتِلَافِ اللَّيْلِ وَالنَّهَارِ لَآيَاتٍ لِّأُولِي الْأَلْبَابِ

190   2:164; 17:12; 45:5

190 In the creation of the heavens and the earth, and in the alternation of night and day, are signs for people of understanding.

١٩١ الَّذِينَ يَذْكُرُونَ اللَّهَ قِيَامًا وَقُعُودًا وَعَلَىٰ جُنُوبِهِمْ وَيَتَفَكَّرُونَ فِي خَلْقِ السَّمَاوَاتِ وَالْأَرْضِ رَبَّنَا مَا خَلَقْتَ هَٰذَا بَاطِلًا سُبْحَانَكَ فَقِنَا عَذَابَ النَّارِ

191   4:103; 673; 10:12; 38:27

191 Those who remember God while standing, and sitting, and on their sides; and they reflect upon the creation of the heavens and the earth: "Our Lord, You did not create this in vain, glory to You, so protect us from the punishment of the Fire."

١٩٢ رَبَّنَا إِنَّكَ مَن تُدْخِلِ النَّارَ فَقَدْ أَخْزَيْتَهُ ۖ وَمَا لِلظَّالِمِينَ مِنْ أَنصَارٍ

192 "Our Lord, whomever You commit to the Fire, You have disgraced. The wrongdoers will have no helpers."

١٩٣ رَبَّنَا إِنَّنَا سَمِعْنَا مُنَادِيًا يُنَادِي لِلْإِيمَانِ أَنْ آمِنُوا بِرَبِّكُمْ فَآمَنَّا ۚ رَبَّنَا فَاغْفِرْ لَنَا ذُنُوبَنَا وَكَفِّرْ عَنَّا سَيِّئَاتِنَا وَتَوَفَّنَا مَعَ الْأَبْرَارِ

193 "Our Lord, we have heard a caller calling to the faith: 'Believe in your Lord,' and we have believed. Our Lord! Forgive us our sins, and remit our misdeeds, and make us die in the company of the virtuous."

١٩٤ رَبَّنَا وَآتِنَا مَا وَعَدتَّنَا عَلَىٰ رُسُلِكَ وَلَا تُخْزِنَا يَوْمَ الْقِيَامَةِ ۗ إِنَّكَ لَا تُخْلِفُ الْمِيعَادَ

194
3:9; 13:31; 30:6; 14:47

194 "Our Lord, and give us what You have promised us through Your messengers, and do not disgrace us on the Day of Resurrection. Surely You never break a promise."

١٩٥ فَاسْتَجَابَ لَهُمْ رَبُّهُمْ أَنِّي لَا أُضِيعُ عَمَلَ عَامِلٍ مِّنكُم مِّن ذَكَرٍ أَوْ أُنثَىٰ ۖ بَعْضُكُم مِّن بَعْضٍ ۖ فَالَّذِينَ هَاجَرُوا وَأُخْرِجُوا مِن دِيَارِهِمْ وَأُوذُوا فِي سَبِيلِي وَقَاتَلُوا وَقُتِلُوا لَأُكَفِّرَنَّ عَنْهُمْ سَيِّئَاتِهِمْ وَلَأُدْخِلَنَّهُمْ جَنَّاتٍ تَجْرِي مِن تَحْتِهَا الْأَنْهَارُ ثَوَابًا مِّنْ عِندِ اللَّهِ ۗ وَاللَّهُ عِندَهُ حُسْنُ الثَّوَابِ

195
4:74; 9:111

195 And so their Lord answered them: "I will not waste the work of any worker among you, whether male or female. You are one of another. For those who emigrated, and were expelled from their homes, and were persecuted because of Me, and fought and were killed—I will remit for them their sins, and will admit them into gardens beneath which rivers flow—a reward from God. With God is the ultimate reward."

١٩٦ لَا يَغُرَّنَّكَ تَقَلُّبُ الَّذِينَ كَفَرُوا فِي الْبِلَادِ

196
pp 40:4

196 Do not be impressed by the disbelievers' movements in the land.

١٩٧ مَتَاعٌ قَلِيلٌ ثُمَّ مَأْوَاهُمْ جَهَنَّمُ ۚ وَبِئْسَ الْمِهَادُ

197 A brief enjoyment, then their abode is Hell. What a miserable resort.

١٩٨ لَٰكِنِ الَّذِينَ اتَّقَوْا رَبَّهُمْ لَهُمْ جَنَّاتٌ تَجْرِي مِن تَحْتِهَا الْأَنْهَارُ خَالِدِينَ فِيهَا نُزُلًا مِّنْ عِندِ اللَّهِ ۗ وَمَا عِندَ اللَّهِ خَيْرٌ لِّلْأَبْرَارِ

198
76:5; 82:13

198 As for those who feared their Lord: for them will be gardens beneath which rivers flow, wherein they will abide forever—hospitality from God. What God possesses is best for the just.

١٩٩ وَإِنَّ مِنْ أَهْلِ الْكِتَابِ لَمَن يُؤْمِنُ بِاللَّهِ وَمَا أُنزِلَ إِلَيْكُمْ وَمَا أُنزِلَ إِلَيْهِمْ خَاشِعِينَ لِلَّهِ لَا يَشْتَرُونَ بِآيَاتِ اللَّهِ ثَمَنًا قَلِيلًا ۗ أُولَٰئِكَ لَهُمْ أَجْرُهُمْ عِندَ رَبِّهِمْ ۗ إِنَّ اللَّهَ سَرِيعُ الْحِسَابِ

199
3:104, 110, 114; 7:157; 9:71

199 Among the People of the Scripture are those who believe in God, and in what was revealed to you, and in what was revealed to them. They are humble before God, and they do not sell God's revelations for a cheap price. These will have their reward with their Lord. God is swift in reckoning.

٢٠٠ يَا أَيُّهَا الَّذِينَ آمَنُوا اصْبِرُوا وَصَابِرُوا وَرَابِطُوا وَاتَّقُوا اللَّهَ لَعَلَّكُمْ تُفْلِحُونَ

200 O you who believe! Be patient, and advocate patience, and be united, and revere God, so that you may thrive.

Sūrah 4: Al-Nisā'

سُورَةُ ٱلنِّسَاء (Women)

بِسْمِ ٱللَّهِ ٱلرَّحْمَٰنِ ٱلرَّحِيمِ

١ يَا أَيُّهَا النَّاسُ اتَّقُوا رَبَّكُمُ الَّذِي خَلَقَكُم مِّن نَّفْسٍ وَاحِدَةٍ وَخَلَقَ مِنْهَا زَوْجَهَا وَبَثَّ مِنْهُمَا رِجَالًا كَثِيرًا وَنِسَاءً ۚ وَاتَّقُوا اللَّهَ الَّذِي تَسَاءَلُونَ بِهِ وَالْأَرْحَامَ ۚ إِنَّ اللَّهَ كَانَ عَلَيْكُمْ رَقِيبًا

1 O people! Fear your Lord, who created you from a single soul, and created from it its mate, and propagated from them many men and women. And revere God whom you ask about, and the parents. Surely, God is Watchful over you.

1
6:98; 7:189; 30:21; 39:6

٢ وَآتُوا الْيَتَامَىٰ أَمْوَالَهُمْ ۖ وَلَا تَتَبَدَّلُوا الْخَبِيثَ بِالطَّيِّبِ ۖ وَلَا تَأْكُلُوا أَمْوَالَهُمْ إِلَىٰ أَمْوَالِكُمْ ۚ إِنَّهُ كَانَ حُوبًا كَبِيرًا

2 And give orphans their properties, and do not substitute the bad for the good. And do not consume their properties by combining them with yours, for that would be a serious sin.

2
4:10, 127; 6:152; 17:34; 89:19

٣ وَإِنْ خِفْتُمْ أَلَّا تُقْسِطُوا فِي الْيَتَامَىٰ فَانكِحُوا مَا طَابَ لَكُم مِّنَ النِّسَاءِ مَثْنَىٰ وَثُلَاثَ وَرُبَاعَ ۖ فَإِنْ خِفْتُمْ أَلَّا تَعْدِلُوا فَوَاحِدَةً أَوْ مَا مَلَكَتْ أَيْمَانُكُمْ ۚ ذَٰلِكَ أَدْنَىٰ أَلَّا تَعُولُوا

3 If you fear you cannot act fairly towards the orphans—then marry the women you like—two, or three, or four. But if you fear you will not be fair, then one, or what you already have. That makes it more likely that you avoid bias.

3
4:24, 127

٤ وَآتُوا النِّسَاءَ صَدُقَاتِهِنَّ نِحْلَةً ۚ فَإِن طِبْنَ لَكُمْ عَن شَيْءٍ مِّنْهُ نَفْسًا فَكُلُوهُ هَنِيئًا مَرِيئًا

4 Give women their dowries graciously. But if they willingly forego some of it, then consume it with enjoyment and pleasure.

4
4:25

٥ وَلَا تُؤْتُوا السُّفَهَاءَ أَمْوَالَكُمُ الَّتِي جَعَلَ اللَّهُ لَكُمْ قِيَامًا وَارْزُقُوهُمْ فِيهَا وَاكْسُوهُمْ وَقُولُوا لَهُمْ قَوْلًا مَعْرُوفًا

5 Do not give the immature your money which God has assigned to you for support. But provide for them from it, and clothe them, and speak to them with kind words.

٦ وَابْتَلُوا الْيَتَامَىٰ حَتَّىٰ إِذَا بَلَغُوا النِّكَاحَ فَإِنْ آنَسْتُم مِّنْهُمْ رُشْدًا فَادْفَعُوا إِلَيْهِمْ أَمْوَالَهُمْ ۖ وَلَا تَأْكُلُوهَا إِسْرَافًا وَبِدَارًا أَن يَكْبَرُوا ۚ وَمَن كَانَ غَنِيًّا فَلْيَسْتَعْفِفْ ۖ وَمَن كَانَ فَقِيرًا فَلْيَأْكُلْ بِالْمَعْرُوفِ ۚ فَإِذَا دَفَعْتُمْ إِلَيْهِمْ أَمْوَالَهُمْ فَأَشْهِدُوا عَلَيْهِمْ ۚ وَكَفَىٰ بِاللَّهِ حَسِيبًا

6 17:34

6 Test the orphans until they reach the age of marriage. If you find them to be mature enough, hand over their properties to them. And do not consume it extravagantly or hastily before they grow up. The rich shall not charge any wage, but the poor may charge fairly. When you hand over their properties to them, have it witnessed for them. God suffices as a Reckoner.

٧ لِّلرِّجَالِ نَصِيبٌ مِّمَّا تَرَكَ الْوَالِدَانِ وَالْأَقْرَبُونَ وَلِلنِّسَاءِ نَصِيبٌ مِّمَّا تَرَكَ الْوَالِدَانِ وَالْأَقْرَبُونَ مِمَّا قَلَّ مِنْهُ أَوْ كَثُرَ ۚ نَصِيبًا مَّفْرُوضًا

7–8 2:215; 4:33

7 Men receive a share of what their parents and relatives leave, and women receive a share of what their parents and relatives leave; be it little or much—a legal share.

٨ وَإِذَا حَضَرَ الْقِسْمَةَ أُولُو الْقُرْبَىٰ وَالْيَتَامَىٰ وَالْمَسَاكِينُ فَارْزُقُوهُم مِّنْهُ وَقُولُوا لَهُمْ قَوْلًا مَّعْرُوفًا

8 If the distribution is attended by the relatives, and the orphans, and the needy, give them something out of it, and speak to them kindly.

٩ وَلْيَخْشَ الَّذِينَ لَوْ تَرَكُوا مِنْ خَلْفِهِمْ ذُرِّيَّةً ضِعَافًا خَافُوا عَلَيْهِمْ فَلْيَتَّقُوا اللَّهَ وَلْيَقُولُوا قَوْلًا سَدِيدًا

9 Those who are concerned about the fate of their weak children, in case they leave them behind, should fear God, and speak appropriate words.

١٠ إِنَّ الَّذِينَ يَأْكُلُونَ أَمْوَالَ الْيَتَامَىٰ ظُلْمًا إِنَّمَا يَأْكُلُونَ فِي بُطُونِهِمْ نَارًا ۖ وَسَيَصْلَوْنَ سَعِيرًا

10 4:2, 127; 6:152; 17:34; 89:19

10 Those who consume the wealth of orphans illicitly consume only fire into their bellies; and they will roast in a Blaze.

١١ يُوصِيكُمُ اللَّهُ فِي أَوْلَادِكُمْ ۖ لِلذَّكَرِ مِثْلُ حَظِّ الْأُنثَيَيْنِ ۚ فَإِن كُنَّ نِسَاءً فَوْقَ اثْنَتَيْنِ فَلَهُنَّ ثُلُثَا مَا تَرَكَ ۖ وَإِن كَانَتْ وَاحِدَةً فَلَهَا النِّصْفُ ۚ وَلِأَبَوَيْهِ لِكُلِّ وَاحِدٍ مِّنْهُمَا السُّدُسُ مِمَّا تَرَكَ إِن كَانَ لَهُ وَلَدٌ ۚ فَإِن لَّمْ يَكُن لَّهُ وَلَدٌ وَوَرِثَهُ أَبَوَاهُ فَلِأُمِّهِ الثُّلُثُ ۚ فَإِن كَانَ لَهُ إِخْوَةٌ فَلِأُمِّهِ السُّدُسُ ۚ مِن بَعْدِ وَصِيَّةٍ يُوصِي بِهَا أَوْ دَيْنٍ ۗ آبَاؤُكُمْ وَأَبْنَاؤُكُمْ لَا تَدْرُونَ أَيُّهُمْ أَقْرَبُ لَكُمْ نَفْعًا ۚ فَرِيضَةً مِّنَ اللَّهِ ۗ إِنَّ اللَّهَ كَانَ عَلِيمًا حَكِيمًا

11–12 4:34, 176

11 God instructs you regarding your children: The male receives the equivalent of the share of two females. If they are daughters, more than two, they get two-thirds of what he leaves. If there is only one, she gets one-half. As for the parents, each gets one-sixth of what he leaves, if he had children. If he had no children, and his parents inherit from him, his mother gets one-third. If he has siblings, his mother gets one-sixth. After fulfilling any bequest and paying off debts. Your parents and your children—you do not know which are closer to you in welfare. This is God's Law. God is Knowing and Judicious.

١٢ وَلَكُمْ نِصْفُ مَا تَرَكَ أَزْوَاجُكُمْ إِنْ لَمْ يَكُنْ لَهُنَّ وَلَدٌ ۚ فَإِنْ كَانَ لَهُنَّ وَلَدٌ فَلَكُمُ الرُّبُعُ مِمَّا تَرَكْنَ ۚ مِنْ بَعْدِ وَصِيَّةٍ يُوصِينَ بِهَا أَوْ دَيْنٍ ۚ وَلَهُنَّ الرُّبُعُ مِمَّا تَرَكْتُمْ إِنْ لَمْ يَكُنْ لَكُمْ وَلَدٌ ۚ فَإِنْ كَانَ لَكُمْ وَلَدٌ فَلَهُنَّ الثُّمُنُ مِمَّا تَرَكْتُم ۚ مِنْ بَعْدِ وَصِيَّةٍ تُوصُونَ بِهَا أَوْ دَيْنٍ ۗ وَإِنْ كَانَ رَجُلٌ يُورَثُ كَلَالَةً أَوِ امْرَأَةٌ وَلَهُ أَخٌ أَوْ أُخْتٌ فَلِكُلِّ وَاحِدٍ مِنْهُمَا السُّدُسُ ۚ فَإِنْ كَانُوا أَكْثَرَ مِنْ ذَلِكَ فَهُمْ شُرَكَاءُ فِي الثُّلُثِ ۚ مِنْ بَعْدِ وَصِيَّةٍ يُوصَىٰ بِهَا أَوْ دَيْنٍ غَيْرَ مُضَارٍّ ۚ وَصِيَّةً مِنَ اللَّهِ ۗ وَاللَّهُ عَلِيمٌ حَلِيمٌ

12 You get one-half of what your wives leave behind, if they had no children. If they had children, you get one-fourth of what they leave. After fulfilling any bequest and paying off debts. They get one-fourth of what you leave behind, if you have no children. If you have children, they get one-eighth of what you leave. After fulfilling any bequest and paying off debts. If a man or woman leaves neither parents nor children, but has a brother or sister, each of them gets one-sixth. If there are more siblings, they share one-third. After fulfilling any bequest and paying off debts, without any prejudice. This is a will from God. God is Knowing and Clement.

١٣ تِلْكَ حُدُودُ اللَّهِ ۚ وَمَنْ يُطِعِ اللَّهَ وَرَسُولَهُ يُدْخِلْهُ جَنَّاتٍ تَجْرِي مِنْ تَحْتِهَا الْأَنْهَارُ خَالِدِينَ فِيهَا ۚ وَذَلِكَ الْفَوْزُ الْعَظِيمُ

13 These are the bounds set by God. Whoever obeys God and His Messenger, He will admit him into Gardens beneath which rivers flow, to abide therein forever. That is the great attainment.

١٤ وَمَنْ يَعْصِ اللَّهَ وَرَسُولَهُ وَيَتَعَدَّ حُدُودَهُ يُدْخِلْهُ نَارًا خَالِدًا فِيهَا وَلَهُ عَذَابٌ مُهِينٌ

14 But whoever disobeys God and His Messenger, and oversteps His bounds, He will admit him into a Fire, wherein he abides forever, and he will have a shameful punishment.

14
72:23

١٥ وَاللَّاتِي يَأْتِينَ الْفَاحِشَةَ مِنْ نِسَائِكُمْ فَاسْتَشْهِدُوا عَلَيْهِنَّ أَرْبَعَةً مِنْكُمْ ۖ فَإِنْ شَهِدُوا فَأَمْسِكُوهُنَّ فِي الْبُيُوتِ حَتَّىٰ يَتَوَفَّاهُنَّ الْمَوْتُ أَوْ يَجْعَلَ اللَّهُ لَهُنَّ سَبِيلًا

15 Those of your women who commit lewdness, you must have four witnesses against them, from among you. If they testify, confine them to the homes until death claims them, or God makes a way for them.

15
24:4, 13

١٦ وَاللَّذَانِ يَأْتِيَانِهَا مِنْكُمْ فَآذُوهُمَا ۖ فَإِنْ تَابَا وَأَصْلَحَا فَأَعْرِضُوا عَنْهُمَا ۗ إِنَّ اللَّهَ كَانَ تَوَّابًا رَحِيمًا

16 If two men among you commit it, punish them both. But if they repent and reform, leave them alone. God is Redeemer, Full of Mercy.

16
24:2

١٧ إِنَّمَا التَّوْبَةُ عَلَى اللَّهِ لِلَّذِينَ يَعْمَلُونَ السُّوءَ بِجَهَالَةٍ ثُمَّ يَتُوبُونَ مِنْ قَرِيبٍ فَأُولَٰئِكَ يَتُوبُ اللَّهُ عَلَيْهِمْ ۗ وَكَانَ اللَّهُ عَلِيمًا حَكِيمًا

17 Repentance is available from God for those who commit evil out of ignorance, and then repent soon after. These—God will relent towards them. God is Knowing and Wise.

17
16:119

١٨ وَلَيْسَتِ التَّوْبَةُ لِلَّذِينَ يَعْمَلُونَ السَّيِّئَاتِ حَتَّىٰ إِذَا حَضَرَ أَحَدَهُمُ الْمَوْتُ قَالَ إِنِّي تُبْتُ الْآنَ وَلَا الَّذِينَ يَمُوتُونَ وَهُمْ كُفَّارٌ ۚ أُولَٰئِكَ أَعْتَدْنَا لَهُمْ عَذَابًا أَلِيمًا

18
6:158; 10:51, 90; 32:29; 40:84

18 But repentance is not available for those who commit evils, until when death approaches one of them, he says, "Now I repent," nor for those who die as disbelievers. These—We have prepared for them a painful torment.

١٩ يَا أَيُّهَا الَّذِينَ آمَنُوا لَا يَحِلُّ لَكُمْ أَنْ تَرِثُوا النِّسَاءَ كَرْهًا ۖ وَلَا تَعْضُلُوهُنَّ لِتَذْهَبُوا بِبَعْضِ مَا آتَيْتُمُوهُنَّ إِلَّا أَنْ يَأْتِينَ بِفَاحِشَةٍ مُبَيِّنَةٍ ۚ وَعَاشِرُوهُنَّ بِالْمَعْرُوفِ ۚ فَإِنْ كَرِهْتُمُوهُنَّ فَعَسَىٰ أَنْ تَكْرَهُوا شَيْئًا وَيَجْعَلَ اللَّهُ فِيهِ خَيْرًا كَثِيرًا

19 O you who believe! It is not permitted for you to inherit women against their will. And do not coerce them in order to take away some of what you had given them, unless they commit a proven adultery. And live with them in kindness. If you dislike them, it may be that you dislike something in which God has placed much good.

٢٠ وَإِنْ أَرَدْتُمُ اسْتِبْدَالَ زَوْجٍ مَكَانَ زَوْجٍ وَآتَيْتُمْ إِحْدَاهُنَّ قِنْطَارًا فَلَا تَأْخُذُوا مِنْهُ شَيْئًا ۚ أَتَأْخُذُونَهُ بُهْتَانًا وَإِثْمًا مُبِينًا

20–21
2:228–231; 65:1–7

20 If you wish to replace one wife with another, and you have given one of them a fortune, take nothing back from it. Would you take it back fraudulently and sinfully?

٢١ وَكَيْفَ تَأْخُذُونَهُ وَقَدْ أَفْضَىٰ بَعْضُكُمْ إِلَىٰ بَعْضٍ وَأَخَذْنَ مِنْكُمْ مِيثَاقًا غَلِيظًا

21 And how can you take it back, when you have been intimate with one another, and they have received from you a solid commitment?

٢٢ وَلَا تَنْكِحُوا مَا نَكَحَ آبَاؤُكُمْ مِنَ النِّسَاءِ إِلَّا مَا قَدْ سَلَفَ ۚ إِنَّهُ كَانَ فَاحِشَةً وَمَقْتًا وَسَاءَ سَبِيلًا

22
2:230

22 Do not marry women whom your fathers married, except what is already past. That is improper, indecent, and a bad custom.

٢٣ حُرِّمَتْ عَلَيْكُمْ أُمَّهَاتُكُمْ وَبَنَاتُكُمْ وَأَخَوَاتُكُمْ وَعَمَّاتُكُمْ وَخَالَاتُكُمْ وَبَنَاتُ الْأَخِ وَبَنَاتُ الْأُخْتِ وَأُمَّهَاتُكُمُ اللَّاتِي أَرْضَعْنَكُمْ وَأَخَوَاتُكُمْ مِنَ الرَّضَاعَةِ وَأُمَّهَاتُ نِسَائِكُمْ وَرَبَائِبُكُمُ اللَّاتِي فِي حُجُورِكُمْ مِنْ نِسَائِكُمُ اللَّاتِي دَخَلْتُمْ بِهِنَّ فَإِنْ لَمْ تَكُونُوا دَخَلْتُمْ بِهِنَّ فَلَا جُنَاحَ عَلَيْكُمْ وَحَلَائِلُ أَبْنَائِكُمُ الَّذِينَ مِنْ أَصْلَابِكُمْ وَأَنْ تَجْمَعُوا بَيْنَ الْأُخْتَيْنِ إِلَّا مَا قَدْ سَلَفَ ۗ إِنَّ اللَّهَ كَانَ غَفُورًا رَحِيمًا

23
33:4, 33, 37

23 Forbidden for you are your mothers, your daughters, your sisters, your paternal aunts, your maternal aunts, your brother's daughters, your sister's daughters, your foster-mothers who nursed you, your sisters through nursing, your wives' mothers, and your stepdaughters in your guardianship—born of wives you have gone into—but if you have not gone into them, there is no blame on you. And the wives of your genetic sons, and marrying two sisters simultaneously. Except what is past. God is Oft-Forgiving, Most Merciful.

٢٤ وَالْمُحْصَنَاتُ مِنَ النِّسَاءِ إِلَّا مَا مَلَكَتْ أَيْمَانُكُمْ ۖ كِتَابَ اللَّهِ عَلَيْكُمْ ۚ وَأُحِلَّ لَكُم مَّا وَرَاءَ ذَٰلِكُمْ أَن تَبْتَغُوا بِأَمْوَالِكُم مُّحْصِنِينَ غَيْرَ مُسَافِحِينَ ۚ فَمَا اسْتَمْتَعْتُم بِهِ مِنْهُنَّ فَآتُوهُنَّ أُجُورَهُنَّ فَرِيضَةً ۚ وَلَا جُنَاحَ عَلَيْكُمْ فِيمَا تَرَاضَيْتُم بِهِ مِن بَعْدِ الْفَرِيضَةِ ۚ إِنَّ اللَّهَ كَانَ عَلِيمًا حَكِيمًا

24 4:3, 24, 129; 5:5; 23:506; 33:50; 49:6; 60:10

24 And all married women, except those you rightfully possess. This is God's decree, binding upon you. Permitted for you are those that lie outside these limits, provided you seek them in legal marriage, with gifts from your property, seeking wedlock, not prostitution. If you wish to enjoy them, then give them their dowry—a legal obligation. You commit no error by agreeing to any change to the dowry. God is All-Knowing, Most Wise.

٢٥ وَمَن لَّمْ يَسْتَطِعْ مِنكُمْ طَوْلًا أَن يَنكِحَ الْمُحْصَنَاتِ الْمُؤْمِنَاتِ فَمِن مَّا مَلَكَتْ أَيْمَانُكُم مِّن فَتَيَاتِكُمُ الْمُؤْمِنَاتِ ۚ وَاللَّهُ أَعْلَمُ بِإِيمَانِكُم ۚ بَعْضُكُم مِّن بَعْضٍ ۚ فَانكِحُوهُنَّ بِإِذْنِ أَهْلِهِنَّ وَآتُوهُنَّ أُجُورَهُنَّ بِالْمَعْرُوفِ مُحْصَنَاتٍ غَيْرَ مُسَافِحَاتٍ وَلَا مُتَّخِذَاتِ أَخْدَانٍ ۚ فَإِذَا أُحْصِنَّ فَإِنْ أَتَيْنَ بِفَاحِشَةٍ فَعَلَيْهِنَّ نِصْفُ مَا عَلَى الْمُحْصَنَاتِ مِنَ الْعَذَابِ ۚ ذَٰلِكَ لِمَنْ خَشِيَ الْعَنَتَ مِنكُمْ ۚ وَأَن تَصْبِرُوا خَيْرٌ لَّكُمْ ۗ وَاللَّهُ غَفُورٌ رَّحِيمٌ

25 4:4

25 If any of you lack the means to marry free believing women, he may marry one of the believing maids under your control. God is well aware of your faith. You are from one another. Marry them with the permission of their guardians, and give them their recompense fairly—to be protected—neither committing adultery, nor taking secret lovers. When they are married, if they commit adultery, their punishment shall be half that of free women. That is for those among you who fear falling into decadence. But to practice self-restraint is better for you. God is Most Forgiving, Most Merciful.

٢٦ يُرِيدُ اللَّهُ لِيُبَيِّنَ لَكُمْ وَيَهْدِيَكُمْ سُنَنَ الَّذِينَ مِن قَبْلِكُمْ وَيَتُوبَ عَلَيْكُمْ ۗ وَاللَّهُ عَلِيمٌ حَكِيمٌ

26 God intends to make things clear to you, and to guide you in the ways of those before you, and to redeem you. God is Most Knowing, Most Wise.

٢٧ وَاللَّهُ يُرِيدُ أَن يَتُوبَ عَلَيْكُمْ وَيُرِيدُ الَّذِينَ يَتَّبِعُونَ الشَّهَوَاتِ أَن تَمِيلُوا مَيْلًا عَظِيمًا

27 God intends to redeem you, but those who follow their desires want you to turn away utterly.

٢٨ يُرِيدُ اللَّهُ أَن يُخَفِّفَ عَنكُمْ ۚ وَخُلِقَ الْإِنسَانُ ضَعِيفًا

28 8:66

28 God intends to lighten your burden, for the human being was created weak.

٢٩ يَا أَيُّهَا الَّذِينَ آمَنُوا لَا تَأْكُلُوا أَمْوَالَكُم بَيْنَكُم بِالْبَاطِلِ إِلَّا أَن تَكُونَ تِجَارَةً عَن تَرَاضٍ مِّنكُمْ ۚ وَلَا تَقْتُلُوا أَنفُسَكُمْ ۚ إِنَّ اللَّهَ كَانَ بِكُمْ رَحِيمًا

29 2:188; 4: 161; 9:34

29 O you who believe! Do not consume each other's wealth illicitly, but trade by mutual consent. And do not kill yourselves, for God is Merciful towards you.

٣٠ وَمَن يَفْعَلْ ذَٰلِكَ عُدْوَانًا وَظُلْمًا فَسَوْفَ نُصْلِيهِ نَارًا ۚ وَكَانَ ذَٰلِكَ عَلَى اللَّهِ يَسِيرًا

30 4:56

30 Whoever does that, out of hostility and wrongdoing, We will cast him into a Fire. And that would be easy for God.

٣١ إِن تَجْتَنِبُوا كَبَائِرَ مَا تُنْهَوْنَ عَنْهُ نُكَفِّرْ عَنكُمْ سَيِّئَاتِكُمْ وَنُدْخِلْكُم مُّدْخَلًا كَرِيمًا

31 42:37; 53:32

31 If you avoid the worst of what you are forbidden, We will remit your sins, and admit you by a Gate of Honor.

٣٢ وَلَا تَتَمَنَّوْا مَا فَضَّلَ اللَّهُ بِهِ بَعْضَكُمْ عَلَىٰ بَعْضٍ ۚ لِّلرِّجَالِ نَصِيبٌ مِّمَّا اكْتَسَبُوا ۖ وَلِلنِّسَاءِ نَصِيبٌ مِّمَّا اكْتَسَبْنَ ۚ وَاسْأَلُوا اللَّهَ مِن فَضْلِهِ ۗ إِنَّ اللَّهَ كَانَ بِكُلِّ شَيْءٍ عَلِيمًا

32 4:34; 33:25

32 Do not covet what God has given to some of you in preference to others. For men is a share of what they have earned, and for women is a share of what they have earned. And ask God of his bounty. God has knowledge of everything.

٣٣ وَلِكُلٍّ جَعَلْنَا مَوَالِيَ مِمَّا تَرَكَ الْوَالِدَانِ وَالْأَقْرَبُونَ ۚ وَالَّذِينَ عَقَدَتْ أَيْمَانُكُمْ فَآتُوهُمْ نَصِيبَهُمْ ۚ إِنَّ اللَّهَ كَانَ عَلَىٰ كُلِّ شَيْءٍ شَهِيدًا

33 2:215; 4:8

33 To everyone We have assigned beneficiaries in what is left by parents and relatives. Those with whom you have made an agreement, give them their share. God is Witness over all things.

٣٤ الرِّجَالُ قَوَّامُونَ عَلَى النِّسَاءِ بِمَا فَضَّلَ اللَّهُ بَعْضَهُمْ عَلَىٰ بَعْضٍ وَبِمَا أَنفَقُوا مِنْ أَمْوَالِهِمْ ۚ فَالصَّالِحَاتُ قَانِتَاتٌ حَافِظَاتٌ لِّلْغَيْبِ بِمَا حَفِظَ اللَّهُ ۚ وَاللَّاتِي تَخَافُونَ نُشُوزَهُنَّ فَعِظُوهُنَّ وَاهْجُرُوهُنَّ فِي الْمَضَاجِعِ وَاضْرِبُوهُنَّ ۖ فَإِنْ أَطَعْنَكُمْ فَلَا تَبْغُوا عَلَيْهِنَّ سَبِيلًا ۗ إِنَّ اللَّهَ كَانَ عَلِيًّا كَبِيرًا

34 2:202, 228; 4:32, 128; 33:35

34 Men are the protectors and maintainers of women, as God has given some of them an advantage over others, and because they spend out of their wealth. The good women are obedient, guarding what God would have them guard. As for those from whom you fear disloyalty, admonish them, and abandon them in their beds, then strike them. But if they obey you, seek no way against them. God is Sublime, Great.

٣٥ وَإِنْ خِفْتُمْ شِقَاقَ بَيْنِهِمَا فَابْعَثُوا حَكَمًا مِّنْ أَهْلِهِ وَحَكَمًا مِّنْ أَهْلِهَا إِن يُرِيدَا إِصْلَاحًا يُوَفِّقِ اللَّهُ بَيْنَهُمَا ۗ إِنَّ اللَّهَ كَانَ عَلِيمًا خَبِيرًا

35 4:128, 130

35 If you fear a breach between the two, appoint an arbiter from his family and an arbiter from her family. If they wish to reconcile, God will bring them together. God is Knowledgeable, Expert.

٣٦ وَاعْبُدُوا اللَّهَ وَلَا تُشْرِكُوا بِهِ شَيْئًا ۖ وَبِالْوَالِدَيْنِ إِحْسَانًا وَبِذِي الْقُرْبَىٰ وَالْيَتَامَىٰ وَالْمَسَاكِينِ وَالْجَارِ ذِي الْقُرْبَىٰ وَالْجَارِ الْجُنُبِ وَالصَّاحِبِ بِالْجَنبِ وَابْنِ السَّبِيلِ وَمَا مَلَكَتْ أَيْمَانُكُمْ ۗ إِنَّ اللَّهَ لَا يُحِبُّ مَن كَانَ مُخْتَالًا فَخُورًا

36 2:83; 17:23

36 Worship God, and ascribe no partners to Him, and be good to the parents, and the relatives, and the orphans, and the poor, and the neighbor next door, and the distant neighbor, and the close associate, and the traveler, and your servants. God does not love the arrogant showoff.

٣٧ الَّذِينَ يَبْخَلُونَ وَيَأْمُرُونَ النَّاسَ بِالْبُخْلِ وَيَكْتُمُونَ مَا آتَاهُمُ اللَّهُ مِن فَضْلِهِ ۗ وَأَعْتَدْنَا لِلْكَافِرِينَ عَذَابًا مُّهِينًا

37 3:180; 9:57; 47:38; 57:24

37 Those who are stingy, and exhort people to stinginess, and conceal what God has given them from His bounty. We have prepared for the disbelievers a disgraceful punishment.

٣٨ وَالَّذِينَ يُنفِقُونَ أَمْوَالَهُمْ رِئَاءَ النَّاسِ وَلَا يُؤْمِنُونَ بِاللَّهِ وَلَا بِالْيَوْمِ الْآخِرِ ۗ وَمَن يَكُنِ الشَّيْطَانُ لَهُ قَرِينًا فَسَاءَ قَرِينًا

38 2:262, 264

38 And those who spend their money to be seen by people, and believe neither in God nor in the Last Day. Whoever has Satan as a companion—what an evil companion.

٣٩ وَمَاذَا عَلَيْهِمْ لَوْ آمَنُوا بِاللَّهِ وَالْيَوْمِ الْآخِرِ وَأَنفَقُوا مِمَّا رَزَقَهُمُ اللَّهُ ۚ وَكَانَ اللَّهُ بِهِمْ عَلِيمًا

39 What would they have lost, had they believed in God and the Last Day, and gave out of what God has provided for them? God knows them very well.

٤٠ إِنَّ اللَّهَ لَا يَظْلِمُ مِثْقَالَ ذَرَّةٍ ۖ وَإِن تَكُ حَسَنَةً يُضَاعِفْهَا وَيُؤْتِ مِن لَّدُنْهُ أَجْرًا عَظِيمًا

40 2:261; 6:160; 21:47; 31:16; 99:7–8

40 God does not commit an atom's weight of injustice; and if there is a good deed, He doubles it, and gives from His Presence a sublime compensation.

٤١ فَكَيْفَ إِذَا جِئْنَا مِن كُلِّ أُمَّةٍ بِشَهِيدٍ وَجِئْنَا بِكَ عَلَىٰ هَٰؤُلَاءِ شَهِيدًا

41 16:89; 28:75

41 Then how will it be, when We bring a witness from every community, and We bring you as a witness against these?

٤٢ يَوْمَئِذٍ يَوَدُّ الَّذِينَ كَفَرُوا وَعَصَوُا الرَّسُولَ لَوْ تُسَوَّىٰ بِهِمُ الْأَرْضُ وَلَا يَكْتُمُونَ اللَّهَ حَدِيثًا

42 78:40

42 On that Day, those who disbelieved and disobeyed the Messenger will wish that the earth were leveled over them. They will conceal nothing from God.

٤٣ يَا أَيُّهَا الَّذِينَ آمَنُوا لَا تَقْرَبُوا الصَّلَاةَ وَأَنتُمْ سُكَارَىٰ حَتَّىٰ تَعْلَمُوا مَا تَقُولُونَ وَلَا جُنُبًا إِلَّا عَابِرِي سَبِيلٍ حَتَّىٰ تَغْتَسِلُوا ۚ وَإِن كُنتُم مَّرْضَىٰ أَوْ عَلَىٰ سَفَرٍ أَوْ جَاءَ أَحَدٌ مِّنكُم مِّنَ الْغَائِطِ أَوْ لَامَسْتُمُ النِّسَاءَ فَلَمْ تَجِدُوا مَاءً فَتَيَمَّمُوا صَعِيدًا طَيِّبًا فَامْسَحُوا بِوُجُوهِكُمْ وَأَيْدِيكُمْ ۗ إِنَّ اللَّهَ كَانَ عَفُوًّا غَفُورًا

43 5:6

43 O you who believe! Do not approach the prayer while you are drunk, so that you know what you say; nor after sexual orgasm—unless you are travelling—until you have bathed. If you are sick, or traveling, or one of you comes from the toilet, or you have had intercourse with women, and cannot find water, find clean sand and wipe your faces and your hands with it. God is Pardoning and Forgiving.

٤٤ أَلَمْ تَرَ إِلَى الَّذِينَ أُوتُوا نَصِيبًا مِّنَ الْكِتَابِ يَشْتَرُونَ الضَّلَالَةَ وَيُرِيدُونَ أَن تَضِلُّوا السَّبِيلَ

44 2:16, 109; 3:23, 69; 4:51; 7:37

44 Have you not considered those who were given a share of the Book? They buy error, and wish you would lose the way.

٤٥ وَاللَّهُ أَعْلَمُ بِأَعْدَائِكُمْ ۚ وَكَفَىٰ بِاللَّهِ وَلِيًّا وَكَفَىٰ بِاللَّهِ نَصِيرًا

45 But God knows your enemies best. God is sufficient as a Protector, and God is sufficient as a Supporter.

٤٦ مِنَ الَّذِينَ هَادُوا يُحَرِّفُونَ الْكَلِمَ عَن مَّوَاضِعِهِ[a] وَيَقُولُونَ سَمِعْنَا وَعَصَيْنَا وَاسْمَعْ غَيْرَ مُسْمَعٍ وَرَاعِنَا لَيًّا بِأَلْسِنَتِهِمْ وَطَعْنًا فِي الدِّينِ ۚ وَلَوْ أَنَّهُمْ قَالُوا سَمِعْنَا وَأَطَعْنَا وَاسْمَعْ وَانْظُرْنَا لَكَانَ خَيْرًا لَهُمْ وَأَقْوَمَ وَلَٰكِن لَّعَنَهُمُ اللَّهُ بِكُفْرِهِمْ فَلَا يُؤْمِنُونَ إِلَّا قَلِيلًا[b]

46
[a] 2:75; 5:13, 41
[b] 2:104; 3:78

46 Among the Jews are some who take words out of context, and say, "We hear and we disobey", and "Hear without listening", and "Observe us," twisting with their tongues and slandering the religion. Had they said, "We hear and we obey", and "Listen", and "Give us your attention," it would have been better for them, and more upright. But God has cursed them for their disbelief; they do not believe except a little.

٤٧ يَا أَيُّهَا الَّذِينَ أُوتُوا الْكِتَابَ آمِنُوا بِمَا نَزَّلْنَا مُصَدِّقًا لِّمَا مَعَكُم مِّن قَبْلِ أَن نَّطْمِسَ وُجُوهًا فَنَرُدَّهَا عَلَىٰ أَدْبَارِهَا أَوْ نَلْعَنَهُمْ كَمَا لَعَنَّا أَصْحَابَ السَّبْتِ ۚ وَكَانَ أَمْرُ اللَّهِ مَفْعُولًا

47
2:65; 5:60; 7:166

47 O you who were given the Book! Believe in what We sent down, confirming what you have, before We obliterate faces and turn them inside out, or curse them as We cursed the Sabbath-breakers. The command of God is always done.

٤٨ إِنَّ اللَّهَ لَا يَغْفِرُ أَن يُشْرَكَ بِهِ وَيَغْفِرُ مَا دُونَ ذَٰلِكَ لِمَن يَشَاءُ ۚ وَمَن يُشْرِكْ بِاللَّهِ فَقَدِ افْتَرَىٰ إِثْمًا عَظِيمًا

48
4:116; 22:31; 31:13

48 God does not forgive association with Him, but He forgives anything less than that to whomever He wills. Whoever associates anything with God has devised a monstrous sin.

٤٩ أَلَمْ تَرَ إِلَى الَّذِينَ يُزَكُّونَ أَنفُسَهُمْ ۚ بَلِ اللَّهُ يُزَكِّي مَن يَشَاءُ وَلَا يُظْلَمُونَ فَتِيلًا

49 Have you not considered those who claim purity for themselves? Rather, God purifies whom He wills, and they will not be wronged a whit.

٥٠ انظُرْ كَيْفَ يَفْتَرُونَ عَلَى اللَّهِ الْكَذِبَ ۖ وَكَفَىٰ بِهِ إِثْمًا مُّبِينًا

50 See how they devise lies against God. That alone is an outright sin.

٥١ أَلَمْ تَرَ إِلَى الَّذِينَ أُوتُوا نَصِيبًا مِّنَ الْكِتَابِ يُؤْمِنُونَ بِالْجِبْتِ وَالطَّاغُوتِ وَيَقُولُونَ لِلَّذِينَ كَفَرُوا هَٰؤُلَاءِ أَهْدَىٰ مِنَ الَّذِينَ آمَنُوا سَبِيلًا

51 Have you not considered those who were given a share of the Book? They believe in superstition and evil powers, and say of those who disbelieve, "These are better guided on the way than the believers."

٥٢ أُولَٰئِكَ الَّذِينَ لَعَنَهُمُ اللَّهُ ۖ وَمَن يَلْعَنِ اللَّهُ فَلَن تَجِدَ لَهُ نَصِيرًا

52 Those are they whom God has cursed. Whomever God curses, you will find no savior for him.

٥٣ أَمْ لَهُمْ نَصِيبٌ مِّنَ الْمُلْكِ فَإِذًا لَّا يُؤْتُونَ النَّاسَ نَقِيرًا

53 Or do they own a share of the kingdom? Then they would not give people a speck.

٥٤ أَمْ يَحْسُدُونَ النَّاسَ عَلَىٰ مَا آتَاهُمُ اللَّهُ مِن فَضْلِهِ ۖ فَقَدْ آتَيْنَا آلَ إِبْرَاهِيمَ الْكِتَابَ وَالْحِكْمَةَ وَآتَيْنَاهُم مُّلْكًا عَظِيمًا

54 2:109

54 Or do they envy the people for what God has given them of His grace? We have given the family of Abraham the Book and wisdom, and We have given them a great kingdom.

٥٥ فَمِنْهُم مَّنْ آمَنَ بِهِ وَمِنْهُم مَّن صَدَّ عَنْهُ ۚ وَكَفَىٰ بِجَهَنَّمَ سَعِيرًا

55 Among them are those who believed in it, and among them are those who held back from it. Hell is a sufficient Inferno.

٥٦ إِنَّ الَّذِينَ كَفَرُوا بِآيَاتِنَا سَوْفَ نُصْلِيهِمْ نَارًا كُلَّمَا نَضِجَتْ جُلُودُهُم بَدَّلْنَاهُمْ جُلُودًا غَيْرَهَا لِيَذُوقُوا الْعَذَابَ ۗ إِنَّ اللَّهَ كَانَ عَزِيزًا حَكِيمًا

56 4:30

56 Those who reject Our revelations—We will scorch them in a Fire. Every time their skins are cooked, We will replace them with other skins, so they will experience the suffering. God is Most Powerful, Most Wise.

٥٧ وَالَّذِينَ آمَنُوا وَعَمِلُوا الصَّالِحَاتِ سَنُدْخِلُهُمْ جَنَّاتٍ تَجْرِي مِن تَحْتِهَا الْأَنْهَارُ خَالِدِينَ فِيهَا أَبَدًا ۖ لَّهُمْ فِيهَا أَزْوَاجٌ مُّطَهَّرَةٌ ۖ وَنُدْخِلُهُمْ ظِلًّا ظَلِيلًا

57 2:25; 3:15; 13:35; 36:56; 77:41

57 As for those who believe and do good deeds, We will admit them into Gardens beneath which rivers flow, abiding therein forever. They will have purified spouses therein, and We will admit them into a shady shade.

٥٨ إِنَّ اللَّهَ يَأْمُرُكُمْ أَن تُؤَدُّوا الْأَمَانَاتِ إِلَىٰ أَهْلِهَا وَإِذَا حَكَمْتُم بَيْنَ النَّاسِ أَن تَحْكُمُوا بِالْعَدْلِ ۚ إِنَّ اللَّهَ نِعِمَّا يَعِظُكُم بِهِ ۗ إِنَّ اللَّهَ كَانَ سَمِيعًا بَصِيرًا

58 2:283; 23:8; 70:32

58 God instructs you to give back things entrusted to you to their owners. And when you judge between people, judge with justice. God's instructions to you are excellent. God is All-Hearing, All-Seeing.

٥٩ يَا أَيُّهَا الَّذِينَ آمَنُوا أَطِيعُوا اللَّهَ وَأَطِيعُوا الرَّسُولَ وَأُولِي الْأَمْرِ مِنكُمْ ۖ فَإِن تَنَازَعْتُمْ فِي شَيْءٍ فَرُدُّوهُ إِلَى اللَّهِ وَالرَّسُولِ إِن كُنتُمْ تُؤْمِنُونَ بِاللَّهِ وَالْيَوْمِ الْآخِرِ ۚ ذَٰلِكَ خَيْرٌ وَأَحْسَنُ تَأْوِيلًا

59 3:122, 152; 8:43; 42:10

59 O you who believe! Obey God and obey the Messenger and those in authority among you. And if you dispute over anything, refer it to God and the Messenger, if you believe in God and the Last Day. That is best, and a most excellent determination.

٦٠ أَلَمْ تَرَ إِلَى الَّذِينَ يَزْعُمُونَ أَنَّهُمْ آمَنُوا بِمَا أُنْزِلَ إِلَيْكَ وَمَا أُنْزِلَ مِنْ قَبْلِكَ يُرِيدُونَ أَنْ يَتَحَاكَمُوا إِلَى الطَّاغُوتِ وَقَدْ أُمِرُوا أَنْ يَكْفُرُوا بِهِ وَيُرِيدُ الشَّيْطَانُ أَنْ يُضِلَّهُمْ ضَلَالًا بَعِيدًا

60 Have you not observed those who claim that they believe in what was revealed to you, and in what was revealed before you, yet they seek Satanic sources for legislation, in spite of being commanded to reject them? Satan means to mislead them far away.

٦١ وَإِذَا قِيلَ لَهُمْ تَعَالَوْا إِلَى مَا أَنْزَلَ اللَّهُ وَإِلَى الرَّسُولِ رَأَيْتَ الْمُنَافِقِينَ يَصُدُّونَ عَنْكَ صُدُودًا | 61
| 63:5

61 And when it is said to them, "Come to what God has revealed, and to the Messenger," you see the hypocrites shunning you completely.

٦٢ فَكَيْفَ إِذَا أَصَابَتْهُمْ مُصِيبَةٌ بِمَا قَدَّمَتْ أَيْدِيهِمْ ثُمَّ جَاءُوكَ يَحْلِفُونَ بِاللَّهِ إِنْ أَرَدْنَا إِلَّا إِحْسَانًا وَتَوْفِيقًا | 62
| 9:17, 107

62 How about when a disaster strikes them because what their hands have put forward, and then they come to you swearing by God: "We only intended goodwill and reconciliation"?

٦٣ أُولَٰئِكَ الَّذِينَ يَعْلَمُ اللَّهُ مَا فِي قُلُوبِهِمْ فَأَعْرِضْ عَنْهُمْ وَعِظْهُمْ وَقُلْ لَهُمْ فِي أَنْفُسِهِمْ قَوْلًا بَلِيغًا

63 They are those whom God knows what is in their hearts. So ignore them, and admonish them, and say to them concerning themselves penetrating words.

٦٤ وَمَا أَرْسَلْنَا مِنْ رَسُولٍ إِلَّا لِيُطَاعَ بِإِذْنِ اللَّهِ ۚ وَلَوْ أَنَّهُمْ إِذْ ظَلَمُوا أَنْفُسَهُمْ جَاءُوكَ فَاسْتَغْفَرُوا اللَّهَ وَاسْتَغْفَرَ لَهُمُ الرَّسُولُ لَوَجَدُوا اللَّهَ تَوَّابًا رَحِيمًا | 64
| 3:135; 9:104; 73:20

64 We did not send any messenger except to be obeyed by God's leave. Had they, when they wronged themselves, come to you, and prayed for God's forgiveness, and the Messenger had prayed for their forgiveness, they would have found God Relenting and Merciful.

٦٥ فَلَا وَرَبِّكَ لَا يُؤْمِنُونَ حَتَّىٰ يُحَكِّمُوكَ فِيمَا شَجَرَ بَيْنَهُمْ ثُمَّ لَا يَجِدُوا فِي أَنْفُسِهِمْ حَرَجًا مِمَّا قَضَيْتَ وَيُسَلِّمُوا تَسْلِيمًا | 65
| 24:51

65 But no, by your Lord, they will not believe until they call you to arbitrate in their disputes, and then find within themselves no resentment regarding your decisions, and submit themselves completely.

٦٦ وَلَوْ أَنَّا كَتَبْنَا عَلَيْهِمْ أَنِ اقْتُلُوا أَنْفُسَكُمْ أَوِ اخْرُجُوا مِنْ دِيَارِكُمْ مَا فَعَلُوهُ إِلَّا قَلِيلٌ مِنْهُمْ ۖ وَلَوْ أَنَّهُمْ فَعَلُوا مَا يُوعَظُونَ بِهِ لَكَانَ خَيْرًا لَهُمْ وَأَشَدَّ تَثْبِيتًا

66 Had We decreed for them: "Kill yourselves," or "Leave your homes," they would not have done it, except for a few of them. But had they done what they were instructed to do, it would have been better for them, and a firmer confirmation.

٦٧ وَإِذًا لَآتَيْنَاهُمْ مِنْ لَدُنَّا أَجْرًا عَظِيمًا

67 And We would have given them from Our presence a rich compensation.

٦٨ وَلَهَدَيْنَاهُمْ صِرَاطًا مُسْتَقِيمًا

68 And We would have guided them on a straight path.

٦٩ وَمَنْ يُطِعِ اللَّهَ وَالرَّسُولَ فَأُولَٰئِكَ مَعَ الَّذِينَ أَنْعَمَ اللَّهُ عَلَيْهِمْ مِنَ النَّبِيِّينَ وَالصِّدِّيقِينَ وَالشُّهَدَاءِ وَالصَّالِحِينَ ۚ وَحَسُنَ أُولَٰئِكَ رَفِيقًا

69
4:13; 24:25; 33:71;
48:17

69 Whoever obeys God and the Messenger—these are with those whom God has blessed—among the prophets, and the sincere, and the martyrs, and the upright. Excellent are those as companions.

٧٠ ذَٰلِكَ الْفَضْلُ مِنَ اللَّهِ ۚ وَكَفَىٰ بِاللَّهِ عَلِيمًا

70 That is the grace from God. God suffices as Knower.

٧١ يَا أَيُّهَا الَّذِينَ آمَنُوا خُذُوا حِذْرَكُمْ فَانْفِرُوا ثُبَاتٍ أَوِ انْفِرُوا جَمِيعًا

71
3:120; 9:50

71 O you who believe! Take your precautions, and mobilize in groups, or mobilize altogether.

٧٢ وَإِنَّ مِنْكُمْ لَمَنْ لَيُبَطِّئَنَّ فَإِنْ أَصَابَتْكُمْ مُصِيبَةٌ قَالَ قَدْ أَنْعَمَ اللَّهُ عَلَيَّ إِذْ لَمْ أَكُنْ مَعَهُمْ شَهِيدًا

72 Among you is he who lags behind. Then, when a calamity befalls you, he says, "God has favored me, that I was not martyred with them."

٧٣ وَلَئِنْ أَصَابَكُمْ فَضْلٌ مِنَ اللَّهِ لَيَقُولَنَّ كَأَنْ لَمْ تَكُنْ بَيْنَكُمْ وَبَيْنَهُ مَوَدَّةٌ يَا لَيْتَنِي كُنْتُ مَعَهُمْ فَأَفُوزَ فَوْزًا عَظِيمًا

73 But when some bounty from God comes to you, he says—as if no affection existed between you and him—"If only I had been with them, I would have achieved a great victory."

٧٤ فَلْيُقَاتِلْ فِي سَبِيلِ اللَّهِ الَّذِينَ يَشْرُونَ الْحَيَاةَ الدُّنْيَا بِالْآخِرَةِ ۚ وَمَنْ يُقَاتِلْ فِي سَبِيلِ اللَّهِ فَيُقْتَلْ أَوْ يَغْلِبْ فَسَوْفَ نُؤْتِيهِ أَجْرًا عَظِيمًا

74
3:1120, 195; 9:50, 111

74 Let those who sell the life of this world for the Hereafter fight in the cause of God. Whoever fights in the cause of God, and then is killed, or achieves victory, We will grant him a great compensation.

٧٥ وَمَا لَكُمْ لَا تُقَاتِلُونَ فِي سَبِيلِ اللَّهِ وَالْمُسْتَضْعَفِينَ مِنَ الرِّجَالِ وَالنِّسَاءِ وَالْوِلْدَانِ الَّذِينَ يَقُولُونَ رَبَّنَا أَخْرِجْنَا مِنْ هَٰذِهِ الْقَرْيَةِ الظَّالِمِ أَهْلُهَا وَاجْعَلْ لَنَا مِنْ لَدُنْكَ وَلِيًّا وَاجْعَلْ لَنَا مِنْ لَدُنْكَ نَصِيرًا

75 And why would you not fight in the cause of God, and the helpless men, and women, and children, cry out, "Our Lord, deliver us from this town whose people are oppressive, and appoint for us from Your Presence a Protector, and appoint for us from Your Presence a Victor."

٧٦ الَّذِينَ آمَنُوا يُقَاتِلُونَ فِي سَبِيلِ اللَّهِ ۖ وَالَّذِينَ كَفَرُوا يُقَاتِلُونَ فِي سَبِيلِ الطَّاغُوتِ فَقَاتِلُوا أَوْلِيَاءَ الشَّيْطَانِ ۖ إِنَّ كَيْدَ الشَّيْطَانِ كَانَ ضَعِيفًا

76 Those who believe fight in the cause of God, while those who disbelieve fight in the cause of Evil. So fight the allies of the Devil. Surely the strategy of the Devil is weak.

٧٧ أَلَمْ تَرَ إِلَى الَّذِينَ قِيلَ لَهُمْ كُفُّوا أَيْدِيَكُمْ وَأَقِيمُوا الصَّلَاةَ وَآتُوا الزَّكَاةَ فَلَمَّا كُتِبَ عَلَيْهِمُ الْقِتَالُ إِذَا فَرِيقٌ مِنْهُمْ يَخْشَوْنَ النَّاسَ كَخَشْيَةِ اللَّهِ أَوْ أَشَدَّ خَشْيَةً ۚ وَقَالُوا رَبَّنَا لِمَ كَتَبْتَ عَلَيْنَا الْقِتَالَ لَوْلَا أَخَّرْتَنَا إِلَىٰ أَجَلٍ قَرِيبٍ ۗ قُلْ مَتَاعُ الدُّنْيَا قَلِيلٌ وَالْآخِرَةُ خَيْرٌ لِمَنِ اتَّقَىٰ وَلَا تُظْلَمُونَ فَتِيلًا

77
2:216, 246; 42:20; 93:4

77 Have you not considered those who were told, "Restrain your hands, and perform your prayers, and spend in regular charity"? But when fighting was ordained for them, a faction of them feared the people as God is ought to be feared, or even more. And they said, "Our Lord, why did You ordain fighting for us? If only You would postpone it for us for a short while." Say, "The enjoyments of this life are brief, but the Hereafter is better for the righteous, and you will not be wronged one bit."

٧٨ أَيْنَمَا تَكُونُوا يُدْرِكْكُمُ الْمَوْتُ وَلَوْ كُنْتُمْ فِي بُرُوجٍ مُشَيَّدَةٍ ۗ وَإِنْ تُصِبْهُمْ حَسَنَةٌ يَقُولُوا هَٰذِهِ مِنْ عِنْدِ اللَّهِ ۖ وَإِنْ تُصِبْهُمْ سَيِّئَةٌ يَقُولُوا هَٰذِهِ مِنْ عِنْدِكَ ۚ قُلْ كُلٌّ مِنْ عِنْدِ اللَّهِ ۖ فَمَالِ هَٰؤُلَاءِ الْقَوْمِ لَا يَكَادُونَ يَفْقَهُونَ حَدِيثًا

78
33:16; 62:8

78 Wherever you may be, death will catch up with you, even if you were in fortified towers. When a good fortune comes their way, they say, "This is from God." But when a misfortune befalls them, they say, "This is from you." Say, "All is from God." So what is the matter with these people, that they hardly understand a thing?

٧٩ مَا أَصَابَكَ مِنْ حَسَنَةٍ فَمِنَ اللَّهِ ۖ وَمَا أَصَابَكَ مِنْ سَيِّئَةٍ فَمِنْ نَفْسِكَ ۚ[a] وَأَرْسَلْنَاكَ لِلنَّاسِ رَسُولًا ۚ وَكَفَىٰ بِاللَّهِ شَهِيدًا[b]

79
[a] 57:22; 64:11
[b] 7:158; 21:107; 24:28

79 Whatever good happens to you is from God, and whatever bad happens to you is from your own self. We sent you to humanity as a messenger, and God is Witness enough.

٨٠ مَنْ يُطِعِ الرَّسُولَ فَقَدْ أَطَاعَ اللَّهَ ۖ وَمَنْ تَوَلَّىٰ فَمَا أَرْسَلْنَاكَ عَلَيْهِمْ حَفِيظًا

80
5:92; 42:48; 64:12

80 Whoever obeys the Messenger is obeying God. And whoever turns away—We did not send you as a watcher over them.

٨١ وَيَقُولُونَ طَاعَةٌ فَإِذَا بَرَزُوا مِنْ عِنْدِكَ بَيَّتَ طَائِفَةٌ مِنْهُمْ غَيْرَ الَّذِي تَقُولُ ۖ وَاللَّهُ يَكْتُبُ مَا يُبَيِّتُونَ ۖ فَأَعْرِضْ عَنْهُمْ وَتَوَكَّلْ عَلَى اللَّهِ ۚ وَكَفَىٰ بِاللَّهِ وَكِيلًا

81 They profess obedience, but when they leave your presence, some of them conspire something contrary to what you said. But God writes down what they conspire. So avoid them, and put your trust in God. God is Guardian enough.

٨٢ أَفَلَا يَتَدَبَّرُونَ الْقُرْآنَ ۚ وَلَوْ كَانَ مِنْ عِنْدِ غَيْرِ اللَّهِ لَوَجَدُوا فِيهِ اخْتِلَافًا كَثِيرًا

82
47:24

82 Do they not ponder the Qur'an? Had it been from any other than God, they would have found in it much discrepancy.

٨٣ وَإِذَا جَاءَهُمْ أَمْرٌ مِنَ الْأَمْنِ أَوِ الْخَوْفِ أَذَاعُوا بِهِ ۖ وَلَوْ رَدُّوهُ إِلَى الرَّسُولِ وَإِلَىٰ أُولِي الْأَمْرِ مِنْهُمْ لَعَلِمَهُ الَّذِينَ يَسْتَنْبِطُونَهُ مِنْهُمْ ۗ وَلَوْلَا فَضْلُ اللَّهِ عَلَيْكُمْ وَرَحْمَتُهُ لَاتَّبَعْتُمُ الشَّيْطَانَ إِلَّا قَلِيلًا

83 4:46, 59; 8:43

83 When some news of security or alarm comes their way, they broadcast it. But had they referred it to the Messenger, and to those in authority among them, those who can draw conclusions from it would have comprehended it. Were it not for God's blessing and mercy upon you, you would have followed the Devil, except for a few.

٨٤ فَقَاتِلْ فِي سَبِيلِ اللَّهِ لَا تُكَلَّفُ إِلَّا نَفْسَكَ ۚ وَحَرِّضِ الْمُؤْمِنِينَ ۖ عَسَى اللَّهُ أَنْ يَكُفَّ بَأْسَ الَّذِينَ كَفَرُوا ۚ وَاللَّهُ أَشَدُّ بَأْسًا وَأَشَدُّ تَنْكِيلًا

84 8:65

84 So fight in the cause of God; you are responsible only for yourself. And rouse the believers. Perhaps God will restrain the might of those who disbelieve. God is Stronger in Might, and More Punishing.

٨٥ مَنْ يَشْفَعْ شَفَاعَةً حَسَنَةً يَكُنْ لَهُ نَصِيبٌ مِنْهَا ۖ وَمَنْ يَشْفَعْ شَفَاعَةً سَيِّئَةً يَكُنْ لَهُ كِفْلٌ مِنْهَا ۗ وَكَانَ اللَّهُ عَلَىٰ كُلِّ شَيْءٍ مُقِيتًا

85 Whoever intercedes for a good cause has a share in it, and whoever intercedes for an evil cause shares in its burdens. God keeps watch over everything.

٨٦ وَإِذَا حُيِّيتُمْ بِتَحِيَّةٍ فَحَيُّوا بِأَحْسَنَ مِنْهَا أَوْ رُدُّوهَا ۗ إِنَّ اللَّهَ كَانَ عَلَىٰ كُلِّ شَيْءٍ حَسِيبًا

86 When you are greeted with a greeting, respond with a better greeting, or return it. God keeps count of everything.

٨٧ اللَّهُ لَا إِلَٰهَ إِلَّا هُوَ ۚ لَيَجْمَعَنَّكُمْ إِلَىٰ يَوْمِ الْقِيَامَةِ لَا رَيْبَ فِيهِ ۗ وَمَنْ أَصْدَقُ مِنَ اللَّهِ حَدِيثًا

87 3:9, 25; 6:12; 42:7; 45:26

87 God—there is no god except He. He will gather you to the Day of Resurrection, in which there is no doubt. And who speaks more truly than God?

٨٨ فَمَا لَكُمْ فِي الْمُنَافِقِينَ فِئَتَيْنِ وَاللَّهُ أَرْكَسَهُمْ بِمَا كَسَبُوا ۚ أَتُرِيدُونَ أَنْ تَهْدُوا مَنْ أَضَلَّ اللَّهُ ۖ وَمَنْ يُضْلِلِ اللَّهُ فَلَنْ تَجِدَ لَهُ سَبِيلًا

88 5:41; 7:1186

88 What is the matter with you, divided into two factions regarding the hypocrites, when God Himself has overwhelmed them on account of what they did? Do you want to guide those whom God has led astray? Whomever God leads astray—you will never find for him a way.

٨٩ وَدُّوا لَوْ تَكْفُرُونَ كَمَا كَفَرُوا فَتَكُونُونَ سَوَاءً ۖ فَلَا تَتَّخِذُوا مِنْهُمْ أَوْلِيَاءَ حَتَّىٰ يُهَاجِرُوا فِي سَبِيلِ اللَّهِ ۚ فَإِنْ تَوَلَّوْا فَخُذُوهُمْ وَاقْتُلُوهُمْ حَيْثُ وَجَدْتُمُوهُمْ ۖ وَلَا تَتَّخِذُوا مِنْهُمْ وَلِيًّا وَلَا نَصِيرًا

89 3:28; 4:139, 144; 5:51; 6:1

89 They would love to see you disbelieve, just as they disbelieve, so you would become equal. So do not befriend any of them, unless they emigrate in the way of God. If they turn away, seize them and execute them wherever you may find them; and do not take from among them allies or supporters.

٩٠ إِلَّا الَّذِينَ يَصِلُونَ إِلَىٰ قَوْمٍ بَيْنَكُمْ وَبَيْنَهُم مِّيثَاقٌ أَوْ جَاءُوكُمْ حَصِرَتْ صُدُورُهُمْ أَن يُقَاتِلُوكُمْ أَوْ يُقَاتِلُوا قَوْمَهُمْ ۚ وَلَوْ شَاءَ اللَّهُ لَسَلَّطَهُمْ عَلَيْكُمْ فَلَقَاتَلُوكُمْ ۚ فَإِنِ اعْتَزَلُوكُمْ فَلَمْ يُقَاتِلُوكُمْ وَأَلْقَوْا إِلَيْكُمُ السَّلَمَ فَمَا جَعَلَ اللَّهُ لَكُمْ عَلَيْهِمْ سَبِيلًا

90 Except those who join people with whom you have a treaty, or those who come to you reluctant to fight you or fight their own people. Had God willed, He would have given them power over you, and they would have fought you. If they withdraw from you, and do not fight you, and offer you peace, then God assigns no excuse for you against them.

٩١ سَتَجِدُونَ آخَرِينَ يُرِيدُونَ أَن يَأْمَنُوكُمْ وَيَأْمَنُوا قَوْمَهُمْ كُلَّ مَا رُدُّوا إِلَى الْفِتْنَةِ أُرْكِسُوا فِيهَا ۚ فَإِن لَّمْ يَعْتَزِلُوكُمْ وَيُلْقُوا إِلَيْكُمُ السَّلَمَ وَيَكُفُّوا أَيْدِيَهُمْ فَخُذُوهُمْ وَاقْتُلُوهُمْ حَيْثُ ثَقِفْتُمُوهُمْ ۚ وَأُولَٰئِكُمْ جَعَلْنَا لَكُمْ عَلَيْهِمْ سُلْطَانًا مُّبِينًا

91
8:57; 9:5; 33:61

91 You will find others who want security from you, and security from their own people. But whenever they are tempted into civil discord, they plunge into it. So if they do not withdraw from you, nor offer you peace, nor restrain their hands, seize them and execute them wherever you find them. Against these, We have given you clear authorization.

٩٢ وَمَا كَانَ لِمُؤْمِنٍ أَن يَقْتُلَ مُؤْمِنًا إِلَّا خَطَأً ۚ وَمَن قَتَلَ مُؤْمِنًا خَطَأً فَتَحْرِيرُ رَقَبَةٍ مُّؤْمِنَةٍ وَدِيَةٌ مُّسَلَّمَةٌ إِلَىٰ أَهْلِهِ إِلَّا أَن يَصَّدَّقُوا ۚ فَإِن كَانَ مِن قَوْمٍ عَدُوٍّ لَّكُمْ وَهُوَ مُؤْمِنٌ فَتَحْرِيرُ رَقَبَةٍ مُّؤْمِنَةٍ ۖ وَإِن كَانَ مِن قَوْمٍ بَيْنَكُمْ وَبَيْنَهُم مِّيثَاقٌ فَدِيَةٌ مُّسَلَّمَةٌ إِلَىٰ أَهْلِهِ وَتَحْرِيرُ رَقَبَةٍ مُّؤْمِنَةٍ ۖ فَمَن لَّمْ يَجِدْ فَصِيَامُ شَهْرَيْنِ مُتَتَابِعَيْنِ تَوْبَةً مِّنَ اللَّهِ ۗ وَكَانَ اللَّهُ عَلِيمًا حَكِيمًا

92 Never should a believer kill another believer, unless by error. Anyone who kills a believer by error must set free a believing slave, and pay compensation to the victim's family, unless they remit it as charity. If the victim belonged to a people who are hostile to you, but is a believer, then the compensation is to free a believing slave. If he belonged to a people with whom you have a treaty, then compensation should be handed over to his family, and a believing slave set free. Anyone who lacks the means must fast for two consecutive months, by way of repentance to God. God is All-Knowing, Most Wise.

٩٣ وَمَن يَقْتُلْ مُؤْمِنًا مُّتَعَمِّدًا فَجَزَاؤُهُ جَهَنَّمُ خَالِدًا فِيهَا وَغَضِبَ اللَّهُ عَلَيْهِ وَلَعَنَهُ وَأَعَدَّ لَهُ عَذَابًا عَظِيمًا

93 Whoever kills a believer deliberately, the penalty for him is Hell, where he will remain forever. And God will be angry with him, and will curse him, and will prepare for him a terrible punishment.

٩٤ يَا أَيُّهَا الَّذِينَ آمَنُوا إِذَا ضَرَبْتُمْ فِي سَبِيلِ اللَّهِ فَتَبَيَّنُوا وَلَا تَقُولُوا لِمَنْ أَلْقَىٰ إِلَيْكُمُ السَّلَامَ لَسْتَ مُؤْمِنًا تَبْتَغُونَ عَرَضَ الْحَيَاةِ الدُّنْيَا فَعِندَ اللَّهِ مَغَانِمُ كَثِيرَةٌ ۚ كَذَٰلِكَ كُنتُم مِّن قَبْلُ فَمَنَّ اللَّهُ عَلَيْكُمْ فَتَبَيَّنُوا ۚ إِنَّ اللَّهَ كَانَ بِمَا تَعْمَلُونَ خَبِيرًا

94
49:6

94 O you who believe! When you journey in the way of God, investigate, and do not say to him who offers you peace, "You are not a believer," aspiring for the goods of this world. With God are abundant riches. You yourselves were like this before, and God bestowed favor on you; so investigate. God is well aware of what you do.

٩٥ لَّا يَسْتَوِي الْقَاعِدُونَ مِنَ الْمُؤْمِنِينَ غَيْرُ أُولِي الضَّرَرِ وَالْمُجَاهِدُونَ فِي سَبِيلِ اللَّهِ بِأَمْوَالِهِمْ وَأَنفُسِهِمْ ۚ فَضَّلَ اللَّهُ الْمُجَاهِدِينَ بِأَمْوَالِهِمْ وَأَنفُسِهِمْ عَلَى الْقَاعِدِينَ دَرَجَةً ۚ وَكُلًّا وَعَدَ اللَّهُ الْحُسْنَىٰ ۚ وَفَضَّلَ اللَّهُ الْمُجَاهِدِينَ عَلَى الْقَاعِدِينَ أَجْرًا عَظِيمًا

95
57:10

95 Not equal are the inactive among the believers—except the disabled—and the strivers in the cause of God with their possessions and their persons. God prefers the strivers with their possessions and their persons above the inactive, by a degree. But God has promised goodness to both. Yet God favors the strivers, over the inactive, with a great reward.

٩٦ دَرَجَاتٍ مِّنْهُ وَمَغْفِرَةً وَرَحْمَةً ۚ وَكَانَ اللَّهُ غَفُورًا رَّحِيمًا

96 Degrees from Him, and forgiveness, and mercy. God is Forgiving and Merciful.

٩٧ إِنَّ الَّذِينَ تَوَفَّاهُمُ الْمَلَائِكَةُ ظَالِمِي أَنفُسِهِمْ قَالُوا فِيمَ كُنتُمْ ۖ قَالُوا كُنَّا مُسْتَضْعَفِينَ فِي الْأَرْضِ ۚ قَالُوا أَلَمْ تَكُنْ أَرْضُ اللَّهِ وَاسِعَةً فَتُهَاجِرُوا فِيهَا ۚ فَأُولَٰئِكَ مَأْوَاهُمْ جَهَنَّمُ ۖ وَسَاءَتْ مَصِيرًا

97
6:39; 8:50; 16:28

97 While the angels are removing the souls of those who have wronged themselves, they will say, "What was the matter with you?" They will say, "We were oppressed in the land." They will say, "Was God's earth not vast enough for you to emigrate in it?" These—their refuge is Hell. What a wretched retreat!

٩٨ إِلَّا الْمُسْتَضْعَفِينَ مِنَ الرِّجَالِ وَالنِّسَاءِ وَالْوِلْدَانِ لَا يَسْتَطِيعُونَ حِيلَةً وَلَا يَهْتَدُونَ سَبِيلًا

98 Except for the weak among men, and women, and children who have no means to act, and no means to find a way out.

٩٩ فَأُولَٰئِكَ عَسَى اللَّهُ أَن يَعْفُوَ عَنْهُمْ ۚ وَكَانَ اللَّهُ عَفُوًّا غَفُورًا

99 These—God may well pardon them. God is Pardoning and Forgiving.

١٠٠ وَمَن يُهَاجِرْ فِي سَبِيلِ اللَّهِ يَجِدْ فِي الْأَرْضِ مُرَاغَمًا كَثِيرًا وَسَعَةً ۚ وَمَن يَخْرُجْ مِن بَيْتِهِ مُهَاجِرًا إِلَى اللَّهِ وَرَسُولِهِ ثُمَّ يُدْرِكْهُ الْمَوْتُ فَقَدْ وَقَعَ أَجْرُهُ عَلَى اللَّهِ ۗ وَكَانَ اللَّهُ غَفُورًا رَّحِيمًا

100
22:58

100 Anyone who emigrates for the sake of God will find on earth many places of refuge, and plentitude. Anyone who leaves his home, emigrating to God and His Messenger, and then is overtaken by death, his compensation falls on God. God is Forgiver, Most Merciful.

١٠١ وَإِذَا ضَرَبْتُمْ فِي الْأَرْضِ فَلَيْسَ عَلَيْكُمْ جُنَاحٌ أَن تَقْصُرُوا مِنَ الصَّلَاةِ إِنْ خِفْتُمْ أَن يَفْتِنَكُمُ الَّذِينَ كَفَرُوا ۚ إِنَّ الْكَافِرِينَ كَانُوا لَكُمْ عَدُوًّا مُّبِينًا

101 2:273

101 When you travel in the land, there is no blame on you for shortening the prayers, if you fear that the disbelievers may harm you. The disbelievers are your manifest enemies.

١٠٢ وَإِذَا كُنتَ فِيهِمْ فَأَقَمْتَ لَهُمُ الصَّلَاةَ فَلْتَقُمْ طَائِفَةٌ مِّنْهُم مَّعَكَ وَلْيَأْخُذُوا أَسْلِحَتَهُمْ فَإِذَا سَجَدُوا فَلْيَكُونُوا مِن وَرَائِكُمْ وَلْتَأْتِ طَائِفَةٌ أُخْرَىٰ لَمْ يُصَلُّوا فَلْيُصَلُّوا مَعَكَ وَلْيَأْخُذُوا حِذْرَهُمْ وَأَسْلِحَتَهُمْ ۗ وَدَّ الَّذِينَ كَفَرُوا لَوْ تَغْفُلُونَ عَنْ أَسْلِحَتِكُمْ وَأَمْتِعَتِكُمْ فَيَمِيلُونَ عَلَيْكُم مَّيْلَةً وَاحِدَةً ۚ وَلَا جُنَاحَ عَلَيْكُمْ إِن كَانَ بِكُمْ أَذًى مِّن مَّطَرٍ أَوْ كُنتُم مَّرْضَىٰ أَن تَضَعُوا أَسْلِحَتَكُمْ ۖ وَخُذُوا حِذْرَكُمْ ۗ إِنَّ اللَّهَ أَعَدَّ لِلْكَافِرِينَ عَذَابًا مُّهِينًا

102 2:239

102 When you are among them, and you stand to lead them in prayer, let a group of them stand with you, and let them hold their weapons. Then, when they have done their prostrations, let them withdraw to the rear, and let another group, that have not prayed yet, come forward and pray with you; and let them take their precautions and their weapons. Those who disbelieve would like you to neglect your weapons and your equipment, so they can attack you in a single assault. You commit no error, if you are hampered by rain or are sick, by putting down your weapons; but take precautions. Indeed, God has prepared for the disbelievers a demeaning punishment.

١٠٣ فَإِذَا قَضَيْتُمُ الصَّلَاةَ فَاذْكُرُوا اللَّهَ قِيَامًا وَقُعُودًا وَعَلَىٰ جُنُوبِكُمْ ۚ فَإِذَا اطْمَأْنَنتُمْ فَأَقِيمُوا الصَّلَاةَ ۚ إِنَّ الصَّلَاةَ كَانَتْ عَلَى الْمُؤْمِنِينَ كِتَابًا مَّوْقُوتًا

103
[a] 3:191; 10:12
[b] 11:114; 17:78; 30:17–18; 11:114

103 When you have completed the prayer, remember God, standing, or sitting, or on your sides. And when you feel secure, perform the prayer. The prayer is obligatory for believers at specific times.

١٠٤ وَلَا تَهِنُوا فِي ابْتِغَاءِ الْقَوْمِ ۖ إِن تَكُونُوا تَأْلَمُونَ فَإِنَّهُمْ يَأْلَمُونَ كَمَا تَأْلَمُونَ ۖ وَتَرْجُونَ مِنَ اللَّهِ مَا لَا يَرْجُونَ ۗ وَكَانَ اللَّهُ عَلِيمًا حَكِيمًا

104 3:139; 47:35

104 And do not falter in the pursuit of the enemy. If you are aching, they are aching as you are aching, but you expect from God what they cannot expect. God is Knowledgeable and Wise.

١٠٥ إِنَّا أَنزَلْنَا إِلَيْكَ الْكِتَابَ بِالْحَقِّ لِتَحْكُمَ بَيْنَ النَّاسِ بِمَا أَرَاكَ اللَّهُ ۚ وَلَا تَكُن لِّلْخَائِنِينَ خَصِيمًا

105 We have revealed to you the Scripture, with the truth, so that you judge between people in accordance with what God has shown you. And do not be an advocate for the traitors.

١٠٦ وَاسْتَغْفِرِ اللَّهَ ۖ إِنَّ اللَّهَ كَانَ غَفُورًا رَّحِيمًا

106 And ask God for forgiveness. God is Forgiver and Merciful.

١٠٧ وَلَا تُجَادِلْ عَنِ الَّذِينَ يَخْتَانُونَ أَنفُسَهُمْ ۚ إِنَّ اللَّهَ لَا يُحِبُّ مَن كَانَ خَوَّانًا أَثِيمًا

107 22:38

107 And do not argue on behalf of those who deceive themselves. God does not love the deceitful sinner.

١٠٨ يَسْتَخْفُونَ مِنَ النَّاسِ وَلَا يَسْتَخْفُونَ مِنَ اللَّهِ وَهُوَ مَعَهُمْ إِذْ يُبَيِّتُونَ مَا لَا يَرْضَىٰ مِنَ الْقَوْلِ ۚ وَكَانَ اللَّهُ بِمَا يَعْمَلُونَ مُحِيطًا

108 They hide from the people, but they cannot hide from God. He is with them, as they plot by night with words He does not approve. God comprehends what they do.

١٠٩ هَا أَنْتُمْ هَٰؤُلَاءِ جَادَلْتُمْ عَنْهُمْ فِي الْحَيَاةِ الدُّنْيَا فَمَنْ يُجَادِلُ اللَّهَ عَنْهُمْ يَوْمَ الْقِيَامَةِ أَمْ مَنْ يَكُونُ عَلَيْهِمْ وَكِيلًا

109 There you are, arguing on their behalf in the present life, but who will argue with God on their behalf on the Day of Resurrection? Or who will be their representative?

١١٠ وَمَنْ يَعْمَلْ سُوءًا أَوْ يَظْلِمْ نَفْسَهُ ثُمَّ يَسْتَغْفِرِ اللَّهَ يَجِدِ اللَّهَ غَفُورًا رَحِيمًا

110
3:135; 9:104

110 Whoever commits evil, or wrongs his soul, then implores God for forgiveness, will find God Forgiving and Merciful.

١١١ وَمَنْ يَكْسِبْ إِثْمًا فَإِنَّمَا يَكْسِبُهُ عَلَىٰ نَفْسِهِ ۚ وَكَانَ اللَّهُ عَلِيمًا حَكِيمًا

111
2:286; 6:164; 41:46

111 And Whoever earns a sin, earns it against himself. God is Aware and Wise.

١١٢ وَمَنْ يَكْسِبْ خَطِيئَةً أَوْ إِثْمًا ثُمَّ يَرْمِ بِهِ بَرِيئًا فَقَدِ احْتَمَلَ بُهْتَانًا وَإِثْمًا مُبِينًا

112
33:58

112 And whoever commits a mistake, or a sin, and then blames it on an innocent person, has taken a slander and a clear sin.

١١٣ وَلَوْلَا فَضْلُ اللَّهِ عَلَيْكَ وَرَحْمَتُهُ لَهَمَّتْ طَائِفَةٌ مِنْهُمْ أَنْ يُضِلُّوكَ وَمَا يُضِلُّونَ إِلَّا أَنْفُسَهُمْ ۖ وَمَا يَضُرُّونَكَ مِنْ شَيْءٍ ۚ وَأَنْزَلَ اللَّهُ عَلَيْكَ الْكِتَابَ وَالْحِكْمَةَ وَعَلَّمَكَ مَا لَمْ تَكُنْ تَعْلَمُ ۚ وَكَانَ فَضْلُ اللَّهِ عَلَيْكَ عَظِيمًا

113
2:135; 3:100, 149; 12:3; 42:52; 96:5

113 Were it not for God's grace towards you, and His mercy, a faction of them would have managed to mislead you. But they only mislead themselves, and they cannot harm you in any way. God has revealed to you the Scripture and wisdom, and has taught you what you did not know. God's goodness towards you is great.

١١٤ لَا خَيْرَ فِي كَثِيرٍ مِنْ نَجْوَاهُمْ إِلَّا مَنْ أَمَرَ بِصَدَقَةٍ أَوْ مَعْرُوفٍ أَوْ إِصْلَاحٍ بَيْنَ النَّاسِ ۚ وَمَنْ يَفْعَلْ ذَٰلِكَ ابْتِغَاءَ مَرْضَاتِ اللَّهِ فَسَوْفَ نُؤْتِيهِ أَجْرًا عَظِيمًا

114
[a] 58:9–10
[b] 49:9–10

114 There is no good in much of their private counsels, except for him who advocates charity, or kindness, or reconciliation between people. Whoever does that, seeking God's approval, We will give him a great compensation.

١١٥ وَمَنْ يُشَاقِقِ الرَّسُولَ مِنْ بَعْدِ مَا تَبَيَّنَ لَهُ الْهُدَىٰ وَيَتَّبِعْ غَيْرَ سَبِيلِ الْمُؤْمِنِينَ نُوَلِّهِ مَا تَوَلَّىٰ وَنُصْلِهِ جَهَنَّمَ ۖ وَسَاءَتْ مَصِيرًا

115
8:13; 47:32

115 Whoever makes a breach with the Messenger, after the guidance has become clear to him, and follows other than the path of the believers, We will direct him in the direction he has chosen, and commit him to Hell—what a terrible destination!

١١٦ إِنَّ اللَّهَ لَا يَغْفِرُ أَنْ يُشْرَكَ بِهِ وَيَغْفِرُ مَا دُونَ ذَٰلِكَ لِمَنْ يَشَاءُ ۚ وَمَنْ يُشْرِكْ بِاللَّهِ فَقَدْ ضَلَّ ضَلَالًا بَعِيدًا

116
4:48

116 God will not forgive that partners be associated with Him; but will forgive anything less than that, to whomever He wills. Anyone who ascribes partners to God has strayed into far error.

١١٧ إِنْ يَدْعُونَ مِنْ دُونِهِ إِلَّا إِنَاثًا وَإِنْ يَدْعُونَ إِلَّا شَيْطَانًا مَرِيدًا

117
17:40; 37:150; 43:19

117 They invoke in His stead only females. In fact, they invoke none but a rebellious devil.

١١٨ لَعَنَهُ اللَّهُ ۘ وَقَالَ لَأَتَّخِذَنَّ مِنْ عِبَادِكَ نَصِيبًا مَفْرُوضًا

118 God has cursed him. And he said, "I will take to myself my due share of Your servants."

١١٩ وَلَأُضِلَّنَّهُمْ وَلَأُمَنِّيَنَّهُمْ وَلَآمُرَنَّهُمْ فَلَيُبَتِّكُنَّ آذَانَ الْأَنْعَامِ وَلَآمُرَنَّهُمْ فَلَيُغَيِّرُنَّ خَلْقَ اللَّهِ ۚ وَمَنْ يَتَّخِذِ الشَّيْطَانَ وَلِيًّا مِنْ دُونِ اللَّهِ فَقَدْ خَسِرَ خُسْرَانًا مُبِينًا

119
2:257; 13:16; 29:41; 39:3; 45:19

119 "And I will mislead them, and I will entice them, and I will prompt them to slit the ears of cattle, and I will prompt them to alter the creation of God." Whoever takes Satan as a lord, instead of God, has surely suffered a profound loss.

١٢٠ يَعِدُهُمْ وَيُمَنِّيهِمْ ۖ وَمَا يَعِدُهُمُ الشَّيْطَانُ إِلَّا غُرُورًا

120
14:22; 17:19

120 He promises them, and he raises their expectations, but Satan promises them nothing but delusions.

١٢١ أُولَٰئِكَ مَأْوَاهُمْ جَهَنَّمُ وَلَا يَجِدُونَ عَنْهَا مَحِيصًا

121 These—their place is Hell, and they will find no escape from it.

١٢٢ وَالَّذِينَ آمَنُوا وَعَمِلُوا الصَّالِحَاتِ سَنُدْخِلُهُمْ جَنَّاتٍ تَجْرِي مِنْ تَحْتِهَا الْأَنْهَارُ خَالِدِينَ فِيهَا أَبَدًا ۖ وَعْدَ اللَّهِ حَقًّا ۚ وَمَنْ أَصْدَقُ مِنَ اللَّهِ قِيلًا

122
2:62; 4:124; 5:69; 31:8–9

122 But as for those who believe and do righteous deeds, We will admit them into gardens beneath which rivers flow, where they will abide forever. The promise of God is true—and who is more truthful in speech than God?

١٢٣ لَيْسَ بِأَمَانِيِّكُمْ وَلَا أَمَانِيِّ أَهْلِ الْكِتَابِ ۗ مَنْ يَعْمَلْ سُوءًا يُجْزَ بِهِ وَلَا يَجِدْ لَهُ مِنْ دُونِ اللَّهِ وَلِيًّا وَلَا نَصِيرًا

123
2:111; 6:70; 10:4

123 It is not in accordance with your wishes, nor in accordance with the wishes of the People of the Scripture. Whoever works evil will pay for it, and will not find for himself, besides God, any protector or savior.

١٢٤ وَمَنْ يَعْمَلْ مِنَ الصَّالِحَاتِ مِنْ ذَكَرٍ أَوْ أُنْثَىٰ وَهُوَ مُؤْمِنٌ فَأُولَٰئِكَ يَدْخُلُونَ الْجَنَّةَ وَلَا يُظْلَمُونَ نَقِيرًا

124
2:62; 4:122; 5:69; 16:97; 31:8–9 21

124 But whoever works righteousness, whether male or female, and is a believer—those will enter Paradise, and will not be wronged a whit.

١٢٥ وَمَنْ أَحْسَنُ دِينًا مِمَّنْ أَسْلَمَ وَجْهَهُ لِلَّهِ وَهُوَ مُحْسِنٌ وَاتَّبَعَ مِلَّةَ إِبْرَاهِيمَ حَنِيفًا ۗ وَاتَّخَذَ اللَّهُ إِبْرَاهِيمَ خَلِيلًا

125 2:112; 31:22

125 And who is better in religion than he who submits himself wholly to God, and is a doer of good, and follows the faith of Abraham the Monotheist? God has chosen Abraham for a friend.

١٢٦ وَلِلَّهِ مَا فِي السَّمَاوَاتِ وَمَا فِي الْأَرْضِ ۚ وَكَانَ اللَّهُ بِكُلِّ شَيْءٍ مُحِيطًا

126 To God belongs what is in the heavens and what is on earth, and God encompasses everything.

١٢٧ وَيَسْتَفْتُونَكَ فِي النِّسَاءِ ۖ قُلِ اللَّهُ يُفْتِيكُمْ فِيهِنَّ وَمَا يُتْلَىٰ عَلَيْكُمْ فِي الْكِتَابِ فِي يَتَامَى النِّسَاءِ اللَّاتِي لَا تُؤْتُونَهُنَّ مَا كُتِبَ لَهُنَّ وَتَرْغَبُونَ أَنْ تَنْكِحُوهُنَّ وَالْمُسْتَضْعَفِينَ مِنَ الْوِلْدَانِ وَأَنْ تَقُومُوا لِلْيَتَامَىٰ بِالْقِسْطِ ۚ وَمَا تَفْعَلُوا مِنْ خَيْرٍ فَإِنَّ اللَّهَ كَانَ بِهِ عَلِيمًا

127 4:2–3; 6:152; 17:34; 89:19

127 They ask you for a ruling about women. Say, "God gives you a ruling about them, and so does what is stated to you in the Book about widowed women from whom you withhold what is decreed for them, yet you desire to marry them, and about helpless children: that you should treat the orphans fairly." Whatever good you do, God knows it.

١٢٨ وَإِنِ امْرَأَةٌ خَافَتْ مِنْ بَعْلِهَا نُشُوزًا أَوْ إِعْرَاضًا فَلَا جُنَاحَ عَلَيْهِمَا أَنْ يُصْلِحَا بَيْنَهُمَا صُلْحًا ۚ وَالصُّلْحُ خَيْرٌ ۗ وَأُحْضِرَتِ الْأَنْفُسُ الشُّحَّ ۚ وَإِنْ تُحْسِنُوا وَتَتَّقُوا فَإِنَّ اللَّهَ كَانَ بِمَا تَعْمَلُونَ خَبِيرًا

128 4:34, 130

128 If a woman fears maltreatment or desertion from her husband, there is no fault in them if they reconcile their differences, for reconciliation is best. Souls are prone to avarice; yet if you do what is good, and practice piety—God is Cognizant of what you do.

١٢٩ وَلَنْ تَسْتَطِيعُوا أَنْ تَعْدِلُوا بَيْنَ النِّسَاءِ وَلَوْ حَرَصْتُمْ ۖ فَلَا تَمِيلُوا كُلَّ الْمَيْلِ فَتَذَرُوهَا كَالْمُعَلَّقَةِ ۚ وَإِنْ تُصْلِحُوا وَتَتَّقُوا فَإِنَّ اللَّهَ كَانَ غَفُورًا رَحِيمًا

129 4:3, 24

129 You will not be able to treat women with equal fairness, no matter how much you desire it. But do not be so biased as to leave another suspended. If you make amends, and act righteously—God is Forgiving and Merciful.

١٣٠ وَإِنْ يَتَفَرَّقَا يُغْنِ اللَّهُ كُلًّا مِنْ سَعَتِهِ ۚ وَكَانَ اللَّهُ وَاسِعًا حَكِيمًا

130 4:34, 130

130 And if they separate, God will enrich each from His abundance. God is Bounteous and Wise.

١٣١ وَلِلَّهِ مَا فِي السَّمَاوَاتِ وَمَا فِي الْأَرْضِ ۗ وَلَقَدْ وَصَّيْنَا الَّذِينَ أُوتُوا الْكِتَابَ مِنْ قَبْلِكُمْ وَإِيَّاكُمْ أَنِ اتَّقُوا اللَّهَ ۚ وَإِنْ تَكْفُرُوا فَإِنَّ لِلَّهِ مَا فِي السَّمَاوَاتِ وَمَا فِي الْأَرْضِ ۚ وَكَانَ اللَّهُ غَنِيًّا حَمِيدًا

131 3:97; 4:170; 14:8; 27:40

131 To God belongs everything in the heavens and everything on earth. We have instructed those who were given the Book before you, and you, to be conscious of God. But if you refuse—to God belongs everything in the heavens and everything on earth. God is in no need, Praiseworthy.

١٣٢ وَلِلَّهِ مَا فِي السَّمَاوَاتِ وَمَا فِي الْأَرْضِ ۚ وَكَفَىٰ بِاللَّهِ وَكِيلًا

132
24:32

132 To God belongs everything in the heavens and everything on earth. God suffices as Manager.

١٣٣ إِنْ يَشَأْ يُذْهِبْكُمْ أَيُّهَا النَّاسُ وَيَأْتِ بِآخَرِينَ ۚ وَكَانَ اللَّهُ عَلَىٰ ذَٰلِكَ قَدِيرًا

133
6:133; 14:19–20; 35:16; 47:38

133 If He wills, He can do away with you, O people, and bring others. God is Able to do that.

١٣٤ مَنْ كَانَ يُرِيدُ ثَوَابَ الدُّنْيَا فَعِنْدَ اللَّهِ ثَوَابُ الدُّنْيَا وَالْآخِرَةِ ۚ وَكَانَ اللَّهُ سَمِيعًا بَصِيرًا

134 Whoever desires the reward of this world—with God is the reward of this world and the next. God is All-Hearing, All-Seeing.

١٣٥ يَا أَيُّهَا الَّذِينَ آمَنُوا كُونُوا قَوَّامِينَ بِالْقِسْطِ شُهَدَاءَ لِلَّهِ وَلَوْ عَلَىٰ أَنْفُسِكُمْ أَوِ الْوَالِدَيْنِ وَالْأَقْرَبِينَ ۚ إِنْ يَكُنْ غَنِيًّا أَوْ فَقِيرًا فَاللَّهُ أَوْلَىٰ بِهِمَا ۖ فَلَا تَتَّبِعُوا الْهَوَىٰ أَنْ تَعْدِلُوا ۚ وَإِنْ تَلْوُوا أَوْ تُعْرِضُوا فَإِنَّ اللَّهَ كَانَ بِمَا تَعْمَلُونَ خَبِيرًا

135
5:8; 22:32, 36

135 O you who believe! Stand firmly for justice, as witnesses to God, even if against yourselves, or your parents, or your relatives. Whether one is rich or poor, God takes care of both. So do not follow your desires, lest you swerve. If you deviate, or turn away—then God is Aware of what you do.

١٣٦ يَا أَيُّهَا الَّذِينَ آمَنُوا آمِنُوا بِاللَّهِ وَرَسُولِهِ وَالْكِتَابِ الَّذِي نَزَّلَ عَلَىٰ رَسُولِهِ وَالْكِتَابِ الَّذِي أَنْزَلَ مِنْ قَبْلُ ۚ وَمَنْ يَكْفُرْ بِاللَّهِ وَمَلَائِكَتِهِ وَكُتُبِهِ وَرُسُلِهِ وَالْيَوْمِ الْآخِرِ فَقَدْ ضَلَّ ضَلَالًا بَعِيدًا

136
2:177, 285

136 O you who believe! Believe in God and His messenger, and the Book He sent down to His messenger, and the Book He sent down before. Whoever rejects God, His angels, His Books, His messengers, and the Last Day, has strayed far in error.

١٣٧ إِنَّ الَّذِينَ آمَنُوا ثُمَّ كَفَرُوا ثُمَّ آمَنُوا ثُمَّ كَفَرُوا ثُمَّ ازْدَادُوا كُفْرًا لَمْ يَكُنِ اللَّهُ لِيَغْفِرَ لَهُمْ وَلَا لِيَهْدِيَهُمْ سَبِيلًا

137
3:90; 4:168

137 Those who believe, then disbelieve, then believe, then disbelieve, then increase in disbelief, God will not forgive them, nor will He guide them to a way.

١٣٨ بَشِّرِ الْمُنَافِقِينَ بِأَنَّ لَهُمْ عَذَابًا أَلِيمًا

138 Inform the hypocrites that they will have a painful punishment.

١٣٩ الَّذِينَ يَتَّخِذُونَ الْكَافِرِينَ أَوْلِيَاءَ مِنْ دُونِ الْمُؤْمِنِينَ ۚ أَيَبْتَغُونَ عِنْدَهُمُ الْعِزَّةَ فَإِنَّ الْعِزَّةَ لِلَّهِ جَمِيعًا

139
3:28; 4:89, 144; 5:51; 6:1

139 Those who ally themselves with the disbelievers instead of the believers. Do they seek glory in them? All glory belongs to God.

١٤٠ وَقَدْ نَزَّلَ عَلَيْكُمْ فِي الْكِتَابِ أَنْ إِذَا سَمِعْتُمْ آيَاتِ اللَّهِ يُكْفَرُ بِهَا وَيُسْتَهْزَأُ بِهَا فَلَا تَقْعُدُوا مَعَهُمْ حَتَّىٰ يَخُوضُوا فِي حَدِيثٍ غَيْرِهِ ۚ إِنَّكُمْ إِذًا مِثْلُهُمْ ۗ إِنَّ اللَّهَ جَامِعُ الْمُنَافِقِينَ وَالْكَافِرِينَ فِي جَهَنَّمَ جَمِيعًا

140
6:68, 91; 9:65; 43:83

140 He has revealed to you in the Book that when you hear God's revelations being rejected, or ridiculed, do not sit with them until they engage in some other subject. Otherwise, you would be like them. God will gather the hypocrites and the disbelievers, into Hell, altogether.

١٤١ الَّذِينَ يَتَرَبَّصُونَ بِكُمْ فَإِنْ كَانَ لَكُمْ فَتْحٌ مِنَ اللَّهِ قَالُوا أَلَمْ نَكُنْ مَعَكُمْ وَإِنْ كَانَ لِلْكَافِرِينَ نَصِيبٌ قَالُوا أَلَمْ نَسْتَحْوِذْ عَلَيْكُمْ وَنَمْنَعْكُمْ مِنَ الْمُؤْمِنِينَ ۚ فَاللَّهُ يَحْكُمُ بَيْنَكُمْ يَوْمَ الْقِيَامَةِ ۗ وَلَنْ يَجْعَلَ اللَّهُ لِلْكَافِرِينَ عَلَى الْمُؤْمِنِينَ سَبِيلًا

141
29:10; 30:47; 57:4

141 Those who lie in wait for you: if you attain victory from God, they say, "Were we not with you?" But if the disbelievers get a turn, they say, "Did we not side with you, and defend you from the believers?" God will judge between you on the Day of Resurrection; and God will give the disbelievers no means of overcoming the believers.

١٤٢ إِنَّ الْمُنَافِقِينَ يُخَادِعُونَ اللَّهَ وَهُوَ خَادِعُهُمْ ᵃ وَإِذَا قَامُوا إِلَى الصَّلَاةِ قَامُوا كُسَالَىٰ يُرَاءُونَ النَّاسَ وَلَا يَذْكُرُونَ اللَّهَ إِلَّا قَلِيلًا ᵇ

142
ᵃ 2:9
ᵇ 9:54; 107:4

142 The hypocrites try to deceive God, but He is deceiving them. And when they stand for prayer, they stand lazily, showing off in front of people, and remembering God only a little.

١٤٣ مُذَبْذَبِينَ بَيْنَ ذَٰلِكَ لَا إِلَىٰ هَٰؤُلَاءِ وَلَا إِلَىٰ هَٰؤُلَاءِ ۚ وَمَنْ يُضْلِلِ اللَّهُ فَلَنْ تَجِدَ لَهُ سَبِيلًا

143 Wavering in between, neither with these, nor with those. Whomever God sends astray, you will never find for him a way.

١٤٤ يَا أَيُّهَا الَّذِينَ آمَنُوا لَا تَتَّخِذُوا الْكَافِرِينَ أَوْلِيَاءَ مِنْ دُونِ الْمُؤْمِنِينَ ۚ أَتُرِيدُونَ أَنْ تَجْعَلُوا لِلَّهِ عَلَيْكُمْ سُلْطَانًا مُبِينًا

144
3:28; 4:89, 139; 5:51; 6:1

144 O you who believe! Do not befriend disbelievers rather than believers. Do you want to give God a clear case against you?

١٤٥ إِنَّ الْمُنَافِقِينَ فِي الدَّرْكِ الْأَسْفَلِ مِنَ النَّارِ وَلَنْ تَجِدَ لَهُمْ نَصِيرًا

145
5:115

145 The hypocrites will be in the lowest level of the Fire, and you will find no helper for them.

١٤٦ إِلَّا الَّذِينَ تَابُوا وَأَصْلَحُوا وَاعْتَصَمُوا بِاللَّهِ وَأَخْلَصُوا دِينَهُمْ لِلَّهِ فَأُولَٰئِكَ مَعَ الْمُؤْمِنِينَ ۖ وَسَوْفَ يُؤْتِ اللَّهُ الْمُؤْمِنِينَ أَجْرًا عَظِيمًا

146
3:89

146 Except those who repent, and reform, and hold fast to God, and dedicate their religion to God alone. These are with the believers; and God will give the believers a great reward.

١٤٧ مَا يَفْعَلُ اللَّهُ بِعَذَابِكُمْ إِنْ شَكَرْتُمْ وَآمَنْتُمْ ۚ وَكَانَ اللَّهُ شَاكِرًا عَلِيمًا

147 What would God accomplish by your punishment, if you have given thanks, and have believed? God is Appreciative and Cognizant.

١٤٨ لَا يُحِبُّ اللَّهُ الْجَهْرَ بِالسُّوءِ مِنَ الْقَوْلِ إِلَّا مَنْ ظُلِمَ ۚ وَكَانَ اللَّهُ سَمِيعًا عَلِيمًا

148 God does not like the public uttering of bad language, unless someone was wronged. God is Hearing and Knowing.

١٤٩ إِنْ تُبْدُوا خَيْرًا أَوْ تُخْفُوهُ أَوْ تَعْفُوا عَنْ سُوءٍ فَإِنَّ اللَّهَ كَانَ عَفُوًّا قَدِيرًا

149 If you let a good deed be shown, or conceal it, or pardon an offense—God is Pardoning and Capable.

١٥٠ إِنَّ الَّذِينَ يَكْفُرُونَ بِاللَّهِ وَرُسُلِهِ وَيُرِيدُونَ أَن يُفَرِّقُوا بَيْنَ اللَّهِ وَرُسُلِهِ وَيَقُولُونَ نُؤْمِنُ بِبَعْضٍ وَنَكْفُرُ بِبَعْضٍ وَيُرِيدُونَ أَن يَتَّخِذُوا بَيْنَ ذَٰلِكَ سَبِيلًا

150 Those who disbelieve in God and His messengers, and want to separate between God and His messengers, and say, "We believe in some, and reject some," and wish to take a path in between.

١٥١ أُولَٰئِكَ هُمُ الْكَافِرُونَ حَقًّا ۚ وَأَعْتَدْنَا لِلْكَافِرِينَ عَذَابًا مُّهِينًا

151 These are the unbelievers, truly. We have prepared for the unbelievers a shameful punishment.

١٥٢ وَالَّذِينَ آمَنُوا بِاللَّهِ وَرُسُلِهِ وَلَمْ يُفَرِّقُوا بَيْنَ أَحَدٍ مِّنْهُمْ أُولَٰئِكَ سَوْفَ يُؤْتِيهِمْ أُجُورَهُمْ ۗ وَكَانَ اللَّهُ غَفُورًا رَّحِيمًا

152
2:136, 285; 3:84

152 As for those who believe in God and His messengers, and make no distinction between any of them—He will give them their rewards. God is Forgiver and Merciful.

١٥٣ يَسْأَلُكَ أَهْلُ الْكِتَابِ أَن تُنَزِّلَ عَلَيْهِمْ كِتَابًا مِّنَ السَّمَاءِ ۚ [a] فَقَدْ سَأَلُوا مُوسَىٰ أَكْبَرَ مِن ذَٰلِكَ فَقَالُوا أَرِنَا اللَّهَ جَهْرَةً فَأَخَذَتْهُمُ الصَّاعِقَةُ بِظُلْمِهِمْ ۚ ثُمَّ اتَّخَذُوا الْعِجْلَ مِن بَعْدِ مَا جَاءَتْهُمُ الْبَيِّنَاتُ فَعَفَوْنَا عَن ذَٰلِكَ ۚ وَآتَيْنَا مُوسَىٰ سُلْطَانًا مُّبِينًا [b]

153
[a] 6:7; 10:76; 15:14; 17:93
[b] 2:51, 92; 7:148; 20:85–98

153 The People of the Scripture challenge you to bring down to them a book from the sky. They had asked Moses for something even greater. They said, "Show us God plainly." The thunderbolt struck them for their wickedness. Then they took the calf for worship, even after the clear proofs had come to them. Yet We pardoned that, and We gave Moses a clear authority.

١٥٤ وَرَفَعْنَا فَوْقَهُمُ الطُّورَ بِمِيثَاقِهِمْ وَقُلْنَا لَهُمُ ادْخُلُوا الْبَابَ سُجَّدًا وَقُلْنَا لَهُمْ لَا تَعْدُوا فِي السَّبْتِ وَأَخَذْنَا مِنْهُم مِّيثَاقًا غَلِيظًا

154
2:63, 93; 7:163, 171

154 And We raised the Mount above them in accordance with their covenant, and We said to them, "Enter the gate humbly", and We said to them, "Do not violate the Sabbath", and We received from them a solemn pledge.

١٥٥ فَبِمَا نَقْضِهِم مِّيثَاقَهُمْ وَكُفْرِهِم بِآيَاتِ اللَّهِ [a] وَقَتْلِهِمُ الْأَنبِيَاءَ بِغَيْرِ حَقٍّ [b] وَقَوْلِهِمْ قُلُوبُنَا غُلْفٌ [c] ۚ بَلْ طَبَعَ اللَّهُ عَلَيْهَا بِكُفْرِهِمْ فَلَا يُؤْمِنُونَ إِلَّا قَلِيلًا

155
[a] 5:13
[b] 2:61, 91; 3:112, 181
[c] 2:88

155 But for their violation of their covenant, and their denial of God's revelations, and their killing of the prophets unjustly, and their saying, "Our minds are closed." In fact, God has sealed them for their disbelief, so they do not believe, except for a few.

١٥٦ وَبِكُفْرِهِمْ وَقَوْلِهِمْ عَلَىٰ مَرْيَمَ بُهْتَانًا عَظِيمًا

156
19:19, 27

156 And for their faithlessness, and their saying against Mary a monstrous slander.

١٥٧ وَقَوْلِهِمْ إِنَّا قَتَلْنَا الْمَسِيحَ عِيسَى ابْنَ مَرْيَمَ رَسُولَ اللَّهِ وَمَا قَتَلُوهُ وَمَا صَلَبُوهُ وَلَٰكِن شُبِّهَ لَهُمْ ۚ وَإِنَّ الَّذِينَ اخْتَلَفُوا فِيهِ لَفِي شَكٍّ مِّنْهُ ۚ مَا لَهُم بِهِ مِنْ عِلْمٍ إِلَّا اتِّبَاعَ الظَّنِّ ۚ وَمَا قَتَلُوهُ يَقِينًا

157 And for their saying, "We have killed the Messiah, Jesus, the son of Mary, the Messenger of God." In fact, they did not kill him, nor did they crucify him, but it appeared to them as if they did. Indeed, those who differ about him are in doubt about it. They have no knowledge of it, except the following of assumptions. Certainly, they did not kill him.

١٥٨ بَل رَّفَعَهُ اللَّهُ إِلَيْهِ ۚ وَكَانَ اللَّهُ عَزِيزًا حَكِيمًا

158 Rather, God raised him up to Himself. God is Mighty and Wise.

158
3:55; 19:33

١٥٩ وَإِن مِّنْ أَهْلِ الْكِتَابِ إِلَّا لَيُؤْمِنَنَّ بِهِ قَبْلَ مَوْتِهِ ۖ وَيَوْمَ الْقِيَامَةِ يَكُونُ عَلَيْهِمْ شَهِيدًا

159 There is none from the People of the Scripture but will believe in him before his death, and on the Day of Resurrection he will be a witness against them.

159
3:55; 5:117

١٦٠ فَبِظُلْمٍ مِّنَ الَّذِينَ هَادُوا حَرَّمْنَا عَلَيْهِمْ طَيِّبَاتٍ أُحِلَّتْ لَهُمْ وَبِصَدِّهِمْ عَن سَبِيلِ اللَّهِ كَثِيرًا

160 Due to wrongdoing on the part of the Jews, We forbade them good things that used to be lawful for them; and for deterring many from God's path.

160
3:93; 6:146; 16:118

١٦١ وَأَخْذِهِمُ الرِّبَا وَقَدْ نُهُوا عَنْهُ وَأَكْلِهِمْ أَمْوَالَ النَّاسِ بِالْبَاطِلِ ۚ وَأَعْتَدْنَا لِلْكَافِرِينَ مِنْهُمْ عَذَابًا أَلِيمًا

161 And for their taking usury, although they were forbidden it; and for their consuming people's wealth dishonestly. We have prepared for the faithless among them a painful torment.

161
2: 275–278

١٦٢ لَّٰكِنِ الرَّاسِخُونَ فِي الْعِلْمِ مِنْهُمْ وَالْمُؤْمِنُونَ يُؤْمِنُونَ بِمَا أُنزِلَ إِلَيْكَ وَمَا أُنزِلَ مِن قَبْلِكَ ۚ وَالْمُقِيمِينَ الصَّلَاةَ ۚ وَالْمُؤْتُونَ الزَّكَاةَ وَالْمُؤْمِنُونَ بِاللَّهِ وَالْيَوْمِ الْآخِرِ أُولَٰئِكَ سَنُؤْتِيهِمْ أَجْرًا عَظِيمًا

162 But those among them firmly rooted in knowledge, and the believers, believe in what was revealed to you, and in what was revealed before you; and the observers of prayers, and the givers of charity, and the believers in God and the Last Day—upon these We will bestow an immense reward.

162
3:7

١٦٣ إِنَّا أَوْحَيْنَا إِلَيْكَ كَمَا أَوْحَيْنَا إِلَىٰ نُوحٍ وَالنَّبِيِّينَ مِن بَعْدِهِ ۚ وَأَوْحَيْنَا إِلَىٰ إِبْرَاهِيمَ وَإِسْمَاعِيلَ وَإِسْحَاقَ وَيَعْقُوبَ وَالْأَسْبَاطِ وَعِيسَىٰ وَأَيُّوبَ وَيُونُسَ وَهَارُونَ وَسُلَيْمَانَ ۚ وَآتَيْنَا دَاوُودَ زَبُورًا

163 We have inspired you, as We had inspired Noah and the prophets after him. And We inspired Abraham, and Ishmael, and Isaac, and Jacob, and the Patriarchs, and Jesus, and Job, and Jonah, and Aaron, and Solomon. And We gave David the Psalms.

١٦٤ وَرُسُلًا قَدْ قَصَصْنَاهُمْ عَلَيْكَ مِنْ قَبْلُ وَرُسُلًا لَمْ نَقْصُصْهُمْ عَلَيْكَ ۚ وَكَلَّمَ اللَّهُ مُوسَىٰ تَكْلِيمًا

164 Some messengers We have already told you about, while some messengers We have not told you about. And God spoke to Moses directly.

164
2:253; 40:78

١٦٥ رُسُلًا مُبَشِّرِينَ وَمُنْذِرِينَ لِئَلَّا يَكُونَ لِلنَّاسِ عَلَى اللَّهِ حُجَّةٌ بَعْدَ الرُّسُلِ ۚ وَكَانَ اللَّهُ عَزِيزًا حَكِيمًا

165 Messengers delivering good news, and bringing warnings; so that people may have no excuse before God after the coming of the messengers. God is Powerful and Wise.

١٦٦ لَٰكِنِ اللَّهُ يَشْهَدُ بِمَا أَنْزَلَ إِلَيْكَ ۖ أَنْزَلَهُ بِعِلْمِهِ ۖ وَالْمَلَائِكَةُ يَشْهَدُونَ ۚ وَكَفَىٰ بِاللَّهِ شَهِيدًا

166 But God bears witness to what He revealed to you. He revealed it with His knowledge. And the angels bear witness. Though God is a sufficient witness.

166
3:18; 13:43; 16:43

١٦٧ إِنَّ الَّذِينَ كَفَرُوا وَصَدُّوا عَنْ سَبِيلِ اللَّهِ قَدْ ضَلُّوا ضَلَالًا بَعِيدًا

167 Those who disbelieve and repel from God's path have gone far astray.

١٦٨ إِنَّ الَّذِينَ كَفَرُوا وَظَلَمُوا لَمْ يَكُنِ اللَّهُ لِيَغْفِرَ لَهُمْ وَلَا لِيَهْدِيَهُمْ طَرِيقًا

168 Those who disbelieve and transgress; God is not about to forgive them, nor will He guide them to any path.

168
3:90; 4:137

١٦٩ إِلَّا طَرِيقَ جَهَنَّمَ خَالِدِينَ فِيهَا أَبَدًا ۚ وَكَانَ ذَٰلِكَ عَلَى اللَّهِ يَسِيرًا

169 Except to the path of Hell, where they will dwell forever. And that is easy for God.

169
4:30; 22:70

١٧٠ يَا أَيُّهَا النَّاسُ قَدْ جَاءَكُمُ الرَّسُولُ بِالْحَقِّ مِنْ رَبِّكُمْ فَآمِنُوا خَيْرًا لَكُمْ ۚ وَإِنْ تَكْفُرُوا فَإِنَّ لِلَّهِ مَا فِي السَّمَاوَاتِ وَالْأَرْضِ ۚ وَكَانَ اللَّهُ عَلِيمًا حَكِيمًا

170 O people! The Messenger has come to you with the truth from your Lord, so believe—that is best for you. But if you disbelieve, to God belongs everything in the heavens and the earth. God is Omniscient and Wise.

١٧١ يَا أَهْلَ الْكِتَابِ لَا تَغْلُوا فِي دِينِكُمْ وَلَا تَقُولُوا عَلَى اللَّهِ إِلَّا الْحَقَّ ۚ إِنَّمَا الْمَسِيحُ عِيسَى ابْنُ مَرْيَمَ رَسُولُ اللَّهِ وَكَلِمَتُهُ أَلْقَاهَا إِلَىٰ مَرْيَمَ وَرُوحٌ مِنْهُ ۖ فَآمِنُوا بِاللَّهِ وَرُسُلِهِ ۖ وَلَا تَقُولُوا ثَلَاثَةٌ ۚ انْتَهُوا خَيْرًا لَكُمْ ۚ إِنَّمَا اللَّهُ إِلَٰهٌ وَاحِدٌ ۖ سُبْحَانَهُ أَنْ يَكُونَ لَهُ وَلَدٌ ۘ لَهُ مَا فِي السَّمَاوَاتِ وَمَا فِي الْأَرْضِ ۗ وَكَفَىٰ بِاللَّهِ وَكِيلًا

171
2:171; 5:73, 77, 116; 6:100; 10:68; 17:40, 111; 19:35; 21:26; 23:91; 25:2

171 O People of the Scripture! Do not exaggerate in your religion, and do not say about God except the truth. The Messiah, Jesus, the son of Mary, is the Messenger of God, and His Word that He conveyed to Mary, and a Spirit from Him. So believe in God and His messengers, and do not say, "Three." Refrain—it is better for you. God is only one God. Glory be to Him—that He should have a son. To Him belongs everything in the heavens and the earth, and God is a sufficient Protector.

	172
١٧٢ لَنْ يَسْتَنْكِفَ الْمَسِيحُ أَنْ يَكُونَ عَبْدًا لِلَّهِ وَلَا الْمَلَائِكَةُ الْمُقَرَّبُونَ ۚ وَمَنْ يَسْتَنْكِفْ عَنْ عِبَادَتِهِ وَيَسْتَكْبِرْ فَسَيَحْشُرُهُمْ إِلَيْهِ جَمِيعًا	5:17, 72

172 The Messiah does not disdain to be a servant of God, nor do the favored angels. Whoever disdains His worship, and is too arrogant—He will round them up to Himself altogether.

	173
١٧٣ فَأَمَّا الَّذِينَ آمَنُوا وَعَمِلُوا الصَّالِحَاتِ فَيُوَفِّيهِمْ أُجُورَهُمْ وَيَزِيدُهُمْ مِنْ فَضْلِهِ ۖ وَأَمَّا الَّذِينَ اسْتَنْكَفُوا وَاسْتَكْبَرُوا فَيُعَذِّبُهُمْ عَذَابًا أَلِيمًا وَلَا يَجِدُونَ لَهُمْ مِنْ دُونِ اللَّهِ وَلِيًّا وَلَا نَصِيرًا	3:56; 5:9–10; 35:30

173 But as for those who believe and do good works, He will pay them their wages in full, and will increase His grace for them. But as for those who disdain and are too proud, He will punish them with an agonizing punishment. And they will find for themselves, apart from God, no lord and no savior.

	174
١٧٤ يَا أَيُّهَا النَّاسُ قَدْ جَاءَكُمْ بُرْهَانٌ مِنْ رَبِّكُمْ وَأَنْزَلْنَا إِلَيْكُمْ نُورًا مُبِينًا	2:201; 7:157; 42:52

174 O people! A proof has come to you from your Lord, and We sent down to you a clear light.

	175
١٧٥ فَأَمَّا الَّذِينَ آمَنُوا بِاللَّهِ وَاعْتَصَمُوا بِهِ فَسَيُدْخِلُهُمْ فِي رَحْمَةٍ مِنْهُ وَفَضْلٍ وَيَهْدِيهِمْ إِلَيْهِ صِرَاطًا مُسْتَقِيمًا	3:101, 103; 4:146; 22:78

175 As for those who believe in God, and hold fast to Him, He will admit them into mercy and grace from Him, and will guide them to Himself in a straight path.

	176
١٧٦ يَسْتَفْتُونَكَ قُلِ اللَّهُ يُفْتِيكُمْ فِي الْكَلَالَةِ ۚ إِنِ امْرُؤٌ هَلَكَ لَيْسَ لَهُ وَلَدٌ وَلَهُ أُخْتٌ فَلَهَا نِصْفُ مَا تَرَكَ ۚ وَهُوَ يَرِثُهَا إِنْ لَمْ يَكُنْ لَهَا وَلَدٌ ۚ فَإِنْ كَانَتَا اثْنَتَيْنِ فَلَهُمَا الثُّلُثَانِ مِمَّا تَرَكَ ۚ وَإِنْ كَانُوا إِخْوَةً رِجَالًا وَنِسَاءً فَلِلذَّكَرِ مِثْلُ حَظِّ الْأُنْثَيَيْنِ ۗ يُبَيِّنُ اللَّهُ لَكُمْ أَنْ تَضِلُّوا ۗ وَاللَّهُ بِكُلِّ شَيْءٍ عَلِيمٌ	4:11

176 They ask you for a ruling. Say, "God gives you a ruling concerning the person who has neither parents nor children." If a man dies, and leaves no children, and he had a sister, she receives one-half of what he leaves. And he inherits from her if she leaves no children. But if there are two sisters, they receive two-thirds of what he leaves. If the siblings are men and women, the male receives the share of two females." God makes things clear for you, lest you err. God is Aware of everything.

Sūrah 5: Al-Mā'idah

سُورَةُ ٱلْمَائِدَة (The Table)

بِسْمِ ٱللَّهِ ٱلرَّحْمَٰنِ ٱلرَّحِيمِ

١ يَا أَيُّهَا الَّذِينَ آمَنُوا أَوْفُوا بِالْعُقُودِ ۚ أُحِلَّتْ لَكُم بَهِيمَةُ الْأَنْعَامِ إِلَّا مَا يُتْلَىٰ عَلَيْكُمْ غَيْرَ مُحِلِّي الصَّيْدِ وَأَنتُمْ حُرُمٌ ۗ إِنَّ اللَّهَ يَحْكُمُ مَا يُرِيدُ

1 — 5:95; 22:27–28

1 O you who believe! Fulfill your commitments. Livestock animals are permitted for you, except those specified to you; but not wild game while you are in pilgrim sanctity. God decrees whatever He wills.

٢ يَا أَيُّهَا الَّذِينَ آمَنُوا لَا تُحِلُّوا شَعَائِرَ اللَّهِ وَلَا الشَّهْرَ الْحَرَامَ وَلَا الْهَدْيَ وَلَا الْقَلَائِدَ وَلَا آمِّينَ الْبَيْتَ الْحَرَامَ يَبْتَغُونَ فَضْلًا مِّن رَّبِّهِمْ وَرِضْوَانًا ۚ وَإِذَا حَلَلْتُمْ فَاصْطَادُوا ۚ وَلَا يَجْرِمَنَّكُمْ شَنَآنُ قَوْمٍ أَن صَدُّوكُمْ عَنِ الْمَسْجِدِ الْحَرَامِ أَن تَعْتَدُوا ۘ وَتَعَاوَنُوا عَلَى الْبِرِّ وَالتَّقْوَىٰ ۖ وَلَا تَعَاوَنُوا عَلَى الْإِثْمِ وَالْعُدْوَانِ ۚ وَاتَّقُوا اللَّهَ ۖ إِنَّ اللَّهَ شَدِيدُ الْعِقَابِ

2 — 2:198; 5:8, 97; 22:32, 36; 48:25

2 O you who believe! Do not violate God's sacraments, nor the Sacred Month, nor the offerings, nor the garlanded, nor those heading for the Sacred House seeking blessings from their Lord and approval. When you have left the pilgrim sanctity, you may hunt. And let not the hatred of people who barred you from the Sacred Mosque incite you to aggression. And cooperate with one another in virtuous conduct and conscience, and do not cooperate with one another in sin and hostility. And fear God. God is severe in punishment.

٣ حُرِّمَتْ عَلَيْكُمُ الْمَيْتَةُ وَالدَّمُ وَلَحْمُ الْخِنزِيرِ وَمَا أُهِلَّ لِغَيْرِ اللَّهِ بِهِ وَالْمُنْخَنِقَةُ وَالْمَوْقُوذَةُ وَالْمُتَرَدِّيَةُ وَالنَّطِيحَةُ وَمَا أَكَلَ السَّبُعُ إِلَّا مَا ذَكَّيْتُمْ وَمَا ذُبِحَ عَلَى النُّصُبِ وَأَن تَسْتَقْسِمُوا بِالْأَزْلَامِ ۚ ذَٰلِكُمْ فِسْقٌ ۗ[a] الْيَوْمَ يَئِسَ الَّذِينَ كَفَرُوا مِن دِينِكُمْ فَلَا تَخْشَوْهُمْ وَاخْشَوْنِ ۚ الْيَوْمَ أَكْمَلْتُ لَكُمْ دِينَكُمْ وَأَتْمَمْتُ عَلَيْكُمْ نِعْمَتِي وَرَضِيتُ لَكُمُ الْإِسْلَامَ دِينًا ۚ[b] فَمَنِ اضْطُرَّ فِي مَخْمَصَةٍ غَيْرَ مُتَجَانِفٍ لِّإِثْمٍ ۙ فَإِنَّ اللَّهَ غَفُورٌ رَّحِيمٌ

3
[a] 2:173; 5:90; 6:145; 16:36, 115; 22:30
[b] 2:131; 3:19

3 Prohibited for you are carrion, blood, the flesh of swine, and animals dedicated to other than God; also the flesh of animals strangled, killed violently, killed by a fall, gored to death, mangled by wild animals—except what you rescue, and animals sacrificed on altars; and the practice of drawing lots. For it is immoral. Today, those who disbelieve have despaired of your religion, so do not fear them, but fear Me. Today I have perfected your religion for you, and have completed My favor upon you, and have approved Islam as a religion for you. But whoever is compelled by hunger, with no intent of wrongdoing—God is Forgiving and Merciful.

Sūrah 5: Al-Māʾidah — 131

٤ يَسْأَلُونَكَ مَاذَا أُحِلَّ لَهُمْ ۖ قُلْ أُحِلَّ لَكُمُ الطَّيِّبَاتُ ۙ وَمَا عَلَّمْتُم مِّنَ الْجَوَارِحِ مُكَلِّبِينَ تُعَلِّمُونَهُنَّ مِمَّا عَلَّمَكُمُ اللَّهُ ۖ فَكُلُوا مِمَّا أَمْسَكْنَ عَلَيْكُمْ وَاذْكُرُوا اسْمَ اللَّهِ عَلَيْهِ ۖ وَاتَّقُوا اللَّهَ ۚ إِنَّ اللَّهَ سَرِيعُ الْحِسَابِ

4 5:87; 6:140; 7:31; 10:59

4 They ask you what is permitted for them. Say, "Permitted for you are all good things, including what trained dogs and falcons catch for you." You train them according to what God has taught you. So eat from what they catch for you, and pronounce God's name over it. And fear God. God is Swift in reckoning.

٥ الْيَوْمَ أُحِلَّ لَكُمُ الطَّيِّبَاتُ ۖ وَطَعَامُ الَّذِينَ أُوتُوا الْكِتَابَ حِلٌّ لَّكُمْ وَطَعَامُكُمْ حِلٌّ لَّهُمْ ۖ وَالْمُحْصَنَاتُ مِنَ الْمُؤْمِنَاتِ وَالْمُحْصَنَاتُ مِنَ الَّذِينَ أُوتُوا الْكِتَابَ مِن قَبْلِكُمْ إِذَا آتَيْتُمُوهُنَّ أُجُورَهُنَّ مُحْصِنِينَ غَيْرَ مُسَافِحِينَ وَلَا مُتَّخِذِي أَخْدَانٍ ۗ وَمَن يَكْفُرْ بِالْإِيمَانِ فَقَدْ حَبِطَ عَمَلُهُ وَهُوَ فِي الْآخِرَةِ مِنَ الْخَاسِرِينَ

5 4:24–25

5 Today all good things are made lawful for you. And the food of those given the Scripture is lawful for you, and your food is lawful for them. So are chaste believing women, and chaste women from the people who were given the Scripture before you, provided you give them their dowries, and take them in marriage, not in adultery, nor as mistresses. But whoever rejects faith, his work will be in vain, and in the Hereafter he will be among the losers.

٦ يَا أَيُّهَا الَّذِينَ آمَنُوا إِذَا قُمْتُمْ إِلَى الصَّلَاةِ فَاغْسِلُوا وُجُوهَكُمْ وَأَيْدِيَكُمْ إِلَى الْمَرَافِقِ وَامْسَحُوا بِرُءُوسِكُمْ وَأَرْجُلَكُمْ إِلَى الْكَعْبَيْنِ ۚ وَإِن كُنتُمْ جُنُبًا فَاطَّهَّرُوا ۚ وَإِن كُنتُم مَّرْضَىٰ أَوْ عَلَىٰ سَفَرٍ أَوْ جَاءَ أَحَدٌ مِّنكُم مِّنَ الْغَائِطِ أَوْ لَامَسْتُمُ النِّسَاءَ فَلَمْ تَجِدُوا مَاءً فَتَيَمَّمُوا صَعِيدًا طَيِّبًا فَامْسَحُوا بِوُجُوهِكُمْ وَأَيْدِيكُم مِّنْهُ ۚ مَا يُرِيدُ اللَّهُ لِيَجْعَلَ عَلَيْكُم مِّنْ حَرَجٍ وَلَٰكِن يُرِيدُ لِيُطَهِّرَكُمْ وَلِيُتِمَّ نِعْمَتَهُ عَلَيْكُمْ لَعَلَّكُمْ تَشْكُرُونَ

6 4:43

6 O you who believe! When you rise to pray, wash your faces and your hands and arms to the elbows, and wipe your heads, and your feet to the ankles. If you had intercourse, then purify yourselves. If you are ill, or travelling, or one of you returns from the toilet, or you had contact with women, and could not find water, then use some clean sand and wipe your faces and hands with it. God does not intend to burden you, but He intends to purify you, and to complete His blessing upon you, that you may be thankful.

٧ وَاذْكُرُوا نِعْمَةَ اللَّهِ عَلَيْكُمْ وَمِيثَاقَهُ الَّذِي وَاثَقَكُم بِهِ إِذْ قُلْتُمْ سَمِعْنَا وَأَطَعْنَا ۖ وَاتَّقُوا اللَّهَ ۚ إِنَّ اللَّهَ عَلِيمٌ بِذَاتِ الصُّدُورِ

7 24:51

7 And Remember God's blessings upon you, and His covenant which He covenanted with you; when you said, "We hear and we obey." And remain conscious of God, for God knows what the hearts contain.

٨ يَا أَيُّهَا الَّذِينَ آمَنُوا كُونُوا قَوَّامِينَ لِلَّهِ شُهَدَاءَ بِالْقِسْطِ ۖ وَلَا يَجْرِمَنَّكُمْ شَنَآنُ قَوْمٍ عَلَىٰ أَلَّا تَعْدِلُوا ۚ اعْدِلُوا هُوَ أَقْرَبُ لِلتَّقْوَىٰ ۖ وَاتَّقُوا اللَّهَ ۚ إِنَّ اللَّهَ خَبِيرٌ بِمَا تَعْمَلُونَ

8 3:18; 4:135; 5:2, 97; 22:32, 36

8 O you who believe! Be upright to God, witnessing with justice; and let not the hatred of a certain people prevent you from acting justly. Adhere to justice, for that is nearer to piety; and fear God. God is informed of what you do.

٩ وَعَدَ اللَّهُ الَّذِينَ آمَنُوا وَعَمِلُوا الصَّالِحَاتِ ۙ لَهُم مَّغْفِرَةٌ وَأَجْرٌ عَظِيمٌ

9–10
3:56; 4:173; 35:30

9 God has promised those who believe and work righteousness: they will have forgiveness and a great reward.

١٠ وَالَّذِينَ كَفَرُوا وَكَذَّبُوا بِآيَاتِنَا أُولَٰئِكَ أَصْحَابُ الْجَحِيمِ

10 As for those who disbelieve and reject Our revelations—these are the inmates of Hell.

١١ يَا أَيُّهَا الَّذِينَ آمَنُوا اذْكُرُوا نِعْمَتَ اللَّهِ عَلَيْكُمْ إِذْ هَمَّ قَوْمٌ أَن يَبْسُطُوا إِلَيْكُمْ أَيْدِيَهُمْ فَكَفَّ أَيْدِيَهُمْ عَنكُمْ ۖ وَاتَّقُوا اللَّهَ ۚ وَعَلَى اللَّهِ فَلْيَتَوَكَّلِ الْمُؤْمِنُونَ

11
48:20, 24

11 O you who believe! Remember God's blessings upon you; when certain people intended to extend their hands against you, and He restrained their hands from you. So reverence God, and in God let the believers put their trust.

١٢ وَلَقَدْ أَخَذَ اللَّهُ مِيثَاقَ بَنِي إِسْرَائِيلَ وَبَعَثْنَا مِنْهُمُ اثْنَيْ عَشَرَ نَقِيبًا ۖ وَقَالَ اللَّهُ إِنِّي مَعَكُمْ ۖ لَئِنْ أَقَمْتُمُ الصَّلَاةَ وَآتَيْتُمُ الزَّكَاةَ وَآمَنتُم بِرُسُلِي وَعَزَّرْتُمُوهُمْ وَأَقْرَضْتُمُ اللَّهَ قَرْضًا حَسَنًا لَّأُكَفِّرَنَّ عَنكُمْ سَيِّئَاتِكُمْ وَلَأُدْخِلَنَّكُمْ جَنَّاتٍ تَجْرِي مِن تَحْتِهَا الْأَنْهَارُ ۚ فَمَن كَفَرَ بَعْدَ ذَٰلِكَ مِنكُمْ فَقَدْ ضَلَّ سَوَاءَ السَّبِيلِ

12
2:40, 62, 83; 4:154; 5:70

12 God received a pledge from the Children of Israel, and We raised among them twelve chiefs. God said, "I am with you; if you perform the prayer, and pay the alms, and believe in My messengers and support them, and lend God a loan of righteousness; I will remit your sins, and admit you into Gardens beneath which rivers flow. But whoever among you disbelieves afterwards has strayed from the right way."

١٣ فَبِمَا نَقْضِهِم مِّيثَاقَهُمْ لَعَنَّاهُمْ وَجَعَلْنَا قُلُوبَهُمْ قَاسِيَةً ۖ يُحَرِّفُونَ الْكَلِمَ عَن مَّوَاضِعِهِ ۙ وَنَسُوا حَظًّا مِّمَّا ذُكِّرُوا بِهِ ۚ وَلَا تَزَالُ تَطَّلِعُ عَلَىٰ خَائِنَةٍ مِّنْهُمْ إِلَّا قَلِيلًا مِّنْهُمْ ۖ فَاعْفُ عَنْهُمْ وَاصْفَحْ ۚ إِنَّ اللَّهَ يُحِبُّ الْمُحْسِنِينَ

13
2:75; 4:46

13 Because of their breaking their pledge, We cursed them, and made their hearts hard. They twist the words out of their context, and they disregarded some of what they were reminded of. You will always witness deceit from them, except for a few of them. But pardon them, and overlook. God loves the doers of good.

١٤ وَمِنَ الَّذِينَ قَالُوا إِنَّا نَصَارَىٰ أَخَذْنَا مِيثَاقَهُمْ فَنَسُوا حَظًّا مِّمَّا ذُكِّرُوا بِهِ فَأَغْرَيْنَا بَيْنَهُمُ الْعَدَاوَةَ وَالْبَغْضَاءَ إِلَىٰ يَوْمِ الْقِيَامَةِ ۚ وَسَوْفَ يُنَبِّئُهُمُ اللَّهُ بِمَا كَانُوا يَصْنَعُونَ

14 And from those who say, "We are Christians," We received their pledge, but they neglected some of what they were reminded of. So We provoked enmity and hatred among them until the Day of Resurrection; God will then inform them of what they used to craft.

١٥ يَا أَهْلَ الْكِتَابِ قَدْ جَاءَكُمْ رَسُولُنَا يُبَيِّنُ لَكُمْ كَثِيرًا مِمَّا كُنْتُمْ تُخْفُونَ مِنَ الْكِتَابِ وَيَعْفُو عَنْ كَثِيرٍ ۚ قَدْ جَاءَكُمْ مِنَ اللَّهِ نُورٌ وَكِتَابٌ مُبِينٌ

15
2:174; 3:23, 37; 6:91

15 O People of the Book! Our Messenger has come to you, clarifying for you much of what you kept hidden of the Book, and overlooking much. A light from God has come to you, and a clear Book.

١٦ يَهْدِي بِهِ اللَّهُ مَنِ اتَّبَعَ رِضْوَانَهُ سُبُلَ السَّلَامِ وَيُخْرِجُهُمْ مِنَ الظُّلُمَاتِ إِلَى النُّورِ بِإِذْنِهِ وَيَهْدِيهِمْ إِلَىٰ صِرَاطٍ مُسْتَقِيمٍ

16
2:257

16 God guides with it whoever follows His approval to the ways of peace, and He brings them out of darkness into light, by His permission, and He guides them in a straight path.

١٧ لَقَدْ كَفَرَ الَّذِينَ قَالُوا إِنَّ اللَّهَ هُوَ الْمَسِيحُ ابْنُ مَرْيَمَ ۚ قُلْ فَمَنْ يَمْلِكُ مِنَ اللَّهِ شَيْئًا إِنْ أَرَادَ أَنْ يُهْلِكَ الْمَسِيحَ ابْنَ مَرْيَمَ وَأُمَّهُ وَمَنْ فِي الْأَرْضِ جَمِيعًا ۗ وَلِلَّهِ مُلْكُ السَّمَاوَاتِ وَالْأَرْضِ وَمَا بَيْنَهُمَا ۚ يَخْلُقُ مَا يَشَاءُ ۚ وَاللَّهُ عَلَىٰ كُلِّ شَيْءٍ قَدِيرٌ

17
4:172; 5:75

17 They disbelieve those who say, "God is the Christ, the son of Mary." Say, "Who can prevent God, if He willed, from annihilating the Christ son of Mary, and his mother, and everyone on earth?" To God belongs the sovereignty of the heavens and the earth and what is between them. He creates whatever He wills, and God has power over everything.

١٨ وَقَالَتِ الْيَهُودُ وَالنَّصَارَىٰ نَحْنُ أَبْنَاءُ اللَّهِ وَأَحِبَّاؤُهُ ۚ قُلْ فَلِمَ يُعَذِّبُكُمْ بِذُنُوبِكُمْ ۖ بَلْ أَنْتُمْ بَشَرٌ مِمَّنْ خَلَقَ ۚ يَغْفِرُ لِمَنْ يَشَاءُ وَيُعَذِّبُ مَنْ يَشَاءُ ۚ وَلِلَّهِ مُلْكُ السَّمَاوَاتِ وَالْأَرْضِ وَمَا بَيْنَهُمَا ۖ وَإِلَيْهِ الْمَصِيرُ

18
2:111, 120, 1352:120; 3:73; 13:37

18 The Jews and the Christians say, "We are the children of God, and His beloved." Say, "Why then does He punish you for your sins?" In fact, you are humans from among those He created. He forgives whom He wills, and He punishes whom He wills. To God belongs the dominion of the heavens and the earth and what lies between them, and to Him is the return.

١٩ يَا أَهْلَ الْكِتَابِ قَدْ جَاءَكُمْ رَسُولُنَا يُبَيِّنُ لَكُمْ عَلَىٰ فَتْرَةٍ مِنَ الرُّسُلِ أَنْ تَقُولُوا مَا جَاءَنَا مِنْ بَشِيرٍ وَلَا نَذِيرٍ ۖ فَقَدْ جَاءَكُمْ بَشِيرٌ وَنَذِيرٌ ۗ وَاللَّهُ عَلَىٰ كُلِّ شَيْءٍ قَدِيرٌ

19 O People of the Book! Our Messenger has come to you, making things clear to you—after a cessation of messengers—so that you cannot say, "No preacher has come to us, and no warner." In fact, a preacher has come to you, and a warner; and God is Capable of everything.

٢٠ وَإِذْ قَالَ مُوسَىٰ لِقَوْمِهِ يَا قَوْمِ اذْكُرُوا نِعْمَةَ اللَّهِ عَلَيْكُمْ إِذْ جَعَلَ فِيكُمْ أَنْبِيَاءَ وَجَعَلَكُمْ مُلُوكًا وَآتَاكُمْ مَا لَمْ يُؤْتِ أَحَدًا مِنَ الْعَالَمِينَ

20
2:40

20 When Moses said to his people, "O my people, remember God's blessings upon you, when He placed prophets among you, and made you kings, and gave you what He never gave any other people."

٢١ يَا قَوْمِ ادْخُلُوا الْأَرْضَ الْمُقَدَّسَةَ الَّتِي كَتَبَ اللَّهُ لَكُمْ وَلَا تَرْتَدُّوا عَلَىٰ أَدْبَارِكُمْ فَتَنقَلِبُوا خَاسِرِينَ

21
2:58; 7:161

21 "O my people, enter the Holy Land which God has assigned for you, and do not turn back, lest you return as losers."

٢٢ قَالُوا يَا مُوسَىٰ إِنَّ فِيهَا قَوْمًا جَبَّارِينَ وَإِنَّا لَن نَّدْخُلَهَا حَتَّىٰ يَخْرُجُوا مِنْهَا فَإِن يَخْرُجُوا مِنْهَا فَإِنَّا دَاخِلُونَ

22 They said, "O Moses, there are tyrannical people in it; we will not enter it until they leave it. If they leave it, we will be entering."

٢٣ قَالَ رَجُلَانِ مِنَ الَّذِينَ يَخَافُونَ أَنْعَمَ اللَّهُ عَلَيْهِمَا ادْخُلُوا عَلَيْهِمُ الْبَابَ فَإِذَا دَخَلْتُمُوهُ فَإِنَّكُمْ غَالِبُونَ ۚ وَعَلَى اللَّهِ فَتَوَكَّلُوا إِن كُنتُم مُّؤْمِنِينَ

23 Two men of those who feared, but whom God had blessed, said, "Go at them by the gate; and when you have entered it, you will prevail. And put your trust in God, if you are believers."

٢٤ قَالُوا يَا مُوسَىٰ إِنَّا لَن نَّدْخُلَهَا أَبَدًا مَّا دَامُوا فِيهَا ۖ فَاذْهَبْ أَنتَ وَرَبُّكَ فَقَاتِلَا إِنَّا هَاهُنَا قَاعِدُونَ

24 They said, "O Moses, we will not enter it, ever, as long as they are in it. So go ahead, you and your Lord, and fight. We are staying right here."

٢٥ قَالَ رَبِّ إِنِّي لَا أَمْلِكُ إِلَّا نَفْسِي وَأَخِي ۖ فَافْرُقْ بَيْنَنَا وَبَيْنَ الْقَوْمِ الْفَاسِقِينَ

25 He said, "My Lord! I have control only over myself and my brother, so separate between us and between the wicked people."

٢٦ قَالَ فَإِنَّهَا مُحَرَّمَةٌ عَلَيْهِمْ ۛ أَرْبَعِينَ سَنَةً ۛ يَتِيهُونَ فِي الْأَرْضِ ۚ فَلَا تَأْسَ عَلَى الْقَوْمِ الْفَاسِقِينَ

26 He said, "It is forbidden for them for forty years. They will wander aimlessly in the land. So do not grieve over the defiant people."

٢٧ وَاتْلُ عَلَيْهِمْ نَبَأَ ابْنَيْ آدَمَ بِالْحَقِّ إِذْ قَرَّبَا قُرْبَانًا فَتُقُبِّلَ مِنْ أَحَدِهِمَا وَلَمْ يُتَقَبَّلْ مِنَ الْآخَرِ قَالَ لَأَقْتُلَنَّكَ ۖ قَالَ إِنَّمَا يَتَقَبَّلُ اللَّهُ مِنَ الْمُتَّقِينَ

27 And relate to them the true story of Adam's two sons: when they offered an offering, and it was accepted from one of them, but it was not accepted from the other. He Said, "I will kill you." He Said, "God accepts only from the righteous."

٢٨ لَئِن بَسَطتَ إِلَيَّ يَدَكَ لِتَقْتُلَنِي مَا أَنَا بِبَاسِطٍ يَدِيَ إِلَيْكَ لِأَقْتُلَكَ ۖ إِنِّي أَخَافُ اللَّهَ رَبَّ الْعَالَمِينَ

28 "If you extend your hand to kill me, I will not extend my hand to kill you; for I fear God, Lord of the Worlds."

٢٩ إِنِّي أُرِيدُ أَن تَبُوءَ بِإِثْمِي وَإِثْمِكَ فَتَكُونَ مِنْ أَصْحَابِ النَّارِ ۚ وَذَٰلِكَ جَزَاءُ الظَّالِمِينَ

29 "I would rather you bear my sin and your sin, and you become among the inmates of the Fire. Such is the reward for the evildoers."

٣٠ فَطَوَّعَتْ لَهُ نَفْسُهُ قَتْلَ أَخِيهِ فَقَتَلَهُ فَأَصْبَحَ مِنَ الْخَاسِرِينَ

30 Then His soul prompted him to kill his brother, so he killed him, and became one of the losers.

٣١ فَبَعَثَ اللَّهُ غُرَابًا يَبْحَثُ فِي الْأَرْضِ لِيُرِيَهُ كَيْفَ يُوَارِي سَوْءَةَ أَخِيهِ ۚ قَالَ يَا وَيْلَتَا أَعَجَزْتُ أَنْ أَكُونَ مِثْلَ هَـٰذَا الْغُرَابِ فَأُوَارِيَ سَوْءَةَ أَخِي ۖ فَأَصْبَحَ مِنَ النَّادِمِينَ

31 Then God sent a raven digging the ground, to show him how to cover his brother's corpse. He said, "Woe to me! I was unable to be like this raven, and bury my brother's corpse." So he became full of regrets.

٣٢ مِنْ أَجْلِ ذَٰلِكَ كَتَبْنَا عَلَىٰ بَنِي إِسْرَائِيلَ أَنَّهُ مَنْ قَتَلَ نَفْسًا بِغَيْرِ نَفْسٍ أَوْ فَسَادٍ فِي الْأَرْضِ فَكَأَنَّمَا قَتَلَ النَّاسَ جَمِيعًا وَمَنْ أَحْيَاهَا فَكَأَنَّمَا أَحْيَا النَّاسَ جَمِيعًا ۚ وَلَقَدْ جَاءَتْهُمْ رُسُلُنَا بِالْبَيِّنَاتِ ثُمَّ إِنَّ كَثِيرًا مِنْهُمْ بَعْدَ ذَٰلِكَ فِي الْأَرْضِ لَمُسْرِفُونَ

32   5:45

32 Because of that We ordained for the Children of Israel: that whoever kills a person—unless it is for murder or corruption on earth—it is as if he killed the whole of mankind; and whoever saves it, it is as if he saved the whole of mankind. Our messengers came to them with clarifications, but even after that, many of them continue to commit excesses in the land.

٣٣ إِنَّمَا جَزَاءُ الَّذِينَ يُحَارِبُونَ اللَّهَ وَرَسُولَهُ وَيَسْعَوْنَ فِي الْأَرْضِ فَسَادًا أَنْ يُقَتَّلُوا أَوْ يُصَلَّبُوا أَوْ تُقَطَّعَ أَيْدِيهِمْ وَأَرْجُلُهُمْ مِنْ خِلَافٍ أَوْ يُنْفَوْا مِنَ الْأَرْضِ ۚ ذَٰلِكَ لَهُمْ خِزْيٌ فِي الدُّنْيَا ۖ وَلَهُمْ فِي الْآخِرَةِ عَذَابٌ عَظِيمٌ

33   7:124; 26:49

33 The punishment for those who fight God and His Messenger, and strive to spread corruption on earth, is that they be killed, or crucified, or have their hands and feet cut off on opposite sides, or be banished from the land. That is to disgrace them in this life; and in the Hereafter they will have a terrible punishment.

٣٤ إِلَّا الَّذِينَ تَابُوا مِنْ قَبْلِ أَنْ تَقْدِرُوا عَلَيْهِمْ ۖ فَاعْلَمُوا أَنَّ اللَّهَ غَفُورٌ رَحِيمٌ

34 Except for those who repent before you apprehend them. So know that God is Forgiving and Merciful.

٣٥ يَا أَيُّهَا الَّذِينَ آمَنُوا اتَّقُوا اللَّهَ وَابْتَغُوا إِلَيْهِ الْوَسِيلَةَ وَجَاهِدُوا فِي سَبِيلِهِ لَعَلَّكُمْ تُفْلِحُونَ

35 O you who believe! Be conscious of God, and seek the means of approach to Him, and strive in His cause, so that you may succeed.

٣٦ إِنَّ الَّذِينَ كَفَرُوا لَوْ أَنَّ لَهُمْ مَا فِي الْأَرْضِ جَمِيعًا وَمِثْلَهُ مَعَهُ لِيَفْتَدُوا بِهِ مِنْ عَذَابِ يَوْمِ الْقِيَامَةِ مَا تُقُبِّلَ مِنْهُمْ ۖ وَلَهُمْ عَذَابٌ أَلِيمٌ

36   3:91; 10:54; 13:18; 39:47

36 As for those who disbelieve, even if they owned everything on earth, and the like of it with it, and they offered it to ransom themselves from the torment of the Day of Resurrection, it will not be accepted from them. For them is a painful punishment.

٣٧ يُرِيدُونَ أَنْ يَخْرُجُوا مِنَ النَّارِ وَمَا هُمْ بِخَارِجِينَ مِنْهَا ۖ وَلَهُمْ عَذَابٌ مُقِيمٌ

37   2:167; 22:22; 32:20

37 They will want to leave the Fire, but they will not leave it. For them is a lasting punishment.

٣٨ وَالسَّارِقُ وَالسَّارِقَةُ فَاقْطَعُوا أَيْدِيَهُمَا جَزَاءً بِمَا كَسَبَا نَكَالًا مِنَ اللَّهِ ۗ وَاللَّهُ عَزِيزٌ حَكِيمٌ

38 As for the thief, whether male or female, cut their hands as a penalty for what they have reaped—a deterrent from God. God is Mighty and Wise.

٣٩ فَمَن تَابَ مِن بَعْدِ ظُلْمِهِ وَأَصْلَحَ فَإِنَّ اللَّهَ يَتُوبُ عَلَيْهِ ۗ إِنَّ اللَّهَ غَفُورٌ رَحِيمٌ

39 But whoever repents after his crime, and reforms, God will accept his repentance. God is Forgiving and Merciful.

٤٠ أَلَمْ تَعْلَمْ أَنَّ اللَّهَ لَهُ مُلْكُ السَّمَاوَاتِ وَالْأَرْضِ يُعَذِّبُ مَن يَشَاءُ وَيَغْفِرُ لِمَن يَشَاءُ ۗ وَاللَّهُ عَلَىٰ كُلِّ شَيْءٍ قَدِيرٌ

40
2:284; 3:129

40 Do you not know that to God belongs the kingdom of the heavens and the earth? He punishes whom He wills, and He forgives whom He wills. And God is Capable of everything.

٤١ يَا أَيُّهَا الرَّسُولُ لَا يَحْزُنكَ الَّذِينَ يُسَارِعُونَ فِي الْكُفْرِ مِنَ الَّذِينَ قَالُوا آمَنَّا بِأَفْوَاهِهِمْ وَلَمْ تُؤْمِن قُلُوبُهُمْ ۛ وَمِنَ الَّذِينَ هَادُوا ۛ سَمَّاعُونَ لِلْكَذِبِ سَمَّاعُونَ لِقَوْمٍ آخَرِينَ لَمْ يَأْتُوكَ ۖ يُحَرِّفُونَ الْكَلِمَ مِن بَعْدِ مَوَاضِعِهِ[a] ۖ يَقُولُونَ إِنْ أُوتِيتُمْ هَٰذَا فَخُذُوهُ وَإِن لَّمْ تُؤْتَوْهُ فَاحْذَرُوا ۚ وَمَن يُرِدِ اللَّهُ فِتْنَتَهُ فَلَن تَمْلِكَ لَهُ مِنَ اللَّهِ شَيْئًا ۚ أُولَٰئِكَ الَّذِينَ لَمْ يُرِدِ اللَّهُ أَن يُطَهِّرَ قُلُوبَهُمْ ۚ لَهُمْ فِي الدُّنْيَا خِزْيٌ ۖ وَلَهُمْ فِي الْآخِرَةِ عَذَابٌ عَظِيمٌ

41
2:8,14; 3:119, 167;
5:61; 48:11
[a] 2:75; 4:46; 5:13

41 O Messenger! Do not let those who are quick to disbelief grieve you—from among those who say with their mouths, "We believe," but their hearts do not believe; and from among the Jews—listeners to lies, listeners to other people who did not come to you. They distort words from their places, and they say, "If you are given this, accept it; but if you are not given it, beware." Whomever God has willed to divert, you have nothing for him from God. Those are they whose hearts God does not intend to purify. For them is disgrace in this world, and for them is a great punishment in the Hereafter.

٤٢ سَمَّاعُونَ لِلْكَذِبِ أَكَّالُونَ لِلسُّحْتِ ۚ[a] فَإِن جَاءُوكَ فَاحْكُم بَيْنَهُمْ أَوْ أَعْرِضْ عَنْهُمْ ۖ وَإِن تُعْرِضْ عَنْهُمْ فَلَن يَضُرُّوكَ شَيْئًا ۖ وَإِنْ حَكَمْتَ فَاحْكُم بَيْنَهُم بِالْقِسْطِ ۚ إِنَّ اللَّهَ يُحِبُّ الْمُقْسِطِينَ[b]

42
[a] 5:62–63
[b] 4:58, 65

42 Listeners to falsehoods, eaters of illicit earnings. If they come to you, judge between them, or turn away from them. If you turn away from them, they will not harm you in the least. But if you judge, judge between them equitably. God loves the equitable.

٤٣ وَكَيْفَ يُحَكِّمُونَكَ وَعِندَهُمُ التَّوْرَاةُ فِيهَا حُكْمُ اللَّهِ ثُمَّ يَتَوَلَّوْنَ مِن بَعْدِ ذَٰلِكَ ۚ وَمَا أُولَٰئِكَ بِالْمُؤْمِنِينَ

43
5:49

43 But why do they come to you for judgment, when they have the Torah, in which is God's Law? Yet they turn away after that. These are not believers.

٤٤ إِنَّا أَنْزَلْنَا التَّوْرَاةَ فِيهَا هُدًى وَنُورٌ ۚ يَحْكُمُ بِهَا النَّبِيُّونَ الَّذِينَ أَسْلَمُوا لِلَّذِينَ هَادُوا وَالرَّبَّانِيُّونَ وَالْأَحْبَارُ بِمَا اسْتُحْفِظُوا مِنْ كِتَابِ اللَّهِ وَكَانُوا عَلَيْهِ شُهَدَاءَ ۚ فَلَا تَخْشَوُا النَّاسَ وَاخْشَوْنِ وَلَا تَشْتَرُوا بِآيَاتِي ثَمَنًا قَلِيلًا ۚ وَمَنْ لَمْ يَحْكُمْ بِمَا أَنْزَلَ اللَّهُ فَأُولَٰئِكَ هُمُ الْكَافِرُونَ

44
4:174; 5:15, 46; 6:91; 7:157; 42:52; 64:8

44 We have revealed the Torah, wherein is guidance and light. The submissive prophets ruled the Jews according to it, so did the rabbis and the scholars, as they were required to protect God's Book, and were witnesses to it. So do not fear people, but fear Me. And do not sell My revelations for a cheap price. Those who do not rule according to what God revealed are the unbelievers.

٤٥ وَكَتَبْنَا عَلَيْهِمْ فِيهَا أَنَّ النَّفْسَ بِالنَّفْسِ وَالْعَيْنَ بِالْعَيْنِ وَالْأَنْفَ بِالْأَنْفِ وَالْأُذُنَ بِالْأُذُنِ وَالسِّنَّ بِالسِّنِّ وَالْجُرُوحَ قِصَاصٌ ۚ فَمَنْ تَصَدَّقَ بِهِ فَهُوَ كَفَّارَةٌ لَهُ ۚ وَمَنْ لَمْ يَحْكُمْ بِمَا أَنْزَلَ اللَّهُ فَأُولَٰئِكَ هُمُ الظَّالِمُونَ

45
5:32

45 And We wrote for them in it: a life for a life, an eye for an eye, a nose for a nose, an ear for an ear, a tooth for a tooth, and an equal wound for a wound; but whoever forgoes it in charity, it will serve as atonement for him. Those who do not rule according to what God revealed are the evildoers.

٤٦ وَقَفَّيْنَا عَلَىٰ آثَارِهِمْ بِعِيسَى ابْنِ مَرْيَمَ مُصَدِّقًا لِمَا بَيْنَ يَدَيْهِ مِنَ التَّوْرَاةِ ۖ وَآتَيْنَاهُ الْإِنْجِيلَ فِيهِ هُدًى وَنُورٌ وَمُصَدِّقًا لِمَا بَيْنَ يَدَيْهِ مِنَ التَّوْرَاةِ وَهُدًى وَمَوْعِظَةً لِلْمُتَّقِينَ

46
3:50; 5:41; 61:6, 91

46 In their footsteps, We sent Jesus son of Mary, fulfilling the Torah that preceded him; and We gave him the Gospel, wherein is guidance and light, and confirming the Torah that preceded him, and guidance and counsel for the righteous.

٤٧ وَلْيَحْكُمْ أَهْلُ الْإِنْجِيلِ بِمَا أَنْزَلَ اللَّهُ فِيهِ ۚ وَمَنْ لَمْ يَحْكُمْ بِمَا أَنْزَلَ اللَّهُ فَأُولَٰئِكَ هُمُ الْفَاسِقُونَ

47
5:68

47 So let the people of the Gospel rule according to what God revealed in it. Those who do not rule according to what God revealed are the sinners.

٤٨ وَأَنْزَلْنَا إِلَيْكَ الْكِتَابَ بِالْحَقِّ مُصَدِّقًا لِمَا بَيْنَ يَدَيْهِ مِنَ الْكِتَابِ وَمُهَيْمِنًا عَلَيْهِ ۖ فَاحْكُمْ بَيْنَهُمْ بِمَا أَنْزَلَ اللَّهُ ۖ وَلَا تَتَّبِعْ أَهْوَاءَهُمْ عَمَّا جَاءَكَ مِنَ الْحَقِّ ۚ [a] لِكُلٍّ جَعَلْنَا مِنْكُمْ شِرْعَةً وَمِنْهَاجًا ۚ وَلَوْ شَاءَ اللَّهُ لَجَعَلَكُمْ أُمَّةً وَاحِدَةً وَلَٰكِنْ لِيَبْلُوَكُمْ فِي مَا آتَاكُمْ ۖ فَاسْتَبِقُوا الْخَيْرَاتِ ۚ إِلَى اللَّهِ مَرْجِعُكُمْ جَمِيعًا فَيُنَبِّئُكُمْ بِمَا كُنْتُمْ فِيهِ تَخْتَلِفُونَ [b]

48
[a] 2:41, 91, 97; 3:3; 35:31
[b] 2:148

48 And We revealed to you the Book, with truth, confirming the Scripture that preceded it, and superseding it. So judge between them according to what God revealed, and do not follow their desires if they differ from the truth that has come to you. For each of you We have assigned a law and a method. Had God willed, He could have made you a single nation, but He tests you through what He has given you. So compete in righteousness. To God is your return, all of you; then He will inform you of what you had disputed.

٤٩ وَأَنِ احْكُم بَيْنَهُم بِمَا أَنزَلَ اللَّهُ وَلَا تَتَّبِعْ أَهْوَاءَهُمْ وَاحْذَرْهُمْ أَن يَفْتِنُوكَ عَنْ بَعْضِ مَا أَنزَلَ اللَّهُ إِلَيْكَ ۖ فَإِن تَوَلَّوْا فَاعْلَمْ أَنَّمَا يُرِيدُ اللَّهُ أَن يُصِيبَهُم بِبَعْضِ ذُنُوبِهِمْ ۗ وَإِنَّ كَثِيرًا مِّنَ النَّاسِ لَفَاسِقُونَ

49
5:43

49 And judge between them according to what God revealed, and do not follow their desires. And beware of them, lest they lure you away from some of what God has revealed to you. But if they turn away, know that God intends to strike them with some of their sins. In fact, a great many people are corrupt.

٥٠ أَفَحُكْمَ الْجَاهِلِيَّةِ يَبْغُونَ ۚ وَمَنْ أَحْسَنُ مِنَ اللَّهِ حُكْمًا لِّقَوْمٍ يُوقِنُونَ

50
3:83

50 Is it the laws of the time of ignorance that they desire? Who is better than God in judgment for people who are certain?

٥١ يَا أَيُّهَا الَّذِينَ آمَنُوا لَا تَتَّخِذُوا الْيَهُودَ وَالنَّصَارَىٰ أَوْلِيَاءَ ۘ بَعْضُهُمْ أَوْلِيَاءُ بَعْضٍ ۚ وَمَن يَتَوَلَّهُم مِّنكُمْ فَإِنَّهُ مِنْهُمْ ۗ إِنَّ اللَّهَ لَا يَهْدِي الْقَوْمَ الظَّالِمِينَ

51
3:28; 4:89, 139 144;
5:55, 57; 60:1, 9, 13

51 O you who believe! Do not take the Jews and the Christians as allies; some of them are allies of one another. Whoever of you allies himself with them is one of them. God does not guide the wrongdoing people.

٥٢ فَتَرَى الَّذِينَ فِي قُلُوبِهِم مَّرَضٌ يُسَارِعُونَ فِيهِمْ يَقُولُونَ نَخْشَىٰ أَن تُصِيبَنَا دَائِرَةٌ ۚ فَعَسَى اللَّهُ أَن يَأْتِيَ بِالْفَتْحِ أَوْ أَمْرٍ مِّنْ عِندِهِ فَيُصْبِحُوا عَلَىٰ مَا أَسَرُّوا فِي أَنفُسِهِمْ نَادِمِينَ

52
7:89

52 You will see those in whose hearts is sickness racing towards them. They say, "We fear the wheel of fate may turn against us." But perhaps God will bring about victory, or some event of His making; thereupon they will regret what they concealed within themselves.

٥٣ وَيَقُولُ الَّذِينَ آمَنُوا أَهَٰؤُلَاءِ الَّذِينَ أَقْسَمُوا بِاللَّهِ جَهْدَ أَيْمَانِهِمْ ۙ إِنَّهُمْ لَمَعَكُمْ ۚ حَبِطَتْ أَعْمَالُهُمْ فَأَصْبَحُوا خَاسِرِينَ

53
9:56–57, 62, 95–96;
16:38

53 Those who believe will say, "Are these the ones who swore by God with their strongest oaths that they are with you?" Their works have failed, so they became losers.

٥٤ يَا أَيُّهَا الَّذِينَ آمَنُوا مَن يَرْتَدَّ مِنكُمْ عَن دِينِهِ فَسَوْفَ يَأْتِي اللَّهُ بِقَوْمٍ يُحِبُّهُمْ وَيُحِبُّونَهُ أَذِلَّةٍ عَلَى الْمُؤْمِنِينَ أَعِزَّةٍ عَلَى الْكَافِرِينَ يُجَاهِدُونَ فِي سَبِيلِ اللَّهِ وَلَا يَخَافُونَ لَوْمَةَ لَائِمٍ ۚ ذَٰلِكَ فَضْلُ اللَّهِ يُؤْتِيهِ مَن يَشَاءُ ۚ وَاللَّهُ وَاسِعٌ عَلِيمٌ

54
2:217; 9:69

54 O you who believe! Whoever of you goes back on his religion—God will bring a people whom He loves and who love Him, kind towards the believers, stern with the disbelievers. They strive in the way of God, and do not fear the blame of the critic. That is the grace of God; He bestows it upon whomever He wills. God is Embracing and Knowing.

Sūrah 5: Al-Mā'idah — 139

٥٥ إِنَّمَا وَلِيُّكُمُ اللَّهُ وَرَسُولُهُ وَالَّذِينَ آمَنُوا الَّذِينَ يُقِيمُونَ الصَّلَاةَ وَيُؤْتُونَ الزَّكَاةَ وَهُمْ رَاكِعُونَ

55 Your allies are God, and His Messenger, and those who believe—those who pray regularly, and give charity, while bowing down.

55
2:257; 3:28; 8:72

٥٦ وَمَن يَتَوَلَّ اللَّهَ وَرَسُولَهُ وَالَّذِينَ آمَنُوا فَإِنَّ حِزْبَ اللَّهِ هُمُ الْغَالِبُونَ

56 Whoever allies himself with God, and His Messenger, and those who believe—surely the Party of God is the victorious.

56
58:19, 21

٥٧ يَا أَيُّهَا الَّذِينَ آمَنُوا لَا تَتَّخِذُوا الَّذِينَ اتَّخَذُوا دِينَكُمْ هُزُوًا وَلَعِبًا مِّنَ الَّذِينَ أُوتُوا الْكِتَابَ مِن قَبْلِكُمْ وَالْكُفَّارَ أَوْلِيَاءَ ۚ وَاتَّقُوا اللَّهَ إِن كُنتُم مُّؤْمِنِينَ

57 O you who believe! Do not befriend those who take your religion in mockery and as a sport, be they from among those who were given the Scripture before you, or the disbelievers. And obey God, if you are believers.

57
3:28; 4:89, 139 144; 5:51; 6:1

٥٨ وَإِذَا نَادَيْتُمْ إِلَى الصَّلَاةِ اتَّخَذُوهَا هُزُوًا وَلَعِبًا ۚ ذَٰلِكَ بِأَنَّهُمْ قَوْمٌ لَّا يَعْقِلُونَ

58 When you call to the prayer, they take it as a joke and a trifle. That is because they are people who do not reason.

٥٩ قُلْ يَا أَهْلَ الْكِتَابِ هَلْ تَنقِمُونَ مِنَّا إِلَّا أَنْ آمَنَّا بِاللَّهِ وَمَا أُنزِلَ إِلَيْنَا وَمَا أُنزِلَ مِن قَبْلُ وَأَنَّ أَكْثَرَكُمْ فَاسِقُونَ

59 Say, "O People of the Scripture! Do you resent us only because we believe in God, and in what was revealed to us, and in what was revealed previously; and most of you are sinners?"

59
7:126; 85:8

٦٠ قُلْ هَلْ أُنَبِّئُكُم بِشَرٍّ مِّن ذَٰلِكَ مَثُوبَةً عِندَ اللَّهِ ۚ مَن لَّعَنَهُ اللَّهُ وَغَضِبَ عَلَيْهِ وَجَعَلَ مِنْهُمُ الْقِرَدَةَ وَالْخَنَازِيرَ وَعَبَدَ الطَّاغُوتَ ۚ أُولَٰئِكَ شَرٌّ مَّكَانًا وَأَضَلُّ عَن سَوَاءِ السَّبِيلِ

60 Say, "Shall I inform you of worse than that for retribution from God? He whom God has cursed, and with whom He became angry; and He turned some of them into apes, and swine, and idol worshipers. These are in a worse position, and further away from the right way."

60
2:65; 7:166; 22:72

٦١ وَإِذَا جَاءُوكُمْ قَالُوا آمَنَّا وَقَد دَّخَلُوا بِالْكُفْرِ وَهُمْ قَدْ خَرَجُوا بِهِ ۚ وَاللَّهُ أَعْلَمُ بِمَا كَانُوا يَكْتُمُونَ

61 When they come to you, they say, "We believe," though they have entered with disbelief, and they have departed with it. But God is well aware of what they hide.

61
2:8,14; 3:119, 167; 5:41; 48:11

٦٢ وَتَرَىٰ كَثِيرًا مِّنْهُمْ يُسَارِعُونَ فِي الْإِثْمِ وَالْعُدْوَانِ وَأَكْلِهِمُ السُّحْتَ ۚ لَبِئْسَ مَا كَانُوا يَعْمَلُونَ

62 You see many of them competing with one another in sin and hostility, and their consuming of what is illicit. What they have been doing is truly evil.

٦٣ لَوْلَا يَنْهَاهُمُ الرَّبَّانِيُّونَ وَالْأَحْبَارُ عَن قَوْلِهِمُ الْإِثْمَ وَأَكْلِهِمُ السُّحْتَ ۚ لَبِئْسَ مَا كَانُوا يَصْنَعُونَ

63 Why do the rabbis and the priests not prevent them from speaking sinfully and from consuming forbidden wealth? Evil is what they have been doing.

63
4:61; 5:42

٦٤ وَقَالَتِ الْيَهُودُ يَدُ اللَّهِ مَغْلُولَةٌ ۚ غُلَّتْ أَيْدِيهِمْ وَلُعِنُوا بِمَا قَالُوا ۘ بَلْ يَدَاهُ مَبْسُوطَتَانِ يُنْفِقُ كَيْفَ يَشَاءُ ۚ وَلَيَزِيدَنَّ كَثِيرًا مِنْهُمْ مَا أُنْزِلَ إِلَيْكَ مِنْ رَبِّكَ طُغْيَانًا وَكُفْرًا ۚ وَأَلْقَيْنَا بَيْنَهُمُ الْعَدَاوَةَ وَالْبَغْضَاءَ إِلَىٰ يَوْمِ الْقِيَامَةِ ۚ كُلَّمَا أَوْقَدُوا نَارًا لِلْحَرْبِ أَطْفَأَهَا اللَّهُ ۚ وَيَسْعَوْنَ فِي الْأَرْضِ فَسَادًا ۚ وَاللَّهُ لَا يُحِبُّ الْمُفْسِدِينَ

64 13:26

64 The Jews say, "God's hand is tied." It is their hands that are tied, and they are cursed for what they say. In fact, His hands are outstretched; He gives as He wills. Certainly, what was revealed to you from your Lord will increase many of them in defiance and blasphemy. And We placed between them enmity and hatred, until the Day of Resurrection. Whenever they kindle the fire of war, God extinguishes it. And they strive to spread corruption on earth. God does not love the corrupters.

٦٥ وَلَوْ أَنَّ أَهْلَ الْكِتَابِ آمَنُوا وَاتَّقَوْا لَكَفَّرْنَا عَنْهُمْ سَيِّئَاتِهِمْ وَلَأَدْخَلْنَاهُمْ جَنَّاتِ النَّعِيمِ

65 3:110

65 Had the People of the Scripture believed and been righteous, We would have remitted their sins, and admitted them into the Gardens of Bliss.

٦٦ وَلَوْ أَنَّهُمْ أَقَامُوا التَّوْرَاةَ وَالْإِنْجِيلَ وَمَا أُنْزِلَ إِلَيْهِمْ مِنْ رَبِّهِمْ لَأَكَلُوا مِنْ فَوْقِهِمْ وَمِنْ تَحْتِ أَرْجُلِهِمْ ۚ [a] مِنْهُمْ أُمَّةٌ مُقْتَصِدَةٌ ۖ وَكَثِيرٌ مِنْهُمْ سَاءَ مَا يَعْمَلُونَ [b]

66
[a] 5:47, 68
[b] 35:32

66 Had they observed the Torah, and the Gospel, and what was revealed to them from their Lord, they would have consumed amply from above them, and from beneath their feet. Among them is a moderate community, but evil is what many of them are doing.

٦٧ يَا أَيُّهَا الرَّسُولُ بَلِّغْ مَا أُنْزِلَ إِلَيْكَ مِنْ رَبِّكَ ۖ وَإِنْ لَمْ تَفْعَلْ فَمَا بَلَّغْتَ رِسَالَتَهُ ۚ وَاللَّهُ يَعْصِمُكَ مِنَ النَّاسِ ۗ إِنَّ اللَّهَ لَا يَهْدِي الْقَوْمَ الْكَافِرِينَ

67 5:92; 24:54; 29:18

67 O Messenger, convey what was revealed to you from your Lord. But if you do not, then you would not have delivered His message. And God will protect you from the people. God does not guide the disbelieving people.

٦٨ قُلْ يَا أَهْلَ الْكِتَابِ لَسْتُمْ عَلَىٰ شَيْءٍ حَتَّىٰ تُقِيمُوا التَّوْرَاةَ وَالْإِنْجِيلَ وَمَا أُنْزِلَ إِلَيْكُمْ مِنْ رَبِّكُمْ ۗ وَلَيَزِيدَنَّ كَثِيرًا مِنْهُمْ مَا أُنْزِلَ إِلَيْكَ مِنْ رَبِّكَ طُغْيَانًا وَكُفْرًا ۖ فَلَا تَأْسَ عَلَى الْقَوْمِ الْكَافِرِينَ

68 5:47, 66; 35:33

68 Say, "O People of the Scripture! You have no basis until you uphold the Torah, and the Gospel, and what is revealed to you from your Lord." But what is revealed to you from your Lord will increase many of them in rebellion and disbelief, so do not be sorry for the disbelieving people.

٦٩ إِنَّ الَّذِينَ آمَنُوا وَالَّذِينَ هَادُوا وَالصَّابِئُونَ وَالنَّصَارَىٰ [a] مَنْ آمَنَ بِاللَّهِ وَالْيَوْمِ الْآخِرِ وَعَمِلَ صَالِحًا فَلَا خَوْفٌ عَلَيْهِمْ وَلَا هُمْ يَحْزَنُونَ [b]

69
pp 2:62
[a] 22:17
[b] 2:277

69 Those who believe, and the Jews, and the Sabians, and the Christians—whoever believes in God and the Last Day, and does what is right—they have nothing to fear, nor shall they grieve.

٧٠ لَقَدْ أَخَذْنَا مِيثَاقَ بَنِي إِسْرَائِيلَ وَأَرْسَلْنَا إِلَيْهِمْ رُسُلًا ۖ كُلَّمَا جَاءَهُمْ رَسُولٌ بِمَا لَا تَهْوَىٰ أَنْفُسُهُمْ فَرِيقًا كَذَّبُوا وَفَرِيقًا يَقْتُلُونَ

70
4:154; 5:12

70 We made a covenant with the Children of Israel, and We sent to them messengers. Whenever a messenger came to them with what their souls did not desire, some of them they accused of lying, and others they put to death.

٧١ وَحَسِبُوا أَلَّا تَكُونَ فِتْنَةٌ فَعَمُوا وَصَمُّوا ثُمَّ تَابَ اللَّهُ عَلَيْهِمْ ثُمَّ عَمُوا وَصَمُّوا كَثِيرٌ مِنْهُمْ ۚ وَاللَّهُ بَصِيرٌ بِمَا يَعْمَلُونَ

71 They assumed there would be no punishment, so they turned blind and deaf. Then God redeemed them, but then again many of them turned blind and deaf. But God is Seeing of what they do.

٧٢ لَقَدْ كَفَرَ الَّذِينَ قَالُوا إِنَّ اللَّهَ هُوَ الْمَسِيحُ ابْنُ مَرْيَمَ ۖ وَقَالَ الْمَسِيحُ يَا بَنِي إِسْرَائِيلَ اعْبُدُوا اللَّهَ رَبِّي وَرَبَّكُمْ ۖ إِنَّهُ مَنْ يُشْرِكْ بِاللَّهِ فَقَدْ حَرَّمَ اللَّهُ عَلَيْهِ الْجَنَّةَ وَمَأْوَاهُ النَّارُ ۖ وَمَا لِلظَّالِمِينَ مِنْ أَنْصَارٍ

72
4:172; 5:17

72 They disbelieve those who say, "God is the Messiah the son of Mary." But the Messiah himself said, "O Children of Israel, worship God, my Lord and your Lord. Whoever associates others with God, God has forbidden him Paradise, and his dwelling is the Fire. The wrongdoers have no saviors."

٧٣ لَقَدْ كَفَرَ الَّذِينَ قَالُوا إِنَّ اللَّهَ ثَالِثُ ثَلَاثَةٍ ۘ وَمَا مِنْ إِلَٰهٍ إِلَّا إِلَٰهٌ وَاحِدٌ ۚ وَإِنْ لَمْ يَنْتَهُوا عَمَّا يَقُولُونَ لَيَمَسَّنَّ الَّذِينَ كَفَرُوا مِنْهُمْ عَذَابٌ أَلِيمٌ

73
4:171; 5:116

73 They disbelieve those who say, "God is the third of three." But there is no deity except the One God. If they do not refrain from what they say, a painful torment will befall those among them who disbelieve.

٧٤ أَفَلَا يَتُوبُونَ إِلَى اللَّهِ وَيَسْتَغْفِرُونَهُ ۚ وَاللَّهُ غَفُورٌ رَحِيمٌ

74
2:192; 8:38

74 Will they not repent to God and ask His forgiveness? God is Forgiving and Merciful.

٧٥ مَا الْمَسِيحُ ابْنُ مَرْيَمَ إِلَّا رَسُولٌ قَدْ خَلَتْ مِنْ قَبْلِهِ الرُّسُلُ وَأُمُّهُ صِدِّيقَةٌ ۖ كَانَا يَأْكُلَانِ الطَّعَامَ ۗ انْظُرْ كَيْفَ نُبَيِّنُ لَهُمُ الْآيَاتِ ثُمَّ انْظُرْ أَنَّىٰ يُؤْفَكُونَ

75
3:144; 5:17; 21:7–8;
25:20

75 The Messiah son of Mary was only a messenger, before whom other Messengers had passed away, and his mother was a woman of truth. They both used to eat food. Note how We make clear the revelations to them; then note how deluded they are.

٧٦ قُلْ أَتَعْبُدُونَ مِنْ دُونِ اللَّهِ مَا لَا يَمْلِكُ لَكُمْ ضَرًّا وَلَا نَفْعًا ۚ وَاللَّهُ هُوَ السَّمِيعُ الْعَلِيمُ

76
6:71; 21:66

76 Say, "Do you worship, besides God, what has no power to harm or benefit you?" But God: He is the Hearer, the Knower.

٧٧ قُلْ يَا أَهْلَ الْكِتَابِ لَا تَغْلُوا فِي دِينِكُمْ غَيْرَ الْحَقِّ وَلَا تَتَّبِعُوا أَهْوَاءَ قَوْمٍ قَدْ ضَلُّوا مِنْ قَبْلُ وَأَضَلُّوا كَثِيرًا وَضَلُّوا عَنْ سَوَاءِ السَّبِيلِ

77
2:171

77 Say, "O People of the Scripture! Do not exaggerate in your religion beyond the truth; and do not follow the opinions of people who went astray before, and misled many, and themselves strayed off the balanced way."

٧٨ لُعِنَ الَّذِينَ كَفَرُوا مِنْ بَنِي إِسْرَائِيلَ عَلَىٰ لِسَانِ دَاوُودَ وَعِيسَى ابْنِ مَرْيَمَ ۚ ذَٰلِكَ بِمَا عَصَوْا وَكَانُوا يَعْتَدُونَ

78 Cursed were those who disbelieved from among the Children of Israel by the tongue of David and Jesus son of Mary. That is because they rebelled and used to transgress.

٧٩ كَانُوا لَا يَتَنَاهَوْنَ عَنْ مُنْكَرٍ فَعَلُوهُ ۚ لَبِئْسَ مَا كَانُوا يَفْعَلُونَ

79 They used not to prevent one another from the wrongs they used to commit. Evil is what they used to do.

٨٠ تَرَىٰ كَثِيرًا مِنْهُمْ يَتَوَلَّوْنَ الَّذِينَ كَفَرُوا ۚ لَبِئْسَ مَا قَدَّمَتْ لَهُمْ أَنْفُسُهُمْ أَنْ سَخِطَ اللَّهُ عَلَيْهِمْ وَفِي الْعَذَابِ هُمْ خَالِدُونَ

80–81
3:28; 4:139, 144; 5:51

80 You will see many of them befriending those who disbelieve. Terrible is what their souls prompts them to do. The wrath of God fell upon them, and in the torment they will remain.

٨١ وَلَوْ كَانُوا يُؤْمِنُونَ بِاللَّهِ وَالنَّبِيِّ وَمَا أُنْزِلَ إِلَيْهِ مَا اتَّخَذُوهُمْ أَوْلِيَاءَ وَلَٰكِنَّ كَثِيرًا مِنْهُمْ فَاسِقُونَ

81 Had they believed in God and the Prophet, and in what was revealed to him, they would not have befriended them. But many of them are immoral.

٨٢ لَتَجِدَنَّ أَشَدَّ النَّاسِ عَدَاوَةً لِلَّذِينَ آمَنُوا الْيَهُودَ وَالَّذِينَ أَشْرَكُوا ۖ وَلَتَجِدَنَّ أَقْرَبَهُمْ مَوَدَّةً لِلَّذِينَ آمَنُوا الَّذِينَ قَالُوا إِنَّا نَصَارَىٰ ۚ ذَٰلِكَ بِأَنَّ مِنْهُمْ قِسِّيسِينَ وَرُهْبَانًا وَأَنَّهُمْ لَا يَسْتَكْبِرُونَ

82 You will find that the people most hostile towards the believers are the Jews and the polytheists. And you will find that the nearest in affection towards the believers are those who say, "We are Christians." That is because among them are priests and monks, and they are not arrogant.

٨٣ وَإِذَا سَمِعُوا مَا أُنْزِلَ إِلَى الرَّسُولِ تَرَىٰ أَعْيُنَهُمْ تَفِيضُ مِنَ الدَّمْعِ مِمَّا عَرَفُوا مِنَ الْحَقِّ ۖ يَقُولُونَ رَبَّنَا آمَنَّا فَاكْتُبْنَا مَعَ الشَّاهِدِينَ

83
17:107–109; 28:52

83 And when they hear what was revealed to the Messenger, you see their eyes overflowing with tears, as they recognize the truth in it. They say, "Our Lord, we have believed, so count us among the witnesses."

٨٤ وَمَا لَنَا لَا نُؤْمِنُ بِاللَّهِ وَمَا جَاءَنَا مِنَ الْحَقِّ وَنَطْمَعُ أَن يُدْخِلَنَا رَبُّنَا مَعَ الْقَوْمِ الصَّالِحِينَ

84 "And why should we not believe in God, and in the truth that has come to us, and hope that our Lord will include us among the righteous people?"

٨٥ فَأَثَابَهُمُ اللَّهُ بِمَا قَالُوا جَنَّاتٍ تَجْرِي مِن تَحْتِهَا الْأَنْهَارُ خَالِدِينَ فِيهَا ۚ وَذَٰلِكَ جَزَاءُ الْمُحْسِنِينَ

85 God will reward them for what they say—Gardens beneath which rivers flow, where they will stay forever. Such is the reward of the righteous.

٨٦ وَالَّذِينَ كَفَرُوا وَكَذَّبُوا بِآيَاتِنَا أُولَٰئِكَ أَصْحَابُ الْجَحِيمِ

86 But as for those who disbelieve and deny Our signs—these are the inmates of the Fire.

٨٧ يَا أَيُّهَا الَّذِينَ آمَنُوا لَا تُحَرِّمُوا طَيِّبَاتِ مَا أَحَلَّ اللَّهُ لَكُمْ وَلَا تَعْتَدُوا ۚ إِنَّ اللَّهَ لَا يُحِبُّ الْمُعْتَدِينَ

87 O you who believe! Do not prohibit the good things God has permitted for you, and do not commit aggression. God does not love the aggressors.

87–88
2:168, 172; 5:4; 7:31, 157; 6:140; 10:59

٨٨ وَكُلُوا مِمَّا رَزَقَكُمُ اللَّهُ حَلَالًا طَيِّبًا ۚ وَاتَّقُوا اللَّهَ الَّذِي أَنتُم بِهِ مُؤْمِنُونَ

88 And eat of the lawful and good things God has provided for you; and be conscious of God, in Whom you are believers.

٨٩ لَا يُؤَاخِذُكُمُ اللَّهُ بِاللَّغْوِ فِي أَيْمَانِكُمْ وَلَٰكِن يُؤَاخِذُكُم بِمَا عَقَّدتُّمُ الْأَيْمَانَ ۖ فَكَفَّارَتُهُ إِطْعَامُ عَشَرَةِ مَسَاكِينَ مِنْ أَوْسَطِ مَا تُطْعِمُونَ أَهْلِيكُمْ أَوْ كِسْوَتُهُمْ أَوْ تَحْرِيرُ رَقَبَةٍ ۖ فَمَن لَّمْ يَجِدْ فَصِيَامُ ثَلَاثَةِ أَيَّامٍ ۚ ذَٰلِكَ كَفَّارَةُ أَيْمَانِكُمْ إِذَا حَلَفْتُمْ ۚ وَاحْفَظُوا أَيْمَانَكُمْ ۚ كَذَٰلِكَ يُبَيِّنُ اللَّهُ لَكُمْ آيَاتِهِ لَعَلَّكُمْ تَشْكُرُونَ

89 God does not hold you accountable for your unintended oaths, but He holds you accountable for your binding oaths. The atonement for it is by feeding ten needy people from the average of what you feed your families, or by clothing them, or by freeing a slave. Anyone who lacks the means shall fast for three days. That is the atonement for breaking your oaths when you have sworn them. So keep your oaths. Thus God makes clear His Revelations to you, that you may be grateful.

89
2:225

٩٠ يَا أَيُّهَا الَّذِينَ آمَنُوا إِنَّمَا الْخَمْرُ وَالْمَيْسِرُ وَالْأَنصَابُ وَالْأَزْلَامُ رِجْسٌ مِّنْ عَمَلِ الشَّيْطَانِ فَاجْتَنِبُوهُ لَعَلَّكُمْ تُفْلِحُونَ

90 O you who believe! Intoxicants, gambling, idolatry, and divination are abominations of Satan's doing. Avoid them, so that you may prosper.

90–91
2:219; 16:36; 22:30; 39:17

٩١ إِنَّمَا يُرِيدُ الشَّيْطَانُ أَن يُوقِعَ بَيْنَكُمُ الْعَدَاوَةَ وَالْبَغْضَاءَ فِي الْخَمْرِ وَالْمَيْسِرِ وَيَصُدَّكُمْ عَن ذِكْرِ اللَّهِ وَعَنِ الصَّلَاةِ ۖ فَهَلْ أَنتُم مُّنتَهُونَ

91 Satan wants to provoke strife and hatred among you through intoxicants and gambling, and to prevent you from the remembrance of God, and from prayer. Will you not desist?

٩٢ وَأَطِيعُوا اللَّهَ وَأَطِيعُوا الرَّسُولَ وَاحْذَرُوا ۚ فَإِن تَوَلَّيْتُمْ فَاعْلَمُوا أَنَّمَا عَلَىٰ رَسُولِنَا الْبَلَاغُ الْمُبِينُ

92 Obey God and obey the Messenger, and be cautious. If you turn away—know that the duty of Our Messenger is clear communication.

92
3:31; 5:67, 99; 8:20; 24:54

٩٣ لَيْسَ عَلَى الَّذِينَ آمَنُوا وَعَمِلُوا الصَّالِحَاتِ جُنَاحٌ فِيمَا طَعِمُوا إِذَا مَا اتَّقَوْا وَآمَنُوا وَعَمِلُوا الصَّالِحَاتِ ثُمَّ اتَّقَوْا وَآمَنُوا ثُمَّ اتَّقَوْا وَأَحْسَنُوا ۗ وَاللَّهُ يُحِبُّ الْمُحْسِنِينَ

93 Those who believe and do righteous deeds will not be blamed for what they may have eaten, provided they obey, and believe, and do good deeds, then maintain piety and faith, then remain righteous and charitable. God loves the charitable.

٩٤ يَا أَيُّهَا الَّذِينَ آمَنُوا لَيَبْلُوَنَّكُمُ اللَّهُ بِشَيْءٍ مِّنَ الصَّيْدِ تَنَالُهُ أَيْدِيكُمْ وَرِمَاحُكُمْ لِيَعْلَمَ اللَّهُ مَن يَخَافُهُ بِالْغَيْبِ ۚ فَمَنِ اعْتَدَىٰ بَعْدَ ذَٰلِكَ فَلَهُ عَذَابٌ أَلِيمٌ

94 O you who believe! God will test you with something of the game your hands and spears obtain, that God may know who fears Him at heart. Whoever commits aggression after that will have a painful punishment.

٩٥ يَا أَيُّهَا الَّذِينَ آمَنُوا لَا تَقْتُلُوا الصَّيْدَ وَأَنتُمْ حُرُمٌ ۚ وَمَن قَتَلَهُ مِنكُم مُّتَعَمِّدًا فَجَزَاءٌ مِّثْلُ مَا قَتَلَ مِنَ النَّعَمِ يَحْكُمُ بِهِ ذَوَا عَدْلٍ مِّنكُمْ هَدْيًا بَالِغَ الْكَعْبَةِ أَوْ كَفَّارَةٌ طَعَامُ مَسَاكِينَ أَوْ عَدْلُ ذَٰلِكَ صِيَامًا لِّيَذُوقَ وَبَالَ أَمْرِهِ ۗ عَفَا اللَّهُ عَمَّا سَلَفَ ۚ وَمَنْ عَادَ فَيَنتَقِمُ اللَّهُ مِنْهُ ۗ وَاللَّهُ عَزِيزٌ ذُو انتِقَامٍ

95 O you who believe! do not kill game while you are in pilgrim sanctity. Whoever of you kills any intentionally, its penalty shall be a domestic animal comparable to what he killed, as determined by two honest persons among you—an offering delivered to the Kaabah. Or he may atone by feeding the needy, or its equivalent in fasting, so that he may taste the consequences of his conduct. God forgives what is past. But whoever repeats, God will take revenge on him. God is Almighty, Avenger.

95–96
5:2; 22:27–28

٩٦ أُحِلَّ لَكُمْ صَيْدُ الْبَحْرِ وَطَعَامُهُ مَتَاعًا لَّكُمْ وَلِلسَّيَّارَةِ ۖ وَحُرِّمَ عَلَيْكُمْ صَيْدُ الْبَرِّ مَا دُمْتُمْ حُرُمًا ۗ وَاتَّقُوا اللَّهَ الَّذِي إِلَيْهِ تُحْشَرُونَ

96 Permitted for you is the catch of sea, and its food—as sustenance for you and for travelers. But forbidden for you is the game of land while you are in pilgrim sanctity. And fear God, to Whom you will be gathered.

٩٧ جَعَلَ اللَّهُ الْكَعْبَةَ الْبَيْتَ الْحَرَامَ قِيَامًا لِّلنَّاسِ وَالشَّهْرَ الْحَرَامَ وَالْهَدْيَ وَالْقَلَائِدَ ۚ ذَٰلِكَ لِتَعْلَمُوا أَنَّ اللَّهَ يَعْلَمُ مَا فِي السَّمَاوَاتِ وَمَا فِي الْأَرْضِ وَأَنَّ اللَّهَ بِكُلِّ شَيْءٍ عَلِيمٌ

97 God has appointed the Kaabah, the Sacred House, a sanctuary for the people, and the Sacred Month, and the offerings, and the garlanded. That you may know that God knows everything in the heavens and the earth, and that God is Cognizant of all things.

97
2:125; 3:96; 5:2; 28:57; 29:67

٩٨ اعْلَمُوا أَنَّ اللَّهَ شَدِيدُ الْعِقَابِ وَأَنَّ اللَّهَ غَفُورٌ رَحِيمٌ

98 Know that God is severe in retribution, and that God is Forgiving and Merciful.

98
6:165; 7:167; 41:43

٩٩ مَا عَلَى الرَّسُولِ إِلَّا الْبَلَاغُ ۗ وَاللَّهُ يَعْلَمُ مَا تُبْدُونَ وَمَا تَكْتُمُونَ

99 The Messenger's sole duty is to convey. God knows what you reveal and what you conceal.

99
5:67; 24:54; 29:18

١٠٠ قُلْ لَا يَسْتَوِي الْخَبِيثُ وَالطَّيِّبُ وَلَوْ أَعْجَبَكَ كَثْرَةُ الْخَبِيثِ ۚ فَاتَّقُوا اللَّهَ يَا أُولِي الْأَلْبَابِ لَعَلَّكُمْ تُفْلِحُونَ

100 Say: "The bad and the good are not equal, even though the abundance of the bad may impress you. So be conscious of God, O you who possess intelligence, that you may succeed."

١٠١ يَا أَيُّهَا الَّذِينَ آمَنُوا لَا تَسْأَلُوا عَنْ أَشْيَاءَ إِنْ تُبْدَ لَكُمْ تَسُؤْكُمْ وَإِنْ تَسْأَلُوا عَنْهَا حِينَ يُنَزَّلُ الْقُرْآنُ تُبْدَ لَكُمْ عَفَا اللَّهُ عَنْهَا ۗ وَاللَّهُ غَفُورٌ حَلِيمٌ

101 O you who believe! Do not ask about things that would trouble you if disclosed to you. But if you were to ask about them while the Qur'an is being revealed, they will become obvious to you. God forgives that. God is Forgiving and Clement.

١٠٢ قَدْ سَأَلَهَا قَوْمٌ مِنْ قَبْلِكُمْ ثُمَّ أَصْبَحُوا بِهَا كَافِرِينَ

102 A people before you asked about them, but then came to reject them.

١٠٣ مَا جَعَلَ اللَّهُ مِنْ بَحِيرَةٍ وَلَا سَائِبَةٍ وَلَا وَصِيلَةٍ وَلَا حَامٍ ۙ وَلَٰكِنَّ الَّذِينَ كَفَرُوا يَفْتَرُونَ عَلَى اللَّهِ الْكَذِبَ ۖ وَأَكْثَرُهُمْ لَا يَعْقِلُونَ

103
6:136

103 God did not institute the superstitions of Bahirah, Saibah, Wasilah, or of Hami; but those who disbelieve fabricate lies about God—most of them do not understand.

١٠٤ وَإِذَا قِيلَ لَهُمْ تَعَالَوْا إِلَىٰ مَا أَنْزَلَ اللَّهُ وَإِلَى الرَّسُولِ قَالُوا حَسْبُنَا مَا وَجَدْنَا عَلَيْهِ آبَاءَنَا ۚ أَوَلَوْ كَانَ آبَاؤُهُمْ لَا يَعْلَمُونَ شَيْئًا وَلَا يَهْتَدُونَ

104
2:170; 10:78; 31:21; 43:22–24

104 And when it is said to them, "Come to what God has revealed, and to the Messenger," they say, "Sufficient for us is what we found our forefathers upon." Even if their forefathers knew nothing, and were not guided?

١٠٥ يَا أَيُّهَا الَّذِينَ آمَنُوا عَلَيْكُمْ أَنْفُسَكُمْ ۖ لَا يَضُرُّكُمْ مَنْ ضَلَّ إِذَا اهْتَدَيْتُمْ ۚ إِلَى اللَّهِ مَرْجِعُكُمْ جَمِيعًا فَيُنَبِّئُكُمْ بِمَا كُنْتُمْ تَعْمَلُونَ

105
6:60; 39:42

105 O you who believe! You are responsible for your own souls. He who has strayed cannot harm you if you are guided. To God is your return, all of you, and He will inform you of what you used to do.

١٠٦ يَا أَيُّهَا الَّذِينَ آمَنُوا شَهَادَةُ بَيْنِكُمْ إِذَا حَضَرَ أَحَدَكُمُ الْمَوْتُ حِينَ الْوَصِيَّةِ اثْنَانِ ذَوَا عَدْلٍ مِّنكُمْ أَوْ آخَرَانِ مِنْ غَيْرِكُمْ إِنْ أَنتُمْ ضَرَبْتُمْ فِي الْأَرْضِ فَأَصَابَتْكُم مُّصِيبَةُ الْمَوْتِ ۚ تَحْبِسُونَهُمَا مِن بَعْدِ الصَّلَاةِ فَيُقْسِمَانِ بِاللَّهِ إِنِ ارْتَبْتُمْ لَا نَشْتَرِي بِهِ ثَمَنًا وَلَوْ كَانَ ذَا قُرْبَىٰ ۙ وَلَا نَكْتُمُ شَهَادَةَ اللَّهِ إِنَّا إِذًا لَّمِنَ الْآثِمِينَ

106–108
2:180–182

106 O you who believe! When death approaches one of you, let two reliable persons from among you act as witnesses to the making of a bequest, or two persons from another people if you are travelling in the land and the event of death approaches you. Engage them after the prayer. If you have doubts, let them swear by God: "We will not sell our testimony for any price, even if he was a near relative, and we will not conceal God's testimony, for then we would be sinners."

١٠٧ فَإِنْ عُثِرَ عَلَىٰ أَنَّهُمَا اسْتَحَقَّا إِثْمًا فَآخَرَانِ يَقُومَانِ مَقَامَهُمَا مِنَ الَّذِينَ اسْتَحَقَّ عَلَيْهِمُ الْأَوْلَيَانِ فَيُقْسِمَانِ بِاللَّهِ لَشَهَادَتُنَا أَحَقُّ مِن شَهَادَتِهِمَا وَمَا اعْتَدَيْنَا إِنَّا إِذًا لَّمِنَ الظَّالِمِينَ

107 If it is discovered that they are guilty of perjury: let two others take their place, two from among those responsible for the claim, and have them swear by God, "Our testimony is more truthful than their testimony, and we will not be biased, for then we would be wrongdoers."

١٠٨ ذَٰلِكَ أَدْنَىٰ أَن يَأْتُوا بِالشَّهَادَةِ عَلَىٰ وَجْهِهَا أَوْ يَخَافُوا أَن تُرَدَّ أَيْمَانٌ بَعْدَ أَيْمَانِهِمْ ۗ وَاتَّقُوا اللَّهَ وَاسْمَعُوا ۗ وَاللَّهُ لَا يَهْدِي الْقَوْمَ الْفَاسِقِينَ

108 That makes it more likely that they will give true testimony, fearing that their oaths might be contradicted by subsequent oaths. So fear God, and listen. God does not guide the disobedient people.

١٠٩ يَوْمَ يَجْمَعُ اللَّهُ الرُّسُلَ فَيَقُولُ مَاذَا أُجِبْتُمْ ۖ قَالُوا لَا عِلْمَ لَنَا ۖ إِنَّكَ أَنتَ عَلَّامُ الْغُيُوبِ

109
5:116; 9:70

109 On the Day when God will gather the messengers, then say, "What response were you given?" They will say, "We have no knowledge; it is You Who are the Knower of the unseen."

١١٠ إِذْ قَالَ اللَّهُ يَا عِيسَى ابْنَ مَرْيَمَ اذْكُرْ نِعْمَتِي عَلَيْكَ وَعَلَىٰ وَالِدَتِكَ إِذْ أَيَّدتُّكَ بِرُوحِ الْقُدُسِ تُكَلِّمُ النَّاسَ فِي الْمَهْدِ وَكَهْلًا ۖ وَإِذْ عَلَّمْتُكَ الْكِتَابَ وَالْحِكْمَةَ وَالتَّوْرَاةَ وَالْإِنجِيلَ ۖ وَإِذْ تَخْلُقُ مِنَ الطِّينِ كَهَيْئَةِ الطَّيْرِ بِإِذْنِي فَتَنفُخُ فِيهَا فَتَكُونُ طَيْرًا بِإِذْنِي ۖ وَتُبْرِئُ الْأَكْمَهَ وَالْأَبْرَصَ بِإِذْنِي ۖ وَإِذْ تُخْرِجُ الْمَوْتَىٰ بِإِذْنِي ۖ وَإِذْ كَفَفْتُ بَنِي إِسْرَائِيلَ عَنكَ إِذْ جِئْتَهُم بِالْبَيِّنَاتِ فَقَالَ الَّذِينَ كَفَرُوا مِنْهُمْ إِنْ هَٰذَا إِلَّا سِحْرٌ مُّبِينٌ

110
2:87, 253; 3:46, 48–49

110 When God will say, "O Jesus son of Mary, recall My favor upon you and upon your mother, how I supported you with the Holy Spirit. You spoke to the people from the crib, and in maturity. How I taught you the Scripture and wisdom, and the Torah and the Gospel. And recall that you molded from clay the shape of a bird, by My leave, and then you breathed into it, and it became a bird, by My leave. And you healed the blind and the leprous, by My leave; and you revived the dead, by My leave. And recall that I restrained the Children of Israel from you when you brought them the clear miracles. But those who disbelieved among them said, 'This is nothing but obvious sorcery.'"

١١١ وَإِذْ أَوْحَيْتُ إِلَى الْحَوَارِيِّينَ أَنْ آمِنُوا بِي وَبِرَسُولِي قَالُوا آمَنَّا وَاشْهَدْ بِأَنَّنَا مُسْلِمُونَ

111 "And when I inspired the disciples: 'Believe in Me and in My Messenger.' They said, 'We have believed, so bear witness that We have submitted.'"

111
3:52

١١٢ إِذْ قَالَ الْحَوَارِيُّونَ يَا عِيسَى ابْنَ مَرْيَمَ هَلْ يَسْتَطِيعُ رَبُّكَ أَنْ يُنَزِّلَ عَلَيْنَا مَائِدَةً مِنَ السَّمَاءِ ۖ قَالَ اتَّقُوا اللَّهَ إِنْ كُنْتُمْ مُؤْمِنِينَ

112 "And when the disciples said, 'O Jesus son of Mary, is your Lord able to bring down for us a feast from heaven?' He said, 'Fear God, if you are believers.'"

١١٣ قَالُوا نُرِيدُ أَنْ نَأْكُلَ مِنْهَا وَتَطْمَئِنَّ قُلُوبُنَا وَنَعْلَمَ أَنْ قَدْ صَدَقْتَنَا وَنَكُونَ عَلَيْهَا مِنَ الشَّاهِدِينَ

113 They said, "We wish to eat from it, so that our hearts may be reassured, and know that you have told us the truth, and be among those who witness it."

١١٤ قَالَ عِيسَى ابْنُ مَرْيَمَ اللَّهُمَّ رَبَّنَا أَنْزِلْ عَلَيْنَا مَائِدَةً مِنَ السَّمَاءِ تَكُونُ لَنَا عِيدًا لِأَوَّلِنَا وَآخِرِنَا وَآيَةً مِنْكَ ۖ وَارْزُقْنَا وَأَنْتَ خَيْرُ الرَّازِقِينَ

114 Jesus son of Mary said, "O God, our Lord, send down for us a table from heaven, to be a festival for us, for the first of us, and the last of us, and a sign from You; and provide for us; You are the Best of providers."

١١٥ قَالَ اللَّهُ إِنِّي مُنَزِّلُهَا عَلَيْكُمْ ۖ فَمَنْ يَكْفُرْ بَعْدُ مِنْكُمْ فَإِنِّي أُعَذِّبُهُ عَذَابًا لَا أُعَذِّبُهُ أَحَدًا مِنَ الْعَالَمِينَ

115 God said, "I will send it down to you. But whoever among you disbelieves thereafter, I will punish him with a punishment the like of which I never punish any other being."

١١٦ وَإِذْ قَالَ اللَّهُ يَا عِيسَى ابْنَ مَرْيَمَ أَأَنْتَ قُلْتَ لِلنَّاسِ اتَّخِذُونِي وَأُمِّيَ إِلَٰهَيْنِ مِنْ دُونِ اللَّهِ ۖ قَالَ سُبْحَانَكَ مَا يَكُونُ لِي أَنْ أَقُولَ مَا لَيْسَ لِي بِحَقٍّ ۚ إِنْ كُنْتُ قُلْتُهُ فَقَدْ عَلِمْتَهُ ۚ تَعْلَمُ مَا فِي نَفْسِي وَلَا أَعْلَمُ مَا فِي نَفْسِكَ ۚ إِنَّكَ أَنْتَ عَلَّامُ الْغُيُوبِ

116
4:171; 5:73, 109; 9:70

116 And God will say, "O Jesus son of Mary, did you say to the people, 'Take me and my mother as gods rather than God?'" He will say, "Glory be to You! It is not for me to say what I have no right to. Had I said it, You would have known it. You know what is in my soul, and I do not know what is in Your soul. You are the Knower of the hidden.

١١٧ مَا قُلْتُ لَهُمْ إِلَّا مَا أَمَرْتَنِي بِهِ أَنِ اعْبُدُوا اللَّهَ رَبِّي وَرَبَّكُمْ ۚ وَكُنْتُ عَلَيْهِمْ شَهِيدًا مَا دُمْتُ فِيهِمْ ۖ فَلَمَّا تَوَفَّيْتَنِي كُنْتَ أَنْتَ الرَّقِيبَ عَلَيْهِمْ ۚ وَأَنْتَ عَلَىٰ كُلِّ شَيْءٍ شَهِيدٌ

117
3:55; 4:159

117 I only told them what You commanded me: that you shall worship God, my Lord and your Lord. And I was a witness over them while I was among them; but when You took me to Yourself, You became the Watcher over them—You are Witness over everything.

١١٨ إِنْ تُعَذِّبْهُمْ فَإِنَّهُمْ عِبَادُكَ ۖ وَإِنْ تَغْفِرْ لَهُمْ فَإِنَّكَ أَنْتَ الْعَزِيزُ الْحَكِيمُ

118 If You punish them, they are Your servants; but if You forgive them, You are the Mighty and Wise."

١١٩ قَالَ اللَّهُ هَٰذَا يَوْمُ يَنْفَعُ الصَّادِقِينَ صِدْقُهُمْ ۚ لَهُمْ جَنَّاتٌ تَجْرِي مِنْ تَحْتِهَا الْأَنْهَارُ خَالِدِينَ فِيهَا أَبَدًا ۚ رَضِيَ اللَّهُ عَنْهُمْ وَرَضُوا عَنْهُ ۚ ذَٰلِكَ الْفَوْزُ الْعَظِيمُ

119 God will say, "This is a Day when the truthful will benefit from their truthfulness." They will have Gardens beneath which rivers flow, wherein they will remain forever. God is pleased with them, and they are pleased with Him. That is the great attainment.

١٢٠ لِلَّهِ مُلْكُ السَّمَاوَاتِ وَالْأَرْضِ وَمَا فِيهِنَّ ۚ وَهُوَ عَلَىٰ كُلِّ شَيْءٍ قَدِيرٌ

120 To God belongs the sovereignty of the heavens and the earth and what lies in them, and He has power over everything.

120
19:65

Sūrah 6: Al-An'ām

سُورَةُ ٱلْأَنْعَامِ (Livestock)

بِسْمِ ٱللَّهِ ٱلرَّحْمَٰنِ ٱلرَّحِيمِ

١ الْحَمْدُ لِلَّهِ الَّذِي خَلَقَ السَّمَاوَاتِ وَالْأَرْضَ وَجَعَلَ الظُّلُمَاتِ وَالنُّورَ ۖ ثُمَّ الَّذِينَ كَفَرُوا بِرَبِّهِمْ يَعْدِلُونَ

1 Praise be to God, Who created the heavens and the earth, and made the darkness and the light. Yet those who disbelieve ascribe equals to their Lord.

1
13:16; 16:17

٢ هُوَ الَّذِي خَلَقَكُمْ مِنْ طِينٍ ثُمَّ قَضَىٰ أَجَلًا ۖ وَأَجَلٌ مُسَمًّى عِنْدَهُ ۖ ثُمَّ أَنْتُمْ تَمْتَرُونَ

2 It is He Who created you from clay, then decided a term—a term determined by Him. Yet you doubt.

2
6:60; 39:42; 40:67

٣ وَهُوَ اللَّهُ فِي السَّمَاوَاتِ وَفِي الْأَرْضِ ۖ يَعْلَمُ سِرَّكُمْ وَجَهْرَكُمْ وَيَعْلَمُ مَا تَكْسِبُونَ

3 He is God in the heavens and the earth. He knows what you keep secret and what you make public; and He knows what you earn.

3
13:13, 42

٤ وَمَا تَأْتِيهِمْ مِنْ آيَةٍ مِنْ آيَاتِ رَبِّهِمْ إِلَّا كَانُوا عَنْهَا مُعْرِضِينَ

4 Not one of their Lord's signs comes to them, but they turn away from it.

4
pp 36:46
12:105; 15:8; 26:5

٥ فَقَدْ كَذَّبُوا بِالْحَقِّ لَمَّا جَاءَهُمْ ۖ فَسَوْفَ يَأْتِيهِمْ أَنْبَاءُ مَا كَانُوا بِهِ يَسْتَهْزِئُونَ

5 They denied the truth when it has come to them; but soon will reach them the news of what they used to ridicule.

5
26:6; 29:68; 39:32

٦ أَلَمْ يَرَوْا كَمْ أَهْلَكْنَا مِن قَبْلِهِم مِّن قَرْنٍ مَّكَّنَّاهُمْ فِي الْأَرْضِ مَا لَمْ نُمَكِّن لَّكُمْ وَأَرْسَلْنَا السَّمَاءَ عَلَيْهِم مِّدْرَارًا وَجَعَلْنَا الْأَنْهَارَ تَجْرِي مِن تَحْتِهِمْ فَأَهْلَكْنَاهُم بِذُنُوبِهِمْ وَأَنشَأْنَا مِن بَعْدِهِمْ قَرْنًا آخَرِينَ

6
19:74; 21:11; 36:31; 38:3; 43:8; 46:26; 50:36

6 Have they not considered how many generations We destroyed before them? We had established them on earth more firmly than We established you, and We sent the clouds pouring down abundant rain on them, and We made rivers flow beneath them. But We destroyed them for their sins, and established other civilizations after them.

٧ وَلَوْ نَزَّلْنَا عَلَيْكَ كِتَابًا فِي قِرْطَاسٍ فَلَمَسُوهُ بِأَيْدِيهِمْ لَقَالَ الَّذِينَ كَفَرُوا إِنْ هَٰذَا إِلَّا سِحْرٌ مُّبِينٌ

7
4:153; 7:146; 10:76, 96–97; 15:14–15; 17:93

7 Had We sent down upon you a book on paper, and they had touched it with their hands, those who disbelieve would have said, "This is nothing but plain magic."

٨ وَقَالُوا لَوْلَا أُنزِلَ عَلَيْهِ مَلَكٌ ۖ وَلَوْ أَنزَلْنَا مَلَكًا لَّقُضِيَ الْأَمْرُ ثُمَّ لَا يُنظَرُونَ

8–9
11:12, 31; 6:111; 15:8; 25:7

8 And they say, "Why was an angel not sent down to him." Had We sent down an angel, the matter would have been settled, and they would not have been reprieved.

٩ وَلَوْ جَعَلْنَاهُ مَلَكًا لَّجَعَلْنَاهُ رَجُلًا وَلَلَبَسْنَا عَلَيْهِم مَّا يَلْبِسُونَ

9
117:95

9 Had We made him an angel, We would have made him a man, and confused them when they are already confused.

١٠ وَلَقَدِ اسْتُهْزِئَ بِرُسُلٍ مِّن قَبْلِكَ فَحَاقَ بِالَّذِينَ سَخِرُوا مِنْهُم مَّا كَانُوا بِهِ يَسْتَهْزِئُونَ

10
11:38; 13:32; 15:11; 21:41; 39:48; 40:83

10 Messengers before you were ridiculed, but those who mocked them became besieged by what they ridiculed.

١١ قُلْ سِيرُوا فِي الْأَرْضِ ثُمَّ انظُرُوا كَيْفَ كَانَ عَاقِبَةُ الْمُكَذِّبِينَ

11
3:137

11 Say, "Travel the earth and observe the final fate of the deniers."

١٢ قُل لِّمَن مَّا فِي السَّمَاوَاتِ وَالْأَرْضِ ۖ قُل لِّلَّهِ ۚ كَتَبَ عَلَىٰ نَفْسِهِ الرَّحْمَةَ ۚ لَيَجْمَعَنَّكُمْ إِلَىٰ يَوْمِ الْقِيَامَةِ لَا رَيْبَ فِيهِ ۚ الَّذِينَ خَسِرُوا أَنفُسَهُمْ فَهُمْ لَا يُؤْمِنُونَ

12
39:49

12 Say, "To whom belongs what is in the heavens and the earth?" Say, "To God." He has inscribed for Himself mercy. He will gather you to the Day of Resurrection, in which there is no doubt. Those who lost their souls do not believe.

١٣ وَلَهُ مَا سَكَنَ فِي اللَّيْلِ وَالنَّهَارِ ۚ وَهُوَ السَّمِيعُ الْعَلِيمُ

13
10:67; 28:73; 30:23

13 To Him belongs whatever rests in the night and the day. He is the Hearing, the Knowing.

١٤ قُلْ أَغَيْرَ اللَّهِ أَتَّخِذُ وَلِيًّا فَاطِرِ السَّمَاوَاتِ وَالْأَرْضِ وَهُوَ يُطْعِمُ وَلَا يُطْعَمُ ۗ قُلْ إِنِّي أُمِرْتُ أَنْ أَكُونَ أَوَّلَ مَنْ أَسْلَمَ ۖ وَلَا تَكُونَنَّ مِنَ الْمُشْرِكِينَ

14
2:101; 6:162–163; 35:15; 51:57

14 Say, "Shall I take for myself a protector other than God, Originator of the heavens and the earth, and He feeds and is not fed?" Say, "I am instructed to be the first of those who submit." And do not be among the idolaters.

١٥ قُلْ إِنِّي أَخَافُ إِنْ عَصَيْتُ رَبِّي عَذَابَ يَوْمٍ عَظِيمٍ

15 Say, "I fear, should I defy my Lord, the punishment of a tremendous Day."

15
10:15; 39:13

١٦ مَّن يُصْرَفْ عَنْهُ يَوْمَئِذٍ فَقَدْ رَحِمَهُ ۚ وَذَٰلِكَ الْفَوْزُ الْمُبِينُ

16 Whoever is spared on that Day—He had mercy on him. That is the clear victory.

16
40:9

١٧ وَإِن يَمْسَسْكَ اللَّهُ بِضُرٍّ فَلَا كَاشِفَ لَهُ إِلَّا هُوَ ۖ وَإِن يَمْسَسْكَ بِخَيْرٍ فَهُوَ عَلَىٰ كُلِّ شَيْءٍ قَدِيرٌ

17 If God touches you with adversity, none can remove it except He. And if He touches you with good—He is Capable of everything.

17
10:107; 35:2

١٨ وَهُوَ الْقَاهِرُ فَوْقَ عِبَادِهِ ۚ وَهُوَ الْحَكِيمُ الْخَبِيرُ

18 He is the Supreme over His servants. He is the Wise, the Expert.

18
6:61

١٩ قُلْ أَيُّ شَيْءٍ أَكْبَرُ شَهَادَةً ۖ قُلِ اللَّهُ ۖ شَهِيدٌ بَيْنِي وَبَيْنَكُمْ ۚ وَأُوحِيَ إِلَيَّ هَٰذَا الْقُرْآنُ لِأُنذِرَكُم بِهِ وَمَن بَلَغَ ۚ أَئِنَّكُمْ لَتَشْهَدُونَ أَنَّ مَعَ اللَّهِ آلِهَةً أُخْرَىٰ ۚ قُل لَّا أَشْهَدُ ۚ قُلْ إِنَّمَا هُوَ إِلَٰهٌ وَاحِدٌ وَإِنَّنِي بَرِيءٌ مِّمَّا تُشْرِكُونَ

19 Say, "What thing is more solemn in testimony?" Say, "God is Witness between you and me. This Qur'an was revealed to me, that I may warn you with it, and whomever it may reach. Do you indeed testify that there are other gods with God?" Say, "I myself do not testify." Say, "He is but One God, and I am innocent of your idolatry."

19
6:92; 42:7

٢٠ الَّذِينَ آتَيْنَاهُمُ الْكِتَابَ يَعْرِفُونَهُ كَمَا يَعْرِفُونَ أَبْنَاءَهُمُ ۘ الَّذِينَ خَسِرُوا أَنفُسَهُمْ فَهُمْ لَا يُؤْمِنُونَ

20 Those to whom We have given the Book recognize it as they recognize their own children; but those who have lost their souls do not believe.

20
2:146; 6:114

٢١ وَمَنْ أَظْلَمُ مِمَّنِ افْتَرَىٰ عَلَى اللَّهِ كَذِبًا أَوْ كَذَّبَ بِآيَاتِهِ ۗ إِنَّهُ لَا يُفْلِحُ الظَّالِمُونَ

21 Who does greater wrong than someone who fabricates lies against God, or denies His revelations? The wrongdoers will not succeed.

21
pp 7:37; 10:17; 29:78

٢٢ وَيَوْمَ نَحْشُرُهُمْ جَمِيعًا ثُمَّ نَقُولُ لِلَّذِينَ أَشْرَكُوا أَيْنَ شُرَكَاؤُكُمُ الَّذِينَ كُنتُمْ تَزْعُمُونَ

22 On the Day when We gather them all together, then say to the idolaters, "Where are your idols, those you used to claim?"

22
pp 10:28
16:27; 18:52; 28:62; 40:73

٢٣ ثُمَّ لَمْ تَكُن فِتْنَتُهُمْ إِلَّا أَن قَالُوا وَاللَّهِ رَبِّنَا مَا كُنَّا مُشْرِكِينَ

23 Then their only argument will be to say, "By God, our Lord, we were not idolaters."

٢٤ انظُرْ كَيْفَ كَذَبُوا عَلَىٰ أَنفُسِهِمْ ۚ وَضَلَّ عَنْهُم مَّا كَانُوا يَفْتَرُونَ

24 Look how they lied to themselves. And what they invented deserted them.

24
7:37, 53; 10:30; 11:21

٢٥ وَمِنْهُم مَّن يَسْتَمِعُ إِلَيْكَ ۖ وَجَعَلْنَا عَلَىٰ قُلُوبِهِمْ أَكِنَّةً أَن يَفْقَهُوهُ وَفِي آذَانِهِمْ وَقْرًا ۚ [a] وَإِن يَرَوْا كُلَّ آيَةٍ لَّا يُؤْمِنُوا بِهَا ۚ حَتَّىٰ إِذَا جَاءُوكَ يُجَادِلُونَكَ يَقُولُ الَّذِينَ كَفَرُوا إِنْ هَٰذَا إِلَّا أَسَاطِيرُ الْأَوَّلِينَ [b]

25 Among them are those who listen to you; but We place covers over their hearts, to prevent them from understanding it, and heaviness in their ears. Even if they see every sign, they will not believe in it. Until, when they come to you, to argue with you, those who disbelieve will say, "These are nothing but myths of the ancients."

25
[a] 10:42; 17:46; 18:57; 27:68; 47:16, 45
[b] 8:31; 16:24; 23:83; 25:55; 27:68; 47:17; 68:15; 83:13

٢٦ وَهُمْ يَنْهَوْنَ عَنْهُ وَيَنْأَوْنَ عَنْهُ ۖ وَإِن يُهْلِكُونَ إِلَّا أَنفُسَهُمْ وَمَا يَشْعُرُونَ

26 They keep others from it, and avoid it themselves; but they ruin only their own souls, and they do not realize.

٢٧ وَلَوْ تَرَىٰ إِذْ وُقِفُوا عَلَى النَّارِ فَقَالُوا يَا لَيْتَنَا نُرَدُّ وَلَا نُكَذِّبَ بِآيَاتِ رَبِّنَا وَنَكُونَ مِنَ الْمُؤْمِنِينَ

27 If only you could see, when they are made to stand before the Fire; they will say, "If only we could be sent back, and not reject the revelations of our Lord, and be among the faithful."

27
7:53; 15:2; 32:12; 35:37

٢٨ بَلْ بَدَا لَهُم مَّا كَانُوا يُخْفُونَ مِن قَبْلُ ۖ وَلَوْ رُدُّوا لَعَادُوا لِمَا نُهُوا عَنْهُ وَإِنَّهُمْ لَكَاذِبُونَ

28 What they used to conceal before will become clear to them. And even if they were sent back, they would revert to what they were forbidden. They are liars.

28
23:75

٢٩ وَقَالُوا إِنْ هِيَ إِلَّا حَيَاتُنَا الدُّنْيَا وَمَا نَحْنُ بِمَبْعُوثِينَ

29 And they say, "There is nothing but our life in this world, and we will not be resurrected."

29
16:38; 23:37; 45:24

٣٠ وَلَوْ تَرَىٰ إِذْ وُقِفُوا عَلَىٰ رَبِّهِمْ ۚ قَالَ أَلَيْسَ هَٰذَا بِالْحَقِّ ۚ قَالُوا بَلَىٰ وَرَبِّنَا ۚ قَالَ فَذُوقُوا الْعَذَابَ بِمَا كُنتُمْ تَكْفُرُونَ

30 If only you could see, when they are stationed before their Lord. He will say, "Is this not real?" They will say, "Yes indeed, by our Lord." He will say, "Then taste the torment for having disbelieved."

30–31
10:53; 34:31; 39:56

٣١ قَدْ خَسِرَ الَّذِينَ كَذَّبُوا بِلِقَاءِ اللَّهِ ۖ حَتَّىٰ إِذَا جَاءَتْهُمُ السَّاعَةُ بَغْتَةً قَالُوا يَا حَسْرَتَنَا عَلَىٰ مَا فَرَّطْنَا فِيهَا وَهُمْ يَحْمِلُونَ أَوْزَارَهُمْ عَلَىٰ ظُهُورِهِمْ ۚ أَلَا سَاءَ مَا يَزِرُونَ

31 Losers are those who deny the encounter with God. Then, when the Hour comes upon them suddenly, they will say, "Alas for us, how we have neglected it." And they will carry their burdens on their backs—evil is what they carry.

٣٢ وَمَا الْحَيَاةُ الدُّنْيَا إِلَّا لَعِبٌ وَلَهْوٌ ۖ وَلَلدَّارُ الْآخِرَةُ خَيْرٌ لِّلَّذِينَ يَتَّقُونَ ۗ أَفَلَا تَعْقِلُونَ

32 The life of this world is nothing but game and distraction, but the Home of the Hereafter is better for those who are righteous. Do you not understand?

32
6:70; 7:51; 29:64; 47:36

٣٣ قَدْ نَعْلَمُ إِنَّهُ لَيَحْزُنُكَ الَّذِي يَقُولُونَ ۖ فَإِنَّهُمْ لَا يُكَذِّبُونَكَ وَلَٰكِنَّ الظَّالِمِينَ بِآيَاتِ اللَّهِ يَجْحَدُونَ

33 We know that what they say grieves you. It is not you they reject, but it is God's revelations that the wicked deny.

33
5:68; 10:65; 15:97; 18:6; 26:3; 27:70–71; 35:8

٣٤ وَلَقَدْ كُذِّبَتْ رُسُلٌ مِنْ قَبْلِكَ فَصَبَرُوا عَلَىٰ مَا كُذِّبُوا وَأُوذُوا حَتَّىٰ أَتَاهُمْ نَصْرُنَا ۚ وَلَا مُبَدِّلَ لِكَلِمَاتِ اللَّهِ ۚ وَلَقَدْ جَاءَكَ مِنْ نَبَإِ الْمُرْسَلِينَ

34 Other messengers before you were rejected, but they endured rejection and persecution until Our help came to them. There can be no change to God's words. News of the Messengers has already reached you.

34
3:184, 186; 6:115; 10:64; 14:12; 35:4, 25

٣٥ وَإِنْ كَانَ كَبُرَ عَلَيْكَ إِعْرَاضُهُمْ فَإِنِ اسْتَطَعْتَ أَنْ تَبْتَغِيَ نَفَقًا فِي الْأَرْضِ أَوْ سُلَّمًا فِي السَّمَاءِ فَتَأْتِيَهُمْ بِآيَةٍ ۚ وَلَوْ شَاءَ اللَّهُ لَجَمَعَهُمْ عَلَى الْهُدَىٰ ۚ فَلَا تَكُونَنَّ مِنَ الْجَاهِلِينَ

35 If you find their rejection hard to bear, then if you can, seek a tunnel into the earth, or a stairway into the heaven, and bring them a sign. Had God willed, He could have gathered them to guidance. So do not be of the ignorant.

35
6:149; 11:117

٣٦ إِنَّمَا يَسْتَجِيبُ الَّذِينَ يَسْمَعُونَ ۘ وَالْمَوْتَىٰ يَبْعَثُهُمُ اللَّهُ ثُمَّ إِلَيْهِ يُرْجَعُونَ

36 Only those who listen will respond. As for the dead, God will resurrect them; then to Him they will be returned.

٣٧ وَقَالُوا لَوْلَا نُزِّلَ عَلَيْهِ آيَةٌ مِنْ رَبِّهِ ۚ قُلْ إِنَّ اللَّهَ قَادِرٌ عَلَىٰ أَنْ يُنَزِّلَ آيَةً وَلَٰكِنَّ أَكْثَرَهُمْ لَا يَعْلَمُونَ

37 And they say, "If only a sign could come down to him from his Lord." Say, "God is Able to send down a sign, but most of them do not know."

37
2:118; 13:7; 21:5; 29:50

٣٨ وَمَا مِنْ دَابَّةٍ فِي الْأَرْضِ وَلَا طَائِرٍ يَطِيرُ بِجَنَاحَيْهِ إِلَّا أُمَمٌ أَمْثَالُكُمْ ۚ ᵃ مَا فَرَّطْنَا فِي الْكِتَابِ مِنْ شَيْءٍ ۚ ᵇ ثُمَّ إِلَىٰ رَبِّهِمْ يُحْشَرُونَ

38 There is no animal on land, nor a bird flying with its wings, but are communities like you. We neglected nothing in the Scripture. Then to their Lord they will be gathered.

38
ᵃ 11:6, 56
ᵇ 16:89

٣٩ وَالَّذِينَ كَذَّبُوا بِآيَاتِنَا صُمٌّ وَبُكْمٌ فِي الظُّلُمَاتِ ۗ مَنْ يَشَأِ اللَّهُ يُضْلِلْهُ وَمَنْ يَشَأْ يَجْعَلْهُ عَلَىٰ صِرَاطٍ مُسْتَقِيمٍ

39 Those who reject Our revelations are deaf and dumb, in total darkness. Whomever God wills, He leaves astray; and whomever He wills, He sets on a straight path.

39
2:18, 171; 6:39; 8:22

٤٠ قُلْ أَرَأَيْتَكُمْ إِنْ أَتَاكُمْ عَذَابُ اللَّهِ أَوْ أَتَتْكُمُ السَّاعَةُ أَغَيْرَ اللَّهِ تَدْعُونَ إِنْ كُنْتُمْ صَادِقِينَ

40 Say, "Have you considered? if God's punishment came upon you, or the Hour overtook you, would you call upon any other than God, if you are sincere?"

40–41
6:43, 47; 10:22–23

٤١ بَلْ إِيَّاهُ تَدْعُونَ فَيَكْشِفُ مَا تَدْعُونَ إِلَيْهِ إِنْ شَاءَ وَتَنْسَوْنَ مَا تُشْرِكُونَ

41 In fact, it is Him you will call upon; and if He wills, he will remove what you called Him for, and you will forget what you idolized.

٤٢ وَلَقَدْ أَرْسَلْنَا إِلَىٰ أُمَمٍ مِنْ قَبْلِكَ فَأَخَذْنَاهُمْ بِالْبَأْسَاءِ وَالضَّرَّاءِ لَعَلَّهُمْ يَتَضَرَّعُونَ

42 We sent messengers to communities before you, and We afflicted them with suffering and hardship, that they may humble themselves.

42
7:94

٤٣ فَلَوْلَا إِذْ جَاءَهُمْ بَأْسُنَا تَضَرَّعُوا وَلَٰكِنْ قَسَتْ قُلُوبُهُمْ وَزَيَّنَ لَهُمُ الشَّيْطَانُ مَا كَانُوا يَعْمَلُونَ

43 If only, when Our calamity came upon them, they humbled themselves. But their hearts hardened, and Satan made their deeds appear good to them.

43
6:40–41; 10:22–23;
17:67; 31:32

٤٤ فَلَمَّا نَسُوا مَا ذُكِّرُوا بِهِ فَتَحْنَا عَلَيْهِمْ أَبْوَابَ كُلِّ شَيْءٍ حَتَّىٰ إِذَا فَرِحُوا بِمَا أُوتُوا أَخَذْنَاهُمْ بَغْتَةً فَإِذَا هُمْ مُبْلِسُونَ

44 Then, when they disregarded what they were reminded of, We opened for them the gates of all things. Until, when they delighted in what they were given, We seized them suddenly; and at once, they were in despair.

44
7:72; 8:7 15:66

٤٥ فَقُطِعَ دَابِرُ الْقَوْمِ الَّذِينَ ظَلَمُوا ۚ وَالْحَمْدُ لِلَّهِ رَبِّ الْعَالَمِينَ

45 Thus the last remnant of the people who did wrong was cut off. And praise be to God, Lord of the Worlds.

45
45:23

٤٦ قُلْ أَرَأَيْتُمْ إِنْ أَخَذَ اللَّهُ سَمْعَكُمْ وَأَبْصَارَكُمْ وَخَتَمَ عَلَىٰ قُلُوبِكُمْ مَنْ إِلَٰهٌ غَيْرُ اللَّهِ يَأْتِيكُمْ بِهِ ۗ انْظُرْ كَيْفَ نُصَرِّفُ الْآيَاتِ ثُمَّ هُمْ يَصْدِفُونَ

46 Say, "Have you considered? If God took away your hearing and your sight, and set a seal on your hearts, what god other than God would restore them to you?" Note how We explain the revelations in various ways, yet they still turn away.

46
2:20; 23:78

٤٧ قُلْ أَرَأَيْتَكُمْ إِنْ أَتَاكُمْ عَذَابُ اللَّهِ بَغْتَةً أَوْ جَهْرَةً هَلْ يُهْلَكُ إِلَّا الْقَوْمُ الظَّالِمُونَ

47 Say, "Have you considered? if God's punishment descended on you suddenly or gradually, would any be destroyed except the wrongdoing people?"

47
6:40; 10:50

٤٨ وَمَا نُرْسِلُ الْمُرْسَلِينَ إِلَّا مُبَشِّرِينَ وَمُنْذِرِينَ ۖ فَمَنْ آمَنَ وَأَصْلَحَ فَلَا خَوْفٌ عَلَيْهِمْ وَلَا هُمْ يَحْزَنُونَ

48 We sent the messengers only as bearers of good news and as warners. Those who believe and reform have nothing to fear, nor shall they grieve.

48
2:213; 4:165; 18:56

٤٩ وَالَّذِينَ كَذَّبُوا بِآيَاتِنَا يَمَسُّهُمُ الْعَذَابُ بِمَا كَانُوا يَفْسُقُونَ

49 But as for those who reject Our revelations, torment will afflict them because of their defiance.

٥٠ قُلْ لَا أَقُولُ لَكُمْ عِندِي خَزَائِنُ اللَّهِ وَلَا أَعْلَمُ الْغَيْبَ وَلَا أَقُولُ لَكُمْ إِنِّي مَلَكٌ ۖ[a] إِنْ أَتَّبِعُ إِلَّا مَا يُوحَىٰ إِلَيَّ ۚ[b] قُلْ هَلْ يَسْتَوِي الْأَعْمَىٰ وَالْبَصِيرُ ۚ[c] أَفَلَا تَتَفَكَّرُونَ

50 Say, "I do not say to you that I possess the treasuries of God, nor do I know the future, nor do I say to you that I am an angel. I only follow what is inspired to me." Say, "Are the blind and the seeing alike? Do you not think?"

50
[a] 6:59; 11:31; 38:9
[b] 10:109; 11:12
[c] 13:16; 35:19; 40:58

٥١ وَأَنذِرْ بِهِ الَّذِينَ يَخَافُونَ أَن يُحْشَرُوا إِلَىٰ رَبِّهِمْ ۙ لَيْسَ لَهُم مِّن دُونِهِ وَلِيٌّ وَلَا شَفِيعٌ لَّعَلَّهُمْ يَتَّقُونَ

51 And warn with it those who fear to be gathered before their Lord—they have no protector or intercessor apart from Him—perhaps they will grow in piety.

51
6:70; 32:4

٥٢ وَلَا تَطْرُدِ الَّذِينَ يَدْعُونَ رَبَّهُم بِالْغَدَاةِ وَالْعَشِيِّ يُرِيدُونَ وَجْهَهُ ۖ مَا عَلَيْكَ مِنْ حِسَابِهِم مِّن شَيْءٍ وَمَا مِنْ حِسَابِكَ عَلَيْهِم مِّن شَيْءٍ فَتَطْرُدَهُمْ فَتَكُونَ مِنَ الظَّالِمِينَ

52 And do not drive away those who call upon their Lord, morning and evening, seeking His attention. You are not accountable for them in any way, nor are they accountable for you in any way. If you drive them away, you would be one of the unjust.

52
6:54; 11:29; 26:114; 18:28

٥٣ وَكَذَٰلِكَ فَتَنَّا بَعْضَهُم بِبَعْضٍ لِّيَقُولُوا أَهَٰؤُلَاءِ مَنَّ اللَّهُ عَلَيْهِم مِّن بَيْنِنَا ۗ أَلَيْسَ اللَّهُ بِأَعْلَمَ بِالشَّاكِرِينَ

53 Thus We try some of them by means of others, that they may say, "Are these the ones whom God has favored from among us?" Is God not aware of the appreciative?

53
19:73; 46:11 30

٥٤ وَإِذَا جَاءَكَ الَّذِينَ يُؤْمِنُونَ بِآيَاتِنَا فَقُلْ سَلَامٌ عَلَيْكُمْ ۖ كَتَبَ رَبُّكُمْ عَلَىٰ نَفْسِهِ الرَّحْمَةَ ۖ أَنَّهُ مَنْ عَمِلَ مِنكُمْ سُوءًا بِجَهَالَةٍ ثُمَّ تَابَ مِن بَعْدِهِ وَأَصْلَحَ فَأَنَّهُ غَفُورٌ رَّحِيمٌ

54 When those who believe in Our revelations come to you, say, "Peace be upon you, your Lord has prescribed mercy for Himself. Whoever among you does wrong out of ignorance, and then repents afterwards and reforms—He is Forgiving and Merciful."

54
6:52; 11:29; 26:114; 18:28

٥٥ وَكَذَٰلِكَ نُفَصِّلُ الْآيَاتِ وَلِتَسْتَبِينَ سَبِيلُ الْمُجْرِمِينَ

55 Thus We explain the revelations, and expose the path of the unrighteous.

٥٦ قُلْ إِنِّي نُهِيتُ أَنْ أَعْبُدَ الَّذِينَ تَدْعُونَ مِن دُونِ اللَّهِ ۚ قُل لَّا أَتَّبِعُ أَهْوَاءَكُمْ ۙ قَدْ ضَلَلْتُ إِذًا وَمَا أَنَا مِنَ الْمُهْتَدِينَ

56 Say, "I am forbidden from worshiping those you pray to besides God." Say, "I will not follow your desires; else I would be lost and not be of those guided."

56
40:66

٥٧ قُلْ إِنِّي عَلَىٰ بَيِّنَةٍ مِّن رَّبِّي وَكَذَّبْتُم بِهِ ۚ مَا عِندِي مَا تَسْتَعْجِلُونَ بِهِ ۚ إِنِ الْحُكْمُ إِلَّا لِلَّهِ ۖ يَقُصُّ الْحَقَّ ۖ وَهُوَ خَيْرُ الْفَاصِلِينَ

57 Say, "I stand on clear evidence from my Lord, and you have rejected Him. I do not possess what you seek me to hasten; the decision belongs solely to God. He states the truth, and He is the Best of Judges."

57–58
11:8; 29:53–54

٥٨ قُلْ لَوْ أَنَّ عِندِي مَا تَسْتَعْجِلُونَ بِهِ لَقُضِيَ الْأَمْرُ بَيْنِي وَبَيْنَكُمْ ۗ وَاللَّهُ أَعْلَمُ بِالظَّالِمِينَ

58 Say, "If I possessed what you seek me to hasten, the matter between you and me would have been settled. God is well aware of the unjust."

٥٩ وَعِندَهُ مَفَاتِحُ الْغَيْبِ لَا يَعْلَمُهَا إِلَّا هُوَ ۚ وَيَعْلَمُ مَا فِي الْبَرِّ وَالْبَحْرِ ۚ وَمَا تَسْقُطُ مِن وَرَقَةٍ إِلَّا يَعْلَمُهَا وَلَا حَبَّةٍ فِي ظُلُمَاتِ الْأَرْضِ وَلَا رَطْبٍ وَلَا يَابِسٍ إِلَّا فِي كِتَابٍ مُّبِينٍ

59
6:50; 27:65; 31:34;
72:26

59 With Him are the keys of the unseen; none knows them except He. And He knows everything on land and in the sea. Not a leaf falls but He knows it; and there is not a single grain in the darkness of earth, nor is there anything wet or dry, but is in a clear record.

٦٠ وَهُوَ الَّذِي يَتَوَفَّاكُم بِاللَّيْلِ وَيَعْلَمُ مَا جَرَحْتُم بِالنَّهَارِ ثُمَّ يَبْعَثُكُمْ فِيهِ لِيُقْضَىٰ أَجَلٌ مُّسَمًّى ۖ ثُمَّ إِلَيْهِ مَرْجِعُكُمْ ثُمَّ يُنَبِّئُكُم بِمَا كُنتُمْ تَعْمَلُونَ

60
5:105; 6:2; 39:42;
40:67; 58:6

60 It is He Who takes you by night, and He knows what you earn by day. Then He raises you up in it, until a fixed term is fulfilled. Then to Him is your return, then He will inform you of what you used to do.

٦١ وَهُوَ الْقَاهِرُ فَوْقَ عِبَادِهِ ۖ وَيُرْسِلُ عَلَيْكُمْ حَفَظَةً حَتَّىٰ إِذَا جَاءَ أَحَدَكُمُ الْمَوْتُ تَوَفَّتْهُ رُسُلُنَا وَهُمْ لَا يُفَرِّطُونَ

61
6:18; 13:11; 82:110–12

61 He is the Conqueror over His servants, and He sends guardians over you, until, when death overtakes one of you, Our envoys take him away, and they never fail.

٦٢ ثُمَّ رُدُّوا إِلَى اللَّهِ مَوْلَاهُمُ الْحَقِّ ۚ أَلَا لَهُ الْحُكْمُ وَهُوَ أَسْرَعُ الْحَاسِبِينَ

62 Then they are brought back to God, their True Master. Unquestionably, His is the judgment, and He is the Swiftest of reckoners.

٦٣ قُلْ مَن يُنَجِّيكُم مِّن ظُلُمَاتِ الْبَرِّ وَالْبَحْرِ تَدْعُونَهُ تَضَرُّعًا وَخُفْيَةً لَّئِنْ أَنجَانَا مِنْ هَٰذِهِ لَنَكُونَنَّ مِنَ الشَّاكِرِينَ

63–64
17:67; 27:63; 29:65;
31:32

63 Say, "Who delivers you from the darkness of land and sea?" You call upon Him humbly and inwardly: "If He delivers us from this, We will surely be among the thankful."

٦٤ قُلِ اللَّهُ يُنَجِّيكُم مِّنْهَا وَمِن كُلِّ كَرْبٍ ثُمَّ أَنتُمْ تُشْرِكُونَ

64 Say, "It is God who delivers you from it, and from every disaster. Yet then you associate others with Him."

٦٥ قُلْ هُوَ الْقَادِرُ عَلَىٰ أَن يَبْعَثَ عَلَيْكُمْ عَذَابًا مِّن فَوْقِكُمْ أَوْ مِن تَحْتِ أَرْجُلِكُمْ أَوْ يَلْبِسَكُمْ شِيَعًا وَيُذِيقَ بَعْضَكُم بَأْسَ بَعْضٍ ۗ انظُرْ كَيْفَ نُصَرِّفُ الْآيَاتِ لَعَلَّهُمْ يَفْقَهُونَ

65
29:55

65 Say, "He is Able to send upon you an affliction, from above you, or from under your feet. Or He can divide you into factions, and make you taste the violence of one another. Note how We explain the revelations, so that they may understand."

٦٦ وَكَذَّبَ بِهِ قَوْمُكَ وَهُوَ الْحَقُّ ۚ قُل لَّسْتُ عَلَيْكُم بِوَكِيلٍ

66 But your people rejected it, though it is the truth. Say, "I am not responsible for you."

٦٧ لِّكُلِّ نَبَإٍ مُّسْتَقَرٌّ ۚ وَسَوْفَ تَعْلَمُونَ

67 For every happening is a finality, and you will surely know.

٦٨ وَإِذَا رَأَيْتَ الَّذِينَ يَخُوضُونَ فِي آيَاتِنَا فَأَعْرِضْ عَنْهُمْ حَتَّىٰ يَخُوضُوا فِي حَدِيثٍ غَيْرِهِ ۚ وَإِمَّا يُنسِيَنَّكَ الشَّيْطَانُ فَلَا تَقْعُدْ بَعْدَ الذِّكْرَىٰ مَعَ الْقَوْمِ الظَّالِمِينَ

68
4:140

68 When you encounter those who gossip about Our revelations, turn away from them, until they engage in another topic. But should Satan make you forget, do not sit after the recollection with the wicked people.

٦٩ وَمَا عَلَى الَّذِينَ يَتَّقُونَ مِنْ حِسَابِهِم مِّن شَيْءٍ وَلَٰكِن ذِكْرَىٰ لَعَلَّهُمْ يَتَّقُونَ

69 The righteous are in no way accountable for them; it is only a reminder, that they may be careful.

٧٠ وَذَرِ الَّذِينَ اتَّخَذُوا دِينَهُمْ لَعِبًا وَلَهْوًا وَغَرَّتْهُمُ الْحَيَاةُ الدُّنْيَا ۚ وَذَكِّرْ بِهِ أَن تُبْسَلَ نَفْسٌ بِمَا كَسَبَتْ لَيْسَ لَهَا مِن دُونِ اللَّهِ وَلِيٌّ وَلَا شَفِيعٌ وَإِن تَعْدِلْ كُلَّ عَدْلٍ لَّا يُؤْخَذْ مِنْهَا ۗ أُولَٰئِكَ الَّذِينَ أُبْسِلُوا بِمَا كَسَبُوا ۖ لَهُمْ شَرَابٌ مِّنْ حَمِيمٍ وَعَذَابٌ أَلِيمٌ بِمَا كَانُوا يَكْفُرُونَ

70
6:32, 51; 7:51; 29:64

70 So leave alone those who take their religion for play and pastime, and whom the worldly life has deceived. But remind with it, lest a soul becomes damned on account of what it has earned. It has no helper or intercessor besides God. Even if it offers every equivalent, none will be accepted from it. These are the ones who are delivered to perdition by their actions. They will have a drink of scalding water, and a painful punishment, because they used to disbelieve.

٧١ قُلْ أَنَدْعُو مِن دُونِ اللَّهِ مَا لَا يَنفَعُنَا وَلَا يَضُرُّنَا وَنُرَدُّ عَلَىٰ أَعْقَابِنَا بَعْدَ إِذْ هَدَانَا اللَّهُ كَالَّذِي اسْتَهْوَتْهُ الشَّيَاطِينُ فِي الْأَرْضِ حَيْرَانَ لَهُ أَصْحَابٌ يَدْعُونَهُ إِلَى الْهُدَى ائْتِنَا ۗ قُلْ إِنَّ هُدَى اللَّهِ هُوَ الْهُدَىٰ ۖ وَأُمِرْنَا لِنُسْلِمَ لِرَبِّ الْعَالَمِينَ

71
5:76; 10:18, 106; 21:66; 22:12; 25:55; 26:72–73; 29:17

71 Say, "Shall we invoke besides God something that can neither benefit us nor harm us, and turn back on our heels after God has guided us; like someone seduced by the devils and confused on earth, who has friends calling him to guidance: 'Come to us'?" Say, "The guidance of God is the guidance, and we are commanded to surrender to the Lord of the Universe."

٧٢ وَأَنْ أَقِيمُوا الصَّلَاةَ وَاتَّقُوهُ ۚ وَهُوَ الَّذِي إِلَيْهِ تُحْشَرُونَ

72 "And to perform the prayers, and to revere Him; it is to Him that you will be gathered."

	٧٣ وَهُوَ الَّذِي خَلَقَ السَّمَاوَاتِ وَالْأَرْضَ بِالْحَقِّ ۖ وَيَوْمَ يَقُولُ كُن فَيَكُونُ ۚ قَوْلُهُ الْحَقُّ ۚ وَلَهُ الْمُلْكُ يَوْمَ يُنفَخُ فِي الصُّورِ ۚ عَالِمُ الْغَيْبِ وَالشَّهَادَةِ ۚ وَهُوَ الْحَكِيمُ الْخَبِيرُ	73 2:117; 3:47, 59; 13:9; 16:40; 29:45; 36:82; 38:27

73 It is He who created the heavens and the earth in truth. On the Day when He says: "Be," it will be. His saying is the truth, and His is the sovereignty on the Day when the trumpet is blown. The Knower of secrets and declarations. He is the Wise, the Expert.

	٧٤ وَإِذْ قَالَ إِبْرَاهِيمُ لِأَبِيهِ آزَرَ أَتَتَّخِذُ أَصْنَامًا آلِهَةً ۖ إِنِّي أَرَاكَ وَقَوْمَكَ فِي ضَلَالٍ مُّبِينٍ	74 29:16

74 Abraham said to his father Azar, "Do you take idols for gods? I see that you and your people are in evident error."

	٧٥ وَكَذَٰلِكَ نُرِي إِبْرَاهِيمَ مَلَكُوتَ السَّمَاوَاتِ وَالْأَرْضِ وَلِيَكُونَ مِنَ الْمُوقِنِينَ	75–78 6:83

75 Thus We showed Abraham the empire of the heavens and the earth, that he might be one of those with certainty.

	٧٦ فَلَمَّا جَنَّ عَلَيْهِ اللَّيْلُ رَأَىٰ كَوْكَبًا ۖ قَالَ هَٰذَا رَبِّي ۖ فَلَمَّا أَفَلَ قَالَ لَا أُحِبُّ الْآفِلِينَ

76 When the night fell over him, he saw a planet. He said, "This is my lord." But when it set, he said, "I do not love those that set."

	٧٧ فَلَمَّا رَأَى الْقَمَرَ بَازِغًا قَالَ هَٰذَا رَبِّي ۖ فَلَمَّا أَفَلَ قَالَ لَئِن لَّمْ يَهْدِنِي رَبِّي لَأَكُونَنَّ مِنَ الْقَوْمِ الضَّالِّينَ

77 Then, when he saw the moon rising, he said, "This is my lord." But when it set, he said, "If my Lord does not guide me, I will be one of the erring people."

	٧٨ فَلَمَّا رَأَى الشَّمْسَ بَازِغَةً قَالَ هَٰذَا رَبِّي هَٰذَا أَكْبَرُ ۖ فَلَمَّا أَفَلَتْ قَالَ يَا قَوْمِ إِنِّي بَرِيءٌ مِّمَّا تُشْرِكُونَ

78 Then, when he saw the sun rising, he said, "This is my lord, this is bigger." But when it set, he said, "O my people, I am innocent of your idolatry.

	٧٩ إِنِّي وَجَّهْتُ وَجْهِيَ لِلَّذِي فَطَرَ السَّمَاوَاتِ وَالْأَرْضَ حَنِيفًا ۖ وَمَا أَنَا مِنَ الْمُشْرِكِينَ	79 4:125; 10:105; 30:30

79 I have directed my attention towards Him Who created the heavens and the earth—a monotheist—and I am not of the idolaters."

	٨٠ وَحَاجَّهُ قَوْمُهُ ۚ قَالَ أَتُحَاجُّونِّي فِي اللَّهِ وَقَدْ هَدَانِ ۚ وَلَا أَخَافُ مَا تُشْرِكُونَ بِهِ إِلَّا أَن يَشَاءَ رَبِّي شَيْئًا ۗ وَسِعَ رَبِّي كُلَّ شَيْءٍ عِلْمًا ۗ أَفَلَا تَتَذَكَّرُونَ

80 And his people argued with him. He said, "Do you argue with me about God, when He has guided me? I do not fear what you associate with Him, unless my Lord wills it. My Lord comprehends all things in knowledge. Will you not reconsider?

	٨١ وَكَيْفَ أَخَافُ مَا أَشْرَكْتُمْ وَلَا تَخَافُونَ أَنَّكُمْ أَشْرَكْتُم بِاللَّهِ مَا لَمْ يُنَزِّلْ بِهِ عَلَيْكُمْ سُلْطَانًا ۚ فَأَيُّ الْفَرِيقَيْنِ أَحَقُّ بِالْأَمْنِ ۖ إِن كُنتُمْ تَعْلَمُونَ	81 3:151; 7:33; 10:106; 12:40 22:71

81 And why should I fear those you associate with Him, and you do not fear associating others with God for which He sent down to you no authority? Which side is more entitled to security, if you are aware?"

٨٢ الَّذِينَ آمَنُوا وَلَمْ يَلْبِسُوا إِيمَانَهُم بِظُلْمٍ أُولَٰئِكَ لَهُمُ الْأَمْنُ وَهُم مُّهْتَدُونَ

82 Those who believe, and do not obscure their faith with wrongdoing—those will have security, and they are guided.

82 10:106; 2:254; 31:13

٨٣ وَتِلْكَ حُجَّتُنَا آتَيْنَاهَا إِبْرَاهِيمَ عَلَىٰ قَوْمِهِ ۚ نَرْفَعُ دَرَجَاتٍ مَّن نَّشَاءُ ۗ إِنَّ رَبَّكَ حَكِيمٌ عَلِيمٌ

83 That was Our argument which We gave to Abraham against his people. We elevate by degrees whomever We will. Your Lord is Wise and Informed.

83 6:75–78

٨٤ وَوَهَبْنَا لَهُ إِسْحَاقَ وَيَعْقُوبَ ۚ كُلًّا هَدَيْنَا ۚ وَنُوحًا هَدَيْنَا مِن قَبْلُ ۖ وَمِن ذُرِّيَّتِهِ دَاوُودَ وَسُلَيْمَانَ وَأَيُّوبَ وَيُوسُفَ وَمُوسَىٰ وَهَارُونَ ۚ وَكَذَٰلِكَ نَجْزِي الْمُحْسِنِينَ

84 And We gave him Isaac and Jacob—each of them We guided. And We guided Noah previously; and from his descendants David, and Solomon, and Job, and Joseph, and Moses, and Aaron. Thus We reward the righteous.

84 19:49; 21:72; 29:27; 38:45

٨٥ وَزَكَرِيَّا وَيَحْيَىٰ وَعِيسَىٰ وَإِلْيَاسَ ۖ كُلٌّ مِّنَ الصَّالِحِينَ

85 And Zechariah, and John, and Jesus, and Elias—every one of them was of the upright.

٨٦ وَإِسْمَاعِيلَ وَالْيَسَعَ وَيُونُسَ وَلُوطًا ۚ وَكُلًّا فَضَّلْنَا عَلَى الْعَالَمِينَ

86 And Ishmael, and Elijah, and Jonah, and Lot—We favored each one of them over all other people.

86 38:48

٨٧ وَمِنْ آبَائِهِمْ وَذُرِّيَّاتِهِمْ وَإِخْوَانِهِمْ ۖ وَاجْتَبَيْنَاهُمْ وَهَدَيْنَاهُمْ إِلَىٰ صِرَاطٍ مُّسْتَقِيمٍ

87 And of their ancestors, and their descendants, and their siblings—We chose them, and guided them to a straight path.

٨٨ ذَٰلِكَ هُدَى اللَّهِ يَهْدِي بِهِ مَن يَشَاءُ مِنْ عِبَادِهِ ۚ وَلَوْ أَشْرَكُوا لَحَبِطَ عَنْهُم مَّا كَانُوا يَعْمَلُونَ

88 Such is God's guidance. He guides with it whomever He wills of His servants. Had they associated, their deeds would have gone in vain.

88 39:65

٨٩ أُولَٰئِكَ الَّذِينَ آتَيْنَاهُمُ الْكِتَابَ وَالْحُكْمَ وَالنُّبُوَّةَ ۚ فَإِن يَكْفُرْ بِهَا هَٰؤُلَاءِ فَقَدْ وَكَّلْنَا بِهَا قَوْمًا لَّيْسُوا بِهَا بِكَافِرِينَ

89 Those are they to whom We gave the Book, and wisdom, and prophethood. If these reject them, We have entrusted them to others who do not reject them.

89 2:225; 3:79; 29:27; 45:16

٩٠ أُولَٰئِكَ الَّذِينَ هَدَى اللَّهُ ۖ فَبِهُدَاهُمُ اقْتَدِهْ ۗ قُل لَّا أَسْأَلُكُمْ عَلَيْهِ أَجْرًا ۖ إِنْ هُوَ إِلَّا ذِكْرَىٰ لِلْعَالَمِينَ

90 Those are they whom God has guided, so follow their guidance. Say, "I ask of you no compensation for it; it is just a reminder for all mankind."

90 38:86

٩١ وَمَا قَدَرُوا اللَّهَ حَقَّ قَدْرِهِ إِذْ قَالُوا مَا أَنزَلَ اللَّهُ عَلَىٰ بَشَرٍ مِّن شَيْءٍ ۗ قُلْ مَنْ أَنزَلَ الْكِتَابَ الَّذِي جَاءَ بِهِ مُوسَىٰ نُورًا وَهُدًى لِّلنَّاسِ ۖ تَجْعَلُونَهُ قَرَاطِيسَ تُبْدُونَهَا وَتُخْفُونَ كَثِيرًا ۖ وَعُلِّمْتُم مَّا لَمْ تَعْلَمُوا أَنتُمْ وَلَا آبَاؤُكُمْ ۖ قُلِ اللَّهُ ۖ ثُمَّ ذَرْهُمْ فِي خَوْضِهِمْ يَلْعَبُونَ

91
5:15; 54:24

91 They do not value God as He should be valued, when they say, "God did not reveal anything to any human being." Say, "Who revealed the Scripture which Moses brought—a light and guidance for humanity?" You put it on scrolls, displaying them, yet concealing much. And you were taught what you did not know—neither you, nor your ancestors. Say, "God;" then leave them toying away in their speculation.

٩٢ وَهَٰذَا كِتَابٌ أَنزَلْنَاهُ مُبَارَكٌ مُّصَدِّقُ الَّذِي بَيْنَ يَدَيْهِ وَلِتُنذِرَ أُمَّ الْقُرَىٰ وَمَنْ حَوْلَهَا ۚ وَالَّذِينَ يُؤْمِنُونَ بِالْآخِرَةِ يُؤْمِنُونَ بِهِ ۖ وَهُمْ عَلَىٰ صَلَاتِهِمْ يُحَافِظُونَ

92
6:19; 42:7

92 This too is a Scripture that We revealed—blessed—verifying what preceded it, that you may warn the Mother of Cities and all around it. Those who believe in the Hereafter believe in it, and are dedicated to their prayers.

٩٣ وَمَنْ أَظْلَمُ مِمَّنِ افْتَرَىٰ عَلَى اللَّهِ كَذِبًا أَوْ قَالَ أُوحِيَ إِلَيَّ وَلَمْ يُوحَ إِلَيْهِ شَيْءٌ وَمَن قَالَ سَأُنزِلُ مِثْلَ مَا أَنزَلَ اللَّهُ ۗ وَلَوْ تَرَىٰ إِذِ الظَّالِمُونَ فِي غَمَرَاتِ الْمَوْتِ وَالْمَلَائِكَةُ بَاسِطُو أَيْدِيهِمْ أَخْرِجُوا أَنفُسَكُمُ ۖ b الْيَوْمَ تُجْزَوْنَ عَذَابَ الْهُونِ بِمَا كُنتُمْ تَقُولُونَ عَلَى اللَّهِ غَيْرَ الْحَقِّ وَكُنتُمْ عَنْ آيَاتِهِ تَسْتَكْبِرُونَ

93
a 2:23, 38; 8:31; 17:88
b 8:50

93 Who does greater wrong than someone who invents falsehood against God, or says, "It was revealed to me," when nothing was revealed to him, or says, "I will reveal the like of what God revealed"? If only you could see the wrongdoers in the floods of death, as the angels with arms outstretched: "Give up your souls. Today you are being repaid with the torment of shame for having said about God other than the truth, and for being too proud to accept His revelations."

٩٤ وَلَقَدْ جِئْتُمُونَا فُرَادَىٰ كَمَا خَلَقْنَاكُمْ أَوَّلَ مَرَّةٍ وَتَرَكْتُم مَّا خَوَّلْنَاكُمْ وَرَاءَ ظُهُورِكُمْ ۖ وَمَا نَرَىٰ مَعَكُمْ شُفَعَاءَكُمُ الَّذِينَ زَعَمْتُمْ أَنَّهُمْ فِيكُمْ شُرَكَاءُ ۚ لَقَد تَّقَطَّعَ بَيْنَكُمْ وَضَلَّ عَنكُم مَّا كُنتُمْ تَزْعُمُونَ

94
2:166; 18:48; 19:80, 95

94 "You have come to Us individually, just as We created you the first time, leaving behind you everything We gave you. We do not see with you your intercessors—those you claimed were your partners. The link between you is cut, and what you had asserted has failed you."

٩٥ إِنَّ اللَّهَ فَالِقُ الْحَبِّ وَالنَّوَىٰ ۖ يُخْرِجُ الْحَيَّ مِنَ الْمَيِّتِ وَمُخْرِجُ الْمَيِّتِ مِنَ الْحَيِّ ۚ ذَٰلِكُمُ اللَّهُ ۖ فَأَنَّىٰ تُؤْفَكُونَ

95
3:27; 10:31; 30:19

95 It is God Who splits the grain and the seed. He brings the living from the dead, and He brings the dead from the living. Such is God. So how could you deviate?

٩٦ فَالِقُ الْإِصْبَاحِ وَجَعَلَ اللَّيْلَ سَكَنًا ᵃ وَالشَّمْسَ وَالْقَمَرَ حُسْبَانًا ᵇ ذَٰلِكَ تَقْدِيرُ الْعَزِيزِ الْعَلِيمِ

96 It is He Who breaks the dawn. And He made the night for rest, and the sun and the moon for calculation. Such is the disposition of the Almighty, the All-Knowing.

ᵃ 10:67; 28:71–73
ᵇ 55:5

٩٧ وَهُوَ الَّذِي جَعَلَ لَكُمُ النُّجُومَ لِتَهْتَدُوا بِهَا فِي ظُلُمَاتِ الْبَرِّ وَالْبَحْرِ ۗ قَدْ فَصَّلْنَا الْآيَاتِ لِقَوْمٍ يَعْلَمُونَ

97 And it is He Who created the stars for you, that you may be guided by them in the darkness of land and sea. We thus explain the revelations for people who know.

16:16; 27:63

٩٨ وَهُوَ الَّذِي أَنشَأَكُم مِّن نَّفْسٍ وَاحِدَةٍ فَمُسْتَقَرٌّ وَمُسْتَوْدَعٌ ۗ قَدْ فَصَّلْنَا الْآيَاتِ لِقَوْمٍ يَفْقَهُونَ

98 And it is He who produced you from a single person, then a repository, then a depository. We have detailed the revelations for people who understand.

4:1; 7:189; 30:21; 39:6

٩٩ وَهُوَ الَّذِي أَنزَلَ مِنَ السَّمَاءِ مَاءً فَأَخْرَجْنَا بِهِ نَبَاتَ كُلِّ شَيْءٍ فَأَخْرَجْنَا مِنْهُ خَضِرًا نُّخْرِجُ مِنْهُ حَبًّا مُّتَرَاكِبًا وَمِنَ النَّخْلِ مِن طَلْعِهَا قِنْوَانٌ دَانِيَةٌ وَجَنَّاتٍ مِّنْ أَعْنَابٍ وَالزَّيْتُونَ وَالرُّمَّانَ مُشْتَبِهًا وَغَيْرَ مُتَشَابِهٍ ۗ انظُرُوا إِلَىٰ ثَمَرِهِ إِذَا أَثْمَرَ وَيَنْعِهِ ۚ إِنَّ فِي ذَٰلِكُمْ لَآيَاتٍ لِّقَوْمٍ يُؤْمِنُونَ

99 And it is He who sends down water from the sky. With it We produce vegetation of all kinds, from which We bring greenery, from which We produce grains in clusters. And palm-trees with hanging clusters, and vineyards, and olives, and pomegranates—similar and dissimilar. Watch their fruits as they grow and ripen. Surely in this are signs for people who believe.

2:22; 7:57; 14:32; 20:53; 50:9

١٠٠ وَجَعَلُوا لِلَّهِ شُرَكَاءَ الْجِنَّ وَخَلَقَهُمْ ۖ وَخَرَقُوا لَهُ بَنِينَ وَبَنَاتٍ بِغَيْرِ عِلْمٍ ۚ سُبْحَانَهُ وَتَعَالَىٰ عَمَّا يَصِفُونَ

100 Yet they attributed to God partners—the sprites—although He created them. And they invented for Him sons and daughters, without any knowledge. Glory be to Him. He is exalted, beyond what they describe.

2:116; 10:68; 17:40, 111; 19:35; 21:26; 23:91; 25:2

١٠١ بَدِيعُ السَّمَاوَاتِ وَالْأَرْضِ ۖ أَنَّىٰ يَكُونُ لَهُ وَلَدٌ وَلَمْ تَكُن لَّهُ صَاحِبَةٌ ۖ وَخَلَقَ كُلَّ شَيْءٍ ۖ وَهُوَ بِكُلِّ شَيْءٍ عَلِيمٌ

101 Originator of the heavens and the earth—how can He have a son when He never had a companion? He created all things, and He has knowledge of all things.

4:171; 19:91; 72:3; 112:3

١٠٢ ذَٰلِكُمُ اللَّهُ رَبُّكُمْ ۖ لَا إِلَٰهَ إِلَّا هُوَ ۖ خَالِقُ كُلِّ شَيْءٍ فَاعْبُدُوهُ ۚ وَهُوَ عَلَىٰ كُلِّ شَيْءٍ وَكِيلٌ

102 Such is God, your Lord. There is no god except He, the Creator of all things; so worship Him. He is responsible for everything.

١٠٣ لَا تُدْرِكُهُ الْأَبْصَارُ وَهُوَ يُدْرِكُ الْأَبْصَارَ ۖ وَهُوَ اللَّطِيفُ الْخَبِيرُ

103 No vision can grasp Him, but His grasp is over all vision. He is the Subtle, the Expert.

75:22–23; 83:15

١٠٤ قَدْ جَاءَكُم بَصَائِرُ مِن رَّبِّكُمْ ۖ فَمَنْ أَبْصَرَ فَلِنَفْسِهِ ۖ وَمَنْ عَمِيَ فَعَلَيْهَا ۚ وَمَا أَنَا عَلَيْكُم بِحَفِيظٍ

104 "Insights have come to you from your Lord. Whoever sees, it is to the benefit of his soul; and whoever remains blind, it is to its detriment. I am not a guardian over you."

١٠٥ وَكَذَٰلِكَ نُصَرِّفُ الْآيَاتِ وَلِيَقُولُوا دَرَسْتَ وَلِنُبَيِّنَهُ لِقَوْمٍ يَعْلَمُونَ

105
16:103; 74:24–26

105 We thus diversify the revelations, lest they say, "You have studied," and to clarify them for people who know.

١٠٦ اتَّبِعْ مَا أُوحِيَ إِلَيْكَ مِن رَّبِّكَ ۖ لَا إِلَٰهَ إِلَّا هُوَ ۖ وَأَعْرِضْ عَنِ الْمُشْرِكِينَ

106
10:109

106 Follow what was revealed to you from your Lord. There is no god but He. And turn away from the polytheists.

١٠٧ وَلَوْ شَاءَ اللَّهُ مَا أَشْرَكُوا ۗ وَمَا جَعَلْنَاكَ عَلَيْهِمْ حَفِيظًا ۖ وَمَا أَنتَ عَلَيْهِم بِوَكِيلٍ

107 Had God willed, they would not have practiced idolatry. We did not appoint you as a guardian over them, and you are not a manager over them.

١٠٨ وَلَا تَسُبُّوا الَّذِينَ يَدْعُونَ مِن دُونِ اللَّهِ فَيَسُبُّوا اللَّهَ عَدْوًا بِغَيْرِ عِلْمٍ ۗ كَذَٰلِكَ زَيَّنَّا لِكُلِّ أُمَّةٍ عَمَلَهُمْ ثُمَّ إِلَىٰ رَبِّهِم مَّرْجِعُهُمْ فَيُنَبِّئُهُم بِمَا كَانُوا يَعْمَلُونَ

108 Do not insult those they call upon besides God, lest they insult God out of hostility and ignorance. We made attractive to every community their deeds. Then to their Lord is their return, and He will inform them of what they used to do.

١٠٩ وَأَقْسَمُوا بِاللَّهِ جَهْدَ أَيْمَانِهِمْ لَئِن جَاءَتْهُمْ آيَةٌ لَّيُؤْمِنُنَّ بِهَا ۚ قُلْ إِنَّمَا الْآيَاتُ عِندَ اللَّهِ ۖ وَمَا يُشْعِرُكُمْ أَنَّهَا إِذَا جَاءَتْ لَا يُؤْمِنُونَ

109
29:50; 35:42

109 They swear by God, with their most solemn oaths, that if a miracle were to come to them, they would believe in it. Say, "The miracles are only with God." But how do you know? Even if it did come, they still would not believe.

١١٠ وَنُقَلِّبُ أَفْئِدَتَهُمْ وَأَبْصَارَهُمْ كَمَا لَمْ يُؤْمِنُوا بِهِ أَوَّلَ مَرَّةٍ وَنَذَرُهُمْ فِي طُغْيَانِهِمْ يَعْمَهُونَ

110
2:15; 7:186; 10:11

110 And We turn away their hearts and their visions, as they refused to believe in it the first time, and We leave them blundering in their rebellion.

١١١ وَلَوْ أَنَّنَا نَزَّلْنَا إِلَيْهِمُ الْمَلَائِكَةَ وَكَلَّمَهُمُ الْمَوْتَىٰ وَحَشَرْنَا عَلَيْهِمْ كُلَّ شَيْءٍ قُبُلًا مَّا كَانُوا لِيُؤْمِنُوا إِلَّا أَن يَشَاءَ اللَّهُ وَلَٰكِنَّ أَكْثَرَهُمْ يَجْهَلُونَ

111
11:12, 6:8–9; 31; 25:7

111 Even if We sent down the angels to them, and the dead spoke to them, and We gathered all things before them, they still would not believe, unless God wills; but most of them are ignorant.

١١٢ وَكَذَلِكَ جَعَلْنَا لِكُلِّ نَبِيٍّ عَدُوًّا شَيَاطِينَ الْإِنْسِ وَالْجِنِّ يُوحِي بَعْضُهُمْ إِلَى بَعْضٍ زُخْرُفَ الْقَوْلِ غُرُورًا ۚ وَلَوْ شَاءَ رَبُّكَ مَا فَعَلُوهُ ۖ فَذَرْهُمْ وَمَا يَفْتَرُونَ

112 2:114; 25:31

112 Likewise, We have assigned for every prophet an enemy—human and jinn devils—inspiring one another with fancy words in order to deceive. But had your Lord willed, they would not have done it. So leave them to their fabrications.

١١٣ وَلِتَصْغَىٰ إِلَيْهِ أَفْئِدَةُ الَّذِينَ لَا يُؤْمِنُونَ بِالْآخِرَةِ وَلِيَرْضَوْهُ وَلِيَقْتَرِفُوا مَا هُمْ مُقْتَرِفُونَ

113 So that the hearts of those who do not believe in the Hereafter may incline to it, and be content with it, and that they may perpetrate whatever they perpetrate.

١١٤ أَفَغَيْرَ اللَّهِ أَبْتَغِي حَكَمًا وَهُوَ الَّذِي أَنْزَلَ إِلَيْكُمُ الْكِتَابَ مُفَصَّلًا ۚ وَالَّذِينَ آتَيْنَاهُمُ الْكِتَابَ يَعْلَمُونَ أَنَّهُ مُنَزَّلٌ مِنْ رَبِّكَ بِالْحَقِّ ۖ فَلَا تَكُونَنَّ مِنَ الْمُمْتَرِينَ

114 2:146; 6:20

114 "Shall I seek a judge other than God, when He is the One who revealed to you the Book, explained in detail?" Those to whom We gave the Book know that it is the truth revealed from your Lord. So do not be of those who doubt.

١١٥ وَتَمَّتْ كَلِمَتُ رَبِّكَ صِدْقًا وَعَدْلًا ۚ لَا مُبَدِّلَ لِكَلِمَاتِهِ ۚ وَهُوَ السَّمِيعُ الْعَلِيمُ

115 6:34

115 The Word of your Lord has been completed, in truth and justice. There is no changing to His words. He is the Hearer, the Knower.

١١٦ وَإِنْ تُطِعْ أَكْثَرَ مَنْ فِي الْأَرْضِ يُضِلُّوكَ عَنْ سَبِيلِ اللَّهِ ۚ إِنْ يَتَّبِعُونَ إِلَّا الظَّنَّ وَإِنْ هُمْ إِلَّا يَخْرُصُونَ

116 10:36, 66; 13:1; 12:103; 37:17; 26:8

116 If you were to obey most of those on earth, they would divert you from God's path. They follow nothing but assumptions, and they only conjecture.

١١٧ إِنَّ رَبَّكَ هُوَ أَعْلَمُ مَنْ يَضِلُّ عَنْ سَبِيلِهِ ۖ وَهُوَ أَعْلَمُ بِالْمُهْتَدِينَ

117 Your Lord knows best who strays from His path, and He knows best the guided ones.

١١٨ فَكُلُوا مِمَّا ذُكِرَ اسْمُ اللَّهِ عَلَيْهِ إِنْ كُنْتُمْ بِآيَاتِهِ مُؤْمِنِينَ

118–119 2:173; 5:3; 6:121, 145; 16:115

118 So eat of that over which the Name of God was pronounced, if you indeed believe in His revelations.

١١٩ وَمَا لَكُمْ أَلَّا تَأْكُلُوا مِمَّا ذُكِرَ اسْمُ اللَّهِ عَلَيْهِ وَقَدْ فَصَّلَ لَكُمْ مَا حَرَّمَ عَلَيْكُمْ إِلَّا مَا اضْطُرِرْتُمْ إِلَيْهِ ۗ وَإِنَّ كَثِيرًا لَيُضِلُّونَ بِأَهْوَائِهِمْ بِغَيْرِ عِلْمٍ ۗ إِنَّ رَبَّكَ هُوَ أَعْلَمُ بِالْمُعْتَدِينَ

119 5:1–3

119 And why should you not eat of that over which the Name of God is pronounced, when He has detailed for you what is prohibited for you, unless you are compelled by necessity? Many lead astray with their opinions, through lack of knowledge. Your Lord knows best the transgressors.

١٢٠ وَذَرُوا ظَاهِرَ الْإِثْمِ وَبَاطِنَهُ ۚ إِنَّ الَّذِينَ يَكْسِبُونَ الْإِثْمَ سَيُجْزَوْنَ بِمَا كَانُوا يَقْتَرِفُونَ	**120** 6:151; 7:33

120 So abandon sin, outward and inward. Those who commit sins will be repaid for what they used to perpetrate.

١٢١ وَلَا تَأْكُلُوا مِمَّا لَمْ يُذْكَرِ اسْمُ اللَّهِ عَلَيْهِ وَإِنَّهُ لَفِسْقٌ ۗ وَإِنَّ الشَّيَاطِينَ لَيُوحُونَ إِلَىٰ أَوْلِيَائِهِمْ لِيُجَادِلُوكُمْ ۖ وَإِنْ أَطَعْتُمُوهُمْ إِنَّكُمْ لَمُشْرِكُونَ	**121** 2:173; 5:3

121 And do not eat from that over which the Name of God was not pronounced, for it is abomination. The devils inspire their followers to argue with you; but if you obey them, you would be polytheists.

١٢٢ أَوَمَنْ كَانَ مَيْتًا فَأَحْيَيْنَاهُ وَجَعَلْنَا لَهُ نُورًا يَمْشِي بِهِ فِي النَّاسِ كَمَنْ مَثَلُهُ فِي الظُّلُمَاتِ لَيْسَ بِخَارِجٍ مِنْهَا ۚ كَذَٰلِكَ زُيِّنَ لِلْكَافِرِينَ مَا كَانُوا يَعْمَلُونَ	**122** 2:257; 57:28

122 Is he who was dead, then We gave him life, and made for him a light by which he walks among the people, like he who is in total darkness, and cannot get out of it? Thus the doings of disbelievers are made to appear good to them.

١٢٣ وَكَذَٰلِكَ جَعَلْنَا فِي كُلِّ قَرْيَةٍ أَكَابِرَ مُجْرِمِيهَا لِيَمْكُرُوا فِيهَا ۖ وَمَا يَمْكُرُونَ إِلَّا بِأَنْفُسِهِمْ وَمَا يَشْعُرُونَ	**123** 34:34; 35:42–43; 43:23

123 And thus We set up in every city its leading wicked sinners, to conspire in it, but they conspire only against themselves, and they do not realize it.

١٢٤ وَإِذَا جَاءَتْهُمْ آيَةٌ قَالُوا لَنْ نُؤْمِنَ حَتَّىٰ نُؤْتَىٰ مِثْلَ مَا أُوتِيَ رُسُلُ اللَّهِ ۘ اللَّهُ أَعْلَمُ حَيْثُ يَجْعَلُ رِسَالَتَهُ ۗ سَيُصِيبُ الَّذِينَ أَجْرَمُوا صَغَارٌ عِنْدَ اللَّهِ وَعَذَابٌ شَدِيدٌ بِمَا كَانُوا يَمْكُرُونَ	**124** 3:183; 17:90, 92; 25:21; 28:48

124 When a sign comes to them, they say, "We will not believe unless we are given the like of what was given to God's messengers." God knows best where to place His message. Humiliation from God and severe torment will afflict the criminals for their scheming.

١٢٥ فَمَنْ يُرِدِ اللَّهُ أَنْ يَهْدِيَهُ يَشْرَحْ صَدْرَهُ لِلْإِسْلَامِ ۖ وَمَنْ يُرِدْ أَنْ يُضِلَّهُ يَجْعَلْ صَدْرَهُ ضَيِّقًا حَرَجًا كَأَنَّمَا يَصَّعَّدُ فِي السَّمَاءِ ۚ كَذَٰلِكَ يَجْعَلُ اللَّهُ الرِّجْسَ عَلَى الَّذِينَ لَا يُؤْمِنُونَ	**125** 10:100; 39:22; 94:1

125 Whomever God desires to guide, He spreads open his heart to Islam; and whomever He desires to misguide, He makes his heart narrow, constricted, as though he were climbing up the sky. God thus lays defilement upon those who do not believe.

١٢٦ وَهَٰذَا صِرَاطُ رَبِّكَ مُسْتَقِيمًا ۗ قَدْ فَصَّلْنَا الْآيَاتِ لِقَوْمٍ يَذَّكَّرُونَ	**126** 6:153

126 This is the straight path of your Lord. We have explained the revelations in detail for people who recollect.

١٢٧ لَهُمْ دَارُ السَّلَامِ عِنْدَ رَبِّهِمْ ۖ وَهُوَ وَلِيُّهُمْ بِمَا كَانُوا يَعْمَلُونَ	

127 For them is the Home of Peace with their Lord, and He is their Master—because of what they used to do.

١٢٨ وَيَوْمَ يَحْشُرُهُمْ جَمِيعًا يَا مَعْشَرَ الْجِنِّ قَدِ اسْتَكْثَرْتُم مِّنَ الْإِنسِ ۖ وَقَالَ أَوْلِيَاؤُهُم مِّنَ الْإِنسِ رَبَّنَا اسْتَمْتَعَ بَعْضُنَا بِبَعْضٍ وَبَلَغْنَا أَجَلَنَا الَّذِي أَجَّلْتَ لَنَا ۚ قَالَ النَّارُ مَثْوَاكُمْ خَالِدِينَ فِيهَا إِلَّا مَا شَاءَ اللَّهُ ۗ إِنَّ رَبَّكَ حَكِيمٌ عَلِيمٌ

128
34:40–42

128 On the Day when He gathers them all together: "O assembly of jinn, you have exploited multitudes of humans." Their adherents among mankind will say, "Our Lord, we have profited from one another, but we have reached the term that you have assigned for us." He will say, "The Fire is your dwelling, wherein you will remain, except as God wills. Your Lord is Wise and Informed."

١٢٩ وَكَذَٰلِكَ نُوَلِّي بَعْضَ الظَّالِمِينَ بَعْضًا بِمَا كَانُوا يَكْسِبُونَ

129
4:115

129 Thus We make some of the wrongdoers befriend one another, because of what they used to do.

١٣٠ يَا مَعْشَرَ الْجِنِّ وَالْإِنسِ أَلَمْ يَأْتِكُمْ رُسُلٌ مِّنكُمْ يَقُصُّونَ عَلَيْكُمْ آيَاتِي وَيُنذِرُونَكُمْ لِقَاءَ يَوْمِكُمْ هَٰذَا ۚ قَالُوا شَهِدْنَا عَلَىٰ أَنفُسِنَا ۖ وَغَرَّتْهُمُ الْحَيَاةُ الدُّنْيَا وَشَهِدُوا عَلَىٰ أَنفُسِهِمْ أَنَّهُمْ كَانُوا كَافِرِينَ

130
39:71; 40:50; 67:8

130 "O assembly of jinn and humans, did there not come to you messengers from among you, relating to you My revelations, and warning you of the meeting of this Day of yours?" They will say, "We testify against ourselves." The life of the world seduced them. They will testify against themselves that they were disbelievers.

١٣١ ذَٰلِكَ أَن لَّمْ يَكُن رَّبُّكَ مُهْلِكَ الْقُرَىٰ بِظُلْمٍ وَأَهْلُهَا غَافِلُونَ

131
11:117; 18:59; 28:59; 46:27

131 That is because your Lord would not destroy towns for injustice while their inhabitants are unaware.

١٣٢ وَلِكُلٍّ دَرَجَاتٌ مِّمَّا عَمِلُوا ۚ وَمَا رَبُّكَ بِغَافِلٍ عَمَّا يَعْمَلُونَ

132
17:21; 46:19

132 They all have ranks according to what they did; and your Lord is not unaware of what they do.

١٣٣ وَرَبُّكَ الْغَنِيُّ ذُو الرَّحْمَةِ ۚ إِن يَشَأْ يُذْهِبْكُمْ وَيَسْتَخْلِفْ مِن بَعْدِكُم مَّا يَشَاءُ كَمَا أَنشَأَكُم مِّن ذُرِّيَّةِ قَوْمٍ آخَرِينَ

133
4:133; 14:19; 35:15–16

133 Your Lord is the Rich Beyond Need, the Possessor of Mercy. If He wills, He can do away with you, and substitute whomever He wills in your place, just as He produced you from the descendants of another people.

١٣٤ إِنَّ مَا تُوعَدُونَ لَآتٍ ۖ وَمَا أَنتُم بِمُعْجِزِينَ

134

134 What you are promised is coming, and you cannot thwart it.

١٣٥ قُلْ يَا قَوْمِ اعْمَلُوا عَلَىٰ مَكَانَتِكُمْ إِنِّي عَامِلٌ ۖ فَسَوْفَ تَعْلَمُونَ مَن تَكُونُ لَهُ عَاقِبَةُ الدَّارِ ۗ إِنَّهُ لَا يُفْلِحُ الظَّالِمُونَ

135
11:93, 121; 39:39

135 Say, "O my people! Work according to your ability, and so will I." You will come to know to whom will belong the sequel of the abode." The wrongdoers will not prevail.

١٣٦ وَجَعَلُوا لِلَّهِ مِمَّا ذَرَأَ مِنَ الْحَرْثِ وَالْأَنْعَامِ نَصِيبًا فَقَالُوا هَٰذَا لِلَّهِ بِزَعْمِهِمْ وَهَٰذَا لِشُرَكَائِنَا ۖ فَمَا كَانَ لِشُرَكَائِهِمْ فَلَا يَصِلُ إِلَى اللَّهِ ۖ وَمَا كَانَ لِلَّهِ فَهُوَ يَصِلُ إِلَىٰ شُرَكَائِهِمْ ۗ سَاءَ مَا يَحْكُمُونَ

136 5:103

136 And they set aside for God a share of the crops and the livestock He created, and they say, "This is for God," according to their claim, "and this is for our idols." But the share of their idols does not reach God, yet the share of God reaches their idols. Evil is their judgment.

١٣٧ وَكَذَٰلِكَ زَيَّنَ لِكَثِيرٍ مِنَ الْمُشْرِكِينَ قَتْلَ أَوْلَادِهِمْ شُرَكَاؤُهُمْ لِيُرْدُوهُمْ وَلِيَلْبِسُوا عَلَيْهِمْ دِينَهُمْ ۖ وَلَوْ شَاءَ اللَّهُ مَا فَعَلُوهُ ۖ فَذَرْهُمْ وَمَا يَفْتَرُونَ

137 6:140, 151

137 Likewise, their idols entice many idolaters to kill their children, in order to lead them to their ruin, and confuse them in their religion. Had God willed, they would not have done it; so leave them to their fraud.

١٣٨ وَقَالُوا هَٰذِهِ أَنْعَامٌ وَحَرْثٌ حِجْرٌ لَا يَطْعَمُهَا إِلَّا مَنْ نَشَاءُ بِزَعْمِهِمْ وَأَنْعَامٌ حُرِّمَتْ ظُهُورُهَا وَأَنْعَامٌ لَا يَذْكُرُونَ اسْمَ اللَّهِ عَلَيْهَا افْتِرَاءً عَلَيْهِ ۚ سَيَجْزِيهِمْ بِمَا كَانُوا يَفْتَرُونَ

138 And they say, "These animals and crops are restricted; none may eat them except those we permit," by their claims, and animals whose backs are forbidden, and animals over which they do not pronounce the name of God—fabricating lies against Him. He will repay them for what they used to invent.

١٣٩ وَقَالُوا مَا فِي بُطُونِ هَٰذِهِ الْأَنْعَامِ خَالِصَةٌ لِذُكُورِنَا وَمُحَرَّمٌ عَلَىٰ أَزْوَاجِنَا ۖ وَإِنْ يَكُنْ مَيْتَةً فَهُمْ فِيهِ شُرَكَاءُ ۚ سَيَجْزِيهِمْ وَصْفَهُمْ ۚ إِنَّهُ حَكِيمٌ عَلِيمٌ

139 And they say, "What lies in the wombs of these animals is exclusively for our males, and prohibited to our wives." But if it is stillborn, they can share in it. He will surely punish them for their allegations. He is Wise and Knowing.

١٤٠ قَدْ خَسِرَ الَّذِينَ قَتَلُوا أَوْلَادَهُمْ سَفَهًا بِغَيْرِ عِلْمٍ وَحَرَّمُوا مَا رَزَقَهُمُ اللَّهُ افْتِرَاءً عَلَى اللَّهِ ۚ قَدْ ضَلُّوا وَمَا كَانُوا مُهْتَدِينَ

140 6:137, 151

140 Lost are those who kill their children foolishly, with no basis in knowledge, and forbid what God has provided for them—innovations about God. They have gone astray. They are not guided.

١٤١ وَهُوَ الَّذِي أَنْشَأَ جَنَّاتٍ مَعْرُوشَاتٍ وَغَيْرَ مَعْرُوشَاتٍ وَالنَّخْلَ وَالزَّرْعَ مُخْتَلِفًا أُكُلُهُ وَالزَّيْتُونَ وَالرُّمَّانَ مُتَشَابِهًا وَغَيْرَ مُتَشَابِهٍ ۚ كُلُوا مِنْ ثَمَرِهِ إِذَا أَثْمَرَ وَآتُوا حَقَّهُ يَوْمَ حَصَادِهِ ۖ وَلَا تُسْرِفُوا ۚ إِنَّهُ لَا يُحِبُّ الْمُسْرِفِينَ

141 2:267

141 It is He who produces gardens, both cultivated and wild, and date-palms, and crops of diverse tastes, and olives and pomegranates, similar and dissimilar. Eat of its fruit when it yields, and give its due on the day of its harvest, and do not waste. He does not love the wasteful.

١٤٢ وَمِنَ الْأَنْعَامِ حَمُولَةً وَفَرْشًا ۚ كُلُوا مِمَّا رَزَقَكُمُ اللَّهُ وَلَا تَتَّبِعُوا خُطُوَاتِ الشَّيْطَانِ ۚ إِنَّهُ لَكُمْ عَدُوٌّ مُبِينٌ

142 2:168

142 Among the livestock are some for transportation, and some for clothing. Eat of what God has provided for you, and do not follow the footsteps of Satan. He is to you an outright enemy.

١٤٣ ثَمَانِيَةَ أَزْوَاجٍ ۖ مِنَ الضَّأْنِ اثْنَيْنِ وَمِنَ الْمَعْزِ اثْنَيْنِ ۗ قُلْ آلذَّكَرَيْنِ حَرَّمَ أَمِ الْأُنْثَيَيْنِ أَمَّا اشْتَمَلَتْ عَلَيْهِ أَرْحَامُ الْأُنْثَيَيْنِ ۖ نَبِّئُونِي بِعِلْمٍ إِنْ كُنْتُمْ صَادِقِينَ

143 39:6

143 Eight pairs: two of the sheep, and two of the goats. Say, "Did He forbid the two males, or the two females, or what the wombs of the two females contain? Inform me with knowledge, if you are truthful."

١٤٤ وَمِنَ الْإِبِلِ اثْنَيْنِ وَمِنَ الْبَقَرِ اثْنَيْنِ ۗ قُلْ آلذَّكَرَيْنِ حَرَّمَ أَمِ الْأُنْثَيَيْنِ أَمَّا اشْتَمَلَتْ عَلَيْهِ أَرْحَامُ الْأُنْثَيَيْنِ ۖ أَمْ كُنْتُمْ شُهَدَاءَ إِذْ وَصَّاكُمُ اللَّهُ بِهَٰذَا ۚ فَمَنْ أَظْلَمُ مِمَّنِ افْتَرَىٰ عَلَى اللَّهِ كَذِبًا لِيُضِلَّ النَّاسَ بِغَيْرِ عِلْمٍ ۗ إِنَّ اللَّهَ لَا يَهْدِي الْقَوْمَ الظَّالِمِينَ

144 And two of the camels, and two of the cattle. Say, "Did He forbid the two males, or the two females, or what the wombs of the two females contain? Were you present when God enjoined this upon you?" Who does greater wrong than he who invents lies and attributes them to God, in order to mislead people without knowledge? God does not guide the wicked people.

١٤٥ قُلْ لَا أَجِدُ فِي مَا أُوحِيَ إِلَيَّ مُحَرَّمًا عَلَىٰ طَاعِمٍ يَطْعَمُهُ إِلَّا أَنْ يَكُونَ مَيْتَةً أَوْ دَمًا مَسْفُوحًا أَوْ لَحْمَ خِنْزِيرٍ فَإِنَّهُ رِجْسٌ أَوْ فِسْقًا أُهِلَّ لِغَيْرِ اللَّهِ بِهِ ۚ فَمَنِ اضْطُرَّ غَيْرَ بَاغٍ وَلَا عَادٍ فَإِنَّ رَبَّكَ غَفُورٌ رَحِيمٌ

145 2:173; 5:3; 6:118–119; 16:115

145 Say, "In what was revealed to me, I find nothing forbidden to a consumer who eats it, except carrion, or spilled blood, or the flesh of swine—because it is impure—or a sinful offering dedicated to other than God. But if someone is compelled by necessity, without being deliberate or malicious—your Lord is Forgiving and Merciful.

١٤٦ وَعَلَى الَّذِينَ هَادُوا حَرَّمْنَا كُلَّ ذِي ظُفُرٍ ۖ وَمِنَ الْبَقَرِ وَالْغَنَمِ حَرَّمْنَا عَلَيْهِمْ شُحُومَهُمَا إِلَّا مَا حَمَلَتْ ظُهُورُهُمَا أَوِ الْحَوَايَا أَوْ مَا اخْتَلَطَ بِعَظْمٍ ۚ ذَٰلِكَ جَزَيْنَاهُمْ بِبَغْيِهِمْ ۖ وَإِنَّا لَصَادِقُونَ

146 16:118

146 For the Jews We forbade everything with claws. As of cattle and sheep: We forbade them their fat, except what adheres to their backs, or the entrails, or what is mixed with bone. This is how We penalized them for their inequity. We are indeed truthful.

١٤٧ فَإِنْ كَذَّبُوكَ فَقُلْ رَبُّكُمْ ذُو رَحْمَةٍ وَاسِعَةٍ وَلَا يُرَدُّ بَأْسُهُ عَنِ الْقَوْمِ الْمُجْرِمِينَ

147 7:156; 12:110; 33:17; 42:8; 76:31

147 If they accuse you of lying, say, "Your Lord is Possessor of infinite mercy, but His wrath cannot be averted from the guilty people."

١٤٨ سَيَقُولُ الَّذِينَ أَشْرَكُوا لَوْ شَاءَ اللَّهُ مَا أَشْرَكْنَا وَلَا آبَاؤُنَا وَلَا حَرَّمْنَا مِن شَيْءٍ ۚ كَذَٰلِكَ كَذَّبَ الَّذِينَ مِن قَبْلِهِمْ حَتَّىٰ ذَاقُوا بَأْسَنَا ۗ قُلْ هَلْ عِندَكُم مِّنْ عِلْمٍ فَتُخْرِجُوهُ لَنَا ۖ إِن تَتَّبِعُونَ إِلَّا الظَّنَّ وَإِنْ أَنتُمْ إِلَّا تَخْرُصُونَ

148 16:35; 43:20

148 The polytheists will say, "Had God willed, we would not have practiced idolatry, nor would have our forefathers, nor would we have prohibited anything." Likewise those before them lied, until they tasted Our might. Say, "Do you have any knowledge that you can produce for us? You follow nothing but conjecture, and you only guess."

١٤٩ قُلْ فَلِلَّهِ الْحُجَّةُ الْبَالِغَةُ ۖ فَلَوْ شَاءَ لَهَدَاكُمْ أَجْمَعِينَ

149 6:35

149 Say, "To God belongs the conclusive argument. Had He willed, He would have guided you all."

١٥٠ قُلْ هَلُمَّ شُهَدَاءَكُمُ الَّذِينَ يَشْهَدُونَ أَنَّ اللَّهَ حَرَّمَ هَٰذَا ۖ فَإِن شَهِدُوا فَلَا تَشْهَدْ مَعَهُمْ ۚ وَلَا تَتَّبِعْ أَهْوَاءَ الَّذِينَ كَذَّبُوا بِآيَاتِنَا وَالَّذِينَ لَا يُؤْمِنُونَ بِالْآخِرَةِ وَهُم بِرَبِّهِمْ يَعْدِلُونَ

150 Say, "Produce your witnesses who would testify that God has prohibited this." If they testify, do not testify with them. And do not follow the whims of those who deny Our revelation, and those who do not believe in the Hereafter, and those who equate others with their Lord.

١٥١ قُلْ تَعَالَوْا أَتْلُ مَا حَرَّمَ رَبُّكُمْ عَلَيْكُمْ ۖ أَلَّا تُشْرِكُوا بِهِ شَيْئًا ۖ وَبِالْوَالِدَيْنِ إِحْسَانًا ۖ وَلَا تَقْتُلُوا أَوْلَادَكُم مِّنْ إِمْلَاقٍ ۖ نَّحْنُ نَرْزُقُكُمْ وَإِيَّاهُمْ ۖ وَلَا تَقْرَبُوا الْفَوَاحِشَ مَا ظَهَرَ مِنْهَا وَمَا بَطَنَ ۖ وَلَا تَقْتُلُوا النَّفْسَ الَّتِي حَرَّمَ اللَّهُ إِلَّا بِالْحَقِّ ۚ ذَٰلِكُمْ وَصَّاكُم بِهِ لَعَلَّكُمْ تَعْقِلُونَ

151 6:120, 137; 7:33; 17:31–32

151 Say, "Come, let me tell you what your Lord has forbidden you: that you associate nothing with Him; that you honor your parents; that you do not kill your children because of poverty—We provide for you and for them; that you do not come near indecencies, whether outward or inward; and that you do not kill the soul which God has sanctified—except in the course of justice. All this He has enjoined upon you, so that you may understand."

١٥٢ وَلَا تَقْرَبُوا مَالَ الْيَتِيمِ إِلَّا بِالَّتِي هِيَ أَحْسَنُ حَتَّىٰ يَبْلُغَ أَشُدَّهُ ۖ وَأَوْفُوا الْكَيْلَ وَالْمِيزَانَ بِالْقِسْطِ ۖ لَا نُكَلِّفُ نَفْسًا إِلَّا وُسْعَهَا ۖ وَإِذَا قُلْتُمْ فَاعْدِلُوا وَلَوْ كَانَ ذَا قُرْبَىٰ ۖ وَبِعَهْدِ اللَّهِ أَوْفُوا ۚ ذَٰلِكُمْ وَصَّاكُم بِهِ لَعَلَّكُمْ تَذَكَّرُونَ

152 4:2, 6, 10, 127; 17:34; 55:8; 89:19

152 And do not come near the property of the orphan, except with the best intentions, until he reaches maturity. And give full weight and full measure, equitably. We do not burden any soul beyond its capacity. And when you speak, be fair, even if it concerns a close relative. And fulfill your covenant with God. All this He has enjoined upon you, so that you may take heed.

١٥٣ وَأَنَّ هَٰذَا صِرَاطِي مُسْتَقِيمًا فَاتَّبِعُوهُ ۖ وَلَا تَتَّبِعُوا السُّبُلَ فَتَفَرَّقَ بِكُمْ عَن سَبِيلِهِ ۚ ذَٰلِكُمْ وَصَّاكُم بِهِ لَعَلَّكُمْ تَتَّقُونَ

153
6:126

153 This is My path, straight, so follow it. And do not follow the other paths, lest they divert you from His path. All this He has enjoined upon you, that you may refrain from wrongdoing.

١٥٤ ثُمَّ آتَيْنَا مُوسَى الْكِتَابَ تَمَامًا عَلَى الَّذِي أَحْسَنَ وَتَفْصِيلًا لِّكُلِّ شَيْءٍ وَهُدًى وَرَحْمَةً لَّعَلَّهُم بِلِقَاءِ رَبِّهِمْ يُؤْمِنُونَ

154 Then We gave Moses the Scripture, perfect for the righteous, and explaining everything clearly, and a beacon, and mercy, that they may believe in the encounter with their Lord.

١٥٥ وَهَٰذَا كِتَابٌ أَنزَلْنَاهُ مُبَارَكٌ فَاتَّبِعُوهُ وَاتَّقُوا لَعَلَّكُمْ تُرْحَمُونَ

155 This too is a blessed Scripture that We revealed; so follow it, and be righteous, that you may receive mercy.

١٥٦ أَن تَقُولُوا إِنَّمَا أُنزِلَ الْكِتَابُ عَلَىٰ طَائِفَتَيْنِ مِن قَبْلِنَا وَإِن كُنَّا عَن دِرَاسَتِهِمْ لَغَافِلِينَ

156 Lest you say, "The Scripture was revealed to two parties before us, and we were unaware of their teachings."

١٥٧ أَوْ تَقُولُوا لَوْ أَنَّا أُنزِلَ عَلَيْنَا الْكِتَابُ لَكُنَّا أَهْدَىٰ مِنْهُمْ ۚ فَقَدْ جَاءَكُم بَيِّنَةٌ مِّن رَّبِّكُمْ وَهُدًى وَرَحْمَةٌ ۚ فَمَنْ أَظْلَمُ مِمَّن كَذَّبَ بِآيَاتِ اللَّهِ وَصَدَفَ عَنْهَا ۗ سَنَجْزِي الَّذِينَ يَصْدِفُونَ عَنْ آيَاتِنَا سُوءَ الْعَذَابِ بِمَا كَانُوا يَصْدِفُونَ

157
35:42

157 Or lest you say, "Had the Scripture been revealed to us, we would have been better guided than they." Clarification has come to you from your Lord, and guidance, and mercy. Who then does greater wrong than he who gives the lie to God's messages, and turns away from them? We will repay those who turn away from Our messages with the worst kind of punishment, because of their turning away.

١٥٨ هَلْ يَنظُرُونَ إِلَّا أَن تَأْتِيَهُمُ الْمَلَائِكَةُ أَوْ يَأْتِيَ رَبُّكَ أَوْ يَأْتِيَ بَعْضُ آيَاتِ رَبِّكَ ۗ يَوْمَ يَأْتِي بَعْضُ آيَاتِ رَبِّكَ لَا يَنفَعُ نَفْسًا إِيمَانُهَا لَمْ تَكُنْ آمَنَتْ مِن قَبْلُ أَوْ كَسَبَتْ فِي إِيمَانِهَا خَيْرًا ۗ قُلِ انتَظِرُوا إِنَّا مُنتَظِرُونَ

158
2:210; 16:33; 40:85

158 Are they waiting for anything but for the angels to come to them, or for your Lord to arrive, or for some of your Lord's signs to come? On the Day when some of your Lord's signs come, no soul will benefit from its faith unless it had believed previously, or had earned goodness through its faith. Say, "Wait, we too are waiting."

١٥٩ إِنَّ الَّذِينَ فَرَّقُوا دِينَهُمْ وَكَانُوا شِيَعًا لَّسْتَ مِنْهُمْ فِي شَيْءٍ ۚ إِنَّمَا أَمْرُهُمْ إِلَى اللَّهِ ثُمَّ يُنَبِّئُهُم بِمَا كَانُوا يَفْعَلُونَ

159
3:105; 21:93; 23:53; 30:31

159 As for those who divided their religion and became sects—you have nothing to do with them. Their case rests with God; then He will inform them of what they used to do.

١٦٠ مَنْ جَاءَ بِالْحَسَنَةِ فَلَهُ عَشْرُ أَمْثَالِهَا ۖ وَمَنْ جَاءَ بِالسَّيِّئَةِ فَلَا يُجْزَىٰ إِلَّا مِثْلَهَا وَهُمْ لَا يُظْلَمُونَ

160 Whoever comes up with a good deed will have ten times its like; and whoever comes up with an evil deed will be repaid only with its equivalent—they will not be wronged.

160
4:40; 10:26; 27:89; 28:84

١٦١ قُلْ إِنَّنِي هَدَانِي رَبِّي إِلَىٰ صِرَاطٍ مُسْتَقِيمٍ دِينًا قِيَمًا مِلَّةَ إِبْرَاهِيمَ حَنِيفًا ۚ وَمَا كَانَ مِنَ الْمُشْرِكِينَ

161 Say, "My Lord has guided me to a straight path, an upright religion, the creed of Abraham the Monotheist, who was not a polytheist."

161
2:135; 3:67, 95; 16:120

١٦٢ قُلْ إِنَّ صَلَاتِي وَنُسُكِي وَمَحْيَايَ وَمَمَاتِي لِلَّهِ رَبِّ الْعَالَمِينَ

162 Say, "My prayer and my worship, and my life and my death, are devoted to God, the Lord of the Worlds.

162–163
2:101; 6:14

١٦٣ لَا شَرِيكَ لَهُ ۖ وَبِذَٰلِكَ أُمِرْتُ وَأَنَا أَوَّلُ الْمُسْلِمِينَ

163 No associate has He. Thus I am commanded, and I am the first of those who submit.

١٦٤ قُلْ أَغَيْرَ اللَّهِ أَبْغِي رَبًّا وَهُوَ رَبُّ كُلِّ شَيْءٍ ۚ وَلَا تَكْسِبُ كُلُّ نَفْسٍ إِلَّا عَلَيْهَا ۚ[a] وَلَا تَزِرُ وَازِرَةٌ وِزْرَ أُخْرَىٰ ۚ[b] ثُمَّ إِلَىٰ رَبِّكُمْ مَرْجِعُكُمْ فَيُنَبِّئُكُمْ بِمَا كُنْتُمْ فِيهِ تَخْتَلِفُونَ

164 Say, "Am I to seek a Lord other than God, when He is the Lord of all things?" No soul gets except what it is due, and no soul bears the burdens of another. Then to your Lord is your return, then He will inform you regarding your disputes.

164
[a] 2:286; 4:111
[b] 6:164; 17:15; 35:18; 39:7; 53:38

١٦٥ وَهُوَ الَّذِي جَعَلَكُمْ خَلَائِفَ الْأَرْضِ[a] وَرَفَعَ بَعْضَكُمْ فَوْقَ بَعْضٍ دَرَجَاتٍ لِيَبْلُوَكُمْ فِي مَا آتَاكُمْ ۗ[b] إِنَّ رَبَّكَ سَرِيعُ الْعِقَابِ وَإِنَّهُ لَغَفُورٌ رَحِيمٌ

165 It is He who made you successors on the earth, and raised some of you in ranks over others, in order to test you through what He has given you. Your Lord is Quick in retribution, and He is Forgiving and Merciful.

165
[a] 7:96, 74; 10:14, 73; 27:62; 35:39
[b] 16:71; 43:32

Sūrah 7: Al-Aʻrāf

سُورَةُ ٱلْأَعْرَافِ (The Elevation)

بِسْمِ ٱللَّهِ ٱلرَّحْمَٰنِ ٱلرَّحِيمِ

١ المص

1 Alif, Lām, Mīm, Ṣād.

٢ كِتَابٌ أُنْزِلَ إِلَيْكَ فَلَا يَكُنْ فِي صَدْرِكَ حَرَجٌ[a] مِنْهُ لِتُنْذِرَ بِهِ وَذِكْرَىٰ لِلْمُؤْمِنِينَ[b]

2 A Scripture was revealed to you, so let there be no anxiety in your heart because of it. You are to warn with it—and a reminder for the believers.

2
[a] 2:147; 3:60; 10:49
[b] 19:97; 36:6

٣ اتَّبِعُوا مَا أُنزِلَ إِلَيْكُم مِّن رَّبِّكُمْ وَلَا تَتَّبِعُوا مِن دُونِهِ أَوْلِيَاءَ ۗ قَلِيلًا مَّا تَذَكَّرُونَ

3 Follow what is revealed to you from your Lord, and do not follow other masters beside Him. Little you recollect.

٤ وَكَم مِّن قَرْيَةٍ أَهْلَكْنَاهَا فَجَاءَهَا بَأْسُنَا بَيَاتًا أَوْ هُمْ قَائِلُونَ

4 How many a town have We destroyed? Our might came upon them by night, or while they were napping.

4
6:10; 7:97–98; 21:11–15; 22:42, 45; 28:58; 46:27

٥ فَمَا كَانَ دَعْوَاهُمْ إِذْ جَاءَهُم بَأْسُنَا إِلَّا أَن قَالُوا إِنَّا كُنَّا ظَالِمِينَ

5 When Our might came upon them, their only cry was, "We were indeed wrongdoers."

5
21:14

٦ فَلَنَسْأَلَنَّ الَّذِينَ أُرْسِلَ إِلَيْهِمْ وَلَنَسْأَلَنَّ الْمُرْسَلِينَ

6 We will question those to whom messengers were sent, and We will question the messengers.

6
15:92–93; 28:65; 43:44

٧ فَلَنَقُصَّنَّ عَلَيْهِم بِعِلْمٍ ۖ وَمَا كُنَّا غَائِبِينَ

7 We will narrate to them with knowledge, for We were never absent.

7
10:61; 11:5; 58:7

٨ وَالْوَزْنُ يَوْمَئِذٍ الْحَقُّ ۚ فَمَن ثَقُلَتْ مَوَازِينُهُ فَأُولَٰئِكَ هُمُ الْمُفْلِحُونَ

8 The scales on that Day will be just. Those whose weights are heavy—it is they who are the successful.

8–9
21:47; 23:103; 101:6–11

٩ وَمَنْ خَفَّتْ مَوَازِينُهُ فَأُولَٰئِكَ الَّذِينَ خَسِرُوا أَنفُسَهُم بِمَا كَانُوا بِآيَاتِنَا يَظْلِمُونَ

9 But as for those whose weights are light—it is they who have lost their souls, because they used to mistreat Our revelations.

١٠ وَلَقَدْ مَكَّنَّاكُمْ فِي الْأَرْضِ وَجَعَلْنَا لَكُمْ فِيهَا مَعَايِشَ ۗ قَلِيلًا مَّا تَشْكُرُونَ

10 We have established you firmly on earth, and made for you in it livelihood—but rarely do you give thanks.

10
15:20

١١ وَلَقَدْ خَلَقْنَاكُمْ ثُمَّ صَوَّرْنَاكُمْ ثُمَّ قُلْنَا لِلْمَلَائِكَةِ اسْجُدُوا لِآدَمَ فَسَجَدُوا إِلَّا إِبْلِيسَ لَمْ يَكُن مِّنَ السَّاجِدِينَ

11 We created you, then We shaped you, then We said to the angels, "Bow down before Adam;" so they bowed down, except for Satan; he was not of those who bowed down.

11
3:6; 23:12–14; 40:64; 64:3; 59:24; 82:7

١٢ قَالَ مَا مَنَعَكَ أَلَّا تَسْجُدَ إِذْ أَمَرْتُكَ ۖ قَالَ أَنَا خَيْرٌ مِّنْهُ خَلَقْتَنِي مِن نَّارٍ وَخَلَقْتَهُ مِن طِينٍ

12 He said, "What prevented you from bowing down when I have commanded you?" He said, "I am better than he; You created me from fire, and You created him from mud."

12
2:34; 15:27, 32; 17:61; 38:75; 55:15

١٣ قَالَ فَاهْبِطْ مِنْهَا فَمَا يَكُونُ لَكَ أَن تَتَكَبَّرَ فِيهَا فَاخْرُجْ إِنَّكَ مِنَ الصَّاغِرِينَ

13 He said, "Get down from it! It is not for you to act arrogantly in it. Get out! You are one of the lowly!"

13
15:34; 38:77

١٤ قَالَ أَنْظِرْنِي إِلَىٰ يَوْمِ يُبْعَثُونَ

14 He said, "Give me respite, until the Day they are resurrected."

14–15
15:36–38; 17:62;
38:79–81

١٥ قَالَ إِنَّكَ مِنَ الْمُنْظَرِينَ

15 He said, "You are of those given respite."

١٦ قَالَ فَبِمَا أَغْوَيْتَنِي لَأَقْعُدَنَّ لَهُمْ صِرَاطَكَ الْمُسْتَقِيمَ

16 He said, "Because you have lured me, I will waylay them on Your straight path.

16
4:118; 15:39; 17:62;
38:82

١٧ ثُمَّ لَآتِيَنَّهُم مِّن بَيْنِ أَيْدِيهِمْ وَمِنْ خَلْفِهِمْ وَعَنْ أَيْمَانِهِمْ وَعَن شَمَائِلِهِمْ ۖ وَلَا تَجِدُ أَكْثَرَهُمْ شَاكِرِينَ

17 Then I will come at them from before them, and from behind them, and from their right, and from their left; and you will not find most of them appreciative."

17
20:117

١٨ قَالَ اخْرُجْ مِنْهَا مَذْءُومًا مَّدْحُورًا ۖ لَّمَن تَبِعَكَ مِنْهُمْ لَأَمْلَأَنَّ جَهَنَّمَ مِنكُمْ أَجْمَعِينَ

18 He said, "Get out of it, despised and vanquished. Whoever among them follows you—I will fill up Hell with you all.

18
15:41–43; 17:63; 38:85

١٩ وَيَا آدَمُ اسْكُنْ أَنتَ وَزَوْجُكَ الْجَنَّةَ فَكُلَا مِنْ حَيْثُ شِئْتُمَا وَلَا تَقْرَبَا هَٰذِهِ الشَّجَرَةَ فَتَكُونَا مِنَ الظَّالِمِينَ

19 And you, Adam, inhabit the Garden, you and your wife, and eat whatever you wish; but do not approach this tree, lest you become sinners."

19
2:35; 20:116–119

٢٠ فَوَسْوَسَ لَهُمَا الشَّيْطَانُ لِيُبْدِيَ لَهُمَا مَا وُورِيَ عَنْهُمَا مِن سَوْآتِهِمَا وَقَالَ مَا نَهَاكُمَا رَبُّكُمَا عَنْ هَٰذِهِ الشَّجَرَةِ إِلَّا أَن تَكُونَا مَلَكَيْنِ أَوْ تَكُونَا مِنَ الْخَالِدِينَ

20 But Satan whispered to them, to reveal to them their nakedness, which was invisible to them. He said, "Your Lord has only forbidden you this tree, lest you become angels, or become immortals."

20
2:36; 7:27; 20:120

٢١ وَقَاسَمَهُمَا إِنِّي لَكُمَا لَمِنَ النَّاصِحِينَ

21 And he swore to them, "I am a sincere advisor to you."

٢٢ فَدَلَّاهُمَا بِغُرُورٍ ۚ فَلَمَّا ذَاقَا الشَّجَرَةَ بَدَتْ لَهُمَا سَوْآتُهُمَا وَطَفِقَا يَخْصِفَانِ عَلَيْهِمَا مِن وَرَقِ الْجَنَّةِ ۖ وَنَادَاهُمَا رَبُّهُمَا أَلَمْ أَنْهَكُمَا عَن تِلْكُمَا الشَّجَرَةِ وَأَقُل لَّكُمَا إِنَّ الشَّيْطَانَ لَكُمَا عَدُوٌّ مُّبِينٌ

22 So he lured them with deceit. And when they tasted the tree, their nakedness became evident to them, and they began covering themselves with the leaves of the Garden. And their Lord called out to them, "Did I not forbid you from this tree, and say to you that Satan is a sworn enemy to you?"

22
2:168; 6:142; 12:5;
17:53; 20:121; 43:62

٢٣ قَالَا رَبَّنَا ظَلَمْنَا أَنفُسَنَا وَإِن لَّمْ تَغْفِرْ لَنَا وَتَرْحَمْنَا لَنَكُونَنَّ مِنَ الْخَاسِرِينَ

23 They said, "Our Lord, we have done wrong to ourselves. Unless You forgive us, and have mercy on us, we will be among the losers."

23
2:37; 7:35; 20:122

٢٤ قَالَ اهْبِطُوا بَعْضُكُمْ لِبَعْضٍ عَدُوٌّ ۖ وَلَكُمْ فِي الْأَرْضِ مُسْتَقَرٌّ وَمَتَاعٌ إِلَىٰ حِينٍ

24 2:38; 20:123

24 He said, "Fall, some of you enemies to one another. On earth you will have residence and livelihood for a while."

٢٥ قَالَ فِيهَا تَحْيَوْنَ وَفِيهَا تَمُوتُونَ وَمِنْهَا تُخْرَجُونَ

25 He said, "In it you will live, and in it you will die, and from it you will be brought out."

٢٦ يَا بَنِي آدَمَ قَدْ أَنزَلْنَا عَلَيْكُمْ لِبَاسًا يُوَارِي سَوْآتِكُمْ وَرِيشًا ۖ وَلِبَاسُ التَّقْوَىٰ ذَٰلِكَ خَيْرٌ ۚ ذَٰلِكَ مِنْ آيَاتِ اللَّهِ لَعَلَّهُمْ يَذَّكَّرُونَ

26 O children of Adam! We have provided you with clothing to cover your bodies, and for luxury. But the clothing of piety—that is best. These are some of God's revelations, so that they may take heed.

٢٧ يَا بَنِي آدَمَ لَا يَفْتِنَنَّكُمُ الشَّيْطَانُ كَمَا أَخْرَجَ أَبَوَيْكُم مِّنَ الْجَنَّةِ يَنزِعُ عَنْهُمَا لِبَاسَهُمَا لِيُرِيَهُمَا سَوْآتِهِمَا ۗ إِنَّهُ يَرَاكُمْ هُوَ وَقَبِيلُهُ مِنْ حَيْثُ لَا تَرَوْنَهُمْ ۗ إِنَّا جَعَلْنَا الشَّيَاطِينَ أَوْلِيَاءَ لِلَّذِينَ لَا يُؤْمِنُونَ

27 2:36; 7:20; 20:120

27 O Children of Adam! Do not let Satan seduce you, as he drove your parents out of the Garden, stripping them of their garments, to show them their nakedness. He sees you, him and his clan, from where you cannot see them. We have made the devils friends of those who do not believe.

٢٨ وَإِذَا فَعَلُوا فَاحِشَةً قَالُوا وَجَدْنَا عَلَيْهَا آبَاءَنَا وَاللَّهُ أَمَرَنَا بِهَا ۗ قُلْ إِنَّ اللَّهَ لَا يَأْمُرُ بِالْفَحْشَاءِ ۖ أَتَقُولُونَ عَلَى اللَّهِ مَا لَا تَعْلَمُونَ

28 2:169–170; 5:104; 43:24

28 And when they commit an indecency, they say, "We found our parents doing this, and God has commanded us to do it." Say, "God does not command indecencies. Are you attributing to God what you do not know?"

٢٩ قُلْ أَمَرَ رَبِّي بِالْقِسْطِ ۖ وَأَقِيمُوا وُجُوهَكُمْ عِندَ كُلِّ مَسْجِدٍ وَادْعُوهُ مُخْلِصِينَ لَهُ الدِّينَ ۚ كَمَا بَدَأَكُمْ تَعُودُونَ

29 40:14

29 Say, "My Lord commands justice, and to stand devoted at every place of worship. So call upon Him, and dedicate your faith to Him alone. Just as He originated you, so you will return."

٣٠ فَرِيقًا هَدَىٰ وَفَرِيقًا حَقَّ عَلَيْهِمُ الضَّلَالَةُ ۗ إِنَّهُمُ اتَّخَذُوا الشَّيَاطِينَ أَوْلِيَاءَ مِن دُونِ اللَّهِ وَيَحْسَبُونَ أَنَّهُم مُّهْتَدُونَ

30 16:36

30 Some He has guided, and some have deserved misguidance. They have adopted the devils for patrons rather than God, and they assume that they are guided.

٣١ يَا بَنِي آدَمَ خُذُوا زِينَتَكُمْ عِندَ كُلِّ مَسْجِدٍ وَكُلُوا وَاشْرَبُوا وَلَا تُسْرِفُوا ۚ إِنَّهُ لَا يُحِبُّ الْمُسْرِفِينَ

31 O Children of Adam! Dress properly at every place of worship, and eat and drink, but do not be excessive. He does not love the excessive.

Sūrah 7: Al-A'rāf

٣٢ قُلْ مَنْ حَرَّمَ زِينَةَ اللَّهِ الَّتِي أَخْرَجَ لِعِبَادِهِ وَالطَّيِّبَاتِ مِنَ الرِّزْقِ ۚ قُلْ هِيَ لِلَّذِينَ آمَنُوا فِي الْحَيَاةِ الدُّنْيَا خَالِصَةً يَوْمَ الْقِيَامَةِ ۗ كَذَٰلِكَ نُفَصِّلُ الْآيَاتِ لِقَوْمٍ يَعْلَمُونَ

32   10:59; 11:20; 16:116

32 Say, "Who forbade God's finery which He has produced for His servants, and the delights of livelihood?" Say, "They are for those who believe, in this present world, but exclusively theirs on the Day of Resurrection." We thus detail the revelations for people who know.

٣٣ قُلْ إِنَّمَا حَرَّمَ رَبِّيَ الْفَوَاحِشَ مَا ظَهَرَ مِنْهَا وَمَا بَطَنَ وَالْإِثْمَ وَالْبَغْيَ بِغَيْرِ الْحَقِّ وَأَنْ تُشْرِكُوا بِاللَّهِ مَا لَمْ يُنَزِّلْ بِهِ سُلْطَانًا وَأَنْ تَقُولُوا عَلَى اللَّهِ مَا لَا تَعْلَمُونَ

33   6:151

33 Say, "My Lord has forbidden immoralities—both open and secret—and sin, and unjustified aggression, and that you associate with God anything for which He revealed no sanction, and that you say about God what you do not know."

٣٤ وَلِكُلِّ أُمَّةٍ أَجَلٌ ۖ فَإِذَا جَاءَ أَجَلُهُمْ لَا يَسْتَأْخِرُونَ سَاعَةً ۖ وَلَا يَسْتَقْدِمُونَ

34   10:49; 15:5; 16:61

34 For every nation is an appointed time. When their time has come, they cannot delay it by one hour, nor can they advance it.

٣٥ يَا بَنِي آدَمَ إِمَّا يَأْتِيَنَّكُمْ رُسُلٌ مِنْكُمْ يَقُصُّونَ عَلَيْكُمْ آيَاتِي ۙ فَمَنِ اتَّقَىٰ وَأَصْلَحَ فَلَا خَوْفٌ عَلَيْهِمْ وَلَا هُمْ يَحْزَنُونَ

35   2:37; 7:23; 20:122

35 O Children of Adam! When messengers from among you come to you, relating to you My revelations—whoever practices piety and reforms—upon them shall be no fear, nor shall they grieve.

٣٦ وَالَّذِينَ كَذَّبُوا بِآيَاتِنَا وَاسْتَكْبَرُوا عَنْهَا أُولَٰئِكَ أَصْحَابُ النَّارِ ۖ هُمْ فِيهَا خَالِدُونَ

36   2:39; 5:10; 7:40

36 But as for those who reject Our revelations, and are too proud to accept them—these are the inmates of the Fire, where they will remain forever.

٣٧ فَمَنْ أَظْلَمُ مِمَّنِ افْتَرَىٰ عَلَى اللَّهِ كَذِبًا أَوْ كَذَّبَ بِآيَاتِهِ ۚ أُولَٰئِكَ يَنَالُهُمْ نَصِيبُهُمْ مِنَ الْكِتَابِ ۖ حَتَّىٰ إِذَا جَاءَتْهُمْ رُسُلُنَا يَتَوَفَّوْنَهُمْ قَالُوا أَيْنَ مَا كُنْتُمْ تَدْعُونَ مِنْ دُونِ اللَّهِ ۖ قَالُوا ضَلُّوا عَنَّا وَشَهِدُوا عَلَىٰ أَنْفُسِهِمْ أَنَّهُمْ كَانُوا كَافِرِينَ

37   pp 6:21; 10:17; 29:78

37 Who does greater wrong than he who invents lies about God, or denies His revelations? These—their share of the decree will reach them. Until, when Our envoys come to them, to take their souls away, they will say, "Where are they whom you used to pray to besides God?" They will say, "They have abandoned us," and they will testify against themselves that they were faithless.

٣٨ قَالَ ادْخُلُوا فِي أُمَمٍ قَدْ خَلَتْ مِنْ قَبْلِكُمْ مِنَ الْجِنِّ وَالْإِنْسِ فِي النَّارِ ۖ كُلَّمَا دَخَلَتْ أُمَّةٌ لَعَنَتْ أُخْتَهَا ۖ حَتَّىٰ إِذَا ادَّارَكُوا فِيهَا جَمِيعًا قَالَتْ أُخْرَاهُمْ لِأُولَاهُمْ رَبَّنَا هَٰؤُلَاءِ أَضَلُّونَا فَآتِهِمْ عَذَابًا ضِعْفًا مِنَ النَّارِ ۖ قَالَ لِكُلٍّ ضِعْفٌ وَلَٰكِنْ لَا تَعْلَمُونَ

38   29:25; 33:67–68; 38:60; 41:29

38 He will say, "Join the crowds of jinn and humans who have gone into the Fire before you." Every time a crowd enters, it will curse its sister-crowd. Until, when they are all in it, the last of them will say to the first of them, "Our Lord, these are the ones who misled us, so inflict on them a double punishment in the Fire." He will say, "Each will have a double, but you do not know."

٣٩ وَقَالَتْ أُولَاهُمْ لِأُخْرَاهُمْ فَمَا كَانَ لَكُمْ عَلَيْنَا مِن فَضْلٍ فَذُوقُوا الْعَذَابَ بِمَا كُنتُمْ تَكْسِبُونَ

39 The first of them will say to the last of them, "You have no advantage over us, so taste the torment for what you used to earn."

٤٠ إِنَّ الَّذِينَ كَذَّبُوا بِآيَاتِنَا وَاسْتَكْبَرُوا عَنْهَا لَا تُفَتَّحُ لَهُمْ أَبْوَابُ السَّمَاءِ وَلَا يَدْخُلُونَ الْجَنَّةَ حَتَّىٰ يَلِجَ الْجَمَلُ فِي سَمِّ الْخِيَاطِ ۚ وَكَذَٰلِكَ نَجْزِي الْمُجْرِمِينَ

40 Those who reject Our revelations and are too arrogant to uphold them—the doors of Heaven will not be opened for them, nor will they enter Paradise, until the camel passes through the eye of the needle. Thus We repay the guilty.

٤١ لَهُم مِّن جَهَنَّمَ مِهَادٌ وَمِن فَوْقِهِمْ غَوَاشٍ ۚ وَكَذَٰلِكَ نَجْزِي الظَّالِمِينَ

41 For them is a couch of hell, and above them are sheets of fire. Thus We repay the wrongdoers.

٤٢ وَالَّذِينَ آمَنُوا وَعَمِلُوا الصَّالِحَاتِ لَا نُكَلِّفُ نَفْسًا إِلَّا وُسْعَهَا أُولَٰئِكَ أَصْحَابُ الْجَنَّةِ ۖ هُمْ فِيهَا خَالِدُونَ

42
2:82, 233

42 As for those who believe and do righteous works—We never burden any soul beyond its capacity—these are the inhabitants of the Garden; abiding therein eternally.

٤٣ وَنَزَعْنَا مَا فِي صُدُورِهِم مِّنْ غِلٍّ تَجْرِي مِن تَحْتِهِمُ الْأَنْهَارُ ۖ وَقَالُوا الْحَمْدُ لِلَّهِ الَّذِي هَدَانَا لِهَٰذَا وَمَا كُنَّا لِنَهْتَدِيَ لَوْلَا أَنْ هَدَانَا اللَّهُ ۖ لَقَدْ جَاءَتْ رُسُلُ رَبِّنَا بِالْحَقِّ ۖ وَنُودُوا أَن تِلْكُمُ الْجَنَّةُ أُورِثْتُمُوهَا بِمَا كُنتُمْ تَعْمَلُونَ

43
15:47–48; 43:72

43 We will remove whatever rancor is in their hearts. Rivers will flow beneath them. And they will say, "Praise be to God, who has guided us to this. Had God not guided us, we would never be guided. The messengers of our Lord did come with the truth." And it will be proclaimed to them, "This is the Garden you are made to inherit, on account of what you used to do."

٤٤ وَنَادَىٰ أَصْحَابُ الْجَنَّةِ أَصْحَابَ النَّارِ أَن قَدْ وَجَدْنَا مَا وَعَدَنَا رَبُّنَا حَقًّا فَهَلْ وَجَدتُّم مَّا وَعَدَ رَبُّكُمْ حَقًّا ۖ قَالُوا نَعَمْ ۚ فَأَذَّنَ مُؤَذِّنٌ بَيْنَهُمْ أَن لَّعْنَةُ اللَّهِ عَلَى الظَّالِمِينَ

44
11:18

44 And the inhabitants of the Garden will call out to the inmates of the Fire, "We found what our Lord promised us to be true; did you find what your Lord promised you to be true?" They will say, "Yes." Thereupon a caller will announce in their midst, "The curse of God is upon the wrongdoers."

٤٥ الَّذِينَ يَصُدُّونَ عَن سَبِيلِ اللَّهِ وَيَبْغُونَهَا عِوَجًا وَهُم بِالْآخِرَةِ كَافِرُونَ

45 "Those who hinder from the path of God, and seek to distort it, and who deny the Hereafter."

45
3:99; 7:86; 11:45; 14:3

٤٦ وَبَيْنَهُمَا حِجَابٌ ۚ وَعَلَى الْأَعْرَافِ رِجَالٌ يَعْرِفُونَ كُلًّا بِسِيمَاهُمْ ۚ وَنَادَوْا أَصْحَابَ الْجَنَّةِ أَن سَلَامٌ عَلَيْكُمْ ۚ لَمْ يَدْخُلُوهَا وَهُمْ يَطْمَعُونَ

46 And between them is a partition, and on the Elevations are men who recognize everyone by their features. They will call to the inhabitants of the Garden, "Peace be upon you." They have not entered it, but they are hoping.

46
3:106; 10:27; 47:30;
54:41; 57:13; 75:22;
80:40; 83:24

٤٧ وَإِذَا صُرِفَتْ أَبْصَارُهُمْ تِلْقَاءَ أَصْحَابِ النَّارِ قَالُوا رَبَّنَا لَا تَجْعَلْنَا مَعَ الْقَوْمِ الظَّالِمِينَ

47 And when their eyes are directed towards the inmates of the Fire, they will say, "Our Lord, do not place us among the wrongdoing people."

٤٨ وَنَادَىٰ أَصْحَابُ الْأَعْرَافِ رِجَالًا يَعْرِفُونَهُم بِسِيمَاهُمْ قَالُوا مَا أَغْنَىٰ عَنكُمْ جَمْعُكُمْ وَمَا كُنتُمْ تَسْتَكْبِرُونَ

48 And the dwellers of the Elevations will call to men they recognize by their features, saying, "Your hoardings did not avail you, nor did your arrogance."

48
6:94; 15:84; 39:50

٤٩ أَهَٰؤُلَاءِ الَّذِينَ أَقْسَمْتُمْ لَا يَنَالُهُمُ اللَّهُ بِرَحْمَةٍ ۚ ادْخُلُوا الْجَنَّةَ لَا خَوْفٌ عَلَيْكُمْ وَلَا أَنتُمْ تَحْزَنُونَ

49 "Are these the ones you swore God will not touch with mercy?" "Enter the Garden; you have nothing to fear, and you will not grieve."

٥٠ وَنَادَىٰ أَصْحَابُ النَّارِ أَصْحَابَ الْجَنَّةِ أَنْ أَفِيضُوا عَلَيْنَا مِنَ الْمَاءِ أَوْ مِمَّا رَزَقَكُمُ اللَّهُ ۚ قَالُوا إِنَّ اللَّهَ حَرَّمَهُمَا عَلَى الْكَافِرِينَ

50 The inmates of the Fire will call on the inhabitants of the Garden, "Pour some water over us, or some of what God has provided for you." They will say, "God has forbidden them for the disbelievers."

٥١ الَّذِينَ اتَّخَذُوا دِينَهُمْ لَهْوًا وَلَعِبًا وَغَرَّتْهُمُ الْحَيَاةُ الدُّنْيَا ۚ فَالْيَوْمَ نَنسَاهُمْ كَمَا نَسُوا لِقَاءَ يَوْمِهِمْ هَٰذَا وَمَا كَانُوا بِآيَاتِنَا يَجْحَدُونَ

51 Those who took their religion lightly, and in jest, and whom the worldly life deceived. Today We will ignore them, as they ignored the meeting on this Day of theirs, and they used to deny Our revelations.

51
6:70; 45:34–35

٥٢ وَلَقَدْ جِئْنَاهُم بِكِتَابٍ فَصَّلْنَاهُ عَلَىٰ عِلْمٍ هُدًى وَرَحْمَةً لِّقَوْمٍ يُؤْمِنُونَ

52 We have given them a Scripture, which We detailed with knowledge—guidance and mercy for people who believe.

٥٣ هَلْ يَنظُرُونَ إِلَّا تَأْوِيلَهُ ۚ يَوْمَ يَأْتِي تَأْوِيلُهُ يَقُولُ الَّذِينَ نَسُوهُ مِن قَبْلُ قَدْ جَاءَتْ رُسُلُ رَبِّنَا بِالْحَقِّ فَهَل لَّنَا مِن شُفَعَاءَ فَيَشْفَعُوا لَنَا أَوْ نُرَدُّ فَنَعْمَلَ غَيْرَ الَّذِي كُنَّا نَعْمَلُ ۚ قَدْ خَسِرُوا أَنفُسَهُمْ وَضَلَّ عَنْهُم مَّا كَانُوا يَفْتَرُونَ

53
9:96; 10:39; 21:28; 26:100; 74:48

53 Are they waiting for anything but its fulfillment? The Day its fulfillment comes true, those who disregarded it before will say, "The messengers of our Lord did come with the truth. Have we any intercessors to intercede for us? Or, could we be sent back, to behave differently from the way we behaved before?" They ruined their souls, and what they used to invent has failed them.

٥٤ إِنَّ رَبَّكُمُ اللَّهُ الَّذِي خَلَقَ السَّمَاوَاتِ وَالْأَرْضَ فِي سِتَّةِ أَيَّامٍ ثُمَّ اسْتَوَىٰ عَلَى الْعَرْشِ يُغْشِي اللَّيْلَ النَّهَارَ يَطْلُبُهُ حَثِيثًا وَالشَّمْسَ وَالْقَمَرَ وَالنُّجُومَ مُسَخَّرَاتٍ بِأَمْرِهِ ۗ أَلَا لَهُ الْخَلْقُ وَالْأَمْرُ ۗ تَبَارَكَ اللَّهُ رَبُّ الْعَالَمِينَ

54
10:3; 11:7; 13:2; 25:59; 32:4; 50:38; 57:4

54 Your Lord is God; He who created the heavens and the earth in six days, then established Himself on the Throne. The night overtakes the day, as it pursues it persistently; and the sun, and the moon, and the stars are subservient by His command. His is the creation, and His is the command. Blessed is God, Lord of all beings.

٥٥ ادْعُوا رَبَّكُمْ تَضَرُّعًا وَخُفْيَةً ۚ إِنَّهُ لَا يُحِبُّ الْمُعْتَدِينَ

55
6:63; 7:205

55 Call upon your Lord humbly and privately. He does not love the aggressors.

٥٦ وَلَا تُفْسِدُوا فِي الْأَرْضِ بَعْدَ إِصْلَاحِهَا وَادْعُوهُ خَوْفًا وَطَمَعًا ۚ إِنَّ رَحْمَتَ اللَّهِ قَرِيبٌ مِّنَ الْمُحْسِنِينَ

56
7:85

56 And do not corrupt on earth after its reformation, and pray to Him with fear and hope. God's mercy is close to the doers of good.

٥٧ وَهُوَ الَّذِي يُرْسِلُ الرِّيَاحَ بُشْرًا بَيْنَ يَدَيْ رَحْمَتِهِ ۖ حَتَّىٰ إِذَا أَقَلَّتْ سَحَابًا ثِقَالًا سُقْنَاهُ لِبَلَدٍ مَّيِّتٍ فَأَنزَلْنَا بِهِ الْمَاءَ فَأَخْرَجْنَا بِهِ مِن كُلِّ الثَّمَرَاتِ ۚ كَذَٰلِكَ نُخْرِجُ الْمَوْتَىٰ لَعَلَّكُمْ تَذَكَّرُونَ

57
25:48; 27:63; 30:46, 48; 35:9; 42:28; 57:4

57 It is He who sends the wind ahead of His mercy. Then, when they have gathered up heavy clouds, We drive them to a dead land, where We make water come down, and with it We bring out all kinds of fruits. Thus We bring out the dead—perhaps you will reflect.

٥٨ وَالْبَلَدُ الطَّيِّبُ يَخْرُجُ نَبَاتُهُ بِإِذْنِ رَبِّهِ ۖ وَالَّذِي خَبُثَ لَا يَخْرُجُ إِلَّا نَكِدًا ۚ كَذَٰلِكَ نُصَرِّفُ الْآيَاتِ لِقَوْمٍ يَشْكُرُونَ

58
35:15

58 As for the good land, it yields its produce by the leave of its Lord. But as for the bad, it produces nothing but hardship and misery. Thus We explain the revelations in various ways for people who are thankful.

٥٩ لَقَدْ أَرْسَلْنَا نُوحًا إِلَىٰ قَوْمِهِ فَقَالَ يَا قَوْمِ اعْبُدُوا اللَّهَ مَا لَكُم مِّنْ إِلَٰهٍ غَيْرُهُ إِنِّي أَخَافُ عَلَيْكُمْ عَذَابَ يَوْمٍ عَظِيمٍ

59 We sent Noah to his people. He said, "O my people! Worship God; you have no god other than Him. I fear for you the punishment of a tremendous Day."

59
11:25; 23:23; 53:52; 71:1–3

٦٠ قَالَ الْمَلَأُ مِن قَوْمِهِ إِنَّا لَنَرَاكَ فِي ضَلَالٍ مُّبِينٍ

60 The dignitaries among his people said, "We see that you are in obvious error."

60
7:66, 75, 88

٦١ قَالَ يَا قَوْمِ لَيْسَ بِي ضَلَالَةٌ وَلَٰكِنِّي رَسُولٌ مِّن رَّبِّ الْعَالَمِينَ

61 He said, "O my people, I am not in error, but I am a messenger from the Lord of the Worlds."

61
7:67

٦٢ أُبَلِّغُكُمْ رِسَالَاتِ رَبِّي وَأَنصَحُ لَكُمْ وَأَعْلَمُ مِنَ اللَّهِ مَا لَا تَعْلَمُونَ

62 "I deliver to you the messages of my Lord, and I advise you, and I know from God what you do not know."

62
7:68

٦٣ أَوَعَجِبْتُمْ أَن جَاءَكُمْ ذِكْرٌ مِّن رَّبِّكُمْ عَلَىٰ رَجُلٍ مِّنكُمْ لِيُنذِرَكُمْ وَلِتَتَّقُوا وَلَعَلَّكُمْ تُرْحَمُونَ

63 "Do you wonder that a reminder has come to you from your Lord, through a man from among you, to warn you, and to lead you to righteousness, so that you may attain mercy?"

63
7:63; 10:2; 50:2; 54:25; 64:6

٦٤ فَكَذَّبُوهُ فَأَنجَيْنَاهُ وَالَّذِينَ مَعَهُ فِي الْفُلْكِ وَأَغْرَقْنَا الَّذِينَ كَذَّبُوا بِآيَاتِنَا ۚ إِنَّهُمْ كَانُوا قَوْمًا عَمِينَ

64 But they called him a liar. So We saved him and those with him in the Ark, and We drowned those who rejected Our revelations. They were blind people.

64
10:73; 21:76; 26:119; 29:14; 54:11

٦٥ وَإِلَىٰ عَادٍ أَخَاهُمْ هُودًا ۗ قَالَ يَا قَوْمِ اعْبُدُوا اللَّهَ مَا لَكُم مِّنْ إِلَٰهٍ غَيْرُهُ ۚ أَفَلَا تَتَّقُونَ

65 And to 'Ād, their brother Hūd. He said, "O my people! Worship God; you have no god other than Him. Will you not take heed?"

65
11:50; 23:32; 46:21; 89:6–8

٦٦ قَالَ الْمَلَأُ الَّذِينَ كَفَرُوا مِن قَوْمِهِ إِنَّا لَنَرَاكَ فِي سَفَاهَةٍ وَإِنَّا لَنَظُنُّكَ مِنَ الْكَاذِبِينَ

66 The elite of his people who disbelieved said, "We see foolishness in you, and we think that you are a liar."

66
7:60, 75, 88

٦٧ قَالَ يَا قَوْمِ لَيْسَ بِي سَفَاهَةٌ وَلَٰكِنِّي رَسُولٌ مِّن رَّبِّ الْعَالَمِينَ

67 He said, "O my people! There is no foolishness in me, but I am a messenger from the Lord of the Worlds.

67
7:61

٦٨ أُبَلِّغُكُمْ رِسَالَاتِ رَبِّي وَأَنَا لَكُمْ نَاصِحٌ أَمِينٌ

68 "I convey to you the messages of my Lord, and I am a trustworthy adviser to you."

68
7:62

٦٩ أَوَعَجِبْتُمْ أَنْ جَاءَكُمْ ذِكْرٌ مِنْ رَبِّكُمْ عَلَىٰ رَجُلٍ مِنْكُمْ لِيُنْذِرَكُمْ ۚ وَاذْكُرُوا إِذْ جَعَلَكُمْ خُلَفَاءَ مِنْ بَعْدِ قَوْمِ نُوحٍ وَزَادَكُمْ فِي الْخَلْقِ بَسْطَةً ۖ فَاذْكُرُوا آلَاءَ اللَّهِ لَعَلَّكُمْ تُفْلِحُونَ	69	7:63, 74

69 "Are you surprised that a reminder has come to you from your Lord, through a man from among you, to warn you? Remember how He made you successors after the people of Noah, and increased you greatly in stature. And remember God's blessings, so that you may prosper."

٧٠ قَالُوا أَجِئْتَنَا لِنَعْبُدَ اللَّهَ وَحْدَهُ وَنَذَرَ مَا كَانَ يَعْبُدُ آبَاؤُنَا ۖ فَأْتِنَا بِمَا تَعِدُنَا إِنْ كُنْتَ مِنَ الصَّادِقِينَ	70	46:22

70 They said, "Did you come to us to make us worship God alone, and abandon what our ancestors used to worship? Then bring us what you threaten us with, if you are truthful."

٧١ قَالَ قَدْ وَقَعَ عَلَيْكُمْ مِنْ رَبِّكُمْ رِجْسٌ وَغَضَبٌ ۖ أَتُجَادِلُونَنِي فِي أَسْمَاءٍ سَمَّيْتُمُوهَا أَنْتُمْ وَآبَاؤُكُمْ مَا نَزَّلَ اللَّهُ بِهَا مِنْ سُلْطَانٍ ۚ فَانْتَظِرُوا إِنِّي مَعَكُمْ مِنَ الْمُنْتَظِرِينَ	71	3:151; 12:40; 53:23

71 He said, "Condemnation and wrath have befallen you from your Lord. Are you arguing with me over names, which you and your ancestors invented, for which God sent down no authority? Just wait; I am waiting with you."

٧٢ فَأَنْجَيْنَاهُ وَالَّذِينَ مَعَهُ بِرَحْمَةٍ مِنَّا وَقَطَعْنَا دَابِرَ الَّذِينَ كَذَّبُوا بِآيَاتِنَا ۖ وَمَا كَانُوا مُؤْمِنِينَ	72	11:58, 66, 94

72 So We saved him and those with him, by mercy from Us, and We cut off the roots of those who rejected Our revelations and were not believers.

٧٣ وَإِلَىٰ ثَمُودَ أَخَاهُمْ صَالِحًا ۗ قَالَ يَا قَوْمِ اعْبُدُوا اللَّهَ مَا لَكُمْ مِنْ إِلَٰهٍ غَيْرُهُ ۖ قَدْ جَاءَتْكُمْ بَيِّنَةٌ مِنْ رَبِّكُمْ ۖ هَٰذِهِ نَاقَةُ اللَّهِ لَكُمْ آيَةً ۖ فَذَرُوهَا تَأْكُلْ فِي أَرْضِ اللَّهِ ۖ وَلَا تَمَسُّوهَا بِسُوءٍ فَيَأْخُذَكُمْ عَذَابٌ أَلِيمٌ	73	11:59; 27:45; 53:51; 54:27; 89:9

73 And to Thamūd, their brother Ṣāliḥ. He said, "O my people! Worship God; you have no god other than Him. Clarification has come to you from your Lord. This she-camel of God is a sign for you. So leave her to graze on God's earth, and do her no harm, lest a painful penalty seizes you."

٧٤ وَاذْكُرُوا إِذْ جَعَلَكُمْ خُلَفَاءَ مِنْ بَعْدِ عَادٍ وَبَوَّأَكُمْ فِي الْأَرْضِ تَتَّخِذُونَ مِنْ سُهُولِهَا قُصُورًا وَتَنْحِتُونَ الْجِبَالَ بُيُوتًا ۖ فَاذْكُرُوا آلَاءَ اللَّهِ وَلَا تَعْثَوْا فِي الْأَرْضِ مُفْسِدِينَ	74	7:69

74 "And remember how He made you successors after 'Ād, and settled you in the land. You make for yourselves mansions on its plains, and carve out dwellings in the mountains. So remember God's benefits, and do not roam the earth corruptingly."

٧٥ قَالَ الْمَلَأُ الَّذِينَ اسْتَكْبَرُوا مِنْ قَوْمِهِ لِلَّذِينَ اسْتُضْعِفُوا لِمَنْ آمَنَ مِنْهُمْ أَتَعْلَمُونَ أَنَّ صَالِحًا مُرْسَلٌ مِنْ رَبِّهِ ۚ قَالُوا إِنَّا بِمَا أُرْسِلَ بِهِ مُؤْمِنُونَ	75	7:60, 66

75 The elite of his people, who were arrogant, said to the common people who had believed, "Do you know that Ṣāliḥ is sent from his Lord?" They said, "We are believers in what he was sent with."

٧٦ قَالَ الَّذِينَ اسْتَكْبَرُوا إِنَّا بِالَّذِي آمَنتُم بِهِ كَافِرُونَ

76 Those who were arrogant said, "We reject what you believe in."

76
11:62; 14:9; 34:34; 43:23

٧٧ فَعَقَرُوا النَّاقَةَ وَعَتَوْا عَنْ أَمْرِ رَبِّهِمْ وَقَالُوا يَا صَالِحُ ائْتِنَا بِمَا تَعِدُنَا إِن كُنتَ مِنَ الْمُرْسَلِينَ

77 So they hamstrung the she-camel, and defied the command of their Lord, and said, "O Ṣāliḥ, bring upon us what you threaten us with, if you are one of the messengers."

77
2:29; 11:64–65

٧٨ فَأَخَذَتْهُمُ الرَّجْفَةُ فَأَصْبَحُوا فِي دَارِهِمْ جَاثِمِينَ

78 Whereupon the quake overtook them, and they became lifeless bodies in their homes.

78
7:91; 11:67

٧٩ فَتَوَلَّىٰ عَنْهُمْ وَقَالَ يَا قَوْمِ لَقَدْ أَبْلَغْتُكُمْ رِسَالَةَ رَبِّي وَنَصَحْتُ لَكُمْ وَلَٰكِن لَّا تُحِبُّونَ النَّاصِحِينَ

79 Then he turned away from them, and said, "O my people, I have delivered to you the message of my Lord, and I have advised you, but you do not like those who give advice."

79
7:93

٨٠ وَلُوطًا إِذْ قَالَ لِقَوْمِهِ أَتَأْتُونَ الْفَاحِشَةَ مَا سَبَقَكُم بِهَا مِنْ أَحَدٍ مِّنَ الْعَالَمِينَ

80 And Lot, when he said to his people, "Do you commit lewdness no people anywhere have ever committed before you?"

80
27:54; 29:28

٨١ إِنَّكُمْ لَتَأْتُونَ الرِّجَالَ شَهْوَةً مِّن دُونِ النِّسَاءِ ۚ بَلْ أَنتُمْ قَوْمٌ مُّسْرِفُونَ

81 "You lust after men rather than women. You are an excessive people."

81
26:165; 2755; 29:29

٨٢ وَمَا كَانَ جَوَابَ قَوْمِهِ إِلَّا أَن قَالُوا أَخْرِجُوهُم مِّن قَرْيَتِكُمْ ۖ إِنَّهُمْ أُنَاسٌ يَتَطَهَّرُونَ

82 And his people's only answer was to say, "Expel them from your town; they are purist people."

82
26:167; 27:56

٨٣ فَأَنجَيْنَاهُ وَأَهْلَهُ إِلَّا امْرَأَتَهُ كَانَتْ مِنَ الْغَابِرِينَ

83 But We saved him and his family, except for his wife; she was of those who lagged behind.

83
11:81; 15:59–60; 27:57; 51:35–36; 66:10

٨٤ وَأَمْطَرْنَا عَلَيْهِم مَّطَرًا ۖ فَانظُرْ كَيْفَ كَانَ عَاقِبَةُ الْمُجْرِمِينَ

84 And We rained down on them a rain; note the consequences for the sinners.

84
11:82; 15:74; 25:40; 26:173; 27:58; 29:34

٨٥ وَإِلَىٰ مَدْيَنَ أَخَاهُمْ شُعَيْبًا ۗ قَالَ يَا قَوْمِ اعْبُدُوا اللَّهَ مَا لَكُم مِّنْ إِلَٰهٍ غَيْرُهُ ۖ قَدْ جَاءَتْكُم بَيِّنَةٌ مِّن رَّبِّكُمْ ۖ فَأَوْفُوا الْكَيْلَ وَالْمِيزَانَ وَلَا تَبْخَسُوا النَّاسَ أَشْيَاءَهُمْ وَلَا تُفْسِدُوا فِي الْأَرْضِ بَعْدَ إِصْلَاحِهَا ۚ ذَٰلِكُمْ خَيْرٌ لَّكُمْ إِن كُنتُم مُّؤْمِنِينَ

85 And to Median, their brother Shuaib. He said, "O my people, worship God; you have no god other than Him. A clear proof has come to you from your Lord. Give full measure and weight, and do not cheat people out of their rights, and do not corrupt the land once it has been set right. This is better for you, if you are believers."

85
11:84; 29:36; 86:26

٨٦ وَلَا تَقْعُدُوا بِكُلِّ صِرَاطٍ تُوعِدُونَ وَتَصُدُّونَ عَن سَبِيلِ اللَّهِ مَنْ آمَنَ بِهِ وَتَبْغُونَهَا عِوَجًا ۚ وَاذْكُرُوا إِذْ كُنتُمْ قَلِيلًا فَكَثَّرَكُمْ ۖ وَانظُرُوا كَيْفَ كَانَ عَاقِبَةُ الْمُفْسِدِينَ

86
8:26

86 "And do not lurk on every path, making threats and turning away from the path of God those who believe in Him, seeking to distort it. And remember how you were few, and how He made you numerous. So note the consequences for the corrupters."

٨٧ وَإِن كَانَ طَائِفَةٌ مِّنكُمْ آمَنُوا بِالَّذِي أُرْسِلْتُ بِهِ وَطَائِفَةٌ لَّمْ يُؤْمِنُوا فَاصْبِرُوا حَتَّىٰ يَحْكُمَ اللَّهُ بَيْنَنَا ۚ وَهُوَ خَيْرُ الْحَاكِمِينَ

87
10:109; 11:94

87 "Since some of you believed in what I was sent with, and some did not believe, be patient until God judges between us; for He is the Best of Judges."

٨٨ قَالَ الْمَلَأُ الَّذِينَ اسْتَكْبَرُوا مِن قَوْمِهِ لَنُخْرِجَنَّكَ يَا شُعَيْبُ وَالَّذِينَ آمَنُوا مَعَكَ مِن قَرْيَتِنَا أَوْ لَتَعُودُنَّ فِي مِلَّتِنَا ۚ قَالَ أَوَلَوْ كُنَّا كَارِهِينَ

88
7:60, 66, 75

88 The arrogant elite among his people said, "O Shuaib, We will evict you from our town, along with those who believe with you, unless you return to our religion." He said, "Even if we are unwilling?"

٨٩ قَدِ افْتَرَيْنَا عَلَى اللَّهِ كَذِبًا إِنْ عُدْنَا فِي مِلَّتِكُم بَعْدَ إِذْ نَجَّانَا اللَّهُ مِنْهَا ۚ وَمَا يَكُونُ لَنَا أَن نَّعُودَ فِيهَا إِلَّا أَن يَشَاءَ اللَّهُ رَبُّنَا ۚ وَسِعَ رَبُّنَا كُلَّ شَيْءٍ عِلْمًا ۚ عَلَى اللَّهِ تَوَكَّلْنَا ۚ رَبَّنَا افْتَحْ بَيْنَنَا وَبَيْنَ قَوْمِنَا بِالْحَقِّ وَأَنتَ خَيْرُ الْفَاتِحِينَ

89
6:52

89 "We would be fabricating falsehood against God, if we were to return to your religion, after God has saved us from it. It is not for us to return to it, unless God, our Lord, wills. Our Lord embraces all things in knowledge. In God we place our trust. Our Lord, decide between us and our people in truth, for You are the Best of Deciders."

٩٠ وَقَالَ الْمَلَأُ الَّذِينَ كَفَرُوا مِن قَوْمِهِ لَئِنِ اتَّبَعْتُمْ شُعَيْبًا إِنَّكُمْ إِذًا لَّخَاسِرُونَ

90
11:101; 23:33

90 The elite of his people who disbelieved said, "If you follow Shuaib, you will be losers."

٩١ فَأَخَذَتْهُمُ الرَّجْفَةُ فَأَصْبَحُوا فِي دَارِهِمْ جَاثِمِينَ

91
7:78; 11:61

91 Thereupon, the quake struck them; and they became lifeless bodies in their homes.

٩٢ الَّذِينَ كَذَّبُوا شُعَيْبًا كَأَن لَّمْ يَغْنَوْا فِيهَا ۚ الَّذِينَ كَذَّبُوا شُعَيْبًا كَانُوا هُمُ الْخَاسِرِينَ

92
11:68, 95

92 Those who rejected Shuaib—as if they never prospered therein. Those who rejected Shuaib—it was they who were the losers.

٩٣ فَتَوَلَّىٰ عَنْهُمْ وَقَالَ يَا قَوْمِ لَقَدْ أَبْلَغْتُكُمْ رِسَالَاتِ رَبِّي وَنَصَحْتُ لَكُمْ ۖ فَكَيْفَ آسَىٰ عَلَىٰ قَوْمٍ كَافِرِينَ

93
7:79

93 So he turned away from them, and said, "O my people, I have delivered to you the messages of my Lord, and I have advised you, so why should I grieve over a disbelieving people?"

Sūrah 7: Al-A'rāf

٩٤ وَمَا أَرْسَلْنَا فِي قَرْيَةٍ مِنْ نَبِيٍّ إِلَّا أَخَذْنَا أَهْلَهَا بِالْبَأْسَاءِ وَالضَّرَّاءِ لَعَلَّهُمْ يَضَّرَّعُونَ

94   6:42

94 We did not send any prophet to any town but We afflicted its people with misery and adversity, so that they may humble themselves.

٩٥ ثُمَّ بَدَّلْنَا مَكَانَ السَّيِّئَةِ الْحَسَنَةَ حَتَّىٰ عَفَوا وَقَالُوا قَدْ مَسَّ آبَاءَنَا الضَّرَّاءُ وَالسَّرَّاءُ فَأَخَذْنَاهُمْ بَغْتَةً وَهُمْ لَا يَشْعُرُونَ

95 Then We substituted prosperity in place of hardship. Until they increased in number, and said, "Adversity and prosperity has touched our ancestors." Then We seized them suddenly, while they were unaware.

٩٦ وَلَوْ أَنَّ أَهْلَ الْقُرَىٰ آمَنُوا وَاتَّقَوْا لَفَتَحْنَا عَلَيْهِمْ بَرَكَاتٍ مِنَ السَّمَاءِ وَالْأَرْضِ وَلَٰكِنْ كَذَّبُوا فَأَخَذْنَاهُمْ بِمَا كَانُوا يَكْسِبُونَ

96 Had the people of the towns believed and turned righteous, We would have opened for them the blessings of the heaven and the earth; but they rejected the truth, so We seized them by what they were doing.

٩٧ أَفَأَمِنَ أَهْلُ الْقُرَىٰ أَنْ يَأْتِيَهُمْ بَأْسُنَا بَيَاتًا وَهُمْ نَائِمُونَ

97–98   7:4; 22:45; 28:58

97 Do the people of the towns feel secure that Our might will not come upon them by night, while they sleep?

٩٨ أَوَأَمِنَ أَهْلُ الْقُرَىٰ أَنْ يَأْتِيَهُمْ بَأْسُنَا ضُحًى وَهُمْ يَلْعَبُونَ

98 Do the people of the towns feel secure that Our might will not come upon them by day, while they play?

٩٩ أَفَأَمِنُوا مَكْرَ اللَّهِ ۚ فَلَا يَأْمَنُ مَكْرَ اللَّهِ إِلَّا الْقَوْمُ الْخَاسِرُونَ

99   43:79

99 Do they feel safe from God's plan? None feel safe from God's plan except the losing people.

١٠٠ أَوَلَمْ يَهْدِ لِلَّذِينَ يَرِثُونَ الْأَرْضَ مِنْ بَعْدِ أَهْلِهَا أَنْ لَوْ نَشَاءُ أَصَبْنَاهُمْ بِذُنُوبِهِمْ ۚ وَنَطْبَعُ عَلَىٰ قُلُوبِهِمْ فَهُمْ لَا يَسْمَعُونَ

100 Is it not guidance for those who inherit the land after its inhabitants, that if We willed, We could strike them for their sins? And seal up their hearts, so that they would not hear?

١٠١ تِلْكَ الْقُرَىٰ نَقُصُّ عَلَيْكَ مِنْ أَنْبَائِهَا ۚ وَلَقَدْ جَاءَتْهُمْ رُسُلُهُمْ بِالْبَيِّنَاتِ فَمَا كَانُوا لِيُؤْمِنُوا بِمَا كَذَّبُوا مِنْ قَبْلُ ۚ كَذَٰلِكَ يَطْبَعُ اللَّهُ عَلَىٰ قُلُوبِ الْكَافِرِينَ

101   6:34; 9:99; 10:77; 11:120; 18:13; 40:22

101 These towns—We narrate to you some of their tales. Their messengers came to them with the clear signs, but they would not believe in what they had rejected previously. Thus God seals the hearts of the disbelievers.

١٠٢ وَمَا وَجَدْنَا لِأَكْثَرِهِم مِّنْ عَهْدٍ ۖ وَإِن وَجَدْنَا أَكْثَرَهُمْ لَفَاسِقِينَ

102 We found most of them untrue to their covenants; We found most of them corrupt.

١٠٣ ثُمَّ بَعَثْنَا مِن بَعْدِهِم مُّوسَىٰ بِآيَاتِنَا إِلَىٰ فِرْعَوْنَ وَمَلَئِهِ فَظَلَمُوا بِهَا ۖ فَانظُرْ كَيْفَ كَانَ عَاقِبَةُ الْمُفْسِدِينَ

103 Then, after them, We sent Moses with Our miracles to Pharaoh and his establishment, but they denounced them. So consider the end of the evildoers.

103
10:75; 11:96; 23:45; 27:13–14; 43:46; 44:17; 89:10

١٠٤ وَقَالَ مُوسَىٰ يَا فِرْعَوْنُ إِنِّي رَسُولٌ مِّن رَّبِّ الْعَالَمِينَ

104 Moses said, "O Pharaoh, I am a messenger from the Lord of the Worlds."

104
20:47; 26:16; 43:46

١٠٥ حَقِيقٌ عَلَىٰ أَن لَّا أَقُولَ عَلَى اللَّهِ إِلَّا الْحَقَّ ۚ قَدْ جِئْتُكُم بِبَيِّنَةٍ مِّن رَّبِّكُمْ فَأَرْسِلْ مَعِيَ بَنِي إِسْرَائِيلَ

105 "It is only proper that I should not say about God anything other than the truth. I have come to you with clear evidence from your Lord, so let the Children of Israel go with me."

105
44:18

١٠٦ قَالَ إِن كُنتَ جِئْتَ بِآيَةٍ فَأْتِ بِهَا إِن كُنتَ مِنَ الصَّادِقِينَ

106 He said, "If you brought a miracle, then present it, if you are truthful."

106
26:30

١٠٧ فَأَلْقَىٰ عَصَاهُ فَإِذَا هِيَ ثُعْبَانٌ مُّبِينٌ

107 So he threw his staff, and it was an apparent serpent.

107–110
20:17–23; 26:32–35; 27:10–14; 28:31–32

١٠٨ وَنَزَعَ يَدَهُ فَإِذَا هِيَ بَيْضَاءُ لِلنَّاظِرِينَ

108 And He pulled out his hand, and it was white to the onlookers.

108
12:32

١٠٩ قَالَ الْمَلَأُ مِن قَوْمِ فِرْعَوْنَ إِنَّ هَٰذَا لَسَاحِرٌ عَلِيمٌ

109 The notables among Pharaoh's people said, "This is really a skilled magician."

109–112
pp 26:34–37
10:76; 38:4

١١٠ يُرِيدُ أَن يُخْرِجَكُم مِّنْ أَرْضِكُمْ ۖ فَمَاذَا تَأْمُرُونَ

110 "He wants to evict you from your land, so what do you recommend?"

110
20:63

١١١ قَالُوا أَرْجِهْ وَأَخَاهُ وَأَرْسِلْ فِي الْمَدَائِنِ حَاشِرِينَ

111 They said, "Put him off, and his brother, and send heralds to the cities."

111
10:79; 20:58–60

١١٢ يَأْتُوكَ بِكُلِّ سَاحِرٍ عَلِيمٍ

112 "And let them bring you every skillful magician."

Sūrah 7: Al-A'rāf — 183

١١٣ وَجَاءَ السَّحَرَةُ فِرْعَوْنَ قَالُوا إِنَّ لَنَا لَأَجْرًا إِن كُنَّا نَحْنُ الْغَالِبِينَ

113–114
pp 26:41–42

113 The magicians came to Pharaoh, and said, "Surely there is a reward for us, if we are the victors."

١١٤ قَالَ نَعَمْ وَإِنَّكُمْ لَمِنَ الْمُقَرَّبِينَ

114 He said, "Yes, and you will be among my favorites."

١١٥ قَالُوا يَا مُوسَىٰ إِمَّا أَن تُلْقِيَ وَإِمَّا أَن نَكُونَ نَحْنُ الْمُلْقِينَ

115–118
10:80–81; 20:65–68;
26:43–45

115 They said, "O Moses! Either you throw, or we are the ones to throw."

١١٦ قَالَ أَلْقُوا ۖ فَلَمَّا أَلْقَوْا سَحَرُوا أَعْيُنَ النَّاسِ وَاسْتَرْهَبُوهُمْ وَجَاءُوا بِسِحْرٍ عَظِيمٍ

116 He said, "You throw!" And when they threw, they beguiled the eyes of the people, and intimidated them, and produced a mighty magic.

١١٧ وَأَوْحَيْنَا إِلَىٰ مُوسَىٰ أَنْ أَلْقِ عَصَاكَ ۖ فَإِذَا هِيَ تَلْقَفُ مَا يَأْفِكُونَ

117 And We inspired Moses: "Throw your staff." And at once, it swallowed what they were faking.

١١٨ فَوَقَعَ الْحَقُّ وَبَطَلَ مَا كَانُوا يَعْمَلُونَ

118 So the truth came to pass, and what they were producing came to nothing.

١١٩ فَغُلِبُوا هُنَالِكَ وَانقَلَبُوا صَاغِرِينَ

119 There they were defeated, and utterly reduced.

١٢٠ وَأُلْقِيَ السَّحَرَةُ سَاجِدِينَ

120–125
10:83; 20:71;
26:46–50

120 And the magicians fell to their knees.

١٢١ قَالُوا آمَنَّا بِرَبِّ الْعَالَمِينَ

121 They said, "We have believed in the Lord of the Worlds."

١٢٢ رَبِّ مُوسَىٰ وَهَارُونَ

122 "The Lord of Moses and Aaron."

١٢٣ قَالَ فِرْعَوْنُ آمَنتُم بِهِ قَبْلَ أَنْ آذَنَ لَكُمْ ۖ إِنَّ هَٰذَا لَمَكْرٌ مَّكَرْتُمُوهُ فِي الْمَدِينَةِ لِتُخْرِجُوا مِنْهَا أَهْلَهَا ۖ فَسَوْفَ تَعْلَمُونَ

123 Pharaoh said, "Did you believe in Him before I have given you permission? This is surely a conspiracy you schemed in the city, in order to expel its people from it. You will surely know."

١٢٤ لَأُقَطِّعَنَّ أَيْدِيَكُمْ وَأَرْجُلَكُم مِّنْ خِلَافٍ ثُمَّ لَأُصَلِّبَنَّكُمْ أَجْمَعِينَ

124–125
pp 26:49–50

124 "I will cut off your hands and your feet on opposite sides; then I will crucify you all."

١٢٥ قَالُوا إِنَّا إِلَىٰ رَبِّنَا مُنقَلِبُونَ

125 They said, "It is to our Lord that we will return."

١٢٦ وَمَا تَنقِمُ مِنَّا إِلَّا أَنْ آمَنَّا بِآيَاتِ رَبِّنَا لَمَّا جَاءَتْنَا ۚ رَبَّنَا أَفْرِغْ عَلَيْنَا صَبْرًا وَتَوَفَّنَا مُسْلِمِينَ

126
5:59; 85:8

126 "You are taking vengeance on us only because we have believed in the signs of our Lord when they have come to us." "Our Lord! Pour out patience upon us, and receive our souls in submission."

١٢٧ وَقَالَ الْمَلَأُ مِن قَوْمِ فِرْعَوْنَ أَتَذَرُ مُوسَىٰ وَقَوْمَهُ لِيُفْسِدُوا فِي الْأَرْضِ وَيَذَرَكَ وَآلِهَتَكَ ۚ قَالَ سَنُقَتِّلُ أَبْنَاءَهُمْ وَنَسْتَحْيِي نِسَاءَهُمْ وَإِنَّا فَوْقَهُمْ قَاهِرُونَ

127
40:26

127 The chiefs of Pharaoh's people said, "Will you let Moses and his people cause trouble in the land, and forsake you and your gods?" He said, "We will kill their sons, and spare their women. We have absolute power over them."

١٢٨ قَالَ مُوسَىٰ لِقَوْمِهِ اسْتَعِينُوا بِاللَّهِ وَاصْبِرُوا ۖ إِنَّ الْأَرْضَ لِلَّهِ يُورِثُهَا مَن يَشَاءُ مِنْ عِبَادِهِ ۖ وَالْعَاقِبَةُ لِلْمُتَّقِينَ

128
7:137; 26:59; 28:5–6

128 Moses said to his people, "Seek help in God, and be patient. The earth belongs to God. He gives it in inheritance to whomever He wills of His servants, and the future belongs to the righteous."

١٢٩ قَالُوا أُوذِينَا مِن قَبْلِ أَن تَأْتِيَنَا وَمِن بَعْدِ مَا جِئْتَنَا ۚ قَالَ عَسَىٰ رَبُّكُمْ أَن يُهْلِكَ عَدُوَّكُمْ وَيَسْتَخْلِفَكُمْ فِي الْأَرْضِ فَيَنظُرَ كَيْفَ تَعْمَلُونَ

129
6:165; 10:14

129 They said, "We were persecuted before you came to us, and after you came to us." He said, "Perhaps your Lord will destroy your enemy, and make you successors in the land; then He will see how you behave."

١٣٠ وَلَقَدْ أَخَذْنَا آلَ فِرْعَوْنَ بِالسِّنِينَ وَنَقْصٍ مِنَ الثَّمَرَاتِ لَعَلَّهُمْ يَذَّكَّرُونَ

130 And We afflicted the people of Pharaoh with barren years, and with shortage of crops, that they may take heed.

١٣١ فَإِذَا جَاءَتْهُمُ الْحَسَنَةُ قَالُوا لَنَا هَٰذِهِ ۖ وَإِن تُصِبْهُمْ سَيِّئَةٌ يَطَّيَّرُوا بِمُوسَىٰ وَمَن مَّعَهُ ۗ أَلَا إِنَّمَا طَائِرُهُمْ عِندَ اللَّهِ وَلَٰكِنَّ أَكْثَرَهُمْ لَا يَعْلَمُونَ

131
4:78; 41:50; 27:46

131 When something good came their way, they said, "This is ours." And when something bad happened to them, they ascribed the evil omen to Moses and those with him. In fact, their omen is with God, but most of them do not know.

١٣٢ وَقَالُوا مَهْمَا تَأْتِنَا بِهِ مِنْ آيَةٍ لِّتَسْحَرَنَا بِهَا فَمَا نَحْنُ لَكَ بِمُؤْمِنِينَ

132
7:146; 54:2

132 And they said, "No matter what sign you bring us, to bewitch us with, we will not believe in you."

١٣٣ فَأَرْسَلْنَا عَلَيْهِمُ الطُّوفَانَ وَالْجَرَادَ وَالْقُمَّلَ وَالضَّفَادِعَ وَالدَّمَ آيَاتٍ مُفَصَّلَاتٍ فَاسْتَكْبَرُوا وَكَانُوا قَوْمًا مُجْرِمِينَ

133 17:101; 27:12; 43:47; 45:31

133 So We let loose upon them the flood, and the locusts, and the lice, and the frogs, and blood—all explicit signs—but they were too arrogant. They were a sinful people.

١٣٤ وَلَمَّا وَقَعَ عَلَيْهِمُ الرِّجْزُ قَالُوا يَا مُوسَى ادْعُ لَنَا رَبَّكَ بِمَا عَهِدَ عِنْدَكَ ۖ لَئِنْ كَشَفْتَ عَنَّا الرِّجْزَ لَنُؤْمِنَنَّ لَكَ وَلَنُرْسِلَنَّ مَعَكَ بَنِي إِسْرَائِيلَ

134 43:49

134 Whenever a plague befell them, they would say, "O Moses, pray to your Lord for us, according to the covenant He made with you. If you lift the plague from us, we will believe in you, and let the Children of Israel go with you."

١٣٥ فَلَمَّا كَشَفْنَا عَنْهُمُ الرِّجْزَ إِلَىٰ أَجَلٍ هُمْ بَالِغُوهُ إِذَا هُمْ يَنْكُثُونَ

135 But when We lifted the plague from them, for a term they were to fulfill, they broke their promise.

١٣٦ فَانْتَقَمْنَا مِنْهُمْ فَأَغْرَقْنَاهُمْ فِي الْيَمِّ بِأَنَّهُمْ كَذَّبُوا بِآيَاتِنَا وَكَانُوا عَنْهَا غَافِلِينَ

136 2:50; 8:54; 17:103; 26:66; 29:40; 51:40; 43:25, 55; 44:24

136 So We took vengeance on them, and drowned them in the sea—because they rejected Our signs, and paid no heed to them.

١٣٧ وَأَوْرَثْنَا الْقَوْمَ الَّذِينَ كَانُوا يُسْتَضْعَفُونَ مَشَارِقَ الْأَرْضِ وَمَغَارِبَهَا الَّتِي بَارَكْنَا فِيهَا ۖ وَتَمَّتْ كَلِمَتُ رَبِّكَ الْحُسْنَىٰ عَلَىٰ بَنِي إِسْرَائِيلَ بِمَا صَبَرُوا ۖ وَدَمَّرْنَا مَا كَانَ يَصْنَعُ فِرْعَوْنُ وَقَوْمُهُ وَمَا كَانُوا يَعْرِشُونَ

137 7:128; 10:93; 26:59; 28:5–6; 44:28

137 And We made the oppressed people inherit the eastern and western parts of the land, which We had blessed. Thus the fair promise of your Lord to the Children of Israel was fulfilled, because of their endurance. And We destroyed what Pharaoh and his people had built, and what they had harvested.

١٣٨ وَجَاوَزْنَا بِبَنِي إِسْرَائِيلَ الْبَحْرَ فَأَتَوْا عَلَىٰ قَوْمٍ يَعْكُفُونَ عَلَىٰ أَصْنَامٍ لَهُمْ ۚ قَالُوا يَا مُوسَى اجْعَلْ لَنَا إِلَٰهًا كَمَا لَهُمْ آلِهَةٌ ۚ قَالَ إِنَّكُمْ قَوْمٌ تَجْهَلُونَ

138 10:90

138 And We delivered the Children of Israel across the sea. And when they came upon a people who were devoted to some statues of theirs, they said, "O Moses, make for us a god, as they have gods." He said, "You are truly an ignorant people."

١٣٩ إِنَّ هَٰؤُلَاءِ مُتَبَّرٌ مَا هُمْ فِيهِ وَبَاطِلٌ مَا كَانُوا يَعْمَلُونَ

139 11:16

139 "What these people are concerned with is perdition, and their deeds are based on falsehoods."

١٤٠ قَالَ أَغَيْرَ اللَّهِ أَبْغِيكُمْ إِلَٰهًا وَهُوَ فَضَّلَكُمْ عَلَى الْعَالَمِينَ

140 2:47; 44:32; 45:16

140 He said, "Shall I seek for you a god other than God, when He has favored you over all other people?"

١٤١ وَإِذْ أَنْجَيْنَاكُم مِّنْ آلِ فِرْعَوْنَ يَسُومُونَكُمْ سُوءَ الْعَذَابِ ۖ يُقَتِّلُونَ أَبْنَاءَكُمْ وَيَسْتَحْيُونَ نِسَاءَكُمْ ۚ وَفِي ذَٰلِكُم بَلَاءٌ مِّن رَّبِّكُمْ عَظِيمٌ

141 2:49; 7:167; 14:6

141 Remember how We saved you from Pharaoh's people, who subjected you to the worst of sufferings—killing your sons and sparing your women. In that was a tremendous trial from your Lord.

١٤٢ وَوَاعَدْنَا مُوسَىٰ ثَلَاثِينَ لَيْلَةً وَأَتْمَمْنَاهَا بِعَشْرٍ فَتَمَّ مِيقَاتُ رَبِّهِ أَرْبَعِينَ لَيْلَةً ۚ وَقَالَ مُوسَىٰ لِأَخِيهِ هَارُونَ اخْلُفْنِي فِي قَوْمِي وَأَصْلِحْ وَلَا تَتَّبِعْ سَبِيلَ الْمُفْسِدِينَ

142 2:51

142 And We appointed to Moses thirty nights, and completed them with ten; and thus the time appointed by his Lord was forty nights. And Moses said to his brother Aaron: "Take my place among my people, and be upright, and do not follow the way of the mischief-makers."

١٤٣ وَلَمَّا جَاءَ مُوسَىٰ لِمِيقَاتِنَا وَكَلَّمَهُ رَبُّهُ قَالَ رَبِّ أَرِنِي أَنظُرْ إِلَيْكَ ۚ قَالَ لَن تَرَانِي وَلَٰكِنِ انظُرْ إِلَى الْجَبَلِ فَإِنِ اسْتَقَرَّ مَكَانَهُ فَسَوْفَ تَرَانِي ۚ فَلَمَّا تَجَلَّىٰ رَبُّهُ لِلْجَبَلِ جَعَلَهُ دَكًّا وَخَرَّ مُوسَىٰ صَعِقًا ۚ فَلَمَّا أَفَاقَ قَالَ سُبْحَانَكَ تُبْتُ إِلَيْكَ وَأَنَا أَوَّلُ الْمُؤْمِنِينَ

143 And when Moses came to Our appointment, and his Lord spoke to him, he said, "My Lord, allow me to look and see You." He said, "You will not see Me, but look at the mountain; if it stays in its place, you will see Me." But when his Lord manifested Himself to the mountain, He turned it into dust, and Moses fell down unconscious. Then, when he recovered, he said, "Glory be to you, I repent to you, and I am the first of the believers."

١٤٤ قَالَ يَا مُوسَىٰ إِنِّي اصْطَفَيْتُكَ عَلَى النَّاسِ بِرِسَالَاتِي وَبِكَلَامِي فَخُذْ مَا آتَيْتُكَ وَكُن مِّنَ الشَّاكِرِينَ

144 2:53

144 He said, "O Moses, I have chosen you over all people for My messages and for My Words. So take what I have given you, and be one of the thankful."

١٤٥ وَكَتَبْنَا لَهُ فِي الْأَلْوَاحِ مِن كُلِّ شَيْءٍ مَّوْعِظَةً وَتَفْصِيلًا لِّكُلِّ شَيْءٍ فَخُذْهَا بِقُوَّةٍ وَأْمُرْ قَوْمَكَ يَأْخُذُوا بِأَحْسَنِهَا ۚ سَأُرِيكُمْ دَارَ الْفَاسِقِينَ

145 And We inscribed for him in the Tablets all kinds of enlightenments, and decisive explanation of all things. "Hold fast to them, and exhort your people to adopt the best of them. I will show you the fate of the sinners."

١٤٦ سَأَصْرِفُ عَنْ آيَاتِيَ الَّذِينَ يَتَكَبَّرُونَ فِي الْأَرْضِ بِغَيْرِ الْحَقِّ وَإِن يَرَوْا كُلَّ آيَةٍ لَّا يُؤْمِنُوا بِهَا وَإِن يَرَوْا سَبِيلَ الرُّشْدِ لَا يَتَّخِذُوهُ سَبِيلًا وَإِن يَرَوْا سَبِيلَ الْغَيِّ يَتَّخِذُوهُ سَبِيلًا ۚ ذَٰلِكَ بِأَنَّهُمْ كَذَّبُوا بِآيَاتِنَا وَكَانُوا عَنْهَا غَافِلِينَ

146 7:132

146 I will turn away from My revelations those who behave proudly on earth without justification. Even if they see every sign, they will not believe in it; and if they see the path of rectitude, they will not

adopt it for a path; and if they see the path of error, they will adopt it for a path. That is because they denied Our revelations, and paid no attention to them.

١٤٧ وَالَّذِينَ كَذَّبُوا بِآيَاتِنَا وَلِقَاءِ الْآخِرَةِ حَبِطَتْ أَعْمَالُهُمْ ۚ هَلْ يُجْزَوْنَ إِلَّا مَا كَانُوا يَعْمَلُونَ

147
18:105

147 Those who deny Our revelations and the meeting of the Hereafter—their deeds will come to nothing. Will they be repaid except according to what they used to do?

١٤٨ وَاتَّخَذَ قَوْمُ مُوسَىٰ مِن بَعْدِهِ مِنْ حُلِيِّهِمْ عِجْلًا جَسَدًا لَّهُ خُوَارٌ ۚ أَلَمْ يَرَوْا أَنَّهُ لَا يُكَلِّمُهُمْ وَلَا يَهْدِيهِمْ سَبِيلًا ۘ اتَّخَذُوهُ وَكَانُوا ظَالِمِينَ

148
20:89

148 In his absence, the people of Moses adopted a calf made from their ornaments—a body which lowed. Did they not see that it could not speak to them, nor guide them in any way? They took it for worship. They were in the wrong.

١٤٩ وَلَمَّا سُقِطَ فِي أَيْدِيهِمْ وَرَأَوْا أَنَّهُمْ قَدْ ضَلُّوا قَالُوا لَئِن لَّمْ يَرْحَمْنَا رَبُّنَا وَيَغْفِرْ لَنَا لَنَكُونَنَّ مِنَ الْخَاسِرِينَ

149
7:23; 11:47

149 Then, when they regretted, and realized that they had erred, they said, "Unless our Lord extends His mercy to us, and forgives us, we will be among the losers."

١٥٠ وَلَمَّا رَجَعَ مُوسَىٰ إِلَىٰ قَوْمِهِ غَضْبَانَ أَسِفًا قَالَ بِئْسَمَا خَلَفْتُمُونِي مِن بَعْدِي ۖ أَعَجِلْتُمْ أَمْرَ رَبِّكُمْ ۖ وَأَلْقَى الْأَلْوَاحَ وَأَخَذَ بِرَأْسِ أَخِيهِ يَجُرُّهُ إِلَيْهِ ۚ قَالَ ابْنَ أُمَّ إِنَّ الْقَوْمَ اسْتَضْعَفُونِي وَكَادُوا يَقْتُلُونَنِي فَلَا تُشْمِتْ بِيَ الْأَعْدَاءَ وَلَا تَجْعَلْنِي مَعَ الْقَوْمِ الظَّالِمِينَ

150
20:86, 92–94

150 And when Moses returned to his people, angry and disappointed, he said, "What an awful thing you did in my absence. Did you forsake the commandments of your Lord so hastily?" And he threw down the tablets; and he took hold of his brother's head, dragging him towards himself. He said, "Son of my mother, the people have overpowered me, and were about to kill me; so do not allow the enemies to gloat over me, and do not count me among the unjust people."

١٥١ قَالَ رَبِّ اغْفِرْ لِي وَلِأَخِي وَأَدْخِلْنَا فِي رَحْمَتِكَ ۖ وَأَنتَ أَرْحَمُ الرَّاحِمِينَ

151

151 He said, "My Lord, forgive me and my brother, and admit us into Your mercy; for you are the Most Merciful of the merciful."

١٥٢ إِنَّ الَّذِينَ اتَّخَذُوا الْعِجْلَ سَيَنَالُهُمْ غَضَبٌ مِّن رَّبِّهِمْ وَذِلَّةٌ فِي الْحَيَاةِ الدُّنْيَا ۚ وَكَذَٰلِكَ نَجْزِي الْمُفْتَرِينَ

152
2:51, 54, 92–93; 4:153

152 Those who idolized the calf have incurred wrath from their Lord, and humiliation in this life. We thus requite the innovators.

١٥٣ وَالَّذِينَ عَمِلُوا السَّيِّئَاتِ ثُمَّ تَابُوا مِن بَعْدِهَا وَآمَنُوا إِنَّ رَبَّكَ مِن بَعْدِهَا لَغَفُورٌ رَّحِيمٌ

153
6:54

153 As for those who commit sins, and then repent afterwards and believe—your Lord, thereafter, is Forgiving and Merciful.

١٥٤ وَلَمَّا سَكَتَ عَن مُّوسَى الْغَضَبُ أَخَذَ الْأَلْوَاحَ ۖ وَفِي نُسْخَتِهَا هُدًى وَرَحْمَةٌ لِّلَّذِينَ هُمْ لِرَبِّهِمْ يَرْهَبُونَ

154–155
20:86–90

154 When the anger abated in Moses, he took up the tablets. In their transcript is guidance and mercy for those in awe of their Lord.

١٥٥ وَاخْتَارَ مُوسَىٰ قَوْمَهُ سَبْعِينَ رَجُلًا لِّمِيقَاتِنَا ۖ فَلَمَّا أَخَذَتْهُمُ الرَّجْفَةُ قَالَ رَبِّ لَوْ شِئْتَ أَهْلَكْتَهُم مِّن قَبْلُ وَإِيَّايَ ۖ أَتُهْلِكُنَا بِمَا فَعَلَ السُّفَهَاءُ مِنَّا ۖ إِنْ هِيَ إِلَّا فِتْنَتُكَ تُضِلُّ بِهَا مَن تَشَاءُ وَتَهْدِي مَن تَشَاءُ ۖ أَنتَ وَلِيُّنَا فَاغْفِرْ لَنَا وَارْحَمْنَا ۖ وَأَنتَ خَيْرُ الْغَافِرِينَ

155 And Moses chose from his people seventy men for Our appointment. When the tremor shook them, he said, "My Lord, had You willed, You could have destroyed them before, and me too. Will you destroy us for what the fools among us have done? This is but Your test—with it You misguide whomever You will, and guide whomever You will. You are our Protector, so forgive us, and have mercy on us. You are the Best of Forgivers."

١٥٦ وَاكْتُبْ لَنَا فِي هَٰذِهِ الدُّنْيَا حَسَنَةً وَفِي الْآخِرَةِ إِنَّا هُدْنَا إِلَيْكَ ۚ قَالَ عَذَابِي أُصِيبُ بِهِ مَنْ أَشَاءُ ۖ وَرَحْمَتِي وَسِعَتْ كُلَّ شَيْءٍ ۚ فَسَأَكْتُبُهَا لِلَّذِينَ يَتَّقُونَ وَيُؤْتُونَ الزَّكَاةَ وَالَّذِينَ هُم بِآيَاتِنَا يُؤْمِنُونَ

156 "And inscribe for us goodness in this world, and in the Hereafter. We have turned to You." He said, "My punishment—I inflict it upon whomever I will, but My mercy encompasses all things. I will specify it for those who act righteously and practice regular charity, and those who believe in Our signs."

١٥٧ الَّذِينَ يَتَّبِعُونَ الرَّسُولَ النَّبِيَّ الْأُمِّيَّ الَّذِي يَجِدُونَهُ مَكْتُوبًا عِندَهُمْ فِي التَّوْرَاةِ وَالْإِنجِيلِ يَأْمُرُهُم بِالْمَعْرُوفِ وَيَنْهَاهُمْ عَنِ الْمُنكَرِ وَيُحِلُّ لَهُمُ الطَّيِّبَاتِ وَيُحَرِّمُ عَلَيْهِمُ الْخَبَائِثَ وَيَضَعُ عَنْهُمْ إِصْرَهُمْ وَالْأَغْلَالَ الَّتِي كَانَتْ عَلَيْهِمْ ۚ فَالَّذِينَ آمَنُوا بِهِ وَعَزَّرُوهُ وَنَصَرُوهُ وَاتَّبَعُوا النُّورَ الَّذِي أُنزِلَ مَعَهُ ۙ أُولَٰئِكَ هُمُ الْمُفْلِحُونَ

157
2:201; 4:174; 42:52

157 Those who follow the Messenger, the Unlettered Prophet, whom they find mentioned in the Torah and the Gospel in their possession. He directs them to righteousness, and deters them from evil, and allows for them all good things, and prohibits for them wickedness, and unloads the burdens and the shackles that are upon them. Those who believe in him, and respect him, and support him, and follow the light that came down with him—these are the successful.

١٥٨ قُلْ يَا أَيُّهَا النَّاسُ إِنِّي رَسُولُ اللَّهِ إِلَيْكُمْ جَمِيعًا الَّذِي لَهُ مُلْكُ السَّمَاوَاتِ وَالْأَرْضِ ۖ لَا إِلَٰهَ إِلَّا هُوَ يُحْيِي وَيُمِيتُ ۖ فَآمِنُوا بِاللَّهِ وَرَسُولِهِ النَّبِيِّ الْأُمِّيِّ الَّذِي يُؤْمِنُ بِاللَّهِ وَكَلِمَاتِهِ وَاتَّبِعُوهُ لَعَلَّكُمْ تَهْتَدُونَ

158
2:107; 9:116; 57:2

158 Say, "O people, I am the Messenger of God to you all—He to whom belongs the kingdom of the heavens and the earth. There is no god but He. He gives life and causes death." So believe in God and His Messenger, the Unlettered Prophet, who believes in God and His words. And follow him, that you may be guided.

Sūrah 7: Al-A'rāf

159 ١٥٩ وَمِن قَوْمِ مُوسَىٰ أُمَّةٌ يَهْدُونَ بِالْحَقِّ وَبِهِ يَعْدِلُونَ
7:181

159 Among the people of Moses is a community that guides by truth, and thereby does justice.

160 ١٦٠ وَقَطَّعْنَاهُمُ اثْنَتَيْ عَشْرَةَ أَسْبَاطًا أُمَمًا ۚ وَأَوْحَيْنَا إِلَىٰ مُوسَىٰ إِذِ اسْتَسْقَاهُ قَوْمُهُ أَنِ اضْرِب بِّعَصَاكَ الْحَجَرَ ۖ فَانبَجَسَتْ مِنْهُ اثْنَتَا عَشْرَةَ عَيْنًا ۖ قَدْ عَلِمَ كُلُّ أُنَاسٍ مَّشْرَبَهُمْ ۚ وَظَلَّلْنَا عَلَيْهِمُ الْغَمَامَ وَأَنزَلْنَا عَلَيْهِمُ الْمَنَّ وَالسَّلْوَىٰ ۖ كُلُوا مِن طَيِّبَاتِ مَا رَزَقْنَاكُمْ ۚ وَمَا ظَلَمُونَا وَلَٰكِن كَانُوا أَنفُسَهُمْ يَظْلِمُونَ
2:60; 7:168

160 We divided them into twelve tribal communities. And We inspired Moses, when his people asked him for something to drink: "Strike the rock with your staff." Whereupon twelve springs gushed from it. Each group recognized its drinking-place. And We shaded them with clouds, and We sent down upon them manna and quails: "Eat of the good things We have provided for you." They did not wrong Us, but they used to wrong their own selves.

161 ١٦١ وَإِذْ قِيلَ لَهُمُ اسْكُنُوا هَٰذِهِ الْقَرْيَةَ وَكُلُوا مِنْهَا حَيْثُ شِئْتُمْ وَقُولُوا حِطَّةٌ وَادْخُلُوا الْبَابَ سُجَّدًا نَّغْفِرْ لَكُمْ خَطِيئَاتِكُمْ ۚ سَنَزِيدُ الْمُحْسِنِينَ
2:58

161 And it was said to them, "Settle this town, and eat therein whatever you wish, and speak modestly, and enter the gate in humility—We will forgive your sins, and will promote the righteous."

162 ١٦٢ فَبَدَّلَ الَّذِينَ ظَلَمُوا مِنْهُمْ قَوْلًا غَيْرَ الَّذِي قِيلَ لَهُمْ فَأَرْسَلْنَا عَلَيْهِمْ رِجْزًا مِّنَ السَّمَاءِ بِمَا كَانُوا يَظْلِمُونَ
pp 2:59

162 But the wicked among them substituted other words for the words given to them; so We sent down upon them a plague from the sky, because of their wrongdoing.

163 ١٦٣ وَاسْأَلْهُمْ عَنِ الْقَرْيَةِ الَّتِي كَانَتْ حَاضِرَةَ الْبَحْرِ إِذْ يَعْدُونَ فِي السَّبْتِ إِذْ تَأْتِيهِمْ حِيتَانُهُمْ يَوْمَ سَبْتِهِمْ شُرَّعًا وَيَوْمَ لَا يَسْبِتُونَ ۙ لَا تَأْتِيهِمْ ۚ كَذَٰلِكَ نَبْلُوهُم بِمَا كَانُوا يَفْسُقُونَ
2:65; 7:166

163 Ask them about the town by the sea, when they violated the Sabbath. When they observed the Sabbath, their fish would come to them abundantly. But when they violated the Sabbath, their fish would not come to them. Thus We tried them because they disobeyed.

164 ١٦٤ وَإِذْ قَالَتْ أُمَّةٌ مِّنْهُمْ لِمَ تَعِظُونَ قَوْمًا ۙ اللَّهُ مُهْلِكُهُمْ أَوْ مُعَذِّبُهُمْ عَذَابًا شَدِيدًا ۖ قَالُوا مَعْذِرَةً إِلَىٰ رَبِّكُمْ وَلَعَلَّهُمْ يَتَّقُونَ

164 And when a group of them said, "Why do you counsel a people whom God will annihilate, or punish with a severe punishment?" They said, "As an excuse to your Lord, and so that they may become righteous."

165 ١٦٥ فَلَمَّا نَسُوا مَا ذُكِّرُوا بِهِ أَنجَيْنَا الَّذِينَ يَنْهَوْنَ عَنِ السُّوءِ وَأَخَذْنَا الَّذِينَ ظَلَمُوا بِعَذَابٍ بَئِيسٍ بِمَا كَانُوا يَفْسُقُونَ
5:13; 6:44

165 Then, when they neglected what they were reminded of, We saved those who prohibited evil, and We seized those who did wrong with a terrible punishment, because of their sinfulness.

١٦٦ فَلَمَّا عَتَوْا عَنْ مَا نُهُوا عَنْهُ قُلْنَا لَهُمْ كُونُوا قِرَدَةً خَاسِئِينَ

166
2:65; 5:60; 7:163

166 Then, when they rebelled against the commands to refrain, We said to them, "Be despicable apes."

١٦٧ وَإِذْ تَأَذَّنَ رَبُّكَ لَيَبْعَثَنَّ عَلَيْهِمْ إِلَىٰ يَوْمِ الْقِيَامَةِ مَنْ يَسُومُهُمْ سُوءَ الْعَذَابِ ۗ إِنَّ رَبَّكَ لَسَرِيعُ الْعِقَابِ ۖ وَإِنَّهُ لَغَفُورٌ رَحِيمٌ

167
2:49; 7:141; 14:6

167 Your Lord has announced that, He would send against them, until the Day of Resurrection, those who would inflict terrible suffering upon them. Your Lord is swift in retribution, yet He is Forgiving and Merciful.

١٦٨ وَقَطَّعْنَاهُمْ فِي الْأَرْضِ أُمَمًا ۖ مِنْهُمُ الصَّالِحُونَ وَمِنْهُمْ دُونَ ذَٰلِكَ ۖ وَبَلَوْنَاهُمْ بِالْحَسَنَاتِ وَالسَّيِّئَاتِ لَعَلَّهُمْ يَرْجِعُونَ

168
2:60; 7:160

168 And We scattered them into communities on earth. Some of them righteous, and some of them short of that. And We tested them with fortunes and misfortunes, so that they may return.

١٦٩ فَخَلَفَ مِنْ بَعْدِهِمْ خَلْفٌ وَرِثُوا الْكِتَابَ يَأْخُذُونَ عَرَضَ هَٰذَا الْأَدْنَىٰ وَيَقُولُونَ سَيُغْفَرُ لَنَا وَإِنْ يَأْتِهِمْ عَرَضٌ مِثْلُهُ يَأْخُذُوهُ ۚ أَلَمْ يُؤْخَذْ عَلَيْهِمْ مِيثَاقُ الْكِتَابِ أَنْ لَا يَقُولُوا عَلَى اللَّهِ إِلَّا الْحَقَّ وَدَرَسُوا مَا فِيهِ ۗ وَالدَّارُ الْآخِرَةُ خَيْرٌ لِلَّذِينَ يَتَّقُونَ ۗ أَفَلَا تَعْقِلُونَ

169
19:59

169 They were succeeded by generations who inherited the Scripture and chose the materials of this world, saying, "We will be forgiven." And should similar materials come their way, they would again seize them. Did they not make a covenant to uphold the Scripture, and to not say about God except the truth? Did they not study its contents? But the Home of the Hereafter is better for the cautious; will you not understand?

١٧٠ وَالَّذِينَ يُمَسِّكُونَ بِالْكِتَابِ وَأَقَامُوا الصَّلَاةَ إِنَّا لَا نُضِيعُ أَجْرَ الْمُصْلِحِينَ

170 Those who adhere to the Scripture, and practice prayer—We will not waste the reward of the reformers.

١٧١ وَإِذْ نَتَقْنَا الْجَبَلَ فَوْقَهُمْ كَأَنَّهُ ظُلَّةٌ وَظَنُّوا أَنَّهُ وَاقِعٌ بِهِمْ خُذُوا مَا آتَيْنَاكُمْ بِقُوَّةٍ وَاذْكُرُوا مَا فِيهِ لَعَلَّكُمْ تَتَّقُونَ

171
2:63, 93; 4:154

171 And when We suspended the mountain over them, as if it was an umbrella, and they thought it would fall on them: "Hold fast to what We have given you, and remember what it contains, so that you may be saved."

١٧٢ وَإِذْ أَخَذَ رَبُّكَ مِنْ بَنِي آدَمَ مِنْ ظُهُورِهِمْ ذُرِّيَّتَهُمْ وَأَشْهَدَهُمْ عَلَىٰ أَنْفُسِهِمْ أَلَسْتُ بِرَبِّكُمْ ۖ قَالُوا بَلَىٰ ۛ شَهِدْنَا ۛ أَنْ تَقُولُوا يَوْمَ الْقِيَامَةِ إِنَّا كُنَّا عَنْ هَٰذَا غَافِلِينَ

172
5:19; 6:130, 155

172 And when Your Lord summoned the descendants of Adam, and made them testify about themselves. "Am I not your Lord?" They said, "Yes, we testify." Thus you cannot say on the Day of Resurrection, "We were unaware of this."

١٧٣ أَوْ تَقُولُوا إِنَّمَا أَشْرَكَ آبَاؤُنَا مِنْ قَبْلُ وَكُنَّا ذُرِّيَّةً مِنْ بَعْدِهِمْ ۖ أَفَتُهْلِكُنَا بِمَا فَعَلَ الْمُبْطِلُونَ

173 Nor can you Say, "Our ancestors practiced idolatry before; and we are their descendants who came after them; will you destroy us for what the falsifiers did?"

173
20:134

١٧٤ وَكَذَلِكَ نُفَصِّلُ الْآيَاتِ وَلَعَلَّهُمْ يَرْجِعُونَ

174 We thus elaborate the revelations, so that they may return.

١٧٥ وَاتْلُ عَلَيْهِمْ نَبَأَ الَّذِي آتَيْنَاهُ آيَاتِنَا فَانْسَلَخَ مِنْهَا فَأَتْبَعَهُ الشَّيْطَانُ فَكَانَ مِنَ الْغَاوِينَ

175 And relate to them the story of him to whom We delivered Our signs, but he detached himself from them, so Satan went after him, and he became one of the perverts.

١٧٦ وَلَوْ شِئْنَا لَرَفَعْنَاهُ بِهَا وَلَكِنَّهُ أَخْلَدَ إِلَى الْأَرْضِ وَاتَّبَعَ هَوَاهُ ۚ فَمَثَلُهُ كَمَثَلِ الْكَلْبِ إِنْ تَحْمِلْ عَلَيْهِ يَلْهَثْ أَوْ تَتْرُكْهُ يَلْهَثْ ۚ ذَلِكَ مَثَلُ الْقَوْمِ الَّذِينَ كَذَّبُوا بِآيَاتِنَا ۚ فَاقْصُصِ الْقَصَصَ لَعَلَّهُمْ يَتَفَكَّرُونَ

176 Had We willed, We could have elevated him through them; but he clung to the ground, and followed his desires. His metaphor is that of a dog: if you chase it, it pants; and if you leave it alone, it pants. Such is the metaphor of the people who deny Our signs. So tell the tale, so that they may ponder.

176
22:72; 29:41; 62:5

١٧٧ سَاءَ مَثَلًا الْقَوْمُ الَّذِينَ كَذَّبُوا بِآيَاتِنَا وَأَنْفُسَهُمْ كَانُوا يَظْلِمُونَ

177 Evil is the metaphor of the people who reject Our signs and wrong themselves.

177
62:5

١٧٨ مَنْ يَهْدِ اللَّهُ فَهُوَ الْمُهْتَدِي ۖ وَمَنْ يُضْلِلْ فَأُولَئِكَ هُمُ الْخَاسِرُونَ

178 Whomever God guides is the guided one. And whomever He sends astray—these are the losers.

178
17:97; 18:17; 39:37

١٧٩ وَلَقَدْ ذَرَأْنَا لِجَهَنَّمَ كَثِيرًا مِنَ الْجِنِّ وَالْإِنْسِ ۖ لَهُمْ قُلُوبٌ لَا يَفْقَهُونَ بِهَا وَلَهُمْ أَعْيُنٌ لَا يُبْصِرُونَ بِهَا وَلَهُمْ آذَانٌ لَا يَسْمَعُونَ بِهَا ۚ أُولَئِكَ كَالْأَنْعَامِ بَلْ هُمْ أَضَلُّ ۚ أُولَئِكَ هُمُ الْغَافِلُونَ

179 We have destined for Hell multitudes of jinn and humans. They have hearts with which they do not understand. They have eyes with which they do not see. They have ears with which they do not hear. These are like cattle. In fact, they are further astray. These are the heedless.

179
2:7; 22:46; 25:44

١٨٠ وَلِلَّهِ الْأَسْمَاءُ الْحُسْنَى فَادْعُوهُ بِهَا ۖ وَذَرُوا الَّذِينَ يُلْحِدُونَ فِي أَسْمَائِهِ ۚ سَيُجْزَوْنَ مَا كَانُوا يَعْمَلُونَ

180 To God belong the Most Beautiful Names, so call Him by them, and disregard those who blaspheme His names. They will be repaid for what they used to do.

180
17:110; 20:8; 59:23

١٨١ وَمِمَّنْ خَلَقْنَا أُمَّةٌ يَهْدُونَ بِالْحَقِّ وَبِهِ يَعْدِلُونَ

181 Among those We created is a community—they guide by truth, and do justice thereby.

181
7:159

١٨٢ وَالَّذِينَ كَذَّبُوا بِآيَاتِنَا سَنَسْتَدْرِجُهُم مِّنْ حَيْثُ لَا يَعْلَمُونَ

182 As for those who reject Our messages, We will gradually lead them from where they do not know.

182 69:44

١٨٣ وَأُمْلِي لَهُمْ ۚ إِنَّ كَيْدِي مَتِينٌ

183 And I will encourage them. My plan is firm.

١٨٤ أَوَلَمْ يَتَفَكَّرُوا ۗ مَا بِصَاحِبِهِم مِّن جِنَّةٍ ۚ إِنْ هُوَ إِلَّا نَذِيرٌ مُّبِينٌ

184 Do they not think? There is no madness in their friend. He is but a plain warner.

184 15:6; 34:46; 44:14; 52:29; 68:2; 81:22

١٨٥ أَوَلَمْ يَنظُرُوا فِي مَلَكُوتِ السَّمَاوَاتِ وَالْأَرْضِ وَمَا خَلَقَ اللَّهُ مِن شَيْءٍ وَأَنْ عَسَىٰ أَن يَكُونَ قَدِ اقْتَرَبَ أَجَلُهُمْ ۖ فَبِأَيِّ حَدِيثٍ بَعْدَهُ يُؤْمِنُونَ

185 Have they not observed the government of the heavens and the earth, and all the things that God created, and that their time may have drawn near? Which message, besides this, will they believe in?

185 45:6; 77:50

١٨٦ مَن يُضْلِلِ اللَّهُ فَلَا هَادِيَ لَهُ ۚ وَيَذَرُهُمْ فِي طُغْيَانِهِمْ يَعْمَهُونَ

186 Whomever God misguides has no guide. And He leaves them blundering in their transgression.

186 13:33; 39:23

١٨٧ يَسْأَلُونَكَ عَنِ السَّاعَةِ أَيَّانَ مُرْسَاهَا ۖ قُلْ إِنَّمَا عِلْمُهَا عِندَ رَبِّي ۖ لَا يُجَلِّيهَا لِوَقْتِهَا إِلَّا هُوَ ۚ ثَقُلَتْ فِي السَّمَاوَاتِ وَالْأَرْضِ ۚ لَا تَأْتِيكُمْ إِلَّا بَغْتَةً ۗ يَسْأَلُونَكَ كَأَنَّكَ حَفِيٌّ عَنْهَا ۖ قُلْ إِنَّمَا عِلْمُهَا عِندَ اللَّهِ وَلَٰكِنَّ أَكْثَرَ النَّاسِ لَا يَعْلَمُونَ

187 They ask you about the Hour, "When will it come?" Say, "Knowledge of it rests with my Lord. None can reveal its coming except He. It weighs heavily on the heavens and the earth. It will not come upon you except suddenly." They ask you as if you are responsible for it. Say, "Knowledge of it rests with God," but most people do not know.

187 22:55; 41:47; 51:12; 79:42–44

١٨٨ قُل لَّا أَمْلِكُ لِنَفْسِي نَفْعًا وَلَا ضَرًّا إِلَّا مَا شَاءَ اللَّهُ ۚ [a] وَلَوْ كُنتُ أَعْلَمُ الْغَيْبَ لَاسْتَكْثَرْتُ مِنَ الْخَيْرِ وَمَا مَسَّنِيَ السُّوءُ ۚ إِنْ أَنَا إِلَّا نَذِيرٌ وَبَشِيرٌ لِّقَوْمٍ يُؤْمِنُونَ [b]

188 Say, "I have no control over any benefit or harm to myself, except as God wills. Had I known the future, I would have acquired much good, and no harm would have touched me. I am only a warner, and a herald of good news to a people who believe."

188
[a] 10:49; 34:42
[b] 6:50; 27:65; 62:26–27

١٨٩ هُوَ الَّذِي خَلَقَكُم مِّن نَّفْسٍ وَاحِدَةٍ وَجَعَلَ مِنْهَا زَوْجَهَا لِيَسْكُنَ إِلَيْهَا ۖ فَلَمَّا تَغَشَّاهَا حَمَلَتْ حَمْلًا خَفِيفًا فَمَرَّتْ بِهِ ۖ فَلَمَّا أَثْقَلَت دَّعَوَا اللَّهَ رَبَّهُمَا لَئِنْ آتَيْتَنَا صَالِحًا لَّنَكُونَنَّ مِنَ الشَّاكِرِينَ

189 It is He who created you from a single person, and made from it its mate, that he may find comfort with her. Then, when he has covered her, she conceives a light load, and she carries it around. But when she has grown heavy, they pray to God their Lord, "if You give us a good child, we will be among the thankful."

189 4:1; 16:72; 30:21; 39:6

Sūrah 7: Al-A'rāf

١٩٠ فَلَمَّا آتَاهُمَا صَالِحًا جَعَلَا لَهُ شُرَكَاءَ فِيمَا آتَاهُمَا ۚ فَتَعَالَى اللَّهُ عَمَّا يُشْرِكُونَ

190 But when He has given them a good child, they attribute partners to Him in what He has given them. God is exalted above what they associate.

١٩١ أَيُشْرِكُونَ مَا لَا يَخْلُقُ شَيْئًا وَهُمْ يُخْلَقُونَ

191
16:20; 25:3

191 Do they idolize those who create nothing, and are themselves created?

١٩٢ وَلَا يَسْتَطِيعُونَ لَهُمْ نَصْرًا وَلَا أَنْفُسَهُمْ يَنْصُرُونَ

192
7:197; 46:28

192 And can neither help them, nor help their own selves?

١٩٣ وَإِنْ تَدْعُوهُمْ إِلَى الْهُدَىٰ لَا يَتَّبِعُوكُمْ ۚ سَوَاءٌ عَلَيْكُمْ أَدَعَوْتُمُوهُمْ أَمْ أَنْتُمْ صَامِتُونَ

193
7:198

193 And if you invite them to guidance, they will not follow you. It is the same for you, whether you invite them, or remain silent.

١٩٤ إِنَّ الَّذِينَ تَدْعُونَ مِنْ دُونِ اللَّهِ عِبَادٌ أَمْثَالُكُمْ ۖ فَادْعُوهُمْ فَلْيَسْتَجِيبُوا لَكُمْ إِنْ كُنْتُمْ صَادِقِينَ

194
46:5

194 Those you call upon besides God are servants like you. So call upon them, and let them answer you, if you are truthful.

١٩٥ أَلَهُمْ أَرْجُلٌ يَمْشُونَ بِهَا ۖ أَمْ لَهُمْ أَيْدٍ يَبْطِشُونَ بِهَا ۖ أَمْ لَهُمْ أَعْيُنٌ يُبْصِرُونَ بِهَا ۖ أَمْ لَهُمْ آذَانٌ يَسْمَعُونَ بِهَا ۗ قُلِ ادْعُوا شُرَكَاءَكُمْ ثُمَّ كِيدُونِ فَلَا تُنْظِرُونِ

195
10:71; 11:54

195 Do they have feet with which they walk? Or do they have hands with which they strike? Or do they have eyes with which they see? Or do they have ears with which they hear? Say, "Call upon your partners, then plot against me, and do not wait."

١٩٦ إِنَّ وَلِيِّيَ اللَّهُ الَّذِي نَزَّلَ الْكِتَابَ ۖ وَهُوَ يَتَوَلَّى الصَّالِحِينَ

196 "My Master is God, He Who sent down the Book, and He takes care of the righteous."

١٩٧ وَالَّذِينَ تَدْعُونَ مِنْ دُونِهِ لَا يَسْتَطِيعُونَ نَصْرَكُمْ وَلَا أَنْفُسَهُمْ يَنْصُرُونَ

197
7:192

197 Those you call upon besides Him cannot help you, nor can they help themselves.

١٩٨ وَإِنْ تَدْعُوهُمْ إِلَى الْهُدَىٰ لَا يَسْمَعُوا ۖ وَتَرَاهُمْ يَنْظُرُونَ إِلَيْكَ وَهُمْ لَا يُبْصِرُونَ

198
7:193

198 And if you call them to guidance, they will not hear. And you see them looking at you, yet they do not see.

١٩٩ خُذِ الْعَفْوَ وَأْمُرْ بِالْعُرْفِ وَأَعْرِضْ عَنِ الْجَاهِلِينَ

199 Be tolerant, and command decency, and avoid the ignorant.

٢٠٠ وَإِمَّا يَنْزَغَنَّكَ مِنَ الشَّيْطَانِ نَزْغٌ فَاسْتَعِذْ بِاللَّهِ ۚ إِنَّهُ سَمِيعٌ عَلِيمٌ

200
pp 41:36

200 And when a suggestion from Satan assails you, take refuge with God. He is Hearing and Knowing.

٢٠١ إِنَّ ٱلَّذِينَ ٱتَّقَوْا إِذَا مَسَّهُمْ طَائِفٌ مِنَ ٱلشَّيْطَانِ تَذَكَّرُوا فَإِذَا هُم مُّبْصِرُونَ

201 Those who are righteous—when an impulse from Satan strikes them, they remind themselves, and immediately see clearly.

٢٠٢ وَإِخْوَانُهُمْ يَمُدُّونَهُمْ فِي ٱلْغَيِّ ثُمَّ لَا يُقْصِرُونَ

202 But their brethren lead them relentlessly into error, and they never stop short.

٢٠٣ وَإِذَا لَمْ تَأْتِهِم بِآيَةٍ قَالُوا لَوْلَا ٱجْتَبَيْتَهَا ۚ قُلْ إِنَّمَا أَتَّبِعُ مَا يُوحَىٰ إِلَيَّ مِن رَّبِّي ۚ هَـٰذَا بَصَائِرُ مِن رَّبِّكُمْ وَهُدًى وَرَحْمَةٌ لِّقَوْمٍ يُؤْمِنُونَ

203
12:111; 16:64; 45:20

203 If you do not produce a miracle for them, they say, "Why don't you improvise one." Say, "I only follow what is inspired to me from my Lord." These are insights from your Lord, and guidance, and mercy, for a people who believe.

٢٠٤ وَإِذَا قُرِئَ ٱلْقُرْآنُ فَٱسْتَمِعُوا لَهُ وَأَنصِتُوا لَعَلَّكُمْ تُرْحَمُونَ

204 When the Qur'an is recited, listen to it, and pay attention, so that you may experience mercy.

٢٠٥ وَٱذْكُر رَّبَّكَ فِي نَفْسِكَ تَضَرُّعًا وَخِيفَةً وَدُونَ ٱلْجَهْرِ مِنَ ٱلْقَوْلِ بِٱلْغُدُوِّ وَٱلْآصَالِ وَلَا تَكُن مِّنَ ٱلْغَافِلِينَ

205
6:63; 7:55; 17:110

205 And remember your Lord within yourself, humbly and fearfully, and quietly, in the morning and the evening, and do not be of the neglectful.

٢٠٦ إِنَّ ٱلَّذِينَ عِندَ رَبِّكَ لَا يَسْتَكْبِرُونَ عَنْ عِبَادَتِهِ وَيُسَبِّحُونَهُ وَلَهُ يَسْجُدُونَ ۩

206
21:19; 16:49; 41:38

206 Those who are in the presence of your Lord are not too proud to worship Him. They recite His praises, and to Him they bow down.

Sūrah 8: Al-Anfāl

سُورَةُ ٱلْأَنْفَالِ (The Spoils)

بِسْمِ ٱللَّهِ ٱلرَّحْمَٰنِ ٱلرَّحِيمِ

١ يَسْأَلُونَكَ عَنِ ٱلْأَنفَالِ ۖ قُلِ ٱلْأَنفَالُ لِلَّهِ وَٱلرَّسُولِ ۖ فَٱتَّقُوا ٱللَّهَ وَأَصْلِحُوا ذَاتَ بَيْنِكُمْ ۖ وَأَطِيعُوا ٱللَّهَ وَرَسُولَهُ إِن كُنتُم مُّؤْمِنِينَ

1
8:41; 59:8

1 They ask you about the bounties. Say, "The bounties are for God and the Messenger." So be mindful of God, and settle your differences, and obey God and His Messenger, if you are believers.

٢ إِنَّمَا الْمُؤْمِنُونَ الَّذِينَ إِذَا ذُكِرَ اللَّهُ وَجِلَتْ قُلُوبُهُمْ وَإِذَا تُلِيَتْ عَلَيْهِمْ آيَاتُهُ زَادَتْهُمْ إِيمَانًا وَعَلَىٰ رَبِّهِمْ يَتَوَكَّلُونَ

2 9:124; 22:35; 47:17

2 The believers are those whose hearts tremble when God is mentioned, and when His revelations are recited to them, they strengthen them in faith, and upon their Lord they rely.

٣ الَّذِينَ يُقِيمُونَ الصَّلَاةَ وَمِمَّا رَزَقْنَاهُمْ يُنْفِقُونَ

3 2:3; 13:22

3 Those who perform the prayer; and from Our provisions to them, they spend.

٤ أُولَٰئِكَ هُمُ الْمُؤْمِنُونَ حَقًّا ۚ لَهُمْ دَرَجَاتٌ عِنْدَ رَبِّهِمْ وَمَغْفِرَةٌ وَرِزْقٌ كَرِيمٌ

4 8:74

4 These are the true believers. They have high standing with their Lord, and forgiveness, and a generous provision.

٥ كَمَا أَخْرَجَكَ رَبُّكَ مِنْ بَيْتِكَ بِالْحَقِّ وَإِنَّ فَرِيقًا مِنَ الْمُؤْمِنِينَ لَكَارِهُونَ

5

5 Even as your Lord brought you out of your home with the truth, some believers were reluctant.

٦ يُجَادِلُونَكَ فِي الْحَقِّ بَعْدَمَا تَبَيَّنَ كَأَنَّمَا يُسَاقُونَ إِلَى الْمَوْتِ وَهُمْ يَنْظُرُونَ

6

6 Arguing with you about the truth after it was made clear, as if they were being driven to death as they looked on.

٧ وَإِذْ يَعِدُكُمُ اللَّهُ إِحْدَى الطَّائِفَتَيْنِ أَنَّهَا لَكُمْ وَتَوَدُّونَ أَنَّ غَيْرَ ذَاتِ الشَّوْكَةِ تَكُونُ لَكُمْ وَيُرِيدُ اللَّهُ أَنْ يُحِقَّ الْحَقَّ بِكَلِمَاتِهِ وَيَقْطَعَ دَابِرَ الْكَافِرِينَ

7 10:81; 42:24

7 God has promised you one of the two groups—that it would be yours—but you wanted the unarmed group to be yours. God intends to prove the truth with His words, and to uproot the disbelievers.

٨ لِيُحِقَّ الْحَقَّ وَيُبْطِلَ الْبَاطِلَ وَلَوْ كَرِهَ الْمُجْرِمُونَ

8 10:82; 42:24

8 In order to confirm the truth and nullify falsehood, even though the guilty dislike it.

٩ إِذْ تَسْتَغِيثُونَ رَبَّكُمْ فَاسْتَجَابَ لَكُمْ أَنِّي مُمِدُّكُمْ بِأَلْفٍ مِنَ الْمَلَائِكَةِ مُرْدِفِينَ

9 3:124–125; 47:11

9 When you appealed to your Lord for help, He answered you, "I am reinforcing you with one thousand angels in succession."

١٠ وَمَا جَعَلَهُ اللَّهُ إِلَّا بُشْرَىٰ وَلِتَطْمَئِنَّ بِهِ قُلُوبُكُمْ ۚ وَمَا النَّصْرُ إِلَّا مِنْ عِنْدِ اللَّهِ ۚ إِنَّ اللَّهَ عَزِيزٌ حَكِيمٌ

10 3:126

10 God only made it a message of hope, and to set your hearts at rest. Victory comes only from God. God is Mighty and Wise.

١١ إِذْ يُغَشِّيكُمُ النُّعَاسَ أَمَنَةً مِنْهُ وَيُنَزِّلُ عَلَيْكُمْ مِنَ السَّمَاءِ مَاءً لِيُطَهِّرَكُمْ بِهِ وَيُذْهِبَ عَنْكُمْ رِجْزَ الشَّيْطَانِ وَلِيَرْبِطَ عَلَىٰ قُلُوبِكُمْ وَيُثَبِّتَ بِهِ الْأَقْدَامَ

11 3:154

11 He made drowsiness overcome you, as a security from Him. And He sent down upon you water from the sky, to cleanse you with it, and to rid you of Satan's pollution, and to fortify your hearts, and to strengthen your foothold.

١٢ إِذْ يُوحِي رَبُّكَ إِلَى الْمَلَائِكَةِ أَنِّي مَعَكُمْ فَثَبِّتُوا الَّذِينَ آمَنُوا ۚ سَأُلْقِي فِي قُلُوبِ الَّذِينَ كَفَرُوا الرُّعْبَ فَاضْرِبُوا فَوْقَ الْأَعْنَاقِ وَاضْرِبُوا مِنْهُمْ كُلَّ بَنَانٍ

12 Your Lord inspired the angels: "I am with you, so support those who believe. I will cast terror into the hearts of those who disbelieve. So strike above the necks, and strike off every fingertip of theirs."

12 — 3:151; 33:26; 59:2; 47:4

١٣ ذَٰلِكَ بِأَنَّهُمْ شَاقُّوا اللَّهَ وَرَسُولَهُ ۚ وَمَن يُشَاقِقِ اللَّهَ وَرَسُولَهُ فَإِنَّ اللَّهَ شَدِيدُ الْعِقَابِ

13 That is because they opposed God and His Messenger. Whoever opposes God and His Messenger—God is severe in retribution.

13 — 59:4

١٤ ذَٰلِكُمْ فَذُوقُوهُ وَأَنَّ لِلْكَافِرِينَ عَذَابَ النَّارِ

14 "Here it is; so taste it." For the disbelievers there is the suffering of the Fire.

١٥ يَا أَيُّهَا الَّذِينَ آمَنُوا إِذَا لَقِيتُمُ الَّذِينَ كَفَرُوا زَحْفًا فَلَا تُوَلُّوهُمُ الْأَدْبَارَ

15 O you who believe! When you meet those who disbelieve on the march, never turn your backs on them.

15 — 8:45

١٦ وَمَن يُوَلِّهِمْ يَوْمَئِذٍ دُبُرَهُ إِلَّا مُتَحَرِّفًا لِقِتَالٍ أَوْ مُتَحَيِّزًا إِلَىٰ فِئَةٍ فَقَدْ بَاءَ بِغَضَبٍ مِنَ اللَّهِ وَمَأْوَاهُ جَهَنَّمُ ۖ وَبِئْسَ الْمَصِيرُ

16 Anyone who turns his back on them on that Day, except while maneuvering for battle, or to join another group, has incurred wrath from God, and his abode is Hell—what a miserable destination!

١٧ فَلَمْ تَقْتُلُوهُمْ وَلَٰكِنَّ اللَّهَ قَتَلَهُمْ ۚ وَمَا رَمَيْتَ إِذْ رَمَيْتَ وَلَٰكِنَّ اللَّهَ رَمَىٰ ۚ وَلِيُبْلِيَ الْمُؤْمِنِينَ مِنْهُ بَلَاءً حَسَنًا ۚ إِنَّ اللَّهَ سَمِيعٌ عَلِيمٌ

17 It was not you who killed them, but it was God who killed them. And it was not you who launched when you launched, but it was God who launched. That He may bestow upon the believers an excellent reward. God is Hearing and Knowing.

١٨ ذَٰلِكُمْ وَأَنَّ اللَّهَ مُوهِنُ كَيْدِ الْكَافِرِينَ

18 Such is the case. God will undermine the strategy of the disbelievers.

18 — 4:76; 7:183; 68:45

١٩ إِن تَسْتَفْتِحُوا فَقَدْ جَاءَكُمُ الْفَتْحُ ۖ وَإِن تَنتَهُوا فَهُوَ خَيْرٌ لَّكُمْ ۖ وَإِن تَعُودُوا نَعُدْ وَلَن تُغْنِيَ عَنكُمْ فِئَتُكُمْ شَيْئًا وَلَوْ كَثُرَتْ وَأَنَّ اللَّهَ مَعَ الْمُؤْمِنِينَ

19 If you desire a verdict, the verdict has come to you. And if you desist, it would be best for you. And if you return, We will return; and your troops, however numerous, will not benefit you. God is with the believers.

19 — 2:192; 7:87; 8:38

٢٠ يَا أَيُّهَا الَّذِينَ آمَنُوا أَطِيعُوا اللَّهَ وَرَسُولَهُ وَلَا تَوَلَّوْا عَنْهُ وَأَنتُمْ تَسْمَعُونَ

20 O you who believe! Obey God and His Messenger, and do not turn away from him when you hear.

20 — 3:32: 5:92; 24:54

٢١ وَلَا تَكُونُوا كَالَّذِينَ قَالُوا سَمِعْنَا وَهُمْ لَا يَسْمَعُونَ

21 And be not like those who say, "We hear," when they do not hear.

21
2:93

٢٢ إِنَّ شَرَّ الدَّوَابِّ عِنْدَ اللَّهِ الصُّمُّ الْبُكْمُ الَّذِينَ لَا يَعْقِلُونَ

22 The worst of animals to God are the deaf and dumb—those who do not reason.

22
2:18, 171; 6:39; 8:22

٢٣ وَلَوْ عَلِمَ اللَّهُ فِيهِمْ خَيْرًا لَأَسْمَعَهُمْ ۖ وَلَوْ أَسْمَعَهُمْ لَتَوَلَّوْا وَهُمْ مُعْرِضُونَ

23 Had God recognized any good in them, He would have made them hear; and had He made them hear, they would have turned away defiantly.

٢٤ يَا أَيُّهَا الَّذِينَ آمَنُوا اسْتَجِيبُوا لِلَّهِ وَلِلرَّسُولِ إِذَا دَعَاكُمْ لِمَا يُحْيِيكُمْ ۖ وَاعْلَمُوا أَنَّ اللَّهَ يَحُولُ بَيْنَ الْمَرْءِ وَقَلْبِهِ وَأَنَّهُ إِلَيْهِ تُحْشَرُونَ

24 O you who believe! Respond to God and to the Messenger when He calls you to what will revive you. And know that God stands between a man and his heart, and that to Him you will be gathered.

24
3:172

٢٥ وَاتَّقُوا فِتْنَةً لَا تُصِيبَنَّ الَّذِينَ ظَلَمُوا مِنْكُمْ خَاصَّةً ۖ وَاعْلَمُوا أَنَّ اللَّهَ شَدِيدُ الْعِقَابِ

25 And beware of discord which does not afflict the wrongdoers among you exclusively; and know that God is severe in retribution.

٢٦ وَاذْكُرُوا إِذْ أَنْتُمْ قَلِيلٌ مُسْتَضْعَفُونَ فِي الْأَرْضِ تَخَافُونَ أَنْ يَتَخَطَّفَكُمُ النَّاسُ فَآوَاكُمْ وَأَيَّدَكُمْ بِنَصْرِهِ وَرَزَقَكُمْ مِنَ الطَّيِّبَاتِ لَعَلَّكُمْ تَشْكُرُونَ

26 And remember when you were few, oppressed in the land, fearing that people may capture you; but He sheltered you, and supported you with His victory, and provided you with good things—so that you may be thankful.

26
3:123; 7:86; 28:57; 29:67

٢٧ يَا أَيُّهَا الَّذِينَ آمَنُوا لَا تَخُونُوا اللَّهَ وَالرَّسُولَ وَتَخُونُوا أَمَانَاتِكُمْ وَأَنْتُمْ تَعْلَمُونَ

27 O you who believe! Do not betray God and the Messenger, nor betray your trusts, while you know.

27
4:58; 8:71; 23:8

٢٨ وَاعْلَمُوا أَنَّمَا أَمْوَالُكُمْ وَأَوْلَادُكُمْ فِتْنَةٌ وَأَنَّ اللَّهَ عِنْدَهُ أَجْرٌ عَظِيمٌ

28 And know that your possessions and your children are a test, and that God possesses an immense reward.

28
3:10; 9:55; 63:9; 64:15

٢٩ يَا أَيُّهَا الَّذِينَ آمَنُوا إِنْ تَتَّقُوا اللَّهَ يَجْعَلْ لَكُمْ فُرْقَانًا وَيُكَفِّرْ عَنْكُمْ سَيِّئَاتِكُمْ وَيَغْفِرْ لَكُمْ ۗ وَاللَّهُ ذُو الْفَضْلِ الْعَظِيمِ

29 O you who believe! If you remain conscious of God, He will give you a criterion, and will remit from you your sins, and will forgive you. God is possessor of infinite grace.

29
2:53; 3:4; 21:48; 25:1; 57:28

٣٠ وَإِذْ يَمْكُرُ بِكَ الَّذِينَ كَفَرُوا لِيُثْبِتُوكَ أَوْ يَقْتُلُوكَ أَوْ يُخْرِجُوكَ ۚ وَيَمْكُرُونَ وَيَمْكُرُ اللَّهُ ۖ وَاللَّهُ خَيْرُ الْمَاكِرِينَ

30 3:59; 7:99

30 When the disbelievers plotted against you, to imprison you, or kill you, or expel you. They planned, and God planned, but God is the Best of planners.

٣١ وَإِذَا تُتْلَىٰ عَلَيْهِمْ آيَاتُنَا قَالُوا قَدْ سَمِعْنَا لَوْ نَشَاءُ لَقُلْنَا مِثْلَ هَٰذَا ۙ إِنْ هَٰذَا إِلَّا أَسَاطِيرُ الْأَوَّلِينَ

31 6:25; 25:5–6

31 And when Our revelations are recited to them, they say, "We have heard. Had we wanted, we could have said the like of this; these are nothing but myths of the ancients."

٣٢ وَإِذْ قَالُوا اللَّهُمَّ إِنْ كَانَ هَٰذَا هُوَ الْحَقَّ مِنْ عِنْدِكَ فَأَمْطِرْ عَلَيْنَا حِجَارَةً مِنَ السَّمَاءِ أَوِ ائْتِنَا بِعَذَابٍ أَلِيمٍ

32 7:70, 77; 10:48; 11:32; 26:187; 29:29

32 And they said, "Our God, if this is the truth from You, then rain down on us stones from the sky, or visit us with a painful affliction."

٣٣ وَمَا كَانَ اللَّهُ لِيُعَذِّبَهُمْ وَأَنْتَ فِيهِمْ ۚ وَمَا كَانَ اللَّهُ مُعَذِّبَهُمْ وَهُمْ يَسْتَغْفِرُونَ

33 But God would not punish them while you are amongst them. And God would not punish them as long as they seek forgiveness.

٣٤ وَمَا لَهُمْ أَلَّا يُعَذِّبَهُمُ اللَّهُ وَهُمْ يَصُدُّونَ عَنِ الْمَسْجِدِ الْحَرَامِ وَمَا كَانُوا أَوْلِيَاءَهُ ۚ إِنْ أَوْلِيَاؤُهُ إِلَّا الْمُتَّقُونَ وَلَٰكِنَّ أَكْثَرَهُمْ لَا يَعْلَمُونَ

34 9:17–8; 22:25; 48:25; 90:2

34 Yet why should God not punish them, when they are turning others away from the Sacred Mosque, although they are not its custodians? Its rightful custodians are the pious; but most of them do not know.

٣٥ وَمَا كَانَ صَلَاتُهُمْ عِنْدَ الْبَيْتِ إِلَّا مُكَاءً وَتَصْدِيَةً ۚ فَذُوقُوا الْعَذَابَ بِمَا كُنْتُمْ تَكْفُرُونَ

35 41:26

35 Their prayer at the House was nothing but whistling and clapping—so taste the punishment for your blasphemy.

٣٦ إِنَّ الَّذِينَ كَفَرُوا يُنْفِقُونَ أَمْوَالَهُمْ لِيَصُدُّوا عَنْ سَبِيلِ اللَّهِ ۚ فَسَيُنْفِقُونَهَا ثُمَّ تَكُونُ عَلَيْهِمْ حَسْرَةً ثُمَّ يُغْلَبُونَ ۗ وَالَّذِينَ كَفَرُوا إِلَىٰ جَهَنَّمَ يُحْشَرُونَ

36 3:12

36 Those who disbelieve spend their wealth to repel from God's path. They will spend it, then it will become a source of sorrow for them, and then they will be defeated. Those who disbelieve will be herded into Hell.

٣٧ لِيَمِيزَ اللَّهُ الْخَبِيثَ مِنَ الطَّيِّبِ وَيَجْعَلَ الْخَبِيثَ بَعْضَهُ عَلَىٰ بَعْضٍ فَيَرْكُمَهُ جَمِيعًا فَيَجْعَلَهُ فِي جَهَنَّمَ ۚ أُولَٰئِكَ هُمُ الْخَاسِرُونَ

37 3:179

37 That God may distinguish the bad from the good, and heap the bad on top of one another, and pile them together, and throw them in Hell. These are the losers.

Sūrah 8: Al-Anfāl

٣٨ قُلْ لِلَّذِينَ كَفَرُوا إِنْ يَنْتَهُوا يُغْفَرْ لَهُمْ مَا قَدْ سَلَفَ وَإِنْ يَعُودُوا فَقَدْ مَضَتْ سُنَّتُ الْأَوَّلِينَ

38–39
2:192–193; 6:74

38 Say to those who disbelieve: if they desist, their past will be forgiven. But if they persist—the practice of the ancients has passed away.

٣٩ وَقَاتِلُوهُمْ حَتَّىٰ لَا تَكُونَ فِتْنَةٌ وَيَكُونَ الدِّينُ كُلُّهُ لِلَّهِ ۚ فَإِنِ انْتَهَوْا فَإِنَّ اللَّهَ بِمَا يَعْمَلُونَ بَصِيرٌ

39 Fight them until there is no more persecution, and religion becomes exclusively for God. But if they desist—God is Seeing of what they do.

٤٠ وَإِنْ تَوَلَّوْا فَاعْلَمُوا أَنَّ اللَّهَ مَوْلَاكُمْ ۚ نِعْمَ الْمَوْلَىٰ وَنِعْمَ النَّصِيرُ

40
22:78

40 And if they turn away, know that God is your Protector. The Best Protector, and the Best Supporter.

٤١ وَاعْلَمُوا أَنَّمَا غَنِمْتُمْ مِنْ شَيْءٍ فَأَنَّ لِلَّهِ خُمُسَهُ وَلِلرَّسُولِ وَلِذِي الْقُرْبَىٰ وَالْيَتَامَىٰ وَالْمَسَاكِينِ وَابْنِ السَّبِيلِ إِنْ كُنْتُمْ آمَنْتُمْ بِاللَّهِ وَمَا أَنْزَلْنَا عَلَىٰ عَبْدِنَا يَوْمَ الْفُرْقَانِ يَوْمَ الْتَقَى الْجَمْعَانِ ۗ وَاللَّهُ عَلَىٰ كُلِّ شَيْءٍ قَدِيرٌ

41
8:1; 59:7

41 And know that whatever spoils you gain, to God belongs its fifth, and to the Messenger, and the relatives, and the orphans, and the poor, and to the wayfarer, provided you believe in God and in what We revealed to Our servant on the Day of Distinction, the day when the two armies met. God is Capable of everything.

٤٢ إِذْ أَنْتُمْ بِالْعُدْوَةِ الدُّنْيَا وَهُمْ بِالْعُدْوَةِ الْقُصْوَىٰ وَالرَّكْبُ أَسْفَلَ مِنْكُمْ ۚ وَلَوْ تَوَاعَدْتُمْ لَاخْتَلَفْتُمْ فِي الْمِيعَادِ ۙ وَلَٰكِنْ لِيَقْضِيَ اللَّهُ أَمْرًا كَانَ مَفْعُولًا لِيَهْلِكَ مَنْ هَلَكَ عَنْ بَيِّنَةٍ وَيَحْيَىٰ مَنْ حَيَّ عَنْ بَيِّنَةٍ ۗ وَإِنَّ اللَّهَ لَسَمِيعٌ عَلِيمٌ

42
8:44

42 Recall when you were on the nearer bank, and they were on the further bank, and the caravan was below you. Had you planned for this meeting, you would have disagreed on the timing, but God was to carry out a predetermined matter, so that those who perish would perish by clear evidence, and those who survive would survive by clear evidence. God is Hearing and Knowing.

٤٣ إِذْ يُرِيكَهُمُ اللَّهُ فِي مَنَامِكَ قَلِيلًا ۖ وَلَوْ أَرَاكَهُمْ كَثِيرًا لَفَشِلْتُمْ وَلَتَنَازَعْتُمْ فِي الْأَمْرِ وَلَٰكِنَّ اللَّهَ سَلَّمَ ۗ إِنَّهُ عَلِيمٌ بِذَاتِ الصُّدُورِ

43
3:152; 4:59; 8:46

43 God made them appear in your dream as few. Had He made them appear as many, you would have lost heart, and disputed in the matter. But God saved the situation. He knows what the hearts contain.

٤٤ وَإِذْ يُرِيكُمُوهُمْ إِذِ الْتَقَيْتُمْ فِي أَعْيُنِكُمْ قَلِيلًا وَيُقَلِّلُكُمْ فِي أَعْيُنِهِمْ لِيَقْضِيَ اللَّهُ أَمْرًا كَانَ مَفْعُولًا ۗ وَإِلَى اللَّهِ تُرْجَعُ الْأُمُورُ

44
3:13

44 When you met, He made them appear as few in your eyes, and made you appear fewer in their eyes, so that God may conclude a predetermined matter. To God all matters revert.

٤٥ يَا أَيُّهَا الَّذِينَ آمَنُوا إِذَا لَقِيتُمْ فِئَةً فَاثْبُتُوا وَاذْكُرُوا اللَّهَ كَثِيرًا لَعَلَّكُمْ تُفْلِحُونَ

45 O you who believe! When you meet a force, stand firm, and remember God much, so that you may prevail.

45
8:15

٤٦ وَأَطِيعُوا اللَّهَ وَرَسُولَهُ وَلَا تَنَازَعُوا فَتَفْشَلُوا وَتَذْهَبَ رِيحُكُمْ ۖ وَاصْبِرُوا ۚ إِنَّ اللَّهَ مَعَ الصَّابِرِينَ

46 And obey God and His Messenger, and do not dispute, lest you falter and lose your courage. And be steadfast. God is with the steadfast.

46
3:103; 4:59; 3:14

٤٧ وَلَا تَكُونُوا كَالَّذِينَ خَرَجُوا مِنْ دِيَارِهِمْ بَطَرًا وَرِئَاءَ النَّاسِ وَيَصُدُّونَ عَنْ سَبِيلِ اللَّهِ ۚ وَاللَّهُ بِمَا يَعْمَلُونَ مُحِيطٌ

47 And do not be like those who left their homes boastfully, showing off before the people, and barring others from the path of God. God comprehends what they do.

٤٨ وَإِذْ زَيَّنَ لَهُمُ الشَّيْطَانُ أَعْمَالَهُمْ وَقَالَ لَا غَالِبَ لَكُمُ الْيَوْمَ مِنَ النَّاسِ وَإِنِّي جَارٌ لَكُمْ ۖ فَلَمَّا تَرَاءَتِ الْفِئَتَانِ نَكَصَ عَلَىٰ عَقِبَيْهِ وَقَالَ إِنِّي بَرِيءٌ مِنْكُمْ إِنِّي أَرَىٰ مَا لَا تَرَوْنَ إِنِّي أَخَافُ اللَّهَ ۚ وَاللَّهُ شَدِيدُ الْعِقَابِ

48
4:120; 14:22; 59:16

48 Satan made their deeds appear good to them, and said, "You cannot be defeated by any people today, and I am at your side." But when the two armies came in sight of one another, he turned on his heels, and said, "I am innocent of you; I see what you do not see; I fear God; God is severe in punishment."

٤٩ إِذْ يَقُولُ الْمُنَافِقُونَ وَالَّذِينَ فِي قُلُوبِهِمْ مَرَضٌ غَرَّ هَٰؤُلَاءِ دِينُهُمْ ۗ وَمَنْ يَتَوَكَّلْ عَلَى اللَّهِ فَإِنَّ اللَّهَ عَزِيزٌ حَكِيمٌ

49
33:12, 32, 60

49 The hypocrites and those in whose hearts is sickness said, "Their religion has deluded these people." But whoever puts his trust in God—God is Mighty and Wise.

٥٠ وَلَوْ تَرَىٰ إِذْ يَتَوَفَّى الَّذِينَ كَفَرُوا ۙ الْمَلَائِكَةُ يَضْرِبُونَ وُجُوهَهُمْ وَأَدْبَارَهُمْ وَذُوقُوا عَذَابَ الْحَرِيقِ

50 If only you could see, as the angels take away those who disbelieve, striking their faces and their backs: "Taste the agony of the Burning."

50
4:97; 6:61, 93; 7:37; 47:27

٥١ ذَٰلِكَ بِمَا قَدَّمَتْ أَيْدِيكُمْ وَأَنَّ اللَّهَ لَيْسَ بِظَلَّامٍ لِلْعَبِيدِ

51 "That is because of what your hands have committed, and because God is not unjust to the servants."

51
3:182; 22:10

٥٢ كَدَأْبِ آلِ فِرْعَوْنَ ۙ وَالَّذِينَ مِنْ قَبْلِهِمْ ۚ كَفَرُوا بِآيَاتِ اللَّهِ فَأَخَذَهُمُ اللَّهُ بِذُنُوبِهِمْ ۗ إِنَّ اللَّهَ قَوِيٌّ شَدِيدُ الْعِقَابِ

52
PP 3:11

52 Like the behavior of the people of Pharaoh, and those before them. They rejected the signs of God, so God seized them for their sins. God is Powerful, Severe in punishment.

٥٣ ذَٰلِكَ بِأَنَّ اللَّهَ لَمْ يَكُ مُغَيِّرًا نِعْمَةً أَنْعَمَهَا عَلَىٰ قَوْمٍ حَتَّىٰ يُغَيِّرُوا مَا بِأَنْفُسِهِمْ ۙ وَأَنَّ اللَّهَ سَمِيعٌ عَلِيمٌ

53 That is because God would never change a blessing He has bestowed on a people unless they change what is within themselves, and because God is Hearing and Knowing.

53
4:79, 114; 13:11; 14:28; 42:30

٥٤ كَدَأْبِ آلِ فِرْعَوْنَ ۙ وَالَّذِينَ مِنْ قَبْلِهِمْ ۚ كَذَّبُوا بِآيَاتِ رَبِّهِمْ فَأَهْلَكْنَاهُمْ بِذُنُوبِهِمْ وَأَغْرَقْنَا آلَ فِرْعَوْنَ ۚ وَكُلٌّ كَانُوا ظَالِمِينَ

54 Such was the case with the people of Pharaoh, and those before them. They denied the signs of their Lord, so We annihilated them for their wrongs, and We drowned the people of Pharaoh—they were all evildoers.

54
3:11; 8:52

٥٥ إِنَّ شَرَّ الدَّوَابِّ عِنْدَ اللَّهِ الَّذِينَ كَفَرُوا فَهُمْ لَا يُؤْمِنُونَ

55 The worst of creatures in God's view are those who disbelieve. They have no faith.

55
2:171; 6:39; 8:22; 10:42

٥٦ الَّذِينَ عَاهَدْتَ مِنْهُمْ ثُمَّ يَنْقُضُونَ عَهْدَهُمْ فِي كُلِّ مَرَّةٍ وَهُمْ لَا يَتَّقُونَ

56 Those of them with whom you made a treaty, but they violate their agreement every time. They are not righteous.

56
2:27, 100; 13:35

٥٧ فَإِمَّا تَثْقَفَنَّهُمْ فِي الْحَرْبِ فَشَرِّدْ بِهِمْ مَنْ خَلْفَهُمْ لَعَلَّهُمْ يَذَّكَّرُونَ

57 If you confront them in battle, make of them a fearsome example for those who follow them, that they may take heed.

57
33:61

٥٨ وَإِمَّا تَخَافَنَّ مِنْ قَوْمٍ خِيَانَةً فَانْبِذْ إِلَيْهِمْ عَلَىٰ سَوَاءٍ ۚ إِنَّ اللَّهَ لَا يُحِبُّ الْخَائِنِينَ

58 If you fear treachery on the part of a people, break off with them in a like manner. God does not like the treacherous.

58
3:175

٥٩ وَلَا يَحْسَبَنَّ الَّذِينَ كَفَرُوا سَبَقُوا ۚ إِنَّهُمْ لَا يُعْجِزُونَ

59 Let not the disbelievers assume that they are ahead. They will not escape.

59
29:4; 24:57

٦٠ وَأَعِدُّوا لَهُمْ مَا اسْتَطَعْتُمْ مِنْ قُوَّةٍ وَمِنْ رِبَاطِ الْخَيْلِ تُرْهِبُونَ بِهِ عَدُوَّ اللَّهِ وَعَدُوَّكُمْ وَآخَرِينَ مِنْ دُونِهِمْ لَا تَعْلَمُونَهُمُ اللَّهُ يَعْلَمُهُمْ ۚ وَمَا تُنْفِقُوا مِنْ شَيْءٍ فِي سَبِيلِ اللَّهِ يُوَفَّ إِلَيْكُمْ وَأَنْتُمْ لَا تُظْلَمُونَ

60 And prepare against them all the power you can muster, and all the cavalry you can mobilize, to terrify thereby God's enemies and your enemies, and others besides them whom you do not know, but God knows them. Whatever you spend in God's way will be repaid to you in full, and you will not be wronged.

60
2:272

٦١ وَإِنْ جَنَحُوا لِلسَّلْمِ فَاجْنَحْ لَهَا وَتَوَكَّلْ عَلَى اللَّهِ ۚ إِنَّهُ هُوَ السَّمِيعُ الْعَلِيمُ

61 But if they incline towards peace, then incline towards it, and put your trust in God. He is the Hearer, the Knower.

61
4:90

٦٢ وَإِنْ يُرِيدُوا أَنْ يَخْدَعُوكَ فَإِنَّ حَسْبَكَ اللَّهُ ۚ هُوَ الَّذِي أَيَّدَكَ بِنَصْرِهِ وَبِالْمُؤْمِنِينَ

62 If they intend to deceive you—God is sufficient for you. It is He who supported you with His aid, and with the believers.

62
2:9; 8:64

٦٣ وَأَلَّفَ بَيْنَ قُلُوبِهِمْ ۚ لَوْ أَنفَقْتَ مَا فِي الْأَرْضِ جَمِيعًا مَّا أَلَّفْتَ بَيْنَ قُلُوبِهِمْ وَلَٰكِنَّ اللَّهَ أَلَّفَ بَيْنَهُمْ ۚ إِنَّهُ عَزِيزٌ حَكِيمٌ

63 And He united their hearts. Had you spent everything on earth, you would not have united their hearts, but God united them together. He is Mighty and Wise.

63
3:103

٦٤ يَا أَيُّهَا النَّبِيُّ حَسْبُكَ اللَّهُ وَمَنِ اتَّبَعَكَ مِنَ الْمُؤْمِنِينَ

64 O prophet! Count on God, and on the believers who have followed you.

64
8:62; 9:59; 39:36; 65:3

٦٥ يَا أَيُّهَا النَّبِيُّ حَرِّضِ الْمُؤْمِنِينَ عَلَى الْقِتَالِ ۚ [a] إِن يَكُن مِّنكُمْ عِشْرُونَ صَابِرُونَ يَغْلِبُوا مِائَتَيْنِ ۚ وَإِن يَكُن مِّنكُم مِّائَةٌ يَغْلِبُوا أَلْفًا مِّنَ الَّذِينَ كَفَرُوا بِأَنَّهُمْ قَوْمٌ لَّا يَفْقَهُونَ [b]

65 O prophet! Rouse the believers to battle. If there are twenty steadfast among you, they will defeat two hundred; and if there are a hundred of you, they will defeat a thousand of those who disbelieve; because they are a people who do not understand.

65
[a] 4:84
[b] 2:249; 5:56

٦٦ الْآنَ خَفَّفَ اللَّهُ عَنكُمْ وَعَلِمَ أَنَّ فِيكُمْ ضَعْفًا ۚ فَإِن يَكُن مِّنكُم مِّائَةٌ صَابِرَةٌ يَغْلِبُوا مِائَتَيْنِ ۚ وَإِن يَكُن مِّنكُمْ أَلْفٌ يَغْلِبُوا أَلْفَيْنِ بِإِذْنِ اللَّهِ ۗ وَاللَّهُ مَعَ الصَّابِرِينَ

66 God has now lightened your burden, knowing that there is weakness in you. If there are a hundred steadfast among you, they will defeat two hundred; and if there are a thousand of you, they will defeat two thousand by God's leave. God is with the steadfast.

66
4:28

٦٧ مَا كَانَ لِنَبِيٍّ أَن يَكُونَ لَهُ أَسْرَىٰ حَتَّىٰ يُثْخِنَ فِي الْأَرْضِ ۚ تُرِيدُونَ عَرَضَ الدُّنْيَا وَاللَّهُ يُرِيدُ الْآخِرَةَ ۗ وَاللَّهُ عَزِيزٌ حَكِيمٌ

67 It is not for a prophet to take prisoners before he has subdued the land. You desire the materials of this world, but God desires the Hereafter. God is Strong and Wise.

67
8:70; 47:4

٦٨ لَّوْلَا كِتَابٌ مِّنَ اللَّهِ سَبَقَ لَمَسَّكُمْ فِيمَا أَخَذْتُمْ عَذَابٌ عَظِيمٌ

68 Were it not for a predetermined decree from God, an awful punishment would have afflicted you for what you have taken.

٦٩ فَكُلُوا مِمَّا غَنِمْتُمْ حَلَالًا طَيِّبًا ۚ وَاتَّقُوا اللَّهَ ۚ إِنَّ اللَّهَ غَفُورٌ رَّحِيمٌ

69 So consume what you have gained, legitimate and wholesome; and remain conscious of God. God is Forgiving and Merciful.

69
2:168; 5:88; 16:114

٧٠ يَا أَيُّهَا النَّبِيُّ قُل لِّمَن فِي أَيْدِيكُم مِّنَ الْأَسْرَىٰ إِن يَعْلَمِ اللَّهُ فِي قُلُوبِكُمْ خَيْرًا يُؤْتِكُمْ خَيْرًا مِّمَّا أُخِذَ مِنكُمْ وَيَغْفِرْ لَكُمْ ۗ وَاللَّهُ غَفُورٌ رَّحِيمٌ

70 O prophet! Say to those you hold prisoners, "If God finds any good in your hearts, He will give you better than what was taken from you, and He will forgive you. God is Forgiving and Merciful."

70
8:67; 47:4

٧١ وَإِنْ يُرِيدُوا خِيَانَتَكَ فَقَدْ خَانُوا اللَّهَ مِنْ قَبْلُ فَأَمْكَنَ مِنْهُمْ ۗ وَاللَّهُ عَلِيمٌ حَكِيمٌ

71   8:27

71 But if they intend to betray you, they have already betrayed God, and He has overpowered them. God is Knowing and Wise.

٧٢ إِنَّ الَّذِينَ آمَنُوا وَهَاجَرُوا وَجَاهَدُوا بِأَمْوَالِهِمْ وَأَنْفُسِهِمْ فِي سَبِيلِ اللَّهِ وَالَّذِينَ آوَوْا وَنَصَرُوا أُولَٰئِكَ بَعْضُهُمْ أَوْلِيَاءُ بَعْضٍ ۚ وَالَّذِينَ آمَنُوا وَلَمْ يُهَاجِرُوا مَا لَكُمْ مِنْ وَلَايَتِهِمْ مِنْ شَيْءٍ حَتَّىٰ يُهَاجِرُوا ۚ وَإِنِ اسْتَنْصَرُوكُمْ فِي الدِّينِ فَعَلَيْكُمُ النَّصْرُ إِلَّا عَلَىٰ قَوْمٍ بَيْنَكُمْ وَبَيْنَهُمْ مِيثَاقٌ ۗ وَاللَّهُ بِمَا تَعْمَلُونَ بَصِيرٌ

72   4:95; 9:20, 41, 44, 81, 88; 49:15

72 Those who believed, and emigrated, and struggled in God's cause with their possessions and their persons, and those who provided shelter and support—these are allies of one another. As for those who believed, but did not emigrate, you owe them no protection, until they have emigrated. But if they ask you for help in religion, you must come to their aid, except against a people with whom you have a treaty. God is Seeing of what you do.

٧٣ وَالَّذِينَ كَفَرُوا بَعْضُهُمْ أَوْلِيَاءُ بَعْضٍ ۚ إِلَّا تَفْعَلُوهُ تَكُنْ فِتْنَةٌ فِي الْأَرْضِ وَفَسَادٌ كَبِيرٌ

73   2:193; 8:39

73 As for those who disbelieve, they are allies of one another. Unless you do this, there will be turmoil in the land, and much corruption.

٧٤ وَالَّذِينَ آمَنُوا وَهَاجَرُوا وَجَاهَدُوا فِي سَبِيلِ اللَّهِ وَالَّذِينَ آوَوْا وَنَصَرُوا أُولَٰئِكَ هُمُ الْمُؤْمِنُونَ حَقًّا ۚ لَهُمْ مَغْفِرَةٌ وَرِزْقٌ كَرِيمٌ

74   2:218; 3:195; 7:157; 8:4; 49:15

74 Those who believed, and emigrated, and struggled for God's cause, and those who gave shelter and support—these are the true believers. They will have forgiveness, and a bountiful provision.

٧٥ وَالَّذِينَ آمَنُوا مِنْ بَعْدُ وَهَاجَرُوا وَجَاهَدُوا مَعَكُمْ فَأُولَٰئِكَ مِنْكُمْ ۚ وَأُولُو الْأَرْحَامِ بَعْضُهُمْ أَوْلَىٰ بِبَعْضٍ فِي كِتَابِ اللَّهِ ۗ إِنَّ اللَّهَ بِكُلِّ شَيْءٍ عَلِيمٌ

75   4:11

75 As for those who believed afterwards, and emigrated and struggled with you—these belong with you. But family members are nearer to one another in the Book of God. God is Cognizant of everything.

Sūrah 9: Al-Tawbah

سُورَةُ ٱلتَّوْبَة (Repentance)

١ بَرَاءَةٌ مِنَ اللَّهِ وَرَسُولِهِ إِلَى الَّذِينَ عَاهَدْتُمْ مِنَ الْمُشْرِكِينَ

1   9:4

1 A declaration of immunity from God and His Messenger to the polytheists with whom you had made a treaty.

٢ فَسِيحُوا فِي الْأَرْضِ أَرْبَعَةَ أَشْهُرٍ وَاعْلَمُوا أَنَّكُمْ غَيْرُ مُعْجِزِي اللَّهِ ۙ وَأَنَّ اللَّهَ مُخْزِي الْكَافِرِينَ

2   2:190; 9:36

2 So travel the land for four months, and know that you cannot escape God, and that God will disgrace the disbelievers.

٣ وَأَذَانٌ مِنَ اللَّهِ وَرَسُولِهِ إِلَى النَّاسِ يَوْمَ الْحَجِّ الْأَكْبَرِ أَنَّ اللَّهَ بَرِيءٌ مِنَ الْمُشْرِكِينَ ۙ وَرَسُولُهُ ۚ فَإِنْ تُبْتُمْ فَهُوَ خَيْرٌ لَكُمْ ۖ وَإِنْ تَوَلَّيْتُمْ فَاعْلَمُوا أَنَّكُمْ غَيْرُ مُعْجِزِي اللَّهِ ۗ وَبَشِّرِ الَّذِينَ كَفَرُوا بِعَذَابٍ أَلِيمٍ

3 And a proclamation from God and His Messenger to the people on the day of the Greater Pilgrimage, that God has disowned the polytheists, and so did His Messenger. If you repent, it will be better for you. But if you turn away, know that you cannot escape God. And announce to those who disbelieve a painful punishment.

٤ إِلَّا الَّذِينَ عَاهَدْتُمْ مِنَ الْمُشْرِكِينَ ثُمَّ لَمْ يَنْقُصُوكُمْ شَيْئًا وَلَمْ يُظَاهِرُوا عَلَيْكُمْ أَحَدًا فَأَتِمُّوا إِلَيْهِمْ عَهْدَهُمْ إِلَىٰ مُدَّتِهِمْ ۚ إِنَّ اللَّهَ يُحِبُّ الْمُتَّقِينَ

4
9:1, 7

4 Except for those among the polytheists with whom you had made a treaty, and did not violate any of its terms, nor aided anyone against you. So fulfill the treaty with them to the end of its term. God loves the righteous.

٥ فَإِذَا انْسَلَخَ الْأَشْهُرُ الْحُرُمُ[a] فَاقْتُلُوا الْمُشْرِكِينَ حَيْثُ وَجَدْتُمُوهُمْ وَخُذُوهُمْ وَاحْصُرُوهُمْ وَاقْعُدُوا لَهُمْ كُلَّ مَرْصَدٍ ۚ فَإِنْ تَابُوا وَأَقَامُوا الصَّلَاةَ وَآتَوُا الزَّكَاةَ فَخَلُّوا سَبِيلَهُمْ[b] ۚ إِنَّ اللَّهَ غَفُورٌ رَحِيمٌ

5
[a] 9:36
[b] 2:191; 4:89; 22:40; 33:61

5 When the Sacred Months have passed, kill the polytheists wherever you find them. And capture them, and besiege them, and lie in wait for them at every ambush. But if they repent, and perform the prayers, and pay the alms, then let them go their way. God is Most Forgiving, Most Merciful.

٦ وَإِنْ أَحَدٌ مِنَ الْمُشْرِكِينَ اسْتَجَارَكَ فَأَجِرْهُ حَتَّىٰ يَسْمَعَ كَلَامَ اللَّهِ ثُمَّ أَبْلِغْهُ مَأْمَنَهُ ۚ ذَٰلِكَ بِأَنَّهُمْ قَوْمٌ لَا يَعْلَمُونَ

6 And if anyone of the polytheists asks you for protection, give him protection so that he may hear the Word of God; then escort him to his place of safety. That is because they are a people who do not know.

٧ كَيْفَ يَكُونُ لِلْمُشْرِكِينَ عَهْدٌ عِنْدَ اللَّهِ وَعِنْدَ رَسُولِهِ إِلَّا الَّذِينَ عَاهَدْتُمْ عِنْدَ الْمَسْجِدِ الْحَرَامِ ۖ فَمَا اسْتَقَامُوا لَكُمْ فَاسْتَقِيمُوا لَهُمْ ۚ إِنَّ اللَّهَ يُحِبُّ الْمُتَّقِينَ

7
9:1, 4

7 How can there be a treaty with the polytheists on the part of God and His Messenger, except for those with whom you made a treaty at the Sacred Mosque? As long as they are upright with you, be upright with them. God loves the pious.

٨ كَيْفَ وَإِنْ يَظْهَرُوا عَلَيْكُمْ لَا يَرْقُبُوا فِيكُمْ إِلًّا وَلَا ذِمَّةً ۚ يُرْضُونَكُمْ بِأَفْوَاهِهِمْ وَتَأْبَىٰ قُلُوبُهُمْ وَأَكْثَرُهُمْ فَاسِقُونَ

8
9:10

8 How? Whenever they overcome you, they respect neither kinship nor treaty with you. They satisfy you with lip service, but their hearts refuse, and most of them are immoral.

٩ اشْتَرَوْا بِآيَاتِ اللَّهِ ثَمَنًا قَلِيلًا فَصَدُّوا عَنْ سَبِيلِهِ ۚ إِنَّهُمْ سَاءَ مَا كَانُوا يَعْمَلُونَ

9 They traded away God's revelations for a cheap price, so they barred others from His path. How evil is what they did.

Sūrah 9: Al-Tawbah — 205

١٠ لَا يَرْقُبُونَ فِي مُؤْمِنٍ إِلًّا وَلَا ذِمَّةً ۚ وَأُولَٰئِكَ هُمُ الْمُعْتَدُونَ

10   9:8

10 Towards a believer they respect neither kinship nor treaty. These are the transgressors.

١١ فَإِن تَابُوا وَأَقَامُوا الصَّلَاةَ وَآتَوُا الزَّكَاةَ فَإِخْوَانُكُمْ فِي الدِّينِ ۗ وَنُفَصِّلُ الْآيَاتِ لِقَوْمٍ يَعْلَمُونَ

11 But if they repent, and perform the prayers, and give the obligatory charity, then they are your brethren in faith. We detail the revelations for a people who know.

١٢ وَإِن نَّكَثُوا أَيْمَانَهُم مِّن بَعْدِ عَهْدِهِمْ وَطَعَنُوا فِي دِينِكُمْ فَقَاتِلُوا أَئِمَّةَ الْكُفْرِ ۙ إِنَّهُمْ لَا أَيْمَانَ لَهُمْ لَعَلَّهُمْ يَنتَهُونَ

12 But if they violate their oaths after their pledge, and attack your religion, then fight the leaders of disbelief—they have no faith—so that they may desist.

١٣ أَلَا تُقَاتِلُونَ قَوْمًا نَّكَثُوا أَيْمَانَهُمْ وَهَمُّوا بِإِخْرَاجِ الرَّسُولِ وَهُم بَدَءُوكُمْ أَوَّلَ مَرَّةٍ ۚ أَتَخْشَوْنَهُمْ ۚ فَاللَّهُ أَحَقُّ أَن تَخْشَوْهُ إِن كُنتُم مُّؤْمِنِينَ

13   8:30; 9:40; 60:1

13 Will you not fight a people who violated their oaths, and planned to exile the Messenger, and initiated hostilities against you? Do you fear them? It is God you should fear, if you are believers.

١٤ قَاتِلُوهُمْ يُعَذِّبْهُمُ اللَّهُ بِأَيْدِيكُمْ وَيُخْزِهِمْ وَيَنصُرْكُمْ عَلَيْهِمْ وَيَشْفِ صُدُورَ قَوْمٍ مُّؤْمِنِينَ

14 Fight them. God will punish them at your hands, and humiliate them, and help you against them, and heal the hearts of a believing people.

١٥ وَيُذْهِبْ غَيْظَ قُلُوبِهِمْ ۗ وَيَتُوبُ اللَّهُ عَلَىٰ مَن يَشَاءُ ۗ وَاللَّهُ عَلِيمٌ حَكِيمٌ

15 And He will remove the anger of their hearts. God redeems whomever He wills. God is Knowledgeable and Wise.

١٦ أَمْ حَسِبْتُمْ أَن تُتْرَكُوا وَلَمَّا يَعْلَمِ اللَّهُ الَّذِينَ جَاهَدُوا مِنكُمْ وَلَمْ يَتَّخِذُوا مِن دُونِ اللَّهِ وَلَا رَسُولِهِ وَلَا الْمُؤْمِنِينَ وَلِيجَةً ۚ وَاللَّهُ خَبِيرٌ بِمَا تَعْمَلُونَ

16   3:142; 29:2

16 Or do you think that you will be left alone, without God identifying which of you will strive, and take no supporters apart from God, His Messenger, and the believers? God is well Aware of what you do.

١٧ مَا كَانَ لِلْمُشْرِكِينَ أَن يَعْمُرُوا مَسَاجِدَ اللَّهِ شَاهِدِينَ عَلَىٰ أَنفُسِهِم بِالْكُفْرِ ۚ أُولَٰئِكَ حَبِطَتْ أَعْمَالُهُمْ وَفِي النَّارِ هُمْ خَالِدُونَ

17   4:62; 9:107

17 It is not for the polytheists to attend God's places of worship while professing their disbelief. These—their works are in vain, and in the Fire they will abide.

١٨ إِنَّمَا يَعْمُرُ مَسَاجِدَ اللَّهِ مَنْ آمَنَ بِاللَّهِ وَالْيَوْمِ الْآخِرِ وَأَقَامَ الصَّلَاةَ وَآتَى الزَّكَاةَ وَلَمْ يَخْشَ إِلَّا اللَّهَ ۖ فَعَسَىٰ أُولَٰئِكَ أَن يَكُونُوا مِنَ الْمُهْتَدِينَ

18 The only people to attend God's places of worship are those who believe in God and the Last Day, and pray regularly, and practice regular charity, and fear none but God. These are most likely to be guided.

١٩ أَجَعَلْتُمْ سِقَايَةَ الْحَاجِّ وَعِمَارَةَ الْمَسْجِدِ الْحَرَامِ كَمَنْ آمَنَ بِاللَّهِ وَالْيَوْمِ الْآخِرِ وَجَاهَدَ فِي سَبِيلِ اللَّهِ ۚ لَا يَسْتَوُونَ عِندَ اللَّهِ ۗ وَاللَّهُ لَا يَهْدِي الْقَوْمَ الظَّالِمِينَ

19 Do you consider giving water to pilgrims and maintaining the Sacred Mosque the same as believing in God and the Last Day and striving in God's path? They are not equal in God's sight. God does not guide the unjust people.

٢٠ الَّذِينَ آمَنُوا وَهَاجَرُوا وَجَاهَدُوا فِي سَبِيلِ اللَّهِ بِأَمْوَالِهِمْ وَأَنفُسِهِمْ أَعْظَمُ دَرَجَةً عِندَ اللَّهِ ۚ وَأُولَٰئِكَ هُمُ الْفَائِزُونَ

20
2:218; 8:72; 16:41; 22:58

20 Those who believe, and emigrate, and strive in God's path with their possessions and their persons, are of a higher rank with God. These are the winners.

٢١ يُبَشِّرُهُمْ رَبُّهُم بِرَحْمَةٍ مِّنْهُ وَرِضْوَانٍ وَجَنَّاتٍ لَّهُمْ فِيهَا نَعِيمٌ مُّقِيمٌ

21–22
2:25; 17:9; 18:2

21 Their Lord announces to them good news of mercy from Him, and acceptance, and gardens wherein they will have lasting bliss.

٢٢ خَالِدِينَ فِيهَا أَبَدًا ۚ إِنَّ اللَّهَ عِندَهُ أَجْرٌ عَظِيمٌ

22 Abiding therein forever. With God is a great reward.

٢٣ يَا أَيُّهَا الَّذِينَ آمَنُوا لَا تَتَّخِذُوا آبَاءَكُمْ وَإِخْوَانَكُمْ أَوْلِيَاءَ إِنِ اسْتَحَبُّوا الْكُفْرَ عَلَى الْإِيمَانِ ۚ وَمَن يَتَوَلَّهُم مِّنكُمْ فَأُولَٰئِكَ هُمُ الظَّالِمُونَ

23
3:28; 4:139, 144; 58:22

23 O you who believe! Do not ally yourselves with your parents and your siblings if they prefer disbelief to belief. Whoever of you allies himself with them—these are the wrongdoers.

٢٤ قُلْ إِن كَانَ آبَاؤُكُمْ وَأَبْنَاؤُكُمْ وَإِخْوَانُكُمْ وَأَزْوَاجُكُمْ وَعَشِيرَتُكُمْ وَأَمْوَالٌ اقْتَرَفْتُمُوهَا وَتِجَارَةٌ تَخْشَوْنَ كَسَادَهَا وَمَسَاكِنُ تَرْضَوْنَهَا أَحَبَّ إِلَيْكُم مِّنَ اللَّهِ وَرَسُولِهِ وَجِهَادٍ فِي سَبِيلِهِ فَتَرَبَّصُوا حَتَّىٰ يَأْتِيَ اللَّهُ بِأَمْرِهِ ۗ وَاللَّهُ لَا يَهْدِي الْقَوْمَ الْفَاسِقِينَ

24
58:22

24 Say, "If your parents, and your children, and your siblings, and your spouses, and your relatives, and the wealth you have acquired, and a business you worry about, and homes you love, are more dear to you than God, and His Messenger, and the struggle in His cause, then wait until God executes His judgment." God does not guide the sinful people.

٢٥ لَقَدْ نَصَرَكُمُ اللَّهُ فِي مَوَاطِنَ كَثِيرَةٍ ۙ وَيَوْمَ حُنَيْنٍ ۙ إِذْ أَعْجَبَتْكُمْ كَثْرَتُكُمْ فَلَمْ تُغْنِ عَنكُمْ شَيْئًا وَضَاقَتْ عَلَيْكُمُ الْأَرْضُ بِمَا رَحُبَتْ ثُمَّ وَلَّيْتُم مُّدْبِرِينَ

25 God has given you victory in numerous regions; but on the day of Hunayn, your great number impressed you, but it availed you nothing; and the land, as spacious as it was, narrowed for you; and you turned your backs in retreat.

٢٦ ثُمَّ أَنزَلَ اللَّهُ سَكِينَتَهُ عَلَىٰ رَسُولِهِ وَعَلَى الْمُؤْمِنِينَ وَأَنزَلَ جُنُودًا لَّمْ تَرَوْهَا وَعَذَّبَ الَّذِينَ كَفَرُوا ۚ وَذَٰلِكَ جَزَاءُ الْكَافِرِينَ

26
9:40; 48:4, 18, 26

26 Then God sent down His serenity upon His Messenger, and upon the believers; and He sent down troops you did not see; and He punished those who disbelieved. Such is the recompense of the disbelievers.

٢٧ ثُمَّ يَتُوبُ اللَّهُ مِن بَعْدِ ذَٰلِكَ عَلَىٰ مَن يَشَاءُ ۗ وَاللَّهُ غَفُورٌ رَّحِيمٌ

27 Then, after that, God will relent towards whomever He wills. God is Forgiving and Merciful.

٢٨ يَا أَيُّهَا الَّذِينَ آمَنُوا إِنَّمَا الْمُشْرِكُونَ نَجَسٌ فَلَا يَقْرَبُوا الْمَسْجِدَ الْحَرَامَ بَعْدَ عَامِهِمْ هَٰذَا ۚ وَإِنْ خِفْتُمْ عَيْلَةً فَسَوْفَ يُغْنِيكُمُ اللَّهُ مِن فَضْلِهِ إِن شَاءَ ۚ إِنَّ اللَّهَ عَلِيمٌ حَكِيمٌ

28
9:95

28 O you who believe! The polytheists are polluted, so let them not approach the Sacred Mosque after this year of theirs. And if you fear poverty, God will enrich you from His grace, if He wills. God is Aware and Wise.

٢٩ قَاتِلُوا الَّذِينَ لَا يُؤْمِنُونَ بِاللَّهِ وَلَا بِالْيَوْمِ الْآخِرِ وَلَا يُحَرِّمُونَ مَا حَرَّمَ اللَّهُ وَرَسُولُهُ وَلَا يَدِينُونَ دِينَ الْحَقِّ مِنَ الَّذِينَ أُوتُوا الْكِتَابَ حَتَّىٰ يُعْطُوا الْجِزْيَةَ عَن يَدٍ وَهُمْ صَاغِرُونَ

29 Fight those who do not believe in God, nor in the Last Day, nor forbid what God and His Messenger have forbidden, nor abide by the religion of truth—from among those who received the Scripture—until they pay the due tax, willingly or unwillingly.

٣٠ وَقَالَتِ الْيَهُودُ عُزَيْرٌ ابْنُ اللَّهِ وَقَالَتِ النَّصَارَى الْمَسِيحُ ابْنُ اللَّهِ ۖ ذَٰلِكَ قَوْلُهُم بِأَفْوَاهِهِمْ ۖ يُضَاهِئُونَ قَوْلَ الَّذِينَ كَفَرُوا مِن قَبْلُ ۚ قَاتَلَهُمُ اللَّهُ ۚ أَنَّىٰ يُؤْفَكُونَ

30
5:18

30 The Jews said, "Ezra is the son of God," and the Christians said, "The Messiah is the son of God." These are their statements, out of their mouths. They emulate the statements of those who blasphemed before. May God assail them! How deceived they are!

٣١ اتَّخَذُوا أَحْبَارَهُمْ وَرُهْبَانَهُمْ أَرْبَابًا مِّن دُونِ اللَّهِ وَالْمَسِيحَ ابْنَ مَرْيَمَ وَمَا أُمِرُوا إِلَّا لِيَعْبُدُوا إِلَٰهًا وَاحِدًا ۖ لَّا إِلَٰهَ إِلَّا هُوَ ۚ سُبْحَانَهُ عَمَّا يُشْرِكُونَ

31
3:64, 79; 12:40; 17:33

31 They have taken their rabbis and their priests as lords instead of God, as well as the Messiah son of Mary. Although they were commanded to worship none but The One God. There is no god except He. Glory be to Him; High above what they associate with Him.

٣٢ يُرِيدُونَ أَن يُطْفِئُوا نُورَ اللَّهِ بِأَفْوَاهِهِمْ وَيَأْبَى اللَّهُ إِلَّا أَن يُتِمَّ نُورَهُ وَلَوْ كَرِهَ الْكَافِرُونَ

32 They want to extinguish God's light with their mouths, but God refuses except to complete His light, even though the disbelievers dislike it.

32
61:8

٣٣ هُوَ الَّذِي أَرْسَلَ رَسُولَهُ بِالْهُدَىٰ وَدِينِ الْحَقِّ لِيُظْهِرَهُ عَلَى الدِّينِ كُلِّهِ وَلَوْ كَرِهَ الْمُشْرِكُونَ

33 It is He who sent His Messenger with the guidance and the religion of truth, in order to make it prevail over all religions, even though the idolaters dislike it.

33
pp *48:28; 61:9*

٣٤ يَا أَيُّهَا الَّذِينَ آمَنُوا إِنَّ كَثِيرًا مِنَ الْأَحْبَارِ وَالرُّهْبَانِ لَيَأْكُلُونَ أَمْوَالَ النَّاسِ بِالْبَاطِلِ وَيَصُدُّونَ عَن سَبِيلِ اللَّهِ ۗ وَالَّذِينَ يَكْنِزُونَ الذَّهَبَ وَالْفِضَّةَ وَلَا يُنفِقُونَهَا فِي سَبِيلِ اللَّهِ فَبَشِّرْهُم بِعَذَابٍ أَلِيمٍ

34 O you who believe! Many of the rabbis and priests consume people's wealth illicitly, and hinder from God's path. Those who hoard gold and silver, and do not spend them in God's cause, inform them of a painful punishment.

34
2:188; 4:29, 161

٣٥ يَوْمَ يُحْمَىٰ عَلَيْهَا فِي نَارِ جَهَنَّمَ فَتُكْوَىٰ بِهَا جِبَاهُهُمْ وَجُنُوبُهُمْ وَظُهُورُهُمْ ۖ هَٰذَا مَا كَنَزْتُمْ لِأَنفُسِكُمْ فَذُوقُوا مَا كُنتُمْ تَكْنِزُونَ

35 On the Day when they will be heated in the Fire of Hell, then their foreheads, and their sides, and their backs will be branded with them: "This is what you hoarded for yourselves; so taste what you used to hoard."

٣٦ إِنَّ عِدَّةَ الشُّهُورِ عِندَ اللَّهِ اثْنَا عَشَرَ شَهْرًا فِي كِتَابِ اللَّهِ يَوْمَ خَلَقَ السَّمَاوَاتِ وَالْأَرْضَ مِنْهَا أَرْبَعَةٌ حُرُمٌ ۚ ذَٰلِكَ الدِّينُ الْقَيِّمُ ۚ فَلَا تَظْلِمُوا فِيهِنَّ أَنفُسَكُمْ ۚ وَقَاتِلُوا الْمُشْرِكِينَ كَافَّةً كَمَا يُقَاتِلُونَكُمْ كَافَّةً ۚ وَاعْلَمُوا أَنَّ اللَّهَ مَعَ الْمُتَّقِينَ

36 The number of months, according to God, is twelve months—in the decree of God—since the Day He created the heavens and the earth, of which four are sacred. This is the correct religion. So do not wrong yourselves during them. And fight the polytheists collectively, as they fight you collectively, and know that God is with the righteous.

36
2:190; 9:2

٣٧ إِنَّمَا النَّسِيءُ زِيَادَةٌ فِي الْكُفْرِ ۖ يُضَلُّ بِهِ الَّذِينَ كَفَرُوا يُحِلُّونَهُ عَامًا وَيُحَرِّمُونَهُ عَامًا لِيُوَاطِئُوا عِدَّةَ مَا حَرَّمَ اللَّهُ فَيُحِلُّوا مَا حَرَّمَ اللَّهُ ۚ زُيِّنَ لَهُمْ سُوءُ أَعْمَالِهِمْ ۗ وَاللَّهُ لَا يَهْدِي الْقَوْمَ الْكَافِرِينَ

37 Postponement is an increase in disbelief—by which those who disbelieve are led astray. They allow it one year, and forbid it another year, in order to conform to the number made sacred by God, thus permitting what God has forbidden. The evil of their deeds seems good to them. God does not guide the disbelieving people.

٣٨ يَا أَيُّهَا الَّذِينَ آمَنُوا مَا لَكُمْ إِذَا قِيلَ لَكُمُ انفِرُوا فِي سَبِيلِ اللَّهِ اثَّاقَلْتُمْ إِلَى الْأَرْضِ ۚ أَرَضِيتُم بِالْحَيَاةِ الدُّنْيَا مِنَ الْآخِرَةِ ۚ فَمَا مَتَاعُ الْحَيَاةِ الدُّنْيَا فِي الْآخِرَةِ إِلَّا قَلِيلٌ

38
3:167; 9:81

38 O you who believe! What is the matter with you, when it is said to you, "Mobilize in the cause of God," you cling heavily to the earth? Do you prefer the present life to the Hereafter? The enjoyment of the present life, compared to the Hereafter, is only a little.

٣٩ إِلَّا تَنفِرُوا يُعَذِّبْكُمْ عَذَابًا أَلِيمًا وَيَسْتَبْدِلْ قَوْمًا غَيْرَكُمْ وَلَا تَضُرُّوهُ شَيْئًا ۗ وَاللَّهُ عَلَىٰ كُلِّ شَيْءٍ قَدِيرٌ

39 Unless you mobilize, He will punish you most painfully, and will replace you with another people, and you will not harm Him at all. God has power over all things.

٤٠ إِلَّا تَنصُرُوهُ فَقَدْ نَصَرَهُ اللَّهُ إِذْ أَخْرَجَهُ الَّذِينَ كَفَرُوا ثَانِيَ اثْنَيْنِ إِذْ هُمَا فِي الْغَارِ إِذْ يَقُولُ لِصَاحِبِهِ لَا تَحْزَنْ إِنَّ اللَّهَ مَعَنَا ۖ فَأَنزَلَ اللَّهُ سَكِينَتَهُ عَلَيْهِ وَأَيَّدَهُ بِجُنُودٍ لَّمْ تَرَوْهَا وَجَعَلَ كَلِمَةَ الَّذِينَ كَفَرُوا السُّفْلَىٰ ۗ وَكَلِمَةُ اللَّهِ هِيَ الْعُلْيَا ۗ وَاللَّهُ عَزِيزٌ حَكِيمٌ

40
9:26; 16:128; 33:9

40 If you do not help him, God has already helped him, when those who disbelieved expelled him, and he was the second of two in the cave. He said to his friend, "Do not worry, God is with us." And God made His tranquility descend upon him, and supported him with forces you did not see, and made the word of those who disbelieved the lowest, while the Word of God is the Highest. God is Mighty and Wise.

٤١ انفِرُوا خِفَافًا وَثِقَالًا وَجَاهِدُوا بِأَمْوَالِكُمْ وَأَنفُسِكُمْ فِي سَبِيلِ اللَّهِ ۚ ذَٰلِكُمْ خَيْرٌ لَّكُمْ إِن كُنتُمْ تَعْلَمُونَ

41
2:184; 61:11

41 Mobilize, light or heavy, and strive with your possessions and your lives in the cause of God. That is better for you, if you only knew.

٤٢ لَوْ كَانَ عَرَضًا قَرِيبًا وَسَفَرًا قَاصِدًا لَّاتَّبَعُوكَ وَلَٰكِن بَعُدَتْ عَلَيْهِمُ الشُّقَّةُ ۚ وَسَيَحْلِفُونَ بِاللَّهِ لَوِ اسْتَطَعْنَا لَخَرَجْنَا مَعَكُمْ يُهْلِكُونَ أَنفُسَهُمْ وَاللَّهُ يَعْلَمُ إِنَّهُمْ لَكَاذِبُونَ

42
3:167; 9:95

42 Had the gain been immediate, and the journey shorter, they would have followed you; but the distance seemed too long for them. Still they swear by God: "Had we been able, we would have marched out with you." They damn their own souls, and God knows that they are lying.

٤٣ عَفَا اللَّهُ عَنكَ لِمَ أَذِنتَ لَهُمْ حَتَّىٰ يَتَبَيَّنَ لَكَ الَّذِينَ صَدَقُوا وَتَعْلَمَ الْكَاذِبِينَ

43–47
9:83

43 May God pardon you! Why did you give them permission before it became clear to you who are the truthful ones, and who are the liars?

٤٤ لَا يَسْتَأْذِنُكَ الَّذِينَ يُؤْمِنُونَ بِاللَّهِ وَالْيَوْمِ الْآخِرِ أَن يُجَاهِدُوا بِأَمْوَالِهِمْ وَأَنفُسِهِمْ ۗ وَاللَّهُ عَلِيمٌ بِالْمُتَّقِينَ

44 Those who believe in God and the Last Day do not ask you for exemption from striving with their possessions and their lives. God is fully aware of the righteous.

٤٥ إِنَّمَا يَسْتَأْذِنُكَ الَّذِينَ لَا يُؤْمِنُونَ بِاللَّهِ وَالْيَوْمِ الْآخِرِ وَارْتَابَتْ قُلُوبُهُمْ فَهُمْ فِي رَيْبِهِمْ يَتَرَدَّدُونَ

45 Only those who do not believe in God and the Last Day ask you for exemption. Their hearts are full of doubts, so they waver in their doubts.

٤٦ وَلَوْ أَرَادُوا الْخُرُوجَ لَأَعَدُّوا لَهُ عُدَّةً وَلَٰكِن كَرِهَ اللَّهُ انبِعَاثَهُمْ فَثَبَّطَهُمْ وَقِيلَ اقْعُدُوا مَعَ الْقَاعِدِينَ

46 Had they wanted to mobilize, they would have made preparations for it; but God disliked their participation, so he held them back, and it was said, "Stay behind with those who stay behind."

٤٧ لَوْ خَرَجُوا فِيكُم مَّا زَادُوكُمْ إِلَّا خَبَالًا وَلَأَوْضَعُوا خِلَالَكُمْ يَبْغُونَكُمُ الْفِتْنَةَ وَفِيكُمْ سَمَّاعُونَ لَهُمْ ۗ وَاللَّهُ عَلِيمٌ بِالظَّالِمِينَ

47 Had they mobilized with you, they would have added only to your difficulties, and they would have spread rumors in your midst, trying to sow discord among you. Some of you are avid listeners to them. God is Aware of the wrongdoers.

٤٨ لَقَدِ ابْتَغَوُا الْفِتْنَةَ مِن قَبْلُ وَقَلَّبُوا لَكَ الْأُمُورَ حَتَّىٰ جَاءَ الْحَقُّ وَظَهَرَ أَمْرُ اللَّهِ وَهُمْ كَارِهُونَ

48 They tried to cause conflict before, and they hatched plots against you, until the truth prevailed, and the command of God became evident—in spite of their dislike.

٤٩ وَمِنْهُم مَّن يَقُولُ ائْذَن لِّي وَلَا تَفْتِنِّي ۚ أَلَا فِي الْفِتْنَةِ سَقَطُوا ۗ وَإِنَّ جَهَنَّمَ لَمُحِيطَةٌ بِالْكَافِرِينَ

49 Among them is he who says, "Excuse me, and do not trouble me." In fact, they sunk into trouble. In fact, Hell will engulf the disbelievers.

49
29:54

٥٠ إِن تُصِبْكَ حَسَنَةٌ تَسُؤْهُمْ ۖ وَإِن تُصِبْكَ مُصِيبَةٌ يَقُولُوا قَدْ أَخَذْنَا أَمْرَنَا مِن قَبْلُ وَيَتَوَلَّوا وَّهُمْ فَرِحُونَ

50 If something good happens to you, it upsets them; and if a calamity befalls you, they say, "We took our precautions in advance," and they depart, happy.

50
3:120; 4:71

٥١ قُل لَّن يُصِيبَنَا إِلَّا مَا كَتَبَ اللَّهُ لَنَا هُوَ مَوْلَانَا ۚ وَعَلَى اللَّهِ فَلْيَتَوَكَّلِ الْمُؤْمِنُونَ

51 Say, "Nothing will happen to us except what God has ordained for us; He is our Protector." In God let the faithful put their trust.

51
57:22

٥٢ قُلْ هَلْ تَرَبَّصُونَ بِنَا إِلَّا إِحْدَى الْحُسْنَيَيْنِ ۖ وَنَحْنُ نَتَرَبَّصُ بِكُمْ أَن يُصِيبَكُمُ اللَّهُ بِعَذَابٍ مِّنْ عِندِهِ أَوْ بِأَيْدِينَا ۖ فَتَرَبَّصُوا إِنَّا مَعَكُم مُّتَرَبِّصُونَ

52 Say, "Are you expecting for us anything other than one of the two excellences? As for us: we are expecting that God will afflict you with a punishment from Himself, or at our hands. So wait, we are waiting with you."

52
6:158; 20:135; 52:31

٥٣ قُلْ أَنْفِقُوا طَوْعًا أَوْ كَرْهًا لَنْ يُتَقَبَّلَ مِنْكُمْ ۖ إِنَّكُمْ كُنْتُمْ قَوْمًا فَاسِقِينَ

53 Say, "Whether you spend willingly or unwillingly, it will not be accepted from you. You are evil people."

٥٤ وَمَا مَنَعَهُمْ أَنْ تُقْبَلَ مِنْهُمْ نَفَقَاتُهُمْ إِلَّا أَنَّهُمْ كَفَرُوا بِاللَّهِ وَبِرَسُولِهِ وَلَا يَأْتُونَ الصَّلَاةَ إِلَّا وَهُمْ كُسَالَىٰ وَلَا يُنْفِقُونَ إِلَّا وَهُمْ كَارِهُونَ

54
4:142

54 What prevents the acceptance of their contributions is nothing but the fact that they disbelieved in God and His Messenger, and that they do not approach the prayer except lazily, and that they do not spend except grudgingly.

٥٥ فَلَا تُعْجِبْكَ أَمْوَالُهُمْ وَلَا أَوْلَادُهُمْ ۚ إِنَّمَا يُرِيدُ اللَّهُ لِيُعَذِّبَهُمْ بِهَا فِي الْحَيَاةِ الدُّنْيَا وَتَزْهَقَ أَنْفُسُهُمْ وَهُمْ كَافِرُونَ

55
3:10; 9:85; 34:35

55 Let neither their possessions nor their children impress you. God intends to torment them through them in this worldly life, and that their souls depart while they are disbelievers.

٥٦ وَيَحْلِفُونَ بِاللَّهِ إِنَّهُمْ لَمِنْكُمْ وَمَا هُمْ مِنْكُمْ وَلَٰكِنَّهُمْ قَوْمٌ يَفْرَقُونَ

56
9:62, 74, 95–95

56 They swear by God that they are of you. But they are not of you. They are divisive people.

٥٧ لَوْ يَجِدُونَ مَلْجَأً أَوْ مَغَارَاتٍ أَوْ مُدَّخَلًا لَوَلَّوْا إِلَيْهِ وَهُمْ يَجْمَحُونَ

57
9:62, 74, 95–96

57 Were they to find a shelter, or a cave, or a hideout, they would go to it, rushing.

٥٨ وَمِنْهُمْ مَنْ يَلْمِزُكَ فِي الصَّدَقَاتِ فَإِنْ أُعْطُوا مِنْهَا رَضُوا وَإِنْ لَمْ يُعْطَوْا مِنْهَا إِذَا هُمْ يَسْخَطُونَ

58
9:79

58 And among them are those who criticize you in regard to charities. If they are given some of it, they become pleased; but if they are not given any, they grow resentful.

٥٩ وَلَوْ أَنَّهُمْ رَضُوا مَا آتَاهُمُ اللَّهُ وَرَسُولُهُ وَقَالُوا حَسْبُنَا اللَّهُ سَيُؤْتِينَا اللَّهُ مِنْ فَضْلِهِ وَرَسُولُهُ إِنَّا إِلَى اللَّهِ رَاغِبُونَ

59
8:64

59 If only they were content with what God and His Messenger have given them, and said, "God is sufficient for us; God will give us of His bounty, and so will His Messenger; to God we eagerly turn."

٦٠ إِنَّمَا الصَّدَقَاتُ لِلْفُقَرَاءِ وَالْمَسَاكِينِ وَالْعَامِلِينَ عَلَيْهَا وَالْمُؤَلَّفَةِ قُلُوبُهُمْ وَفِي الرِّقَابِ وَالْغَارِمِينَ وَفِي سَبِيلِ اللَّهِ وَابْنِ السَّبِيلِ ۖ فَرِيضَةً مِنَ اللَّهِ ۗ وَاللَّهُ عَلِيمٌ حَكِيمٌ

60 Charities are for the poor, and the destitute, and those who administer them, and for reconciling hearts, and for freeing slaves, and for those in debt, and in the path of God, and for the traveler in need—an obligation from God. God is All-Knowing, Most Wise.

٦١ وَمِنْهُمُ الَّذِينَ يُؤْذُونَ النَّبِيَّ وَيَقُولُونَ هُوَ أُذُنٌ ۚ قُلْ أُذُنُ خَيْرٍ لَكُمْ يُؤْمِنُ بِاللَّهِ وَيُؤْمِنُ لِلْمُؤْمِنِينَ وَرَحْمَةٌ لِلَّذِينَ آمَنُوا مِنْكُمْ ۚ وَالَّذِينَ يُؤْذُونَ رَسُولَ اللَّهِ لَهُمْ عَذَابٌ أَلِيمٌ

61
33:57

61 And among them are those who insult the Prophet, and say, "He is all ears." Say, "He listens for your own good. He believes in God, and trusts the believers, and is mercy for those of you who believe." Those who insult the Messenger of God will have a painful penalty.

٦٢ يَحْلِفُونَ بِاللَّهِ لَكُمْ لِيُرْضُوكُمْ وَاللَّهُ وَرَسُولُهُ أَحَقُّ أَنْ يُرْضُوهُ إِنْ كَانُوا مُؤْمِنِينَ

62
9:57, 74, 95–96

62 They swear to you by God to please you. But it is more proper for them to please God and His Messenger, if they are believers.

٦٣ أَلَمْ يَعْلَمُوا أَنَّهُ مَنْ يُحَادِدِ اللَّهَ وَرَسُولَهُ فَأَنَّ لَهُ نَارَ جَهَنَّمَ خَالِدًا فِيهَا ۚ ذَٰلِكَ الْخِزْيُ الْعَظِيمُ

63
58:5, 20

63 Do they not know that whoever opposes God and His Messenger, will have the Fire of Hell, abiding in it forever? That is the supreme disgrace.

٦٤ يَحْذَرُ الْمُنَافِقُونَ أَنْ تُنَزَّلَ عَلَيْهِمْ سُورَةٌ تُنَبِّئُهُمْ بِمَا فِي قُلُوبِهِمْ ۚ قُلِ اسْتَهْزِئُوا إِنَّ اللَّهَ مُخْرِجٌ مَا تَحْذَرُونَ

64
9:86, 127; 47:20

64 The hypocrites worry lest a chapter may be revealed about them, informing them of what is in their hearts. Say, "Go on mocking; God will bring out what you fear."

٦٥ وَلَئِنْ سَأَلْتَهُمْ لَيَقُولُنَّ إِنَّمَا كُنَّا نَخُوضُ وَنَلْعَبُ ۚ قُلْ أَبِاللَّهِ وَآيَاتِهِ وَرَسُولِهِ كُنْتُمْ تَسْتَهْزِئُونَ

65
6:68, 91; 47:29; 52:11; 43:83; 70:42

65 If you ask them, they will say, "We were just joking and playing." Say, "Were you making jokes about God, His revelations, and His Messenger?"

٦٦ لَا تَعْتَذِرُوا قَدْ كَفَرْتُمْ بَعْدَ إِيمَانِكُمْ ۚ إِنْ نَعْفُ عَنْ طَائِفَةٍ مِنْكُمْ نُعَذِّبْ طَائِفَةً بِأَنَّهُمْ كَانُوا مُجْرِمِينَ

66
3:86, 90; 4:137; 9:106; 63:3

66 Do not apologize. You have disbelieved after your belief. If We pardon some of you, We will punish others, because they are guilty.

٦٧ الْمُنَافِقُونَ وَالْمُنَافِقَاتُ بَعْضُهُمْ مِنْ بَعْضٍ ۚ يَأْمُرُونَ بِالْمُنْكَرِ وَيَنْهَوْنَ عَنِ الْمَعْرُوفِ وَيَقْبِضُونَ أَيْدِيَهُمْ ۚ نَسُوا اللَّهَ فَنَسِيَهُمْ ۗ إِنَّ الْمُنَافِقِينَ هُمُ الْفَاسِقُونَ

67

67 The hypocrite men and hypocrite women are of one another. They advocate evil, and prohibit righteousness, and withhold their hands. They forgot God, so He forgot them. The hypocrites are the sinners.

٦٨ وَعَدَ اللَّهُ الْمُنَافِقِينَ وَالْمُنَافِقَاتِ وَالْكُفَّارَ نَارَ جَهَنَّمَ خَالِدِينَ فِيهَا ۚ هِيَ حَسْبُهُمْ ۚ وَلَعَنَهُمُ اللَّهُ ۖ وَلَهُمْ عَذَابٌ مُقِيمٌ

68
4:140; 48:6

68 God has promised the hypocrite men and hypocrite women, and the disbelievers, the Fire of Hell, abiding therein forever. It is their due. And God has cursed them. They will have a lasting punishment.

٦٩ كَالَّذِينَ مِنْ قَبْلِكُمْ كَانُوا أَشَدَّ مِنْكُمْ قُوَّةً وَأَكْثَرَ أَمْوَالًا وَأَوْلَادًا فَاسْتَمْتَعُوا بِخَلَاقِهِمْ فَاسْتَمْتَعْتُمْ بِخَلَاقِكُمْ كَمَا اسْتَمْتَعَ الَّذِينَ مِنْ قَبْلِكُمْ بِخَلَاقِهِمْ وَخُضْتُمْ كَالَّذِي خَاضُوا ۚ أُولَٰئِكَ حَبِطَتْ أَعْمَالُهُمْ فِي الدُّنْيَا وَالْآخِرَةِ ۖ وَأُولَٰئِكَ هُمُ الْخَاسِرُونَ

69 2:217; 5:54; 47:13

69 Like those before you. They were more powerful than you, and had more wealth and children. They enjoyed their share, and you enjoyed your share, as those before you enjoyed their share. And you indulged, as they indulged. It is they whose works will fail in this world and in the Hereafter. It is they who are the losers.

٧٠ أَلَمْ يَأْتِهِمْ نَبَأُ الَّذِينَ مِنْ قَبْلِهِمْ قَوْمِ نُوحٍ وَعَادٍ وَثَمُودَ وَقَوْمِ إِبْرَاهِيمَ وَأَصْحَابِ مَدْيَنَ وَالْمُؤْتَفِكَاتِ ۚ أَتَتْهُمْ رُسُلُهُمْ بِالْبَيِّنَاتِ ۖ فَمَا كَانَ اللَّهُ لِيَظْلِمَهُمْ وَلَٰكِنْ كَانُوا أَنْفُسَهُمْ يَظْلِمُونَ

70 3:183; 5:32; 14:9; 43:76

70 Have they not heard the stories of those before them? The people of Noah, and ʿĀd, and Thamūd; and the people of Abraham, and the inhabitants of Median, and the Overturned Cities? Their messengers came to them with the clear proofs. God never wronged them, but they used to wrong their own selves.

٧١ وَالْمُؤْمِنُونَ وَالْمُؤْمِنَاتُ بَعْضُهُمْ أَوْلِيَاءُ بَعْضٍ ۚ يَأْمُرُونَ بِالْمَعْرُوفِ وَيَنْهَوْنَ عَنِ الْمُنْكَرِ وَيُقِيمُونَ الصَّلَاةَ وَيُؤْتُونَ الزَّكَاةَ وَيُطِيعُونَ اللَّهَ وَرَسُولَهُ ۚ أُولَٰئِكَ سَيَرْحَمُهُمُ اللَّهُ ۗ إِنَّ اللَّهَ عَزِيزٌ حَكِيمٌ

71 3:104

71 The believing men and believing women are friends of one another. They advocate virtue, forbid evil, perform the prayers, practice charity, and obey God and His Messenger. These—God will have mercy on them. God is Noble and Wise.

٧٢ وَعَدَ اللَّهُ الْمُؤْمِنِينَ وَالْمُؤْمِنَاتِ جَنَّاتٍ تَجْرِي مِنْ تَحْتِهَا الْأَنْهَارُ خَالِدِينَ فِيهَا وَمَسَاكِنَ طَيِّبَةً فِي جَنَّاتِ عَدْنٍ ۚ وَرِضْوَانٌ مِنَ اللَّهِ أَكْبَرُ ۚ ذَٰلِكَ هُوَ الْفَوْزُ الْعَظِيمُ

72 4:9; 48:29; 61:12

72 God promises the believers, men and women, gardens beneath which rivers flow, abiding therein forever, and fine homes in the Gardens of Eden. But approval from God is even greater. That is the supreme achievement.

٧٣ يَا أَيُّهَا النَّبِيُّ جَاهِدِ الْكُفَّارَ وَالْمُنَافِقِينَ وَاغْلُظْ عَلَيْهِمْ ۚ وَمَأْوَاهُمْ جَهَنَّمُ ۖ وَبِئْسَ الْمَصِيرُ

73 9:123; 25:52; 66:9

73 O Prophet! Strive against the disbelievers and the hypocrites, and be stern with them. Their abode is Hell—what a miserable destination!

٧٤ يَحْلِفُونَ بِاللَّهِ مَا قَالُوا وَلَقَدْ قَالُوا كَلِمَةَ الْكُفْرِ وَكَفَرُوا بَعْدَ إِسْلَامِهِمْ وَهَمُّوا بِمَا لَمْ يَنَالُوا ۚ وَمَا نَقَمُوا إِلَّا أَنْ أَغْنَاهُمُ اللَّهُ وَرَسُولُهُ مِنْ فَضْلِهِ ۚ فَإِنْ يَتُوبُوا يَكُ خَيْرًا لَهُمْ ۖ وَإِنْ يَتَوَلَّوْا يُعَذِّبْهُمُ اللَّهُ عَذَابًا أَلِيمًا فِي الدُّنْيَا وَالْآخِرَةِ ۚ وَمَا لَهُمْ فِي الْأَرْضِ مِنْ وَلِيٍّ وَلَا نَصِيرٍ

74
[a] 9:62, 57, 95–96
[b] 7:126; 22:40; 85:8

74 They swear by God that they said nothing; but they did utter the word of blasphemy, and they renounced faith after their submission. And they plotted what they could not attain. They were resentful only because God and His Messenger have enriched them out of His grace. If they repent, it would be best for them; but if they turn away, God will afflict them with a painful punishment—in this life and in the Hereafter—and they will have on earth no protector and no savior.

٧٥ وَمِنْهُم مَّنْ عَاهَدَ اللَّهَ لَئِنْ آتَانَا مِن فَضْلِهِ لَنَصَّدَّقَنَّ وَلَنَكُونَنَّ مِنَ الصَّالِحِينَ

75 Among them are those who promised God: "If He gives us of His bounty, we will donate and be among the upright."

75
63:5

٧٦ فَلَمَّا آتَاهُم مِّن فَضْلِهِ بَخِلُوا بِهِ وَتَوَلَّوا وَّهُم مُّعْرِضُونَ

76 But when He has given them of His bounty, they became stingy with it, and turned away in aversion.

76
3:180

٧٧ فَأَعْقَبَهُمْ نِفَاقًا فِي قُلُوبِهِمْ إِلَىٰ يَوْمِ يَلْقَوْنَهُ بِمَا أَخْلَفُوا اللَّهَ مَا وَعَدُوهُ وَبِمَا كَانُوا يَكْذِبُونَ

77 So He penalized them with hypocrisy in their hearts, until the Day they face Him—because they broke their promise to God, and because they used to lie.

٧٨ أَلَمْ يَعْلَمُوا أَنَّ اللَّهَ يَعْلَمُ سِرَّهُمْ وَنَجْوَاهُمْ وَأَنَّ اللَّهَ عَلَّامُ الْغُيُوبِ

78 Do they not know that God knows their secrets and their conspiracies? And that God is the Knower of the unseen?

78
2:33; 5:9; 43:80; 58:7

٧٩ الَّذِينَ يَلْمِزُونَ الْمُطَّوِّعِينَ مِنَ الْمُؤْمِنِينَ فِي الصَّدَقَاتِ وَالَّذِينَ لَا يَجِدُونَ إِلَّا جُهْدَهُمْ فَيَسْخَرُونَ مِنْهُمْ ۙ سَخِرَ اللَّهُ مِنْهُمْ وَلَهُمْ عَذَابٌ أَلِيمٌ

79 Those who criticize the believers who give charity voluntarily, and ridicule those who find nothing to give except their own efforts—God ridicules them. They will have a painful punishment.

79
9:58; 49:11

٨٠ اسْتَغْفِرْ لَهُمْ أَوْ لَا تَسْتَغْفِرْ لَهُمْ إِن تَسْتَغْفِرْ لَهُمْ سَبْعِينَ مَرَّةً فَلَن يَغْفِرَ اللَّهُ لَهُمْ ۚ ذَٰلِكَ بِأَنَّهُمْ كَفَرُوا بِاللَّهِ وَرَسُولِهِ ۗ وَاللَّهُ لَا يَهْدِي الْقَوْمَ الْفَاسِقِينَ

80 Whether you ask forgiveness for them, or do not ask forgiveness for them—even if you ask forgiveness for them seventy times, God will not forgive them. That is because they disbelieved in God and His Messenger. God does not guide the immoral people.

80
9:113; 63:6

٨١ فَرِحَ الْمُخَلَّفُونَ بِمَقْعَدِهِمْ خِلَافَ رَسُولِ اللَّهِ وَكَرِهُوا أَن يُجَاهِدُوا بِأَمْوَالِهِمْ وَأَنفُسِهِمْ فِي سَبِيلِ اللَّهِ وَقَالُوا لَا تَنفِرُوا فِي الْحَرِّ ۗ قُلْ نَارُ جَهَنَّمَ أَشَدُّ حَرًّا ۚ لَّوْ كَانُوا يَفْقَهُونَ

81 Those who stayed behind rejoiced at their staying behind the Messenger of God. And they hated to strive with their wealth and their lives in God's way. And they said, "Do not venture out in the heat." Say, "The Fire of Hell is much hotter, if they only understood."

81
[a] 9:38
[b] 4:56; 7:15–16; 18:29; 22:19–21; 47:15

٨٢ فَلْيَضْحَكُوا قَلِيلًا وَلْيَبْكُوا كَثِيرًا جَزَاءً بِمَا كَانُوا يَكْسِبُونَ

82 Let them laugh a little, and weep much; in recompense for what they used to earn.

٨٣ فَإِن رَّجَعَكَ اللَّهُ إِلَىٰ طَائِفَةٍ مِّنْهُمْ فَاسْتَأْذَنُوكَ لِلْخُرُوجِ فَقُل لَّن تَخْرُجُوا مَعِيَ أَبَدًا وَلَن تُقَاتِلُوا مَعِيَ عَدُوًّا ۖ إِنَّكُمْ رَضِيتُم بِالْقُعُودِ أَوَّلَ مَرَّةٍ فَاقْعُدُوا مَعَ الْخَالِفِينَ

83 If God brings you back to a party of them, and they ask your permission to go out, say, "You will not go out with me, ever, nor will you ever fight an enemy with me. You were content to sit back the first time, so sit back with those who stay behind."

83
9:43–47

٨٤ وَلَا تُصَلِّ عَلَىٰ أَحَدٍ مِنْهُمْ مَاتَ أَبَدًا وَلَا تَقُمْ عَلَىٰ قَبْرِهِ ۖ إِنَّهُمْ كَفَرُوا بِاللَّهِ وَرَسُولِهِ وَمَاتُوا وَهُمْ فَاسِقُونَ

84 You are never to pray over anyone of them who dies, nor are you to stand at his graveside. They rejected God and His Messenger, and died while they were sinners.

٨٥ وَلَا تُعْجِبْكَ أَمْوَالُهُمْ وَأَوْلَادُهُمْ ۚ إِنَّمَا يُرِيدُ اللَّهُ أَنْ يُعَذِّبَهُمْ بِهَا فِي الدُّنْيَا وَتَزْهَقَ أَنْفُسُهُمْ وَهُمْ كَافِرُونَ

85
3:10; 9:55; 34:35

85 Do not let their possessions and their children impress you. God desires to torment them through them in this world, and their souls expire while they are disbelievers.

٨٦ وَإِذَا أُنْزِلَتْ سُورَةٌ أَنْ آمِنُوا بِاللَّهِ وَجَاهِدُوا مَعَ رَسُولِهِ اسْتَأْذَنَكَ أُولُو الطَّوْلِ مِنْهُمْ وَقَالُوا ذَرْنَا نَكُنْ مَعَ الْقَاعِدِينَ

86–87
9:64, 83; 33:19; 47:20

86 When a chapter is revealed, stating: "Believe in God and strive with His Messenger," the prominent among them ask you for exemption. They say, "Allow us to stay with those who stay behind."

٨٧ رَضُوا بِأَنْ يَكُونُوا مَعَ الْخَوَالِفِ وَطُبِعَ عَلَىٰ قُلُوبِهِمْ فَهُمْ لَا يَفْقَهُونَ

87 They prefer to be with those who stay behind. Their hearts were sealed, so they do not understand.

٨٨ لَٰكِنِ الرَّسُولُ وَالَّذِينَ آمَنُوا مَعَهُ جَاهَدُوا بِأَمْوَالِهِمْ وَأَنْفُسِهِمْ ۚ وَأُولَٰئِكَ لَهُمُ الْخَيْرَاتُ ۖ وَأُولَٰئِكَ هُمُ الْمُفْلِحُونَ

88
4:95; 8:72; 9:20, 41, 44, 81; 49:15

88 But the Messenger and those who believe with him struggle with their possessions and their lives. These have deserved the good things. These are the successful.

٨٩ أَعَدَّ اللَّهُ لَهُمْ جَنَّاتٍ تَجْرِي مِنْ تَحْتِهَا الْأَنْهَارُ خَالِدِينَ فِيهَا ۚ ذَٰلِكَ الْفَوْزُ الْعَظِيمُ

89 God has prepared for them gardens beneath which rivers flow, wherein they will abide forever. That is the great victory.

٩٠ وَجَاءَ الْمُعَذِّرُونَ مِنَ الْأَعْرَابِ لِيُؤْذَنَ لَهُمْ وَقَعَدَ الَّذِينَ كَذَبُوا اللَّهَ وَرَسُولَهُ ۚ سَيُصِيبُ الَّذِينَ كَفَرُوا مِنْهُمْ عَذَابٌ أَلِيمٌ

90
9:94; 33:20

90 Some of the Desert-Arabs came to make excuses, asking to be granted exemption, while those who were untrue to God and His Messenger stayed behind. A painful punishment will afflict those among them who disbelieved.

٩١ لَيْسَ عَلَى الضُّعَفَاءِ وَلَا عَلَى الْمَرْضَىٰ وَلَا عَلَى الَّذِينَ لَا يَجِدُونَ مَا يُنْفِقُونَ حَرَجٌ إِذَا نَصَحُوا لِلَّهِ وَرَسُولِهِ ۚ مَا عَلَى الْمُحْسِنِينَ مِنْ سَبِيلٍ ۚ وَاللَّهُ غَفُورٌ رَحِيمٌ

91
48:17

91 There is no blame on the weak, nor on the sick, nor on those who have nothing to give, provided they are true to God and His Messenger. In no way can the righteous be blamed. God is Forgiving and Merciful.

٩٢ وَلَا عَلَى الَّذِينَ إِذَا مَا أَتَوْكَ لِتَحْمِلَهُمْ قُلْتَ لَا أَجِدُ مَا أَحْمِلُكُمْ عَلَيْهِ تَوَلَّوا وَأَعْيُنُهُمْ تَفِيضُ مِنَ الدَّمْعِ حَزَنًا أَلَّا يَجِدُوا مَا يُنْفِقُونَ

92 Nor on those who approach you, wishing to ride with you, and you said, "I have nothing to carry you on." So they went away, with their eyes overflowing with tears, sorrowing for not finding the means to spend.

٩٣ إِنَّمَا السَّبِيلُ عَلَى الَّذِينَ يَسْتَأْذِنُونَكَ وَهُمْ أَغْنِيَاءُ ۚ رَضُوا بِأَنْ يَكُونُوا مَعَ الْخَوَالِفِ وَطَبَعَ اللَّهُ عَلَىٰ قُلُوبِهِمْ فَهُمْ لَا يَعْلَمُونَ

93
9:83, 86–87; 33:19

93 But blame is on those who ask you for exemption, although they are rich. They are content to be with those who stay behind. God has sealed their hearts, so they do not know.

٩٤ يَعْتَذِرُونَ إِلَيْكُمْ إِذَا رَجَعْتُمْ إِلَيْهِمْ ۚ قُلْ لَا تَعْتَذِرُوا لَنْ نُؤْمِنَ لَكُمْ قَدْ نَبَّأَنَا اللَّهُ مِنْ أَخْبَارِكُمْ ۚ وَسَيَرَى اللَّهُ عَمَلَكُمْ وَرَسُولُهُ ثُمَّ تُرَدُّونَ إِلَىٰ عَالِمِ الْغَيْبِ وَالشَّهَادَةِ فَيُنَبِّئُكُمْ بِمَا كُنْتُمْ تَعْمَلُونَ

94
9:90, 105

94 They present excuses to you when you return to them. Say, "Do not offer excuses; we do not trust you; God has informed us of you. And God will watch your actions, and so will the Messenger; then you will be returned to the Knower of the Invisible and the Visible, and He will inform you of what you used to do."

٩٥ سَيَحْلِفُونَ بِاللَّهِ لَكُمْ إِذَا انْقَلَبْتُمْ إِلَيْهِمْ لِتُعْرِضُوا عَنْهُمْ ۖ فَأَعْرِضُوا عَنْهُمْ ۖ إِنَّهُمْ رِجْسٌ ۖ وَمَأْوَاهُمْ جَهَنَّمُ جَزَاءً بِمَا كَانُوا يَكْسِبُونَ

95
3:167; 9:28, 42; 57, 62, 74

95 They will swear to you by God, when you return to them, that you may leave them alone. So leave them alone. They are a disgrace, and their destiny is Hell; a reward for what they used to earn.

٩٦ يَحْلِفُونَ لَكُمْ لِتَرْضَوْا عَنْهُمْ ۖ فَإِنْ تَرْضَوْا عَنْهُمْ فَإِنَّ اللَّهَ لَا يَرْضَىٰ عَنِ الْقَوْمِ الْفَاسِقِينَ

96
9:62

96 They will swear to you that you may accept them. But even if you accept them, God does not accept the wicked people.

٩٧ الْأَعْرَابُ أَشَدُّ كُفْرًا وَنِفَاقًا وَأَجْدَرُ أَلَّا يَعْلَمُوا حُدُودَ مَا أَنْزَلَ اللَّهُ عَلَىٰ رَسُولِهِ ۗ وَاللَّهُ عَلِيمٌ حَكِيمٌ

97
49:14

97 The Desert-Arabs are the most steeped in disbelief and hypocrisy, and the most likely to ignore the limits that God revealed to His Messenger. God is Knowing and Wise.

٩٨ وَمِنَ الْأَعْرَابِ مَنْ يَتَّخِذُ مَا يُنْفِقُ مَغْرَمًا وَيَتَرَبَّصُ بِكُمُ الدَّوَائِرَ ۚ عَلَيْهِمْ دَائِرَةُ السَّوْءِ ۗ وَاللَّهُ سَمِيعٌ عَلِيمٌ

98 And among the Desert-Arabs are those who consider their contribution to be a fine. And they wait for a reversal of your fortunes. Upon them will fall the cycle of misfortune. God is Hearing and Knowing.

٩٩ وَمِنَ الْأَعْرَابِ مَن يُؤْمِنُ بِاللَّهِ وَالْيَوْمِ الْآخِرِ وَيَتَّخِذُ مَا يُنفِقُ قُرُبَاتٍ عِندَ اللَّهِ وَصَلَوَاتِ الرَّسُولِ ۚ أَلَا إِنَّهَا قُرْبَةٌ لَّهُمْ ۚ سَيُدْخِلُهُمُ اللَّهُ فِي رَحْمَتِهِ ۗ إِنَّ اللَّهَ غَفُورٌ رَّحِيمٌ

99
9:103

99 Yet among the Desert-Arabs are those who believe in God and the Last Day, and consider their contribution to be a means towards God, and the prayers of the Messenger. Surely it will draw them closer, and God will admit them into His mercy. God is Forgiving and Compassionate.

١٠٠ وَالسَّابِقُونَ الْأَوَّلُونَ مِنَ الْمُهَاجِرِينَ وَالْأَنصَارِ وَالَّذِينَ اتَّبَعُوهُم بِإِحْسَانٍ رَّضِيَ اللَّهُ عَنْهُمْ وَرَضُوا عَنْهُ وَأَعَدَّ لَهُمْ جَنَّاتٍ تَجْرِي تَحْتَهَا الْأَنْهَارُ خَالِدِينَ فِيهَا أَبَدًا ۚ ذَٰلِكَ الْفَوْزُ الْعَظِيمُ

100
8:74; 9:117

100 The Pioneers—The first of the Migrants and the Supporters, and those who followed them in righteousness. God is pleased with them, and they are pleased with Him. He has prepared for them Gardens beneath which rivers flow, where they will abide forever. That is the sublime triumph.

١٠١ وَمِمَّنْ حَوْلَكُم مِّنَ الْأَعْرَابِ مُنَافِقُونَ ۖ وَمِنْ أَهْلِ الْمَدِينَةِ ۖ مَرَدُوا عَلَى النِّفَاقِ لَا تَعْلَمُهُمْ ۖ نَحْنُ نَعْلَمُهُمْ ۚ سَنُعَذِّبُهُم مَّرَّتَيْنِ ثُمَّ يُرَدُّونَ إِلَىٰ عَذَابٍ عَظِيمٍ

101
9:120

101 Among the Desert-Arabs around you there are some hypocrites, and among the inhabitants of Medina too. They have become adamant in hypocrisy. You do not know them, but We know them. We will punish them twice; then they will be returned to a severe torment.

١٠٢ وَآخَرُونَ اعْتَرَفُوا بِذُنُوبِهِمْ خَلَطُوا عَمَلًا صَالِحًا وَآخَرَ سَيِّئًا عَسَى اللَّهُ أَن يَتُوبَ عَلَيْهِمْ ۚ إِنَّ اللَّهَ غَفُورٌ رَّحِيمٌ

102

102 Others have confessed their sins, having mixed good deeds with bad deeds. Perhaps God will redeem them. God is Forgiving and Merciful.

١٠٣ خُذْ مِنْ أَمْوَالِهِمْ صَدَقَةً تُطَهِّرُهُمْ وَتُزَكِّيهِم بِهَا وَصَلِّ عَلَيْهِمْ ۖ إِنَّ صَلَاتَكَ سَكَنٌ لَّهُمْ ۗ وَاللَّهُ سَمِيعٌ عَلِيمٌ

103
9:99

103 Receive contributions from their wealth, to purify them and sanctify them with it; and pray for them. Your prayer is comfort for them. God is Hearing and Knowing.

١٠٤ أَلَمْ يَعْلَمُوا أَنَّ اللَّهَ هُوَ يَقْبَلُ التَّوْبَةَ عَنْ عِبَادِهِ وَيَأْخُذُ الصَّدَقَاتِ وَأَنَّ اللَّهَ هُوَ التَّوَّابُ الرَّحِيمُ

104
4:64; 42:25

104 Do they not know that God accepts the repentance of His servants, and that He receives the contributions, and that God is the Acceptor of Repentance, the Merciful?

١٠٥ وَقُلِ اعْمَلُوا فَسَيَرَى اللَّهُ عَمَلَكُمْ وَرَسُولُهُ وَالْمُؤْمِنُونَ ۖ وَسَتُرَدُّونَ إِلَىٰ عَالِمِ الْغَيْبِ وَالشَّهَادَةِ فَيُنَبِّئُكُم بِمَا كُنتُمْ تَعْمَلُونَ

105
9:94

105 Say, "Work. God will see your work, and so will His Messenger, and the believers. Then you will be returned to the Knower of secrets and declarations, and He will inform you of what you used to do."

١٠٦ وَآخَرُونَ مُرْجَوْنَ لِأَمْرِ اللَّهِ إِمَّا يُعَذِّبُهُمْ وَإِمَّا يَتُوبُ عَلَيْهِمْ ۗ وَاللَّهُ عَلِيمٌ حَكِيمٌ

106 — 9:66

106 Others are held in suspense, awaiting God's decree, as to whether He will punish them, or accept their repentance. God is Aware and Wise.

١٠٧ وَالَّذِينَ اتَّخَذُوا مَسْجِدًا ضِرَارًا وَكُفْرًا وَتَفْرِيقًا بَيْنَ الْمُؤْمِنِينَ وَإِرْصَادًا لِمَنْ حَارَبَ اللَّهَ وَرَسُولَهُ مِن قَبْلُ ۚ وَلَيَحْلِفُنَّ إِنْ أَرَدْنَا إِلَّا الْحُسْنَىٰ ۖ وَاللَّهُ يَشْهَدُ إِنَّهُمْ لَكَاذِبُونَ

107 — 4:62; 9:17

107 Then there are those who establish a mosque to cause harm, and disbelief, and disunity among the believers, and as an outpost for those who fight God and His Messenger. They will swear: "Our intentions are nothing but good." But God bears witness that they are liars.

١٠٨ لَا تَقُمْ فِيهِ أَبَدًا ۚ لَمَسْجِدٌ أُسِّسَ عَلَى التَّقْوَىٰ مِنْ أَوَّلِ يَوْمٍ أَحَقُّ أَن تَقُومَ فِيهِ ۚ فِيهِ رِجَالٌ يُحِبُّونَ أَن يَتَطَهَّرُوا ۚ وَاللَّهُ يُحِبُّ الْمُطَّهِّرِينَ

108 Do not stand in it, ever. A mosque founded upon piety from the first day is worthier of your standing in it. In it are men who love to be purified. God loves those who purify themselves.

١٠٩ أَفَمَنْ أَسَّسَ بُنْيَانَهُ عَلَىٰ تَقْوَىٰ مِنَ اللَّهِ وَرِضْوَانٍ خَيْرٌ أَم مَّنْ أَسَّسَ بُنْيَانَهُ عَلَىٰ شَفَا جُرُفٍ هَارٍ فَانْهَارَ بِهِ فِي نَارِ جَهَنَّمَ ۗ وَاللَّهُ لَا يَهْدِي الْقَوْمَ الظَّالِمِينَ

109 — 3:103, 162

109 Is he who founds his structure upon piety and acceptance from God better, or he who founds his structure on the brink of a cliff that is about to tumble, so it tumbles with him into the Fire of Hell? God does not guide the unjust people.

١١٠ لَا يَزَالُ بُنْيَانُهُمُ الَّذِي بَنَوْا رِيبَةً فِي قُلُوبِهِمْ إِلَّا أَن تَقَطَّعَ قُلُوبُهُمْ ۗ وَاللَّهُ عَلِيمٌ حَكِيمٌ

110 The structure which they built will remain questionable in their hearts, until their hearts are stopped. God is Knowing and Wise.

١١١ إِنَّ اللَّهَ اشْتَرَىٰ مِنَ الْمُؤْمِنِينَ أَنفُسَهُمْ وَأَمْوَالَهُم بِأَنَّ لَهُمُ الْجَنَّةَ ۚ يُقَاتِلُونَ فِي سَبِيلِ اللَّهِ فَيَقْتُلُونَ وَيُقْتَلُونَ ۖ وَعْدًا عَلَيْهِ حَقًّا فِي التَّوْرَاةِ وَالْإِنجِيلِ وَالْقُرْآنِ ۚ وَمَنْ أَوْفَىٰ بِعَهْدِهِ مِنَ اللَّهِ ۚ فَاسْتَبْشِرُوا بِبَيْعِكُمُ الَّذِي بَايَعْتُم بِهِ ۚ وَذَٰلِكَ هُوَ الْفَوْزُ الْعَظِيمُ

111 — 3:195; 4:74; 6:10

111 God has purchased from the believers their lives and their properties in exchange for Paradise. They fight in God's way, and they kill and get killed. It is a promise binding on Him in the Torah, and the Gospel, and the Qur'an. And who is more true to his promise than God? So rejoice in making such an exchange—that is the supreme triumph.

١١٢ التَّائِبُونَ الْعَابِدُونَ الْحَامِدُونَ السَّائِحُونَ الرَّاكِعُونَ السَّاجِدُونَ الْآمِرُونَ بِالْمَعْرُوفِ وَالنَّاهُونَ عَنِ الْمُنكَرِ وَالْحَافِظُونَ لِحُدُودِ اللَّهِ ۗ وَبَشِّرِ الْمُؤْمِنِينَ

112 Those who repent, those who worship, those who praise, those who journey, those who kneel, those who bow down, those who advocate righteousness and forbid evil, and those who keep God's limits—give good news to the believers.

١١٣ مَا كَانَ لِلنَّبِيِّ وَالَّذِينَ آمَنُوا أَن يَسْتَغْفِرُوا لِلْمُشْرِكِينَ وَلَوْ كَانُوا أُولِي قُرْبَىٰ مِن بَعْدِ مَا تَبَيَّنَ لَهُمْ أَنَّهُمْ أَصْحَابُ الْجَحِيمِ

113   63:6

113 It is not for the Prophet and those who believe to ask forgiveness for the polytheists, even if they are near relatives, after it has become clear to them that they are people of Hellfire.

١١٤ وَمَا كَانَ اسْتِغْفَارُ إِبْرَاهِيمَ لِأَبِيهِ إِلَّا عَن مَّوْعِدَةٍ وَعَدَهَا إِيَّاهُ فَلَمَّا تَبَيَّنَ لَهُ أَنَّهُ عَدُوٌّ لِّلَّهِ تَبَرَّأَ مِنْهُ ۚ إِنَّ إِبْرَاهِيمَ لَأَوَّاهٌ حَلِيمٌ

114   14:41; 19:47; 26:86; 60:4

114 Abraham asked forgiveness for his father only because of a promise he had made to him. But when it became clear to him that he was an enemy of God, he disowned him. Abraham was kind and clement.

١١٥ وَمَا كَانَ اللَّهُ لِيُضِلَّ قَوْمًا بَعْدَ إِذْ هَدَاهُمْ حَتَّىٰ يُبَيِّنَ لَهُم مَّا يَتَّقُونَ ۚ إِنَّ اللَّهَ بِكُلِّ شَيْءٍ عَلِيمٌ

115 God would never lead a people astray, after He had guided them, until He makes clear to them what they should guard against. God has knowledge of all things.

١١٦ إِنَّ اللَّهَ لَهُ مُلْكُ السَّمَاوَاتِ وَالْأَرْضِ ۖ يُحْيِي وَيُمِيتُ ۚ وَمَا لَكُم مِّن دُونِ اللَّهِ مِن وَلِيٍّ وَلَا نَصِيرٍ

116   2:107; 7:158

116 To God belongs the dominion of the heavens and the earth. He gives life, and He causes death. And besides God, you have neither protector, nor supporter.

١١٧ لَّقَد تَّابَ اللَّهُ عَلَى النَّبِيِّ وَالْمُهَاجِرِينَ وَالْأَنصَارِ الَّذِينَ اتَّبَعُوهُ فِي سَاعَةِ الْعُسْرَةِ مِن بَعْدِ مَا كَادَ يَزِيغُ قُلُوبُ فَرِيقٍ مِّنْهُمْ ثُمَّ تَابَ عَلَيْهِمْ ۚ إِنَّهُ بِهِمْ رَءُوفٌ رَّحِيمٌ

117   9:100

117 God has redeemed the Prophet, and the Emigrants, and the Supporters—those who followed him in the hour of difficulty—after the hearts of some of them almost swerved. Then He pardoned them. He is Kind towards them, Compassionate.

١١٨ وَعَلَى الثَّلَاثَةِ الَّذِينَ خُلِّفُوا حَتَّىٰ إِذَا ضَاقَتْ عَلَيْهِمُ الْأَرْضُ بِمَا رَحُبَتْ وَضَاقَتْ عَلَيْهِمْ أَنفُسُهُمْ وَظَنُّوا أَن لَّا مَلْجَأَ مِنَ اللَّهِ إِلَّا إِلَيْهِ ثُمَّ تَابَ عَلَيْهِمْ لِيَتُوبُوا ۚ إِنَّ اللَّهَ هُوَ التَّوَّابُ الرَّحِيمُ

118 Also towards the three who were left behind. Then, when the earth, as vast as it is, closed in on them, and their very souls closed in on them, and they realized that there was no refuge from God, except in Him, He redeemed them, so that they may repent. God is the Redeemer, the Merciful.

١١٩ يَا أَيُّهَا الَّذِينَ آمَنُوا اتَّقُوا اللَّهَ وَكُونُوا مَعَ الصَّادِقِينَ

119   59:8

119 O you who believe! Be conscious of God, and be with the sincere.

١٢٠ مَا كَانَ لِأَهْلِ الْمَدِينَةِ وَمَنْ حَوْلَهُمْ مِنَ الْأَعْرَابِ أَنْ يَتَخَلَّفُوا عَنْ رَسُولِ اللَّهِ وَلَا يَرْغَبُوا بِأَنْفُسِهِمْ عَنْ نَفْسِهِ ۚ ذَٰلِكَ بِأَنَّهُمْ لَا يُصِيبُهُمْ ظَمَأٌ وَلَا نَصَبٌ وَلَا مَخْمَصَةٌ فِي سَبِيلِ اللَّهِ وَلَا يَطَئُونَ مَوْطِئًا يَغِيظُ الْكُفَّارَ وَلَا يَنَالُونَ مِنْ عَدُوٍّ نَيْلًا إِلَّا كُتِبَ لَهُمْ بِهِ عَمَلٌ صَالِحٌ ۚ إِنَّ اللَّهَ لَا يُضِيعُ أَجْرَ الْمُحْسِنِينَ

120 9:101

120 It is not for the inhabitants of Medina and the Desert-Arabs around them to stay behind the Messenger of God, nor to prefer themselves to him. That is because they never suffer any thirst, nor fatigue, nor hunger in the cause of God, nor do they take one step that enrages the disbelievers, nor do they gain anything from an enemy, but it is recorded to their credit as a righteous deed. God does not waste the reward of the righteous.

١٢١ وَلَا يُنْفِقُونَ نَفَقَةً صَغِيرَةً وَلَا كَبِيرَةً وَلَا يَقْطَعُونَ وَادِيًا إِلَّا كُتِبَ لَهُمْ لِيَجْزِيَهُمُ اللَّهُ أَحْسَنَ مَا كَانُوا يَعْمَلُونَ

121 2:272–273; 8:60; 35:29

121 Nor do they spend any expenditure, small or large, nor do they cross any valley, but it is recorded to their credit. That God may reward them in accordance with the best of their deeds.

١٢٢ وَمَا كَانَ الْمُؤْمِنُونَ لِيَنْفِرُوا كَافَّةً ۚ فَلَوْلَا نَفَرَ مِنْ كُلِّ فِرْقَةٍ مِنْهُمْ طَائِفَةٌ لِيَتَفَقَّهُوا فِي الدِّينِ وَلِيُنْذِرُوا قَوْمَهُمْ إِذَا رَجَعُوا إِلَيْهِمْ لَعَلَّهُمْ يَحْذَرُونَ

122 It is not advisable for the believers to march out altogether. Of every division that marches out, let a group remain behind, to gain understanding of the religion, and to notify their people when they have returned to them, that they may beware.

١٢٣ يَا أَيُّهَا الَّذِينَ آمَنُوا قَاتِلُوا الَّذِينَ يَلُونَكُمْ مِنَ الْكُفَّارِ وَلْيَجِدُوا فِيكُمْ غِلْظَةً ۚ وَاعْلَمُوا أَنَّ اللَّهَ مَعَ الْمُتَّقِينَ

123 9:73; 25:52; 66:9

123 O you who believe! Fight those of the disbelievers who attack you, and let them find severity in you, and know that God is with the righteous.

١٢٤ وَإِذَا مَا أُنْزِلَتْ سُورَةٌ فَمِنْهُمْ مَنْ يَقُولُ أَيُّكُمْ زَادَتْهُ هَٰذِهِ إِيمَانًا ۚ فَأَمَّا الَّذِينَ آمَنُوا فَزَادَتْهُمْ إِيمَانًا وَهُمْ يَسْتَبْشِرُونَ

124 8:2

124 Whenever a chapter is revealed, some of them say, "Which of you has this increased in faith?" As for those who believe: it increases them in faith, and they rejoice.

١٢٥ وَأَمَّا الَّذِينَ فِي قُلُوبِهِمْ مَرَضٌ فَزَادَتْهُمْ رِجْسًا إِلَىٰ رِجْسِهِمْ وَمَاتُوا وَهُمْ كَافِرُونَ

125 2:10; 47:29; 74:31

125 But as for those in whose hearts is sickness: it adds disgrace to their disgrace, and they die as unbelievers.

١٢٦ أَوَلَا يَرَوْنَ أَنَّهُمْ يُفْتَنُونَ فِي كُلِّ عَامٍ مَرَّةً أَوْ مَرَّتَيْنِ ثُمَّ لَا يَتُوبُونَ وَلَا هُمْ يَذَّكَّرُونَ

126 Do they not see that they are tested once or twice every year? Yet they do not repent, and they do not learn.

١٢٧ وَإِذَا مَا أُنزِلَتْ سُورَةٌ نَّظَرَ بَعْضُهُمْ إِلَىٰ بَعْضٍ هَلْ يَرَاكُم مِّنْ أَحَدٍ ثُمَّ انصَرَفُوا ۚ صَرَفَ اللَّهُ قُلُوبَهُم بِأَنَّهُمْ قَوْمٌ لَّا يَفْقَهُونَ

127 9:64

127 And whenever a chapter is revealed, they look at one another, "Does anyone see you?" Then they slip away. God has diverted their hearts, because they are a people who do not understand.

١٢٨ لَقَدْ جَاءَكُمْ رَسُولٌ مِّنْ أَنفُسِكُمْ عَزِيزٌ عَلَيْهِ مَا عَنِتُّمْ حَرِيصٌ عَلَيْكُم بِالْمُؤْمِنِينَ رَءُوفٌ رَّحِيمٌ

128 3:164

128 There has come to you a messenger from among yourselves, concerned over your suffering, anxious over you. Towards the believers, he is compassionate and merciful.

١٢٩ فَإِن تَوَلَّوْا فَقُلْ حَسْبِيَ اللَّهُ لَا إِلَٰهَ إِلَّا هُوَ ۖ عَلَيْهِ تَوَكَّلْتُ ۖ وَهُوَ رَبُّ الْعَرْشِ الْعَظِيمِ

129 11:54–56

129 If they turn away, say, "God is enough for me; there is no god except He; in Him I have put my trust; He is the Lord of the Sublime Throne."

Sūrah 10: Yūnus

سُورَةُ يُونُس (Jonah)

بِسْمِ ٱللَّهِ ٱلرَّحْمَٰنِ ٱلرَّحِيمِ

١ الر ۚ تِلْكَ آيَاتُ الْكِتَابِ الْحَكِيمِ

1

1 Alif, Lām, Rā'. These are the Verses of the Wise Book.

٢ أَكَانَ لِلنَّاسِ عَجَبًا أَنْ أَوْحَيْنَا إِلَىٰ رَجُلٍ مِّنْهُمْ أَنْ أَنذِرِ النَّاسَ وَبَشِّرِ الَّذِينَ آمَنُوا أَنَّ لَهُمْ قَدَمَ صِدْقٍ عِندَ رَبِّهِمْ ۗ قَالَ الْكَافِرُونَ إِنَّ هَٰذَا لَسَاحِرٌ مُّبِينٌ

2 7:63, 69; 38:4; 50:2; 54:55

2 Is it a wonder to the people that We inspired a man from among them: "Warn mankind, and give good news to those who believe that they are on a sound footing with their Lord"? The disbelievers said, "This is a manifest sorcerer."

٣ إِنَّ رَبَّكُمُ اللَّهُ الَّذِي خَلَقَ السَّمَاوَاتِ وَالْأَرْضَ فِي سِتَّةِ أَيَّامٍ ثُمَّ اسْتَوَىٰ عَلَى الْعَرْشِ ۖ يُدَبِّرُ الْأَمْرَ ۖ مَا مِن شَفِيعٍ إِلَّا مِن بَعْدِ إِذْنِهِ ۚ ذَٰلِكُمُ اللَّهُ رَبُّكُمْ فَاعْبُدُوهُ ۚ أَفَلَا تَذَكَّرُونَ

3 7:54; 10:3; 13:2; 11:7; 20:5; 25:29; 32:4; 57:4

3 Your Lord is God, who created the heavens and the earth in six days, then settled over the Throne, governing all things. There is no intercessor except after His permission. Such is God, your Lord—so serve Him. Will you not reflect?

٤ إِلَيْهِ مَرْجِعُكُمْ جَمِيعًا ۖ وَعْدَ اللَّهِ حَقًّا ۚ إِنَّهُ يَبْدَأُ الْخَلْقَ ثُمَّ يُعِيدُهُ لِيَجْزِيَ الَّذِينَ آمَنُوا وَعَمِلُوا الصَّالِحَاتِ بِالْقِسْطِ ۚ [a] وَالَّذِينَ كَفَرُوا لَهُمْ شَرَابٌ مِّنْ حَمِيمٍ وَعَذَابٌ أَلِيمٌ بِمَا كَانُوا يَكْفُرُونَ [b]

4
[a] 30:45; 34:4
[b] 6:70; 47:15; 55:44; 56:54

4 To Him is your return, altogether. The promise of God is true. He originates creation, and then He repeats it, to reward those who believe and do good deeds with equity. As for those who disbelieve, for them is a drink of boiling water, and agonizing torment, on account of their disbelief.

٥ هُوَ الَّذِي جَعَلَ الشَّمْسَ ضِيَاءً وَالْقَمَرَ نُورًا وَقَدَّرَهُ مَنَازِلَ لِتَعْلَمُوا عَدَدَ السِّنِينَ وَالْحِسَابَ ۚ مَا خَلَقَ اللَّهُ ذَٰلِكَ إِلَّا بِالْحَقِّ ۚ يُفَصِّلُ الْآيَاتِ لِقَوْمٍ يَعْلَمُونَ

5 6:96; 17:12; 25:61; 71:16

5 It is He who made the sun radiant, and the moon a light, and determined phases for it—that you may know the number of years and the calculation. God did not create all this except with truth. He details the revelations for a people who know.

٦ إِنَّ فِي اخْتِلَافِ اللَّيْلِ وَالنَّهَارِ وَمَا خَلَقَ اللَّهُ فِي السَّمَاوَاتِ وَالْأَرْضِ لَآيَاتٍ لِقَوْمٍ يَتَّقُونَ

6 2:164

6 In the alternation of night and day, and in what God created in the heavens and the earth, are signs for people who are aware.

٧ إِنَّ الَّذِينَ لَا يَرْجُونَ لِقَاءَنَا وَرَضُوا بِالْحَيَاةِ الدُّنْيَا وَاطْمَأَنُّوا بِهَا وَالَّذِينَ هُمْ عَنْ آيَاتِنَا غَافِلُونَ

7 Those who do not hope to meet Us, and are content with the worldly life, and are at ease in it, and those who pay no heed to Our signs.

٨ أُولَٰئِكَ مَأْوَاهُمُ النَّارُ بِمَا كَانُوا يَكْسِبُونَ

8 These—their dwelling is the Fire—on account of what they used to do.

٩ إِنَّ الَّذِينَ آمَنُوا وَعَمِلُوا الصَّالِحَاتِ يَهْدِيهِمْ رَبُّهُمْ بِإِيمَانِهِمْ ۖ تَجْرِي مِنْ تَحْتِهِمُ الْأَنْهَارُ فِي جَنَّاتِ النَّعِيمِ

9 As for those who believe and do good deeds, their Lord guides them in their faith. Rivers will flow beneath them in the Gardens of Bliss.

١٠ دَعْوَاهُمْ فِيهَا سُبْحَانَكَ اللَّهُمَّ وَتَحِيَّتُهُمْ فِيهَا سَلَامٌ ۚ وَآخِرُ دَعْوَاهُمْ أَنِ الْحَمْدُ لِلَّهِ رَبِّ الْعَالَمِينَ

10 13:23–24; 14:23; 16:32; 33:44; 36:58; 50:34; 56:91

10 Their call therein is, "Glory be to You, our God." And their greeting therein is, "Peace." And the last of their call is, "Praise be to God, Lord of the Worlds."

١١ وَلَوْ يُعَجِّلُ اللَّهُ لِلنَّاسِ الشَّرَّ اسْتِعْجَالَهُمْ بِالْخَيْرِ لَقُضِيَ إِلَيْهِمْ أَجَلُهُمْ ۖ فَنَذَرُ الَّذِينَ لَا يَرْجُونَ لِقَاءَنَا فِي طُغْيَانِهِمْ يَعْمَهُونَ

11 6:110; 17:11; 21:37; 41:49

11 If God were to accelerate the ill for the people, as they wish to accelerate the good, their term would have been fulfilled. But We leave those who do not expect Our encounter to blunder in their excesses.

١٢ وَإِذَا مَسَّ الْإِنْسَانَ الضُّرُّ دَعَانَا لِجَنْبِهِ أَوْ قَاعِدًا أَوْ قَائِمًا فَلَمَّا كَشَفْنَا عَنْهُ ضُرَّهُ مَرَّ كَأَنْ لَمْ يَدْعُنَا إِلَىٰ ضُرٍّ مَسَّهُ ۚ كَذَٰلِكَ زُيِّنَ لِلْمُسْرِفِينَ مَا كَانُوا يَعْمَلُونَ

12 30:33; 39:8, 49; 41:51

12 Whenever adversity touches the human being, he prays to Us—reclining on his side, or sitting, or standing. But when We have relieved his adversity from him, he goes away, as though he had never called on Us for trouble that had afflicted him. Thus the deeds of the transgressors appear good to them.

١٣ وَلَقَدْ أَهْلَكْنَا الْقُرُونَ مِن قَبْلِكُمْ لَمَّا ظَلَمُوا ۙ وَجَاءَتْهُمْ رُسُلُهُم بِالْبَيِّنَاتِ وَمَا كَانُوا لِيُؤْمِنُوا ۚ كَذَٰلِكَ نَجْزِي الْقَوْمَ الْمُجْرِمِينَ

13 7:4; 8:54; 21:11; 22:45

13 We destroyed generations before you when they did wrong. Their messengers came to them with clear signs, but they would not believe. Thus We requite the sinful people.

١٤ ثُمَّ جَعَلْنَاكُمْ خَلَائِفَ فِي الْأَرْضِ مِن بَعْدِهِمْ لِنَنظُرَ كَيْفَ تَعْمَلُونَ

14 6:165; 7:129

14 Then We made you successors on earth after them, to see how you would behave.

١٥ وَإِذَا تُتْلَىٰ عَلَيْهِمْ آيَاتُنَا بَيِّنَاتٍ ۙ قَالَ الَّذِينَ لَا يَرْجُونَ لِقَاءَنَا ائْتِ بِقُرْآنٍ غَيْرِ هَٰذَا أَوْ بَدِّلْهُ ۚ قُلْ مَا يَكُونُ لِي أَنْ أُبَدِّلَهُ مِن تِلْقَاءِ نَفْسِي ۖ إِنْ أَتَّبِعُ إِلَّا مَا يُوحَىٰ إِلَيَّ ۖ إِنِّي أَخَافُ إِنْ عَصَيْتُ رَبِّي عَذَابَ يَوْمٍ عَظِيمٍ

15 6:15; 17:73; 25:21; 53:3–4

15 And when Our clear revelations are recited to them, those who do not hope to meet Us say, "Bring a Qur'an other than this, or change it." Say, "It is not for me to change it of my own accord. I only follow what is revealed to me. I fear, if I disobeyed my Lord, the torment of a terrible Day."

١٦ قُل لَّوْ شَاءَ اللَّهُ مَا تَلَوْتُهُ عَلَيْكُمْ وَلَا أَدْرَاكُم بِهِ ۖ فَقَدْ لَبِثْتُ فِيكُمْ عُمُرًا مِّن قَبْلِهِ ۚ أَفَلَا تَعْقِلُونَ

16 23:69

16 Say, "Had God willed, I would not have recited it to you, and He would not have made it known to you. I have lived among you for a lifetime before it. Do you not understand?"

١٧ فَمَنْ أَظْلَمُ مِمَّنِ افْتَرَىٰ عَلَى اللَّهِ كَذِبًا أَوْ كَذَّبَ بِآيَاتِهِ ۚ إِنَّهُ لَا يُفْلِحُ الْمُجْرِمُونَ

17 6:21

17 Who does greater wrong than someone who fabricates lies about God, or denies His revelations? The guilty will never prosper.

١٨ وَيَعْبُدُونَ مِن دُونِ اللَّهِ مَا لَا يَضُرُّهُمْ وَلَا يَنفَعُهُمْ وَيَقُولُونَ هَٰؤُلَاءِ شُفَعَاؤُنَا عِندَ اللَّهِ ۚ قُلْ أَتُنَبِّئُونَ اللَّهَ بِمَا لَا يَعْلَمُ فِي السَّمَاوَاتِ وَلَا فِي الْأَرْضِ ۚ سُبْحَانَهُ وَتَعَالَىٰ عَمَّا يُشْرِكُونَ

18 6:71; 10:106; 21:66; 25:55; 26:72; 29:17

18 And they worship, besides God, what neither harms them nor benefits them. And they say, "These are our intercessors with God." Say, "Are you informing God about what He does not know in the heavens or on earth?" Glorified be He, High above the associations they make.

١٩ وَمَا كَانَ النَّاسُ إِلَّا أُمَّةً وَاحِدَةً فَاخْتَلَفُوا ۚ وَلَوْلَا كَلِمَةٌ سَبَقَتْ مِن رَّبِّكَ لَقُضِيَ بَيْنَهُمْ فِيمَا فِيهِ يَخْتَلِفُونَ

19 2:213; 11:110

19 Mankind was a single community; then they differed. Were it not for a prior decree from your Lord, the matters over which they had disputed would have been settled.

٢٠ وَيَقُولُونَ لَوْلَا أُنزِلَ عَلَيْهِ آيَةٌ مِّن رَّبِّهِ ۖ فَقُلْ إِنَّمَا الْغَيْبُ لِلَّهِ فَانتَظِرُوا إِنِّي مَعَكُم مِّنَ الْمُنتَظِرِينَ

20 6:37, 59, 158

20 And they say, "If only a miracle was sent down to him from his Lord." Say, "The realm of the unseen belongs to God; so wait, I am waiting with you."

٢١ وَإِذَا أَذَقْنَا النَّاسَ رَحْمَةً مِنْ بَعْدِ ضَرَّاءَ مَسَّتْهُمْ إِذَا لَهُمْ مَكْرٌ فِي آيَاتِنَا ۚ قُلِ اللَّهُ أَسْرَعُ مَكْرًا ۚ إِنَّ رُسُلَنَا يَكْتُبُونَ مَا تَمْكُرُونَ

21 / 11:9

21 When We make the people taste mercy after some adversity has touched them, they begin to scheme against Our revelations. Say, "God is swifter in scheming." Our envoys are writing down what you scheme.

٢٢ هُوَ الَّذِي يُسَيِّرُكُمْ فِي الْبَرِّ وَالْبَحْرِ ۖ حَتَّىٰ إِذَا كُنْتُمْ فِي الْفُلْكِ وَجَرَيْنَ بِهِمْ بِرِيحٍ طَيِّبَةٍ وَفَرِحُوا بِهَا جَاءَتْهَا رِيحٌ عَاصِفٌ وَجَاءَهُمُ الْمَوْجُ مِنْ كُلِّ مَكَانٍ وَظَنُّوا أَنَّهُمْ أُحِيطَ بِهِمْ ۙ دَعَوُا اللَّهَ مُخْلِصِينَ لَهُ الدِّينَ لَئِنْ أَنْجَيْتَنَا مِنْ هَٰذِهِ لَنَكُونَنَّ مِنَ الشَّاكِرِينَ

22 / 29:65

22 It is He who transports you across land and sea. Until, when you are on ships, sailing in a favorable wind, and rejoicing in it, a raging wind arrives. The waves surge over them from every side, and they realize that they are besieged. Thereupon they pray to God, professing sincere devotion to Him: "If You save us from this, we will be among the appreciative."

٢٣ فَلَمَّا أَنْجَاهُمْ إِذَا هُمْ يَبْغُونَ فِي الْأَرْضِ بِغَيْرِ الْحَقِّ ۗ يَا أَيُّهَا النَّاسُ إِنَّمَا بَغْيُكُمْ عَلَىٰ أَنْفُسِكُمْ ۖ مَتَاعَ الْحَيَاةِ الدُّنْيَا ۖ ثُمَّ إِلَيْنَا مَرْجِعُكُمْ فَنُنَبِّئُكُمْ بِمَا كُنْتُمْ تَعْمَلُونَ

23 / 10:70

23 But then, when He has saved them, they commit violations on earth, and oppose justice. O people! Your violations are against your own souls. It is the enjoyment of the present life. Then to Us is your return, and We will inform you of what you used to do.

٢٤ إِنَّمَا مَثَلُ الْحَيَاةِ الدُّنْيَا كَمَاءٍ أَنْزَلْنَاهُ مِنَ السَّمَاءِ فَاخْتَلَطَ بِهِ نَبَاتُ الْأَرْضِ مِمَّا يَأْكُلُ النَّاسُ وَالْأَنْعَامُ حَتَّىٰ إِذَا أَخَذَتِ الْأَرْضُ زُخْرُفَهَا وَازَّيَّنَتْ وَظَنَّ أَهْلُهَا أَنَّهُمْ قَادِرُونَ عَلَيْهَا أَتَاهَا أَمْرُنَا لَيْلًا أَوْ نَهَارًا فَجَعَلْنَاهَا حَصِيدًا كَأَنْ لَمْ تَغْنَ بِالْأَمْسِ ۚ كَذَٰلِكَ نُفَصِّلُ الْآيَاتِ لِقَوْمٍ يَتَفَكَّرُونَ

24 / 18:45; 57:20

24 The likeness of the present life is this: water that We send down from the sky is absorbed by the plants of the earth, from which the people and the animals eat. Until, when the earth puts on its fine appearance, and is beautified, and its inhabitants think that they have mastered it, Our command descends upon it by night or by day, and We turn it into stubble, as if it had not flourished the day before. We thus clarify the revelations for people who reflect.

٢٥ وَاللَّهُ يَدْعُو إِلَىٰ دَارِ السَّلَامِ وَيَهْدِي مَنْ يَشَاءُ إِلَىٰ صِرَاطٍ مُسْتَقِيمٍ

25 / 1:6; 2:142, 213; 6:127

25 God invites to the Home of Peace, and guides whomever He wills to a straight path.

٢٦ لِلَّذِينَ أَحْسَنُوا الْحُسْنَىٰ وَزِيَادَةٌ ۖ وَلَا يَرْهَقُ وُجُوهَهُمْ قَتَرٌ وَلَا ذِلَّةٌ ۚ أُولَٰئِكَ أَصْحَابُ الْجَنَّةِ ۖ هُمْ فِيهَا خَالِدُونَ

26 / 6:160; 55:60

26 For those who have done good is goodness, and more. Neither gloom nor shame will come over their faces. These are the inhabitants of Paradise, abiding therein forever.

٢٧ وَالَّذِينَ كَسَبُوا السَّيِّئَاتِ جَزَاءُ سَيِّئَةٍ بِمِثْلِهَا وَتَرْهَقُهُمْ ذِلَّةٌ ۖ مَا لَهُمْ مِنَ اللَّهِ مِنْ عَاصِمٍ ۖ كَأَنَّمَا أُغْشِيَتْ وُجُوهُهُمْ قِطَعًا مِنَ اللَّيْلِ مُظْلِمًا ۚ أُولَٰئِكَ أَصْحَابُ النَّارِ ۖ هُمْ فِيهَا خَالِدُونَ

27 As for those who have earned evil deeds: a reward of similar evil, and shame will cover them. They will have no defense against God—as if their faces are covered with dark patches of night. These are the inmates of the Fire, abiding therein forever.

٢٨ وَيَوْمَ نَحْشُرُهُمْ جَمِيعًا ثُمَّ نَقُولُ لِلَّذِينَ أَشْرَكُوا مَكَانَكُمْ أَنْتُمْ وَشُرَكَاؤُكُمْ ۚ فَزَيَّلْنَا بَيْنَهُمْ ۖ وَقَالَ شُرَكَاؤُهُمْ مَا كُنْتُمْ إِيَّانَا تَعْبُدُونَ

28
6:128

28 On the Day when We will gather them altogether, then say to those who ascribed partners, "To your place, you and your partners." Then We will separate between them, and their partners will say, "It was not us you were worshiping."

٢٩ فَكَفَىٰ بِاللَّهِ شَهِيدًا بَيْنَنَا وَبَيْنَكُمْ إِنْ كُنَّا عَنْ عِبَادَتِكُمْ لَغَافِلِينَ

29 "God is sufficient witness between us and you. We were unaware of your worshiping us."

٣٠ هُنَالِكَ تَبْلُو كُلُّ نَفْسٍ مَا أَسْلَفَتْ ۚ وَرُدُّوا إِلَى اللَّهِ مَوْلَاهُمُ الْحَقِّ ۖ وَضَلَّ عَنْهُمْ مَا كَانُوا يَفْتَرُونَ

30
17:13; 75:13; 86:9

30 There, every soul will experience what it had done previously; and they will be returned to God, their True Master; and what they used to invent will fail them.

٣١ قُلْ مَنْ يَرْزُقُكُمْ مِنَ السَّمَاءِ وَالْأَرْضِ أَمَّنْ يَمْلِكُ السَّمْعَ وَالْأَبْصَارَ وَمَنْ يُخْرِجُ الْحَيَّ مِنَ الْمَيِّتِ وَيُخْرِجُ الْمَيِّتَ مِنَ الْحَيِّ وَمَنْ يُدَبِّرُ الْأَمْرَ ۚ فَسَيَقُولُونَ اللَّهُ ۚ فَقُلْ أَفَلَا تَتَّقُونَ

31
23:84–85; 43:9, 43, 87

31 Say, "Who provides for you from the heaven and the earth? And who controls the hearing and the sight? And who produces the living from the dead, and produces the dead from the living? And who governs the Order?" They will say, "God." Say, "Will you not be careful?"

٣٢ فَذَٰلِكُمُ اللَّهُ رَبُّكُمُ الْحَقُّ ۖ فَمَاذَا بَعْدَ الْحَقِّ إِلَّا الضَّلَالُ ۖ فَأَنَّىٰ تُصْرَفُونَ

32 Such is God, your Lord—the True. What is there, beyond the truth, except falsehood? How are you turned away?

٣٣ كَذَٰلِكَ حَقَّتْ كَلِمَتُ رَبِّكَ عَلَى الَّذِينَ فَسَقُوا أَنَّهُمْ لَا يُؤْمِنُونَ

33
10:96; 40:5

33 Thus your Lord's Word proved true against those who disobeyed, for they do not believe.

٣٤ قُلْ هَلْ مِنْ شُرَكَائِكُمْ مَنْ يَبْدَأُ الْخَلْقَ ثُمَّ يُعِيدُهُ ۚ قُلِ اللَّهُ يَبْدَأُ الْخَلْقَ ثُمَّ يُعِيدُهُ ۖ فَأَنَّىٰ تُؤْفَكُونَ

34
16:17; 25:3; 29:13;
30:40; 35:3

34 Say, "Can any of your partners initiate creation, and then repeat it?" Say, "God initiates creation, and then repeats it. How are you so deluded?"

٣٥ قُلْ هَلْ مِنْ شُرَكَائِكُمْ مَنْ يَهْدِي إِلَى الْحَقِّ ۚ قُلِ اللَّهُ يَهْدِي لِلْحَقِّ ۗ أَفَمَنْ يَهْدِي إِلَى الْحَقِّ أَحَقُّ أَنْ يُتَّبَعَ أَمَّنْ لَا يَهِدِّي إِلَّا أَنْ يُهْدَىٰ ۖ فَمَا لَكُمْ كَيْفَ تَحْكُمُونَ

35 Say, "Can any of your partners guide to the truth?" Say, "God guides to the truth. Is He who guides to the truth more worthy of being followed, or he who does not guide, unless he himself is guided? What is the matter with you? How do you judge?"

٣٦ وَمَا يَتَّبِعُ أَكْثَرُهُمْ إِلَّا ظَنًّا ۚ إِنَّ الظَّنَّ لَا يُغْنِي مِنَ الْحَقِّ شَيْئًا ۚ إِنَّ اللَّهَ عَلِيمٌ بِمَا يَفْعَلُونَ

36
6:116; 53:28

36 Most of them follow nothing but assumptions; and assumptions avail nothing against the truth. God is fully aware of what they do.

٣٧ وَمَا كَانَ هَٰذَا الْقُرْآنُ أَنْ يُفْتَرَىٰ مِنْ دُونِ اللَّهِ وَلَٰكِنْ تَصْدِيقَ الَّذِي بَيْنَ يَدَيْهِ وَتَفْصِيلَ الْكِتَابِ لَا رَيْبَ فِيهِ مِنْ رَبِّ الْعَالَمِينَ

37
10:38; 12:111;
16:210–211; 17:105

37 This Qur'an could not have been produced by anyone other than God. In fact, it is a confirmation of what preceded it, and an elaboration of the Book. There is no doubt about it—it is from the Lord of the Universe.

٣٨ أَمْ يَقُولُونَ افْتَرَاهُ ۖ قُلْ فَأْتُوا بِسُورَةٍ مِثْلِهِ وَادْعُوا مَنِ اسْتَطَعْتُمْ مِنْ دُونِ اللَّهِ إِنْ كُنْتُمْ صَادِقِينَ

38
2:23; 11:13; 17:88;
46:8

38 Or do they say, "He has forged it"? Say, "Then produce a single chapter like it, and call upon whomever you can, apart from God, if you are truthful."

٣٩ بَلْ كَذَّبُوا بِمَا لَمْ يُحِيطُوا بِعِلْمِهِ وَلَمَّا يَأْتِهِمْ تَأْوِيلُهُ ۚ كَذَٰلِكَ كَذَّبَ الَّذِينَ مِنْ قَبْلِهِمْ ۖ فَانْظُرْ كَيْفَ كَانَ عَاقِبَةُ الظَّالِمِينَ

39
7:53; 27:84

39 In fact, they deny what is beyond the limits of their knowledge, and whose explanation has not yet reached them. Thus those before them refused to believe. So note the consequences for the wrongdoers.

٤٠ وَمِنْهُمْ مَنْ يُؤْمِنُ بِهِ وَمِنْهُمْ مَنْ لَا يُؤْمِنُ بِهِ ۚ وَرَبُّكَ أَعْلَمُ بِالْمُفْسِدِينَ

40 Among them are those who believe in it, and among them are those who do not believe in it. Your Lord is fully aware of the mischief-makers.

٤١ وَإِنْ كَذَّبُوكَ فَقُلْ لِي عَمَلِي وَلَكُمْ عَمَلُكُمْ ۖ أَنْتُمْ بَرِيئُونَ مِمَّا أَعْمَلُ وَأَنَا بَرِيءٌ مِمَّا تَعْمَلُونَ

41
2:139; 28:55; 42:15;
109:2–5

41 If they accuse you of lying, say, "I have my deeds, and you have your deeds. You are quit of what I do, and I am quit of what you do."

٤٢ وَمِنْهُمْ مَنْ يَسْتَمِعُونَ إِلَيْكَ ۚ أَفَأَنْتَ تُسْمِعُ الصُّمَّ وَلَوْ كَانُوا لَا يَعْقِلُونَ

42
27:80

42 And among them are those who listen to you. But can you make the deaf hear, even though they do not understand?

٤٣ وَمِنْهُمْ مَنْ يَنْظُرُ إِلَيْكَ ۚ أَفَأَنْتَ تَهْدِي الْعُمْيَ وَلَوْ كَانُوا لَا يُبْصِرُونَ

43 And among them are those who look at you. But can you guide the blind, even though they do not see?

٤٤ إِنَّ اللَّهَ لَا يَظْلِمُ النَّاسَ شَيْئًا وَلَٰكِنَّ النَّاسَ أَنفُسَهُمْ يَظْلِمُونَ	44 3:117; 10:44; 11:101; 29:40
44 God does not wrong the people in the least, but the people wrong their own selves.	
٤٥ وَيَوْمَ يَحْشُرُهُمْ كَأَن لَّمْ يَلْبَثُوا إِلَّا سَاعَةً مِّنَ النَّهَارِ يَتَعَارَفُونَ بَيْنَهُمْ ۚ قَدْ خَسِرَ الَّذِينَ كَذَّبُوا بِلِقَاءِ اللَّهِ وَمَا كَانُوا مُهْتَدِينَ	45 20:103; 23:113; 30:55; 46:35; 79:46
45 On the Day when He rounds them up—as if they had tarried only one hour of a day—they will recognize one another. Those who denied the meeting with God will be the losers. They were not guided.	
٤٦ وَإِمَّا نُرِيَنَّكَ بَعْضَ الَّذِي نَعِدُهُمْ أَوْ نَتَوَفَّيَنَّكَ فَإِلَيْنَا مَرْجِعُهُمْ ثُمَّ اللَّهُ شَهِيدٌ عَلَىٰ مَا يَفْعَلُونَ	46 13:40; 40:77; 43:42
46 Whether We show you some of what We promise them, or take you, to Us is their return. God is witness to everything they do.	
٤٧ وَلِكُلِّ أُمَّةٍ رَّسُولٌ ۖ فَإِذَا جَاءَ رَسُولُهُمْ قُضِيَ بَيْنَهُم بِالْقِسْطِ وَهُمْ لَا يُظْلَمُونَ	47 13:7; 16:36; 35:24
47 Every community has a messenger. When their messenger has come, judgment will be passed between them with fairness, and they will not be wronged.	
٤٨ وَيَقُولُونَ مَتَىٰ هَٰذَا الْوَعْدُ إِن كُنتُمْ صَادِقِينَ	48 21:28; 27:71; 34:29
48 And they say, "When will this promise be fulfilled, if you are truthful?"	
٤٩ قُل لَّا أَمْلِكُ لِنَفْسِي ضَرًّا وَلَا نَفْعًا إِلَّا مَا شَاءَ اللَّهُ ۗ لِكُلِّ أُمَّةٍ أَجَلٌ ۚ إِذَا جَاءَ أَجَلُهُمْ فَلَا يَسْتَأْخِرُونَ سَاعَةً ۖ وَلَا يَسْتَقْدِمُونَ	49 15:5; 23:43; 34:42; 63:11; 71:4
49 Say, "I have no power to harm or benefit myself, except as God wills. To every nation is an appointed time. Then, when their time arrives, they can neither postpone it by one hour, nor advance it.	
٥٠ قُلْ أَرَأَيْتُمْ إِنْ أَتَاكُمْ عَذَابُهُ بَيَاتًا أَوْ نَهَارًا مَّاذَا يَسْتَعْجِلُ مِنْهُ الْمُجْرِمُونَ	50 6:47; 7:4, 97; 10:24; 12:107; 42:18; 50:14
50 Say, "Have you considered? If His punishment overtakes you by night or by day, what part of it will the guilty seek to hasten?"	
٥١ أَثُمَّ إِذَا مَا وَقَعَ آمَنتُم بِهِ ۚ آلْآنَ وَقَدْ كُنتُم بِهِ تَسْتَعْجِلُونَ	51 4:18; 10:51; 40:84,85
51 "Then, when it falls, will you believe in it? Now? When before you tried to hasten it?"	
٥٢ ثُمَّ قِيلَ لِلَّذِينَ ظَلَمُوا ذُوقُوا عَذَابَ الْخُلْدِ هَلْ تُجْزَوْنَ إِلَّا بِمَا كُنتُمْ تَكْسِبُونَ	52 40:17
52 Then it will be said to those who did wrong, "Taste the torment of eternity. Will you be rewarded except for what you used to do?"	
٥٣ وَيَسْتَنبِئُونَكَ أَحَقٌّ هُوَ ۖ قُلْ إِي وَرَبِّي إِنَّهُ لَحَقٌّ ۖ وَمَا أَنتُم بِمُعْجِزِينَ	53 6:30, 134; 10:55; 46:34
53 And they inquire of you, "Is it true?" Say, "Yes, by my Lord, it is true, and you cannot evade it."	

٥٤ وَلَوْ أَنَّ لِكُلِّ نَفْسٍ ظَلَمَتْ مَا فِي الْأَرْضِ لَافْتَدَتْ بِهِ ۗ وَأَسَرُّوا النَّدَامَةَ لَمَّا رَأَوُا الْعَذَابَ ۖ وَقُضِيَ بَيْنَهُم بِالْقِسْطِ ۚ وَهُمْ لَا يُظْلَمُونَ

54   5:36; 13:18; 34:33; 39:47

54 Had every soul which had done wrong possessed everything on earth, it would offer it as a ransom. They will hide the remorse when they witness the suffering, and it will be judged between them equitably, and they will not be wronged.

٥٥ أَلَا إِنَّ لِلَّهِ مَا فِي السَّمَاوَاتِ وَالْأَرْضِ ۗ أَلَا إِنَّ وَعْدَ اللَّهِ حَقٌّ وَلَٰكِنَّ أَكْثَرَهُمْ لَا يَعْلَمُونَ

55   16:38; 30:6

55 Assuredly, to God belongs everything in the heavens and the earth. Assuredly, the promise of God is true. But most of them do not know.

٥٦ هُوَ يُحْيِي وَيُمِيتُ وَإِلَيْهِ تُرْجَعُونَ

56 He gives life and causes death, and to Him you will be returned.

٥٧ يَا أَيُّهَا النَّاسُ قَدْ جَاءَتْكُم مَّوْعِظَةٌ مِّن رَّبِّكُمْ وَشِفَاءٌ لِّمَا فِي الصُّدُورِ وَهُدًى وَرَحْمَةٌ لِّلْمُؤْمِنِينَ

57   3:138; 11:120; 17:82; 24:34

57 O people! There has come to you advice from your Lord, and healing for what is in the hearts, and guidance and mercy for the believers.

٥٨ قُلْ بِفَضْلِ اللَّهِ وَبِرَحْمَتِهِ فَبِذَٰلِكَ فَلْيَفْرَحُوا هُوَ خَيْرٌ مِّمَّا يَجْمَعُونَ

58 Say, "In God's grace and mercy let them rejoice. That is better than what they hoard."

٥٩ قُلْ أَرَأَيْتُم مَّا أَنزَلَ اللَّهُ لَكُم مِّن رِّزْقٍ فَجَعَلْتُم مِّنْهُ حَرَامًا وَحَلَالًا قُلْ آللَّهُ أَذِنَ لَكُمْ ۖ أَمْ عَلَى اللَّهِ تَفْتَرُونَ

59   5:87; 6:140; 16:116

59 Say, "Have you considered the sustenance God has sent down for you, some of which you made unlawful, and some lawful?" Say, "Did God give you permission, or do you fabricate lies and attribute them to God?"

٦٠ وَمَا ظَنُّ الَّذِينَ يَفْتَرُونَ عَلَى اللَّهِ الْكَذِبَ يَوْمَ الْقِيَامَةِ ۗ إِنَّ اللَّهَ لَذُو فَضْلٍ عَلَى النَّاسِ وَلَٰكِنَّ أَكْثَرَهُمْ لَا يَشْكُرُونَ

60   2:243; 27:73; 40:61

60 What will they think—those who fabricate lies and attribute them to God—on the Day of Resurrection? God is bountiful towards the people, but most of them do not give thanks.

٦١ وَمَا تَكُونُ فِي شَأْنٍ وَمَا تَتْلُو مِنْهُ مِن قُرْآنٍ وَلَا تَعْمَلُونَ مِنْ عَمَلٍ إِلَّا كُنَّا عَلَيْكُمْ شُهُودًا إِذْ تُفِيضُونَ فِيهِ ۚ وَمَا يَعْزُبُ عَن رَّبِّكَ مِن مِّثْقَالِ ذَرَّةٍ فِي الْأَرْضِ وَلَا فِي السَّمَاءِ وَلَا أَصْغَرَ مِن ذَٰلِكَ وَلَا أَكْبَرَ إِلَّا فِي كِتَابٍ مُّبِينٍ

61   11:5; 34:3; 99:7–8

61 You do not get into any situation, nor do you recite any Qur'an, nor do you do anything, but We are watching over you as you undertake it. Not even the weight of an atom, on earth or in the sky, escapes your Lord, nor is there anything smaller or larger, but is in a clear record.

٦٢ أَلَا إِنَّ أَوْلِيَاءَ اللَّهِ لَا خَوْفٌ عَلَيْهِمْ وَلَا هُمْ يَحْزَنُونَ

62 Unquestionably, God's friends have nothing to fear, nor shall they grieve.

62
8:34; 45:19

٦٣ الَّذِينَ آمَنُوا وَكَانُوا يَتَّقُونَ

63 Those who believe and are aware.

٦٤ لَهُمُ الْبُشْرَىٰ فِي الْحَيَاةِ الدُّنْيَا وَفِي الْآخِرَةِ ۚ لَا تَبْدِيلَ لِكَلِمَاتِ اللَّهِ ۚ ذَٰلِكَ هُوَ الْفَوْزُ الْعَظِيمُ

64 For them is good news in this life, and in the Hereafter. There is no alteration to the words of God. That is the supreme triumph.

64
6:34; 39:17; 41:30

٦٥ وَلَا يَحْزُنْكَ قَوْلُهُمْ ۘ إِنَّ الْعِزَّةَ لِلَّهِ جَمِيعًا ۚ هُوَ السَّمِيعُ الْعَلِيمُ

65 And let not their sayings dishearten you. All power is God's. He is the Hearer, the Knower.

65
36:76

٦٦ أَلَا إِنَّ لِلَّهِ مَنْ فِي السَّمَاوَاتِ وَمَنْ فِي الْأَرْضِ ۗ وَمَا يَتَّبِعُ الَّذِينَ يَدْعُونَ مِنْ دُونِ اللَّهِ شُرَكَاءَ ۚ إِنْ يَتَّبِعُونَ إِلَّا الظَّنَّ وَإِنْ هُمْ إِلَّا يَخْرُصُونَ

66 Certainly, to God belongs everyone in the heavens and everyone on earth. Those who invoke other than God do not follow partners; they follow only assumptions, and they only guess.

66
6:116, 148

٦٧ هُوَ الَّذِي جَعَلَ لَكُمُ اللَّيْلَ لِتَسْكُنُوا فِيهِ وَالنَّهَارَ مُبْصِرًا ۚ إِنَّ فِي ذَٰلِكَ لَآيَاتٍ لِقَوْمٍ يَسْمَعُونَ

67 It is He who made the night for your rest, and the daylight for visibility. Surely in that are signs for people who listen.

67
6:13; 27:86; 40:61

٦٨ قَالُوا اتَّخَذَ اللَّهُ وَلَدًا ۗ سُبْحَانَهُ ۖ هُوَ الْغَنِيُّ ۖ لَهُ مَا فِي السَّمَاوَاتِ وَمَا فِي الْأَرْضِ ۚ إِنْ عِنْدَكُمْ مِنْ سُلْطَانٍ بِهَٰذَا ۚ أَتَقُولُونَ عَلَى اللَّهِ مَا لَا تَعْلَمُونَ

68 And they said, "God has taken a son." Be He glorified. He is the Self-Sufficient. His is everything in the heavens and everything on earth. Do you have any proof for this? Or are you saying about God what you do not know?

68
2:116; 4:171; 6:100; 17:40, 111; 19:35; 21:26; 23:91; 25:2

٦٩ قُلْ إِنَّ الَّذِينَ يَفْتَرُونَ عَلَى اللَّهِ الْكَذِبَ لَا يُفْلِحُونَ

69 Say, "Those who fabricate lies about God will not succeed."

69
6:21; 16:116

٧٠ مَتَاعٌ فِي الدُّنْيَا ثُمَّ إِلَيْنَا مَرْجِعُهُمْ ثُمَّ نُذِيقُهُمُ الْعَذَابَ الشَّدِيدَ بِمَا كَانُوا يَكْفُرُونَ

70 Some enjoyment in this world; then to Us is their return; then We will make them taste the severe punishment on account of their disbelief.

70
2:36; 16:117

٧١ وَاتْلُ عَلَيْهِمْ نَبَأَ نُوحٍ إِذْ قَالَ لِقَوْمِهِ يَا قَوْمِ إِنْ كَانَ كَبُرَ عَلَيْكُمْ مَقَامِي وَتَذْكِيرِي بِآيَاتِ اللَّهِ فَعَلَى اللَّهِ تَوَكَّلْتُ فَأَجْمِعُوا أَمْرَكُمْ وَشُرَكَاءَكُمْ ثُمَّ لَا يَكُنْ أَمْرُكُمْ عَلَيْكُمْ غُمَّةً ثُمَّ اقْضُوا إِلَيَّ وَلَا تُنْظِرُونِ

71 And relate to them the story of Noah, when he said to his people, "O my people, if my presence among you and my reminding you of God's signs is too much for you, then in God I have put my trust. So come to a decision, you and your partners, and do not let the matter perplex you; then carry out your decision on me, and do not hold back."

71–73
7:59–64

٧٢ فَإِن تَوَلَّيْتُمْ فَمَا سَأَلْتُكُم مِّنْ أَجْرٍ ۖ إِنْ أَجْرِيَ إِلَّا عَلَى اللَّهِ ۖ وَأُمِرْتُ أَنْ أَكُونَ مِنَ الْمُسْلِمِينَ

72 "But if you turn away, I have not asked you for any wage. My wage falls only on God, and I was commanded to be of those who submit."

٧٣ فَكَذَّبُوهُ فَنَجَّيْنَاهُ وَمَن مَّعَهُ فِي الْفُلْكِ وَجَعَلْنَاهُمْ خَلَائِفَ وَأَغْرَقْنَا الَّذِينَ كَذَّبُوا بِآيَاتِنَا ۖ فَانظُرْ كَيْفَ كَانَ عَاقِبَةُ الْمُنذَرِينَ

73 — 7:64; 21:76; 26:119; 29:14; 54:11

73 But they denounced him, so We saved him and those with him in the Ark, and We made them successors, and We drowned those who rejected Our signs. So consider the fate of those who were warned.

٧٤ ثُمَّ بَعَثْنَا مِن بَعْدِهِ رُسُلًا إِلَىٰ قَوْمِهِمْ فَجَاءُوهُم بِالْبَيِّنَاتِ فَمَا كَانُوا لِيُؤْمِنُوا بِمَا كَذَّبُوا بِهِ مِن قَبْلُ ۚ كَذَٰلِكَ نَطْبَعُ عَلَىٰ قُلُوبِ الْمُعْتَدِينَ

74 — 7:101

74 Then, after him, We sent messengers to their people. They came to them with the clear proofs, but they would not believe in anything they had already rejected. Thus We set a seal on the hearts of the hostile.

٧٥ ثُمَّ بَعَثْنَا مِن بَعْدِهِم مُّوسَىٰ وَهَارُونَ إِلَىٰ فِرْعَوْنَ وَمَلَئِهِ بِآيَاتِنَا فَاسْتَكْبَرُوا وَكَانُوا قَوْمًا مُّجْرِمِينَ

75 — 7:103; 11:96; 23:45; 27:13–14

75 Then, after them, We sent Moses and Aaron with Our proofs to Pharaoh and his dignitaries. But they acted arrogantly. They were sinful people.

٧٦ فَلَمَّا جَاءَهُمُ الْحَقُّ مِنْ عِندِنَا قَالُوا إِنَّ هَٰذَا لَسِحْرٌ مُّبِينٌ

76 — 7:109; 27:13; 28:36, 48; 40:23; 43:30; 46:7

76 And when the truth came to them from Us, they said, "This is clearly sorcery."

٧٧ قَالَ مُوسَىٰ أَتَقُولُونَ لِلْحَقِّ لَمَّا جَاءَكُمْ ۖ أَسِحْرٌ هَٰذَا وَلَا يُفْلِحُ السَّاحِرُونَ

77 Moses said, "Is this what you say of the truth when it has come to you? Is this sorcery? Sorcerers do not succeed."

٧٨ قَالُوا أَجِئْتَنَا لِتَلْفِتَنَا عَمَّا وَجَدْنَا عَلَيْهِ آبَاءَنَا وَتَكُونَ لَكُمَا الْكِبْرِيَاءُ فِي الْأَرْضِ وَمَا نَحْنُ لَكُمَا بِمُؤْمِنِينَ

78 — 7:70; 11:62, 87; 14:10

78 They said, "Did you come to us to divert us from what we found our ancestors following, and so that you become prominent in the land? We will never believe in you."

٧٩ وَقَالَ فِرْعَوْنُ ائْتُونِي بِكُلِّ سَاحِرٍ عَلِيمٍ

79 — 7:111; 20:58–60; 26:36–38

79 Pharaoh said, "Bring me every experienced sorcerer."

٨٠ فَلَمَّا جَاءَ السَّحَرَةُ قَالَ لَهُم مُّوسَىٰ أَلْقُوا مَا أَنتُم مُّلْقُونَ

80 — 7:113–116; 20:65; 26:41–43

80 And when the sorcerers came, Moses said to them, "Throw whatever you have to throw."

٨١ فَلَمَّا أَلْقَوْا قَالَ مُوسَىٰ مَا جِئْتُمْ بِهِ السِّحْرُ ۖ إِنَّ اللَّهَ سَيُبْطِلُهُ ۖ إِنَّ اللَّهَ لَا يُصْلِحُ عَمَلَ الْمُفْسِدِينَ

81 7:116–118; 20:67–69

81 And when they threw, Moses said, "What you produced is sorcery, and God will make it fail. God does not foster the efforts of the corrupt."

٨٢ وَيُحِقُّ اللَّهُ الْحَقَّ بِكَلِمَاتِهِ وَلَوْ كَرِهَ الْمُجْرِمُونَ

82 8:8

82 "And God upholds the truth with His words, even though the sinners detest it."

٨٣ فَمَا آمَنَ لِمُوسَىٰ إِلَّا ذُرِّيَّةٌ مِنْ قَوْمِهِ عَلَىٰ خَوْفٍ مِنْ فِرْعَوْنَ وَمَلَئِهِمْ أَنْ يَفْتِنَهُمْ ۚ وَإِنَّ فِرْعَوْنَ لَعَالٍ فِي الْأَرْضِ وَإِنَّهُ لَمِنَ الْمُسْرِفِينَ

83 7:120–124

83 But none believed in Moses except some children of his people, for fear that Pharaoh and his chiefs would persecute them. Pharaoh was high and mighty in the land. He was a tyrant.

٨٤ وَقَالَ مُوسَىٰ يَا قَوْمِ إِنْ كُنْتُمْ آمَنْتُمْ بِاللَّهِ فَعَلَيْهِ تَوَكَّلُوا إِنْ كُنْتُمْ مُسْلِمِينَ

84 Moses said, "O my people, if you have believed in God, then put your trust in Him, if you have submitted."

٨٥ فَقَالُوا عَلَى اللَّهِ تَوَكَّلْنَا رَبَّنَا لَا تَجْعَلْنَا فِتْنَةً لِلْقَوْمِ الظَّالِمِينَ

85 60:5

85 They said, "In God we have put our trust. Our Lord, do not make us victims of the oppressive people."

٨٦ وَنَجِّنَا بِرَحْمَتِكَ مِنَ الْقَوْمِ الْكَافِرِينَ

86 2:49

86 "And deliver us, by Your mercy, from the disbelieving people."

٨٧ وَأَوْحَيْنَا إِلَىٰ مُوسَىٰ وَأَخِيهِ أَنْ تَبَوَّآ لِقَوْمِكُمَا بِمِصْرَ بُيُوتًا وَاجْعَلُوا بُيُوتَكُمْ قِبْلَةً وَأَقِيمُوا الصَّلَاةَ ۗ وَبَشِّرِ الْمُؤْمِنِينَ

87 And We inspired Moses and his brother, "Settle your people in Egypt, and make your homes places of worship, and perform the prayer, and give good news to the believers."

٨٨ وَقَالَ مُوسَىٰ رَبَّنَا إِنَّكَ آتَيْتَ فِرْعَوْنَ وَمَلَأَهُ زِينَةً وَأَمْوَالًا فِي الْحَيَاةِ الدُّنْيَا رَبَّنَا لِيُضِلُّوا عَنْ سَبِيلِكَ ۖ رَبَّنَا اطْمِسْ عَلَىٰ أَمْوَالِهِمْ وَاشْدُدْ عَلَىٰ قُلُوبِهِمْ فَلَا يُؤْمِنُوا حَتَّىٰ يَرَوُا الْعَذَابَ الْأَلِيمَ

88 Moses said, "Our Lord, you have given Pharaoh and his chiefs splendor and wealth in the worldly life. Our Lord, for them to lead away from Your path. Our Lord, obliterate their wealth, and harden their hearts, they will not believe until they see the painful torment."

٨٩ قَالَ قَدْ أُجِيبَتْ دَعْوَتُكُمَا فَاسْتَقِيمَا وَلَا تَتَّبِعَانِّ سَبِيلَ الَّذِينَ لَا يَعْلَمُونَ

89 He said, "Your prayer has been answered, so go straight, and do not follow the path of those who do not know."

٩٠ وَجَاوَزْنَا بِبَنِي إِسْرَائِيلَ الْبَحْرَ فَأَتْبَعَهُمْ فِرْعَوْنُ وَجُنُودُهُ بَغْيًا وَعَدْوًا ۖ حَتَّىٰ إِذَا أَدْرَكَهُ الْغَرَقُ قَالَ آمَنْتُ أَنَّهُ لَا إِلَٰهَ إِلَّا الَّذِي آمَنَتْ بِهِ بَنُو إِسْرَائِيلَ وَأَنَا مِنَ الْمُسْلِمِينَ

90   7:138; 20:77; 85:17

90 And We delivered the Children of Israel across the sea. Pharaoh and his troops pursued them, defiantly and aggressively. Until, when he was about to drown, he said, "I believe that there is no god except the One the Children of Israel believe in, and I am of those who submit."

٩١ آلْآنَ وَقَدْ عَصَيْتَ قَبْلُ وَكُنْتَ مِنَ الْمُفْسِدِينَ

91 Now? When you have rebelled before, and been of the mischief-makers?

٩٢ فَالْيَوْمَ نُنَجِّيكَ بِبَدَنِكَ لِتَكُونَ لِمَنْ خَلْفَكَ آيَةً ۚ وَإِنَّ كَثِيرًا مِنَ النَّاسِ عَنْ آيَاتِنَا لَغَافِلُونَ

92 Today We will preserve your body, so that you become a sign for those after you. But most people are heedless of Our signs.

٩٣ وَلَقَدْ بَوَّأْنَا بَنِي إِسْرَائِيلَ مُبَوَّأَ صِدْقٍ وَرَزَقْنَاهُمْ مِنَ الطَّيِّبَاتِ فَمَا اخْتَلَفُوا حَتَّىٰ جَاءَهُمُ الْعِلْمُ ۚ إِنَّ رَبَّكَ يَقْضِي بَيْنَهُمْ يَوْمَ الْقِيَامَةِ فِيمَا كَانُوا فِيهِ يَخْتَلِفُونَ

93   7:137; 26:59

93 And We settled the Children of Israel in a position of honor, and provided them with good things. They did not differ until knowledge came to them. Your Lord will judge between them on the Day of Resurrection regarding their differences.

٩٤ فَإِنْ كُنْتَ فِي شَكٍّ مِمَّا أَنْزَلْنَا إِلَيْكَ فَاسْأَلِ الَّذِينَ يَقْرَءُونَ الْكِتَابَ مِنْ قَبْلِكَ ۚ لَقَدْ جَاءَكَ الْحَقُّ مِنْ رَبِّكَ فَلَا تَكُونَنَّ مِنَ الْمُمْتَرِينَ

94   17:101; 43:45

94 If you are in doubt about what We revealed to you, ask those who read the Scripture before you. The truth has come to you from your Lord, so do not be of those who doubt.

٩٥ وَلَا تَكُونَنَّ مِنَ الَّذِينَ كَذَّبُوا بِآيَاتِ اللَّهِ فَتَكُونَ مِنَ الْخَاسِرِينَ

95 And do not be of those who deny God's revelations, lest you become one of the losers.

٩٦ إِنَّ الَّذِينَ حَقَّتْ عَلَيْهِمْ كَلِمَتُ رَبِّكَ لَا يُؤْمِنُونَ

96–97   2:6; 6:4; 10:33

96 Those against whom your Lord's Word is justified will not believe.

٩٧ وَلَوْ جَاءَتْهُمْ كُلُّ آيَةٍ حَتَّىٰ يَرَوُا الْعَذَابَ الْأَلِيمَ

97 Even if every sign comes to them—until they see the painful punishment.

٩٨ فَلَوْلَا كَانَتْ قَرْيَةٌ آمَنَتْ فَنَفَعَهَا إِيمَانُهَا إِلَّا قَوْمَ يُونُسَ لَمَّا آمَنُوا كَشَفْنَا عَنْهُمْ عَذَابَ الْخِزْيِ فِي الْحَيَاةِ الدُّنْيَا وَمَتَّعْنَاهُمْ إِلَىٰ حِينٍ

98 If only there was one town that believed and benefited by its belief. Except for the people of Jonah. When they believed, We removed from them the suffering of disgrace in the worldly life, and We gave them comfort for a while.

٩٩ وَلَوْ شَاءَ رَبُّكَ لَآمَنَ مَنْ فِي الْأَرْضِ كُلُّهُمْ جَمِيعًا ۚ أَفَأَنْتَ تُكْرِهُ النَّاسَ حَتَّىٰ يَكُونُوا مُؤْمِنِينَ

99   6:35, 107; 12:103; 16:37; 32:13

99 Had your Lord willed, everyone on earth would have believed. Will you compel people to become believers?

١٠٠ وَمَا كَانَ لِنَفْسٍ أَنْ تُؤْمِنَ إِلَّا بِإِذْنِ اللَّهِ ۚ وَيَجْعَلُ الرِّجْسَ عَلَى الَّذِينَ لَا يَعْقِلُونَ

100   6:125

100 No soul can believe except by God's leave; and He lays disgrace upon those who refuse to understand.

١٠١ قُلِ انْظُرُوا مَاذَا فِي السَّمَاوَاتِ وَالْأَرْضِ ۚ وَمَا تُغْنِي الْآيَاتُ وَالنُّذُرُ عَنْ قَوْمٍ لَا يُؤْمِنُونَ

101   45:3; 54:5

101 Say, "Look at what is in the heavens and the earth." But signs and warnings are of no avail for people who do not believe.

١٠٢ فَهَلْ يَنْتَظِرُونَ إِلَّا مِثْلَ أَيَّامِ الَّذِينَ خَلَوْا مِنْ قَبْلِهِمْ ۚ قُلْ فَانْتَظِرُوا إِنِّي مَعَكُمْ مِنَ الْمُنْتَظِرِينَ

102   41:53

102 Do they expect anything but the likes of the days of those who passed away before them? Say, "Then wait, I will be waiting with you."

١٠٣ ثُمَّ نُنَجِّي رُسُلَنَا وَالَّذِينَ آمَنُوا ۚ كَذَٰلِكَ حَقًّا عَلَيْنَا نُنْجِ الْمُؤْمِنِينَ

103 Then We save Our messengers and those who believe. It is binding on Us to save the believers.

١٠٤ قُلْ يَا أَيُّهَا النَّاسُ إِنْ كُنْتُمْ فِي شَكٍّ مِنْ دِينِي فَلَا أَعْبُدُ الَّذِينَ تَعْبُدُونَ مِنْ دُونِ اللَّهِ وَلَٰكِنْ أَعْبُدُ اللَّهَ الَّذِي يَتَوَفَّاكُمْ ۖ وَأُمِرْتُ أَنْ أَكُونَ مِنَ الْمُؤْمِنِينَ

104 Say, "O people, if you are in doubt about my religion—I do not serve those you serve apart from God. But I serve God, the one who will terminate your lives. And I was commanded to be of the believers."

١٠٥ وَأَنْ أَقِمْ وَجْهَكَ لِلدِّينِ حَنِيفًا وَلَا تَكُونَنَّ مِنَ الْمُشْرِكِينَ

105   6:79; 7:29; 30:30

105 And dedicate yourself to the true religion—a monotheist—and never be of the polytheists.

١٠٦ وَلَا تَدْعُ مِنْ دُونِ اللَّهِ مَا لَا يَنْفَعُكَ وَلَا يَضُرُّكَ ۖ فَإِنْ فَعَلْتَ فَإِنَّكَ إِذًا مِنَ الظَّالِمِينَ

106   6:71; 10:18; 21:66; 25:55; 26:71–72; 29:17

106 And do not call, apart from God, on what neither benefits you nor harms you. If you do, you are then one of the wrongdoers.

١٠٧ وَإِنْ يَمْسَسْكَ اللَّهُ بِضُرٍّ فَلَا كَاشِفَ لَهُ إِلَّا هُوَ ۖ وَإِنْ يُرِدْكَ بِخَيْرٍ فَلَا رَادَّ لِفَضْلِهِ ۚ يُصِيبُ بِهِ مَنْ يَشَاءُ مِنْ عِبَادِهِ ۚ وَهُوَ الْغَفُورُ الرَّحِيمُ

107 If God afflicts you with harm, none can remove it except He. And if He wants good for you, none can repel His grace. He makes it reach whomever He wills of His servants. He is the Forgiver, the Merciful.

١٠٨ قُلْ يَا أَيُّهَا النَّاسُ قَدْ جَاءَكُمُ الْحَقُّ مِنْ رَبِّكُمْ ۖ فَمَنِ اهْتَدَىٰ فَإِنَّمَا يَهْتَدِي لِنَفْسِهِ ۖ وَمَنْ ضَلَّ فَإِنَّمَا يَضِلُّ عَلَيْهَا ۖ وَمَا أَنَا عَلَيْكُمْ بِوَكِيلٍ

108   4:170, 174; 27:92; 39:41

108 Say, "O people, the truth has come to you from your Lord. Whoever accepts guidance is guided for his own soul; and whoever strays only strays to its detriment. I am not a guardian over you."

١٠٩ وَٱتَّبِعْ مَا يُوحَىٰ إِلَيْكَ وَٱصْبِرْ حَتَّىٰ يَحْكُمَ ٱللَّهُ ۚ وَهُوَ خَيْرُ ٱلْحَاكِمِينَ

109 And follow what is revealed to you, and be patient until God issues His judgment, for He is the Best of judges.

109 — 6:50, 106; 33:2; 13:41

Sūrah 11: Hūd

هُود سُوْرَةُ (Hūd)

بِسْمِ ٱللَّهِ ٱلرَّحْمَٰنِ ٱلرَّحِيمِ

١ الر ۚ كِتَابٌ أُحْكِمَتْ آيَاتُهُ ثُمَّ فُصِّلَتْ مِن لَّدُنْ حَكِيمٍ خَبِيرٍ

1 Alif, Lām, Rā'. A Scripture whose Verses were perfected, then elaborated, from One who is Wise and Informed.

1 — 3:7; 22:52; 47:20

٢ أَلَّا تَعْبُدُوا إِلَّا ٱللَّهَ ۚ إِنَّنِي لَكُم مِّنْهُ نَذِيرٌ وَبَشِيرٌ

2 That you shall worship none but God. "I am a warner to you from Him, and a bearer of good news."

2 — 11:25; 41:13; 46:21

٣ وَأَنِ ٱسْتَغْفِرُوا رَبَّكُمْ ثُمَّ تُوبُوا إِلَيْهِ يُمَتِّعْكُم مَّتَاعًا حَسَنًا إِلَىٰ أَجَلٍ مُّسَمًّى وَيُؤْتِ كُلَّ ذِي فَضْلٍ فَضْلَهُ ۖ وَإِن تَوَلَّوْا فَإِنِّي أَخَافُ عَلَيْكُمْ عَذَابَ يَوْمٍ كَبِيرٍ

3 "And ask your Lord for forgiveness, and repent to Him. He will provide you with good sustenance until a stated term, and will bestow His grace on every possessor of virtue. But if you turn away, then I fear for you the punishment of a grievous Day."

3 — 2:36; 71:9–11

٤ إِلَى ٱللَّهِ مَرْجِعُكُمْ ۖ وَهُوَ عَلَىٰ كُلِّ شَيْءٍ قَدِيرٌ

4 "To God is your return, and He is Capable of all things."

4 — 2:156; 5:48; 6:60, 164; 39:7

٥ أَلَا إِنَّهُمْ يَثْنُونَ صُدُورَهُمْ لِيَسْتَخْفُوا مِنْهُ ۚ أَلَا حِينَ يَسْتَغْشُونَ ثِيَابَهُمْ يَعْلَمُ مَا يُسِرُّونَ وَمَا يُعْلِنُونَ ۚ إِنَّهُ عَلِيمٌ بِذَاتِ ٱلصُّدُورِ

5 They wrap their chests to hide from Him. But even as they cover themselves with their clothes, He knows what they conceal and what they reveal. He knows what lies within the hearts.

5 — 7:7; 10:61; 50:16

٦ وَمَا مِن دَابَّةٍ فِي ٱلْأَرْضِ إِلَّا عَلَى ٱللَّهِ رِزْقُهَا وَيَعْلَمُ مُسْتَقَرَّهَا وَمُسْتَوْدَعَهَا ۚ كُلٌّ فِي كِتَابٍ مُّبِينٍ

6 There is no moving creature on earth but its sustenance depends on God. And He knows where it lives and where it rests. Everything is in a Clear Book.

6 — 6:98; 29:60

٧ وَهُوَ الَّذِي خَلَقَ السَّمَاوَاتِ وَالْأَرْضَ فِي سِتَّةِ أَيَّامٍ وَكَانَ عَرْشُهُ عَلَى الْمَاءِ لِيَبْلُوَكُمْ أَيُّكُمْ أَحْسَنُ عَمَلًا ۗ وَلَئِنْ قُلْتَ إِنَّكُمْ مَبْعُوثُونَ مِنْ بَعْدِ الْمَوْتِ لَيَقُولَنَّ الَّذِينَ كَفَرُوا إِنْ هَٰذَا إِلَّا سِحْرٌ مُبِينٌ	7	2:255; 7:54; 10:3; 67:2

7 It is He who created the heavens and the earth in six days—and His Throne was upon the waters—in order to test you—which of you is best in conduct. And if you were to say, "You will be resurrected after death," those who disbelieve would say, "This is nothing but plain witchcraft."

٨ وَلَئِنْ أَخَّرْنَا عَنْهُمُ الْعَذَابَ إِلَىٰ أُمَّةٍ مَعْدُودَةٍ لَيَقُولُنَّ مَا يَحْبِسُهُ ۗ أَلَا يَوْمَ يَأْتِيهِمْ لَيْسَ مَصْرُوفًا عَنْهُمْ وَحَاقَ بِهِمْ مَا كَانُوا بِهِ يَسْتَهْزِئُونَ	8	11:104

8 And if We postponed their punishment until a stated time, they would say, "What holds it back?" On the Day when it reaches them, it will not be averted from them, and what they used to ridicule will besiege them.

٩ وَلَئِنْ أَذَقْنَا الْإِنْسَانَ مِنَّا رَحْمَةً ثُمَّ نَزَعْنَاهَا مِنْهُ إِنَّهُ لَيَئُوسٌ كَفُورٌ	9	10:21; 30:36; 41:47; 100:6

9 If We give the human being a taste of mercy from Us, and then withdraw it from him, he becomes despairing and ungrateful.

١٠ وَلَئِنْ أَذَقْنَاهُ نَعْمَاءَ بَعْدَ ضَرَّاءَ مَسَّتْهُ لَيَقُولَنَّ ذَهَبَ السَّيِّئَاتُ عَنِّي ۚ إِنَّهُ لَفَرِحٌ فَخُورٌ	10	17:75; 41:50

10 And if We give him a taste of prosperity, after some adversity has afflicted him, he will say, "Troubles have gone away from me." He becomes excited and proud.

١١ إِلَّا الَّذِينَ صَبَرُوا وَعَمِلُوا الصَّالِحَاتِ أُولَٰئِكَ لَهُمْ مَغْفِرَةٌ وَأَجْرٌ كَبِيرٌ	11	95:6; 103:3

11 Except those who are patient and do good deeds—these will have forgiveness and a great reward.

١٢ فَلَعَلَّكَ تَارِكٌ بَعْضَ مَا يُوحَىٰ إِلَيْكَ وَضَائِقٌ بِهِ صَدْرُكَ أَنْ يَقُولُوا لَوْلَا أُنْزِلَ عَلَيْهِ كَنْزٌ أَوْ جَاءَ مَعَهُ مَلَكٌ ۚ إِنَّمَا أَنْتَ نَذِيرٌ ۚ وَاللَّهُ عَلَىٰ كُلِّ شَيْءٍ وَكِيلٌ	12	7:2

12 Perhaps you wish to disregard some of what is revealed to you, and you may be stressed because of it, since they say, "If only a treasure was sent down to him, or an angel came with him." You are only a warner, and God is Responsible for all things.

١٣ أَمْ يَقُولُونَ افْتَرَاهُ ۖ قُلْ فَأْتُوا بِعَشْرِ سُوَرٍ مِثْلِهِ مُفْتَرَيَاتٍ وَادْعُوا مَنِ اسْتَطَعْتُمْ مِنْ دُونِ اللَّهِ إِنْ كُنْتُمْ صَادِقِينَ	13	2:23; 10:38; 17:88

13 Or do they say, "He invented it?" Say, "Then produce ten chapters like it, invented, and call upon whomever you can, besides God, if you are truthful."

١٤ فَإِلَّمْ يَسْتَجِيبُوا لَكُمْ فَاعْلَمُوا أَنَّمَا أُنْزِلَ بِعِلْمِ اللَّهِ وَأَنْ لَا إِلَٰهَ إِلَّا هُوَ ۖ فَهَلْ أَنْتُمْ مُسْلِمُونَ	14

14 But if they fail to answer you, know that it was revealed with God's knowledge, and that there is no god but He. Will you then submit?

١٥ مَن كَانَ يُرِيدُ الْحَيَاةَ الدُّنْيَا وَزِينَتَهَا نُوَفِّ إِلَيْهِمْ أَعْمَالَهُمْ فِيهَا وَهُمْ فِيهَا لَا يُبْخَسُونَ

15 Whoever desires the worldly life and its glitter—We will fully recompense them for their deeds therein, and therein they will not be defrauded.

15
3:145; 17:18; 42:20

١٦ أُولَٰئِكَ الَّذِينَ لَيْسَ لَهُمْ فِي الْآخِرَةِ إِلَّا النَّارُ ۖ وَحَبِطَ مَا صَنَعُوا فِيهَا وَبَاطِلٌ مَا كَانُوا يَعْمَلُونَ

16 These—they will have nothing but the Fire in the Hereafter. Their deeds are in vain therein, and their works are null.

16
2:217

١٧ أَفَمَن كَانَ عَلَىٰ بَيِّنَةٍ مِّن رَّبِّهِ وَيَتْلُوهُ شَاهِدٌ مِّنْهُ وَمِن قَبْلِهِ كِتَابُ مُوسَىٰ إِمَامًا وَرَحْمَةً ۚ أُولَٰئِكَ يُؤْمِنُونَ بِهِ ۚ وَمَن يَكْفُرْ بِهِ مِنَ الْأَحْزَابِ فَالنَّارُ مَوْعِدُهُ ۚ فَلَا تَكُ فِي مِرْيَةٍ مِّنْهُ ۚ إِنَّهُ الْحَقُّ مِن رَّبِّكَ وَلَٰكِنَّ أَكْثَرَ النَّاسِ لَا يُؤْمِنُونَ

17 Is he who possesses a clear proof from his Lord, recited by a witness from Him, and before it the Book of Moses, a guide and a mercy? These believe in it. But whoever defies it from among the various factions, the Fire is his promise. So have no doubt about it. It is the truth from your Lord, but most people do not believe.

17
6:19; 46:12

١٨ وَمَنْ أَظْلَمُ مِمَّنِ افْتَرَىٰ عَلَى اللَّهِ كَذِبًا ۚ أُولَٰئِكَ يُعْرَضُونَ عَلَىٰ رَبِّهِمْ وَيَقُولُ الْأَشْهَادُ هَٰؤُلَاءِ الَّذِينَ كَذَبُوا عَلَىٰ رَبِّهِمْ ۚ أَلَا لَعْنَةُ اللَّهِ عَلَى الظَّالِمِينَ

18 Who does greater wrong than he who fabricates lies about God? These will be presented before their Lord, and the witnesses will say, "These are they who lied about their Lord." Indeed, the curse of God is upon the wrongdoers.

18
6:21

١٩ الَّذِينَ يَصُدُّونَ عَن سَبِيلِ اللَّهِ وَيَبْغُونَهَا عِوَجًا وَهُم بِالْآخِرَةِ هُمْ كَافِرُونَ

19 Those who hinder others from the path of God, and seek to make it crooked; and regarding the Hereafter, they are in denial.

19
7:45; 16:88

٢٠ أُولَٰئِكَ لَمْ يَكُونُوا مُعْجِزِينَ فِي الْأَرْضِ وَمَا كَانَ لَهُم مِّن دُونِ اللَّهِ مِنْ أَوْلِيَاءَ ۘ يُضَاعَفُ لَهُمُ الْعَذَابُ ۚ مَا كَانُوا يَسْتَطِيعُونَ السَّمْعَ وَمَا كَانُوا يُبْصِرُونَ

20 These will not escape on earth, and they have no protectors besides God. The punishment will be doubled for them. They have failed to hear, and they have failed to see.

20
7:38; 16:88; 25:69; 46:32

٢١ أُولَٰئِكَ الَّذِينَ خَسِرُوا أَنفُسَهُمْ وَضَلَّ عَنْهُم مَّا كَانُوا يَفْتَرُونَ

21 Those are the ones who lost their souls, and what they had invented has strayed away from them.

21
7:53

٢٢ لَا جَرَمَ أَنَّهُمْ فِي الْآخِرَةِ هُمُ الْأَخْسَرُونَ

22 Without a doubt, in the Hereafter, they will be the biggest losers.

22
3:85; 16:109; 27:5

٢٣ إِنَّ الَّذِينَ آمَنُوا وَعَمِلُوا الصَّالِحَاتِ وَأَخْبَتُوا إِلَىٰ رَبِّهِمْ أُولَٰئِكَ أَصْحَابُ الْجَنَّةِ ۖ هُمْ فِيهَا خَالِدُونَ

23 As for those who believe and do good deeds, and humble themselves before their Lord—these are the inhabitants of Paradise, where they will abide forever.

23
22:34, 54

٢٤ مَثَلُ الْفَرِيقَيْنِ كَالْأَعْمَىٰ وَالْأَصَمِّ وَالْبَصِيرِ وَالسَّمِيعِ ۚ هَلْ يَسْتَوِيَانِ مَثَلًا ۚ أَفَلَا تَذَكَّرُونَ

24 The parable of the two groups is that of the blind and the deaf, and the seeing and the hearing. Are they equal in comparison? Will you not reflect?

24
13:19; 35:19–23

٢٥ وَلَقَدْ أَرْسَلْنَا نُوحًا إِلَىٰ قَوْمِهِ إِنِّي لَكُمْ نَذِيرٌ مُبِينٌ

25 We sent Noah to his people, "I am to you a clear warner."

25–49
7:59–64; 11:12; 23:23

٢٦ أَنْ لَا تَعْبُدُوا إِلَّا اللَّهَ ۖ إِنِّي أَخَافُ عَلَيْكُمْ عَذَابَ يَوْمٍ أَلِيمٍ

26 "That you shall worship none but God. I fear for you the agony of a painful Day."

٢٧ فَقَالَ الْمَلَأُ الَّذِينَ كَفَرُوا مِنْ قَوْمِهِ مَا نَرَاكَ إِلَّا بَشَرًا مِثْلَنَا وَمَا نَرَاكَ اتَّبَعَكَ إِلَّا الَّذِينَ هُمْ أَرَاذِلُنَا بَادِيَ الرَّأْيِ وَمَا نَرَىٰ لَكُمْ عَلَيْنَا مِنْ فَضْلٍ بَلْ نَظُنُّكُمْ كَاذِبِينَ

27 The notables who disbelieved among his people said, "We see in you nothing but a man like us, and we see that only the worst among us have followed you, those of immature judgment. And we see that you have no advantage over us. In fact, we think you are liars."

27
23:24

٢٨ قَالَ يَا قَوْمِ أَرَأَيْتُمْ إِنْ كُنْتُ عَلَىٰ بَيِّنَةٍ مِنْ رَبِّي وَآتَانِي رَحْمَةً مِنْ عِنْدِهِ فَعُمِّيَتْ عَلَيْكُمْ أَنُلْزِمُكُمُوهَا وَأَنْتُمْ لَهَا كَارِهُونَ

28 He said, "O my people, Have you considered? If I stand on clear evidence from my Lord, and He has given me a mercy from Himself, but you were blind to it, can we compel you to accept it, even though you dislike it?"

٢٩ وَيَا قَوْمِ لَا أَسْأَلُكُمْ عَلَيْهِ مَالًا ۖ إِنْ أَجْرِيَ إِلَّا عَلَى اللَّهِ ۚ وَمَا أَنَا بِطَارِدِ الَّذِينَ آمَنُوا ۚ إِنَّهُمْ مُلَاقُو رَبِّهِمْ وَلَٰكِنِّي أَرَاكُمْ قَوْمًا تَجْهَلُونَ

29 "O my people! I ask of you no money for it. My reward lies only with God. And I am not about to dismiss those who believed; they will surely meet their Lord. And I see that you are ignorant people."

29
6:90; 11:51; 25:57; 26:109; 34:47

٣٠ وَيَا قَوْمِ مَنْ يَنْصُرُنِي مِنَ اللَّهِ إِنْ طَرَدْتُهُمْ ۚ أَفَلَا تَذَكَّرُونَ

30 "O my people! Who will support me against God, if I dismiss them? Will you not give a thought?"

٣١ وَلَا أَقُولُ لَكُمْ عِنْدِي خَزَائِنُ اللَّهِ وَلَا أَعْلَمُ الْغَيْبَ وَلَا أَقُولُ إِنِّي مَلَكٌ وَلَا أَقُولُ لِلَّذِينَ تَزْدَرِي أَعْيُنُكُمْ لَنْ يُؤْتِيَهُمُ اللَّهُ خَيْرًا ۖ اللَّهُ أَعْلَمُ بِمَا فِي أَنْفُسِهِمْ ۖ إِنِّي إِذًا لَمِنَ الظَّالِمِينَ

31 "I do not say to you that I possess the treasures of God, nor do I know the future, nor do I say that I am an angel. Nor do I say of those who are despicable in your eyes that God will never give them any good. God is Aware of what lies in their souls. If I did, I would be one of the wrongdoers."

٣٢ قَالُوا يَا نُوحُ قَدْ جَادَلْتَنَا فَأَكْثَرْتَ جِدَالَنَا فَأْتِنَا بِمَا تَعِدُنَا إِن كُنتَ مِنَ الصَّادِقِينَ

32 They said, "O Noah, you have argued with us, and argued a great deal. Now bring upon us what you threaten us with, if you are truthful."

٣٣ قَالَ إِنَّمَا يَأْتِيكُم بِهِ اللَّهُ إِن شَاءَ وَمَا أَنتُم بِمُعْجِزِينَ

33 He said, "It is God who will bring it upon you, if He wills, and you will not be able to escape."

33
6:124

٣٤ وَلَا يَنفَعُكُمْ نُصْحِي إِنْ أَرَدتُّ أَنْ أَنصَحَ لَكُمْ إِن كَانَ اللَّهُ يُرِيدُ أَن يُغْوِيَكُمْ ۚ هُوَ رَبُّكُمْ وَإِلَيْهِ تُرْجَعُونَ

34 "My advice will not benefit you, much as I may want to advise you, if God desires to confound you. He is your Lord, and to Him you will be returned."

٣٥ أَمْ يَقُولُونَ افْتَرَاهُ ۖ قُلْ إِنِ افْتَرَيْتُهُ فَعَلَيَّ إِجْرَامِي وَأَنَا بَرِيءٌ مِّمَّا تُجْرِمُونَ

35 Or do they say, "He made it up?" Say, "If I made it up, upon me falls my crime, and I am innocent of the crimes you commit."

٣٦ وَأُوحِيَ إِلَىٰ نُوحٍ أَنَّهُ لَن يُؤْمِنَ مِن قَوْمِكَ إِلَّا مَن قَدْ آمَنَ فَلَا تَبْتَئِسْ بِمَا كَانُوا يَفْعَلُونَ

36 And it was revealed to Noah: "None of your people will believe, except those who have already believed, so do not grieve over what they do."

٣٧ وَاصْنَعِ الْفُلْكَ بِأَعْيُنِنَا وَوَحْيِنَا وَلَا تُخَاطِبْنِي فِي الَّذِينَ ظَلَمُوا ۚ إِنَّهُم مُّغْرَقُونَ

37 "And build the Ark, under Our eyes, and with Our inspiration, and do not address Me regarding those who did wrong; they are to be drowned."

37
23:27

٣٨ وَيَصْنَعُ الْفُلْكَ وَكُلَّمَا مَرَّ عَلَيْهِ مَلَأٌ مِّن قَوْمِهِ سَخِرُوا مِنْهُ ۚ قَالَ إِن تَسْخَرُوا مِنَّا فَإِنَّا نَسْخَرُ مِنكُمْ كَمَا تَسْخَرُونَ

38 As he was building the ark, whenever some of his people passed by him, they ridiculed him. He said, "If you ridicule us, we will ridicule you, just as you ridicule."

38
83:29–34

٣٩ فَسَوْفَ تَعْلَمُونَ مَن يَأْتِيهِ عَذَابٌ يُخْزِيهِ وَيَحِلُّ عَلَيْهِ عَذَابٌ مُّقِيمٌ

39 "You will surely know upon whom will come a torment that will abase him, and upon whom will fall a lasting torment."

39
11:93; 39:39

٤٠ حَتَّىٰ إِذَا جَاءَ أَمْرُنَا وَفَارَ التَّنُّورُ قُلْنَا احْمِلْ فِيهَا مِن كُلٍّ زَوْجَيْنِ اثْنَيْنِ وَأَهْلَكَ إِلَّا مَن سَبَقَ عَلَيْهِ الْقَوْلُ وَمَنْ آمَنَ ۚ وَمَا آمَنَ مَعَهُ إِلَّا قَلِيلٌ

40 Until, when Our command came, and the volcano erupted, We said, "Board into it a pair of every kind, and your family—except those against whom the sentence has already been passed—and those who have believed." But those who believed with him were only a few.

40
23:27

٤١ وَقَالَ ارْكَبُوا فِيهَا بِسْمِ اللَّهِ مَجْرَاهَا وَمُرْسَاهَا ۚ إِنَّ رَبِّي لَغَفُورٌ رَحِيمٌ	41 23:28–29; 43:12–14

41 He said, "Embark in it. In the name of God shall be its sailing and its anchorage. My Lord is indeed Forgiving and Merciful."

٤٢ وَهِيَ تَجْرِي بِهِمْ فِي مَوْجٍ كَالْجِبَالِ وَنَادَىٰ نُوحٌ ابْنَهُ وَكَانَ فِي مَعْزِلٍ يَا بُنَيَّ ارْكَب مَّعَنَا وَلَا تَكُن مَّعَ الْكَافِرِينَ	42 54:11–15; 69:11–12

42 And so it sailed with them amidst waves like hills. And Noah called to his son, who had kept away, "O my son! Embark with us, and do not be with the disbelievers."

٤٣ قَالَ سَآوِي إِلَىٰ جَبَلٍ يَعْصِمُنِي مِنَ الْمَاءِ ۚ قَالَ لَا عَاصِمَ الْيَوْمَ مِنْ أَمْرِ اللَّهِ إِلَّا مَن رَّحِمَ ۚ وَحَالَ بَيْنَهُمَا الْمَوْجُ فَكَانَ مِنَ الْمُغْرَقِينَ

43 He said, "I will take refuge on a mountain—it will protect me from the water." He said, "There is no protection from God's decree today, except for him on whom He has mercy." And the waves surged between them, and he was among the drowned.

٤٤ وَقِيلَ يَا أَرْضُ ابْلَعِي مَاءَكِ وَيَا سَمَاءُ أَقْلِعِي وَغِيضَ الْمَاءُ وَقُضِيَ الْأَمْرُ وَاسْتَوَتْ عَلَى الْجُودِيِّ ۖ وَقِيلَ بُعْدًا لِّلْقَوْمِ الظَّالِمِينَ

44 And it was said, "O earth, swallow your waters," and "O heaven, clear up." And the waters receded, and the event was concluded, and it settled on Judi, and it was proclaimed: "Away with the wicked people."

٤٥ وَنَادَىٰ نُوحٌ رَّبَّهُ فَقَالَ رَبِّ إِنَّ ابْنِي مِنْ أَهْلِي وَإِنَّ وَعْدَكَ الْحَقُّ وَأَنتَ أَحْكَمُ الْحَاكِمِينَ	45 95:8

45 And Noah called to his Lord. He said, "O My Lord, my son is of my family, and Your promise is true, and You are the Wisest of the wise."

٤٦ قَالَ يَا نُوحُ إِنَّهُ لَيْسَ مِنْ أَهْلِكَ ۖ إِنَّهُ عَمَلٌ غَيْرُ صَالِحٍ ۖ فَلَا تَسْأَلْنِ مَا لَيْسَ لَكَ بِهِ عِلْمٌ ۖ إِنِّي أَعِظُكَ أَن تَكُونَ مِنَ الْجَاهِلِينَ

46 He said, "O Noah, he is not of your family. It is an unrighteous deed. So do not ask Me about something you know nothing about. I admonish you, lest you be one of the ignorant."

٤٧ قَالَ رَبِّ إِنِّي أَعُوذُ بِكَ أَنْ أَسْأَلَكَ مَا لَيْسَ لِي بِهِ عِلْمٌ ۖ وَإِلَّا تَغْفِرْ لِي وَتَرْحَمْنِي أَكُن مِّنَ الْخَاسِرِينَ	47 7:23, 149

47 He said, "O My Lord, I seek refuge with You, from asking You about what I have no knowledge of. Unless You forgive me, and have mercy on me, I will be one of the losers."

٤٨ قِيلَ يَا نُوحُ اهْبِطْ بِسَلَامٍ مِّنَّا وَبَرَكَاتٍ عَلَيْكَ وَعَلَىٰ أُمَمٍ مِّمَّن مَّعَكَ ۚ وَأُمَمٌ سَنُمَتِّعُهُمْ ثُمَّ يَمَسُّهُم مِّنَّا عَذَابٌ أَلِيمٌ	48 37:75–79

48 It was said, "O Noah, disembark with peace from Us; and with blessings upon you, and upon communities from those with you. And other communities We will grant prosperity, and then a painful torment from Us will befall them."

٤٩ تِلْكَ مِنْ أَنْبَاءِ الْغَيْبِ نُوحِيهَا إِلَيْكَ ۖ مَا كُنْتَ تَعْلَمُهَا أَنْتَ وَلَا قَوْمُكَ مِنْ قَبْلِ هَٰذَا ۖ فَاصْبِرْ ۖ إِنَّ الْعَاقِبَةَ لِلْمُتَّقِينَ

49   3:44; 12:102; 28:44–46

49 These are some stories from the past that we reveal to you. Neither you, nor your people knew them before this. So be patient. The future belongs to the pious.

٥٠ وَإِلَىٰ عَادٍ أَخَاهُمْ هُودًا ۚ قَالَ يَا قَوْمِ اعْبُدُوا اللَّهَ مَا لَكُمْ مِنْ إِلَٰهٍ غَيْرُهُ ۖ إِنْ أَنْتُمْ إِلَّا مُفْتَرُونَ

50–60   7:65–60

50 And to 'Ād, their brother Hūd. He said, "O my people, worship God, you have no other god besides Him. You do nothing but invent lies."

٥١ يَا قَوْمِ لَا أَسْأَلُكُمْ عَلَيْهِ أَجْرًا ۖ إِنْ أَجْرِيَ إِلَّا عَلَى الَّذِي فَطَرَنِي ۚ أَفَلَا تَعْقِلُونَ

51   6:90; 11:29; 25:57; 26:109; 34:47

51 "O my people, I ask you no wage for it; my wage lies with Him who originated me. Do you not understand?"

٥٢ وَيَا قَوْمِ اسْتَغْفِرُوا رَبَّكُمْ ثُمَّ تُوبُوا إِلَيْهِ يُرْسِلِ السَّمَاءَ عَلَيْكُمْ مِدْرَارًا وَيَزِدْكُمْ قُوَّةً إِلَىٰ قُوَّتِكُمْ وَلَا تَتَوَلَّوْا مُجْرِمِينَ

52 "O my people, ask forgiveness from your Lord, and repent to Him. He will release the sky pouring down upon you, and will add strength to your strength. And do not turn away and be wicked."

٥٣ قَالُوا يَا هُودُ مَا جِئْتَنَا بِبَيِّنَةٍ وَمَا نَحْنُ بِتَارِكِي آلِهَتِنَا عَنْ قَوْلِكَ وَمَا نَحْنُ لَكَ بِمُؤْمِنِينَ

53   7:70

53 They said, "O Hūd, you did not bring us any evidence, and we are not about to abandon our gods at your word, and we are not believers in you."

٥٤ إِنْ نَقُولُ إِلَّا اعْتَرَاكَ بَعْضُ آلِهَتِنَا بِسُوءٍ ۗ قَالَ إِنِّي أُشْهِدُ اللَّهَ وَاشْهَدُوا أَنِّي بَرِيءٌ مِمَّا تُشْرِكُونَ

54 "We only say that some of our gods have possessed you with evil." He said, "I call God to witness, and you to witness, that I am innocent of what you associate.

٥٥ مِنْ دُونِهِ ۖ فَكِيدُونِي جَمِيعًا ثُمَّ لَا تُنْظِرُونِ

55   7:195; 10:71

55 Besides Him. So scheme against me, all of you, and do not hesitate.

٥٦ إِنِّي تَوَكَّلْتُ عَلَى اللَّهِ رَبِّي وَرَبِّكُمْ ۚ مَا مِنْ دَابَّةٍ إِلَّا هُوَ آخِذٌ بِنَاصِيَتِهَا ۚ إِنَّ رَبِّي عَلَىٰ صِرَاطٍ مُسْتَقِيمٍ

56   6:38; 11:6; 29:60

56 I have placed my trust in God, my Lord and your Lord. There is not a creature but He holds it by the forelock. My Lord is on a straight path.

٥٧ فَإِنْ تَوَلَّوْا فَقَدْ أَبْلَغْتُكُمْ مَا أُرْسِلْتُ بِهِ إِلَيْكُمْ ۚ وَيَسْتَخْلِفُ رَبِّي قَوْمًا غَيْرَكُمْ وَلَا تَضُرُّونَهُ شَيْئًا ۚ إِنَّ رَبِّي عَلَىٰ كُلِّ شَيْءٍ حَفِيظٌ

57   46:23

57 If you turn away, I have conveyed to you what I was sent to you with; and my Lord will replace you with another people, and you will not cause Him any harm. My Lord is Guardian over all things."

٥٨ وَلَمَّا جَاءَ أَمْرُنَا نَجَّيْنَا هُودًا وَالَّذِينَ آمَنُوا مَعَهُ بِرَحْمَةٍ مِنَّا وَنَجَّيْنَاهُمْ مِنْ عَذَابٍ غَلِيظٍ

58 And when Our decree came, We saved Hūd and those who believed with him, by a mercy from Us, and We delivered them from a harsh punishment.

58
11:66, 94; 41:16;
51:41–42; 64:19–20;
69:6–7

٥٩ وَتِلْكَ عَادٌ ۖ جَحَدُوا بِآيَاتِ رَبِّهِمْ وَعَصَوْا رُسُلَهُ وَاتَّبَعُوا أَمْرَ كُلِّ جَبَّارٍ عَنِيدٍ

59 That was 'Ād; they denied the signs of their Lord, and defied His messengers, and followed the lead of every stubborn tyrant.

٦٠ وَأُتْبِعُوا فِي هَٰذِهِ الدُّنْيَا لَعْنَةً وَيَوْمَ الْقِيَامَةِ ۗ أَلَا إِنَّ عَادًا كَفَرُوا رَبَّهُمْ ۗ أَلَا بُعْدًا لِعَادٍ قَوْمِ هُودٍ

60 And they were pursued by a curse in this world, and on the Day of Resurrection. Indeed, 'Ād blasphemed against their Lord—so away with 'Ād, the people of Hūd.

60
11:99; 24:23; 28:42

٦١ وَإِلَىٰ ثَمُودَ أَخَاهُمْ صَالِحًا ۚ قَالَ يَا قَوْمِ اعْبُدُوا اللَّهَ مَا لَكُمْ مِنْ إِلَٰهٍ غَيْرُهُ ۖ هُوَ أَنْشَأَكُمْ مِنَ الْأَرْضِ وَاسْتَعْمَرَكُمْ فِيهَا فَاسْتَغْفِرُوهُ ثُمَّ تُوبُوا إِلَيْهِ ۚ إِنَّ رَبِّي قَرِيبٌ مُجِيبٌ

61 And to Thamūd, their brother Ṣāliḥ. He said, "O my people, worship God, you have no god other than Him. He initiated you from the earth, and settled you in it. So seek His forgiveness, and repent to Him. My Lord is Near and Responsive."

61
7:73; 27:45

٦٢ قَالُوا يَا صَالِحُ قَدْ كُنْتَ فِينَا مَرْجُوًّا قَبْلَ هَٰذَا ۖ أَتَنْهَانَا أَنْ نَعْبُدَ مَا يَعْبُدُ آبَاؤُنَا وَإِنَّنَا لَفِي شَكٍّ مِمَّا تَدْعُونَا إِلَيْهِ مُرِيبٍ

62 They said, "O Ṣāliḥ, we had hopes in you before this. Are you trying to prevent us from worshiping what our parents worship? We are in serious doubt regarding what you are calling us to."

62
10:78

٦٣ قَالَ يَا قَوْمِ أَرَأَيْتُمْ إِنْ كُنْتُ عَلَىٰ بَيِّنَةٍ مِنْ رَبِّي وَآتَانِي مِنْهُ رَحْمَةً فَمَنْ يَنْصُرُنِي مِنَ اللَّهِ إِنْ عَصَيْتُهُ ۖ فَمَا تَزِيدُونَنِي غَيْرَ تَخْسِيرٍ

63 He said, "O my people, have you considered? If I stand upon clear evidence from my Lord, and He has given me mercy from Him, who would protect me from God, if I disobeyed Him? You add nothing for me except loss."

٦٤ وَيَا قَوْمِ هَٰذِهِ نَاقَةُ اللَّهِ لَكُمْ آيَةً فَذَرُوهَا تَأْكُلْ فِي أَرْضِ اللَّهِ وَلَا تَمَسُّوهَا بِسُوءٍ فَيَأْخُذَكُمْ عَذَابٌ قَرِيبٌ

64 "O my people, this is the she-camel of God, a sign for you. Let her graze on God's land, and do not harm her, lest an imminent punishment overtakes you."

64
7:73

٦٥ فَعَقَرُوهَا فَقَالَ تَمَتَّعُوا فِي دَارِكُمْ ثَلَاثَةَ أَيَّامٍ ۖ ذَٰلِكَ وَعْدٌ غَيْرُ مَكْذُوبٍ

65 But they hamstrung her, and so He said, "Enjoy yourselves in your homes for three days. This is a prophecy that is infallible."

65
7:77

٦٦ فَلَمَّا جَاءَ أَمْرُنَا نَجَّيْنَا صَالِحًا وَالَّذِينَ آمَنُوا مَعَهُ بِرَحْمَةٍ مِنَّا وَمِنْ خِزْيِ يَوْمِئِذٍ ۗ إِنَّ رَبَّكَ هُوَ الْقَوِيُّ الْعَزِيزُ

66 Then, when Our command came, We saved Ṣāliḥ and those who believed with him, by a mercy from Us, from the disgrace of that day. Your Lord is the Strong, the Mighty.

66
11:58, 94

٦٧ وَأَخَذَ الَّذِينَ ظَلَمُوا الصَّيْحَةُ فَأَصْبَحُوا فِي دِيَارِهِمْ جَاثِمِينَ

67 And the Scream struck those who transgressed, and they became motionless bodies in their homes.

67
15:83; 54:31

٦٨ كَأَنْ لَمْ يَغْنَوْا فِيهَا ۗ أَلَا إِنَّ ثَمُودَ كَفَرُوا رَبَّهُمْ ۗ أَلَا بُعْدًا لِثَمُودَ

68 As if they had never prospered therein. Indeed, Thamūd rejected their Lord, so away with Thamūd.

68
11:95

٦٩ وَلَقَدْ جَاءَتْ رُسُلُنَا إِبْرَاهِيمَ بِالْبُشْرَىٰ قَالُوا سَلَامًا ۖ قَالَ سَلَامٌ ۖ فَمَا لَبِثَ أَنْ جَاءَ بِعِجْلٍ حَنِيذٍ

69 Our messengers came to Abraham with good news. They said, "Peace." He said, "Peace." Soon after, he came with a roasted calf.

69
15:51; 29:31; 51:28

٧٠ فَلَمَّا رَأَىٰ أَيْدِيَهُمْ لَا تَصِلُ إِلَيْهِ نَكِرَهُمْ وَأَوْجَسَ مِنْهُمْ خِيفَةً ۚ قَالُوا لَا تَخَفْ إِنَّا أُرْسِلْنَا إِلَىٰ قَوْمِ لُوطٍ

70 But when he saw their hands not reaching towards it, he became suspicious of them, and conceived a fear of them. They said, "Do not fear, we were sent to the people of Lot."

70–73
15:54–56; 51:28–30

٧١ وَامْرَأَتُهُ قَائِمَةٌ فَضَحِكَتْ فَبَشَّرْنَاهَا بِإِسْحَاقَ وَمِنْ وَرَاءِ إِسْحَاقَ يَعْقُوبَ

71 His wife was standing by, so she laughed. And We gave her good news of Isaac; and after Isaac, Jacob.

٧٢ قَالَتْ يَا وَيْلَتَىٰ أَأَلِدُ وَأَنَا عَجُوزٌ وَهَٰذَا بَعْلِي شَيْخًا ۖ إِنَّ هَٰذَا لَشَيْءٌ عَجِيبٌ

72 She said, "Alas for me. Shall I give birth, when I am an old woman, and this, my husband, is an old man? This is truly a strange thing."

٧٣ قَالُوا أَتَعْجَبِينَ مِنْ أَمْرِ اللَّهِ ۖ رَحْمَتُ اللَّهِ وَبَرَكَاتُهُ عَلَيْكُمْ أَهْلَ الْبَيْتِ ۚ إِنَّهُ حَمِيدٌ مَجِيدٌ

73 They said, "Do you marvel at the decree of God? The mercy and blessings of God are upon you, O people of the house. He is Praiseworthy and Glorious."

٧٤ فَلَمَّا ذَهَبَ عَنْ إِبْرَاهِيمَ الرَّوْعُ وَجَاءَتْهُ الْبُشْرَىٰ يُجَادِلُنَا فِي قَوْمِ لُوطٍ

74 When Abraham's fear subsided, and the good news had reached him, he started pleading with Us concerning the people of Lot.

74–76
15:57–60; 29:31–32; 51:31–34

٧٥ إِنَّ إِبْرَاهِيمَ لَحَلِيمٌ أَوَّاهٌ مُنِيبٌ

75 Abraham was gentle, kind, penitent.

٧٦ يَا إِبْرَاهِيمُ أَعْرِضْ عَنْ هَٰذَا ۖ إِنَّهُ قَدْ جَاءَ أَمْرُ رَبِّكَ ۖ وَإِنَّهُمْ آتِيهِمْ عَذَابٌ غَيْرُ مَرْدُودٍ

76 "O Abraham, refrain from this. The command of your Lord has come; they have incurred an irreversible punishment."

٧٧ وَلَمَّا جَاءَتْ رُسُلُنَا لُوطًا سِيءَ بِهِمْ وَضَاقَ بِهِمْ ذَرْعًا وَقَالَ هَٰذَا يَوْمٌ عَصِيبٌ

77
15:61; 29:33

77 And when Our envoys came to Lot, he was anxious for them, and concerned for them. He said, "This is a dreadful day."

٧٨ وَجَاءَهُ قَوْمُهُ يُهْرَعُونَ إِلَيْهِ وَمِنْ قَبْلُ كَانُوا يَعْمَلُونَ السَّيِّئَاتِ ۚ قَالَ يَا قَوْمِ هَٰؤُلَاءِ بَنَاتِي هُنَّ أَطْهَرُ لَكُمْ ۖ فَاتَّقُوا اللَّهَ وَلَا تُخْزُونِ فِي ضَيْفِي ۖ أَلَيْسَ مِنْكُمْ رَجُلٌ رَشِيدٌ

78
7:80–82; 15:67–72; 29:28–30; 54:37

78 And his people came rushing towards him—they were in the habit of committing sins. He said, "O my people, these are my daughters; they are purer for you. So fear God, and do not embarrass me before my guests. Is there not one reasonable man among you?"

٧٩ قَالُوا لَقَدْ عَلِمْتَ مَا لَنَا فِي بَنَاتِكَ مِنْ حَقٍّ وَإِنَّكَ لَتَعْلَمُ مَا نُرِيدُ

79 They said, "You know well that we have no right to your daughters, and you know well what we want."

٨٠ قَالَ لَوْ أَنَّ لِي بِكُمْ قُوَّةً أَوْ آوِي إِلَىٰ رُكْنٍ شَدِيدٍ

80 He said, "If only I had the strength to stop you, or could rely on some strong support."

٨١ قَالُوا يَا لُوطُ إِنَّا رُسُلُ رَبِّكَ لَنْ يَصِلُوا إِلَيْكَ ۖ فَأَسْرِ بِأَهْلِكَ بِقِطْعٍ مِنَ اللَّيْلِ وَلَا يَلْتَفِتْ مِنْكُمْ أَحَدٌ إِلَّا امْرَأَتَكَ ۖ إِنَّهُ مُصِيبُهَا مَا أَصَابَهُمْ ۚ إِنَّ مَوْعِدَهُمُ الصُّبْحُ ۚ أَلَيْسَ الصُّبْحُ بِقَرِيبٍ

81
7:83; 15:73–75; 29:33; 37:133–135; 54:34, 38

81 They said, "O Lot, we are the envoys of your Lord; they will not reach you. So set out with your family during the cover of the night, and let none of you look back, except for your wife. She will be struck by what will strike them. Their appointed time is the morning. Is not the morning near?"

٨٢ فَلَمَّا جَاءَ أَمْرُنَا جَعَلْنَا عَالِيَهَا سَافِلَهَا وَأَمْطَرْنَا عَلَيْهَا حِجَارَةً مِنْ سِجِّيلٍ مَنْضُودٍ

82
pp 15:74
7:84; 25:40; 26:173; 27:58; 29:34; 51:32–33

82 And when Our command came about, We turned it upside down, and We rained down on it stones of baked clay.

٨٣ مُسَوَّمَةً عِنْدَ رَبِّكَ ۖ وَمَا هِيَ مِنَ الظَّالِمِينَ بِبَعِيدٍ

83 Marked from your Lord, and never far from the wrongdoers.

٨٤ وَإِلَىٰ مَدْيَنَ أَخَاهُمْ شُعَيْبًا ۚ قَالَ يَا قَوْمِ اعْبُدُوا اللَّهَ مَا لَكُمْ مِنْ إِلَٰهٍ غَيْرُهُ ۖ وَلَا تَنْقُصُوا الْمِكْيَالَ وَالْمِيزَانَ ۚ إِنِّي أَرَاكُمْ بِخَيْرٍ وَإِنِّي أَخَافُ عَلَيْكُمْ عَذَابَ يَوْمٍ مُحِيطٍ

84
7:85; 29:36

84 And to Median, their brother Shu'ayb. He said, "O my people, worship God; you have no god other than Him. And do not short measure or short weight. I see you in good circumstances, but I fear for you the agony of an encompassing Day."

٨٥ وَيَا قَوْمِ أَوْفُوا الْمِكْيَالَ وَالْمِيزَانَ بِالْقِسْطِ ۖ وَلَا تَبْخَسُوا النَّاسَ أَشْيَاءَهُمْ وَلَا تَعْثَوْا فِي الْأَرْضِ مُفْسِدِينَ

85 6:152; 7:85; 11:116; 17:35; 26:181–183

85 "O my people! Give full measure and full weight, in all fairness, and do not cheat the people out of their rights, and do not spread corruption in the land.

٨٦ بَقِيَّتُ اللَّهِ خَيْرٌ لَكُمْ إِنْ كُنْتُمْ مُؤْمِنِينَ ۚ وَمَا أَنَا عَلَيْكُمْ بِحَفِيظٍ

86 What is left by God is best for you, if you are believers. And I am not a guardian over you."

٨٧ قَالُوا يَا شُعَيْبُ أَصَلَاتُكَ تَأْمُرُكَ أَنْ نَتْرُكَ مَا يَعْبُدُ آبَاؤُنَا أَوْ أَنْ نَفْعَلَ فِي أَمْوَالِنَا مَا نَشَاءُ ۖ إِنَّكَ لَأَنْتَ الْحَلِيمُ الرَّشِيدُ

87 They said, "O Shuʿayb, does your prayer command you that we abandon what our ancestors worshiped, or doing with our wealth what we want? You are the one who is intelligent and wise."

٨٨ قَالَ يَا قَوْمِ أَرَأَيْتُمْ إِنْ كُنْتُ عَلَىٰ بَيِّنَةٍ مِنْ رَبِّي وَرَزَقَنِي مِنْهُ رِزْقًا حَسَنًا ۚ وَمَا أُرِيدُ أَنْ أُخَالِفَكُمْ إِلَىٰ مَا أَنْهَاكُمْ عَنْهُ ۚ إِنْ أُرِيدُ إِلَّا الْإِصْلَاحَ مَا اسْتَطَعْتُ ۚ وَمَا تَوْفِيقِي إِلَّا بِاللَّهِ ۚ عَلَيْهِ تَوَكَّلْتُ وَإِلَيْهِ أُنِيبُ

88 2:44; 61:3

88 He said, "O my people, have you considered? What if I have clear evidence from my Lord, and He has given me good livelihood from Himself? I have no desire to do what I forbid you from doing. I desire nothing but reform, as far as I can. My success lies only with God. In Him I trust, and to Him I turn."

٨٩ وَيَا قَوْمِ لَا يَجْرِمَنَّكُمْ شِقَاقِي أَنْ يُصِيبَكُمْ مِثْلُ مَا أَصَابَ قَوْمَ نُوحٍ أَوْ قَوْمَ هُودٍ أَوْ قَوْمَ صَالِحٍ ۚ وَمَا قَوْمُ لُوطٍ مِنْكُمْ بِبَعِيدٍ

89 "O my people, let not your hostility towards me cause you to suffer what was suffered by the people of Noah, or the people of Hūd, or the people of Ṣāliḥ. The people of Lot are not far away from you."

٩٠ وَاسْتَغْفِرُوا رَبَّكُمْ ثُمَّ تُوبُوا إِلَيْهِ ۚ إِنَّ رَبِّي رَحِيمٌ وَدُودٌ

90 "And ask your Lord for forgiveness, and repent to Him. My Lord is Merciful and Loving."

٩١ قَالُوا يَا شُعَيْبُ مَا نَفْقَهُ كَثِيرًا مِمَّا تَقُولُ وَإِنَّا لَنَرَاكَ فِينَا ضَعِيفًا ۖ وَلَوْلَا رَهْطُكَ لَرَجَمْنَاكَ ۖ وَمَا أَنْتَ عَلَيْنَا بِعَزِيزٍ

91 They said, "O Shuʿayb, we do not understand much of what you say, and we see that you are weak among us. Were it not for your tribe, we would have stoned you. You are of no value to us."

٩٢ قَالَ يَا قَوْمِ أَرَهْطِي أَعَزُّ عَلَيْكُمْ مِنَ اللَّهِ وَاتَّخَذْتُمُوهُ وَرَاءَكُمْ ظِهْرِيًّا ۖ إِنَّ رَبِّي بِمَا تَعْمَلُونَ مُحِيطٌ

92 He said, "O my people, is my tribe more important to you than God? And you have turned your backs on Him? My Lord comprehends everything you do."

٩٣ وَيَا قَوْمِ اعْمَلُوا عَلَىٰ مَكَانَتِكُمْ إِنِّي عَامِلٌ ۖ سَوْفَ تَعْلَمُونَ مَن يَأْتِيهِ عَذَابٌ يُخْزِيهِ وَمَنْ هُوَ كَاذِبٌ ۖ وَارْتَقِبُوا إِنِّي مَعَكُمْ رَقِيبٌ	93	6:135; 11:39, 121; 39:39

93 "O my people, do as you may, and so will I. You will know to whom will come a punishment that will shame him, and who is a liar. So look out; I am on the lookout with you."

٩٤ وَلَمَّا جَاءَ أَمْرُنَا نَجَّيْنَا شُعَيْبًا وَالَّذِينَ آمَنُوا مَعَهُ بِرَحْمَةٍ مِّنَّا وَأَخَذَتِ الَّذِينَ ظَلَمُوا الصَّيْحَةُ فَأَصْبَحُوا فِي دِيَارِهِمْ جَاثِمِينَ	94	11:58, 66

94 And when Our command came, We saved Shu'ayb and those who believed with him, by mercy from Us, and the Blast struck the wrongdoers, and they became motionless bodies in their homes.

٩٥ كَأَن لَّمْ يَغْنَوْا فِيهَا ۗ أَلَا بُعْدًا لِّمَدْيَنَ كَمَا بَعِدَتْ ثَمُودُ	95	11:68

95 As though they never flourished therein. Away with Median, as was done away with Thamūd.

٩٦ وَلَقَدْ أَرْسَلْنَا مُوسَىٰ بِآيَاتِنَا وَسُلْطَانٍ مُّبِينٍ	96	40:23

96 And We sent Moses with Our signs and a clear mandate.

٩٧ إِلَىٰ فِرْعَوْنَ وَمَلَئِهِ فَاتَّبَعُوا أَمْرَ فِرْعَوْنَ ۖ وَمَا أَمْرُ فِرْعَوْنَ بِرَشِيدٍ	97

97 To Pharaoh and his nobles, but they followed the command of Pharaoh, and the command of Pharaoh was not wise.

٩٨ يَقْدُمُ قَوْمَهُ يَوْمَ الْقِيَامَةِ فَأَوْرَدَهُمُ النَّارَ ۖ وَبِئْسَ الْوِرْدُ الْمَوْرُودُ	98	7:103–136

98 He will precede his people on the Day of Resurrection, and will lead them into the Fire. Miserable is the place he placed them in.

٩٩ وَأُتْبِعُوا فِي هَٰذِهِ لَعْنَةً وَيَوْمَ الْقِيَامَةِ ۚ بِئْسَ الرِّفْدُ الْمَرْفُودُ	99	11:60; 24:23; 28:42

99 They were followed by a curse in this, and on the Day of Resurrection. Miserable is the path they followed.

١٠٠ ذَٰلِكَ مِنْ أَنبَاءِ الْقُرَىٰ نَقُصُّهُ عَلَيْكَ ۖ مِنْهَا قَائِمٌ وَحَصِيدٌ	100

100 These are of the reports of the towns—We relate them to you. Some are still standing, and some have withered away.

١٠١ وَمَا ظَلَمْنَاهُمْ وَلَٰكِن ظَلَمُوا أَنفُسَهُمْ ۖ فَمَا أَغْنَتْ عَنْهُمْ آلِهَتُهُمُ الَّتِي يَدْعُونَ مِن دُونِ اللَّهِ مِن شَيْءٍ لَّمَّا جَاءَ أَمْرُ رَبِّكَ ۖ وَمَا زَادُوهُمْ غَيْرَ تَتْبِيبٍ	101	7:90; 111:1–2

101 We did not wrong them, but they wronged themselves. Their gods, whom they invoked besides God, availed them nothing when the command of your Lord arrived. In fact, they added only to their ruin.

١٠٢ وَكَذَٰلِكَ أَخْذُ رَبِّكَ إِذَا أَخَذَ الْقُرَىٰ وَهِيَ ظَالِمَةٌ ۚ إِنَّ أَخْذَهُ أَلِيمٌ شَدِيدٌ	102

102 Such is the grip of your Lord when He seizes the towns in the midst of their sins. His grip is most painful, most severe.

١٠٣ إِنَّ فِي ذَٰلِكَ لَآيَةً لِّمَنْ خَافَ عَذَابَ الْآخِرَةِ ۚ ذَٰلِكَ يَوْمٌ مَّجْمُوعٌ لَّهُ النَّاسُ وَذَٰلِكَ يَوْمٌ مَّشْهُودٌ

103 In that is a sign for whoever fears the punishment of the Hereafter. That is a Day for which humanity will be gathered together—that is a Day to be witnessed.

١٠٤ وَمَا نُؤَخِّرُهُ إِلَّا لِأَجَلٍ مَّعْدُودٍ

104
11:8

104 We only postpone it until a predetermined time.

١٠٥ يَوْمَ يَأْتِ لَا تَكَلَّمُ نَفْسٌ إِلَّا بِإِذْنِهِ ۚ فَمِنْهُمْ شَقِيٌّ وَسَعِيدٌ

105 On the Day when it arrives, no soul will speak without His permission. Some will be miserable, and some will be happy.

١٠٦ فَأَمَّا الَّذِينَ شَقُوا فَفِي النَّارِ لَهُمْ فِيهَا زَفِيرٌ وَشَهِيقٌ

106
21:99; 25:11

106 As for those who are miserable, they will be in the Fire. They will have therein sighing and wailing.

١٠٧ خَالِدِينَ فِيهَا مَا دَامَتِ السَّمَاوَاتُ وَالْأَرْضُ إِلَّا مَا شَاءَ رَبُّكَ ۚ إِنَّ رَبَّكَ فَعَّالٌ لِّمَا يُرِيدُ

107
6:128

107 Remaining therein for as long as the heavens and the earth endure, except as your Lord wills. Your Lord is Doer of whatever He wills.

١٠٨ وَأَمَّا الَّذِينَ سُعِدُوا فَفِي الْجَنَّةِ خَالِدِينَ فِيهَا مَا دَامَتِ السَّمَاوَاتُ وَالْأَرْضُ إِلَّا مَا شَاءَ رَبُّكَ ۖ عَطَاءً غَيْرَ مَجْذُوذٍ

108 And as for those who are happy, they will be in Paradise, remaining therein for as long as the heavens and the earth endure, except as your Lord wills—a reward without end.

١٠٩ فَلَا تَكُ فِي مِرْيَةٍ مِّمَّا يَعْبُدُ هَٰؤُلَاءِ ۚ مَا يَعْبُدُونَ إِلَّا كَمَا يَعْبُدُ آبَاؤُهُم مِّن قَبْلُ ۚ وَإِنَّا لَمُوَفُّوهُمْ نَصِيبَهُمْ غَيْرَ مَنقُوصٍ

109
2:147; 7:37

109 So be not in doubt regarding what these people worship. They worship only as their ancestors worshiped before. We will pay them their due in full, without any reduction.

١١٠ وَلَقَدْ آتَيْنَا مُوسَى الْكِتَابَ فَاخْتُلِفَ فِيهِ ۚ وَلَوْلَا كَلِمَةٌ سَبَقَتْ مِن رَّبِّكَ لَقُضِيَ بَيْنَهُمْ ۚ وَإِنَّهُمْ لَفِي شَكٍّ مِّنْهُ مُرِيبٍ

110
10:19; 41:45; 42:14

110 We gave Moses the Scripture, but it was disputed. Were it not for a prior word from your Lord, it would have been settled between them. They are in serious doubt concerning it.

١١١ وَإِنَّ كُلًّا لَّمَّا لَيُوَفِّيَنَّهُمْ رَبُّكَ أَعْمَالَهُمْ ۚ إِنَّهُ بِمَا يَعْمَلُونَ خَبِيرٌ

111 Your Lord will repay each one of them in full for their deeds. He is Aware of everything they do.

١١٢ فَاسْتَقِمْ كَمَا أُمِرْتَ وَمَن تَابَ مَعَكَ وَلَا تَطْغَوْا ۚ إِنَّهُ بِمَا تَعْمَلُونَ بَصِيرٌ

112
42:15

112 So be upright, as you are commanded, along with those who repented with you, and do not transgress. He is Seeing of everything you do.

١١٣ وَلَا تَرْكَنُوا إِلَى الَّذِينَ ظَلَمُوا فَتَمَسَّكُمُ النَّارُ وَمَا لَكُمْ مِنْ دُونِ اللَّهِ مِنْ أَوْلِيَاءَ ثُمَّ لَا تُنْصَرُونَ

113 17:74

113 And do not incline towards those who do wrong, or the Fire may touch you; and you will have no protectors besides God, and you will not be saved.

١١٤ وَأَقِمِ الصَّلَاةَ طَرَفَيِ النَّهَارِ وَزُلَفًا مِنَ اللَّيْلِ ۚ إِنَّ الْحَسَنَاتِ يُذْهِبْنَ السَّيِّئَاتِ ۚ ذَٰلِكَ ذِكْرَىٰ لِلذَّاكِرِينَ

114 17:78; 20:130; 50:39; 52:48; 76:24

114 Perform the prayer at the borders of the day, and during the approaches of the night. The good deeds take away the bad deeds. This is a reminder for those who remember.

١١٥ وَاصْبِرْ فَإِنَّ اللَّهَ لَا يُضِيعُ أَجْرَ الْمُحْسِنِينَ

115 And be patient. God will not waste the reward of the virtuous.

١١٦ فَلَوْلَا كَانَ مِنَ الْقُرُونِ مِنْ قَبْلِكُمْ أُولُو بَقِيَّةٍ يَنْهَوْنَ عَنِ الْفَسَادِ فِي الْأَرْضِ إِلَّا قَلِيلًا مِمَّنْ أَنْجَيْنَا مِنْهُمْ ۗ وَاتَّبَعَ الَّذِينَ ظَلَمُوا مَا أُتْرِفُوا فِيهِ وَكَانُوا مُجْرِمِينَ

116 11:85; 21:13

116 If only there were, among the generations before you, people with wisdom, who spoke against corruption on earth—except for the few whom We saved. But the wrongdoers pursued the luxuries they were indulged in, and thus became guilty.

١١٧ وَمَا كَانَ رَبُّكَ لِيُهْلِكَ الْقُرَىٰ بِظُلْمٍ وَأَهْلُهَا مُصْلِحُونَ

117 6:131; 18:59; 28:59; 46:27

117 Your Lord would never destroy the towns wrongfully, while their inhabitants are righteous.

١١٨ وَلَوْ شَاءَ رَبُّكَ لَجَعَلَ النَّاسَ أُمَّةً وَاحِدَةً ۖ وَلَا يَزَالُونَ مُخْتَلِفِينَ

118 6:35, 149

118 Had your Lord willed, He could have made humanity one community, but they continue to differ.

١١٩ إِلَّا مَنْ رَحِمَ رَبُّكَ ۚ وَلِذَٰلِكَ خَلَقَهُمْ ۗ وَتَمَّتْ كَلِمَةُ رَبِّكَ لَأَمْلَأَنَّ جَهَنَّمَ مِنَ الْجِنَّةِ وَالنَّاسِ أَجْمَعِينَ

119 Except those on whom your Lord has mercy—for that reason He created them. The Word of your Lord is final: "I will fill Hell with jinn and humans, altogether."

١٢٠ وَكُلًّا نَقُصُّ عَلَيْكَ مِنْ أَنْبَاءِ الرُّسُلِ مَا نُثَبِّتُ بِهِ فُؤَادَكَ ۚ وَجَاءَكَ فِي هَٰذِهِ الْحَقُّ وَمَوْعِظَةٌ وَذِكْرَىٰ لِلْمُؤْمِنِينَ

120 6:34; 7:101; 9:99; 18:13

120 Everything We narrate to you of the history of the messengers is to strengthen your heart therewith. The truth has come to you in this, and a lesson, and a reminder for the believers.

١٢١ وَقُلْ لِلَّذِينَ لَا يُؤْمِنُونَ اعْمَلُوا عَلَىٰ مَكَانَتِكُمْ إِنَّا عَامِلُونَ

121 6:135; 11:93; 39:39

121 And say to those who do not believe, "Act according to your ability; and so will we."

١٢٢ وَانْتَظِرُوا إِنَّا مُنْتَظِرُونَ

122 "And wait; we too are waiting."

١٢٣ وَلِلَّهِ غَيْبُ ٱلسَّمَاوَاتِ وَٱلْأَرْضِ وَإِلَيْهِ يُرْجَعُ ٱلْأَمْرُ كُلُّهُ فَٱعْبُدْهُ وَتَوَكَّلْ عَلَيْهِ ۚ وَمَا رَبُّكَ بِغَافِلٍ عَمَّا تَعْمَلُونَ

123 To God belongs the future of the heavens and the earth, and to Him all authority goes back. So worship Him, and rely on Him. Your Lord is never unaware of what you do.

Sūrah 12: Yūsuf

سُورَةُ يُوسُف (Joseph)

بِسْمِ ٱللَّهِ ٱلرَّحْمَٰنِ ٱلرَّحِيمِ

١ الر ۚ تِلْكَ آيَاتُ ٱلْكِتَابِ ٱلْمُبِينِ 1 Alif, Lām, Rā'. These are the Verses of the Clear Book.	**1** 28:2
٢ إِنَّا أَنْزَلْنَاهُ قُرْآنًا عَرَبِيًّا لَعَلَّكُمْ تَعْقِلُونَ 2 We have revealed it an Arabic Qur'an, so that you may understand.	**2** 13:37; 20:3; 41:3, 44; 42:7; 43:3
٣ نَحْنُ نَقُصُّ عَلَيْكَ أَحْسَنَ ٱلْقَصَصِ بِمَا أَوْحَيْنَا إِلَيْكَ هَٰذَا ٱلْقُرْآنَ وَإِنْ كُنْتَ مِنْ قَبْلِهِ لَمِنَ ٱلْغَافِلِينَ 3 We narrate to you the most accurate history, by revealing to you this Qur'an. Although, prior to it, you were of the unaware.	**3** 12:111; 18:13; 39:23
٤ إِذْ قَالَ يُوسُفُ لِأَبِيهِ يَا أَبَتِ إِنِّي رَأَيْتُ أَحَدَ عَشَرَ كَوْكَبًا وَٱلشَّمْسَ وَٱلْقَمَرَ رَأَيْتُهُمْ لِي سَاجِدِينَ 4 When Joseph said to his father, "O my father, I saw eleven planets, and the sun, and the moon; I saw them bowing down to me."	
٥ قَالَ يَا بُنَيَّ لَا تَقْصُصْ رُؤْيَاكَ عَلَىٰ إِخْوَتِكَ فَيَكِيدُوا لَكَ كَيْدًا ۖ إِنَّ ٱلشَّيْطَانَ لِلْإِنْسَانِ عَدُوٌّ مُبِينٌ 5 He said, "O my son, do not relate your vision to your brothers, lest they plot and scheme against you. Satan is man's sworn enemy.	**5** 12:100
٦ وَكَذَٰلِكَ يَجْتَبِيكَ رَبُّكَ وَيُعَلِّمُكَ مِنْ تَأْوِيلِ ٱلْأَحَادِيثِ وَيُتِمُّ نِعْمَتَهُ عَلَيْكَ وَعَلَىٰ آلِ يَعْقُوبَ كَمَا أَتَمَّهَا عَلَىٰ أَبَوَيْكَ مِنْ قَبْلُ إِبْرَاهِيمَ وَإِسْحَاقَ ۚ إِنَّ رَبَّكَ عَلِيمٌ حَكِيمٌ 6 And thus your Lord will choose you, and will teach you the interpretation of events, and will complete His blessing upon you and upon the family of Jacob, as He has completed it before upon your forefathers Abraham and Isaac. Your Lord is Knowing and Wise.	**6** 12:21, 41, 101
٧ لَقَدْ كَانَ فِي يُوسُفَ وَإِخْوَتِهِ آيَاتٌ لِلسَّائِلِينَ 7 In Joseph and his brothers are lessons for the seekers.	
٨ إِذْ قَالُوا لَيُوسُفُ وَأَخُوهُ أَحَبُّ إِلَىٰ أَبِينَا مِنَّا وَنَحْنُ عُصْبَةٌ إِنَّ أَبَانَا لَفِي ضَلَالٍ مُبِينٍ 8 When they said, "Joseph and his brother are dearer to our father than we are, although we are a whole group. Our father is obviously in the wrong.	**8** 12:95

٩ اقْتُلُوا يُوسُفَ أَوِ اطْرَحُوهُ أَرْضًا يَخْلُ لَكُمْ وَجْهُ أَبِيكُمْ وَتَكُونُوا مِنْ بَعْدِهِ قَوْمًا صَالِحِينَ

9 "Kill Joseph, or throw him somewhere in the land, and your father's attention will be yours. Afterwards, you will be decent people."

١٠ قَالَ قَائِلٌ مِنْهُمْ لَا تَقْتُلُوا يُوسُفَ وَأَلْقُوهُ فِي غَيَابَتِ الْجُبِّ يَلْتَقِطْهُ بَعْضُ السَّيَّارَةِ إِنْ كُنْتُمْ فَاعِلِينَ

10 One of them said, "Do not kill Joseph, but throw him into the bottom of the well; some caravan may pick him up—if you must do something."

١١ قَالُوا يَا أَبَانَا مَا لَكَ لَا تَأْمَنَّا عَلَىٰ يُوسُفَ وَإِنَّا لَهُ لَنَاصِحُونَ

11
12:64

11 They said, "Father, why do you not trust us with Joseph, although we care for him?"

١٢ أَرْسِلْهُ مَعَنَا غَدًا يَرْتَعْ وَيَلْعَبْ وَإِنَّا لَهُ لَحَافِظُونَ

12 "Send him with us tomorrow, that he may roam and play; we will take care of him."

١٣ قَالَ إِنِّي لَيَحْزُنُنِي أَنْ تَذْهَبُوا بِهِ وَأَخَافُ أَنْ يَأْكُلَهُ الذِّئْبُ وَأَنْتُمْ عَنْهُ غَافِلُونَ

13 He said, "It worries me that you would take him away. And I fear the wolf may eat him while you are careless of him."

١٤ قَالُوا لَئِنْ أَكَلَهُ الذِّئْبُ وَنَحْنُ عُصْبَةٌ إِنَّا إِذًا لَخَاسِرُونَ

14 They said, "If the wolf ate him, and we are many, we would be good for nothing."

١٥ فَلَمَّا ذَهَبُوا بِهِ وَأَجْمَعُوا أَنْ يَجْعَلُوهُ فِي غَيَابَتِ الْجُبِّ ۚ وَأَوْحَيْنَا إِلَيْهِ لَتُنَبِّئَنَّهُمْ بِأَمْرِهِمْ هَٰذَا وَهُمْ لَا يَشْعُرُونَ

15
12:77, 89

15 So they went away with him, and agreed to put him at the bottom of the well. And We inspired him, "You will inform them of this deed of theirs when they are unaware."

١٦ وَجَاءُوا أَبَاهُمْ عِشَاءً يَبْكُونَ

16 And they came to their father in the evening weeping.

١٧ قَالُوا يَا أَبَانَا إِنَّا ذَهَبْنَا نَسْتَبِقُ وَتَرَكْنَا يُوسُفَ عِنْدَ مَتَاعِنَا فَأَكَلَهُ الذِّئْبُ ۖ وَمَا أَنْتَ بِمُؤْمِنٍ لَنَا وَلَوْ كُنَّا صَادِقِينَ

17 They said, "O father, we went off racing one another, and left Joseph by our belongings; and the wolf ate him. But you will not believe us, even though we are being truthful."

١٨ وَجَاءُوا عَلَىٰ قَمِيصِهِ بِدَمٍ كَذِبٍ ۚ قَالَ بَلْ سَوَّلَتْ لَكُمْ أَنْفُسُكُمْ أَمْرًا ۖ فَصَبْرٌ جَمِيلٌ ۖ وَاللَّهُ الْمُسْتَعَانُ عَلَىٰ مَا تَصِفُونَ

18
12:83

18 And they brought his shirt, with fake blood on it. He said, "Your souls enticed you to do something. But patience is beautiful, and God is my Help against what you describe."

١٩ وَجَاءَتْ سَيَّارَةٌ فَأَرْسَلُوا وَارِدَهُمْ فَأَدْلَىٰ دَلْوَهُۥ ۖ قَالَ يَٰبُشْرَىٰ هَٰذَا غُلَٰمٌ ۚ وَأَسَرُّوهُ بِضَٰعَةً ۚ وَٱللَّهُ عَلِيمٌۢ بِمَا يَعْمَلُونَ

19 A caravan passed by, and they sent their water-carrier. He lowered his bucket, and said, "Good news. Here is a boy." And they hid him as merchandise. But God was aware of what they did.

٢٠ وَشَرَوْهُ بِثَمَنٍۭ بَخْسٍ دَرَٰهِمَ مَعْدُودَةٍ وَكَانُوا فِيهِ مِنَ ٱلزَّٰهِدِينَ

20 And they sold him for a cheap price—a few coins—they considered him to be of little value.

٢١ وَقَالَ ٱلَّذِى ٱشْتَرَىٰهُ مِن مِّصْرَ لِٱمْرَأَتِهِۦٓ أَكْرِمِى مَثْوَىٰهُ عَسَىٰٓ أَن يَنفَعَنَآ أَوْ نَتَّخِذَهُۥ وَلَدًا ۚ وَكَذَٰلِكَ مَكَّنَّا لِيُوسُفَ فِى ٱلْأَرْضِ وَلِنُعَلِّمَهُۥ مِن تَأْوِيلِ ٱلْأَحَادِيثِ ۚ وَٱللَّهُ غَالِبٌ عَلَىٰٓ أَمْرِهِۦ وَلَٰكِنَّ أَكْثَرَ ٱلنَّاسِ لَا يَعْلَمُونَ

21
12:6, 41, 56, 101

21 The Egyptian who bought him said to his wife, "Take good care of him; he may be useful to us, or we may adopt him as a son." We thus established Joseph in the land, to teach him the interpretation of events. God has control over His affairs, but most people do not know.

٢٢ وَلَمَّا بَلَغَ أَشُدَّهُۥٓ ءَاتَيْنَٰهُ حُكْمًا وَعِلْمًا ۚ وَكَذَٰلِكَ نَجْزِى ٱلْمُحْسِنِينَ

22 When he reached his maturity, We gave him wisdom and knowledge. We thus reward the righteous.

٢٣ وَرَٰوَدَتْهُ ٱلَّتِى هُوَ فِى بَيْتِهَا عَن نَّفْسِهِۦ وَغَلَّقَتِ ٱلْأَبْوَٰبَ وَقَالَتْ هَيْتَ لَكَ ۚ قَالَ مَعَاذَ ٱللَّهِ ۖ إِنَّهُۥ رَبِّىٓ أَحْسَنَ مَثْوَاىَ ۖ إِنَّهُۥ لَا يُفْلِحُ ٱلظَّٰلِمُونَ

23 She in whose house he was living tried to seduce him. She shut the doors, and said, "I am yours." He said, "God forbid! He is my Lord. He has given me a good home. Sinners never succeed."

٢٤ وَلَقَدْ هَمَّتْ بِهِۦ ۖ وَهَمَّ بِهَا لَوْلَآ أَن رَّءَا بُرْهَٰنَ رَبِّهِۦ ۚ كَذَٰلِكَ لِنَصْرِفَ عَنْهُ ٱلسُّوٓءَ وَٱلْفَحْشَآءَ ۚ إِنَّهُۥ مِنْ عِبَادِنَا ٱلْمُخْلَصِينَ

24 She desired him, and he desired her, had he not seen the proof of his Lord. It was thus that We diverted evil and indecency away from him. He was one of Our loyal servants.

٢٥ وَٱسْتَبَقَا ٱلْبَابَ وَقَدَّتْ قَمِيصَهُۥ مِن دُبُرٍ وَأَلْفَيَا سَيِّدَهَا لَدَى ٱلْبَابِ ۚ قَالَتْ مَا جَزَآءُ مَنْ أَرَادَ بِأَهْلِكَ سُوٓءًا إِلَّآ أَن يُسْجَنَ أَوْ عَذَابٌ أَلِيمٌ

25 As they raced towards the door, she tore his shirt from behind. At the door, they ran into her husband. She said, "What is the penalty for him who desired to dishonor your wife, except imprisonment or a painful punishment?"

٢٦ قَالَ هِىَ رَٰوَدَتْنِى عَن نَّفْسِى ۚ وَشَهِدَ شَاهِدٌ مِّنْ أَهْلِهَآ إِن كَانَ قَمِيصُهُۥ قُدَّ مِن قُبُلٍ فَصَدَقَتْ وَهُوَ مِنَ ٱلْكَٰذِبِينَ

26
12:32

26 He said, "It was she who tried to seduce me." A witness from her household suggested: "If his shirt is torn from the front: then she has told the truth, and he is the liar.

٢٧ وَإِن كَانَ قَمِيصُهُ قُدَّ مِن دُبُرٍ فَكَذَبَتْ وَهُوَ مِنَ الصَّادِقِينَ

27 But if his shirt is torn from the back: then she has lied, and he is the truthful."

٢٨ فَلَمَّا رَأَىٰ قَمِيصَهُ قُدَّ مِن دُبُرٍ قَالَ إِنَّهُ مِن كَيْدِكُنَّ ۖ إِنَّ كَيْدَكُنَّ عَظِيمٌ

28 And when he saw that his shirt was torn from the back, he said, "This is a woman's scheme. Your scheming is serious indeed."

٢٩ يُوسُفُ أَعْرِضْ عَنْ هَٰذَا ۚ وَاسْتَغْفِرِي لِذَنبِكِ ۖ إِنَّكِ كُنتِ مِنَ الْخَاطِئِينَ

29 "Joseph, turn away from this. And you, woman, ask forgiveness for your sin; you are indeed in the wrong."

٣٠ وَقَالَ نِسْوَةٌ فِي الْمَدِينَةِ امْرَأَتُ الْعَزِيزِ تُرَاوِدُ فَتَاهَا عَن نَّفْسِهِ ۖ قَدْ شَغَفَهَا حُبًّا ۖ إِنَّا لَنَرَاهَا فِي ضَلَالٍ مُّبِينٍ

30 Some ladies in the city said, "The governor's wife is trying to seduce her servant. She is deeply in love with him. We see she has gone astray."

٣١ فَلَمَّا سَمِعَتْ بِمَكْرِهِنَّ أَرْسَلَتْ إِلَيْهِنَّ وَأَعْتَدَتْ لَهُنَّ مُتَّكَأً وَآتَتْ كُلَّ وَاحِدَةٍ مِّنْهُنَّ سِكِّينًا وَقَالَتِ اخْرُجْ عَلَيْهِنَّ ۖ فَلَمَّا رَأَيْنَهُ أَكْبَرْنَهُ وَقَطَّعْنَ أَيْدِيَهُنَّ وَقُلْنَ حَاشَ لِلَّهِ مَا هَٰذَا بَشَرًا إِنْ هَٰذَا إِلَّا مَلَكٌ كَرِيمٌ

31 And when she heard of their gossip, she invited them, and prepared for them a banquet, and she gave each one of them a knife. She said, "Come out before them." And when they saw him, they marveled at him, and cut their hands. They said, "Good God, this is not a human, this must be a precious angel."

٣٢ قَالَتْ فَذَٰلِكُنَّ الَّذِي لُمْتُنَّنِي فِيهِ ۖ وَلَقَدْ رَاوَدتُّهُ عَن نَّفْسِهِ فَاسْتَعْصَمَ ۖ وَلَئِن لَّمْ يَفْعَلْ مَا آمُرُهُ لَيُسْجَنَنَّ وَلَيَكُونًا مِّنَ الصَّاغِرِينَ

32
12:26

32 She said, "Here he is, the one you blamed me for. I did try to seduce him, but he resisted. But if he does not do what I tell him to do, he will be imprisoned, and will be one of the despised."

٣٣ قَالَ رَبِّ السِّجْنُ أَحَبُّ إِلَيَّ مِمَّا يَدْعُونَنِي إِلَيْهِ ۖ وَإِلَّا تَصْرِفْ عَنِّي كَيْدَهُنَّ أَصْبُ إِلَيْهِنَّ وَأَكُن مِّنَ الْجَاهِلِينَ

33 He said, "My Lord, prison is more desirable to me than what they call me to. Unless You turn their scheming away from me, I may yield to them, and become one of the ignorant."

٣٤ فَاسْتَجَابَ لَهُ رَبُّهُ فَصَرَفَ عَنْهُ كَيْدَهُنَّ ۚ إِنَّهُ هُوَ السَّمِيعُ الْعَلِيمُ

34 Thereupon his Lord answered him, and diverted their scheming away from him. He is the Hearer, the Knower.

٣٥ ثُمَّ بَدَا لَهُم مِّن بَعْدِ مَا رَأَوُا الْآيَاتِ لَيَسْجُنُنَّهُ حَتَّىٰ حِينٍ

35 Then it occurred to them, after they had seen the signs, to imprison him for a while.

٣٦ وَدَخَلَ مَعَهُ السِّجْنَ فَتَيَانِ ۖ قَالَ أَحَدُهُمَا إِنِّي أَرَانِي أَعْصِرُ خَمْرًا ۖ وَقَالَ الْآخَرُ إِنِّي أَرَانِي أَحْمِلُ فَوْقَ رَأْسِي خُبْزًا تَأْكُلُ الطَّيْرُ مِنْهُ ۖ نَبِّئْنَا بِتَأْوِيلِهِ ۖ إِنَّا نَرَاكَ مِنَ الْمُحْسِنِينَ

36 Two youth entered the prison with him. One of them said, "I see myself pressing wine." The other said, "I see myself carrying bread on my head, from which the birds are eating. Tell us their interpretation—we see that you are one of the righteous."

٣٧ قَالَ لَا يَأْتِيكُمَا طَعَامٌ تُرْزَقَانِهِ إِلَّا نَبَّأْتُكُمَا بِتَأْوِيلِهِ قَبْلَ أَنْ يَأْتِيَكُمَا ۚ ذَٰلِكُمَا مِمَّا عَلَّمَنِي رَبِّي ۚ إِنِّي تَرَكْتُ مِلَّةَ قَوْمٍ لَا يُؤْمِنُونَ بِاللَّهِ وَهُمْ بِالْآخِرَةِ هُمْ كَافِرُونَ

37 He said, "No food is served to you, but I have informed you about it before you have received it. That is some of what my Lord has taught me. I have forsaken the tradition of people who do not believe in God; and regarding the Hereafter, they are deniers."

٣٨ وَاتَّبَعْتُ مِلَّةَ آبَائِي إِبْرَاهِيمَ وَإِسْحَاقَ وَيَعْقُوبَ ۚ مَا كَانَ لَنَا أَنْ نُشْرِكَ بِاللَّهِ مِنْ شَيْءٍ ۚ ذَٰلِكَ مِنْ فَضْلِ اللَّهِ عَلَيْنَا وَعَلَى النَّاسِ وَلَٰكِنَّ أَكْثَرَ النَّاسِ لَا يَشْكُرُونَ

38
13:16; 27:59; 38:65; 39:4

38 "And I have followed the faith of my forefathers, Abraham, and Isaac, and Jacob. It is not for us to associate anything with God. This is by virtue of God's grace upon us and upon the people, but most people do not give thanks.

٣٩ يَا صَاحِبَيِ السِّجْنِ أَأَرْبَابٌ مُتَفَرِّقُونَ خَيْرٌ أَمِ اللَّهُ الْوَاحِدُ الْقَهَّارُ

39 "O My fellow inmates, are diverse lords better, or God, the One, the Supreme?"

٤٠ مَا تَعْبُدُونَ مِنْ دُونِهِ إِلَّا أَسْمَاءً سَمَّيْتُمُوهَا أَنْتُمْ وَآبَاؤُكُمْ مَا أَنْزَلَ اللَّهُ بِهَا مِنْ سُلْطَانٍ ۚ إِنِ الْحُكْمُ إِلَّا لِلَّهِ ۚ أَمَرَ أَلَّا تَعْبُدُوا إِلَّا إِيَّاهُ ۚ ذَٰلِكَ الدِّينُ الْقَيِّمُ وَلَٰكِنَّ أَكْثَرَ النَّاسِ لَا يَعْلَمُونَ

40
7:71; 53:23

40 "You do not worship, besides Him, except names you have named, you and your ancestors, for which God has sent down no authority. Judgment belongs to none but God. He has commanded that you worship none but Him. This is the right religion, but most people do not know.

٤١ يَا صَاحِبَيِ السِّجْنِ أَمَّا أَحَدُكُمَا فَيَسْقِي رَبَّهُ خَمْرًا ۖ وَأَمَّا الْآخَرُ فَيُصْلَبُ فَتَأْكُلُ الطَّيْرُ مِنْ رَأْسِهِ ۚ قُضِيَ الْأَمْرُ الَّذِي فِيهِ تَسْتَفْتِيَانِ

41
12:6, 21, 101

41 "O my fellow inmates! One of you will serve his master wine; while the other will be crucified, and the birds will eat from his head. Thus the matter you are inquiring about is settled."

٤٢ وَقَالَ لِلَّذِي ظَنَّ أَنَّهُ نَاجٍ مِنْهُمَا اذْكُرْنِي عِنْدَ رَبِّكَ فَأَنْسَاهُ الشَّيْطَانُ ذِكْرَ رَبِّهِ فَلَبِثَ فِي السِّجْنِ بِضْعَ سِنِينَ

42 And he said to the one he thought would be released, "Mention me to your master." But Satan caused him to forget mentioning him to his master, so he remained in prison for several years.

٤٣ وَقَالَ الْمَلِكُ إِنِّي أَرَىٰ سَبْعَ بَقَرَاتٍ سِمَانٍ يَأْكُلُهُنَّ سَبْعٌ عِجَافٌ وَسَبْعَ سُنبُلَاتٍ خُضْرٍ وَأُخَرَ يَابِسَاتٍ ۖ يَا أَيُّهَا الْمَلَأُ أَفْتُونِي فِي رُؤْيَايَ إِن كُنتُمْ لِلرُّؤْيَا تَعْبُرُونَ

43 The king said, "I see seven fat cows being eaten by seven lean ones, and seven green spikes, and others dried up. O elders, explain to me my vision, if you are able to interpret visions."

٤٤ قَالُوا أَضْغَاثُ أَحْلَامٍ ۖ وَمَا نَحْنُ بِتَأْوِيلِ الْأَحْلَامِ بِعَالِمِينَ

44 They said, "Jumbles of dreams, and we know nothing of the interpretation of dreams."

٤٥ وَقَالَ الَّذِي نَجَا مِنْهُمَا وَادَّكَرَ بَعْدَ أُمَّةٍ أَنَا أُنَبِّئُكُم بِتَأْوِيلِهِ فَأَرْسِلُونِ

45 The one who was released said, having remembered after a time, "I will inform you of its interpretation, so send me out."

٤٦ يُوسُفُ أَيُّهَا الصِّدِّيقُ أَفْتِنَا فِي سَبْعِ بَقَرَاتٍ سِمَانٍ يَأْكُلُهُنَّ سَبْعٌ عِجَافٌ وَسَبْعِ سُنبُلَاتٍ خُضْرٍ وَأُخَرَ يَابِسَاتٍ لَّعَلِّي أَرْجِعُ إِلَى النَّاسِ لَعَلَّهُمْ يَعْلَمُونَ

46 "Joseph, O man of truth, inform us concerning seven fat cows being eaten by seven lean ones, and seven green spikes, and others dried up, so that I may return to the people, so that they may know."

٤٧ قَالَ تَزْرَعُونَ سَبْعَ سِنِينَ دَأَبًا فَمَا حَصَدتُّمْ فَذَرُوهُ فِي سُنبُلِهِ إِلَّا قَلِيلًا مِّمَّا تَأْكُلُونَ

47 He said, "You will farm for seven consecutive years. But whatever you harvest, leave it in its spikes, except for the little that you eat."

٤٨ ثُمَّ يَأْتِي مِن بَعْدِ ذَٰلِكَ سَبْعٌ شِدَادٌ يَأْكُلْنَ مَا قَدَّمْتُمْ لَهُنَّ إِلَّا قَلِيلًا مِّمَّا تُحْصِنُونَ

48 Then after that will come seven difficult ones, which will consume what you have stored for them, except for the little that you have preserved.

٤٩ ثُمَّ يَأْتِي مِن بَعْدِ ذَٰلِكَ عَامٌ فِيهِ يُغَاثُ النَّاسُ وَفِيهِ يَعْصِرُونَ

49 Then after that will come a year that brings relief to the people, and during which they will press.

٥٠ وَقَالَ الْمَلِكُ ائْتُونِي بِهِ ۖ فَلَمَّا جَاءَهُ الرَّسُولُ قَالَ ارْجِعْ إِلَىٰ رَبِّكَ فَاسْأَلْهُ مَا بَالُ النِّسْوَةِ اللَّاتِي قَطَّعْنَ أَيْدِيَهُنَّ ۚ إِنَّ رَبِّي بِكَيْدِهِنَّ عَلِيمٌ

50 The king said, "Bring him to me." And when the envoy came to him, he said, "Go back to your master, and ask him about the intentions of the women who cut their hands; my Lord is well aware of their schemes."

٥١ قَالَ مَا خَطْبُكُنَّ إِذْ رَاوَدتُّنَّ يُوسُفَ عَن نَّفْسِهِ ۚ قُلْنَ حَاشَ لِلَّهِ مَا عَلِمْنَا عَلَيْهِ مِن سُوءٍ ۚ قَالَتِ امْرَأَتُ الْعَزِيزِ الْآنَ حَصْحَصَ الْحَقُّ أَنَا رَاوَدتُّهُ عَن نَّفْسِهِ وَإِنَّهُ لَمِنَ الصَّادِقِينَ

51 He said, "What was the matter with you, women, when you tried to seduce Joseph?" They said, "God forbid! We knew of no evil committed by him." The governor's wife then said, "Now the truth is out. It was I who tried to seduce him, and he is telling the truth."

٥٢ ذَٰلِكَ لِيَعْلَمَ أَنِّي لَمْ أَخُنْهُ بِالْغَيْبِ وَأَنَّ اللَّهَ لَا يَهْدِي كَيْدَ الْخَائِنِينَ

52 "This is that he may know that I did not betray him in secret, and that God does not guide the scheming of the betrayers."

٥٣ وَمَا أُبَرِّئُ نَفْسِي ۚ إِنَّ النَّفْسَ لَأَمَّارَةٌ بِالسُّوءِ إِلَّا مَا رَحِمَ رَبِّي ۚ إِنَّ رَبِّي غَفُورٌ رَحِيمٌ

53 "Yet I do not claim to be innocent. The soul commands evil, except those on whom my Lord has mercy. Truly my Lord is Forgiving and Merciful."

٥٤ وَقَالَ الْمَلِكُ ائْتُونِي بِهِ أَسْتَخْلِصْهُ لِنَفْسِي ۖ فَلَمَّا كَلَّمَهُ قَالَ إِنَّكَ الْيَوْمَ لَدَيْنَا مَكِينٌ أَمِينٌ

54 The king said, "Bring him to me, and I will reserve him for myself." And when he spoke to him, he said, "This day you are with us established and secure."

٥٥ قَالَ اجْعَلْنِي عَلَىٰ خَزَائِنِ الْأَرْضِ ۖ إِنِّي حَفِيظٌ عَلِيمٌ

55 He said, "Put me in charge of the storehouses of the land; I am honest and knowledgeable."

٥٦ وَكَذَٰلِكَ مَكَّنَّا لِيُوسُفَ فِي الْأَرْضِ يَتَبَوَّأُ مِنْهَا حَيْثُ يَشَاءُ ۚ نُصِيبُ بِرَحْمَتِنَا مَن نَّشَاءُ ۖ وَلَا نُضِيعُ أَجْرَ الْمُحْسِنِينَ

56 And thus We established Joseph in the land, to live therein wherever he wished. We touch with Our mercy whomever We will, and We never waste the reward of the righteous.

56
21:21

٥٧ وَلَأَجْرُ الْآخِرَةِ خَيْرٌ لِّلَّذِينَ آمَنُوا وَكَانُوا يَتَّقُونَ

57 But the reward of the Hereafter is better for those who believe and observed piety.

٥٨ وَجَاءَ إِخْوَةُ يُوسُفَ فَدَخَلُوا عَلَيْهِ فَعَرَفَهُمْ وَهُمْ لَهُ مُنكِرُونَ

58 And Joseph's brothers came, and entered into his presence. He recognized them, but they did not recognize him.

٥٩ وَلَمَّا جَهَّزَهُم بِجَهَازِهِمْ قَالَ ائْتُونِي بِأَخٍ لَّكُم مِّنْ أَبِيكُمْ ۚ أَلَا تَرَوْنَ أَنِّي أُوفِي الْكَيْلَ وَأَنَا خَيْرُ الْمُنزِلِينَ

59 When he provided them with their provisions, he said, "Bring me a brother of yours from your father. Do you not see that I fill up the measure, and I am the best of hosts?"

٦٠ فَإِن لَّمْ تَأْتُونِي بِهِ فَلَا كَيْلَ لَكُمْ عِندِي وَلَا تَقْرَبُونِ

60 "But if you do not bring him to me, you will have no measure from me, and you will not come near me."

٦١ قَالُوا سَنُرَاوِدُ عَنْهُ أَبَاهُ وَإِنَّا لَفَاعِلُونَ

61 They said, "We will solicit him from his father. We will surely do."

٦٢ وَقَالَ لِفِتْيَانِهِ اجْعَلُوا بِضَاعَتَهُمْ فِي رِحَالِهِمْ لَعَلَّهُمْ يَعْرِفُونَهَا إِذَا انْقَلَبُوا إِلَىٰ أَهْلِهِمْ لَعَلَّهُمْ يَرْجِعُونَ

62 He said to his servants, "Put their goods in their saddlebags; perhaps they will recognize them when they return to their families, and maybe they will come back."

٦٣ فَلَمَّا رَجَعُوا إِلَىٰ أَبِيهِمْ قَالُوا يَا أَبَانَا مُنِعَ مِنَّا الْكَيْلُ فَأَرْسِلْ مَعَنَا أَخَانَا نَكْتَلْ وَإِنَّا لَهُ لَحَافِظُونَ

63 When they returned to their father, they said, "O father, we were denied measure, but send our brother with us, and we will obtain measure. We will take care of him."

٦٤ قَالَ هَلْ آمَنُكُمْ عَلَيْهِ إِلَّا كَمَا أَمِنْتُكُمْ عَلَىٰ أَخِيهِ مِنْ قَبْلُ ۖ فَاللَّهُ خَيْرٌ حَافِظًا ۖ وَهُوَ أَرْحَمُ الرَّاحِمِينَ

64 He said, "Shall I trust you with him, as I trusted you with his brother before? God is the Best Guardian, and He is the Most Merciful of the merciful."

64
12:11

٦٥ وَلَمَّا فَتَحُوا مَتَاعَهُمْ وَجَدُوا بِضَاعَتَهُمْ رُدَّتْ إِلَيْهِمْ ۖ قَالُوا يَا أَبَانَا مَا نَبْغِي ۖ هَٰذِهِ بِضَاعَتُنَا رُدَّتْ إِلَيْنَا ۖ وَنَمِيرُ أَهْلَنَا وَنَحْفَظُ أَخَانَا وَنَزْدَادُ كَيْلَ بَعِيرٍ ۖ ذَٰلِكَ كَيْلٌ يَسِيرٌ

65 And when they opened their baggage, they found that their goods were returned to them. They said, "Father, what more do we want? Here are our goods, returned to us. We will provide for our family, and protect our brother, and have an additional camel-load. This is easy commerce."

٦٦ قَالَ لَنْ أُرْسِلَهُ مَعَكُمْ حَتَّىٰ تُؤْتُونِ مَوْثِقًا مِنَ اللَّهِ لَتَأْتُنَّنِي بِهِ إِلَّا أَنْ يُحَاطَ بِكُمْ ۖ فَلَمَّا آتَوْهُ مَوْثِقَهُمْ قَالَ اللَّهُ عَلَىٰ مَا نَقُولُ وَكِيلٌ

66 He said, "I will not send him with you, unless you give me a pledge before God that you will bring him back to me, unless you get trapped." And when they gave him their pledge, he said, "God is witness to what we say."

٦٧ وَقَالَ يَا بَنِيَّ لَا تَدْخُلُوا مِنْ بَابٍ وَاحِدٍ وَادْخُلُوا مِنْ أَبْوَابٍ مُتَفَرِّقَةٍ ۖ وَمَا أُغْنِي عَنْكُمْ مِنَ اللَّهِ مِنْ شَيْءٍ ۖ إِنِ الْحُكْمُ إِلَّا لِلَّهِ ۖ عَلَيْهِ تَوَكَّلْتُ ۖ وَعَلَيْهِ فَلْيَتَوَكَّلِ الْمُتَوَكِّلُونَ

67 And he said, "O my sons, do not enter by one gate, but enter by different gates. I cannot avail you anything against God. The decision rests only with God. On Him I rely, and on Him let the reliant rely."

٦٨ وَلَمَّا دَخَلُوا مِنْ حَيْثُ أَمَرَهُمْ أَبُوهُمْ مَا كَانَ يُغْنِي عَنْهُمْ مِنَ اللَّهِ مِنْ شَيْءٍ إِلَّا حَاجَةً فِي نَفْسِ يَعْقُوبَ قَضَاهَا ۚ وَإِنَّهُ لَذُو عِلْمٍ لِمَا عَلَّمْنَاهُ وَلَٰكِنَّ أَكْثَرَ النَّاسِ لَا يَعْلَمُونَ

68 And when they entered as their father had instructed them, it did not avail them anything against God; it was just a need in the soul of Jacob, which he carried out. He was a person of knowledge inasmuch as We had taught him, but most people do not know.

٦٩ وَلَمَّا دَخَلُوا عَلَىٰ يُوسُفَ آوَىٰ إِلَيْهِ أَخَاهُ ۖ قَالَ إِنِّي أَنَا أَخُوكَ فَلَا تَبْتَئِسْ بِمَا كَانُوا يَعْمَلُونَ

69 And when they entered into the presence of Joseph, he embraced his brother, and said, "I am your brother; do not be saddened by what they used to do."

٧٠ فَلَمَّا جَهَّزَهُم بِجَهَازِهِمْ جَعَلَ السِّقَايَةَ فِي رَحْلِ أَخِيهِ ثُمَّ أَذَّنَ مُؤَذِّنٌ أَيَّتُهَا الْعِيرُ إِنَّكُمْ لَسَارِقُونَ

70 Then, when he provided them with their provisions, he placed the drinking-cup in his brother's saddlebag. Then an announcer called out, "O people of the caravan, you are thieves."

٧١ قَالُوا وَأَقْبَلُوا عَلَيْهِم مَّاذَا تَفْقِدُونَ

71 They said, as they came towards them, "What are you missing?"

٧٢ قَالُوا نَفْقِدُ صُوَاعَ الْمَلِكِ وَلِمَن جَاءَ بِهِ حِمْلُ بَعِيرٍ وَأَنَا بِهِ زَعِيمٌ

72 They said, "We are missing the king's goblet. Whoever brings it will have a camel-load; and I personally guarantee it."

٧٣ قَالُوا تَاللَّهِ لَقَدْ عَلِمْتُم مَّا جِئْنَا لِنُفْسِدَ فِي الْأَرْضِ وَمَا كُنَّا سَارِقِينَ

73 They said, "By God, you know we did not come to cause trouble in the land, and we are not thieves."

٧٤ قَالُوا فَمَا جَزَاؤُهُ إِن كُنتُمْ كَاذِبِينَ

74 They said, "What shall be his punishment, if you are lying?"

٧٥ قَالُوا جَزَاؤُهُ مَن وُجِدَ فِي رَحْلِهِ فَهُوَ جَزَاؤُهُ ۚ كَذَٰلِكَ نَجْزِي الظَّالِمِينَ

75 They said, "His punishment, if it is found in his bag: he will belong to you. Thus we penalize the guilty."

٧٦ فَبَدَأَ بِأَوْعِيَتِهِمْ قَبْلَ وِعَاءِ أَخِيهِ ثُمَّ اسْتَخْرَجَهَا مِن وِعَاءِ أَخِيهِ ۚ كَذَٰلِكَ كِدْنَا لِيُوسُفَ ۖ مَا كَانَ لِيَأْخُذَ أَخَاهُ فِي دِينِ الْمَلِكِ إِلَّا أَن يَشَاءَ اللَّهُ ۚ نَرْفَعُ دَرَجَاتٍ مَّن نَّشَاءُ ۗ وَفَوْقَ كُلِّ ذِي عِلْمٍ عَلِيمٌ

76 So he began with their bags, before his brother's bag. Then he pulled it out of his brother's bag. Thus We devised a plan for Joseph; he could not have detained his brother under the king's law, unless God so willed. We elevate by degrees whomever We will; and above every person of knowledge, there is one more learned.

٧٧ قَالُوا إِن يَسْرِقْ فَقَدْ سَرَقَ أَخٌ لَّهُ مِن قَبْلُ ۚ فَأَسَرَّهَا يُوسُفُ فِي نَفْسِهِ وَلَمْ يُبْدِهَا لَهُمْ ۚ قَالَ أَنتُمْ شَرٌّ مَّكَانًا ۖ وَاللَّهُ أَعْلَمُ بِمَا تَصِفُونَ

77 They said, "If he has stolen, a brother of his has stolen before." But Joseph kept it to himself, and did not reveal it to them. He said, "You are in a worse situation, and God is Aware of what you allege."

77
12:15, 89

٧٨ قَالُوا يَا أَيُّهَا الْعَزِيزُ إِنَّ لَهُ أَبًا شَيْخًا كَبِيرًا فَخُذْ أَحَدَنَا مَكَانَهُ ۖ إِنَّا نَرَاكَ مِنَ الْمُحْسِنِينَ

78 They said, "O noble prince, he has a father, a very old man, so take one of us in his place. We see that you are a good person."

٧٩ قَالَ مَعَاذَ اللَّهِ أَن نَّأْخُذَ إِلَّا مَن وَجَدْنَا مَتَاعَنَا عِندَهُ إِنَّا إِذًا لَّظَالِمُونَ

79 He said, "God forbid that we should arrest anyone except him in whose possession we found our property; for then we would be unjust."

٨٠ فَلَمَّا اسْتَيْأَسُوا مِنْهُ خَلَصُوا نَجِيًّا ۖ قَالَ كَبِيرُهُمْ أَلَمْ تَعْلَمُوا أَنَّ أَبَاكُمْ قَدْ أَخَذَ عَلَيْكُم مَّوْثِقًا مِّنَ اللَّهِ وَمِن قَبْلُ مَا فَرَّطتُمْ فِي يُوسُفَ ۖ فَلَنْ أَبْرَحَ الْأَرْضَ حَتَّىٰ يَأْذَنَ لِي أَبِي أَوْ يَحْكُمَ اللَّهُ لِي ۖ وَهُوَ خَيْرُ الْحَاكِمِينَ

80 And when they despaired of him, they conferred privately. Their eldest said, "Don't you know that your father received a pledge from you before God, and in the past you failed with regard to Joseph? I will not leave this land until my father permits me, or God decides for me; for He is the Best of Deciders."

٨١ ارْجِعُوا إِلَىٰ أَبِيكُمْ فَقُولُوا يَا أَبَانَا إِنَّ ابْنَكَ سَرَقَ وَمَا شَهِدْنَا إِلَّا بِمَا عَلِمْنَا وَمَا كُنَّا لِلْغَيْبِ حَافِظِينَ

81 "Go back to your father, and say, 'Our father, your son has stolen. We testify only to what we know, and we could not have prevented the unforeseen.'"

٨٢ وَاسْأَلِ الْقَرْيَةَ الَّتِي كُنَّا فِيهَا وَالْعِيرَ الَّتِي أَقْبَلْنَا فِيهَا ۖ وَإِنَّا لَصَادِقُونَ

82 "Ask the town where we were, and the caravan in which we came. We are being truthful."

٨٣ قَالَ بَلْ سَوَّلَتْ لَكُمْ أَنفُسُكُمْ أَمْرًا ۖ فَصَبْرٌ جَمِيلٌ ۖ عَسَى اللَّهُ أَن يَأْتِيَنِي بِهِمْ جَمِيعًا ۚ إِنَّهُ هُوَ الْعَلِيمُ الْحَكِيمُ

83 He said, "Rather, your souls have contrived something for you. Patience is a virtue. Perhaps God will bring them all back to me. He is the Knowing, the Wise."

83
12:18

٨٤ وَتَوَلَّىٰ عَنْهُمْ وَقَالَ يَا أَسَفَىٰ عَلَىٰ يُوسُفَ وَابْيَضَّتْ عَيْنَاهُ مِنَ الْحُزْنِ فَهُوَ كَظِيمٌ

84 Then he turned away from them, and said, "O my bitterness for Joseph." And his eyes turned white from sorrow, and he became depressed.

٨٥ قَالُوا تَاللَّهِ تَفْتَأُ تَذْكُرُ يُوسُفَ حَتَّىٰ تَكُونَ حَرَضًا أَوْ تَكُونَ مِنَ الْهَالِكِينَ

85 They said, "By God, you will not stop remembering Joseph, until you have ruined your health, or you have passed away."

٨٦ قَالَ إِنَّمَا أَشْكُو بَثِّي وَحُزْنِي إِلَى اللَّهِ وَأَعْلَمُ مِنَ اللَّهِ مَا لَا تَعْلَمُونَ

86 He said, "I only complain of my grief and sorrow to God, and I know from God what you do not know."

٨٧ يَا بَنِيَّ اذْهَبُوا فَتَحَسَّسُوا مِن يُوسُفَ وَأَخِيهِ وَلَا تَيْأَسُوا مِن رَّوْحِ اللَّهِ ۖ إِنَّهُ لَا يَيْأَسُ مِن رَّوْحِ اللَّهِ إِلَّا الْقَوْمُ الْكَافِرُونَ

87 "O my sons, go and inquire about Joseph and his brother, and do not despair of God's comfort. None despairs of God's comfort except the disbelieving people."

٨٨ فَلَمَّا دَخَلُوا عَلَيْهِ قَالُوا يَا أَيُّهَا الْعَزِيزُ مَسَّنَا وَأَهْلَنَا الضُّرُّ وَجِئْنَا بِبِضَاعَةٍ مُزْجَاةٍ فَأَوْفِ لَنَا الْكَيْلَ وَتَصَدَّقْ عَلَيْنَا ۖ إِنَّ اللَّهَ يَجْزِي الْمُتَصَدِّقِينَ

88 Then, when they entered into his presence, they said, "Mighty governor, adversity has befallen us, and our family. We have brought scant merchandise. But give us full measure, and be charitable towards us—God rewards the charitable."

٨٩ قَالَ هَلْ عَلِمْتُمْ مَا فَعَلْتُمْ بِيُوسُفَ وَأَخِيهِ إِذْ أَنْتُمْ جَاهِلُونَ

89 He said, "Do you realize what you did with Joseph and his brother, in your ignorance?"

89
12:15, 77

٩٠ قَالُوا أَإِنَّكَ لَأَنْتَ يُوسُفُ ۖ قَالَ أَنَا يُوسُفُ وَهَٰذَا أَخِي ۖ قَدْ مَنَّ اللَّهُ عَلَيْنَا ۖ إِنَّهُ مَنْ يَتَّقِ وَيَصْبِرْ فَإِنَّ اللَّهَ لَا يُضِيعُ أَجْرَ الْمُحْسِنِينَ

90 They said, "Is that you, Joseph?" He said, "I am Joseph, and this is my brother. God has been gracious to us. He who practices piety and patience—God never fails to reward the righteous."

٩١ قَالُوا تَاللَّهِ لَقَدْ آثَرَكَ اللَّهُ عَلَيْنَا وَإِنْ كُنَّا لَخَاطِئِينَ

91 They said, "By God, God has preferred you over us. We were definitely in the wrong."

٩٢ قَالَ لَا تَثْرِيبَ عَلَيْكُمُ الْيَوْمَ ۖ يَغْفِرُ اللَّهُ لَكُمْ ۖ وَهُوَ أَرْحَمُ الرَّاحِمِينَ

92 He said, "There is no blame upon you today. God will forgive you. He is the Most Merciful of the merciful."

٩٣ اذْهَبُوا بِقَمِيصِي هَٰذَا فَأَلْقُوهُ عَلَىٰ وَجْهِ أَبِي يَأْتِ بَصِيرًا وَأْتُونِي بِأَهْلِكُمْ أَجْمَعِينَ

93 "Take this shirt of mine, and lay it over my father's face, and he will recover his sight. And bring your whole family to me."

٩٤ وَلَمَّا فَصَلَتِ الْعِيرُ قَالَ أَبُوهُمْ إِنِّي لَأَجِدُ رِيحَ يُوسُفَ ۖ لَوْلَا أَنْ تُفَنِّدُونِ

94 As the caravan set out, their father said, "I sense the presence of Joseph, though you may think I am senile."

٩٥ قَالُوا تَاللَّهِ إِنَّكَ لَفِي ضَلَالِكَ الْقَدِيمِ

95 They said, "By God, you are still in your old confusion."

95
12:8

٩٦ فَلَمَّا أَنْ جَاءَ الْبَشِيرُ أَلْقَاهُ عَلَىٰ وَجْهِهِ فَارْتَدَّ بَصِيرًا ۖ قَالَ أَلَمْ أَقُلْ لَكُمْ إِنِّي أَعْلَمُ مِنَ اللَّهِ مَا لَا تَعْلَمُونَ

96 Then, when the bearer of good news arrived, he laid it over his face, and he regained his sight. He said, "Did I not say to you that I know from God what you do not know?"

٩٧ قَالُوا يَا أَبَانَا اسْتَغْفِرْ لَنَا ذُنُوبَنَا إِنَّا كُنَّا خَاطِئِينَ

97 They said, "Father, pray for the forgiveness of our sins; we were indeed at fault."

٩٨ قَالَ سَوْفَ أَسْتَغْفِرُ لَكُمْ رَبِّي ۖ إِنَّهُ هُوَ الْغَفُورُ الرَّحِيمُ

98 He said, "I will ask my Lord to forgive you. He is the Forgiver, the Most Merciful."

٩٩ فَلَمَّا دَخَلُوا عَلَىٰ يُوسُفَ آوَىٰ إِلَيْهِ أَبَوَيْهِ وَقَالَ ادْخُلُوا مِصْرَ إِنْ شَاءَ اللَّهُ آمِنِينَ

99 Then, when they entered into the presence of Joseph, he embraced his parents, and said, "Enter Egypt, God willing, safe and secure."

١٠٠ وَرَفَعَ أَبَوَيْهِ عَلَى الْعَرْشِ وَخَرُّوا لَهُ سُجَّدًا ۖ وَقَالَ يَا أَبَتِ هَٰذَا تَأْوِيلُ رُؤْيَايَ مِنْ قَبْلُ قَدْ جَعَلَهَا رَبِّي حَقًّا ۖ وَقَدْ أَحْسَنَ بِي إِذْ أَخْرَجَنِي مِنَ السِّجْنِ وَجَاءَ بِكُمْ مِنَ الْبَدْوِ مِنْ بَعْدِ أَنْ نَزَغَ الشَّيْطَانُ بَيْنِي وَبَيْنَ إِخْوَتِي ۚ إِنَّ رَبِّي لَطِيفٌ لِمَا يَشَاءُ ۚ إِنَّهُ هُوَ الْعَلِيمُ الْحَكِيمُ

100
12:5

100 And he elevated his parents on the throne, and they fell prostrate before him. He said, "Father, this is the fulfillment of my vision of long ago. My Lord has made it come true. He has blessed me, when he released me from prison, and brought you out of the wilderness, after the devil had sown conflict between me and my brothers. My Lord is Most Kind towards whomever He wills. He is the All-knowing, the Most Wise."

١٠١ رَبِّ قَدْ آتَيْتَنِي مِنَ الْمُلْكِ وَعَلَّمْتَنِي مِنْ تَأْوِيلِ الْأَحَادِيثِ ۚ فَاطِرَ السَّمَاوَاتِ وَالْأَرْضِ أَنْتَ وَلِيِّي فِي الدُّنْيَا وَالْآخِرَةِ ۖ تَوَفَّنِي مُسْلِمًا وَأَلْحِقْنِي بِالصَّالِحِينَ

101
12:6, 21, 41

101 "My Lord, You have given me some authority, and taught me some interpretation of events. Initiator of the heavens and the earth; You are my Protector in this life and in the Hereafter. Receive my soul in submission, and unite me with the righteous."

١٠٢ ذَٰلِكَ مِنْ أَنْبَاءِ الْغَيْبِ نُوحِيهِ إِلَيْكَ ۖ وَمَا كُنْتَ لَدَيْهِمْ إِذْ أَجْمَعُوا أَمْرَهُمْ وَهُمْ يَمْكُرُونَ

102
3:44; 11:49

102 This is news from the past that We reveal to you. You were not present with them when they plotted and agreed on a plan.

١٠٣ وَمَا أَكْثَرُ النَّاسِ وَلَوْ حَرَصْتَ بِمُؤْمِنِينَ

103
2:256; 10:86; 16:37

103 But most people, for all your eagerness, are not believers.

١٠٤ وَمَا تَسْأَلُهُمْ عَلَيْهِ مِنْ أَجْرٍ ۚ إِنْ هُوَ إِلَّا ذِكْرٌ لِلْعَالَمِينَ

104
6:90; 38:86

104 You ask them no wage for it. It is only a reminder for all mankind.

١٠٥ وَكَأَيِّنْ مِنْ آيَةٍ فِي السَّمَاوَاتِ وَالْأَرْضِ يَمُرُّونَ عَلَيْهَا وَهُمْ عَنْهَا مُعْرِضُونَ

105
6:4; 12:105; 15:8; 26:5; 36:46

105 How many a sign in the heavens and the earth do they pass by, paying no attention to them?

١٠٦ وَمَا يُؤْمِنُ أَكْثَرُهُمْ بِاللَّهِ إِلَّا وَهُمْ مُشْرِكُونَ

106
29:61, 63

106 And most of them do not believe in God unless they associate others.

١٠٧ أَفَأَمِنُوا أَن تَأْتِيَهُمْ غَاشِيَةٌ مِنْ عَذَابِ اللَّهِ أَوْ تَأْتِيَهُمُ السَّاعَةُ بَغْتَةً وَهُمْ لَا يَشْعُرُونَ

107 Do they feel secure that a covering of God's punishment will not come upon them, or that the Hour will not come upon them suddenly, while they are unaware?

107
16:45; 43:66; 47:18; 88:1

١٠٨ قُلْ هَٰذِهِ سَبِيلِي أَدْعُو إِلَى اللَّهِ ۚ عَلَىٰ بَصِيرَةٍ أَنَا وَمَنِ اتَّبَعَنِي ۖ وَسُبْحَانَ اللَّهِ وَمَا أَنَا مِنَ الْمُشْرِكِينَ

108 Say, "This is my way; I invite to God, based on clear knowledge—I and whoever follows me. Glory be to God; and I am not of the polytheists."

108
13:36; 22:67; 28:87; 40:42; 41:33

١٠٩ وَمَا أَرْسَلْنَا مِنْ قَبْلِكَ إِلَّا رِجَالًا نُوحِي إِلَيْهِمْ مِنْ أَهْلِ الْقُرَىٰ ۗ أَفَلَمْ يَسِيرُوا فِي الْأَرْضِ فَيَنْظُرُوا كَيْفَ كَانَ عَاقِبَةُ الَّذِينَ مِنْ قَبْلِهِمْ ۗ وَلَدَارُ الْآخِرَةِ خَيْرٌ لِلَّذِينَ اتَّقَوْا ۗ أَفَلَا تَعْقِلُونَ

109 We did not send before you except men, whom We inspired, from the people of the towns. Have they not roamed the earth and seen the consequences for those before them? The Home of the Hereafter is better for those who are righteous. Do you not understand?

109
16:43; 21:7, 25; 22:46; 47:10

١١٠ حَتَّىٰ إِذَا اسْتَيْأَسَ الرُّسُلُ وَظَنُّوا أَنَّهُمْ قَدْ كُذِبُوا جَاءَهُمْ نَصْرُنَا فَنُجِّيَ مَنْ نَشَاءُ ۖ وَلَا يُرَدُّ بَأْسُنَا عَنِ الْقَوْمِ الْمُجْرِمِينَ

110 Until, when the messengers have despaired, and thought that they were rejected, Our help came to them. We save whomever We will, and Our severity is not averted from the guilty people.

110
6:34

١١١ لَقَدْ كَانَ فِي قَصَصِهِمْ عِبْرَةٌ لِأُولِي الْأَلْبَابِ ۗ مَا كَانَ حَدِيثًا يُفْتَرَىٰ وَلَٰكِنْ تَصْدِيقَ الَّذِي بَيْنَ يَدَيْهِ وَتَفْصِيلَ كُلِّ شَيْءٍ وَهُدًى وَرَحْمَةً لِقَوْمٍ يُؤْمِنُونَ

111 In their stories is a lesson for those who possess intelligence. This is not a fabricated tale, but a confirmation of what came before it, and a detailed explanation of all things, and guidance, and mercy for people who believe.

111
10:37; 12:3

Sūrah 13: Al-Ra'd

سُورَةُ ٱلرَّعْد (Thunder)

بِسْمِ ٱللَّهِ ٱلرَّحْمَٰنِ ٱلرَّحِيمِ

١ المر ۚ تِلْكَ آيَاتُ الْكِتَابِ ۗ وَالَّذِي أُنْزِلَ إِلَيْكَ مِنْ رَبِّكَ الْحَقُّ وَلَٰكِنَّ أَكْثَرَ النَّاسِ لَا يُؤْمِنُونَ

1 Alif, Lām, Mīm, Rā'. These are the signs of the Scripture. What is revealed to you from your Lord is the truth, but most people do not believe.

Sūrah 13: Al-Ra'd

٢ اللَّهُ الَّذِي رَفَعَ السَّمَاوَاتِ بِغَيْرِ عَمَدٍ تَرَوْنَهَا ۖ ثُمَّ اسْتَوَىٰ عَلَى الْعَرْشِ ۖ وَسَخَّرَ الشَّمْسَ وَالْقَمَرَ ۖ كُلٌّ يَجْرِي لِأَجَلٍ مُسَمًّى ۚ يُدَبِّرُ الْأَمْرَ يُفَصِّلُ الْآيَاتِ لَعَلَّكُم بِلِقَاءِ رَبِّكُمْ تُوقِنُونَ

2 7:54; 22:5, 65; 31:10; 35:13; 52:5; 55:7; 79:27

2 God is He who raised the heavens without pillars that you can see, and then settled on the Throne. And He regulated the sun and the moon, each running for a specified period. He manages all affairs, and He explains the signs, that you may be certain of the meeting with your Lord.

٣ وَهُوَ الَّذِي مَدَّ الْأَرْضَ وَجَعَلَ فِيهَا رَوَاسِيَ وَأَنْهَارًا ۖ وَمِن كُلِّ الثَّمَرَاتِ جَعَلَ فِيهَا زَوْجَيْنِ اثْنَيْنِ ۖ يُغْشِي اللَّيْلَ النَّهَارَ ۚ إِنَّ فِي ذَٰلِكَ لَآيَاتٍ لِّقَوْمٍ يَتَفَكَّرُونَ

3 2:22; 15:19; 20:53; 41:10; 50:7; 51:48, 49

3 And it is He who spread the earth, and placed in it mountains and rivers. And He placed in it two kinds of every fruit. He causes the night to overlap the day. In that are signs for people who reflect.

٤ وَفِي الْأَرْضِ قِطَعٌ مُّتَجَاوِرَاتٌ وَجَنَّاتٌ مِّنْ أَعْنَابٍ وَزَرْعٌ وَنَخِيلٌ صِنْوَانٌ وَغَيْرُ صِنْوَانٍ يُسْقَىٰ بِمَاءٍ وَاحِدٍ وَنُفَضِّلُ بَعْضَهَا عَلَىٰ بَعْضٍ فِي الْأُكُلِ ۚ إِنَّ فِي ذَٰلِكَ لَآيَاتٍ لِّقَوْمٍ يَعْقِلُونَ

4 6:99, 141; 23:19; 36:33

4 On earth are adjacent terrains, and gardens of vines, and crops, and date-palms, from the same root or from distinct roots, irrigated with the same water. We make some taste better than others. In that are proofs for people who reason.

٥ وَإِن تَعْجَبْ فَعَجَبٌ قَوْلُهُمْ أَإِذَا كُنَّا تُرَابًا أَإِنَّا لَفِي خَلْقٍ جَدِيدٍ ۗ أُولَٰئِكَ الَّذِينَ كَفَرُوا بِرَبِّهِمْ ۖ وَأُولَٰئِكَ الْأَغْلَالُ فِي أَعْنَاقِهِمْ ۖ وَأُولَٰئِكَ أَصْحَابُ النَّارِ ۖ هُمْ فِيهَا خَالِدُونَ

5 17:98; 23:82; 36:78; 37:12–17; 40:71; 56:47

5 Should you wonder—the real wonder is their saying: "When we have become dust, will we be in a new creation?" Those are they who defied their Lord. Those are they who will have yokes around their necks. Those are the inhabitants of the Fire, where they will remain forever.

٦ وَيَسْتَعْجِلُونَكَ بِالسَّيِّئَةِ قَبْلَ الْحَسَنَةِ وَقَدْ خَلَتْ مِن قَبْلِهِمُ الْمَثُلَاتُ ۗ[a] وَإِنَّ رَبَّكَ لَذُو مَغْفِرَةٍ لِّلنَّاسِ عَلَىٰ ظُلْمِهِمْ ۖ وَإِنَّ رَبَّكَ لَشَدِيدُ الْعِقَابِ[b]

6
[a] 22:47; 29:53–54; 38:16; 42:18
[b] 6:1147, 156; 7:167; 15:49–50

6 And they urge you to hasten evil before good, though examples have passed away before them. Your Lord is full of forgiveness towards the people for their wrongdoings, yet your Lord is severe in retribution.

٧ وَيَقُولُ الَّذِينَ كَفَرُوا لَوْلَا أُنزِلَ عَلَيْهِ آيَةٌ مِّن رَّبِّهِ ۗ إِنَّمَا أَنتَ مُنذِرٌ ۖ وَلِكُلِّ قَوْمٍ هَادٍ

7 2:272; 6:37; 10:47; 13:40; 16:36; 35:24

7 Those who disbelieve say, "Why was a miracle not sent down to him from his Lord?" You are only a warner, and to every community is a guide.

٨ اللَّهُ يَعْلَمُ مَا تَحْمِلُ كُلُّ أُنثَىٰ وَمَا تَغِيضُ الْأَرْحَامُ وَمَا تَزْدَادُ ۖ وَكُلُّ شَيْءٍ عِندَهُ بِمِقْدَارٍ

8 3:6; 31:34; 35:11; 41:47; 53:23

8 God knows what every female bears, and every increase and decrease of the wombs. With Him, everything is by measure.

٩ عَالِمُ الْغَيْبِ وَالشَّهَادَةِ الْكَبِيرُ الْمُتَعَالِ

9 2:117; 3:47, 59; 6:73; 16:40

9 The Knower of the Invisible and the Visible; the Grand, the Supreme.

١٠ سَوَاءٌ مِنكُم مَّنْ أَسَرَّ الْقَوْلَ وَمَن جَهَرَ بِهِ وَمَنْ هُوَ مُسْتَخْفٍ بِاللَّيْلِ وَسَارِبٌ بِالنَّهَارِ

10 It is the same; whether one of you conceals his speech, or declares it; whether he goes into hiding by night, or goes out by day.

10 2:33; 6:3; 67:13

١١ لَهُ مُعَقِّبَاتٌ مِّن بَيْنِ يَدَيْهِ وَمِنْ خَلْفِهِ يَحْفَظُونَهُ مِنْ أَمْرِ اللَّهِ ᵃ إِنَّ اللَّهَ لَا يُغَيِّرُ مَا بِقَوْمٍ حَتَّىٰ يُغَيِّرُوا مَا بِأَنفُسِهِمْ ۗ وَإِذَا أَرَادَ اللَّهُ بِقَوْمٍ سُوءًا فَلَا مَرَدَّ لَهُ ᵇ وَمَا لَهُم مِّن دُونِهِ مِن وَالٍ

11 He has a succession; before him and behind him, protecting him by God's command. God does not change the condition of a people until they change what is within themselves. And if God wills any hardship for a people, there is no turning it back; and apart from Him they have no protector.

11
ᵃ 8:53; 42:30
ᵇ 6:147

١٢ هُوَ الَّذِي يُرِيكُمُ الْبَرْقَ خَوْفًا وَطَمَعًا وَيُنشِئُ السَّحَابَ الثِّقَالَ

12 It is He who shows you the lightening, causing fear and hope. And He produces the heavy clouds.

12 30:24

١٣ وَيُسَبِّحُ الرَّعْدُ بِحَمْدِهِ وَالْمَلَائِكَةُ مِنْ خِيفَتِهِ وَيُرْسِلُ الصَّوَاعِقَ فَيُصِيبُ بِهَا مَن يَشَاءُ وَهُمْ يُجَادِلُونَ فِي اللَّهِ وَهُوَ شَدِيدُ الْمِحَالِ

13 The thunder praises His glory, and so do the angels, in awe of Him. And He sends the thunderbolts, striking with them whomever He wills. Yet they argue about God, while He is Tremendous in might.

13 2:19; 6:3

١٤ لَهُ دَعْوَةُ الْحَقِّ ۖ وَالَّذِينَ يَدْعُونَ مِن دُونِهِ لَا يَسْتَجِيبُونَ لَهُم بِشَيْءٍ إِلَّا كَبَاسِطِ كَفَّيْهِ إِلَى الْمَاءِ لِيَبْلُغَ فَاهُ وَمَا هُوَ بِبَالِغِهِ ۚ وَمَا دُعَاءُ الْكَافِرِينَ إِلَّا فِي ضَلَالٍ

14 To Him belongs the call to truth. Those they call upon besides Him do not respond to them with anything—except as someone who stretches his hands towards water, so that it may reach his mouth, but it does not reach it. The prayers of the unbelievers are only in vain.

14 7:194; 40:50

١٥ وَلِلَّهِ يَسْجُدُ مَن فِي السَّمَاوَاتِ وَالْأَرْضِ طَوْعًا وَكَرْهًا وَظِلَالُهُم بِالْغُدُوِّ وَالْآصَالِ ۩

15 To God prostrates everyone in the heavens and the earth, willingly or unwillingly, as do their shadows, in the morning and in the evening.

15 3:83; 16:48–49; 22:18; 41:11

١٦ قُلْ مَن رَّبُّ السَّمَاوَاتِ وَالْأَرْضِ قُلِ اللَّهُ ۚ قُلْ أَفَاتَّخَذْتُم مِّن دُونِهِ أَوْلِيَاءَ لَا يَمْلِكُونَ لِأَنفُسِهِمْ نَفْعًا وَلَا ضَرًّا ۚ قُلْ هَلْ يَسْتَوِي الْأَعْمَىٰ وَالْبَصِيرُ أَمْ هَلْ تَسْتَوِي الظُّلُمَاتُ وَالنُّورُ ۗ أَمْ جَعَلُوا لِلَّهِ شُرَكَاءَ خَلَقُوا كَخَلْقِهِ فَتَشَابَهَ الْخَلْقُ عَلَيْهِمْ ۚ قُلِ اللَّهُ خَالِقُ كُلِّ شَيْءٍ وَهُوَ الْوَاحِدُ الْقَهَّارُ

16 Say, "Who is the Lord of the heavens and the earth?" Say, "God." Say, "Have you taken besides Him protectors, who have no power to profit or harm even themselves?" Say, "Are the blind and the seeing equal? Or are darkness and light equal? Or have they assigned to God associates, who created the likes of His creation, so that the creations seemed to them alike? Say, "God is the Creator of all things, and He is The One, the Irresistible."

16 6:1, 50, 71; 25:3; 35:19–22

١٧ أَنْزَلَ مِنَ السَّمَاءِ مَاءً فَسَالَتْ أَوْدِيَةٌ بِقَدَرِهَا فَاحْتَمَلَ السَّيْلُ زَبَدًا رَابِيًا ۚ وَمِمَّا يُوقِدُونَ عَلَيْهِ فِي النَّارِ ابْتِغَاءَ حِلْيَةٍ أَوْ مَتَاعٍ زَبَدٌ مِثْلُهُ ۚ كَذَٰلِكَ يَضْرِبُ اللَّهُ الْحَقَّ وَالْبَاطِلَ ۚ فَأَمَّا الزَّبَدُ فَيَذْهَبُ جُفَاءً ۖ وَأَمَّا مَا يَنْفَعُ النَّاسَ فَيَمْكُثُ فِي الْأَرْضِ ۚ كَذَٰلِكَ يَضْرِبُ اللَّهُ الْأَمْثَالَ

17 2318; 42:27; 43:11

17 He sends down water from the sky, and riverbeds flow according to their capacity. The current carries swelling froth. And from what they heat in fire of ornaments or utensils comes a similar froth. Thus God exemplifies truth and falsehood. As for the froth, it is swept away, but what benefits the people remains in the ground. Thus God presents the analogies.

١٨ لِلَّذِينَ اسْتَجَابُوا لِرَبِّهِمُ الْحُسْنَىٰ ۚ وَالَّذِينَ لَمْ يَسْتَجِيبُوا لَهُ لَوْ أَنَّ لَهُمْ مَا فِي الْأَرْضِ جَمِيعًا وَمِثْلَهُ مَعَهُ لَافْتَدَوْا بِهِ ۚ أُولَٰئِكَ لَهُمْ سُوءُ الْحِسَابِ وَمَأْوَاهُمْ جَهَنَّمُ ۖ وَبِئْسَ الْمِهَادُ

18 5:36; 10:54; 39:47

18 For those who respond to their Lord is the best. But as for those who do not respond to Him, even if they possessed everything on earth, and twice as much, they could not redeem themselves with it. Those will have the worst reckoning; and their home is Hell—a miserable destination.

١٩ أَفَمَنْ يَعْلَمُ أَنَّمَا أُنْزِلَ إِلَيْكَ مِنْ رَبِّكَ الْحَقُّ كَمَنْ هُوَ أَعْمَىٰ ۚ إِنَّمَا يَتَذَكَّرُ أُولُو الْأَلْبَابِ

19 Is he who knows that what was revealed to you from your Lord is the truth, like him who is blind? Only those who reason will remember.

٢٠ الَّذِينَ يُوفُونَ بِعَهْدِ اللَّهِ وَلَا يَنْقُضُونَ الْمِيثَاقَ

20 3:76; 6:152; 16:91; 48:10

20 Those who fulfill the promise to God, and do not violate the agreement.

٢١ وَالَّذِينَ يَصِلُونَ مَا أَمَرَ اللَّهُ بِهِ أَنْ يُوصَلَ وَيَخْشَوْنَ رَبَّهُمْ وَيَخَافُونَ سُوءَ الْحِسَابِ

21 And those who join what God has commanded to be joined, and fear their Lord, and dread the dire reckoning.

٢٢ وَالَّذِينَ صَبَرُوا ابْتِغَاءَ وَجْهِ رَبِّهِمْ وَأَقَامُوا الصَّلَاةَ وَأَنْفَقُوا مِمَّا رَزَقْنَاهُمْ سِرًّا وَعَلَانِيَةً وَيَدْرَءُونَ بِالْحَسَنَةِ السَّيِّئَةَ أُولَٰئِكَ لَهُمْ عُقْبَى الدَّارِ

22 2:274; 14:31; 16:75

22 And those who patiently seek the presence of their Lord, and pray regularly, and spend from Our provisions to them, secretly and openly, and repel evil with good. These will have the Ultimate Home.

٢٣ جَنَّاتُ عَدْنٍ يَدْخُلُونَهَا وَمَنْ صَلَحَ مِنْ آبَائِهِمْ وَأَزْوَاجِهِمْ وَذُرِّيَّاتِهِمْ ۖ وَالْمَلَائِكَةُ يَدْخُلُونَ عَلَيْهِمْ مِنْ كُلِّ بَابٍ

23 10:10; 40:8

23 Everlasting Gardens, which they will enter, along with the righteous among their parents, and their spouses, and their descendants. And the angels will enter upon them from every gate.

٢٤ سَلَامٌ عَلَيْكُم بِمَا صَبَرْتُمْ ۚ فَنِعْمَ عُقْبَى الدَّارِ

24 "Peace be upon you, because you endured patiently. How excellent is the Final Home."

24
10:10; 19:6; 33:44;
65:25–26

٢٥ وَالَّذِينَ يَنقُضُونَ عَهْدَ اللَّهِ مِن بَعْدِ مِيثَاقِهِ وَيَقْطَعُونَ مَا أَمَرَ اللَّهُ بِهِ أَن يُوصَلَ وَيُفْسِدُونَ فِي الْأَرْضِ ۙ أُولَٰئِكَ لَهُمُ اللَّعْنَةُ وَلَهُمْ سُوءُ الدَّارِ

25 As for those who violate the promise to God, after pledging to keep it, and sever what God has commanded to be joined, and spread corruption on earth—these, the curse will be upon them, and they will have the Worst Home.

25
2:27

٢٦ اللَّهُ يَبْسُطُ الرِّزْقَ لِمَن يَشَاءُ وَيَقْدِرُ ۚ وَفَرِحُوا بِالْحَيَاةِ الدُّنْيَا وَمَا الْحَيَاةُ الدُّنْيَا فِي الْآخِرَةِ إِلَّا مَتَاعٌ

26 God dispenses the provisions to whomever He wills, and restricts. And they delight in the worldly life; yet the worldly life, compared to the Hereafter, is only enjoyment.

26
6:64; 39:52; 42:27

٢٧ وَيَقُولُ الَّذِينَ كَفَرُوا لَوْلَا أُنزِلَ عَلَيْهِ آيَةٌ مِّن رَّبِّهِ ۗ قُلْ إِنَّ اللَّهَ يُضِلُّ مَن يَشَاءُ وَيَهْدِي إِلَيْهِ مَنْ أَنَابَ

27 Those who disbelieve say, "If only a miracle was sent down to him from his Lord." Say, "God leads astray whomever He wills, and He guides to Himself whoever repents."

27
6:37; 10:20; 17:59;
29:50–51

٢٨ الَّذِينَ آمَنُوا وَتَطْمَئِنُّ قُلُوبُهُم بِذِكْرِ اللَّهِ ۗ أَلَا بِذِكْرِ اللَّهِ تَطْمَئِنُّ الْقُلُوبُ

28 Those who believe, and whose hearts find comfort in the remembrance of God. Surely, it is in the remembrance of God that hearts find comfort."

28
89:27–30

٢٩ الَّذِينَ آمَنُوا وَعَمِلُوا الصَّالِحَاتِ طُوبَىٰ لَهُمْ وَحُسْنُ مَآبٍ

29 For those who believe and do righteous deeds—for them is happiness and a beautiful return.

٣٠ كَذَٰلِكَ أَرْسَلْنَاكَ فِي أُمَّةٍ قَدْ خَلَتْ مِن قَبْلِهَا أُمَمٌ لِّتَتْلُوَ عَلَيْهِمُ الَّذِي أَوْحَيْنَا إِلَيْكَ وَهُمْ يَكْفُرُونَ بِالرَّحْمَٰنِ ۚ قُلْ هُوَ رَبِّي لَا إِلَٰهَ إِلَّا هُوَ عَلَيْهِ تَوَكَّلْتُ وَإِلَيْهِ مَتَابِ

30 Thus We sent you among a community before which other communities have passed away, that you may recite to them what We revealed to you. Yet they deny the Benevolent One. Say, "He is my Lord; there is no god but He; in Him I trust, and to Him is my repentance."

30
21:25

٣١ وَلَوْ أَنَّ قُرْآنًا سُيِّرَتْ بِهِ الْجِبَالُ أَوْ قُطِّعَتْ بِهِ الْأَرْضُ أَوْ كُلِّمَ بِهِ الْمَوْتَىٰ ۗ بَل لِّلَّهِ الْأَمْرُ جَمِيعًا ۗ أَفَلَمْ يَيْأَسِ الَّذِينَ آمَنُوا أَن لَّوْ يَشَاءُ اللَّهُ لَهَدَى النَّاسَ جَمِيعًا ۗ وَلَا يَزَالُ الَّذِينَ كَفَرُوا تُصِيبُهُم بِمَا صَنَعُوا قَارِعَةٌ أَوْ تَحُلُّ قَرِيبًا مِّن دَارِهِمْ حَتَّىٰ يَأْتِيَ وَعْدُ اللَّهِ ۚ إِنَّ اللَّهَ لَا يُخْلِفُ الْمِيعَادَ

31 Even if there were a Qur'an, by which mountains could be set in motion, or by which the earth could be shattered, or by which the dead could be made to speak. In fact, every decision rests with God.

31
15:14

Did the believers not give up and realize that had God willed, He would have guided all humanity? Disasters will continue to strike those who disbelieve, because of their deeds, or they fall near their homes, until God's promise comes true. God never breaks a promise.

٣٢ وَلَقَدِ اسْتُهْزِئَ بِرُسُلٍ مِنْ قَبْلِكَ فَأَمْلَيْتُ لِلَّذِينَ كَفَرُوا ثُمَّ أَخَذْتُهُمْ ۖ فَكَيْفَ كَانَ عِقَابِ

32 Messengers before you were ridiculed, but I granted the disbelievers respite, and then I seized them. What a punishment it was!

32
6:10; 15:11; 21:41;
22:44, 48; 36:30

٣٣ أَفَمَنْ هُوَ قَائِمٌ عَلَىٰ كُلِّ نَفْسٍ بِمَا كَسَبَتْ ۗ وَجَعَلُوا لِلَّهِ شُرَكَاءَ قُلْ سَمُّوهُمْ ۚ أَمْ تُنَبِّئُونَهُ بِمَا لَا يَعْلَمُ فِي الْأَرْضِ أَمْ بِظَاهِرٍ مِنَ الْقَوْلِ ۗ بَلْ زُيِّنَ لِلَّذِينَ كَفَرُوا مَكْرُهُمْ وَصُدُّوا عَنِ السَّبِيلِ ۗ وَمَنْ يُضْلِلِ اللَّهُ فَمَا لَهُ مِنْ هَادٍ

33 Is He who is watchful over the deeds of every soul? Yet they ascribe associates to God. Say, "Name them! Or are you informing Him of something on earth He does not know, or is it a show of words?" In fact, the scheming of those who disbelieve is made to appear good to them, and they are averted from the path. Whomever God misguides has no guide.

33
49:16

٣٤ لَهُمْ عَذَابٌ فِي الْحَيَاةِ الدُّنْيَا ۖ وَلَعَذَابُ الْآخِرَةِ أَشَقُّ ۖ وَمَا لَهُمْ مِنَ اللَّهِ مِنْ وَاقٍ

34 There is for them torment in the worldly life, but the torment of the Hereafter is harsher. And they have no defender against God.

٣٥ مَثَلُ الْجَنَّةِ الَّتِي وُعِدَ الْمُتَّقُونَ ۖ تَجْرِي مِنْ تَحْتِهَا الْأَنْهَارُ ۖ أُكُلُهَا دَائِمٌ وَظِلُّهَا ۚ تِلْكَ عُقْبَى الَّذِينَ اتَّقَوْا ۖ وَعُقْبَى الْكَافِرِينَ النَّارُ

35 The likeness of the Garden promised to the righteous: rivers flowing beneath it; its food is perpetual, and so is its shade. Such is the sequel for those who guard against evil, but the sequel of the disbelievers is the Fire.

35
47:15

٣٦ وَالَّذِينَ آتَيْنَاهُمُ الْكِتَابَ يَفْرَحُونَ بِمَا أُنْزِلَ إِلَيْكَ ۖ وَمِنَ الْأَحْزَابِ مَنْ يُنْكِرُ بَعْضَهُ ۚ قُلْ إِنَّمَا أُمِرْتُ أَنْ أَعْبُدَ اللَّهَ وَلَا أُشْرِكَ بِهِ ۚ إِلَيْهِ أَدْعُو وَإِلَيْهِ مَآبِ

36 Those to whom We gave the Scripture rejoice in what was revealed to you, while some factions reject parts of it. Say, "I am commanded to worship God, and to never associate anything with Him. To Him I invite, and to Him is my return."

36
2:121; 3:133, 199;
6:114; 12:108; 28:52;
29:47

٣٧ وَكَذَٰلِكَ أَنْزَلْنَاهُ حُكْمًا عَرَبِيًّا ۚ وَلَئِنِ اتَّبَعْتَ أَهْوَاءَهُمْ بَعْدَمَا جَاءَكَ مِنَ الْعِلْمِ مَا لَكَ مِنَ اللَّهِ مِنْ وَلِيٍّ وَلَا وَاقٍ

37 Thus We revealed it an Arabic code of law. Were you to follow their desires, after the knowledge that has come to you, you would have neither ally nor defender against God.

37
2:111, 120, 135, 145;
3:73; 5:18

٣٨ وَلَقَدْ أَرْسَلْنَا رُسُلًا مِّن قَبْلِكَ وَجَعَلْنَا لَهُمْ أَزْوَاجًا وَذُرِّيَّةً ۚ وَمَا كَانَ لِرَسُولٍ أَن يَأْتِيَ بِآيَةٍ إِلَّا بِإِذْنِ اللَّهِ ۗ لِكُلِّ أَجَلٍ كِتَابٌ

38 We sent messengers before you, and We assigned for them wives and offspring. No messenger could bring a sign except with the permission of God. For every era is a scripture.

38
14:11; 17:94; 21:8; 25:20; 40:78

٣٩ يَمْحُو اللَّهُ مَا يَشَاءُ وَيُثْبِتُ ۖ وَعِندَهُ أُمُّ الْكِتَابِ

39 God abolishes whatever He wills, and He affirms. With Him is the source of the Scripture.

39
2:106; 16:101; 17:86

٤٠ وَإِن مَّا نُرِيَنَّكَ بَعْضَ الَّذِي نَعِدُهُمْ أَوْ نَتَوَفَّيَنَّكَ فَإِنَّمَا عَلَيْكَ الْبَلَاغُ وَعَلَيْنَا الْحِسَابُ

40 Whether We show you some of what We have promised them, or We cause you to die—your duty is to inform, and Ours is the reckoning.

40
40:46

٤١ أَوَلَمْ يَرَوْا أَنَّا نَأْتِي الْأَرْضَ نَنقُصُهَا مِنْ أَطْرَافِهَا ۚ وَاللَّهُ يَحْكُمُ لَا مُعَقِّبَ لِحُكْمِهِ ۚ وَهُوَ سَرِيعُ الْحِسَابِ

41 Do they not see how We deal with the earth, diminishing it at its edges? God judges; and nothing can hold back His judgment. And He is quick to settle accounts.

41
6:3; 21:44

٤٢ وَقَدْ مَكَرَ الَّذِينَ مِن قَبْلِهِمْ فَلِلَّهِ الْمَكْرُ جَمِيعًا ۖ يَعْلَمُ مَا تَكْسِبُ كُلُّ نَفْسٍ ۗ وَسَيَعْلَمُ الْكُفَّارُ لِمَنْ عُقْبَى الدَّارِ

42 Those before them planned, but the entire plan is up to God. He knows what every soul earns. Those who disbelieve will know to whom the Ultimate Home is.

42
3:54; 7:99; 8:30; 14:46; 16:26, 45; 27:50

٤٣ وَيَقُولُ الَّذِينَ كَفَرُوا لَسْتَ مُرْسَلًا ۚ قُلْ كَفَىٰ بِاللَّهِ شَهِيدًا بَيْنِي وَبَيْنَكُمْ وَمَنْ عِندَهُ عِلْمُ الْكِتَابِ

43 Those who disbelieve say, "You are not a messenger." Say, "God is a sufficient witness between me and you, and whoever has knowledge of the Scripture."

43
3:18; 4:166; 16:43; 17:95

Sūrah 14: Ibrāhīm

سُورَةُ إِبْرَاهِيم (Abraham)

بِسْمِ ٱللَّهِ ٱلرَّحْمَٰنِ ٱلرَّحِيمِ

١ الر ۚ كِتَابٌ أَنزَلْنَاهُ إِلَيْكَ لِتُخْرِجَ النَّاسَ مِنَ الظُّلُمَاتِ إِلَى النُّورِ بِإِذْنِ رَبِّهِمْ إِلَىٰ صِرَاطِ الْعَزِيزِ الْحَمِيدِ

1 Alif, Lām, Rā'. A Scripture that We revealed to you, that you may bring humanity from darkness to light—with the permission of their Lord—to the path of the Almighty, the Praiseworthy.

1
57:9; 65:11

٢ اللَّهِ الَّذِي لَهُ مَا فِي السَّمَاوَاتِ وَمَا فِي الْأَرْضِ ۗ وَوَيْلٌ لِلْكَافِرِينَ مِنْ عَذَابٍ شَدِيدٍ

2 14:33; 31:10

2 God—to whom belongs what is in the heavens and the earth. And woe to the disbelievers from a severe torment.

٣ الَّذِينَ يَسْتَحِبُّونَ الْحَيَاةَ الدُّنْيَا عَلَى الْآخِرَةِ وَيَصُدُّونَ عَنْ سَبِيلِ اللَّهِ وَيَبْغُونَهَا عِوَجًا ۚ أُولَٰئِكَ فِي ضَلَالٍ بَعِيدٍ

3 7:45; 16:107

3 Those who prefer the present life to the Hereafter, and repel from the path of God, and seek to make it crooked—these are far astray.

٤ وَمَا أَرْسَلْنَا مِنْ رَسُولٍ إِلَّا بِلِسَانِ قَوْمِهِ لِيُبَيِّنَ لَهُمْ ۖ فَيُضِلُّ اللَّهُ مَنْ يَشَاءُ وَيَهْدِي مَنْ يَشَاءُ ۚ وَهُوَ الْعَزِيزُ الْحَكِيمُ

4 16:103; 19:97; 26:192; 46:12

4 We never sent any messenger except in the language of his people, to make things clear for them. God leads astray whom He wills, and guides whom He wills. He is the Mighty, the Wise.

٥ وَلَقَدْ أَرْسَلْنَا مُوسَىٰ بِآيَاتِنَا أَنْ أَخْرِجْ قَوْمَكَ مِنَ الظُّلُمَاتِ إِلَى النُّورِ وَذَكِّرْهُمْ بِأَيَّامِ اللَّهِ ۚ إِنَّ فِي ذَٰلِكَ لَآيَاتٍ لِكُلِّ صَبَّارٍ شَكُورٍ

5 11:96

5 We sent Moses with Our signs: "Bring your people out of darkness into light, and remind them of the Days of God." In that are signs for every patient and thankful person."

٦ وَإِذْ قَالَ مُوسَىٰ لِقَوْمِهِ اذْكُرُوا نِعْمَةَ اللَّهِ عَلَيْكُمْ إِذْ أَنْجَاكُمْ مِنْ آلِ فِرْعَوْنَ يَسُومُونَكُمْ سُوءَ الْعَذَابِ وَيُذَبِّحُونَ أَبْنَاءَكُمْ وَيَسْتَحْيُونَ نِسَاءَكُمْ ۚ وَفِي ذَٰلِكُمْ بَلَاءٌ مِنْ رَبِّكُمْ عَظِيمٌ

6 2:49; 7:141, 167; 14:6; 28:4

6 Moses said to his people, "Remember God's blessings upon you, as He delivered you from the people of Pharaoh, who inflicted on you terrible suffering, slaughtering your sons while sparing your daughters. In that was a serious trial from your Lord."

٧ وَإِذْ تَأَذَّنَ رَبُّكُمْ لَئِنْ شَكَرْتُمْ لَأَزِيدَنَّكُمْ ۖ وَلَئِنْ كَفَرْتُمْ إِنَّ عَذَابِي لَشَدِيدٌ

7 7:167

7 And when your Lord proclaimed: "If you give thanks, I will grant you increase; but if you are ungrateful, My punishment is severe."

٨ وَقَالَ مُوسَىٰ إِنْ تَكْفُرُوا أَنْتُمْ وَمَنْ فِي الْأَرْضِ جَمِيعًا فَإِنَّ اللَّهَ لَغَنِيٌّ حَمِيدٌ

8 4:131

8 And Moses said, "Even if you are ungrateful, together with everyone on earth—God is in no need, Worthy of Praise."

٩ أَلَمْ يَأْتِكُمْ نَبَأُ الَّذِينَ مِنْ قَبْلِكُمْ قَوْمِ نُوحٍ وَعَادٍ وَثَمُودَ ۛ وَالَّذِينَ مِنْ بَعْدِهِمْ ۛ لَا يَعْلَمُهُمْ إِلَّا اللَّهُ ۚ جَاءَتْهُمْ رُسُلُهُمْ بِالْبَيِّنَاتِ فَرَدُّوا أَيْدِيَهُمْ فِي أَفْوَاهِهِمْ وَقَالُوا إِنَّا كَفَرْنَا بِمَا أُرْسِلْتُمْ بِهِ وَإِنَّا لَفِي شَكٍّ مِمَّا تَدْعُونَنَا إِلَيْهِ مُرِيبٍ

9 9:70; 11:62, 89; 22:42; 38:12

9 Has not the story reached you, of those before you, the people of Noah, and 'Ād, and Thamūd—and those after them? None knows them except God. Their messengers came to them with the clear proofs, but they tried to silence them, and said, "We reject what you are sent with, and we are in serious doubt regarding what you are calling us to."

١٠ قَالَتْ رُسُلُهُمْ أَفِي اللَّهِ شَكٌّ فَاطِرِ السَّمَاوَاتِ وَالْأَرْضِ ۖ يَدْعُوكُمْ لِيَغْفِرَ لَكُم مِّن ذُنُوبِكُمْ وَيُؤَخِّرَكُمْ إِلَىٰ أَجَلٍ مُّسَمًّى ۚ قَالُوا إِنْ أَنتُمْ إِلَّا بَشَرٌ مِّثْلُنَا تُرِيدُونَ أَن تَصُدُّونَا عَمَّا كَانَ يَعْبُدُ آبَاؤُنَا فَأْتُونَا بِسُلْطَانٍ مُّبِينٍ

10 10:78; 46:31; 71:4

10 Their messengers said, "Is there any doubt about God, Maker of the heavens and the earth? He calls you to forgive you your sins, and to defer you until a stated term." They said, "You are only humans like us; you want to turn us away from what our ancestors worshiped; so bring us a clear proof."

١١ قَالَتْ لَهُمْ رُسُلُهُمْ إِن نَّحْنُ إِلَّا بَشَرٌ مِّثْلُكُمْ وَلَٰكِنَّ اللَّهَ يَمُنُّ عَلَىٰ مَن يَشَاءُ مِنْ عِبَادِهِ ۖ وَمَا كَانَ لَنَا أَن نَّأْتِيَكُم بِسُلْطَانٍ إِلَّا بِإِذْنِ اللَّهِ ۚ وَعَلَى اللَّهِ فَلْيَتَوَكَّلِ الْمُؤْمِنُونَ

11 13:38; 18:110; 41:6

11 Their messengers said to them, "We are only humans like you, but God favors whomever He wills from among His servants. We cannot possibly show you any proof, except by leave of God. In God let the faithful put their trust."

١٢ وَمَا لَنَا أَلَّا نَتَوَكَّلَ عَلَى اللَّهِ وَقَدْ هَدَانَا سُبُلَنَا ۚ وَلَنَصْبِرَنَّ عَلَىٰ مَا آذَيْتُمُونَا ۚ وَعَلَى اللَّهِ فَلْيَتَوَكَّلِ الْمُتَوَكِّلُونَ

12 "And why should we not trust in God, when He has guided us in our ways? We will persevere in the face of your persecution. And upon God the reliant should rely."

١٣ وَقَالَ الَّذِينَ كَفَرُوا لِرُسُلِهِمْ لَنُخْرِجَنَّكُم مِّنْ أَرْضِنَا أَوْ لَتَعُودُنَّ فِي مِلَّتِنَا ۖ[a] فَأَوْحَىٰ إِلَيْهِمْ رَبُّهُمْ لَنُهْلِكَنَّ الظَّالِمِينَ[b]

13
[a] 7:88; 8:30; 17:76; 27:56
[b] 7:128, 137; 37:1171–173; 40:51; 58:21

13 Those who disbelieved said to their messengers, "We will expel you from our land, unless you return to our religion." And their Lord inspired them: "We will destroy the wrongdoers."

١٤ وَلَنُسْكِنَنَّكُمُ الْأَرْضَ مِن بَعْدِهِمْ ۚ ذَٰلِكَ لِمَنْ خَافَ مَقَامِي وَخَافَ وَعِيدِ

14 7:137; 17:104; 28:5

14 "And We will settle you in the land after them. That is for him who fears My Majesty, and fears My threats."

١٥ وَاسْتَفْتَحُوا وَخَابَ كُلُّ جَبَّارٍ عَنِيدٍ

15 And they prayed for victory, and every stubborn tyrant came to disappointment.

١٦ مِّن وَرَائِهِ جَهَنَّمُ وَيُسْقَىٰ مِن مَّاءٍ صَدِيدٍ

16 45:9

16 Beyond him lies Hell, and he will be given to drink putrid water.

١٧ يَتَجَرَّعُهُ وَلَا يَكَادُ يُسِيغُهُ وَيَأْتِيهِ الْمَوْتُ مِن كُلِّ مَكَانٍ وَمَا هُوَ بِمَيِّتٍ ۖ وَمِن وَرَائِهِ عَذَابٌ غَلِيظٌ

17 He will guzzle it, but he will not swallow it. Death will come at him from every direction, but he will not die. And beyond this is relentless suffering.

١٨ مَثَلُ ٱلَّذِينَ كَفَرُوا بِرَبِّهِمْ ۖ أَعْمَالُهُمْ كَرَمَادٍ ٱشْتَدَّتْ بِهِ ٱلرِّيحُ فِي يَوْمٍ عَاصِفٍ ۖ لَّا يَقْدِرُونَ مِمَّا كَسَبُوا عَلَىٰ شَيْءٍ ۚ ذَٰلِكَ هُوَ ٱلضَّلَٰلُ ٱلْبَعِيدُ

18 2:264; 10:22; 24:39

18 The likeness of those who disbelieve in their Lord: their works are like ashes, in a fierce wind, on a stormy day. They have no control over anything they have earned. That is the utmost misguidance.

١٩ أَلَمْ تَرَ أَنَّ ٱللَّهَ خَلَقَ ٱلسَّمَٰوَٰتِ وَٱلْأَرْضَ بِٱلْحَقِّ ۚ إِن يَشَأْ يُذْهِبْكُمْ وَيَأْتِ بِخَلْقٍ جَدِيدٍ

19 4:133; 6:133; 35:16; 47:38

19 Do you not see that God created the heavens and the earth with truth? If He wills, He can do away with you, and bring a new creation.

٢٠ وَمَا ذَٰلِكَ عَلَى ٱللَّهِ بِعَزِيزٍ

20

20 And that is not difficult for God.

٢١ وَبَرَزُوا لِلَّهِ جَمِيعًا فَقَالَ ٱلضُّعَفَٰٓؤُا۟ لِلَّذِينَ ٱسْتَكْبَرُوٓا۟ إِنَّا كُنَّا لَكُمْ تَبَعًا فَهَلْ أَنتُم مُّغْنُونَ عَنَّا مِنْ عَذَابِ ٱللَّهِ مِن شَيْءٍ ۚ قَالُوا۟ لَوْ هَدَىٰنَا ٱللَّهُ لَهَدَيْنَٰكُمْ ۖ سَوَآءٌ عَلَيْنَآ أَجَزِعْنَآ أَمْ صَبَرْنَا مَا لَنَا مِن مَّحِيصٍ

21 40:47–48

21 They will emerge before God, altogether. The weak will say to those who were proud, "We were your followers, can you protect us at all against God's punishment?" They will say, "Had God guided us, we would have guided you. It is the same for us; whether we mourn, or are patient; there is no asylum for us."

٢٢ وَقَالَ ٱلشَّيْطَٰنُ لَمَّا قُضِيَ ٱلْأَمْرُ إِنَّ ٱللَّهَ وَعَدَكُمْ وَعْدَ ٱلْحَقِّ وَوَعَدتُّكُمْ فَأَخْلَفْتُكُمْ ۖ وَمَا كَانَ لِيَ عَلَيْكُم مِّن سُلْطَٰنٍ إِلَّآ أَن دَعَوْتُكُمْ فَٱسْتَجَبْتُمْ لِي ۖ فَلَا تَلُومُونِي وَلُومُوٓا۟ أَنفُسَكُم ۖ مَّآ أَنَا۠ بِمُصْرِخِكُمْ وَمَآ أَنتُم بِمُصْرِخِيَّ ۖ إِنِّي كَفَرْتُ بِمَآ أَشْرَكْتُمُونِ مِن قَبْلُ ۗ إِنَّ ٱلظَّٰلِمِينَ لَهُمْ عَذَابٌ أَلِيمٌ

22 4:120, 122; 113:31

22 And Satan will say, when the issue is settled, "God has promised you the promise of truth, and I promised you, but I failed you. I had no authority over you, except that I called you, and you answered me. So do not blame me, but blame yourselves. I cannot come to your aid, nor can you come to my aid. I reject your associating with me in the past. The wrongdoers will have a torment most painful."

٢٣ وَأُدْخِلَ ٱلَّذِينَ ءَامَنُوا۟ وَعَمِلُوا۟ ٱلصَّٰلِحَٰتِ جَنَّٰتٍ تَجْرِي مِن تَحْتِهَا ٱلْأَنْهَٰرُ خَٰلِدِينَ فِيهَا بِإِذْنِ رَبِّهِمْ ۖ تَحِيَّتُهُمْ فِيهَا سَلَٰمٌ

23 10:10; 13:23–24; 25:75; 19:6; 33:44; 39:73; 65:25–26

23 But those who believed and did good deeds will be admitted into gardens beneath which rivers flow, to remain therein forever, by leave of their Lord. Their greeting therein will be: "Peace."

٢٤ أَلَمْ تَرَ كَيْفَ ضَرَبَ ٱللَّهُ مَثَلًا كَلِمَةً طَيِّبَةً كَشَجَرَةٍ طَيِّبَةٍ أَصْلُهَا ثَابِتٌ وَفَرْعُهَا فِي ٱلسَّمَآءِ

24 14:26; 29:43; 59:21

24 Do you not see how God presents a parable? A good word is like a good tree—its root is firm, and its branches are in the sky.

٢٥ تُؤْتِىٓ أُكُلَهَا كُلَّ حِينٍۭ بِإِذْنِ رَبِّهَا ۗ وَيَضْرِبُ ٱللَّهُ ٱلْأَمْثَالَ لِلنَّاسِ لَعَلَّهُمْ يَتَذَكَّرُونَ

25 39:27; 59:21

25 It yields its fruits every season by the will of its Lord. God presents the parables to the people, so that they may reflect.

٢٦ وَمَثَلُ كَلِمَةٍ خَبِيثَةٍ كَشَجَرَةٍ خَبِيثَةٍ اجْتُثَّتْ مِنْ فَوْقِ الْأَرْضِ مَا لَهَا مِنْ قَرَارٍ

26 And the parable of a bad word is that of a bad tree—it is uprooted from the ground; it has no stability.

26
14:24

٢٧ يُثَبِّتُ اللَّهُ الَّذِينَ آمَنُوا بِالْقَوْلِ الثَّابِتِ فِي الْحَيَاةِ الدُّنْيَا وَفِي الْآخِرَةِ ۖ وَيُضِلُّ اللَّهُ الظَّالِمِينَ ۚ وَيَفْعَلُ اللَّهُ مَا يَشَاءُ

27 God gives firmness to those who believe, with the firm word, in this life, and in the Hereafter. And God leads the wicked astray. God does whatever He wills.

٢٨ أَلَمْ تَرَ إِلَى الَّذِينَ بَدَّلُوا نِعْمَتَ اللَّهِ كُفْرًا وَأَحَلُّوا قَوْمَهُمْ دَارَ الْبَوَارِ

28 Have you not seen those who exchanged the blessing of God with blasphemy, and landed their people into the house of perdition?

28
2:211; 8:53

٢٩ جَهَنَّمَ يَصْلَوْنَهَا ۖ وَبِئْسَ الْقَرَارُ

29 Hell—they will roast in it. What a miserable settlement.

29
4:115; 38:56; 58:8

٣٠ وَجَعَلُوا لِلَّهِ أَنْدَادًا لِيُضِلُّوا عَنْ سَبِيلِهِ ۗ[a] قُلْ تَمَتَّعُوا فَإِنَّ مَصِيرَكُمْ إِلَى النَّارِ[b]

30 And they set up rivals to God, in order to lead away from His path. Say, "Enjoy yourselves; your destination is the Fire."

30
[a] 2:48, 254; 34:33; 41:9; 57:15
[b] 3:196–197; 10:70; 31:24; 39:8

٣١ قُلْ لِعِبَادِيَ الَّذِينَ آمَنُوا يُقِيمُوا الصَّلَاةَ وَيُنْفِقُوا مِمَّا رَزَقْنَاهُمْ سِرًّا وَعَلَانِيَةً مِنْ قَبْلِ أَنْ يَأْتِيَ يَوْمٌ لَا بَيْعٌ فِيهِ وَلَا خِلَالٌ

31 Tell My servants who have believed to perform the prayers, and to give from what We have given them, secretly and publicly, before a Day comes in which there is neither trading nor friendship.

31
2:254; 36:47; 63:10

٣٢ اللَّهُ الَّذِي خَلَقَ السَّمَاوَاتِ وَالْأَرْضَ وَأَنْزَلَ مِنَ السَّمَاءِ مَاءً فَأَخْرَجَ بِهِ مِنَ الثَّمَرَاتِ رِزْقًا لَكُمْ ۖ وَسَخَّرَ لَكُمُ الْفُلْكَ لِتَجْرِيَ فِي الْبَحْرِ بِأَمْرِهِ ۖ وَسَخَّرَ لَكُمُ الْأَنْهَارَ

32 God is He Who created the heavens and the earth, and sends down water from the sky, and with it produces fruits for your sustenance. And He committed the ships to your service, sailing through the sea by His command, and He committed the rivers to your service.

32
2:22, 164; 6:99

٣٣ وَسَخَّرَ لَكُمُ الشَّمْسَ وَالْقَمَرَ دَائِبَيْنِ ۖ وَسَخَّرَ لَكُمُ اللَّيْلَ وَالنَّهَارَ

33 And He committed the sun and the moon to your service, both continuously pursuing their courses, and He committed the night and the day to your service.

33
14:2; 31:10

٣٤ وَآتَاكُمْ مِنْ كُلِّ مَا سَأَلْتُمُوهُ ۚ وَإِنْ تَعُدُّوا نِعْمَتَ اللَّهِ لَا تُحْصُوهَا ۗ إِنَّ الْإِنْسَانَ لَظَلُومٌ كَفَّارٌ

34 And He has given you something of all what you asked. And if you were to count God's blessings, you would not be able to enumerate them. The human being is unfair and ungrateful.

34
16:18

Sūrah 14: Ibrāhīm

٣٥ وَإِذْ قَالَ إِبْرَاهِيمُ رَبِّ اجْعَلْ هَٰذَا الْبَلَدَ آمِنًا وَاجْنُبْنِي وَبَنِيَّ أَنْ نَعْبُدَ الْأَصْنَامَ

35   2:126; 28:57

35 Recall that Abraham said, "O my Lord, make this land peaceful, and keep me and my sons from worshiping idols."

٣٦ رَبِّ إِنَّهُنَّ أَضْلَلْنَ كَثِيرًا مِنَ النَّاسِ ۖ فَمَنْ تَبِعَنِي فَإِنَّهُ مِنِّي ۖ وَمَنْ عَصَانِي فَإِنَّكَ غَفُورٌ رَحِيمٌ

36 "My Lord, they have led many people astray. Whoever follows me belongs with me; and whoever disobeys me—You are Forgiving and Merciful.

٣٧ رَبَّنَا إِنِّي أَسْكَنْتُ مِنْ ذُرِّيَّتِي بِوَادٍ غَيْرِ ذِي زَرْعٍ عِنْدَ بَيْتِكَ الْمُحَرَّمِ رَبَّنَا لِيُقِيمُوا الصَّلَاةَ فَاجْعَلْ أَفْئِدَةً مِنَ النَّاسِ تَهْوِي إِلَيْهِمْ وَارْزُقْهُمْ مِنَ الثَّمَرَاتِ لَعَلَّهُمْ يَشْكُرُونَ

37   2:125; 14:40

37 "Our Lord, I have settled some of my offspring in a valley of no vegetation, by Your Sacred House, our Lord, so that they may perform the prayers. So make the hearts of some people incline towards them, and provide them with fruits, that they may be thankful."

٣٨ رَبَّنَا إِنَّكَ تَعْلَمُ مَا نُخْفِي وَمَا نُعْلِنُ ۗ وَمَا يَخْفَىٰ عَلَى اللَّهِ مِنْ شَيْءٍ فِي الْأَرْضِ وَلَا فِي السَّمَاءِ

38 "Our Lord, You know what we conceal and what we reveal. And nothing is hidden from God, on earth or in the heaven."

٣٩ الْحَمْدُ لِلَّهِ الَّذِي وَهَبَ لِي عَلَى الْكِبَرِ إِسْمَاعِيلَ وَإِسْحَاقَ ۚ إِنَّ رَبِّي لَسَمِيعُ الدُّعَاءِ

39 "Praise be to God, Who has given me, in my old age, Ishmael and Isaac. My Lord is the Hearer of Prayers."

٤٠ رَبِّ اجْعَلْنِي مُقِيمَ الصَّلَاةِ وَمِنْ ذُرِّيَّتِي ۚ رَبَّنَا وَتَقَبَّلْ دُعَاءِ

40 "My Lord, make me one who performs the prayer, and from my offspring. Our Lord, accept my supplication."

٤١ رَبَّنَا اغْفِرْ لِي وَلِوَالِدَيَّ وَلِلْمُؤْمِنِينَ يَوْمَ يَقُومُ الْحِسَابُ

41   9:114

41 "Our Lord, forgive me, and my parents, and the believers, on the Day the Reckoning takes place."

٤٢ وَلَا تَحْسَبَنَّ اللَّهَ غَافِلًا عَمَّا يَعْمَلُ الظَّالِمُونَ ۚ إِنَّمَا يُؤَخِّرُهُمْ لِيَوْمٍ تَشْخَصُ فِيهِ الْأَبْصَارُ

42   11:104; 21:97

42 Do not ever think that God is unaware of what the wrongdoers do. He only defers them until a Day when the sights stare.

٤٣ مُهْطِعِينَ مُقْنِعِي رُءُوسِهِمْ لَا يَرْتَدُّ إِلَيْهِمْ طَرْفُهُمْ ۖ وَأَفْئِدَتُهُمْ هَوَاءٌ

43   50:44; 54:7; 70:36, 43

43 Their necks outstretched, their heads upraised, their gaze unblinking, their hearts void.

٤٤ وَأَنْذِرِ النَّاسَ يَوْمَ يَأْتِيهِمُ الْعَذَابُ فَيَقُولُ الَّذِينَ ظَلَمُوا رَبَّنَا أَخِّرْنَا إِلَىٰ أَجَلٍ قَرِيبٍ نُجِبْ دَعْوَتَكَ وَنَتَّبِعِ الرُّسُلَ ۗ أَوَلَمْ تَكُونُوا أَقْسَمْتُمْ مِنْ قَبْلُ مَا لَكُمْ مِنْ زَوَالٍ

44   4:77; 63:10

44 And warn mankind of the Day when the punishment will come upon them, and the wicked will say, "Our Lord, defer us for a little while, and we will answer Your call and follow the messengers." Did you not swear before that there will be no passing away for you?

٤٥ وَسَكَنتُمْ فِي مَسَاكِنِ الَّذِينَ ظَلَمُوا أَنفُسَهُمْ وَتَبَيَّنَ لَكُمْ كَيْفَ فَعَلْنَا بِهِمْ وَضَرَبْنَا لَكُمُ الْأَمْثَالَ

45 And you inhabited the homes of those who wronged themselves, and it became clear to you how We dealt with them, and We cited for you the examples.

45
20:128; 28:58; 29:38; 32:26

٤٦ وَقَدْ مَكَرُوا مَكْرَهُمْ وَعِندَ اللَّهِ مَكْرُهُمْ وَإِن كَانَ مَكْرُهُمْ لِتَزُولَ مِنْهُ الْجِبَالُ

46 They planned their plans, but their plans are known to God, even if their plans can eliminate mountains.

46
3:54; 7:99; 8:30; 13:42; 16:26, 45; 27:50

٤٧ فَلَا تَحْسَبَنَّ اللَّهَ مُخْلِفَ وَعْدِهِ رُسُلَهُ ۗ إِنَّ اللَّهَ عَزِيزٌ ذُو انتِقَامٍ

47 Do not ever think that God will break His promise to His messengers. God is Strong, Able to Avenge.

47
3:9, 194; 13:31; 30:6

٤٨ يَوْمَ تُبَدَّلُ الْأَرْضُ غَيْرَ الْأَرْضِ وَالسَّمَاوَاتُ ۖ وَبَرَزُوا لِلَّهِ الْوَاحِدِ الْقَهَّارِ

48 On the Day when the earth is changed into another earth, and the heavens, and they will emerge before God, the One, the Irresistible.

٤٩ وَتَرَى الْمُجْرِمِينَ يَوْمَئِذٍ مُّقَرَّنِينَ فِي الْأَصْفَادِ

49 On that Day, you will see the sinners bound together in chains.

49
25:13; 38:38

٥٠ سَرَابِيلُهُم مِّن قَطِرَانٍ وَتَغْشَىٰ وُجُوهَهُمُ النَّارُ

50 Their garments made of tar, and the Fire covering their faces.

50
21:39; 23:104

٥١ لِيَجْزِيَ اللَّهُ كُلَّ نَفْسٍ مَّا كَسَبَتْ ۚ إِنَّ اللَّهَ سَرِيعُ الْحِسَابِ

51 That God may repay each soul according to what it has earned. God is Quick in reckoning.

51
20:15; 40:17; 45:22

٥٢ هَٰذَا بَلَاغٌ لِّلنَّاسِ وَلِيُنذَرُوا بِهِ وَلِيَعْلَمُوا أَنَّمَا هُوَ إِلَٰهٌ وَاحِدٌ وَلِيَذَّكَّرَ أُولُو الْأَلْبَابِ

52 This is a proclamation for mankind, that they may be warned thereby, and know that He is One God, and that people of understanding may remember.

52
6:19

Sūrah 15: Al-Ḥijr

سُورَةُ ٱلْحِجْر (The Rock)

بِسْمِ ٱللَّهِ ٱلرَّحْمَٰنِ ٱلرَّحِيمِ

١ الر ۚ تِلْكَ آيَاتُ الْكِتَابِ وَقُرْآنٍ مُّبِينٍ

1 Alif, Lām, Rā'. These are the Verses of the Book; a Qur'an that makes things clear.

٢ رُّبَمَا يَوَدُّ الَّذِينَ كَفَرُوا لَوْ كَانُوا مُسْلِمِينَ

2 Perhaps those who disbelieve will wish they had been Muslims.

2
6:27, 31; 25:27

٣ ذَرْهُمْ يَأْكُلُوا وَيَتَمَتَّعُوا وَيُلْهِهِمُ الْأَمَلُ ۖ فَسَوْفَ يَعْلَمُونَ

3 Leave them to eat, and enjoy, and be lulled by hope. They will find out.

3
14:30; 39:8; 43:83;
47:12; 52:45; 77:46

٤ وَمَا أَهْلَكْنَا مِنْ قَرْيَةٍ إِلَّا وَلَهَا كِتَابٌ مَعْلُومٌ

4 We have never destroyed a town unless it had a set time.

4
17:58; 18:59

٥ مَا تَسْبِقُ مِنْ أُمَّةٍ أَجَلَهَا وَمَا يَسْتَأْخِرُونَ

5 No nation can bring its time forward, nor can they delay it.

5
7:34; 10:49; 15:5;
16:61; 23:43

٦ وَقَالُوا يَا أَيُّهَا الَّذِي نُزِّلَ عَلَيْهِ الذِّكْرُ إِنَّكَ لَمَجْنُونٌ

6 And they said, "O you who received the message, you are insane."

6
7:184; 26:27; 34:46;
52:29; 68:2, 51; 81:22

٧ لَوْ مَا تَأْتِينَا بِالْمَلَائِكَةِ إِنْ كُنْتَ مِنَ الصَّادِقِينَ

7 Why do you not bring us the angels, if you are truthful?"

7–8
6:8; 11:12, 17:92; 31;
25:7

٨ مَا نُنَزِّلُ الْمَلَائِكَةَ إِلَّا بِالْحَقِّ وَمَا كَانُوا إِذًا مُنْظَرِينَ

8 We do not send the angels down except with reason, and they will not be held back.

٩ إِنَّا نَحْنُ نَزَّلْنَا الذِّكْرَ وَإِنَّا لَهُ لَحَافِظُونَ

9 Surely We revealed the Message, and We will surely preserve it.

١٠ وَلَقَدْ أَرْسَلْنَا مِنْ قَبْلِكَ فِي شِيَعِ الْأَوَّلِينَ

10 We sent others before you, to the former communities.

10
36:30; 43:6

١١ وَمَا يَأْتِيهِمْ مِنْ رَسُولٍ إِلَّا كَانُوا بِهِ يَسْتَهْزِئُونَ

11 But no messenger came to them, but they ridiculed him.

11
13:32; 21:41

١٢ كَذَٰلِكَ نَسْلُكُهُ فِي قُلُوبِ الْمُجْرِمِينَ

12 Thus We slip it into the hearts of the guilty.

12
26:200

١٣ لَا يُؤْمِنُونَ بِهِ ۖ وَقَدْ خَلَتْ سُنَّةُ الْأَوَّلِينَ

13 They do not believe in it, though the ways of the ancients have passed away.

١٤ وَلَوْ فَتَحْنَا عَلَيْهِمْ بَابًا مِنَ السَّمَاءِ فَظَلُّوا فِيهِ يَعْرُجُونَ

14 Even if We opened for them a gateway into the sky, and they began to ascend through it.

14
6:35, 111; 13:31

١٥ لَقَالُوا إِنَّمَا سُكِّرَتْ أَبْصَارُنَا بَلْ نَحْنُ قَوْمٌ مَسْحُورُونَ

15 They would still say, "Our eyes are hallucinating; in fact, we are people bewitched."

١٦ وَلَقَدْ جَعَلْنَا فِي السَّمَاءِ بُرُوجًا[a] وَزَيَّنَّاهَا لِلنَّاظِرِينَ[b]

16 We placed constellations in the sky, and made them beautiful to the beholders.

16
[a] 25:61; 50:6; 85:1
[b] 37:6; 57:5

١٧ وَحَفِظْنَاهَا مِنْ كُلِّ شَيْطَانٍ رَجِيمٍ

17 And We guarded them from every outcast devil.

17–18
37:7; 41:12; 67:5; 72:8–9

١٨ إِلَّا مَنِ اسْتَرَقَ السَّمْعَ فَأَتْبَعَهُ شِهَابٌ مُبِينٌ

18 Except one who steals a hearing, and is followed by a visible projectile.

١٩ وَالْأَرْضَ مَدَدْنَاهَا وَأَلْقَيْنَا فِيهَا رَوَاسِيَ وَأَنْبَتْنَا فِيهَا مِنْ كُلِّ شَيْءٍ مَوْزُونٍ

19 We spread the earth, and placed stabilizers in it, and in it We grew all things in proper measure.

19
13:3

٢٠ وَجَعَلْنَا لَكُمْ فِيهَا مَعَايِشَ وَمَنْ لَسْتُمْ لَهُ بِرَازِقِينَ

20 And in it We created livelihoods for you, and for those for whom you are not the providers.

20
7:10

٢١ وَإِنْ مِنْ شَيْءٍ إِلَّا عِنْدَنَا خَزَائِنُهُ وَمَا نُنَزِّلُهُ إِلَّا بِقَدَرٍ مَعْلُومٍ

21 There is not a thing but with Us are its stores, and We send it down only in precise measure.

٢٢ وَأَرْسَلْنَا الرِّيَاحَ لَوَاقِحَ فَأَنْزَلْنَا مِنَ السَّمَاءِ مَاءً فَأَسْقَيْنَاكُمُوهُ وَمَا أَنْتُمْ لَهُ بِخَازِنِينَ

22 We send the fertilizing winds; and send down water from the sky, and give it to you to drink, and you are not the ones who store it.

22
25:48; 30:48; 35:9

٢٣ وَإِنَّا لَنَحْنُ نُحْيِي وَنُمِيتُ[a] وَنَحْنُ الْوَارِثُونَ[b]

23 It is We who give life and cause death, and We are the Inheritors.

23
[a] 2:28, 258; 40:11; 44:8; 50:43
[b] 19:40

٢٤ وَلَقَدْ عَلِمْنَا الْمُسْتَقْدِمِينَ مِنْكُمْ وَلَقَدْ عَلِمْنَا الْمُسْتَأْخِرِينَ

24 And We know those of you who go forward, and We know those who lag behind.

٢٥ وَإِنَّ رَبَّكَ هُوَ يَحْشُرُهُمْ ۚ إِنَّهُ حَكِيمٌ عَلِيمٌ

25 It is your Lord who will gather them together. He is the Wise, the Knowing.

٢٦ وَلَقَدْ خَلَقْنَا الْإِنْسَانَ مِنْ صَلْصَالٍ مِنْ حَمَإٍ مَسْنُونٍ

26 We created the human being from clay, from molded mud.

26
15:28, 33; 55:14

٢٧ وَالْجَانَّ خَلَقْنَاهُ مِنْ قَبْلُ مِنْ نَارِ السَّمُومِ

27 And the jinn We created before, from piercing fire.

٢٨ وَإِذْ قَالَ رَبُّكَ لِلْمَلَائِكَةِ إِنِّي خَالِقٌ بَشَرًا مِنْ صَلْصَالٍ مِنْ حَمَإٍ مَسْنُونٍ	28–29 15:26, 33; 38:71; 55:14

28 Your Lord said to the angels, "I am creating a human being from clay, from molded mud."

٢٩ فَإِذَا سَوَّيْتُهُ وَنَفَخْتُ فِيهِ مِنْ رُوحِي فَقَعُوا لَهُ سَاجِدِينَ	

29 "When I have formed him, and breathed into him of My spirit, fall down prostrating before him."

٣٠ فَسَجَدَ الْمَلَائِكَةُ كُلُّهُمْ أَجْمَعُونَ	30 2:34; 7:11; 17:61; 18:50; 38:73

30 So the angels prostrated themselves, all together.

٣١ إِلَّا إِبْلِيسَ أَبَىٰ أَنْ يَكُونَ مَعَ السَّاجِدِينَ	31 7:12; 17:61; 38:75

31 Except for Satan. He refused to be among those who prostrated themselves.

٣٢ قَالَ يَا إِبْلِيسُ مَا لَكَ أَلَّا تَكُونَ مَعَ السَّاجِدِينَ	

32 He said, "O Satan, what kept you from being among those who prostrated themselves?"

٣٣ قَالَ لَمْ أَكُنْ لِأَسْجُدَ لِبَشَرٍ خَلَقْتَهُ مِنْ صَلْصَالٍ مِنْ حَمَإٍ مَسْنُونٍ	33 15:26, 28; 55:14; 38:76

33 He said, "I am not about to prostrate myself before a human being, whom You created from clay, from molded mud."

٣٤ قَالَ فَاخْرُجْ مِنْهَا فَإِنَّكَ رَجِيمٌ	34 7:13; 38:77

34 He said, "Then get out of here, for you are an outcast".

٣٥ وَإِنَّ عَلَيْكَ اللَّعْنَةَ إِلَىٰ يَوْمِ الدِّينِ	35 38:78

35 "And the curse will be upon you until the Day of Judgment."

٣٦ قَالَ رَبِّ فَأَنْظِرْنِي إِلَىٰ يَوْمِ يُبْعَثُونَ	36–38 7:14; 17:62; 38:79–81

36 He said, "My Lord, reprieve me until the Day they are resurrected."

٣٧ قَالَ فَإِنَّكَ مِنَ الْمُنْظَرِينَ	

37 He said, "You are of those reprieved."

٣٨ إِلَىٰ يَوْمِ الْوَقْتِ الْمَعْلُومِ	

38 "Until the Day of the time appointed."

٣٩ قَالَ رَبِّ بِمَا أَغْوَيْتَنِي لَأُزَيِّنَنَّ لَهُمْ فِي الْأَرْضِ وَلَأُغْوِيَنَّهُمْ أَجْمَعِينَ	39 38:82

39 He said, "My Lord, since You have lured me away, I will glamorize for them on earth, and I will lure them all away."

٤٠ إِلَّا عِبَادَكَ مِنْهُمُ الْمُخْلَصِينَ	40 34:20; 38:83

40 "Except for Your sincere servants among them."

٤١ قَالَ هَٰذَا صِرَاطٌ عَلَيَّ مُسْتَقِيمٌ

41 He said, "This is a right way with Me."

٤٢ إِنَّ عِبَادِي لَيْسَ لَكَ عَلَيْهِمْ سُلْطَانٌ إِلَّا مَنِ اتَّبَعَكَ مِنَ الْغَاوِينَ

42 "Over My servants you have no authority, except for the sinners who follow you."

42 — 7:18; 17:63; 38:85

٤٣ وَإِنَّ جَهَنَّمَ لَمَوْعِدُهُمْ أَجْمَعِينَ

43 And Hell is the meeting-place for them all.

٤٤ لَهَا سَبْعَةُ أَبْوَابٍ لِكُلِّ بَابٍ مِنْهُمْ جُزْءٌ مَقْسُومٌ

44 "It has seven doors; for each door is an assigned class."

٤٥ إِنَّ الْمُتَّقِينَ فِي جَنَّاتٍ وَعُيُونٍ

45 But the righteous will be in gardens with springs.

45 — 51:15

٤٦ ادْخُلُوهَا بِسَلَامٍ آمِنِينَ

46 "Enter it in peace and security."

٤٧ وَنَزَعْنَا مَا فِي صُدُورِهِمْ مِنْ غِلٍّ إِخْوَانًا عَلَىٰ سُرُرٍ مُتَقَابِلِينَ

47 And We will remove all ill-feelings from their hearts—brothers and sisters, on couches facing one another.

47 — 7:43; 56:15; 59:10,

٤٨ لَا يَمَسُّهُمْ فِيهَا نَصَبٌ وَمَا هُمْ مِنْهَا بِمُخْرَجِينَ

48 No fatigue will ever touch them therein, nor will they be asked to leave it.

48 — 35:35

٤٩ نَبِّئْ عِبَادِي أَنِّي أَنَا الْغَفُورُ الرَّحِيمُ

49 Inform My servants that I am the Forgiver, the Merciful.

٥٠ وَأَنَّ عَذَابِي هُوَ الْعَذَابُ الْأَلِيمُ

50 And that My punishment is the painful punishment.

٥١ وَنَبِّئْهُمْ عَنْ ضَيْفِ إِبْرَاهِيمَ

51 And inform them of the guests of Abraham.

51 — 11:69

٥٢ إِذْ دَخَلُوا عَلَيْهِ فَقَالُوا سَلَامًا قَالَ إِنَّا مِنْكُمْ وَجِلُونَ

52 When they entered upon him, and said, "Peace." He said, "We are wary of you."

52 — 51:25; 11:69

٥٣ قَالُوا لَا تَوْجَلْ إِنَّا نُبَشِّرُكَ بِغُلَامٍ عَلِيمٍ

53 They said, "Do not fear; we bring you good news of a boy endowed with knowledge."

53 — 29:31; 52:28; 11:70

٥٤ قَالَ أَبَشَّرْتُمُونِي عَلَىٰ أَنْ مَسَّنِيَ الْكِبَرُ فَبِمَ تُبَشِّرُونَ

54 He said, "Do you bring me good news, when old age has overtaken me? What good news do you bring?"

54 — 11:71–73; 51:29

٥٥ قَالُوا بَشَّرْنَاكَ بِالْحَقِّ فَلَا تَكُن مِّنَ الْقَانِطِينَ		
55 They said, "We bring you good news in truth, so do not despair."		
٥٦ قَالَ وَمَن يَقْنَطُ مِن رَّحْمَةِ رَبِّهِ إِلَّا الضَّالُّونَ		56
56 He said, "And who despairs of his Lord's mercy but the lost?"		12:87; 39:53
٥٧ قَالَ فَمَا خَطْبُكُمْ أَيُّهَا الْمُرْسَلُونَ		57
57 He said, "So what is your business, O envoys?"		11:74; 29:31; 51:31
٥٨ قَالُوا إِنَّا أُرْسِلْنَا إِلَىٰ قَوْمٍ مُّجْرِمِينَ		58
58 They said, "We were sent to a sinful people."		11:66
٥٩ إِلَّا آلَ لُوطٍ إِنَّا لَمُنَجُّوهُمْ أَجْمَعِينَ		59–60
59 "Except for the family of Lot; we will save them all."		7:83; 11:81; 51:35–36; 66:10
٦٠ إِلَّا امْرَأَتَهُ قَدَّرْنَا ۙ إِنَّهَا لَمِنَ الْغَابِرِينَ		
60 "Except for his wife." We have determined that she will be of those who lag behind.		
٦١ فَلَمَّا جَاءَ آلَ لُوطٍ الْمُرْسَلُونَ		61
61 And when the envoys came to the family of Lot.		11:77; 51:25
٦٢ قَالَ إِنَّكُمْ قَوْمٌ مُّنكَرُونَ		
62 He said, "You are a people unknown to me."		
٦٣ قَالُوا بَلْ جِئْنَاكَ بِمَا كَانُوا فِيهِ يَمْتَرُونَ		63
63 They said, "We bring you what they have doubts about."		29:29; 54:36
٦٤ وَأَتَيْنَاكَ بِالْحَقِّ وَإِنَّا لَصَادِقُونَ		
64 "We bring you the truth, and we are truthful."		
٦٥ فَأَسْرِ بِأَهْلِكَ بِقِطْعٍ مِّنَ اللَّيْلِ وَاتَّبِعْ أَدْبَارَهُمْ وَلَا يَلْتَفِتْ مِنكُمْ أَحَدٌ وَامْضُوا حَيْثُ تُؤْمَرُونَ		65
65 "Travel with your family at the dead of the night, and follow up behind them, and let none of you look back, and proceed as commanded."		11:81
٦٦ وَقَضَيْنَا إِلَيْهِ ذَٰلِكَ الْأَمْرَ أَنَّ دَابِرَ هَٰؤُلَاءِ مَقْطُوعٌ مُّصْبِحِينَ		
66 And We informed him of Our decree: the last remnant of these will be uprooted by early morning.		
٦٧ وَجَاءَ أَهْلُ الْمَدِينَةِ يَسْتَبْشِرُونَ		67–72
67 And the people of the town came joyfully.		11:78–79
٦٨ قَالَ إِنَّ هَٰؤُلَاءِ ضَيْفِي فَلَا تَفْضَحُونِ		
68 He said, "These are my guests, so do not embarrass me."		

69 وَاتَّقُوا اللَّهَ وَلَا تُخْزُونِ

69 "And fear God, and do not disgrace me."

70 قَالُوا أَوَلَمْ نَنْهَكَ عَنِ الْعَالَمِينَ

70 They said, "Did we not forbid you from strangers?"

71 قَالَ هَؤُلَاءِ بَنَاتِي إِنْ كُنْتُمْ فَاعِلِينَ

71 He said, "These are my daughters, if you must."

72 لَعَمْرُكَ إِنَّهُمْ لَفِي سَكْرَتِهِمْ يَعْمَهُونَ

72 By your life, they were blundering in their drunkenness.

73 فَأَخَذَتْهُمُ الصَّيْحَةُ مُشْرِقِينَ

73 So the Blast struck them at sunrise. **73** 11:81; 15:83

74 فَجَعَلْنَا عَالِيَهَا سَافِلَهَا وَأَمْطَرْنَا عَلَيْهِمْ حِجَارَةً مِنْ سِجِّيلٍ

74 And We turned it upside down, and rained down upon them stones of baked clay. **74** pp 11:82

75 إِنَّ فِي ذَلِكَ لَآيَاتٍ لِلْمُتَوَسِّمِينَ

75 Surely in that are lessons for those who read signs.

76 وَإِنَّهَا لَبِسَبِيلٍ مُقِيمٍ

76 And it is on an existing road.

77 إِنَّ فِي ذَلِكَ لَآيَةً لِلْمُؤْمِنِينَ

77 Surely in that is a sign for the believers.

78 وَإِنْ كَانَ أَصْحَابُ الْأَيْكَةِ لَظَالِمِينَ

78 The people of the Woods were also wrongdoers. **78** 26:176

79 فَانْتَقَمْنَا مِنْهُمْ وَإِنَّهُمَا لَبِإِمَامٍ مُبِينٍ

79 So We took revenge upon them. Both are clearly documented. **79** 17:71

80 وَلَقَدْ كَذَّبَ أَصْحَابُ الْحِجْرِ الْمُرْسَلِينَ

80 The people of the Rock also rejected the messengers. **80** 26:141

81 وَآتَيْنَاهُمْ آيَاتِنَا فَكَانُوا عَنْهَا مُعْرِضِينَ

81 We gave them Our revelations, but they turned away from them.

82 وَكَانُوا يَنْحِتُونَ مِنَ الْجِبَالِ بُيُوتًا آمِنِينَ

82 They used to carve homes in the mountains, feeling secure. **82** 7:74; 26:149; 89:9

83 فَأَخَذَتْهُمُ الصَّيْحَةُ مُصْبِحِينَ

83 But the Blast struck them in the morning. **83** 11:67; 15:73

84 فَمَا أَغْنَى عَنْهُمْ مَا كَانُوا يَكْسِبُونَ

84 All they had acquired was of no avail to them.

٨٥ وَمَا خَلَقْنَا السَّمَاوَاتِ وَالْأَرْضَ وَمَا بَيْنَهُمَا إِلَّا بِالْحَقِّ ۗ وَإِنَّ السَّاعَةَ لَآتِيَةٌ ۖ[a] فَاصْفَحِ الصَّفْحَ الْجَمِيلَ[b]

85 [a] 20:15; 22:7; 34:3; 40:59
[b] 2:109; 43:89

85 We did not create the heavens and the earth, and what lies between them, except with truth. The Hour is coming, so forgive with gracious forgiveness.

٨٦ إِنَّ رَبَّكَ هُوَ الْخَلَّاقُ الْعَلِيمُ

86 Your Lord is the All-Knowing Creator.

٨٧ وَلَقَدْ آتَيْنَاكَ سَبْعًا مِنَ الْمَثَانِي وَالْقُرْآنَ الْعَظِيمَ

87 We have given you seven of the pairs, and the Grand Qur'an.

٨٨ لَا تَمُدَّنَّ عَيْنَيْكَ إِلَىٰ مَا مَتَّعْنَا بِهِ أَزْوَاجًا مِنْهُمْ وَلَا تَحْزَنْ عَلَيْهِمْ وَاخْفِضْ جَنَاحَكَ لِلْمُؤْمِنِينَ

88 17:24; 20:131; 26:215

88 Do not extend your eyes towards what We have bestowed on some couples of them to enjoy, and do not grieve over them, and lower your wing to the believers.

٨٩ وَقُلْ إِنِّي أَنَا النَّذِيرُ الْمُبِينُ

89 And say, "I am the clear warner."

٩٠ كَمَا أَنْزَلْنَا عَلَى الْمُقْتَسِمِينَ

90 7:49; 14:44; 16:38; 27:49

90 Just as We sent down to the separatists.

٩١ الَّذِينَ جَعَلُوا الْقُرْآنَ عِضِينَ

91 Those who made the Qur'an obsolete.

٩٢ فَوَرَبِّكَ لَنَسْأَلَنَّهُمْ أَجْمَعِينَ

92 By your Lord, we will question them all.

٩٣ عَمَّا كَانُوا يَعْمَلُونَ

93 About what they used to do.

٩٤ فَاصْدَعْ بِمَا تُؤْمَرُ وَأَعْرِضْ عَنِ الْمُشْرِكِينَ

94 6:106; 32:30; 33:48; 53:29

94 So proclaim openly what you are commanded, and turn away from the polytheists.

٩٥ إِنَّا كَفَيْنَاكَ الْمُسْتَهْزِئِينَ

95 2:137; 39:36

95 We are enough for you against the mockers.

٩٦ الَّذِينَ يَجْعَلُونَ مَعَ اللَّهِ إِلَٰهًا آخَرَ ۚ فَسَوْفَ يَعْلَمُونَ

96 Those who set up another god with God. They will come to know.

٩٧ وَلَقَدْ نَعْلَمُ أَنَّكَ يَضِيقُ صَدْرُكَ بِمَا يَقُولُونَ

97 6:33; 10:65; 11:12; 18:6; 26:3

97 We are aware that your heart is strained by what they say.

٩٨ فَسَبِّحْ بِحَمْدِ رَبِّكَ وَكُن مِّنَ السَّاجِدِينَ

98 So glorify the praise of your Lord, and be among those who bow down.

٩٩ وَاعْبُدْ رَبَّكَ حَتَّىٰ يَأْتِيَكَ الْيَقِينُ

99 And worship your Lord in order to attain certainty.

Sūrah 16: Al-Naḥl

سُورَةُ ٱلنَّحْل (The Bee)

بِسْمِ ٱللَّهِ ٱلرَّحْمَٰنِ ٱلرَّحِيمِ

١ أَتَىٰ أَمْرُ اللَّهِ فَلَا تَسْتَعْجِلُوهُ ۚ سُبْحَانَهُ وَتَعَالَىٰ عَمَّا يُشْرِكُونَ

1 The command of God has come, so do not rush it. Glory be to Him; exalted above what they associate.

٢ يُنَزِّلُ الْمَلَائِكَةَ بِالرُّوحِ مِنْ أَمْرِهِ عَلَىٰ مَن يَشَاءُ مِنْ عِبَادِهِ أَنْ أَنذِرُوا أَنَّهُ لَا إِلَٰهَ إِلَّا أَنَا فَاتَّقُونِ

2 He sends down the angels with the Spirit by His command, upon whom He wills of His servants: "Give warning that there is no god but Me, and fear Me."

2
16:101; 40:15; 42:52

٣ خَلَقَ السَّمَاوَاتِ وَالْأَرْضَ بِالْحَقِّ ۚ تَعَالَىٰ عَمَّا يُشْرِكُونَ

3 He created the heavens and the earth with justice. He is exalted above the associations they attribute.

3
13:16; 35:40; 46:4

٤ خَلَقَ الْإِنسَانَ مِن نُّطْفَةٍ فَإِذَا هُوَ خَصِيمٌ مُّبِينٌ

4 He created the human being from a drop of fluid, yet he becomes an open adversary.

4
36:77; 53:43:58; 45; 76:2; 80:17

٥ وَالْأَنْعَامَ خَلَقَهَا ۗ لَكُمْ فِيهَا دِفْءٌ وَمَنَافِعُ وَمِنْهَا تَأْكُلُونَ

5 And the livestock—He created them for you. In them are warmth and benefits for you, and of them you eat.

5–6
6:142; 16:80; 23:21; 40:79

٦ وَلَكُمْ فِيهَا جَمَالٌ حِينَ تُرِيحُونَ وَحِينَ تَسْرَحُونَ

6 And there is beauty in them for you, when you bring them home, and when you drive them to pasture.

٧ وَتَحْمِلُ أَثْقَالَكُمْ إِلَىٰ بَلَدٍ لَّمْ تَكُونُوا بَالِغِيهِ إِلَّا بِشِقِّ الْأَنفُسِ ۚ إِنَّ رَبَّكُمْ لَرَءُوفٌ رَّحِيمٌ

7 And they carry your loads to territory you could not have reached without great hardship. Your Lord is Clement and Merciful.

٨ وَالْخَيْلَ وَالْبِغَالَ وَالْحَمِيرَ لِتَرْكَبُوهَا وَزِينَةً ۚ وَيَخْلُقُ مَا لَا تَعْلَمُونَ

8 And the horses, and the mules, and the donkeys—for you to ride, and for luxury. And He creates what you do not know.

8
36:36

٩ وَعَلَى اللَّهِ قَصْدُ السَّبِيلِ وَمِنْهَا جَائِرٌ ۚ وَلَوْ شَاءَ لَهَدَاكُمْ أَجْمَعِينَ	9	6:35; 32:13

9 It is for God to point out the paths, but some of them are flawed. Had He willed, He could have guided you all.

١٠ هُوَ الَّذِي أَنْزَلَ مِنَ السَّمَاءِ مَاءً ۖ لَكُمْ مِنْهُ شَرَابٌ وَمِنْهُ شَجَرٌ فِيهِ تُسِيمُونَ	10	56:68–70

10 It is He Who sends down for you from the sky water. From it is drink, and with it grows vegetation for grazing.

١١ يُنْبِتُ لَكُمْ بِهِ الزَّرْعَ وَالزَّيْتُونَ وَالنَّخِيلَ وَالْأَعْنَابَ وَمِنْ كُلِّ الثَّمَرَاتِ ۗ إِنَّ فِي ذَٰلِكَ لَآيَةً لِقَوْمٍ يَتَفَكَّرُونَ	11	20:53–54; 32:27; 50:9–11

11 And He produces for you grains with it, and olives, and date-palms, and grapes, and all kinds of fruits. Surely in that is a sign for people who think.

١٢ وَسَخَّرَ لَكُمُ اللَّيْلَ وَالنَّهَارَ وَالشَّمْسَ وَالْقَمَرَ ۖ وَالنُّجُومُ مُسَخَّرَاتٌ بِأَمْرِهِ ۗ إِنَّ فِي ذَٰلِكَ لَآيَاتٍ لِقَوْمٍ يَعْقِلُونَ	12	7:54; 13:2; 14:33

12 And He regulated for you the night and the day; and the sun, and the moon, and the stars are disposed by His command. Surely in that are signs for people who ponder.

١٣ وَمَا ذَرَأَ لَكُمْ فِي الْأَرْضِ مُخْتَلِفًا أَلْوَانُهُ ۗ إِنَّ فِي ذَٰلِكَ لَآيَةً لِقَوْمٍ يَذَّكَّرُونَ	13	35:27; 36:37–39; 39:21

13 And whatsoever He created for you on earth is of diverse colors. Surely in that is a sign for people who are mindful.

١٤ وَهُوَ الَّذِي سَخَّرَ الْبَحْرَ لِتَأْكُلُوا مِنْهُ لَحْمًا طَرِيًّا وَتَسْتَخْرِجُوا مِنْهُ حِلْيَةً تَلْبَسُونَهَا وَتَرَى الْفُلْكَ مَوَاخِرَ فِيهِ وَلِتَبْتَغُوا مِنْ فَضْلِهِ وَلَعَلَّكُمْ تَشْكُرُونَ	14	2:164; 5:96; 35:12; 45:12; 55:22

14 And it is He who made the sea to serve you, that you may eat from it tender meat, and extract from it ornaments that you wear. And you see the ships plowing through it, as you seek His bounties, so that you may give thanks.

١٥ وَأَلْقَىٰ فِي الْأَرْضِ رَوَاسِيَ أَنْ تَمِيدَ بِكُمْ وَأَنْهَارًا وَسُبُلًا لَعَلَّكُمْ تَهْتَدُونَ	15	13:3; 21:31; 31:10; 77:27

15 And he cast mountains on the earth, lest it shifts with you; and rivers, and roads, so that you may be guided.

١٦ وَعَلَامَاتٍ ۚ وَبِالنَّجْمِ هُمْ يَهْتَدُونَ	16	6:97; 16:20

16 And landmarks. And by the stars they guide themselves.

١٧ أَفَمَنْ يَخْلُقُ كَمَنْ لَا يَخْلُقُ ۗ أَفَلَا تَذَكَّرُونَ	17	10:34; 13:16; 31:11

17 Is He who creates like him who does not create? Will you not take a lesson?

١٨ وَإِنْ تَعُدُّوا نِعْمَةَ اللَّهِ لَا تُحْصُوهَا ۗ إِنَّ اللَّهَ لَغَفُورٌ رَحِيمٌ	18	14:34

18 And if you tried to enumerate the favors of God, you will not be able to count them. God is Forgiving and Merciful.

١٩ وَاللَّهُ يَعْلَمُ مَا تُسِرُّونَ وَمَا تُعْلِنُونَ

19 And God knows what you hide and what you disclose.

19   16:23; 64:4

٢٠ وَالَّذِينَ يَدْعُونَ مِنْ دُونِ اللَّهِ لَا يَخْلُقُونَ شَيْئًا وَهُمْ يُخْلَقُونَ

20 Those they invoke besides God create nothing, but are themselves created.

20   6:97; 16:16

٢١ أَمْوَاتٌ غَيْرُ أَحْيَاءٍ ۖ وَمَا يَشْعُرُونَ أَيَّانَ يُبْعَثُونَ

21 They are dead, not alive; and they do not know when they will be resurrected.

٢٢ إِلَٰهُكُمْ إِلَٰهٌ وَاحِدٌ ۚ فَالَّذِينَ لَا يُؤْمِنُونَ بِالْآخِرَةِ قُلُوبُهُمْ مُنْكِرَةٌ وَهُمْ مُسْتَكْبِرُونَ

22 Your God is one God. As for those who do not believe in the Hereafter, their hearts are in denial, and they are arrogant.

٢٣ لَا جَرَمَ أَنَّ اللَّهَ يَعْلَمُ مَا يُسِرُّونَ وَمَا يُعْلِنُونَ ۚ إِنَّهُ لَا يُحِبُّ الْمُسْتَكْبِرِينَ

23 Without a doubt, God knows what they conceal and what they reveal. He does not like the arrogant.

23   16:19

٢٤ وَإِذَا قِيلَ لَهُمْ مَاذَا أَنْزَلَ رَبُّكُمْ ۙ قَالُوا أَسَاطِيرُ الْأَوَّلِينَ

24 And when it is said to them, "What has your Lord sent down?" They say, "Legends of the ancients."

24
a 16:30
b 8:31; 23:83; 25:5; 27:68; 46:17; 68:15

٢٥ لِيَحْمِلُوا أَوْزَارَهُمْ كَامِلَةً يَوْمَ الْقِيَامَةِ ۙ وَمِنْ أَوْزَارِ الَّذِينَ يُضِلُّونَهُمْ بِغَيْرِ عِلْمٍ ۗ أَلَا سَاءَ مَا يَزِرُونَ

25 So let them carry their loads complete on the Day of Resurrection, and some of the loads of those they misguided without knowledge. Evil is what they carry.

25   6:31; 29:13; 83:13

٢٦ قَدْ مَكَرَ الَّذِينَ مِنْ قَبْلِهِمْ فَأَتَى اللَّهُ بُنْيَانَهُمْ مِنَ الْقَوَاعِدِ فَخَرَّ عَلَيْهِمُ السَّقْفُ مِنْ فَوْقِهِمْ وَأَتَاهُمُ الْعَذَابُ مِنْ حَيْثُ لَا يَشْعُرُونَ

26 Those before them also schemed, but God took their structures from the foundations, and the roof caved in on them. The punishment came at them from where they did not perceive.

26   3:54; 7:99; 8:30; 13:42; 14:46; 16:45; 27:50–52

٢٧ ثُمَّ يَوْمَ الْقِيَامَةِ يُخْزِيهِمْ وَيَقُولُ أَيْنَ شُرَكَائِيَ الَّذِينَ كُنْتُمْ تُشَاقُّونَ فِيهِمْ ۚ قَالَ الَّذِينَ أُوتُوا الْعِلْمَ إِنَّ الْخِزْيَ الْيَوْمَ وَالسُّوءَ عَلَى الْكَافِرِينَ

27 Then, on the Day of Resurrection, He will disgrace them, and say, "Where are My associates for whose sake you used to dispute?" Those who were given knowledge will say, "Today shame and misery are upon the disbelievers."

27   6:22; 10:28; 28:62; 40:73–74

٢٨ الَّذِينَ تَتَوَفَّاهُمُ الْمَلَائِكَةُ ظَالِمِي أَنْفُسِهِمْ ۖ فَأَلْقَوُا السَّلَمَ مَا كُنَّا نَعْمَلُ مِنْ سُوءٍ ۚ بَلَىٰ إِنَّ اللَّهَ عَلِيمٌ بِمَا كُنْتُمْ تَعْمَلُونَ

28 Those wronging their souls while the angels are taking them away—they will propose peace: "We did no wrong." Yes you did. God is aware of what you used to do."

28   4:97; 6:39; 8:50; 16:32, 86

٢٩ فَادْخُلُوا أَبْوَابَ جَهَنَّمَ خَالِدِينَ فِيهَا ۖ فَلَبِئْسَ مَثْوَى الْمُتَكَبِّرِينَ

29 Enter the gates of Hell, to dwell therein forever. Miserable is the residence of the arrogant.

29
15:44; 39:72; 40:76

٣٠ وَقِيلَ لِلَّذِينَ اتَّقَوْا مَاذَا أَنزَلَ رَبُّكُمْ ۚ قَالُوا خَيْرًا ۗ [a] لِّلَّذِينَ أَحْسَنُوا فِي هَٰذِهِ الدُّنْيَا حَسَنَةٌ ۚ [b] وَلَدَارُ الْآخِرَةِ خَيْرٌ ۚ وَلَنِعْمَ دَارُ الْمُتَّقِينَ

30 And it will be said to those who maintained piety, "What has your Lord revealed?" They will say, "Goodness." To those who do good in this world is goodness, and the Home of the Hereafter is even better. How wonderful is the residence of the pious.

30
[a] 16:24, 4
[b] 10:26; 28:84; 39:10; 55:60

٣١ جَنَّاتُ عَدْنٍ يَدْخُلُونَهَا تَجْرِي مِن تَحْتِهَا الْأَنْهَارُ ۖ لَهُمْ فِيهَا مَا يَشَاءُونَ ۚ كَذَٰلِكَ يَجْزِي اللَّهُ الْمُتَّقِينَ

31 The Gardens of Perpetuity, which they will enter, beneath which rivers flow, where they will have whatever they desire. Thus God rewards the pious.

٣٢ الَّذِينَ تَتَوَفَّاهُمُ الْمَلَائِكَةُ طَيِّبِينَ ۙ يَقُولُونَ سَلَامٌ عَلَيْكُمُ ادْخُلُوا الْجَنَّةَ بِمَا كُنتُمْ تَعْمَلُونَ

32 Those who are in a wholesome state when the angels take them— will say, "Peace be upon you; enter Paradise, for what you used to do."

32
10:10; 13:23–24; 16:28

٣٣ هَلْ يَنظُرُونَ إِلَّا أَن تَأْتِيَهُمُ الْمَلَائِكَةُ أَوْ يَأْتِيَ أَمْرُ رَبِّكَ ۚ كَذَٰلِكَ فَعَلَ الَّذِينَ مِن قَبْلِهِمْ ۚ وَمَا ظَلَمَهُمُ اللَّهُ وَلَٰكِن كَانُوا أَنفُسَهُمْ يَظْلِمُونَ

33 Are they but waiting for the angels to come to them, or for the command of your Lord to arrive? Those before them did likewise. God did not wrong them, but they used to wrong their own souls.

33
2:210; 6:158; 15:8; 78:38

٣٤ فَأَصَابَهُمْ سَيِّئَاتُ مَا عَمِلُوا وَحَاقَ بِهِم مَّا كَانُوا بِهِ يَسْتَهْزِئُونَ

34 So the evils of their deeds assailed them, and what they used to ridicule engulfed them.

34
39:48, 51; 45:33

٣٥ وَقَالَ الَّذِينَ أَشْرَكُوا لَوْ شَاءَ اللَّهُ مَا عَبَدْنَا مِن دُونِهِ مِن شَيْءٍ نَّحْنُ وَلَا آبَاؤُنَا وَلَا حَرَّمْنَا مِن دُونِهِ مِن شَيْءٍ ۚ كَذَٰلِكَ فَعَلَ الَّذِينَ مِن قَبْلِهِمْ ۚ فَهَلْ عَلَى الرُّسُلِ إِلَّا الْبَلَاغُ الْمُبِينُ

35 The idolaters say, "Had God willed, we would not have worshiped anything besides Him, neither us, nor our ancestors, nor would we have prohibited anything besides His prohibitions." Those before them did likewise. Are the messengers responsible for anything but clear communication?

35
6:148; 3:20; 43:20

٣٦ وَلَقَدْ بَعَثْنَا فِي كُلِّ أُمَّةٍ رَّسُولًا أَنِ اعْبُدُوا اللَّهَ وَاجْتَنِبُوا الطَّاغُوتَ ۖ فَمِنْهُم مَّنْ هَدَى اللَّهُ وَمِنْهُم مَّنْ حَقَّتْ عَلَيْهِ الضَّلَالَةُ ۚ فَسِيرُوا فِي الْأَرْضِ فَانظُرُوا كَيْفَ كَانَ عَاقِبَةُ الْمُكَذِّبِينَ

36 To every community We sent a messenger: "Worship God, and avoid idolatry." Some of them God guided, while others deserved misguidance. So travel through the earth, and see what the fate of the deniers was.

36
2:219; 5:90–91; 13:7; 22:30; 39:17

Sūrah 16: Al-Naḥl — 283

٣٧ إِنْ تَحْرِصْ عَلَىٰ هُدَاهُمْ فَإِنَّ اللَّهَ لَا يَهْدِي مَن يُضِلُّ ۖ وَمَا لَهُم مِّن نَّاصِرِينَ

37 Even though you may be concerned about their guidance, God does not guide those who misguide. And they will have no saviors.

37
2:256; 10:99; 12:103; 30:29

٣٨ وَأَقْسَمُوا بِاللَّهِ جَهْدَ أَيْمَانِهِمْ ۙ لَا يَبْعَثُ اللَّهُ مَن يَمُوتُ ۚ بَلَىٰ وَعْدًا عَلَيْهِ حَقًّا وَلَٰكِنَّ أَكْثَرَ النَّاسِ لَا يَعْلَمُونَ

38 And they swear by God with their most solemn oaths, "God will not resurrect anyone who dies." Yes indeed, it is a promise binding on Him, but most people do not know.

38
5:53; 9:56-57, 62; 17:51; 64:7

٣٩ لِيُبَيِّنَ لَهُمُ الَّذِي يَخْتَلِفُونَ فِيهِ وَلِيَعْلَمَ الَّذِينَ كَفَرُوا أَنَّهُمْ كَانُوا كَاذِبِينَ

39 To clarify for them what they differed about, and for the faithless to know that they were liars.

٤٠ إِنَّمَا قَوْلُنَا لِشَيْءٍ إِذَا أَرَدْنَاهُ أَن نَّقُولَ لَهُ كُن فَيَكُونُ

40 When We intend for something to happen, We say to it, "Be," and it becomes.

40
2:117; 3:4, 59; 13:9; 36:82

٤١ وَالَّذِينَ هَاجَرُوا فِي اللَّهِ مِن بَعْدِ مَا ظُلِمُوا لَنُبَوِّئَنَّهُمْ فِي الدُّنْيَا حَسَنَةً ۖ وَلَأَجْرُ الْآخِرَةِ أَكْبَرُ ۚ لَوْ كَانُوا يَعْلَمُونَ

41 Those who emigrate for God's sake after being persecuted, We will settle them in a good place in this world; but the reward of the Hereafter is greater, if they only knew.

41
2:218; 3:157; 9:20; 22:58

٤٢ الَّذِينَ صَبَرُوا وَعَلَىٰ رَبِّهِمْ يَتَوَكَّلُونَ

42 Those who endure patiently, and in their Lord they put their trust.

42
29:59

٤٣ وَمَا أَرْسَلْنَا مِن قَبْلِكَ إِلَّا رِجَالًا نُّوحِي إِلَيْهِمْ ۚ فَاسْأَلُوا أَهْلَ الذِّكْرِ إِن كُنتُمْ لَا تَعْلَمُونَ

43 We did not send before you except men whom We inspired. So ask the people of knowledge, if you do not know.

43
10:2; 12:109; 21:7

٤٤ بِالْبَيِّنَاتِ وَالزُّبُرِ ۗ وَأَنزَلْنَا إِلَيْكَ الذِّكْرَ لِتُبَيِّنَ لِلنَّاسِ مَا نُزِّلَ إِلَيْهِمْ وَلَعَلَّهُمْ يَتَفَكَّرُونَ

44 With the clarifications and the scriptures. And We revealed to you the Reminder, that you may clarify to the people what was revealed to them, and that they may reflect.

٤٥ أَفَأَمِنَ الَّذِينَ مَكَرُوا السَّيِّئَاتِ أَن يَخْسِفَ اللَّهُ بِهِمُ الْأَرْضَ أَوْ يَأْتِيَهُمُ الْعَذَابُ مِنْ حَيْثُ لَا يَشْعُرُونَ

45 Do those who scheme evils feel secure that God will not cause the earth to cave in with them, or that the punishment will not come upon them from where they do not perceive?

45
3:54; 12:107; 16:26; 28:81; 67:16

٤٦ أَوْ يَأْخُذَهُمْ فِي تَقَلُّبِهِمْ فَمَا هُم بِمُعْجِزِينَ

46 Or that He will not seize them during their activities? And they will not be able to prevent it.

٤٧ أَوْ يَأْخُذَهُمْ عَلَىٰ تَخَوُّفٍ فَإِنَّ رَبَّكُمْ لَرَءُوفٌ رَحِيمٌ

47 Or that He will not seize them while in dread? Your Lord is Gentle and Merciful.

٤٨ أَوَلَمْ يَرَوْا إِلَىٰ مَا خَلَقَ اللَّهُ مِنْ شَيْءٍ يَتَفَيَّأُ ظِلَالُهُ عَنِ الْيَمِينِ وَالشَّمَائِلِ سُجَّدًا لِلَّهِ وَهُمْ دَاخِرُونَ

48 Have they not observed what God has created? Their shadows revolve from the right and the left, bowing to God as they shrink away.

48
13:15; 22:18

٤٩ وَلِلَّهِ يَسْجُدُ مَا فِي السَّمَاوَاتِ وَمَا فِي الْأَرْضِ مِنْ دَابَّةٍ وَالْمَلَائِكَةُ وَهُمْ لَا يَسْتَكْبِرُونَ

49 To God bows down everything in the heavens and everything on earth—every living creature, and the angels, and without being proud.

٥٠ يَخَافُونَ رَبَّهُمْ مِنْ فَوْقِهِمْ وَيَفْعَلُونَ مَا يُؤْمَرُونَ ۩

50 They fear their Lord above them, and they do what they are commanded.

٥١ وَقَالَ اللَّهُ لَا تَتَّخِذُوا إِلَٰهَيْنِ اثْنَيْنِ ۖ إِنَّمَا هُوَ إِلَٰهٌ وَاحِدٌ ۖ فَإِيَّايَ فَارْهَبُونِ

51 God has said: "Do not take two gods; He is only One God; so fear only Me."

51
5:116

٥٢ وَلَهُ مَا فِي السَّمَاوَاتِ وَالْأَرْضِ وَلَهُ الدِّينُ وَاصِبًا ۚ أَفَغَيْرَ اللَّهِ تَتَّقُونَ

52 To Him belongs everything in the heavens and the earth; and to Him obedience is due always. Do you, then, fear anyone other than God?

٥٣ وَمَا بِكُمْ مِنْ نِعْمَةٍ فَمِنَ اللَّهِ ۖ ᵃ ثُمَّ إِذَا مَسَّكُمُ الضُّرُّ فَإِلَيْهِ تَجْأَرُونَ ᵇ

53 Whatever blessing you have is from God. And when harm touches you, it is to Him that you groan.

53
ᵃ 93:11
ᵇ 30:33

٥٤ ثُمَّ إِذَا كَشَفَ الضُّرَّ عَنْكُمْ إِذَا فَرِيقٌ مِنْكُمْ بِرَبِّهِمْ يُشْرِكُونَ

54 But when He lifts the harm from you, some of you associate others with their Lord.

٥٥ لِيَكْفُرُوا بِمَا آتَيْنَاهُمْ ۚ فَتَمَتَّعُوا ۖ فَسَوْفَ تَعْلَمُونَ

55 To show ingratitude for what We have given them. Enjoy yourselves. You will soon know.

55
6:136; 14:30; 39:8

٥٦ وَيَجْعَلُونَ لِمَا لَا يَعْلَمُونَ نَصِيبًا مِمَّا رَزَقْنَاهُمْ ۗ تَاللَّهِ لَتُسْأَلُنَّ عَمَّا كُنْتُمْ تَفْتَرُونَ

56 And they allocate, to something they do not know, a share of what We have provided for them. By God, you will be questioned about what you have been inventing.

56
6:136; 29:13

٥٧ وَيَجْعَلُونَ لِلَّهِ الْبَنَاتِ سُبْحَانَهُ ۙ وَلَهُمْ مَا يَشْتَهُونَ

57 And they attribute to God daughters—exalted is He—and for themselves what they desire.

57
17:40; 37:149; 43:16, 19; 52:39; 53:21

٥٨ وَإِذَا بُشِّرَ أَحَدُهُم بِٱلْأُنثَىٰ ظَلَّ وَجْهُهُۥ مُسْوَدًّا وَهُوَ كَظِيمٌ

58 And when one of them is given news of a female infant, his face darkens, and he chokes with grief.

58
43:17; 81:8

٥٩ يَتَوَارَىٰ مِنَ ٱلْقَوْمِ مِن سُوءِ مَا بُشِّرَ بِهِۦٓ ۚ أَيُمْسِكُهُۥ عَلَىٰ هُونٍ أَمْ يَدُسُّهُۥ فِى ٱلتُّرَابِ ۗ أَلَا سَآءَ مَا يَحْكُمُونَ

59 He hides from the people because of the bad news given to him. Shall he keep it in humiliation, or bury it in the dust? Evil is the decision they make.

59
6:137; 81:8

٦٠ لِلَّذِينَ لَا يُؤْمِنُونَ بِٱلْءَاخِرَةِ مَثَلُ ٱلسَّوْءِ ۖ وَلِلَّهِ ٱلْمَثَلُ ٱلْأَعْلَىٰ ۚ وَهُوَ ٱلْعَزِيزُ ٱلْحَكِيمُ

60 Those who do not believe in the Hereafter set a bad example, while God sets the Highest Example. He is the Mighty, the Wise.

٦١ وَلَوْ يُؤَاخِذُ ٱللَّهُ ٱلنَّاسَ بِظُلْمِهِم مَّا تَرَكَ عَلَيْهَا مِن دَآبَّةٍ وَلَٰكِن يُؤَخِّرُهُمْ إِلَىٰٓ أَجَلٍ مُّسَمًّى ۖ فَإِذَا جَآءَ أَجَلُهُمْ لَا يَسْتَـْٔخِرُونَ سَاعَةً ۖ وَلَا يَسْتَقْدِمُونَ

61 If God were to hold mankind for their injustices, He would not leave upon it a single creature, but He postpones them until an appointed time. Then, when their time arrives, they will not delay it by one hour, nor will they advance it.

61
14:42; 18:58; 35:45; 82:10–12

٦٢ وَيَجْعَلُونَ لِلَّهِ مَا يَكْرَهُونَ وَتَصِفُ أَلْسِنَتُهُمُ ٱلْكَذِبَ أَنَّ لَهُمُ ٱلْحُسْنَىٰ ۖ لَا جَرَمَ أَنَّ لَهُمُ ٱلنَّارَ وَأَنَّهُم مُّفْرَطُونَ

62 And they attribute to God what they themselves dislike, while their tongues utter the lie that theirs is the goodness. Without a doubt, for them is the Fire, and they will be neglected.

٦٣ تَٱللَّهِ لَقَدْ أَرْسَلْنَآ إِلَىٰٓ أُمَمٍ مِّن قَبْلِكَ فَزَيَّنَ لَهُمُ ٱلشَّيْطَٰنُ أَعْمَٰلَهُمْ فَهُوَ وَلِيُّهُمُ ٱلْيَوْمَ وَلَهُمْ عَذَابٌ أَلِيمٌ

63 By God, We sent messengers to communities before you, but Satan made their deeds appear alluring to them. He is their master today, and they will have a painful punishment.

٦٤ وَمَآ أَنزَلْنَا عَلَيْكَ ٱلْكِتَٰبَ إِلَّا لِتُبَيِّنَ لَهُمُ ٱلَّذِى ٱخْتَلَفُوا۟ فِيهِ ۙ وَهُدًى وَرَحْمَةً لِّقَوْمٍ يُؤْمِنُونَ

64 We revealed to you the Scripture only to clarify for them what they differ about, and guidance and mercy for people who believe.

64
7:203; 12:111; 16:89; 27:76

٦٥ وَٱللَّهُ أَنزَلَ مِنَ ٱلسَّمَآءِ مَآءً فَأَحْيَا بِهِ ٱلْأَرْضَ بَعْدَ مَوْتِهَآ ۚ إِنَّ فِى ذَٰلِكَ لَءَايَةً لِّقَوْمٍ يَسْمَعُونَ

65 God sends down water from the sky, with which He revives the earth after its death. In this is a sign for people who listen.

65
2:164

٦٦ وَإِنَّ لَكُمْ فِى ٱلْأَنْعَٰمِ لَعِبْرَةً ۖ نُّسْقِيكُم مِّمَّا فِى بُطُونِهِۦ مِنۢ بَيْنِ فَرْثٍ وَدَمٍ لَّبَنًا خَالِصًا سَآئِغًا لِّلشَّٰرِبِينَ

66 And there is a lesson for you in cattle: We give you a drink from their bellies, from between waste and blood, pure milk, refreshing to the drinkers.

66
23:21

٦٧ وَمِن ثَمَرَاتِ النَّخِيلِ وَالْأَعْنَابِ تَتَّخِذُونَ مِنْهُ سَكَرًا وَرِزْقًا حَسَنًا ۗ إِنَّ فِي ذَٰلِكَ لَآيَةً لِّقَوْمٍ يَعْقِلُونَ

67 And from the fruits of date-palms and grapevines, you derive sugar and wholesome food. In this is a sign for people who understand.

67 — 2:219; 4:43; 5:90

٦٨ وَأَوْحَىٰ رَبُّكَ إِلَى النَّحْلِ أَنِ اتَّخِذِي مِنَ الْجِبَالِ بُيُوتًا وَمِنَ الشَّجَرِ وَمِمَّا يَعْرِشُونَ

68 And your Lord inspired the bee: "Set up hives in the mountains, and in the trees, and in what they construct."

٦٩ ثُمَّ كُلِي مِن كُلِّ الثَّمَرَاتِ فَاسْلُكِي سُبُلَ رَبِّكِ ذُلُلًا ۚ يَخْرُجُ مِن بُطُونِهَا شَرَابٌ مُّخْتَلِفٌ أَلْوَانُهُ فِيهِ شِفَاءٌ لِّلنَّاسِ ۗ إِنَّ فِي ذَٰلِكَ لَآيَةً لِّقَوْمٍ يَتَفَكَّرُونَ

69 Then eat of all the fruits, and go along the pathways of your Lord, with precision. From their bellies emerges a fluid of diverse colors, containing healing for the people. Surely in this is a sign for people who reflect.

٧٠ وَاللَّهُ خَلَقَكُمْ ثُمَّ يَتَوَفَّاكُمْ ۚ وَمِنكُم مَّن يُرَدُّ إِلَىٰ أَرْذَلِ الْعُمُرِ لِكَيْ لَا يَعْلَمَ بَعْدَ عِلْمٍ شَيْئًا ۚ إِنَّ اللَّهَ عَلِيمٌ قَدِيرٌ

70 God created you; then He takes you away. Some of you will be brought back to the worst age, so that he will no longer know anything, after having acquired knowledge. God is Omniscient and Omnipotent.

70 — 22:5; 36:68

٧١ وَاللَّهُ فَضَّلَ بَعْضَكُمْ عَلَىٰ بَعْضٍ فِي الرِّزْقِ ۚ فَمَا الَّذِينَ فُضِّلُوا بِرَادِّي رِزْقِهِمْ عَلَىٰ مَا مَلَكَتْ أَيْمَانُهُمْ فَهُمْ فِيهِ سَوَاءٌ ۚ أَفَبِنِعْمَةِ اللَّهِ يَجْحَدُونَ

71 God has favored some of you over others in livelihood. Those who are favored would not give their properties to their servants, to the extent of making them partners in it. Will they then renounce God's blessings?

71 — 17:21; 30:28

٧٢ وَاللَّهُ جَعَلَ لَكُم مِّنْ أَنفُسِكُمْ أَزْوَاجًا وَجَعَلَ لَكُم مِّنْ أَزْوَاجِكُم بَنِينَ وَحَفَدَةً وَرَزَقَكُم مِّنَ الطَّيِّبَاتِ ۚ أَفَبِالْبَاطِلِ يُؤْمِنُونَ وَبِنِعْمَتِ اللَّهِ هُمْ يَكْفُرُونَ

72 God has given you mates from among yourselves; and has produced for you, from your mates, children and grandchildren; and has provided you with good things. Will they then believe in falsehood, and refuse God's favors?

72 — 4:1; 7:189; 30:21; 39:6; 42:11

٧٣ وَيَعْبُدُونَ مِن دُونِ اللَّهِ مَا لَا يَمْلِكُ لَهُمْ رِزْقًا مِّنَ السَّمَاوَاتِ وَالْأَرْضِ شَيْئًا وَلَا يَسْتَطِيعُونَ

73 And yet they serve besides God what possesses no provisions for them in the heavens, nor on earth, nor are they capable.

73 — 29:17; 67:21

٧٤ فَلَا تَضْرِبُوا لِلَّهِ الْأَمْثَالَ ۚ إِنَّ اللَّهَ يَعْلَمُ وَأَنتُمْ لَا تَعْلَمُونَ

74 So do not cite the examples for God. God knows, and you do not know.

74 — 42:11

٧٥ ضَرَبَ اللَّهُ مَثَلًا عَبْدًا مَمْلُوكًا لَا يَقْدِرُ عَلَىٰ شَيْءٍ وَمَن رَّزَقْنَاهُ مِنَّا رِزْقًا حَسَنًا فَهُوَ يُنفِقُ مِنْهُ سِرًّا وَجَهْرًا ۖ هَلْ يَسْتَوُونَ ۚ الْحَمْدُ لِلَّهِ ۚ بَلْ أَكْثَرُهُمْ لَا يَعْلَمُونَ

75 — 39:29

75 God cites the example of a bonded slave, who has no power over anything; and someone to whom We have given plentiful provision, from which he gives secretly and openly. Are they equal in comparison? All praise belongs to God, but most of them do not know.

٧٦ وَضَرَبَ اللَّهُ مَثَلًا رَّجُلَيْنِ أَحَدُهُمَا أَبْكَمُ لَا يَقْدِرُ عَلَىٰ شَيْءٍ وَهُوَ كَلٌّ عَلَىٰ مَوْلَاهُ أَيْنَمَا يُوَجِّههُّ لَا يَأْتِ بِخَيْرٍ ۖ هَلْ يَسْتَوِي هُوَ وَمَن يَأْمُرُ بِالْعَدْلِ ۙ وَهُوَ عَلَىٰ صِرَاطٍ مُّسْتَقِيمٍ

76 — 67:22

76 And God cites the example of two men: one of them dumb, unable to do anything, and is a burden on his master; whichever way he directs him, he achieves nothing good. Is he equal to him who commands justice, and is on a straight path?

٧٧ وَلِلَّهِ غَيْبُ السَّمَاوَاتِ وَالْأَرْضِ ۚ وَمَا أَمْرُ السَّاعَةِ إِلَّا كَلَمْحِ الْبَصَرِ أَوْ هُوَ أَقْرَبُ ۚ إِنَّ اللَّهَ عَلَىٰ كُلِّ شَيْءٍ قَدِيرٌ

77 — 10:24; 22:47; 54:50; 70:6–7

77 To God belongs the unseen of the heavens and the earth. The coming of the Hour is only as the twinkling of the eye, or even nearer. God has power over everything.

٧٨ وَاللَّهُ أَخْرَجَكُم مِّن بُطُونِ أُمَّهَاتِكُمْ لَا تَعْلَمُونَ شَيْئًا وَجَعَلَ لَكُمُ السَّمْعَ وَالْأَبْصَارَ وَالْأَفْئِدَةَ ۙ لَعَلَّكُمْ تَشْكُرُونَ

78 — 10:31; 23:78; 67:23

78 God brought you out of your mothers' wombs, not knowing anything; and He gave you the hearing, and the eyesight, and the brains; that you may give thanks.

٧٩ أَلَمْ يَرَوْا إِلَى الطَّيْرِ مُسَخَّرَاتٍ فِي جَوِّ السَّمَاءِ مَا يُمْسِكُهُنَّ إِلَّا اللَّهُ ۗ إِنَّ فِي ذَٰلِكَ لَآيَاتٍ لِّقَوْمٍ يُؤْمِنُونَ

79 — 67:19

79 Have they not seen the birds, flying in the midst of the sky? None sustains them except God. In this are signs for people who believe.

٨٠ وَاللَّهُ جَعَلَ لَكُم مِّن بُيُوتِكُمْ سَكَنًا وَجَعَلَ لَكُم مِّن جُلُودِ الْأَنْعَامِ بُيُوتًا تَسْتَخِفُّونَهَا يَوْمَ ظَعْنِكُمْ وَيَوْمَ إِقَامَتِكُمْ ۙ وَمِنْ أَصْوَافِهَا وَأَوْبَارِهَا وَأَشْعَارِهَا أَثَاثًا وَمَتَاعًا إِلَىٰ حِينٍ

80

80 And God has given you in your homes habitats for you, and has provided for you out of the hides of livestock portable homes for you, so you can use them when you travel, and when you camp; and from their wool, and fur, and hair, furnishings and comfort for a while.

٨١ وَاللَّهُ جَعَلَ لَكُم مِّمَّا خَلَقَ ظِلَالًا وَجَعَلَ لَكُم مِّنَ الْجِبَالِ أَكْنَانًا وَجَعَلَ لَكُمْ سَرَابِيلَ تَقِيكُمُ الْحَرَّ وَسَرَابِيلَ تَقِيكُم بَأْسَكُمْ ۚ كَذَٰلِكَ يُتِمُّ نِعْمَتَهُ عَلَيْكُمْ لَعَلَّكُمْ تُسْلِمُونَ

81 — 21:80

81 And God has made for you shade out of what He has created, and has given you resorts in the mountains, and has given you garments to protect you from the heat, and garments to protect you from your violence. Thus He completes His blessings upon you, so that you may submit.

٨٢ فَإِنْ تَوَلَّوْا فَإِنَّمَا عَلَيْكَ الْبَلَاغُ الْمُبِينُ

82 But if they turn away, your only duty is clear communication.

٨٣ يَعْرِفُونَ نِعْمَتَ اللَّهِ ثُمَّ يُنْكِرُونَهَا وَأَكْثَرُهُمُ الْكَافِرُونَ

83 They recognize God's blessing, but then deny it, as most of them are ungrateful.

٨٤ وَيَوْمَ نَبْعَثُ مِنْ كُلِّ أُمَّةٍ شَهِيدًا ثُمَّ لَا يُؤْذَنُ لِلَّذِينَ كَفَرُوا وَلَا هُمْ يُسْتَعْتَبُونَ

84 On the Day when We raise up a witness from every community—those who disbelieved will not be permitted, nor will they be excused.

84
14:28; 41:24

٨٥ وَإِذَا رَأَى الَّذِينَ ظَلَمُوا الْعَذَابَ فَلَا يُخَفَّفُ عَنْهُمْ وَلَا هُمْ يُنْظَرُونَ

85 When those who did wrong see the punishment, it will not be lightened for them, nor will they be reprieved.

85
2:162; 3:88

٨٦ وَإِذَا رَأَى الَّذِينَ أَشْرَكُوا شُرَكَاءَهُمْ قَالُوا رَبَّنَا هَٰؤُلَاءِ شُرَكَاؤُنَا الَّذِينَ كُنَّا نَدْعُو مِنْ دُونِكَ فَأَلْقَوْا إِلَيْهِمُ الْقَوْلَ إِنَّكُمْ لَكَاذِبُونَ

86 And when the idolaters see their associates, they will say, "Our Lord, these are our associates whom we used to invoke besides You." They will strike back at them with the saying, "Surely you are liars."

86
10:28; 28:64

٨٧ وَأَلْقَوْا إِلَى اللَّهِ يَوْمَئِذٍ السَّلَمَ وَضَلَّ عَنْهُمْ مَا كَانُوا يَفْتَرُونَ

87 On that Day they will offer their submission to God, and what they had invented will abandon them.

87
16:28

٨٨ الَّذِينَ كَفَرُوا وَصَدُّوا عَنْ سَبِيلِ اللَّهِ زِدْنَاهُمْ عَذَابًا فَوْقَ الْعَذَابِ بِمَا كَانُوا يُفْسِدُونَ

88 Those who disbelieve and obstruct from God's path—We will add punishment to their punishment, on account of the mischief they used to make.

88
11:20; 38:61; 78:30

٨٩ وَيَوْمَ نَبْعَثُ فِي كُلِّ أُمَّةٍ شَهِيدًا عَلَيْهِمْ مِنْ أَنْفُسِهِمْ وَجِئْنَا بِكَ شَهِيدًا عَلَىٰ هَٰؤُلَاءِ [a] وَنَزَّلْنَا عَلَيْكَ الْكِتَابَ تِبْيَانًا لِكُلِّ شَيْءٍ وَهُدًى وَرَحْمَةً وَبُشْرَىٰ لِلْمُسْلِمِينَ [b]

89 On the Day when We raise in every community a witness against them, from among them, and bring you as a witness against these. We have revealed to you the Book, as an explanation of all things, and guidance, and mercy and good news for those who submit.

89
[a] 4:41; 7:6
[b] 6:38; 17:82; 28:75

٩٠ إِنَّ اللَّهَ يَأْمُرُ بِالْعَدْلِ وَالْإِحْسَانِ وَإِيتَاءِ ذِي الْقُرْبَىٰ وَيَنْهَىٰ عَنِ الْفَحْشَاءِ وَالْمُنْكَرِ وَالْبَغْيِ يَعِظُكُمْ لَعَلَّكُمْ تَذَكَّرُونَ

90 God commands justice, and goodness, and generosity towards relatives. And He forbids immorality, and injustice, and oppression. He advises you, so that you may take heed.

90
4:58; 5:8

٩١ وَأَوْفُوا بِعَهْدِ اللَّهِ إِذَا عَاهَدتُّمْ وَلَا تَنقُضُوا الْأَيْمَانَ بَعْدَ تَوْكِيدِهَا وَقَدْ جَعَلْتُمُ اللَّهَ عَلَيْكُمْ كَفِيلًا ۚ إِنَّ اللَّهَ يَعْلَمُ مَا تَفْعَلُونَ

91   3:76; 13:20; 17:38

91 Fulfill God's covenant when you make a covenant, and do not break your oaths after ratifying them. You have made God your guarantor, and God knows what you do.

٩٢ وَلَا تَكُونُوا كَالَّتِي نَقَضَتْ غَزْلَهَا مِن بَعْدِ قُوَّةٍ أَنكَاثًا تَتَّخِذُونَ أَيْمَانَكُمْ دَخَلًا بَيْنَكُمْ أَن تَكُونَ أُمَّةٌ هِيَ أَرْبَىٰ مِنْ أُمَّةٍ ۚ إِنَّمَا يَبْلُوكُمُ اللَّهُ بِهِ ۚ وَلَيُبَيِّنَنَّ لَكُمْ يَوْمَ الْقِيَامَةِ مَا كُنتُمْ فِيهِ تَخْتَلِفُونَ

92 And do not be like her who unravels her yarn, breaking it into pieces, after she has spun it strongly. Nor use your oaths as means of deception among you, because one community is more prosperous than another. God is testing you thereby. On the Day of Resurrection, He will make clear to you everything you had disputed about.

٩٣ وَلَوْ شَاءَ اللَّهُ لَجَعَلَكُمْ أُمَّةً وَاحِدَةً وَلَٰكِن يُضِلُّ مَن يَشَاءُ وَيَهْدِي مَن يَشَاءُ ۚ وَلَتُسْأَلُنَّ عَمَّا كُنتُمْ تَعْمَلُونَ

93   5:48; 6:35; 11:118; 42:8

93 Had God willed, He would have made you one congregation, but He leaves astray whom He wills, and He guides whom He wills. And you will surely be questioned about what you used to do.

٩٤ وَلَا تَتَّخِذُوا أَيْمَانَكُمْ دَخَلًا بَيْنَكُمْ فَتَزِلَّ قَدَمٌ بَعْدَ ثُبُوتِهَا وَتَذُوقُوا السُّوءَ بِمَا صَدَدتُّمْ عَن سَبِيلِ اللَّهِ ۖ وَلَكُمْ عَذَابٌ عَظِيمٌ

94 And do not use your oaths to deceive one another, so that a foot may not slip after being firm, and you taste misery because you hindered from God's path, and incur a terrible torment.

٩٥ وَلَا تَشْتَرُوا بِعَهْدِ اللَّهِ ثَمَنًا قَلِيلًا ۚ إِنَّمَا عِندَ اللَّهِ هُوَ خَيْرٌ لَّكُمْ إِن كُنتُمْ تَعْلَمُونَ

95   2:184; 3:77, 187

95 And do not exchange God's covenant for a small price. What is with God is better for you, if you only knew.

٩٦ مَا عِندَكُمْ يَنفَدُ ۖ وَمَا عِندَ اللَّهِ بَاقٍ ۗ وَلَنَجْزِيَنَّ الَّذِينَ صَبَرُوا أَجْرَهُم بِأَحْسَنِ مَا كَانُوا يَعْمَلُونَ

96   20:131; 28:60; 38:54

96 What you have runs out, but what is with God remains. We will reward those who are patient according to the best of their deeds.

٩٧ مَنْ عَمِلَ صَالِحًا مِّن ذَكَرٍ أَوْ أُنثَىٰ وَهُوَ مُؤْمِنٌ فَلَنُحْيِيَنَّهُ حَيَاةً طَيِّبَةً ۖ وَلَنَجْزِيَنَّهُمْ أَجْرَهُم بِأَحْسَنِ مَا كَانُوا يَعْمَلُونَ

97   2:62; 4:124; 5:69; 31:8–9

97 Whoever works righteousness, whether male or female, while being a believer, We will grant him a good life—and We will reward them according to the best of what they used to do.

٩٨ فَإِذَا قَرَأْتَ الْقُرْآنَ فَاسْتَعِذْ بِاللَّهِ مِنَ الشَّيْطَانِ الرَّجِيمِ

98 When you read the Qur'an, seek refuge with God from Satan the outcast.

٩٩ إِنَّهُ لَيْسَ لَهُ سُلْطَانٌ عَلَى الَّذِينَ آمَنُوا وَعَلَىٰ رَبِّهِمْ يَتَوَكَّلُونَ

99 14:22; 14:42

99 He has no authority over those who believe and trust in their Lord.

١٠٠ إِنَّمَا سُلْطَانُهُ عَلَى الَّذِينَ يَتَوَلَّوْنَهُ وَالَّذِينَ هُم بِهِ مُشْرِكُونَ

100

100 His authority is only over those who follow him, and those who associate others with Him.

١٠١ وَإِذَا بَدَّلْنَا آيَةً مَّكَانَ آيَةٍ ۙ وَاللَّهُ أَعْلَمُ بِمَا يُنَزِّلُ قَالُوا إِنَّمَا أَنتَ مُفْتَرٍ ۚ بَلْ أَكْثَرُهُمْ لَا يَعْلَمُونَ

101 2:106; 13:39; 17:86

101 When We substitute a verse in place of another verse—and God knows best what He reveals—they say, "You are an impostor." But most of them do not know.

١٠٢ قُلْ نَزَّلَهُ رُوحُ الْقُدُسِ مِن رَّبِّكَ بِالْحَقِّ لِيُثَبِّتَ الَّذِينَ آمَنُوا وَهُدًى وَبُشْرَىٰ لِلْمُسْلِمِينَ

102 2:97; 26:193–194

102 Say, "The Holy Spirit has brought it down from your Lord, truthfully, in order to stabilize those who believe, and as guidance and good news for those who submit."

١٠٣ وَلَقَدْ نَعْلَمُ أَنَّهُمْ يَقُولُونَ إِنَّمَا يُعَلِّمُهُ بَشَرٌ ۗ لِّسَانُ الَّذِي يُلْحِدُونَ إِلَيْهِ أَعْجَمِيٌّ وَهَٰذَا لِسَانٌ عَرَبِيٌّ مُّبِينٌ

103 6:105; 25:5; 41:44

103 We are well aware that they say, "It is a human being who is teaching him." But the tongue of him they allude to is foreign, while this is a clear Arabic tongue.

١٠٤ إِنَّ الَّذِينَ لَا يُؤْمِنُونَ بِآيَاتِ اللَّهِ لَا يَهْدِيهِمُ اللَّهُ وَلَهُمْ عَذَابٌ أَلِيمٌ

104

104 Those who do not believe in God's revelations—God will not guide them, and for them is a painful punishment.

١٠٥ إِنَّمَا يَفْتَرِي الْكَذِبَ الَّذِينَ لَا يُؤْمِنُونَ بِآيَاتِ اللَّهِ ۖ وَأُولَٰئِكَ هُمُ الْكَاذِبُونَ

105

105 It is those who do not believe in God's revelations who fabricate falsehood. These are the liars.

١٠٦ مَن كَفَرَ بِاللَّهِ مِن بَعْدِ إِيمَانِهِ إِلَّا مَنْ أُكْرِهَ وَقَلْبُهُ مُطْمَئِنٌّ بِالْإِيمَانِ وَلَٰكِن مَّن شَرَحَ بِالْكُفْرِ صَدْرًا فَعَلَيْهِمْ غَضَبٌ مِّنَ اللَّهِ وَلَهُمْ عَذَابٌ عَظِيمٌ

106 3:86, 90; 9:74, 66

106 Whoever renounces faith in God after having believed—except for someone who is compelled, while his heart rests securely in faith—but whoever willingly opens up his heart to disbelief—upon them falls wrath from God, and for them is a tremendous torment.

١٠٧ ذَٰلِكَ بِأَنَّهُمُ اسْتَحَبُّوا الْحَيَاةَ الدُّنْيَا عَلَى الْآخِرَةِ وَأَنَّ اللَّهَ لَا يَهْدِي الْقَوْمَ الْكَافِرِينَ

107 14:3

107 That is because they have preferred the worldly life to the Hereafter, and because God does not guide the people who refuse.

١٠٨ أُولَٰئِكَ الَّذِينَ طَبَعَ اللَّهُ عَلَىٰ قُلُوبِهِمْ وَسَمْعِهِمْ وَأَبْصَارِهِمْ ۖ وَأُولَٰئِكَ هُمُ الْغَافِلُونَ

108 2:7; 36:9; 45:23

108 It is they whom God has sealed their hearts, and their hearing, and their sight. It is they who are the heedless.

١٠٩ لَا جَرَمَ أَنَّهُمْ فِي الْآخِرَةِ هُمُ الْخَاسِرُونَ

109
11:22

109 There is no doubt that in the Hereafter they will be the losers.

١١٠ ثُمَّ إِنَّ رَبَّكَ لِلَّذِينَ هَاجَرُوا مِنْ بَعْدِ مَا فُتِنُوا ثُمَّ جَاهَدُوا وَصَبَرُوا إِنَّ رَبَّكَ مِنْ بَعْدِهَا لَغَفُورٌ رَحِيمٌ

110
3:125

110 But then your Lord—for those who emigrated after being persecuted, then struggled and persevered—your Lord thereafter is Forgiving and Merciful.

١١١ يَوْمَ تَأْتِي كُلُّ نَفْسٍ تُجَادِلُ عَنْ نَفْسِهَا وَتُوَفَّىٰ كُلُّ نَفْسٍ مَا عَمِلَتْ وَهُمْ لَا يُظْلَمُونَ

111
2:281

111 On the Day when every soul will come pleading for itself, and every soul will be paid in full for what it has done, and they will not be wronged.

١١٢ وَضَرَبَ اللَّهُ مَثَلًا قَرْيَةً كَانَتْ آمِنَةً مُطْمَئِنَّةً يَأْتِيهَا رِزْقُهَا رَغَدًا مِنْ كُلِّ مَكَانٍ فَكَفَرَتْ بِأَنْعُمِ اللَّهِ فَأَذَاقَهَا اللَّهُ لِبَاسَ الْجُوعِ وَالْخَوْفِ بِمَا كَانُوا يَصْنَعُونَ

112
2:126

112 And God cites the example of a town that was secure and peaceful, with its livelihood coming to it abundantly from every direction. But then it turned unappreciative of God's blessings, so God made it taste the robe of hunger and fear, because of what they used to craft.

١١٣ وَلَقَدْ جَاءَهُمْ رَسُولٌ مِنْهُمْ فَكَذَّبُوهُ فَأَخَذَهُمُ الْعَذَابُ وَهُمْ ظَالِمُونَ

113 A messenger from among them had come to them, but they denounced him, so the punishment seized them in the midst of their wrongdoing.

١١٤ فَكُلُوا مِمَّا رَزَقَكُمُ اللَّهُ حَلَالًا طَيِّبًا وَاشْكُرُوا نِعْمَتَ اللَّهِ إِنْ كُنْتُمْ إِيَّاهُ تَعْبُدُونَ

114
2:172; 5:88

114 Eat of the lawful and good things God has provided for you, and be thankful for God's blessings, if it is Him that you serve.

١١٥ إِنَّمَا حَرَّمَ عَلَيْكُمُ الْمَيْتَةَ وَالدَّمَ وَلَحْمَ الْخِنْزِيرِ وَمَا أُهِلَّ لِغَيْرِ اللَّهِ بِهِ ۖ فَمَنِ اضْطُرَّ غَيْرَ بَاغٍ وَلَا عَادٍ فَإِنَّ اللَّهَ غَفُورٌ رَحِيمٌ

115
2:173; 5:3; 6:145

115 He has forbidden you carrion, and blood, and the flesh of swine, and anything consecrated to other than God. But if anyone is compelled by necessity, without being deliberate or malicious, then God is Forgiving and Merciful.

١١٦ وَلَا تَقُولُوا لِمَا تَصِفُ أَلْسِنَتُكُمُ الْكَذِبَ هَٰذَا حَلَالٌ وَهَٰذَا حَرَامٌ لِتَفْتَرُوا عَلَى اللَّهِ الْكَذِبَ ۚ إِنَّ الَّذِينَ يَفْتَرُونَ عَلَى اللَّهِ الْكَذِبَ لَا يُفْلِحُونَ

116
5:87; 10:59

116 And do not say of falsehood asserted by your tongues, "This is lawful, and this is unlawful," in order to invent lies and attribute them to God. Those who invent lies and attribute them to God will not succeed.

١١٧ مَتَاعٌ قَلِيلٌ وَلَهُمْ عَذَابٌ أَلِيمٌ

117
2:36; 10:70

117 A brief enjoyment—then they will have a painful punishment.

١١٨ وَعَلَى الَّذِينَ هَادُوا حَرَّمْنَا مَا قَصَصْنَا عَلَيْكَ مِن قَبْلُ ۖ وَمَا ظَلَمْنَاهُمْ وَلَٰكِن كَانُوا أَنفُسَهُمْ يَظْلِمُونَ

118 6:146

118 For those who are Jews, We have prohibited what We related to you before. We did not wrong them, but they used to wrong their own selves.

١١٩ ثُمَّ إِنَّ رَبَّكَ لِلَّذِينَ عَمِلُوا السُّوءَ بِجَهَالَةٍ ثُمَّ تَابُوا مِن بَعْدِ ذَٰلِكَ وَأَصْلَحُوا إِنَّ رَبَّكَ مِن بَعْدِهَا لَغَفُورٌ رَّحِيمٌ

119 6:54

119 But towards those who do wrongs in ignorance, and then repent afterwards and reform, your Lord thereafter is Forgiving and Merciful.

١٢٠ إِنَّ إِبْرَاهِيمَ كَانَ أُمَّةً قَانِتًا لِلَّهِ حَنِيفًا وَلَمْ يَكُ مِنَ الْمُشْرِكِينَ

120 2:124

120 Abraham was an exemplary leader, devoted to God, a monotheist, and was not of the polytheists.

١٢١ شَاكِرًا لِّأَنْعُمِهِ ۚ اجْتَبَاهُ وَهَدَاهُ إِلَىٰ صِرَاطٍ مُّسْتَقِيمٍ

121 3:33; 6:87; 19:58

121 Thankful for His blessings. He chose him, and guided him to a straight path.

١٢٢ وَآتَيْنَاهُ فِي الدُّنْيَا حَسَنَةً ۖ وَإِنَّهُ فِي الْآخِرَةِ لَمِنَ الصَّالِحِينَ

122 3:95

122 And We gave him goodness in this world, and in the Hereafter he will be among the righteous.

١٢٣ ثُمَّ أَوْحَيْنَا إِلَيْكَ أَنِ اتَّبِعْ مِلَّةَ إِبْرَاهِيمَ حَنِيفًا ۖ وَمَا كَانَ مِنَ الْمُشْرِكِينَ

123 2:130, 135; 3:95; 4:123; 6:161; 12:38; 16:123; 22:78

123 Then We inspired you: "Follow the religion of Abraham, the Monotheist. He was not an idol-worshiper."

١٢٤ إِنَّمَا جُعِلَ السَّبْتُ عَلَى الَّذِينَ اخْتَلَفُوا فِيهِ ۚ وَإِنَّ رَبَّكَ لَيَحْكُمُ بَيْنَهُمْ يَوْمَ الْقِيَامَةِ فِيمَا كَانُوا فِيهِ يَخْتَلِفُونَ

124 The Sabbath was decreed only for those who differed about it. Your Lord will judge between them on the Day of Resurrection regarding their differences.

١٢٥ ادْعُ إِلَىٰ سَبِيلِ رَبِّكَ بِالْحِكْمَةِ وَالْمَوْعِظَةِ الْحَسَنَةِ ۖ وَجَادِلْهُم بِالَّتِي هِيَ أَحْسَنُ ۚ إِنَّ رَبَّكَ هُوَ أَعْلَمُ بِمَن ضَلَّ عَن سَبِيلِهِ ۖ وَهُوَ أَعْلَمُ بِالْمُهْتَدِينَ

125 29:46; 41:34

125 Invite to the way of your Lord with wisdom and good advice, and debate with them in the most dignified manner. Your Lord is aware of those who stray from His path, and He is aware of those who are guided.

١٢٦ وَإِنْ عَاقَبْتُمْ فَعَاقِبُوا بِمِثْلِ مَا عُوقِبْتُم بِهِ ۖ وَلَئِن صَبَرْتُمْ لَهُوَ خَيْرٌ لِّلصَّابِرِينَ

126 5:45; 42:40–41

126 If you were to retaliate, retaliate to the same degree as the injury done to you. But if you resort to patience—it is better for the patient.

١٢٧ وَاصْبِرْ وَمَا صَبْرُكَ إِلَّا بِاللَّهِ ۚ وَلَا تَحْزَنْ عَلَيْهِمْ وَلَا تَكُ فِي ضَيْقٍ مِّمَّا يَمْكُرُونَ

127 So be patient. Your patience is solely from God. And do not grieve over them, and do not be stressed by their schemes.

127
41:35

١٢٨ إِنَّ اللَّهَ مَعَ الَّذِينَ اتَّقَوا وَّالَّذِينَ هُم مُّحْسِنُونَ

128 God is with those who are righteous and those who are virtuous.

128
9:40

Sūrah 17: Al-Isrā'

سُورَةُ ٱلْإِسْرَاء (The Night Journey)

بِسْمِ ٱللَّهِ ٱلرَّحْمَٰنِ ٱلرَّحِيمِ

١ سُبْحَانَ الَّذِي أَسْرَىٰ بِعَبْدِهِ لَيْلًا مِّنَ الْمَسْجِدِ الْحَرَامِ إِلَى الْمَسْجِدِ الْأَقْصَى الَّذِي بَارَكْنَا حَوْلَهُ لِنُرِيَهُ مِنْ آيَاتِنَا ۚ إِنَّهُ هُوَ السَّمِيعُ الْبَصِيرُ

1 Glory to Him who journeyed His servant by night, from the Sacred Mosque, to the Farthest Mosque, whose precincts We have blessed, in order to show him of Our wonders. He is the Listener, the Beholder.

٢ وَآتَيْنَا مُوسَى الْكِتَابَ وَجَعَلْنَاهُ هُدًى لِّبَنِي إِسْرَائِيلَ[a] أَلَّا تَتَّخِذُوا مِن دُونِي وَكِيلًا[b]

2 And We gave Moses the Scripture, and made it a guide for the Children of Israel: Take none for protector other than Me.

2
[a] 28:43; 32:23–24; 40:53
[b] 3:173; 10:3; 10:71; 11:56; 14:12; 65:3; 67:29

٣ ذُرِّيَّةَ مَنْ حَمَلْنَا مَعَ نُوحٍ ۚ إِنَّهُ كَانَ عَبْدًا شَكُورًا

3 The descendants of those We carried with Noah. He was an appreciative servant.

3
19:58; 36:41

٤ وَقَضَيْنَا إِلَىٰ بَنِي إِسْرَائِيلَ فِي الْكِتَابِ لَتُفْسِدُنَّ فِي الْأَرْضِ مَرَّتَيْنِ وَلَتَعْلُنَّ عُلُوًّا كَبِيرًا

4 And We conveyed to the Children of Israel in the Scripture: You will commit evil on earth twice, and you will rise to a great height.

٥ فَإِذَا جَاءَ وَعْدُ أُولَاهُمَا بَعَثْنَا عَلَيْكُمْ عِبَادًا لَّنَا أُولِي بَأْسٍ شَدِيدٍ فَجَاسُوا خِلَالَ الدِّيَارِ ۚ وَكَانَ وَعْدًا مَّفْعُولًا

5 When the first of the two promises came true, We sent against you servants of Ours, possessing great might, and they ransacked your homes. It was a promise fulfilled.

5
17:7

٦ ثُمَّ رَدَدْنَا لَكُمُ الْكَرَّةَ عَلَيْهِمْ وَأَمْدَدْنَاكُم بِأَمْوَالٍ وَبَنِينَ وَجَعَلْنَاكُمْ أَكْثَرَ نَفِيرًا

6 Then We gave you back your turn against them, and supplied you with wealth and children, and made you more numerous.

٧ إِنْ أَحْسَنتُمْ أَحْسَنتُمْ لِأَنفُسِكُمْ ۖ وَإِنْ أَسَأْتُمْ فَلَهَا ۚ فَإِذَا جَاءَ وَعْدُ الْآخِرَةِ لِيَسُوءُوا وُجُوهَكُمْ وَلِيَدْخُلُوا الْمَسْجِدَ كَمَا دَخَلُوهُ أَوَّلَ مَرَّةٍ وَلِيُتَبِّرُوا مَا عَلَوْا تَتْبِيرًا		7 17:5; 30:44; 41:46; 45:15; 99:7–8

7 If you work righteousness, you work righteousness for yourselves; and if you commit evil, you do so against yourselves. Then, when the second promise comes true, they will make your faces filled with sorrow, and enter the Temple as they entered it the first time, and utterly destroy all that falls into their power.

٨ عَسَىٰ رَبُّكُمْ أَنْ يَرْحَمَكُمْ ۚ وَإِنْ عُدتُّمْ عُدْنَا ۘ وَجَعَلْنَا جَهَنَّمَ لِلْكَافِرِينَ حَصِيرًا	8 8:19

8 Perhaps your Lord will have mercy on you. But if you revert, We will revert. We have made Hell a prison for the disbelievers.

٩ إِنَّ هَٰذَا الْقُرْآنَ يَهْدِي لِلَّتِي هِيَ أَقْوَمُ وَيُبَشِّرُ الْمُؤْمِنِينَ الَّذِينَ يَعْمَلُونَ الصَّالِحَاتِ أَنَّ لَهُمْ أَجْرًا كَبِيرًا	9 18:1–2

9 This Qur'an guides to what is most upright; and it gives good news to the believers who do good deeds, that they will have a great reward.

١٠ وَأَنَّ الَّذِينَ لَا يُؤْمِنُونَ بِالْآخِرَةِ أَعْتَدْنَا لَهُمْ عَذَابًا أَلِيمًا

10 And those who do not believe in the Hereafter—We have prepared for them a painful punishment.

١١ وَيَدْعُ الْإِنسَانُ بِالشَّرِّ دُعَاءَهُ بِالْخَيْرِ ۖ وَكَانَ الْإِنسَانُ عَجُولًا	11 10:11

11 The human being prays for evil as he prays for good. The human being is very hasty.

١٢ وَجَعَلْنَا اللَّيْلَ وَالنَّهَارَ آيَتَيْنِ ۖ فَمَحَوْنَا آيَةَ اللَّيْلِ وَجَعَلْنَا آيَةَ النَّهَارِ مُبْصِرَةً لِتَبْتَغُوا فَضْلًا مِنْ رَبِّكُمْ وَلِتَعْلَمُوا عَدَدَ السِّنِينَ وَالْحِسَابَ ۚ وَكُلَّ شَيْءٍ فَصَّلْنَاهُ تَفْصِيلًا	12 3:190; 10:5–6; 36:37; 41:37

12 We have made the night and the day two wonders. We erased the wonder of the night, and made the wonder of the day revealing, that you may seek bounty from your Lord, and know the number of years, and the calculation. We have explained all things in detail.

١٣ وَكُلَّ إِنسَانٍ أَلْزَمْنَاهُ طَائِرَهُ فِي عُنُقِهِ ۖ وَنُخْرِجُ لَهُ يَوْمَ الْقِيَامَةِ كِتَابًا يَلْقَاهُ مَنشُورًا	13–14 10:30; 18:49; 69:19– 23, 25–32; 81:10

13 For every person We have attached his fate to his neck. And on the Day of Resurrection, We will bring out for him a book which he will find spread open.

١٤ اقْرَأْ كِتَابَكَ كَفَىٰ بِنَفْسِكَ الْيَوْمَ عَلَيْكَ حَسِيبًا

14 "Read your book; today there will be none but yourself to call you to account."

١٥ مَنِ اهْتَدَىٰ فَإِنَّمَا يَهْتَدِي لِنَفْسِهِ ۖ وَمَنْ ضَلَّ فَإِنَّمَا يَضِلُّ عَلَيْهَا ۚ وَلَا تَزِرُ وَازِرَةٌ وِزْرَ أُخْرَىٰ [a] وَمَا كُنَّا مُعَذِّبِينَ حَتَّىٰ نَبْعَثَ رَسُولًا [b]	15 [a] 10:108; 6:104; 10:108; 30:44; 41:46 [b] 4:165; 20:208; 28:47

15 Whoever is guided—is guided for his own good. And whoever goes astray—goes astray to his detriment. No burdened soul carries the burdens of another, nor do We ever punish until We have sent a messenger.

١٦ وَإِذَا أَرَدْنَا أَن نُّهْلِكَ قَرْيَةً أَمَرْنَا مُتْرَفِيهَا فَفَسَقُوا فِيهَا فَحَقَّ عَلَيْهَا الْقَوْلُ فَدَمَّرْنَاهَا تَدْمِيرًا

16 When We decide to destroy a town, We command its affluent ones, they transgress in it, so the word becomes justified against it, and We destroy it completely.

16
34:34–35

١٧ وَكَمْ أَهْلَكْنَا مِنَ الْقُرُونِ مِن بَعْدِ نُوحٍ ۗ وَكَفَىٰ بِرَبِّكَ بِذُنُوبِ عِبَادِهِ خَبِيرًا بَصِيرًا

17 How many generations have We destroyed after Noah? Your Lord is sufficient as Knower and Beholder of the sins of his servants.

17
19:74, 98; 20:128; 32:26; 38:3; 44:37

١٨ مَّن كَانَ يُرِيدُ الْعَاجِلَةَ عَجَّلْنَا لَهُ فِيهَا مَا نَشَاءُ لِمَن نُّرِيدُ ثُمَّ جَعَلْنَا لَهُ جَهَنَّمَ يَصْلَاهَا مَذْمُومًا مَّدْحُورًا

18 Whoever desires the fleeting life, We expedite for him what We decide to give him, to whomever We desire. Then We consign him to Hell, where he will roast, condemned and defeated.

18
3:145

١٩ وَمَنْ أَرَادَ الْآخِرَةَ وَسَعَىٰ لَهَا سَعْيَهَا وَهُوَ مُؤْمِنٌ فَأُولَٰئِكَ كَانَ سَعْيُهُم مَّشْكُورًا

19 But whoever desires the Hereafter, and pursues it as it should be pursued, while he is a believer; these—their effort will be appreciated.

19
40:40

٢٠ كُلًّا نُّمِدُّ هَٰؤُلَاءِ وَهَٰؤُلَاءِ مِنْ عَطَاءِ رَبِّكَ ۚ وَمَا كَانَ عَطَاءُ رَبِّكَ مَحْظُورًا

20 To all—these and those—We extend from the gifts of your Lord. The gifts of your Lord are not restricted.

٢١ انظُرْ كَيْفَ فَضَّلْنَا بَعْضَهُمْ عَلَىٰ بَعْضٍ ۚ وَلَلْآخِرَةُ أَكْبَرُ دَرَجَاتٍ وَأَكْبَرُ تَفْضِيلًا

21 See how We have favored some of them over others; yet the Hereafter is greater in ranks, and greater in favors.

21
3:163; 16:71

٢٢ لَّا تَجْعَلْ مَعَ اللَّهِ إِلَٰهًا آخَرَ فَتَقْعُدَ مَذْمُومًا مَّخْذُولًا

22 Do not set up another god with God, lest you become condemned and damned.

22
17: 39

٢٣ وَقَضَىٰ رَبُّكَ أَلَّا تَعْبُدُوا إِلَّا إِيَّاهُ وَبِالْوَالِدَيْنِ إِحْسَانًا ۚ إِمَّا يَبْلُغَنَّ عِندَكَ الْكِبَرَ أَحَدُهُمَا أَوْ كِلَاهُمَا فَلَا تَقُل لَّهُمَا أُفٍّ وَلَا تَنْهَرْهُمَا وَقُل لَّهُمَا قَوْلًا كَرِيمًا

23 Your Lord has commanded that you worship none but Him, and that you be good to your parents. If either of them or both of them reach old age with you, do not say to them a word of disrespect, nor scold them, but say to them kind words.

23
2:83; 4:36; 29:8; 31:145; 45:17

٢٤ وَاخْفِضْ لَهُمَا جَنَاحَ الذُّلِّ مِنَ الرَّحْمَةِ وَقُل رَّبِّ ارْحَمْهُمَا كَمَا رَبَّيَانِي صَغِيرًا

24 And lower to them the wing of humility, out of mercy, and say, "My Lord, have mercy on them, as they raised me when I was a child."

24
15:88; 26:215

٢٥ رَّبُّكُمْ أَعْلَمُ بِمَا فِي نُفُوسِكُمْ ۚ إِن تَكُونُوا صَالِحِينَ فَإِنَّهُ كَانَ لِلْأَوَّابِينَ غَفُورًا

25 Your Lord knows best what is in your minds. If you are righteous—He is Forgiving to the obedient.

٢٦ وَآتِ ذَا الْقُرْبَىٰ حَقَّهُ وَالْمِسْكِينَ وَابْنَ السَّبِيلِ وَلَا تُبَذِّرْ تَبْذِيرًا	26	2:83; 4:36; 30:38

26 And give the relative his rights, and the poor, and the wayfarer, and do not squander wastefully.

٢٧ إِنَّ الْمُبَذِّرِينَ كَانُوا إِخْوَانَ الشَّيَاطِينِ ۖ وَكَانَ الشَّيْطَانُ لِرَبِّهِ كَفُورًا		

27 The extravagant are brethren of the devils, and the devil is ever ungrateful to his Lord.

٢٨ وَإِمَّا تُعْرِضَنَّ عَنْهُمُ ابْتِغَاءَ رَحْمَةٍ مِنْ رَبِّكَ تَرْجُوهَا فَقُلْ لَهُمْ قَوْلًا مَيْسُورًا	28	2:263

28 But if you turn away from them, seeking mercy from your Lord which you hope for, then say to them words of comfort.

٢٩ وَلَا تَجْعَلْ يَدَكَ مَغْلُولَةً إِلَىٰ عُنُقِكَ وَلَا تَبْسُطْهَا كُلَّ الْبَسْطِ فَتَقْعُدَ مَلُومًا مَحْسُورًا	29	5:64; 25:67

29 And do not keep your hand tied to your neck, nor spread it out fully, lest you end up liable and regretful.

٣٠ إِنَّ رَبَّكَ يَبْسُطُ الرِّزْقَ لِمَنْ يَشَاءُ وَيَقْدِرُ ۚ إِنَّهُ كَانَ بِعِبَادِهِ خَبِيرًا بَصِيرًا	30	13:26

30 Your Lord expands the provision for whomever He wills, and restricts it. He is fully Informed, Observant of His servants.

٣١ وَلَا تَقْتُلُوا أَوْلَادَكُمْ خَشْيَةَ إِمْلَاقٍ ۖ نَحْنُ نَرْزُقُهُمْ وَإِيَّاكُمْ ۚ إِنَّ قَتْلَهُمْ كَانَ خِطْئًا كَبِيرًا	31–32	6:151; 7:33

31 And do not kill your children for fear of poverty. We provide for them, and for you. Killing them is a grave sin.

٣٢ وَلَا تَقْرَبُوا الزِّنَا ۖ إِنَّهُ كَانَ فَاحِشَةً وَسَاءَ سَبِيلًا	

32 And do not come near adultery. It is immoral, and an evil way.

٣٣ وَلَا تَقْتُلُوا النَّفْسَ الَّتِي حَرَّمَ اللَّهُ إِلَّا بِالْحَقِّ ۗ وَمَنْ قُتِلَ مَظْلُومًا فَقَدْ جَعَلْنَا لِوَلِيِّهِ سُلْطَانًا فَلَا يُسْرِفْ فِي الْقَتْلِ ۖ إِنَّهُ كَانَ مَنْصُورًا	33	2:178; 6:151

33 And do not kill the soul which God has made sacred, except in the course of justice. If someone is killed unjustly, We have given his next of kin certain authority. But he should not be excessive in killing, for he will be supported.

٣٤ وَلَا تَقْرَبُوا مَالَ الْيَتِيمِ إِلَّا بِالَّتِي هِيَ أَحْسَنُ حَتَّىٰ يَبْلُغَ أَشُدَّهُ ۚ وَأَوْفُوا بِالْعَهْدِ ۖ إِنَّ الْعَهْدَ كَانَ مَسْئُولًا	34	4:2, 6, 10, 127; 6:152

34 And do not go near the orphan's property, except with the best of intentions, until he has reached his maturity. And honor your pledge, because the pledge involves responsibility.

٣٥ وَأَوْفُوا الْكَيْلَ إِذَا كِلْتُمْ وَزِنُوا بِالْقِسْطَاسِ الْمُسْتَقِيمِ ۚ ذَٰلِكَ خَيْرٌ وَأَحْسَنُ تَأْوِيلًا	35	26:181

35 And give full measure when you measure, and weigh with accurate scales. That is fair, and the best determination.

٣٦ وَلَا تَقْفُ مَا لَيْسَ لَكَ بِهِ عِلْمٌ ۚ إِنَّ السَّمْعَ وَالْبَصَرَ وَالْفُؤَادَ كُلُّ أُولَٰئِكَ كَانَ عَنْهُ مَسْئُولًا	

36 And do not occupy yourself with what you have no knowledge of. The hearing, and the sight, and the brains—all these will be questioned.

٣٧ وَلَا تَمْشِ فِي الْأَرْضِ مَرَحًا ۖ إِنَّكَ لَن تَخْرِقَ الْأَرْضَ وَلَن تَبْلُغَ الْجِبَالَ طُولًا

37 And do not walk proudly on earth. You can neither pierce the earth, nor can you match the mountains in height.

37
31:18; 40:75; 57:23

٣٨ كُلُّ ذَٰلِكَ كَانَ سَيِّئُهُ عِندَ رَبِّكَ مَكْرُوهًا

38 The evil of all these is disliked by your Lord.

٣٩ ذَٰلِكَ مِمَّا أَوْحَىٰ إِلَيْكَ رَبُّكَ مِنَ الْحِكْمَةِ ۗ وَلَا تَجْعَلْ مَعَ اللَّهِ إِلَٰهًا آخَرَ فَتُلْقَىٰ فِي جَهَنَّمَ مَلُومًا مَّدْحُورًا

39 That is some of the wisdom your Lord has revealed to you. Do not set up with God another god, or else you will be thrown in Hell, rebuked and banished.

39
17: 22

٤٠ أَفَأَصْفَاكُمْ رَبُّكُم بِالْبَنِينَ وَاتَّخَذَ مِنَ الْمَلَائِكَةِ إِنَاثًا ۚ إِنَّكُمْ لَتَقُولُونَ قَوْلًا عَظِيمًا

40 Has your Lord favored you with sons, while choosing for Himself daughters from among the angels? You are indeed saying a terrible thing.

40
4:171; 6:100; 10:68;
37:149–153; 43:16–19;
17:111; 43:16

٤١ وَلَقَدْ صَرَّفْنَا فِي هَٰذَا الْقُرْآنِ لِيَذَّكَّرُوا وَمَا يَزِيدُهُمْ إِلَّا نُفُورًا

41 We have explained in this Qur'an in various ways, that they may remember, but it only adds to their rebellion.

41
17:89; 18:54; 20:113

٤٢ قُل لَّوْ كَانَ مَعَهُ آلِهَةٌ كَمَا يَقُولُونَ إِذًا لَّابْتَغَوْا إِلَىٰ ذِي الْعَرْشِ سَبِيلًا

42 Say, "If there were other gods with Him, as they say, they would have sought a way to the Lord of the Throne."

42
17:75; 21:22

٤٣ سُبْحَانَهُ وَتَعَالَىٰ عَمَّا يَقُولُونَ عُلُوًّا كَبِيرًا

43 Be He glorified. He is exalted, far above what they say.

43
10:18; 16:1; 30:40;
39:67

٤٤ تُسَبِّحُ لَهُ السَّمَاوَاتُ السَّبْعُ وَالْأَرْضُ وَمَن فِيهِنَّ ۚ وَإِن مِّن شَيْءٍ إِلَّا يُسَبِّحُ بِحَمْدِهِ وَلَٰكِن لَّا تَفْقَهُونَ تَسْبِيحَهُمْ ۗ إِنَّهُ كَانَ حَلِيمًا غَفُورًا

44 Praising Him are the seven heavens, and the earth, and everyone in them. There is not a thing that does not glorify Him with praise, but you do not understand their praises. He is indeed Forbearing and Forgiving.

44
24:41; 59:24

٤٥ وَإِذَا قَرَأْتَ الْقُرْآنَ جَعَلْنَا بَيْنَكَ وَبَيْنَ الَّذِينَ لَا يُؤْمِنُونَ بِالْآخِرَةِ حِجَابًا مَّسْتُورًا

45 When you read the Qur'an, We place between you and those who do not believe in the Hereafter an invisible barrier.

45
31:7; 36:9; 41:4

٤٦ وَجَعَلْنَا عَلَىٰ قُلُوبِهِمْ أَكِنَّةً أَن يَفْقَهُوهُ وَفِي آذَانِهِمْ وَقْرًا ۚ وَإِذَا ذَكَرْتَ رَبَّكَ فِي الْقُرْآنِ وَحْدَهُ وَلَّوْا عَلَىٰ أَدْبَارِهِمْ نُفُورًا

46 And We drape veils over their hearts, preventing them from understanding it, and heaviness in their ears. And when you mention your Lord alone in the Qur'an, they turn their backs in aversion.

46
6:25; 18:57; 41:5;
40:12

٤٧ نَحْنُ أَعْلَمُ بِمَا يَسْتَمِعُونَ بِهِ إِذْ يَسْتَمِعُونَ إِلَيْكَ وَإِذْ هُمْ نَجْوَىٰ إِذْ يَقُولُ الظَّالِمُونَ إِن تَتَّبِعُونَ إِلَّا رَجُلًا مَّسْحُورًا

47 21:2

47 We know well what they listen to, when they listen to you, as they conspire, when the wrongdoers say, "You only follow a man bewitched."

٤٨ انظُرْ كَيْفَ ضَرَبُوا لَكَ الْأَمْثَالَ فَضَلُّوا فَلَا يَسْتَطِيعُونَ سَبِيلًا

48 Note what they compared you to. They are lost, and unable to find a way.

٤٩ وَقَالُوا أَإِذَا كُنَّا عِظَامًا وَرُفَاتًا أَإِنَّا لَمَبْعُوثُونَ خَلْقًا جَدِيدًا

49 13:5; 17:98

49 And they say, "When we have become bones and fragments, shall we really be resurrected as a new creation?"

٥٠ قُلْ كُونُوا حِجَارَةً أَوْ حَدِيدًا

50 10:4; 36:78

50 Say, "Even if you become rocks or iron.

٥١ أَوْ خَلْقًا مِّمَّا يَكْبُرُ فِي صُدُورِكُمْ ۚ فَسَيَقُولُونَ مَن يُعِيدُنَا ۖ قُلِ الَّذِي فَطَرَكُمْ أَوَّلَ مَرَّةٍ ۚ فَسَيُنْغِضُونَ إِلَيْكَ رُءُوسَهُمْ وَيَقُولُونَ مَتَىٰ هُوَ ۖ قُلْ عَسَىٰ أَن يَكُونَ قَرِيبًا

51 Or some substance, which, in your minds, is even harder." Then they will say, "Who will restore us?" Say, "The One who originated you the first time." Then they will nod their heads at you, and say, "When will it be?" Say, "Perhaps it will be soon."

٥٢ يَوْمَ يَدْعُوكُمْ فَتَسْتَجِيبُونَ بِحَمْدِهِ وَتَظُنُّونَ إِن لَّبِثْتُمْ إِلَّا قَلِيلًا

52 On the Day when He calls you, you will respond with His praise, and you will realize that you stayed only a little.

٥٣ وَقُل لِّعِبَادِي يَقُولُوا الَّتِي هِيَ أَحْسَنُ ۚ إِنَّ الشَّيْطَانَ يَنزَغُ بَيْنَهُمْ ۚ إِنَّ الشَّيْطَانَ كَانَ لِلْإِنسَانِ عَدُوًّا مُّبِينًا

53 7:22, 200

53 Tell My servants to say what is best. Satan sows discord among them. Satan is to man an open enemy.

٥٤ رَّبُّكُمْ أَعْلَمُ بِكُمْ ۖ إِن يَشَأْ يَرْحَمْكُمْ أَوْ إِن يَشَأْ يُعَذِّبْكُمْ ۚ وَمَا أَرْسَلْنَاكَ عَلَيْهِمْ وَكِيلًا

54 2:284; 3:129; 29:21

54 Your Lord knows you best. If He wills, He will have mercy on you; and if He wills, He will punish you. We did not send you as their advocate.

٥٥ وَرَبُّكَ أَعْلَمُ بِمَن فِي السَّمَاوَاتِ وَالْأَرْضِ ۗ وَلَقَدْ فَضَّلْنَا بَعْضَ النَّبِيِّينَ عَلَىٰ بَعْضٍ ۖ وَآتَيْنَا دَاوُودَ زَبُورًا

55 2:253; 27:15

55 Your Lord knows well everyone in the heavens and the earth. We have given some prophets advantage over others; and to David We gave the Psalms.

٥٦ قُلِ ادْعُوا الَّذِينَ زَعَمْتُم مِّن دُونِهِ فَلَا يَمْلِكُونَ كَشْفَ الضُّرِّ عَنكُمْ وَلَا تَحْوِيلًا

56 34:22; 39:38

56 Say, "Call upon those you claim besides Him. They have no power to relieve your adversity, nor can they change it."

٥٧ أُولَٰئِكَ الَّذِينَ يَدْعُونَ يَبْتَغُونَ إِلَىٰ رَبِّهِمُ الْوَسِيلَةَ أَيُّهُمْ أَقْرَبُ وَيَرْجُونَ رَحْمَتَهُ وَيَخَافُونَ عَذَابَهُ ۚ إِنَّ عَذَابَ رَبِّكَ كَانَ مَحْذُورًا

57 5:35

57 Those they call upon are themselves seeking means of access to their Lord, vying to be nearer, and hoping for His mercy, and fearing His punishment. The punishment of your Lord is to be dreaded.

٥٨ وَإِنْ مِنْ قَرْيَةٍ إِلَّا نَحْنُ مُهْلِكُوهَا قَبْلَ يَوْمِ الْقِيَامَةِ أَوْ مُعَذِّبُوهَا عَذَابًا شَدِيدًا ۚ كَانَ ذَٰلِكَ فِي الْكِتَابِ مَسْطُورًا

58 6:131; 11:17; 28:59; 65:8–9

58 There is no city but We will destroy before the Day of Resurrection, or punish it with a severe punishment. This is inscribed in the Book.

٥٩ وَمَا مَنَعَنَا أَنْ نُرْسِلَ بِالْآيَاتِ إِلَّا أَنْ كَذَّبَ بِهَا الْأَوَّلُونَ ۚ وَآتَيْنَا ثَمُودَ النَّاقَةَ مُبْصِرَةً فَظَلَمُوا بِهَا ۚ وَمَا نُرْسِلُ بِالْآيَاتِ إِلَّا تَخْوِيفًا

59 7:73, 77

59 Nothing prevents Us from sending miraculous signs, except that the ancients called them lies. We gave Thamood the she-camel, a visible sign, but they mistreated her. We do not send the signs except to instill reverence.

٦٠ وَإِذْ قُلْنَا لَكَ إِنَّ رَبَّكَ أَحَاطَ بِالنَّاسِ ۚ وَمَا جَعَلْنَا الرُّؤْيَا الَّتِي أَرَيْنَاكَ إِلَّا فِتْنَةً لِلنَّاسِ وَالشَّجَرَةَ الْمَلْعُونَةَ فِي الْقُرْآنِ ۚ وَنُخَوِّفُهُمْ فَمَا يَزِيدُهُمْ إِلَّا طُغْيَانًا كَبِيرًا

60 37:62

60 We said to you that your Lord encompasses humanity. We did not make the vision We showed you, except as a test for the people, and the tree cursed in the Qur'an. We frighten them, but that only increases their defiance.

٦١ وَإِذْ قُلْنَا لِلْمَلَائِكَةِ اسْجُدُوا لِآدَمَ فَسَجَدُوا إِلَّا إِبْلِيسَ قَالَ أَأَسْجُدُ لِمَنْ خَلَقْتَ طِينًا

61 2:34; 7:11; 15:26; 38:71

61 When We said to the angels, "Bow down before Adam," they bowed down, except for Satan. He said, "Shall I bow down before someone You created from mud?"

٦٢ قَالَ أَرَأَيْتَكَ هَٰذَا الَّذِي كَرَّمْتَ عَلَيَّ لَئِنْ أَخَّرْتَنِ إِلَىٰ يَوْمِ الْقِيَامَةِ لَأَحْتَنِكَنَّ ذُرِّيَّتَهُ إِلَّا قَلِيلًا

62 7:16; 15:39

62 He said, "Do You see this one whom You have honored more than me? If You reprieve me until the Day of Resurrection, I will bring his descendants under my sway, except for a few."

٦٣ قَالَ اذْهَبْ فَمَنْ تَبِعَكَ مِنْهُمْ فَإِنَّ جَهَنَّمَ جَزَاؤُكُمْ جَزَاءً مَوْفُورًا

63 7:18; 15:41–43; 38:84–85

63 He said, "Begone! Whoever of them follows you—Hell is your reward, an ample reward."

٦٤ وَاسْتَفْزِزْ مَنِ اسْتَطَعْتَ مِنْهُمْ بِصَوْتِكَ وَأَجْلِبْ عَلَيْهِمْ بِخَيْلِكَ وَرَجِلِكَ وَشَارِكْهُمْ فِي الْأَمْوَالِ وَالْأَوْلَادِ وَعِدْهُمْ ۚ وَمَا يَعِدُهُمُ الشَّيْطَانُ إِلَّا غُرُورًا

64 "And entice whomever of them you can with your voice, and rally against them your cavalry and your infantry, and share with them in wealth and children, and make promises to them." But Satan promises them nothing but delusion.

٦٥ إِنَّ عِبَادِي لَيْسَ لَكَ عَلَيْهِمْ سُلْطَانٌ ۚ وَكَفَىٰ بِرَبِّكَ وَكِيلًا

65 7:18; 15:42; 38:85

65 "As for My devotees, you have no authority over them." Your Lord is an adequate Guardian.

٦٦ رَبُّكُمُ الَّذِي يُزْجِي لَكُمُ الْفُلْكَ فِي الْبَحْرِ لِتَبْتَغُوا مِنْ فَضْلِهِ ۚ إِنَّهُ كَانَ بِكُمْ رَحِيمًا

66 16:4; 35:12

66 Your Lord is He who propels for you the ships at sea, that you may seek of His bounty. He is towards you Most Merciful.

٦٧ وَإِذَا مَسَّكُمُ الضُّرُّ فِي الْبَحْرِ ضَلَّ مَنْ تَدْعُونَ إِلَّا إِيَّاهُ ۖ فَلَمَّا نَجَّاكُمْ إِلَى الْبَرِّ أَعْرَضْتُمْ ۚ وَكَانَ الْإِنْسَانُ كَفُورًا

67 29:65

67 When harm afflicts you at sea, those you pray to vanish, except for Him. But when He saves you to land, you turn away. The human being is ever thankless.

٦٨ أَفَأَمِنْتُمْ أَنْ يَخْسِفَ بِكُمْ جَانِبَ الْبَرِّ أَوْ يُرْسِلَ عَلَيْكُمْ حَاصِبًا ثُمَّ لَا تَجِدُوا لَكُمْ وَكِيلًا

68 34:9; 67:16

68 Are you confident that He will not cause a track of land to cave in beneath you, or unleash a tornado against you, and then you find no protector?

٦٩ أَمْ أَمِنْتُمْ أَنْ يُعِيدَكُمْ فِيهِ تَارَةً أُخْرَىٰ فَيُرْسِلَ عَلَيْكُمْ قَاصِفًا مِنَ الرِّيحِ فَيُغْرِقَكُمْ بِمَا كَفَرْتُمْ ۙ ثُمَّ لَا تَجِدُوا لَكُمْ عَلَيْنَا بِهِ تَبِيعًا

69 Or are you confident that He will not return you to it once again, and unleash a hurricane against you, and drown you for your ingratitude? Then you will find no helper against Us.

٧٠ وَلَقَدْ كَرَّمْنَا بَنِي آدَمَ وَحَمَلْنَاهُمْ فِي الْبَرِّ وَالْبَحْرِ وَرَزَقْنَاهُمْ مِنَ الطَّيِّبَاتِ وَفَضَّلْنَاهُمْ عَلَىٰ كَثِيرٍ مِمَّنْ خَلَقْنَا تَفْضِيلًا

70 10:22; 23:22; 43:12

70 We have honored the Children of Adam, and carried them on land and sea, and provided them with good things, and greatly favored them over many of those We created.

٧١ يَوْمَ نَدْعُو كُلَّ أُنَاسٍ بِإِمَامِهِمْ ۖ فَمَنْ أُوتِيَ كِتَابَهُ بِيَمِينِهِ فَأُولَٰئِكَ يَقْرَءُونَ كِتَابَهُمْ وَلَا يُظْلَمُونَ فَتِيلًا

71 15:79; 36:12; 45:28; 69:19–24; 84:7–9

71 On the Day when We call every people with their leader. Whoever is given his record in his right hand—these will read their record, and they will not be wronged one bit.

٧٢ وَمَنْ كَانَ فِي هَٰذِهِ أَعْمَىٰ فَهُوَ فِي الْآخِرَةِ أَعْمَىٰ وَأَضَلُّ سَبِيلًا

72 22:46

72 But whoever is blind in this, he will be blind in the Hereafter, and further astray from the way.

٧٣ وَإِنْ كَادُوا لَيَفْتِنُونَكَ عَنِ الَّذِي أَوْحَيْنَا إِلَيْكَ لِتَفْتَرِيَ عَلَيْنَا غَيْرَهُ ۖ وَإِذًا لَاتَّخَذُوكَ خَلِيلًا

73 5:49; 10:15

73 They almost lured you away from what We have revealed to you, so that you would invent something else in Our name. In that case, they would have taken you for a friend.

٧٤ وَلَوْلَا أَنْ ثَبَّتْنَاكَ لَقَدْ كِدْتَ تَرْكَنُ إِلَيْهِمْ شَيْئًا قَلِيلًا

74 Had We not given you stability, you might have inclined towards them a little.

74
11:113

٧٥ إِذًا لَأَذَقْنَاكَ ضِعْفَ الْحَيَاةِ وَضِعْفَ الْمَمَاتِ ثُمَّ لَا تَجِدُ لَكَ عَلَيْنَا نَصِيرًا

75 Then We would have made you taste double in life, and double at death; then you would have found for yourself no helper against Us.

75
17:42

٧٦ وَإِنْ كَادُوا لَيَسْتَفِزُّونَكَ مِنَ الْأَرْضِ لِيُخْرِجُوكَ مِنْهَا ۖ وَإِذًا لَا يَلْبَثُونَ خِلَافَكَ إِلَّا قَلِيلًا

76 They almost provoked you, to expel you from the land. In that case, they would not have lasted after you, except briefly.

76
8:30; 14:13; 17:103

٧٧ سُنَّةَ مَنْ قَدْ أَرْسَلْنَا قَبْلَكَ مِنْ رُسُلِنَا ۖ وَلَا تَجِدُ لِسُنَّتِنَا تَحْوِيلًا

77 The tradition of the messengers We sent before you—you will find no change in Our rules.

77
3:137; 8:38; 33:62; 35:43

٧٨ أَقِمِ الصَّلَاةَ لِدُلُوكِ الشَّمْسِ إِلَىٰ غَسَقِ اللَّيْلِ وَقُرْآنَ الْفَجْرِ ۖ إِنَّ قُرْآنَ الْفَجْرِ كَانَ مَشْهُودًا

78 Perform the prayer at the decline of the sun, until the darkness of the night; and the Qur'an at dawn. The Qur'an at dawn is witnessed.

78
4:103; 11:114

٧٩ وَمِنَ اللَّيْلِ فَتَهَجَّدْ بِهِ نَافِلَةً لَكَ عَسَىٰ أَنْ يَبْعَثَكَ رَبُّكَ مَقَامًا مَحْمُودًا

79 And keep vigil with it during parts of the night, as an extra prayer. Perhaps your Lord will raise you to a laudable position.

٨٠ وَقُلْ رَبِّ أَدْخِلْنِي مُدْخَلَ صِدْقٍ وَأَخْرِجْنِي مُخْرَجَ صِدْقٍ وَاجْعَلْ لِي مِنْ لَدُنْكَ سُلْطَانًا نَصِيرًا

80 And say, "My Lord, lead me in through an entry of truth, and lead me out through an exit of truth, and grant me from You a supporting power."

٨١ وَقُلْ جَاءَ الْحَقُّ وَزَهَقَ الْبَاطِلُ ۚ إِنَّ الْبَاطِلَ كَانَ زَهُوقًا

81 And say, "The truth has come, and falsehood has withered away; for falsehood is bound to wither away."

81
8:8; 21:18; 34:49; 42:24

٨٢ وَنُنَزِّلُ مِنَ الْقُرْآنِ مَا هُوَ شِفَاءٌ وَرَحْمَةٌ لِلْمُؤْمِنِينَ ۙ وَلَا يَزِيدُ الظَّالِمِينَ إِلَّا خَسَارًا

82 We send down in the Qur'an healing and mercy for the believers, but it increases the wrongdoers only in loss.

82
3:138; 10:57; 11:120; 24:34; 41:44

٨٣ وَإِذَا أَنْعَمْنَا عَلَى الْإِنْسَانِ أَعْرَضَ وَنَأَىٰ بِجَانِبِهِ ۖ وَإِذَا مَسَّهُ الشَّرُّ كَانَ يَئُوسًا

83 When We bless the human being, he turns away and distances himself. But when adversity touches him, he is in despair.

83
10:12; 11:9; 30:33; 39:41; 41:49, 51

٨٤ قُلْ كُلٌّ يَعْمَلُ عَلَىٰ شَاكِلَتِهِ فَرَبُّكُمْ أَعْلَمُ بِمَنْ هُوَ أَهْدَىٰ سَبِيلًا

84 Say, "Each does according to his disposition. Your Lord knows best who is better guided in the way."

٨٥ وَيَسْأَلُونَكَ عَنِ الرُّوحِ ۖ قُلِ الرُّوحُ مِنْ أَمْرِ رَبِّي وَمَا أُوتِيتُمْ مِنَ الْعِلْمِ إِلَّا قَلِيلًا

85 And they ask you about the Spirit. Say, "The Spirit belongs to the domain of my Lord; and you were given only little knowledge."

85
16:2

Sūrah 17: Al-Isrā' — 303

٨٦ وَلَئِن شِئْنَا لَنَذْهَبَنَّ بِالَّذِي أَوْحَيْنَا إِلَيْكَ ثُمَّ لَا تَجِدُ لَكَ بِهِ عَلَيْنَا وَكِيلًا

86 17:69

86 If We willed, We could take away what We revealed to you. Then you will find for yourself no protecting guardian against Us.

٨٧ إِلَّا رَحْمَةً مِّن رَّبِّكَ ۚ إِنَّ فَضْلَهُ كَانَ عَلَيْكَ كَبِيرًا

87 28:46, 86; 44:5

87 Except through a mercy from your Lord. His favors upon you have been great.

٨٨ قُل لَّئِنِ اجْتَمَعَتِ الْإِنسُ وَالْجِنُّ عَلَىٰ أَن يَأْتُوا بِمِثْلِ هَٰذَا الْقُرْآنِ لَا يَأْتُونَ بِمِثْلِهِ وَلَوْ كَانَ بَعْضُهُمْ لِبَعْضٍ ظَهِيرًا

88 2:23; 10:37; 11:13

88 Say, "If mankind and jinn came together to produce the like of this Qur'an, they could never produce the like of it, even if they backed up one another."

٨٩ وَلَقَدْ صَرَّفْنَا لِلنَّاسِ فِي هَٰذَا الْقُرْآنِ مِن كُلِّ مَثَلٍ فَأَبَىٰ أَكْثَرُ النَّاسِ إِلَّا كُفُورًا

89 17:41; 18:54; 20:113; 47:3

89 We have displayed for mankind in this Qur'an every kind of similitude, but most people insist on denying the truth.

٩٠ وَقَالُوا لَن نُّؤْمِنَ لَكَ حَتَّىٰ تَفْجُرَ لَنَا مِنَ الْأَرْضِ يَنبُوعًا

90

90 And they said, "We will not believe in you unless you make a spring burst from the ground for us.

٩١ أَوْ تَكُونَ لَكَ جَنَّةٌ مِّن نَّخِيلٍ وَعِنَبٍ فَتُفَجِّرَ الْأَنْهَارَ خِلَالَهَا تَفْجِيرًا

91 25:8

91 Or you have a garden of palms and vines; then cause rivers to gush pouring through them.

٩٢ أَوْ تُسْقِطَ السَّمَاءَ كَمَا زَعَمْتَ عَلَيْنَا كِسَفًا أَوْ تَأْتِيَ بِاللَّهِ وَالْمَلَائِكَةِ قَبِيلًا

92 26:187; 34:9

92 Or make the sky fall on us in pieces, as you claim, or bring God and the angels before us.

٩٣ أَوْ يَكُونَ لَكَ بَيْتٌ مِّن زُخْرُفٍ أَوْ تَرْقَىٰ فِي السَّمَاءِ وَلَن نُّؤْمِنَ لِرُقِيِّكَ حَتَّىٰ تُنَزِّلَ عَلَيْنَا كِتَابًا نَّقْرَؤُهُ ۗ قُلْ سُبْحَانَ رَبِّي هَلْ كُنتُ إِلَّا بَشَرًا رَّسُولًا

93 43:33–35

93 Or you possess a house of gold. Or you ascend into the sky. Even then, we will not believe in your ascension, unless you bring down for us a book that we can read." Say, "Glory be to my Lord. Am I anything but a human messenger?"

٩٤ وَمَا مَنَعَ النَّاسَ أَن يُؤْمِنُوا إِذْ جَاءَهُمُ الْهُدَىٰ إِلَّا أَن قَالُوا أَبَعَثَ اللَّهُ بَشَرًا رَّسُولًا

94 14:10; 23:34, 47; 25:20; 54:24; 64:6

94 Nothing prevented the people from believing, when guidance has come to them, except that they said, "Did God send a human messenger?"

٩٥ قُل لَّوْ كَانَ فِي الْأَرْضِ مَلَائِكَةٌ يَمْشُونَ مُطْمَئِنِّينَ لَنَزَّلْنَا عَلَيْهِم مِّنَ السَّمَاءِ مَلَكًا رَّسُولًا

95 6:8; 15:7; 21:7; 25:20–21

95 Say, "If there were angels on earth, walking around in peace, We would have sent down to them from heaven an angel messenger."

٩٦ قُلْ كَفَىٰ بِاللَّهِ شَهِيدًا بَيْنِي وَبَيْنَكُمْ ۚ إِنَّهُ كَانَ بِعِبَادِهِ خَبِيرًا بَصِيرًا

96 Say, "God is enough witness between you and me. He is fully aware of His servants, and He sees them well."

96
13:43

٩٧ وَمَنْ يَهْدِ اللَّهُ فَهُوَ الْمُهْتَدِ ۖ وَمَنْ يُضْلِلْ فَلَنْ تَجِدَ لَهُمْ أَوْلِيَاءَ مِنْ دُونِهِ ۖ وَنَحْشُرُهُمْ يَوْمَ الْقِيَامَةِ عَلَىٰ وُجُوهِهِمْ عُمْيًا وَبُكْمًا وَصُمًّا ۖ مَأْوَاهُمْ جَهَنَّمُ ۖ كُلَّمَا خَبَتْ زِدْنَاهُمْ سَعِيرًا

97 Whomever God guides is the guided one. And whomever He leaves astray—for them you will find no protectors apart from Him. And We will gather them on the Day of Resurrection, on their faces, blind, dumb, and deaf. Their abode is Hell; whenever it abates, We intensify the blaze for them.

97
7:178; 18:17; 39:36

٩٨ ذَٰلِكَ جَزَاؤُهُمْ بِأَنَّهُمْ كَفَرُوا بِآيَاتِنَا وَقَالُوا أَإِذَا كُنَّا عِظَامًا وَرُفَاتًا أَإِنَّا لَمَبْعُوثُونَ خَلْقًا جَدِيدًا

98 This is their repayment for having blasphemed against Our revelations, and having said, "Shall we, when we have become bones and fragments, be resurrected as a new creation?"

98
13:5; 17:49; 23:82;
37:12–17; 56:47

٩٩ أَوَلَمْ يَرَوْا أَنَّ اللَّهَ الَّذِي خَلَقَ السَّمَاوَاتِ وَالْأَرْضَ قَادِرٌ عَلَىٰ أَنْ يَخْلُقَ مِثْلَهُمْ وَجَعَلَ لَهُمْ أَجَلًا لَا رَيْبَ فِيهِ فَأَبَى الظَّالِمُونَ إِلَّا كُفُورًا

99 Do they not consider that God, Who created the heavens and the earth, is Able to create the likes of them? He has assigned for them a term, in which there is no doubt. But the wrongdoers persist in denying the truth.

99
36:81

١٠٠ قُلْ لَوْ أَنْتُمْ تَمْلِكُونَ خَزَائِنَ رَحْمَةِ رَبِّي إِذًا لَأَمْسَكْتُمْ خَشْيَةَ الْإِنْفَاقِ ۚ وَكَانَ الْإِنْسَانُ قَتُورًا

100 Say, "If you possessed the treasuries of my Lord's mercy, you would have withheld them for fear of spending." The human being has always been stingy.

100
70:19–22

١٠١ وَلَقَدْ آتَيْنَا مُوسَىٰ تِسْعَ آيَاتٍ بَيِّنَاتٍ ۖ فَاسْأَلْ بَنِي إِسْرَائِيلَ إِذْ جَاءَهُمْ فَقَالَ لَهُ فِرْعَوْنُ إِنِّي لَأَظُنُّكَ يَا مُوسَىٰ مَسْحُورًا

101 We gave Moses nine clear signs—ask the Children of Israel. When he went to them, Pharaoh said to him, "I think that you, Moses, are bewitched."

101
2:211; 7:103; 27:12

١٠٢ قَالَ لَقَدْ عَلِمْتَ مَا أَنْزَلَ هَٰؤُلَاءِ إِلَّا رَبُّ السَّمَاوَاتِ وَالْأَرْضِ بَصَائِرَ وَإِنِّي لَأَظُنُّكَ يَا فِرْعَوْنُ مَثْبُورًا

102 He said, "You know that none sent these down except the Lord of the heavens and the earth—eye openers; and I think that you, Pharaoh, are doomed."

١٠٣ فَأَرَادَ أَنْ يَسْتَفِزَّهُمْ مِنَ الْأَرْضِ فَأَغْرَقْنَاهُ وَمَنْ مَعَهُ جَمِيعًا

103 He resolved to scare them off the land, but We drowned him, and those with him, altogether.

١٠٤ وَقُلْنَا مِنْ بَعْدِهِ لِبَنِي إِسْرَائِيلَ اسْكُنُوا الْأَرْضَ فَإِذَا جَاءَ وَعْدُ الْآخِرَةِ جِئْنَا بِكُمْ لَفِيفًا	**104** 8:30; 14:14; 17:76

104 After him, We said to the Children of Israel, "Inhabit the land, and when the promise of the Hereafter arrives, We will bring you all together."

١٠٥ وَبِالْحَقِّ أَنْزَلْنَاهُ وَبِالْحَقِّ نَزَلَ ۗ وَمَا أَرْسَلْنَاكَ إِلَّا مُبَشِّرًا وَنَذِيرًا	**105** 10:94

105 With the truth We sent it down, and with the truth it descended. We sent you only as a bearer of good news and a warner.

١٠٦ وَقُرْآنًا فَرَقْنَاهُ لِتَقْرَأَهُ عَلَى النَّاسِ عَلَىٰ مُكْثٍ وَنَزَّلْنَاهُ تَنْزِيلًا	**106** 25:32; 44:4; 73:4

106 A Qur'an which We unfolded gradually, that you may recite to the people over time. And We revealed it in stages.

١٠٧ قُلْ آمِنُوا بِهِ أَوْ لَا تُؤْمِنُوا ۚ إِنَّ الَّذِينَ أُوتُوا الْعِلْمَ مِنْ قَبْلِهِ إِذَا يُتْلَىٰ عَلَيْهِمْ يَخِرُّونَ لِلْأَذْقَانِ سُجَّدًا	**107–109** 5:82; 28:52

107 Say, "Believe in it, or do not believe." Those who were given knowledge before it, when it is recited to them, they fall to their chins, prostrating.

١٠٨ وَيَقُولُونَ سُبْحَانَ رَبِّنَا إِنْ كَانَ وَعْدُ رَبِّنَا لَمَفْعُولًا

108 And they say, "Glory to our Lord. The promise of our Lord is fulfilled."

١٠٩ وَيَخِرُّونَ لِلْأَذْقَانِ يَبْكُونَ وَيَزِيدُهُمْ خُشُوعًا ۩

109 And they fall to their chins, weeping, and it adds to their humility.

١١٠ قُلِ ادْعُوا اللَّهَ أَوِ ادْعُوا الرَّحْمَٰنَ ۖ أَيًّا مَا تَدْعُوا فَلَهُ الْأَسْمَاءُ الْحُسْنَىٰ ۚ وَلَا تَجْهَرْ بِصَلَاتِكَ وَلَا تُخَافِتْ بِهَا وَابْتَغِ بَيْنَ ذَٰلِكَ سَبِيلًا	**110** 7:180; 20:8; 25:60; 55:1–4; 59:22–23

110 Say, "Call Him God, or call Him the Most Merciful. Whichever name you use, to Him belong the Best Names." And be neither loud in your prayer, nor silent in it, but follow a course in between.

١١١ وَقُلِ الْحَمْدُ لِلَّهِ الَّذِي لَمْ يَتَّخِذْ وَلَدًا وَلَمْ يَكُنْ لَهُ شَرِيكٌ فِي الْمُلْكِ وَلَمْ يَكُنْ لَهُ وَلِيٌّ مِنَ الذُّلِّ ۖ وَكَبِّرْهُ تَكْبِيرًا	**111** 2:116; 4:171; 6:101; 10:68; 17:40; 19:35; 23:91; 25:2; 72:3

111 And say, "Praise be to God, who has not begotten a son, nor has He a partner in sovereignty, nor has He an ally out of weakness, and glorify Him constantly."

Sūrah 18: Al-Kahf

سُورَةُ ٱلْكَهْفِ (The Cave)

بِسْمِ ٱللَّهِ ٱلرَّحْمَٰنِ ٱلرَّحِيمِ

١ ٱلْحَمْدُ لِلَّهِ ٱلَّذِي أَنزَلَ عَلَىٰ عَبْدِهِ ٱلْكِتَٰبَ وَلَمْ يَجْعَل لَّهُ عِوَجَا

1 Praise be to God, who revealed the Book to His servant, and allowed in it no distortion.

1 39:27–28

٢ قَيِّمًا لِّيُنذِرَ بَأْسًا شَدِيدًا مِّن لَّدُنْهُ وَيُبَشِّرَ ٱلْمُؤْمِنِينَ ٱلَّذِينَ يَعْمَلُونَ ٱلصَّٰلِحَٰتِ أَنَّ لَهُمْ أَجْرًا حَسَنًا

2 Valuable—to warn of severe punishment from Himself; and to deliver good news to the believers who do righteous deeds, that they will have an excellent reward.

2 17:9; 19:97; 98:1

٣ مَّٰكِثِينَ فِيهِ أَبَدًا

3 In which they will abide forever.

٤ وَيُنذِرَ ٱلَّذِينَ قَالُوا ٱتَّخَذَ ٱللَّهُ وَلَدًا

4 And to warn those who say, "God has begotten a son."

4–5 17:39–40; 19:88

٥ مَّا لَهُم بِهِۦ مِنْ عِلْمٍ وَلَا لِءَابَائِهِمْ كَبُرَتْ كَلِمَةً تَخْرُجُ مِنْ أَفْوَٰهِهِمْ إِن يَقُولُونَ إِلَّا كَذِبًا

5 They have no knowledge of this, nor did their forefathers. Grave is the word that comes out of their mouths. They say nothing but a lie.

5 17:40

٦ فَلَعَلَّكَ بَٰخِعٌ نَّفْسَكَ عَلَىٰٓ ءَاثَٰرِهِمْ إِن لَّمْ يُؤْمِنُوا بِهَٰذَا ٱلْحَدِيثِ أَسَفًا

6 Perhaps you may destroy yourself with grief, chasing after them, if they do not believe in this information.

6 5:68; 6:33; 15:88, 97; 26:3

٧ إِنَّا جَعَلْنَا مَا عَلَى ٱلْأَرْضِ زِينَةً لَّهَا لِنَبْلُوَهُمْ أَيُّهُمْ أَحْسَنُ عَمَلًا

7 We made what is upon the earth an ornament for it, to test them as to which of them is best in conduct.

7 18:46; 16:8; 67:1–2

٨ وَإِنَّا لَجَٰعِلُونَ مَا عَلَيْهَا صَعِيدًا جُرُزًا

8 And We will turn what is on it into barren waste.

8 32:27

٩ أَمْ حَسِبْتَ أَنَّ أَصْحَٰبَ ٱلْكَهْفِ وَٱلرَّقِيمِ كَانُوا مِنْ ءَايَٰتِنَا عَجَبًا

9 Did you know that the People of the Cave and the Inscription were of Our wondrous signs?

١٠ إِذْ أَوَى ٱلْفِتْيَةُ إِلَى ٱلْكَهْفِ فَقَالُوا رَبَّنَآ ءَاتِنَا مِن لَّدُنكَ رَحْمَةً وَهَيِّئْ لَنَا مِنْ أَمْرِنَا رَشَدًا

10 When the youths took shelter in the cave, they said, "Our Lord, give us mercy from Yourself, and bless our affair with guidance."

١١ فَضَرَبْنَا عَلَىٰٓ ءَاذَانِهِمْ فِي ٱلْكَهْفِ سِنِينَ عَدَدًا

11 Then We sealed their ears in the cave for a number of years.

11 18:25

١٢ ثُمَّ بَعَثْنَاهُمْ لِنَعْلَمَ أَيُّ الْحِزْبَيْنِ أَحْصَىٰ لِمَا لَبِثُوا أَمَدًا	12	18:19, 125–126

12 Then We awakened them to know which of the two groups could better calculate the length of their stay.

١٣ نَحْنُ نَقُصُّ عَلَيْكَ نَبَأَهُم بِالْحَقِّ ۚ إِنَّهُمْ فِتْيَةٌ آمَنُوا بِرَبِّهِمْ وَزِدْنَاهُمْ هُدًى	13	9:124; 47:17; 48:4

13 We relate to you their story in truth. They were youths who believed in their Lord, and We increased them in guidance.

١٤ وَرَبَطْنَا عَلَىٰ قُلُوبِهِمْ إِذْ قَامُوا فَقَالُوا رَبُّنَا رَبُّ السَّمَاوَاتِ وَالْأَرْضِ لَن نَّدْعُوَ مِن دُونِهِ إِلَٰهًا ۖ لَّقَدْ قُلْنَا إِذًا شَطَطًا	14	72:4

14 And We strengthened their hearts, when they stood up and said, "Our Lord is the Lord of the heavens and the earth; we will not call on any god besides Him, for then we would have spoken an outrage."

١٥ هَٰؤُلَاءِ قَوْمُنَا اتَّخَذُوا مِن دُونِهِ آلِهَةً ۖ لَّوْلَا يَأْتُونَ عَلَيْهِم بِسُلْطَانٍ بَيِّنٍ ۖ فَمَنْ أَظْلَمُ مِمَّنِ افْتَرَىٰ عَلَى اللَّهِ كَذِبًا	15	11:18; 39:32

15 "These people, our people, have taken to themselves gods other than Him. Why do they not bring a clear proof concerning them? Who, then, does greater wrong than he who invents lies and attributes them to God?"

١٦ وَإِذِ اعْتَزَلْتُمُوهُمْ وَمَا يَعْبُدُونَ إِلَّا اللَّهَ فَأْوُوا إِلَى الْكَهْفِ يَنشُرْ لَكُمْ رَبُّكُم مِّن رَّحْمَتِهِ وَيُهَيِّئْ لَكُم مِّنْ أَمْرِكُم مِّرْفَقًا	16	19:48–49

16 "Now that you have withdrawn from them, and from what they worship besides God, take shelter in the cave. And your Lord will unfold His mercy for you, and will set your affair towards ease."

١٧ وَتَرَى الشَّمْسَ إِذَا طَلَعَت تَّزَاوَرُ عَن كَهْفِهِمْ ذَاتَ الْيَمِينِ وَإِذَا غَرَبَت تَّقْرِضُهُمْ ذَاتَ الشِّمَالِ وَهُمْ فِي فَجْوَةٍ مِّنْهُ ۚ ذَٰلِكَ مِنْ آيَاتِ اللَّهِ ۗ مَن يَهْدِ اللَّهُ فَهُوَ الْمُهْتَدِ ۖ وَمَن يُضْلِلْ فَلَن تَجِدَ لَهُ وَلِيًّا مُّرْشِدًا	17	7:178; 17:97

17 You would have seen the sun, when it rose, veering away from their cave towards the right, and when it sets, moving away from them to the left, as they lay in the midst of the cave. That was one of God's wonders. He whom God guides is truly guided; but he whom He misguides, for him you will find no directing friend.

١٨ وَتَحْسَبُهُمْ أَيْقَاظًا وَهُمْ رُقُودٌ ۚ وَنُقَلِّبُهُمْ ذَاتَ الْيَمِينِ وَذَاتَ الشِّمَالِ ۖ وَكَلْبُهُم بَاسِطٌ ذِرَاعَيْهِ بِالْوَصِيدِ ۚ لَوِ اطَّلَعْتَ عَلَيْهِمْ لَوَلَّيْتَ مِنْهُمْ فِرَارًا وَلَمُلِئْتَ مِنْهُمْ رُعْبًا	18

18 You would think them awake, although they were asleep. And We turned them over to the right, and to the left, with their dog stretching its paws across the threshold. Had you looked at them, you would have turned away from them in flight, and been filled with fear of them.

١٩ وَكَذَٰلِكَ بَعَثْنَاهُمْ لِيَتَسَاءَلُوا بَيْنَهُمْ ۚ قَالَ قَائِلٌ مِنْهُمْ كَمْ لَبِثْتُمْ ۖ قَالُوا لَبِثْنَا يَوْمًا أَوْ بَعْضَ يَوْمٍ ۚ قَالُوا رَبُّكُمْ أَعْلَمُ بِمَا لَبِثْتُمْ فَابْعَثُوا أَحَدَكُمْ بِوَرِقِكُمْ هَٰذِهِ إِلَى الْمَدِينَةِ فَلْيَنظُرْ أَيُّهَا أَزْكَىٰ طَعَامًا فَلْيَأْتِكُمْ بِرِزْقٍ مِنْهُ وَلْيَتَلَطَّفْ وَلَا يُشْعِرَنَّ بِكُمْ أَحَدًا

19 18:12, 25–26

19 Even so, We awakened them, so that they may ask one another. A speaker among them said, "How long have you stayed?" They said, "We have stayed a day, or part of a day." They said, "Your Lord knows best how long you have stayed." "Send one of you to the city, with this money of yours, and let him see which food is most suitable, and let him bring you some provision thereof. And let him be gentle, and let no one become aware of you."

٢٠ إِنَّهُمْ إِنْ يَظْهَرُوا عَلَيْكُمْ يَرْجُمُوكُمْ أَوْ يُعِيدُوكُمْ فِي مِلَّتِهِمْ وَلَنْ تُفْلِحُوا إِذًا أَبَدًا

20 "If they discover you, they will stone you, or force you back into their religion; then you will never be saved."

٢١ وَكَذَٰلِكَ أَعْثَرْنَا عَلَيْهِمْ لِيَعْلَمُوا أَنَّ وَعْدَ اللَّهِ حَقٌّ وَأَنَّ السَّاعَةَ لَا رَيْبَ فِيهَا إِذْ يَتَنَازَعُونَ بَيْنَهُمْ أَمْرَهُمْ ۖ فَقَالُوا ابْنُوا عَلَيْهِمْ بُنْيَانًا ۖ رَبُّهُمْ أَعْلَمُ بِهِمْ ۚ قَالَ الَّذِينَ غَلَبُوا عَلَىٰ أَمْرِهِمْ لَنَتَّخِذَنَّ عَلَيْهِمْ مَسْجِدًا

21 So it was, that We caused them to be discovered, that they would know that the promise of God is true, and that of the Hour there is no doubt. As they were disputing their case among themselves, they said, "Build over them a building." Their Lord knows best about them. Those who prevailed over their case said, "We will set up over them a place of worship."

٢٢ سَيَقُولُونَ ثَلَاثَةٌ رَابِعُهُمْ كَلْبُهُمْ وَيَقُولُونَ خَمْسَةٌ سَادِسُهُمْ كَلْبُهُمْ رَجْمًا بِالْغَيْبِ ۖ وَيَقُولُونَ سَبْعَةٌ وَثَامِنُهُمْ كَلْبُهُمْ ۚ قُلْ رَبِّي أَعْلَمُ بِعِدَّتِهِمْ مَا يَعْلَمُهُمْ إِلَّا قَلِيلٌ ۗ فَلَا تُمَارِ فِيهِمْ إِلَّا مِرَاءً ظَاهِرًا وَلَا تَسْتَفْتِ فِيهِمْ مِنْهُمْ أَحَدًا

22 They will say, "Three, and their fourth being their dog." And they will say, "Five, and their sixth being their dog," guessing at the unknown. And they will say, "Seven, and their eighth being their dog." Say, "My Lord knows best their number." None knows them except a few. So do not argue concerning them except with an obvious argument, and do not consult any of them about them.

٢٣ وَلَا تَقُولَنَّ لِشَيْءٍ إِنِّي فَاعِلٌ ذَٰلِكَ غَدًا

23 And never say about anything, "I will do that tomorrow."

٢٤ إِلَّا أَنْ يَشَاءَ اللَّهُ ۚ وَاذْكُرْ رَبَّكَ إِذَا نَسِيتَ وَقُلْ عَسَىٰ أَنْ يَهْدِيَنِ رَبِّي لِأَقْرَبَ مِنْ هَٰذَا رَشَدًا

24 6:68; 8:63; 58:19

24 Without saying, "If God wills." And remember your Lord if you forget, and say, "Perhaps my Lord will guide me to nearer than this in integrity."

٢٥ وَلَبِثُوا فِي كَهْفِهِمْ ثَلَاثَ مِائَةٍ سِنِينَ وَازْدَادُوا تِسْعًا

25 18:11

25 And they stayed in their cave for three hundred years, adding nine.

٢٦ قُلِ اللَّهُ أَعْلَمُ بِمَا لَبِثُوا ۖ لَهُ غَيْبُ السَّمَاوَاتِ وَالْأَرْضِ ۖ أَبْصِرْ بِهِ وَأَسْمِعْ ۚ مَا لَهُم مِّن دُونِهِ مِن وَلِيٍّ وَلَا يُشْرِكُ فِي حُكْمِهِ أَحَدًا[b]

26 Say, "God knows best how long they stayed." His is the mystery of the heavens and the earth. By Him you see and hear. They have no guardian apart from Him, and He shares His Sovereignty with no one.

26
[a] 6:59; 11:123; 13:9; 27:65
[b] 2:257; 10:62; 47:11

٢٧ وَاتْلُ مَا أُوحِيَ إِلَيْكَ مِن كِتَابِ رَبِّكَ[a] ۖ لَا مُبَدِّلَ لِكَلِمَاتِهِ[b] وَلَن تَجِدَ مِن دُونِهِ مُلْتَحَدًا[c]

27 And recite what was revealed to you from the Book of your Lord. There is no changing His words, and you will find no refuge except in Him.

27
[a] 2:121; 27:92; 29:45; 35:29
[b] 6:34, 115; 10:15; 16:101
[c] 7:180; 41:40; 72:21–22

٢٨ وَاصْبِرْ نَفْسَكَ مَعَ الَّذِينَ يَدْعُونَ رَبَّهُم بِالْغَدَاةِ وَالْعَشِيِّ يُرِيدُونَ وَجْهَهُ ۖ وَلَا تَعْدُ عَيْنَاكَ عَنْهُمْ تُرِيدُ زِينَةَ الْحَيَاةِ الدُّنْيَا[a] ۖ وَلَا تُطِعْ مَنْ أَغْفَلْنَا قَلْبَهُ عَن ذِكْرِنَا وَاتَّبَعَ هَوَاهُ وَكَانَ أَمْرُهُ فُرُطًا[b]

28 And content yourself with those who pray to their Lord morning and evening, desiring His Presence. And do not turn your eyes away from them, desiring the glitter of this world. And do not obey him whose heart We have made heedless of Our remembrance—so he follows his own desires—and his priorities are confused.

28
[a] 6:52
[b] 33:48; 76:24

٢٩ وَقُلِ الْحَقُّ مِن رَّبِّكُمْ ۖ فَمَن شَاءَ فَلْيُؤْمِن وَمَن شَاءَ فَلْيَكْفُرْ ۚ إِنَّا أَعْتَدْنَا لِلظَّالِمِينَ نَارًا أَحَاطَ بِهِمْ سُرَادِقُهَا ۚ وَإِن يَسْتَغِيثُوا يُغَاثُوا بِمَاءٍ كَالْمُهْلِ يَشْوِي الْوُجُوهَ ۚ بِئْسَ الشَّرَابُ وَسَاءَتْ مُرْتَفَقًا

29 And say, "The truth is from your Lord. Whoever wills—let him believe. And whoever wills—let him disbelieve". We have prepared for the unjust a Fire, whose curtains will hem them in. And when they cry for relief, they will be relieved with water like molten brass, which scalds the faces. What a miserable drink, and what a terrible place.

29–30
19:53

٣٠ إِنَّ الَّذِينَ آمَنُوا وَعَمِلُوا الصَّالِحَاتِ إِنَّا لَا نُضِيعُ أَجْرَ مَنْ أَحْسَنَ عَمَلًا

30 As for those who believe and lead a righteous life—We will not waste the reward of those who work righteousness.

30
3:195, 171

٣١ أُولَٰئِكَ لَهُمْ جَنَّاتُ عَدْنٍ تَجْرِي مِن تَحْتِهِمُ الْأَنْهَارُ يُحَلَّوْنَ فِيهَا مِنْ أَسَاوِرَ مِن ذَهَبٍ وَيَلْبَسُونَ ثِيَابًا خُضْرًا مِّن سُندُسٍ وَإِسْتَبْرَقٍ مُّتَّكِئِينَ فِيهَا عَلَى الْأَرَائِكِ ۚ نِعْمَ الثَّوَابُ وَحَسُنَتْ مُرْتَفَقًا

31 These will have the Gardens of Eden, beneath which rivers flow. Reclining on comfortable furnishings, they will be adorned with bracelets of gold, and will wear green garments of silk and brocade. What a wonderful reward, and what an excellent resting-place.

31
22:23; 35:33; 44:53; 76:21

٣٢ وَاضْرِبْ لَهُم مَّثَلًا رَّجُلَيْنِ جَعَلْنَا لِأَحَدِهِمَا جَنَّتَيْنِ مِنْ أَعْنَابٍ وَحَفَفْنَاهُمَا بِنَخْلٍ وَجَعَلْنَا بَيْنَهُمَا زَرْعًا

32 And cite for them the parable of two men. To one of them We gave two gardens of vine, and We surrounded them with palm-trees, and We placed between them crops.

32–42
68:17–32; 40:67; 86:5–7

٣٣ كِلْتَا الْجَنَّتَيْنِ آتَتْ أُكُلَهَا وَلَمْ تَظْلِم مِنْهُ شَيْئًا ۚ وَفَجَّرْنَا خِلَالَهُمَا نَهَرًا

33 Both gardens produced their harvest in full, and suffered no loss. And We made a river flow through them.

٣٤ وَكَانَ لَهُ ثَمَرٌ فَقَالَ لِصَاحِبِهِ وَهُوَ يُحَاوِرُهُ أَنَا أَكْثَرُ مِنكَ مَالًا وَأَعَزُّ نَفَرًا

34 And thus he had abundant fruits. He said to his friend, as he conversed with him, "I am wealthier than you, and greater in manpower."

٣٥ وَدَخَلَ جَنَّتَهُ وَهُوَ ظَالِمٌ لِنَفْسِهِ قَالَ مَا أَظُنُّ أَن تَبِيدَ هَٰذِهِ أَبَدًا

35 And he entered his garden, wronging himself. He said, "I do not think this will ever perish."

٣٦ وَمَا أَظُنُّ السَّاعَةَ قَائِمَةً وَلَئِن رُّدِدتُّ إِلَىٰ رَبِّي لَأَجِدَنَّ خَيْرًا مِّنْهَا مُنقَلَبًا

36 "And I do not think the Hour is coming. And even if I am returned to my Lord, I will find something better than this in return."

٣٧ قَالَ لَهُ صَاحِبُهُ وَهُوَ يُحَاوِرُهُ أَكَفَرْتَ بِالَّذِي خَلَقَكَ مِن تُرَابٍ ثُمَّ مِن نُّطْفَةٍ ثُمَّ سَوَّاكَ رَجُلًا

37 His friend said to him, as he conversed with him, "Are you being ungrateful to Him who created you from dust, then from a sperm-drop, then evolved you into a man?

٣٨ لَّٰكِنَّا هُوَ اللَّهُ رَبِّي وَلَا أُشْرِكُ بِرَبِّي أَحَدًا

38 But as for me, He is God, my Lord, and I never associate with my Lord anyone.

٣٩ وَلَوْلَا إِذْ دَخَلْتَ جَنَّتَكَ قُلْتَ مَا شَاءَ اللَّهُ لَا قُوَّةَ إِلَّا بِاللَّهِ ۚ إِن تَرَنِ أَنَا أَقَلَّ مِنكَ مَالًا وَوَلَدًا

39 When you entered your garden, why did you not say, "As God wills; there is no power except through God"? Although you see me inferior to you in wealth and children.

٤٠ فَعَسَىٰ رَبِّي أَن يُؤْتِيَنِ خَيْرًا مِّن جَنَّتِكَ وَيُرْسِلَ عَلَيْهَا حُسْبَانًا مِّنَ السَّمَاءِ فَتُصْبِحَ صَعِيدًا زَلَقًا

40 Perhaps my Lord will give me something better than your garden, and release upon it thunderbolts from the sky, so it becomes barren waste.

٤١ أَوْ يُصْبِحَ مَاؤُهَا غَوْرًا فَلَن تَسْتَطِيعَ لَهُ طَلَبًا

41 Or its water will sink into the ground, and you will be unable to draw it."

٤٢ وَأُحِيطَ بِثَمَرِهِ فَأَصْبَحَ يُقَلِّبُ كَفَّيْهِ عَلَىٰ مَا أَنفَقَ فِيهَا وَهِيَ خَاوِيَةٌ عَلَىٰ عُرُوشِهَا وَيَقُولُ يَا لَيْتَنِي لَمْ أُشْرِكْ بِرَبِّي أَحَدًا

42 And ruin closed in on his crops, and so he began wringing his hands over what he had invested in it, as it lays fallen upon its trellises. And he was saying, "I wish I never associated anyone with my Lord."

٤٣ وَلَمْ تَكُن لَّهُۥ فِئَةٌ يَنصُرُونَهُۥ مِن دُونِ ٱللَّهِ وَمَا كَانَ مُنتَصِرًا

43 He had no faction to help him besides God, and he was helpless.

43
28:81; 42:46

٤٤ هُنَالِكَ ٱلْوَلَٰيَةُ لِلَّهِ ٱلْحَقِّ ۚ هُوَ خَيْرٌ ثَوَابًا وَخَيْرٌ عُقْبًا

44 That is because authority belongs to God, the True. He is Best in rewarding, and Best in requiting.

44
10:30; 47:11

٤٥ وَٱضْرِبْ لَهُم مَّثَلَ ٱلْحَيَوٰةِ ٱلدُّنْيَا كَمَآءٍ أَنزَلْنَٰهُ مِنَ ٱلسَّمَآءِ فَٱخْتَلَطَ بِهِۦ نَبَاتُ ٱلْأَرْضِ فَأَصْبَحَ هَشِيمًا تَذْرُوهُ ٱلرِّيَٰحُ ۗ وَكَانَ ٱللَّهُ عَلَىٰ كُلِّ شَىْءٍ مُّقْتَدِرًا

45 And cite for them the parable of the present life: it is like water that We send down from the sky; the plants of the earth absorb it; but then it becomes debris, scattered by the wind. God has absolute power over everything.

45
10:24

٤٦ ٱلْمَالُ وَٱلْبَنُونَ زِينَةُ ٱلْحَيَوٰةِ ٱلدُّنْيَا ۖ وَٱلْبَٰقِيَٰتُ ٱلصَّٰلِحَٰتُ خَيْرٌ عِندَ رَبِّكَ ثَوَابًا وَخَيْرٌ أَمَلًا

46 Wealth and children are the adornments of the present life. But the things that last, the virtuous deeds, are better with your Lord for reward, and better for hope.

46
3:14; 34:37; 64:15

٤٧ وَيَوْمَ نُسَيِّرُ ٱلْجِبَالَ وَتَرَى ٱلْأَرْضَ بَارِزَةً وَحَشَرْنَٰهُمْ فَلَمْ نُغَادِرْ مِنْهُمْ أَحَدًا

47 On the Day when We set the mountains in motion; and you see the earth emerging; and We gather them together, and leave none of them behind.

47
52:10; 78:20; 81:3

٤٨ وَعُرِضُوا عَلَىٰ رَبِّكَ صَفًّا لَّقَدْ جِئْتُمُونَا كَمَا خَلَقْنَٰكُمْ أَوَّلَ مَرَّةٍ ۚ بَلْ زَعَمْتُمْ أَلَّن نَّجْعَلَ لَكُم مَّوْعِدًا

48 They will be presented before your Lord in a row. "You have come to Us as We created you the first time. Although you claimed We would not set a meeting for you."

48
69:18

٤٩ وَوُضِعَ ٱلْكِتَٰبُ فَتَرَى ٱلْمُجْرِمِينَ مُشْفِقِينَ مِمَّا فِيهِ وَيَقُولُونَ يَٰوَيْلَتَنَا مَالِ هَٰذَا ٱلْكِتَٰبِ لَا يُغَادِرُ صَغِيرَةً وَلَا كَبِيرَةً إِلَّآ أَحْصَىٰهَا ۚ وَوَجَدُوا مَا عَمِلُوا حَاضِرًا ۗ وَلَا يَظْلِمُ رَبُّكَ أَحَدًا

49 And the book will be placed, and you will see the sinners fearful of its contents. And they will say, "Woe to us! What is with this book that leaves nothing, small or big, but it has enumerated it?" They will find everything they had done present. Your Lord does not wrong anyone.

49
42:22; 45:29; 99:6

٥٠ وَإِذْ قُلْنَا لِلْمَلَٰٓئِكَةِ ٱسْجُدُوا لِءَادَمَ فَسَجَدُوٓا إِلَّآ إِبْلِيسَ كَانَ مِنَ ٱلْجِنِّ فَفَسَقَ عَنْ أَمْرِ رَبِّهِۦ ۗ أَفَتَتَّخِذُونَهُۥ وَذُرِّيَّتَهُۥٓ أَوْلِيَآءَ مِن دُونِى وَهُمْ لَكُمْ عَدُوٌّۢ ۚ بِئْسَ لِلظَّٰلِمِينَ بَدَلًا

50 We said to the angels, "Bow down to Adam." So they bowed down, except for Satan. He was of the jinn, and he defied the command of his Lord. Will you take him and his offspring as lords instead of Me, when they are an enemy to you? Evil is the exchange for the wrongdoers.

50
2:34; 7:12; 15:30;
17:61; 38:75

٥١ مَّآ أَشْهَدتُّهُمْ خَلْقَ ٱلسَّمَٰوَٰتِ وَٱلْأَرْضِ وَلَا خَلْقَ أَنفُسِهِمْ وَمَا كُنتُ مُتَّخِذَ ٱلْمُضِلِّينَ عَضُدًا

51 I did not call them to witness the creation of the heavens and the earth, nor their own creation; and I do not take the misleaders for assistants.

٥٢ وَيَوْمَ يَقُولُ نَادُوا شُرَكَائِيَ الَّذِينَ زَعَمْتُمْ فَدَعَوْهُمْ فَلَمْ يَسْتَجِيبُوا لَهُمْ وَجَعَلْنَا بَيْنَهُمْ مَوْبِقًا	52	6:22

52 On the Day when He will say, "Call on My partners whom you have claimed." They will call on them, but they will not answer them. And We will place between them a barrier.

٥٣ وَرَأَى الْمُجْرِمُونَ النَّارَ فَظَنُّوا أَنَّهُمْ مُوَاقِعُوهَا وَلَمْ يَجِدُوا عَنْهَا مَصْرِفًا	53	102:6–7

53 And the sinners will see the Fire, and will realize that they will tumble into it. They will find no deliverance from it.

٥٤ وَلَقَدْ صَرَّفْنَا فِي هَٰذَا الْقُرْآنِ لِلنَّاسِ مِنْ كُلِّ مَثَلٍ ۚ وَكَانَ الْإِنْسَانُ أَكْثَرَ شَيْءٍ جَدَلًا	54	17:89

54 We have elaborated in this Qur'an for the people every kind of example, but the human being is a most argumentative being.

٥٥ وَمَا مَنَعَ النَّاسَ أَنْ يُؤْمِنُوا إِذْ جَاءَهُمُ الْهُدَىٰ وَيَسْتَغْفِرُوا رَبَّهُمْ إِلَّا أَنْ تَأْتِيَهُمْ سُنَّةُ الْأَوَّلِينَ أَوْ يَأْتِيَهُمُ الْعَذَابُ قُبُلًا	55	17:94

55 What prevented people from accepting faith, when guidance has come to them, and from seeking their Lord's forgiveness? Unless they are waiting for the precedent of the ancients to befall them, or to have the punishment come upon them face to face.

٥٦ وَمَا نُرْسِلُ الْمُرْسَلِينَ إِلَّا مُبَشِّرِينَ وَمُنْذِرِينَ ۚ وَيُجَادِلُ الَّذِينَ كَفَرُوا بِالْبَاطِلِ لِيُدْحِضُوا بِهِ الْحَقَّ ۖ وَاتَّخَذُوا آيَاتِي وَمَا أُنْذِرُوا هُزُوًا	56	6:25; 17:46

56 We send the messengers only as deliverers of good news and warners. Those who disbelieve argue with false argument, in order to defeat the truth thereby. They take My Verses, and the warnings, for a joke.

٥٧ وَمَنْ أَظْلَمُ مِمَّنْ ذُكِّرَ بِآيَاتِ رَبِّهِ فَأَعْرَضَ عَنْهَا وَنَسِيَ مَا قَدَّمَتْ يَدَاهُ ۚ إِنَّا جَعَلْنَا عَلَىٰ قُلُوبِهِمْ أَكِنَّةً أَنْ يَفْقَهُوهُ وَفِي آذَانِهِمْ وَقْرًا ۖ وَإِنْ تَدْعُهُمْ إِلَى الْهُدَىٰ فَلَنْ يَهْتَدُوا إِذًا أَبَدًا	57	2:7; 17:45; 45:23; 63:3

57 Who does greater wrong than he, who, when reminded of his Lord's revelations, turns away from them, and forgets what his hands have put forward? We have placed coverings over their hearts, lest they understand it, and heaviness in their ears. And if you call them to guidance, they will not be guided, ever.

٥٨ وَرَبُّكَ الْغَفُورُ ذُو الرَّحْمَةِ ۖ لَوْ يُؤَاخِذُهُمْ بِمَا كَسَبُوا لَعَجَّلَ لَهُمُ الْعَذَابَ ۚ بَلْ لَهُمْ مَوْعِدٌ لَنْ يَجِدُوا مِنْ دُونِهِ مَوْئِلًا	58	16:61; 35:45

58 Your Lord is the Forgiver, Possessor of Mercy. Were He to call them to account for what they have earned, He would have hastened the punishment for them. But they have an appointment from which they will find no escape.

٥٩ وَتِلْكَ الْقُرَىٰ أَهْلَكْنَاهُمْ لَمَّا ظَلَمُوا وَجَعَلْنَا لِمَهْلِكِهِمْ مَوْعِدًا	59	6:131; 10:13; 17:17

59 And these towns—We destroyed them when they committed injustices, and We set for their destruction an appointed time.

٦٠ وَإِذْ قَالَ مُوسَىٰ لِفَتَاهُ لَا أَبْرَحُ حَتَّىٰ أَبْلُغَ مَجْمَعَ الْبَحْرَيْنِ أَوْ أَمْضِيَ حُقُبًا

60 Recall when Moses said to his servant, "I will not give up until I reach the junction of the two rivers, even if it takes me years."

60
25:53; 27:61; 35:12; 55:19

٦١ فَلَمَّا بَلَغَا مَجْمَعَ بَيْنِهِمَا نَسِيَا حُوتَهُمَا فَاتَّخَذَ سَبِيلَهُ فِي الْبَحْرِ سَرَبًا

61 Then, when they reached the junction between them, they forgot about their fish. It found its way into the river, slipping away.

٦٢ فَلَمَّا جَاوَزَا قَالَ لِفَتَاهُ آتِنَا غَدَاءَنَا لَقَدْ لَقِينَا مِنْ سَفَرِنَا هَٰذَا نَصَبًا

62 When they went further, he said to his servant, "Bring us our lunch; we were exposed in our travel to much fatigue."

٦٣ قَالَ أَرَأَيْتَ إِذْ أَوَيْنَا إِلَى الصَّخْرَةِ فَإِنِّي نَسِيتُ الْحُوتَ وَمَا أَنْسَانِيهُ إِلَّا الشَّيْطَانُ أَنْ أَذْكُرَهُ ۚ وَاتَّخَذَ سَبِيلَهُ فِي الْبَحْرِ عَجَبًا

63 He said, "Do you remember when we rested by the rock? I forgot about the fish. It was only the devil who made me forget it. And so it found its way to the river, amazingly."

63
6:68; 58:19

٦٤ قَالَ ذَٰلِكَ مَا كُنَّا نَبْغِ ۚ فَارْتَدَّا عَلَىٰ آثَارِهِمَا قَصَصًا

64 He said, "This is what we were seeking." And so they turned back retracing their steps.

٦٥ فَوَجَدَا عَبْدًا مِنْ عِبَادِنَا آتَيْنَاهُ رَحْمَةً مِنْ عِنْدِنَا وَعَلَّمْنَاهُ مِنْ لَدُنَّا عِلْمًا

65 Then they came upon a servant of Ours, whom We had blessed with mercy from Us, and had taught him knowledge from Our Own.

٦٦ قَالَ لَهُ مُوسَىٰ هَلْ أَتَّبِعُكَ عَلَىٰ أَنْ تُعَلِّمَنِ مِمَّا عُلِّمْتَ رُشْدًا

66 Moses said to him, "May I follow you, so that you may teach me some of the guidance you were taught?"

٦٧ قَالَ إِنَّكَ لَنْ تَسْتَطِيعَ مَعِيَ صَبْرًا

67 He said, "You will not be able to endure with me.

٦٨ وَكَيْفَ تَصْبِرُ عَلَىٰ مَا لَمْ تُحِطْ بِهِ خُبْرًا

68 And how will you endure what you have no knowledge of?"

٦٩ قَالَ سَتَجِدُنِي إِنْ شَاءَ اللَّهُ صَابِرًا وَلَا أَعْصِي لَكَ أَمْرًا

69 He said, "You will find me, God willing, patient; and I will not disobey you in any order of yours."

٧٠ قَالَ فَإِنِ اتَّبَعْتَنِي فَلَا تَسْأَلْنِي عَنْ شَيْءٍ حَتَّىٰ أُحْدِثَ لَكَ مِنْهُ ذِكْرًا

70 He said, "If you follow me, do not ask me about anything, until I myself make mention of it to you."

٧١ فَانْطَلَقَا حَتَّىٰ إِذَا رَكِبَا فِي السَّفِينَةِ خَرَقَهَا ۖ قَالَ أَخَرَقْتَهَا لِتُغْرِقَ أَهْلَهَا لَقَدْ جِئْتَ شَيْئًا إِمْرًا

71 So they set out. Until, when they had boarded the boat, he holed it. He said, "Did you hole it, to drown its passengers? You have done something awful."

٧٢ قَالَ أَلَمْ أَقُلْ إِنَّكَ لَن تَسْتَطِيعَ مَعِيَ صَبْرًا

72 He said, "Did I not tell you that you will not be able to endure with me?"

٧٣ قَالَ لَا تُؤَاخِذْنِي بِمَا نَسِيتُ وَلَا تُرْهِقْنِي مِنْ أَمْرِي عُسْرًا

73 He said, "Do not rebuke me for forgetting, and do not make my course difficult for me."

٧٤ فَانطَلَقَا حَتَّىٰ إِذَا لَقِيَا غُلَامًا فَقَتَلَهُ قَالَ أَقَتَلْتَ نَفْسًا زَكِيَّةً بِغَيْرِ نَفْسٍ لَّقَدْ جِئْتَ شَيْئًا نُّكْرًا

74 Then they set out. Until, when they encountered a boy, he killed him. He said, "Did you kill a pure soul, who killed no one? You have done something terrible."

٧٥ قَالَ أَلَمْ أَقُل لَّكَ إِنَّكَ لَن تَسْتَطِيعَ مَعِيَ صَبْرًا

75 He said, "Did I not tell you that you will not be able to endure with me?"

٧٦ قَالَ إِن سَأَلْتُكَ عَن شَيْءٍ بَعْدَهَا فَلَا تُصَاحِبْنِي ۖ قَدْ بَلَغْتَ مِن لَّدُنِّي عُذْرًا

76 He said, "If I ask you about anything after this, then do not keep company with me. You have received excuses from me."

٧٧ فَانطَلَقَا حَتَّىٰ إِذَا أَتَيَا أَهْلَ قَرْيَةٍ اسْتَطْعَمَا أَهْلَهَا فَأَبَوْا أَن يُضَيِّفُوهُمَا فَوَجَدَا فِيهَا جِدَارًا يُرِيدُ أَن يَنقَضَّ فَأَقَامَهُ ۖ قَالَ لَوْ شِئْتَ لَاتَّخَذْتَ عَلَيْهِ أَجْرًا

77 So they set out. Until, when they reached the people of a town, they asked them for food, but they refused to offer them hospitality. There they found a wall about to collapse, and he repaired it. He said, "If you wanted, you could have obtained a payment for it."

٧٨ قَالَ هَٰذَا فِرَاقُ بَيْنِي وَبَيْنِكَ ۚ سَأُنَبِّئُكَ بِتَأْوِيلِ مَا لَمْ تَسْتَطِع عَّلَيْهِ صَبْرًا

78 He said, "This is the parting between you and me. I will tell you the interpretation of what you were unable to endure.

٧٩ أَمَّا السَّفِينَةُ فَكَانَتْ لِمَسَاكِينَ يَعْمَلُونَ فِي الْبَحْرِ فَأَرَدتُّ أَنْ أَعِيبَهَا وَكَانَ وَرَاءَهُم مَّلِكٌ يَأْخُذُ كُلَّ سَفِينَةٍ غَصْبًا

79 As for the boat, it belonged to paupers working at sea. I wanted to damage it because there was a king coming after them seizing every boat by force.

٨٠ وَأَمَّا الْغُلَامُ فَكَانَ أَبَوَاهُ مُؤْمِنَيْنِ فَخَشِينَا أَن يُرْهِقَهُمَا طُغْيَانًا وَكُفْرًا

80 As for the boy, his parents were believers, and we feared he would overwhelm them with oppression and disbelief.

٨١ فَأَرَدْنَا أَن يُبْدِلَهُمَا رَبُّهُمَا خَيْرًا مِّنْهُ زَكَاةً وَأَقْرَبَ رُحْمًا

81 So we wanted their Lord to replace him with someone better in purity, and closer to mercy.

٨٢ وَأَمَّا الْجِدَارُ فَكَانَ لِغُلَامَيْنِ يَتِيمَيْنِ فِي الْمَدِينَةِ وَكَانَ تَحْتَهُ كَنزٌ لَّهُمَا وَكَانَ أَبُوهُمَا صَالِحًا فَأَرَادَ رَبُّكَ أَن يَبْلُغَا أَشُدَّهُمَا وَيَسْتَخْرِجَا كَنزَهُمَا رَحْمَةً مِّن رَّبِّكَ ۚ وَمَا فَعَلْتُهُ عَنْ أَمْرِي ۚ ذَٰلِكَ تَأْوِيلُ مَا لَمْ تَسْطِع عَّلَيْهِ صَبْرًا

82 And as for the wall, it belonged to two orphaned boys in the city. Beneath it was a treasure that belonged to them. Their father was a righteous man. Your Lord wanted them to reach their maturity, and then extract their treasure—as a mercy from your Lord. I did not do it of my own accord. This is the interpretation of what you were unable to endure."

٨٣ وَيَسْأَلُونَكَ عَن ذِي الْقَرْنَيْنِ ۖ قُلْ سَأَتْلُو عَلَيْكُم مِّنْهُ ذِكْرًا

83 And they ask you about Zul-Qarnain. Say, "I will tell you something about him."

٨٤ إِنَّا مَكَّنَّا لَهُ فِي الْأَرْضِ وَآتَيْنَاهُ مِن كُلِّ شَيْءٍ سَبَبًا

84 We established him on earth, and gave him all kinds of means.

٨٥ فَأَتْبَعَ سَبَبًا

85 He pursued a certain course.

85
pp 18:89, 92

٨٦ حَتَّىٰ إِذَا بَلَغَ مَغْرِبَ الشَّمْسِ وَجَدَهَا تَغْرُبُ فِي عَيْنٍ حَمِئَةٍ وَوَجَدَ عِندَهَا قَوْمًا ۗ قُلْنَا يَا ذَا الْقَرْنَيْنِ إِمَّا أَن تُعَذِّبَ وَإِمَّا أَن تَتَّخِذَ فِيهِمْ حُسْنًا

86 Until, when he reached the setting of the sun, he found it setting in a murky spring, and found a people in its vicinity. We said, "O Zul-Qarnain, you may either inflict a penalty, or else treat them kindly."

٨٧ قَالَ أَمَّا مَن ظَلَمَ فَسَوْفَ نُعَذِّبُهُ ثُمَّ يُرَدُّ إِلَىٰ رَبِّهِ فَيُعَذِّبُهُ عَذَابًا نُّكْرًا

87 He said, "As for him who does wrong, we will penalize him, then he will be returned to his Lord, and He will punish him with an unheard-of torment.

٨٨ وَأَمَّا مَنْ آمَنَ وَعَمِلَ صَالِحًا فَلَهُ جَزَاءً الْحُسْنَىٰ ۖ وَسَنَقُولُ لَهُ مِنْ أَمْرِنَا يُسْرًا

88 "But as for him who believes and acts righteously, he will have the finest reward, and We will speak to him of Our command with ease."

٨٩ ثُمَّ أَتْبَعَ سَبَبًا

89 Then he pursued a course.

89
pp 18:85, 92

٩٠ حَتَّىٰ إِذَا بَلَغَ مَطْلِعَ الشَّمْسِ وَجَدَهَا تَطْلُعُ عَلَىٰ قَوْمٍ لَّمْ نَجْعَل لَّهُم مِّن دُونِهَا سِتْرًا

90 Until, when he reached the rising of the sun, he found it rising on a people for whom We had provided no shelter from it.

٩١ كَذَٰلِكَ وَقَدْ أَحَطْنَا بِمَا لَدَيْهِ خُبْرًا

91 And so it was. We had full knowledge of what he had.

92

٩٢ ثُمَّ أَتْبَعَ سَبَبًا

92 Then he pursued a course.

pp 18:85, 89

٩٣ حَتَّىٰ إِذَا بَلَغَ بَيْنَ السَّدَّيْنِ وَجَدَ مِنْ دُونِهِمَا قَوْمًا لَا يَكَادُونَ يَفْقَهُونَ قَوْلًا

93 Until, when he reached the point separating the two barriers, he found beside them a people who could barely understand what is said.

٩٤ قَالُوا يَا ذَا الْقَرْنَيْنِ إِنَّ يَأْجُوجَ وَمَأْجُوجَ مُفْسِدُونَ فِي الْأَرْضِ فَهَلْ نَجْعَلُ لَكَ خَرْجًا عَلَىٰ أَنْ تَجْعَلَ بَيْنَنَا وَبَيْنَهُمْ سَدًّا

94 They said, "O Zul-Qarnain, the Gog and Magog are spreading chaos in the land. Can we pay you, to build between us and them a wall?"

٩٥ قَالَ مَا مَكَّنِّي فِيهِ رَبِّي خَيْرٌ فَأَعِينُونِي بِقُوَّةٍ أَجْعَلْ بَيْنَكُمْ وَبَيْنَهُمْ رَدْمًا

95 He said, "What my Lord has empowered me with is better. But assist me with strength, and I will build between you and them a dam.

٩٦ آتُونِي زُبَرَ الْحَدِيدِ ۖ حَتَّىٰ إِذَا سَاوَىٰ بَيْنَ الصَّدَفَيْنِ قَالَ انْفُخُوا ۖ حَتَّىٰ إِذَا جَعَلَهُ نَارًا قَالَ آتُونِي أُفْرِغْ عَلَيْهِ قِطْرًا

96 "Bring me blocks of iron." So that, when he had leveled up between the two cliffs, he said, "Blow." And having turned it into a fire, he said, "Bring me tar to pour over it."

٩٧ فَمَا اسْطَاعُوا أَنْ يَظْهَرُوهُ وَمَا اسْتَطَاعُوا لَهُ نَقْبًا

97 So they were unable to climb it, and they could not penetrate it.

٩٨ قَالَ هَٰذَا رَحْمَةٌ مِنْ رَبِّي ۖ فَإِذَا جَاءَ وَعْدُ رَبِّي جَعَلَهُ دَكَّاءَ ۖ وَكَانَ وَعْدُ رَبِّي حَقًّا

98 He said, "This is a mercy from my Lord. But when the promise of my Lord comes true, He will turn it into rubble, and the promise of my Lord is always true."

٩٩ وَتَرَكْنَا بَعْضَهُمْ يَوْمَئِذٍ يَمُوجُ فِي بَعْضٍ ۖ وَنُفِخَ فِي الصُّورِ فَجَمَعْنَاهُمْ جَمْعًا

99 On that Day, We will leave them surging upon one another. And the Trumpet will be blown, and We will gather them together.

١٠٠ وَعَرَضْنَا جَهَنَّمَ يَوْمَئِذٍ لِلْكَافِرِينَ عَرْضًا

100 On that Day, We will present the disbelievers to Hell, all displayed.

100
18:48; 40:46; 46:20

١٠١ الَّذِينَ كَانَتْ أَعْيُنُهُمْ فِي غِطَاءٍ عَنْ ذِكْرِي وَكَانُوا لَا يَسْتَطِيعُونَ سَمْعًا

101 Those whose eyes were screened to My message, and were unable to hear.

101
45:23

١٠٢ أَفَحَسِبَ الَّذِينَ كَفَرُوا أَنْ يَتَّخِذُوا عِبَادِي مِنْ دُونِي أَوْلِيَاءَ ۚ إِنَّا أَعْتَدْنَا جَهَنَّمَ لِلْكَافِرِينَ نُزُلًا

102 Do those who disbelieve think that they can take My servants for masters instead of Me? We have prepared Hell for the hospitality of the faithless.

١٠٣ قُلْ هَلْ نُنَبِّئُكُمْ بِالْأَخْسَرِينَ أَعْمَالًا

103–104
14:18; 24:39; 25:23–24

103 Say, "Shall We inform you of the greatest losers in their works?"

١٠٤ الَّذِينَ ضَلَّ سَعْيُهُمْ فِي الْحَيَاةِ الدُّنْيَا وَهُمْ يَحْسَبُونَ أَنَّهُمْ يُحْسِنُونَ صُنْعًا

104 "Those whose efforts in this world are misguided, while they assume that they are doing well."

١٠٥ أُولَٰئِكَ الَّذِينَ كَفَرُوا بِآيَاتِ رَبِّهِمْ وَلِقَائِهِ فَحَبِطَتْ أَعْمَالُهُمْ فَلَا نُقِيمُ لَهُمْ يَوْمَ الْقِيَامَةِ وَزْنًا

105
7:147

105 It is they who rejected the communications of their Lord, and the encounter with Him. So their works are in vain. And on the Day of Resurrection, We will consider them of no weight.

١٠٦ ذَٰلِكَ جَزَاؤُهُمْ جَهَنَّمُ بِمَا كَفَرُوا وَاتَّخَذُوا آيَاتِي وَرُسُلِي هُزُوًا

s106
45:35

106 That is their requital—Hell—on account of their disbelief, and their taking My revelations and My messengers in mockery.

١٠٧ إِنَّ الَّذِينَ آمَنُوا وَعَمِلُوا الصَّالِحَاتِ كَانَتْ لَهُمْ جَنَّاتُ الْفِرْدَوْسِ نُزُلًا

107 As for those who believe and do righteous deeds, they will have the Gardens of Paradise for hospitality.

١٠٨ خَالِدِينَ فِيهَا لَا يَبْغُونَ عَنْهَا حِوَلًا

108 Abiding therein forever, without desiring any change therefrom.

١٠٩ قُلْ لَوْ كَانَ الْبَحْرُ مِدَادًا لِكَلِمَاتِ رَبِّي لَنَفِدَ الْبَحْرُ قَبْلَ أَنْ تَنْفَدَ كَلِمَاتُ رَبِّي وَلَوْ جِئْنَا بِمِثْلِهِ مَدَدًا

109
31:27

109 Say, "If the ocean were ink for the words of my Lord, the ocean would run out, before the words of my Lord run out," even if We were to bring the like of it in addition to it.

١١٠ قُلْ إِنَّمَا أَنَا بَشَرٌ مِثْلُكُمْ يُوحَىٰ إِلَيَّ أَنَّمَا إِلَٰهُكُمْ إِلَٰهٌ وَاحِدٌ ۖ فَمَنْ كَانَ يَرْجُو لِقَاءَ رَبِّهِ فَلْيَعْمَلْ عَمَلًا صَالِحًا وَلَا يُشْرِكْ بِعِبَادَةِ رَبِّهِ أَحَدًا

110
41:6; 21:108

110 Say, "I am only a human being like you, being inspired that your god is One God. Whoever hopes to meet his Lord, let him work righteousness, and never associate anyone with the service of his Lord."

Sūrah 19: Maryam

سُورَةُ مَرْيَم (Mary)

بِسْمِ ٱللَّهِ ٱلرَّحْمَٰنِ ٱلرَّحِيمِ

١ كهيعص

1 Kāf, Hā', Yā', 'Ayn, Ṣād.

٢ ذِكْرُ رَحْمَتِ رَبِّكَ عَبْدَهُ زَكَرِيَّا

2 A mention of the mercy of your Lord towards His servant Zechariah.

٣ إِذْ نَادَىٰ رَبَّهُ نِدَاءً خَفِيًّا

3 When he called on his Lord, a call in seclusion.

3
3:38

٤ قَالَ رَبِّ إِنِّي وَهَنَ ٱلْعَظْمُ مِنِّي وَٱشْتَعَلَ ٱلرَّأْسُ شَيْبًا وَلَمْ أَكُن بِدُعَائِكَ رَبِّ شَقِيًّا

4 He said, "My Lord, my bones have become feeble, and my hair is aflame with gray, and never, Lord, have I been disappointed in my prayer to you.

4–5
3:40; 19:8

٥ وَإِنِّي خِفْتُ ٱلْمَوَالِيَ مِن وَرَائِي وَكَانَتِ ٱمْرَأَتِي عَاقِرًا فَهَبْ لِي مِن لَّدُنكَ وَلِيًّا

5 "And I fear for my dependents after me, and my wife is barren. So grant me, from Yourself, an heir.

٦ يَرِثُنِي وَيَرِثُ مِنْ آلِ يَعْقُوبَ وَٱجْعَلْهُ رَبِّ رَضِيًّا

6 To inherit me, and inherit from the House of Jacob, and make him, my Lord, pleasing."

٧ يَا زَكَرِيَّا إِنَّا نُبَشِّرُكَ بِغُلَامٍ ٱسْمُهُ يَحْيَىٰ لَمْ نَجْعَل لَّهُ مِن قَبْلُ سَمِيًّا

7 "O Zechariah, We give you good news of a son, whose name is John, a name We have never given before."

7
3:39; 4:160; 6:146

٨ قَالَ رَبِّ أَنَّىٰ يَكُونُ لِي غُلَامٌ وَكَانَتِ ٱمْرَأَتِي عَاقِرًا وَقَدْ بَلَغْتُ مِنَ ٱلْكِبَرِ عِتِيًّا

8 He said, "My Lord, how can I have a son, when my wife is barren, and I have become decrepit with old age?"

8
3:40

٩ قَالَ كَذَٰلِكَ قَالَ رَبُّكَ هُوَ عَلَيَّ هَيِّنٌ[a] وَقَدْ خَلَقْتُكَ مِن قَبْلُ وَلَمْ تَكُ شَيْئًا[b]

9 He said, "It will be so, your Lord says, 'it is easy for me, and I created you before, when you were nothing.'"

9
[a] 19:21
[b] 19:67; 76:1

١٠ قَالَ رَبِّ ٱجْعَل لِّي آيَةً ۚ قَالَ آيَتُكَ أَلَّا تُكَلِّمَ ٱلنَّاسَ ثَلَاثَ لَيَالٍ سَوِيًّا

10 He said, "My Lord, give me a sign." He said, "Your sign is that you will not speak to the people for three nights straight."

10–11
3:41

١١ فَخَرَجَ عَلَىٰ قَوْمِهِ مِنَ ٱلْمِحْرَابِ فَأَوْحَىٰ إِلَيْهِمْ أَن سَبِّحُوا بُكْرَةً وَعَشِيًّا

11 And he came out to his people, from the sanctuary, and signaled to them to praise morning and evening.

١٢ يَا يَحْيَىٰ خُذِ الْكِتَابَ بِقُوَّةٍ ۖ وَآتَيْنَاهُ الْحُكْمَ صَبِيًّا

12 "O John, hold on to the Scripture firmly," and We gave him wisdom in his youth.

١٣ وَحَنَانًا مِّن لَّدُنَّا وَزَكَاةً ۖ وَكَانَ تَقِيًّا

13 And tenderness from Us, and innocence. He was devout.

١٤ وَبَرًّا بِوَالِدَيْهِ وَلَمْ يَكُن جَبَّارًا عَصِيًّا

14 And kind to his parents; and he was not a disobedient tyrant.

١٥ وَسَلَامٌ عَلَيْهِ يَوْمَ وُلِدَ وَيَوْمَ يَمُوتُ وَيَوْمَ يُبْعَثُ حَيًّا

15 And peace be upon him the day he was born, and the day he dies, and the Day he is raised alive.

١٦ وَاذْكُرْ فِي الْكِتَابِ مَرْيَمَ إِذِ انتَبَذَتْ مِنْ أَهْلِهَا مَكَانًا شَرْقِيًّا

16 And mention in the Scripture Mary, when she withdrew from her people to an eastern location.

١٧ فَاتَّخَذَتْ مِن دُونِهِمْ حِجَابًا فَأَرْسَلْنَا إِلَيْهَا رُوحَنَا فَتَمَثَّلَ لَهَا بَشَرًا سَوِيًّا

17 She screened herself away from them, and We sent to her Our spirit, and He appeared to her as an immaculate human.

17–19
3:45

١٨ قَالَتْ إِنِّي أَعُوذُ بِالرَّحْمَٰنِ مِنكَ إِن كُنتَ تَقِيًّا

18 She said, "I take refuge from you in the Most Merciful, should you be righteous."

١٩ قَالَ إِنَّمَا أَنَا رَسُولُ رَبِّكِ لِأَهَبَ لَكِ غُلَامًا زَكِيًّا

19 He said, "I am only the messenger of your Lord, to give you the gift of a pure son."

٢٠ قَالَتْ أَنَّىٰ يَكُونُ لِي غُلَامٌ وَلَمْ يَمْسَسْنِي بَشَرٌ وَلَمْ أَكُ بَغِيًّا

20 She said, "How can I have a son, when no man has touched me, and I was never unchaste?"

20
3:47

٢١ قَالَ كَذَٰلِكِ قَالَ رَبُّكِ هُوَ عَلَيَّ هَيِّنٌ ۖ وَلِنَجْعَلَهُ آيَةً لِّلنَّاسِ وَرَحْمَةً مِّنَّا ۚ وَكَانَ أَمْرًا مَّقْضِيًّا

21 He said, "Thus said your Lord, 'It is easy for Me, and We will make him a sign for humanity, and a mercy from Us. It is a matter already decided.'"

21
19:9

٢٢ فَحَمَلَتْهُ فَانتَبَذَتْ بِهِ مَكَانًا قَصِيًّا

22 So she carried him, and secluded herself with him in a remote place.

٢٣ فَأَجَاءَهَا الْمَخَاضُ إِلَىٰ جِذْعِ النَّخْلَةِ قَالَتْ يَا لَيْتَنِي مِتُّ قَبْلَ هَٰذَا وَكُنتُ نَسْيًا مَّنسِيًّا

23 The labor-pains came upon her, by the trunk of a palm-tree. She said, "I wish I had died before this, and been completely forgotten."

٢٤ فَنَادَاهَا مِنْ تَحْتِهَا أَلَّا تَحْزَنِي قَدْ جَعَلَ رَبُّكِ تَحْتَكِ سَرِيًّا

24 Whereupon he called her from beneath her: "Do not worry; your Lord has placed a stream beneath you.

٢٥ وَهُزِّي إِلَيْكِ بِجِذْعِ النَّخْلَةِ تُسَاقِطْ عَلَيْكِ رُطَبًا جَنِيًّا

25 And shake the trunk of the palm-tree towards you, and it will drop ripe dates by you."

٢٦ فَكُلِي وَاشْرَبِي وَقَرِّي عَيْنًا ۖ فَإِمَّا تَرَيِنَّ مِنَ الْبَشَرِ أَحَدًا فَقُولِي إِنِّي نَذَرْتُ لِلرَّحْمَٰنِ صَوْمًا فَلَنْ أُكَلِّمَ الْيَوْمَ إِنْسِيًّا

26 "So eat, and drink, and be consoled. And if you see any human, say, 'I have vowed a fast to the Most Gracious, so I will not speak to any human today.'"

٢٧ فَأَتَتْ بِهِ قَوْمَهَا تَحْمِلُهُ ۖ قَالُوا يَا مَرْيَمُ لَقَدْ جِئْتِ شَيْئًا فَرِيًّا

27 Then she came to her people, carrying him. They said, "O Mary, you have done something terrible.

27–28
4:156; 19:89

٢٨ يَا أُخْتَ هَارُونَ مَا كَانَ أَبُوكِ امْرَأَ سَوْءٍ وَمَا كَانَتْ أُمُّكِ بَغِيًّا

28 O sister of Aaron, your father was not an evil man, and your mother was not a whore."

٢٩ فَأَشَارَتْ إِلَيْهِ ۖ قَالُوا كَيْفَ نُكَلِّمُ مَنْ كَانَ فِي الْمَهْدِ صَبِيًّا

29 So she pointed to him. They said, "How can we speak to an infant in the crib?"

٣٠ قَالَ إِنِّي عَبْدُ اللَّهِ آتَانِيَ الْكِتَابَ وَجَعَلَنِي نَبِيًّا

30 He said, "I am the servant of God. He has given me the Scripture, and made me a prophet.

٣١ وَجَعَلَنِي مُبَارَكًا أَيْنَ مَا كُنْتُ وَأَوْصَانِي بِالصَّلَاةِ وَالزَّكَاةِ مَا دُمْتُ حَيًّا

31 And has made me blessed wherever I may be; and has enjoined on me prayer and charity, so long as I live.

٣٢ وَبَرًّا بِوَالِدَتِي وَلَمْ يَجْعَلْنِي جَبَّارًا شَقِيًّا

32 And kind to my mother, and He did not make me a disobedient rebel.

٣٣ وَالسَّلَامُ عَلَيَّ يَوْمَ وُلِدْتُ وَيَوْمَ أَمُوتُ وَيَوْمَ أُبْعَثُ حَيًّا

33 So Peace is upon me the day I was born, and the day I die, and the Day I get resurrected alive."

٣٤ ذَٰلِكَ عِيسَى ابْنُ مَرْيَمَ ۚ قَوْلَ الْحَقِّ الَّذِي فِيهِ يَمْتَرُونَ

34 That is Jesus son of Mary—the Word of truth about which they doubt.

34
3:60

٣٥ مَا كَانَ لِلَّهِ أَن يَتَّخِذَ مِن وَلَدٍ ۖ سُبْحَانَهُ ۚ إِذَا قَضَىٰ أَمْرًا فَإِنَّمَا يَقُولُ لَهُ كُن فَيَكُونُ

35 It is not for God to have a child—glory be to Him. To have anything done, He says to it, "Be," and it becomes.

35
2:116; 4:171

٣٦ وَإِنَّ اللَّهَ رَبِّي وَرَبُّكُمْ فَاعْبُدُوهُ ۚ هَٰذَا صِرَاطٌ مُّسْتَقِيمٌ

36 "God is my Lord and your Lord, so worship Him. That is a straight path."

36
3:51; 5:72; 43:64

٣٧ فَاخْتَلَفَ الْأَحْزَابُ مِن بَيْنِهِمْ ۖ فَوَيْلٌ لِّلَّذِينَ كَفَرُوا مِن مَّشْهَدِ يَوْمٍ عَظِيمٍ

37 But the various factions differed among themselves. So woe to those who disbelieve from the scene of a tremendous Day.

37
43:65

٣٨ أَسْمِعْ بِهِمْ وَأَبْصِرْ يَوْمَ يَأْتُونَنَا ۖ لَٰكِنِ الظَّالِمُونَ الْيَوْمَ فِي ضَلَالٍ مُّبِينٍ

38 Listen to them and watch for them the Day they come to Us. But the wrongdoers today are completely lost.

٣٩ وَأَنذِرْهُمْ يَوْمَ الْحَسْرَةِ إِذْ قُضِيَ الْأَمْرُ وَهُمْ فِي غَفْلَةٍ وَهُمْ لَا يُؤْمِنُونَ

39 And warn them of the Day of Regret, when the matter will be concluded. Yet they are heedless, and they do not believe.

39
40:18

٤٠ إِنَّا نَحْنُ نَرِثُ الْأَرْضَ وَمَنْ عَلَيْهَا وَإِلَيْنَا يُرْجَعُونَ

40 It is We who will inherit the earth and everyone on it, and to Us they will be returned.

40
15:23

٤١ وَاذْكُرْ فِي الْكِتَابِ إِبْرَاهِيمَ ۚ إِنَّهُ كَانَ صِدِّيقًا نَّبِيًّا

41 And mention in the Scripture Abraham. He was a man of truth, a prophet.

41
19:56

٤٢ إِذْ قَالَ لِأَبِيهِ يَا أَبَتِ لِمَ تَعْبُدُ مَا لَا يَسْمَعُ وَلَا يُبْصِرُ وَلَا يُغْنِي عَنكَ شَيْئًا

42 He said to his father, "O my father, why do you worship what can neither hear, nor see, nor benefit you in any way?

42
6:74; 21:51–522;
26:70; 37:85; 43:26

٤٣ يَا أَبَتِ إِنِّي قَدْ جَاءَنِي مِنَ الْعِلْمِ مَا لَمْ يَأْتِكَ فَاتَّبِعْنِي أَهْدِكَ صِرَاطًا سَوِيًّا

43 O my father, there has come to me knowledge that never came to you. So follow me, and I will guide you along a straight way.

٤٤ يَا أَبَتِ لَا تَعْبُدِ الشَّيْطَانَ ۖ إِنَّ الشَّيْطَانَ كَانَ لِلرَّحْمَٰنِ عَصِيًّا

44 O my father, do not worship the devil. The devil is disobedient to the Most Gracious.

44
36:60

٤٥ يَا أَبَتِ إِنِّي أَخَافُ أَن يَمَسَّكَ عَذَابٌ مِّنَ الرَّحْمَٰنِ فَتَكُونَ لِلشَّيْطَانِ وَلِيًّا

45 O my father, I fear that a punishment from the Most Gracious will afflict you, and you become an ally of the devil."

٤٦ قَالَ أَرَاغِبٌ أَنتَ عَنْ آلِهَتِي يَا إِبْرَاهِيمُ ۖ لَئِن لَّمْ تَنتَهِ لَأَرْجُمَنَّكَ ۖ وَاهْجُرْنِي مَلِيًّا

46 He said, "Are you renouncing my gods, O Abraham? If you do not desist, I will stone you. So leave me alone for a while."

٤٧ قَالَ سَلَامٌ عَلَيْكَ ۖ سَأَسْتَغْفِرُ لَكَ رَبِّي ۖ إِنَّهُ كَانَ بِي حَفِيًّا

47 He said, "Peace be upon you. I will ask my Lord to forgive you; He has been Kind to me.

٤٨ وَأَعْتَزِلُكُمْ وَمَا تَدْعُونَ مِنْ دُونِ اللَّهِ وَأَدْعُو رَبِّي عَسَىٰ أَلَّا أَكُونَ بِدُعَاءِ رَبِّي شَقِيًّا

48 And I will withdraw from you, and from what you pray to instead of God. And I will pray to my Lord, and I hope I will not be disappointed in my prayer to my Lord."

48
43:26–27

٤٩ فَلَمَّا اعْتَزَلَهُمْ وَمَا يَعْبُدُونَ مِنْ دُونِ اللَّهِ وَهَبْنَا لَهُ إِسْحَاقَ وَيَعْقُوبَ ۖ وَكُلًّا جَعَلْنَا نَبِيًّا

49 When he withdrew from them, and from what they worship besides God, We granted him Isaac and Jacob. And each We made a prophet.

49
6:84; 21:72; 29:27

٥٠ وَوَهَبْنَا لَهُمْ مِنْ رَحْمَتِنَا وَجَعَلْنَا لَهُمْ لِسَانَ صِدْقٍ عَلِيًّا

50 And We gave them freely of Our mercy, and gave them a noble reputation of truth.

٥١ وَاذْكُرْ فِي الْكِتَابِ مُوسَىٰ ۚ إِنَّهُ كَانَ مُخْلَصًا وَكَانَ رَسُولًا نَبِيًّا

51 And mention in the Scripture Moses. He was dedicated. He was a messenger and a prophet.

٥٢ وَنَادَيْنَاهُ مِنْ جَانِبِ الطُّورِ الْأَيْمَنِ وَقَرَّبْنَاهُ نَجِيًّا

52 And We called him from the right side of the Mount, and brought him near in communion.

52
20:12; 26:10; 79:16

٥٣ وَوَهَبْنَا لَهُ مِنْ رَحْمَتِنَا أَخَاهُ هَارُونَ نَبِيًّا

53 And We granted him, out of Our mercy, his brother Aaron, a prophet.

53
20:29–30; 25:35

٥٤ وَاذْكُرْ فِي الْكِتَابِ إِسْمَاعِيلَ ۚ إِنَّهُ كَانَ صَادِقَ الْوَعْدِ وَكَانَ رَسُولًا نَبِيًّا

54 And mention in the Scripture Ishmael. He was true to his promise, and was a messenger, a prophet.

54
21:85; 38:48

٥٥ وَكَانَ يَأْمُرُ أَهْلَهُ بِالصَّلَاةِ وَالزَّكَاةِ وَكَانَ عِنْدَ رَبِّهِ مَرْضِيًّا

55 And he used to enjoin on his people prayer and charity, and he was pleasing to his Lord.

٥٦ وَاذْكُرْ فِي الْكِتَابِ إِدْرِيسَ ۚ إِنَّهُ كَانَ صِدِّيقًا نَبِيًّا

56 And mention in the Scripture Enoch. He was a man of truth, a prophet.

56
19:41; 21:85

٥٧ وَرَفَعْنَاهُ مَكَانًا عَلِيًّا

57 And We raised him to a high position.

٥٨ أُولَٰئِكَ الَّذِينَ أَنْعَمَ اللَّهُ عَلَيْهِم مِّنَ النَّبِيِّينَ مِن ذُرِّيَّةِ آدَمَ وَمِمَّنْ حَمَلْنَا مَعَ نُوحٍ وَمِن ذُرِّيَّةِ إِبْرَاهِيمَ وَإِسْرَائِيلَ وَمِمَّنْ هَدَيْنَا وَاجْتَبَيْنَا ۚ إِذَا تُتْلَىٰ عَلَيْهِمْ آيَاتُ الرَّحْمَٰنِ خَرُّوا سُجَّدًا وَبُكِيًّا ۩

58 3:33; 6:84–87; 16:121; 17:3; 57:26

58 These are some of the prophets God has blessed, from the descendants of Adam, and from those We carried with Noah, and from the descendants of Abraham and Israel, and from those We guided and selected. Whenever the revelations of the Most Gracious are recited to them, they would fall down, prostrating and weeping.

٥٩ فَخَلَفَ مِن بَعْدِهِمْ خَلْفٌ أَضَاعُوا الصَّلَاةَ وَاتَّبَعُوا الشَّهَوَاتِ ۖ فَسَوْفَ يَلْقَوْنَ غَيًّا

59 7:169; 107:5

59 But they were succeeded by generations who lost the prayers and followed their appetites. They will meet perdition.

٦٠ إِلَّا مَن تَابَ وَآمَنَ وَعَمِلَ صَالِحًا فَأُولَٰئِكَ يَدْخُلُونَ الْجَنَّةَ وَلَا يُظْلَمُونَ شَيْئًا

60 Except for those who repent, and believe, and act righteously. These will enter Paradise, and will not be wronged in the least.

٦١ جَنَّاتِ عَدْنٍ الَّتِي وَعَدَ الرَّحْمَٰنُ عِبَادَهُ بِالْغَيْبِ ۚ إِنَّهُ كَانَ وَعْدُهُ مَأْتِيًّا

61 The Gardens of Eden, promised by the Most Merciful to His servants in the Unseen. His promise will certainly come true.

٦٢ لَا يَسْمَعُونَ فِيهَا لَغْوًا إِلَّا سَلَامًا ۖ وَلَهُمْ رِزْقُهُمْ فِيهَا بُكْرَةً وَعَشِيًّا

62 13:23–24; 14:23; 56:26

62 They will hear no nonsense therein, but only peace. And they will have their provision therein, morning and evening.

٦٣ تِلْكَ الْجَنَّةُ الَّتِي نُورِثُ مِنْ عِبَادِنَا مَن كَانَ تَقِيًّا

63 Such is Paradise which We will give as inheritance to those of Our servants who are devout.

٦٤ وَمَا نَتَنَزَّلُ إِلَّا بِأَمْرِ رَبِّكَ ۖ لَهُ مَا بَيْنَ أَيْدِينَا وَمَا خَلْفَنَا وَمَا بَيْنَ ذَٰلِكَ ۚ وَمَا كَانَ رَبُّكَ نَسِيًّا

64 41:30

64 "We do not descend except by the command of your Lord. His is what is before us, and what is behind us, and what is between them. Your Lord is never forgetful."

٦٥ رَبُّ السَّمَاوَاتِ وَالْأَرْضِ وَمَا بَيْنَهُمَا فَاعْبُدْهُ وَاصْطَبِرْ لِعِبَادَتِهِ ۚ هَلْ تَعْلَمُ لَهُ سَمِيًّا

65 Lord of the heavens and the earth and what is between them. So worship Him, and persevere in His service. Do you know of anyone equal to Him?

٦٦ وَيَقُولُ الْإِنسَانُ أَإِذَا مَا مِتُّ لَسَوْفَ أُخْرَجُ حَيًّا

66 13:5; 37:78–79

66 And the human being says, "When I am dead, will I be brought back alive?"

٦٧ أَوَلَا يَذْكُرُ الْإِنسَانُ أَنَّا خَلَقْنَاهُ مِن قَبْلُ وَلَمْ يَكُ شَيْئًا

67 19:29; 76:1

67 Does the human being not remember that We created him before, when he was nothing?

٦٨ فَوَرَبِّكَ لَنَحْشُرَنَّهُمْ وَالشَّيَاطِينَ ثُمَّ لَنُحْضِرَنَّهُمْ حَوْلَ جَهَنَّمَ جِثِيًّا

68 By your Lord, We will round them up, and the devils, then We will bring them around Hell, on their knees.

68
37:22; 45:28

٦٩ ثُمَّ لَنَنزِعَنَّ مِن كُلِّ شِيعَةٍ أَيُّهُمْ أَشَدُّ عَلَى الرَّحْمَٰنِ عِتِيًّا

69 Then, out of every sect, We will snatch those most defiant to the Most Merciful.

٧٠ ثُمَّ لَنَحْنُ أَعْلَمُ بِالَّذِينَ هُمْ أَوْلَىٰ بِهَا صِلِيًّا

70 We are fully aware of those most deserving to scorch in it.

٧١ وَإِن مِّنكُمْ إِلَّا وَارِدُهَا ۚ كَانَ عَلَىٰ رَبِّكَ حَتْمًا مَّقْضِيًّا

71 There is not one of you but will go down to it. This has been an unavoidable decree of your Lord.

71
11:98; 19:86; 21:86, 99

٧٢ ثُمَّ نُنَجِّي الَّذِينَ اتَّقَوا وَّنَذَرُ الظَّالِمِينَ فِيهَا جِثِيًّا

72 Then We will rescue those who were devout, and leave the wrong-doers in it, on their knees.

٧٣ وَإِذَا تُتْلَىٰ عَلَيْهِمْ آيَاتُنَا بَيِّنَاتٍ قَالَ الَّذِينَ كَفَرُوا لِلَّذِينَ آمَنُوا أَيُّ الْفَرِيقَيْنِ خَيْرٌ مَّقَامًا وَأَحْسَنُ نَدِيًّا

73 When Our clear revelations are recited to them, those who disbelieve say to those who believe, "Which of the two parties is better in position, and superior in influence?"

٧٤ وَكَمْ أَهْلَكْنَا قَبْلَهُم مِّن قَرْنٍ هُمْ أَحْسَنُ أَثَاثًا وَرِئْيًا

74 How many a generation have We destroyed before them, who surpassed them in riches and splendor?

74
6:6; 17:17; 19:98

٧٥ قُلْ مَن كَانَ فِي الضَّلَالَةِ فَلْيَمْدُدْ لَهُ الرَّحْمَٰنُ مَدًّا ۚ حَتَّىٰ إِذَا رَأَوْا مَا يُوعَدُونَ إِمَّا الْعَذَابَ وَإِمَّا السَّاعَةَ فَسَيَعْلَمُونَ مَنْ هُوَ شَرٌّ مَّكَانًا وَأَضْعَفُ جُندًا

75 Say, "Whoever is in error, the Most Merciful will lead him on." Until, when they see what they were promised—either the punishment, or the Hour. Then they will know who was in worse position and weaker in forces.

75
72:24

٧٦ وَيَزِيدُ اللَّهُ الَّذِينَ اهْتَدَوْا هُدًى ۗ وَالْبَاقِيَاتُ الصَّالِحَاتُ خَيْرٌ عِندَ رَبِّكَ ثَوَابًا وَخَيْرٌ مَّرَدًّا

76 God increases in guidance those who accept guidance. And the things that endure—the righteous deeds—have the best reward with your Lord, and the best outcome.

76
47:17

٧٧ أَفَرَأَيْتَ الَّذِي كَفَرَ بِآيَاتِنَا وَقَالَ لَأُوتَيَنَّ مَالًا وَوَلَدًا

77 Have you seen him who denied Our revelations, and said, "I will be given wealth and children"?

77
23:56

٧٨ أَطَّلَعَ الْغَيْبَ أَمِ اتَّخَذَ عِندَ الرَّحْمَٰنِ عَهْدًا

78 Did he look into the future, or did he receive a promise from the Most Merciful?

٧٩ كَلَّا ۚ سَنَكْتُبُ مَا يَقُولُ وَنَمُدُّ لَهُ مِنَ الْعَذَابِ مَدًّا

79 No indeed! We will write what he says, and will keep extending the agony for him.

٨٠ وَنَرِثُهُ مَا يَقُولُ وَيَأْتِينَا فَرْدًا

80 Then We will inherit from him what he speaks of, and he will come to Us alone.

٨١ وَاتَّخَذُوا مِنْ دُونِ اللَّهِ آلِهَةً لِيَكُونُوا لَهُمْ عِزًّا

81 And they took, besides God, other gods, to be for them a source of strength.

81
36:47

٨٢ كَلَّا ۚ سَيَكْفُرُونَ بِعِبَادَتِهِمْ وَيَكُونُونَ عَلَيْهِمْ ضِدًّا

82 By no means! They will reject their worship of them, and become opponents to them.

٨٣ أَلَمْ تَرَ أَنَّا أَرْسَلْنَا الشَّيَاطِينَ عَلَى الْكَافِرِينَ تَؤُزُّهُمْ أَزًّا

83 Have you not considered how We dispatch the devils against the disbelievers, exciting them with incitement?

83
17:64; 43:36

٨٤ فَلَا تَعْجَلْ عَلَيْهِمْ ۖ إِنَّمَا نَعُدُّ لَهُمْ عَدًّا

84 So do not hurry against them. We are counting for them a countdown.

٨٥ يَوْمَ نَحْشُرُ الْمُتَّقِينَ إِلَى الرَّحْمَٰنِ وَفْدًا

85 On the Day when We will gather the righteous to the Most Merciful, as guests.

٨٦ وَنَسُوقُ الْمُجْرِمِينَ إِلَىٰ جَهَنَّمَ وِرْدًا

86 And herd the sinners into hell, like animals to water.

86
11:98; 19:71

٨٧ لَا يَمْلِكُونَ الشَّفَاعَةَ إِلَّا مَنِ اتَّخَذَ عِنْدَ الرَّحْمَٰنِ عَهْدًا

87 They will have no power of intercession, except for someone who has an agreement with the Most Merciful.

87
2:48, 123, 255;
20:109; 21:28; 34:23;
53:26; 74:48

٨٨ وَقَالُوا اتَّخَذَ الرَّحْمَٰنُ وَلَدًا

88 And they say, "The Most Merciful has begotten a son."

88
18:4–9

٨٩ لَقَدْ جِئْتُمْ شَيْئًا إِدًّا

89 You have come up with something monstrous.

89
18:71; 19:27

٩٠ تَكَادُ السَّمَاوَاتُ يَتَفَطَّرْنَ مِنْهُ وَتَنْشَقُّ الْأَرْضُ وَتَخِرُّ الْجِبَالُ هَدًّا

90 At which the heavens almost rupture, and the earth splits, and the mountains fall and crumble.

٩١ أَنْ دَعَوْا لِلرَّحْمَٰنِ وَلَدًا

91 Because they attribute a son to the Most Merciful.

91
2:116

٩٢ وَمَا يَنبَغِي لِلرَّحْمَٰنِ أَن يَتَّخِذَ وَلَدًا

92 It is not fitting for the Most Merciful to have a son.

٩٣ إِن كُلُّ مَن فِي السَّمَاوَاتِ وَالْأَرْضِ إِلَّا آتِي الرَّحْمَٰنِ عَبْدًا

93 There is none in the heavens and the earth but will come to the Most Merciful as a servant.

٩٤ لَّقَدْ أَحْصَاهُمْ وَعَدَّهُمْ عَدًّا

94 He has enumerated them, and counted them one by one.

94
72:28; 78:29

٩٥ وَكُلُّهُمْ آتِيهِ يَوْمَ الْقِيَامَةِ فَرْدًا

95 And each one of them will come to Him on the Day of Resurrection alone.

٩٦ إِنَّ الَّذِينَ آمَنُوا وَعَمِلُوا الصَّالِحَاتِ سَيَجْعَلُ لَهُمُ الرَّحْمَٰنُ وُدًّا

96 Those who believe and do righteous deeds, the Most Merciful will give them love.

٩٧ فَإِنَّمَا يَسَّرْنَاهُ بِلِسَانِكَ لِتُبَشِّرَ بِهِ الْمُتَّقِينَ وَتُنذِرَ بِهِ قَوْمًا لُّدًّا

97 We made it easy in your tongue, in order to deliver good news to the righteous, and to warn with it a hostile people.

٩٨ وَكَمْ أَهْلَكْنَا قَبْلَهُم مِّن قَرْنٍ هَلْ تُحِسُّ مِنْهُم مِّنْ أَحَدٍ أَوْ تَسْمَعُ لَهُمْ رِكْزًا

98 How many a generation have We destroyed before them? Can you feel a single one of them, or hear from them the slightest whisper?

Sūrah 20: Ṭā-Hā

سُورَةُ طه (Ṭā' Hā')

بِسْمِ اللَّهِ الرَّحْمَٰنِ الرَّحِيمِ

١ طه

1 Ṭā', Hā'.

٢ مَا أَنزَلْنَا عَلَيْكَ الْقُرْآنَ لِتَشْقَىٰ

2 We did not reveal the Qur'an to you to make you suffer.

2–3
79:45; 81:27–28

٣ إِلَّا تَذْكِرَةً لِّمَن يَخْشَىٰ

3 But only as a reminder for him who fears.

3
50:45

٤ تَنزِيلًا مِّمَّنْ خَلَقَ الْأَرْضَ وَالسَّمَاوَاتِ الْعُلَى

4 A revelation from He who created the earth and the high heavens.

4
19:41; 26:192; 39:1

٥ الرَّحْمَٰنُ عَلَى الْعَرْشِ اسْتَوَىٰ

5 The Most Merciful; on the Throne He settled.

5
7:54

Sūrah 20: Ṭā-Hā — 327

٦ لَهُ مَا فِي السَّمَاوَاتِ وَمَا فِي الْأَرْضِ وَمَا بَيْنَهُمَا وَمَا تَحْتَ الثَّرَىٰ

6 To Him belongs everything in the heavens and the earth, and everything between them, and everything beneath the soil.

6
7:54; 10:3; 11:7; 13:2; 32:4; 57:4

٧ وَإِنْ تَجْهَرْ بِالْقَوْلِ فَإِنَّهُ يَعْلَمُ السِّرَّ وَأَخْفَىٰ

7 If you speak aloud—He knows the secret, and the most hidden.

7
16:19; 25:6; 47:26; 67:13

٨ اللَّهُ لَا إِلَٰهَ إِلَّا هُوَ ۖ لَهُ الْأَسْمَاءُ الْحُسْنَىٰ

8 God, there is no god but He, His are the Most Beautiful Names.

8
7:180; 17:110; 59:24

٩ وَهَلْ أَتَاكَ حَدِيثُ مُوسَىٰ

9 Has the story of Moses reached you?

9
pp 79:15

١٠ إِذْ رَأَىٰ نَارًا فَقَالَ لِأَهْلِهِ امْكُثُوا إِنِّي آنَسْتُ نَارًا لَعَلِّي آتِيكُمْ مِنْهَا بِقَبَسٍ أَوْ أَجِدُ عَلَى النَّارِ هُدًى

10 When he saw a fire, he said to his family, "Stay; I have noticed a fire; Perhaps I can bring you a torch therefrom, or find some guidance by the fire."

10
27:7; 28:29

١١ فَلَمَّا أَتَاهَا نُودِيَ يَا مُوسَىٰ

11 Then, when he reached it, he was called, "O Moses.

11
27:8; 28:30; 79:16

١٢ إِنِّي أَنَا رَبُّكَ فَاخْلَعْ نَعْلَيْكَ ۖ إِنَّكَ بِالْوَادِ الْمُقَدَّسِ طُوًى

12 I—I am your Lord. Take off your shoes. You are in the sacred valley of Tuwa.

١٣ وَأَنَا اخْتَرْتُكَ فَاسْتَمِعْ لِمَا يُوحَىٰ

13 I have chosen you, so listen to what is revealed.

13
7:114

١٤ إِنَّنِي أَنَا اللَّهُ لَا إِلَٰهَ إِلَّا أَنَا فَاعْبُدْنِي وَأَقِمِ الصَّلَاةَ لِذِكْرِي

14 I—I am God. There is no God but I. So serve Me, and practice the prayer for My remembrance.

١٥ إِنَّ السَّاعَةَ آتِيَةٌ أَكَادُ أُخْفِيهَا لِتُجْزَىٰ كُلُّ نَفْسٍ بِمَا تَسْعَىٰ

15 The Hour is coming—but I keep it almost hidden—so that each soul will be paid for what it endeavors.

15
14:51

١٦ فَلَا يَصُدَّنَّكَ عَنْهَا مَنْ لَا يُؤْمِنُ بِهَا وَاتَّبَعَ هَوَاهُ فَتَرْدَىٰ

16 And do not let him who denies it and follows his desire turn you away from it, lest you fall.

١٧ وَمَا تِلْكَ بِيَمِينِكَ يَا مُوسَىٰ

17 And what is that in your right-hand, O Moses?"

١٨ قَالَ هِيَ عَصَايَ أَتَوَكَّأُ عَلَيْهَا وَأَهُشُّ بِهَا عَلَىٰ غَنَمِي وَلِيَ فِيهَا مَآرِبُ أُخْرَىٰ

18 He said, "This is my staff. I lean on it, and herd my sheep with it, and I have other uses for it."

19 He said, "Throw it, O Moses."	١٩ قَالَ أَلْقِهَا يَا مُوسَىٰ	**19–20** 26:32; 27:10; 28:31
20 So he threw it—thereupon it became a moving serpent.	٢٠ فَأَلْقَاهَا فَإِذَا هِيَ حَيَّةٌ تَسْعَىٰ	
21 He said, "Take hold of it, and do not fear. We will restore it to its original condition.	٢١ قَالَ خُذْهَا وَلَا تَخَفْ ۖ سَنُعِيدُهَا سِيرَتَهَا الْأُولَىٰ	
22 And press your hand to your side; it will come out white, without a blemish—another sign.	٢٢ وَاضْمُمْ يَدَكَ إِلَىٰ جَنَاحِكَ تَخْرُجْ بَيْضَاءَ مِنْ غَيْرِ سُوءٍ آيَةً أُخْرَىٰ	**22–23** 26:33; 27:12; 28:32
23 That We may show you some of Our greatest signs.	٢٣ لِنُرِيَكَ مِنْ آيَاتِنَا الْكُبْرَى	
24 Go to Pharaoh; He has transgressed."	٢٤ اذْهَبْ إِلَىٰ فِرْعَوْنَ إِنَّهُ طَغَىٰ	**24** pp 79:17
25 He said, "My Lord, put my heart at peace for me.	٢٥ قَالَ رَبِّ اشْرَحْ لِي صَدْرِي	
26 And ease my task for me.	٢٦ وَيَسِّرْ لِي أَمْرِي	
27 And untie the knot from my tongue.	٢٧ وَاحْلُلْ عُقْدَةً مِنْ لِسَانِي	**27** 37:114
28 So they can understand my speech.	٢٨ يَفْقَهُوا قَوْلِي	
29 And appoint an assistant for me, from my family.	٢٩ وَاجْعَلْ لِي وَزِيرًا مِنْ أَهْلِي	**29–30** 20:42; 25:35
30 Aaron, my brother.	٣٠ هَارُونَ أَخِي	
31 Strengthen me with him.	٣١ اشْدُدْ بِهِ أَزْرِي	**31** 27:35
32 And have him share in my mission.	٣٢ وَأَشْرِكْهُ فِي أَمْرِي	
33 That we may glorify You much.	٣٣ كَيْ نُسَبِّحَكَ كَثِيرًا	
34 And remember You much.	٣٤ وَنَذْكُرَكَ كَثِيرًا	

٣٥ إِنَّكَ كُنتَ بِنَا بَصِيرًا

35 You are always watching over us."

٣٦ قَالَ قَدْ أُوتِيتَ سُؤْلَكَ يَا مُوسَىٰ

36 He said, "You are granted your request, O Moses.

٣٧ وَلَقَدْ مَنَنَّا عَلَيْكَ مَرَّةً أُخْرَىٰ

37 We had favored you another time.

٣٨ إِذْ أَوْحَيْنَا إِلَىٰ أُمِّكَ مَا يُوحَىٰ

38
28:7

38 When We inspired your mother with the inspiration.

٣٩ أَنِ اقْذِفِيهِ فِي التَّابُوتِ فَاقْذِفِيهِ فِي الْيَمِّ فَلْيُلْقِهِ الْيَمُّ بِالسَّاحِلِ يَأْخُذْهُ عَدُوٌّ لِي وَعَدُوٌّ لَهُ ۚ وَأَلْقَيْتُ عَلَيْكَ مَحَبَّةً مِنِّي وَلِتُصْنَعَ عَلَىٰ عَيْنِي

39
28:8, 34

39 'Put him in the chest; then cast him into the river. The river will wash him to shore, where an enemy of Mine and an enemy of his will pick him up. And I have bestowed upon you love from Me, so that you may be reared before My eye.

٤٠ إِذْ تَمْشِي أُخْتُكَ فَتَقُولُ هَلْ أَدُلُّكُمْ عَلَىٰ مَن يَكْفُلُهُ ۖ فَرَجَعْنَاكَ إِلَىٰ أُمِّكَ كَيْ تَقَرَّ عَيْنُهَا وَلَا تَحْزَنَ ۚ وَقَتَلْتَ نَفْسًا فَنَجَّيْنَاكَ مِنَ الْغَمِّ وَفَتَنَّاكَ فُتُونًا ۚ[a] فَلَبِثْتَ سِنِينَ فِي أَهْلِ مَدْيَنَ ثُمَّ جِئْتَ عَلَىٰ قَدَرٍ يَا مُوسَىٰ[b]

40
[a] 28:11–13, 33
[b] 28:27

40 When your sister walked along, and said, 'Shall I tell you about someone who will take care of him?' So We returned you to your mother, that she may be comforted, and not sorrow. And you killed a person, but We saved you from stress; and We tested you thoroughly. And you stayed years among the people of Median. Then you came back, as ordained, O Moses.

٤١ وَاصْطَنَعْتُكَ لِنَفْسِي

41 And I made you for Myself.

٤٢ اذْهَبْ أَنتَ وَأَخُوكَ بِآيَاتِي وَلَا تَنِيَا فِي ذِكْرِي

42
17:101; 20:29–30;
27:12

42 Go, you and your brother, with My signs, and do not neglect My remembrance.

٤٣ اذْهَبَا إِلَىٰ فِرْعَوْنَ إِنَّهُ طَغَىٰ

43 Go to Pharaoh. He has tyrannized.

٤٤ فَقُولَا لَهُ قَوْلًا لَيِّنًا لَعَلَّهُ يَتَذَكَّرُ أَوْ يَخْشَىٰ

44 But speak to him nicely. Perhaps he will remember, or have some fear."

٤٥ قَالَا رَبَّنَا إِنَّنَا نَخَافُ أَن يَفْرُطَ عَلَيْنَا أَوْ أَن يَطْغَىٰ

45 They said, "Lord, we fear he may persecute us, or become violent."

٤٦ قَالَ لَا تَخَافَا ۖ إِنَّنِي مَعَكُمَا أَسْمَعُ وَأَرَىٰ

46 He said, "Do not fear, I am with you, I hear and I see."

46
26:15

٤٧ فَأْتِيَاهُ فَقُولَا إِنَّا رَسُولَا رَبِّكَ فَأَرْسِلْ مَعَنَا بَنِي إِسْرَائِيلَ وَلَا تُعَذِّبْهُمْ ۖ قَدْ جِئْنَاكَ بِآيَةٍ مِنْ رَبِّكَ ۖ وَالسَّلَامُ عَلَىٰ مَنِ اتَّبَعَ الْهُدَىٰ

47 Approach him and say, 'We are the messengers of your Lord; so let the Children of Israel go with us, and do not torment them. We bring you a sign from your Lord, and peace be upon him who follows guidance.

47
7:104; 26:16; 43:46

٤٨ إِنَّا قَدْ أُوحِيَ إِلَيْنَا أَنَّ الْعَذَابَ عَلَىٰ مَنْ كَذَّبَ وَتَوَلَّىٰ

48 It was revealed to us that the punishment falls upon him who disbelieves and turns away.'"

٤٩ قَالَ فَمَنْ رَبُّكُمَا يَا مُوسَىٰ

49 He said, "Who is your Lord, O Moses."

49–50
26:23–24

٥٠ قَالَ رَبُّنَا الَّذِي أَعْطَىٰ كُلَّ شَيْءٍ خَلْقَهُ ثُمَّ هَدَىٰ

50 He said, "Our Lord is He who gave everything its existence, then guided it."

٥١ قَالَ فَمَا بَالُ الْقُرُونِ الْأُولَىٰ

51 He said, "What about the first generations?"

٥٢ قَالَ عِلْمُهَا عِنْدَ رَبِّي فِي كِتَابٍ ۖ لَا يَضِلُّ رَبِّي وَلَا يَنْسَى

52 He said, "Knowledge thereof is with my Lord, in a Book. My Lord never errs, nor does He forget."

٥٣ الَّذِي جَعَلَ لَكُمُ الْأَرْضَ مَهْدًا وَسَلَكَ لَكُمْ فِيهَا سُبُلًا وَأَنْزَلَ مِنَ السَّمَاءِ مَاءً فَأَخْرَجْنَا بِهِ أَزْوَاجًا مِنْ نَبَاتٍ شَتَّىٰ

53 He who made the earth a habitat for you; and traced in it routes for you; and sent down water from the sky, with which We produce pairs of diverse plants.

53
43:10

٥٤ كُلُوا وَارْعَوْا أَنْعَامَكُمْ ۗ إِنَّ فِي ذَٰلِكَ لَآيَاتٍ لِأُولِي النُّهَىٰ

54 Eat and pasture your livestock. In that are signs for those with understanding.

54
32:27; 79:31–33

٥٥ مِنْهَا خَلَقْنَاكُمْ وَفِيهَا نُعِيدُكُمْ وَمِنْهَا نُخْرِجُكُمْ تَارَةً أُخْرَىٰ

55 From it We created you, and into it We will return you, and from it We will bring you out another time.

55
71:18

٥٦ وَلَقَدْ أَرَيْنَاهُ آيَاتِنَا كُلَّهَا فَكَذَّبَ وَأَبَىٰ

56 We showed him Our signs, all of them, but he denied and refused.

56
79:20–21

٥٧ قَالَ أَجِئْتَنَا لِتُخْرِجَنَا مِنْ أَرْضِنَا بِسِحْرِكَ يَا مُوسَىٰ

57 He said, "Did you come to us to drive us out of our land with your magic, O Moses?

57
7:109–110; 20:63

٥٨ فَلَنَأْتِيَنَّكَ بِسِحْرٍ مِثْلِهِ فَاجْعَلْ بَيْنَنَا وَبَيْنَكَ مَوْعِدًا لَا نُخْلِفُهُ نَحْنُ وَلَا أَنتَ مَكَانًا سُوًى

58 We will produce for you magic like it; so make an appointment between us and you, which we will not miss—neither us, nor you—in a central place."

58   7:111; 10:79; 26:36–37

٥٩ قَالَ مَوْعِدُكُمْ يَوْمُ الزِّينَةِ وَأَن يُحْشَرَ النَّاسُ ضُحًى

59 He said, "Your appointment is the day of the festival, so let the people be gathered together at mid-morning."

59   26:37

٦٠ فَتَوَلَّىٰ فِرْعَوْنُ فَجَمَعَ كَيْدَهُ ثُمَّ أَتَىٰ

60 Pharaoh turned away, put together his plan, and then came back.

60   20:64, 69

٦١ قَالَ لَهُم مُّوسَىٰ وَيْلَكُمْ لَا تَفْتَرُوا عَلَى اللَّهِ كَذِبًا فَيُسْحِتَكُم بِعَذَابٍ وَقَدْ خَابَ مَنِ افْتَرَىٰ

61 Moses said to them, "Woe to you. Do not fabricate lies against God, or He will destroy you with a punishment. He who invents lies will fail."

٦٢ فَتَنَازَعُوا أَمْرَهُم بَيْنَهُمْ وَأَسَرُّوا النَّجْوَىٰ

62 They disagreed among themselves over their affair, and conferred secretly.

٦٣ قَالُوا إِنْ هَٰذَانِ لَسَاحِرَانِ يُرِيدَانِ أَن يُخْرِجَاكُم مِّنْ أَرْضِكُم بِسِحْرِهِمَا وَيَذْهَبَا بِطَرِيقَتِكُمُ الْمُثْلَىٰ

63 They said, "These two are magicians who want to drive you out of your land with their magic, and to abolish your exemplary way of life.

63   7:109; 10:76; 20:57; 26:34

٦٤ فَأَجْمِعُوا كَيْدَكُمْ ثُمَّ ائْتُوا صَفًّا وَقَدْ أَفْلَحَ الْيَوْمَ مَنِ اسْتَعْلَىٰ

64 So settle your plan, and come as one front. Today, whoever gains the upper hand will succeed."

٦٥ قَالُوا يَا مُوسَىٰ إِمَّا أَن تُلْقِيَ وَإِمَّا أَن نَّكُونَ أَوَّلَ مَنْ أَلْقَىٰ

65 They said, "O Moses, either you throw, or we will be the first to throw."

65   7:115; 26:43–45

٦٦ قَالَ بَلْ أَلْقُوا فَإِذَا حِبَالُهُمْ وَعِصِيُّهُمْ يُخَيَّلُ إِلَيْهِ مِن سِحْرِهِمْ أَنَّهَا تَسْعَىٰ

66 He said, "You throw." And suddenly, their ropes and sticks appeared to him, because of their magic, to be crawling swiftly.

66   7:116; 10:80; 26:43

٦٧ فَأَوْجَسَ فِي نَفْسِهِ خِيفَةً مُّوسَىٰ

67 So Moses felt apprehensive within himself.

٦٨ قُلْنَا لَا تَخَفْ إِنَّكَ أَنتَ الْأَعْلَىٰ

68 We said, "Do not be afraid, you are the uppermost.

٦٩ وَأَلْقِ مَا فِي يَمِينِكَ تَلْقَفْ مَا صَنَعُوا إِنَّمَا صَنَعُوا كَيْدُ سَاحِرٍ وَلَا يُفْلِحُ السَّاحِرُ حَيْثُ أَتَىٰ

69 Now throw down what is in your right hand—it will swallow what they have crafted. What they have crafted is only a magician's trickery. But the magician will not succeed, no matter what he does."

69   7:117; 26:45

٧٠ فَأُلْقِيَ السَّحَرَةُ سُجَّدًا قَالُوا آمَنَّا بِرَبِّ هَارُونَ وَمُوسَىٰ

70 And the magicians fell down prostrate. They said, "We have believed in the Lord of Aaron and Moses."

70
7:120–122; 26:46–48

٧١ قَالَ آمَنتُمْ لَهُ قَبْلَ أَنْ آذَنَ لَكُمْ ۖ إِنَّهُ لَكَبِيرُكُمُ الَّذِي عَلَّمَكُمُ السِّحْرَ ۖ فَلَأُقَطِّعَنَّ أَيْدِيَكُمْ وَأَرْجُلَكُم مِّنْ خِلَافٍ وَلَأُصَلِّبَنَّكُمْ فِي جُذُوعِ النَّخْلِ وَلَتَعْلَمُنَّ أَيُّنَا أَشَدُّ عَذَابًا وَأَبْقَىٰ

71 He said, "Did you believe in him before I have given you permission? He must be your chief, who has taught you magic. I will cut off your hands and your feet on alternate sides, and I will crucify you on the trunks of the palm-trees. Then you will know which of us is more severe in punishment, and more lasting."

71
7:123; 26:49

٧٢ قَالُوا لَن نُّؤْثِرَكَ عَلَىٰ مَا جَاءَنَا مِنَ الْبَيِّنَاتِ وَالَّذِي فَطَرَنَا ۖ فَاقْضِ مَا أَنتَ قَاضٍ ۖ إِنَّمَا تَقْضِي هَٰذِهِ الْحَيَاةَ الدُّنْيَا

72 They said, "We will not prefer you to the proofs that have come to us, and Him who created us. So issue whatever judgment you wish to issue. You can only rule in this lowly life.

٧٣ إِنَّا آمَنَّا بِرَبِّنَا لِيَغْفِرَ لَنَا خَطَايَانَا وَمَا أَكْرَهْتَنَا عَلَيْهِ مِنَ السِّحْرِ ۗ وَاللَّهُ خَيْرٌ وَأَبْقَىٰ

73 We have believed in our Lord, so that He may forgive us our sins, and the magic you have compelled us to practice. God is Better, and more Lasting."

٧٤ إِنَّهُ مَن يَأْتِ رَبَّهُ مُجْرِمًا فَإِنَّ لَهُ جَهَنَّمَ لَا يَمُوتُ فِيهَا وَلَا يَحْيَىٰ

74 Whoever comes to his Lord guilty, for him is Hell, where he neither dies nor lives.

74
4:56; 14:15–17;
87:12–13

٧٥ وَمَن يَأْتِهِ مُؤْمِنًا قَدْ عَمِلَ الصَّالِحَاتِ فَأُولَٰئِكَ لَهُمُ الدَّرَجَاتُ الْعُلَىٰ

75 But whoever comes to Him a believer, having worked righteousness—these will have the highest ranks.

٧٦ جَنَّاتُ عَدْنٍ تَجْرِي مِن تَحْتِهَا الْأَنْهَارُ خَالِدِينَ فِيهَا ۚ وَذَٰلِكَ جَزَاءُ مَن تَزَكَّىٰ

76 The Gardens of Perpetuity, beneath which rivers flow, dwelling therein forever. That is the reward for him who purifies himself.

٧٧ وَلَقَدْ أَوْحَيْنَا إِلَىٰ مُوسَىٰ أَنْ أَسْرِ بِعِبَادِي فَاضْرِبْ لَهُمْ طَرِيقًا فِي الْبَحْرِ يَبَسًا لَّا تَخَافُ دَرَكًا وَلَا تَخْشَىٰ

77 And We inspired Moses: "Travel by night with My servants, and strike for them a dry path across the sea, not fearing being overtaken, nor worrying."

77
10:90; 26:52; 44:23

٧٨ فَأَتْبَعَهُمْ فِرْعَوْنُ بِجُنُودِهِ فَغَشِيَهُم مِّنَ الْيَمِّ مَا غَشِيَهُمْ

78 Pharaoh pursued them with his troops, but the sea overwhelmed them, and completely engulfed them.

78
7:136; 10:90

٧٩ وَأَضَلَّ فِرْعَوْنُ قَوْمَهُ وَمَا هَدَىٰ

79 Pharaoh misled his people, and did not guide them.

٨٠ يَا بَنِي إِسْرَائِيلَ قَدْ أَنْجَيْنَاكُمْ مِنْ عَدُوِّكُمْ وَوَاعَدْنَاكُمْ جَانِبَ الطُّورِ الْأَيْمَنَ وَنَزَّلْنَا عَلَيْكُمُ الْمَنَّ وَالسَّلْوَىٰ

80
2:49; 7:141, 160; 40:30

80 O Children of Israel! We have delivered you from your enemy, and promised you by the right side of the Mount, and sent down to you manna and quails.

٨١ كُلُوا مِنْ طَيِّبَاتِ مَا رَزَقْنَاكُمْ وَلَا تَطْغَوْا فِيهِ فَيَحِلَّ عَلَيْكُمْ غَضَبِي ۖ وَمَنْ يَحْلِلْ عَلَيْهِ غَضَبِي فَقَدْ هَوَىٰ

81 Eat of the good things We have provided for you, but do not be excessive therein, lest My wrath descends upon you. He upon whom My wrath descends has fallen.

٨٢ وَإِنِّي لَغَفَّارٌ لِمَنْ تَابَ وَآمَنَ وَعَمِلَ صَالِحًا ثُمَّ اهْتَدَىٰ

82 And I am Forgiving towards him who repents, believes, acts righteously, and then remains guided.

٨٣ وَمَا أَعْجَلَكَ عَنْ قَوْمِكَ يَا مُوسَىٰ

83
2:51; 4:153; 7:148

83 "And what made you rush ahead of your people, O Moses?"

٨٤ قَالَ هُمْ أُولَاءِ عَلَىٰ أَثَرِي وَعَجِلْتُ إِلَيْكَ رَبِّ لِتَرْضَىٰ

84 He said, "They are following in my footsteps; and I hurried on to You, my Lord, that you may be pleased."

٨٥ قَالَ فَإِنَّا قَدْ فَتَنَّا قَوْمَكَ مِنْ بَعْدِكَ وَأَضَلَّهُمُ السَّامِرِيُّ

85
20:87, 95–96

85 He said, "We have tested your people in your absence, and the Samarian misled them."

٨٦ فَرَجَعَ مُوسَىٰ إِلَىٰ قَوْمِهِ غَضْبَانَ أَسِفًا ۚ قَالَ يَا قَوْمِ أَلَمْ يَعِدْكُمْ رَبُّكُمْ وَعْدًا حَسَنًا ۚ أَفَطَالَ عَلَيْكُمُ الْعَهْدُ أَمْ أَرَدْتُمْ أَنْ يَحِلَّ عَلَيْكُمْ غَضَبٌ مِنْ رَبِّكُمْ فَأَخْلَفْتُمْ مَوْعِدِي

86
7:150

86 So Moses returned to his people, angry and disappointed. He said, "O my people, did your Lord not promise you a good promise? Was the time too long for you? Or did you want wrath from your Lord to descend upon you, so you broke your promise to me?"

٨٧ قَالُوا مَا أَخْلَفْنَا مَوْعِدَكَ بِمَلْكِنَا وَلَٰكِنَّا حُمِّلْنَا أَوْزَارًا مِنْ زِينَةِ الْقَوْمِ فَقَذَفْنَاهَا فَكَذَٰلِكَ أَلْقَى السَّامِرِيُّ

87
20:85, 95–96

87 They said, "We did not break our promise to you by our choice, but we were made to carry loads of the people's ornaments, and we cast them in. That was what the Samarian suggested."

٨٨ فَأَخْرَجَ لَهُمْ عِجْلًا جَسَدًا لَهُ خُوَارٌ فَقَالُوا هَٰذَا إِلَٰهُكُمْ وَإِلَٰهُ مُوسَىٰ فَنَسِيَ

88
7:147

88 So he produced for them a calf—a mere body which lowed. And they said, "This is your god, and the god of Moses, but he has forgotten."

٨٩ أَفَلَا يَرَوْنَ أَلَّا يَرْجِعُ إِلَيْهِمْ قَوْلًا وَلَا يَمْلِكُ لَهُمْ ضَرًّا وَلَا نَفْعًا

89 Did they not see that it cannot return a word to them, and has no power to harm them or benefit them?

٩٠ وَلَقَدْ قَالَ لَهُمْ هَارُونُ مِنْ قَبْلُ يَا قَوْمِ إِنَّمَا فُتِنْتُمْ بِهِ ۖ وَإِنَّ رَبَّكُمُ الرَّحْمَٰنُ فَاتَّبِعُونِي وَأَطِيعُوا أَمْرِي

90 Aaron had said to them before, "O my people, you are being tested by this. And your Lord is the Merciful, so follow me, and obey my command."

٩١ قَالُوا لَنْ نَبْرَحَ عَلَيْهِ عَاكِفِينَ حَتَّىٰ يَرْجِعَ إِلَيْنَا مُوسَىٰ

91 They said, "We will not give up our devotion to it, until Moses returns to us."

٩٢ قَالَ يَا هَارُونُ مَا مَنَعَكَ إِذْ رَأَيْتَهُمْ ضَلُّوا

92 He said, "O Aaron, what prevented you, when you saw them going astray.

٩٣ أَلَّا تَتَّبِعَنِ ۖ أَفَعَصَيْتَ أَمْرِي

93 From following me? Did you disobey my command?"

٩٤ قَالَ يَا ابْنَ أُمَّ لَا تَأْخُذْ بِلِحْيَتِي وَلَا بِرَأْسِي ۖ إِنِّي خَشِيتُ أَنْ تَقُولَ فَرَّقْتَ بَيْنَ بَنِي إِسْرَائِيلَ وَلَمْ تَرْقُبْ قَوْلِي

94 He said, "Son of my mother, do not seize me by my beard or my head. I feared you would say, 'You have caused division among the Children of Israel, and did not regard my word.'"

٩٥ قَالَ فَمَا خَطْبُكَ يَا سَامِرِيُّ

95 He said, "What do you have to say, O Samarian?"

95-96
20:85, 87

٩٦ قَالَ بَصُرْتُ بِمَا لَمْ يَبْصُرُوا بِهِ فَقَبَضْتُ قَبْضَةً مِنْ أَثَرِ الرَّسُولِ فَنَبَذْتُهَا وَكَذَٰلِكَ سَوَّلَتْ لِي نَفْسِي

96 He said, "I saw what they did not see, so I grasped a handful from the Messenger's traces, and I flung it away. Thus my soul prompted me."

٩٧ قَالَ فَاذْهَبْ فَإِنَّ لَكَ فِي الْحَيَاةِ أَنْ تَقُولَ لَا مِسَاسَ ۖ وَإِنَّ لَكَ مَوْعِدًا لَنْ تُخْلَفَهُ ۖ وَانْظُرْ إِلَىٰ إِلَٰهِكَ الَّذِي ظَلْتَ عَلَيْهِ عَاكِفًا ۖ لَنُحَرِّقَنَّهُ ثُمَّ لَنَنْسِفَنَّهُ فِي الْيَمِّ نَسْفًا

97 He said, "Begone! Your lot in this life is to say, 'No contact.' And you have an appointment that you will not miss. Now look at your god that you remained devoted to—we will burn it up, and then blow it away into the sea, as powder."

٩٨ إِنَّمَا إِلَٰهُكُمُ اللَّهُ الَّذِي لَا إِلَٰهَ إِلَّا هُوَ ۚ وَسِعَ كُلَّ شَيْءٍ عِلْمًا

98 Surely your god is God, the One besides whom there is no other god. He comprehends everything in knowledge.

٩٩ كَذَٰلِكَ نَقُصُّ عَلَيْكَ مِنْ أَنْبَاءِ مَا قَدْ سَبَقَ ۚ وَقَدْ آتَيْنَاكَ مِنْ لَدُنَّا ذِكْرًا

99 Thus We narrate to you reports of times gone by; and We have given you a message from Our Presence.

99
4:164; 7:101; 11:120; 14:9; 40:78

١٠٠ مَنْ أَعْرَضَ عَنْهُ فَإِنَّهُ يَحْمِلُ يَوْمَ الْقِيَامَةِ وِزْرًا

100 Whoever turns away from it will carry on the Day of Resurrection a burden.

100
16:25; 29:13; 35:18

١٠١ خَالِدِينَ فِيهِ ۖ وَسَاءَ لَهُمْ يَوْمَ الْقِيَامَةِ حِمْلًا

101 Abiding therein forever. And wretched is their burden on the Day of Resurrection.

١٠٢ يَوْمَ يُنْفَخُ فِي الصُّورِ ۚ وَنَحْشُرُ الْمُجْرِمِينَ يَوْمَئِذٍ زُرْقًا

102 On the Day when the Trumpet is blown—We will gather the sinners on that Day, blue.

١٠٣ يَتَخَافَتُونَ بَيْنَهُمْ إِنْ لَبِثْتُمْ إِلَّا عَشْرًا

103 Murmuring among themselves: "You have lingered only for ten."

103
10:45

١٠٤ نَحْنُ أَعْلَمُ بِمَا يَقُولُونَ إِذْ يَقُولُ أَمْثَلُهُمْ طَرِيقَةً إِنْ لَبِثْتُمْ إِلَّا يَوْمًا

104 We are fully aware of what they say, when the most exemplary of them in conduct will say, "You have lingered only a day."

١٠٥ وَيَسْأَلُونَكَ عَنِ الْجِبَالِ فَقُلْ يَنْسِفُهَا رَبِّي نَسْفًا

105 And they ask you about the mountains. Say, "My Lord will crumble them utterly."

105
8:3; 18:47; 52:10; 69:14; 77:10

١٠٦ فَيَذَرُهَا قَاعًا صَفْصَفًا

106 And leave them desolate waste.

١٠٧ لَا تَرَىٰ فِيهَا عِوَجًا وَلَا أَمْتًا

107 You will see in them neither crookedness, nor deviation."

١٠٨ يَوْمَئِذٍ يَتَّبِعُونَ الدَّاعِيَ لَا عِوَجَ لَهُ ۖ وَخَشَعَتِ الْأَصْوَاتُ لِلرَّحْمَٰنِ فَلَا تَسْمَعُ إِلَّا هَمْسًا

108 On that Day, they will follow the caller, without any deviation. Voices will be hushed before the Merciful, and you will hear nothing but murmur.

108
17:52; 50:41–42; 54:6–7

١٠٩ يَوْمَئِذٍ لَا تَنْفَعُ الشَّفَاعَةُ إِلَّا مَنْ أَذِنَ لَهُ الرَّحْمَٰنُ وَرَضِيَ لَهُ قَوْلًا

109 On that Day, intercession will not avail, except for him permitted by the Merciful, and whose words He has approved.

109
2:48, 123, 255; 19:87; 21:28; 34:23; 53:26; 74:48

١١٠ يَعْلَمُ مَا بَيْنَ أَيْدِيهِمْ وَمَا خَلْفَهُمْ وَلَا يُحِيطُونَ بِهِ عِلْمًا

110 He knows what is before them and what is behind them, and they cannot comprehend Him in their knowledge.

110
2:255; 22:76

١١١ وَعَنَتِ الْوُجُوهُ لِلْحَيِّ الْقَيُّومِ ۖ وَقَدْ خَابَ مَنْ حَمَلَ ظُلْمًا

111 Faces will be humbled before the Living, the Eternal. Whoever carries injustice will despair.

١١٢ وَمَن يَعْمَلْ مِنَ الصَّالِحَاتِ وَهُوَ مُؤْمِنٌ فَلَا يَخَافُ ظُلْمًا وَلَا هَضْمًا

112 But whoever has done righteous deeds, while being a believer—will fear neither injustice, nor grievance.

١١٣ وَكَذَٰلِكَ أَنزَلْنَاهُ قُرْآنًا عَرَبِيًّا وَصَرَّفْنَا فِيهِ مِنَ الْوَعِيدِ لَعَلَّهُمْ يَتَّقُونَ أَوْ يُحْدِثُ لَهُمْ ذِكْرًا

113
12:2; 42:7

113 Thus We have revealed it an Arabic Qur'an, and We have diversified the warnings in it, that perhaps they would become righteous, or it may produce a lesson for them.

١١٤ فَتَعَالَى اللَّهُ الْمَلِكُ الْحَقُّ ۗ وَلَا تَعْجَلْ بِالْقُرْآنِ مِن قَبْلِ أَن يُقْضَىٰ إِلَيْكَ وَحْيُهُ ۖ وَقُل رَّبِّ زِدْنِي عِلْمًا

114
75:16

114 Exalted is God, the True King. Do not be hasty with the Qur'an before its inspiration to you is concluded, and say, "My Lord, increase me in knowledge."

١١٥ وَلَقَدْ عَهِدْنَا إِلَىٰ آدَمَ مِن قَبْلُ فَنَسِيَ وَلَمْ نَجِدْ لَهُ عَزْمًا

115
2:35; 7:19; 36:60

115 And We covenanted with Adam before, but he forgot, and We found in him no resolve.

١١٦ وَإِذْ قُلْنَا لِلْمَلَائِكَةِ اسْجُدُوا لِآدَمَ فَسَجَدُوا إِلَّا إِبْلِيسَ أَبَىٰ

116
2:34; 7:11, 22; 15:31, 30–31; 38:73–74

116 And when We said to the angels, "Bow down to Adam." They bowed down, except for Satan; he refused.

١١٧ فَقُلْنَا يَا آدَمُ إِنَّ هَٰذَا عَدُوٌّ لَّكَ وَلِزَوْجِكَ فَلَا يُخْرِجَنَّكُمَا مِنَ الْجَنَّةِ فَتَشْقَىٰ

117 We said, "O Adam, this is an enemy to you and to your wife. So do not let him make you leave the Garden, for then you will suffer.

١١٨ إِنَّ لَكَ أَلَّا تَجُوعَ فِيهَا وَلَا تَعْرَىٰ

118 In it you will never go hungry, nor be naked.

١١٩ وَأَنَّكَ لَا تَظْمَأُ فِيهَا وَلَا تَضْحَىٰ

119 Nor will you be thirsty in it, nor will you swelter."

١٢٠ فَوَسْوَسَ إِلَيْهِ الشَّيْطَانُ قَالَ يَا آدَمُ هَلْ أَدُلُّكَ عَلَىٰ شَجَرَةِ الْخُلْدِ وَمُلْكٍ لَّا يَبْلَىٰ

120
2:36; 7:20; 70:20, 27

120 But Satan whispered to him. He said, "O Adam, shall I show you the Tree of Immortality, and a kingdom that never decays?"

١٢١ فَأَكَلَا مِنْهَا فَبَدَتْ لَهُمَا سَوْآتُهُمَا وَطَفِقَا يَخْصِفَانِ عَلَيْهِمَا مِن وَرَقِ الْجَنَّةِ ۚ وَعَصَىٰ آدَمُ رَبَّهُ فَغَوَىٰ

121
7:22

121 And so they ate from it; whereupon their bodies became visible to them, and they started covering themselves with the leaves of the Garden. Thus Adam disobeyed his Lord, and fell.

	122
١٢٢ ثُمَّ اجْتَبَاهُ رَبُّهُ فَتَابَ عَلَيْهِ وَهَدَىٰ	2:37; 7:23, 25

122 But then his Lord recalled him, and pardoned him, and guided him.

	123
١٢٣ قَالَ اهْبِطَا مِنْهَا جَمِيعًا ۖ بَعْضُكُمْ لِبَعْضٍ عَدُوٌّ ۖ فَإِمَّا يَأْتِيَنَّكُم مِّنِّي هُدًى فَمَنِ اتَّبَعَ هُدَايَ فَلَا يَضِلُّ وَلَا يَشْقَىٰ	2:36; 7:24

123 He said, "Go down from it, altogether; some of you enemies of some others. But whenever guidance comes to you from Me, whoever follows My guidance, will not go astray, nor suffer.

	124
١٢٤ وَمَنْ أَعْرَضَ عَن ذِكْرِي فَإِنَّ لَهُ مَعِيشَةً ضَنكًا وَنَحْشُرُهُ يَوْمَ الْقِيَامَةِ أَعْمَىٰ	13:57

124 But whoever turns away from My Reminder, for him is a confined life. And We will raise him on the Day of Resurrection blind."

١٢٥ قَالَ رَبِّ لِمَ حَشَرْتَنِي أَعْمَىٰ وَقَدْ كُنتُ بَصِيرًا

125 He will say, "My Lord, why did You raise me blind, though I was seeing?"

١٢٦ قَالَ كَذَٰلِكَ أَتَتْكَ آيَاتُنَا فَنَسِيتَهَا ۖ وَكَذَٰلِكَ الْيَوْمَ تُنسَىٰ

126 He will say, "Just as Our revelations came to you, and you forgot them, today you will be forgotten."

١٢٧ وَكَذَٰلِكَ نَجْزِي مَنْ أَسْرَفَ وَلَمْ يُؤْمِن بِآيَاتِ رَبِّهِ ۚ وَلَعَذَابُ الْآخِرَةِ أَشَدُّ وَأَبْقَىٰ

127 Thus We recompense him who transgresses and does not believe in the revelations of his Lord. The punishment of the Hereafter is more severe, and more lasting.

	128
١٢٨ أَفَلَمْ يَهْدِ لَهُمْ كَمْ أَهْلَكْنَا قَبْلَهُم مِّنَ الْقُرُونِ يَمْشُونَ فِي مَسَاكِنِهِمْ ۗ إِنَّ فِي ذَٰلِكَ لَآيَاتٍ لِّأُولِي النُّهَىٰ	6:6; 14:45; 17:17; 32:26; 36:31

128 Is it not instructive to them, how many generations before them We destroyed, in whose settlements they walk? Surely in that are signs for people of understanding.

١٢٩ وَلَوْلَا كَلِمَةٌ سَبَقَتْ مِن رَّبِّكَ لَكَانَ لِزَامًا وَأَجَلٌ مُّسَمًّى

129 Were it not for a word that issued from your Lord, the inevitable would have happened, but there is an appointed term.

	130
١٣٠ فَاصْبِرْ عَلَىٰ مَا يَقُولُونَ وَسَبِّحْ بِحَمْدِ رَبِّكَ قَبْلَ طُلُوعِ الشَّمْسِ وَقَبْلَ غُرُوبِهَا ۖ وَمِنْ آنَاءِ اللَّيْلِ فَسَبِّحْ وَأَطْرَافَ النَّهَارِ لَعَلَّكَ تَرْضَىٰ	50:39; 52:48

130 So bear patiently what they say, and celebrate the praises of your Lord before the rising of the sun, and before its setting. And during the hours of the night glorify Him, and at the borders of the day, that you may be satisfied.

١٣١ وَلَا تَمُدَّنَّ عَيْنَيْكَ إِلَىٰ مَا مَتَّعْنَا بِهِ أَزْوَاجًا مِّنْهُمْ زَهْرَةَ الْحَيَاةِ الدُّنْيَا لِنَفْتِنَهُمْ فِيهِ ۚ وَرِزْقُ رَبِّكَ خَيْرٌ وَأَبْقَىٰ

131 And do not extend your glance towards what We have given some classes of them to enjoy—the splendor of the life of this world—that We may test them thereby. Your Lord's provision is better, and more lasting.

15:88; 16:96

١٣٢ وَأْمُرْ أَهْلَكَ بِالصَّلَاةِ وَاصْطَبِرْ عَلَيْهَا ۖ لَا نَسْأَلُكَ رِزْقًا ۖ نَّحْنُ نَرْزُقُكَ ۗ وَالْعَاقِبَةُ لِلتَّقْوَىٰ

132 And exhort your people to pray, and patiently adhere to it. We ask of you no sustenance, but it is We who sustain you. The good ending is that for righteousness.

١٣٣ وَقَالُوا لَوْلَا يَأْتِينَا بِآيَةٍ مِّن رَّبِّهِ ۚ أَوَلَمْ تَأْتِهِم بَيِّنَةُ مَا فِي الصُّحُفِ الْأُولَىٰ

133 And they say, "Why does he not bring us a miracle from his Lord?" Were they not given enough miracles in the former scriptures?

2:118; 21:5; 6:37; 13:7; 29:50

١٣٤ وَلَوْ أَنَّا أَهْلَكْنَاهُم بِعَذَابٍ مِّن قَبْلِهِ لَقَالُوا رَبَّنَا لَوْلَا أَرْسَلْتَ إِلَيْنَا رَسُولًا فَنَتَّبِعَ آيَاتِكَ مِن قَبْلِ أَن نَّذِلَّ وَنَخْزَىٰ

134 Had We destroyed them with a punishment before him, they would have said, "Our Lord, if only You had sent us a messenger, we would have followed Your revelations before we were humiliated and disgraced."

17:15; 26:208; 28:46

١٣٥ قُلْ كُلٌّ مُّتَرَبِّصٌ فَتَرَبَّصُوا ۖ فَسَتَعْلَمُونَ مَنْ أَصْحَابُ الصِّرَاطِ السَّوِيِّ وَمَنِ اهْتَدَىٰ

135 Say, "Everybody is waiting, so wait. You will know who the people of the straight path are, and who is rightly-guided."

9:52, 98

Sūrah 21: Al-Anbiyā'

سُورَةُ ٱلْأَنْبِيَاءِ (The Prophets)

بِسْمِ ٱللَّهِ ٱلرَّحْمَٰنِ ٱلرَّحِيمِ

١ اقْتَرَبَ لِلنَّاسِ حِسَابُهُمْ وَهُمْ فِي غَفْلَةٍ مُّعْرِضُونَ

1 Mankind's reckoning has drawn near, but they turn away heedlessly.

33:63; 42:17; 54:1

٢ مَا يَأْتِيهِم مِّن ذِكْرٍ مِّن رَّبِّهِم مُّحْدَثٍ إِلَّا اسْتَمَعُوهُ وَهُمْ يَلْعَبُونَ

2 No fresh reminder comes to them from their Lord, but they listen to it playfully.

6:25; 17:47; 26:5

٣ لَاهِيَةً قُلُوبُهُمْ ۗ وَأَسَرُّوا النَّجْوَى الَّذِينَ ظَلَمُوا هَلْ هَٰذَا إِلَّا بَشَرٌ مِّثْلُكُمْ ۖ [a] أَفَتَأْتُونَ السِّحْرَ وَأَنتُمْ تُبْصِرُونَ [b]

3 Their hearts distracted, the wrongdoers confer secretly, "Is this anything but a mortal like you? Will you take to sorcery, with open-eyes?"

[a] 14:10; 17:94; 23:33; 51:52; 54:24; 64:6
[b] 51:52; 74:24

٤ قَالَ رَبِّي يَعْلَمُ الْقَوْلَ فِي السَّمَاءِ وَالْأَرْضِ ۖ وَهُوَ السَّمِيعُ الْعَلِيمُ

4 He said, "My Lord knows what is said in the heaven and the earth; and He is the Hearer, the Knower."

4
25:6

٥ بَلْ قَالُوا أَضْغَاثُ أَحْلَامٍ بَلِ افْتَرَاهُ بَلْ هُوَ شَاعِرٌ[a] فَلْيَأْتِنَا بِآيَةٍ كَمَا أُرْسِلَ الْأَوَّلُونَ[b]

5 And they said, "A jumble of dreams," and, "He made it up," and, "He is a poet," "let him bring us a sign, like those sent to the ancients."

5
[a] 10:37; 36:69; 69:41
[b] 10:97; 20:133

٦ مَا آمَنَتْ قَبْلَهُمْ مِنْ قَرْيَةٍ أَهْلَكْنَاهَا ۖ أَفَهُمْ يُؤْمِنُونَ

6 None of the towns We destroyed before them had believed. Will they, then, believe?

6
21:11

٧ وَمَا أَرْسَلْنَا قَبْلَكَ إِلَّا رِجَالًا نُوحِي إِلَيْهِمْ ۖ فَاسْأَلُوا أَهْلَ الذِّكْرِ إِنْ كُنْتُمْ لَا تَعْلَمُونَ

7 We did not send before you except men, whom We inspired. Ask the people of knowledge, if you do not know.

7
12:109; 16:43

٨ وَمَا جَعَلْنَاهُمْ جَسَدًا لَا يَأْكُلُونَ الطَّعَامَ وَمَا كَانُوا خَالِدِينَ

8 We did not make them mere bodies that ate no food, nor were they immortal.

8
5:75; 23:33; 25:7

٩ ثُمَّ صَدَقْنَاهُمُ الْوَعْدَ فَأَنْجَيْنَاهُمْ وَمَنْ نَشَاءُ وَأَهْلَكْنَا الْمُسْرِفِينَ

9 Then We fulfilled Our promise to them, and We saved them together with whomever We willed, and We destroyed the extravagant.

9
3:152; 12:110; 14:47; 21:9; 79:15

١٠ لَقَدْ أَنْزَلْنَا إِلَيْكُمْ كِتَابًا فِيهِ ذِكْرُكُمْ ۖ أَفَلَا تَعْقِلُونَ

10 We have sent down to you a Book, containing your message. Do you not understand?

10
23:71

١١ وَكَمْ قَصَمْنَا مِنْ قَرْيَةٍ كَانَتْ ظَالِمَةً وَأَنْشَأْنَا بَعْدَهَا قَوْمًا آخَرِينَ

11 How many a guilty town have We crushed, and established thereafter another people?

11
17:17; 21:6; 22:45; 65:8–9

١٢ فَلَمَّا أَحَسُّوا بَأْسَنَا إِذَا هُمْ مِنْهَا يَرْكُضُونَ

12 Then, when they sensed Our might, they started running away from it.

١٣ لَا تَرْكُضُوا وَارْجِعُوا إِلَىٰ مَا أُتْرِفْتُمْ فِيهِ وَمَسَاكِنِكُمْ لَعَلَّكُمْ تُسْأَلُونَ

13 Do not run, but come back to your luxuries, and to your homes, that you may be questioned.

13
11:116

١٤ قَالُوا يَا وَيْلَنَا إِنَّا كُنَّا ظَالِمِينَ

14 They said, "Woe to us; we were unfair."

١٥ فَمَا زَالَتْ تِلْكَ دَعْوَاهُمْ حَتَّىٰ جَعَلْنَاهُمْ حَصِيدًا خَامِدِينَ

15 This continued to be their cry, until We made them silent ashes.

15
10:24; 11:100

١٦ وَمَا خَلَقْنَا السَّمَاءَ وَالْأَرْضَ وَمَا بَيْنَهُمَا لَاعِبِينَ	16 23:115
16 We did not create the sky and the earth and what is between them for amusement.	
١٧ لَوْ أَرَدْنَا أَن نَّتَّخِذَ لَهْوًا لَّاتَّخَذْنَاهُ مِن لَّدُنَّا إِن كُنَّا فَاعِلِينَ	17
17 If We wanted amusement, We could have found it within Us, were We to do so.	
١٨ بَلْ نَقْذِفُ بِالْحَقِّ عَلَى الْبَاطِلِ فَيَدْمَغُهُ فَإِذَا هُوَ زَاهِقٌ ۚ وَلَكُمُ الْوَيْلُ مِمَّا تَصِفُونَ	18 17:81; 34:48; 42:24
18 In fact, We hurl the truth against falsehood, and it crushes it, so it vanishes. Woe unto you, for what you describe.	
١٩ وَلَهُ مَن فِي السَّمَاوَاتِ وَالْأَرْضِ ۚ وَمَنْ عِندَهُ لَا يَسْتَكْبِرُونَ عَنْ عِبَادَتِهِ وَلَا يَسْتَحْسِرُونَ	19 4:172; 7:206; 41:38
19 To Him belongs everyone in the heavens and the earth. Those near Him are not too proud to worship Him, nor do they waver.	
٢٠ يُسَبِّحُونَ اللَّيْلَ وَالنَّهَارَ لَا يَفْتُرُونَ	20 7:206; 41:38
20 They praise night and day, without ever tiring.	
٢١ أَمِ اتَّخَذُوا آلِهَةً مِّنَ الْأَرْضِ هُمْ يُنشِرُونَ	21 25:3
21 Or have they taken to themselves gods from the earth who resurrect?	
٢٢ لَوْ كَانَ فِيهِمَا آلِهَةٌ إِلَّا اللَّهُ لَفَسَدَتَا ۚ فَسُبْحَانَ اللَّهِ رَبِّ الْعَرْشِ عَمَّا يَصِفُونَ	22 21:24; 23:71, 91
22 If there were in them gods other than God, they would have gone to ruin. So glory be to God, Lord of the Throne, beyond what they allege.	
٢٣ لَا يُسْأَلُ عَمَّا يَفْعَلُ وَهُمْ يُسْأَلُونَ	23
23 He will not be questioned about what He does, but they will be questioned.	
٢٤ أَمِ اتَّخَذُوا مِن دُونِهِ آلِهَةً ۖ قُلْ هَاتُوا بُرْهَانَكُمْ ۖ هَٰذَا ذِكْرُ مَن مَّعِيَ وَذِكْرُ مَن قَبْلِي ۗ بَلْ أَكْثَرُهُمْ لَا يَعْلَمُونَ الْحَقَّ ۖ فَهُم مُّعْرِضُونَ	24 21:22; 42:6, 9
24 Or have they taken, besides Him, other gods? Say, "Bring your proof. This is a message for those with me, and a message of those before me." But most of them do not know the truth, so they turn away.	
٢٥ وَمَا أَرْسَلْنَا مِن قَبْلِكَ مِن رَّسُولٍ إِلَّا نُوحِي إِلَيْهِ أَنَّهُ لَا إِلَٰهَ إِلَّا أَنَا فَاعْبُدُونِ	25 12:109; 13:30; 16:43
25 We never sent a messenger before you without inspiring him that: "There is no god but I, so worship Me."	
٢٦ وَقَالُوا اتَّخَذَ الرَّحْمَٰنُ وَلَدًا ۗ سُبْحَانَهُ ۚ بَلْ عِبَادٌ مُّكْرَمُونَ	26 2:116; 4:171; 6:100; 10:68; 17:40, 111; 19:35; 23:91; 25:2
26 And they say, "The Most Merciful has taken to himself a son." Be He glorified; they are but honored servants.	

٢٧ لَا يَسْبِقُونَهُ بِالْقَوْلِ وَهُمْ بِأَمْرِهِ يَعْمَلُونَ

27 They never speak before He has spoken, and they only act on His command.

٢٨ يَعْلَمُ مَا بَيْنَ أَيْدِيهِمْ وَمَا خَلْفَهُمْ وَلَا يَشْفَعُونَ إِلَّا لِمَنِ ارْتَضَىٰ وَهُم مِّنْ خَشْيَتِهِ مُشْفِقُونَ

28 He knows what is before them, and what is behind them; and they do not intercede except for him whom He approves; and they tremble in awe of Him.

28
2:48, 123, 255; 19:87; 20:109; 21:28; 34:23; 53:26; 74:48

٢٩ وَمَن يَقُلْ مِنْهُمْ إِنِّي إِلَٰهٌ مِّن دُونِهِ فَذَٰلِكَ نَجْزِيهِ جَهَنَّمَ ۚ كَذَٰلِكَ نَجْزِي الظَّالِمِينَ

29 And whoever of them says, "I am a god besides Him," We will reward him with Hell. Thus We reward the wrongdoers.

29
3:79

٣٠ أَوَلَمْ يَرَ الَّذِينَ كَفَرُوا أَنَّ السَّمَاوَاتِ وَالْأَرْضَ كَانَتَا رَتْقًا فَفَتَقْنَاهُمَا ۖ وَجَعَلْنَا مِنَ الْمَاءِ كُلَّ شَيْءٍ حَيٍّ ۖ أَفَلَا يُؤْمِنُونَ

30 Do the disbelievers not see that the heavens and the earth were one mass, and We tore them apart? And We made from water every living thing. Will they not believe?

٣١ وَجَعَلْنَا فِي الْأَرْضِ رَوَاسِيَ أَن تَمِيدَ بِهِمْ وَجَعَلْنَا فِيهَا فِجَاجًا سُبُلًا لَّعَلَّهُمْ يَهْتَدُونَ

31 And We placed on earth stabilizers, lest it sways with them, and We placed therein signposts and passages, that they may be guided.

31
16:15

٣٢ وَجَعَلْنَا السَّمَاءَ سَقْفًا مَّحْفُوظًا ۖ وَهُمْ عَنْ آيَاتِهَا مُعْرِضُونَ

32 And We made the sky a protected roof; yet they turn away from its wonders.

32
15:17; 52:5

٣٣ وَهُوَ الَّذِي خَلَقَ اللَّيْلَ وَالنَّهَارَ وَالشَّمْسَ وَالْقَمَرَ ۖ كُلٌّ فِي فَلَكٍ يَسْبَحُونَ

33 It is He who created the night and the day, and the sun and the moon; each floating in an orbit.

33
36:40

٣٤ وَمَا جَعَلْنَا لِبَشَرٍ مِّن قَبْلِكَ الْخُلْدَ ۖ أَفَإِن مِّتَّ فَهُمُ الْخَالِدُونَ

34 We did not grant immortality to any human being before you. Should you die, are they then the immortal?

34
3:185; 4:78; 29:57; 39:3

٣٥ كُلُّ نَفْسٍ ذَائِقَةُ الْمَوْتِ ۗ وَنَبْلُوكُم بِالشَّرِّ وَالْخَيْرِ فِتْنَةً ۖ وَإِلَيْنَا تُرْجَعُونَ

35 Every soul will taste death. We burden you with adversity and prosperity—a test. And to Us you will be returned.

35
3:185; 29:57; 52:26

٣٦ وَإِذَا رَآكَ الَّذِينَ كَفَرُوا إِن يَتَّخِذُونَكَ إِلَّا هُزُوًا أَهَٰذَا الَّذِي يَذْكُرُ آلِهَتَكُمْ وَهُم بِذِكْرِ الرَّحْمَٰنِ هُمْ كَافِرُونَ

36 When those who disbelieve see you, they treat you only with ridicule: "Is this the one who mentions your gods?" And they reject the mention of the Merciful.

36
25:41

٣٧ خُلِقَ الْإِنْسَانُ مِنْ عَجَلٍ ۚ سَأُرِيكُمْ آيَاتِي فَلَا تَسْتَعْجِلُونِ

37 The human being was created of haste. I will show you My signs, so do not seek to rush Me.

37
17:11

٣٨ وَيَقُولُونَ مَتَىٰ هَٰذَا الْوَعْدُ إِنْ كُنْتُمْ صَادِقِينَ

38 And they say, "When will this promise come true, if you are truthful?"

38
10:48; 27:71; 34:29

٣٩ لَوْ يَعْلَمُ الَّذِينَ كَفَرُوا حِينَ لَا يَكُفُّونَ عَنْ وُجُوهِهِمُ النَّارَ وَلَا عَنْ ظُهُورِهِمْ وَلَا هُمْ يُنْصَرُونَ

39 If those who disbelieve only knew, when they cannot keep the fire off their faces and off their backs, and they will not be helped.

39
14:50; 18:29

٤٠ بَلْ تَأْتِيهِمْ بَغْتَةً فَتَبْهَتُهُمْ فَلَا يَسْتَطِيعُونَ رَدَّهَا وَلَا هُمْ يُنْظَرُونَ

40 In fact, it will come upon them suddenly, and bewilder them. They will not be able to repel it, and they will not be reprieved.

٤١ وَلَقَدِ اسْتُهْزِئَ بِرُسُلٍ مِنْ قَبْلِكَ فَحَاقَ بِالَّذِينَ سَخِرُوا مِنْهُمْ مَا كَانُوا بِهِ يَسْتَهْزِئُونَ

41 Messengers before you were also ridiculed, but those who jeered were surrounded by what they had ridiculed.

41
6:10; 13:32; 15:11; 21:41; 35:25–26; 41:43

٤٢ قُلْ مَنْ يَكْلَؤُكُمْ بِاللَّيْلِ وَالنَّهَارِ مِنَ الرَّحْمَٰنِ ۗ بَلْ هُمْ عَنْ ذِكْرِ رَبِّهِمْ مُعْرِضُونَ

42 Say, "Who guards you against the Merciful by night and by day?" But they turn away from the mention of their Lord.

42
5:17; 33:17; 48:11

٤٣ أَمْ لَهُمْ آلِهَةٌ تَمْنَعُهُمْ مِنْ دُونِنَا ۚ لَا يَسْتَطِيعُونَ نَصْرَ أَنْفُسِهِمْ وَلَا هُمْ مِنَّا يُصْحَبُونَ

43 Or do they have gods who can defend them against Us? They cannot help themselves, nor will they be protected from Us.

43
7:191, 197; 26:92

٤٤ بَلْ مَتَّعْنَا هَٰؤُلَاءِ وَآبَاءَهُمْ حَتَّىٰ طَالَ عَلَيْهِمُ الْعُمُرُ ۗ[a] أَفَلَا يَرَوْنَ أَنَّا نَأْتِي الْأَرْضَ نَنْقُصُهَا مِنْ أَطْرَافِهَا ۚ أَفَهُمُ الْغَالِبُونَ[b]

44 We have given these enjoyments, and their ancestors, until time grew long upon them. Do they not see how We gradually reduce the land from its extremities? Are they then the victors?

44
[a] 3:178; 43:29; 25:18
[b] 13:31, 41; 46:27

٤٥ قُلْ إِنَّمَا أُنْذِرُكُمْ بِالْوَحْيِ ۚ وَلَا يَسْمَعُ الصُّمُّ الدُّعَاءَ إِذَا مَا يُنْذَرُونَ

45 Say, "I am warning you through inspiration." But the deaf cannot hear the call when they are being warned.

٤٦ وَلَئِنْ مَسَّتْهُمْ نَفْحَةٌ مِنْ عَذَابِ رَبِّكَ لَيَقُولُنَّ يَا وَيْلَنَا إِنَّا كُنَّا ظَالِمِينَ

46 And when a breath of your Lord's punishment touches them, they say, "Woe to us, we were truly wicked."

46
7:5; 21:12

٤٧ وَنَضَعُ الْمَوَازِينَ الْقِسْطَ لِيَوْمِ الْقِيَامَةِ فَلَا تُظْلَمُ نَفْسٌ شَيْئًا ۖ وَإِنْ كَانَ مِثْقَالَ حَبَّةٍ مِنْ خَرْدَلٍ أَتَيْنَا بِهَا ۗ وَكَفَىٰ بِنَا حَاسِبِينَ

47 We will set up the scales of justice for the Day of Resurrection, so that no soul will suffer the least injustice. And even if it be the weight of a mustard-seed, We will bring it up. Sufficient are We as Reckoners.

47
4:40; 7:8–9; 23:101–103; 31:16; 101:6–9

٤٨ وَلَقَدْ آتَيْنَا مُوسَىٰ وَهَارُونَ الْفُرْقَانَ وَضِيَاءً وَذِكْرًا لِلْمُتَّقِينَ

48 We gave Moses and Aaron the Criterion, and illumination, and a reminder for the righteous.

48
2:52; 3:4

٤٩ الَّذِينَ يَخْشَوْنَ رَبَّهُمْ بِالْغَيْبِ وَهُمْ مِنَ السَّاعَةِ مُشْفِقُونَ

49 Those who fear their Lord in private, and are apprehensive of the Hour.

٥٠ وَهَٰذَا ذِكْرٌ مُبَارَكٌ أَنْزَلْنَاهُ ۚ أَفَأَنْتُمْ لَهُ مُنْكِرُونَ

50 This too is a blessed message that We revealed. Are you going to deny it?

50
6:92, 155; 38:29

٥١ وَلَقَدْ آتَيْنَا إِبْرَاهِيمَ رُشْدَهُ مِنْ قَبْلُ وَكُنَّا بِهِ عَالِمِينَ

51 We gave Abraham his integrity formerly, and We knew him well.

٥٢ إِذْ قَالَ لِأَبِيهِ وَقَوْمِهِ مَا هَٰذِهِ التَّمَاثِيلُ الَّتِي أَنْتُمْ لَهَا عَاكِفُونَ

52 When he said to his father and his people, "What are these statues to which you are devoted?"

52
6:74; 26:70; 29:16; 37:85

٥٣ قَالُوا وَجَدْنَا آبَاءَنَا لَهَا عَابِدِينَ

53 They said, "We found our parents worshiping them."

53
26:74; 31:21; 43:22

٥٤ قَالَ لَقَدْ كُنْتُمْ أَنْتُمْ وَآبَاؤُكُمْ فِي ضَلَالٍ مُبِينٍ

54 He said, "You and your parents are in evident error."

54
6:74

٥٥ قَالُوا أَجِئْتَنَا بِالْحَقِّ أَمْ أَنْتَ مِنَ اللَّاعِبِينَ

55 They said, "Are you telling us the truth, or are you just playing?"

٥٦ قَالَ بَلْ رَبُّكُمْ رَبُّ السَّمَاوَاتِ وَالْأَرْضِ الَّذِي فَطَرَهُنَّ وَأَنَا عَلَىٰ ذَٰلِكُمْ مِنَ الشَّاهِدِينَ

56 He said, "Your Lord is the Lord of the heavens and the earth, the One who created them, and I bear witness to that.

٥٧ وَتَاللَّهِ لَأَكِيدَنَّ أَصْنَامَكُمْ بَعْدَ أَنْ تُوَلُّوا مُدْبِرِينَ

57 "By God, I will have a plan for your statues after you have gone away."

57
37:91

٥٨ فَجَعَلَهُمْ جُذَاذًا إِلَّا كَبِيرًا لَهُمْ لَعَلَّهُمْ إِلَيْهِ يَرْجِعُونَ

58 So he reduced them into pieces, except for their biggest, that they may return to it.

58
37:91–93

٥٩ قَالُوا مَنْ فَعَلَ هَٰذَا بِآلِهَتِنَا إِنَّهُ لَمِنَ الظَّالِمِينَ

59 They said, "Who did this to our gods? He is certainly one of the wrongdoers."

٦٠ قَالُوا سَمِعْنَا فَتًى يَذْكُرُهُمْ يُقَالُ لَهُ إِبْرَاهِيمُ

60 They said, "We heard a youth mentioning them. He is called Abraham."

٦١ قَالُوا فَأْتُوا بِهِ عَلَىٰ أَعْيُنِ النَّاسِ لَعَلَّهُمْ يَشْهَدُونَ

61 They said, "Bring him before the eyes of the people, so that they may witness."

٦٢ قَالُوا أَأَنتَ فَعَلْتَ هَٰذَا بِآلِهَتِنَا يَا إِبْرَاهِيمُ

62 They said, "Are you the one who did this to our gods, O Abraham?"

٦٣ قَالَ بَلْ فَعَلَهُ كَبِيرُهُمْ هَٰذَا فَاسْأَلُوهُمْ إِن كَانُوا يَنطِقُونَ

63 He said, "But it was this biggest of them that did it. Ask them, if they can speak."

63–65
37:91–93

٦٤ فَرَجَعُوا إِلَىٰ أَنفُسِهِمْ فَقَالُوا إِنَّكُمْ أَنتُمُ الظَّالِمُونَ

64 Then they turned to one another, and said, "You yourselves are the wrongdoers."

٦٥ ثُمَّ نُكِسُوا عَلَىٰ رُءُوسِهِمْ لَقَدْ عَلِمْتَ مَا هَٰؤُلَاءِ يَنطِقُونَ

65 But they reverted to their old ideas: "You certainly know that these do not speak."

٦٦ قَالَ أَفَتَعْبُدُونَ مِن دُونِ اللَّهِ مَا لَا يَنفَعُكُمْ شَيْئًا وَلَا يَضُرُّكُمْ

66 He said, "Do you worship, instead of God, what can neither benefit you in anything, nor harm you?

66
6:71; 10:18, 106;
25:55; 26:72; 29:17;
37:95–96

٦٧ أُفٍّ لَّكُمْ وَلِمَا تَعْبُدُونَ مِن دُونِ اللَّهِ ۖ أَفَلَا تَعْقِلُونَ

67 Fie on you, and on what you worship instead of God. Do you not understand?"

٦٨ قَالُوا حَرِّقُوهُ وَانصُرُوا آلِهَتَكُمْ إِن كُنتُمْ فَاعِلِينَ

68 They said, "Burn him and support your gods, if you are going to act."

68
29:24; 37:97

٦٩ قُلْنَا يَا نَارُ كُونِي بَرْدًا وَسَلَامًا عَلَىٰ إِبْرَاهِيمَ

69 We said, "O fire, be coolness and safety upon Abraham."

٧٠ وَأَرَادُوا بِهِ كَيْدًا فَجَعَلْنَاهُمُ الْأَخْسَرِينَ

70 They planned to harm him, but We made them the worst losers.

70
37:98; 52:42; 86:15

٧١ وَنَجَّيْنَاهُ وَلُوطًا إِلَى الْأَرْضِ الَّتِي بَارَكْنَا فِيهَا لِلْعَالَمِينَ

71 And We delivered him, and Lot, to the land that We blessed for all people.

71
29:26; 37:99

٧٢ وَوَهَبْنَا لَهُ إِسْحَاقَ وَيَعْقُوبَ نَافِلَةً ۖ وَكُلًّا جَعَلْنَا صَالِحِينَ

72 And We granted him Isaac and Jacob as a gift; and each We made righteous.

72
6:84; 11:71; 19:49;
29:27; 37:112

٧٣ وَجَعَلْنَاهُمْ أَئِمَّةً يَهْدُونَ بِأَمْرِنَا وَأَوْحَيْنَا إِلَيْهِمْ فِعْلَ الْخَيْرَاتِ وَإِقَامَ الصَّلَاةِ وَإِيتَاءَ الزَّكَاةِ ۖ وَكَانُوا لَنَا عَابِدِينَ

73 And We made them leaders, guiding by Our command; and We inspired them to do good works, and to observe the prayer, and to give out charity. They were devoted servants to Us.

٧٤ وَلُوطًا آتَيْنَاهُ حُكْمًا وَعِلْمًا وَنَجَّيْنَاهُ مِنَ الْقَرْيَةِ الَّتِي كَانَت تَّعْمَلُ الْخَبَائِثَ ۗ إِنَّهُمْ كَانُوا قَوْمَ سَوْءٍ فَاسِقِينَ

74
12:22; 21:79; 28:14

74 And Lot—We gave him judgment and knowledge, and We delivered him from the town that practiced the abominations. They were wicked and perverted people.

٧٥ وَأَدْخَلْنَاهُ فِي رَحْمَتِنَا ۖ إِنَّهُ مِنَ الصَّالِحِينَ

75
21:86

75 And We admitted him into Our mercy; for He was one of the righteous.

٧٦ وَنُوحًا إِذْ نَادَىٰ مِن قَبْلُ فَاسْتَجَبْنَا لَهُ فَنَجَّيْنَاهُ وَأَهْلَهُ مِنَ الْكَرْبِ الْعَظِيمِ

76
37:75–76; 71:26–27

76 And Noah, when he called before. So We answered him, and delivered him and his family from the great disaster.

٧٧ وَنَصَرْنَاهُ مِنَ الْقَوْمِ الَّذِينَ كَذَّبُوا بِآيَاتِنَا ۚ إِنَّهُمْ كَانُوا قَوْمَ سَوْءٍ فَأَغْرَقْنَاهُمْ أَجْمَعِينَ

77
7:64

77 And We supported him against the people who rejected Our signs. They were an evil people, so We drowned them all.

٧٨ وَدَاوُودَ وَسُلَيْمَانَ إِذْ يَحْكُمَانِ فِي الْحَرْثِ إِذْ نَفَشَتْ فِيهِ غَنَمُ الْقَوْمِ وَكُنَّا لِحُكْمِهِمْ شَاهِدِينَ

78 And David and Solomon, when they gave judgment in the case of the field, when some people's sheep wandered therein by night; and We were witnesses to their judgment.

٧٩ فَفَهَّمْنَاهَا سُلَيْمَانَ ۚ وَكُلًّا آتَيْنَا حُكْمًا وَعِلْمًا ۚ وَسَخَّرْنَا مَعَ دَاوُودَ الْجِبَالَ يُسَبِّحْنَ وَالطَّيْرَ ۚ وَكُنَّا فَاعِلِينَ

79
34:10; 38:18

79 And so We made Solomon understand it, and to each We gave wisdom and knowledge. And We subjected the mountains along with David to sing Our praises, and the birds as well—surely We did.

٨٠ وَعَلَّمْنَاهُ صَنْعَةَ لَبُوسٍ لَّكُمْ لِتُحْصِنَكُم مِّن بَأْسِكُمْ ۖ فَهَلْ أَنتُمْ شَاكِرُونَ

80
2:251; 16:81; 34:10

80 And We taught him the making of shields for you, to protect you from your violence. Are you, then, appreciative?

٨١ وَلِسُلَيْمَانَ الرِّيحَ عَاصِفَةً تَجْرِي بِأَمْرِهِ إِلَى الْأَرْضِ الَّتِي بَارَكْنَا فِيهَا ۚ وَكُنَّا بِكُلِّ شَيْءٍ عَالِمِينَ

81
34:12; 38:36

81 And to Solomon the stormy wind, blowing at His command towards the land that We have blessed. We are aware of everything.

٨٢ وَمِنَ الشَّيَاطِينِ مَن يَغُوصُونَ لَهُ وَيَعْمَلُونَ عَمَلًا دُونَ ذَٰلِكَ ۖ وَكُنَّا لَهُمْ حَافِظِينَ

82
21:83; 34:12; 38:37

82 And of the devils were some that dived for him, and performed other, lesser tasks. But We kept them restrained.

٨٣ وَأَيُّوبَ إِذْ نَادَىٰ رَبَّهُ أَنِّي مَسَّنِيَ الضُّرُّ وَأَنتَ أَرْحَمُ الرَّاحِمِينَ

83 And Job, when he cried out to his Lord: "Great harm has afflicted me, and you are the Most Merciful of the merciful."

83
38:41

٨٤ فَاسْتَجَبْنَا لَهُ فَكَشَفْنَا مَا بِهِ مِن ضُرٍّ ۖ وَآتَيْنَاهُ أَهْلَهُ وَمِثْلَهُم مَّعَهُمْ رَحْمَةً مِّنْ عِندِنَا وَذِكْرَىٰ لِلْعَابِدِينَ

84 So We answered him, lifted his suffering, and restored his family to him, and their like with them—a mercy from Us, and a reminder for the worshipers.

84
38:43

٨٥ وَإِسْمَاعِيلَ وَإِدْرِيسَ وَذَا الْكِفْلِ ۖ كُلٌّ مِّنَ الصَّابِرِينَ

85 And Ishmael, and Enoch, and Ezekiel; each was one of the steadfast.

85
38:48

٨٦ وَأَدْخَلْنَاهُمْ فِي رَحْمَتِنَا ۖ إِنَّهُم مِّنَ الصَّالِحِينَ

86 And We admitted them into Our mercy. They were among the righteous.

86
21:75

٨٧ وَذَا النُّونِ إِذ ذَّهَبَ مُغَاضِبًا فَظَنَّ أَن لَّن نَّقْدِرَ عَلَيْهِ فَنَادَىٰ فِي الظُّلُمَاتِ أَن لَّا إِلَٰهَ إِلَّا أَنتَ سُبْحَانَكَ إِنِّي كُنتُ مِنَ الظَّالِمِينَ

87 And Jonah, when he stormed out in fury, thinking We had no power over him. But then He cried out in the darkness, "There is no god but You! Glory to You! I was one of the wrongdoers!"

87
37:142; 68:48

٨٨ فَاسْتَجَبْنَا لَهُ وَنَجَّيْنَاهُ مِنَ الْغَمِّ ۚ وَكَذَٰلِكَ نُنجِي الْمُؤْمِنِينَ

88 So We answered him, and saved him from the affliction. Thus We save the faithful.

٨٩ وَزَكَرِيَّا إِذْ نَادَىٰ رَبَّهُ رَبِّ لَا تَذَرْنِي فَرْدًا وَأَنتَ خَيْرُ الْوَارِثِينَ

89 And Zechariah, when he called out to his Lord, "My Lord, do not leave me alone, even though you are the Best of heirs."

89
3:38; 19:3–6

٩٠ فَاسْتَجَبْنَا لَهُ وَوَهَبْنَا لَهُ يَحْيَىٰ وَأَصْلَحْنَا لَهُ زَوْجَهُ ۚ إِنَّهُمْ كَانُوا يُسَارِعُونَ فِي الْخَيْرَاتِ وَيَدْعُونَنَا رَغَبًا وَرَهَبًا ۖ وَكَانُوا لَنَا خَاشِعِينَ

90 So We answered him, and gave him John. And We cured his wife for him. They used to vie in doing righteous deeds, and used to call on Us in love and awe, and they used to humble themselves to Us.

90
3:39; 19:7

٩١ وَالَّتِي أَحْصَنَتْ فَرْجَهَا فَنَفَخْنَا فِيهَا مِن رُّوحِنَا وَجَعَلْنَاهَا وَابْنَهَا آيَةً لِّلْعَالَمِينَ

91 And she who guarded her virginity. We breathed into her of Our spirit, and made her and her son a sign to the world.

91
19:16; 23:50; 66:12

٩٢ إِنَّ هَٰذِهِ أُمَّتُكُمْ أُمَّةً وَاحِدَةً وَأَنَا رَبُّكُمْ فَاعْبُدُونِ

92 This community of yours is one community, and I am your Lord, so worship Me.

92
2:213; 10:19; 23:52; 66:12

٩٣ وَتَقَطَّعُوا أَمْرَهُم بَيْنَهُمْ ۖ كُلٌّ إِلَيْنَا رَاجِعُونَ

93 But they splintered themselves into factions. They will all return to Us.

93
23:53

٩٤ فَمَن يَعْمَلْ مِنَ الصَّالِحَاتِ وَهُوَ مُؤْمِنٌ فَلَا كُفْرَانَ لِسَعْيِهِ وَإِنَّا لَهُ كَاتِبُونَ

94 Whoever does righteous deeds, and is a believer, his effort will not be denied. We are writing it down for him.

٩٥ وَحَرَامٌ عَلَىٰ قَرْيَةٍ أَهْلَكْنَاهَا أَنَّهُمْ لَا يَرْجِعُونَ

95 There is a ban on the town that We had destroyed—that they will not return.

95
36:31

٩٦ حَتَّىٰ إِذَا فُتِحَتْ يَأْجُوجُ وَمَأْجُوجُ وَهُم مِّن كُلِّ حَدَبٍ يَنسِلُونَ

96 Until, when Gog and Magog are let loose, and they swarm down from every mound.

96
18:98; 22:6

٩٧ وَاقْتَرَبَ الْوَعْدُ الْحَقُّ فَإِذَا هِيَ شَاخِصَةٌ أَبْصَارُ الَّذِينَ كَفَرُوا يَا وَيْلَنَا قَدْ كُنَّا فِي غَفْلَةٍ مِّنْ هَٰذَا بَلْ كُنَّا ظَالِمِينَ

97 The promise of truth has drawn near. The eyes of those who disbelieved will stare in horror: "Woe to us. We were oblivious to this. In fact, we were wrongdoers."

97
22:2; 14:42

٩٨ إِنَّكُمْ وَمَا تَعْبُدُونَ مِن دُونِ اللَّهِ حَصَبُ جَهَنَّمَ أَنتُمْ لَهَا وَارِدُونَ

98 You and what you worship besides God are fuel for Hell. You will descend into it.

98
2:24

٩٩ لَوْ كَانَ هَٰؤُلَاءِ آلِهَةً مَّا وَرَدُوهَا ۖ وَكُلٌّ فِيهَا خَالِدُونَ

99 Had these been gods, they would not have descended into it. All will abide in it.

١٠٠ لَهُمْ فِيهَا زَفِيرٌ وَهُمْ فِيهَا لَا يَسْمَعُونَ

100 In it they will wail. In it they will not hear.

١٠١ إِنَّ الَّذِينَ سَبَقَتْ لَهُم مِّنَّا الْحُسْنَىٰ أُولَٰئِكَ عَنْهَا مُبْعَدُونَ

101 As for those who deserved goodness from Us—these will be kept away from it.

101
10:16; 55:60

١٠٢ لَا يَسْمَعُونَ حَسِيسَهَا ۖ وَهُمْ فِي مَا اشْتَهَتْ أَنفُسُهُمْ خَالِدُونَ

102 They will not hear its hissing, and they will forever abide in what their hearts desire.

102
41:31; 43:71

١٠٣ لَا يَحْزُنُهُمُ الْفَزَعُ الْأَكْبَرُ وَتَتَلَقَّاهُمُ الْمَلَائِكَةُ هَٰذَا يَوْمُكُمُ الَّذِي كُنتُمْ تُوعَدُونَ

103 The Supreme Fear will not worry them, and the angels will receive them: "This is your Day which you were promised."

103
13:23; 16:32; 41:33

١٠٤ يَوْمَ نَطْوِي السَّمَاءَ كَطَيِّ السِّجِلِّ لِلْكُتُبِ ۚ كَمَا بَدَأْنَا أَوَّلَ خَلْقٍ نُعِيدُهُ ۚ وَعْدًا عَلَيْنَا ۚ إِنَّا كُنَّا فَاعِلِينَ 104 On the Day when We fold the heaven, like the folding of a book. Just as We began the first creation, We will repeat it—a promise binding on Us. We will act.	**104** 39:67
١٠٥ وَلَقَدْ كَتَبْنَا فِي الزَّبُورِ مِنْ بَعْدِ الذِّكْرِ أَنَّ الْأَرْضَ يَرِثُهَا عِبَادِيَ الصَّالِحُونَ 105 We have written in the Psalms, after the Reminder, that the earth will be inherited by My righteous servants.	**105** 7:128, 137; 33:27; 39:74
١٠٦ إِنَّ فِي هَٰذَا لَبَلَاغًا لِقَوْمٍ عَابِدِينَ 106 Indeed, in this is a message for people who worship.	
١٠٧ وَمَا أَرْسَلْنَاكَ إِلَّا رَحْمَةً لِلْعَالَمِينَ 107 We did not send you except as mercy to mankind.	**107** 4:79; 7:158; 21:107; 24:28
١٠٨ قُلْ إِنَّمَا يُوحَىٰ إِلَيَّ أَنَّمَا إِلَٰهُكُمْ إِلَٰهٌ وَاحِدٌ ۖ فَهَلْ أَنْتُمْ مُسْلِمُونَ 108 Say, "It is revealed to me that your God is One God. Are you going to submit?"	**108** 18:110; 41:6
١٠٩ فَإِنْ تَوَلَّوْا فَقُلْ آذَنْتُكُمْ عَلَىٰ سَوَاءٍ ۖ وَإِنْ أَدْرِي أَقَرِيبٌ أَمْ بَعِيدٌ مَا تُوعَدُونَ 109 But if they turn away, say, "I have informed you sufficiently. Although I do not know whether what you are promised is near or far."	
١١٠ إِنَّهُ يَعْلَمُ الْجَهْرَ مِنَ الْقَوْلِ وَيَعْلَمُ مَا تَكْتُمُونَ 110 He knows what is said openly, and He knows what you conceal.	**110** 2:33; 20:7; 24:29; 29:23; 50:16
١١١ وَإِنْ أَدْرِي لَعَلَّهُ فِتْنَةٌ لَكُمْ وَمَتَاعٌ إِلَىٰ حِينٍ 111 "And I do not know whether it is perhaps a trial for you, and an enjoyment for a while."	
١١٢ قَالَ رَبِّ احْكُمْ بِالْحَقِّ ۗ وَرَبُّنَا الرَّحْمَٰنُ الْمُسْتَعَانُ عَلَىٰ مَا تَصِفُونَ 112 He said, "My Lord, judge with justice." And, "Our Lord is the Gracious, Whose help is sought against what you allege."	**112** 12:18; 16:62, 116

Sūrah 22: Al-Ḥajj

سُورَةُ ٱلْحَجّ (The Pilgrimage)

بِسْمِ ٱللَّهِ ٱلرَّحْمَـٰنِ ٱلرَّحِيمِ

١ يَا أَيُّهَا النَّاسُ اتَّقُوا رَبَّكُمْ ۚ إِنَّ زَلْزَلَةَ السَّاعَةِ شَيْءٌ عَظِيمٌ

1 — 56:4; 69:14; 99:1

1 O people, be conscious of your Lord. The quaking of the Hour is a tremendous thing.

٢ يَوْمَ تَرَوْنَهَا تَذْهَلُ كُلُّ مُرْضِعَةٍ عَمَّا أَرْضَعَتْ وَتَضَعُ كُلُّ ذَاتِ حَمْلٍ حَمْلَهَا وَتَرَى النَّاسَ سُكَارَىٰ وَمَا هُم بِسُكَارَىٰ وَلَـٰكِنَّ عَذَابَ اللَّهِ شَدِيدٌ

2 — 7:187; 21:97

2 On the Day when you will see it: every nursing mother will discard her infant, and every pregnant woman will abort her load, and you will see the people drunk, even though they are not drunk—but the punishment of God is severe.

٣ وَمِنَ النَّاسِ مَن يُجَادِلُ فِي اللَّهِ بِغَيْرِ عِلْمٍ وَيَتَّبِعُ كُلَّ شَيْطَانٍ مَرِيدٍ

3 — 22:8; 31:20; 42:16

3 Among the people is he who argues about God without knowledge, and follows every defiant devil.

٤ كُتِبَ عَلَيْهِ أَنَّهُ مَن تَوَلَّاهُ فَأَنَّهُ يُضِلُّهُ وَيَهْدِيهِ إِلَىٰ عَذَابِ السَّعِيرِ

4 — 81:12

4 It was decreed for him, that whoever follows him—he will misguide him, and lead him to the torment of the Blaze.

٥ يَا أَيُّهَا النَّاسُ إِن كُنتُمْ فِي رَيْبٍ مِنَ الْبَعْثِ فَإِنَّا خَلَقْنَاكُم مِن تُرَابٍ ثُمَّ مِن نُطْفَةٍ ثُمَّ مِنْ عَلَقَةٍ ثُمَّ مِن مُضْغَةٍ مُخَلَّقَةٍ وَغَيْرِ مُخَلَّقَةٍ لِنُبَيِّنَ لَكُمْ ۚ وَنُقِرُّ فِي الْأَرْحَامِ مَا نَشَاءُ إِلَىٰ أَجَلٍ مُسَمًّى ثُمَّ نُخْرِجُكُمْ طِفْلًا ثُمَّ لِتَبْلُغُوا أَشُدَّكُمْ ۖ وَمِنكُم مَن يُتَوَفَّىٰ وَمِنكُم مَن يُرَدُّ إِلَىٰ أَرْذَلِ الْعُمُرِ لِكَيْلَا يَعْلَمَ مِن بَعْدِ عِلْمٍ شَيْئًا ۚ [a] وَتَرَى الْأَرْضَ هَامِدَةً فَإِذَا أَنزَلْنَا عَلَيْهَا الْمَاءَ اهْتَزَّتْ وَرَبَتْ وَأَنبَتَتْ مِن كُلِّ زَوْجٍ بَهِيجٍ [b]

5
[a] 2:76; 18:37; 23:12–16; 30:27; 36:78; 40:67; 71:13–14; 96:2
[b] 30:19, 50; 41:39; 50:11

5 O people! If you are in doubt about the Resurrection—We created you from dust, then from a small drop, then from a clinging clot, then from a lump of flesh, partly developed and partly undeveloped. In order to clarify things for you. And We settle in the wombs whatever We will for a designated term, and then We bring you out as infants, until you reach your full strength. And some of you will pass away, and some of you will be returned to the vilest age, so that he may not know, after having known. And you see the earth still; but when We send down water on it, it vibrates, and swells, and grows all kinds of lovely pairs.

٦ ذَٰلِكَ بِأَنَّ اللَّهَ هُوَ الْحَقُّ وَأَنَّهُ يُحْيِي الْمَوْتَىٰ وَأَنَّهُ عَلَىٰ كُلِّ شَيْءٍ قَدِيرٌ

6 — 46:33

6 That is because God is the truth, and because He gives life to the dead, and because He is Capable of everything.

٧ وَأَنَّ السَّاعَةَ آتِيَةٌ لَا رَيْبَ فِيهَا وَأَنَّ اللَّهَ يَبْعَثُ مَن فِي الْقُبُورِ

7 — 15:85; 40:59

7 And because the Hour is coming—there is no doubt about it—and because God will resurrect those in the graves.

٨ وَمِنَ النَّاسِ مَن يُجَادِلُ فِي اللَّهِ بِغَيْرِ عِلْمٍ وَلَا هُدًى وَلَا كِتَابٍ مُّنِيرٍ

8 And among the people is he who argues about God without knowledge, or guidance, or an enlightening scripture.

8
22:3; 31:20; 42:16

٩ ثَانِيَ عِطْفِهِ لِيُضِلَّ عَن سَبِيلِ اللَّهِ ۖ لَهُ فِي الدُّنْيَا خِزْيٌ ۖ وَنُذِيقُهُ يَوْمَ الْقِيَامَةِ عَذَابَ الْحَرِيقِ

9 Turning aside in contempt, to lead away from the path of God. He will have humiliation in this world, and on the Day of Resurrection We will make him taste the agony of burning.

١٠ ذَٰلِكَ بِمَا قَدَّمَتْ يَدَاكَ وَأَنَّ اللَّهَ لَيْسَ بِظَلَّامٍ لِّلْعَبِيدِ

10 That is for what your hands have advanced, and because God is not unjust to the servants.

10
3:182; 8:51; 22:10

١١ وَمِنَ النَّاسِ مَن يَعْبُدُ اللَّهَ عَلَىٰ حَرْفٍ ۖ فَإِنْ أَصَابَهُ خَيْرٌ اطْمَأَنَّ بِهِ ۖ وَإِنْ أَصَابَتْهُ فِتْنَةٌ انقَلَبَ عَلَىٰ وَجْهِهِ خَسِرَ الدُّنْيَا وَالْآخِرَةَ ۚ ذَٰلِكَ هُوَ الْخُسْرَانُ الْمُبِينُ

11 And among the people is he who worships God on edge. When something good comes his way, he is content with it. But when an ordeal strikes him, he makes a turnaround. He loses this world and the next. That is the obvious loss.

١٢ يَدْعُو مِن دُونِ اللَّهِ مَا لَا يَضُرُّهُ وَمَا لَا يَنفَعُهُ ۚ ذَٰلِكَ هُوَ الضَّلَالُ الْبَعِيدُ

12 He invokes, instead of God, what can neither harm him nor benefit him. That is the far straying.

12–13
5:76; 6:71; 10:18, 106; 21:66; 22:12; 26:72

١٣ يَدْعُو لَمَن ضَرُّهُ أَقْرَبُ مِن نَّفْعِهِ ۚ لَبِئْسَ الْمَوْلَىٰ وَلَبِئْسَ الْعَشِيرُ

13 He invokes one whose harm is closer than his benefit. What a miserable master. What a miserable companion.

١٤ إِنَّ اللَّهَ يُدْخِلُ الَّذِينَ آمَنُوا وَعَمِلُوا الصَّالِحَاتِ جَنَّاتٍ تَجْرِي مِن تَحْتِهَا الْأَنْهَارُ ۚ إِنَّ اللَّهَ يَفْعَلُ مَا يُرِيدُ

14 God will admit those who believe and do righteous deeds into Gardens beneath which rivers flow. God does whatever He wills.

14
22:23, 50, 56

١٥ مَن كَانَ يَظُنُّ أَن لَّن يَنصُرَهُ اللَّهُ فِي الدُّنْيَا وَالْآخِرَةِ فَلْيَمْدُدْ بِسَبَبٍ إِلَى السَّمَاءِ ثُمَّ لْيَقْطَعْ فَلْيَنظُرْ هَلْ يُذْهِبَنَّ كَيْدُهُ مَا يَغِيظُ

15 Whoever thinks that God will not help him in this life and in the Hereafter—let him turn to heaven, then sever, and see if his cunning eliminates what enrages him.

١٦ وَكَذَٰلِكَ أَنزَلْنَاهُ آيَاتٍ بَيِّنَاتٍ وَأَنَّ اللَّهَ يَهْدِي مَن يُرِيدُ

16 Thus We revealed it as clarifying signs, and God guides whomever He wills.

١٧ إِنَّ الَّذِينَ آمَنُوا وَالَّذِينَ هَادُوا وَالصَّابِئِينَ وَالنَّصَارَىٰ وَالْمَجُوسَ وَالَّذِينَ أَشْرَكُوا إِنَّ اللَّهَ يَفْصِلُ بَيْنَهُمْ يَوْمَ الْقِيَامَةِ ۚ إِنَّ اللَّهَ عَلَىٰ كُلِّ شَيْءٍ شَهِيدٌ

17 2:62; 5:69

17 Those who believe, and those who are Jewish, and the Sabeans, and the Christians, and the Zoroastrians, and the Polytheists—God will judge between them on the Day of Resurrection. God is witness to all things.

١٨ أَلَمْ تَرَ أَنَّ اللَّهَ يَسْجُدُ لَهُ مَنْ فِي السَّمَاوَاتِ وَمَنْ فِي الْأَرْضِ وَالشَّمْسُ وَالْقَمَرُ وَالنُّجُومُ وَالْجِبَالُ وَالشَّجَرُ وَالدَّوَابُّ وَكَثِيرٌ مِنَ النَّاسِ ۖ وَكَثِيرٌ حَقَّ عَلَيْهِ الْعَذَابُ ۗ وَمَنْ يُهِنِ اللَّهُ فَمَا لَهُ مِنْ مُكْرِمٍ ۚ إِنَّ اللَّهَ يَفْعَلُ مَا يَشَاءُ ۩

18 13:15; 16:49; 55:6

18 Do you not realize that to God prostrates everyone in the heavens and everyone on earth, and the sun, and the moon, and the stars, and the mountains, and the trees, and the animals, and many of the people? But many are justly deserving of punishment. Whomever God shames, there is none to honor him. God does whatever He wills.

١٩ هَٰذَانِ خَصْمَانِ اخْتَصَمُوا فِي رَبِّهِمْ ۖ فَالَّذِينَ كَفَرُوا قُطِّعَتْ لَهُمْ ثِيَابٌ مِنْ نَارٍ يُصَبُّ مِنْ فَوْقِ رُءُوسِهِمُ الْحَمِيمُ

19 14:50; 44:48

19 Here are two adversaries feuding regarding their Lord. As for those who disbelieve, garments of fire will be tailored for them, and scalding water will be poured over their heads.

٢٠ يُصْهَرُ بِهِ مَا فِي بُطُونِهِمْ وَالْجُلُودُ

20 47:15

20 Melting their insides and their skins.

٢١ وَلَهُمْ مَقَامِعُ مِنْ حَدِيدٍ

21

21 And they will have maces of iron.

٢٢ كُلَّمَا أَرَادُوا أَنْ يَخْرُجُوا مِنْهَا مِنْ غَمٍّ أُعِيدُوا فِيهَا وَذُوقُوا عَذَابَ الْحَرِيقِ

22 5:37; 32:20

22 Whenever they try to escape the gloom, they will be driven back to it: "Taste the suffering of burning."

٢٣ إِنَّ اللَّهَ يُدْخِلُ الَّذِينَ آمَنُوا وَعَمِلُوا الصَّالِحَاتِ جَنَّاتٍ تَجْرِي مِنْ تَحْتِهَا الْأَنْهَارُ يُحَلَّوْنَ فِيهَا مِنْ أَسَاوِرَ مِنْ ذَهَبٍ وَلُؤْلُؤًا ۖ وَلِبَاسُهُمْ فِيهَا حَرِيرٌ

23 17:70; 22:14, 50; 35:33; 76:21

23 But God will admit those who believe and do good deeds into Gardens beneath which rivers flow. They will be decorated therein with bracelets of gold and pearls, and their garments therein will be of silk.

٢٤ وَهُدُوا إِلَى الطَّيِّبِ مِنَ الْقَوْلِ وَهُدُوا إِلَىٰ صِرَاطِ الْحَمِيدِ

24 They were guided to purity of speech. They were guided to the path of the Most Praised.

٢٥ إِنَّ الَّذِينَ كَفَرُوا وَيَصُدُّونَ عَن سَبِيلِ اللَّهِ وَالْمَسْجِدِ الْحَرَامِ الَّذِي جَعَلْنَاهُ لِلنَّاسِ سَوَاءً الْعَاكِفُ فِيهِ وَالْبَادِ ۚ وَمَن يُرِدْ فِيهِ بِإِلْحَادٍ بِظُلْمٍ نُذِقْهُ مِنْ عَذَابٍ أَلِيمٍ

25 As for those who disbelieve and repel from God's path and from the Sacred Mosque—which We have designated for all mankind equally, whether residing therein or passing through—and whoever seeks to commit sacrilege therein—We will make him taste of a painful punishment.

٢٦ وَإِذْ بَوَّأْنَا لِإِبْرَاهِيمَ مَكَانَ الْبَيْتِ أَن لَّا تُشْرِكْ بِي شَيْئًا وَطَهِّرْ بَيْتِيَ لِلطَّائِفِينَ وَالْقَائِمِينَ وَالرُّكَّعِ السُّجُودِ

26
2:125

26 We showed Abraham the location of the House: "Do not associate anything with Me; and purify My House for those who circle around, and those who stand to pray, and those who kneel and prostrate."

٢٧ وَأَذِّن فِي النَّاسِ بِالْحَجِّ يَأْتُوكَ رِجَالًا وَعَلَىٰ كُلِّ ضَامِرٍ يَأْتِينَ مِن كُلِّ فَجٍّ عَمِيقٍ

27
2:158, 196; 3:97

27 And announce the pilgrimage to humanity. They will come to you on foot, and on every transport. They will come from every distant point.

٢٨ لِيَشْهَدُوا مَنَافِعَ لَهُمْ وَيَذْكُرُوا اسْمَ اللَّهِ فِي أَيَّامٍ مَّعْلُومَاتٍ عَلَىٰ مَا رَزَقَهُم مِّن بَهِيمَةِ الْأَنْعَامِ ۖ فَكُلُوا مِنْهَا وَأَطْعِمُوا الْبَائِسَ الْفَقِيرَ

28
22:34

28 That they may witness the benefits for themselves, and celebrate the name of God during the appointed days, for providing them with the animal livestock. So eat from it, and feed the unfortunate poor.

٢٩ ثُمَّ لْيَقْضُوا تَفَثَهُمْ وَلْيُوفُوا نُذُورَهُمْ وَلْيَطَّوَّفُوا بِالْبَيْتِ الْعَتِيقِ

29
3:96

29 Then let them perform their acts of cleansing, and fulfill their vows, and circle around the Ancient House.

٣٠ ذَٰلِكَ وَمَن يُعَظِّمْ حُرُمَاتِ اللَّهِ فَهُوَ خَيْرٌ لَّهُ عِندَ رَبِّهِ ۗ وَأُحِلَّتْ لَكُمُ الْأَنْعَامُ إِلَّا مَا يُتْلَىٰ عَلَيْكُمْ ۖ فَاجْتَنِبُوا الرِّجْسَ مِنَ الْأَوْثَانِ وَاجْتَنِبُوا قَوْلَ الزُّورِ

30
2:219; 5:90–91; 14:35; 16:36; 39:17

30 All that. Whoever venerates the sanctities of God—it is good for him with his Lord. All livestock are permitted to you, except what is recited to you. So stay away from the abomination of idols, and stay away from perjury.

٣١ حُنَفَاءَ لِلَّهِ غَيْرَ مُشْرِكِينَ بِهِ ۚ وَمَن يُشْرِكْ بِاللَّهِ فَكَأَنَّمَا خَرَّ مِنَ السَّمَاءِ فَتَخْطَفُهُ الطَّيْرُ أَوْ تَهْوِي بِهِ الرِّيحُ فِي مَكَانٍ سَحِيقٍ

31
98:5

31 Being true to God, without associating anything with Him. Whoever associates anything with God—it is as though he has fallen from the sky, and is snatched by the birds, or is swept away by the wind to a distant abyss.

Sūrah 22: Al-Ḥajj

٣٢ ذَٰلِكَ وَمَن يُعَظِّمْ شَعَائِرَ اللَّهِ فَإِنَّهَا مِن تَقْوَى الْقُلُوبِ	32	2:158; 5:2; 22:36, 37

32 So it is. Whoever venerates the rites of God—it is from the piety of the hearts.

٣٣ لَكُمْ فِيهَا مَنَافِعُ إِلَىٰ أَجَلٍ مُّسَمًّى ثُمَّ مَحِلُّهَا إِلَى الْبَيْتِ الْعَتِيقِ	33	2:196; 48:25

33 In them are benefits for you until a certain time. Then their place is by the Ancient House.

٣٤ وَلِكُلِّ أُمَّةٍ جَعَلْنَا مَنسَكًا لِّيَذْكُرُوا اسْمَ اللَّهِ عَلَىٰ مَا رَزَقَهُم مِّن بَهِيمَةِ الْأَنْعَامِ ۗ فَإِلَٰهُكُمْ إِلَٰهٌ وَاحِدٌ فَلَهُ أَسْلِمُوا ۗ وَبَشِّرِ الْمُخْبِتِينَ	34	2:200; 22:28

34 We have appointed a rite for every nation, that they may commemorate God's name over the livestock He has provided for them. Your God is One God, so to Him submit, and announce good news to the humble.

٣٥ الَّذِينَ إِذَا ذُكِرَ اللَّهُ وَجِلَتْ قُلُوبُهُمْ وَالصَّابِرِينَ عَلَىٰ مَا أَصَابَهُمْ وَالْمُقِيمِي الصَّلَاةِ وَمِمَّا رَزَقْنَاهُمْ يُنفِقُونَ	35	8:2; 23:60; 39:23

35 Those whose hearts tremble when God is mentioned, and those who endure what has befallen them, and those who perform the prayer and spend from what We have provided for them.

٣٦ وَالْبُدْنَ جَعَلْنَاهَا لَكُم مِّن شَعَائِرِ اللَّهِ لَكُمْ فِيهَا خَيْرٌ ۖ فَاذْكُرُوا اسْمَ اللَّهِ عَلَيْهَا صَوَافَّ ۖ فَإِذَا وَجَبَتْ جُنُوبُهَا فَكُلُوا مِنْهَا وَأَطْعِمُوا الْقَانِعَ وَالْمُعْتَرَّ ۚ كَذَٰلِكَ سَخَّرْنَاهَا لَكُمْ لَعَلَّكُمْ تَشْكُرُونَ	36	5:2; 22:32

36 We have made the animal offerings among the rites of God for you. In them is goodness for you. So pronounce God's name upon them as they line up. Then, when they have fallen on their sides, eat of them and feed the contented and the beggar. Thus We have subjected them to you, that you may be thankful.

٣٧ لَن يَنَالَ اللَّهَ لُحُومُهَا وَلَا دِمَاؤُهَا وَلَٰكِن يَنَالُهُ التَّقْوَىٰ مِنكُمْ ۚ كَذَٰلِكَ سَخَّرَهَا لَكُمْ لِتُكَبِّرُوا اللَّهَ عَلَىٰ مَا هَدَاكُمْ ۗ وَبَشِّرِ الْمُحْسِنِينَ	37	2:177, 189; 22:32

37 Neither their flesh, nor their blood, ever reaches God. What reaches Him is the righteousness from you. Thus He subdued them to you, that you may glorify God for guiding you. And give good news to the charitable.

٣٨ إِنَّ اللَّهَ يُدَافِعُ عَنِ الَّذِينَ آمَنُوا ۗ إِنَّ اللَّهَ لَا يُحِبُّ كُلَّ خَوَّانٍ كَفُورٍ	38	4:107

38 God defends those who believe. God does not love any ungrateful traitor.

٣٩ أُذِنَ لِلَّذِينَ يُقَاتَلُونَ بِأَنَّهُمْ ظُلِمُوا ۚ وَإِنَّ اللَّهَ عَلَىٰ نَصْرِهِمْ لَقَدِيرٌ	39	2:190

39 Permission is given to those who are fought against, and God is Able to give them victory.

٤٠ الَّذِينَ أُخْرِجُوا مِن دِيَارِهِم بِغَيْرِ حَقٍّ إِلَّا أَن يَقُولُوا رَبُّنَا اللَّهُ ۗ وَلَوْلَا دَفْعُ اللَّهِ النَّاسَ بَعْضَهُم بِبَعْضٍ لَّهُدِّمَتْ صَوَامِعُ وَبِيَعٌ وَصَلَوَاتٌ وَمَسَاجِدُ يُذْكَرُ فِيهَا اسْمُ اللَّهِ كَثِيرًا ۗ وَلَيَنصُرَنَّ اللَّهُ مَن يَنصُرُهُ ۗ إِنَّ اللَّهَ لَقَوِيٌّ عَزِيزٌ	40 47:7–8	

40 Those who were unjustly evicted from their homes, merely for saying, "Our Lord is God." Were it not that God repels people by means of others: monasteries, churches, synagogues, and mosques—where the name of God is mentioned much—would have been demolished. God supports whoever supports Him. God is Strong and Mighty.

٤١ الَّذِينَ إِن مَّكَّنَّاهُمْ فِي الْأَرْضِ أَقَامُوا الصَّلَاةَ وَآتَوُا الزَّكَاةَ وَأَمَرُوا بِالْمَعْرُوفِ وَنَهَوْا عَنِ الْمُنكَرِ ۗ وَلِلَّهِ عَاقِبَةُ الْأُمُورِ	41 24:55

41 Those who, when We empower them in the land, observe the prayer, and give regular charity, and command what is right, and forbid what is wrong. To God belongs the outcome of events.

٤٢ وَإِن يُكَذِّبُوكَ فَقَدْ كَذَّبَتْ قَبْلَهُمْ قَوْمُ نُوحٍ وَعَادٌ وَثَمُودُ	42–43 9:70; 10:39; 11:120; 14:9; 26:141; 35:4; 41:43

42 If they deny you—before them the people of Noah, and 'Ād, and Thamūd also denied.

٤٣ وَقَوْمُ إِبْرَاهِيمَ وَقَوْمُ لُوطٍ	

43 And the people of Abraham, and the people of Lot.

٤٤ وَأَصْحَابُ مَدْيَنَ ۖ وَكُذِّبَ مُوسَىٰ فَأَمْلَيْتُ لِلْكَافِرِينَ ثُمَّ أَخَذْتُهُمْ ۖ فَكَيْفَ كَانَ نَكِيرِ	44 22:48

44 And the inhabitants of Median. And Moses was denied. Then I reprieved those who disbelieved, but then I seized them. So how was My rejection?

٤٥ فَكَأَيِّن مِّن قَرْيَةٍ أَهْلَكْنَاهَا وَهِيَ ظَالِمَةٌ فَهِيَ خَاوِيَةٌ عَلَىٰ عُرُوشِهَا وَبِئْرٍ مُّعَطَّلَةٍ وَقَصْرٍ مَّشِيدٍ	45 8:54; 10:13; 11:102; 21:11; 22:48; 65:8–10

45 How many a town have We destroyed while it was doing wrong? They lie in ruins; with stilled wells, and lofty mansions.

٤٦ أَفَلَمْ يَسِيرُوا فِي الْأَرْضِ فَتَكُونَ لَهُمْ قُلُوبٌ يَعْقِلُونَ بِهَا أَوْ آذَانٌ يَسْمَعُونَ بِهَا ۖ فَإِنَّهَا لَا تَعْمَى الْأَبْصَارُ وَلَـٰكِن تَعْمَى الْقُلُوبُ الَّتِي فِي الصُّدُورِ	46 12:109; 17:72

46 Have they not journeyed in the land, and had minds to reason with, or ears to listen with? It is not the eyes that go blind, but it is the hearts, within the chests, that go blind.

٤٧ وَيَسْتَعْجِلُونَكَ بِالْعَذَابِ وَلَن يُخْلِفَ اللَّهُ وَعْدَهُ ۚ [a] وَإِنَّ يَوْمًا عِندَ رَبِّكَ كَأَلْفِ سَنَةٍ مِّمَّا تَعُدُّونَ [b]	47 [a] 10:50–51; 29:53–54 [b] 32:5; 70:4

47 And they ask you to hasten the punishment. But God never breaks His promise. A day with your Lord is like a thousand years of your count.

٤٨ وَكَأَيِّن مِّن قَرْيَةٍ أَمْلَيْتُ لَهَا وَهِيَ ظَالِمَةٌ ثُمَّ أَخَذْتُهَا وَإِلَيَّ الْمَصِيرُ	48 13:32; 22:44

48 How many a town have I reprieved, although it was unjust? Then I seized it. To Me is the destination.

٤٩ قُلْ يَا أَيُّهَا النَّاسُ إِنَّمَا أَنَا لَكُمْ نَذِيرٌ مُبِينٌ

49 Say, "O people, I am only a plain warner to you."

٥٠ فَالَّذِينَ آمَنُوا وَعَمِلُوا الصَّالِحَاتِ لَهُمْ مَغْفِرَةٌ وَرِزْقٌ كَرِيمٌ

50 Those who believe and work righteousness—for them is forgiveness and a generous provision.

50
22:14, 23

٥١ وَالَّذِينَ سَعَوْا فِي آيَاتِنَا مُعَاجِزِينَ أُولَٰئِكَ أَصْحَابُ الْجَحِيمِ

51 But those who strive against Our revelations—these are the inmates of Hell.

51
34:5, 38

٥٢ وَمَا أَرْسَلْنَا مِنْ قَبْلِكَ مِنْ رَسُولٍ وَلَا نَبِيٍّ إِلَّا إِذَا تَمَنَّىٰ أَلْقَى الشَّيْطَانُ فِي أُمْنِيَّتِهِ فَيَنْسَخُ اللَّهُ مَا يُلْقِي الشَّيْطَانُ ثُمَّ يُحْكِمُ اللَّهُ آيَاتِهِ ۗ وَاللَّهُ عَلِيمٌ حَكِيمٌ

52 We never sent a messenger before you, or a prophet, but when he had a desire Satan interfered in his wishes. But God nullifies what Satan interjects, and God affirms His revelations. God is Omniscient and Wise.

52
3:7; 4:119; 22:53

٥٣ لِيَجْعَلَ مَا يُلْقِي الشَّيْطَانُ فِتْنَةً لِلَّذِينَ فِي قُلُوبِهِمْ مَرَضٌ وَالْقَاسِيَةِ قُلُوبُهُمْ ۗ وَإِنَّ الظَّالِمِينَ لَفِي شِقَاقٍ بَعِيدٍ

53 In order to make Satan's suggestions a trial for those whose hearts are diseased, and those whose hearts are hardened. The wrongdoers are in profound discord.

٥٤ وَلِيَعْلَمَ الَّذِينَ أُوتُوا الْعِلْمَ أَنَّهُ الْحَقُّ مِنْ رَبِّكَ فَيُؤْمِنُوا بِهِ فَتُخْبِتَ لَهُ قُلُوبُهُمْ ۗ وَإِنَّ اللَّهَ لَهَادِ الَّذِينَ آمَنُوا إِلَىٰ صِرَاطٍ مُسْتَقِيمٍ

54 And so that those endowed with knowledge may know that it is the truth from your Lord, and so believe in it, and their hearts soften to it. God guides those who believe to a straight path.

٥٥ وَلَا يَزَالُ الَّذِينَ كَفَرُوا فِي مِرْيَةٍ مِنْهُ حَتَّىٰ تَأْتِيَهُمُ السَّاعَةُ بَغْتَةً أَوْ يَأْتِيَهُمْ عَذَابُ يَوْمٍ عَقِيمٍ

55 Those who disbelieve will continue to be hesitant about it, until the Hour comes upon them suddenly, or there comes to them the torment of a desolate Day.

55
7:187

٥٦ الْمُلْكُ يَوْمَئِذٍ لِلَّهِ يَحْكُمُ بَيْنَهُمْ ۚ فَالَّذِينَ آمَنُوا وَعَمِلُوا الصَّالِحَاتِ فِي جَنَّاتِ النَّعِيمِ

56 Sovereignty on that Day belongs to God; He will judge between them. Those who believe and do good deeds will be in the Gardens of Bliss.

56
6:73; 25:26; 40:16

٥٧ وَالَّذِينَ كَفَرُوا وَكَذَّبُوا بِآيَاتِنَا فَأُولَٰئِكَ لَهُمْ عَذَابٌ مُهِينٌ

57 But those who disbelieve and reject Our revelations—these will have a humiliating punishment.

٥٨ وَالَّذِينَ هَاجَرُوا فِي سَبِيلِ اللَّهِ ثُمَّ قُتِلُوا أَوْ مَاتُوا لَيَرْزُقَنَّهُمُ اللَّهُ رِزْقًا حَسَنًا ۚ وَإِنَّ اللَّهَ لَهُوَ خَيْرُ الرَّازِقِينَ

58 Those who emigrate in God's cause, then get killed, or die, God will provide them with fine provisions. God is the Best of Providers.

58 2:218; 3:157, 169; 4:100; 9:20; 16:41

٥٩ لَيُدْخِلَنَّهُم مُّدْخَلًا يَرْضَوْنَهُ ۗ وَإِنَّ اللَّهَ لَعَلِيمٌ حَلِيمٌ

59 He will admit them an admittance that will please them. God is Knowing and Clement.

٦٠ ذَٰلِكَ وَمَنْ عَاقَبَ بِمِثْلِ مَا عُوقِبَ بِهِ ثُمَّ بُغِيَ عَلَيْهِ لَيَنصُرَنَّهُ اللَّهُ ۗ إِنَّ اللَّهَ لَعَفُوٌّ غَفُورٌ

60 That is so! Whoever retaliates similarly to the affliction he was made to suffer, and then he is wronged again, God will definitely assist him. God is Pardoning and Forgiving.

60 16:126

٦١ ذَٰلِكَ بِأَنَّ اللَّهَ يُولِجُ اللَّيْلَ فِي النَّهَارِ وَيُولِجُ النَّهَارَ فِي اللَّيْلِ وَأَنَّ اللَّهَ سَمِيعٌ بَصِيرٌ

61 That is because God merges the night into the day, and He merges the day into the night, and because God is Hearing and Seeing.

61 31:29

٦٢ ذَٰلِكَ بِأَنَّ اللَّهَ هُوَ الْحَقُّ وَأَنَّ مَا يَدْعُونَ مِن دُونِهِ هُوَ الْبَاطِلُ وَأَنَّ اللَّهَ هُوَ الْعَلِيُّ الْكَبِيرُ

62 That is because God is the Reality, and what they invoke besides Him is vanity, and because God is the Sublime, the Grand.

٦٣ أَلَمْ تَرَ أَنَّ اللَّهَ أَنزَلَ مِنَ السَّمَاءِ مَاءً فَتُصْبِحُ الْأَرْضُ مُخْضَرَّةً ۗ إِنَّ اللَّهَ لَطِيفٌ خَبِيرٌ

63 Do you not see that God sends down water from the sky, and the land becomes green? God is Kind and Aware.

63 41:39; 50:9–11

٦٤ لَّهُ مَا فِي السَّمَاوَاتِ وَمَا فِي الْأَرْضِ ۗ وَإِنَّ اللَّهَ لَهُوَ الْغَنِيُّ الْحَمِيدُ

64 To Him belongs everything in the heavens and everything on earth. God is the Rich, the Praised.

٦٥ أَلَمْ تَرَ أَنَّ اللَّهَ سَخَّرَ لَكُم مَّا فِي الْأَرْضِ وَالْفُلْكَ تَجْرِي فِي الْبَحْرِ بِأَمْرِهِ وَيُمْسِكُ السَّمَاءَ أَن تَقَعَ عَلَى الْأَرْضِ إِلَّا بِإِذْنِهِ ۗ إِنَّ اللَّهَ بِالنَّاسِ لَرَءُوفٌ رَّحِيمٌ[b]

65 Do you not see that God made everything on earth subservient to you? How the ships sail at sea by His command? That He holds up the sky lest it falls on earth—except by His permission? God is Gracious towards the people, Most Merciful.

65
[a] 2:164; 31:20; 45:13
[b] 21:32; 34:9; 35:14; 78:12

٦٦ وَهُوَ الَّذِي أَحْيَاكُمْ ثُمَّ يُمِيتُكُمْ ثُمَّ يُحْيِيكُمْ ۗ إِنَّ الْإِنسَانَ لَكَفُورٌ

66 And it is He who gives you life, then makes you die, then revives you. The human being is unappreciative.

66 2:28; 26:81; 30:40; 45:26

Sūrah 22: Al-Ḥajj — 357

٦٧ لِكُلِّ أُمَّةٍ جَعَلْنَا مَنسَكًا هُمْ نَاسِكُوهُ ۖ فَلَا يُنَازِعُنَّكَ فِي الْأَمْرِ ۚ وَادْعُ إِلَىٰ رَبِّكَ ۖ إِنَّكَ لَعَلَىٰ هُدًى مُّسْتَقِيمٍ

67
16:125; 23:73; 28:87; 42:15, 52

67 For every congregation We have appointed acts of devotion, which they observe. So do not let them dispute with you in this matter. And invite to your Lord; you are upon a straight guidance.

٦٨ وَإِن جَادَلُوكَ فَقُلِ اللَّهُ أَعْلَمُ بِمَا تَعْمَلُونَ

68
26:188; 39:70

68 But if they dispute with you, say, "God is fully aware of what you do."

٦٩ اللَّهُ يَحْكُمُ بَيْنَكُمْ يَوْمَ الْقِيَامَةِ فِيمَا كُنتُمْ فِيهِ تَخْتَلِفُونَ

69
2:113

69 God will judge between you on the Day of Resurrection regarding what you disagree about.

٧٠ أَلَمْ تَعْلَمْ أَنَّ اللَّهَ يَعْلَمُ مَا فِي السَّمَاءِ وَالْأَرْضِ ۗ إِنَّ ذَٰلِكَ فِي كِتَابٍ ۚ إِنَّ ذَٰلِكَ عَلَى اللَّهِ يَسِيرٌ

70 Do you not know that God knows everything in the heavens and the earth? This is in a book. That is easy for God.

٧١ وَيَعْبُدُونَ مِن دُونِ اللَّهِ مَا لَمْ يُنَزِّلْ بِهِ سُلْطَانًا وَمَا لَيْسَ لَهُم بِهِ عِلْمٌ ۗ وَمَا لِلظَّالِمِينَ مِن نَّصِيرٍ

71
7:33; 12:40

71 Yet they worship, besides God, things for which He sent down no warrant, and what they have no knowledge of. There is no savior for the transgressors.

٧٢ وَإِذَا تُتْلَىٰ عَلَيْهِمْ آيَاتُنَا بَيِّنَاتٍ تَعْرِفُ فِي وُجُوهِ الَّذِينَ كَفَرُوا الْمُنكَرَ ۖ يَكَادُونَ يَسْطُونَ بِالَّذِينَ يَتْلُونَ عَلَيْهِمْ آيَاتِنَا ۗ قُلْ أَفَأُنَبِّئُكُم بِشَرٍّ مِّن ذَٰلِكُمُ ۗ النَّارُ وَعَدَهَا اللَّهُ الَّذِينَ كَفَرُوا ۖ وَبِئْسَ الْمَصِيرُ

72 And when Our Clear Verses are recited to them, you will recognize disgust on the faces of those who disbelieve. They nearly assault those who recite to them Our Verses. Say, "Shall I inform you of something worse than that? The Fire! God has promised it to those who disbelieve. And what a wretched outcome!"

٧٣ يَا أَيُّهَا النَّاسُ ضُرِبَ مَثَلٌ فَاسْتَمِعُوا لَهُ ۚ إِنَّ الَّذِينَ تَدْعُونَ مِن دُونِ اللَّهِ لَن يَخْلُقُوا ذُبَابًا وَلَوِ اجْتَمَعُوا لَهُ ۖ وَإِن يَسْلُبْهُمُ الذُّبَابُ شَيْئًا لَّا يَسْتَنقِذُوهُ مِنْهُ ۚ ضَعُفَ الطَّالِبُ وَالْمَطْلُوبُ

73
7:191; 16:17

73 O people! A parable is presented, so listen to it: Those you invoke besides God will never create a fly, even if they banded together for that purpose. And if the fly steals anything from them, they cannot recover it from it. Weak are the pursuer and the pursued.

٧٤ مَا قَدَرُوا اللَّهَ حَقَّ قَدْرِهِ ۗ إِنَّ اللَّهَ لَقَوِيٌّ عَزِيزٌ

74
6:91; 39:67

74 They do not value God as He should be valued. God is Strong and Powerful.

٧٥ اللَّهُ يَصْطَفِي مِنَ الْمَلَائِكَةِ رُسُلًا وَمِنَ النَّاسِ ۚ إِنَّ اللَّهَ سَمِيعٌ بَصِيرٌ

75 God chooses messengers from among the angels, and from among the people. God is Hearing and Seeing.

٧٦ يَعْلَمُ مَا بَيْنَ أَيْدِيهِمْ وَمَا خَلْفَهُمْ ۗ وَإِلَى اللَّهِ تُرْجَعُ الْأُمُورُ

76 He knows what is before them, and what is behind them. To God all matters are referred.

٧٧ يَا أَيُّهَا الَّذِينَ آمَنُوا ارْكَعُوا وَاسْجُدُوا وَاعْبُدُوا رَبَّكُمْ وَافْعَلُوا الْخَيْرَ لَعَلَّكُمْ تُفْلِحُونَ ۩

77 O you who believe! Kneel, and prostrate, and worship your Lord, and do good deeds, so that you may succeed.

٧٨ وَجَاهِدُوا فِي اللَّهِ حَقَّ جِهَادِهِ ۚ هُوَ اجْتَبَاكُمْ وَمَا جَعَلَ عَلَيْكُمْ فِي الدِّينِ مِنْ حَرَجٍ ۚ [a] مِلَّةَ أَبِيكُمْ إِبْرَاهِيمَ ۚ هُوَ سَمَّاكُمُ الْمُسْلِمِينَ مِنْ قَبْلُ وَفِي هَٰذَا لِيَكُونَ الرَّسُولُ شَهِيدًا عَلَيْكُمْ وَتَكُونُوا شُهَدَاءَ عَلَى النَّاسِ ۚ [b] فَأَقِيمُوا الصَّلَاةَ وَآتُوا الزَّكَاةَ وَاعْتَصِمُوا بِاللَّهِ هُوَ مَوْلَاكُمْ ۖ فَنِعْمَ الْمَوْلَىٰ وَنِعْمَ النَّصِيرُ

78
[a] 4:28; 5:6
[b] 2:128, 143; 6:78; 48:8

78 And strive for God, with the striving due to Him. He has chosen you, and has not burdened you in religion—the faith of your father Abraham. It is he who named you Muslims before, and in this. So that the Messenger may be a witness over you, and you may be witnesses over the people. So pray regularly, and give regular charity, and cleave to God. He is your Protector. What an excellent Protector, and what an excellent Helper.

Sūrah 23: Al-Mu'minūn

سُورَةُ ٱلْمُؤْمِنُون (The Believers)

بِسْمِ ٱللَّهِ ٱلرَّحْمَٰنِ ٱلرَّحِيمِ

١ قَدْ أَفْلَحَ الْمُؤْمِنُونَ

1 Successful are the believers.

1
33:47

٢ الَّذِينَ هُمْ فِي صَلَاتِهِمْ خَاشِعُونَ

2 Those who are humble in their prayers.

2
2:45; 33:55

٣ وَالَّذِينَ هُمْ عَنِ اللَّغْوِ مُعْرِضُونَ

3 Those who avoid nonsense.

3
28:55

٤ وَالَّذِينَ هُمْ لِلزَّكَاةِ فَاعِلُونَ

4 Those who work for charity.

4
18:81; 24:21; 87:14; 91:9

٥ وَالَّذِينَ هُمْ لِفُرُوجِهِمْ حَافِظُونَ

5 Those who safeguard their chastity.

5–6
70:29–30

٦ إِلَّا عَلَىٰ أَزْوَاجِهِمْ أَوْ مَا مَلَكَتْ أَيْمَانُهُمْ فَإِنَّهُمْ غَيْرُ مَلُومِينَ

6 Except from their spouses, or their dependents—for they are free from blame.

٧ فَمَنِ ابْتَغَىٰ وَرَاءَ ذَٰلِكَ فَأُولَٰئِكَ هُمُ الْعَادُونَ

7 But whoever seeks anything beyond that—these are the transgressors.

7
70:31

٨ وَالَّذِينَ هُمْ لِأَمَانَاتِهِمْ وَعَهْدِهِمْ رَاعُونَ

8 Those who are faithful to their trusts and pledges.

8
2:282; 4:58; 8:27;
17:34; 70:32

٩ وَالَّذِينَ هُمْ عَلَىٰ صَلَوَاتِهِمْ يُحَافِظُونَ

9 Those who safeguard their prayers.

9
2:238; 6:92; 70:34

١٠ أُولَٰئِكَ هُمُ الْوَارِثُونَ

10 These are the inheritors.

١١ الَّذِينَ يَرِثُونَ الْفِرْدَوْسَ هُمْ فِيهَا خَالِدُونَ

11 Who will inherit Paradise, wherein they will dwell forever.

11
7:43; 19:63

١٢ وَلَقَدْ خَلَقْنَا الْإِنْسَانَ مِنْ سُلَالَةٍ مِنْ طِينٍ

12 We created man from an extract of clay.

12–14
18:37; 22:5; 32:7–9;
40:67; 71:13–14;
75:36–37; 86:5–6

١٣ ثُمَّ جَعَلْنَاهُ نُطْفَةً فِي قَرَارٍ مَكِينٍ

13 Then We made him a seed, in a secure repository.

١٤ ثُمَّ خَلَقْنَا النُّطْفَةَ عَلَقَةً فَخَلَقْنَا الْعَلَقَةَ مُضْغَةً فَخَلَقْنَا الْمُضْغَةَ عِظَامًا فَكَسَوْنَا الْعِظَامَ لَحْمًا ثُمَّ أَنْشَأْنَاهُ خَلْقًا آخَرَ ۚ فَتَبَارَكَ اللَّهُ أَحْسَنُ الْخَالِقِينَ

14 Then We developed the seed into a clot. Then We developed the clot into a lump. Then We developed the lump into bones. Then We clothed the bones with flesh. Then We produced it into another creature. Most Blessed is God, the Best of Creators.

١٥ ثُمَّ إِنَّكُمْ بَعْدَ ذَٰلِكَ لَمَيِّتُونَ

15 Then, after that, you will die.

15–16
2:28; 40:11

١٦ ثُمَّ إِنَّكُمْ يَوْمَ الْقِيَامَةِ تُبْعَثُونَ

16 Then, on the Day of Resurrection, you will be resurrected.

١٧ وَلَقَدْ خَلَقْنَا فَوْقَكُمْ سَبْعَ طَرَائِقَ وَمَا كُنَّا عَنِ الْخَلْقِ غَافِلِينَ

17 We created above you seven pathways, and We are never heedless of the creation.

17
67:3; 71:15

١٨ وَأَنْزَلْنَا مِنَ السَّمَاءِ مَاءً بِقَدَرٍ فَأَسْكَنَّاهُ فِي الْأَرْضِ ۖ وَإِنَّا عَلَىٰ ذَهَابٍ بِهِ لَقَادِرُونَ

18 And We sent down water from the sky in proper quantity, and settled it in the ground, and We are Able to take it away.

18
15:21; 39:21; 43:11

١٩ فَأَنشَأْنَا لَكُم بِهِ جَنَّاتٍ مِّن نَّخِيلٍ وَأَعْنَابٍ لَّكُمْ فِيهَا فَوَاكِهُ كَثِيرَةٌ وَمِنْهَا تَأْكُلُونَ

19 With it We produce for you gardens of palms and vines, yielding abundant fruit for you to eat.

19 16:11; 36:34; 55:11

٢٠ وَشَجَرَةً تَخْرُجُ مِن طُورِ سَيْنَاءَ تَنبُتُ بِالدُّهْنِ وَصِبْغٍ لِّلْآكِلِينَ

20 And a tree springing out of Mount Sinai, producing oil, and seasoning for those who eat.

٢١ وَإِنَّ لَكُمْ فِي الْأَنْعَامِ لَعِبْرَةً نُّسْقِيكُم مِّمَّا فِي بُطُونِهَا وَلَكُمْ فِيهَا مَنَافِعُ كَثِيرَةٌ وَمِنْهَا تَأْكُلُونَ

21 And there is a lesson for you in livestock: We give you to drink from what is in their bellies, and you have many benefits in them, and from them you eat.

21 16:66

٢٢ وَعَلَيْهَا وَعَلَى الْفُلْكِ تُحْمَلُونَ

22 And on them, and on the ships, you are transported.

22 16:7; 36:71–72; 40:80; 43:12

٢٣ وَلَقَدْ أَرْسَلْنَا نُوحًا إِلَىٰ قَوْمِهِ فَقَالَ يَا قَوْمِ اعْبُدُوا اللَّهَ مَا لَكُم مِّنْ إِلَٰهٍ غَيْرُهُ أَفَلَا تَتَّقُونَ

23 We sent Noah to his people. He said, "O my people, worship God, you have no deity other than Him. Will you not take heed?"

23 7:59; 23:32

٢٤ فَقَالَ الْمَلَأُ الَّذِينَ كَفَرُوا مِن قَوْمِهِ مَا هَٰذَا إِلَّا بَشَرٌ مِّثْلُكُمْ يُرِيدُ أَن يَتَفَضَّلَ عَلَيْكُمْ وَلَوْ شَاءَ اللَّهُ لَأَنزَلَ مَلَائِكَةً مَّا سَمِعْنَا بِهَٰذَا فِي آبَائِنَا الْأَوَّلِينَ

24 But the notables of his people, who disbelieved, said, "This is nothing but a human like you, who wants to gain superiority over you. Had God willed, He would have sent down angels. We never heard of this from our forefathers of old.

24 11:27

٢٥ إِنْ هُوَ إِلَّا رَجُلٌ بِهِ جِنَّةٌ فَتَرَبَّصُوا بِهِ حَتَّىٰ حِينٍ

25 He is nothing but a man possessed. Just ignore him for a while."

٢٦ قَالَ رَبِّ انصُرْنِي بِمَا كَذَّبُونِ

26 He said, "My Lord, help me, for they have rejected me."

٢٧ فَأَوْحَيْنَا إِلَيْهِ أَنِ اصْنَعِ الْفُلْكَ بِأَعْيُنِنَا وَوَحْيِنَا فَإِذَا جَاءَ أَمْرُنَا وَفَارَ التَّنُّورُ فَاسْلُكْ فِيهَا مِن كُلٍّ زَوْجَيْنِ اثْنَيْنِ وَأَهْلَكَ إِلَّا مَن سَبَقَ عَلَيْهِ الْقَوْلُ مِنْهُمْ وَلَا تُخَاطِبْنِي فِي الَّذِينَ ظَلَمُوا إِنَّهُم مُّغْرَقُونَ

27 So We inspired him: "Build the Ark under Our observation and by Our inspiration. And when Our decree comes to pass, and the oven boils over, load into it two pairs of every kind, together with your family, except those of them against whom the word has already been pronounced. And do not speak to me concerning those who did wrong; for they are to be drowned."

27 11:37, 40

٢٨ فَإِذَا اسْتَوَيْتَ أَنتَ وَمَن مَّعَكَ عَلَى الْفُلْكِ فَقُلِ الْحَمْدُ لِلَّهِ الَّذِي نَجَّانَا مِنَ الْقَوْمِ الظَّالِمِينَ

28 Then, when you and those with you are settled in the Ark, say, "Praise be to God, who has saved us from the wrongdoing people."

28 11:44

٢٩ وَقُل رَّبِّ أَنزِلْنِي مُنزَلًا مُّبَارَكًا وَأَنتَ خَيْرُ الْمُنزِلِينَ	**29** 11:48

29 And say, "My Lord, land me with a blessed landing, as you are the best of transporters."

٣٠ إِنَّ فِي ذَٰلِكَ لَآيَاتٍ وَإِن كُنَّا لَمُبْتَلِينَ	**30**

30 Surely in that are signs. We are always testing.

٣١ ثُمَّ أَنشَأْنَا مِن بَعْدِهِمْ قَرْنًا آخَرِينَ	**31** 6:6; 21:11; 23:42; 28:45

31 Then, after them, We established another generation.

٣٢ فَأَرْسَلْنَا فِيهِمْ رَسُولًا مِّنْهُمْ أَنِ اعْبُدُوا اللَّهَ مَا لَكُم مِّنْ إِلَٰهٍ غَيْرُهُ ۖ أَفَلَا تَتَّقُونَ	**32** 7:65; 23:23

32 And We sent among them a messenger from themselves: "Serve God. You have no god other than Him. Will you not be cautious?"

٣٣ وَقَالَ الْمَلَأُ مِن قَوْمِهِ الَّذِينَ كَفَرُوا وَكَذَّبُوا بِلِقَاءِ الْآخِرَةِ وَأَتْرَفْنَاهُمْ فِي الْحَيَاةِ الدُّنْيَا مَا هَٰذَا إِلَّا بَشَرٌ مِّثْلُكُمْ يَأْكُلُ مِمَّا تَأْكُلُونَ مِنْهُ وَيَشْرَبُ مِمَّا تَشْرَبُونَ	**33–34** 11:27

33 But the dignitaries of his people, those who disbelieved and denied the meeting of the Hereafter, and We had indulged them in the present life, said, "This is nothing but a human like you; he eats what you eat, and he drinks what you drink.

٣٤ وَلَئِنْ أَطَعْتُم بَشَرًا مِّثْلَكُمْ إِنَّكُمْ إِذًا لَّخَاسِرُونَ	

34 If you obey a human being like yourselves, then you will be losers.

٣٥ أَيَعِدُكُمْ أَنَّكُمْ إِذَا مِتُّمْ وَكُنتُمْ تُرَابًا وَعِظَامًا أَنَّكُم مُّخْرَجُونَ	**35** 13:5; 23:82

35 Does he promise you that when you have died and become dust and bones, you will be brought out?

٣٦ هَيْهَاتَ هَيْهَاتَ لِمَا تُوعَدُونَ	**36**

36 Farfetched, farfetched is what you are promised.

٣٧ إِنْ هِيَ إِلَّا حَيَاتُنَا الدُّنْيَا نَمُوتُ وَنَحْيَا وَمَا نَحْنُ بِمَبْعُوثِينَ	**37** 6:29; 16:38; 45:24

37 There is nothing but our life in this world. We die, and we live, and we are not resurrected.

٣٨ إِنْ هُوَ إِلَّا رَجُلٌ افْتَرَىٰ عَلَى اللَّهِ كَذِبًا وَمَا نَحْنُ لَهُ بِمُؤْمِنِينَ	**38** 42:24

38 He is nothing but a man, making up lies about God. We have no faith in him."

٣٩ قَالَ رَبِّ انصُرْنِي بِمَا كَذَّبُونِ	**39** 23:26

39 He said, "My Lord, help me, for they have rejected me."

٤٠ قَالَ عَمَّا قَلِيلٍ لَّيُصْبِحُنَّ نَادِمِينَ	**40**

40 He said, "Soon they will be filled with regret."

٤١ فَأَخَذَتْهُمُ الصَّيْحَةُ بِالْحَقِّ فَجَعَلْنَاهُمْ غُثَاءً ۚ فَبُعْدًا لِلْقَوْمِ الظَّالِمِينَ

41 Then the Blast struck them, justifiably, and We turned them into scum. So away with the wicked people.

41
11:44

٤٢ ثُمَّ أَنشَأْنَا مِن بَعْدِهِمْ قُرُونًا آخَرِينَ

42 Then, after them, We raised other generations.

42
6:6; 21:11; 23:31; 28:45

٤٣ مَا تَسْبِقُ مِنْ أُمَّةٍ أَجَلَهَا وَمَا يَسْتَأْخِرُونَ

43 No nation can advance its time, nor can they postpone it.

٤٤ ثُمَّ أَرْسَلْنَا رُسُلَنَا تَتْرَىٰ ۖ كُلَّ مَا جَاءَ أُمَّةً رَسُولُهَا كَذَّبُوهُ ۚ فَأَتْبَعْنَا بَعْضَهُم بَعْضًا وَجَعَلْنَاهُمْ أَحَادِيثَ ۚ فَبُعْدًا لِقَوْمٍ لَا يُؤْمِنُونَ

44 Then We sent Our messengers in succession. Every time a messenger came to his community, they called him a liar. So We made them follow one another, and made them history. So away with a people who do not believe.

44
34:34; 43:23

٤٥ ثُمَّ أَرْسَلْنَا مُوسَىٰ وَأَخَاهُ هَارُونَ بِآيَاتِنَا وَسُلْطَانٍ مُبِينٍ

45 Then We sent Moses and his brother Aaron, with Our signs and a clear authority.

45
7:103; 10:75; 11:96

٤٦ إِلَىٰ فِرْعَوْنَ وَمَلَئِهِ فَاسْتَكْبَرُوا وَكَانُوا قَوْمًا عَالِينَ

46 To Pharaoh and his nobles, but they turned arrogant. They were oppressive people.

46
7:103; 10:75; 11:97; 40:24

٤٧ فَقَالُوا أَنُؤْمِنُ لِبَشَرَيْنِ مِثْلِنَا وَقَوْمُهُمَا لَنَا عَابِدُونَ

47 They said, "Are we to believe in two mortals like us, and their people are our slaves?"

٤٨ فَكَذَّبُوهُمَا فَكَانُوا مِنَ الْمُهْلَكِينَ

48 So they called them liars, and thus were among those destroyed.

٤٩ وَلَقَدْ آتَيْنَا مُوسَى الْكِتَابَ لَعَلَّهُمْ يَهْتَدُونَ

49 And We gave Moses the Scripture, that they may be guided.

49
2:53

٥٠ وَجَعَلْنَا ابْنَ مَرْيَمَ وَأُمَّهُ آيَةً وَآوَيْنَاهُمَا إِلَىٰ رَبْوَةٍ ذَاتِ قَرَارٍ وَمَعِينٍ

50 And We made Mary's son and his mother a sign, and We sheltered them on high ground with security and flowing springs.

50
19:21; 21:91

٥١ يَا أَيُّهَا الرُّسُلُ كُلُوا مِنَ الطَّيِّبَاتِ وَاعْمَلُوا صَالِحًا ۖ إِنِّي بِمَا تَعْمَلُونَ عَلِيمٌ

51 O messengers, eat of the good things, and act with integrity. I am aware of what you do.

51
2:172; 21:92

٥٢ وَإِنَّ هَٰذِهِ أُمَّتُكُمْ أُمَّةً وَاحِدَةً وَأَنَا رَبُّكُمْ فَاتَّقُونِ

52 This nation of yours is one nation, and I am your Lord, so fear Me.

52
21:91–92

٥٣ فَتَقَطَّعُوا أَمْرَهُم بَيْنَهُمْ زُبُرًا ۖ كُلُّ حِزْبٍ بِمَا لَدَيْهِمْ فَرِحُونَ	53	2:213; 10:19; 21:93

53 But they tore themselves into sects; each party happy with what they have.

٥٤ فَذَرْهُمْ فِي غَمْرَتِهِمْ حَتَّىٰ حِينٍ	54	5:11; 15:3; 23:63

54 So leave them in their bewilderment until a time.

٥٥ أَيَحْسَبُونَ أَنَّمَا نُمِدُّهُم بِهِ مِن مَّالٍ وَبَنِينَ	55	18:36

55 Do they assume that, in furnishing them with wealth and children.

٥٦ نُسَارِعُ لَهُمْ فِي الْخَيْرَاتِ ۚ بَل لَّا يَشْعُرُونَ	56	19:77

56 We race to give them the good things? In fact, they have no idea.

٥٧ إِنَّ الَّذِينَ هُم مِّنْ خَشْيَةِ رَبِّهِم مُّشْفِقُونَ	57	21:28

57 Those who, from awe of their Lord, are fearful.

٥٨ وَالَّذِينَ هُم بِآيَاتِ رَبِّهِمْ يُؤْمِنُونَ	58

58 And those who believe in their Lord's Verses.

٥٩ وَالَّذِينَ هُم بِرَبِّهِمْ لَا يُشْرِكُونَ	59

59 And those who associate no partners with their Lord.

٦٠ وَالَّذِينَ يُؤْتُونَ مَا آتَوا وَّقُلُوبُهُمْ وَجِلَةٌ أَنَّهُمْ إِلَىٰ رَبِّهِمْ رَاجِعُونَ	60

60 And those who give what they give, while their hearts quake, knowing that to their Lord they will return.

٦١ أُولَٰئِكَ يُسَارِعُونَ فِي الْخَيْرَاتِ وَهُمْ لَهَا سَابِقُونَ	61

61 It is they who race towards goodness. It is they who will reach it first.

٦٢ وَلَا نُكَلِّفُ نَفْسًا إِلَّا وُسْعَهَا ۖ وَلَدَيْنَا كِتَابٌ يَنطِقُ بِالْحَقِّ ۚ وَهُمْ لَا يُظْلَمُونَ	62	17:13; 18:49; 45:29

62 We never burden any soul beyond its capacity. And with Us is a record that tells the truth, and they will not be wronged.

٦٣ بَلْ قُلُوبُهُمْ فِي غَمْرَةٍ مِّنْ هَٰذَا وَلَهُمْ أَعْمَالٌ مِّن دُونِ ذَٰلِكَ هُمْ لَهَا عَامِلُونَ	63	51:11

63 But their hearts are puzzled because of this; and they have deeds that do not conform to this, which they continue to perpetrate.

٦٤ حَتَّىٰ إِذَا أَخَذْنَا مُتْرَفِيهِم بِالْعَذَابِ إِذَا هُمْ يَجْأَرُونَ	64–65	18:29; 35:36

64 Until, when We seize the decadent among them with torment, they begin to groan.

٦٥ لَا تَجْأَرُوا الْيَوْمَ ۖ إِنَّكُم مِّنَّا لَا تُنصَرُونَ	

65 Do not groan today. You will receive no help from Us.

٦٦ قَدْ كَانَتْ آيَاتِي تُتْلَىٰ عَلَيْكُمْ فَكُنتُمْ عَلَىٰ أَعْقَابِكُمْ تَنكِصُونَ	66	31:7; 45:8

66 My Verses were recited to you, but you turned back on your heels.

٦٧ مُسْتَكْبِرِينَ بِهِ سَامِرًا تَهْجُرُونَ

67 Arrogant towards it—talked nonsense about it—disregarded it.

٦٨ أَفَلَمْ يَدَّبَّرُوا الْقَوْلَ أَمْ جَاءَهُم مَّا لَمْ يَأْتِ آبَاءَهُمُ الْأَوَّلِينَ

68 Have they not pondered the Word? Or has there come to them what came not to their forefathers of old?

٦٩ أَمْ لَمْ يَعْرِفُوا رَسُولَهُمْ فَهُمْ لَهُ مُنكِرُونَ

69 Or is it that they did not recognize their messenger, so they are denying him?

69
10:16

٧٠ أَمْ يَقُولُونَ بِهِ جِنَّةٌ ۚ بَلْ جَاءَهُم بِالْحَقِّ وَأَكْثَرُهُمْ لِلْحَقِّ كَارِهُونَ

70 Or do they say, "He is possessed?" In fact, he brought them the truth, but most of them hate the truth.

70
7:184; 23:25; 34:8; 51:52; 52:29; 81:22

٧١ وَلَوِ اتَّبَعَ الْحَقُّ أَهْوَاءَهُمْ لَفَسَدَتِ السَّمَاوَاتُ وَالْأَرْضُ وَمَن فِيهِنَّ ۚ بَلْ أَتَيْنَاهُم بِذِكْرِهِمْ فَهُمْ عَن ذِكْرِهِم مُّعْرِضُونَ

71 If the truth conformed to their desires, the heavens, the earth, and everyone in them would have gone to ruin. In fact, We have given them their message, but they keep avoiding their message.

71
21:22

٧٢ أَمْ تَسْأَلُهُمْ خَرْجًا فَخَرَاجُ رَبِّكَ خَيْرٌ ۖ وَهُوَ خَيْرُ الرَّازِقِينَ

72 Or are you asking them for a payment? The revenue from your Lord is better, and He is the Best of providers.

72
10:72; 11:29; 42:23

٧٣ وَإِنَّكَ لَتَدْعُوهُمْ إِلَىٰ صِرَاطٍ مُّسْتَقِيمٍ

73 You are inviting them to a straight path.

73
22:67

٧٤ وَإِنَّ الَّذِينَ لَا يُؤْمِنُونَ بِالْآخِرَةِ عَنِ الصِّرَاطِ لَنَاكِبُونَ

74 But those who do not believe in the Hereafter are swerving from the path.

74
30:16

٧٥ وَلَوْ رَحِمْنَاهُمْ وَكَشَفْنَا مَا بِهِم مِّن ضُرٍّ لَّلَجُّوا فِي طُغْيَانِهِمْ يَعْمَهُونَ

75 Even if We had mercy on them, and relieved their problems, they would still blindly persist in their defiance.

75
10:12

٧٦ وَلَقَدْ أَخَذْنَاهُم بِالْعَذَابِ فَمَا اسْتَكَانُوا لِرَبِّهِمْ وَمَا يَتَضَرَّعُونَ

76 We have already gripped them with suffering, but they did not surrender to their Lord, nor did they humble themselves.

76
6:42

٧٧ حَتَّىٰ إِذَا فَتَحْنَا عَلَيْهِم بَابًا ذَا عَذَابٍ شَدِيدٍ إِذَا هُمْ فِيهِ مُبْلِسُونَ

77 Until, when We have opened before them a gate of intense agony, at once they will despair.

٧٨ وَهُوَ الَّذِي أَنشَأَ لَكُمُ السَّمْعَ وَالْأَبْصَارَ وَالْأَفْئِدَةَ ۚ قَلِيلًا مَّا تَشْكُرُونَ

78 It is He who produced for you the hearing, and the eyesight, and the feelings. But little gratitude you show.

78
10:31; 16:78; 32:9; 67:23

٧٩ وَهُوَ الَّذِي ذَرَأَكُمْ فِي الْأَرْضِ وَإِلَيْهِ تُحْشَرُونَ

79 And it is He who multiplied you on earth, and to Him you will be gathered.

79
30:20; 42:11; 67:24

٨٠ وَهُوَ الَّذِي يُحْيِي وَيُمِيتُ[a] وَلَهُ اخْتِلَافُ اللَّيْلِ وَالنَّهَارِ ۚ أَفَلَا تَعْقِلُونَ[b]

80 And it is He who gives life and brings death, and to Him is the alternation of night and day. Do you not understand?

80
[a] 2:28; 22:26
[b] 10:6; 28:71–73; 36:37; 41:37

٨١ بَلْ قَالُوا مِثْلَ مَا قَالَ الْأَوَّلُونَ

81 But they say the like of what the ancients said.

٨٢ قَالُوا أَإِذَا مِتْنَا وَكُنَّا تُرَابًا وَعِظَامًا أَإِنَّا لَمَبْعُوثُونَ

82 They say, "After we have died, and become dust and bones, will we be resurrected?

82
13:5; 23:35

٨٣ لَقَدْ وُعِدْنَا نَحْنُ وَآبَاؤُنَا هَٰذَا مِنْ قَبْلُ إِنْ هَٰذَا إِلَّا أَسَاطِيرُ الْأَوَّلِينَ

83 We were promised this before—we and our ancestors—these are nothing but legends of the ancients."

83
pp 27:68

٨٤ قُلْ لِمَنِ الْأَرْضُ وَمَنْ فِيهَا إِنْ كُنْتُمْ تَعْلَمُونَ

84 Say, "To whom does the earth belong, and everyone in it, if you happen to know?"

84–89
10:31; 36:83

٨٥ سَيَقُولُونَ لِلَّهِ ۚ قُلْ أَفَلَا تَذَكَّرُونَ

85 They will say, "To God." Say, "Will you not reflect?"

٨٦ قُلْ مَنْ رَبُّ السَّمَاوَاتِ السَّبْعِ وَرَبُّ الْعَرْشِ الْعَظِيمِ

86 Say, "Who is the Lord of the seven heavens, and Lord of the Splendid Throne?"

٨٧ سَيَقُولُونَ لِلَّهِ ۚ قُلْ أَفَلَا تَتَّقُونَ

87 They will say, "To God." Say, "Will you not become righteous?"

٨٨ قُلْ مَنْ بِيَدِهِ مَلَكُوتُ كُلِّ شَيْءٍ وَهُوَ يُجِيرُ وَلَا يُجَارُ عَلَيْهِ إِنْ كُنْتُمْ تَعْلَمُونَ

88 Say, "In whose hand is the dominion of all things, and He protects and cannot be protected from, if you happen to know?"

٨٩ سَيَقُولُونَ لِلَّهِ ۚ قُلْ فَأَنَّىٰ تُسْحَرُونَ

89 They will say, "To God." Say, "Then are you bewitched?"

٩٠ بَلْ أَتَيْنَاهُمْ بِالْحَقِّ وَإِنَّهُمْ لَكَاذِبُونَ

90 In fact, We have given them the truth, and they are liars.

٩١ مَا اتَّخَذَ اللَّهُ مِن وَلَدٍ وَمَا كَانَ مَعَهُ مِنْ إِلَٰهٍ ۚ إِذًا لَّذَهَبَ كُلُّ إِلَٰهٍ بِمَا خَلَقَ وَلَعَلَا بَعْضُهُمْ عَلَىٰ بَعْضٍ ۚ سُبْحَانَ اللَّهِ عَمَّا يَصِفُونَ

91   2:116; 17:42; 21:22

91 God has never begotten a son, nor is there any god besides Him. Otherwise, each god would have taken away what it has created, and some of them would have gained supremacy over others. Glory be to God, far beyond what they describe.

٩٢ عَالِمِ الْغَيْبِ وَالشَّهَادَةِ فَتَعَالَىٰ عَمَّا يُشْرِكُونَ

92 The Knower of the hidden and the manifest. He is exalted, far above what they associate.

٩٣ قُل رَّبِّ إِمَّا تُرِيَنِّي مَا يُوعَدُونَ

93   10:46; 13:40; 40:77; 43:41

93 Say, "My Lord, if You would show me what they are promised.

٩٤ رَبِّ فَلَا تَجْعَلْنِي فِي الْقَوْمِ الظَّالِمِينَ

94 My Lord, do not place me among the wicked people."

٩٥ وَإِنَّا عَلَىٰ أَن نُّرِيَكَ مَا نَعِدُهُمْ لَقَادِرُونَ

95 We are surely Able to show you what We promise them.

٩٦ ادْفَعْ بِالَّتِي هِيَ أَحْسَنُ السَّيِّئَةَ ۚ نَحْنُ أَعْلَمُ بِمَا يَصِفُونَ

96   16:125

96 Repel evil by what is better. We are aware of what they describe.

٩٧ وَقُل رَّبِّ أَعُوذُ بِكَ مِنْ هَمَزَاتِ الشَّيَاطِينِ

97 And say, "My Lord, I seek refuge with You from the urgings of the devils.

٩٨ وَأَعُوذُ بِكَ رَبِّ أَن يَحْضُرُونِ

98 And I seek refuge with You, my Lord, lest they become present."

٩٩ حَتَّىٰ إِذَا جَاءَ أَحَدَهُمُ الْمَوْتُ قَالَ رَبِّ ارْجِعُونِ

99   63:10–11

99 Until, when death comes to one of them, he says, "My Lord, send me back.

١٠٠ لَعَلِّي أَعْمَلُ صَالِحًا فِيمَا تَرَكْتُ ۚ كَلَّا ۚ إِنَّهَا كَلِمَةٌ هُوَ قَائِلُهَا ۖ وَمِن وَرَائِهِم بَرْزَخٌ إِلَىٰ يَوْمِ يُبْعَثُونَ

100 That I may do right in what I have neglected." By no means! It is just a word that he utters. And behind them is a barrier, until the Day they are resurrected.

١٠١ فَإِذَا نُفِخَ فِي الصُّورِ فَلَا أَنسَابَ بَيْنَهُمْ يَوْمَئِذٍ وَلَا يَتَسَاءَلُونَ

101   37:27; 52:25; 80:33–36

101 When the Horn is blown, no relations between them will exist on that Day, and they will not ask after one another.

Sūrah 23: Al-Muʾminūn

١٠٢ فَمَن ثَقُلَتْ مَوَازِينُهُ فَأُولَٰئِكَ هُمُ الْمُفْلِحُونَ

102 Those whose scales are heavy—those are the successful.

102–103
7:8–9

١٠٣ وَمَنْ خَفَّتْ مَوَازِينُهُ فَأُولَٰئِكَ الَّذِينَ خَسِرُوا أَنفُسَهُمْ فِي جَهَنَّمَ خَالِدُونَ

103 But those whose scales are light—those are they who have lost their souls; in Hell they will dwell forever.

١٠٤ تَلْفَحُ وُجُوهَهُمُ النَّارُ وَهُمْ فِيهَا كَالِحُونَ

104 The Fire lashes their faces, and therein they grimace.

104
14:50; 21:39; 27:90;
33:66; 39:24

١٠٥ أَلَمْ تَكُنْ آيَاتِي تُتْلَىٰ عَلَيْكُمْ فَكُنتُم بِهَا تُكَذِّبُونَ

105 "Were not My revelations recited to you, and you kept on rejecting them?"

١٠٦ قَالُوا رَبَّنَا غَلَبَتْ عَلَيْنَا شِقْوَتُنَا وَكُنَّا قَوْمًا ضَالِّينَ

106 They will say, "Our Lord, our wretchedness prevailed over us, and we were a people astray.

106
67:11

١٠٧ رَبَّنَا أَخْرِجْنَا مِنْهَا فَإِنْ عُدْنَا فَإِنَّا ظَالِمُونَ

107 Our Lord! Bring us out of this. If we ever returned, we would truly be evil."

107
2:167; 5:37; 22:22;
32:20

١٠٨ قَالَ اخْسَئُوا فِيهَا وَلَا تُكَلِّمُونِ

108 He will say, "Be despised therein, and do not speak to Me.

١٠٩ إِنَّهُ كَانَ فَرِيقٌ مِّنْ عِبَادِي يَقُولُونَ رَبَّنَا آمَنَّا فَاغْفِرْ لَنَا وَارْحَمْنَا وَأَنتَ خَيْرُ الرَّاحِمِينَ

109 There was a group of My servants who would say, 'Our Lord, we have believed, so forgive us, and have mercy on us; You are the Best of the merciful.'

١١٠ فَاتَّخَذْتُمُوهُمْ سِخْرِيًّا حَتَّىٰ أَنسَوْكُمْ ذِكْرِي وَكُنتُم مِّنْهُمْ تَضْحَكُونَ

110 But you made them a target of ridicule, until they made you forget My remembrance; and you used to laugh at them.

110
83:29–30

١١١ إِنِّي جَزَيْتُهُمُ الْيَوْمَ بِمَا صَبَرُوا أَنَّهُمْ هُمُ الْفَائِزُونَ

111 Today, I have rewarded them for their endurance. They are the ones who are the triumphant."

١١٢ قَالَ كَمْ لَبِثْتُمْ فِي الْأَرْضِ عَدَدَ سِنِينَ

112 He will say, "How many years did you remain on earth?"

112–114
10:45; 20:102–104;
30:55

١١٣ قَالُوا لَبِثْنَا يَوْمًا أَوْ بَعْضَ يَوْمٍ فَاسْأَلِ الْعَادِّينَ

113 They will say, "We remained a day, or part of a day; but ask those who keep count."

١١٤ قَالَ إِن لَّبِثْتُمْ إِلَّا قَلِيلًا ۖ لَّوْ أَنَّكُمْ كُنتُمْ تَعْلَمُونَ

114 He will say, "You remained only for a little while, if you only knew.

١١٥ أَفَحَسِبْتُمْ أَنَّمَا خَلَقْنَاكُمْ عَبَثًا وَأَنَّكُمْ إِلَيْنَا لَا تُرْجَعُونَ

115 Did you think that We created you in vain, and that to Us you will not be returned?"

115
21:16; 75:36

١١٦ فَتَعَالَى اللَّهُ الْمَلِكُ الْحَقُّ ۖ لَا إِلَٰهَ إِلَّا هُوَ رَبُّ الْعَرْشِ الْكَرِيمِ

116 So Exalted is God, the Ruler, the Real. There is no god except He, the Lord of the Noble Throne.

١١٧ وَمَن يَدْعُ مَعَ اللَّهِ إِلَٰهًا آخَرَ لَا بُرْهَانَ لَهُ بِهِ فَإِنَّمَا حِسَابُهُ عِندَ رَبِّهِ ۚ إِنَّهُ لَا يُفْلِحُ الْكَافِرُونَ

117 Whoever invokes another god besides God—he has no proof thereof—his reckoning rests with his Lord. The disbelievers will not succeed.

117
22:71

١١٨ وَقُل رَّبِّ اغْفِرْ وَارْحَمْ وَأَنتَ خَيْرُ الرَّاحِمِينَ

118 And say, "My Lord, forgive and have mercy, for You are the Best of the merciful."

Sūrah 24: Al-Nūr

سُورَةُ ٱلنُّور (The Light)

بِسْمِ ٱللَّهِ ٱلرَّحْمَـٰنِ ٱلرَّحِيمِ

١ سُورَةٌ أَنزَلْنَاهَا وَفَرَضْنَاهَا وَأَنزَلْنَا فِيهَا آيَاتٍ بَيِّنَاتٍ لَّعَلَّكُمْ تَذَكَّرُونَ

1 A chapter that We have revealed, and made obligatory, and revealed in it clear Verses, that you may take heed.

٢ الزَّانِيَةُ وَالزَّانِي فَاجْلِدُوا كُلَّ وَاحِدٍ مِّنْهُمَا مِائَةَ جَلْدَةٍ ۖ وَلَا تَأْخُذْكُم بِهِمَا رَأْفَةٌ فِي دِينِ اللَّهِ إِن كُنتُمْ تُؤْمِنُونَ بِاللَّهِ وَالْيَوْمِ الْآخِرِ ۖ وَلْيَشْهَدْ عَذَابَهُمَا طَائِفَةٌ مِّنَ الْمُؤْمِنِينَ

2
4:16

2 The adulteress and the adulterer—whip each one of them a hundred lashes, and let no pity towards them overcome you regarding God's Law, if you believe in God and the Last Day. And let a group of believers witness their punishment.

٣ الزَّانِي لَا يَنكِحُ إِلَّا زَانِيَةً أَوْ مُشْرِكَةً وَالزَّانِيَةُ لَا يَنكِحُهَا إِلَّا زَانٍ أَوْ مُشْرِكٌ ۚ وَحُرِّمَ ذَٰلِكَ عَلَى الْمُؤْمِنِينَ

3
24:26

3 The adulterer shall marry none but an adulteress or an idolatress; and the adulteress shall marry none but an adulterer or an idolater. That has been prohibited for the believers.

٤ وَالَّذِينَ يَرْمُونَ الْمُحْصَنَاتِ ثُمَّ لَمْ يَأْتُوا بِأَرْبَعَةِ شُهَدَاءَ فَاجْلِدُوهُمْ ثَمَانِينَ جَلْدَةً وَلَا تَقْبَلُوا لَهُمْ شَهَادَةً أَبَدًا ۚ وَأُولَٰئِكَ هُمُ الْفَاسِقُونَ

4 24:6, 13, 23

4 Those who accuse chaste women, then cannot bring four witnesses, whip them eighty lashes, and do not ever accept their testimony. For these are the immoral.

٥ إِلَّا الَّذِينَ تَابُوا مِنْ بَعْدِ ذَٰلِكَ وَأَصْلَحُوا فَإِنَّ اللَّهَ غَفُورٌ رَحِيمٌ

5 2:160; 3:89

5 Except for those who repent afterwards, and reform; for God is Forgiving and Merciful.

٦ وَالَّذِينَ يَرْمُونَ أَزْوَاجَهُمْ وَلَمْ يَكُنْ لَهُمْ شُهَدَاءُ إِلَّا أَنْفُسُهُمْ فَشَهَادَةُ أَحَدِهِمْ أَرْبَعُ شَهَادَاتٍ بِاللَّهِ ۙ إِنَّهُ لَمِنَ الصَّادِقِينَ

6 24:4, 13, 23

6 As for those who accuse their own spouses, but have no witnesses except themselves, the testimony of one of them is equivalent to four testimonies, if he swears by God that he is truthful.

٧ وَالْخَامِسَةُ أَنَّ لَعْنَتَ اللَّهِ عَلَيْهِ إِنْ كَانَ مِنَ الْكَاذِبِينَ

7 And the fifth time, that God's curse be upon him, if he is a liar.

٨ وَيَدْرَأُ عَنْهَا الْعَذَابَ أَنْ تَشْهَدَ أَرْبَعَ شَهَادَاتٍ بِاللَّهِ ۙ إِنَّهُ لَمِنَ الْكَاذِبِينَ

8 But punishment shall be averted from her, if she swears four times by God, that he is a liar.

٩ وَالْخَامِسَةَ أَنَّ غَضَبَ اللَّهِ عَلَيْهَا إِنْ كَانَ مِنَ الصَّادِقِينَ

9 And the fifth time, that God's wrath be upon her, if he is truthful.

١٠ وَلَوْلَا فَضْلُ اللَّهِ عَلَيْكُمْ وَرَحْمَتُهُ وَأَنَّ اللَّهَ تَوَّابٌ حَكِيمٌ

10 24:20

10 Were it not for God's grace upon you, and His mercy, and that God is Conciliatory and Wise.

١١ إِنَّ الَّذِينَ جَاءُوا بِالْإِفْكِ عُصْبَةٌ مِنْكُمْ ۚ لَا تَحْسَبُوهُ شَرًّا لَكُمْ ۖ بَلْ هُوَ خَيْرٌ لَكُمْ ۚ لِكُلِّ امْرِئٍ مِنْهُمْ مَا اكْتَسَبَ مِنَ الْإِثْمِ ۚ وَالَّذِي تَوَلَّىٰ كِبْرَهُ مِنْهُمْ لَهُ عَذَابٌ عَظِيمٌ

11 Those who perpetrated the slander are a band of you. Do not consider it bad for you, but it is good for you. Each person among them bears his share in the sin. As for him who played the major role—for him is a terrible punishment.

١٢ لَوْلَا إِذْ سَمِعْتُمُوهُ ظَنَّ الْمُؤْمِنُونَ وَالْمُؤْمِنَاتُ بِأَنْفُسِهِمْ خَيْرًا وَقَالُوا هَٰذَا إِفْكٌ مُبِينٌ

12 24:16

12 Why, when you heard about it, the believing men and women did not think well of one another, and say, "This is an obvious lie"?

١٣ لَوْلَا جَاءُوا عَلَيْهِ بِأَرْبَعَةِ شُهَدَاءَ ۚ فَإِذْ لَمْ يَأْتُوا بِالشُّهَدَاءِ فَأُولَٰئِكَ عِنْدَ اللَّهِ هُمُ الْكَاذِبُونَ

13 24:4, 6, 23

13 Why did they not bring four witnesses to testify to it? If they fail to bring the witnesses, then in God's sight, they are liars.

١٤ وَلَوْلَا فَضْلُ اللَّهِ عَلَيْكُمْ وَرَحْمَتُهُ فِي الدُّنْيَا وَالْآخِرَةِ لَمَسَّكُمْ فِي مَا أَفَضْتُمْ فِيهِ عَذَابٌ عَظِيمٌ

14 Were it not for God's favor upon you, and His mercy, in this world and the Hereafter, you would have suffered a great punishment for what you have ventured into.

١٥ إِذْ تَلَقَّوْنَهُ بِأَلْسِنَتِكُمْ وَتَقُولُونَ بِأَفْوَاهِكُمْ مَا لَيْسَ لَكُمْ بِهِ عِلْمٌ وَتَحْسَبُونَهُ هَيِّنًا وَهُوَ عِنْدَ اللَّهِ عَظِيمٌ

15 When you rumored it with your tongues, and spoke with your mouths what you had no knowledge of, and you considered it trivial; but according to God, it is serious.

١٦ وَلَوْلَا إِذْ سَمِعْتُمُوهُ قُلْتُمْ مَا يَكُونُ لَنَا أَنْ نَتَكَلَّمَ بِهَذَا سُبْحَانَكَ هَذَا بُهْتَانٌ عَظِيمٌ

16 When you heard it, you should have said, "It is not for us to repeat this. By Your glory, this is a serious slander."

16
24:12

١٧ يَعِظُكُمُ اللَّهُ أَنْ تَعُودُوا لِمِثْلِهِ أَبَدًا إِنْ كُنْتُمْ مُؤْمِنِينَ

17 God cautions you never to return to the like of it, if you are believers.

١٨ وَيُبَيِّنُ اللَّهُ لَكُمُ الْآيَاتِ ۚ وَاللَّهُ عَلِيمٌ حَكِيمٌ

18 God explains the Verses to you. God is Knowing and Wise.

١٩ إِنَّ الَّذِينَ يُحِبُّونَ أَنْ تَشِيعَ الْفَاحِشَةُ فِي الَّذِينَ آمَنُوا لَهُمْ عَذَابٌ أَلِيمٌ فِي الدُّنْيَا وَالْآخِرَةِ ۚ وَاللَّهُ يَعْلَمُ وَأَنْتُمْ لَا تَعْلَمُونَ

19 Those who love to see immorality spread among the believers—for them is a painful punishment, in this life and in the Hereafter. God knows, and you do not know.

٢٠ وَلَوْلَا فَضْلُ اللَّهِ عَلَيْكُمْ وَرَحْمَتُهُ وَأَنَّ اللَّهَ رَءُوفٌ رَحِيمٌ

20 Were it not for God's grace upon you, and His mercy, and that God is Clement and Merciful.

20
24:10

٢١ يَا أَيُّهَا الَّذِينَ آمَنُوا لَا تَتَّبِعُوا خُطُوَاتِ الشَّيْطَانِ ۚ وَمَنْ يَتَّبِعْ خُطُوَاتِ الشَّيْطَانِ فَإِنَّهُ يَأْمُرُ بِالْفَحْشَاءِ وَالْمُنْكَرِ ۚ وَلَوْلَا فَضْلُ اللَّهِ عَلَيْكُمْ وَرَحْمَتُهُ مَا زَكَىٰ مِنْكُمْ مِنْ أَحَدٍ أَبَدًا وَلَكِنَّ اللَّهَ يُزَكِّي مَنْ يَشَاءُ ۗ وَاللَّهُ سَمِيعٌ عَلِيمٌ

21 O you who believe! Do not follow Satan's footsteps. Whoever follows Satan's footsteps—he advocates obscenity and immorality. Were it not for God's grace towards you, and His mercy, not one of you would have been pure, ever. But God purifies whomever He wills. God is All-Hearing, All-Knowing.

21
2:168, 268; 4:49

٢٢ وَلَا يَأْتَلِ أُولُو الْفَضْلِ مِنْكُمْ وَالسَّعَةِ أَنْ يُؤْتُوا أُولِي الْقُرْبَىٰ وَالْمَسَاكِينَ وَالْمُهَاجِرِينَ فِي سَبِيلِ اللَّهِ[a] وَلْيَعْفُوا وَلْيَصْفَحُوا ۗ أَلَا تُحِبُّونَ أَنْ يَغْفِرَ اللَّهُ لَكُمْ ۗ وَاللَّهُ غَفُورٌ رَحِيمٌ[b]

22 Those of you who have affluence and means should not refuse to give to the relatives, and the needy, and the emigrants for the sake of God. And let them pardon, and let them overlook. Do you not love for God to pardon you? God is All-Forgiving, Most Merciful.

22
[a] 2:226
[b] 64:14

٢٣ إِنَّ الَّذِينَ يَرْمُونَ الْمُحْصَنَاتِ الْغَافِلَاتِ الْمُؤْمِنَاتِ لُعِنُوا فِي الدُّنْيَا وَالْآخِرَةِ وَلَهُمْ عَذَابٌ عَظِيمٌ	23	24:4, 6, 13

23 Those who slander honorable, innocent, believing women are cursed in this life and in the Hereafter. They will have a terrible punishment.

٢٤ يَوْمَ تَشْهَدُ عَلَيْهِمْ أَلْسِنَتُهُمْ وَأَيْدِيهِمْ وَأَرْجُلُهُمْ بِمَا كَانُوا يَعْمَلُونَ	24	36:65; 41:20

24 On the Day when their tongues, and their hands, and their feet will testify against them regarding what they used to do.

٢٥ يَوْمَئِذٍ يُوَفِّيهِمُ اللَّهُ دِينَهُمُ الْحَقَّ وَيَعْلَمُونَ أَنَّ اللَّهَ هُوَ الْحَقُّ الْمُبِينُ	25	3:161, 185

25 On that Day, God will pay them their account in full, and they will know that God is the Evident Reality.

٢٦ الْخَبِيثَاتُ لِلْخَبِيثِينَ وَالْخَبِيثُونَ لِلْخَبِيثَاتِ ۖ وَالطَّيِّبَاتُ لِلطَّيِّبِينَ وَالطَّيِّبُونَ لِلطَّيِّبَاتِ ۚ أُولَٰئِكَ مُبَرَّءُونَ مِمَّا يَقُولُونَ ۖ لَهُم مَّغْفِرَةٌ وَرِزْقٌ كَرِيمٌ	26	24:3

26 Bad women are for bad men, and bad men are for bad women, and good women are for good men, and good men are for good women. Those are acquitted of what they say. There is forgiveness for them, and a generous provision.

٢٧ يَا أَيُّهَا الَّذِينَ آمَنُوا لَا تَدْخُلُوا بُيُوتًا غَيْرَ بُيُوتِكُمْ حَتَّىٰ تَسْتَأْنِسُوا وَتُسَلِّمُوا عَلَىٰ أَهْلِهَا ۚ ذَٰلِكُمْ خَيْرٌ لَّكُمْ لَعَلَّكُمْ تَذَكَّرُونَ	27–28	24:28; 33:53

27 O you who believe! Do not enter homes other than your own, until you have asked permission and greeted their occupants. That is better for you, that you may be aware.

٢٨ فَإِن لَّمْ تَجِدُوا فِيهَا أَحَدًا فَلَا تَدْخُلُوهَا حَتَّىٰ يُؤْذَنَ لَكُمْ ۖ وَإِن قِيلَ لَكُمُ ارْجِعُوا فَارْجِعُوا ۖ هُوَ أَزْكَىٰ لَكُمْ ۚ وَاللَّهُ بِمَا تَعْمَلُونَ عَلِيمٌ

28 And if you find no one in them, do not enter them until you are given permission. And if it is said to you, "Turn back," then turn back. That is more proper for you. God is aware of what you do.

٢٩ لَّيْسَ عَلَيْكُمْ جُنَاحٌ أَن تَدْخُلُوا بُيُوتًا غَيْرَ مَسْكُونَةٍ فِيهَا مَتَاعٌ لَّكُمْ ۚ وَاللَّهُ يَعْلَمُ مَا تُبْدُونَ وَمَا تَكْتُمُونَ

29 There is no blame on you for entering uninhabited houses, in which are belongings of yours. God knows what you reveal and what you conceal.

٣٠ قُل لِّلْمُؤْمِنِينَ يَغُضُّوا مِنْ أَبْصَارِهِمْ وَيَحْفَظُوا فُرُوجَهُمْ ۚ ذَٰلِكَ أَزْكَىٰ لَهُمْ ۗ إِنَّ اللَّهَ خَبِيرٌ بِمَا يَصْنَعُونَ	30	23:5; 33:35; 70:29

30 Tell the believing men to restrain their looks, and to guard their privates. That is purer for them. God is cognizant of what they do.

٣١ وَقُل لِّلْمُؤْمِنَاتِ يَغْضُضْنَ مِنْ أَبْصَارِهِنَّ وَيَحْفَظْنَ فُرُوجَهُنَّ وَلَا يُبْدِينَ زِينَتَهُنَّ إِلَّا مَا ظَهَرَ مِنْهَا ۖ وَلْيَضْرِبْنَ بِخُمُرِهِنَّ عَلَىٰ جُيُوبِهِنَّ ۖ وَلَا يُبْدِينَ زِينَتَهُنَّ إِلَّا لِبُعُولَتِهِنَّ أَوْ آبَائِهِنَّ أَوْ آبَاءِ بُعُولَتِهِنَّ أَوْ أَبْنَائِهِنَّ أَوْ أَبْنَاءِ بُعُولَتِهِنَّ أَوْ إِخْوَانِهِنَّ أَوْ بَنِي إِخْوَانِهِنَّ أَوْ بَنِي أَخَوَاتِهِنَّ أَوْ نِسَائِهِنَّ أَوْ مَا مَلَكَتْ أَيْمَانُهُنَّ أَوِ التَّابِعِينَ غَيْرِ أُولِي الْإِرْبَةِ مِنَ الرِّجَالِ أَوِ الطِّفْلِ الَّذِينَ لَمْ يَظْهَرُوا عَلَىٰ عَوْرَاتِ النِّسَاءِ ۖ وَلَا يَضْرِبْنَ بِأَرْجُلِهِنَّ لِيُعْلَمَ مَا يُخْفِينَ مِنْ زِينَتِهِنَّ ۚ وَتُوبُوا إِلَى اللَّهِ جَمِيعًا أَيُّهَ الْمُؤْمِنُونَ لَعَلَّكُمْ تُفْلِحُونَ

31 23:56; 24:60; 40:19; 70:29–30

31 And tell the believing women to restrain their looks, and to guard their privates, and not display their beauty except what is apparent thereof, and to draw their coverings over their breasts, and not expose their beauty except to their husbands, their fathers, their husbands' fathers, their sons, their husbands' sons, their brothers, their brothers' sons, their sisters' sons, their women, what their right hands possess, their male attendants who have no sexual desires, or children who are not yet aware of the nakedness of women. And they should not strike their feet to draw attention to their hidden beauty. And repent to God, all of you believers, so that you may succeed.

٣٢ وَأَنكِحُوا الْأَيَامَىٰ مِنكُمْ وَالصَّالِحِينَ مِنْ عِبَادِكُمْ وَإِمَائِكُمْ ۚ إِن يَكُونُوا فُقَرَاءَ يُغْنِهِمُ اللَّهُ مِن فَضْلِهِ ۗ وَاللَّهُ وَاسِعٌ عَلِيمٌ

32 2:221; 60:10

32 And wed the singles among you, and those who are fit among your servants and maids. If they are poor, God will enrich them from His bounty. God is All-Encompassing, All-Knowing.

٣٣ وَلْيَسْتَعْفِفِ الَّذِينَ لَا يَجِدُونَ نِكَاحًا حَتَّىٰ يُغْنِيَهُمُ اللَّهُ مِن فَضْلِهِ ۗ وَالَّذِينَ يَبْتَغُونَ الْكِتَابَ مِمَّا مَلَكَتْ أَيْمَانُكُمْ فَكَاتِبُوهُمْ إِنْ عَلِمْتُمْ فِيهِمْ خَيْرًا ۖ وَآتُوهُم مِّن مَّالِ اللَّهِ الَّذِي آتَاكُمْ ۚ وَلَا تُكْرِهُوا فَتَيَاتِكُمْ عَلَى الْبِغَاءِ إِنْ أَرَدْنَ تَحَصُّنًا لِّتَبْتَغُوا عَرَضَ الْحَيَاةِ الدُّنْيَا ۚ وَمَن يُكْرِههُّنَّ فَإِنَّ اللَّهَ مِن بَعْدِ إِكْرَاهِهِنَّ غَفُورٌ رَحِيمٌ

33 And let those who do not find the means to marry abstain, until God enriches them from His bounty. If any of your servants wish to be freed, grant them their wish, if you recognize some good in them. And give them of God's wealth which he has given you. And do not compel your girls to prostitution, seeking the materials of this life, if they desire to remain chaste. Should anyone compel them—after their compulsion, God is Forgiving and Merciful.

٣٤ وَلَقَدْ أَنزَلْنَا إِلَيْكُمْ آيَاتٍ مُّبَيِّنَاتٍ وَمَثَلًا مِّنَ الَّذِينَ خَلَوْا مِن قَبْلِكُمْ وَمَوْعِظَةً لِّلْمُتَّقِينَ

34 24:1

34 We have sent down to you clarifying revelations, and examples of those who passed on before you, and advice for the righteous.

٣٥ اللَّهُ نُورُ السَّمَاوَاتِ وَالْأَرْضِ ۚ مَثَلُ نُورِهِ كَمِشْكَاةٍ فِيهَا مِصْبَاحٌ ۖ الْمِصْبَاحُ فِي زُجَاجَةٍ ۖ الزُّجَاجَةُ كَأَنَّهَا كَوْكَبٌ دُرِّيٌّ يُوقَدُ مِنْ شَجَرَةٍ مُبَارَكَةٍ زَيْتُونَةٍ لَا شَرْقِيَّةٍ وَلَا غَرْبِيَّةٍ يَكَادُ زَيْتُهَا يُضِيءُ وَلَوْ لَمْ تَمْسَسْهُ نَارٌ ۚ نُورٌ عَلَىٰ نُورٍ ۗ يَهْدِي اللَّهُ لِنُورِهِ مَنْ يَشَاءُ ۚ وَيَضْرِبُ اللَّهُ الْأَمْثَالَ لِلنَّاسِ ۗ وَاللَّهُ بِكُلِّ شَيْءٍ عَلِيمٌ

35 God is the Light of the heavens and the earth. The allegory of His light is that of a pillar on which is a lamp. The lamp is within a glass. The glass is like a brilliant planet, fueled by a blessed tree, an olive tree, neither eastern nor western. Its oil would almost illuminate, even if no fire has touched it. Light upon Light. God guides to His light whomever He wills. God thus cites the parables for the people. God is cognizant of everything.

٣٦ فِي بُيُوتٍ أَذِنَ اللَّهُ أَنْ تُرْفَعَ وَيُذْكَرَ فِيهَا اسْمُهُ يُسَبِّحُ لَهُ فِيهَا بِالْغُدُوِّ وَالْآصَالِ

36 In houses which God has permitted to be raised, and His name is celebrated therein. He is glorified therein, morning and evening.

٣٧ رِجَالٌ لَا تُلْهِيهِمْ تِجَارَةٌ وَلَا بَيْعٌ عَنْ ذِكْرِ اللَّهِ وَإِقَامِ الصَّلَاةِ وَإِيتَاءِ الزَّكَاةِ ۙ يَخَافُونَ يَوْمًا تَتَقَلَّبُ فِيهِ الْقُلُوبُ وَالْأَبْصَارُ

37
15:3; 62:9; 63:9

37 By men who neither trading nor commerce distracts them from God's remembrance, and from performing the prayers, and from giving alms. They fear a Day when hearts and sights are overturned.

٣٨ لِيَجْزِيَهُمُ اللَّهُ أَحْسَنَ مَا عَمِلُوا وَيَزِيدَهُمْ مِنْ فَضْلِهِ ۗ وَاللَّهُ يَرْزُقُ مَنْ يَشَاءُ بِغَيْرِ حِسَابٍ

38
6:160; 10:26

38 God will reward them according to the best of what they did, and He will increase them from His bounty. God provides for whomever He wills without reckoning.

٣٩ وَالَّذِينَ كَفَرُوا أَعْمَالُهُمْ كَسَرَابٍ بِقِيعَةٍ يَحْسَبُهُ الظَّمْآنُ مَاءً حَتَّىٰ إِذَا جَاءَهُ لَمْ يَجِدْهُ شَيْئًا وَوَجَدَ اللَّهَ عِنْدَهُ فَوَفَّاهُ حِسَابَهُ ۗ وَاللَّهُ سَرِيعُ الْحِسَابِ

39
14:18; 25:23

39 As for those who disbelieve, their works are like a mirage in a desert. The thirsty assumes it is to be water. Until, when he has reached it, he finds it to be nothing, but there he finds God, Who settles his account in full. God is swift in reckoning.

٤٠ أَوْ كَظُلُمَاتٍ فِي بَحْرٍ لُجِّيٍّ يَغْشَاهُ مَوْجٌ مِنْ فَوْقِهِ مَوْجٌ مِنْ فَوْقِهِ سَحَابٌ ۚ ظُلُمَاتٌ بَعْضُهَا فَوْقَ بَعْضٍ إِذَا أَخْرَجَ يَدَهُ لَمْ يَكَدْ يَرَاهَا ۗ وَمَنْ لَمْ يَجْعَلِ اللَّهُ لَهُ نُورًا فَمَا لَهُ مِنْ نُورٍ

40 Or like utter darkness in a vast ocean, covered by waves, above which are waves, above which is fog. Darkness upon darkness. If he brings out his hand, he will hardly see it. He to whom God has not granted a light has no light.

٤١ أَلَمْ تَرَ أَنَّ اللَّهَ يُسَبِّحُ لَهُ مَنْ فِي السَّمَاوَاتِ وَالْأَرْضِ وَالطَّيْرُ صَافَّاتٍ ۖ كُلٌّ قَدْ عَلِمَ صَلَاتَهُ وَتَسْبِيحَهُ ۗ وَاللَّهُ عَلِيمٌ بِمَا يَفْعَلُونَ

41
16:79; 17:44

41 Do you not realize that God is glorified by whatever is in the heavens and the earth, and even by the birds in formation? Each knows its prayer and its manner of praise. God knows well what they do.

٤٢ وَلِلَّهِ مُلْكُ السَّمَاوَاتِ وَالْأَرْضِ ۖ وَإِلَى اللَّهِ الْمَصِيرُ

42 To God belongs the dominion of the heavens and the earth, and to God is the ultimate return.

٤٣ أَلَمْ تَرَ أَنَّ اللَّهَ يُزْجِي سَحَابًا ثُمَّ يُؤَلِّفُ بَيْنَهُ ثُمَّ يَجْعَلُهُ رُكَامًا فَتَرَى الْوَدْقَ يَخْرُجُ مِنْ خِلَالِهِ وَيُنَزِّلُ مِنَ السَّمَاءِ مِنْ جِبَالٍ فِيهَا مِنْ بَرَدٍ فَيُصِيبُ بِهِ مَنْ يَشَاءُ وَيَصْرِفُهُ عَنْ مَنْ يَشَاءُ ۖ يَكَادُ سَنَا بَرْقِهِ يَذْهَبُ بِالْأَبْصَارِ

43
30:48

43 Have you not seen how God propels the clouds, then brings them together, then piles them into a heap, and you see rain drops emerging from its midst? How He brings down loads of hail from the sky, striking with it whomever He wills, and diverting it from whomever He wills? The flash of its lightning almost snatches the sight away.

٤٤ يُقَلِّبُ اللَّهُ اللَّيْلَ وَالنَّهَارَ ۚ إِنَّ فِي ذَٰلِكَ لَعِبْرَةً لِأُولِي الْأَبْصَارِ

44
2:164; 3:190

44 God alternates the night and the day. In that is a lesson for those who have insight.

٤٥ وَاللَّهُ خَلَقَ كُلَّ دَابَّةٍ مِنْ مَاءٍ ۖ فَمِنْهُمْ مَنْ يَمْشِي عَلَىٰ بَطْنِهِ وَمِنْهُمْ مَنْ يَمْشِي عَلَىٰ رِجْلَيْنِ وَمِنْهُمْ مَنْ يَمْشِي عَلَىٰ أَرْبَعٍ ۚ يَخْلُقُ اللَّهُ مَا يَشَاءُ ۚ إِنَّ اللَّهَ عَلَىٰ كُلِّ شَيْءٍ قَدِيرٌ

45 God created every living creature from water. Some of them crawl on their bellies, and some walk on two feet, and others walk on four. God creates whatever He wills. God is Capable of everything.

٤٦ لَقَدْ أَنْزَلْنَا آيَاتٍ مُبَيِّنَاتٍ ۚ وَاللَّهُ يَهْدِي مَنْ يَشَاءُ إِلَىٰ صِرَاطٍ مُسْتَقِيمٍ

46
24:34

46 We sent down enlightening revelations, and God guides whomever He wills to a straight path.

٤٧ وَيَقُولُونَ آمَنَّا بِاللَّهِ وَبِالرَّسُولِ وَأَطَعْنَا ثُمَّ يَتَوَلَّىٰ فَرِيقٌ مِنْهُمْ مِنْ بَعْدِ ذَٰلِكَ ۚ وَمَا أُولَٰئِكَ بِالْمُؤْمِنِينَ

47 And they say, "We have believed in God and the Messenger, and we obey," but some of them turn away afterwards. These are not believers.

٤٨ وَإِذَا دُعُوا إِلَى اللَّهِ وَرَسُولِهِ لِيَحْكُمَ بَيْنَهُمْ إِذَا فَرِيقٌ مِنْهُمْ مُعْرِضُونَ

48
3:23

48 And when they are called to God and His Messenger, in order to judge between them, some of them refuse.

٤٩ وَإِنْ يَكُنْ لَهُمُ الْحَقُّ يَأْتُوا إِلَيْهِ مُذْعِنِينَ

49 But if justice is on their side, they accept it willingly.

٥٠ أَفِي قُلُوبِهِمْ مَرَضٌ أَمِ ارْتَابُوا أَمْ يَخَافُونَ أَنْ يَحِيفَ اللَّهُ عَلَيْهِمْ وَرَسُولُهُ ۚ بَلْ أُولَٰئِكَ هُمُ الظَّالِمُونَ

50 Is there sickness in their hearts? Or are they suspicious? Or do they fear that God may do them injustice? Or His Messenger? In fact, they themselves are the unjust.

٥١ إِنَّمَا كَانَ قَوْلَ الْمُؤْمِنِينَ إِذَا دُعُوا إِلَى اللَّهِ وَرَسُولِهِ لِيَحْكُمَ بَيْنَهُمْ أَنْ يَقُولُوا سَمِعْنَا وَأَطَعْنَا ۚ وَأُولَٰئِكَ هُمُ الْمُفْلِحُونَ

51–52
2:285; 4:13; 5:7 33:71

51 The response of the believers, when they are called to God and His Messenger in order to judge between them, is to say, "We hear and we obey." These are the successful.

٥٢ وَمَنْ يُطِعِ اللَّهَ وَرَسُولَهُ وَيَخْشَ اللَّهَ وَيَتَّقْهِ فَأُولَٰئِكَ هُمُ الْفَائِزُونَ

52 Whoever obeys God and His Messenger, and fears God, and is conscious of Him—these are the winners.

٥٣ وَأَقْسَمُوا بِاللَّهِ جَهْدَ أَيْمَانِهِمْ لَئِنْ أَمَرْتَهُمْ لَيَخْرُجُنَّ ۖ قُلْ لَا تُقْسِمُوا ۖ طَاعَةٌ مَعْرُوفَةٌ ۚ إِنَّ اللَّهَ خَبِيرٌ بِمَا تَعْمَلُونَ

53
5:53; 9:42, 95

53 And they swear by God with their solemn oaths, that if you commanded them, they would mobilize. Say, "Do not swear. Obedience will be recognized. God is experienced with what you do."

٥٤ قُلْ أَطِيعُوا اللَّهَ وَأَطِيعُوا الرَّسُولَ ۖ فَإِنْ تَوَلَّوْا فَإِنَّمَا عَلَيْهِ مَا حُمِّلَ وَعَلَيْكُمْ مَا حُمِّلْتُمْ ۖ وَإِنْ تُطِيعُوهُ تَهْتَدُوا ۚ وَمَا عَلَى الرَّسُولِ إِلَّا الْبَلَاغُ الْمُبِينُ

54
3:32; 5:92; 8:20; 64:12

54 Say, "Obey God and obey the Messenger." But if they turn away, then he is responsible for his obligations, and you are responsible for your obligations. And if you obey him, you will be guided. It is only incumbent on the Messenger to deliver the Clarifying Message.

٥٥ وَعَدَ اللَّهُ الَّذِينَ آمَنُوا مِنْكُمْ وَعَمِلُوا الصَّالِحَاتِ لَيَسْتَخْلِفَنَّهُمْ فِي الْأَرْضِ كَمَا اسْتَخْلَفَ الَّذِينَ مِنْ قَبْلِهِمْ وَلَيُمَكِّنَنَّ لَهُمْ دِينَهُمُ الَّذِي ارْتَضَىٰ لَهُمْ وَلَيُبَدِّلَنَّهُمْ مِنْ بَعْدِ خَوْفِهِمْ أَمْنًا ۚ يَعْبُدُونَنِي لَا يُشْرِكُونَ بِي شَيْئًا ۚ وَمَنْ كَفَرَ بَعْدَ ذَٰلِكَ فَأُولَٰئِكَ هُمُ الْفَاسِقُونَ

55
6:133; 7:129; 24:41; 57:7; 64:12

55 God has promised those of you who believe and do righteous deeds, that He will make them successors on earth, as He made those before them successors, and He will establish for them their religion—which He has approved for them—and He will substitute security in place of their fear. They worship Me, never associating anything with Me. But whoever disbelieves after that—these are the sinners.

٥٦ وَأَقِيمُوا الصَّلَاةَ وَآتُوا الزَّكَاةَ وَأَطِيعُوا الرَّسُولَ لَعَلَّكُمْ تُرْحَمُونَ

56
9:71

56 Pray regularly, and give regular charity, and obey the Messenger, so that you may receive mercy.

٥٧ لَا تَحْسَبَنَّ الَّذِينَ كَفَرُوا مُعْجِزِينَ فِي الْأَرْضِ ۚ وَمَأْوَاهُمُ النَّارُ ۖ وَلَبِئْسَ الْمَصِيرُ

57
6:134; 8:59; 9:2–3; 10:53; 11:20; 29:21–22; 42:31

57 Never think that those who disbelieve can escape on earth. Their place is the Fire; a miserable destination.

٥٨ يَا أَيُّهَا الَّذِينَ آمَنُوا لِيَسْتَأْذِنكُمُ الَّذِينَ مَلَكَتْ أَيْمَانُكُمْ وَالَّذِينَ لَمْ يَبْلُغُوا الْحُلُمَ مِنكُمْ ثَلَاثَ مَرَّاتٍ ۚ مِّن قَبْلِ صَلَاةِ الْفَجْرِ وَحِينَ تَضَعُونَ ثِيَابَكُم مِّنَ الظَّهِيرَةِ وَمِن بَعْدِ صَلَاةِ الْعِشَاءِ ۚ ثَلَاثُ عَوْرَاتٍ لَّكُمْ ۚ لَيْسَ عَلَيْكُمْ وَلَا عَلَيْهِمْ جُنَاحٌ بَعْدَهُنَّ ۚ طَوَّافُونَ عَلَيْكُم بَعْضُكُمْ عَلَىٰ بَعْضٍ ۚ كَذَٰلِكَ يُبَيِّنُ اللَّهُ لَكُمُ الْآيَاتِ ۗ وَاللَّهُ عَلِيمٌ حَكِيمٌ

58 O you who believe! Permission must be requested by your servants and those of you who have not reached puberty. On three occasions: before the Dawn Prayer, and at noon when you change your clothes, and after the Evening Prayer. These are three occasions of privacy for you. At other times, it is not wrong for you or them to intermingle with one another. God thus clarifies the revelations for you. God is Knowledgeable and Wise.

٥٩ وَإِذَا بَلَغَ الْأَطْفَالُ مِنكُمُ الْحُلُمَ فَلْيَسْتَأْذِنُوا كَمَا اسْتَأْذَنَ الَّذِينَ مِن قَبْلِهِمْ ۚ كَذَٰلِكَ يُبَيِّنُ اللَّهُ لَكُمْ آيَاتِهِ ۗ وَاللَّهُ عَلِيمٌ حَكِيمٌ

59 When the children among you reach puberty, they must ask permission, as those before them asked permission. God thus clarifies His revelations for you. God is Knowledgeable and Wise.

٦٠ وَالْقَوَاعِدُ مِنَ النِّسَاءِ اللَّاتِي لَا يَرْجُونَ نِكَاحًا فَلَيْسَ عَلَيْهِنَّ جُنَاحٌ أَن يَضَعْنَ ثِيَابَهُنَّ غَيْرَ مُتَبَرِّجَاتٍ بِزِينَةٍ ۖ وَأَن يَسْتَعْفِفْنَ خَيْرٌ لَّهُنَّ ۗ وَاللَّهُ سَمِيعٌ عَلِيمٌ

60
24:31

60 Women past the age of childbearing, who have no desire for marriage, commit no wrong by taking off their outer clothing, provided they do not flaunt their finery. But to maintain modesty is better for them. God is Hearing and Knowing.

٦١ لَّيْسَ عَلَى الْأَعْمَىٰ حَرَجٌ وَلَا عَلَى الْأَعْرَجِ حَرَجٌ وَلَا عَلَى الْمَرِيضِ حَرَجٌ وَلَا عَلَىٰ أَنفُسِكُمْ أَن تَأْكُلُوا مِن بُيُوتِكُمْ أَوْ بُيُوتِ آبَائِكُمْ أَوْ بُيُوتِ أُمَّهَاتِكُمْ أَوْ بُيُوتِ إِخْوَانِكُمْ أَوْ بُيُوتِ أَخَوَاتِكُمْ أَوْ بُيُوتِ أَعْمَامِكُمْ أَوْ بُيُوتِ عَمَّاتِكُمْ أَوْ بُيُوتِ أَخْوَالِكُمْ أَوْ بُيُوتِ خَالَاتِكُمْ أَوْ مَا مَلَكْتُم مَّفَاتِحَهُ أَوْ صَدِيقِكُمْ ۚ لَيْسَ عَلَيْكُمْ جُنَاحٌ أَن تَأْكُلُوا جَمِيعًا أَوْ أَشْتَاتًا ۚ فَإِذَا دَخَلْتُم بُيُوتًا فَسَلِّمُوا عَلَىٰ أَنفُسِكُمْ تَحِيَّةً مِّنْ عِندِ اللَّهِ مُبَارَكَةً طَيِّبَةً ۚ كَذَٰلِكَ يُبَيِّنُ اللَّهُ لَكُمُ الْآيَاتِ لَعَلَّكُمْ تَعْقِلُونَ

61
48:17

61 There is no blame on the blind, nor any blame on the lame, nor any blame on the sick, nor on yourselves for eating at your homes, or your fathers' homes, or your mothers' homes, or your brothers' homes, or your sisters' homes, or the homes of your paternal uncles, or the homes of your paternal aunts, or the homes of your maternal uncles, or the homes of your maternal aunts, or those whose keys you own, or the homes of your friends. You commit no wrong by eating together or separately. But when you enter any home, greet one another with a greeting from God, blessed and good. God thus explains the revelations for you, so that you may understand.

٦٢ إِنَّمَا الْمُؤْمِنُونَ الَّذِينَ آمَنُوا بِاللَّهِ وَرَسُولِهِ وَإِذَا كَانُوا مَعَهُ عَلَىٰ أَمْرٍ جَامِعٍ لَمْ يَذْهَبُوا حَتَّىٰ يَسْتَأْذِنُوهُ ۚ إِنَّ الَّذِينَ يَسْتَأْذِنُونَكَ أُولَٰئِكَ الَّذِينَ يُؤْمِنُونَ بِاللَّهِ وَرَسُولِهِ ۚ فَإِذَا اسْتَأْذَنُوكَ لِبَعْضِ شَأْنِهِمْ فَأْذَن لِّمَن شِئْتَ مِنْهُمْ وَاسْتَغْفِرْ لَهُمُ اللَّهَ ۚ إِنَّ اللَّهَ غَفُورٌ رَّحِيمٌ

62

9:44, 45, 83

62 The believers are those who believe in God and His Messenger, and when they are with him for a matter of common interest, they do not leave until they have asked him for permission. Those who ask your permission are those who believe in God and His Messenger. So when they ask your permission to attend to some affair of theirs, give permission to any of them you wish, and ask God's forgiveness for them. God is Forgiving and Merciful.

٦٣ لَا تَجْعَلُوا دُعَاءَ الرَّسُولِ بَيْنَكُمْ كَدُعَاءِ بَعْضِكُم بَعْضًا ۚ قَدْ يَعْلَمُ اللَّهُ الَّذِينَ يَتَسَلَّلُونَ مِنكُمْ لِوَاذًا ۚ فَلْيَحْذَرِ الَّذِينَ يُخَالِفُونَ عَنْ أَمْرِهِ أَن تُصِيبَهُمْ فِتْنَةٌ أَوْ يُصِيبَهُمْ عَذَابٌ أَلِيمٌ

63

49:2–3

63 Do not address the Messenger in the same manner you address one another. God knows those of you who slip away using flimsy excuses. So let those who oppose his orders beware, lest an ordeal strikes them, or a painful punishment befalls them.

٦٤ أَلَا إِنَّ لِلَّهِ مَا فِي السَّمَاوَاتِ وَالْأَرْضِ ۖ قَدْ يَعْلَمُ مَا أَنتُمْ عَلَيْهِ وَيَوْمَ يُرْجَعُونَ إِلَيْهِ فَيُنَبِّئُهُم بِمَا عَمِلُوا ۗ وَاللَّهُ بِكُلِّ شَيْءٍ عَلِيمٌ

64

33:18; 75:13

64 Surely, to God belongs everything in the heavens and the earth. He knows what you are about. And on the Day they are returned to Him, He will inform them of what they did. God has full knowledge of all things.

Sūrah 25: Al-Furqān

سُورَةُ ٱلْفُرْقَانِ (The Criterion)

بِسْمِ ٱللَّهِ ٱلرَّحْمَٰنِ ٱلرَّحِيمِ

١ تَبَارَكَ الَّذِي نَزَّلَ الْفُرْقَانَ عَلَىٰ عَبْدِهِ لِيَكُونَ لِلْعَالَمِينَ نَذِيرًا

1

2:53; 3:4; 21:48

1 Blessed is He who sent down the Criterion upon His servant, to be a warning to humanity.

٢ الَّذِي لَهُ مُلْكُ السَّمَاوَاتِ وَالْأَرْضِ ۖ وَلَمْ يَتَّخِذْ وَلَدًا وَلَمْ يَكُن لَّهُ شَرِيكٌ فِي الْمُلْكِ وَخَلَقَ كُلَّ شَيْءٍ فَقَدَّرَهُ تَقْدِيرًا [b]

2

[a] 3:26; 5:40; 6:73; 24:42; 35:13; 67:1
[b] 2:116; 6:101; 17:111; 19:88–89; 23:91; 72:3; 112:3–4

2 He to whom belongs the kingdom of the heavens and the earth, who took to Himself no son, who never had a partner in His kingship; who created everything and determined its measure.

٣ وَاتَّخَذُوا مِن دُونِهِ آلِهَةً لَّا يَخْلُقُونَ شَيْئًا وَهُمْ يُخْلَقُونَ وَلَا يَمْلِكُونَ لِأَنفُسِهِمْ ضَرًّا وَلَا نَفْعًا وَلَا يَمْلِكُونَ مَوْتًا وَلَا حَيَاةً وَلَا نُشُورًا

3 And yet, instead of Him, they produce for themselves gods that create nothing, but are themselves created; that have no power to harm or benefit themselves; and no power over life, death, or resurrection.

3
7:191; 13:16; 16:20; 21:21; 22:73; 35:40

٤ وَقَالَ الَّذِينَ كَفَرُوا إِنْ هَٰذَا إِلَّا إِفْكٌ افْتَرَاهُ وَأَعَانَهُ عَلَيْهِ قَوْمٌ آخَرُونَ ۖ فَقَدْ جَاءُوا ظُلْمًا وَزُورًا

4 Those who disbelieve say, "This is nothing but a lie that he made up, and others have helped him at it." They have committed an injustice and a perjury.

4
10:38; 34:43; 46:11

٥ وَقَالُوا أَسَاطِيرُ الْأَوَّلِينَ اكْتَتَبَهَا فَهِيَ تُمْلَىٰ عَلَيْهِ بُكْرَةً وَأَصِيلًا

5 And they say, "Tales of the ancients; he wrote them down; they are dictated to him morning and evening."

5
6:25; 16:24; 23:83; 68:15; 83:1

٦ قُلْ أَنزَلَهُ الَّذِي يَعْلَمُ السِّرَّ فِي السَّمَاوَاتِ وَالْأَرْضِ ۚ إِنَّهُ كَانَ غَفُورًا رَّحِيمًا

6 Say, "It was revealed by He who knows the Secret in the heavens and the earth. He is always Forgiving and Merciful."

6
21:4; 20:7; 43:80; 67:3

٧ وَقَالُوا مَالِ هَٰذَا الرَّسُولِ يَأْكُلُ الطَّعَامَ وَيَمْشِي فِي الْأَسْوَاقِ ۙ لَوْلَا أُنزِلَ إِلَيْهِ مَلَكٌ فَيَكُونَ مَعَهُ نَذِيرًا

7 And they say, "What sort of messenger is this, who eats food, and walks in the marketplaces? If only an angel was sent down with him, to be alongside him a warner."

7
5:75; 14:10; 17:94; 21:8; 23:33, 47; 25:20

٨ أَوْ يُلْقَىٰ إِلَيْهِ كَنزٌ أَوْ تَكُونُ لَهُ جَنَّةٌ يَأْكُلُ مِنْهَا ۚ وَقَالَ الظَّالِمُونَ إِن تَتَّبِعُونَ إِلَّا رَجُلًا مَّسْحُورًا

8 Or, "If only a treasure was dropped on him." Or, "If only he had a garden from which he eats." The evildoers also say, "You are following but a man under spell."

8
6:76; 17:47; 20:69

٩ انظُرْ كَيْفَ ضَرَبُوا لَكَ الْأَمْثَالَ فَضَلُّوا فَلَا يَسْتَطِيعُونَ سَبِيلًا

9 Look how they invent examples for you. They have gone astray, and cannot find a way.

9
17:48

١٠ تَبَارَكَ الَّذِي إِن شَاءَ جَعَلَ لَكَ خَيْرًا مِّن ذَٰلِكَ جَنَّاتٍ تَجْرِي مِن تَحْتِهَا الْأَنْهَارُ وَيَجْعَل لَّكَ قُصُورًا

10 Blessed is He who, if He wills, can provide you with better than that—gardens beneath which rivers flow—and He will give you palaces.

10
67:1

١١ بَلْ كَذَّبُوا بِالسَّاعَةِ ۖ وَأَعْتَدْنَا لِمَن كَذَّبَ بِالسَّاعَةِ سَعِيرًا

11 In fact, they have denied the Hour, and We have prepared for those who deny the Hour a Blaze.

11
45:32, 35

١٢ إِذَا رَأَتْهُم مِّن مَّكَانٍ بَعِيدٍ سَمِعُوا لَهَا تَغَيُّظًا وَزَفِيرًا

12 When it sees them from a distant place, they will hear it raging and roaring.

12
67:7

١٣ وَإِذَا أُلْقُوا مِنْهَا مَكَانًا ضَيِّقًا مُقَرَّنِينَ دَعَوْا هُنَالِكَ ثُبُورًا	13–14 84:11	

13 And when they are thrown into it, into a tight place, shackled, they will plead there for death.

١٤ لَا تَدْعُوا الْيَوْمَ ثُبُورًا وَاحِدًا وَادْعُوا ثُبُورًا كَثِيرًا

14 "Do not plead for one death today, but plead for a great many deaths."

١٥ قُلْ أَذَٰلِكَ خَيْرٌ أَمْ جَنَّةُ الْخُلْدِ الَّتِي وُعِدَ الْمُتَّقُونَ ۚ كَانَتْ لَهُمْ جَزَاءً وَمَصِيرًا   15 37:62

15 Say, "Is this better, or the Garden of Eternity promised to the righteous? It is for them a reward and a destination.

١٦ لَهُمْ فِيهَا مَا يَشَاءُونَ خَالِدِينَ ۚ كَانَ عَلَىٰ رَبِّكَ وَعْدًا مَسْئُولًا

16 They will have therein whatever they desire, forever. That is upon your Lord a binding promise.

١٧ وَيَوْمَ يَحْشُرُهُمْ وَمَا يَعْبُدُونَ مِنْ دُونِ اللَّهِ فَيَقُولُ أَأَنْتُمْ أَضْلَلْتُمْ عِبَادِي هَٰؤُلَاءِ أَمْ هُمْ ضَلُّوا السَّبِيلَ   17–19 10:28–30; 34:40–42

17 On the Day when He gathers them, and what they worshiped besides God, He will say, "Was it you who misled these servants of Mine, or was it they who lost the way?"

١٨ قَالُوا سُبْحَانَكَ مَا كَانَ يَنْبَغِي لَنَا أَنْ نَتَّخِذَ مِنْ دُونِكَ مِنْ أَوْلِيَاءَ وَلَٰكِنْ مَتَّعْتَهُمْ وَآبَاءَهُمْ حَتَّىٰ نَسُوا الذِّكْرَ وَكَانُوا قَوْمًا بُورًا

18 They will say, "Glory be to You. It was not for us to take any lords besides You. But you gave them enjoyments, and their ancestors, until they forgot the Message, and became ruined people."

١٩ فَقَدْ كَذَّبُوكُمْ بِمَا تَقُولُونَ فَمَا تَسْتَطِيعُونَ صَرْفًا وَلَا نَصْرًا ۚ وَمَنْ يَظْلِمْ مِنْكُمْ نُذِقْهُ عَذَابًا كَبِيرًا   19 2:254; 10:106; 31:13

19 They have denied you because of what you say; so you can neither avert, nor help. Whoever among you commits injustice, We will make him taste a grievous punishment.

٢٠ وَمَا أَرْسَلْنَا قَبْلَكَ مِنَ الْمُرْسَلِينَ إِلَّا إِنَّهُمْ لَيَأْكُلُونَ الطَّعَامَ وَيَمْشُونَ فِي الْأَسْوَاقِ [a] وَجَعَلْنَا بَعْضَكُمْ لِبَعْضٍ فِتْنَةً أَتَصْبِرُونَ [b] وَكَانَ رَبُّكَ بَصِيرًا   20 [a] 23:33; 25:7 [b] 6:53

20 We never sent any messengers before you, but they ate food and walked in the marketplaces. And We made some of you tempters for one another—will you be patient? Your Lord is always Observing.

٢١ وَقَالَ الَّذِينَ لَا يَرْجُونَ لِقَاءَنَا لَوْلَا أُنْزِلَ عَلَيْنَا الْمَلَائِكَةُ أَوْ نَرَىٰ رَبَّنَا ۗ لَقَدِ اسْتَكْبَرُوا فِي أَنْفُسِهِمْ وَعَتَوْا عُتُوًّا كَبِيرًا   21 6:124; 15:8; 17:90–92

21 Those who do not expect to meet Us say, "If only the angels were sent down to us, or we could see our Lord." They have grown arrogant within themselves, and have become excessively defiant.

٢٢ يَوْمَ يَرَوْنَ الْمَلَائِكَةَ لَا بُشْرَىٰ يَوْمَئِذٍ لِلْمُجْرِمِينَ وَيَقُولُونَ حِجْرًا مَحْجُورًا

22 On the Day when they see the angels—there will be no good news for sinners on that Day; and they will say, "A protective refuge."

22
6:93; 8:56; 47:27–28

٢٣ وَقَدِمْنَا إِلَىٰ مَا عَمِلُوا مِنْ عَمَلٍ فَجَعَلْنَاهُ هَبَاءً مَنْثُورًا

23 We will proceed to the works they did, and will turn them into scattered dust.

٢٤ أَصْحَابُ الْجَنَّةِ يَوْمَئِذٍ خَيْرٌ مُسْتَقَرًّا وَأَحْسَنُ مَقِيلًا

24 The companions of Paradise on that Day will be better lodged, and more fairly accommodated.

24
24:66

٢٥ وَيَوْمَ تَشَقَّقُ السَّمَاءُ بِالْغَمَامِ وَنُزِّلَ الْمَلَائِكَةُ تَنْزِيلًا

25 The Day when the sky is cleft with clouds, and the angels are sent down in streams.

25
2:210; 55:37; 69:16; 81:1; 88:1

٢٦ الْمُلْكُ يَوْمَئِذٍ الْحَقُّ لِلرَّحْمَٰنِ ۚ وَكَانَ يَوْمًا عَلَى الْكَافِرِينَ عَسِيرًا

26 On that Day, true sovereignty will belong to the Merciful, and it will be a difficult Day for the disbelievers.

26
6:73; 40:16; 54:8; 74:9

٢٧ وَيَوْمَ يَعَضُّ الظَّالِمُ عَلَىٰ يَدَيْهِ يَقُولُ يَا لَيْتَنِي اتَّخَذْتُ مَعَ الرَّسُولِ سَبِيلًا

27 On that Day, the wrongdoer will bite his hands, and say, "If only I had followed the way with the Messenger.

٢٨ يَا وَيْلَتَىٰ لَيْتَنِي لَمْ أَتَّخِذْ فُلَانًا خَلِيلًا

28 Oh, woe to me; I wish I never took so-and-so for a friend.

٢٩ لَقَدْ أَضَلَّنِي عَنِ الذِّكْرِ بَعْدَ إِذْ جَاءَنِي ۗ وَكَانَ الشَّيْطَانُ لِلْإِنْسَانِ خَذُولًا

29 He led me away from the Message after it had come to me; for Satan has always been a betrayer of man."

29
12:42; 25:18; 58:19

٣٠ وَقَالَ الرَّسُولُ يَا رَبِّ إِنَّ قَوْمِي اتَّخَذُوا هَٰذَا الْقُرْآنَ مَهْجُورًا

30 And the Messenger will say, "My Lord, my people have abandoned this Qur'an."

٣١ وَكَذَٰلِكَ جَعَلْنَا لِكُلِّ نَبِيٍّ عَدُوًّا مِنَ الْمُجْرِمِينَ ۗ وَكَفَىٰ بِرَبِّكَ هَادِيًا وَنَصِيرًا

31 Likewise, to every prophet We assign enemies from among the wicked. But your Lord suffices as a Guide and Savior.

31
6:112

٣٢ وَقَالَ الَّذِينَ كَفَرُوا لَوْلَا نُزِّلَ عَلَيْهِ الْقُرْآنُ جُمْلَةً وَاحِدَةً ۚ[a] كَذَٰلِكَ لِنُثَبِّتَ بِهِ فُؤَادَكَ ۖ وَرَتَّلْنَاهُ تَرْتِيلًا[b]

32 Those who disbelieve say, "Why was the Qur'an not revealed to him at once?" Thus in order to strengthen your heart thereby, and We revealed it in stages.

32
[a] 17:106
[b] 73:4

| | ٣٣ وَلَا يَأْتُونَكَ بِمَثَلٍ إِلَّا جِئْنَاكَ بِالْحَقِّ وَأَحْسَنَ تَفْسِيرًا | 33 75:19 |

33 Whatever argument they come to you with, We provide you with the truth, and a better exposition.

| | ٣٤ الَّذِينَ يُحْشَرُونَ عَلَىٰ وُجُوهِهِمْ إِلَىٰ جَهَنَّمَ أُولَٰئِكَ شَرٌّ مَكَانًا وَأَضَلُّ سَبِيلًا | 34 17:97; 33:66; 54:48 |

34 Those who are herded into Hell on their faces—those are in a worse position, and further astray from the way.

| | ٣٥ وَلَقَدْ آتَيْنَا مُوسَى الْكِتَابَ وَجَعَلْنَا مَعَهُ أَخَاهُ هَارُونَ وَزِيرًا | 35 20:29 |

35 We gave Moses the Scripture, and appointed his brother Aaron as his assistant.

| | ٣٦ فَقُلْنَا اذْهَبَا إِلَى الْقَوْمِ الَّذِينَ كَذَّبُوا بِآيَاتِنَا فَدَمَّرْنَاهُمْ تَدْمِيرًا | 36 |

36 We said, "Go to the people who rejected Our signs," and We destroyed them completely.

| | ٣٧ وَقَوْمَ نُوحٍ لَمَّا كَذَّبُوا الرُّسُلَ أَغْرَقْنَاهُمْ وَجَعَلْنَاهُمْ لِلنَّاسِ آيَةً ۖ وَأَعْتَدْنَا لِلظَّالِمِينَ عَذَابًا أَلِيمًا | 37 7:64 |

37 And the people of Noah: when they rejected the messengers, We drowned them, and made them a lesson for mankind. We have prepared for the wrongdoers a painful retribution.

| | ٣٨ وَعَادًا وَثَمُودَ وَأَصْحَابَ الرَّسِّ وَقُرُونًا بَيْنَ ذَٰلِكَ كَثِيرًا | 38 |

38 And 'Ād, and Thamūd, and the inhabitants of Arras, and many generations in between.

| | ٣٩ وَكُلًّا ضَرَبْنَا لَهُ الْأَمْثَالَ ۖ وَكُلًّا تَبَّرْنَا تَتْبِيرًا | 39 17:7 |

39 To each We presented the parables; and each We devastated utterly.

| | ٤٠ وَلَقَدْ أَتَوْا عَلَى الْقَرْيَةِ الَّتِي أُمْطِرَتْ مَطَرَ السَّوْءِ ۚ أَفَلَمْ يَكُونُوا يَرَوْنَهَا ۚ بَلْ كَانُوا لَا يَرْجُونَ نُشُورًا | 40 26:173 |

40 And they came upon the city that was drenched by the terrible rain. Did they not see it? But they do not expect resurrection.

| | ٤١ وَإِذَا رَأَوْكَ إِنْ يَتَّخِذُونَكَ إِلَّا هُزُوًا أَهَٰذَا الَّذِي بَعَثَ اللَّهُ رَسُولًا | 41 14:36; 21:36 |

41 And when they see you, they take you for nothing but mockery: "Is this the one God sent as a messenger?"

| | ٤٢ إِنْ كَادَ لَيُضِلُّنَا عَنْ آلِهَتِنَا لَوْلَا أَنْ صَبَرْنَا عَلَيْهَا ۚ وَسَوْفَ يَعْلَمُونَ حِينَ يَرَوْنَ الْعَذَابَ مَنْ أَضَلُّ سَبِيلًا | 42 38:5–6 |

42 "He nearly led us away from our gods, had we not patiently adhered to them." But they will know, when they witness the torment, who is further away from the way.

| | ٤٣ أَرَأَيْتَ مَنِ اتَّخَذَ إِلَٰهَهُ هَوَاهُ أَفَأَنْتَ تَكُونُ عَلَيْهِ وَكِيلًا | 43 45:23 |

43 Have you seen him who chose his desire as his god? Would you be an agent for him?

٤٤ أَمْ تَحْسَبُ أَنَّ أَكْثَرَهُمْ يَسْمَعُونَ أَوْ يَعْقِلُونَ ۚ إِنْ هُمْ إِلَّا كَالْأَنْعَامِ ۖ بَلْ هُمْ أَضَلُّ سَبِيلًا

44 Or do you assume that most of them hear or understand? They are just like cattle, but even more errant in their way.

44
7:179

٤٥ أَلَمْ تَرَ إِلَىٰ رَبِّكَ كَيْفَ مَدَّ الظِّلَّ وَلَوْ شَاءَ لَجَعَلَهُ سَاكِنًا ثُمَّ جَعَلْنَا الشَّمْسَ عَلَيْهِ دَلِيلًا

45 Do you not see how your Lord extends the shadow? Had He willed, He could have made it still. And We made the sun a pointer to it.

٤٦ ثُمَّ قَبَضْنَاهُ إِلَيْنَا قَبْضًا يَسِيرًا

46 Then We withdraw it towards Us gradually.

٤٧ وَهُوَ الَّذِي جَعَلَ لَكُمُ اللَّيْلَ لِبَاسًا وَالنَّوْمَ سُبَاتًا وَجَعَلَ النَّهَارَ نُشُورًا

47 And it is He who made the night a covering for you, and sleep for rest; and He made the day a revival.

47
10:67; 17:12; 78:9

٤٨ وَهُوَ الَّذِي أَرْسَلَ الرِّيَاحَ بُشْرًا بَيْنَ يَدَيْ رَحْمَتِهِ ۚ وَأَنْزَلْنَا مِنَ السَّمَاءِ مَاءً طَهُورًا

48 And it is He who sends the winds, bringing advance news of His mercy; and We send down from the sky pure water.

48
7:57; 27:63; 30:46; 42:28

٤٩ لِنُحْيِيَ بِهِ بَلْدَةً مَيْتًا وَنُسْقِيَهُ مِمَّا خَلَقْنَا أَنْعَامًا وَأَنَاسِيَّ كَثِيرًا

49 To revive dead lands thereby, and to provide drink for the multitude of animals and humans We created.

49
50:11

٥٠ وَلَقَدْ صَرَّفْنَاهُ بَيْنَهُمْ لِيَذَّكَّرُوا فَأَبَىٰ أَكْثَرُ النَّاسِ إِلَّا كُفُورًا

50 We have circulated it among them, that they may reflect, but most people persist in thanklessness.

50
17:41

٥١ وَلَوْ شِئْنَا لَبَعَثْنَا فِي كُلِّ قَرْيَةٍ نَذِيرًا

51 Had We willed, We could have sent to every town a warner.

٥٢ فَلَا تُطِعِ الْكَافِرِينَ وَجَاهِدْهُمْ بِهِ جِهَادًا كَبِيرًا

52 So do not obey the disbelievers, but strive against them with it, a mighty struggle.

٥٣ وَهُوَ الَّذِي مَرَجَ الْبَحْرَيْنِ هَٰذَا عَذْبٌ فُرَاتٌ وَهَٰذَا مِلْحٌ أُجَاجٌ وَجَعَلَ بَيْنَهُمَا بَرْزَخًا وَحِجْرًا مَحْجُورًا

53 And it is He who merged the two seas; this one fresh and sweet, and that one salty and bitter; and He placed between them a barrier, and an impassable boundary.

53
27:61; 35:12; 55:19

٥٤ وَهُوَ الَّذِي خَلَقَ مِنَ الْمَاءِ بَشَرًا فَجَعَلَهُ نَسَبًا وَصِهْرًا ۗ وَكَانَ رَبُّكَ قَدِيرًا

54 And it is He who, from fluid, created the human being. Then He made relationships through marriage and mating. Your Lord is Omnipotent.

54
75:37–39

٥٥ وَيَعْبُدُونَ مِن دُونِ اللَّهِ مَا لَا يَنفَعُهُمْ وَلَا يَضُرُّهُمْ ۗ وَكَانَ الْكَافِرُ عَلَىٰ رَبِّهِ ظَهِيرًا

55 And yet, instead of God, they serve what neither profits them nor harms them. The disbeliever has always turned his back on his Lord.

55
6:71; 10:18, 106; 21:66; 26:72; 29:17; 36:74–75

٥٦ وَمَا أَرْسَلْنَاكَ إِلَّا مُبَشِّرًا وَنَذِيرًا

56 We sent you only as a herald of good news and a warner.

٥٧ قُلْ مَا أَسْأَلُكُمْ عَلَيْهِ مِنْ أَجْرٍ إِلَّا مَن شَاءَ أَن يَتَّخِذَ إِلَىٰ رَبِّهِ سَبِيلًا

57 Say, "I ask of you no payment for this—only that whoever wills may take a path to his Lord."

57
11:29

٥٨ وَتَوَكَّلْ عَلَى الْحَيِّ الَّذِي لَا يَمُوتُ وَسَبِّحْ بِحَمْدِهِ ۚ وَكَفَىٰ بِهِ بِذُنُوبِ عِبَادِهِ خَبِيرًا

58 And put your trust in the Living, the One who never dies; and celebrate His praise. He suffices as the All-Informed Knower of the faults of His creatures.

58
17:17

٥٩ الَّذِي خَلَقَ السَّمَاوَاتِ وَالْأَرْضَ وَمَا بَيْنَهُمَا فِي سِتَّةِ أَيَّامٍ ثُمَّ اسْتَوَىٰ عَلَى الْعَرْشِ ۚ الرَّحْمَـٰنُ فَاسْأَلْ بِهِ خَبِيرًا

59 He who created the heavens and the earth and everything between them in six days, then settled on the Throne. The Most Merciful. Ask about Him a well-informed.

59
7:54

٦٠ وَإِذَا قِيلَ لَهُمُ اسْجُدُوا لِلرَّحْمَـٰنِ قَالُوا وَمَا الرَّحْمَـٰنُ أَنَسْجُدُ لِمَا تَأْمُرُنَا وَزَادَهُمْ نُفُورًا

60 And when it is said to them, "Bow down to the Merciful," they say, "And what is the Merciful? Are we to bow down to whatever you command us?" And it increases their aversion.

60
17:110

٦١ تَبَارَكَ الَّذِي جَعَلَ فِي السَّمَاءِ بُرُوجًا وَجَعَلَ فِيهَا سِرَاجًا وَقَمَرًا مُّنِيرًا

61 Blessed is He who placed constellations in the sky, and placed in it a lamp, and an illuminating moon.

61
15:16; 85:1

٦٢ وَهُوَ الَّذِي جَعَلَ اللَّيْلَ وَالنَّهَارَ خِلْفَةً لِّمَنْ أَرَادَ أَن يَذَّكَّرَ أَوْ أَرَادَ شُكُورًا

62 And it is He who made the night and the day alternate—for whoever desires to reflect, or desires to show gratitude.

٦٣ وَعِبَادُ الرَّحْمَـٰنِ الَّذِينَ يَمْشُونَ عَلَى الْأَرْضِ هَوْنًا وَإِذَا خَاطَبَهُمُ الْجَاهِلُونَ قَالُوا سَلَامًا

63 The servants of the Merciful are those who walk the earth in humility, and when the ignorant address them, they say, "Peace."

63
17:37; 19:47; 25:72

٦٤ وَالَّذِينَ يَبِيتُونَ لِرَبِّهِمْ سُجَّدًا وَقِيَامًا

64 And those who pass the night prostrating themselves to their Lord and standing up.

64
32:16; 39:9; 51:16–18

٦٥ وَالَّذِينَ يَقُولُونَ رَبَّنَا اصْرِفْ عَنَّا عَذَابَ جَهَنَّمَ ۖ إِنَّ عَذَابَهَا كَانَ غَرَامًا

65 And those who say, "Our Lord, avert from us the suffering of Hell, for its suffering is continuous.

٦٦ إِنَّهَا سَاءَتْ مُسْتَقَرًّا وَمُقَامًا

66 It is indeed a miserable residence and destination."

66
25:24

٦٧ وَالَّذِينَ إِذَا أَنفَقُوا لَمْ يُسْرِفُوا وَلَمْ يَقْتُرُوا وَكَانَ بَيْنَ ذَٰلِكَ قَوَامًا

67 And those who, when they spend, are neither wasteful nor stingy, but choose a middle course between that.

67
17:29

٦٨ وَالَّذِينَ لَا يَدْعُونَ مَعَ اللَّهِ إِلَٰهًا آخَرَ وَلَا يَقْتُلُونَ النَّفْسَ الَّتِي حَرَّمَ اللَّهُ إِلَّا بِالْحَقِّ وَلَا يَزْنُونَ ۚ وَمَن يَفْعَلْ ذَٰلِكَ يَلْقَ أَثَامًا

68 And those who do not implore besides God any other god, and do not kill the soul which God has made sacred—except in the pursuit of justice—and do not commit adultery. Whoever does that will face penalties.

٦٩ يُضَاعَفْ لَهُ الْعَذَابُ يَوْمَ الْقِيَامَةِ وَيَخْلُدْ فِيهِ مُهَانًا

69 The punishment will be doubled for him on the Day of Resurrection, and he will dwell therein in humiliation forever.

٧٠ إِلَّا مَن تَابَ وَآمَنَ وَعَمِلَ عَمَلًا صَالِحًا فَأُولَٰئِكَ يُبَدِّلُ اللَّهُ سَيِّئَاتِهِمْ حَسَنَاتٍ ۗ وَكَانَ اللَّهُ غَفُورًا رَّحِيمًا

70 Except for those who repent, and believe, and do good deeds. These—God will replace their bad deeds with good deeds. God is ever Forgiving and Merciful.

70
19:60

٧١ وَمَن تَابَ وَعَمِلَ صَالِحًا فَإِنَّهُ يَتُوبُ إِلَى اللَّهِ مَتَابًا

71 Whoever repents and acts righteously—has inclined towards God with repentance.

٧٢ وَالَّذِينَ لَا يَشْهَدُونَ الزُّورَ وَإِذَا مَرُّوا بِاللَّغْوِ مَرُّوا كِرَامًا

72 And those who do not bear false witness; and when they come across indecencies, they pass by with dignity.

72
22:30; 25:63

٧٣ وَالَّذِينَ إِذَا ذُكِّرُوا بِآيَاتِ رَبِّهِمْ لَمْ يَخِرُّوا عَلَيْهَا صُمًّا وَعُمْيَانًا

73 And those who, when reminded of the revelations of their Lord, do not fall before them deaf and blind.

73
8:2; 9:124; 39:23

٧٤ وَالَّذِينَ يَقُولُونَ رَبَّنَا هَبْ لَنَا مِنْ أَزْوَاجِنَا وَذُرِّيَّاتِنَا قُرَّةَ أَعْيُنٍ وَاجْعَلْنَا لِلْمُتَّقِينَ إِمَامًا

74 And those who say, "Our Lord, grant us delight in our spouses and our children, and make us a good example for the righteous."

٧٥ أُولَٰئِكَ يُجْزَوْنَ الْغُرْفَةَ بِمَا صَبَرُوا وَيُلَقَّوْنَ فِيهَا تَحِيَّةً وَسَلَامًا

75 Those will be awarded the Chamber for their patience, and will be greeted therein with greetings and peace.

75
29:58; 34:37; 39:20

٧٦ خَالِدِينَ فِيهَا ۚ حَسُنَتْ مُسْتَقَرًّا وَمُقَامًا

76 Abiding therein forever—it is an excellent residence and destination.

٧٧ قُلْ مَا يَعْبَؤُا۟ بِكُمْ رَبِّى لَوْلَا دُعَاؤُكُمْ ۖ فَقَدْ كَذَّبْتُمْ فَسَوْفَ يَكُونُ لِزَامًا

77 Say, "What are you to my Lord without your prayers? You have denied the truth, and the inevitable will happen."

Sūrah 26: Al-Shu'arā'

سُورَةُ ٱلشُّعَرَاء (The Poets)

بِسْمِ ٱللَّهِ ٱلرَّحْمَٰنِ ٱلرَّحِيمِ

١ طسم

1 Ṭā', Sīn, Mīm.

٢ تِلْكَ آيَاتُ ٱلْكِتَابِ ٱلْمُبِينِ

2 These are the Verses of the Clarifying Book.

٣ لَعَلَّكَ بَاخِعٌ نَفْسَكَ أَلَّا يَكُونُوا۟ مُؤْمِنِينَ

3
15:88, 97; 18:6; 35:8

3 Perhaps you will destroy yourself with grief, because they do not become believers.

٤ إِن نَّشَأْ نُنَزِّلْ عَلَيْهِم مِّنَ ٱلسَّمَاءِ آيَةً فَظَلَّتْ أَعْنَاقُهُمْ لَهَا خَاضِعِينَ

4 If We will, We can send down upon them a sign from heaven, at which their necks will stay bent in humility.

٥ وَمَا يَأْتِيهِم مِّن ذِكْرٍ مِّنَ ٱلرَّحْمَٰنِ مُحْدَثٍ إِلَّا كَانُوا۟ عَنْهُ مُعْرِضِينَ

5
6:4; 21:2; 36:46

5 No fresh reminder comes to them from the Most Merciful, but they turn their backs at it.

٦ فَقَدْ كَذَّبُوا۟ فَسَيَأْتِيهِمْ أَنۢبَٰٓؤُا۟ مَا كَانُوا۟ بِهِۦ يَسْتَهْزِءُونَ

6
6:5

6 They have denied the truth, but soon will come to them the news of what they ridiculed.

٧ أَوَلَمْ يَرَوْا۟ إِلَى ٱلْأَرْضِ كَمْ أَنۢبَتْنَا فِيهَا مِن كُلِّ زَوْجٍ كَرِيمٍ

7
2:21–22; 22:5; 31:10; 50:7

7 Have they not seen the earth, and how many beautiful pairs We produced therein?

٨ إِنَّ فِى ذَٰلِكَ لَآيَةً ۖ وَمَا كَانَ أَكْثَرُهُم مُّؤْمِنِينَ

8 Surely in this is a sign, but most of them are not believers.

٩ وَإِنَّ رَبَّكَ لَهُوَ ٱلْعَزِيزُ ٱلرَّحِيمُ

9 Most surely, your Lord is the Almighty, the Merciful.

١٠ وَإِذْ نَادَىٰ رَبُّكَ مُوسَىٰٓ أَنِ ٱئْتِ ٱلْقَوْمَ ٱلظَّٰلِمِينَ

10–11
7:103; 19:52

10 Your Lord called to Moses, "Go to the tyrannical people.

١١ قَوْمَ فِرْعَوْنَ ۚ أَلَا يَتَّقُونَ

11 The people of Pharaoh. Will they not fear?"

١٢ قَالَ رَبِّ إِنِّي أَخَافُ أَنْ يُكَذِّبُونِ		**12**
12 He said, "My Lord, I fear they will reject me.		28:33–34

١٣ وَيَضِيقُ صَدْرِي وَلَا يَنطَلِقُ لِسَانِي فَأَرْسِلْ إِلَىٰ هَارُونَ

13 And I become stressed, and my tongue is not fluent, so send Aaron too.

١٤ وَلَهُمْ عَلَيَّ ذَنبٌ فَأَخَافُ أَن يَقْتُلُونِ

14 And they have a charge against me, so I fear they will kill me."

١٥ قَالَ كَلَّا ۖ فَاذْهَبَا بِآيَاتِنَا ۖ إِنَّا مَعَكُم مُّسْتَمِعُونَ		**15**
15 He said, "No. Go, both of you, with Our proofs. We will be with you, listening.		20:46; 28:35

١٦ فَأْتِيَا فِرْعَوْنَ فَقُولَا إِنَّا رَسُولُ رَبِّ الْعَالَمِينَ		**16–17**
16 Go to Pharaoh, and say, 'We are the Messengers of the Lord of the Worlds.		7:104; 20:47; 44:18

١٧ أَنْ أَرْسِلْ مَعَنَا بَنِي إِسْرَائِيلَ

17 Let the Children of Israel go with us.'"

١٨ قَالَ أَلَمْ نُرَبِّكَ فِينَا وَلِيدًا وَلَبِثْتَ فِينَا مِنْ عُمُرِكَ سِنِينَ		**18**
18 He said, "Did we not raise you among us as a child, and you stayed among us for many of your years?		28:9

١٩ وَفَعَلْتَ فَعْلَتَكَ الَّتِي فَعَلْتَ وَأَنتَ مِنَ الْكَافِرِينَ		**19**
19 And you committed that deed you committed, and you were ungrateful."		28:15, 28

٢٠ قَالَ فَعَلْتُهَا إِذًا وَأَنَا مِنَ الضَّالِّينَ

20 He said, "I did it then, when I was of those astray.

٢١ فَفَرَرْتُ مِنكُمْ لَمَّا خِفْتُكُمْ فَوَهَبَ لِي رَبِّي حُكْمًا وَجَعَلَنِي مِنَ الْمُرْسَلِينَ		**21**
21 And I fled from you when I feared you; but my Lord gave me wisdom, and made me one of the messengers.		28:20–21; 28:18

٢٢ وَتِلْكَ نِعْمَةٌ تَمُنُّهَا عَلَيَّ أَنْ عَبَّدتَّ بَنِي إِسْرَائِيلَ

22 Is that the favor you taunt me with, although you have enslaved the Children of Israel?"

٢٣ قَالَ فِرْعَوْنُ وَمَا رَبُّ الْعَالَمِينَ		**23**
23 Pharaoh said, "And what is the Lord of the Worlds?"		20:49–50; 25:60

٢٤ قَالَ رَبُّ السَّمَاوَاتِ وَالْأَرْضِ وَمَا بَيْنَهُمَا ۖ إِن كُنتُم مُّوقِنِينَ		**24**
24 He said, "The Lord of the heavens and the earth, and everything between them, if you are aware."		19:65; 44:7

٢٥ قَالَ لِمَنْ حَوْلَهُ أَلَا تَسْتَمِعُونَ

25 He said to those around him, "Do you not hear?"

٢٦ قَالَ رَبُّكُمْ وَرَبُّ آبَائِكُمُ الْأَوَّلِينَ

26 He said, "Your Lord and the Lord of your ancestors of old."

٢٧ قَالَ إِنَّ رَسُولَكُمُ الَّذِي أُرْسِلَ إِلَيْكُمْ لَمَجْنُونٌ

27 He said, "This messenger of yours, who is sent to you, is crazy."

27
7:184

٢٨ قَالَ رَبُّ الْمَشْرِقِ وَالْمَغْرِبِ وَمَا بَيْنَهُمَا ۖ إِنْ كُنْتُمْ تَعْقِلُونَ

28 He said, "Lord of the East and the West, and everything between them, if you understand."

28
2:115; 26:24; 73:9

٢٩ قَالَ لَئِنِ اتَّخَذْتَ إِلَٰهًا غَيْرِي لَأَجْعَلَنَّكَ مِنَ الْمَسْجُونِينَ

29 He said, "If you accept any god other than me, I will make you a prisoner."

29
28:38; 79:24

٣٠ قَالَ أَوَلَوْ جِئْتُكَ بِشَيْءٍ مُبِينٍ

30 He said, "What if I bring you something convincing?"

٣١ قَالَ فَأْتِ بِهِ إِنْ كُنْتَ مِنَ الصَّادِقِينَ

31 He said, "Bring it, if you are being truthful."

31
7:106

٣٢ فَأَلْقَىٰ عَصَاهُ فَإِذَا هِيَ ثُعْبَانٌ مُبِينٌ

32 So he cast his staff; and it was a serpent, plain to see.

32–37
7:107–112; 20:26–27;
27:10–14; 28:31–32

٣٣ وَنَزَعَ يَدَهُ فَإِذَا هِيَ بَيْضَاءُ لِلنَّاظِرِينَ

33 And he pulled his hand; and it was white, for all to see.

٣٤ قَالَ لِلْمَلَإِ حَوْلَهُ إِنَّ هَٰذَا لَسَاحِرٌ عَلِيمٌ

34 He said to the dignitaries around him, "This is a skilled magician.

٣٥ يُرِيدُ أَنْ يُخْرِجَكُمْ مِنْ أَرْضِكُمْ بِسِحْرِهِ فَمَاذَا تَأْمُرُونَ

35 He intends to drive you out of your land with his magic, so what do you recommend?"

٣٦ قَالُوا أَرْجِهْ وَأَخَاهُ وَابْعَثْ فِي الْمَدَائِنِ حَاشِرِينَ

36 They said, "Delay him and his brother, and send recruiters to the cities.

٣٧ يَأْتُوكَ بِكُلِّ سَحَّارٍ عَلِيمٍ

37 To bring you every experienced magician."

٣٨ فَجُمِعَ السَّحَرَةُ لِمِيقَاتِ يَوْمٍ مَعْلُومٍ

38 So the magicians were gathered for the appointment on a specified day.

وَقِيلَ لِلنَّاسِ هَلْ أَنتُم مُّجْتَمِعُونَ ٣٩

39 And it was said to the people, "Are you all gathered?

لَعَلَّنَا نَتَّبِعُ السَّحَرَةَ إِن كَانُوا هُمُ الْغَالِبِينَ ٤٠

40 That we may follow the magicians, if they are the winners."

فَلَمَّا جَاءَ السَّحَرَةُ قَالُوا لِفِرْعَوْنَ أَئِنَّ لَنَا لَأَجْرًا إِن كُنَّا نَحْنُ الْغَالِبِينَ ٤١

41 When the magicians arrived, they said to Pharaoh, "Is there a reward for us, if we are the winners?"

41–42
PP 7:113–114

قَالَ نَعَمْ وَإِنَّكُمْ إِذًا لَّمِنَ الْمُقَرَّبِينَ ٤٢

42 He said, "Yes, and you will be among those favored."

قَالَ لَهُم مُّوسَىٰ أَلْقُوا مَا أَنتُم مُّلْقُونَ ٤٣

43 Moses said to them, "Present what you intend to present."

43–45
7:115–118; 10:80–81;
20:65–68

فَأَلْقَوْا حِبَالَهُمْ وَعِصِيَّهُمْ وَقَالُوا بِعِزَّةِ فِرْعَوْنَ إِنَّا لَنَحْنُ الْغَالِبُونَ ٤٤

44 So they threw their ropes and their sticks, and said, "By the majesty of Pharaoh, we will be the winners."

فَأَلْقَىٰ مُوسَىٰ عَصَاهُ فَإِذَا هِيَ تَلْقَفُ مَا يَأْفِكُونَ ٤٥

45 Then Moses threw his staff, and behold, it began swallowing their trickery.

فَأُلْقِيَ السَّحَرَةُ سَاجِدِينَ ٤٦

46 And the magicians fell down prostrating.

46–50
7:120–125; 20:71

قَالُوا آمَنَّا بِرَبِّ الْعَالَمِينَ ٤٧

47 They said, "We have believed in the Lord of the Worlds.

رَبِّ مُوسَىٰ وَهَارُونَ ٤٨

48 The Lord of Moses and Aaron."

قَالَ آمَنتُمْ لَهُ قَبْلَ أَنْ آذَنَ لَكُمْ ۖ إِنَّهُ لَكَبِيرُكُمُ الَّذِي عَلَّمَكُمُ السِّحْرَ فَلَسَوْفَ تَعْلَمُونَ ۚ لَأُقَطِّعَنَّ أَيْدِيَكُمْ وَأَرْجُلَكُم مِّنْ خِلَافٍ وَلَأُصَلِّبَنَّكُمْ أَجْمَعِينَ ٤٩

49–50
7:124–125

49 He said, "Did you believe in Him before I have given you permission? He must be your chief, who taught you magic. You will soon know. I will cut off your hands and feet on opposite sides, and I will crucify you all."

قَالُوا لَا ضَيْرَ ۖ إِنَّا إِلَىٰ رَبِّنَا مُنقَلِبُونَ ٥٠

50 They said, "No problem. To our Lord we will return.

إِنَّا نَطْمَعُ أَن يَغْفِرَ لَنَا رَبُّنَا خَطَايَانَا أَن كُنَّا أَوَّلَ الْمُؤْمِنِينَ ٥١

51 We are eager for our Lord to forgive us our sins, since we are the first of the believers."

٥٢ وَأَوْحَيْنَا إِلَىٰ مُوسَىٰ أَنْ أَسْرِ بِعِبَادِي إِنَّكُم مُّتَّبَعُونَ	**52** 20:77; 44:23

52 And We inspired Moses: "Travel with My servants by night. You will be followed."

٥٣ فَأَرْسَلَ فِرْعَوْنُ فِي الْمَدَائِنِ حَاشِرِينَ

53 Pharaoh sent heralds to the cities.

٥٤ إِنَّ هَٰؤُلَاءِ لَشِرْذِمَةٌ قَلِيلُونَ

54 "These are a small gang.

٥٥ وَإِنَّهُمْ لَنَا لَغَائِظُونَ

55 And they are enraging us.

٥٦ وَإِنَّا لَجَمِيعٌ حَاذِرُونَ   **56**
                                   54:44

56 But we are a vigilant multitude."

٥٧ فَأَخْرَجْنَاهُم مِّن جَنَّاتٍ وَعُيُونٍ   **57**
                                              44:25

57 So We drove them out of gardens and springs.

٥٨ وَكُنُوزٍ وَمَقَامٍ كَرِيمٍ

58 And treasures and noble dwellings.

٥٩ كَذَٰلِكَ وَأَوْرَثْنَاهَا بَنِي إِسْرَائِيلَ   **59**
                                                    7:137; 28:5; 42:36;
                                                    44:28

59 So it was. And We made the Children of Israel inherit them.

٦٠ فَأَتْبَعُوهُم مُّشْرِقِينَ   **60**
                                  10:90; 20:78

60 And they pursued them at sunrise.

٦١ فَلَمَّا تَرَاءَى الْجَمْعَانِ قَالَ أَصْحَابُ مُوسَىٰ إِنَّا لَمُدْرَكُونَ

61 When the two groups sighted each other, the followers of Moses said, "We are being overtaken."

٦٢ قَالَ كَلَّا ۖ إِنَّ مَعِيَ رَبِّي سَيَهْدِينِ

62 He said, "No; my Lord is with me, He will guide me."

٦٣ فَأَوْحَيْنَا إِلَىٰ مُوسَىٰ أَنِ اضْرِب بِّعَصَاكَ الْبَحْرَ ۖ فَانفَلَقَ فَكَانَ كُلُّ فِرْقٍ كَالطَّوْدِ الْعَظِيمِ   **63–66**
                                                                                                                            2:50; 10:90; 20:77

63 We inspired Moses: "Strike the sea with your staff." Whereupon it parted, and each part was like a huge hill.

٦٤ وَأَزْلَفْنَا ثَمَّ الْآخَرِينَ

64 And there We brought the others near.

٦٥ وَأَنجَيْنَا مُوسَىٰ وَمَن مَّعَهُ أَجْمَعِينَ

65 And We saved Moses and those with him, all together.

٦٦ ثُمَّ أَغْرَقْنَا الْآخَرِينَ

66 Then We drowned the others.

٦٧ إِنَّ فِي ذَٰلِكَ لَآيَةً ۖ وَمَا كَانَ أَكْثَرُهُم مُّؤْمِنِينَ

67 In that there is a sign, but most of them are not believers.

٦٨ وَإِنَّ رَبَّكَ لَهُوَ الْعَزِيزُ الرَّحِيمُ

68 Surely, your Lord is the Almighty, the Merciful.

٦٩ وَاتْلُ عَلَيْهِمْ نَبَأَ إِبْرَاهِيمَ

69 And relate to them the story of Abraham.

٧٠ إِذْ قَالَ لِأَبِيهِ وَقَوْمِهِ مَا تَعْبُدُونَ

70 When he said to his father and his people, "What do you worship?"

70
6:74; 19:42; 21:52; 37:85

٧١ قَالُوا نَعْبُدُ أَصْنَامًا فَنَظَلُّ لَهَا عَاكِفِينَ

71 They said, "We worship idols, and we remain devoted to them."

٧٢ قَالَ هَلْ يَسْمَعُونَكُمْ إِذْ تَدْعُونَ

72 He said, "Do they hear you when you pray?

72–73
6:71; 10:18, 106; 21:66; 22:12; 25:55; 29:17

٧٣ أَوْ يَنفَعُونَكُمْ أَوْ يَضُرُّونَ

73 Or do they benefit you, or harm you?"

٧٤ قَالُوا بَلْ وَجَدْنَا آبَاءَنَا كَذَٰلِكَ يَفْعَلُونَ

74 They said, "But we found our ancestors doing so."

74
10:78; 21:53

٧٥ قَالَ أَفَرَأَيْتُم مَّا كُنتُمْ تَعْبُدُونَ

75 He said, "Have you considered what you worship.

٧٦ أَنتُمْ وَآبَاؤُكُمُ الْأَقْدَمُونَ

76 You and your ancient ancestors?

٧٧ فَإِنَّهُمْ عَدُوٌّ لِّي إِلَّا رَبَّ الْعَالَمِينَ

77 They are enemies to me, but not so the Lord of the Worlds.

٧٨ الَّذِي خَلَقَنِي فَهُوَ يَهْدِينِ

78 He who created me, and guides me.

78
37:99; 43:27

٧٩ وَالَّذِي هُوَ يُطْعِمُنِي وَيَسْقِينِ

79 He who feeds me, and waters me.

٨٠ وَإِذَا مَرِضْتُ فَهُوَ يَشْفِينِ

80 And when I get sick, He heals me.

٨١ وَالَّذِي يُمِيتُنِي ثُمَّ يُحْيِينِ

81 He who makes me die, and then revives me.

81
2:28; 22:66; 30:40

٨٢ وَالَّذِي أَطْمَعُ أَنْ يَغْفِرَ لِي خَطِيئَتِي يَوْمَ الدِّينِ

82 He who, I hope, will forgive my sins on the Day of the Reckoning."

٨٣ رَبِّ هَبْ لِي حُكْمًا وَأَلْحِقْنِي بِالصَّالِحِينَ

83 "My Lord! Grant me wisdom, and include me with the righteous.

٨٤ وَاجْعَلْ لِي لِسَانَ صِدْقٍ فِي الْآخِرِينَ

84 And give me a reputation of truth among the others.

٨٥ وَاجْعَلْنِي مِنْ وَرَثَةِ جَنَّةِ النَّعِيمِ

85 And make me of the inheritors of the Garden of Bliss.

٨٦ وَاغْفِرْ لِأَبِي إِنَّهُ كَانَ مِنَ الضَّالِّينَ

86 And forgive my father—he was one of the misguided.

86
14:41; 19:47; 60:4

٨٧ وَلَا تُخْزِنِي يَوْمَ يُبْعَثُونَ

87 And do not disgrace me on the Day they are resurrected.

87
3:194

٨٨ يَوْمَ لَا يَنْفَعُ مَالٌ وَلَا بَنُونَ

88 The Day when neither wealth nor children will help.

٨٩ إِلَّا مَنْ أَتَى اللَّهَ بِقَلْبٍ سَلِيمٍ

89 Except for him who comes to God with a sound heart."

٩٠ وَأُزْلِفَتِ الْجَنَّةُ لِلْمُتَّقِينَ

90 And Paradise will be brought near for the righteous.

90
50:31; 81:13

٩١ وَبُرِّزَتِ الْجَحِيمُ لِلْغَاوِينَ

91 And the Blaze will be displayed to the deviators.

91
79:36

٩٢ وَقِيلَ لَهُمْ أَيْنَ مَا كُنْتُمْ تَعْبُدُونَ

92 And it will be said to them, "Where are those you used to worship?"

92–93
7:37, 192; 40:73

٩٣ مِنْ دُونِ اللَّهِ هَلْ يَنْصُرُونَكُمْ أَوْ يَنْتَصِرُونَ

93 Besides God? Can they help you, or help themselves?"

٩٤ فَكُبْكِبُوا فِيهَا هُمْ وَالْغَاوُونَ

94 Then they will be toppled into it, together with the seducers.

94
27:90

٩٥ وَجُنُودُ إِبْلِيسَ أَجْمَعُونَ

95 And the soldiers of Satan, all of them.

٩٦ قَالُوا وَهُمْ فِيهَا يَخْتَصِمُونَ

96 They will say, as they feud in it.

٩٧ تَاللَّهِ إِنْ كُنَّا لَفِي ضَلَالٍ مُبِينٍ

97 "By God, We were in evident error.

٩٨ إِذْ نُسَوِّيكُم بِرَبِّ الْعَالَمِينَ

98 For equating you with the Lord of the Worlds.

٩٩ وَمَا أَضَلَّنَا إِلَّا الْمُجْرِمُونَ

99 No one misled us except the sinners.

١٠٠ فَمَا لَنَا مِن شَافِعِينَ

100 Now we have no intercessors.

١٠١ وَلَا صَدِيقٍ حَمِيمٍ

101 And no sincere friend.

١٠٢ فَلَوْ أَنَّ لَنَا كَرَّةً فَنَكُونَ مِنَ الْمُؤْمِنِينَ

102
2:167; 39:58

102 If only we could have another chance, we would be among the faithful."

١٠٣ إِنَّ فِي ذَٰلِكَ لَآيَةً ۖ وَمَا كَانَ أَكْثَرُهُم مُّؤْمِنِينَ

103 Surely in this is a sign, but most of them are not believers.

١٠٤ وَإِنَّ رَبَّكَ لَهُوَ الْعَزِيزُ الرَّحِيمُ

104 Your Lord is the Almighty, the Merciful.

١٠٥ كَذَّبَتْ قَوْمُ نُوحٍ الْمُرْسَلِينَ

105
7:59; 22:42

105 The people of Noah disbelieved the messengers.

١٠٦ إِذْ قَالَ لَهُمْ أَخُوهُمْ نُوحٌ أَلَا تَتَّقُونَ

106 Their brother Noah said to them, "Do you not fear?

١٠٧ إِنِّي لَكُمْ رَسُولٌ أَمِينٌ

107–109
pp 26:125–127, 143–145, 162–164, 178–180

107 I am to you a faithful messenger.

١٠٨ فَاتَّقُوا اللَّهَ وَأَطِيعُونِ

108 So fear God, and obey me.

١٠٩ وَمَا أَسْأَلُكُمْ عَلَيْهِ مِنْ أَجْرٍ ۖ إِنْ أَجْرِيَ إِلَّا عَلَىٰ رَبِّ الْعَالَمِينَ

109 I ask of you no payment for this. My payment is only from the Lord of the Worlds.

١١٠ فَاتَّقُوا اللَّهَ وَأَطِيعُونِ

110 So fear God, and obey me."

١١١ قَالُوا أَنُؤْمِنُ لَكَ وَاتَّبَعَكَ الْأَرْذَلُونَ

111–113
6:52; 11:27

111 They said, "Shall we believe in you, when it is the lowliest who follow you?"

١١٢ قَالَ وَمَا عِلْمِي بِمَا كَانُوا يَعْمَلُونَ

112 He said, "What do I know about what they do?

١١٣ إِنْ حِسَابُهُمْ إِلَّا عَلَىٰ رَبِّي ۖ لَوْ تَشْعُرُونَ

113 Their account rests only with my Lord, if you have sense.

١١٤ وَمَا أَنَا بِطَارِدِ الْمُؤْمِنِينَ

114 And I am not about to drive away the believers.

114
15:89

١١٥ إِنْ أَنَا إِلَّا نَذِيرٌ مُبِينٌ

115 I am only a clear warner."

١١٦ قَالُوا لَئِنْ لَمْ تَنْتَهِ يَا نُوحُ لَتَكُونَنَّ مِنَ الْمَرْجُومِينَ

116 They said, "If you do not refrain, O Noah, you will be stoned."

116
19:46; 26:167; 36:19; 71:5–7

١١٧ قَالَ رَبِّ إِنَّ قَوْمِي كَذَّبُونِ

117 He said, "My Lord, my people have denied me.

١١٨ فَافْتَحْ بَيْنِي وَبَيْنَهُمْ فَتْحًا وَنَجِّنِي وَمَنْ مَعِيَ مِنَ الْمُؤْمِنِينَ

118 So judge between me and them decisively, and deliver me and the believers who are with me.

١١٩ فَأَنْجَيْنَاهُ وَمَنْ مَعَهُ فِي الْفُلْكِ الْمَشْحُونِ

119 So We delivered him and those with him in the laden Ark.

119–120
7:64

١٢٠ ثُمَّ أَغْرَقْنَا بَعْدُ الْبَاقِينَ

120 Then We drowned the rest.

١٢١ إِنَّ فِي ذَٰلِكَ لَآيَةً ۖ وَمَا كَانَ أَكْثَرُهُمْ مُؤْمِنِينَ

121 In that is a sign, but most of them are not believers.

١٢٢ وَإِنَّ رَبَّكَ لَهُوَ الْعَزِيزُ الرَّحِيمُ

122 Your Lord is the Almighty, the Merciful.

١٢٣ كَذَّبَتْ عَادٌ الْمُرْسَلِينَ

123 'Ād disbelieved the messengers.

123
7:65; 22:42

١٢٤ إِذْ قَالَ لَهُمْ أَخُوهُمْ هُودٌ أَلَا تَتَّقُونَ

124 When their brother Hūd said to them, "Do you not fear?

١٢٥ إِنِّي لَكُمْ رَسُولٌ أَمِينٌ

125 I am to you a faithful messenger.

125–127
pp 26:107–109, 143–145, 162–164, 178–180

١٢٦ فَاتَّقُوا اللَّهَ وَأَطِيعُونِ

126 So fear God, and obey me.

١٢٧ وَمَا أَسْأَلُكُمْ عَلَيْهِ مِنْ أَجْرٍ ۖ إِنْ أَجْرِيَ إِلَّا عَلَىٰ رَبِّ الْعَالَمِينَ

127 I ask of you no payment for this. My payment is only from the Lord of the Worlds.

۱۲۸ أَتَبْنُونَ بِكُلِّ رِيعٍ آيَةً تَعْبَثُونَ

128 Do you build a monument on every height for vanity's sake?

۱۲۹ وَتَتَّخِذُونَ مَصَانِعَ لَعَلَّكُمْ تَخْلُدُونَ

129 And you set up fortresses, hoping to live forever?

۱۳۰ وَإِذَا بَطَشْتُمْ بَطَشْتُمْ جَبَّارِينَ

130 And when you strike, you strike mercilessly?

۱۳۱ فَاتَّقُوا اللَّهَ وَأَطِيعُونِ

131 So fear God, and obey me.

۱۳۲ وَاتَّقُوا الَّذِي أَمَدَّكُم بِمَا تَعْلَمُونَ

132 And reverence Him, who supplied you with everything you know.

132–134
17:6; 23:55; 71:12

۱۳۳ أَمَدَّكُم بِأَنْعَامٍ وَبَنِينَ

133 He supplied you with livestock and children.

۱۳٤ وَجَنَّاتٍ وَعُيُونٍ

134 And gardens and springs.

۱۳٥ إِنِّي أَخَافُ عَلَيْكُمْ عَذَابَ يَوْمٍ عَظِيمٍ

135 I fear for you the punishment of an awesome Day."

۱۳٦ قَالُوا سَوَاءٌ عَلَيْنَا أَوَعَظْتَ أَمْ لَمْ تَكُنْ مِنَ الْوَاعِظِينَ

136 They said, "It is the same for us, whether you lecture us, or do not lecture.

136
2:6; 36:10

۱۳۷ إِنْ هَذَا إِلَّا خُلُقُ الْأَوَّلِينَ

137 This is nothing but morals of the ancients.

۱۳۸ وَمَا نَحْنُ بِمُعَذَّبِينَ

138 And we will not be punished."

۱۳۹ فَكَذَّبُوهُ فَأَهْلَكْنَاهُمْ ۗ إِنَّ فِي ذَلِكَ لَآيَةً ۖ وَمَا كَانَ أَكْثَرُهُم مُّؤْمِنِينَ

139 So they denied him, and We destroyed them. Surely in this is a sign, but most of them are not believers.

۱٤۰ وَإِنَّ رَبَّكَ لَهُوَ الْعَزِيزُ الرَّحِيمُ

140 Your Lord is the Almighty, the Merciful.

۱٤۱ كَذَّبَتْ ثَمُودُ الْمُرْسَلِينَ

141 Thamūd disbelieved the messengers.

141
7:73; 15:80; 22:42

۱٤۲ إِذْ قَالَ لَهُمْ أَخُوهُمْ صَالِحٌ أَلَا تَتَّقُونَ

142 When their brother Ṣāliḥ said to them, "Do you not fear?

143 إِنِّي لَكُمْ رَسُولٌ أَمِينٌ	**143–145** pp 26:107–109, 125–127, 162–164, 178–180

143 I am to you a faithful messenger.

144 فَاتَّقُوا اللَّهَ وَأَطِيعُونِ

144 So fear God, and obey me.

145 وَمَا أَسْأَلُكُمْ عَلَيْهِ مِنْ أَجْرٍ ۖ إِنْ أَجْرِيَ إِلَّا عَلَىٰ رَبِّ الْعَالَمِينَ

145 I ask of you no payment for it. My payment is only from the Lord of the Worlds.

146 أَتُتْرَكُونَ فِي مَا هَاهُنَا آمِنِينَ	**146–149** 44:25–27

146 Will you be left secure in what is here?

147 فِي جَنَّاتٍ وَعُيُونٍ

147 In gardens and springs?

148 وَزُرُوعٍ وَنَخْلٍ طَلْعُهَا هَضِيمٌ

148 And fields, and palm-trees whose fruits are delicious?

149 وَتَنْحِتُونَ مِنَ الْجِبَالِ بُيُوتًا فَارِهِينَ

149 And you skillfully carve houses in the mountains?

150 فَاتَّقُوا اللَّهَ وَأَطِيعُونِ

150 So fear God, and obey me.

151 وَلَا تُطِيعُوا أَمْرَ الْمُسْرِفِينَ

151 And do not obey the command of the extravagant.

152 الَّذِينَ يُفْسِدُونَ فِي الْأَرْضِ وَلَا يُصْلِحُونَ	**152** 2:11; 7:142; 27:48

152 Who spread turmoil on earth, and do not reform."

153 قَالُوا إِنَّمَا أَنْتَ مِنَ الْمُسَحَّرِينَ	**153** pp 26:185

153 They said, "You are surely one of the bewitched.

154 مَا أَنْتَ إِلَّا بَشَرٌ مِثْلُنَا فَأْتِ بِآيَةٍ إِنْ كُنْتَ مِنَ الصَّادِقِينَ

154 You are nothing but a man like us. So bring us a sign, if you are truthful.

155 قَالَ هَٰذِهِ نَاقَةٌ لَهَا شِرْبٌ وَلَكُمْ شِرْبُ يَوْمٍ مَعْلُومٍ	**155** 7:78; 11:67; 54:30

155 He said, "This is a she-camel; she has her turn of drinking, and you have your turn of drinking—on a specified day.

156 وَلَا تَمَسُّوهَا بِسُوءٍ فَيَأْخُذَكُمْ عَذَابُ يَوْمٍ عَظِيمٍ

156 And do not touch her with harm, lest the punishment of a great day seizes you."

١٥٧ فَعَقَرُوهَا فَأَصْبَحُوا نَادِمِينَ	**157**	
157 But they slaughtered her, and became full of remorse.	90:14	

١٥٨ فَأَخَذَهُمُ الْعَذَابُ ۗ إِنَّ فِي ذَٰلِكَ لَآيَةً ۖ وَمَا كَانَ أَكْثَرُهُم مُّؤْمِنِينَ

158 So the punishment overtook them. Surely in this is a sign, but most of them are not believers.

١٥٩ وَإِنَّ رَبَّكَ لَهُوَ الْعَزِيزُ الرَّحِيمُ

159 Your Lord is the Almighty, the Merciful.

١٦٠ كَذَّبَتْ قَوْمُ لُوطٍ الْمُرْسَلِينَ	**160**	
160 The people of Lot disbelieved the messengers.	7:80	

١٦١ إِذْ قَالَ لَهُمْ أَخُوهُمْ لُوطٌ أَلَا تَتَّقُونَ

161 When their brother Lot said to them, "Do you not fear?

١٦٢ إِنِّي لَكُمْ رَسُولٌ أَمِينٌ	**162–164**	
162 I am to you a faithful messenger.	pp 26:105–107, 127–129, 143–145 178–180	

١٦٣ فَاتَّقُوا اللَّهَ وَأَطِيعُونِ

163 So fear God, and obey me.

١٦٤ وَمَا أَسْأَلُكُمْ عَلَيْهِ مِنْ أَجْرٍ ۖ إِنْ أَجْرِيَ إِلَّا عَلَىٰ رَبِّ الْعَالَمِينَ

164 I ask of you no payment for it. My payment is only from the Lord of the Worlds.

١٦٥ أَتَأْتُونَ الذُّكْرَانَ مِنَ الْعَالَمِينَ	**165**	
165 Do you approach the males of the world?	7:80; 27:55; 29:28	

١٦٦ وَتَذَرُونَ مَا خَلَقَ لَكُمْ رَبُّكُم مِّنْ أَزْوَاجِكُم ۚ بَلْ أَنتُمْ قَوْمٌ عَادُونَ

166 And forsake the wives your Lord created for you? Indeed, you are intrusive people."

١٦٧ قَالُوا لَئِن لَّمْ تَنتَهِ يَا لُوطُ لَتَكُونَنَّ مِنَ الْمُخْرَجِينَ	**167**	
167 They said, "Unless you refrain, O Lot, you will be expelled."	7:82	

١٦٨ قَالَ إِنِّي لِعَمَلِكُم مِّنَ الْقَالِينَ

168 He said, "I certainly deplore your conduct."

١٦٩ رَبِّ نَجِّنِي وَأَهْلِي مِمَّا يَعْمَلُونَ

169 "My Lord, save me and my family from what they do."

١٧٠ فَنَجَّيْنَاهُ وَأَهْلَهُ أَجْمَعِينَ	**170**	
170 So We saved him and his family, altogether.	37:134	

١٧١ إِلَّا عَجُوزًا فِي الْغَابِرِينَ

171 Except for an old woman among those who tarried.

	١٧٢ ثُمَّ دَمَّرْنَا الْآخَرِينَ	**172**
172 Then We destroyed the others.		37:136
	١٧٣ وَأَمْطَرْنَا عَلَيْهِم مَّطَرًا ۖ فَسَاءَ مَطَرُ الْمُنذَرِينَ	**173**
173 And We rained down on them a rain. Dreadful is the rain of those forewarned.		7:84; 27:58
	١٧٤ إِنَّ فِي ذَٰلِكَ لَآيَةً ۖ وَمَا كَانَ أَكْثَرُهُم مُّؤْمِنِينَ	
174 Surely in this is a sign, but most of them are not believers.		
	١٧٥ وَإِنَّ رَبَّكَ لَهُوَ الْعَزِيزُ الرَّحِيمُ	
175 Your Lord is the Almighty, the Merciful.		
	١٧٦ كَذَّبَ أَصْحَابُ الْأَيْكَةِ الْمُرْسَلِينَ	**176**
176 The People of the Woods disbelieved the messengers.		15:78
	١٧٧ إِذْ قَالَ لَهُمْ شُعَيْبٌ أَلَا تَتَّقُونَ	**177**
177 When Shuaib said to them, "Do you not fear?		7:85
	١٧٨ إِنِّي لَكُمْ رَسُولٌ أَمِينٌ	**178–180**
178 I am to you a trustworthy messenger.		pp 26:105–107, 127–129, 143–145, 163–165
	١٧٩ فَاتَّقُوا اللَّهَ وَأَطِيعُونِ	
179 So fear God, and obey me.		
	١٨٠ وَمَا أَسْأَلُكُمْ عَلَيْهِ مِنْ أَجْرٍ ۖ إِنْ أَجْرِيَ إِلَّا عَلَىٰ رَبِّ الْعَالَمِينَ	
180 I ask of you no payment for it. My payment is only from the Lord of the Worlds.		
	١٨١ أَوْفُوا الْكَيْلَ وَلَا تَكُونُوا مِنَ الْمُخْسِرِينَ	**181–183**
181 Give full measure, and do not cheat.		6:152; 7:85; 11:84; 17:35
	١٨٢ وَزِنُوا بِالْقِسْطَاسِ الْمُسْتَقِيمِ	
182 And weigh with accurate scales.		
	١٨٣ وَلَا تَبْخَسُوا النَّاسَ أَشْيَاءَهُمْ وَلَا تَعْثَوْا فِي الْأَرْضِ مُفْسِدِينَ	
183 And do not defraud people of their belongings, and do not work corruption in the land.		
	١٨٤ وَاتَّقُوا الَّذِي خَلَقَكُمْ وَالْجِبِلَّةَ الْأَوَّلِينَ	
184 And fear Him who created you and the masses of old."		
	١٨٥ قَالُوا إِنَّمَا أَنتَ مِنَ الْمُسَحَّرِينَ	**185**
185 They said, "You are one of those bewitched.		pp 26:153

١٨٦ وَمَا أَنتَ إِلَّا بَشَرٌ مِّثْلُنَا وَإِن نَّظُنُّكَ لَمِنَ الْكَاذِبِينَ

186 And you are nothing but a man like us; and we think that you are a liar.

١٨٧ فَأَسْقِطْ عَلَيْنَا كِسَفًا مِّنَ السَّمَاءِ إِن كُنتَ مِنَ الصَّادِقِينَ

187 So bring down on us pieces from the sky, if you are truthful."

187
17:92; 34:9; 52:44

١٨٨ قَالَ رَبِّي أَعْلَمُ بِمَا تَعْمَلُونَ

188 He said, "My Lord is Well Aware of what you do."

188
22:68

١٨٩ فَكَذَّبُوهُ فَأَخَذَهُمْ عَذَابُ يَوْمِ الظُّلَّةِ ۚ إِنَّهُ كَانَ عَذَابَ يَوْمٍ عَظِيمٍ

189 But they denied him. So the punishment of the day of gloom gripped them. It was the punishment of a great day.

١٩٠ إِنَّ فِي ذَٰلِكَ لَآيَةً ۖ وَمَا كَانَ أَكْثَرُهُم مُّؤْمِنِينَ

190 Surely in this is a sign, but most of them are not believers.

١٩١ وَإِنَّ رَبَّكَ لَهُوَ الْعَزِيزُ الرَّحِيمُ

191 Your Lord is the Almighty, the Merciful.

١٩٢ وَإِنَّهُ لَتَنزِيلُ رَبِّ الْعَالَمِينَ

192 It is a revelation from the Lord of the Worlds.

١٩٣ نَزَلَ بِهِ الرُّوحُ الْأَمِينُ

193 The Honest Spirit came down with it.

193
16:2; 40:15

١٩٤ عَلَىٰ قَلْبِكَ لِتَكُونَ مِنَ الْمُنذِرِينَ

194 Upon your heart, that you may be one of the warners.

١٩٥ بِلِسَانٍ عَرَبِيٍّ مُّبِينٍ

195 In a clear Arabic tongue.

195
11:2

١٩٦ وَإِنَّهُ لَفِي زُبُرِ الْأَوَّلِينَ

196 And it is in the scriptures of the ancients.

196
3:184; 16:43; 20:33; 35:25

١٩٧ أَوَلَمْ يَكُن لَّهُمْ آيَةً أَن يَعْلَمَهُ عُلَمَاءُ بَنِي إِسْرَائِيلَ

197 Is it not a sign for them that the scholars of the Children of Israel recognized it?

197
10:94; 16:43; 17:101

١٩٨ وَلَوْ نَزَّلْنَاهُ عَلَىٰ بَعْضِ الْأَعْجَمِينَ

198 Had We revealed it to one of the foreigners.

198
41:44

١٩٩ فَقَرَأَهُ عَلَيْهِم مَّا كَانُوا بِهِ مُؤْمِنِينَ

199 And he had recited it to them, they still would not have believed in it.

٢٠٠ كَذَٰلِكَ سَلَكْنَاهُ فِي قُلُوبِ الْمُجْرِمِينَ

200 Thus We make it pass through the hearts of the guilty.

200
10:96; 15:12

٢٠١ لَا يُؤْمِنُونَ بِهِ حَتَّىٰ يَرَوُا الْعَذَابَ الْأَلِيمَ

201 They will not believe in it until they witness the painful punishment.

٢٠٢ فَيَأْتِيَهُم بَغْتَةً وَهُمْ لَا يَشْعُرُونَ

202 It will come to them suddenly, while they are unaware.

٢٠٣ فَيَقُولُوا هَلْ نَحْنُ مُنظَرُونَ

203 Then they will say, "Are we given any respite?"

٢٠٤ أَفَبِعَذَابِنَا يَسْتَعْجِلُونَ

204 Do they seek to hasten Our punishment?

٢٠٥ أَفَرَأَيْتَ إِن مَّتَّعْنَاهُمْ سِنِينَ

205–207
19:75; 72:24

205 Have you considered: if We let them enjoy themselves for some years.

٢٠٦ ثُمَّ جَاءَهُم مَّا كَانُوا يُوعَدُونَ

206 Then there comes to them what they were promised.

٢٠٧ مَا أَغْنَىٰ عَنْهُم مَّا كَانُوا يُمَتَّعُونَ

207 Of what avail to them will be their past enjoyments?

٢٠٨ وَمَا أَهْلَكْنَا مِن قَرْيَةٍ إِلَّا لَهَا مُنذِرُونَ

208
17:15; 20:134; 28:46

208 Never did We destroy a town, but it had warners.

٢٠٩ ذِكْرَىٰ وَمَا كُنَّا ظَالِمِينَ

209 As a reminder—We are never unjust.

٢١٠ وَمَا تَنَزَّلَتْ بِهِ الشَّيَاطِينُ

210
26:221

210 It was not the devils that revealed it.

٢١١ وَمَا يَنبَغِي لَهُمْ وَمَا يَسْتَطِيعُونَ

211 It is not in their interests, nor in their power.

٢١٢ إِنَّهُمْ عَنِ السَّمْعِ لَمَعْزُولُونَ

212 They are barred from hearing.

٢١٣ فَلَا تَدْعُ مَعَ اللَّهِ إِلَٰهًا آخَرَ فَتَكُونَ مِنَ الْمُعَذَّبِينَ

213
23:117; 28:88

213 So do not pray to another god with God, else you will be of those tormented.

٢١٤ وَأَنذِرْ عَشِيرَتَكَ الْأَقْرَبِينَ

214 And warn your close relatives.

٢١٥ وَاخْفِضْ جَنَاحَكَ لِمَنِ اتَّبَعَكَ مِنَ الْمُؤْمِنِينَ

215
15:88; 17:24

215 And lower your wing to those of the believers who follow you.

216 فَإِنْ عَصَوْكَ فَقُلْ إِنِّي بَرِيءٌ مِمَّا تَعْمَلُونَ

216 And if they disobey you, say, "I am innocent of what you do."

216
10:41

217 وَتَوَكَّلْ عَلَى الْعَزِيزِ الرَّحِيمِ

217 And put your trust in the Almighty, the Merciful.

218 الَّذِي يَرَاكَ حِينَ تَقُومُ

218 He Who sees you when you rise.

219 وَتَقَلُّبَكَ فِي السَّاجِدِينَ

219 And your devotions amidst the worshipers.

220 إِنَّهُ هُوَ السَّمِيعُ الْعَلِيمُ

220 He is indeed the Hearer, the Aware.

221 هَلْ أُنَبِّئُكُمْ عَلَىٰ مَنْ تَنَزَّلُ الشَّيَاطِينُ

221 Shall I inform you upon whom the devils descend?

222 تَنَزَّلُ عَلَىٰ كُلِّ أَفَّاكٍ أَثِيمٍ

222 They descend upon every sinful liar.

223 يُلْقُونَ السَّمْعَ وَأَكْثَرُهُمْ كَاذِبُونَ

223 They give ear, and most of them are liars.

224 وَالشُّعَرَاءُ يَتَّبِعُهُمُ الْغَاوُونَ

224 And as for the poets—the deviators follow them.

224
15:42; 21:5; 36:96;
37:36; 69:41

225 أَلَمْ تَرَ أَنَّهُمْ فِي كُلِّ وَادٍ يَهِيمُونَ

225 Do you not see how they ramble in every style?

226 وَأَنَّهُمْ يَقُولُونَ مَا لَا يَفْعَلُونَ

226 And how they say what they do not do?

226
42:41–42; 61:2

227 إِلَّا الَّذِينَ آمَنُوا وَعَمِلُوا الصَّالِحَاتِ وَذَكَرُوا اللَّهَ كَثِيرًا وَانْتَصَرُوا مِنْ بَعْدِ مَا ظُلِمُوا ۗ وَسَيَعْلَمُ الَّذِينَ ظَلَمُوا أَيَّ مُنْقَلَبٍ يَنْقَلِبُونَ

227 Except for those who believe, and do good deeds, and remember God frequently, and defend themselves after they are wronged. As for those who do wrong, they will know by what overturning they will be overturned.

Sūrah 27: Al-Naml

سُورَةُ ٱلنَّمْل (The Ant)

بِسْمِ ٱللَّهِ ٱلرَّحْمَٰنِ ٱلرَّحِيمِ

١ طس ۚ تِلْكَ آيَاتُ الْقُرْآنِ وَكِتَابٍ مُبِينٍ

1 Ta, Seen. These are the Signs of the Qur'an—a book that makes things clear.

٢ هُدًى وَبُشْرَىٰ لِلْمُؤْمِنِينَ

2 Guidance and good news for the believers.

2:97; 16:89

٣ الَّذِينَ يُقِيمُونَ الصَّلَاةَ وَيُؤْتُونَ الزَّكَاةَ وَهُم بِالْآخِرَةِ هُمْ يُوقِنُونَ

3 Those who observe the prayers, and give charity regularly, and are certain of the Hereafter.

2:3, 23; 31:4

٤ إِنَّ الَّذِينَ لَا يُؤْمِنُونَ بِالْآخِرَةِ زَيَّنَّا لَهُمْ أَعْمَالَهُمْ فَهُمْ يَعْمَهُونَ

4 As for those who do not believe in the Hereafter: We made their deeds appear good to them, so they wander aimlessly.

6:108

٥ أُولَٰئِكَ الَّذِينَ لَهُمْ سُوءُ الْعَذَابِ وَهُمْ فِي الْآخِرَةِ هُمُ الْأَخْسَرُونَ

5 It is they who will receive the grievous punishment—and in the Hereafter they will be the greatest losers.

11:22

٦ وَإِنَّكَ لَتُلَقَّى الْقُرْآنَ مِن لَّدُنْ حَكِيمٍ عَلِيمٍ

6 You are receiving the Qur'an from an All-Wise, All-Knowing.

٧ إِذْ قَالَ مُوسَىٰ لِأَهْلِهِ إِنِّي آنَسْتُ نَارًا سَآتِيكُم مِّنْهَا بِخَبَرٍ أَوْ آتِيكُم بِشِهَابٍ قَبَسٍ لَّعَلَّكُمْ تَصْطَلُونَ

7 When Moses said to his family, "I have glimpsed a fire. I will bring you some news from it; or bring you a firebrand, that you may warm yourselves."

20:10; 28:29

٨ فَلَمَّا جَاءَهَا نُودِيَ أَن بُورِكَ مَن فِي النَّارِ وَمَنْ حَوْلَهَا وَسُبْحَانَ اللَّهِ رَبِّ الْعَالَمِينَ

8 Then, when he reached it, he was called: "Blessed is He who is within the fire, and He who is around it, and glorified be God, Lord of the Worlds.

20:11; 28:30

٩ يَا مُوسَىٰ إِنَّهُ أَنَا اللَّهُ الْعَزِيزُ الْحَكِيمُ

9 O Moses, it is I, God, the Almighty, the Wise.

10:107; 20:17–21; 26:32; 28:31

١٠ وَأَلْقِ عَصَاكَ ۚ فَلَمَّا رَآهَا تَهْتَزُّ كَأَنَّهَا جَانٌّ وَلَّىٰ مُدْبِرًا وَلَمْ يُعَقِّبْ ۚ يَا مُوسَىٰ لَا تَخَفْ إِنِّي لَا يَخَافُ لَدَيَّ الْمُرْسَلُونَ

10 Throw down your staff." But when he saw it quivering, as though it were a demon, he turned around not looking back. "O Moses, do not fear; the messengers do not fear in My presence.

28:31

١١ إِلَّا مَن ظَلَمَ ثُمَّ بَدَّلَ حُسْنًا بَعْدَ سُوءٍ فَإِنِّي غَفُورٌ رَحِيمٌ

11 But whoever has done wrong, and then substituted goodness in place of evil. I am Forgiving and Merciful.

١٢ وَأَدْخِلْ يَدَكَ فِي جَيْبِكَ تَخْرُجْ بَيْضَاءَ مِنْ غَيْرِ سُوءٍ فِي تِسْعِ آيَاتٍ إِلَىٰ فِرْعَوْنَ وَقَوْمِهِ ۚ إِنَّهُمْ كَانُوا قَوْمًا فَاسِقِينَ

12 Put your hand inside your pocket, and it will come out white, without blemish—among nine miracles to Pharaoh and his people, for they are immoral people."

12   7:108; 20:22; 26:33; 28:32

١٣ فَلَمَّا جَاءَتْهُمْ آيَاتُنَا مُبْصِرَةً قَالُوا هَٰذَا سِحْرٌ مُبِينٌ

13 Yet when Our enlightening signs came to them, they said, "This is obvious witchcraft."

13   10:76

١٤ وَجَحَدُوا بِهَا وَاسْتَيْقَنَتْهَا أَنفُسُهُمْ ظُلْمًا وَعُلُوًّا ۚ فَانظُرْ كَيْفَ كَانَ عَاقِبَةُ الْمُفْسِدِينَ

14 And they rejected them, although their souls were certain of them, out of wickedness and pride. So see how the outcome was for the mischief-makers.

١٥ وَلَقَدْ آتَيْنَا دَاوُودَ وَسُلَيْمَانَ عِلْمًا ۖ وَقَالَا الْحَمْدُ لِلَّهِ الَّذِي فَضَّلَنَا عَلَىٰ كَثِيرٍ مِنْ عِبَادِهِ الْمُؤْمِنِينَ

15 And We gave David and Solomon knowledge. They said, "Praise God, who has favored us over many of His believing servants."

15   17:55; 21:79

١٦ وَوَرِثَ سُلَيْمَانُ دَاوُودَ ۖ وَقَالَ يَا أَيُّهَا النَّاسُ عُلِّمْنَا مَنطِقَ الطَّيْرِ وَأُوتِينَا مِن كُلِّ شَيْءٍ ۖ إِنَّ هَٰذَا لَهُوَ الْفَضْلُ الْمُبِينُ

16 And Solomon succeeded David. He said, "O people, we were taught the language of birds, and we were given from everything. This is indeed a real blessing."

16   19:6

١٧ وَحُشِرَ لِسُلَيْمَانَ جُنُودُهُ مِنَ الْجِنِّ وَالْإِنسِ وَالطَّيْرِ فَهُمْ يُوزَعُونَ

17 To the service of Solomon were mobilized his troops of sprites, and men, and birds—all held in strict order.

١٨ حَتَّىٰ إِذَا أَتَوْا عَلَىٰ وَادِ النَّمْلِ قَالَتْ نَمْلَةٌ يَا أَيُّهَا النَّمْلُ ادْخُلُوا مَسَاكِنَكُمْ لَا يَحْطِمَنَّكُمْ سُلَيْمَانُ وَجُنُودُهُ وَهُمْ لَا يَشْعُرُونَ

18 Until, when they came upon the Valley of Ants, an ant said, "O ants! Go into your nests, lest Solomon and his troops crush you without noticing."

١٩ فَتَبَسَّمَ ضَاحِكًا مِّن قَوْلِهَا وَقَالَ رَبِّ أَوْزِعْنِي أَنْ أَشْكُرَ نِعْمَتَكَ الَّتِي أَنْعَمْتَ عَلَيَّ وَعَلَىٰ وَالِدَيَّ وَأَنْ أَعْمَلَ صَالِحًا تَرْضَاهُ وَأَدْخِلْنِي بِرَحْمَتِكَ فِي عِبَادِكَ الصَّالِحِينَ

19 He smiled and laughed at her words, and said, "My Lord, direct me to be thankful for the blessings you have bestowed upon me and upon my parents, and to do good works that please You. And admit me, by Your grace, into the company of Your virtuous servants."

٢٠ وَتَفَقَّدَ الطَّيْرَ فَقَالَ مَا لِيَ لَا أَرَى الْهُدْهُدَ أَمْ كَانَ مِنَ الْغَائِبِينَ

20 Then he inspected the birds, and said, "Why do I not see the hoopoe? Or is he among the absentees?

٢١ لَأُعَذِّبَنَّهُ عَذَابًا شَدِيدًا أَوْ لَأَذْبَحَنَّهُ أَوْ لَيَأْتِيَنِّي بِسُلْطَانٍ مُبِينٍ

21 I will punish him most severely, or slay him, unless he gives me a valid excuse."

٢٢ فَمَكَثَ غَيْرَ بَعِيدٍ فَقَالَ أَحَطتُ بِمَا لَمْ تُحِطْ بِهِ وَجِئْتُكَ مِن سَبَإٍ بِنَبَإٍ يَقِينٍ

22 But he did not stay for long. He said, "I have learnt something you did not know. I have come to you from Sheba, with reliable information.

٢٣ إِنِّي وَجَدتُّ امْرَأَةً تَمْلِكُهُمْ وَأُوتِيَتْ مِن كُلِّ شَيْءٍ وَلَهَا عَرْشٌ عَظِيمٌ

23 I found a woman ruling over them, and she was given of everything, and she has a magnificent throne.

٢٤ وَجَدتُّهَا وَقَوْمَهَا يَسْجُدُونَ لِلشَّمْسِ مِن دُونِ اللَّهِ وَزَيَّنَ لَهُمُ الشَّيْطَانُ أَعْمَالَهُمْ فَصَدَّهُمْ عَنِ السَّبِيلِ فَهُمْ لَا يَهْتَدُونَ

24–25
41:37

24 I found her and her people worshiping the sun, instead of God. Satan made their conduct appear good to them, and diverted them from the path, so they are not guided.

٢٥ أَلَّا يَسْجُدُوا لِلَّهِ الَّذِي يُخْرِجُ الْخَبْءَ فِي السَّمَاوَاتِ وَالْأَرْضِ وَيَعْلَمُ مَا تُخْفُونَ وَمَا تُعْلِنُونَ

25 If only they would worship God, who brings to light the mysteries of the heavens and the earth, and knows what you conceal and what you reveal.

٢٦ اللَّهُ لَا إِلَٰهَ إِلَّا هُوَ رَبُّ الْعَرْشِ الْعَظِيمِ ۩

26
11:5; 41:37

26 God—There is no god but He, the Lord of the Sublime Throne."

٢٧ قَالَ سَنَنظُرُ أَصَدَقْتَ أَمْ كُنتَ مِنَ الْكَاذِبِينَ

27 He said, "We will see, whether you have spoken the truth, or whether you are a liar.

٢٨ اذْهَب بِّكِتَابِي هَٰذَا فَأَلْقِهْ إِلَيْهِمْ ثُمَّ تَوَلَّ عَنْهُمْ فَانظُرْ مَاذَا يَرْجِعُونَ

28 Go with this letter of mine, and deliver it to them; then withdraw from them, and see how they respond."

٢٩ قَالَتْ يَا أَيُّهَا الْمَلَأُ إِنِّي أُلْقِيَ إِلَيَّ كِتَابٌ كَرِيمٌ

29 She said, "O Counselors, a gracious letter was delivered to me.

٣٠ إِنَّهُ مِن سُلَيْمَانَ وَإِنَّهُ بِسْمِ اللَّهِ الرَّحْمَٰنِ الرَّحِيمِ

30
1:1

30 It is from Solomon, and it is, 'In the Name of God, the Gracious, the Merciful.

٣١ أَلَّا تَعْلُوا عَلَيَّ وَأْتُونِي مُسْلِمِينَ

31 Do not defy me, and come to me submissively.'"

٣٢ قَالَتْ يَا أَيُّهَا الْمَلَأُ أَفْتُونِي فِي أَمْرِي مَا كُنتُ قَاطِعَةً أَمْرًا حَتَّىٰ تَشْهَدُونِ

32 She said, "O counselors, advise me in this matter of mine. I never make a decision unless you are present."

٣٣ قَالُوا نَحْنُ أُولُو قُوَّةٍ وَأُولُو بَأْسٍ شَدِيدٍ وَالْأَمْرُ إِلَيْكِ فَانظُرِي مَاذَا تَأْمُرِينَ

33 They said, "We are a people of might and great courage, but the decision is yours, so consider what you wish to command."

33
17:5; 48:16

٣٤ قَالَتْ إِنَّ الْمُلُوكَ إِذَا دَخَلُوا قَرْيَةً أَفْسَدُوهَا وَجَعَلُوا أَعِزَّةَ أَهْلِهَا أَذِلَّةً ۖ وَكَذَٰلِكَ يَفْعَلُونَ

34 She said, "When kings enter a city, they devastate it, and subjugate its dignified people. Thus they always do.

34
3:26; 27:37; 63:8

٣٥ وَإِنِّي مُرْسِلَةٌ إِلَيْهِم بِهَدِيَّةٍ فَنَاظِرَةٌ بِمَ يَرْجِعُ الْمُرْسَلُونَ

35 I am sending them a gift, and will see what the envoys bring back."

٣٦ فَلَمَّا جَاءَ سُلَيْمَانَ قَالَ أَتُمِدُّونَنِ بِمَالٍ فَمَا آتَانِيَ اللَّهُ خَيْرٌ مِّمَّا آتَاكُم بَلْ أَنتُم بِهَدِيَّتِكُمْ تَفْرَحُونَ

36 When he came to Solomon, he said, "Are you supplying me with money? What God has given me is better than what He has given you. It is you who delight in your gift.

٣٧ ارْجِعْ إِلَيْهِمْ فَلَنَأْتِيَنَّهُم بِجُنُودٍ لَّا قِبَلَ لَهُم بِهَا وَلَنُخْرِجَنَّهُم مِّنْهَا أَذِلَّةً وَهُمْ صَاغِرُونَ

37 Go back to them. We will come upon them with troops they cannot resist; and we will expel them from there, disgraced and humiliated."

٣٨ قَالَ يَا أَيُّهَا الْمَلَأُ أَيُّكُمْ يَأْتِينِي بِعَرْشِهَا قَبْلَ أَن يَأْتُونِي مُسْلِمِينَ

38 He said, "O notables, which one of you will bring me her throne before they come to me in submission?"

٣٩ قَالَ عِفْرِيتٌ مِّنَ الْجِنِّ أَنَا آتِيكَ بِهِ قَبْلَ أَن تَقُومَ مِن مَّقَامِكَ ۖ وَإِنِّي عَلَيْهِ لَقَوِيٌّ أَمِينٌ

39 An imp of the sprites said, "I will bring it to you before you rise from your seat. I am strong and reliable enough to do it."

٤٠ قَالَ الَّذِي عِندَهُ عِلْمٌ مِّنَ الْكِتَابِ أَنَا آتِيكَ بِهِ قَبْلَ أَن يَرْتَدَّ إِلَيْكَ طَرْفُكَ ۚ فَلَمَّا رَآهُ مُسْتَقِرًّا عِندَهُ قَالَ هَٰذَا مِن فَضْلِ رَبِّي لِيَبْلُوَنِي أَأَشْكُرُ أَمْ أَكْفُرُ ۖ وَمَن شَكَرَ فَإِنَّمَا يَشْكُرُ لِنَفْسِهِ ۖ ᵃ وَمَن كَفَرَ فَإِنَّ رَبِّي غَنِيٌّ كَرِيمٌ ᵇ

40
ᵃ 17:7; 41:46
ᵇ 14:8; 47:38; 64:6

40 He who had knowledge from the Book said, "I will bring it to you before your glance returns to you." And when he saw it settled before him, he said, "This is from the grace of my Lord, to test me, whether I am grateful or ungrateful. He who is grateful, his gratitude is to his own credit; but he who is ungrateful—my Lord is Independent and Generous."

٤١ قَالَ نَكِّرُوا لَهَا عَرْشَهَا نَنظُرْ أَتَهْتَدِي أَمْ تَكُونُ مِنَ الَّذِينَ لَا يَهْتَدُونَ

41 He said, "Disguise her throne for her, and we shall see whether she will be guided, or remains one of the misguided."

٤٢ فَلَمَّا جَاءَتْ قِيلَ أَهَٰكَذَا عَرْشُكِ ۖ قَالَتْ كَأَنَّهُ هُوَ ۚ وَأُوتِينَا الْعِلْمَ مِن قَبْلِهَا وَكُنَّا مُسْلِمِينَ

42 When she arrived, it was said, "Is your throne like this?" She said, "As if this is it." "We were given knowledge before her, and we were submissive."

٤٣ وَصَدَّهَا مَا كَانَت تَّعْبُدُ مِن دُونِ اللَّهِ ۖ إِنَّهَا كَانَتْ مِن قَوْمٍ كَافِرِينَ

43 But she was prevented by what she worshiped besides God; she belonged to a disbelieving people.

٤٤ قِيلَ لَهَا ادْخُلِي الصَّرْحَ ۖ فَلَمَّا رَأَتْهُ حَسِبَتْهُ لُجَّةً وَكَشَفَتْ عَن سَاقَيْهَا ۚ قَالَ إِنَّهُ صَرْحٌ مُّمَرَّدٌ مِّن قَوَارِيرَ ۗ قَالَتْ رَبِّ إِنِّي ظَلَمْتُ نَفْسِي وَأَسْلَمْتُ مَعَ سُلَيْمَانَ لِلَّهِ رَبِّ الْعَالَمِينَ

44 It was said to her, "Go inside the palace." And when she saw it, she thought it was a deep pond, and she bared her legs. He said, "It is a palace paved with glass." She said, "My Lord, I have done wrong to myself, and I have submitted with Solomon, to God, Lord of the Worlds."

٤٥ وَلَقَدْ أَرْسَلْنَا إِلَىٰ ثَمُودَ أَخَاهُمْ صَالِحًا أَنِ اعْبُدُوا اللَّهَ فَإِذَا هُمْ فَرِيقَانِ يَخْتَصِمُونَ

45 And We sent to Thamūd their brother Ṣāliḥ: "Worship God." But they became two disputing factions.

45
7:73

٤٦ قَالَ يَا قَوْمِ لِمَ تَسْتَعْجِلُونَ بِالسَّيِّئَةِ قَبْلَ الْحَسَنَةِ ۖ لَوْلَا تَسْتَغْفِرُونَ اللَّهَ لَعَلَّكُمْ تُرْحَمُونَ

46 He said, "O my people, why are you quick to do evil rather than good? If only you would seek God's forgiveness, so that you may be shown mercy."

46
7:131; 36:18

٤٧ قَالُوا اطَّيَّرْنَا بِكَ وَبِمَن مَّعَكَ ۚ قَالَ طَائِرُكُمْ عِندَ اللَّهِ ۖ بَلْ أَنتُمْ قَوْمٌ تُفْتَنُونَ

47 They said, "We consider you an ill omen, and those with you." He said, "Your omen is with God. In fact, you are a people being tested."

47
4:78; 36:18–19

٤٨ وَكَانَ فِي الْمَدِينَةِ تِسْعَةُ رَهْطٍ يُفْسِدُونَ فِي الْأَرْضِ وَلَا يُصْلِحُونَ

48 In the city was a gang of nine who made mischief in the land and did no good.

٤٩ قَالُوا تَقَاسَمُوا بِاللَّهِ لَنُبَيِّتَنَّهُ وَأَهْلَهُ ثُمَّ لَنَقُولَنَّ لِوَلِيِّهِ مَا شَهِدْنَا مَهْلِكَ أَهْلِهِ وَإِنَّا لَصَادِقُونَ

49 They said, "Swear by God to one another that we will attack him and his family by night, and then tell his guardian, 'We did not witness the murder of his family, and we are being truthful.'"

٥٠ وَمَكَرُوا مَكْرًا وَمَكَرْنَا مَكْرًا وَهُمْ لَا يَشْعُرُونَ

50 They planned a plan, and We planned a plan, but they did not notice.

50
3:54; 7:99; 8:30

٥١ فَانظُرْ كَيْفَ كَانَ عَاقِبَةُ مَكْرِهِمْ أَنَّا دَمَّرْنَاهُمْ وَقَوْمَهُمْ أَجْمَعِينَ	**51** 17:16

51 So note the outcome of their planning; We destroyed them and their people, altogether.

٥٢ فَتِلْكَ بُيُوتُهُمْ خَاوِيَةً بِمَا ظَلَمُوا ۗ إِنَّ فِي ذَٰلِكَ لَآيَةً لِّقَوْمٍ يَعْلَمُونَ	**52** 2:259

52 Here are their homes, in ruins, on account of their iniquities. Surely in this is a sign for people who know.

٥٣ وَأَنجَيْنَا الَّذِينَ آمَنُوا وَكَانُوا يَتَّقُونَ	**53**

53 And We saved those who believed and were pious.

٥٤ وَلُوطًا إِذْ قَالَ لِقَوْمِهِ أَتَأْتُونَ الْفَاحِشَةَ وَأَنتُمْ تُبْصِرُونَ	**54** 7:80

54 And Lot, when he said to his people, "Do you commit lewdness with open eyes?

٥٥ أَئِنَّكُمْ لَتَأْتُونَ الرِّجَالَ شَهْوَةً مِّن دُونِ النِّسَاءِ ۚ بَلْ أَنتُمْ قَوْمٌ تَجْهَلُونَ	**55** 7:81 26:165; 29:29

55 Do you lust after men instead of women? You are truly ignorant people."

٥٦ فَمَا كَانَ جَوَابَ قَوْمِهِ إِلَّا أَن قَالُوا أَخْرِجُوا آلَ لُوطٍ مِّن قَرْيَتِكُمْ ۖ إِنَّهُمْ أُنَاسٌ يَتَطَهَّرُونَ	**56** 7:82

56 But the only response of his people was to say, "Expel the family of Lot from your town. They are purist people."

٥٧ فَأَنجَيْنَاهُ وَأَهْلَهُ إِلَّا امْرَأَتَهُ قَدَّرْنَاهَا مِنَ الْغَابِرِينَ	**57** 7:83

57 So We saved him and his family, except for his wife, whom We destined to be among the laggards.

٥٨ وَأَمْطَرْنَا عَلَيْهِم مَّطَرًا ۖ فَسَاءَ مَطَرُ الْمُنذَرِينَ	**58** 7:84; 26:173

58 And We rained upon them a rain. Miserable was the rain of those forewarned.

٥٩ قُلِ الْحَمْدُ لِلَّهِ وَسَلَامٌ عَلَىٰ عِبَادِهِ الَّذِينَ اصْطَفَىٰ ۗ آللَّهُ خَيْرٌ أَمَّا يُشْرِكُونَ	**59**

59 Say, "Praise God, and peace be upon His servants whom He has selected. Is God better, or what they associate?"

٦٠ أَمَّنْ خَلَقَ السَّمَاوَاتِ وَالْأَرْضَ وَأَنزَلَ لَكُم مِّنَ السَّمَاءِ مَاءً فَأَنبَتْنَا بِهِ حَدَائِقَ ذَاتَ بَهْجَةٍ مَّا كَانَ لَكُمْ أَن تُنبِتُوا شَجَرَهَا ۗ أَإِلَٰهٌ مَّعَ اللَّهِ ۚ بَلْ هُمْ قَوْمٌ يَعْدِلُونَ	**60**

60 Or, who created the heavens and the earth, and rains down water from the sky for you? With it We produce gardens full of beauty, whose trees you could not have produced. Is there another god with God? But they are a people who equate.

٦١ أَمَّن جَعَلَ الْأَرْضَ قَرَارًا وَجَعَلَ خِلَالَهَا أَنْهَارًا وَجَعَلَ لَهَا رَوَاسِيَ وَجَعَلَ بَيْنَ الْبَحْرَيْنِ حَاجِزًا ۗ أَإِلَٰهٌ مَّعَ اللَّهِ ۚ بَلْ أَكْثَرُهُمْ لَا يَعْلَمُونَ	**61** 25:53; 35:12; 55:19

61 Or, who made the earth habitable, and made rivers flow through it, and set mountains on it, and placed a partition between the two seas? Is there another god with God? But most of them do not know.

٦٢ أَمَّن يُجِيبُ الْمُضْطَرَّ إِذَا دَعَاهُ وَيَكْشِفُ السُّوءَ وَيَجْعَلُكُمْ خُلَفَاءَ الْأَرْضِ ۗ أَإِلَٰهٌ مَّعَ اللَّهِ ۚ قَلِيلًا مَّا تَذَكَّرُونَ

62   2:186; 6:41; 11:61

62 Or, who answers the one in need when he prays to Him, and relieves adversity, and makes you successors on earth? Is there another god with God? How hardly you pay attention.

٦٣ أَمَّن يَهْدِيكُمْ فِي ظُلُمَاتِ الْبَرِّ وَالْبَحْرِ وَمَن يُرْسِلُ الرِّيَاحَ بُشْرًا بَيْنَ يَدَيْ رَحْمَتِهِ ۗ أَإِلَٰهٌ مَّعَ اللَّهِ ۚ تَعَالَى اللَّهُ عَمَّا يُشْرِكُونَ

63   6:63, 97; 7:57; 25:48

63 Or, who guides you through the darkness of land and sea, and who sends the winds as heralds of His mercy? Is there another god with God? Most exalted is God, above what they associate.

٦٤ أَمَّن يَبْدَأُ الْخَلْقَ ثُمَّ يُعِيدُهُ وَمَن يَرْزُقُكُم مِّنَ السَّمَاءِ وَالْأَرْضِ ۗ أَإِلَٰهٌ مَّعَ اللَّهِ ۚ قُلْ هَاتُوا بُرْهَانَكُمْ إِن كُنتُمْ صَادِقِينَ

64   10:4

64 Or, who originates the creation and then repeats it, and who gives you livelihood from the sky and the earth? Is there another god with God? Say, "Produce your evidence, if you are truthful."

٦٥ قُل لَّا يَعْلَمُ مَن فِي السَّمَاوَاتِ وَالْأَرْضِ الْغَيْبَ إِلَّا اللَّهُ ۚ وَمَا يَشْعُرُونَ أَيَّانَ يُبْعَثُونَ

65   6:59

65 Say, "No one in the heavens or on earth knows the future except God; and they do not perceive when they will be resurrected."

٦٦ بَلِ ادَّارَكَ عِلْمُهُمْ فِي الْآخِرَةِ ۚ بَلْ هُمْ فِي شَكٍّ مِّنْهَا ۖ بَلْ هُم مِّنْهَا عَمُونَ

66 In fact, their knowledge of the Hereafter is confused. In fact, they are in doubt about it. In fact, they are blind to it.

٦٧ وَقَالَ الَّذِينَ كَفَرُوا أَإِذَا كُنَّا تُرَابًا وَآبَاؤُنَا أَئِنَّا لَمُخْرَجُونَ

67   13:5; 23:82; 37:16

67 Those who disbelieve say, "When we have become dust, and our ancestors, shall we be brought out?

٦٨ لَقَدْ وُعِدْنَا هَٰذَا نَحْنُ وَآبَاؤُنَا مِن قَبْلُ إِنْ هَٰذَا إِلَّا أَسَاطِيرُ الْأَوَّلِينَ

68   pp 23:83

68 We were promised that before, we and our ancestors—these are nothing but legends of the ancients."

٦٩ قُلْ سِيرُوا فِي الْأَرْضِ فَانظُرُوا كَيْفَ كَانَ عَاقِبَةُ الْمُجْرِمِينَ

69   3:137

69 Say, travel through the earth, and observe the fate of the guilty."

٧٠ وَلَا تَحْزَنْ عَلَيْهِمْ وَلَا تَكُن فِي ضَيْقٍ مِّمَّا يَمْكُرُونَ

70   10:65; 16:127

70 But do not grieve over them, and do not be troubled by what they plot.

٧١ وَيَقُولُونَ مَتَىٰ هَٰذَا الْوَعْدُ إِن كُنتُمْ صَادِقِينَ

71   10:48

71 And they say, "When is this promise, if you are truthful?"

٧٢ قُلْ عَسَىٰ أَن يَكُونَ رَدِفَ لَكُم بَعْضُ الَّذِي تَسْتَعْجِلُونَ

72 Say, "Perhaps some of what you are impatient for has drawn near."

٧٣ وَإِنَّ رَبَّكَ لَذُو فَضْلٍ عَلَى النَّاسِ وَلَٰكِنَّ أَكْثَرَهُمْ لَا يَشْكُرُونَ

73 Your Lord is gracious towards humanity, but most of them are not thankful.

73
2:243; 10:60; 40:61

٧٤ وَإِنَّ رَبَّكَ لَيَعْلَمُ مَا تُكِنُّ صُدُورُهُمْ وَمَا يُعْلِنُونَ

74 And your Lord knows what their hearts conceal, and what they reveal.

74
PP 28:69

٧٥ وَمَا مِنْ غَائِبَةٍ فِي السَّمَاءِ وَالْأَرْضِ إِلَّا فِي كِتَابٍ مُبِينٍ

75 There is no mystery in the heaven and the earth, but it is in a Clear Book.

٧٦ إِنَّ هَٰذَا الْقُرْآنَ يَقُصُّ عَلَىٰ بَنِي إِسْرَائِيلَ أَكْثَرَ الَّذِي هُمْ فِيهِ يَخْتَلِفُونَ

76 This Qur'an relates to the Children of Israel most of what they differ about.

٧٧ وَإِنَّهُ لَهُدًى وَرَحْمَةٌ لِلْمُؤْمِنِينَ

77 And it is guidance and mercy for the believers.

٧٨ إِنَّ رَبَّكَ يَقْضِي بَيْنَهُمْ بِحُكْمِهِ ۚ وَهُوَ الْعَزِيزُ الْعَلِيمُ

78 Your Lord will judge between them by His wisdom. He is the Almighty, the All-Knowing.

78
2:113; 10:93

٧٩ فَتَوَكَّلْ عَلَى اللَّهِ ۖ إِنَّكَ عَلَى الْحَقِّ الْمُبِينِ

79 So rely on God. You are upon the clear truth.

٨٠ إِنَّكَ لَا تُسْمِعُ الْمَوْتَىٰ وَلَا تُسْمِعُ الصُّمَّ الدُّعَاءَ إِذَا وَلَّوْا مُدْبِرِينَ

80 You cannot make the dead hear, nor can you make the deaf hear the call if they turn their backs and flee.

80
6:36; 10:42; 27:81; 30:52; 43:40

٨١ وَمَا أَنْتَ بِهَادِي الْعُمْيِ عَنْ ضَلَالَتِهِمْ ۖ إِنْ تُسْمِعُ إِلَّا مَنْ يُؤْمِنُ بِآيَاتِنَا فَهُمْ مُسْلِمُونَ

81 Nor can you guide the blind out of their straying. You can make no one listen, except those who believe in Our verses; for they are Muslims.

٨٢ وَإِذَا وَقَعَ الْقَوْلُ عَلَيْهِمْ أَخْرَجْنَا لَهُمْ دَابَّةً مِنَ الْأَرْضِ تُكَلِّمُهُمْ أَنَّ النَّاسَ كَانُوا بِآيَاتِنَا لَا يُوقِنُونَ

82 And when the Word has fallen on them, We will bring out for them from the earth a creature which will say to them that the people are uncertain of Our revelations.

٨٣ وَيَوْمَ نَحْشُرُ مِنْ كُلِّ أُمَّةٍ فَوْجًا مِمَّنْ يُكَذِّبُ بِآيَاتِنَا فَهُمْ يُوزَعُونَ

83 On the Day when We gather from every community a group of those who rejected Our revelations; and they will be restrained.

83
6:22, 38; 18:47

٨٤ حَتَّىٰ إِذَا جَاءُوا قَالَ أَكَذَّبْتُمْ بِآيَاتِي وَلَمْ تُحِيطُوا بِهَا عِلْمًا أَمَّاذَا كُنْتُمْ تَعْمَلُونَ

84 Until, when they arrive, He will say, "Did you reject My revelations without comprehending them? Or what is it you were doing?"

84
10:39

٨٥ وَوَقَعَ الْقَوْلُ عَلَيْهِم بِمَا ظَلَمُوا فَهُمْ لَا يَنطِقُونَ

85 The Word will come down upon them for their wrongdoing, and they will not speak.

٨٦ أَلَمْ يَرَوْا أَنَّا جَعَلْنَا اللَّيْلَ لِيَسْكُنُوا فِيهِ وَالنَّهَارَ مُبْصِرًا ۚ إِنَّ فِي ذَٰلِكَ لَآيَاتٍ لِّقَوْمٍ يُؤْمِنُونَ

86
10:67; 17:12

86 Do they not see that We made the night for them to rest therein, and the day for visibility? Surely in that are signs for people who believe.

٨٧ وَيَوْمَ يُنفَخُ فِي الصُّورِ فَفَزِعَ مَن فِي السَّمَاوَاتِ وَمَن فِي الْأَرْضِ إِلَّا مَن شَاءَ اللَّهُ ۚ وَكُلٌّ أَتَوْهُ دَاخِرِينَ

87
6:73; 34:51; 37:18

87 On the Day when the Trumpet is blown, everyone in the heavens and the earth will be horrified, except whomever God wills; and everyone will come before Him in humility.

٨٨ وَتَرَى الْجِبَالَ تَحْسَبُهَا جَامِدَةً وَهِيَ تَمُرُّ مَرَّ السَّحَابِ ۚ صُنْعَ اللَّهِ الَّذِي أَتْقَنَ كُلَّ شَيْءٍ ۚ إِنَّهُ خَبِيرٌ بِمَا تَفْعَلُونَ

88
18:47; 52:10; 78:20; 81:3

88 And you see the mountains, and imagine them fixed, yet they pass, as the passing of the clouds—the making of God, who has perfected everything. He is fully Informed of what you do.

٨٩ مَن جَاءَ بِالْحَسَنَةِ فَلَهُ خَيْرٌ مِّنْهَا ᵃ وَهُم مِّن فَزَعٍ يَوْمَئِذٍ آمِنُونَ ᵇ

89
ᵃ 4:40; 6:160; 34:37
ᵇ 21:105; 27:89

89 Whoever brings a virtue will receive better than it—and they will be safe from the horrors of that Day.

٩٠ وَمَن جَاءَ بِالسَّيِّئَةِ فَكُبَّتْ وُجُوهُهُمْ فِي النَّارِ هَلْ تُجْزَوْنَ إِلَّا مَا كُنتُمْ تَعْمَلُونَ

90
6:160; 26:94; 28:84

90 But whoever brings evil—their faces will be tumbled into the Fire. Will you be rewarded except for what you used to do?

٩١ إِنَّمَا أُمِرْتُ أَنْ أَعْبُدَ رَبَّ هَٰذِهِ الْبَلْدَةِ الَّذِي حَرَّمَهَا وَلَهُ كُلُّ شَيْءٍ ۖ وَأُمِرْتُ أَنْ أَكُونَ مِنَ الْمُسْلِمِينَ

91
6:14

91 "I was commanded to worship the Lord of this town, who has sanctified it, and to Whom everything belongs; and I was commanded to be of those who submit.

٩٢ وَأَنْ أَتْلُوَ الْقُرْآنَ ۖ فَمَنِ اهْتَدَىٰ فَإِنَّمَا يَهْتَدِي لِنَفْسِهِ ۖ وَمَن ضَلَّ فَقُلْ إِنَّمَا أَنَا مِنَ الْمُنذِرِينَ

92
10:108

92 And to recite the Qur'an." Whoever is guided—is guided to his own advantage. And whoever goes astray, then say, "I am one of the warners."

٩٣ وَقُلِ الْحَمْدُ لِلَّهِ سَيُرِيكُمْ آيَاتِهِ فَتَعْرِفُونَهَا ۚ وَمَا رَبُّكَ بِغَافِلٍ عَمَّا تَعْمَلُونَ

93
2:74; 14:42; 21:37; 41:53

93 And say, "Praise belongs to God; He will show you His signs, and you will recognize them. Your Lord is not heedless of what you do."

Sūrah 28: Al-Qaṣaṣ

سُورَةُ ٱلْقَصَصِ (The Stories)

بِسْمِ ٱللَّهِ ٱلرَّحْمَـٰنِ ٱلرَّحِيمِ

١ طسم

1 Ṭā', Sīn, Mīm.

٢ تِلْكَ ءَايَـٰتُ ٱلْكِتَـٰبِ ٱلْمُبِينِ

2
pp 12:1

2 These are the Verses of the Clear Book.

٣ نَتْلُواْ عَلَيْكَ مِن نَّبَإِ مُوسَىٰ وَفِرْعَوْنَ بِٱلْحَقِّ لِقَوْمٍ يُؤْمِنُونَ

3
2:252; 3:108; 45:6

3 We narrate to you from the history of Moses and Pharaoh—in truth—for people who believe.

٤ إِنَّ فِرْعَوْنَ عَلَا فِي ٱلْأَرْضِ وَجَعَلَ أَهْلَهَا شِيَعًا يَسْتَضْعِفُ طَائِفَةً مِّنْهُمْ يُذَبِّحُ أَبْنَاءَهُمْ وَيَسْتَحْيِي نِسَاءَهُمْ ۚ إِنَّهُ كَانَ مِنَ ٱلْمُفْسِدِينَ

4
2:49; 7:127, 141; 10:83; 14:6; 23:45; 44:31

4 Pharaoh exalted himself in the land, and divided its people into factions. He persecuted a group of them, slaughtering their sons, while sparing their daughters. He was truly a corrupter.

٥ وَنُرِيدُ أَن نَّمُنَّ عَلَى ٱلَّذِينَ ٱسْتُضْعِفُوا فِي ٱلْأَرْضِ وَنَجْعَلَهُمْ أَئِمَّةً وَنَجْعَلَهُمُ ٱلْوَٰرِثِينَ

5
7:137; 26:59

5 But We desired to favor those who were oppressed in the land, and to make them leaders, and to make them the inheritors.

٦ وَنُمَكِّنَ لَهُمْ فِي ٱلْأَرْضِ وَنُرِيَ فِرْعَوْنَ وَهَـٰمَـٰنَ وَجُنُودَهُمَا مِنْهُم مَّا كَانُوا يَحْذَرُونَ

6 And to establish them in the land; and to show Pharaoh, Hamaan, and their troops, the very thing they feared.

٧ وَأَوْحَيْنَا إِلَىٰ أُمِّ مُوسَىٰ أَنْ أَرْضِعِيهِ ۖ فَإِذَا خِفْتِ عَلَيْهِ فَأَلْقِيهِ فِي ٱلْيَمِّ وَلَا تَخَافِي وَلَا تَحْزَنِي ۖ إِنَّا رَادُّوهُ إِلَيْكِ وَجَاعِلُوهُ مِنَ ٱلْمُرْسَلِينَ

7
20:38

7 We inspired the mother of Moses: "Nurse him; then, when you fear for him, cast him into the river, and do not fear, nor grieve; We will return him to you, and make him one of the messengers."

٨ فَٱلْتَقَطَهُ ءَالُ فِرْعَوْنَ لِيَكُونَ لَهُمْ عَدُوًّا وَحَزَنًا ۗ إِنَّ فِرْعَوْنَ وَهَـٰمَـٰنَ وَجُنُودَهُمَا كَانُوا خَـٰطِئِينَ

8
20:39; 71:25

8 Pharaoh's household picked him up, to be an opponent and a sorrow for them. Pharaoh, Hamaan, and their troops were sinners.

٩ وَقَالَتِ ٱمْرَأَتُ فِرْعَوْنَ قُرَّتُ عَيْنٍ لِّي وَلَكَ ۖ لَا تَقْتُلُوهُ عَسَىٰ أَن يَنفَعَنَا أَوْ نَتَّخِذَهُ وَلَدًا وَهُمْ لَا يَشْعُرُونَ

9 Pharaoh's wife said, "An eye's delight for me and for you. Do not kill him; perhaps he will be useful to us, or we may adopt him as a son." But they did not foresee.

١٠ وَأَصْبَحَ فُؤَادُ أُمِّ مُوسَىٰ فَارِغًا ۖ إِن كَادَتْ لَتُبْدِي بِهِ لَوْلَا أَن رَّبَطْنَا عَلَىٰ قَلْبِهَا لِتَكُونَ مِنَ الْمُؤْمِنِينَ

10 The heart of Moses' mother became vacant. She was about to disclose him, had We not steadied her heart, that she may remain a believer.

١١ وَقَالَتْ لِأُخْتِهِ قُصِّيهِ ۖ فَبَصُرَتْ بِهِ عَن جُنُبٍ وَهُمْ لَا يَشْعُرُونَ

11 She said to his sister, "Trail him." So she watched him from afar, and they were unaware.

11
10:53, 55; 20:40; 30:6

١٢ وَحَرَّمْنَا عَلَيْهِ الْمَرَاضِعَ مِن قَبْلُ فَقَالَتْ هَلْ أَدُلُّكُمْ عَلَىٰ أَهْلِ بَيْتٍ يَكْفُلُونَهُ لَكُمْ وَهُمْ لَهُ نَاصِحُونَ

12 We forbade him breastfeeding at first. So she said, "Shall I tell you about a family that can raise him for you, and will look after him?"

١٣ فَرَدَدْنَاهُ إِلَىٰ أُمِّهِ كَيْ تَقَرَّ عَيْنُهَا وَلَا تَحْزَنَ وَلِتَعْلَمَ أَنَّ وَعْدَ اللَّهِ حَقٌّ وَلَٰكِنَّ أَكْثَرَهُمْ لَا يَعْلَمُونَ

13 Thus We returned him to his mother, that she may be comforted, and not grieve, and know that God's promise is true. But most of them do not know.

١٤ وَلَمَّا بَلَغَ أَشُدَّهُ وَاسْتَوَىٰ آتَيْنَاهُ حُكْمًا وَعِلْمًا ۚ وَكَذَٰلِكَ نَجْزِي الْمُحْسِنِينَ

14 And when he reached his maturity, and became established, We gave him wisdom and knowledge. Thus do We reward the virtuous.

١٥ وَدَخَلَ الْمَدِينَةَ عَلَىٰ حِينِ غَفْلَةٍ مِّنْ أَهْلِهَا فَوَجَدَ فِيهَا رَجُلَيْنِ يَقْتَتِلَانِ هَٰذَا مِن شِيعَتِهِ وَهَٰذَا مِنْ عَدُوِّهِ ۖ فَاسْتَغَاثَهُ الَّذِي مِن شِيعَتِهِ عَلَى الَّذِي مِنْ عَدُوِّهِ فَوَكَزَهُ مُوسَىٰ فَقَضَىٰ عَلَيْهِ ۖ قَالَ هَٰذَا مِنْ عَمَلِ الشَّيْطَانِ ۖ إِنَّهُ عَدُوٌّ مُّضِلٌّ مُّبِينٌ

15
20:40; 26:15; 28:33

15 Once he entered the city, unnoticed by its people. He found in it two men fighting—one of his own sect, and one from his enemies. The one of his sect solicited his assistance against the one from his enemies; so Moses punched him, and put an end to him. He said, "This is of Satan's doing; he is an enemy that openly misleads."

١٦ قَالَ رَبِّ إِنِّي ظَلَمْتُ نَفْسِي فَاغْفِرْ لِي فَغَفَرَ لَهُ ۚ إِنَّهُ هُوَ الْغَفُورُ الرَّحِيمُ

16 He said, "My Lord, I have wronged myself, so forgive me." So He forgave him. He is the Forgiver, the Merciful.

١٧ قَالَ رَبِّ بِمَا أَنْعَمْتَ عَلَيَّ فَلَنْ أَكُونَ ظَهِيرًا لِّلْمُجْرِمِينَ

17 He said, "My Lord, in as much as you have favored me, I will never be a supporter of the criminals."

١٨ فَأَصْبَحَ فِي الْمَدِينَةِ خَائِفًا يَتَرَقَّبُ فَإِذَا الَّذِي اسْتَنصَرَهُ بِالْأَمْسِ يَسْتَصْرِخُهُ ۚ قَالَ لَهُ مُوسَىٰ إِنَّكَ لَغَوِيٌّ مُّبِينٌ

18
28:21

18 The next morning, he went about in the city, fearful and vigilant, when the man who had sought his assistance the day before was shouting out to him. Moses said to him, "You are clearly a troublemaker."

١٩ فَلَمَّا أَنْ أَرَادَ أَنْ يَبْطِشَ بِالَّذِي هُوَ عَدُوٌّ لَهُمَا قَالَ يَا مُوسَىٰ أَتُرِيدُ أَنْ تَقْتُلَنِي كَمَا قَتَلْتَ نَفْسًا بِالْأَمْسِ ۖ إِنْ تُرِيدُ إِلَّا أَنْ تَكُونَ جَبَّارًا فِي الْأَرْضِ وَمَا تُرِيدُ أَنْ تَكُونَ مِنَ الْمُصْلِحِينَ

19 As he was about to strike the one who was their enemy, he said, "O Moses, do you intend to kill me, as you killed someone yesterday? You only want to be a bully in the land, and do not want to be a peacemaker."

٢٠ وَجَاءَ رَجُلٌ مِنْ أَقْصَى الْمَدِينَةِ يَسْعَىٰ قَالَ يَا مُوسَىٰ إِنَّ الْمَلَأَ يَأْتَمِرُونَ بِكَ لِيَقْتُلُوكَ فَاخْرُجْ إِنِّي لَكَ مِنَ النَّاصِحِينَ

20
36:20

20 And a man came from the farthest part of the city running. He said, "O Moses, the authorities are considering killing you, so leave; I am giving you good advice."

٢١ فَخَرَجَ مِنْهَا خَائِفًا يَتَرَقَّبُ ۖ قَالَ رَبِّ نَجِّنِي مِنَ الْقَوْمِ الظَّالِمِينَ

21
28:18

21 So he left, fearful and vigilant. He said, "My Lord, deliver me from the wrongdoing people."

٢٢ وَلَمَّا تَوَجَّهَ تِلْقَاءَ مَدْيَنَ قَالَ عَسَىٰ رَبِّي أَنْ يَهْدِيَنِي سَوَاءَ السَّبِيلِ

22 As he headed towards Median, he said, "Perhaps my Lord will guide me to the right way."

٢٣ وَلَمَّا وَرَدَ مَاءَ مَدْيَنَ وَجَدَ عَلَيْهِ أُمَّةً مِنَ النَّاسِ يَسْقُونَ وَوَجَدَ مِنْ دُونِهِمُ امْرَأَتَيْنِ تَذُودَانِ ۖ قَالَ مَا خَطْبُكُمَا ۖ قَالَتَا لَا نَسْقِي حَتَّىٰ يُصْدِرَ الرِّعَاءُ ۖ وَأَبُونَا شَيْخٌ كَبِيرٌ

23 And when he arrived at the waters of Median, he found there a crowd of people drawing water, and he noticed two women waiting on the side. He said, "What is the matter with you?" They said, "We cannot draw water until the shepherds depart, and our father is a very old man."

٢٤ فَسَقَىٰ لَهُمَا ثُمَّ تَوَلَّىٰ إِلَى الظِّلِّ فَقَالَ رَبِّ إِنِّي لِمَا أَنْزَلْتَ إِلَيَّ مِنْ خَيْرٍ فَقِيرٌ

24 So he drew water for them, and then withdrew to the shade, and said, "My Lord, I am in dire need of whatever good you might send down to me."

٢٥ فَجَاءَتْهُ إِحْدَاهُمَا تَمْشِي عَلَى اسْتِحْيَاءٍ قَالَتْ إِنَّ أَبِي يَدْعُوكَ لِيَجْزِيَكَ أَجْرَ مَا سَقَيْتَ لَنَا ۚ فَلَمَّا جَاءَهُ وَقَصَّ عَلَيْهِ الْقَصَصَ قَالَ لَا تَخَفْ ۖ نَجَوْتَ مِنَ الْقَوْمِ الظَّالِمِينَ

25 Then, one of the two women approached him, walking bashfully. She said, "My father is calling you, to reward you for drawing water for us." And when he came to him, and told him the story, he said, "Do not fear, you have escaped from the wrongdoing people."

٢٦ قَالَتْ إِحْدَاهُمَا يَا أَبَتِ اسْتَأْجِرْهُ ۖ إِنَّ خَيْرَ مَنِ اسْتَأْجَرْتَ الْقَوِيُّ الْأَمِينُ

26 One of the two women said, "Father, hire him; the best employee for you is the strong and trustworthy."

٢٧ قَالَ إِنِّي أُرِيدُ أَنْ أُنكِحَكَ إِحْدَى ابْنَتَيَّ هَاتَيْنِ عَلَىٰ أَن تَأْجُرَنِي ثَمَانِيَ حِجَجٍ ۖ فَإِنْ أَتْمَمْتَ عَشْرًا فَمِنْ عِندِكَ ۖ وَمَا أُرِيدُ أَنْ أَشُقَّ عَلَيْكَ ۚ سَتَجِدُنِي إِن شَاءَ اللَّهُ مِنَ الصَّالِحِينَ

27 He said, "I want to marry you to one of these two daughters of mine, provided you work for me for eight years. But if you complete ten, that is up to you. I do not intend to impose any hardship on you. You will find me, God willing, one of the righteous."

٢٨ قَالَ ذَٰلِكَ بَيْنِي وَبَيْنَكَ ۖ أَيَّمَا الْأَجَلَيْنِ قَضَيْتُ فَلَا عُدْوَانَ عَلَيَّ ۖ وَاللَّهُ عَلَىٰ مَا نَقُولُ وَكِيلٌ

28
12:66

28 He said, "Let this be an agreement between you and me. Whichever of the two terms I fulfill, there shall be no reprisal against me; and God is witness over what we say."

٢٩ فَلَمَّا قَضَىٰ مُوسَى الْأَجَلَ وَسَارَ بِأَهْلِهِ آنَسَ مِن جَانِبِ الطُّورِ نَارًا قَالَ لِأَهْلِهِ امْكُثُوا إِنِّي آنَسْتُ نَارًا لَّعَلِّي آتِيكُم مِّنْهَا بِخَبَرٍ أَوْ جَذْوَةٍ مِّنَ النَّارِ لَعَلَّكُمْ تَصْطَلُونَ

29
20:10; 26:20; 27:7; 79:16

29 When Moses had completed the term, and departed with his family, he noticed a fire by the side of the Mount. He said to his family, "Stay here, I have glimpsed a fire. Perhaps I can bring you some information from there, or an ember from the fire, that you may warm yourselves."

٣٠ فَلَمَّا أَتَاهَا نُودِيَ مِن شَاطِئِ الْوَادِ الْأَيْمَنِ فِي الْبُقْعَةِ الْمُبَارَكَةِ مِنَ الشَّجَرَةِ أَن يَا مُوسَىٰ إِنِّي أَنَا اللَّهُ رَبُّ الْعَالَمِينَ

30 When he reached it, he was called from the right side of the valley, at the Blessed Spot, from the bush: "O Moses, it is I, God, the Lord of the Worlds.

٣١ وَأَنْ أَلْقِ عَصَاكَ ۖ فَلَمَّا رَآهَا تَهْتَزُّ كَأَنَّهَا جَانٌّ وَلَّىٰ مُدْبِرًا وَلَمْ يُعَقِّبْ ۚ يَا مُوسَىٰ أَقْبِلْ وَلَا تَخَفْ ۖ إِنَّكَ مِنَ الْآمِنِينَ

31
7:107; 20:7; 27:10

31 Throw down your staff." And when he saw it wiggling, as if it were possessed, he turned his back to flee, and did not look back. "O Moses, come forward, and do not fear, you are perfectly safe.

٣٢ اسْلُكْ يَدَكَ فِي جَيْبِكَ تَخْرُجْ بَيْضَاءَ مِنْ غَيْرِ سُوءٍ وَاضْمُمْ إِلَيْكَ جَنَاحَكَ مِنَ الرَّهْبِ ۖ فَذَانِكَ بُرْهَانَانِ مِن رَّبِّكَ إِلَىٰ فِرْعَوْنَ وَمَلَئِهِ ۚ إِنَّهُمْ كَانُوا قَوْمًا فَاسِقِينَ

32
7:108; 20:22; 26:33; 27:12

32 Put your hand inside your pocket, and it will come out white, without blemish. And press your arm to your side, against fear. These are two proofs from your Lord, to Pharaoh and his dignitaries. They are truly sinful people."

٣٣ قَالَ رَبِّ إِنِّي قَتَلْتُ مِنْهُمْ نَفْسًا فَأَخَافُ أَن يَقْتُلُونِ

33
20:40; 23:3; 26:14; 28:15

33 He said, "My Lord, I have killed one of them, and I fear they will kill me.

٣٤ وَأَخِي هَارُونُ هُوَ أَفْصَحُ مِنِّي لِسَانًا فَأَرْسِلْهُ مَعِيَ رِدْءًا يُصَدِّقُنِي ۖ إِنِّي أَخَافُ أَن يُكَذِّبُونِ	34	20:29; 25:35; 26:12

34 And my brother Aaron, he is more eloquent than me, so send him with me, to help me, and to confirm my words, for I fear they will reject me."

٣٥ قَالَ سَنَشُدُّ عَضُدَكَ بِأَخِيكَ وَنَجْعَلُ لَكُمَا سُلْطَانًا فَلَا يَصِلُونَ إِلَيْكُمَا ۚ بِآيَاتِنَا أَنتُمَا وَمَنِ اتَّبَعَكُمَا الْغَالِبُونَ	35	4:153; 20:31; 23:45

35 He said, "We will strengthen your arm with your brother, and We will give you authority, so they will not touch you. By virtue of Our signs, you and those who follow you will be the triumphant."

٣٦ فَلَمَّا جَاءَهُم مُّوسَىٰ بِآيَاتِنَا بَيِّنَاتٍ قَالُوا مَا هَٰذَا إِلَّا سِحْرٌ مُّفْتَرًى وَمَا سَمِعْنَا بِهَٰذَا فِي آبَائِنَا الْأَوَّلِينَ	36	10:76

36 But when Moses came to them with Our signs, clear and manifest, they said, "This is nothing but fabricated magic, and We never heard of this from our ancestors of old."

٣٧ وَقَالَ مُوسَىٰ رَبِّي أَعْلَمُ بِمَن جَاءَ بِالْهُدَىٰ مِنْ عِندِهِ وَمَن تَكُونُ لَهُ عَاقِبَةُ الدَّارِ ۖ إِنَّهُ لَا يُفْلِحُ الظَّالِمُونَ	37	28:85

37 Moses said, "My Lord is well aware of him who brings guidance from Him, and him who will have the sequel of the abode. The wrongdoers will not succeed."

٣٨ وَقَالَ فِرْعَوْنُ يَا أَيُّهَا الْمَلَأُ مَا عَلِمْتُ لَكُم مِّنْ إِلَٰهٍ غَيْرِي فَأَوْقِدْ لِي يَا هَامَانُ عَلَى الطِّينِ فَاجْعَل لِّي صَرْحًا لَّعَلِّي أَطَّلِعُ إِلَىٰ إِلَٰهِ مُوسَىٰ وَإِنِّي لَأَظُنُّهُ مِنَ الْكَاذِبِينَ	38	26:29; 40:36; 79:24

38 Pharaoh said, "O nobles, I know of no god for you other than me. So fire-up the bricks for me O Hamaan, and build me a tower, that I may ascend to the God of Moses, though I think he is a liar."

٣٩ وَاسْتَكْبَرَ هُوَ وَجُنُودُهُ فِي الْأَرْضِ بِغَيْرِ الْحَقِّ وَظَنُّوا أَنَّهُمْ إِلَيْنَا لَا يُرْجَعُونَ	39	23:46; 29:39; 41:15

39 He and his troops acted arrogantly in the land, with no justification. They thought they would not be returned to Us.

٤٠ فَأَخَذْنَاهُ وَجُنُودَهُ فَنَبَذْنَاهُمْ فِي الْيَمِّ ۖ فَانظُرْ كَيْفَ كَانَ عَاقِبَةُ الظَّالِمِينَ	40	7:136; 51:40

40 So We seized him, and his troops, and We threw them into the sea. Observe, therefore, what was the end of the oppressors.

٤١ وَجَعَلْنَاهُمْ أَئِمَّةً يَدْعُونَ إِلَى النَّارِ ۖ وَيَوْمَ الْقِيَامَةِ لَا يُنصَرُونَ	41	2:221; 49:4

41 And We made them leaders calling to the Fire. And on Resurrection Day, they will not be saved.

٤٢ وَأَتْبَعْنَاهُمْ فِي هَٰذِهِ الدُّنْيَا لَعْنَةً ۖ وَيَوْمَ الْقِيَامَةِ هُم مِّنَ الْمَقْبُوحِينَ	42	11:60, 99; 24:23; 33:57

42 And We pursued them in this world with a curse. And on Resurrection Day, they will be among the despised.

٤٣ وَلَقَدْ آتَيْنَا مُوسَى الْكِتَابَ مِنْ بَعْدِ مَا أَهْلَكْنَا الْقُرُونَ الْأُولَىٰ بَصَائِرَ لِلنَّاسِ وَهُدًى وَرَحْمَةً لَعَلَّهُمْ يَتَذَكَّرُونَ

43   2:53; 7:203; 45:20

43 We gave Moses the Scripture after We had annihilated the previous generations; as an illumination for mankind, and guidance, and mercy, so that they may remember.

٤٤ وَمَا كُنْتَ بِجَانِبِ الْغَرْبِيِّ إِذْ قَضَيْنَا إِلَىٰ مُوسَى الْأَمْرَ وَمَا كُنْتَ مِنَ الشَّاهِدِينَ

44   3:44; 11:49; 12:102

44 You were not on the Western Side when We decreed the command to Moses, nor were you among the witnesses.

٤٥ وَلَٰكِنَّا أَنْشَأْنَا قُرُونًا فَتَطَاوَلَ عَلَيْهِمُ الْعُمُرُ ۚ وَمَا كُنْتَ ثَاوِيًا فِي أَهْلِ مَدْيَنَ تَتْلُو عَلَيْهِمْ آيَاتِنَا وَلَٰكِنَّا كُنَّا مُرْسِلِينَ

45

45 But We established many generations, and time took its toll on them. Nor were you among the people of Median, reciting Our revelations to them. But We kept sending messengers.

٤٦ وَمَا كُنْتَ بِجَانِبِ الطُّورِ إِذْ نَادَيْنَا وَلَٰكِنْ رَحْمَةً مِنْ رَبِّكَ لِتُنْذِرَ قَوْمًا مَا أَتَاهُمْ مِنْ نَذِيرٍ مِنْ قَبْلِكَ لَعَلَّهُمْ يَتَذَكَّرُونَ

46   20:134; 26:208; 32:3; 36:6

46 Nor were you by the side of the Mount when We proclaimed. Rather, it was a mercy from your Lord, that you may warn people who received no warner before you, so that they may take heed.

٤٧ وَلَوْلَا أَنْ تُصِيبَهُمْ مُصِيبَةٌ بِمَا قَدَّمَتْ أَيْدِيهِمْ فَيَقُولُوا رَبَّنَا لَوْلَا أَرْسَلْتَ إِلَيْنَا رَسُولًا فَنَتَّبِعَ آيَاتِكَ وَنَكُونَ مِنَ الْمُؤْمِنِينَ

47

47 Otherwise, if a calamity befell them as a result of what their hands have perpetrated, they would say, "Our Lord, if only You had sent us a messenger, we would have followed Your revelations, and been among the believers."

٤٨ فَلَمَّا جَاءَهُمُ الْحَقُّ مِنْ عِنْدِنَا قَالُوا لَوْلَا أُوتِيَ مِثْلَ مَا أُوتِيَ مُوسَىٰ ۚ أَوَلَمْ يَكْفُرُوا بِمَا أُوتِيَ مُوسَىٰ مِنْ قَبْلُ ۖ قَالُوا سِحْرَانِ تَظَاهَرَا وَقَالُوا إِنَّا بِكُلٍّ كَافِرُونَ

48   6:124; 10:76; 40:25

48 But when the truth came to them from Us, they said, "If only he was given the like of what was given to Moses." Did they not disbelieve in what was given to Moses in the past? They said, "Two works of magic backing one another." And they said, "We are disbelieving in both."

٤٩ قُلْ فَأْتُوا بِكِتَابٍ مِنْ عِنْدِ اللَّهِ هُوَ أَهْدَىٰ مِنْهُمَا أَتَّبِعْهُ إِنْ كُنْتُمْ صَادِقِينَ

49   2:23; 10:38; 11:13; 52:34

49 Say, "Then bring a scripture from God, more conductive to guidance than both, and I will follow it, if you are truthful."

٥٠ فَإِنْ لَمْ يَسْتَجِيبُوا لَكَ فَاعْلَمْ أَنَّمَا يَتَّبِعُونَ أَهْوَاءَهُمْ ۚ وَمَنْ أَضَلُّ مِمَّنِ اتَّبَعَ هَوَاهُ بِغَيْرِ هُدًى مِنَ اللَّهِ ۚ إِنَّ اللَّهَ لَا يَهْدِي الْقَوْمَ الظَّالِمِينَ

50   11:14

50 But if they fail to respond to you, know that they follow their fancies. And who is more lost than him who follows his fancy without guidance from God? God does not guide the unjust people.

٥١ وَلَقَدْ وَصَّلْنَا لَهُمُ الْقَوْلَ لَعَلَّهُمْ يَتَذَكَّرُونَ

51 We have delivered the Word to them, that they may remember.

٥٢ الَّذِينَ آتَيْنَاهُمُ الْكِتَابَ مِنْ قَبْلِهِ هُمْ بِهِ يُؤْمِنُونَ

52 Those to whom We gave the Scripture before it believe in it.

52
2:121; 5:83; 6:114; 17:109; 29:47

٥٣ وَإِذَا يُتْلَىٰ عَلَيْهِمْ قَالُوا آمَنَّا بِهِ إِنَّهُ الْحَقُّ مِنْ رَبِّنَا إِنَّا كُنَّا مِنْ قَبْلِهِ مُسْلِمِينَ

53 When it is recited to them, they say, "We have believed in it; it is the truth from our Lord; we were Muslims prior to it."

٥٤ أُولَٰئِكَ يُؤْتَوْنَ أَجْرَهُمْ مَرَّتَيْنِ بِمَا صَبَرُوا وَيَدْرَءُونَ بِالْحَسَنَةِ السَّيِّئَةَ وَمِمَّا رَزَقْنَاهُمْ يُنْفِقُونَ

54 These will be given their reward twice, because they persevered; and they counter evil with good; and from Our provisions to them, they give.

54
33:31

٥٥ وَإِذَا سَمِعُوا اللَّغْوَ أَعْرَضُوا عَنْهُ وَقَالُوا لَنَا أَعْمَالُنَا وَلَكُمْ أَعْمَالُكُمْ سَلَامٌ عَلَيْكُمْ لَا نَبْتَغِي الْجَاهِلِينَ

55 And when they hear vain talk, they avoid it, and say, "We have our deeds, and you have your deeds; peace be upon you; we do not desire the ignorant."

55
25:72; 23:3

٥٦ إِنَّكَ لَا تَهْدِي مَنْ أَحْبَبْتَ وَلَٰكِنَّ اللَّهَ يَهْدِي مَنْ يَشَاءُ [a] وَهُوَ أَعْلَمُ بِالْمُهْتَدِينَ [b]

56 You cannot guide whom you love, but God guides whom He wills, and He knows best those who are guided.

56
[a] 2:272; 5:41; 6:117
[b] 16:37; 53:30

٥٧ وَقَالُوا إِنْ نَتَّبِعِ الْهُدَىٰ مَعَكَ نُتَخَطَّفْ مِنْ أَرْضِنَا أَوَلَمْ نُمَكِّنْ لَهُمْ حَرَمًا آمِنًا يُجْبَىٰ إِلَيْهِ ثَمَرَاتُ كُلِّ شَيْءٍ رِزْقًا مِنْ لَدُنَّا وَلَٰكِنَّ أَكْثَرَهُمْ لَا يَعْلَمُونَ

57 And they say, "If we follow the guidance with you, we will be snatched from our land." Did We not establish for them a Safe Sanctuary, to which are brought all kinds of fruits, as provision from Ourselves? But most of them do not know.

57
2:125; 8:26; 29:67

٥٨ وَكَمْ أَهْلَكْنَا مِنْ قَرْيَةٍ بَطِرَتْ مَعِيشَتَهَا فَتِلْكَ مَسَاكِنُهُمْ لَمْ تُسْكَنْ مِنْ بَعْدِهِمْ إِلَّا قَلِيلًا وَكُنَّا نَحْنُ الْوَارِثِينَ

58 And how many a city did We destroy for turning unappreciative of its livelihood? Here are their homes, uninhabited after them, except for a few. And We became the Inheritors.

58
74; 10:13; 22:45; 27:52 47:13

٥٩ وَمَا كَانَ رَبُّكَ مُهْلِكَ الْقُرَىٰ حَتَّىٰ يَبْعَثَ فِي أُمِّهَا رَسُولًا يَتْلُو عَلَيْهِمْ آيَاتِنَا وَمَا كُنَّا مُهْلِكِي الْقُرَىٰ إِلَّا وَأَهْلُهَا ظَالِمُونَ

59 Your Lord never destroys cities without first sending a messenger in their midst, reciting to them Our revelations. And We never destroy the cities, unless their people are wrongdoers.

59
6:47; 17:15; 46:35

٦٠ وَمَا أُوتِيتُم مِّن شَيْءٍ فَمَتَاعُ الْحَيَاةِ الدُّنْيَا وَزِينَتُهَا ۚ وَمَا عِندَ اللَّهِ خَيْرٌ وَأَبْقَىٰ ۚ أَفَلَا تَعْقِلُونَ

60 — 43:35

60 Whatever thing you are given is but the material of this world, and its glitter. But what is with God is better, and longer lasting. Do you not comprehend?

٦١ أَفَمَن وَعَدْنَاهُ وَعْدًا حَسَنًا فَهُوَ لَاقِيهِ كَمَن مَّتَّعْنَاهُ مَتَاعَ الْحَيَاةِ الدُّنْيَا ثُمَّ هُوَ يَوْمَ الْقِيَامَةِ مِنَ الْمُحْضَرِينَ

61 — 30:16; 34:36

61 Can someone to whom We have made a fine promise—which he will attain—be equal to someone to whom We have given enjoyments in this world, but who will be, on Resurrection Day, among the arraigned?

٦٢ وَيَوْمَ يُنَادِيهِمْ فَيَقُولُ أَيْنَ شُرَكَائِيَ الَّذِينَ كُنتُمْ تَزْعُمُونَ

62 — 6:22; 10:28; 28:74

62 On the Day when He will call to them, and say, "Where are My associates whom you used to claim?"

٦٣ قَالَ الَّذِينَ حَقَّ عَلَيْهِمُ الْقَوْلُ رَبَّنَا هَٰؤُلَاءِ الَّذِينَ أَغْوَيْنَا أَغْوَيْنَاهُمْ كَمَا غَوَيْنَا ۖ تَبَرَّأْنَا إِلَيْكَ ۖ مَا كَانُوا إِيَّانَا يَعْبُدُونَ

63 — 17:16; 37:31–32

63 Those against whom the sentence is justified will say, "Our Lord, these are they whom we misled. We misled them, as we were misled. We beg Your forgiveness; it was not us they used to worship."

٦٤ وَقِيلَ ادْعُوا شُرَكَاءَكُمْ فَدَعَوْهُمْ فَلَمْ يَسْتَجِيبُوا لَهُمْ وَرَأَوُا الْعَذَابَ ۚ لَوْ أَنَّهُمْ كَانُوا يَهْتَدُونَ

64 — 7:194; 18:52

64 And it will be said, "Call on your partners." And they will call on them, but they will not respond to them. And they will see the suffering. If only they were guided.

٦٥ وَيَوْمَ يُنَادِيهِمْ فَيَقُولُ مَاذَا أَجَبْتُمُ الْمُرْسَلِينَ

65 — 5:109

65 On the Day when He will call to them, and say, "What did you answer the Messengers?"

٦٦ فَعَمِيَتْ عَلَيْهِمُ الْأَنبَاءُ يَوْمَئِذٍ فَهُمْ لَا يَتَسَاءَلُونَ

66

66 They will be blinded by the facts on that Day, and they will not question each other.

٦٧ فَأَمَّا مَن تَابَ وَآمَنَ وَعَمِلَ صَالِحًا فَعَسَىٰ أَن يَكُونَ مِنَ الْمُفْلِحِينَ

67 — 19:60

67 But he who repents, and believes, and does righteous deeds, may well be among the winners.

٦٨ وَرَبُّكَ يَخْلُقُ مَا يَشَاءُ وَيَخْتَارُ ۗ مَا كَانَ لَهُمُ الْخِيَرَةُ ۚ سُبْحَانَ اللَّهِ وَتَعَالَىٰ عَمَّا يُشْرِكُونَ

68 — 3:47

68 Your Lord creates whatever He wills, and He chooses. The choice is not theirs. Glory be to God, and exalted be He above the associations they make.

٦٩ وَرَبُّكَ يَعْلَمُ مَا تُكِنُّ صُدُورُهُمْ وَمَا يُعْلِنُونَ	**69** PP 27:74

69 And your Lord knows what their hearts conceal, and what they reveal.

٧٠ وَهُوَ اللَّهُ لَا إِلَٰهَ إِلَّا هُوَ ۖ لَهُ الْحَمْدُ فِي الْأُولَىٰ وَالْآخِرَةِ ۖ وَلَهُ الْحُكْمُ وَإِلَيْهِ تُرْجَعُونَ	**70** 2:255; 3:2; 59:22

70 And He is God. There is no god but He. To Him belongs all praise in this life, and in the next. And His is the decision, and to Him you will be returned.

٧١ قُلْ أَرَأَيْتُمْ إِنْ جَعَلَ اللَّهُ عَلَيْكُمُ اللَّيْلَ سَرْمَدًا إِلَىٰ يَوْمِ الْقِيَامَةِ مَنْ إِلَٰهٌ غَيْرُ اللَّهِ يَأْتِيكُمْ بِضِيَاءٍ ۖ أَفَلَا تَسْمَعُونَ	**71–72** 6:14, 114, 164; 7:140; 35:3

71 Say, "Have you considered? Had God made the night perpetual over you until the Day of Resurrection, which god other than God will bring you illumination? Do you not hear?"

٧٢ قُلْ أَرَأَيْتُمْ إِنْ جَعَلَ اللَّهُ عَلَيْكُمُ النَّهَارَ سَرْمَدًا إِلَىٰ يَوْمِ الْقِيَامَةِ مَنْ إِلَٰهٌ غَيْرُ اللَّهِ يَأْتِيكُمْ بِلَيْلٍ تَسْكُنُونَ فِيهِ ۖ أَفَلَا تُبْصِرُونَ	

72 Say, "Have you considered? Had God made the day perpetual over you until the Day of Resurrection, which god other than God will bring you night to rest in? Do you not see?"

٧٣ وَمِنْ رَحْمَتِهِ جَعَلَ لَكُمُ اللَّيْلَ وَالنَّهَارَ لِتَسْكُنُوا فِيهِ وَلِتَبْتَغُوا مِنْ فَضْلِهِ وَلَعَلَّكُمْ تَشْكُرُونَ	**73** 10:67; 30:32

73 It is out of His mercy that He made for you the night and the day, that you may rest in it, and seek some of His bounty; and that you may give thanks.

٧٤ وَيَوْمَ يُنَادِيهِمْ فَيَقُولُ أَيْنَ شُرَكَائِيَ الَّذِينَ كُنْتُمْ تَزْعُمُونَ	**74** 6:22; 10:28; 28:62

74 On the Day when He will call to them, and say, "Where are My associates whom you used to claim?"

٧٥ وَنَزَعْنَا مِنْ كُلِّ أُمَّةٍ شَهِيدًا فَقُلْنَا هَاتُوا بُرْهَانَكُمْ فَعَلِمُوا أَنَّ الْحَقَّ لِلَّهِ وَضَلَّ عَنْهُمْ مَا كَانُوا يَفْتَرُونَ	**75** 4:41; 16:84

75 And We will draw out from every community a witness, and say, "Produce your evidence." Then they will realize that the truth is God's, and those they used to invent have forsaken them.

٧٦ إِنَّ قَارُونَ كَانَ مِنْ قَوْمِ مُوسَىٰ فَبَغَىٰ عَلَيْهِمْ ۖ وَآتَيْنَاهُ مِنَ الْكُنُوزِ مَا إِنَّ مَفَاتِحَهُ لَتَنُوءُ بِالْعُصْبَةِ أُولِي الْقُوَّةِ إِذْ قَالَ لَهُ قَوْمُهُ لَا تَفْرَحْ ۖ إِنَّ اللَّهَ لَا يُحِبُّ الْفَرِحِينَ	**76** 11:10; 13:26; 40:75; 57:23

76 Quaroon belonged to the clan of Moses, but he oppressed them. We had given him treasures, the keys of which would weigh down a group of strong men. His people said to him, "Do not exult; God does not love the exultant.

٧٧ وَابْتَغِ فِيمَا آتَاكَ اللَّهُ الدَّارَ الْآخِرَةَ ۖ وَلَا تَنسَ نَصِيبَكَ مِنَ الدُّنْيَا ۖ وَأَحْسِن كَمَا أَحْسَنَ اللَّهُ إِلَيْكَ ۖ وَلَا تَبْغِ الْفَسَادَ فِي الْأَرْضِ ۖ إِنَّ اللَّهَ لَا يُحِبُّ الْمُفْسِدِينَ

77 But seek, with what God has given you, the Home of the Hereafter, and do not neglect your share of this world. And be charitable, as God has been charitable to you. And do not seek corruption in the land. God does not like the seekers of corruption."

٧٨ قَالَ إِنَّمَا أُوتِيتُهُ عَلَىٰ عِلْمٍ عِندِي ۚ أَوَلَمْ يَعْلَمْ أَنَّ اللَّهَ قَدْ أَهْلَكَ مِن قَبْلِهِ مِنَ الْقُرُونِ مَنْ هُوَ أَشَدُّ مِنْهُ قُوَّةً وَأَكْثَرُ جَمْعًا ۚ وَلَا يُسْأَلُ عَن ذُنُوبِهِمُ الْمُجْرِمُونَ

78 10:13; 39:49

78 He said, "I was given all this on account of knowledge I possess." Did he not know that God destroyed many generations before him, who were stronger than he, and possessed greater riches? But the guilty will not be asked about their sins.

٧٩ فَخَرَجَ عَلَىٰ قَوْمِهِ فِي زِينَتِهِ ۖ قَالَ الَّذِينَ يُرِيدُونَ الْحَيَاةَ الدُّنْيَا يَا لَيْتَ لَنَا مِثْلَ مَا أُوتِيَ قَارُونُ إِنَّهُ لَذُو حَظٍّ عَظِيمٍ

79 And he went out before his people in his splendor. Those who desired the worldly life said, "If only we possessed the likes of what Quaroon was given. He is indeed very fortunate."

٨٠ وَقَالَ الَّذِينَ أُوتُوا الْعِلْمَ وَيْلَكُمْ ثَوَابُ اللَّهِ خَيْرٌ لِّمَنْ آمَنَ وَعَمِلَ صَالِحًا وَلَا يُلَقَّاهَا إِلَّا الصَّابِرُونَ

80 But those who were given knowledge said, "Woe to you! The reward of God is better for those who believe and do righteous deeds." Yet none attains it except the steadfast.

٨١ فَخَسَفْنَا بِهِ وَبِدَارِهِ الْأَرْضَ فَمَا كَانَ لَهُ مِن فِئَةٍ يَنصُرُونَهُ مِن دُونِ اللَّهِ وَمَا كَانَ مِنَ الْمُنتَصِرِينَ

81 16:45; 18:43; 42:46; 67:20

81 So We caused the earth to cave in on him and his mansion. He had no company to save him from God, and he could not defend himself.

٨٢ وَأَصْبَحَ الَّذِينَ تَمَنَّوْا مَكَانَهُ بِالْأَمْسِ يَقُولُونَ وَيْكَأَنَّ اللَّهَ يَبْسُطُ الرِّزْقَ لِمَن يَشَاءُ مِنْ عِبَادِهِ وَيَقْدِرُ ۖ لَوْلَا أَن مَّنَّ اللَّهُ عَلَيْنَا لَخَسَفَ بِنَا ۖ وَيْكَأَنَّهُ لَا يُفْلِحُ الْكَافِرُونَ

82 13:26; 29:62; 34:39

82 Those who had wished they were in his position the day before were saying, "Indeed, it is God who spreads the bounty to whomever He wills of His servants, and restricts it. Had God not been gracious to us, He would have caved in on us. No wonder the ungrateful never prosper."

٨٣ تِلْكَ الدَّارُ الْآخِرَةُ نَجْعَلُهَا لِلَّذِينَ لَا يُرِيدُونَ عُلُوًّا فِي الْأَرْضِ وَلَا فَسَادًا ۚ وَالْعَاقِبَةُ لِلْمُتَّقِينَ

83 That Home of the Hereafter—We assign it for those who seek no superiority on earth, nor corruption. And the outcome is for the cautious.

٨٤ مَن جَاءَ بِالْحَسَنَةِ فَلَهُ خَيْرٌ مِّنْهَا ۖ وَمَن جَاءَ بِالسَّيِّئَةِ فَلَا يُجْزَى الَّذِينَ عَمِلُوا السَّيِّئَاتِ إِلَّا مَا كَانُوا يَعْمَلُونَ

84 6:160; 27:89

84 Whoever brings a virtue will receive better than it. But whoever brings evil—the evildoers will be rewarded only according to what they used to do.

٨٥ إِنَّ الَّذِي فَرَضَ عَلَيْكَ الْقُرْآنَ لَرَادُّكَ إِلَىٰ مَعَادٍ ۚ قُل رَّبِّي أَعْلَمُ مَن جَاءَ بِالْهُدَىٰ وَمَنْ هُوَ فِي ضَلَالٍ مُّبِينٍ

85 28:37

85 He Who ordained the Qur'an for you will return you Home. Say, "My Lord knows best who comes with guidance, and who is in manifest error."

٨٦ وَمَا كُنتَ تَرْجُو أَن يُلْقَىٰ إِلَيْكَ الْكِتَابُ إِلَّا رَحْمَةً مِّن رَّبِّكَ ۖ فَلَا تَكُونَنَّ ظَهِيرًا لِّلْكَافِرِينَ

86 You did not expect the Scripture to be transmitted to you, except as mercy from your Lord. Therefore, do not be a supporter of the disbelievers.

٨٧ وَلَا يَصُدُّنَّكَ عَنْ آيَاتِ اللَّهِ بَعْدَ إِذْ أُنزِلَتْ إِلَيْكَ ۖ وَادْعُ إِلَىٰ رَبِّكَ ۖ وَلَا تَكُونَنَّ مِنَ الْمُشْرِكِينَ

87 And do not let them divert you from God's revelations after they have been revealed to you. And pray to your Lord, and never be of the polytheists.

٨٨ وَلَا تَدْعُ مَعَ اللَّهِ إِلَٰهًا آخَرَ ۘ لَا إِلَٰهَ إِلَّا هُوَ ۚ ᵃ كُلُّ شَيْءٍ هَالِكٌ إِلَّا وَجْهَهُ ۚ لَهُ الْحُكْمُ وَإِلَيْهِ تُرْجَعُونَ ᵇ

88
ᵃ 23:117; 25:68; 26:213; 55:26; 72:18
ᵇ 18:26; 55:26–27

88 And do not invoke with God any other god. There is no god but He. All things perish, except His presence. His is the judgment, and to Him you will be returned.

Sūrah 29: Al-'Ankabūt

سُورَةُ ٱلْعَنكَبُوت (The Spider)

بِسْمِ ٱللَّهِ ٱلرَّحْمَٰنِ ٱلرَّحِيمِ

١ الم

1 Alif, Lām, Mīm.

٢ أَحَسِبَ النَّاسُ أَن يُتْرَكُوا أَن يَقُولُوا آمَنَّا وَهُمْ لَا يُفْتَنُونَ

2 2:214; 3:142; 5:71; 9:16; 47:31

2 Have the people supposed that they will be left alone to say, "We believe," without being put to the test?

٣ وَلَقَدْ فَتَنَّا الَّذِينَ مِن قَبْلِهِمْ ۖ فَلَيَعْلَمَنَّ اللَّهُ الَّذِينَ صَدَقُوا وَلَيَعْلَمَنَّ الْكَاذِبِينَ

3 We have tested those before them. God will surely know the truthful, and He will surely know the liars.

٤ أَمْ حَسِبَ الَّذِينَ يَعْمَلُونَ السَّيِّئَاتِ أَنْ يَسْبِقُونَا ۚ سَاءَ مَا يَحْكُمُونَ

4 Or do those who commit sins think they can fool Us? Terrible is their opinion!

4
8:59

٥ مَنْ كَانَ يَرْجُو لِقَاءَ اللَّهِ فَإِنَّ أَجَلَ اللَّهِ لَآتٍ ۚ وَهُوَ السَّمِيعُ الْعَلِيمُ

5 Whoever looks forward to the meeting with God—the appointed time of God is coming. He is the All-Hearing, the All-Knowing.

٦ وَمَنْ جَاهَدَ فَإِنَّمَا يُجَاهِدُ لِنَفْسِهِ ۚ إِنَّ اللَّهَ لَغَنِيٌّ عَنِ الْعَالَمِينَ

6 Whoever strives, strives only for himself. God is Independent of the beings.

٧ وَالَّذِينَ آمَنُوا وَعَمِلُوا الصَّالِحَاتِ لَنُكَفِّرَنَّ عَنْهُمْ سَيِّئَاتِهِمْ وَلَنَجْزِيَنَّهُمْ أَحْسَنَ الَّذِي كَانُوا يَعْمَلُونَ

7 Those who believe and do righteous deeds—We will remit their sins, and We will reward them according to the best of what they used to do.

7
5:12; 3:195; 39:35; 47:2; 48:5; 65:5

٨ وَوَصَّيْنَا الْإِنْسَانَ بِوَالِدَيْهِ حُسْنًا ۖ وَإِنْ جَاهَدَاكَ لِتُشْرِكَ بِي مَا لَيْسَ لَكَ بِهِ عِلْمٌ فَلَا تُطِعْهُمَا ۚ إِلَيَّ مَرْجِعُكُمْ فَأُنَبِّئُكُمْ بِمَا كُنْتُمْ تَعْمَلُونَ

8 We have advised the human being to be good to his parents. But if they urge you to associate with Me something you have no knowledge of, do not obey them. To Me is your return; and I will inform you of what you used to do.

8
31:15

٩ وَالَّذِينَ آمَنُوا وَعَمِلُوا الصَّالِحَاتِ لَنُدْخِلَنَّهُمْ فِي الصَّالِحِينَ

9 Those who believe and do good works—We will admit them into the company of the righteous.

9
12:101

١٠ وَمِنَ النَّاسِ مَنْ يَقُولُ آمَنَّا بِاللَّهِ فَإِذَا أُوذِيَ فِي اللَّهِ جَعَلَ فِتْنَةَ النَّاسِ كَعَذَابِ اللَّهِ[a] وَلَئِنْ جَاءَ نَصْرٌ مِنْ رَبِّكَ لَيَقُولُنَّ إِنَّا كُنَّا مَعَكُمْ ۚ أَوَلَيْسَ اللَّهُ بِأَعْلَمَ بِمَا فِي صُدُورِ الْعَالَمِينَ[b]

10 Among the people is he who says, "We have believed in God." Yet when he is harmed on God's account, he equates the people's persecution with God's retribution. And if help comes from your Lord, he says, "We were actually with you." Is not God aware of what is inside the hearts of the people?

10
[a] 4:73–74, 141; 22:11
[b] 4:72–73

١١ وَلَيَعْلَمَنَّ اللَّهُ الَّذِينَ آمَنُوا وَلَيَعْلَمَنَّ الْمُنَافِقِينَ

11 God certainly knows those who believe, and He certainly knows the hypocrites.

11
3:142, 166; 29:3

١٢ وَقَالَ الَّذِينَ كَفَرُوا لِلَّذِينَ آمَنُوا اتَّبِعُوا سَبِيلَنَا وَلْنَحْمِلْ خَطَايَاكُمْ وَمَا هُمْ بِحَامِلِينَ مِنْ خَطَايَاهُمْ مِنْ شَيْءٍ ۖ إِنَّهُمْ لَكَاذِبُونَ

12 Those who disbelieve say to those who believe, "Follow our way, and we will carry your sins." In no way can they carry any of their sins. They are liars.

١٣ وَلَيَحْمِلُنَّ أَثْقَالَهُمْ وَأَثْقَالًا مَعَ أَثْقَالِهِمْ ۖ وَلَيُسْأَلُنَّ يَوْمَ الْقِيَامَةِ عَمَّا كَانُوا يَفْتَرُونَ

13 They will carry their own loads, and other loads with their own. And they will be questioned on the Day of Resurrection concerning what they used to fabricate.

13
16:25, 56

١٤ وَلَقَدْ أَرْسَلْنَا نُوحًا إِلَىٰ قَوْمِهِ فَلَبِثَ فِيهِمْ أَلْفَ سَنَةٍ إِلَّا خَمْسِينَ عَامًا فَأَخَذَهُمُ الطُّوفَانُ وَهُمْ ظَالِمُونَ

14 We sent Noah to his people, and He stayed among them for a thousand years minus fifty years. Then the Deluge swept them; for they were wrongdoers.

14–15
7:59–64; 11:25; 23:23; 36:41–42

١٥ فَأَنجَيْنَاهُ وَأَصْحَابَ السَّفِينَةِ وَجَعَلْنَاهَا آيَةً لِلْعَالَمِينَ

15 But We saved him, together with the company of the Ark, and We made it a sign for all peoples.

١٦ وَإِبْرَاهِيمَ إِذْ قَالَ لِقَوْمِهِ اعْبُدُوا اللَّهَ وَاتَّقُوهُ ۖ ذَٰلِكُمْ خَيْرٌ لَكُمْ إِن كُنتُمْ تَعْلَمُونَ

16 And Abraham, when he said to his people, "Worship God, and fear Him. That is better for you, if you only knew.

16
6:74

١٧ إِنَّمَا تَعْبُدُونَ مِن دُونِ اللَّهِ أَوْثَانًا وَتَخْلُقُونَ إِفْكًا ۚ إِنَّ الَّذِينَ تَعْبُدُونَ مِن دُونِ اللَّهِ لَا يَمْلِكُونَ لَكُمْ رِزْقًا فَابْتَغُوا عِندَ اللَّهِ الرِّزْقَ وَاعْبُدُوهُ وَاشْكُرُوا لَهُ ۖ إِلَيْهِ تُرْجَعُونَ

17 You worship idols besides God, and you fabricate falsehoods. Those you worship, instead of God, cannot provide you with livelihood. So seek your livelihood from God, and worship Him, and thank Him. To Him you will be returned."

17
10:18, 106; 21:66; 25:55; 26:72–73

١٨ وَإِن تُكَذِّبُوا فَقَدْ كَذَّبَ أُمَمٌ مِّن قَبْلِكُمْ ۖ وَمَا عَلَى الرَّسُولِ إِلَّا الْبَلَاغُ الْمُبِينُ

18 If you disbelieve, communities before you have also disbelieved. The Messenger is only responsible for clear transmission.

18
10:39; 22:42

١٩ أَوَلَمْ يَرَوْا كَيْفَ يُبْدِئُ اللَّهُ الْخَلْقَ ثُمَّ يُعِيدُهُ ۚ إِنَّ ذَٰلِكَ عَلَى اللَّهِ يَسِيرٌ

19 Have they not seen how God originates the creation, and then reproduces it? This is easy for God.

19
10:4

٢٠ قُلْ سِيرُوا فِي الْأَرْضِ فَانظُرُوا كَيْفَ بَدَأَ الْخَلْقَ ۚ ثُمَّ اللَّهُ يُنشِئُ النَّشْأَةَ الْآخِرَةَ ۚ إِنَّ اللَّهَ عَلَىٰ كُلِّ شَيْءٍ قَدِيرٌ

20 Say, "Roam the earth, and observe how He originated the creation." Then God will bring about the next existence. God has power over all things.

٢١ يُعَذِّبُ مَن يَشَاءُ وَيَرْحَمُ مَن يَشَاءُ ۖ وَإِلَيْهِ تُقْلَبُونَ

21 He punishes whom He wills, and He grants mercy to whom He wills, and to Him you will be restored.

21
2:284

٢٢ وَمَا أَنْتُمْ بِمُعْجِزِينَ فِي الْأَرْضِ وَلَا فِي السَّمَاءِ ۖ وَمَا لَكُمْ مِنْ دُونِ اللَّهِ مِنْ وَلِيٍّ وَلَا نَصِيرٍ

22 You cannot escape, on earth or in the heaven; and you have no protector and no savior besides God.

22
11:20; 55:33

٢٣ وَالَّذِينَ كَفَرُوا بِآيَاتِ اللَّهِ وَلِقَائِهِ أُولَٰئِكَ يَئِسُوا مِنْ رَحْمَتِي وَأُولَٰئِكَ لَهُمْ عَذَابٌ أَلِيمٌ

23 Those who disbelieved in God's signs and His encounter—these have despaired of My mercy. For them is a painful torment.

٢٤ فَمَا كَانَ جَوَابَ قَوْمِهِ إِلَّا أَنْ قَالُوا اقْتُلُوهُ أَوْ حَرِّقُوهُ فَأَنْجَاهُ اللَّهُ مِنَ النَّارِ ۚ إِنَّ فِي ذَٰلِكَ لَآيَاتٍ لِقَوْمٍ يُؤْمِنُونَ

24 But the only response from his people was their saying, "Kill him, or burn him." But God saved him from the fire. Surely in that are signs for people who believe.

24
21:69

٢٥ وَقَالَ إِنَّمَا اتَّخَذْتُمْ مِنْ دُونِ اللَّهِ أَوْثَانًا مَوَدَّةَ بَيْنِكُمْ فِي الْحَيَاةِ الدُّنْيَا ۖ ثُمَّ يَوْمَ الْقِيَامَةِ يَكْفُرُ بَعْضُكُمْ بِبَعْضٍ وَيَلْعَنُ بَعْضُكُمْ بَعْضًا وَمَأْوَاكُمُ النَّارُ وَمَا لَكُمْ مِنْ نَاصِرِينَ

25 And he said, "You have chosen idols instead of God, out of affection for one another in the worldly life. But then, on the Day of Resurrection, you will disown one another, and curse one another. Your destiny is Hell, and you will have no saviors."

25
7:38; 19:82

٢٦ فَآمَنَ لَهُ لُوطٌ ۘ وَقَالَ إِنِّي مُهَاجِرٌ إِلَىٰ رَبِّي ۖ إِنَّهُ هُوَ الْعَزِيزُ الْحَكِيمُ

26 Then Lot believed in him, and said, "I am emigrating to my Lord. He is the Noble, the Wise."

٢٧ وَوَهَبْنَا لَهُ إِسْحَاقَ وَيَعْقُوبَ وَجَعَلْنَا فِي ذُرِّيَّتِهِ النُّبُوَّةَ وَالْكِتَابَ وَآتَيْنَاهُ أَجْرَهُ فِي الدُّنْيَا ۖ وَإِنَّهُ فِي الْآخِرَةِ لَمِنَ الصَّالِحِينَ

27 And We granted him Isaac and Jacob, and conferred on his descendants the Prophethood and the Book, and gave him his reward in this life; and in the Hereafter he will be among the upright.

27
2:225; 3:79; 5:89;
6:84, 89; 19:49; 21:72;
57:26

٢٨ وَلُوطًا إِذْ قَالَ لِقَوْمِهِ إِنَّكُمْ لَتَأْتُونَ الْفَاحِشَةَ مَا سَبَقَكُمْ بِهَا مِنْ أَحَدٍ مِنَ الْعَالَمِينَ

28 And Lot, when he said to his people, "You are committing an obscenity not perpetrated before you by anyone in the whole world.

28
7:80; 27:54

٢٩ أَئِنَّكُمْ لَتَأْتُونَ الرِّجَالَ وَتَقْطَعُونَ السَّبِيلَ وَتَأْتُونَ فِي نَادِيكُمُ الْمُنْكَرَ ۖ فَمَا كَانَ جَوَابَ قَوْمِهِ إِلَّا أَنْ قَالُوا ائْتِنَا بِعَذَابِ اللَّهِ إِنْ كُنْتَ مِنَ الصَّادِقِينَ

29 You approach men, and cut off the way, and commit lewdness in your gatherings." But the only response from his people was to say, "Bring upon us God's punishment, if you are truthful."

29
7:81; 15:63; 26:165;
27:55

٣٠ قَالَ رَبِّ انْصُرْنِي عَلَى الْقَوْمِ الْمُفْسِدِينَ

30 He said, "My Lord, help me against the people of corruption."

٣١ وَلَمَّا جَاءَتْ رُسُلُنَا إِبْرَاهِيمَ بِالْبُشْرَىٰ قَالُوا إِنَّا مُهْلِكُو أَهْلِ هَٰذِهِ الْقَرْيَةِ ۖ إِنَّ أَهْلَهَا كَانُوا ظَالِمِينَ

31 And when Our envoys brought Abraham the good news, they said, "We are going to destroy the people of this town; its people are wrong-doers."

31
11:69, 74; 15:51–56;
51:24–30

٣٢ قَالَ إِنَّ فِيهَا لُوطًا ۚ قَالُوا نَحْنُ أَعْلَمُ بِمَن فِيهَا ۖ لَنُنَجِّيَنَّهُ وَأَهْلَهُ إِلَّا امْرَأَتَهُ كَانَتْ مِنَ الْغَابِرِينَ

32 He said, "Yet Lot is in it." They said, "We are well aware of who is in it. We will save him, and his family, except for his wife, who will remain behind."

32
7:83; 11:77; 15:61

٣٣ وَلَمَّا أَن جَاءَتْ رُسُلُنَا لُوطًا سِيءَ بِهِمْ وَضَاقَ بِهِمْ ذَرْعًا وَقَالُوا لَا تَخَفْ وَلَا تَحْزَنْ ۖ إِنَّا مُنَجُّوكَ وَأَهْلَكَ إِلَّا امْرَأَتَكَ كَانَتْ مِنَ الْغَابِرِينَ

33 Then, when Our envoys came to Lot, they were mistreated, and he was troubled and distressed on their account. They said, "Do not fear, nor grieve. We will save you and your family, except for your wife, who will remain behind."

٣٤ إِنَّا مُنزِلُونَ عَلَىٰ أَهْلِ هَٰذِهِ الْقَرْيَةِ رِجْزًا مِّنَ السَّمَاءِ بِمَا كَانُوا يَفْسُقُونَ

34 "We will bring down upon the people of this town a scourge from heaven, because of their wickedness."

34
7:84

٣٥ وَلَقَد تَّرَكْنَا مِنْهَا آيَةً بَيِّنَةً لِّقَوْمٍ يَعْقِلُونَ

35 And We left behind a clear trace of it, for people who understand.

35
11:83; 51:37

٣٦ وَإِلَىٰ مَدْيَنَ أَخَاهُمْ شُعَيْبًا فَقَالَ يَا قَوْمِ اعْبُدُوا اللَّهَ وَارْجُوا الْيَوْمَ الْآخِرَ وَلَا تَعْثَوْا فِي الْأَرْضِ مُفْسِدِينَ

36 And to Median, their brother Shuaib. He said, "O my people, worship God and anticipate the Last Day, and do not spread corruption in the land."

36–37
7:85–93; 11:84

٣٧ فَكَذَّبُوهُ فَأَخَذَتْهُمُ الرَّجْفَةُ فَأَصْبَحُوا فِي دَارِهِمْ جَاثِمِينَ

37 But they rejected him, so the tremor overtook them, and they were left motionless in their homes.

٣٨ وَعَادًا وَثَمُودَ وَقَد تَّبَيَّنَ لَكُم مِّن مَّسَاكِنِهِمْ ۖ وَزَيَّنَ لَهُمُ الشَّيْطَانُ أَعْمَالَهُمْ فَصَدَّهُمْ عَنِ السَّبِيلِ وَكَانُوا مُسْتَبْصِرِينَ

38 And 'Ād and Thamūd. It has become clear to you from their dwellings. Satan embellished for them their deeds, barring them from the path, even though they could see.

38
7:65–72, 73–79;
11:67–68

٣٩ وَقَارُونَ وَفِرْعَوْنَ وَهَامَانَ ۖ وَلَقَدْ جَاءَهُم مُّوسَىٰ بِالْبَيِّنَاتِ فَاسْتَكْبَرُوا فِي الْأَرْضِ وَمَا كَانُوا سَابِقِينَ

39 And Qārūn, and Pharaoh, and Hāman—Moses went to them with clear arguments, but they acted arrogantly in the land. And they could not get ahead.

39
28:39; 76–84; 40:24, 36

٤٠ فَكُلًّا أَخَذْنَا بِذَنبِهِ ۖ فَمِنْهُم مَّنْ أَرْسَلْنَا عَلَيْهِ حَاصِبًا وَمِنْهُم مَّنْ أَخَذَتْهُ الصَّيْحَةُ وَمِنْهُم مَّنْ خَسَفْنَا بِهِ الْأَرْضَ وَمِنْهُم مَّنْ أَغْرَقْنَا ۚ وَمَا كَانَ اللَّهُ لِيَظْلِمَهُمْ وَلَٰكِن كَانُوا أَنفُسَهُمْ يَظْلِمُونَ

40 7:64; 10:73; 11:67, 94; 15:73, 83; 17:68; 54:34

40 Each We seized by his sin. Against some We sent a sandstorm. Some were struck by the Blast. Some We caused the ground to cave in beneath them. And some We drowned. It was not God who wronged them, but it was they who wronged their own selves.

٤١ مَثَلُ الَّذِينَ اتَّخَذُوا مِن دُونِ اللَّهِ أَوْلِيَاءَ كَمَثَلِ الْعَنكَبُوتِ اتَّخَذَتْ بَيْتًا ۖ وَإِنَّ أَوْهَنَ الْبُيُوتِ لَبَيْتُ الْعَنكَبُوتِ ۖ لَوْ كَانُوا يَعْلَمُونَ

41 7:176; 22:72; 62:5

41 The likeness of those who take to themselves protectors other than God is that of the spider. It builds a house. But the most fragile of houses is the spider's house. If they only knew.

٤٢ إِنَّ اللَّهَ يَعْلَمُ مَا يَدْعُونَ مِن دُونِهِ مِن شَيْءٍ ۚ وَهُوَ الْعَزِيزُ الْحَكِيمُ

42 God knows what they invoke besides Him. He is the Almighty, the Wise.

٤٣ وَتِلْكَ الْأَمْثَالُ نَضْرِبُهَا لِلنَّاسِ ۖ وَمَا يَعْقِلُهَا إِلَّا الْعَالِمُونَ

43 14:24; 59:21

43 These examples—We put them forward to the people; but none grasps them except the learned.

٤٤ خَلَقَ اللَّهُ السَّمَاوَاتِ وَالْأَرْضَ بِالْحَقِّ ۚ إِنَّ فِي ذَٰلِكَ لَآيَةً لِّلْمُؤْمِنِينَ

44 God created the heavens and the earth with truth. Surely in that is a sign for the believers.

٤٥ اتْلُ مَا أُوحِيَ إِلَيْكَ مِنَ الْكِتَابِ وَأَقِمِ الصَّلَاةَ ۖ إِنَّ الصَّلَاةَ تَنْهَىٰ عَنِ الْفَحْشَاءِ وَالْمُنكَرِ ۗ وَلَذِكْرُ اللَّهِ أَكْبَرُ ۗ وَاللَّهُ يَعْلَمُ مَا تَصْنَعُونَ

45 2:45; 6:73

45 Recite what is revealed to you of the Scripture, and perform the prayer. The prayer prevents indecencies and evils. And the remembrance of God is greater. And God knows what you do.

٤٦ وَلَا تُجَادِلُوا أَهْلَ الْكِتَابِ إِلَّا بِالَّتِي هِيَ أَحْسَنُ إِلَّا الَّذِينَ ظَلَمُوا مِنْهُمْ ۖ وَقُولُوا آمَنَّا بِالَّذِي أُنزِلَ إِلَيْنَا وَأُنزِلَ إِلَيْكُمْ وَإِلَٰهُنَا وَإِلَٰهُكُمْ وَاحِدٌ وَنَحْنُ لَهُ مُسْلِمُونَ

46 2:139; 16:125

46 And do not argue with the People of the Scripture except in the best manner possible, except those who do wrong among them. And say, "We believe in what was revealed to us, and in what was revealed to you; and our God and your God is One; and to Him we are submissive."

٤٧ وَكَذَٰلِكَ أَنزَلْنَا إِلَيْكَ الْكِتَابَ ۚ فَالَّذِينَ آتَيْنَاهُمُ الْكِتَابَ يُؤْمِنُونَ بِهِ ۖ وَمِنْ هَٰؤُلَاءِ مَن يُؤْمِنُ بِهِ ۚ وَمَا يَجْحَدُ بِآيَاتِنَا إِلَّا الْكَافِرُونَ

47 28:52

47 Likewise, We revealed to you the Scripture. Those to whom We gave the Scripture believe in it, and some of these believe in it. None renounce Our communications except the disbelievers.

٤٨ وَمَا كُنتَ تَتْلُو مِن قَبْلِهِ مِن كِتَابٍ وَلَا تَخُطُّهُ بِيَمِينِكَ ۖ إِذًا لَّارْتَابَ الْمُبْطِلُونَ

48 You did not read any scripture before this, nor did you write it down with your right hand; otherwise the falsifiers would have doubted.

48
7:173; 30:58; 40:78; 45:27

٤٩ بَلْ هُوَ آيَاتٌ بَيِّنَاتٌ فِي صُدُورِ الَّذِينَ أُوتُوا الْعِلْمَ ۚ وَمَا يَجْحَدُ بِآيَاتِنَا إِلَّا الظَّالِمُونَ

49 In fact, it is clear signs in the hearts of those given knowledge. No one renounce Our signs except the unjust.

٥٠ وَقَالُوا لَوْلَا أُنزِلَ عَلَيْهِ آيَاتٌ مِّن رَّبِّهِ ۖ قُلْ إِنَّمَا الْآيَاتُ عِندَ اللَّهِ وَإِنَّمَا أَنَا نَذِيرٌ مُّبِينٌ

50 And they said, "If only a miracle from his Lord was sent down to him." Say, "Miracles are only with God, and I am only a clear warner."

50
6:37; 13:7

٥١ أَوَلَمْ يَكْفِهِمْ أَنَّا أَنزَلْنَا عَلَيْكَ الْكِتَابَ يُتْلَىٰ عَلَيْهِمْ ۚ إِنَّ فِي ذَٰلِكَ لَرَحْمَةً وَذِكْرَىٰ لِقَوْمٍ يُؤْمِنُونَ

51 Does it not suffice them that We revealed to you the Scripture, which is recited to them? In that is mercy and a reminder for people who believe.

٥٢ قُلْ كَفَىٰ بِاللَّهِ بَيْنِي وَبَيْنَكُمْ شَهِيدًا ۖ يَعْلَمُ مَا فِي السَّمَاوَاتِ وَالْأَرْضِ ۗ وَالَّذِينَ آمَنُوا بِالْبَاطِلِ وَكَفَرُوا بِاللَّهِ أُولَٰئِكَ هُمُ الْخَاسِرُونَ

52 Say, "God suffices as witness between you and me. He knows everything in the heavens and the Earth. Those who believe in vanity and reject God—it is they who are the losers."

52
13:43

٥٣ وَيَسْتَعْجِلُونَكَ بِالْعَذَابِ ۚ وَلَوْلَا أَجَلٌ مُّسَمًّى لَّجَاءَهُمُ الْعَذَابُ وَلَيَأْتِيَنَّهُم بَغْتَةً وَهُمْ لَا يَشْعُرُونَ

53 And they urge you to hasten the punishment. Were it not for a specified time, the punishment would have come to them. But it will come upon them suddenly, while they are unaware.

53
6:13, 57; 10:50; 22:47; 26:204; 37:176

٥٤ يَسْتَعْجِلُونَكَ بِالْعَذَابِ وَإِنَّ جَهَنَّمَ لَمُحِيطَةٌ بِالْكَافِرِينَ

54 They urge you to hasten the punishment. But Hell will engulf the disbelievers.

54
9:49

٥٥ يَوْمَ يَغْشَاهُمُ الْعَذَابُ مِن فَوْقِهِمْ وَمِن تَحْتِ أَرْجُلِهِمْ وَيَقُولُ ذُوقُوا مَا كُنتُمْ تَعْمَلُونَ

55 On the Day when the punishment will envelop them, from above them, and from beneath their feet, He will say, "Taste what you used to do!"

55
39:16

٥٦ يَا عِبَادِيَ الَّذِينَ آمَنُوا إِنَّ أَرْضِي وَاسِعَةٌ فَإِيَّايَ فَاعْبُدُونِ

56 O My servants who have believed: My earth is vast, so worship Me alone.

56
4:97, 100; 39:10

٥٧ كُلُّ نَفْسٍ ذَائِقَةُ الْمَوْتِ ۖ ثُمَّ إِلَيْنَا تُرْجَعُونَ

57 Every soul will taste death. Then to Us you will be returned.

57
3:185; 21:35

٥٨ وَالَّذِينَ آمَنُوا وَعَمِلُوا الصَّالِحَاتِ لَنُبَوِّئَنَّهُم مِّنَ الْجَنَّةِ غُرَفًا تَجْرِي مِن تَحْتِهَا الْأَنْهَارُ خَالِدِينَ فِيهَا ۚ نِعْمَ أَجْرُ الْعَامِلِينَ

58 | 25:75; 39:16

58 Those who believe and work righteousness—We will settle them in Paradise, in mansions under which rivers flow, dwelling therein forever. Excellent is the compensation for the workers.

٥٩ الَّذِينَ صَبَرُوا وَعَلَىٰ رَبِّهِمْ يَتَوَكَّلُونَ

59 | 16:42

59 Those who endure patiently, and in their Lord they trust.

٦٠ وَكَأَيِّن مِّن دَابَّةٍ لَّا تَحْمِلُ رِزْقَهَا اللَّهُ يَرْزُقُهَا وَإِيَّاكُمْ ۚ وَهُوَ السَّمِيعُ الْعَلِيمُ

60 | 11:6

60 How many a creature there is that does not carry its provision? God provides for them, and for you. He is the Hearer, the Knowledgeable.

٦١ وَلَئِن سَأَلْتَهُم مَّنْ خَلَقَ السَّمَاوَاتِ وَالْأَرْضَ وَسَخَّرَ الشَّمْسَ وَالْقَمَرَ لَيَقُولُنَّ اللَّهُ ۖ فَأَنَّىٰ يُؤْفَكُونَ

61 | 31:25; 39:38; 43:9

61 And if you asked them, "Who created the heavens and the earth and regulated the sun and the moon?" They would say, "God." Why then do they deviate?

٦٢ اللَّهُ يَبْسُطُ الرِّزْقَ لِمَن يَشَاءُ مِنْ عِبَادِهِ وَيَقْدِرُ لَهُ ۚ إِنَّ اللَّهَ بِكُلِّ شَيْءٍ عَلِيمٌ

62 | 13:26; 34:39

62 God expands the provision for whomever He wills of His servants, and restricts it. God is Cognizant of all things.

٦٣ وَلَئِن سَأَلْتَهُم مَّن نَّزَّلَ مِنَ السَّمَاءِ مَاءً فَأَحْيَا بِهِ الْأَرْضَ مِن بَعْدِ مَوْتِهَا لَيَقُولُنَّ اللَّهُ ۚ قُلِ الْحَمْدُ لِلَّهِ ۚ بَلْ أَكْثَرُهُمْ لَا يَعْقِلُونَ

63 | 2:164

63 And if you asked them, "Who sends water down from the sky, with which He revives the earth after it had died?" They would say, "God." Say, "Praise be to God." But most of them do not understand.

٦٤ وَمَا هَٰذِهِ الْحَيَاةُ الدُّنْيَا إِلَّا لَهْوٌ وَلَعِبٌ ۚ وَإِنَّ الدَّارَ الْآخِرَةَ لَهِيَ الْحَيَوَانُ ۚ لَوْ كَانُوا يَعْلَمُونَ

64 | 6:32, 70; 7:51; 47:36; 57:20

64 The life of this world is nothing but diversion and play, and the Home of the Hereafter is the Life, if they only knew.

٦٥ فَإِذَا رَكِبُوا فِي الْفُلْكِ دَعَوُا اللَّهَ مُخْلِصِينَ لَهُ الدِّينَ فَلَمَّا نَجَّاهُمْ إِلَى الْبَرِّ إِذَا هُمْ يُشْرِكُونَ

65 | 6:63; 10:22; 16:53; 17:67

65 When they embark on a vessel, they pray to God, devoting their faith to Him; but once He has delivered them safely to land, they attribute partners to Him.

٦٦ لِيَكْفُرُوا بِمَا آتَيْنَاهُمْ وَلِيَتَمَتَّعُوا ۖ فَسَوْفَ يَعْلَمُونَ

66

66 To be ungrateful for what We have given them, and to enjoy themselves. They will surely come to know.

٦٧ أَوَلَمْ يَرَوْا أَنَّا جَعَلْنَا حَرَمًا آمِنًا وَيُتَخَطَّفُ النَّاسُ مِنْ حَوْلِهِمْ ۚ أَفَبِالْبَاطِلِ يُؤْمِنُونَ وَبِنِعْمَةِ اللَّهِ يَكْفُرُونَb

67
a 2:125; 3:97; 5:97; 106:3–4
b 2:125; 8:26; 28:57; 106:4

67 Do they not see that We established a Secure Sanctuary, while all around them the people are being carried away? Do they believe in falsehood, and reject the blessings of God?

٦٨ وَمَنْ أَظْلَمُ مِمَّنِ افْتَرَىٰ عَلَى اللَّهِ كَذِبًا أَوْ كَذَّبَ بِالْحَقِّ لَمَّا جَاءَهُ ۚ أَلَيْسَ فِي جَهَنَّمَ مَثْوًى لِلْكَافِرِينَ

68 And who does greater wrong than he who fabricates lies and attributes them to God, or calls the truth a lie when it has come to him? Is there not in Hell a dwelling for the blasphemers?

68
6:5, 21; 39:32

٦٩ وَالَّذِينَ جَاهَدُوا فِينَا لَنَهْدِيَنَّهُمْ سُبُلَنَا ۚ وَإِنَّ اللَّهَ لَمَعَ الْمُحْسِنِينَ

69 As for those who strive for Us—We will guide them in Our ways. God is with the doers of good.

Sūrah 30: Al-Rūm

سُورَةُ ٱلرُّومِ (The Romans)

بِسْمِ ٱللَّهِ ٱلرَّحْمَـٰنِ ٱلرَّحِيمِ

١ الم

1 Alif, Lām, Mīm.

٢ غُلِبَتِ الرُّومُ

2 The Romans have been defeated.

٣ فِي أَدْنَى الْأَرْضِ وَهُم مِّنْ بَعْدِ غَلَبِهِمْ سَيَغْلِبُونَ

3 In a nearby territory. But following their defeat, they will be victorious.

٤ فِي بِضْعِ سِنِينَ ۗ لِلَّهِ الْأَمْرُ مِنْ قَبْلُ وَمِنْ بَعْدُ ۚ وَيَوْمَئِذٍ يَفْرَحُ الْمُؤْمِنُونَ

4 In a few years. The matter is up to God, in the past, and in the future. On that day, the believers will rejoice.

٥ بِنَصْرِ اللَّهِ ۚ يَنصُرُ مَن يَشَاءُ ۖ وَهُوَ الْعَزِيزُ الرَّحِيمُ

5 In God's support. He supports whomever He wills. He is the Almighty, the Merciful.

٦ وَعْدَ اللَّهِ ۖ لَا يُخْلِفُ اللَّهُ وَعْدَهُ وَلَٰكِنَّ أَكْثَرَ النَّاسِ لَا يَعْلَمُونَ

6 The promise of God—God never breaks His promise, but most people do not know.

6
3:9; 10:55; 13:31;
30:60; 14:47; 39:20

٧ يَعْلَمُونَ ظَاهِرًا مِّنَ الْحَيَاةِ الدُّنْيَا وَهُمْ عَنِ الْآخِرَةِ هُمْ غَافِلُونَ

7 They know an outer aspect of the worldly life, but they are heedless of the Hereafter.

٨ أَوَلَمْ يَتَفَكَّرُوا فِي أَنْفُسِهِمْ ۗ مَا خَلَقَ اللَّهُ السَّمَاوَاتِ وَالْأَرْضَ وَمَا بَيْنَهُمَا إِلَّا بِالْحَقِّ وَأَجَلٍ مُسَمًّى ۗ وَإِنَّ كَثِيرًا مِنَ النَّاسِ بِلِقَاءِ رَبِّهِمْ لَكَافِرُونَ

8 3:191; 6:73; 15:85; 38:27; 44:39; 46:3

8 Do they not reflect within themselves? God did not create the heavens and the earth, and what is between them, except with reason, and for a specific duration. But most people, regarding meeting their Lord, are disbelievers.

٩ أَوَلَمْ يَسِيرُوا فِي الْأَرْضِ فَيَنْظُرُوا كَيْفَ كَانَ عَاقِبَةُ الَّذِينَ مِنْ قَبْلِهِمْ ۚ كَانُوا أَشَدَّ مِنْهُمْ قُوَّةً وَأَثَارُوا الْأَرْضَ وَعَمَرُوهَا أَكْثَرَ مِمَّا عَمَرُوهَا وَجَاءَتْهُمْ رُسُلُهُمْ بِالْبَيِّنَاتِ ۖ فَمَا كَانَ اللَّهُ لِيَظْلِمَهُمْ وَلَٰكِنْ كَانُوا أَنْفُسَهُمْ يَظْلِمُونَ

9 3:137; 12:109; 35:44; 40:21

9 Have they not travelled the earth and seen how those before them ended up? They were more powerful than them, and they cultivated the land and developed it more than they developed it, and their messengers came to them with clear signs. God would never wrong them, but they used to wrong themselves.

١٠ ثُمَّ كَانَ عَاقِبَةَ الَّذِينَ أَسَاءُوا السُّوأَىٰ أَنْ كَذَّبُوا بِآيَاتِ اللَّهِ وَكَانُوا بِهَا يَسْتَهْزِئُونَ

10 41:27

10 Then, evil was the end of those who committed evil. That is because they rejected God's revelations, and used to ridicule them.

١١ اللَّهُ يَبْدَأُ الْخَلْقَ ثُمَّ يُعِيدُهُ ثُمَّ إِلَيْهِ تُرْجَعُونَ

11 10:4; 30:27

11 God originates creation, and then repeats it. Then to Him you will be returned.

١٢ وَيَوْمَ تَقُومُ السَّاعَةُ يُبْلِسُ الْمُجْرِمُونَ

12 On the Day when the Hour takes place, the guilty will despair.

١٣ وَلَمْ يَكُنْ لَهُمْ مِنْ شُرَكَائِهِمْ شُفَعَاءُ وَكَانُوا بِشُرَكَائِهِمْ كَافِرِينَ

13 2:48

13 They will have no intercessors from among their idols, and they will disown their partners.

١٤ وَيَوْمَ تَقُومُ السَّاعَةُ يَوْمَئِذٍ يَتَفَرَّقُونَ

14 On the Day when the Hour takes place—on that Day they will separate.

١٥ فَأَمَّا الَّذِينَ آمَنُوا وَعَمِلُوا الصَّالِحَاتِ فَهُمْ فِي رَوْضَةٍ يُحْبَرُونَ

15 As for those who believed and did good deeds—they will be delighted in meadows.

١٦ وَأَمَّا الَّذِينَ كَفَرُوا وَكَذَّبُوا بِآيَاتِنَا وَلِقَاءِ الْآخِرَةِ فَأُولَٰئِكَ فِي الْعَذَابِ مُحْضَرُونَ

16 23:74; 29:61

16 But as for those who disbelieved, and rejected Our signs and the encounter of the Hereafter—those will be hauled into the torment.

١٧ فَسُبْحَانَ اللَّهِ حِينَ تُمْسُونَ وَحِينَ تُصْبِحُونَ

17 So glorify God when you retire at night, and when you rise in the morning.

١٨ وَلَهُ الْحَمْدُ فِي السَّمَاوَاتِ وَالْأَرْضِ وَعَشِيًّا وَحِينَ تُظْهِرُونَ

18 His is the praise in the heavens and on earth, and in the evening, and when you reach midday.

١٩ يُخْرِجُ الْحَيَّ مِنَ الْمَيِّتِ وَيُخْرِجُ الْمَيِّتَ مِنَ الْحَيِّ وَيُحْيِي الْأَرْضَ بَعْدَ مَوْتِهَا ۚ وَكَذَٰلِكَ تُخْرَجُونَ

19 He brings the living out of the dead, and He brings the dead out of the living, and He revives the land after it had died. Likewise you will be resurrected.

19
3:27; 6:95; 10:31; 16:11; 22:2

٢٠ وَمِنْ آيَاتِهِ أَنْ خَلَقَكُمْ مِنْ تُرَابٍ ثُمَّ إِذَا أَنْتُمْ بَشَرٌ تَنْتَشِرُونَ

20 And of His signs is that He created you from dust; and behold, you become humans spreading out.

20
20:55

٢١ وَمِنْ آيَاتِهِ أَنْ خَلَقَ لَكُمْ مِنْ أَنْفُسِكُمْ أَزْوَاجًا لِتَسْكُنُوا إِلَيْهَا وَجَعَلَ بَيْنَكُمْ مَوَدَّةً وَرَحْمَةً ۚ إِنَّ فِي ذَٰلِكَ لَآيَاتٍ لِقَوْمٍ يَتَفَكَّرُونَ

21 And of His signs is that He created for you mates from among yourselves, so that you may find tranquility in them; and He planted love and compassion between you. In this are signs for people who reflect.

21
7:189; 16:72

٢٢ وَمِنْ آيَاتِهِ خَلْقُ السَّمَاوَاتِ وَالْأَرْضِ وَاخْتِلَافُ أَلْسِنَتِكُمْ وَأَلْوَانِكُمْ ۚ إِنَّ فِي ذَٰلِكَ لَآيَاتٍ لِلْعَالِمِينَ

22 And of His signs is the creation of the heavens and the earth, and the diversity of your languages and colors. In this are signs for those who know.

22
2:164; 17:12; 35:27–28

٢٣ وَمِنْ آيَاتِهِ مَنَامُكُمْ بِاللَّيْلِ وَالنَّهَارِ وَابْتِغَاؤُكُمْ مِنْ فَضْلِهِ ۚ إِنَّ فِي ذَٰلِكَ لَآيَاتٍ لِقَوْمٍ يَسْمَعُونَ

23 And of His signs are your sleep by night and day, and your pursuit of His bounty. In this are signs for people who listen.

23
10:67; 17:12; 27:86; 28:71–73

٢٤ وَمِنْ آيَاتِهِ يُرِيكُمُ الْبَرْقَ خَوْفًا وَطَمَعًا وَيُنَزِّلُ مِنَ السَّمَاءِ مَاءً فَيُحْيِي بِهِ الْأَرْضَ بَعْدَ مَوْتِهَا ۚ إِنَّ فِي ذَٰلِكَ لَآيَاتٍ لِقَوْمٍ يَعْقِلُونَ

24 And of His signs is that He shows you the lightning, causing fear and hope. And He brings down water from the sky, and with it He revives the earth after it was dead. In this are signs for people who understand.

24
13:12

٢٥ وَمِنْ آيَاتِهِ أَنْ تَقُومَ السَّمَاءُ وَالْأَرْضُ بِأَمْرِهِ ۚ ثُمَّ إِذَا دَعَاكُمْ دَعْوَةً مِنَ الْأَرْضِ إِذَا أَنْتُمْ تَخْرُجُونَ

25 And of His signs is that the heaven and the earth stand at His disposal. And then, when He calls you out of the earth, you will emerge at once.

25
13:2; 21:31; 31:10; 35:41

٢٦ وَلَهُ مَن فِى السَّمَاوَاتِ وَالْأَرْضِ ۖ كُلٌّ لَّهُ قَانِتُونَ

26 To Him belongs everyone in the heavens and the earth. All are submissive to Him.

٢٧ وَهُوَ الَّذِى يَبْدَأُ الْخَلْقَ ثُمَّ يُعِيدُهُ وَهُوَ أَهْوَنُ عَلَيْهِ ۚ وَلَهُ الْمَثَلُ الْأَعْلَىٰ فِى السَّمَاوَاتِ وَالْأَرْضِ ۚ وَهُوَ الْعَزِيزُ الْحَكِيمُ

27
10:4; 30:11

27 It is He who initiates creation, and then repeats it, something easy for Him. His is the highest attribute, in the heavens and the earth. He is the Almighty, the Wise.

٢٨ ضَرَبَ لَكُم مَّثَلًا مِّنْ أَنفُسِكُمْ ۖ هَل لَّكُم مِّن مَّا مَلَكَتْ أَيْمَانُكُم مِّن شُرَكَاءَ فِى مَا رَزَقْنَاكُمْ فَأَنتُمْ فِيهِ سَوَاءٌ تَخَافُونَهُمْ كَخِيفَتِكُمْ أَنفُسَكُمْ ۚ كَذَٰلِكَ نُفَصِّلُ الْآيَاتِ لِقَوْمٍ يَعْقِلُونَ

28
16:71

28 He illustrates an example for you, from your own selves: do you make your servants full partners in the wealth We have given you? Do you revere them as you revere one another? We thus explain the revelations for a people who understand.

٢٩ بَلِ اتَّبَعَ الَّذِينَ ظَلَمُوا أَهْوَاءَهُم بِغَيْرِ عِلْمٍ ۖ فَمَن يَهْدِى مَنْ أَضَلَّ اللَّهُ ۖ وَمَا لَهُم مِّن نَّاصِرِينَ

29
2:120

29 Yet the wrongdoers follow their desires without knowledge. But who can guide whom God leaves astray? They will have no helpers.

٣٠ فَأَقِمْ وَجْهَكَ لِلدِّينِ حَنِيفًا ۚ فِطْرَتَ اللَّهِ الَّتِى فَطَرَ النَّاسَ عَلَيْهَا ۚ لَا تَبْدِيلَ لِخَلْقِ اللَّهِ ۚ ذَٰلِكَ الدِّينُ الْقَيِّمُ وَلَٰكِنَّ أَكْثَرَ النَّاسِ لَا يَعْلَمُونَ

30
10:105; 6:79; 7:29

30 So devote yourself to the religion of monotheism—the natural instinct God has instilled in mankind. There is no altering God's creation. This is the true religion, but most people do not know.

٣١ مُنِيبِينَ إِلَيْهِ وَاتَّقُوهُ وَأَقِيمُوا الصَّلَاةَ وَلَا تَكُونُوا مِنَ الْمُشْرِكِينَ

31 Turning towards Him—and be conscious of Him, and perform the prayer, and do not be of the idolaters.

٣٢ مِنَ الَّذِينَ فَرَّقُوا دِينَهُمْ وَكَانُوا شِيَعًا ۖ كُلُّ حِزْبٍ بِمَا لَدَيْهِمْ فَرِحُونَ

32 Of those who divided their religion, and became sects; each faction pleased with what they have.

٣٣ وَإِذَا مَسَّ النَّاسَ ضُرٌّ دَعَوْا رَبَّهُم مُّنِيبِينَ إِلَيْهِ ثُمَّ إِذَا أَذَاقَهُم مِّنْهُ رَحْمَةً إِذَا فَرِيقٌ مِّنْهُم بِرَبِّهِمْ يُشْرِكُونَ

33
10:21; 16:53; 29:65; 29:8

33 When affliction touches the people, they call on their Lord, turning to Him in repentance. But then, when He gives them a taste of His mercy, some of them attribute partners to their Lord.

٣٤ لِيَكْفُرُوا بِمَا آتَيْنَاهُمْ ۚ فَتَمَتَّعُوا فَسَوْفَ تَعْلَمُونَ

34
16:55; 29:66

34 To show ingratitude for what We have given them. Indulge yourselves—you will surely know.

٣٥ أَمْ أَنزَلْنَا عَلَيْهِمْ سُلْطَانًا فَهُوَ يَتَكَلَّمُ بِمَا كَانُوا بِهِ يُشْرِكُونَ

35 Have We sent down to them any authority, which speaks in support of their idols?

35 — 3:151; 37:156

٣٦ وَإِذَا أَذَقْنَا النَّاسَ رَحْمَةً فَرِحُوا بِهَا ۖ وَإِن تُصِبْهُمْ سَيِّئَةٌ بِمَا قَدَّمَتْ أَيْدِيهِمْ إِذَا هُمْ يَقْنَطُونَ

36 When We give people a taste of mercy, they rejoice in it. But when adversity befalls them, because of what their hands have perpetrated, they begin to despair.

36 — 119; 17:83; 41:49; 42:48

٣٧ أَوَلَمْ يَرَوْا أَنَّ اللَّهَ يَبْسُطُ الرِّزْقَ لِمَن يَشَاءُ وَيَقْدِرُ ۚ إِنَّ فِي ذَٰلِكَ لَآيَاتٍ لِّقَوْمٍ يُؤْمِنُونَ

37 Do they not see that God expands the provision for whomever He wills, or restricts it? Surely in this are signs for people who believe.

37 — 13:26; 39:52

٣٨ فَآتِ ذَا الْقُرْبَىٰ حَقَّهُ وَالْمِسْكِينَ وَابْنَ السَّبِيلِ ۚ ذَٰلِكَ خَيْرٌ لِّلَّذِينَ يُرِيدُونَ وَجْهَ اللَّهِ ۖ وَأُولَٰئِكَ هُمُ الْمُفْلِحُونَ

38 So give the relative his rights, and the destitute, and the wayfarer. That is best for those who seek God's presence. Those are the prosperous.

38 — 2:83; 4:36; 17:26

٣٩ وَمَا آتَيْتُم مِّن رِّبًا لِّيَرْبُوَ فِي أَمْوَالِ النَّاسِ فَلَا يَرْبُو عِندَ اللَّهِ ۖ وَمَا آتَيْتُم مِّن زَكَاةٍ تُرِيدُونَ وَجْهَ اللَّهِ فَأُولَٰئِكَ هُمُ الْمُضْعِفُونَ

39 The usury you practice, seeking thereby to multiply people's wealth, will not multiply with God. But what you give in charity, desiring God's approval—these are the multipliers.

39 — 2:275–276; 3:130; 4:161

٤٠ اللَّهُ الَّذِي خَلَقَكُمْ ثُمَّ رَزَقَكُمْ ثُمَّ يُمِيتُكُمْ ثُمَّ يُحْيِيكُمْ ۖ هَلْ مِن شُرَكَائِكُم مَّن يَفْعَلُ مِن ذَٰلِكُم مِّن شَيْءٍ ۚ سُبْحَانَهُ وَتَعَالَىٰ عَمَّا يُشْرِكُونَ

40 God is He who created you, then provides for you, then makes you die, then brings you back to life. Can any of your idols do any of that? Glorified is He, and Exalted above what they associate.

40 — 2:28; 22:66; 26:81; 45:26

٤١ ظَهَرَ الْفَسَادُ فِي الْبَرِّ وَالْبَحْرِ بِمَا كَسَبَتْ أَيْدِي النَّاسِ لِيُذِيقَهُم بَعْضَ الَّذِي عَمِلُوا لَعَلَّهُمْ يَرْجِعُونَ

41 Corruption has appeared on land and sea, because of what people's hands have earned, in order to make them taste some of what they have done, so that they might return.

٤٢ قُلْ سِيرُوا فِي الْأَرْضِ فَانظُرُوا كَيْفَ كَانَ عَاقِبَةُ الَّذِينَ مِن قَبْلُ ۚ كَانَ أَكْثَرُهُم مُّشْرِكِينَ

42 Say, "Roam the earth, and observe the fate of those who came before. Most of them were idolaters."

42 — 3:137

٤٣ فَأَقِمْ وَجْهَكَ لِلدِّينِ الْقَيِّمِ مِن قَبْلِ أَن يَأْتِيَ يَوْمٌ لَّا مَرَدَّ لَهُ مِنَ اللَّهِ ۖ يَوْمَئِذٍ يَصَّدَّعُونَ

43 So devote yourself to the upright religion, before there comes from God a Day that cannot be averted. On that Day, they will be shocked.

Sūrah 30: Al-Rūm

٤٤ مَنْ كَفَرَ فَعَلَيْهِ كُفْرُهُ ۖ وَمَنْ عَمِلَ صَالِحًا فَلِأَنْفُسِهِمْ يَمْهَدُونَ

44 Whoever disbelieves, upon him falls his disbelief. And whoever acts righteously—they are preparing for themselves.

44
17:7; 41:46; 45:15

٤٥ لِيَجْزِيَ الَّذِينَ آمَنُوا وَعَمِلُوا الصَّالِحَاتِ مِنْ فَضْلِهِ ۗ إِنَّهُ لَا يُحِبُّ الْكَافِرِينَ

45 So that He may reward those who have believed and done the righteous deeds out of His bounty. Indeed, He does not love the ungrateful.

45
10:4; 14:51; 33:24; 34:4

٤٦ وَمِنْ آيَاتِهِ أَنْ يُرْسِلَ الرِّيَاحَ مُبَشِّرَاتٍ وَلِيُذِيقَكُمْ مِنْ رَحْمَتِهِ وَلِتَجْرِيَ الْفُلْكُ بِأَمْرِهِ وَلِتَبْتَغُوا مِنْ فَضْلِهِ وَلَعَلَّكُمْ تَشْكُرُونَ

46 And of His signs is that He sends the winds bearing good news, to give you a taste of His mercy, and so that the ships may sail by His command, and so that you may seek of His bounty, and so that you may give thanks.

46
2:164; 7:57; 25:48; 27:63

٤٧ وَلَقَدْ أَرْسَلْنَا مِنْ قَبْلِكَ رُسُلًا إِلَىٰ قَوْمِهِمْ فَجَاءُوهُمْ بِالْبَيِّنَاتِ فَانْتَقَمْنَا مِنَ الَّذِينَ أَجْرَمُوا ۖ وَكَانَ حَقًّا عَلَيْنَا نَصْرُ الْمُؤْمِنِينَ

47 Before you, We sent messengers to their people. They came to them with clear proofs. Then We took revenge on those who sinned. It is incumbent on Us to help the believers.

47
10:101–103; 12:110; 32:22

٤٨ اللَّهُ الَّذِي يُرْسِلُ الرِّيَاحَ فَتُثِيرُ سَحَابًا فَيَبْسُطُهُ فِي السَّمَاءِ كَيْفَ يَشَاءُ وَيَجْعَلُهُ كِسَفًا فَتَرَى الْوَدْقَ يَخْرُجُ مِنْ خِلَالِهِ ۖ فَإِذَا أَصَابَ بِهِ مَنْ يَشَاءُ مِنْ عِبَادِهِ إِذَا هُمْ يَسْتَبْشِرُونَ

48 God is He who sends the winds. They stir up clouds. Then He spreads them in the sky as He wills. And He breaks them apart. Then you see rain drops issuing from their midst. Then, when He makes it fall upon whom He wills of His servants, behold, they rejoice.

48
24:43

٤٩ وَإِنْ كَانُوا مِنْ قَبْلِ أَنْ يُنَزَّلَ عَلَيْهِمْ مِنْ قَبْلِهِ لَمُبْلِسِينَ

49 Although they were before this—before it was sent down upon them—in despair.

٥٠ فَانْظُرْ إِلَىٰ آثَارِ رَحْمَتِ اللَّهِ كَيْفَ يُحْيِي الْأَرْضَ بَعْدَ مَوْتِهَا ۚ إِنَّ ذَٰلِكَ لَمُحْيِي الْمَوْتَىٰ ۖ وَهُوَ عَلَىٰ كُلِّ شَيْءٍ قَدِيرٌ

50 So observe the effects of God's mercy—how He revives the earth after it was dead. Indeed, He is the Reviver of the dead. He is Capable of everything.

50
2:164; 30:19, 24; 41:39; 42:9

٥١ وَلَئِنْ أَرْسَلْنَا رِيحًا فَرَأَوْهُ مُصْفَرًّا لَظَلُّوا مِنْ بَعْدِهِ يَكْفُرُونَ

51 But if We send a wind, and they see it turning things yellow, they would continue thereafter to disbelieve.

51
3:117; 39:21; 57:20

٥٢ فَإِنَّكَ لَا تُسْمِعُ الْمَوْتَىٰ وَلَا تُسْمِعُ الصُّمَّ الدُّعَاءَ إِذَا وَلَّوْا مُدْبِرِينَ

52 You cannot make the dead hear, nor can you make the deaf hear the call when they turn away.

52
27:80

٥٣ وَمَا أَنتَ بِهَادِ الْعُمْيِ عَن ضَلَالَتِهِمْ ۖ إِن تُسْمِعُ إِلَّا مَن يُؤْمِنُ بِآيَاتِنَا فَهُم مُّسْلِمُونَ

53 Nor can you guide the blind out of their error. You can make hear only those who believe in Our signs, and so have submitted.

53
24:27–28

٥٤ اللَّهُ الَّذِي خَلَقَكُم مِّن ضَعْفٍ ثُمَّ جَعَلَ مِن بَعْدِ ضَعْفٍ قُوَّةً ثُمَّ جَعَلَ مِن بَعْدِ قُوَّةٍ ضَعْفًا وَشَيْبَةً ۚ يَخْلُقُ مَا يَشَاءُ ۖ وَهُوَ الْعَلِيمُ الْقَدِيرُ

54 God is He Who created you weak, then after weakness gave you strength, then after strength gave you weakness and gray hair. He creates whatever He wills. He is the Omniscient, the Omnipotent.

٥٥ وَيَوْمَ تَقُومُ السَّاعَةُ يُقْسِمُ الْمُجْرِمُونَ مَا لَبِثُوا غَيْرَ سَاعَةٍ ۚ كَذَٰلِكَ كَانُوا يُؤْفَكُونَ

55 On the Day when the Hour takes place, the sinners will swear they had stayed but an hour. Thus they were deluded.

55
10:45

٥٦ وَقَالَ الَّذِينَ أُوتُوا الْعِلْمَ وَالْإِيمَانَ لَقَدْ لَبِثْتُمْ فِي كِتَابِ اللَّهِ إِلَىٰ يَوْمِ الْبَعْثِ ۖ فَهَٰذَا يَوْمُ الْبَعْثِ وَلَٰكِنَّكُمْ كُنتُمْ لَا تَعْلَمُونَ

56 But those endowed with knowledge and faith will say, "You remained in God's Book until the Day of Resurrection. This is the Day of Resurrection, but you did not know."

٥٧ فَيَوْمَئِذٍ لَّا يَنفَعُ الَّذِينَ ظَلَمُوا مَعْذِرَتُهُمْ وَلَا هُمْ يُسْتَعْتَبُونَ

57 On that Day, the sinners' excuses will not benefit them, nor will they be excused.

57
16:84; 40:52; 77:35

٥٨ وَلَقَدْ ضَرَبْنَا لِلنَّاسِ فِي هَٰذَا الْقُرْآنِ مِن كُلِّ مَثَلٍ ۚ وَلَئِن جِئْتَهُم بِآيَةٍ لَّيَقُولَنَّ الَّذِينَ كَفَرُوا إِنْ أَنتُمْ إِلَّا مُبْطِلُونَ

58 We have cited in this Qur'an for the people every sort of parable. But even if you bring them a miracle, those who disbelieve will say, "You are nothing but fakers."

58
17:89; 18:54; 39:27

٥٩ كَذَٰلِكَ يَطْبَعُ اللَّهُ عَلَىٰ قُلُوبِ الَّذِينَ لَا يَعْلَمُونَ

59 God thus seals the hearts of those who do not know.

59
2:7

٦٠ فَاصْبِرْ إِنَّ وَعْدَ اللَّهِ حَقٌّ ۖ وَلَا يَسْتَخِفَّنَّكَ الَّذِينَ لَا يُوقِنُونَ

60 So be patient. The promise of God is true. And do not let those who lack certainty belittle you.

60
30:6

Sūrah 31: Luqmān

سُورَةُ لُقْمَان (Luqman)

بِسْمِ ٱللَّهِ ٱلرَّحْمَٰنِ ٱلرَّحِيمِ

١ الم

1–5
2:1–5

1 Alif, Lām, Mīm.

٢ تِلْكَ آيَاتُ الْكِتَابِ الْحَكِيمِ

2 These are the Verses of the Wise Book.

٣ هُدًى وَرَحْمَةً لِلْمُحْسِنِينَ

3 A guide and a mercy for the righteous.

٤ الَّذِينَ يُقِيمُونَ الصَّلَاةَ وَيُؤْتُونَ الزَّكَاةَ وَهُم بِالْآخِرَةِ هُمْ يُوقِنُونَ

4 Those who observe the prayer, and pay the obligatory charity, and are certain of the Hereafter.

٥ أُولَٰئِكَ عَلَىٰ هُدًى مِّن رَّبِّهِمْ ۖ وَأُولَٰئِكَ هُمُ الْمُفْلِحُونَ

5
pp 2:5

5 These are upon guidance from their Lord. These are the successful.

٦ وَمِنَ النَّاسِ مَن يَشْتَرِي لَهْوَ الْحَدِيثِ لِيُضِلَّ عَن سَبِيلِ اللَّهِ بِغَيْرِ عِلْمٍ وَيَتَّخِذَهَا هُزُوًا ۚ أُولَٰئِكَ لَهُمْ عَذَابٌ مُّهِينٌ

6
2:16, 175; 3:177

6 Among the people is he who trades in distracting tales; intending, without knowledge, to lead away from God's way, and to make a mockery of it. These will have a humiliating punishment.

٧ وَإِذَا تُتْلَىٰ عَلَيْهِ آيَاتُنَا وَلَّىٰ مُسْتَكْبِرًا كَأَن لَّمْ يَسْمَعْهَا كَأَنَّ فِي أُذُنَيْهِ وَقْرًا ۖ فَبَشِّرْهُ بِعَذَابٍ أَلِيمٍ

7
23:66; 45:8

7 And when Our Verses are recited to him, he turns away in pride, as though he did not hear them, as though there is deafness in his ears. So inform him of a painful punishment.

٨ إِنَّ الَّذِينَ آمَنُوا وَعَمِلُوا الصَّالِحَاتِ لَهُمْ جَنَّاتُ النَّعِيمِ

8
4:122

8 As for those who believe and do good deeds—for them are the Gardens of Bliss.

٩ خَالِدِينَ فِيهَا ۖ وَعْدَ اللَّهِ حَقًّا ۚ وَهُوَ الْعَزِيزُ الْحَكِيمُ

9 Dwelling therein forever. The promise of God is true. He is the Mighty, the Wise.

١٠ خَلَقَ السَّمَاوَاتِ بِغَيْرِ عَمَدٍ تَرَوْنَهَا ۖ وَأَلْقَىٰ فِي الْأَرْضِ رَوَاسِيَ أَن تَمِيدَ بِكُمْ وَبَثَّ فِيهَا مِن كُلِّ دَابَّةٍ ۚ وَأَنزَلْنَا مِنَ السَّمَاءِ مَاءً فَأَنبَتْنَا فِيهَا مِن كُلِّ زَوْجٍ كَرِيمٍ

10
13:2; 14:2, 33; 16:15; 21:31; 26:7

10 He created the heavens without pillars that you can see, and placed stabilizers on earth lest it shifts with you, and scattered throughout it all kinds of creatures. And from the sky We sent down water, and caused to grow therein of every noble pair.

١١ هَٰذَا خَلْقُ اللَّهِ فَأَرُونِي مَاذَا خَلَقَ الَّذِينَ مِن دُونِهِ ۚ بَلِ الظَّالِمُونَ فِي ضَلَالٍ مُّبِينٍ

11 Such is God's creation. Now show me what those besides Him have created. In fact, the wicked are in obvious error.

13:16; 35:40; 46:4

١٢ وَلَقَدْ آتَيْنَا لُقْمَانَ الْحِكْمَةَ أَنِ اشْكُرْ لِلَّهِ ۚ وَمَن يَشْكُرْ فَإِنَّمَا يَشْكُرُ لِنَفْسِهِ ۖ وَمَن كَفَرَ فَإِنَّ اللَّهَ غَنِيٌّ حَمِيدٌ

12 We endowed Luqman with wisdom: "Give thanks to God." Whoever is appreciative—is appreciative for the benefit of his own soul. And whoever is unappreciative—God is Sufficient and Praiseworthy.

4:131; 27:40

١٣ وَإِذْ قَالَ لُقْمَانُ لِابْنِهِ وَهُوَ يَعِظُهُ يَا بُنَيَّ لَا تُشْرِكْ بِاللَّهِ ۖ إِنَّ الشِّرْكَ لَظُلْمٌ عَظِيمٌ

13 When Luqman said to his son, as he advised him, "O my son, do not associate anything with God, for idolatry is a terrible wrong."

6:82

١٤ وَوَصَّيْنَا الْإِنسَانَ بِوَالِدَيْهِ حَمَلَتْهُ أُمُّهُ وَهْنًا عَلَىٰ وَهْنٍ وَفِصَالُهُ فِي عَامَيْنِ أَنِ اشْكُرْ لِي وَلِوَالِدَيْكَ إِلَيَّ الْمَصِيرُ

14 We have entrusted the human being with the care of his parents. His mother carried him through hardship upon hardship, weaning him in two years. So, give thanks to Me, and to your parents. To Me is the destination.

2:233; 29:8; 46:15

١٥ وَإِن جَاهَدَاكَ عَلَىٰ أَن تُشْرِكَ بِي مَا لَيْسَ لَكَ بِهِ عِلْمٌ فَلَا تُطِعْهُمَا ۖ وَصَاحِبْهُمَا فِي الدُّنْيَا مَعْرُوفًا ۖ وَاتَّبِعْ سَبِيلَ مَنْ أَنَابَ إِلَيَّ ۚ ثُمَّ إِلَيَّ مَرْجِعُكُمْ فَأُنَبِّئُكُم بِمَا كُنتُمْ تَعْمَلُونَ

15 But if they strive to have you associate with Me something of which you have no knowledge, do not obey them. But keep them company in this life, in kindness, and follow the path of him who turns to Me. Then to Me is your return; and I will inform you of what you used to do.

29:8

١٦ يَا بُنَيَّ إِنَّهَا إِن تَكُ مِثْقَالَ حَبَّةٍ مِّنْ خَرْدَلٍ فَتَكُن فِي صَخْرَةٍ أَوْ فِي السَّمَاوَاتِ أَوْ فِي الْأَرْضِ يَأْتِ بِهَا اللَّهُ ۚ إِنَّ اللَّهَ لَطِيفٌ خَبِيرٌ

16 "O my son, even if it were the weight of a mustard-seed, in a rock, or in the heavens, or on earth, God will bring it to light. God is Kind and Expert.

21:47

١٧ يَا بُنَيَّ أَقِمِ الصَّلَاةَ وَأْمُرْ بِالْمَعْرُوفِ وَانْهَ عَنِ الْمُنكَرِ وَاصْبِرْ عَلَىٰ مَا أَصَابَكَ ۖ إِنَّ ذَٰلِكَ مِنْ عَزْمِ الْأُمُورِ

17 O my son, observe the prayer, advocate righteousness, forbid evil, and be patient over what has befallen you. These are of the most honorable traits.

١٨ وَلَا تُصَعِّرْ خَدَّكَ لِلنَّاسِ وَلَا تَمْشِ فِي الْأَرْضِ مَرَحًا ۖ إِنَّ اللَّهَ لَا يُحِبُّ كُلَّ مُخْتَالٍ فَخُورٍ

18 And do not treat people with arrogance, nor walk proudly on earth. God does not love the arrogant showoffs.

7:13; 17:37; 40:75; 57:23

Sūrah 31: Luqmān

١٩ وَاقْصِدْ فِي مَشْيِكَ وَاغْضُضْ مِن صَوْتِكَ ۚ إِنَّ أَنكَرَ الْأَصْوَاتِ لَصَوْتُ الْحَمِيرِ

19 And moderate your stride, and lower your voice. The most repulsive of voices is the donkey's voice."

19
49:3

٢٠ أَلَمْ تَرَوْا أَنَّ اللَّهَ سَخَّرَ لَكُم مَّا فِي السَّمَاوَاتِ وَمَا فِي الْأَرْضِ وَأَسْبَغَ عَلَيْكُمْ نِعَمَهُ ظَاهِرَةً وَبَاطِنَةً ۗ وَمِنَ النَّاسِ مَن يُجَادِلُ فِي اللَّهِ بِغَيْرِ عِلْمٍ وَلَا هُدًى وَلَا كِتَابٍ مُّنِيرٍ

20 Do you not see how God placed at your service everything in the heavens and the earth? How He showered you with His blessings, both outward and inward? Yet among the people is he who argues about God without knowledge, without guidance, and without an enlightening Scripture.

20
22:65; 22:8; 45:13

٢١ وَإِذَا قِيلَ لَهُمُ اتَّبِعُوا مَا أَنزَلَ اللَّهُ قَالُوا بَلْ نَتَّبِعُ مَا وَجَدْنَا عَلَيْهِ آبَاءَنَا ۚ أَوَلَوْ كَانَ الشَّيْطَانُ يَدْعُوهُمْ إِلَىٰ عَذَابِ السَّعِيرِ

21 And when it is said to them, "Follow what God has revealed," they say, "Rather, we follow what we found our parents devoted to." Even if Satan is calling them to the suffering of the Blaze?

21
2:170; 5:1:104; 10:78

٢٢ وَمَن يُسْلِمْ وَجْهَهُ إِلَى اللَّهِ وَهُوَ مُحْسِنٌ فَقَدِ اسْتَمْسَكَ بِالْعُرْوَةِ الْوُثْقَىٰ ۗ وَإِلَى اللَّهِ عَاقِبَةُ الْأُمُورِ

22 Whoever submits himself wholly to God, and is a doer of good, has grasped the most trustworthy handle. With God rests the outcome of all events.

22
2:112; 4:125

٢٣ وَمَن كَفَرَ فَلَا يَحْزُنكَ كُفْرُهُ ۚ إِلَيْنَا مَرْجِعُهُمْ فَنُنَبِّئُهُم بِمَا عَمِلُوا ۚ إِنَّ اللَّهَ عَلِيمٌ بِذَاتِ الصُّدُورِ

23 Whoever disbelieves—let not his disbelief sadden you. To Us is their return. Then We will inform them of what they did. God knows what lies within the hearts.

23
10:65

٢٤ نُمَتِّعُهُمْ قَلِيلًا ثُمَّ نَضْطَرُّهُمْ إِلَىٰ عَذَابٍ غَلِيظٍ

24 We give them a little comfort; then We compel them to a harsh torment.

24
2:126

٢٥ وَلَئِن سَأَلْتَهُم مَّنْ خَلَقَ السَّمَاوَاتِ وَالْأَرْضَ لَيَقُولُنَّ اللَّهُ ۚ قُلِ الْحَمْدُ لِلَّهِ ۚ بَلْ أَكْثَرُهُمْ لَا يَعْلَمُونَ

25 And if you ask them, "Who created the heavens and the earth?" They will say, "God." Say, "Praise be to God." But most of them do not know.

25
29:61; 39:38

٢٦ لِلَّهِ مَا فِي السَّمَاوَاتِ وَالْأَرْضِ ۚ إِنَّ اللَّهَ هُوَ الْغَنِيُّ الْحَمِيدُ

26 To God belongs everything in the heavens and the earth. God is the Rich, the Praised.

26
4:131; 22:64

٢٧ وَلَوْ أَنَّمَا فِي الْأَرْضِ مِن شَجَرَةٍ أَقْلَامٌ وَالْبَحْرُ يَمُدُّهُ مِن بَعْدِهِ سَبْعَةُ أَبْحُرٍ مَّا نَفِدَتْ كَلِمَاتُ اللَّهِ ۗ إِنَّ اللَّهَ عَزِيزٌ حَكِيمٌ

27 If all the trees on earth were pens, filled by the ocean, with seven more oceans besides, the Words of God would not run out. God is Majestic and Wise.

27
18:109

٢٨ مَا خَلْقُكُمْ وَلَا بَعْثُكُمْ إِلَّا كَنَفْسٍ وَاحِدَةٍ ۗ إِنَّ اللَّهَ سَمِيعٌ بَصِيرٌ

28 Your creation and your resurrection are only as a single soul. God is Hearing and Seeing.

28 — 2:73

٢٩ أَلَمْ تَرَ أَنَّ اللَّهَ يُولِجُ اللَّيْلَ فِي النَّهَارِ وَيُولِجُ النَّهَارَ فِي اللَّيْلِ وَسَخَّرَ الشَّمْسَ وَالْقَمَرَ كُلٌّ يَجْرِي إِلَىٰ أَجَلٍ مُسَمًّى وَأَنَّ اللَّهَ بِمَا تَعْمَلُونَ خَبِيرٌ

29 Have you not seen how God merges the night into the day, and merges the day into the night? That He subjected the sun and the moon, each running for a stated term? And that God is Cognizant of everything you do?

29 — 3:27; 35:13; 13:2; 22:61; 35:13; 39:5

٣٠ ذَٰلِكَ بِأَنَّ اللَّهَ هُوَ الْحَقُّ وَأَنَّ مَا يَدْعُونَ مِنْ دُونِهِ الْبَاطِلُ وَأَنَّ اللَّهَ هُوَ الْعَلِيُّ الْكَبِيرُ

30 That is because God is the Reality, and what they worship besides Him is falsehood, and because God is the Exalted, the Supreme.

30 — 22:6, 62

٣١ أَلَمْ تَرَ أَنَّ الْفُلْكَ تَجْرِي فِي الْبَحْرِ بِنِعْمَتِ اللَّهِ لِيُرِيَكُمْ مِنْ آيَاتِهِ ۚ إِنَّ فِي ذَٰلِكَ لَآيَاتٍ لِكُلِّ صَبَّارٍ شَكُورٍ

31 Have you not seen how the ships sail through the sea, by the grace of God, to show you of His wonders? In that are signs for every persevering, thankful person.

31 — 2:164

٣٢ وَإِذَا غَشِيَهُمْ مَوْجٌ كَالظُّلَلِ دَعَوُا اللَّهَ مُخْلِصِينَ لَهُ الدِّينَ فَلَمَّا نَجَّاهُمْ إِلَى الْبَرِّ فَمِنْهُمْ مُقْتَصِدٌ ۚ وَمَا يَجْحَدُ بِآيَاتِنَا إِلَّا كُلُّ خَتَّارٍ كَفُورٍ

32 When waves, like canopies, cover them, they call upon God, devoting their religion to Him. But when He has delivered them to dry land, some of them waver. No one renounces Our revelations except the treacherous blasphemer.

32 — 6:63; 10:22; 17:33, 67; 29:65

٣٣ يَا أَيُّهَا النَّاسُ اتَّقُوا رَبَّكُمْ وَاخْشَوْا يَوْمًا لَا يَجْزِي وَالِدٌ عَنْ وَلَدِهِ وَلَا مَوْلُودٌ هُوَ جَازٍ عَنْ وَالِدِهِ شَيْئًا ۚ إِنَّ وَعْدَ اللَّهِ حَقٌّ ۖ فَلَا تَغُرَّنَّكُمُ الْحَيَاةُ الدُّنْيَا وَلَا يَغُرَّنَّكُمْ بِاللَّهِ الْغَرُورُ

33 O people! Be conscious of your Lord, and dread a Day when no parent can avail his child, nor can a child avail his parent, in anything. The promise of God is true. Therefore, do not let this life deceive you, nor let illusions deceive you regarding God.

33 — 2:48, 123

٣٤ إِنَّ اللَّهَ عِنْدَهُ عِلْمُ السَّاعَةِ وَيُنَزِّلُ الْغَيْثَ وَيَعْلَمُ مَا فِي الْأَرْحَامِ ۖ وَمَا تَدْرِي نَفْسٌ مَاذَا تَكْسِبُ غَدًا ۖ وَمَا تَدْرِي نَفْسٌ بِأَيِّ أَرْضٍ تَمُوتُ ۚ إِنَّ اللَّهَ عَلِيمٌ خَبِيرٌ

34 With God rests the knowledge of the Hour. He sends down the rain, and He knows what the wombs contain. No soul knows what it will reap tomorrow, and no soul knows in what land it will die. God is All-Knowing, Well-Informed.

34 — 6:59; 7:187; 13:8; 35:11; 42:28

Sūrah 32: Al-Sajdah

سُوۡرَةُ ٱلسَّجۡدَة (Prostration)

بِسۡمِ ٱللَّهِ ٱلرَّحۡمَٰنِ ٱلرَّحِيمِ

١ الم

1 Alif, Lām, Mīm.

٢ تَنزِيلُ ٱلۡكِتَٰبِ لَا رَيۡبَ فِيهِ مِن رَّبِّ ٱلۡعَٰلَمِينَ

2 The revelation of the Book, without a doubt, is from the Lord of the Universe.

2:2

٣ أَمۡ يَقُولُونَ ٱفۡتَرَىٰهُ ۚ بَلۡ هُوَ ٱلۡحَقُّ مِن رَّبِّكَ لِتُنذِرَ قَوۡمًا مَّآ أَتَىٰهُم مِّن نَّذِيرٍ مِّن قَبۡلِكَ لَعَلَّهُمۡ يَهۡتَدُونَ

3 Yet they say, "He made it up." In fact, it is the Truth from your Lord, to warn a people who received no warner before you, that they may be guided.

28:46; 34:44; 36:6

٤ ٱللَّهُ ٱلَّذِي خَلَقَ ٱلسَّمَٰوَٰتِ وَٱلۡأَرۡضَ وَمَا بَيۡنَهُمَا فِي سِتَّةِ أَيَّامٍ ثُمَّ ٱسۡتَوَىٰ عَلَى ٱلۡعَرۡشِ ۖ مَا لَكُم مِّن دُونِهِۦ مِن وَلِيٍّ وَلَا شَفِيعٍ ۚ أَفَلَا تَتَذَكَّرُونَ

4 God is He who created the heavens and the earth and everything between them in six days, and then established Himself on the Throne. Apart from Him, you have no master and no intercessor. Will you not reflect?

7:54

٥ يُدَبِّرُ ٱلۡأَمۡرَ مِنَ ٱلسَّمَآءِ إِلَى ٱلۡأَرۡضِ ثُمَّ يَعۡرُجُ إِلَيۡهِ فِي يَوۡمٍ كَانَ مِقۡدَارُهُۥٓ أَلۡفَ سَنَةٍ مِّمَّا تَعُدُّونَ

5 He regulates all affairs, from the heavens, to the earth. Then it ascends to Him on a Day the length of which is a thousand years by your count.

22:47; 70:4

٦ ذَٰلِكَ عَٰلِمُ ٱلۡغَيۡبِ وَٱلشَّهَٰدَةِ ٱلۡعَزِيزُ ٱلرَّحِيمُ

6 That is the Knower of the Invisible and the Visible, the Powerful, the Merciful.

٧ ٱلَّذِيٓ أَحۡسَنَ كُلَّ شَيۡءٍ خَلَقَهُۥ ۖ وَبَدَأَ خَلۡقَ ٱلۡإِنسَٰنِ مِن طِينٍ

7 He who perfected everything He created, and originated the creation of man from clay.

18:37

٨ ثُمَّ جَعَلَ نَسۡلَهُۥ مِن سُلَٰلَةٍ مِّن مَّآءٍ مَّهِينٍ

8 Then made his reproduction from an extract of an insignificant fluid.

43:52; 77:20

٩ ثُمَّ سَوَّىٰهُ وَنَفَخَ فِيهِ مِن رُّوحِهِۦ ۖ وَجَعَلَ لَكُمُ ٱلسَّمۡعَ وَٱلۡأَبۡصَٰرَ وَٱلۡأَفۡـِٔدَةَ ۚ قَلِيلًا مَّا تَشۡكُرُونَ

9 Then He proportioned him, and breathed into him of His Spirit. Then He gave you the hearing, and the eyesight, and the brains—but rarely do you give thanks.

15:28; 23:78; 67:23

١٠ وَقَالُوا أَإِذَا ضَلَلْنَا فِي الْأَرْضِ أَإِنَّا لَفِي خَلْقٍ جَدِيدٍ ۚ بَلْ هُم بِلِقَاءِ رَبِّهِمْ كَافِرُونَ

10 And they say, "When we are lost into the earth, shall we be in a new creation?" In fact, they deny the meeting with their Lord.

10
13:5

١١ قُلْ يَتَوَفَّاكُم مَّلَكُ الْمَوْتِ الَّذِي وُكِّلَ بِكُمْ ثُمَّ إِلَىٰ رَبِّكُمْ تُرْجَعُونَ

11 Say, "The angel of death put in charge of you will reclaim you. Then to your Lord you will be returned."

11
4:97; 6:61, 93; 7:38;
8:50; 47:27

١٢ وَلَوْ تَرَىٰ إِذِ الْمُجْرِمُونَ نَاكِسُو رُءُوسِهِمْ عِندَ رَبِّهِمْ رَبَّنَا أَبْصَرْنَا وَسَمِعْنَا فَارْجِعْنَا نَعْمَلْ صَالِحًا إِنَّا مُوقِنُونَ

12 If only you could see the guilty, bowing their heads before their Lord: "Our Lord, we have seen and we have heard, so send us back, and we will act righteously; we are now convinced."

١٣ وَلَوْ شِئْنَا لَآتَيْنَا كُلَّ نَفْسٍ هُدَاهَا وَلَٰكِنْ حَقَّ الْقَوْلُ مِنِّي لَأَمْلَأَنَّ جَهَنَّمَ مِنَ الْجِنَّةِ وَالنَّاسِ أَجْمَعِينَ

13 Had We willed, We could have given every soul its guidance, but the declaration from Me will come true: "I will fill Hell with jinn and humans, altogether."

13
6:35; 7:18

١٤ فَذُوقُوا بِمَا نَسِيتُمْ لِقَاءَ يَوْمِكُمْ هَٰذَا إِنَّا نَسِينَاكُمْ ۖ وَذُوقُوا عَذَابَ الْخُلْدِ بِمَا كُنتُمْ تَعْمَلُونَ

14 So taste, because you forgot the meeting of this Day of yours; We have forgotten you; so taste the eternal torment for what you used to do.

14
7:51; 45:34

١٥ إِنَّمَا يُؤْمِنُ بِآيَاتِنَا الَّذِينَ إِذَا ذُكِّرُوا بِهَا خَرُّوا سُجَّدًا وَسَبَّحُوا بِحَمْدِ رَبِّهِمْ وَهُمْ لَا يَسْتَكْبِرُونَ ۩

15 They believe in Our communications, those who, when reminded of them, fall down prostrate, and glorify their Lord with praise, and are not proud.

١٦ تَتَجَافَىٰ جُنُوبُهُمْ عَنِ الْمَضَاجِعِ يَدْعُونَ رَبَّهُمْ خَوْفًا وَطَمَعًا وَمِمَّا رَزَقْنَاهُمْ يُنفِقُونَ

16 Their sides shun their beds, as they pray to their Lord, out of reverence and hope; and from Our provisions to them, they give.

16
7:56; 21:90

١٧ فَلَا تَعْلَمُ نَفْسٌ مَّا أُخْفِيَ لَهُم مِّن قُرَّةِ أَعْيُنٍ جَزَاءً بِمَا كَانُوا يَعْمَلُونَ

17 No soul knows what eye's delight awaits them—a reward for what they used to do.

١٨ أَفَمَن كَانَ مُؤْمِنًا كَمَن كَانَ فَاسِقًا ۚ لَّا يَسْتَوُونَ

18 Is someone who is faithful like someone who is a sinner? They are not equal.

١٩ أَمَّا الَّذِينَ آمَنُوا وَعَمِلُوا الصَّالِحَاتِ فَلَهُمْ جَنَّاتُ الْمَأْوَىٰ نُزُلًا بِمَا كَانُوا يَعْمَلُونَ

19 As for those who believe and do righteous deeds, for them are the Gardens of Shelter—hospitality for what they used to do.

٢٠ وَأَمَّا الَّذِينَ فَسَقُوا فَمَأْوَاهُمُ النَّارُ ۖ كُلَّمَا أَرَادُوا أَن يَخْرُجُوا مِنْهَا أُعِيدُوا فِيهَا وَقِيلَ لَهُمْ ذُوقُوا عَذَابَ النَّارِ الَّذِي كُنتُم بِهِ تُكَذِّبُونَ

20 2:167; 5:37; 22:22

20 But as for those who transgressed, their shelter is the Fire. Every time they try to get out of it, they will be brought back into it, and it will be said to them, "Taste the suffering of the Fire which you used to deny."

٢١ وَلَنُذِيقَنَّهُم مِّنَ الْعَذَابِ الْأَدْنَىٰ دُونَ الْعَذَابِ الْأَكْبَرِ لَعَلَّهُمْ يَرْجِعُونَ

21 We will make them taste the lesser torment, prior to the greater torment, so that they may return.

٢٢ وَمَنْ أَظْلَمُ مِمَّن ذُكِّرَ بِآيَاتِ رَبِّهِ ثُمَّ أَعْرَضَ عَنْهَا ۚ إِنَّا مِنَ الْمُجْرِمِينَ مُنتَقِمُونَ

22 18:57; 30:47; 43:41; 44:16

22 Who is more wrong than he, who, when reminded of his Lord's revelations, turns away from them? We will certainly wreak vengeance upon the criminals.

٢٣ وَلَقَدْ آتَيْنَا مُوسَى الْكِتَابَ فَلَا تَكُن فِي مِرْيَةٍ مِّن لِّقَائِهِ ۖ وَجَعَلْنَاهُ هُدًى لِّبَنِي إِسْرَائِيلَ

23 2:53, 147; 6:154; 11:17; 41:54

23 We gave Moses the Book; so do not be in doubt regarding His encounter; and We made it a guidance for the Children of Israel.

٢٤ وَجَعَلْنَا مِنْهُمْ أَئِمَّةً يَهْدُونَ بِأَمْرِنَا لَمَّا صَبَرُوا ۖ وَكَانُوا بِآيَاتِنَا يُوقِنُونَ

24 2:124; 21:73; 28:5

24 And We appointed leaders from among them, guiding by Our command, as long as they persevered and were certain of Our communications.

٢٥ إِنَّ رَبَّكَ هُوَ يَفْصِلُ بَيْنَهُمْ يَوْمَ الْقِيَامَةِ فِيمَا كَانُوا فِيهِ يَخْتَلِفُونَ

25 Your Lord will judge between them on the Day of Resurrection regarding everything they had disputed.

٢٦ أَوَلَمْ يَهْدِ لَهُمْ كَمْ أَهْلَكْنَا مِن قَبْلِهِم مِّنَ الْقُرُونِ يَمْشُونَ فِي مَسَاكِنِهِمْ ۚ إِنَّ فِي ذَٰلِكَ لَآيَاتٍ ۖ أَفَلَا يَسْمَعُونَ

26 19:98; 20:128

26 Is it not a lesson for them, how many generations We have destroyed before them, in whose habitations they walk? Surely in that are signs. Do they not hear?

٢٧ أَوَلَمْ يَرَوْا أَنَّا نَسُوقُ الْمَاءَ إِلَى الْأَرْضِ الْجُرُزِ فَنُخْرِجُ بِهِ زَرْعًا تَأْكُلُ مِنْهُ أَنْعَامُهُمْ وَأَنفُسُهُمْ ۖ أَفَلَا يُبْصِرُونَ

27 7:57; 10:24; 20:53–54; 79:33

27 Do they not see how We conduct the water to a dry land, and with it We produce vegetation, from which their livestock eat, and themselves? Do they not see?

٢٨ وَيَقُولُونَ مَتَىٰ هَٰذَا الْفَتْحُ إِن كُنتُمْ صَادِقِينَ

28 10:48

28 And they say, "When is this victory, if you are truthful?"

٢٩ قُلْ يَوْمَ الْفَتْحِ لَا يَنفَعُ الَّذِينَ كَفَرُوا إِيمَانُهُمْ وَلَا هُمْ يُنظَرُونَ

29–30 2:162; 6:158

29 Say, "On the day of victory, the faith of those who disbelieved will be of no avail to them, and they will not be granted respite."

٣٠ فَأَعْرِضْ عَنْهُمْ وَانتَظِرْ إِنَّهُم مُّنتَظِرُونَ

30 So turn away from them, and wait. They too are waiting.

30
6:158

Sūrah 33: Al-Aḥzāb

سُورَةُ ٱلْأَحْزَابِ (The Confiderates)

بِسْمِ ٱللَّهِ ٱلرَّحْمَٰنِ ٱلرَّحِيمِ

١ يَا أَيُّهَا النَّبِيُّ اتَّقِ اللَّهَ وَلَا تُطِعِ الْكَافِرِينَ وَالْمُنَافِقِينَ ۗ إِنَّ اللَّهَ كَانَ عَلِيمًا حَكِيمًا

1 O Prophet! Fear God, and do not obey the unbelievers and the hypocrites. God is Knowledgeable and Wise.

1
25:52; 33:48

٢ وَاتَّبِعْ مَا يُوحَىٰ إِلَيْكَ مِن رَّبِّكَ ۚ إِنَّ اللَّهَ كَانَ بِمَا تَعْمَلُونَ خَبِيرًا

2 And follow what is revealed to you from your Lord. God is fully aware of what you do.

2
6:50, 106; 10:109

٣ وَتَوَكَّلْ عَلَى اللَّهِ ۚ وَكَفَىٰ بِاللَّهِ وَكِيلًا

3 And put your trust in God. God is enough as a trustee.

٤ مَا جَعَلَ اللَّهُ لِرَجُلٍ مِّن قَلْبَيْنِ فِي جَوْفِهِ ۚ وَمَا جَعَلَ أَزْوَاجَكُمُ اللَّائِي تُظَاهِرُونَ مِنْهُنَّ أُمَّهَاتِكُمْ ۚ وَمَا جَعَلَ أَدْعِيَاءَكُمْ أَبْنَاءَكُمْ ۚ ذَٰلِكُمْ قَوْلُكُم بِأَفْوَاهِكُمْ ۖ وَاللَّهُ يَقُولُ الْحَقَّ وَهُوَ يَهْدِي السَّبِيلَ

4 God did not place two hearts inside any man's body. Nor did He make your wives whom you equate with your mothers, your actual mothers. Nor did He make your adopted sons, your actual sons. These are your words coming out of your mouths. God speaks the truth, and guides to the path.

4
58:2–3

٥ ادْعُوهُمْ لِآبَائِهِمْ هُوَ أَقْسَطُ عِندَ اللَّهِ ۚ فَإِن لَّمْ تَعْلَمُوا آبَاءَهُمْ فَإِخْوَانُكُمْ فِي الدِّينِ وَمَوَالِيكُمْ ۚ وَلَيْسَ عَلَيْكُمْ جُنَاحٌ فِيمَا أَخْطَأْتُم بِهِ وَلَٰكِن مَّا تَعَمَّدَتْ قُلُوبُكُمْ ۚ وَكَانَ اللَّهُ غَفُورًا رَّحِيمًا

5 Call them after their fathers; that is more equitable with God. But if you do not know their fathers, then your brethren in faith and your friends. There is no blame on you if you err therein, barring what your hearts premeditates. God is Forgiving and Merciful.

٦ النَّبِيُّ أَوْلَىٰ بِالْمُؤْمِنِينَ مِنْ أَنفُسِهِمْ ۖ وَأَزْوَاجُهُ أُمَّهَاتُهُمْ ۗ وَأُولُو الْأَرْحَامِ بَعْضُهُمْ أَوْلَىٰ بِبَعْضٍ فِي كِتَابِ اللَّهِ مِنَ الْمُؤْمِنِينَ وَالْمُهَاجِرِينَ إِلَّا أَن تَفْعَلُوا إِلَىٰ أَوْلِيَائِكُم مَّعْرُوفًا ۚ كَانَ ذَٰلِكَ فِي الْكِتَابِ مَسْطُورًا

6
8:75

6 The Prophet is more caring of the believers than they are of themselves, and his wives are mothers to them. And blood-relatives are closer to one another in God's Book than the believers or the emigrants, though you should do good to your friends. That is inscribed in the Book.

٧ وَإِذْ أَخَذْنَا مِنَ النَّبِيِّينَ مِيثَاقَهُمْ وَمِنكَ وَمِن نُّوحٍ وَإِبْرَاهِيمَ وَمُوسَىٰ وَعِيسَى ابْنِ مَرْيَمَ ۖ وَأَخَذْنَا مِنْهُم مِّيثَاقًا غَلِيظًا

7 3:81; 4:154

7 Recall that We received a pledge from the prophets, and from you, and from Noah, and Abraham, and Moses, and Jesus son of Mary. We received from them a solemn pledge.

٨ لِّيَسْأَلَ الصَّادِقِينَ عَن صِدْقِهِمْ ۚ وَأَعَدَّ لِلْكَافِرِينَ عَذَابًا أَلِيمًا

8 That He may ask the sincere about their sincerity. He has prepared for the disbelievers a painful punishment.

٩ يَا أَيُّهَا الَّذِينَ آمَنُوا اذْكُرُوا نِعْمَةَ اللَّهِ عَلَيْكُمْ إِذْ جَاءَتْكُمْ جُنُودٌ فَأَرْسَلْنَا عَلَيْهِمْ رِيحًا وَجُنُودًا لَّمْ تَرَوْهَا ۚ وَكَانَ اللَّهُ بِمَا تَعْمَلُونَ بَصِيرًا

9 8:12; 9:26, 40

9 O you who believe! Remember God's blessings upon you, when forces came against you, and We sent against them a wind, and forces you did not see. God is Observant of what you do.

١٠ إِذْ جَاءُوكُم مِّن فَوْقِكُمْ وَمِنْ أَسْفَلَ مِنكُمْ وَإِذْ زَاغَتِ الْأَبْصَارُ وَبَلَغَتِ الْقُلُوبُ الْحَنَاجِرَ وَتَظُنُّونَ بِاللَّهِ الظُّنُونَا

10 When they came upon you, from above you, and from beneath you; and the eyes became dazed, and the hearts reached the throats, and you harbored doubts about God.

١١ هُنَالِكَ ابْتُلِيَ الْمُؤْمِنُونَ وَزُلْزِلُوا زِلْزَالًا شَدِيدًا

11 There and then the believers were tested, and were shaken most severely.

١٢ وَإِذْ يَقُولُ الْمُنَافِقُونَ وَالَّذِينَ فِي قُلُوبِهِم مَّرَضٌ مَّا وَعَدَنَا اللَّهُ وَرَسُولُهُ إِلَّا غُرُورًا

12 8:49

12 When the hypocrites and those in whose hearts is sickness said, "God and His Messenger promised us nothing but illusion."

١٣ وَإِذْ قَالَت طَّائِفَةٌ مِّنْهُمْ يَا أَهْلَ يَثْرِبَ لَا مُقَامَ لَكُمْ فَارْجِعُوا ۚ وَيَسْتَأْذِنُ فَرِيقٌ مِّنْهُمُ النَّبِيَّ يَقُولُونَ إِنَّ بُيُوتَنَا عَوْرَةٌ وَمَا هِيَ بِعَوْرَةٍ ۖ إِن يُرِيدُونَ إِلَّا فِرَارًا

13 And when a group of them said, "O people of Yathrib, you cannot make a stand, so retreat." And a faction of them asked the Prophet to excuse them, saying, "Our homes are exposed," although they were not exposed. They only wanted to flee.

١٤ وَلَوْ دُخِلَتْ عَلَيْهِم مِّنْ أَقْطَارِهَا ثُمَّ سُئِلُوا الْفِتْنَةَ لَآتَوْهَا وَمَا تَلَبَّثُوا بِهَا إِلَّا يَسِيرًا

14 Had it been invaded from its sides, and they were asked to dissent, they would have done so with little hesitation.

١٥ وَلَقَدْ كَانُوا عَاهَدُوا اللَّهَ مِن قَبْلُ لَا يُوَلُّونَ الْأَدْبَارَ ۚ وَكَانَ عَهْدُ اللَّهِ مَسْئُولًا

15 Although they had made a pledge to God, in the past, that they will not turn their backs. A pledge to God is a responsibility.

١٦ قُلْ لَنْ يَنْفَعَكُمُ الْفِرَارُ إِنْ فَرَرْتُمْ مِنَ الْمَوْتِ أَوِ الْقَتْلِ وَإِذًا لَا تُمَتَّعُونَ إِلَّا قَلِيلًا

16 Say, "Flight will not benefit you, if you flee from death or killing, even then you will be given only brief enjoyment."

16
2:243

١٧ قُلْ مَنْ ذَا الَّذِي يَعْصِمُكُمْ مِنَ اللَّهِ إِنْ أَرَادَ بِكُمْ سُوءًا أَوْ أَرَادَ بِكُمْ رَحْمَةً ۚ وَلَا يَجِدُونَ لَهُمْ مِنْ دُونِ اللَّهِ وَلِيًّا وَلَا نَصِيرًا

17 Say, "Who is it who will shield you from God, if He intends adversity for you, or intends mercy for you?" Besides God, they will find for themselves neither friend nor helper.

17
3:17; 10:27; 13:11; 40:33; 70:22–35

١٨ قَدْ يَعْلَمُ اللَّهُ الْمُعَوِّقِينَ مِنْكُمْ وَالْقَائِلِينَ لِإِخْوَانِهِمْ هَلُمَّ إِلَيْنَا ۖ وَلَا يَأْتُونَ الْبَأْسَ إِلَّا قَلِيلًا

18 God already knows the hinderers among you, and those who say to their brethren, "Come and join us." Rarely do they mobilize for battle.

١٩ أَشِحَّةً عَلَيْكُمْ ۖ فَإِذَا جَاءَ الْخَوْفُ رَأَيْتَهُمْ يَنْظُرُونَ إِلَيْكَ تَدُورُ أَعْيُنُهُمْ كَالَّذِي يُغْشَىٰ عَلَيْهِ مِنَ الْمَوْتِ ۖ فَإِذَا ذَهَبَ الْخَوْفُ سَلَقُوكُمْ بِأَلْسِنَةٍ حِدَادٍ أَشِحَّةً عَلَى الْخَيْرِ ۚ أُولَٰئِكَ لَمْ يُؤْمِنُوا فَأَحْبَطَ اللَّهُ أَعْمَالَهُمْ ۚ وَكَانَ ذَٰلِكَ عَلَى اللَّهِ يَسِيرًا

19 Being stingy towards you. And when fear approaches, you see them staring at you—their eyes rolling—like someone fainting at death. Then, when panic is over, they whip you with sharp tongues. They resent you any good. These have never believed, so God has nullified their works; a matter easy for God.

19
47:9, 28, 32

٢٠ يَحْسَبُونَ الْأَحْزَابَ لَمْ يَذْهَبُوا ۖ وَإِنْ يَأْتِ الْأَحْزَابُ يَوَدُّوا لَوْ أَنَّهُمْ بَادُونَ فِي الْأَعْرَابِ يَسْأَلُونَ عَنْ أَنْبَائِكُمْ ۚ وَلَوْ كَانُوا فِيكُمْ مَا قَاتَلُوا إِلَّا قَلِيلًا

20 They assumed that the confederates had not withdrawn. But were the confederates to advance, they would wish they were in the desert with the Bedouins, inquiring about your news. And if they were among you, they would have done little fighting.

٢١ لَقَدْ كَانَ لَكُمْ فِي رَسُولِ اللَّهِ أُسْوَةٌ حَسَنَةٌ لِمَنْ كَانَ يَرْجُو اللَّهَ وَالْيَوْمَ الْآخِرَ وَذَكَرَ اللَّهَ كَثِيرًا

21 You have an excellent example in the Messenger of God; for anyone who seeks God and the Last Day, and remembers God frequently.

21
60:4

٢٢ وَلَمَّا رَأَى الْمُؤْمِنُونَ الْأَحْزَابَ قَالُوا هَٰذَا مَا وَعَدَنَا اللَّهُ وَرَسُولُهُ وَصَدَقَ اللَّهُ وَرَسُولُهُ ۚ وَمَا زَادَهُمْ إِلَّا إِيمَانًا وَتَسْلِيمًا

22 And when the believers saw the confederates, they said, "This is what God and His messenger have promised us; and God and His messenger have told the truth." And it only increased them in faith and submission.

22
3:152; 21:9; 30:6

٢٣ مِنَ الْمُؤْمِنِينَ رِجَالٌ صَدَقُوا مَا عَاهَدُوا اللَّهَ عَلَيْهِ ۖ فَمِنْهُم مَّن قَضَىٰ نَحْبَهُ وَمِنْهُم مَّن يَنتَظِرُ ۖ وَمَا بَدَّلُوا تَبْدِيلًا

23 Of the believers are men who are true to what they pledged to God. Some of them have fulfilled their vows; and some are still waiting, and never wavering.

٢٤ لِّيَجْزِيَ اللَّهُ الصَّادِقِينَ بِصِدْقِهِمْ وَيُعَذِّبَ الْمُنَافِقِينَ إِن شَاءَ أَوْ يَتُوبَ عَلَيْهِمْ ۚ إِنَّ اللَّهَ كَانَ غَفُورًا رَّحِيمًا

24
9:66

24 That God may reward the truthful for their truthfulness; and punish the hypocrites, if He wills, or pardon them. God is Forgiving and Merciful.

٢٥ وَرَدَّ اللَّهُ الَّذِينَ كَفَرُوا بِغَيْظِهِمْ لَمْ يَنَالُوا خَيْرًا ۚ وَكَفَى اللَّهُ الْمُؤْمِنِينَ الْقِتَالَ ۚ وَكَانَ اللَّهُ قَوِيًّا عَزِيزًا

25 God repelled the disbelievers in their rage; they gained no advantage. God thus spared the believers combat. God is Strong and Mighty.

٢٦ وَأَنزَلَ الَّذِينَ ظَاهَرُوهُم مِّنْ أَهْلِ الْكِتَابِ مِن صَيَاصِيهِمْ وَقَذَفَ فِي قُلُوبِهِمُ الرُّعْبَ فَرِيقًا تَقْتُلُونَ وَتَأْسِرُونَ فَرِيقًا

26
3:151; 8:12

26 And He brought down from their strongholds those of the People of the Book who backed them, and He threw terror into their hearts. Some of them you killed, and others you took captive.

٢٧ وَأَوْرَثَكُمْ أَرْضَهُمْ وَدِيَارَهُمْ وَأَمْوَالَهُمْ وَأَرْضًا لَّمْ تَطَئُوهَا ۚ وَكَانَ اللَّهُ عَلَىٰ كُلِّ شَيْءٍ قَدِيرًا

27 And He made you inherit their land, and their homes, and their possessions, and a region you have never stepped on. God has power over all things.

٢٨ يَا أَيُّهَا النَّبِيُّ قُل لِّأَزْوَاجِكَ إِن كُنتُنَّ تُرِدْنَ الْحَيَاةَ الدُّنْيَا وَزِينَتَهَا فَتَعَالَيْنَ أُمَتِّعْكُنَّ وَأُسَرِّحْكُنَّ سَرَاحًا جَمِيلًا

28
11:15; 33:49

28 O Prophet! Say to your wives, "If you desire the life of this world and its finery, then let me compensate you, and release you kindly.

٢٩ وَإِن كُنتُنَّ تُرِدْنَ اللَّهَ وَرَسُولَهُ وَالدَّارَ الْآخِرَةَ فَإِنَّ اللَّهَ أَعَدَّ لِلْمُحْسِنَاتِ مِنكُنَّ أَجْرًا عَظِيمًا

29 But if you desire God, His Messenger, and the Home of the Hereafter, then God has prepared for the righteous among you a magnificent compensation."

٣٠ يَا نِسَاءَ النَّبِيِّ مَن يَأْتِ مِنكُنَّ بِفَاحِشَةٍ مُّبَيِّنَةٍ يُضَاعَفْ لَهَا الْعَذَابُ ضِعْفَيْنِ ۚ وَكَانَ ذَٰلِكَ عَلَى اللَّهِ يَسِيرًا

30
65:1

30 O wives of the Prophet! Whoever of you commits a proven indecency, the punishment for her will be doubled. And that would be easy for God.

٣١ وَمَن يَقْنُتْ مِنكُنَّ لِلَّهِ وَرَسُولِهِ وَتَعْمَلْ صَالِحًا نُؤْتِهَا أَجْرَهَا مَرَّتَيْنِ وَأَعْتَدْنَا لَهَا رِزْقًا كَرِيمًا

31 But whoever of you remains obedient to God and His Messenger, and acts righteously, We will give her a double reward; and We have prepared for her a generous provision.

31
28:54

٣٢ يَا نِسَاءَ النَّبِيِّ لَسْتُنَّ كَأَحَدٍ مِّنَ النِّسَاءِ ۚ إِنِ اتَّقَيْتُنَّ فَلَا تَخْضَعْنَ بِالْقَوْلِ فَيَطْمَعَ الَّذِي فِي قَلْبِهِ مَرَضٌ وَقُلْنَ قَوْلًا مَّعْرُوفًا

32 O wives of the Prophet! You are not like any other women, if you observe piety. So do not speak too softly, lest the sick at heart lusts after you, but speak in an appropriate manner.

٣٣ وَقَرْنَ فِي بُيُوتِكُنَّ وَلَا تَبَرَّجْنَ تَبَرُّجَ الْجَاهِلِيَّةِ الْأُولَىٰ ۖ وَأَقِمْنَ الصَّلَاةَ وَآتِينَ الزَّكَاةَ وَأَطِعْنَ اللَّهَ وَرَسُولَهُ ۚ إِنَّمَا يُرِيدُ اللَّهُ لِيُذْهِبَ عَنكُمُ الرِّجْسَ أَهْلَ الْبَيْتِ وَيُطَهِّرَكُمْ تَطْهِيرًا

33 And settle in your homes; and do not display yourselves, as in the former days of ignorance. And perform the prayer, and give regular charity, and obey God and His Messenger. God desires to remove all impurity from you, O People of the Household, and to purify you thoroughly.

٣٤ وَاذْكُرْنَ مَا يُتْلَىٰ فِي بُيُوتِكُنَّ مِنْ آيَاتِ اللَّهِ وَالْحِكْمَةِ ۚ إِنَّ اللَّهَ كَانَ لَطِيفًا خَبِيرًا

34 And remember what is recited in your homes of God's revelations and wisdom. God is Kind and Informed.

٣٥ إِنَّ الْمُسْلِمِينَ وَالْمُسْلِمَاتِ وَالْمُؤْمِنِينَ وَالْمُؤْمِنَاتِ وَالْقَانِتِينَ وَالْقَانِتَاتِ وَالصَّادِقِينَ وَالصَّادِقَاتِ وَالصَّابِرِينَ وَالصَّابِرَاتِ وَالْخَاشِعِينَ وَالْخَاشِعَاتِ وَالْمُتَصَدِّقِينَ وَالْمُتَصَدِّقَاتِ وَالصَّائِمِينَ وَالصَّائِمَاتِ وَالْحَافِظِينَ فُرُوجَهُمْ وَالْحَافِظَاتِ وَالذَّاكِرِينَ اللَّهَ كَثِيرًا وَالذَّاكِرَاتِ أَعَدَّ اللَّهُ لَهُم مَّغْفِرَةً وَأَجْرًا عَظِيمًا

35
2:202; 4:32, 34;
24:30; 26:68

35 Muslim men and Muslim women, believing men and believing women, obedient men and obedient women, truthful men and truthful women, patient men and patient women, humble men and humble women, charitable men and charitable women, fasting men and fasting women, men who guard their chastity and women who guard, men who remember God frequently and women who remember—God has prepared for them a pardon, and an immense reward.

٣٦ وَمَا كَانَ لِمُؤْمِنٍ وَلَا مُؤْمِنَةٍ إِذَا قَضَى اللَّهُ وَرَسُولُهُ أَمْرًا أَن يَكُونَ لَهُمُ الْخِيَرَةُ مِنْ أَمْرِهِمْ ۗ وَمَن يَعْصِ اللَّهَ وَرَسُولَهُ فَقَدْ ضَلَّ ضَلَالًا مُّبِينًا

36
24:63; 28:68

36 It is not for any believer, man or woman, when God and His Messenger have decided a matter, to have liberty of choice in their decision. Whoever disobeys God and His Messenger has gone far astray.

٣٧ وَإِذْ تَقُولُ لِلَّذِي أَنْعَمَ اللَّهُ عَلَيْهِ وَأَنْعَمْتَ عَلَيْهِ أَمْسِكْ عَلَيْكَ زَوْجَكَ وَاتَّقِ اللَّهَ وَتُخْفِي فِي نَفْسِكَ مَا اللَّهُ مُبْدِيهِ وَتَخْشَى النَّاسَ وَاللَّهُ أَحَقُّ أَنْ تَخْشَاهُ ۖ فَلَمَّا قَضَىٰ زَيْدٌ مِنْهَا وَطَرًا زَوَّجْنَاكَهَا لِكَيْ لَا يَكُونَ عَلَى الْمُؤْمِنِينَ حَرَجٌ فِي أَزْوَاجِ أَدْعِيَائِهِمْ إِذَا قَضَوْا مِنْهُنَّ وَطَرًا ۚ وَكَانَ أَمْرُ اللَّهِ مَفْعُولًا

37 When you said to him whom God had blessed, and you had favored, "Keep your wife to yourself, and fear God." But you hid within yourself what God was to reveal. And you feared the people, but it was God you were supposed to fear. Then, when Zaid ended his relationship with her, We gave her to you in marriage, that there may be no restriction for believers regarding the wives of their adopted sons, when their relationship has ended. The command of God was fulfilled.

٣٨ مَا كَانَ عَلَى النَّبِيِّ مِنْ حَرَجٍ فِيمَا فَرَضَ اللَّهُ لَهُ ۖ سُنَّةَ اللَّهِ فِي الَّذِينَ خَلَوْا مِنْ قَبْلُ ۚ وَكَانَ أَمْرُ اللَّهِ قَدَرًا مَقْدُورًا

38 There is no blame on the Prophet regarding what God has ordained for him. Such is the pattern of God among those who passed before. The command of God is an absolute decree.

٣٩ الَّذِينَ يُبَلِّغُونَ رِسَالَاتِ اللَّهِ وَيَخْشَوْنَهُ وَلَا يَخْشَوْنَ أَحَدًا إِلَّا اللَّهَ ۗ وَكَفَىٰ بِاللَّهِ حَسِيبًا

39 Those who deliver the messages of God, and fear Him, and never fear anyone except God. God is sufficient as a reckoner.

٤٠ مَا كَانَ مُحَمَّدٌ أَبَا أَحَدٍ مِنْ رِجَالِكُمْ وَلَٰكِنْ رَسُولَ اللَّهِ وَخَاتَمَ النَّبِيِّينَ ۗ وَكَانَ اللَّهُ بِكُلِّ شَيْءٍ عَلِيمًا

40 Muhammad is not the father of any of your men; but he is the Messenger of God, and the seal of the prophets. God is Cognizant of everything.

٤١ يَا أَيُّهَا الَّذِينَ آمَنُوا اذْكُرُوا اللَّهَ ذِكْرًا كَثِيرًا

41 O you who believe, remember God with frequent remembrance.

٤٢ وَسَبِّحُوهُ بُكْرَةً وَأَصِيلًا

42 And glorify Him morning and evening.

٤٣ هُوَ الَّذِي يُصَلِّي عَلَيْكُمْ وَمَلَائِكَتُهُ لِيُخْرِجَكُمْ مِنَ الظُّلُمَاتِ إِلَى النُّورِ ۚ وَكَانَ بِالْمُؤْمِنِينَ رَحِيمًا

43 It is He who reaches out to you, and His angels, to bring you out of darkness into the light. And He is Ever-Merciful towards the believers.

43
33:56

٤٤ تَحِيَّتُهُمْ يَوْمَ يَلْقَوْنَهُ سَلَامٌ ۚ وَأَعَدَّ لَهُمْ أَجْرًا كَرِيمًا

44 Their greeting on the Day they meet Him is, "Peace," and He has prepared for them a generous reward.

٤٥ يَا أَيُّهَا النَّبِيُّ إِنَّا أَرْسَلْنَاكَ شَاهِدًا وَمُبَشِّرًا وَنَذِيرًا

45 O prophet! We have sent you as a witness, and a bearer of good news, and a warner.

45
48:8

٤٦ وَدَاعِيًا إِلَى اللَّهِ بِإِذْنِهِ وَسِرَاجًا مُنِيرًا

46 And a caller towards God by His leave, and an illuminating beacon.

٤٧ وَبَشِّرِ الْمُؤْمِنِينَ بِأَنَّ لَهُم مِّنَ اللَّهِ فَضْلًا كَبِيرًا

47 And give the believers the good news that for them is a great reward.

47
23:1; 42:22

٤٨ وَلَا تُطِعِ الْكَافِرِينَ وَالْمُنَافِقِينَ وَدَعْ أَذَاهُمْ وَتَوَكَّلْ عَلَى اللَّهِ ۚ وَكَفَىٰ بِاللَّهِ وَكِيلًا

48 And do not obey the blasphemers and the hypocrites, and ignore their insults, and rely on God. God is a sufficient protector.

48
25:52; 33:1

٤٩ يَا أَيُّهَا الَّذِينَ آمَنُوا إِذَا نَكَحْتُمُ الْمُؤْمِنَاتِ ثُمَّ طَلَّقْتُمُوهُنَّ مِن قَبْلِ أَن تَمَسُّوهُنَّ فَمَا لَكُمْ عَلَيْهِنَّ مِنْ عِدَّةٍ تَعْتَدُّونَهَا ۖ فَمَتِّعُوهُنَّ وَسَرِّحُوهُنَّ سَرَاحًا جَمِيلًا

49 O you who believe! When you marry believing women, but then divorce them before you have touched them, there is no waiting period for you to observe in respect to them; but compensate them, and release them in a graceful manner.

٥٠ يَا أَيُّهَا النَّبِيُّ إِنَّا أَحْلَلْنَا لَكَ أَزْوَاجَكَ اللَّاتِي آتَيْتَ أُجُورَهُنَّ وَمَا مَلَكَتْ يَمِينُكَ مِمَّا أَفَاءَ اللَّهُ عَلَيْكَ وَبَنَاتِ عَمِّكَ وَبَنَاتِ عَمَّاتِكَ وَبَنَاتِ خَالِكَ وَبَنَاتِ خَالَاتِكَ اللَّاتِي هَاجَرْنَ مَعَكَ وَامْرَأَةً مُّؤْمِنَةً إِن وَهَبَتْ نَفْسَهَا لِلنَّبِيِّ إِنْ أَرَادَ النَّبِيُّ أَن يَسْتَنكِحَهَا خَالِصَةً لَّكَ مِن دُونِ الْمُؤْمِنِينَ ۗ قَدْ عَلِمْنَا مَا فَرَضْنَا عَلَيْهِمْ فِي أَزْوَاجِهِمْ وَمَا مَلَكَتْ أَيْمَانُهُمْ لِكَيْلَا يَكُونَ عَلَيْكَ حَرَجٌ ۗ وَكَانَ اللَّهُ غَفُورًا رَّحِيمًا

50 O Prophet! We have permitted to you your wives to whom you have given their dowries, and those you already have, as granted to you by God, and the daughters of your paternal uncle, and the daughters of your paternal aunts, and the daughters of your maternal uncle, and the daughters of your maternal aunts who emigrated with you, and a believing woman who has offered herself to the Prophet, if the Prophet desires to marry her, exclusively for you, and not for the believers. We know what We have ordained for them regarding their wives and those their right-hands possess. This is to spare you any difficulty. God is Forgiving and Merciful.

٥١ تُرْجِي مَن تَشَاءُ مِنْهُنَّ وَتُؤْوِي إِلَيْكَ مَن تَشَاءُ ۖ وَمَنِ ابْتَغَيْتَ مِمَّنْ عَزَلْتَ فَلَا جُنَاحَ عَلَيْكَ ۚ ذَٰلِكَ أَدْنَىٰ أَن تَقَرَّ أَعْيُنُهُنَّ وَلَا يَحْزَنَّ وَيَرْضَيْنَ بِمَا آتَيْتَهُنَّ كُلُّهُنَّ ۚ وَاللَّهُ يَعْلَمُ مَا فِي قُلُوبِكُمْ ۚ وَكَانَ اللَّهُ عَلِيمًا حَلِيمًا

51 You may defer any of them you wish, and receive any of them you wish. Should you desire any of those you had deferred, there is no blame on you. This is more proper, so that they will be comforted, and not be grieved, and be content with what you have given each one of them. God knows what is within your hearts. God is Omniscient and Clement.

٥٢ لَا يَحِلُّ لَكَ النِّسَاءُ مِنْ بَعْدُ وَلَا أَنْ تَبَدَّلَ بِهِنَّ مِنْ أَزْوَاجٍ وَلَوْ أَعْجَبَكَ حُسْنُهُنَّ إِلَّا مَا مَلَكَتْ يَمِينُكَ ۗ وَكَانَ اللَّهُ عَلَىٰ كُلِّ شَيْءٍ رَقِيبًا

52 Beyond that, no other women are permissible for you, nor can you exchange them for other wives, even if you admire their beauty, except those you already have. God is Watchful over all things.

٥٣ يَا أَيُّهَا الَّذِينَ آمَنُوا لَا تَدْخُلُوا بُيُوتَ النَّبِيِّ إِلَّا أَنْ يُؤْذَنَ لَكُمْ إِلَىٰ طَعَامٍ غَيْرَ نَاظِرِينَ إِنَاهُ وَلَٰكِنْ إِذَا دُعِيتُمْ فَادْخُلُوا فَإِذَا طَعِمْتُمْ فَانْتَشِرُوا وَلَا مُسْتَأْنِسِينَ لِحَدِيثٍ ۚ إِنَّ ذَٰلِكُمْ كَانَ يُؤْذِي النَّبِيَّ فَيَسْتَحْيِي مِنْكُمْ ۖ وَاللَّهُ لَا يَسْتَحْيِي مِنَ الْحَقِّ ۚ وَإِذَا سَأَلْتُمُوهُنَّ مَتَاعًا فَاسْأَلُوهُنَّ مِنْ وَرَاءِ حِجَابٍ ۚ ذَٰلِكُمْ أَطْهَرُ لِقُلُوبِكُمْ وَقُلُوبِهِنَّ ۚ وَمَا كَانَ لَكُمْ أَنْ تُؤْذُوا رَسُولَ اللَّهِ وَلَا أَنْ تَنْكِحُوا أَزْوَاجَهُ مِنْ بَعْدِهِ أَبَدًا ۚ إِنَّ ذَٰلِكُمْ كَانَ عِنْدَ اللَّهِ عَظِيمًا

53 O you who believe! Do not enter the homes of the Prophet, unless you are given permission to come for a meal; and do not wait for its preparation. And when you are invited, go in. And when you have eaten, disperse, without lingering for conversation. This irritates the Prophet, and he shies away from you, but God does not shy away from the truth. And when you ask his wives for something, ask them from behind a screen; that is purer for your hearts and their hearts. You must never offend the Messenger of God, nor must you ever marry his wives after him, for that would be an enormity with God.

53
24:27; 33:59

٥٤ إِنْ تُبْدُوا شَيْئًا أَوْ تُخْفُوهُ فَإِنَّ اللَّهَ كَانَ بِكُلِّ شَيْءٍ عَلِيمًا

54 Whether you declare a thing, or hide it, God is Aware of all things.

٥٥ لَا جُنَاحَ عَلَيْهِنَّ فِي آبَائِهِنَّ وَلَا أَبْنَائِهِنَّ وَلَا إِخْوَانِهِنَّ وَلَا أَبْنَاءِ إِخْوَانِهِنَّ وَلَا أَبْنَاءِ أَخَوَاتِهِنَّ وَلَا نِسَائِهِنَّ وَلَا مَا مَلَكَتْ أَيْمَانُهُنَّ ۗ وَاتَّقِينَ اللَّهَ ۚ إِنَّ اللَّهَ كَانَ عَلَىٰ كُلِّ شَيْءٍ شَهِيدًا

55 There is no blame on them concerning their fathers, or their sons, or their brothers, or their brothers' sons, or their sisters' sons, or their women, or their female servants. But they should remain conscious of God. God is Witness over all things.

55
24:31

٥٦ إِنَّ اللَّهَ وَمَلَائِكَتَهُ يُصَلُّونَ عَلَى النَّبِيِّ ۚ يَا أَيُّهَا الَّذِينَ آمَنُوا صَلُّوا عَلَيْهِ وَسَلِّمُوا تَسْلِيمًا

56 God and His angels give blessings to the Prophet. O you who believe, call for blessings on him, and greet him with a prayer of peace.

56
33:43

٥٧ إِنَّ الَّذِينَ يُؤْذُونَ اللَّهَ وَرَسُولَهُ لَعَنَهُمُ اللَّهُ فِي الدُّنْيَا وَالْآخِرَةِ وَأَعَدَّ لَهُمْ عَذَابًا مُهِينًا

57 Those who insult God and His Messenger, God has cursed them in this life and in the Hereafter, and has prepared for them a demeaning punishment.

57
9:61

٥٨ وَالَّذِينَ يُؤْذُونَ الْمُؤْمِنِينَ وَالْمُؤْمِنَاتِ بِغَيْرِ مَا اكْتَسَبُوا فَقَدِ احْتَمَلُوا بُهْتَانًا وَإِثْمًا مُبِينًا

58 Those who harm believing men and believing women, for acts they did not commit, bear the burden of perjury and a flagrant sin.

58
24:11, 23

٥٩ يَا أَيُّهَا النَّبِيُّ قُل لِّأَزْوَاجِكَ وَبَنَاتِكَ وَنِسَاءِ الْمُؤْمِنِينَ يُدْنِينَ عَلَيْهِنَّ مِن جَلَابِيبِهِنَّ ۚ ذَٰلِكَ أَدْنَىٰ أَن يُعْرَفْنَ فَلَا يُؤْذَيْنَ ۗ وَكَانَ اللَّهُ غَفُورًا رَّحِيمًا

59 O Prophet! Tell your wives, and your daughters, and the women of the believers, to lengthen their garments. That is more proper, so they will be recognized and not harassed. God is Forgiving and Merciful.

33:53; 40:31

٦٠ لَّئِن لَّمْ يَنتَهِ الْمُنَافِقُونَ وَالَّذِينَ فِي قُلُوبِهِم مَّرَضٌ وَالْمُرْجِفُونَ فِي الْمَدِينَةِ لَنُغْرِيَنَّكَ بِهِمْ ثُمَّ لَا يُجَاوِرُونَكَ فِيهَا إِلَّا قَلِيلًا

60 If the hypocrites, and those with sickness in their hearts, and the rumormongers in the City, do not desist, We will incite you against them; then they will not be your neighbors there except for a short while.

٦١ مَّلْعُونِينَ ۖ أَيْنَمَا ثُقِفُوا أُخِذُوا وَقُتِّلُوا تَقْتِيلًا

61 They are cursed; wherever they are found, they should be captured and killed outright.

61
2:191; 3:112; 4:89; 8:57; 9:5

٦٢ سُنَّةَ اللَّهِ فِي الَّذِينَ خَلَوْا مِن قَبْلُ ۖ وَلَن تَجِدَ لِسُنَّةِ اللَّهِ تَبْدِيلًا

62 Such has been God's precedent with those who passed away before. You will find no change in God's system.

62
3:137; 48:23

٦٣ يَسْأَلُكَ النَّاسُ عَنِ السَّاعَةِ ۖ قُلْ إِنَّمَا عِلْمُهَا عِندَ اللَّهِ ۚ وَمَا يُدْرِيكَ لَعَلَّ السَّاعَةَ تَكُونُ قَرِيبًا

63 The people ask you about the Hour. Say, "The knowledge thereof rests with God. But what do you know? Perhaps the hour is near."

63
7:187; 21:1

٦٤ إِنَّ اللَّهَ لَعَنَ الْكَافِرِينَ وَأَعَدَّ لَهُمْ سَعِيرًا

64 God has cursed the disbelievers, and has prepared for them a Blaze.

٦٥ خَالِدِينَ فِيهَا أَبَدًا ۖ لَّا يَجِدُونَ وَلِيًّا وَلَا نَصِيرًا

65 Dwelling therein forever, not finding a protector or a savior.

٦٦ يَوْمَ تُقَلَّبُ وُجُوهُهُمْ فِي النَّارِ يَقُولُونَ يَا لَيْتَنَا أَطَعْنَا اللَّهَ وَأَطَعْنَا الرَّسُولَا

66 The Day when their faces are flipped into the Fire, they will say, "If only we had obeyed God and obeyed the Messenger."

٦٧ وَقَالُوا رَبَّنَا إِنَّا أَطَعْنَا سَادَتَنَا وَكُبَرَاءَنَا فَأَضَلُّونَا السَّبِيلَا

67 And they will say, "Lord, we have obeyed our superiors and our dignitaries, but they led us away from the way.

67
7:38

٦٨ رَبَّنَا آتِهِمْ ضِعْفَيْنِ مِنَ الْعَذَابِ وَالْعَنْهُمْ لَعْنًا كَبِيرًا

68 Lord, give them double the punishment, and curse them with a great curse."

٦٩ يَا أَيُّهَا الَّذِينَ آمَنُوا لَا تَكُونُوا كَالَّذِينَ آذَوْا مُوسَىٰ فَبَرَّأَهُ اللَّهُ مِمَّا قَالُوا ۚ وَكَانَ عِندَ اللَّهِ وَجِيهًا

69 O you who believe! Do not be like those who abused Moses; but God cleared him of what they said. He was distinguished with God.

69
61:5

٧٠ يَا أَيُّهَا الَّذِينَ آمَنُوا اتَّقُوا اللَّهَ وَقُولُوا قَوْلًا سَدِيدًا

70 O you who believe! Be conscious of God, and speak in a straight-forward manner.

٧١ يُصْلِحْ لَكُمْ أَعْمَالَكُمْ وَيَغْفِرْ لَكُمْ ذُنُوبَكُمْ ۗ وَمَنْ يُطِعِ اللَّهَ وَرَسُولَهُ فَقَدْ فَازَ فَوْزًا عَظِيمًا

71
4:13, 69; 24:52; 48:17

71 He will rectify your conduct for you, and will forgive you your sins. Whoever obeys God and His Messenger has won a great victory.

٧٢ إِنَّا عَرَضْنَا الْأَمَانَةَ عَلَى السَّمَاوَاتِ وَالْأَرْضِ وَالْجِبَالِ فَأَبَيْنَ أَنْ يَحْمِلْنَهَا وَأَشْفَقْنَ مِنْهَا وَحَمَلَهَا الْإِنْسَانُ ۖ إِنَّهُ كَانَ ظَلُومًا جَهُولًا

72 We offered the Trust to the heavens, and the earth, and the mountains; but they refused to bear it, and were apprehensive of it; but the human being accepted it. He was unfair and ignorant.

٧٣ لِيُعَذِّبَ اللَّهُ الْمُنَافِقِينَ وَالْمُنَافِقَاتِ وَالْمُشْرِكِينَ وَالْمُشْرِكَاتِ وَيَتُوبَ اللَّهُ عَلَى الْمُؤْمِنِينَ وَالْمُؤْمِنَاتِ ۗ وَكَانَ اللَّهُ غَفُورًا رَحِيمًا

73
48:5

73 God will punish the hypocrites, men and women, and the idolaters, men and women. And God will redeem the believers, men and women. God is Ever-Forgiving, Most Merciful.

Sūrah 34: Saba'

سُوْرَةُ سَبَأٍ (Sheba)

بِسْمِ اللَّهِ الرَّحْمَٰنِ الرَّحِيمِ

١ الْحَمْدُ لِلَّهِ الَّذِي لَهُ مَا فِي السَّمَاوَاتِ وَمَا فِي الْأَرْضِ وَلَهُ الْحَمْدُ فِي الْآخِرَةِ ۚ وَهُوَ الْحَكِيمُ الْخَبِيرُ

1 Praise be to God, to Whom belongs everything in the heavens and the earth; and praise be to Him in the Hereafter. He is the Wise, the Expert.

٢ يَعْلَمُ مَا يَلِجُ فِي الْأَرْضِ وَمَا يَخْرُجُ مِنْهَا وَمَا يَنْزِلُ مِنَ السَّمَاءِ وَمَا يَعْرُجُ فِيهَا ۚ وَهُوَ الرَّحِيمُ الْغَفُورُ

2
23:18; 29:21; 32:5

2 He knows what penetrates into the earth, and what comes out of it, and what descends from the sky, and what ascends to it. He is the Merciful, the Forgiving.

٣ وَقَالَ الَّذِينَ كَفَرُوا لَا تَأْتِينَا السَّاعَةُ ۖ قُلْ بَلَىٰ وَرَبِّي لَتَأْتِيَنَّكُمْ عَالِمِ الْغَيْبِ ۖ لَا يَعْزُبُ عَنْهُ مِثْقَالُ ذَرَّةٍ فِي السَّمَاوَاتِ وَلَا فِي الْأَرْضِ وَلَا أَصْغَرُ مِنْ ذَٰلِكَ وَلَا أَكْبَرُ إِلَّا فِي كِتَابٍ مُبِينٍ

3
6:59; 10:61; 16:38

3 Those who disbelieve say, "The Hour will not come upon us." Say, "Yes indeed, by my Lord, it will come upon you. He is the Knower of the unseen." Not an atom's weight in the heavens and the earth, or anything smaller or larger, escapes His knowledge. All are in a Clear Record.

٤ لِيَجْزِيَ الَّذِينَ آمَنُوا وَعَمِلُوا الصَّالِحَاتِ ۚ أُولَٰئِكَ لَهُم مَّغْفِرَةٌ وَرِزْقٌ كَرِيمٌ

4 That He may recompense those who believe and do good works. Those will have forgiveness, and a generous provision.

4 — 10:4; 30:45

٥ وَالَّذِينَ سَعَوْا فِي آيَاتِنَا مُعَاجِزِينَ أُولَٰئِكَ لَهُمْ عَذَابٌ مِّن رِّجْزٍ أَلِيمٌ

5 As for those who strive against Our revelations, seeking to undermine them—for them is a punishment of a painful plague.

5 — 22:51; 34:38

٦ وَيَرَى الَّذِينَ أُوتُوا الْعِلْمَ الَّذِي أُنزِلَ إِلَيْكَ مِن رَّبِّكَ هُوَ الْحَقَّ وَيَهْدِي إِلَىٰ صِرَاطِ الْعَزِيزِ الْحَمِيدِ

6 Those who received knowledge know that what is revealed to you from your Lord is the truth; and it guides to the path of the Majestic, the Praiseworthy.

6 — 22:54; 29:49

٧ وَقَالَ الَّذِينَ كَفَرُوا هَلْ نَدُلُّكُمْ عَلَىٰ رَجُلٍ يُنَبِّئُكُمْ إِذَا مُزِّقْتُمْ كُلَّ مُمَزَّقٍ إِنَّكُمْ لَفِي خَلْقٍ جَدِيدٍ

7 Those who disbelieved said, "Shall we point out to you a man, who will tell you that, once torn into shreds, you will be in a new creation?

٨ أَفْتَرَىٰ عَلَى اللَّهِ كَذِبًا أَم بِهِ جِنَّةٌ ۗ بَلِ الَّذِينَ لَا يُؤْمِنُونَ بِالْآخِرَةِ فِي الْعَذَابِ وَالضَّلَالِ الْبَعِيدِ

8 Did he invent a lie about God, or is there madness in him?" Indeed, those who do not believe in the Hereafter are in torment, and far astray.

8 — 7:184; 23:25, 70

٩ أَفَلَمْ يَرَوْا إِلَىٰ مَا بَيْنَ أَيْدِيهِمْ وَمَا خَلْفَهُم مِّنَ السَّمَاءِ وَالْأَرْضِ ۚ إِن نَّشَأْ نَخْسِفْ بِهِمُ الْأَرْضَ أَوْ نُسْقِطْ عَلَيْهِمْ كِسَفًا مِّنَ السَّمَاءِ ۚ إِنَّ فِي ذَٰلِكَ لَآيَةً لِّكُلِّ عَبْدٍ مُّنِيبٍ

9 Do they not reflect upon what lies before them and behind them, of the heaven and the earth? If We will, We can make the earth cave in beneath them, or make pieces of the sky fall down on them. In that is a sign for every devout servant.

9 — 7:158; 16:187; 17:92; 26:187; 50:6; 52:44

١٠ وَلَقَدْ آتَيْنَا دَاوُودَ مِنَّا فَضْلًا ۖ يَا جِبَالُ أَوِّبِي مَعَهُ وَالطَّيْرَ ۖ وَأَلَنَّا لَهُ الْحَدِيدَ

10 We bestowed upon David favor from Us: "O mountains, and birds: echo with him." And We softened iron for him.

10–11 — 17:55; 21:78–80; 27:15

١١ أَنِ اعْمَلْ سَابِغَاتٍ وَقَدِّرْ فِي السَّرْدِ ۖ وَاعْمَلُوا صَالِحًا ۖ إِنِّي بِمَا تَعْمَلُونَ بَصِيرٌ

11 "Make coats of armor, and measure the links well; and work righteousness. I am Observant of everything you do."

١٢ وَلِسُلَيْمَانَ الرِّيحَ غُدُوُّهَا شَهْرٌ وَرَوَاحُهَا شَهْرٌ ۖ وَأَسَلْنَا لَهُ عَيْنَ الْقِطْرِ ۖ وَمِنَ الْجِنِّ مَن يَعْمَلُ بَيْنَ يَدَيْهِ بِإِذْنِ رَبِّهِ ۖ وَمَن يَزِغْ مِنْهُمْ عَنْ أَمْرِنَا نُذِقْهُ مِنْ عَذَابِ السَّعِيرِ

12 And for Solomon the wind—its outward journey was one month, and its return journey was one month. And We made a spring of tar flow for him. And there were sprites that worked under him, by the leave of his Lord. But whoever of them swerved from Our command, We make him taste of the punishment of the Inferno.

12 — 21:81; 38:36

١٣ يَعْمَلُونَ لَهُ مَا يَشَاءُ مِنْ مَحَارِيبَ وَتَمَاثِيلَ وَجِفَانٍ كَالْجَوَابِ وَقُدُورٍ رَاسِيَاتٍ ۚ اعْمَلُوا آلَ دَاوُودَ شُكْرًا ۚ وَقَلِيلٌ مِنْ عِبَادِيَ الشَّكُورُ

13 They made for him whatever he wished: sanctuaries, statues, bowls like pools, and heavy cauldrons. "O House of David, work with appreciation," but a few of My servants are appreciative.

١٤ فَلَمَّا قَضَيْنَا عَلَيْهِ الْمَوْتَ مَا دَلَّهُمْ عَلَىٰ مَوْتِهِ إِلَّا دَابَّةُ الْأَرْضِ تَأْكُلُ مِنْسَأَتَهُ ۖ فَلَمَّا خَرَّ تَبَيَّنَتِ الْجِنُّ أَنْ لَوْ كَانُوا يَعْلَمُونَ الْغَيْبَ مَا لَبِثُوا فِي الْعَذَابِ الْمُهِينِ

14 Then, when We decreed death for him, nothing indicated his death to them except an earthworm eating at his staff. Then, when he fell down, it became clear to the sprites that, had they known the unseen, they would not have remained in the demeaning torment.

١٥ لَقَدْ كَانَ لِسَبَإٍ فِي مَسْكَنِهِمْ آيَةٌ ۖ جَنَّتَانِ عَنْ يَمِينٍ وَشِمَالٍ ۖ كُلُوا مِنْ رِزْقِ رَبِّكُمْ وَاشْكُرُوا لَهُ ۚ بَلْدَةٌ طَيِّبَةٌ وَرَبٌّ غَفُورٌ

15 In Sheba's homeland there used to be a wonder: two gardens, on the right, and on the left. "Eat of your Lord's provision, and give thanks to Him." A good land, and a forgiving Lord.

١٦ فَأَعْرَضُوا فَأَرْسَلْنَا عَلَيْهِمْ سَيْلَ الْعَرِمِ وَبَدَّلْنَاهُمْ بِجَنَّتَيْهِمْ جَنَّتَيْنِ ذَوَاتَيْ أُكُلٍ خَمْطٍ وَأَثْلٍ وَشَيْءٍ مِنْ سِدْرٍ قَلِيلٍ

16 But they turned away, so We unleashed against them the flood of the dam; and We substituted their two gardens with two gardens of bitter fruits, thorny shrubs, and meager harvest.

١٧ ذَٰلِكَ جَزَيْنَاهُمْ بِمَا كَفَرُوا ۖ وَهَلْ نُجَازِي إِلَّا الْكَفُورَ

17 We thus penalized them for their ingratitude. Would We penalize any but the ungrateful?

17
35:36

١٨ وَجَعَلْنَا بَيْنَهُمْ وَبَيْنَ الْقُرَى الَّتِي بَارَكْنَا فِيهَا قُرًى ظَاهِرَةً وَقَدَّرْنَا فِيهَا السَّيْرَ ۖ سِيرُوا فِيهَا لَيَالِيَ وَأَيَّامًا آمِنِينَ

18 Between them and the towns We had blessed, We placed prominent towns, and We made the travel between them easy. "Travel between them by night and day, in safety."

١٩ فَقَالُوا رَبَّنَا بَاعِدْ بَيْنَ أَسْفَارِنَا وَظَلَمُوا أَنْفُسَهُمْ فَجَعَلْنَاهُمْ أَحَادِيثَ وَمَزَّقْنَاهُمْ كُلَّ مُمَزَّقٍ ۚ إِنَّ فِي ذَٰلِكَ لَآيَاتٍ لِكُلِّ صَبَّارٍ شَكُورٍ

19 But they said, "Our Lord, lengthen the distances of our journeys." They wronged themselves; so We made them history, and We scattered them in every direction. In this are lessons for every steadfast and appreciative person.

٢٠ وَلَقَدْ صَدَّقَ عَلَيْهِمْ إِبْلِيسُ ظَنَّهُ فَاتَّبَعُوهُ إِلَّا فَرِيقًا مِنَ الْمُؤْمِنِينَ

20
15:40

20 Satan was correct in his assessment of them. They followed him, except for a group of believers.

٢١ وَمَا كَانَ لَهُ عَلَيْهِم مِّن سُلْطَانٍ إِلَّا لِنَعْلَمَ مَن يُؤْمِنُ بِالْآخِرَةِ مِمَّنْ هُوَ مِنْهَا فِي شَكٍّ ۗ وَرَبُّكَ عَلَىٰ كُلِّ شَيْءٍ حَفِيظٌ

21 14:22

21 He had no authority over them; except that We willed to distinguish him who believes in the Hereafter, from him who is doubtful about it. Your Lord is Guardian over all things.

٢٢ قُلِ ادْعُوا الَّذِينَ زَعَمْتُم مِّن دُونِ اللَّهِ ۖ لَا يَمْلِكُونَ مِثْقَالَ ذَرَّةٍ فِي السَّمَاوَاتِ وَلَا فِي الْأَرْضِ وَمَا لَهُمْ فِيهِمَا مِن شِرْكٍ وَمَا لَهُ مِنْهُم مِّن ظَهِيرٍ

22 17:56

22 Say, "Call upon those whom you claim besides God. They possess not an atom's weight in the heavens or the earth, and they possess no share of either, and He has no backers from among them."

٢٣ وَلَا تَنفَعُ الشَّفَاعَةُ عِندَهُ إِلَّا لِمَنْ أَذِنَ لَهُ ۚ حَتَّىٰ إِذَا فُزِّعَ عَن قُلُوبِهِمْ قَالُوا مَاذَا قَالَ رَبُّكُمْ ۖ قَالُوا الْحَقَّ ۖ وَهُوَ الْعَلِيُّ الْكَبِيرُ

23 2:255; 20:109

23 Intercession with Him is of no value, except for someone He has permitted. Until, when fear has subsided from their hearts, they will say, "What did your Lord say?" They will say, "The truth, and He is the High, the Great."

٢٤ قُلْ مَن يَرْزُقُكُم مِّنَ السَّمَاوَاتِ وَالْأَرْضِ ۖ قُلِ اللَّهُ ۖ وَإِنَّا أَوْ إِيَّاكُمْ لَعَلَىٰ هُدًى أَوْ فِي ضَلَالٍ مُّبِينٍ

24 10:31

24 Say, "Who provides for you from the heavens and the earth?" Say, "God. And Either you, or we, are rightly guided, or in evident error."

٢٥ قُل لَّا تُسْأَلُونَ عَمَّا أَجْرَمْنَا وَلَا نُسْأَلُ عَمَّا تَعْمَلُونَ

25 11:35

25 Say, "You will not be asked about our misdeeds, nor will we be asked about what you do."

٢٦ قُلْ يَجْمَعُ بَيْنَنَا رَبُّنَا ثُمَّ يَفْتَحُ بَيْنَنَا بِالْحَقِّ وَهُوَ الْفَتَّاحُ الْعَلِيمُ

26 7:89

26 Say, "Our Lord will bring us together; then He will judge between us equitably. He is the All-Knowing Judge."

٢٧ قُلْ أَرُونِيَ الَّذِينَ أَلْحَقْتُم بِهِ شُرَكَاءَ ۖ كَلَّا ۚ بَلْ هُوَ اللَّهُ الْعَزِيزُ الْحَكِيمُ

27

27 Say, "Show me those you have attached to Him as associates. No indeed! But He is God, the Powerful, the Wise."

٢٨ وَمَا أَرْسَلْنَاكَ إِلَّا كَافَّةً لِّلنَّاسِ بَشِيرًا وَنَذِيرًا وَلَٰكِنَّ أَكْثَرَ النَّاسِ لَا يَعْلَمُونَ

28 4:79; 7:158; 21:107

28 We sent you only universally to all people, a herald and warner, but most people do not know.

٢٩ وَيَقُولُونَ مَتَىٰ هَٰذَا الْوَعْدُ إِن كُنتُمْ صَادِقِينَ

29 10:48

29 And they say, "When is this promise due, if you are truthful?"

٣٠ قُل لَّكُم مِّيعَادُ يَوْمٍ لَّا تَسْتَأْخِرُونَ عَنْهُ سَاعَةً وَلَا تَسْتَقْدِمُونَ

30 7:34; 10:49

30 Say, "You are promised a Day, which you cannot postpone by one hour, nor bring forward."

٣١ وَقَالَ الَّذِينَ كَفَرُوا لَن نُّؤْمِنَ بِهَٰذَا الْقُرْآنِ وَلَا بِالَّذِي بَيْنَ يَدَيْهِ ۗ وَلَوْ تَرَىٰ إِذِ الظَّالِمُونَ مَوْقُوفُونَ عِندَ رَبِّهِمْ يَرْجِعُ بَعْضُهُمْ إِلَىٰ بَعْضٍ الْقَوْلَ يَقُولُ الَّذِينَ اسْتُضْعِفُوا لِلَّذِينَ اسْتَكْبَرُوا لَوْلَا أَنتُمْ لَكُنَّا مُؤْمِنِينَ

31
6:30

31 Those who disbelieve say, "We will never believe in this Qur'an, nor in what came before it." If you could only see the wrongdoers, captive before their Lord, throwing back allegations at one another. Those who were oppressed will say to those who were arrogant, "Were it not for you, we would have been believers."

٣٢ قَالَ الَّذِينَ اسْتَكْبَرُوا لِلَّذِينَ اسْتُضْعِفُوا أَنَحْنُ صَدَدْنَاكُمْ عَنِ الْهُدَىٰ بَعْدَ إِذْ جَاءَكُم ۖ بَلْ كُنتُم مُّجْرِمِينَ

32 Those who were arrogant will say to those who were oppressed, "Was it us who turned you away from guidance when it came to you? No indeed, you yourselves were sinful."

٣٣ وَقَالَ الَّذِينَ اسْتُضْعِفُوا لِلَّذِينَ اسْتَكْبَرُوا بَلْ مَكْرُ اللَّيْلِ وَالنَّهَارِ إِذْ تَأْمُرُونَنَا أَن نَّكْفُرَ بِاللَّهِ وَنَجْعَلَ لَهُ أَندَادًا ۚ وَأَسَرُّوا النَّدَامَةَ لَمَّا رَأَوُا الْعَذَابَ وَجَعَلْنَا الْأَغْلَالَ فِي أَعْنَاقِ الَّذِينَ كَفَرُوا ۚ هَلْ يُجْزَوْنَ إِلَّا مَا كَانُوا يَعْمَلُونَ

33
14:21; 13:5; 36:8;
40:47, 71

33 And those who were oppressed will say to those who were arrogant, "It was your scheming by night and day; as you instructed us to reject God, and to set up rivals to Him." They will hide their remorse when they see the retribution. We will put yokes around the necks of those who disbelieved. Will they be repaid for anything other than what they used to do?

٣٤ وَمَا أَرْسَلْنَا فِي قَرْيَةٍ مِّن نَّذِيرٍ إِلَّا قَالَ مُتْرَفُوهَا إِنَّا بِمَا أُرْسِلْتُم بِهِ كَافِرُونَ

34
17:16; 23:44; 43:23–24

34 We sent no warner to any town, without its affluent saying, "We reject what you are sent with."

٣٥ وَقَالُوا نَحْنُ أَكْثَرُ أَمْوَالًا وَأَوْلَادًا وَمَا نَحْنُ بِمُعَذَّبِينَ

35
57:20; 63:9

35 And they say, "We have more wealth and more children, and we will not be punished."

٣٦ قُلْ إِنَّ رَبِّي يَبْسُطُ الرِّزْقَ لِمَن يَشَاءُ وَيَقْدِرُ وَلَٰكِنَّ أَكْثَرَ النَّاسِ لَا يَعْلَمُونَ

36
13:26; 34:39

36 Say, "My Lord spreads out His bounty to whomever He wills, or restricts it; but most people do not know."

٣٧ وَمَا أَمْوَالُكُمْ وَلَا أَوْلَادُكُم بِالَّتِي تُقَرِّبُكُمْ عِندَنَا زُلْفَىٰ إِلَّا مَنْ آمَنَ وَعَمِلَ صَالِحًا فَأُولَٰئِكَ لَهُمْ جَزَاءُ الضِّعْفِ بِمَا عَمِلُوا وَهُمْ فِي الْغُرُفَاتِ آمِنُونَ

37
3:10; 39:3

37 It is neither your wealth nor your children that bring you closer to Us, but it is he who believes and does good deeds. These will have a double reward for what they did; and they will reside in the Chambers, in peace and security.

٣٨ وَالَّذِينَ يَسْعَوْنَ فِي آيَاتِنَا مُعَاجِزِينَ أُولَٰئِكَ فِي الْعَذَابِ مُحْضَرُونَ

38 But those who work against Our revelations, seeking to undermine them—those will be summoned to the punishment.

38
22:51; 34:5

٣٩ قُلْ إِنَّ رَبِّي يَبْسُطُ الرِّزْقَ لِمَنْ يَشَاءُ مِنْ عِبَادِهِ وَيَقْدِرُ لَهُ ۚ وَمَا أَنْفَقْتُمْ مِنْ شَيْءٍ فَهُوَ يُخْلِفُهُ ۖ وَهُوَ خَيْرُ الرَّازِقِينَ

39 Say, "My Lord extends the provision to whomever He wills of His servants, or withholds it. Anything you spend, He will replace it. He is the Best of providers."

39
13:26; 29:62; 34:36

٤٠ وَيَوْمَ يَحْشُرُهُمْ جَمِيعًا ثُمَّ يَقُولُ لِلْمَلَائِكَةِ أَهَٰؤُلَاءِ إِيَّاكُمْ كَانُوا يَعْبُدُونَ

40 On the Day when He gathers them all together, then say to the angels, "Was it you these used to worship?"

40
10:28; 25:19

٤١ قَالُوا سُبْحَانَكَ أَنْتَ وَلِيُّنَا مِنْ دُونِهِمْ ۖ بَلْ كَانُوا يَعْبُدُونَ الْجِنَّ ۖ أَكْثَرُهُمْ بِهِمْ مُؤْمِنُونَ

41 They will say, "Be You glorified; You are our Master, not them. In fact, they used to worship the jinn, and most of them had faith in them."

41

٤٢ فَالْيَوْمَ لَا يَمْلِكُ بَعْضُكُمْ لِبَعْضٍ نَفْعًا وَلَا ضَرًّا وَنَقُولُ لِلَّذِينَ ظَلَمُوا ذُوقُوا عَذَابَ النَّارِ الَّتِي كُنْتُمْ بِهَا تُكَذِّبُونَ

42 "Today, none of you has the power to profit or harm the other." And We will say to those who did wrong, "Taste the agony of the Fire which you used to deny."

42
7:188; 10:49

٤٣ وَإِذَا تُتْلَىٰ عَلَيْهِمْ آيَاتُنَا بَيِّنَاتٍ قَالُوا مَا هَٰذَا إِلَّا رَجُلٌ يُرِيدُ أَنْ يَصُدَّكُمْ عَمَّا كَانَ يَعْبُدُ آبَاؤُكُمْ وَقَالُوا مَا هَٰذَا إِلَّا إِفْكٌ مُفْتَرًى ۚ وَقَالَ الَّذِينَ كَفَرُوا لِلْحَقِّ لَمَّا جَاءَهُمْ إِنْ هَٰذَا إِلَّا سِحْرٌ مُبِينٌ

43 And when Our enlightening Verses are recited to them, they say, "This is nothing but a man who wants to divert you from what your ancestors used to worship." And they say, "This is nothing but a fabricated lie." And when the Truth comes to them, the blasphemers say of the Truth, "This is nothing but plain magic."

43
10:78; 14:10; 25:4

٤٤ وَمَا آتَيْنَاهُمْ مِنْ كُتُبٍ يَدْرُسُونَهَا ۖ وَمَا أَرْسَلْنَا إِلَيْهِمْ قَبْلَكَ مِنْ نَذِيرٍ

44 But We gave them no book to study, and We did not send them any warner before you.

44
35:40; 43:21; 46:4; 68:37

٤٥ وَكَذَّبَ الَّذِينَ مِنْ قَبْلِهِمْ وَمَا بَلَغُوا مِعْشَارَ مَا آتَيْنَاهُمْ فَكَذَّبُوا رُسُلِي ۖ فَكَيْفَ كَانَ نَكِيرِ

45 Those before them also denied the Truth, yet they have not attained one-tenth of what We had given them. They rejected My messengers, so how was My disapproval?

45
10:39

٤٦ قُلْ إِنَّمَا أَعِظُكُم بِوَاحِدَةٍ ۖ أَن تَقُومُوا لِلَّهِ مَثْنَىٰ وَفُرَادَىٰ ثُمَّ تَتَفَكَّرُوا ۚ مَا بِصَاحِبِكُم مِّن جِنَّةٍ ۚ إِنْ هُوَ إِلَّا نَذِيرٌ لَّكُم بَيْنَ يَدَيْ عَذَابٍ شَدِيدٍ

46 7:184; 23:70

46 Say, "I offer you a single advice: devote yourselves to God, in pairs, or individually; and reflect. There is no madness in your friend. He is just a warner to you, before the advent of a severe punishment."

٤٧ قُلْ مَا سَأَلْتُكُم مِّنْ أَجْرٍ فَهُوَ لَكُمْ ۖ إِنْ أَجْرِيَ إِلَّا عَلَى اللَّهِ ۖ وَهُوَ عَلَىٰ كُلِّ شَيْءٍ شَهِيدٌ

47 10:72; 11:8

47 Say, "Whatever compensation I have asked of you, is yours. My compensation comes only from God, and He is Witness over all things."

٤٨ قُلْ إِنَّ رَبِّي يَقْذِفُ بِالْحَقِّ عَلَّامُ الْغُيُوبِ

48

48 Say, "My Lord projects the truth. He is the Knower of the Unseen."

٤٩ قُلْ جَاءَ الْحَقُّ وَمَا يُبْدِئُ الْبَاطِلُ وَمَا يُعِيدُ

49

49 Say, "The Truth has come; while falsehood can neither originate, nor regenerate."

٥٠ قُلْ إِن ضَلَلْتُ فَإِنَّمَا أَضِلُّ عَلَىٰ نَفْسِي ۖ وَإِنِ اهْتَدَيْتُ فَبِمَا يُوحِي إِلَيَّ رَبِّي ۚ إِنَّهُ سَمِيعٌ قَرِيبٌ

50 10:108; 17:15; 27:92; 39:41

50 Say, "If I err, I err only to my own loss; but if I am guided, it is by what my Lord inspires me. He is Hearing and Near."

٥١ وَلَوْ تَرَىٰ إِذْ فَزِعُوا فَلَا فَوْتَ وَأُخِذُوا مِن مَّكَانٍ قَرِيبٍ

51 27:87

51 If you could only see when they are terrified, and there is no escape, and they are seized from a nearby place.

٥٢ وَقَالُوا آمَنَّا بِهِ وَأَنَّىٰ لَهُمُ التَّنَاوُشُ مِن مَّكَانٍ بَعِيدٍ

52

52 And they say, "We have believed in it." But how can they attain it from a distant place?

٥٣ وَقَدْ كَفَرُوا بِهِ مِن قَبْلُ ۖ وَيَقْذِفُونَ بِالْغَيْبِ مِن مَّكَانٍ بَعِيدٍ

53

53 They have rejected it in the past, and made allegations from a far-off place.

٥٤ وَحِيلَ بَيْنَهُمْ وَبَيْنَ مَا يَشْتَهُونَ كَمَا فُعِلَ بِأَشْيَاعِهِم مِّن قَبْلُ ۚ إِنَّهُمْ كَانُوا فِي شَكٍّ مُّرِيبٍ

54 11:62; 54:51

54 A barrier will be placed between them and what they desire, as was done formerly with their counterparts. They were in disturbing doubt.

Sūrah 35: Fāṭir

سُوْرَةُ فَاطِر (Originator)

بِسْمِ اللَّهِ الرَّحْمَٰنِ الرَّحِيمِ

١ الْحَمْدُ لِلَّهِ فَاطِرِ السَّمَاوَاتِ وَالْأَرْضِ جَاعِلِ الْمَلَائِكَةِ رُسُلًا أُولِي أَجْنِحَةٍ مَثْنَىٰ وَثُلَاثَ وَرُبَاعَ ۚ يَزِيدُ فِي الْخَلْقِ مَا يَشَاءُ ۚ إِنَّ اللَّهَ عَلَىٰ كُلِّ شَيْءٍ قَدِيرٌ

1 — 22:75

1 Praise be to God, Originator of the heavens and the earth, Maker of the angels messengers with wings—double, triple, and quadruple. He adds to creation as He wills. God is Able to do all things.

٢ مَا يَفْتَحِ اللَّهُ لِلنَّاسِ مِنْ رَحْمَةٍ فَلَا مُمْسِكَ لَهَا ۖ وَمَا يُمْسِكْ فَلَا مُرْسِلَ لَهُ مِنْ بَعْدِهِ ۚ وَهُوَ الْعَزِيزُ الْحَكِيمُ

2 — 6:17; 10:107; 33:17; 39:38; 48:11

2 Whatever mercy God unfolds for the people, none can withhold it. And if He withholds it, none can release it thereafter. He is the Exalted in Power, Full of Wisdom.

٣ يَا أَيُّهَا النَّاسُ اذْكُرُوا نِعْمَتَ اللَّهِ عَلَيْكُمْ ۚ هَلْ مِنْ خَالِقٍ غَيْرُ اللَّهِ يَرْزُقُكُمْ مِنَ السَّمَاءِ وَالْأَرْضِ ۚ لَا إِلَٰهَ إِلَّا هُوَ ۖ فَأَنَّىٰ تُؤْفَكُونَ

3 — 10:31; 13:16; 25:3

3 O people! Remember God's blessings upon you. Is there a creator other than God who provides for you from the heaven and the earth? There is no god but He. So how are you misled?

٤ وَإِنْ يُكَذِّبُوكَ فَقَدْ كُذِّبَتْ رُسُلٌ مِنْ قَبْلِكَ ۚ وَإِلَى اللَّهِ تُرْجَعُ الْأُمُورُ

4 — 3:184; 6:34; 10:39; 35:25; 41:43

4 If they reject you, messengers before you were also rejected. To God all matters are returned.

٥ يَا أَيُّهَا النَّاسُ إِنَّ وَعْدَ اللَّهِ حَقٌّ ۖ فَلَا تَغُرَّنَّكُمُ الْحَيَاةُ الدُّنْيَا ۖ وَلَا يَغُرَّنَّكُمْ بِاللَّهِ الْغَرُورُ

5 O people! The promise of God is true; so let not the lowly life seduce you, and let not the Tempter tempt you away from God.

٦ إِنَّ الشَّيْطَانَ لَكُمْ عَدُوٌّ فَاتَّخِذُوهُ عَدُوًّا ۚ إِنَّمَا يَدْعُو حِزْبَهُ لِيَكُونُوا مِنْ أَصْحَابِ السَّعِيرِ

6 — 7:22; 18:50; 22:4

6 Satan is an enemy to you, so treat him as an enemy. He only invites his gang to be among the inmates of the Inferno.

٧ الَّذِينَ كَفَرُوا لَهُمْ عَذَابٌ شَدِيدٌ ۖ وَالَّذِينَ آمَنُوا وَعَمِلُوا الصَّالِحَاتِ لَهُمْ مَغْفِرَةٌ وَأَجْرٌ كَبِيرٌ

7 Those who disbelieve will suffer a harsh punishment, but those who believe and do righteous deeds will have forgiveness and a great reward.

٨ أَفَمَنْ زُيِّنَ لَهُ سُوءُ عَمَلِهِ فَرَآهُ حَسَنًا ۖ فَإِنَّ اللَّهَ يُضِلُّ مَنْ يَشَاءُ وَيَهْدِي مَنْ يَشَاءُ ۖ [a] فَلَا تَذْهَبْ نَفْسُكَ عَلَيْهِمْ حَسَرَاتٍ ۚ إِنَّ اللَّهَ عَلِيمٌ بِمَا يَصْنَعُونَ [b]

8
[a] 14:4; 16:93; 26:3; 74:31
[b] 6:33; 18:6

8 What of him whose evil deed was made attractive to him, and so he regards it as good? God leads astray whomever He wills, and He guides whomever He wills. Therefore, do not waste yourself sorrowing over them. God knows exactly what they do.

٩ وَاللَّهُ الَّذِي أَرْسَلَ الرِّيَاحَ فَتُثِيرُ سَحَابًا فَسُقْنَاهُ إِلَىٰ بَلَدٍ مَّيِّتٍ فَأَحْيَيْنَا بِهِ الْأَرْضَ بَعْدَ مَوْتِهَا ۚ كَذَٰلِكَ النُّشُورُ

9 7:57; 30:48; 32:27

9 God is He who sends the winds, which agitate clouds, which We drive to a dead land, and thereby revive the ground after it had died. Likewise is the Resurrection.

١٠ مَن كَانَ يُرِيدُ الْعِزَّةَ فَلِلَّهِ الْعِزَّةُ جَمِيعًا ۚ إِلَيْهِ يَصْعَدُ الْكَلِمُ الطَّيِّبُ وَالْعَمَلُ الصَّالِحُ يَرْفَعُهُ ۚ وَالَّذِينَ يَمْكُرُونَ السَّيِّئَاتِ لَهُمْ عَذَابٌ شَدِيدٌ ۖ وَمَكْرُ أُولَٰئِكَ هُوَ يَبُورُ

10
a 4:139; 10:65; 63:8
b 16:45; 35:45; 40:45

10 Whoever desires honor—all honor belongs to God. To Him ascends speech that is pure, and He elevates righteous conduct. As for those who plot evil, a terrible punishment awaits them, and the planning of these will fail.

١١ وَاللَّهُ خَلَقَكُم مِّن تُرَابٍ ثُمَّ مِن نُّطْفَةٍ ثُمَّ جَعَلَكُمْ أَزْوَاجًا ۚ وَمَا تَحْمِلُ مِنْ أُنثَىٰ وَلَا تَضَعُ إِلَّا بِعِلْمِهِ ۚ وَمَا يُعَمَّرُ مِن مُّعَمَّرٍ وَلَا يُنقَصُ مِنْ عُمُرِهِ إِلَّا فِي كِتَابٍ ۚ إِنَّ ذَٰلِكَ عَلَى اللَّهِ يَسِيرٌ

11 13:8; 18:37; 22:5; 31:34

11 God created you from dust, then from a small drop; then He made you pairs. No female conceives, or delivers, except with His knowledge. No living thing advances in years, or its life is shortened, except it be in a Record. That is surely easy for God.

١٢ وَمَا يَسْتَوِي الْبَحْرَانِ هَٰذَا عَذْبٌ فُرَاتٌ سَائِغٌ شَرَابُهُ وَهَٰذَا مِلْحٌ أُجَاجٌ ۖ وَمِن كُلٍّ تَأْكُلُونَ لَحْمًا طَرِيًّا وَتَسْتَخْرِجُونَ حِلْيَةً تَلْبَسُونَهَا ۖ وَتَرَى الْفُلْكَ فِيهِ مَوَاخِرَ لِتَبْتَغُوا مِن فَضْلِهِ وَلَعَلَّكُمْ تَشْكُرُونَ

12 16:14; 17:66; 25:53; 55:19

12 The two seas are not the same. One is fresh, sweet, good to drink, while the other is salty and bitter. Yet from each you eat tender meat, and extract jewelry which you wear. And you see the ships plowing through them, so that you may seek of His bounty, so that you may give thanks.

١٣ يُولِجُ اللَّيْلَ فِي النَّهَارِ وَيُولِجُ النَّهَارَ فِي اللَّيْلِ وَسَخَّرَ الشَّمْسَ وَالْقَمَرَ كُلٌّ يَجْرِي لِأَجَلٍ مُّسَمًّى ۚ ذَٰلِكُمُ اللَّهُ رَبُّكُمْ لَهُ الْمُلْكُ ۚ وَالَّذِينَ تَدْعُونَ مِن دُونِهِ مَا يَمْلِكُونَ مِن قِطْمِيرٍ

13
a 3:27; 13:2; 31:29; 39:5
b 17:56; 34:22

13 He merges the night into the day, and He merges the day into the night; and He regulates the sun and the moon, each running for a stated term. Such is God, your Lord; His is the sovereignty. As for those you call upon besides Him, they do not possess a speck.

١٤ إِن تَدْعُوهُمْ لَا يَسْمَعُوا دُعَاءَكُمْ وَلَوْ سَمِعُوا مَا اسْتَجَابُوا لَكُمْ ۖ وَيَوْمَ الْقِيَامَةِ يَكْفُرُونَ بِشِرْكِكُمْ ۚ وَلَا يُنَبِّئُكَ مِثْلُ خَبِيرٍ

14 If you pray to them, they cannot hear your prayer. And even if they heard, they would not answer you. And on the Day of Resurrection, they will reject your partnership. None informs you like an Expert.

١٥ يَا أَيُّهَا النَّاسُ أَنتُمُ الْفُقَرَاءُ إِلَى اللَّهِ ۖ وَاللَّهُ هُوَ الْغَنِيُّ الْحَمِيدُ

15 4:131; 14:8; 47:38; 64:6

15 O people! It is you who are the poor, in need of God; while God is the Rich, the Praiseworthy.

	16
١٦ إِن يَشَأْ يُذْهِبْكُمْ وَيَأْتِ بِخَلْقٍ جَدِيدٍ	4:132; 6:133; 14:19

16 If He wills, He can do away with you, and produce a new creation.

١٧ وَمَا ذَٰلِكَ عَلَى اللَّهِ بِعَزِيزٍ

17 And that would not be difficult for God.

	18
١٨ وَلَا تَزِرُ وَازِرَةٌ وِزْرَ أُخْرَىٰ ۚ وَإِن تَدْعُ مُثْقَلَةٌ إِلَىٰ حِمْلِهَا لَا يُحْمَلْ مِنْهُ شَيْءٌ وَلَوْ كَانَ ذَا قُرْبَىٰ ۗ إِنَّمَا تُنذِرُ الَّذِينَ يَخْشَوْنَ رَبَّهُم بِالْغَيْبِ وَأَقَامُوا الصَّلَاةَ ۚ وَمَن تَزَكَّىٰ فَإِنَّمَا يَتَزَكَّىٰ لِنَفْسِهِ ۚ وَإِلَى اللَّهِ الْمَصِيرُ	6:164; 17:15; 39:7

18 No burdened soul can carry the burden of another. Even if one weighted down calls for help with its burden, nothing can be lifted from it, even if they were related. You are to warn those who fear their Lord inwardly, and perform the prayer. He who purifies himself purifies himself for his own good. To God is the ultimate return.

	19
١٩ وَمَا يَسْتَوِي الْأَعْمَىٰ وَالْبَصِيرُ	6:50; 11:24; 13:16

19 Not equal are the blind and the seeing.

٢٠ وَلَا الظُّلُمَاتُ وَلَا النُّورُ

20 Nor are the darkness and the light.

٢١ وَلَا الظِّلُّ وَلَا الْحَرُورُ

21 Nor are the shade and the torrid heat.

٢٢ وَمَا يَسْتَوِي الْأَحْيَاءُ وَلَا الْأَمْوَاتُ ۚ إِنَّ اللَّهَ يُسْمِعُ مَن يَشَاءُ ۖ وَمَا أَنتَ بِمُسْمِعٍ مَّن فِي الْقُبُورِ

22 Nor are equal the living and the dead. God causes whomever He wills to hear, but you cannot make those in the graves hear.

٢٣ إِنْ أَنتَ إِلَّا نَذِيرٌ

23 You are only a warner.

	24
٢٤ إِنَّا أَرْسَلْنَاكَ بِالْحَقِّ بَشِيرًا وَنَذِيرًا ۚ وَإِن مِّنْ أُمَّةٍ إِلَّا خَلَا فِيهَا نَذِيرٌ	2:119; 13:7

24 We sent you with the truth; a bearer of good news, and a warner. There is no community but a warner has passed through it.

	25
٢٥ وَإِن يُكَذِّبُوكَ فَقَدْ كَذَّبَ الَّذِينَ مِن قَبْلِهِم جَاءَتْهُمْ رُسُلُهُم بِالْبَيِّنَاتِ وَبِالزُّبُرِ وَبِالْكِتَابِ الْمُنِيرِ	3:184; 6:34; 35:4

25 If they disbelieve you, those before them also disbelieved. Their messengers came to them with the clear proofs, with the Psalms, and with the Enlightening Scripture.

٢٦ ثُمَّ أَخَذْتُ الَّذِينَ كَفَرُوا ۖ فَكَيْفَ كَانَ نَكِيرِ

26 Then I seized those who disbelieved—so how was My rejection?

	27
٢٧ أَلَمْ تَرَ أَنَّ اللَّهَ أَنزَلَ مِنَ السَّمَاءِ مَاءً فَأَخْرَجْنَا بِهِ ثَمَرَاتٍ مُّخْتَلِفًا أَلْوَانُهَا ۚ وَمِنَ الْجِبَالِ جُدَدٌ بِيضٌ وَحُمْرٌ مُّخْتَلِفٌ أَلْوَانُهَا وَغَرَابِيبُ سُودٌ	6:99; 30:22

27 Have you not seen that God sends down water from the sky? With it We produce fruits of various colors. And in the mountains are streaks of white and red—varying in their hue—and pitch-black.

٢٨ وَمِنَ النَّاسِ وَالدَّوَابِّ وَالْأَنْعَامِ مُخْتَلِفٌ أَلْوَانُهُ كَذَٰلِكَ ۗ إِنَّمَا يَخْشَى اللَّهَ مِنْ عِبَادِهِ الْعُلَمَاءُ ۗ إِنَّ اللَّهَ عَزِيزٌ غَفُورٌ

28   30:22

28 Likewise, human beings, animals, and livestock come in various colors. From among His servants, the learned fear God. God is Almighty, Oft-Forgiving.

٢٩ إِنَّ الَّذِينَ يَتْلُونَ كِتَابَ اللَّهِ وَأَقَامُوا الصَّلَاةَ وَأَنْفَقُوا مِمَّا رَزَقْنَاهُمْ سِرًّا وَعَلَانِيَةً يَرْجُونَ تِجَارَةً لَنْ تَبُورَ

29   2:274; 13:22; 14:31

29 Those who recite the Book of God, and perform the prayer, and spend of what We have provided for them, secretly and publicly, expect a trade that will not fail.

٣٠ لِيُوَفِّيَهُمْ أُجُورَهُمْ وَيَزِيدَهُمْ مِنْ فَضْلِهِ ۚ إِنَّهُ غَفُورٌ شَكُورٌ

30   3:57; 4:173; 24:38; 42:26

30 He will pay them their dues in full, and will increase them from His bounty. He is Forgiving and Appreciative.

٣١ وَالَّذِي أَوْحَيْنَا إِلَيْكَ مِنَ الْكِتَابِ هُوَ الْحَقُّ مُصَدِّقًا لِمَا بَيْنَ يَدَيْهِ ۗ إِنَّ اللَّهَ بِعِبَادِهِ لَخَبِيرٌ بَصِيرٌ

31   5:48

31 What We inspired in you, of the Book, is the truth, confirming what preceded it. God is Well-Informed of His servants, All-Seeing.

٣٢ ثُمَّ أَوْرَثْنَا الْكِتَابَ الَّذِينَ اصْطَفَيْنَا مِنْ عِبَادِنَا ۖ فَمِنْهُمْ ظَالِمٌ لِنَفْسِهِ وَمِنْهُمْ مُقْتَصِدٌ وَمِنْهُمْ سَابِقٌ بِالْخَيْرَاتِ بِإِذْنِ اللَّهِ ۚ ذَٰلِكَ هُوَ الْفَضْلُ الْكَبِيرُ

32   40:53; 42:14

32 Then We passed the Book to those of Our servants whom We chose. Some of them wrong their souls, and some follow a middle course, and some are in the foremost in good deeds by God's leave; that is the greatest blessing.

٣٣ جَنَّاتُ عَدْنٍ يَدْخُلُونَهَا يُحَلَّوْنَ فِيهَا مِنْ أَسَاوِرَ مِنْ ذَهَبٍ وَلُؤْلُؤًا ۖ وَلِبَاسُهُمْ فِيهَا حَرِيرٌ

33   22:23

33 The Gardens of Eden, which they will enter. They will be adorned therein with gold bracelets and pearls, and their garments therein will be of silk.

٣٤ وَقَالُوا الْحَمْدُ لِلَّهِ الَّذِي أَذْهَبَ عَنَّا الْحَزَنَ ۖ إِنَّ رَبَّنَا لَغَفُورٌ شَكُورٌ

34

34 And they will say, "Praise God, who has lifted all sorrow from us. Our Lord is Most Forgiving, Most Appreciative.

٣٥ الَّذِي أَحَلَّنَا دَارَ الْمُقَامَةِ مِنْ فَضْلِهِ لَا يَمَسُّنَا فِيهَا نَصَبٌ وَلَا يَمَسُّنَا فِيهَا لُغُوبٌ

35   15:48; 23:64

35 He Who settled us in the Home of Permanence, by His grace, where boredom will not touch us, and fatigue will not afflict us."

٣٦ وَالَّذِينَ كَفَرُوا لَهُمْ نَارُ جَهَنَّمَ لَا يُقْضَىٰ عَلَيْهِمْ فَيَمُوتُوا وَلَا يُخَفَّفُ عَنْهُمْ مِنْ عَذَابِهَا ۚ كَذَٰلِكَ نَجْزِي كُلَّ كَفُورٍ

36

36 As for those who disbelieve, for them is the Fire of Hell, wherein they will never be finished off and die, nor will its punishment be lightened for them. Thus We will repay every ingrate.

٣٧ وَهُمْ يَصْطَرِخُونَ فِيهَا رَبَّنَا أَخْرِجْنَا نَعْمَلْ صَالِحًا غَيْرَ الَّذِي كُنَّا نَعْمَلُ ۚ أَوَلَمْ نُعَمِّرْكُم مَّا يَتَذَكَّرُ فِيهِ مَن تَذَكَّرَ وَجَاءَكُمُ النَّذِيرُ ۖ فَذُوقُوا فَمَا لِلظَّالِمِينَ مِن نَّصِيرٍ

37   7:53

37 And they will scream therein, "Our Lord, let us out, and we will act righteously, differently from the way we used to act." Did We not give you a life long enough, in which anyone who wanted to understand would have understood? And the warner did come to you. So taste. The evildoers will have no helper.

٣٨ إِنَّ اللَّهَ عَالِمُ غَيْبِ السَّمَاوَاتِ وَالْأَرْضِ ۚ إِنَّهُ عَلِيمٌ بِذَاتِ الصُّدُورِ

38   49:18

38 God is the Knower of the future of the heavens and the earth. He knows what the hearts contain.

٣٩ هُوَ الَّذِي جَعَلَكُمْ خَلَائِفَ فِي الْأَرْضِ ۚ فَمَن كَفَرَ فَعَلَيْهِ كُفْرُهُ ۖ وَلَا يَزِيدُ الْكَافِرِينَ كُفْرُهُمْ عِندَ رَبِّهِمْ إِلَّا مَقْتًا ۖ وَلَا يَزِيدُ الْكَافِرِينَ كُفْرُهُمْ إِلَّا خَسَارًا

39   30:44; 40:10, 35; 61:3

39 It is He who made you successors on earth. Whoever disbelieves, his disbelief will recoil upon him. The disbelief of the disbelievers adds only to their Lord's disfavor of them. The disbelief of the disbelievers adds only to their perdition.

٤٠ قُلْ أَرَأَيْتُمْ شُرَكَاءَكُمُ الَّذِينَ تَدْعُونَ مِن دُونِ اللَّهِ أَرُونِي مَاذَا خَلَقُوا مِنَ الْأَرْضِ أَمْ لَهُمْ شِرْكٌ فِي السَّمَاوَاتِ أَمْ آتَيْنَاهُمْ كِتَابًا فَهُمْ عَلَىٰ بَيِّنَتٍ مِّنْهُ ۚ بَلْ إِن يَعِدُ الظَّالِمُونَ بَعْضُهُم بَعْضًا إِلَّا غُرُورًا

40   34:44; 46:4; 31:11

40 Say, "Have you considered those partners of yours that you worship instead of God? Show me what they have created on earth. Or do they have any share in the heavens?" Or have We given them a book whose clear teachings they follow? In fact, the wrongdoers promise one another nothing but delusions.

٤١ إِنَّ اللَّهَ يُمْسِكُ السَّمَاوَاتِ وَالْأَرْضَ أَن تَزُولَا ۚ وَلَئِن زَالَتَا إِنْ أَمْسَكَهُمَا مِنْ أَحَدٍ مِّن بَعْدِهِ ۚ إِنَّهُ كَانَ حَلِيمًا غَفُورًا

41   22:65

41 God holds the heavens and the earth, lest they fall apart. And were they to fall apart, there is none to hold them together except He. He is Most Clement, Most Forgiving.

٤٢ وَأَقْسَمُوا بِاللَّهِ جَهْدَ أَيْمَانِهِمْ لَئِن جَاءَهُمْ نَذِيرٌ لَّيَكُونُنَّ أَهْدَىٰ مِنْ إِحْدَى الْأُمَمِ ۖ فَلَمَّا جَاءَهُمْ نَذِيرٌ مَّا زَادَهُمْ إِلَّا نُفُورًا

42   6:157; 37:167

42 And they swore by God with their solemn oaths, that if a warner came to them, they would be more guided than any other people. Yet when a warner came to them, it only increased them in aversion.

٤٣ اسْتِكْبَارًا فِي الْأَرْضِ وَمَكْرَ السَّيِّئِ ۚ وَلَا يَحِيقُ الْمَكْرُ السَّيِّئُ إِلَّا بِأَهْلِهِ ۚ فَهَلْ يَنظُرُونَ إِلَّا سُنَّتَ الْأَوَّلِينَ ۚ فَلَن تَجِدَ لِسُنَّتِ اللَّهِ تَبْدِيلًا ۖ وَلَن تَجِدَ لِسُنَّتِ اللَّهِ تَحْوِيلًا

43   17:77; 33:62; 48:23

43 Priding themselves on earth, and scheming evil. But evil scheming overwhelms none but its authors. Do they expect anything but the precedent of the ancients? You will not find any change in God's practice, and you will not find any substitute to God's practice.

٤٤ أَوَلَمْ يَسِيرُوا فِي الْأَرْضِ فَيَنظُرُوا كَيْفَ كَانَ عَاقِبَةُ الَّذِينَ مِن قَبْلِهِمْ وَكَانُوا أَشَدَّ مِنْهُمْ قُوَّةً ۚ وَمَا كَانَ اللَّهُ لِيُعْجِزَهُ مِن شَيْءٍ فِي السَّمَاوَاتِ وَلَا فِي الْأَرْضِ ۚ إِنَّهُ كَانَ عَلِيمًا قَدِيرًا

44
12:109

44 Have they not journeyed in the land and observed the fate of those who preceded them? They were superior to them in strength. But nothing can defeat God in the heavens or on Earth. He is indeed Omniscient and Omnipotent.

٤٥ وَلَوْ يُؤَاخِذُ اللَّهُ النَّاسَ بِمَا كَسَبُوا مَا تَرَكَ عَلَىٰ ظَهْرِهَا مِن دَابَّةٍ وَلَٰكِن يُؤَخِّرُهُمْ إِلَىٰ أَجَلٍ مُّسَمًّى ۖ فَإِذَا جَاءَ أَجَلُهُمْ فَإِنَّ اللَّهَ كَانَ بِعِبَادِهِ بَصِيرًا

45
16:61; 18:58

45 If God were to punish the people for what they have earned, He would not leave a single living creature on its surface. But He defers them until a stated time. Then, when their time has arrived—God is Observant of His creatures.

Sūrah 36: Yā-Sīn

سُوْرَةُ يس (Yā-Sīn)

بِسْمِ اللَّهِ الرَّحْمَٰنِ الرَّحِيمِ

١ يس

1 Yā, Sīn.

٢ وَالْقُرْآنِ الْحَكِيمِ

2–3
2:252

2 By the Wise Qur'an.

٣ إِنَّكَ لَمِنَ الْمُرْسَلِينَ

3 You are one of the messengers.

٤ عَلَىٰ صِرَاطٍ مُّسْتَقِيمٍ

4 On a straight path.

٥ تَنزِيلَ الْعَزِيزِ الرَّحِيمِ

5 The revelation of the Almighty, the Merciful.

٦ لِتُنذِرَ قَوْمًا مَّا أُنذِرَ آبَاؤُهُمْ فَهُمْ غَافِلُونَ

6
28:46; 32:3; 34:44

6 To warn a people whose ancestors were not warned, and so they are unaware.

٧ لَقَدْ حَقَّ الْقَوْلُ عَلَىٰ أَكْثَرِهِمْ فَهُمْ لَا يُؤْمِنُونَ

7
10:33; 10:96; 28:63; 36:70; 41:25

7 The Word was realized against most of them, for they do not believe.

٨ إِنَّا جَعَلْنَا فِي أَعْنَاقِهِمْ أَغْلَالًا فَهِيَ إِلَى الْأَذْقَانِ فَهُم مُّقْمَحُونَ

8 We placed shackles around their necks, up to their chins, so they are stiff-necked.

13:5; 34:33

٩ وَجَعَلْنَا مِن بَيْنِ أَيْدِيهِمْ سَدًّا وَمِنْ خَلْفِهِمْ سَدًّا فَأَغْشَيْنَاهُمْ فَهُمْ لَا يُبْصِرُونَ

9 And We placed a barrier in front of them, and a barrier behind them, and We have enshrouded them, so they cannot see.

2:7; 16:108; 45:23

١٠ وَسَوَاءٌ عَلَيْهِمْ أَأَنذَرْتَهُمْ أَمْ لَمْ تُنذِرْهُمْ لَا يُؤْمِنُونَ

10 It is the same for them, whether you warn them, or do not warn them—they will not believe.

2:6; 26:136

١١ إِنَّمَا تُنذِرُ مَنِ اتَّبَعَ الذِّكْرَ وَخَشِيَ الرَّحْمَٰنَ بِالْغَيْبِ ۖ فَبَشِّرْهُ بِمَغْفِرَةٍ وَأَجْرٍ كَرِيمٍ

11 You warn only him who follows the Message, and fears the Most Gracious inwardly. So give him good news of forgiveness, and a generous reward.

35:18

١٢ إِنَّا نَحْنُ نُحْيِي الْمَوْتَىٰ وَنَكْتُبُ مَا قَدَّمُوا وَآثَارَهُمْ ۚ وَكُلَّ شَيْءٍ أَحْصَيْنَاهُ فِي إِمَامٍ مُّبِينٍ

12 It is We who revive the dead; and We write down what they have forwarded, and their traces. We have tallied all things in a Clear Record.

17:71; 18:49; 43:80; 50:18

١٣ وَاضْرِبْ لَهُم مَّثَلًا أَصْحَابَ الْقَرْيَةِ إِذْ جَاءَهَا الْمُرْسَلُونَ

13 And cite for them the parable of the landlords of the town—when the messengers came to it.

١٤ إِذْ أَرْسَلْنَا إِلَيْهِمُ اثْنَيْنِ فَكَذَّبُوهُمَا فَعَزَّزْنَا بِثَالِثٍ فَقَالُوا إِنَّا إِلَيْكُم مُّرْسَلُونَ

14 We sent them two messengers, but they denied them both, so We reinforced them with a third. They said, "We are messengers to you."

١٥ قَالُوا مَا أَنتُمْ إِلَّا بَشَرٌ مِّثْلُنَا وَمَا أَنزَلَ الرَّحْمَٰنُ مِن شَيْءٍ إِنْ أَنتُمْ إِلَّا تَكْذِبُونَ

15 They said, "You are nothing but humans like us, and the Gracious did not send down anything; you are only lying."

17:94

١٦ قَالُوا رَبُّنَا يَعْلَمُ إِنَّا إِلَيْكُمْ لَمُرْسَلُونَ

16 They said, "Our Lord knows that we are messengers to you.

١٧ وَمَا عَلَيْنَا إِلَّا الْبَلَاغُ الْمُبِينُ

17 And our only duty is clear communication."

١٨ قَالُوا إِنَّا تَطَيَّرْنَا بِكُمْ ۖ لَئِن لَّمْ تَنتَهُوا لَنَرْجُمَنَّكُمْ وَلَيَمَسَّنَّكُم مِّنَّا عَذَابٌ أَلِيمٌ

18 They said, "We see an evil omen in you; if you do not give up, we will stone you, and a painful punishment from us will befall you."

18–19
7:131; 27:47

١٩ قَالُوا طَائِرُكُم مَّعَكُمْ ۚ أَئِن ذُكِّرْتُم ۚ بَلْ أَنتُمْ قَوْمٌ مُّسْرِفُونَ

19 They said, "Your evil omen is upon you. Is it because you were reminded? But you are an extravagant people."

٢٠ وَجَاءَ مِنْ أَقْصَى الْمَدِينَةِ رَجُلٌ يَسْعَىٰ قَالَ يَا قَوْمِ اتَّبِعُوا الْمُرْسَلِينَ

20 Then a man came running from the remotest part of the city. He said, "O my people, follow the messengers.

20
28:20

٢١ اتَّبِعُوا مَنْ لَا يَسْأَلُكُمْ أَجْرًا وَهُمْ مُهْتَدُونَ

21 Follow those who ask you of no wage, and are themselves guided.

21
11:29

٢٢ وَمَا لِيَ لَا أَعْبُدُ الَّذِي فَطَرَنِي وَإِلَيْهِ تُرْجَعُونَ

22 "And why should I not worship Him Who created me, and to Whom you will be returned?

22
43:26

٢٣ أَأَتَّخِذُ مِنْ دُونِهِ آلِهَةً إِنْ يُرِدْنِ الرَّحْمَٰنُ بِضُرٍّ لَا تُغْنِ عَنِّي شَفَاعَتُهُمْ شَيْئًا وَلَا يُنْقِذُونِ

23 Shall I take other gods instead of Him? If the Merciful desires harm for me, their intercession will not avail me at all, nor will they save me.

23
6:41; 10:18, 106;
17:56; 39:38

٢٤ إِنِّي إِذًا لَفِي ضَلَالٍ مُبِينٍ

24 In that case, I would be completely lost.

٢٥ إِنِّي آمَنْتُ بِرَبِّكُمْ فَاسْمَعُونِ

25 I have believed in your Lord, so listen to me."

٢٦ قِيلَ ادْخُلِ الْجَنَّةَ ۖ قَالَ يَا لَيْتَ قَوْمِي يَعْلَمُونَ

26 It was said, "Enter Paradise." He said, "If only my people knew.

٢٧ بِمَا غَفَرَ لِي رَبِّي وَجَعَلَنِي مِنَ الْمُكْرَمِينَ

27 How my Lord has forgiven me, and made me one of the honored."

٢٨ وَمَا أَنْزَلْنَا عَلَىٰ قَوْمِهِ مِنْ بَعْدِهِ مِنْ جُنْدٍ مِنَ السَّمَاءِ وَمَا كُنَّا مُنْزِلِينَ

28 After him, We sent down no hosts from heaven to his people; nor would We ever send any down.

٢٩ إِنْ كَانَتْ إِلَّا صَيْحَةً وَاحِدَةً فَإِذَا هُمْ خَامِدُونَ

29 It was just one Cry, and they were stilled.

29
36:49, 53

٣٠ يَا حَسْرَةً عَلَى الْعِبَادِ مَا يَأْتِيهِمْ مِنْ رَسُولٍ إِلَّا كَانُوا بِهِ يَسْتَهْزِئُونَ

30 Alas for the servants. No messenger ever came to them, but they ridiculed him.

30
15:11

٣١ أَلَمْ يَرَوْا كَمْ أَهْلَكْنَا قَبْلَهُمْ مِنَ الْقُرُونِ أَنَّهُمْ إِلَيْهِمْ لَا يَرْجِعُونَ

31 Have they not considered how many generations We destroyed before them; and that unto them they will not return?

31
6:6; 21:95

٣٢ وَإِنْ كُلٌّ لَمَّا جَمِيعٌ لَدَيْنَا مُحْضَرُونَ

32 All of them, every single one of them, will be arraigned before Us.

٣٣ وَآيَةٌ لَهُمُ الْأَرْضُ الْمَيْتَةُ أَحْيَيْنَاهَا وَأَخْرَجْنَا مِنْهَا حَبًّا فَمِنْهُ يَأْكُلُونَ

33 And there is a sign for them in the dead land: We give it life, and produce from it grains from which they eat.

33
13:4; 25:48

٣٤ وَجَعَلْنَا فِيهَا جَنَّاتٍ مِنْ نَخِيلٍ وَأَعْنَابٍ وَفَجَّرْنَا فِيهَا مِنَ الْعُيُونِ

34 And We place in it gardens of palm-trees and vines, and cause springs to gush out of it.

34
17:91; 22:19

٣٥ لِيَأْكُلُوا مِنْ ثَمَرِهِ وَمَا عَمِلَتْهُ أَيْدِيهِمْ ۖ أَفَلَا يَشْكُرُونَ

35 That they may eat from its fruits, although their hands did not make it. Will they not be appreciative?

٣٦ سُبْحَانَ الَّذِي خَلَقَ الْأَزْوَاجَ كُلَّهَا مِمَّا تُنْبِتُ الْأَرْضُ وَمِنْ أَنْفُسِهِمْ وَمِمَّا لَا يَعْلَمُونَ

36 Glory be to Him who created all the pairs; of what the earth produces, and of their own selves, and of what they do not know.

36
16:8; 42:11; 43:12; 51:49; 78:8

٣٧ وَآيَةٌ لَهُمُ اللَّيْلُ نَسْلَخُ مِنْهُ النَّهَارَ فَإِذَا هُمْ مُظْلِمُونَ

37 Another sign for them is the night: We strip the day out of it—and they are in darkness.

37
3:27

٣٨ وَالشَّمْسُ تَجْرِي لِمُسْتَقَرٍّ لَهَا ۚ ذَٰلِكَ تَقْدِيرُ الْعَزِيزِ الْعَلِيمِ

38 And the sun runs towards its destination. Such is the design of the Almighty, the All-Knowing.

38
36:23

٣٩ وَالْقَمَرَ قَدَّرْنَاهُ مَنَازِلَ حَتَّىٰ عَادَ كَالْعُرْجُونِ الْقَدِيمِ

39 And the moon: We have disposed it in phases, until it returns like the old twig.

٤٠ لَا الشَّمْسُ يَنْبَغِي لَهَا أَنْ تُدْرِكَ الْقَمَرَ وَلَا اللَّيْلُ سَابِقُ النَّهَارِ ۚ وَكُلٌّ فِي فَلَكٍ يَسْبَحُونَ

40 The sun is not to overtake the moon, nor is the night to outpace the day. Each floats in an orbit.

40
21:33

٤١ وَآيَةٌ لَهُمْ أَنَّا حَمَلْنَا ذُرِّيَّتَهُمْ فِي الْفُلْكِ الْمَشْحُونِ

41 Another sign for them is that We carried their offspring in the laden Ark.

41
17:3; 19:58; 26:119

٤٢ وَخَلَقْنَا لَهُمْ مِنْ مِثْلِهِ مَا يَرْكَبُونَ

42 And We created for them the like of it, in which they ride.

42
23:22; 40:80; 43:12

٤٣ وَإِنْ نَشَأْ نُغْرِقْهُمْ فَلَا صَرِيخَ لَهُمْ وَلَا هُمْ يُنْقَذُونَ

43 If We will, We can drown them—with no screaming to be heard from them, nor will they be saved.

43
6:123

٤٤ إِلَّا رَحْمَةً مِنَّا وَمَتَاعًا إِلَىٰ حِينٍ

44 Except by a mercy from Us, and enjoyment for a while.

٤٥ وَإِذَا قِيلَ لَهُمُ اتَّقُوا مَا بَيْنَ أَيْدِيكُمْ وَمَا خَلْفَكُمْ لَعَلَّكُمْ تُرْحَمُونَ

45 18:58

45 Yet when it is said to them, "Beware of what lies before you, and what lies behind you, that you may receive mercy."

٤٦ وَمَا تَأْتِيهِم مِّنْ آيَةٍ مِّنْ آيَاتِ رَبِّهِمْ إِلَّا كَانُوا عَنْهَا مُعْرِضِينَ

46 6:4; 26:5

46 Yet never came to them a sign of their Lord's signs, but they turned away from it.

٤٧ وَإِذَا قِيلَ لَهُمْ أَنفِقُوا مِمَّا رَزَقَكُمُ اللَّهُ قَالَ الَّذِينَ كَفَرُوا لِلَّذِينَ آمَنُوا أَنُطْعِمُ مَن لَّوْ يَشَاءُ اللَّهُ أَطْعَمَهُ إِنْ أَنتُمْ إِلَّا فِي ضَلَالٍ مُّبِينٍ

47 2:254; 14:31; 63:10; 19:81

47 And when it is said to them, "Spend of what God has provided for you," those who disbelieve say to those who believe, "Shall we feed someone whom God could feed, if He so willed? You must be deeply misguided."

٤٨ وَيَقُولُونَ مَتَىٰ هَٰذَا الْوَعْدُ إِن كُنتُمْ صَادِقِينَ

48 10:48

48 And they say, "When will this promise be, if you are truthful?"

٤٩ مَا يَنظُرُونَ إِلَّا صَيْحَةً وَاحِدَةً تَأْخُذُهُمْ وَهُمْ يَخِصِّمُونَ

49 36:29, 53

49 All they can expect is a single blast, which will seize them while they feud.

٥٠ فَلَا يَسْتَطِيعُونَ تَوْصِيَةً وَلَا إِلَىٰ أَهْلِهِمْ يَرْجِعُونَ

50

50 They will not be able to make a will, nor will they return to their families.

٥١ وَنُفِخَ فِي الصُّورِ فَإِذَا هُم مِّنَ الْأَجْدَاثِ إِلَىٰ رَبِّهِمْ يَنسِلُونَ

51 18:99; 21:96; 54:7; 70:43

51 The Trumpet will be blown, then behold, they will rush from the tombs to their Lord.

٥٢ قَالُوا يَا وَيْلَنَا مَن بَعَثَنَا مِن مَّرْقَدِنَا ۗ هَٰذَا مَا وَعَدَ الرَّحْمَٰنُ وَصَدَقَ الْمُرْسَلُونَ

52 33:22

52 They will say, "Woe to us! Who resurrected us from our resting-place?" This is what the Most Gracious had promised, and the messengers have spoken the truth."

٥٣ إِن كَانَتْ إِلَّا صَيْحَةً وَاحِدَةً فَإِذَا هُمْ جَمِيعٌ لَّدَيْنَا مُحْضَرُونَ

53 36:29, 49

53 It will be but a single scream; and behold, they will all be brought before Us.

٥٤ فَالْيَوْمَ لَا تُظْلَمُ نَفْسٌ شَيْئًا وَلَا تُجْزَوْنَ إِلَّا مَا كُنتُمْ تَعْمَلُونَ

54

54 On that Day, no soul will be wronged in the least, and you will be recompensed only for what you used to do.

٥٥ إِنَّ أَصْحَابَ الْجَنَّةِ الْيَوْمَ فِي شُغُلٍ فَاكِهُونَ

55 44:27; 52:18

55 The inhabitants of Paradise, on that Day, will be happily busy.

٥٦ هُمْ وَأَزْوَاجُهُمْ فِي ظِلَالٍ عَلَى الْأَرَائِكِ مُتَّكِئُونَ	**56** 18:31

56 They and their spouses, in shades, reclining on couches.

٥٧ لَهُمْ فِيهَا فَاكِهَةٌ وَلَهُمْ مَا يَدَّعُونَ	**57** 44:55; 56:32

57 They will have therein fruits. They will have whatever they call for.

٥٨ سَلَامٌ قَوْلًا مِنْ رَبٍّ رَحِيمٍ	**58** 10:10

58 Peace—a saying from a Most Merciful Lord.

٥٩ وَامْتَازُوا الْيَوْمَ أَيُّهَا الْمُجْرِمُونَ

59 But step aside today, you criminals.

٦٠ أَلَمْ أَعْهَدْ إِلَيْكُمْ يَا بَنِي آدَمَ أَنْ لَا تَعْبُدُوا الشَّيْطَانَ ۖ إِنَّهُ لَكُمْ عَدُوٌّ مُبِينٌ	**60** 19:44

60 Did I not covenant with you, O Children of Adam, that you shall not serve the devil? That he is your sworn enemy?

٦١ وَأَنِ اعْبُدُونِي ۚ هَٰذَا صِرَاطٌ مُسْتَقِيمٌ

61 And that you shall serve Me? This is a straight path.

٦٢ وَلَقَدْ أَضَلَّ مِنْكُمْ جِبِلًّا كَثِيرًا ۖ أَفَلَمْ تَكُونُوا تَعْقِلُونَ

62 He has misled a great multitude of you. Did you not understand?

٦٣ هَٰذِهِ جَهَنَّمُ الَّتِي كُنْتُمْ تُوعَدُونَ

63 This is Hellfire, which you were promised.

٦٤ اصْلَوْهَا الْيَوْمَ بِمَا كُنْتُمْ تَكْفُرُونَ

64 Roast in it today, because you persistently disbelieved.

٦٥ الْيَوْمَ نَخْتِمُ عَلَىٰ أَفْوَاهِهِمْ وَتُكَلِّمُنَا أَيْدِيهِمْ وَتَشْهَدُ أَرْجُلُهُمْ بِمَا كَانُوا يَكْسِبُونَ	**65** 24:24; 41:20

65 On this Day, We will seal their mouths, and their hands will speak to Us, and their feet will testify to everything they had done.

٦٦ وَلَوْ نَشَاءُ لَطَمَسْنَا عَلَىٰ أَعْيُنِهِمْ فَاسْتَبَقُوا الصِّرَاطَ فَأَنَّىٰ يُبْصِرُونَ

66 If We will, We can blind their eyes as they rush towards the path—but how will they see?

٦٧ وَلَوْ نَشَاءُ لَمَسَخْنَاهُمْ عَلَىٰ مَكَانَتِهِمْ فَمَا اسْتَطَاعُوا مُضِيًّا وَلَا يَرْجِعُونَ

67 And if We will, We can cripple them in their place; so they can neither move forward, nor go back.

٦٨ وَمَنْ نُعَمِّرْهُ نُنَكِّسْهُ فِي الْخَلْقِ ۖ أَفَلَا يَعْقِلُونَ	**68** 16:70; 22:5; 92:4-5

68 Whomever We grant old age, We reverse his development. Do they not understand?

٦٩ وَمَا عَلَّمْنَاهُ الشِّعْرَ وَمَا يَنْبَغِي لَهُ ۚ إِنْ هُوَ إِلَّا ذِكْرٌ وَقُرْآنٌ مُبِينٌ	**69** 21:5; 26:224; 37:36; 52:30; 69:41

69 We did not teach him poetry, nor is it proper for him. It is only a reminder, and a Clear Qur'an.

٧٠ لِيُنذِرَ مَن كَانَ حَيًّا وَيَحِقَّ الْقَوْلُ عَلَى الْكَافِرِينَ

70 That he may warn whoever is alive, and prove the Word against the faithless.

70
36:7

٧١ أَوَلَمْ يَرَوْا أَنَّا خَلَقْنَا لَهُم مِّمَّا عَمِلَتْ أَيْدِينَا أَنْعَامًا فَهُمْ لَهَا مَالِكُونَ

71 Have they not seen that We created for them, of Our Handiwork, livestock that they own?

٧٢ وَذَلَّلْنَاهَا لَهُمْ فَمِنْهَا رَكُوبُهُمْ وَمِنْهَا يَأْكُلُونَ

72 And We subdued them for them. Some they ride, and some they eat.

٧٣ وَلَهُمْ فِيهَا مَنَافِعُ وَمَشَارِبُ ۖ أَفَلَا يَشْكُرُونَ

73 And they have in them other benefits, and drinks. Will they not give thanks?

٧٤ وَاتَّخَذُوا مِن دُونِ اللَّهِ آلِهَةً لَعَلَّهُمْ يُنصَرُونَ

74 Yet they have taken to themselves gods other than God, that perhaps they may be helped.

74
19:81

٧٥ لَا يَسْتَطِيعُونَ نَصْرَهُمْ وَهُمْ لَهُمْ جُندٌ مُّحْضَرُونَ

75 They cannot help them, although they are arrayed as troops for them.

٧٦ فَلَا يَحْزُنكَ قَوْلُهُمْ ۘ إِنَّا نَعْلَمُ مَا يُسِرُّونَ وَمَا يُعْلِنُونَ

76 So let their words not sadden you. We know what they conceal, and what they reveal.

76
10:65

٧٧ أَوَلَمْ يَرَ الْإِنسَانُ أَنَّا خَلَقْنَاهُ مِن نُّطْفَةٍ فَإِذَا هُوَ خَصِيمٌ مُّبِينٌ

77 Does the human being not consider that We created him from a seed? Yet he becomes a fierce adversary.

77
16:4

٧٨ وَضَرَبَ لَنَا مَثَلًا وَنَسِيَ خَلْقَهُ ۖ قَالَ مَن يُحْيِي الْعِظَامَ وَهِيَ رَمِيمٌ

78 And he produces arguments against Us, and he forgets his own creation. He says, "Who will revive the bones when they have decayed?"

78
13:5

٧٩ قُلْ يُحْيِيهَا الَّذِي أَنشَأَهَا أَوَّلَ مَرَّةٍ ۖ وَهُوَ بِكُلِّ خَلْقٍ عَلِيمٌ

79 Say, "He who initiated them in the first instance will revive them. He has knowledge of every creation."

79
17:51; 10:4

٨٠ الَّذِي جَعَلَ لَكُم مِّنَ الشَّجَرِ الْأَخْضَرِ نَارًا فَإِذَا أَنتُم مِّنْهُ تُوقِدُونَ

80 He who produced fuel for you from the green trees, with which you kindle a fire.

٨١ أَوَلَيْسَ ٱلَّذِي خَلَقَ ٱلسَّمَاوَاتِ وَٱلْأَرْضَ بِقَادِرٍ عَلَىٰ أَن يَخْلُقَ مِثْلَهُم ۚ بَلَىٰ وَهُوَ ٱلْخَلَّاقُ ٱلْعَلِيمُ

81 Is not He who created the heavens and the earth able to create the like of them? Certainly. He is the Supreme All-Knowing Creator.

81
17:99

٨٢ إِنَّمَا أَمْرُهُ إِذَا أَرَادَ شَيْئًا أَن يَقُولَ لَهُ كُن فَيَكُونُ

82 His command, when He wills a thing, is to say to it, "Be," and it comes to be.

82
2:117; 16:40

٨٣ فَسُبْحَانَ ٱلَّذِي بِيَدِهِ مَلَكُوتُ كُلِّ شَيْءٍ وَإِلَيْهِ تُرْجَعُونَ

83 So glory be to Him in whose hand is the dominion of everything, and to Him you will be returned.

83
23:88; 43:85; 67:1

Sūrah 37: Al-Ṣaffāt

سُورَةُ ٱلصَّافَّات (The Aligners)

بِسْمِ ٱللَّهِ ٱلرَّحْمَٰنِ ٱلرَّحِيمِ

١ وَٱلصَّافَّاتِ صَفًّا

1 By the aligners aligning.

٢ فَٱلزَّاجِرَاتِ زَجْرًا

2 And the drivers driving.

٣ فَٱلتَّالِيَاتِ ذِكْرًا

3 And the reciters of the Reminder.

٤ إِنَّ إِلَٰهَكُمْ لَوَاحِدٌ

4 Your God is indeed One.

٥ رَبُّ ٱلسَّمَاوَاتِ وَٱلْأَرْضِ وَمَا بَيْنَهُمَا وَرَبُّ ٱلْمَشَارِقِ

5 Lord of the heavens and the earth, and everything between them; and Lord of the Easts.

٦ إِنَّا زَيَّنَّا ٱلسَّمَاءَ ٱلدُّنْيَا بِزِينَةٍ ٱلْكَوَاكِبِ

6 We have adorned the lower heaven with the beauty of the planets.

6–10
15:16–18; 26:210–222;
41:12; 67:5; 72:8–9

٧ وَحِفْظًا مِّن كُلِّ شَيْطَانٍ مَّارِدٍ

7 And guarded it against every defiant devil.

٨ لَا يَسَّمَّعُونَ إِلَى ٱلْمَلَإِ ٱلْأَعْلَىٰ وَيُقْذَفُونَ مِن كُلِّ جَانِبٍ

8 They cannot eavesdrop on the Supernal Elite, for they get bombarded from every side.

ذُحُورًا ۖ وَلَهُمْ عَذَابٌ وَاصِبٌ ٩

9 Repelled—they will have a lingering torment.

إِلَّا مَنْ خَطِفَ الْخَطْفَةَ فَأَتْبَعَهُ شِهَابٌ ثَاقِبٌ ١٠

10 Except for him who snatches a fragment—he gets pursued by a piercing projectile.

10
86:3

فَاسْتَفْتِهِمْ أَهُمْ أَشَدُّ خَلْقًا أَمْ مَنْ خَلَقْنَا ۚ إِنَّا خَلَقْنَاهُم مِّن طِينٍ لَّازِبٍ ١١

11 Inquire of them, "Are they more difficult to create, or the others We created?" We created them from sticky clay.

11
40:57; 79:27

بَلْ عَجِبْتَ وَيَسْخَرُونَ ١٢

12 But you wonder, and they ridicule.

وَإِذَا ذُكِّرُوا لَا يَذْكُرُونَ ١٣

13 And when reminded, they pay no attention.

وَإِذَا رَأَوْا آيَةً يَسْتَسْخِرُونَ ١٤

14 And when they see a sign, they ridicule.

وَقَالُوا إِنْ هَٰذَا إِلَّا سِحْرٌ مُّبِينٌ ١٥

15 And they say, "This is nothing but plain magic.

15
10:76

أَإِذَا مِتْنَا وَكُنَّا تُرَابًا وَعِظَامًا أَإِنَّا لَمَبْعُوثُونَ ١٦

16 When we have died and become dust and bones, shall we be resurrected?

16
23:82; 27:67; 56:47

أَوَآبَاؤُنَا الْأَوَّلُونَ ١٧

17 And our ancestors of old?"

قُلْ نَعَمْ وَأَنتُمْ دَاخِرُونَ ١٨

18 Say, "Yes indeed, and you will be totally subdued."

18
27:87

فَإِنَّمَا هِيَ زَجْرَةٌ وَاحِدَةٌ فَإِذَا هُمْ يَنظُرُونَ ١٩

19 It will be a single nudge, and they will be staring.

وَقَالُوا يَا وَيْلَنَا هَٰذَا يَوْمُ الدِّينِ ٢٠

20 They will say, "Woe to us. This is the Day of Judgment."

هَٰذَا يَوْمُ الْفَصْلِ الَّذِي كُنتُم بِهِ تُكَذِّبُونَ ٢١

21 "This is the Day of Separation which you used to deny.

21
44:40; 77:38

احْشُرُوا الَّذِينَ ظَلَمُوا وَأَزْوَاجَهُمْ وَمَا كَانُوا يَعْبُدُونَ ٢٢

22 Gather those who did wrong, and their mates, and what they used to worship.

22
81:7; 21:98

مِن دُونِ اللَّهِ فَاهْدُوهُمْ إِلَىٰ صِرَاطِ الْجَحِيمِ ٢٣

23 Besides God, and lead them to the way to Hell.

٢٤ وَقِفُوهُمْ ۖ إِنَّهُم مَّسْـُٔولُونَ

24 And stop them. They are to be questioned."

٢٥ مَا لَكُمْ لَا تَنَاصَرُونَ

25 What is the matter with you? Why do you not help one another?

٢٦ بَلْ هُمُ ٱلْيَوْمَ مُسْتَسْلِمُونَ

26 In fact, on that Day, they will be submissive.

٢٧ وَأَقْبَلَ بَعْضُهُمْ عَلَىٰ بَعْضٍ يَتَسَآءَلُونَ

27 They will come to one another, questioning one another.

27
37:50; 52:25

٢٨ قَالُوٓا۟ إِنَّكُمْ كُنتُمْ تَأْتُونَنَا عَنِ ٱلْيَمِينِ

28 They will say, "You used to come at us from the right."

٢٩ قَالُوا۟ بَل لَّمْ تَكُونُوا۟ مُؤْمِنِينَ

29 They will say, "You yourselves were not believers.

٣٠ وَمَا كَانَ لَنَا عَلَيْكُم مِّن سُلْطَٰنٍ ۖ بَلْ كُنتُمْ قَوْمًا طَٰغِينَ

30 We had no authority over you. You yourselves were rebellious people.

٣١ فَحَقَّ عَلَيْنَا قَوْلُ رَبِّنَآ ۖ إِنَّا لَذَآئِقُونَ

31 The Word of our Lord has been realized against us. We are tasting it.

31–32
7:16; 15:39; 28:63; 38:82

٣٢ فَأَغْوَيْنَٰكُمْ إِنَّا كُنَّا غَاوِينَ

32 We seduced you. We were seducers."

٣٣ فَإِنَّهُمْ يَوْمَئِذٍ فِى ٱلْعَذَابِ مُشْتَرِكُونَ

33 On that Day, they will share in the punishment.

33
43:39

٣٤ إِنَّا كَذَٰلِكَ نَفْعَلُ بِٱلْمُجْرِمِينَ

34 Thus We deal with the sinners.

٣٥ إِنَّهُمْ كَانُوٓا۟ إِذَا قِيلَ لَهُمْ لَآ إِلَٰهَ إِلَّا ٱللَّهُ يَسْتَكْبِرُونَ

35 When it was said to them, "There is no god except God," they grew arrogant.

٣٦ وَيَقُولُونَ أَئِنَّا لَتَارِكُوٓا۟ ءَالِهَتِنَا لِشَاعِرٍ مَّجْنُونٍۭ

36 And said, "Are we to abandon our gods for a mad poet?"

36
7:70; 11:53

٣٧ بَلْ جَآءَ بِٱلْحَقِّ وَصَدَّقَ ٱلْمُرْسَلِينَ

37 In fact, he came with the truth, and he confirmed the messengers.

٣٨ إِنَّكُمْ لَذَآئِقُو ٱلْعَذَابِ ٱلْأَلِيمِ

38 Most assuredly, you will taste the painful punishment.

39
10:52

٣٩ وَمَا تُجْزَوْنَ إِلَّا مَا كُنتُمْ تَعْمَلُونَ

39 And you will be repaid only for what you used to do.

٤٠ إِلَّا عِبَادَ اللَّهِ الْمُخْلَصِينَ

40 Except for God's sincere servants.

٤١ أُولَٰئِكَ لَهُمْ رِزْقٌ مَعْلُومٌ

41 For them is a known provision.

٤٢ فَوَاكِهُ وَهُم مُّكْرَمُونَ

42 Fruits; and they will be honored.

٤٣ فِي جَنَّاتِ النَّعِيمِ

43 In the Gardens of Bliss.

٤٤ عَلَىٰ سُرُرٍ مُّتَقَابِلِينَ

44 On furnishings, facing one another.

44
15:47

٤٥ يُطَافُ عَلَيْهِم بِكَأْسٍ مِّن مَّعِينٍ

45 They will be offered a cup of pure drink.

45
43:71; 52:23; 56:18; 76:5

٤٦ بَيْضَاءَ لَذَّةٍ لِّلشَّارِبِينَ

46 White; a delight to those who drink.

٤٧ لَا فِيهَا غَوْلٌ وَلَا هُمْ عَنْهَا يُنزَفُونَ

47 Never polluted, and never intoxicating.

47
56:19

٤٨ وَعِندَهُمْ قَاصِرَاتُ الطَّرْفِ عِينٌ

48 With them will be bashful women with lovely eyes.

48
38:52; 55:56; 56:22

٤٩ كَأَنَّهُنَّ بَيْضٌ مَّكْنُونٌ

49 As if they were closely guarded pearls.

٥٠ فَأَقْبَلَ بَعْضُهُمْ عَلَىٰ بَعْضٍ يَتَسَاءَلُونَ

50 Then they will approach one another, questioning.

50
37:27; 55:56; 56:23

٥١ قَالَ قَائِلٌ مِّنْهُمْ إِنِّي كَانَ لِي قَرِينٌ

51 One of them will say, "I used to have a friend.

51
112:3

٥٢ يَقُولُ أَإِنَّكَ لَمِنَ الْمُصَدِّقِينَ

52 Who used to say, 'Are you of those who believe?

٥٣ أَإِذَا مِتْنَا وَكُنَّا تُرَابًا وَعِظَامًا أَإِنَّا لَمَدِينُونَ

53 That after we die and become dust and bones, we will be called to account?'"

53
13:5; 37:16

٥٤ قَالَ هَلْ أَنتُم مُّطَّلِعُونَ

54 He will say, "Will you have a look?"

٥٥ فَاطَّلَعَ فَرَآهُ فِي سَوَاءِ الْجَحِيمِ

55 He will look, and will see him in the pit of Hell.

٥٦ قَالَ تَاللَّهِ إِنْ كِدْتَ لَتُرْدِينِ

56 He will say, "By God, you almost ruined me.

٥٧ وَلَوْلَا نِعْمَةُ رَبِّي لَكُنْتُ مِنَ الْمُحْضَرِينَ

57 Were it not for the grace of my Lord, I would have been among the arraigned."

٥٨ أَفَمَا نَحْنُ بِمَيِّتِينَ

58 "We will not die.

58
44:56

٥٩ إِلَّا مَوْتَتَنَا الْأُولَىٰ وَمَا نَحْنُ بِمُعَذَّبِينَ

59 Except for our first death, and we will not be punished."

59
44:56

٦٠ إِنَّ هَٰذَا لَهُوَ الْفَوْزُ الْعَظِيمُ

60 This is the supreme triumph.

٦١ لِمِثْلِ هَٰذَا فَلْيَعْمَلِ الْعَامِلُونَ

61 For the like of this let the workers work.

٦٢ أَذَٰلِكَ خَيْرٌ نُزُلًا أَمْ شَجَرَةُ الزَّقُّومِ

62 Is this a better hospitality, or the Tree of Bitterness?

62
17:60; 25:15; 37:64; 56:52

٦٣ إِنَّا جَعَلْنَاهَا فِتْنَةً لِلظَّالِمِينَ

63 We made it an ordeal for the unjust.

٦٤ إِنَّهَا شَجَرَةٌ تَخْرُجُ فِي أَصْلِ الْجَحِيمِ

64 It is a tree that grows from the bottom of Hell.

64–66
37:62; 44:43–44; 56:52

٦٥ طَلْعُهَا كَأَنَّهُ رُءُوسُ الشَّيَاطِينِ

65 Its fruits are like the devils' heads.

٦٦ فَإِنَّهُمْ لَآكِلُونَ مِنْهَا فَمَالِئُونَ مِنْهَا الْبُطُونَ

66 They will eat from it, and fill their bellies with it.

66
56:52–54; 66:67

٦٧ ثُمَّ إِنَّ لَهُمْ عَلَيْهَا لَشَوْبًا مِنْ حَمِيمٍ

67 Then, on top of it, they will have a brew of boiling liquid.

٦٨ ثُمَّ إِنَّ مَرْجِعَهُمْ لَإِلَى الْجَحِيمِ

68 Then their return will be to the Blaze.

٦٩ إِنَّهُمْ أَلْفَوْا آبَاءَهُمْ ضَالِّينَ

69 They had found their parents astray.

69–70
2:170; 5:104; 23:43; 43:22

	٧٠ فَهُمْ عَلَىٰ آثَارِهِمْ يُهْرَعُونَ	
70 And rushed along in their footsteps.		
	٧١ وَلَقَدْ ضَلَّ قَبْلَهُمْ أَكْثَرُ الْأَوَّلِينَ	
71 And most of the ancients before them went astray.		
	٧٢ وَلَقَدْ أَرْسَلْنَا فِيهِمْ مُنْذِرِينَ	
72 Even though We sent messengers to warn them.		
	٧٣ فَانْظُرْ كَيْفَ كَانَ عَاقِبَةُ الْمُنْذَرِينَ	**73** 10:73
73 So observe the end of those who were warned.		
	٧٤ إِلَّا عِبَادَ اللَّهِ الْمُخْلَصِينَ	
74 Except for the sincere servants of God.		
	٧٥ وَلَقَدْ نَادَانَا نُوحٌ فَلَنِعْمَ الْمُجِيبُونَ	**75** 21:76; 37:115
75 And Noah called out to Us, and We are the Best of responders.		
	٧٦ وَنَجَّيْنَاهُ وَأَهْلَهُ مِنَ الْكَرْبِ الْعَظِيمِ	**76** 21:76
76 And We saved him and his family from the great calamity.		
	٧٧ وَجَعَلْنَا ذُرِّيَّتَهُ هُمُ الْبَاقِينَ	
77 And We made his descendants the survivors.		
	٧٨ وَتَرَكْنَا عَلَيْهِ فِي الْآخِرِينَ	
78 And We left mention of him among those who succeeded.		
	٧٩ سَلَامٌ عَلَىٰ نُوحٍ فِي الْعَالَمِينَ	
79 Peace be upon Noah among all people.		
	٨٠ إِنَّا كَذَٰلِكَ نَجْزِي الْمُحْسِنِينَ	
80 We thus reward the righteous.		
	٨١ إِنَّهُ مِنْ عِبَادِنَا الْمُؤْمِنِينَ	
81 He was one of Our believing servants.		
	٨٢ ثُمَّ أَغْرَقْنَا الْآخَرِينَ	**82** 7:64; 21:77; 26:120
82 Then We drowned the others.		
	٨٣ وَإِنَّ مِنْ شِيعَتِهِ لَإِبْرَاهِيمَ	
83 Of his kind was Abraham.		
	٨٤ إِذْ جَاءَ رَبَّهُ بِقَلْبٍ سَلِيمٍ	**84** 26:89
84 When he came to his Lord with a sound heart.		
	٨٥ إِذْ قَالَ لِأَبِيهِ وَقَوْمِهِ مَاذَا تَعْبُدُونَ	**85–87** 26:70
85 He said to his father and his people, "What are you worshiping?"		

٨٦ أَئِفْكًا آلِهَةً دُونَ اللَّهِ تُرِيدُونَ	
86 Is it falsified gods, instead of God, that you want?	
٨٧ فَمَا ظَنُّكُم بِرَبِّ الْعَالَمِينَ	
87 So what is your opinion about the Lord of the Worlds?"	
٨٨ فَنَظَرَ نَظْرَةً فِي النُّجُومِ	
88 Then he took a glance at the stars.	
٨٩ فَقَالَ إِنِّي سَقِيمٌ	
89 And said, "I am sick."	
٩٠ فَتَوَلَّوْا عَنْهُ مُدْبِرِينَ	
90 But they turned their backs on him, and went away.	
٩١ فَرَاغَ إِلَىٰ آلِهَتِهِمْ فَقَالَ أَلَا تَأْكُلُونَ	**91–93**
91 Then he turned to their gods, and said, "will you not eat?	21:58
٩٢ مَا لَكُمْ لَا تَنطِقُونَ	
92 What is it with you, that you do not speak?"	
٩٣ فَرَاغَ عَلَيْهِمْ ضَرْبًا بِالْيَمِينِ	
93 Then he turned on them, striking with his right hand.	
٩٤ فَأَقْبَلُوا إِلَيْهِ يَزِفُّونَ	
94 And they came running towards him.	
٩٥ قَالَ أَتَعْبُدُونَ مَا تَنْحِتُونَ	
95 He said, "Do you worship what you carve?	
٩٦ وَاللَّهُ خَلَقَكُمْ وَمَا تَعْمَلُونَ	
96 When God created you, and what you manufacture?"	
٩٧ قَالُوا ابْنُوا لَهُ بُنْيَانًا فَأَلْقُوهُ فِي الْجَحِيمِ	**97**
97 They said, "Build a pyre for him, and throw him into the furnace."	21:68–70; 29:24
٩٨ فَأَرَادُوا بِهِ كَيْدًا فَجَعَلْنَاهُمُ الْأَسْفَلِينَ	
98 They wished him ill, but We made them the losers.	
٩٩ وَقَالَ إِنِّي ذَاهِبٌ إِلَىٰ رَبِّي سَيَهْدِينِ	
99 He said, "I am going towards my Lord, and He will guide me."	
١٠٠ رَبِّ هَبْ لِي مِنَ الصَّالِحِينَ	**100**
100 "My Lord, give me one of the righteous."	37:112
١٠١ فَبَشَّرْنَاهُ بِغُلَامٍ حَلِيمٍ	**101**
101 So We gave him good news of a clement boy.	11:71; 15:53; 51:28

١٠٢ فَلَمَّا بَلَغَ مَعَهُ السَّعْيَ قَالَ يَا بُنَيَّ إِنِّي أَرَىٰ فِي الْمَنَامِ أَنِّي أَذْبَحُكَ فَانظُرْ مَاذَا تَرَىٰ ۚ قَالَ يَا أَبَتِ افْعَلْ مَا تُؤْمَرُ ۖ سَتَجِدُنِي إِن شَاءَ اللَّهُ مِنَ الصَّابِرِينَ

102 Then, when he was old enough to accompany him, he said, "O My son, I see in a dream that I am sacrificing you; see what you think." He said, "O my Father, do as you are commanded; you will find me, God willing, one of the steadfast."

١٠٣ فَلَمَّا أَسْلَمَا وَتَلَّهُ لِلْجَبِينِ

103 Then, when they had submitted, and he put his forehead down.

١٠٤ وَنَادَيْنَاهُ أَن يَا إِبْرَاهِيمُ

104 We called out to him, "O Abraham!

١٠٥ قَدْ صَدَّقْتَ الرُّؤْيَا ۚ إِنَّا كَذَٰلِكَ نَجْزِي الْمُحْسِنِينَ

105 You have fulfilled the vision." Thus We reward the doers of good.

١٠٦ إِنَّ هَٰذَا لَهُوَ الْبَلَاءُ الْمُبِينُ

106 This was certainly an evident test.

١٠٧ وَفَدَيْنَاهُ بِذِبْحٍ عَظِيمٍ

107 And We redeemed him with a great sacrifice.

١٠٨ وَتَرَكْنَا عَلَيْهِ فِي الْآخِرِينَ

108 And We left with him for later generations.

١٠٩ سَلَامٌ عَلَىٰ إِبْرَاهِيمَ

109 Peace be upon Abraham.

١١٠ كَذَٰلِكَ نَجْزِي الْمُحْسِنِينَ

110 Thus We reward the doers of good.

١١١ إِنَّهُ مِنْ عِبَادِنَا الْمُؤْمِنِينَ

111 He was one of Our believing servants.

١١٢ وَبَشَّرْنَاهُ بِإِسْحَاقَ نَبِيًّا مِنَ الصَّالِحِينَ

112 And We gave him good news of Isaac, a prophet, one of the righteous.

112
19:49; 21:72; 37:101–102

١١٣ وَبَارَكْنَا عَلَيْهِ وَعَلَىٰ إِسْحَاقَ ۚ وَمِن ذُرِّيَّتِهِمَا مُحْسِنٌ وَظَالِمٌ لِّنَفْسِهِ مُبِينٌ

113 And We blessed him, and Isaac. But among their descendants are some who are righteous, and some who are clearly unjust to themselves.

١١٤ وَلَقَدْ مَنَنَّا عَلَىٰ مُوسَىٰ وَهَارُونَ

114 And We blessed Moses and Aaron.

114
20:37

١١٥ وَنَجَّيْنَاهُمَا وَقَوْمَهُمَا مِنَ الْكَرْبِ الْعَظِيمِ

115 And We delivered them and their people from the terrible disaster.

115
2:50; 21:76

١١٦ وَنَصَرْنَاهُمْ فَكَانُوا هُمُ الْغَالِبِينَ	**116**	28:35; 37:171

116 And We supported them, and so they were the victors.

١١٧ وَآتَيْنَاهُمَا الْكِتَابَ الْمُسْتَبِينَ	**117**	6:154; 21:48; 23:49

117 And We gave them the Clarifying Scripture.

١١٨ وَهَدَيْنَاهُمَا الصِّرَاطَ الْمُسْتَقِيمَ

118 And We guided them upon the straight path.

١١٩ وَتَرَكْنَا عَلَيْهِمَا فِي الْآخِرِينَ

119 And We left with them for later generations.

١٢٠ سَلَامٌ عَلَىٰ مُوسَىٰ وَهَارُونَ

120 Peace be upon Moses and Aaron.

١٢١ إِنَّا كَذَٰلِكَ نَجْزِي الْمُحْسِنِينَ

121 Thus We reward the righteous.

١٢٢ إِنَّهُمَا مِنْ عِبَادِنَا الْمُؤْمِنِينَ

122 They were of Our believing servants.

١٢٣ وَإِنَّ إِلْيَاسَ لَمِنَ الْمُرْسَلِينَ

123 Also Elijah was one of the messengers.

١٢٤ إِذْ قَالَ لِقَوْمِهِ أَلَا تَتَّقُونَ

124 He said to his people, "Do you not fear?

١٢٥ أَتَدْعُونَ بَعْلًا وَتَذَرُونَ أَحْسَنَ الْخَالِقِينَ

125 Do you call on Baal, and forsake the Best of creators?

١٢٦ اللَّهَ رَبَّكُمْ وَرَبَّ آبَائِكُمُ الْأَوَّلِينَ

126 God is your Lord, and the Lord of your ancestors."

١٢٧ فَكَذَّبُوهُ فَإِنَّهُمْ لَمُحْضَرُونَ

127 But they called him a liar, and thus they will be brought forward.

١٢٨ إِلَّا عِبَادَ اللَّهِ الْمُخْلَصِينَ

128 Except for God's sincere servants.

١٢٩ وَتَرَكْنَا عَلَيْهِ فِي الْآخِرِينَ

129 And We left with him for later generations.

١٣٠ سَلَامٌ عَلَىٰ إِلْ يَاسِينَ

130 Peace be upon the House of Elijah.

١٣١ إِنَّا كَذَٰلِكَ نَجْزِي الْمُحْسِنِينَ

131 Thus We reward the virtuous.

١٣٢ إِنَّهُ مِنْ عِبَادِنَا الْمُؤْمِنِينَ

132 He was one of Our believing servants.

١٣٣ وَإِنَّ لُوطًا لَمِنَ الْمُرْسَلِينَ

133 And Lot was one of the messengers.

١٣٤ إِذْ نَجَّيْنَاهُ وَأَهْلَهُ أَجْمَعِينَ

134 We saved him and his family, all of them.

134
26:170

١٣٥ إِلَّا عَجُوزًا فِي الْغَابِرِينَ

135 Except for an old woman who lagged behind.

١٣٦ ثُمَّ دَمَّرْنَا الْآخَرِينَ

136 Then We annihilated the others.

136
26:172

١٣٧ وَإِنَّكُمْ لَتَمُرُّونَ عَلَيْهِمْ مُصْبِحِينَ

137 You pass by them in the morning.

١٣٨ وَبِاللَّيْلِ ۗ أَفَلَا تَعْقِلُونَ

138 And at night. Do you not understand?

١٣٩ وَإِنَّ يُونُسَ لَمِنَ الْمُرْسَلِينَ

139 And Jonah was one of the messengers.

١٤٠ إِذْ أَبَقَ إِلَى الْفُلْكِ الْمَشْحُونِ

140 When he fled to the laden boat.

١٤١ فَسَاهَمَ فَكَانَ مِنَ الْمُدْحَضِينَ

141 He gambled and lost.

١٤٢ فَالْتَقَمَهُ الْحُوتُ وَهُوَ مُلِيمٌ

142 Then the fish swallowed him, and he was to blame.

١٤٣ فَلَوْلَا أَنَّهُ كَانَ مِنَ الْمُسَبِّحِينَ

143 Had he not been one of those who praised.

143–144
21:87–88; 68:48

١٤٤ لَلَبِثَ فِي بَطْنِهِ إِلَىٰ يَوْمِ يُبْعَثُونَ

144 He would have stayed in its belly until the Day they are raised.

١٤٥ فَنَبَذْنَاهُ بِالْعَرَاءِ وَهُوَ سَقِيمٌ

145 Then We threw him into the wilderness, and he was sick.

١٤٦ وَأَنْبَتْنَا عَلَيْهِ شَجَرَةً مِنْ يَقْطِينٍ

146 And We made a gourd tree grow over him.

١٤٧ وَأَرْسَلْنَاهُ إِلَىٰ مِائَةِ أَلْفٍ أَوْ يَزِيدُونَ

147 Then We sent him to a hundred thousand, or more.

١٤٨ فَآمَنُوا فَمَتَّعْنَاهُمْ إِلَىٰ حِينٍ

148 And they believed, so We gave them enjoyment for a while.

148
10:98

١٤٩ فَاسْتَفْتِهِمْ أَلِرَبِّكَ الْبَنَاتُ وَلَهُمُ الْبَنُونَ

149 Ask them, "Are the daughters for your Lord, while for them the sons?"

149–154
16:57–59; 17:40; 43:16; 52:39; 39:4; 53:21

١٥٠ أَمْ خَلَقْنَا الْمَلَائِكَةَ إِنَاثًا وَهُمْ شَاهِدُونَ

150 Or did We create the angels females, as they witnessed?"

١٥١ أَلَا إِنَّهُمْ مِنْ إِفْكِهِمْ لَيَقُولُونَ

151 No indeed! It is one of their lies when they say.

١٥٢ وَلَدَ اللَّهُ وَإِنَّهُمْ لَكَاذِبُونَ

152 "God has begotten." They are indeed lying.

١٥٣ أَصْطَفَى الْبَنَاتِ عَلَى الْبَنِينَ

153 So He preferred girls over boys?

١٥٤ مَا لَكُمْ كَيْفَ تَحْكُمُونَ

154 What is the matter with you? How do you judge?

١٥٥ أَفَلَا تَذَكَّرُونَ

155 Will you not reflect?

١٥٦ أَمْ لَكُمْ سُلْطَانٌ مُبِينٌ

156 Or do you have some clear proof?

١٥٧ فَأْتُوا بِكِتَابِكُمْ إِنْ كُنْتُمْ صَادِقِينَ

157 Then bring your book, if you are telling the truth.

157
6:100

١٥٨ وَجَعَلُوا بَيْنَهُ وَبَيْنَ الْجِنَّةِ نَسَبًا ۚ وَلَقَدْ عَلِمَتِ الْجِنَّةُ إِنَّهُمْ لَمُحْضَرُونَ

158 And they invented a relationship between Him and the jinn. But the jinn know that they will be arraigned.

١٥٩ سُبْحَانَ اللَّهِ عَمَّا يَصِفُونَ

159 God be glorified, far above what they allege.

١٦٠ إِلَّا عِبَادَ اللَّهِ الْمُخْلَصِينَ

160 Except for God's sincere servants.

١٦١ فَإِنَّكُمْ وَمَا تَعْبُدُونَ

161 Surely, you and what you serve.

١٦٢ مَا أَنْتُمْ عَلَيْهِ بِفَاتِنِينَ

162 Cannot seduce away from Him.

١٦٣ إِلَّا مَنْ هُوَ صَالِ الْجَحِيمِ

163 Except for he who will be roasting in Hell.

164 "There is not one of us but has an assigned position.

١٦٤ وَمَا مِنَّا إِلَّا لَهُ مَقَامٌ مَعْلُومٌ

165 And we are the arrangers.

١٦٥ وَإِنَّا لَنَحْنُ الصَّافُّونَ

166 And we are the glorifiers."

١٦٦ وَإِنَّا لَنَحْنُ الْمُسَبِّحُونَ

167 Even though they used to say.

١٦٧ وَإِنْ كَانُوا لَيَقُولُونَ

168 "Had we received advice from the ancients.

١٦٨ لَوْ أَنَّ عِنْدَنَا ذِكْرًا مِنَ الْأَوَّلِينَ

169 We would have been God's faithful servants."

١٦٩ لَكُنَّا عِبَادَ اللَّهِ الْمُخْلَصِينَ

170 But they rejected it, so they will find out.

١٧٠ فَكَفَرُوا بِهِ ۖ فَسَوْفَ يَعْلَمُونَ

171 Our Word has already gone out to our servant messengers.

١٧١ وَلَقَدْ سَبَقَتْ كَلِمَتُنَا لِعِبَادِنَا الْمُرْسَلِينَ

171–173
5:56; 30:47; 37:116;
40:51; 58:21
pp 37:178

172 It is they who will be supported.

١٧٢ إِنَّهُمْ لَهُمُ الْمَنْصُورُونَ

173 And Our troops will be the victors.

١٧٣ وَإِنَّ جُنْدَنَا لَهُمُ الْغَالِبُونَ

173
pp 37:178

174 So disregard them for a while.

١٧٤ فَتَوَلَّ عَنْهُمْ حَتَّىٰ حِينٍ

175 And watch them—they will soon see.

١٧٥ وَأَبْصِرْهُمْ فَسَوْفَ يُبْصِرُونَ

176 Are they seeking to hasten Our punishment?

١٧٦ أَفَبِعَذَابِنَا يَسْتَعْجِلُونَ

176
10:50; 13:6; 26:204

177 When it descends into their yard, miserable will be the morning of those forewarned.

١٧٧ فَإِذَا نَزَلَ بِسَاحَتِهِمْ فَسَاءَ صَبَاحُ الْمُنْذَرِينَ

178 So avoid them for a while.

١٧٨ وَتَوَلَّ عَنْهُمْ حَتَّىٰ حِينٍ

178
pp 37:174

١٧٩ وَأَبْصِرْ فَسَوْفَ يُبْصِرُونَ

179 And watch—they will soon see.

١٨٠ سُبْحَانَ رَبِّكَ رَبِّ الْعِزَّةِ عَمَّا يَصِفُونَ

180 Exalted be your Lord, the Lord of Glory, beyond their allegations.

١٨١ وَسَلَامٌ عَلَى الْمُرْسَلِينَ

181 And peace be upon the messengers.

181
pp 27:59

١٨٢ وَالْحَمْدُ لِلَّهِ رَبِّ الْعَالَمِينَ

182 And praise be to God, the Lord of the Worlds.

182
pp 1:2

Sūrah 38: Ṣād

سُورَةُ ص (Ṣād)

بِسْمِ اللَّهِ الرَّحْمَٰنِ الرَّحِيمِ

١ ص ۚ وَالْقُرْآنِ ذِي الذِّكْرِ

1 Ṣād. By the renowned Qur'an.

٢ بَلِ الَّذِينَ كَفَرُوا فِي عِزَّةٍ وَشِقَاقٍ

2 Those who disbelieve are steeped in arrogance and defiance.

٣ كَمْ أَهْلَكْنَا مِن قَبْلِهِم مِّن قَرْنٍ فَنَادَوا وَّلَاتَ حِينَ مَنَاصٍ

3 How many generations have We destroyed before them? They cried out when it was too late to escape.

3
6:6; 14:9; 17:17; 22:45

٤ وَعَجِبُوا أَن جَاءَهُم مُّنذِرٌ مِّنْهُمْ ۖ وَقَالَ الْكَافِرُونَ هَٰذَا سَاحِرٌ كَذَّابٌ

4 And they marveled that a warner has come to them from among them. The disbelievers said, "This is a lying magician."

4
7:63; 10:2; 50:2

٥ أَجَعَلَ الْآلِهَةَ إِلَٰهًا وَاحِدًا ۖ إِنَّ هَٰذَا لَشَيْءٌ عُجَابٌ

5 "Did he turn all the gods into one God? This is something strange."

5–6
25:42

٦ وَانطَلَقَ الْمَلَأُ مِنْهُمْ أَنِ امْشُوا وَاصْبِرُوا عَلَىٰ آلِهَتِكُمْ ۖ إِنَّ هَٰذَا لَشَيْءٌ يُرَادُ

6 The notables among them announced: "Go on, and hold fast to your gods. This is something planned.

6
25:42

٧ مَا سَمِعْنَا بِهَٰذَا فِي الْمِلَّةِ الْآخِرَةِ إِنْ هَٰذَا إِلَّا اخْتِلَاقٌ

7 We never heard of this in the former faith. This is nothing but a fabrication.

7
23:24; 28:36

٨ أَأُنزِلَ عَلَيْهِ الذِّكْرُ مِن بَيْنِنَا ۚ بَلْ هُمْ فِي شَكٍّ مِّن ذِكْرِي ۖ بَل لَّمَّا يَذُوقُوا عَذَابِ

8 Was the message sent down to him, out of all of us?" In fact, they are doubtful of My warning. In fact, they have not yet tasted My punishment.

٩ أَمْ عِندَهُمْ خَزَائِنُ رَحْمَةِ رَبِّكَ الْعَزِيزِ الْوَهَّابِ

9 Or do they possess the treasuries of the mercy of your Lord—the Majestic, the Giver?

9
6:50; 17:100; 43:32; 52:37

١٠ أَمْ لَهُم مُّلْكُ السَّمَاوَاتِ وَالْأَرْضِ وَمَا بَيْنَهُمَا ۖ فَلْيَرْتَقُوا فِي الْأَسْبَابِ

10 Or do they possess the sovereignty of the heavens and the earth and what is between them? Then let them ascend the ropes.

١١ جُندٌ مَّا هُنَالِكَ مَهْزُومٌ مِّنَ الْأَحْزَابِ

11 An army of confederates will be defeated there.

١٢ كَذَّبَتْ قَبْلَهُمْ قَوْمُ نُوحٍ وَعَادٌ وَفِرْعَوْنُ ذُو الْأَوْتَادِ

12 Before them the people of Noah denied the truth; as did 'Ād, and Pharaoh of the Stakes.

12–14
22:42–44; 26:105; 40:5; 50:12–14; 54:9

١٣ وَثَمُودُ وَقَوْمُ لُوطٍ وَأَصْحَابُ الْأَيْكَةِ ۚ أُولَٰئِكَ الْأَحْزَابُ

13 And Thamūd, and the people of Lot, and the dwellers of the Woods—these were the confederates.

١٤ إِن كُلٌّ إِلَّا كَذَّبَ الرُّسُلَ فَحَقَّ عِقَابِ

14 None of them but denied the messengers, so My retribution was deserved.

١٥ وَمَا يَنظُرُ هَٰؤُلَاءِ إِلَّا صَيْحَةً وَاحِدَةً مَّا لَهَا مِن فَوَاقٍ

15 These can expect only a single scream, from which there is no recovery.

15
36:29, 49, 53

١٦ وَقَالُوا رَبَّنَا عَجِّل لَّنَا قِطَّنَا قَبْلَ يَوْمِ الْحِسَابِ

16 And they say, "Our Lord, hasten Your writ upon us, before the Day of Account."

16
6:57; 10:15; 13:6; 22:47

١٧ اصْبِرْ عَلَىٰ مَا يَقُولُونَ وَاذْكُرْ عَبْدَنَا دَاوُودَ ذَا الْأَيْدِ ۖ إِنَّهُ أَوَّابٌ

17 Be patient in the face of what they say, and mention Our servant David, the resourceful. He was obedient.

١٨ إِنَّا سَخَّرْنَا الْجِبَالَ مَعَهُ يُسَبِّحْنَ بِالْعَشِيِّ وَالْإِشْرَاقِ

18 We committed the mountains to glorify with him, in the evening and at daybreak.

18
21:79; 34:10

١٩ وَالطَّيْرَ مَحْشُورَةً ۖ كُلٌّ لَّهُ أَوَّابٌ

19 And the birds, gathered together. All obedient to him.

٢٠ وَشَدَدْنَا مُلْكَهُ وَآتَيْنَاهُ الْحِكْمَةَ وَفَصْلَ الْخِطَابِ

20 And We strengthened his kingdom, and gave him wisdom and decisive speech.

20
2:251

٢١ وَهَلْ أَتَاكَ نَبَأُ الْخَصْمِ إِذْ تَسَوَّرُوا الْمِحْرَابَ

21 Has the story of the two disputants reached you? When they scaled the sanctuary?

٢٢ إِذْ دَخَلُوا عَلَىٰ دَاوُودَ فَفَزِعَ مِنْهُمْ ۖ قَالُوا لَا تَخَفْ ۖ خَصْمَانِ بَغَىٰ بَعْضُنَا عَلَىٰ بَعْضٍ فَاحْكُم بَيْنَنَا بِالْحَقِّ وَلَا تُشْطِطْ وَاهْدِنَا إِلَىٰ سَوَاءِ الصِّرَاطِ

22 When they entered upon David, and he was startled by them. They said, "Do not fear. Two disputants; one of us has wronged the other; so judge between us fairly, and do not be biased, and guide us to the straight way."

٢٣ إِنَّ هَٰذَا أَخِي لَهُ تِسْعٌ وَتِسْعُونَ نَعْجَةً وَلِيَ نَعْجَةٌ وَاحِدَةٌ فَقَالَ أَكْفِلْنِيهَا وَعَزَّنِي فِي الْخِطَابِ

23 "This brother of mine has ninety-nine ewes, and I have one ewe, and he said, 'Entrust it to me,' and he pressured me with words."

٢٤ قَالَ لَقَدْ ظَلَمَكَ بِسُؤَالِ نَعْجَتِكَ إِلَىٰ نِعَاجِهِ ۖ وَإِنَّ كَثِيرًا مِّنَ الْخُلَطَاءِ لَيَبْغِي بَعْضُهُمْ عَلَىٰ بَعْضٍ إِلَّا الَّذِينَ آمَنُوا وَعَمِلُوا الصَّالِحَاتِ وَقَلِيلٌ مَّا هُمْ ۗ وَظَنَّ دَاوُودُ أَنَّمَا فَتَنَّاهُ فَاسْتَغْفَرَ رَبَّهُ وَخَرَّ رَاكِعًا وَأَنَابَ ۩

24 He said, "He has done you wrong by asking your ewe in addition to his ewes. Many partners take advantage of one another, except those who believe and do good deeds, but these are so few." David realized that We were testing him, so he sought forgiveness from his Lord, and fell down to his knees, and repented.

٢٥ فَغَفَرْنَا لَهُ ذَٰلِكَ ۖ وَإِنَّ لَهُ عِندَنَا لَزُلْفَىٰ وَحُسْنَ مَآبٍ

25 So We forgave him that. And for him is nearness to Us, and a good place of return.

٢٦ يَا دَاوُودُ إِنَّا جَعَلْنَاكَ خَلِيفَةً فِي الْأَرْضِ فَاحْكُم بَيْنَ النَّاسِ بِالْحَقِّ وَلَا تَتَّبِعِ الْهَوَىٰ فَيُضِلَّكَ عَن سَبِيلِ اللَّهِ ۚ إِنَّ الَّذِينَ يَضِلُّونَ عَن سَبِيلِ اللَّهِ لَهُمْ عَذَابٌ شَدِيدٌ بِمَا نَسُوا يَوْمَ الْحِسَابِ

26 "O David, We made you a ruler in the land, so judge between the people with justice, and do not follow desire, lest it diverts you from God's path. Those who stray from God's path will have a painful punishment, for having ignored the Day of Account."

٢٧ وَمَا خَلَقْنَا السَّمَاءَ وَالْأَرْضَ وَمَا بَيْنَهُمَا بَاطِلًا ۚ ذَٰلِكَ ظَنُّ الَّذِينَ كَفَرُوا ۚ فَوَيْلٌ لِّلَّذِينَ كَفَرُوا مِنَ النَّارِ

27 3;191; 15:85; 23:115; 44:38

27 We did not create the heaven and the earth and everything between them in vain. That is the assumption of those who disbelieve—so woe to those who disbelieve because of the Fire.

٢٨ أَمْ نَجْعَلُ الَّذِينَ آمَنُوا وَعَمِلُوا الصَّالِحَاتِ كَالْمُفْسِدِينَ فِي الْأَرْضِ أَمْ نَجْعَلُ الْمُتَّقِينَ كَالْفُجَّارِ

28 45:21; 68:35

28 Or are We to treat those who believe and do righteous deeds like those who make trouble on earth? Or are We to treat the pious like the shameless?

٢٩ كِتَابٌ أَنزَلْنَاهُ إِلَيْكَ مُبَارَكٌ لِّيَدَّبَّرُوا آيَاتِهِ وَلِيَتَذَكَّرَ أُولُو الْأَلْبَابِ		29 3:7; 6:92; 6:92, 155; 21:50; 44:3; 97:1

29 A blessed Book that We sent down to you, that they may ponder its Verses, and for those with intelligence to take heed.

٣٠ وَوَهَبْنَا لِدَاوُودَ سُلَيْمَانَ ۚ نِعْمَ الْعَبْدُ ۖ إِنَّهُ أَوَّابٌ		30 27:15–16

30 And We granted David, Solomon, an excellent servant. He was penitent.

٣١ إِذْ عُرِضَ عَلَيْهِ بِالْعَشِيِّ الصَّافِنَاتُ الْجِيَادُ

31 When the beautiful horses were paraded before him in the evening.

٣٢ فَقَالَ إِنِّي أَحْبَبْتُ حُبَّ الْخَيْرِ عَن ذِكْرِ رَبِّي حَتَّىٰ تَوَارَتْ بِالْحِجَابِ

32 He said, "I have preferred the love of niceties to the remembrance of my Lord—until it disappeared behind the veil.

٣٣ رُدُّوهَا عَلَيَّ ۖ فَطَفِقَ مَسْحًا بِالسُّوقِ وَالْأَعْنَاقِ

33 Bring them back to me." And he began caressing their legs and necks.

٣٤ وَلَقَدْ فَتَنَّا سُلَيْمَانَ وَأَلْقَيْنَا عَلَىٰ كُرْسِيِّهِ جَسَدًا ثُمَّ أَنَابَ

34 We tested Solomon, and placed a body on his throne; then he repented.

٣٥ قَالَ رَبِّ اغْفِرْ لِي وَهَبْ لِي مُلْكًا لَّا يَنبَغِي لِأَحَدٍ مِّن بَعْدِي ۖ إِنَّكَ أَنتَ الْوَهَّابُ

35 He said, "My Lord, forgive me, and grant me a kingdom never to be attained by anyone after me. You are the Giver."

٣٦ فَسَخَّرْنَا لَهُ الرِّيحَ تَجْرِي بِأَمْرِهِ رُخَاءً حَيْثُ أَصَابَ		36–37 21:81–82; 34:12

36 So We placed the wind at his service, blowing gently by his command, wherever he directed.

٣٧ وَالشَّيَاطِينَ كُلَّ بَنَّاءٍ وَغَوَّاصٍ		37 21:82

37 And the demons—every builder and diver.

٣٨ وَآخَرِينَ مُقَرَّنِينَ فِي الْأَصْفَادِ

38 And others fettered in chains.

٣٩ هَٰذَا عَطَاؤُنَا فَامْنُنْ أَوْ أَمْسِكْ بِغَيْرِ حِسَابٍ

39 "This is Our gift; so give generously, or withhold; without account."

٤٠ وَإِنَّ لَهُ عِندَنَا لَزُلْفَىٰ وَحُسْنَ مَآبٍ

40 For him is nearness to Us, and a beautiful resort.

٤١ وَاذْكُرْ عَبْدَنَا أَيُّوبَ إِذْ نَادَىٰ رَبَّهُ أَنِّي مَسَّنِيَ الشَّيْطَانُ بِنُصْبٍ وَعَذَابٍ		41 21:83

41 And mention Our servant Job, when he called out to his Lord, "Satan has afflicted me with hardship and pain."

٤٢ ارْكُضْ بِرِجْلِكَ ۖ هَـٰذَا مُغْتَسَلٌ بَارِدٌ وَشَرَابٌ

42 "Stamp with your foot—here is cool water to wash with, and to drink."

٤٣ وَوَهَبْنَا لَهُ أَهْلَهُ وَمِثْلَهُم مَّعَهُمْ رَحْمَةً مِّنَّا وَذِكْرَىٰ لِأُولِي الْأَلْبَابِ

43 And We restored his family for him, and their like with them; as a mercy from Us, and a lesson for those who possess insight.

43
21:84

٤٤ وَخُذْ بِيَدِكَ ضِغْثًا فَاضْرِب بِّهِ وَلَا تَحْنَثْ ۗ إِنَّا وَجَدْنَاهُ صَابِرًا ۚ نِّعْمَ الْعَبْدُ ۖ إِنَّهُ أَوَّابٌ

44 "Take with your hand a bundle, and strike with it, and do not break your oath." We found him patient. What an excellent servant! He was obedient.

٤٥ وَاذْكُرْ عِبَادَنَا إِبْرَاهِيمَ وَإِسْحَاقَ وَيَعْقُوبَ أُولِي الْأَيْدِي وَالْأَبْصَارِ

45 And mention Our servants Abraham, Isaac, and Jacob—endowed with ability and vision.

45
6:84

٤٦ إِنَّا أَخْلَصْنَاهُم بِخَالِصَةٍ ذِكْرَى الدَّارِ

46 We distinguished them with a distinct quality: the remembrance of the Home.

٤٧ وَإِنَّهُمْ عِندَنَا لَمِنَ الْمُصْطَفَيْنَ الْأَخْيَارِ

47 To Us they are among the chosen, the outstanding.

٤٨ وَاذْكُرْ إِسْمَاعِيلَ وَالْيَسَعَ وَذَا الْكِفْلِ ۖ وَكُلٌّ مِّنَ الْأَخْيَارِ

48 And mention Ishmael, Elisha, and Ezekiel; all are among the outstanding.

48
6:86; 21:85

٤٩ هَـٰذَا ذِكْرٌ ۚ وَإِنَّ لِلْمُتَّقِينَ لَحُسْنَ مَآبٍ

49 This is a reminder. The devout will have a good place of return.

٥٠ جَنَّاتِ عَدْنٍ مُّفَتَّحَةً لَّهُمُ الْأَبْوَابُ

50 The Gardens of Eden, with their doors wide-open for them.

٥١ مُتَّكِئِينَ فِيهَا يَدْعُونَ فِيهَا بِفَاكِهَةٍ كَثِيرَةٍ وَشَرَابٍ

51 Relaxing therein, and calling for abundant fruit and beverage.

51
36:57; 44:55

٥٢ وَعِندَهُمْ قَاصِرَاتُ الطَّرْفِ أَتْرَابٌ

52 With them will be attendants with modest gaze, of same age.

52
37:48; 55:56

٥٣ هَـٰذَا مَا تُوعَدُونَ لِيَوْمِ الْحِسَابِ

53 This is what you are promised for the Day of Account.

٥٤ إِنَّ هَـٰذَا لَرِزْقُنَا مَا لَهُ مِن نَّفَادٍ

54 Such is Our bounty, inexhaustible.

54
11:108; 16:96

٥٥ هَٰذَا ۚ وَإِنَّ لِلطَّاغِينَ لَشَرَّ مَآبٍ

55 All This. But the transgressors will have a miserable return.

٥٦ جَهَنَّمَ يَصْلَوْنَهَا فَبِئْسَ الْمِهَادُ

56 Hell; in which they will roast; what a miserable abode!

56
14:29; 58:8

٥٧ هَٰذَا فَلْيَذُوقُوهُ حَمِيمٌ وَغَسَّاقٌ

57 All this. Let them taste it—boiling and bitter cold.

57
6:70; 78:24

٥٨ وَآخَرُ مِنْ شَكْلِهِ أَزْوَاجٌ

58 And similar torments of diverse kinds.

٥٩ هَٰذَا فَوْجٌ مُقْتَحِمٌ مَعَكُمْ ۖ لَا مَرْحَبًا بِهِمْ ۚ إِنَّهُمْ صَالُو النَّارِ

59 "This is a crowd rushing headlong with you." There is no welcome for them. They will be scorched by the Fire.

59
4:115; 4:29

٦٠ قَالُوا بَلْ أَنْتُمْ لَا مَرْحَبًا بِكُمْ ۖ أَنْتُمْ قَدَّمْتُمُوهُ لَنَا ۖ فَبِئْسَ الْقَرَارُ

60 They will say, "But it is you! There is no welcome for you! It is you who brought it upon us! What a miserable end!"

٦١ قَالُوا رَبَّنَا مَنْ قَدَّمَ لَنَا هَٰذَا فَزِدْهُ عَذَابًا ضِعْفًا فِي النَّارِ

61 They will say, "Our Lord, whoever brought this upon us, give him double torment in the Fire."

61
7:38; 33:68

٦٢ وَقَالُوا مَا لَنَا لَا نَرَىٰ رِجَالًا كُنَّا نَعُدُّهُمْ مِنَ الْأَشْرَارِ

62 And they will say, "What is it with us that we do not see men we used to count among the wicked?

٦٣ أَتَّخَذْنَاهُمْ سِخْرِيًّا أَمْ زَاغَتْ عَنْهُمُ الْأَبْصَارُ

63 Did we take them for mockery, or have our eyes swerved from them?

٦٤ إِنَّ ذَٰلِكَ لَحَقٌّ تَخَاصُمُ أَهْلِ النَّارِ

64 This is certainly true—the feuding of the people of the Fire.

٦٥ قُلْ إِنَّمَا أَنَا مُنْذِرٌ ۖ وَمَا مِنْ إِلَٰهٍ إِلَّا اللَّهُ الْوَاحِدُ الْقَهَّارُ

65 Say, "I am only a warner, and there is no god except God—the One, the Conqueror.

٦٦ رَبُّ السَّمَاوَاتِ وَالْأَرْضِ وَمَا بَيْنَهُمَا الْعَزِيزُ الْغَفَّارُ

66 The Lord of the heavens and the earth, and everything between them; the Mighty, the Forgiver."

٦٧ قُلْ هُوَ نَبَأٌ عَظِيمٌ

67 Say, "It is a message of great importance.

٦٨ أَنْتُمْ عَنْهُ مُعْرِضُونَ

68 From which you are turning away.

	٦٩ مَا كَانَ لِيَ مِنْ عِلْمٍ بِالْمَلَإِ الْأَعْلَىٰ إِذْ يَخْتَصِمُونَ	**69** 3:44; 11:49; 12:89

69 I have no knowledge of the Highest Assembly as they dispute.

| | ٧٠ إِنْ يُوحَىٰ إِلَيَّ إِلَّا أَنَّمَا أَنَا نَذِيرٌ مُبِينٌ | |

70 It is only revealed to me that I am a clear warner."

| | ٧١ إِذْ قَالَ رَبُّكَ لِلْمَلَائِكَةِ إِنِّي خَالِقٌ بَشَرًا مِنْ طِينٍ | **71**
15:28 |

71 Your Lord said to the angels, "I am creating a human being from clay.

| | ٧٢ فَإِذَا سَوَّيْتُهُ وَنَفَخْتُ فِيهِ مِنْ رُوحِي فَقَعُوا لَهُ سَاجِدِينَ | |

72 When I have formed him, and breathed into him of My spirit, fall prostrate before him.

| | ٧٣ فَسَجَدَ الْمَلَائِكَةُ كُلُّهُمْ أَجْمَعُونَ | **73**
15:30 |

73 So the angels fell prostrate, all of them.

| | ٧٤ إِلَّا إِبْلِيسَ اسْتَكْبَرَ وَكَانَ مِنَ الْكَافِرِينَ | |

74 Except for Satan. He was too proud, and one of the faithless.

| | ٧٥ قَالَ يَا إِبْلِيسُ مَا مَنَعَكَ أَنْ تَسْجُدَ لِمَا خَلَقْتُ بِيَدَيَّ ۖ أَسْتَكْبَرْتَ أَمْ كُنْتَ مِنَ الْعَالِينَ | **75**
2:34; 7:12; 15:30; 17:61 |

75 He said, "O Satan, what prevented you from prostrating before what I created with My Own hands? Are you too proud, or were you one of the exalted?"

| | ٧٦ قَالَ أَنَا خَيْرٌ مِنْهُ ۖ خَلَقْتَنِي مِنْ نَارٍ وَخَلَقْتَهُ مِنْ طِينٍ | **76**
2:34 |

76 He said, "I am better than he; You created me from fire, and You created him from clay."

| | ٧٧ قَالَ فَاخْرُجْ مِنْهَا فَإِنَّكَ رَجِيمٌ | **77**
7:13; 15:34 |

77 He said, "Then get out of here! You are an outcast!

| | ٧٨ وَإِنَّ عَلَيْكَ لَعْنَتِي إِلَىٰ يَوْمِ الدِّينِ | **78**
15:35 |

78 And My curse will be upon you until the Day of Judgment."

| | ٧٩ قَالَ رَبِّ فَأَنْظِرْنِي إِلَىٰ يَوْمِ يُبْعَثُونَ | **79–81**
7:14; 15:36–38 |

79 He said, "Lord, defer me until the Day they are resurrected."

| | ٨٠ قَالَ فَإِنَّكَ مِنَ الْمُنْظَرِينَ | |

80 He said, "You are one of those deferred.

| | ٨١ إِلَىٰ يَوْمِ الْوَقْتِ الْمَعْلُومِ | |

81 Until the Day of the Time Appointed."

| | ٨٢ قَالَ فَبِعِزَّتِكَ لَأُغْوِيَنَّهُمْ أَجْمَعِينَ | **82**
7:16; 15:39; 17:64; 38:31–32 |

82 He said, "By Your majesty, I will seduce them all.

83 إِلَّا عِبَادَكَ مِنْهُمُ الْمُخْلَصِينَ

83 Except for your loyal servants among them."

      83
      15:40

٨٤ قَالَ فَالْحَقُّ وَالْحَقَّ أَقُولُ

84 He said, "The truth is, and I say the truth.

٨٥ لَأَمْلَأَنَّ جَهَنَّمَ مِنكَ وَمِمَّن تَبِعَكَ مِنْهُمْ أَجْمَعِينَ

85 I will fill Hell with you, and with every one of them who follows you."

      85
      7:18

٨٦ قُل مَّا أَسْأَلُكُمْ عَلَيْهِ مِنْ أَجْرٍ وَمَا أَنَا مِنَ الْمُتَكَلِّفِينَ

86 Say, "I ask of you no wage for this, and I am not a pretender.

      86
      6:90; 11:29

٨٧ إِنْ هُوَ إِلَّا ذِكْرٌ لِّلْعَالَمِينَ

87 It is but a reminder to mankind.

٨٨ وَلَتَعْلَمُنَّ نَبَأَهُ بَعْدَ حِينٍ

88 And you will know its message after a while."

Sūrah 39: Al-Zumar

سُورَةُ ٱلزُّمَر (Throngs)

بِسْمِ ٱللَّهِ ٱلرَّحْمَٰنِ ٱلرَّحِيمِ

١ تَنزِيلُ الْكِتَابِ مِنَ اللَّهِ الْعَزِيزِ الْحَكِيمِ

1 The revelation of the Book is from God, the Mighty and Wise.

      1
      pp 45:2

٢ إِنَّا أَنزَلْنَا إِلَيْكَ الْكِتَابَ بِالْحَقِّ فَاعْبُدِ اللَّهَ مُخْلِصًا لَّهُ الدِّينَ

2 We sent down to you the Book with the truth, so serve God, devoting your religion to Him.

      2
      39:14; 98:5

٣ أَلَا لِلَّهِ الدِّينُ الْخَالِصُ ۚ وَالَّذِينَ اتَّخَذُوا مِن دُونِهِ أَوْلِيَاءَ مَا نَعْبُدُهُمْ إِلَّا لِيُقَرِّبُونَا إِلَى اللَّهِ زُلْفَىٰ إِنَّ اللَّهَ يَحْكُمُ بَيْنَهُمْ فِي مَا هُمْ فِيهِ يَخْتَلِفُونَ ۗ إِنَّ اللَّهَ لَا يَهْدِي مَنْ هُوَ كَاذِبٌ كَفَّارٌ

3 Is not to God that sincere faith is due? As for those who take guardians besides Him, "We only worship them that they may bring us nearer to God." God will judge between them regarding their differences. God does not guide the lying blasphemer.

      3
      2:113; 39:46

٤ لَّوْ أَرَادَ اللَّهُ أَن يَتَّخِذَ وَلَدًا لَّاصْطَفَىٰ مِمَّا يَخْلُقُ مَا يَشَاءُ ۚ سُبْحَانَهُ ۖ هُوَ اللَّهُ الْوَاحِدُ الْقَهَّارُ

4 If God wanted to have a son, He could have selected from His creation at will. Glory be to Him. He is God, the One, the Prevailing.

      4
      2:116; 16:57; 37:149

٥ خَلَقَ السَّمَاوَاتِ وَالْأَرْضَ بِالْحَقِّ ۖ يُكَوِّرُ اللَّيْلَ عَلَى النَّهَارِ وَيُكَوِّرُ النَّهَارَ عَلَى اللَّيْلِ ۖ وَسَخَّرَ الشَّمْسَ وَالْقَمَرَ ۖ كُلٌّ يَجْرِي لِأَجَلٍ مُسَمًّى ۗ أَلَا هُوَ الْعَزِيزُ الْغَفَّارُ

5
3:27; 13:2; 31:29; 35:13

5 He created the heavens and the earth with reason. He wraps the night around the day, and He wraps the day around the night. And He regulates the sun and the moon, each running along a specific course. He is indeed the Almighty, the Forgiver.

٦ خَلَقَكُم مِّن نَّفْسٍ وَاحِدَةٍ ثُمَّ جَعَلَ مِنْهَا زَوْجَهَا وَأَنزَلَ لَكُم مِّنَ الْأَنْعَامِ ثَمَانِيَةَ أَزْوَاجٍ ۚ يَخْلُقُكُمْ فِي بُطُونِ أُمَّهَاتِكُمْ خَلْقًا مِّن بَعْدِ خَلْقٍ فِي ظُلُمَاتٍ ثَلَاثٍ ۚ ذَٰلِكُمُ اللَّهُ رَبُّكُمْ لَهُ الْمُلْكُ ۖ لَا إِلَٰهَ إِلَّا هُوَ ۖ فَأَنَّىٰ تُصْرَفُونَ

6
[a] 4:1; 7:189
[b] 6:143
[c] 16:78; 22:5; 23:13; 53:23

6 He created you from one person, then made from it its mate, and brought down livestock for you—eight kinds in pairs. He creates you in the wombs of your mothers, in successive formations, in a triple darkness. Such is God, your Lord. His is the kingdom. There is no god but He. So what made you deviate?

٧ إِن تَكْفُرُوا فَإِنَّ اللَّهَ غَنِيٌّ عَنكُمْ ۖ وَلَا يَرْضَىٰ لِعِبَادِهِ الْكُفْرَ ۖ وَإِن تَشْكُرُوا يَرْضَهُ لَكُمْ ۗ وَلَا تَزِرُ وَازِرَةٌ وِزْرَ أُخْرَىٰ ۗ ثُمَّ إِلَىٰ رَبِّكُم مَّرْجِعُكُمْ فَيُنَبِّئُكُم بِمَا كُنتُمْ تَعْمَلُونَ ۚ إِنَّهُ عَلِيمٌ بِذَاتِ الصُّدُورِ

7
[a] 6:164; 10:68; 35:15; 47:38
[b] 16:25

7 If you disbelieve, God is Independent of you, yet He does not approve ingratitude on the part of His servants. And if you are thankful, He will approve that in you. No bearer of burden can bear the burden of another. Then to your Lord is your return; and He will inform you of what you used to do. He is aware of what the hearts contain.

٨ وَإِذَا مَسَّ الْإِنسَانَ ضُرٌّ دَعَا رَبَّهُ مُنِيبًا إِلَيْهِ ثُمَّ إِذَا خَوَّلَهُ نِعْمَةً مِّنْهُ نَسِيَ مَا كَانَ يَدْعُو إِلَيْهِ مِن قَبْلُ وَجَعَلَ لِلَّهِ أَندَادًا لِّيُضِلَّ عَن سَبِيلِهِ ۚ قُلْ تَمَتَّعْ بِكُفْرِكَ قَلِيلًا ۖ إِنَّكَ مِنْ أَصْحَابِ النَّارِ

8
10:12; 16:53; 30:33; 39:49

8 When some adversity touches the human being, he prays to his Lord, repenting to Him. But then, when He confers on him a grace of His, he forgets what he was praying for before, and he attributes rivals to God, in order to lead astray from His way. Say, "Enjoy your disbelief for a little while; you will be among the inmates of the Fire."

٩ أَمَّنْ هُوَ قَانِتٌ آنَاءَ اللَّيْلِ سَاجِدًا وَقَائِمًا يَحْذَرُ الْآخِرَةَ وَيَرْجُو رَحْمَةَ رَبِّهِ ۗ قُلْ هَلْ يَسْتَوِي الَّذِينَ يَعْلَمُونَ وَالَّذِينَ لَا يَعْلَمُونَ ۗ إِنَّمَا يَتَذَكَّرُ أُولُو الْأَلْبَابِ

9 Is he who worships devoutly during the watches of the night, prostrating himself and standing up, mindful of the Hereafter, and placing his hope in the mercy of his Lord? Say, "Are those who know and those who do not know equal?" Only those possessed of reason will remember.

١٠ قُلْ يَا عِبَادِ الَّذِينَ آمَنُوا اتَّقُوا رَبَّكُمْ ۚ لِلَّذِينَ أَحْسَنُوا فِي هَٰذِهِ الدُّنْيَا حَسَنَةٌ ۗa وَأَرْضُ اللَّهِ وَاسِعَةٌ ۗ إِنَّمَا يُوَفَّى الصَّابِرُونَ أَجْرَهُم بِغَيْرِ حِسَابٍb

10
a 3:56, 30, 41; 7:156
b 4:97; 29:56

10 Say, "O My devotees who have believed, keep your duty to your Lord. For those who do good in this world, is goodness. And God's earth is vast. The steadfast will be paid their wages in full, without reckoning."

١١ قُلْ إِنِّي أُمِرْتُ أَنْ أَعْبُدَ اللَّهَ مُخْلِصًا لَّهُ الدِّينَ

11
7:29; 39:14; 39:14; 98:5

11 Say, "I was commanded to serve God, devoting my religion exclusively to Him.

١٢ وَأُمِرْتُ لِأَنْ أَكُونَ أَوَّلَ الْمُسْلِمِينَ

12
6:14, 163; 10:72

12 And I was commanded to be the first of those who submit."

١٣ قُلْ إِنِّي أَخَافُ إِنْ عَصَيْتُ رَبِّي عَذَابَ يَوْمٍ عَظِيمٍ

13
6:15; 10:15

13 Say, "I fear, if I disobeyed my Lord, the punishment of a horrendous Day."

١٤ قُلِ اللَّهَ أَعْبُدُ مُخْلِصًا لَّهُ دِينِي

14
7:29; 39:14; 39:11; 98:5

14 Say, "It is God I worship, sincere in my faith in Him."

١٥ فَاعْبُدُوا مَا شِئْتُم مِّن دُونِهِ ۗ قُلْ إِنَّ الْخَاسِرِينَ الَّذِينَ خَسِرُوا أَنفُسَهُمْ وَأَهْلِيهِمْ يَوْمَ الْقِيَامَةِ ۗ أَلَا ذَٰلِكَ هُوَ الْخُسْرَانُ الْمُبِينُ

15
6:12; 10:45; 42:45

15 "But you can worship whatever you wish besides Him." Say, "The losers are those who lose their souls and their people on the Day of Resurrection." That is indeed the obvious loss.

١٦ لَهُم مِّن فَوْقِهِمْ ظُلَلٌ مِّنَ النَّارِ وَمِن تَحْتِهِمْ ظُلَلٌ ۚ ذَٰلِكَ يُخَوِّفُ اللَّهُ بِهِ عِبَادَهُ ۚ يَا عِبَادِ فَاتَّقُونِ

16
21:39; 29:55

16 They will have layers of Fire above them, and layers beneath them. That is how God strikes fear into His servants—"O My servants! Beware of Me!"

١٧ وَالَّذِينَ اجْتَنَبُوا الطَّاغُوتَ أَن يَعْبُدُوهَا وَأَنَابُوا إِلَى اللَّهِ لَهُمُ الْبُشْرَىٰ ۚ فَبَشِّرْ عِبَادِ

17
2:219; 5:90–91; 16:36; 22:30

17 As for those who avoid the worship of idols, and devote themselves to God—theirs is the good news. So give good news to My servants.

١٨ الَّذِينَ يَسْتَمِعُونَ الْقَوْلَ فَيَتَّبِعُونَ أَحْسَنَهُ ۚ أُولَٰئِكَ الَّذِينَ هَدَاهُمُ اللَّهُ ۖ وَأُولَٰئِكَ هُمْ أُولُو الْأَلْبَابِ

18
39:55

18 Those who listen to the Word, and follow the best of it. These are they whom God has guided. These are they who possess intellect.

١٩ أَفَمَنْ حَقَّ عَلَيْهِ كَلِمَةُ الْعَذَابِ أَفَأَنتَ تُنقِذُ مَن فِي النَّارِ

19
10:33; 36:7; 39:71

19 What about someone who has deserved the sentence of punishment? Is it you who can save those in the Fire?

٢٠ لَكِنِ الَّذِينَ اتَّقَوْا رَبَّهُمْ لَهُمْ غُرَفٌ مِنْ فَوْقِهَا غُرَفٌ مَبْنِيَّةٌ تَجْرِي مِنْ تَحْتِهَا الْأَنْهَارُ ۖ وَعْدَ اللَّهِ ۖ لَا يُخْلِفُ اللَّهُ الْمِيعَادَ

20 But those who fear their Lord will have mansions upon mansions, built high, with streams flowing beneath them. The promise of God; and God never breaks a promise.

25:75; 29:58; 34:37; 61:12

٢١ أَلَمْ تَرَ أَنَّ اللَّهَ أَنْزَلَ مِنَ السَّمَاءِ مَاءً فَسَلَكَهُ يَنَابِيعَ فِي الْأَرْضِ ثُمَّ يُخْرِجُ بِهِ زَرْعًا مُخْتَلِفًا أَلْوَانُهُ ثُمَّ يَهِيجُ فَتَرَاهُ مُصْفَرًّا ثُمَّ يَجْعَلُهُ حُطَامًا ۚ إِنَّ فِي ذَٰلِكَ لَذِكْرَىٰ لِأُولِي الْأَلْبَابِ

21 Have you not considered how God sends down water from the sky, then He makes it flow into underground wells, then He produces with it plants of various colors, then they wither and you see them yellowing, then He turns them into debris? Surely in this is a reminder for those with understanding.

10:24; 18:45; 23:18; 30:22, 51; 57:20

٢٢ أَفَمَنْ شَرَحَ اللَّهُ صَدْرَهُ لِلْإِسْلَامِ فَهُوَ عَلَىٰ نُورٍ مِنْ رَبِّهِ ۚ فَوَيْلٌ لِلْقَاسِيَةِ قُلُوبُهُمْ مِنْ ذِكْرِ اللَّهِ ۚ أُولَٰئِكَ فِي ضَلَالٍ مُبِينٍ

22 What about someone whose heart God has opened to Islam, so that he follows a light from His Lord? Woe to those whose hearts are hardened against the mention of God. Those are in manifest error.

6:125

٢٣ اللَّهُ نَزَّلَ أَحْسَنَ الْحَدِيثِ كِتَابًا مُتَشَابِهًا مَثَانِيَ تَقْشَعِرُّ مِنْهُ جُلُودُ الَّذِينَ يَخْشَوْنَ رَبَّهُمْ ثُمَّ تَلِينُ جُلُودُهُمْ وَقُلُوبُهُمْ إِلَىٰ ذِكْرِ اللَّهِ ۚ ذَٰلِكَ هُدَى اللَّهِ يَهْدِي بِهِ مَنْ يَشَاءُ ۚ وَمَنْ يُضْلِلِ اللَّهُ فَمَا لَهُ مِنْ هَادٍ

23 God has sent down the best of narrations: A Scripture consistent and paired. The skins of those who reverence their Lord shiver from it, then their skins and their hearts soften up to the remembrance of God. Such is God's guidance; He guides with it whomever He wills. But whomever God leaves astray, for him there is no guide.

3:7; 16:37

٢٤ أَفَمَنْ يَتَّقِي بِوَجْهِهِ سُوءَ الْعَذَابِ يَوْمَ الْقِيَامَةِ ۚ وَقِيلَ لِلظَّالِمِينَ ذُوقُوا مَا كُنْتُمْ تَكْسِبُونَ

24 What about someone who covers his face against the terrible misery of the Day of Resurrection? To the evildoers it will be said, "Taste what you used to earn."

٢٥ كَذَّبَ الَّذِينَ مِنْ قَبْلِهِمْ فَأَتَاهُمُ الْعَذَابُ مِنْ حَيْثُ لَا يَشْعُرُونَ

25 Those before them also denied the truth, so the penalty came upon them from where they did not perceive.

10:39; 16:26

٢٦ فَأَذَاقَهُمُ اللَّهُ الْخِزْيَ فِي الْحَيَاةِ الدُّنْيَا ۖ وَلَعَذَابُ الْآخِرَةِ أَكْبَرُ ۚ لَوْ كَانُوا يَعْلَمُونَ

26 God made them taste disgrace in the present life, but the punishment of the Hereafter is worse, if they only knew.

٢٧ وَلَقَدْ ضَرَبْنَا لِلنَّاسِ فِي هَٰذَا الْقُرْآنِ مِنْ كُلِّ مَثَلٍ لَعَلَّهُمْ يَتَذَكَّرُونَ

27 We have cited in this Qur'an for mankind every ideal, that they may take heed.

14:25; 17:89; 18:54; 30:58

٢٨ قُرْآنًا عَرَبِيًّا غَيْرَ ذِي عِوَجٍ لَّعَلَّهُمْ يَتَّقُونَ

28 An Arabic Qur'an, without any defect, so they may become righteous.

28
12:2; 18:1; 20:113; 26:195; 41:44; 43:3

٢٩ ضَرَبَ اللَّهُ مَثَلًا رَّجُلًا فِيهِ شُرَكَاءُ مُتَشَاكِسُونَ وَرَجُلًا سَلَمًا لِّرَجُلٍ هَلْ يَسْتَوِيَانِ مَثَلًا ۚ الْحَمْدُ لِلَّهِ ۚ بَلْ أَكْثَرُهُمْ لَا يَعْلَمُونَ

29 God cites the example of a man shared by partners at odds, and a man belonging exclusively to one man. Are they equal in status? Praise be to God, but most of them do not know.

٣٠ إِنَّكَ مَيِّتٌ وَإِنَّهُم مَّيِّتُونَ

30 You will die, and they will die.

٣١ ثُمَّ إِنَّكُمْ يَوْمَ الْقِيَامَةِ عِندَ رَبِّكُمْ تَخْتَصِمُونَ

31 Then, on the Day of Resurrection, you will be quarrelling before your Lord.

٣٢ فَمَنْ أَظْلَمُ مِمَّن كَذَبَ عَلَى اللَّهِ وَكَذَّبَ بِالصِّدْقِ إِذْ جَاءَهُ ۚ أَلَيْسَ فِي جَهَنَّمَ مَثْوًى لِّلْكَافِرِينَ

32 Who is more evil than he who lies about God, and denies the truth when it has come to him? Is there not in Hell room for the ungrateful?

32
29:68

٣٣ وَالَّذِي جَاءَ بِالصِّدْقِ وَصَدَّقَ بِهِ ۙ أُولَٰئِكَ هُمُ الْمُتَّقُونَ

33 But he who promotes the truth, and testifies to it—these are the righteous.

٣٤ لَهُم مَّا يَشَاءُونَ عِندَ رَبِّهِمْ ۚ ذَٰلِكَ جَزَاءُ الْمُحْسِنِينَ

34 They will have whatever they please with their Lord. Such is the reward for the virtuous.

٣٥ لِيُكَفِّرَ اللَّهُ عَنْهُمْ أَسْوَأَ الَّذِي عَمِلُوا وَيَجْزِيَهُمْ أَجْرَهُم بِأَحْسَنِ الَّذِي كَانُوا يَعْمَلُونَ

35 God will acquit them of the worst of their deeds, and will reward them according to the best of what they used to do.

35
16:97

٣٦ أَلَيْسَ اللَّهُ بِكَافٍ عَبْدَهُ ۖ[a] وَيُخَوِّفُونَكَ بِالَّذِينَ مِن دُونِهِ ۚ وَمَن يُضْلِلِ اللَّهُ فَمَا لَهُ مِنْ هَادٍ[b]

36 Is God not enough for His servant? And they frighten you with those besides Him. Whomever God sends astray, for him there is no guide.

36
[a] 2:137; 8:64
[b] 3:175

٣٧ وَمَن يَهْدِ اللَّهُ فَمَا لَهُ مِن مُّضِلٍّ ۗ أَلَيْسَ اللَّهُ بِعَزِيزٍ ذِي انتِقَامٍ

37 And whomever God guides, for him there is no misleader. Is God not Powerful and Vengeful?

37
7:178; 17:97; 18:17

٣٨ وَلَئِن سَأَلْتَهُم مَّنْ خَلَقَ السَّمَاوَاتِ وَالْأَرْضَ لَيَقُولُنَّ اللَّهُ ۚ قُلْ أَفَرَأَيْتُم مَّا تَدْعُونَ مِن دُونِ اللَّهِ إِنْ أَرَادَنِيَ اللَّهُ بِضُرٍّ هَلْ هُنَّ كَاشِفَاتُ ضُرِّهِ أَوْ أَرَادَنِي بِرَحْمَةٍ هَلْ هُنَّ مُمْسِكَاتُ رَحْمَتِهِ ۚ قُلْ حَسْبِيَ اللَّهُ ۖ عَلَيْهِ يَتَوَكَّلُ الْمُتَوَكِّلُونَ

[a] 29:61; 31:25; 43:9
[b] 6:17; 10:107; 26:72–73; 35:2

38 And if you asked them, "Who created the heavens and the earth?" they would say, "God." Say, "Have you seen those you pray to instead of God? If God willed any harm for me, can they lift His harm? And if He willed a blessing for me, can they hold back His mercy?" Say, "God suffices for me. On Him the reliant rely."

٣٩ قُلْ يَا قَوْمِ اعْمَلُوا عَلَىٰ مَكَانَتِكُمْ إِنِّي عَامِلٌ ۖ فَسَوْفَ تَعْلَمُونَ

11:93, 121; 6:135

39 Say: "O my people, work according to your ability; and so will I. Then you will know.

٤٠ مَن يَأْتِيهِ عَذَابٌ يُخْزِيهِ وَيَحِلُّ عَلَيْهِ عَذَابٌ مُّقِيمٌ

40 Who will receive a humiliating punishment, and on whom will fall a lasting torment."

٤١ إِنَّا أَنزَلْنَا عَلَيْكَ الْكِتَابَ لِلنَّاسِ بِالْحَقِّ ۖ فَمَنِ اهْتَدَىٰ فَلِنَفْسِهِ ۖ وَمَن ضَلَّ فَإِنَّمَا يَضِلُّ عَلَيْهَا ۖ وَمَا أَنتَ عَلَيْهِم بِوَكِيلٍ

10:108

41 We sent down upon you the Book for mankind in truth. He who follows guidance does so for the good of his soul. And he who strays in error does so to its detriment. You are not their overseer.

٤٢ اللَّهُ يَتَوَفَّى الْأَنفُسَ حِينَ مَوْتِهَا وَالَّتِي لَمْ تَمُتْ فِي مَنَامِهَا ۖ فَيُمْسِكُ الَّتِي قَضَىٰ عَلَيْهَا الْمَوْتَ وَيُرْسِلُ الْأُخْرَىٰ إِلَىٰ أَجَلٍ مُّسَمًّى ۚ إِنَّ فِي ذَٰلِكَ لَآيَاتٍ لِّقَوْمٍ يَتَفَكَّرُونَ

6:60

42 God takes the souls at the time of their death, and those that have not died during their sleep. He retains those for which He has decreed death, and He releases the others until a predetermined time. In that are signs for people who reflect.

٤٣ أَمِ اتَّخَذُوا مِن دُونِ اللَّهِ شُفَعَاءَ ۚ قُلْ أَوَلَوْ كَانُوا لَا يَمْلِكُونَ شَيْئًا وَلَا يَعْقِلُونَ

43–44
10:18; 21:24; 42:9

43 Or have they chosen intercessors other than God? Say, "Even though they have no power over anything, and are devoid of reason?"

٤٤ قُل لِّلَّهِ الشَّفَاعَةُ جَمِيعًا ۖ لَّهُ مُلْكُ السَّمَاوَاتِ وَالْأَرْضِ ۖ ثُمَّ إِلَيْهِ تُرْجَعُونَ

44 Say, "All intercession is up to God. To Him belongs the kingdom of the heavens and the earth. Then to Him you will be returned."

٤٥ وَإِذَا ذُكِرَ اللَّهُ وَحْدَهُ اشْمَأَزَّتْ قُلُوبُ الَّذِينَ لَا يُؤْمِنُونَ بِالْآخِرَةِ ۖ وَإِذَا ذُكِرَ الَّذِينَ مِن دُونِهِ إِذَا هُمْ يَسْتَبْشِرُونَ

17:46; 40:12

45 When God alone is mentioned, the hearts of those who do not believe in the Hereafter shrink with resentment. But when those other than Him are mentioned, they become filled with joy.

٤٦ قُلِ اللَّهُمَّ فَاطِرَ السَّمَاوَاتِ وَالْأَرْضِ عَالِمَ الْغَيْبِ وَالشَّهَادَةِ أَنْتَ تَحْكُمُ بَيْنَ عِبَادِكَ فِي مَا كَانُوا فِيهِ يَخْتَلِفُونَ

46 39:3

46 Say, "Our God, Initiator of the heavens and the earth, Knower of all secrets and declarations. You will judge between your servants regarding what they had differed about."

٤٧ وَلَوْ أَنَّ لِلَّذِينَ ظَلَمُوا مَا فِي الْأَرْضِ جَمِيعًا وَمِثْلَهُ مَعَهُ لَافْتَدَوْا بِهِ مِنْ سُوءِ الْعَذَابِ يَوْمَ الْقِيَامَةِ ۚ وَبَدَا لَهُمْ مِنَ اللَّهِ مَا لَمْ يَكُونُوا يَحْتَسِبُونَ

47 3:91; 5:36; 10:54; 13:18

47 If those who did wrong owned everything on earth, and the like of it with it, they would redeem themselves with it from the terrible suffering on the Day of Resurrection. But there will appear to them from God what they never anticipated.

٤٨ وَبَدَا لَهُمْ سَيِّئَاتُ مَا كَسَبُوا وَحَاقَ بِهِمْ مَا كَانُوا بِهِ يَسْتَهْزِئُونَ

48 6:10; 16:34; 45:33

48 There will appear to them the evils of their deeds, and they will be surrounded by what they used to ridicule.

٤٩ فَإِذَا مَسَّ الْإِنْسَانَ ضُرٌّ دَعَانَا ثُمَّ إِذَا خَوَّلْنَاهُ نِعْمَةً مِنَّا قَالَ إِنَّمَا أُوتِيتُهُ عَلَىٰ عِلْمٍ ۚ بَلْ هِيَ فِتْنَةٌ وَلَٰكِنَّ أَكْثَرَهُمْ لَا يَعْلَمُونَ

49 10:12; 16:53; 30:33; 39:8

49 When adversity touches the human being, he calls on Us. But then, when We favor him with a blessing from Us, he says, "I have attained this by virtue of my knowledge." However, it is a test, but most of them do not know.

٥٠ قَدْ قَالَهَا الَّذِينَ مِنْ قَبْلِهِمْ فَمَا أَغْنَىٰ عَنْهُمْ مَا كَانُوا يَكْسِبُونَ

50

50 Those before them said it, but what they had earned did not avail them.

٥١ فَأَصَابَهُمْ سَيِّئَاتُ مَا كَسَبُوا ۚ وَالَّذِينَ ظَلَمُوا مِنْ هَٰؤُلَاءِ سَيُصِيبُهُمْ سَيِّئَاتُ مَا كَسَبُوا وَمَا هُمْ بِمُعْجِزِينَ

51 4:79; 6:134; 16:34; 28:47; 42:30

51 The evils of their deeds caught up with them. And the wrongdoers among these will also be afflicted by the evils of what they earned, and they cannot prevent it.

٥٢ أَوَلَمْ يَعْلَمُوا أَنَّ اللَّهَ يَبْسُطُ الرِّزْقَ لِمَنْ يَشَاءُ وَيَقْدِرُ ۚ إِنَّ فِي ذَٰلِكَ لَآيَاتٍ لِقَوْمٍ يُؤْمِنُونَ

52 13:26; 30:37

52 Do they not know that God extends the provision to whomever He wills, and constricts it? In that are signs for people who believe.

٥٣ قُلْ يَا عِبَادِيَ الَّذِينَ أَسْرَفُوا عَلَىٰ أَنْفُسِهِمْ لَا تَقْنَطُوا مِنْ رَحْمَةِ اللَّهِ ۚ إِنَّ اللَّهَ يَغْفِرُ الذُّنُوبَ جَمِيعًا ۚ إِنَّهُ هُوَ الْغَفُورُ الرَّحِيمُ

53 12:87; 15:56

53 Say, "O My servants who have transgressed against themselves: do not despair of God's mercy, for God forgives all sins. He is indeed the Forgiver, the Clement."

٥٤ وَأَنِيبُوا إِلَىٰ رَبِّكُمْ وَأَسْلِمُوا لَهُ مِن قَبْلِ أَن يَأْتِيَكُمُ الْعَذَابُ ثُمَّ لَا تُنصَرُونَ

54 And turn to your Lord, and submit to Him, before the retribution comes upon you. Then you will not be helped.

٥٥ وَاتَّبِعُوا أَحْسَنَ مَا أُنزِلَ إِلَيْكُم مِّن رَّبِّكُم مِّن قَبْلِ أَن يَأْتِيَكُمُ الْعَذَابُ بَغْتَةً وَأَنتُمْ لَا تَشْعُرُونَ

55 And follow the best of what was revealed to you from your Lord, before the punishment comes upon you suddenly, while you are unaware.

55
16:97; 39:18

٥٦ أَن تَقُولَ نَفْسٌ يَا حَسْرَتَا عَلَىٰ مَا فَرَّطتُ فِي جَنبِ اللَّهِ وَإِن كُنتُ لَمِنَ السَّاخِرِينَ

56 So that a soul may not say, "How sorry I am, for having neglected my duty to God, and for having been of the scoffers."

56
6:31

٥٧ أَوْ تَقُولَ لَوْ أَنَّ اللَّهَ هَدَانِي لَكُنتُ مِنَ الْمُتَّقِينَ

57 Or say, "Had God guided me; I would have been of the pious."

٥٨ أَوْ تَقُولَ حِينَ تَرَى الْعَذَابَ لَوْ أَنَّ لِي كَرَّةً فَأَكُونَ مِنَ الْمُحْسِنِينَ

58 Or say, when it sees the penalty, "If only I had another chance, I would be of the virtuous."

58
2:167; 26:102

٥٩ بَلَىٰ قَدْ جَاءَتْكَ آيَاتِي فَكَذَّبْتَ بِهَا وَاسْتَكْبَرْتَ وَكُنتَ مِنَ الْكَافِرِينَ

59 Yes indeed! My Verses did come to you, but you called them lies, turned arrogant, and were of the faithless.

٦٠ وَيَوْمَ الْقِيَامَةِ تَرَى الَّذِينَ كَذَبُوا عَلَى اللَّهِ وُجُوهُهُم مُّسْوَدَّةٌ ۚ أَلَيْسَ فِي جَهَنَّمَ مَثْوًى لِّلْمُتَكَبِّرِينَ

60 On the Day of Resurrection, you will see those who told lies about God with their faces blackened. Is there not a place in Hell for the arrogant?

60
3:106

٦١ وَيُنَجِّي اللَّهُ الَّذِينَ اتَّقَوْا بِمَفَازَتِهِمْ لَا يَمَسُّهُمُ السُّوءُ وَلَا هُمْ يَحْزَنُونَ

61 And God will save those who maintained righteousness to their place of salvation. No harm will touch them, nor will they grieve.

61
3:188; 16:29; 29:68; 39:72

٦٢ اللَّهُ خَالِقُ كُلِّ شَيْءٍ ۖ وَهُوَ عَلَىٰ كُلِّ شَيْءٍ وَكِيلٌ

62 God is the Creator of all things, and He is in Charge of all things.

٦٣ لَّهُ مَقَالِيدُ السَّمَاوَاتِ وَالْأَرْضِ ۗ وَالَّذِينَ كَفَرُوا بِآيَاتِ اللَّهِ أُولَٰئِكَ هُمُ الْخَاسِرُونَ

63 To Him belong the reins of the heavens and the earth. But those who blaspheme against the revelations of God—it is they who are the losers.

63
42:12

٦٤ قُلْ أَفَغَيْرَ اللَّهِ تَأْمُرُونِّي أَعْبُدُ أَيُّهَا الْجَاهِلُونَ

64 Say, "Is it other than God you instruct me to worship, you ignorant ones?"

٦٥ وَلَقَدْ أُوحِيَ إِلَيْكَ وَإِلَى الَّذِينَ مِنْ قَبْلِكَ لَئِنْ أَشْرَكْتَ لَيَحْبَطَنَّ عَمَلُكَ وَلَتَكُونَنَّ مِنَ الْخَاسِرِينَ[b]

65 It was revealed to you, and to those before you, that if you idolize, your works will be in vain, and you will be of the losers.

65
[a] 42:3
[b] 5:5

٦٦ بَلِ اللَّهَ فَاعْبُدْ وَكُنْ مِنَ الشَّاكِرِينَ

66 Rather, worship God, and be of the appreciative.

٦٧ وَمَا قَدَرُوا اللَّهَ حَقَّ قَدْرِهِ وَالْأَرْضُ جَمِيعًا قَبْضَتُهُ يَوْمَ الْقِيَامَةِ وَالسَّمَاوَاتُ مَطْوِيَّاتٌ بِيَمِينِهِ ۚ سُبْحَانَهُ وَتَعَالَى عَمَّا يُشْرِكُونَ

67 They have not esteemed God as He ought to be esteemed. The entire earth will be in His grip on the Day of Resurrection, and the heavens will be folded in His right. Immaculate is He, and Transcendent He is beyond the associations they make.

67
21:104; 22:74

٦٨ وَنُفِخَ فِي الصُّورِ فَصَعِقَ مَنْ فِي السَّمَاوَاتِ وَمَنْ فِي الْأَرْضِ إِلَّا مَنْ شَاءَ اللَّهُ ۖ ثُمَّ نُفِخَ فِيهِ أُخْرَىٰ فَإِذَا هُمْ قِيَامٌ يَنْظُرُونَ

68 And the Trumpet will be sounded, whereupon everyone in the heavens and the earth will be stunned, except whomever God wills. Then it will be sounded another time, whereupon they will rise up, looking on.

68
18:99; 36:51

٦٩ وَأَشْرَقَتِ الْأَرْضُ بِنُورِ رَبِّهَا وَوُضِعَ الْكِتَابُ وَجِيءَ بِالنَّبِيِّينَ وَالشُّهَدَاءِ وَقُضِيَ بَيْنَهُمْ بِالْحَقِّ وَهُمْ لَا يُظْلَمُونَ

69 And the earth will shine with the Light of its Lord; and the Book will be put in place; and the prophets and the witnesses will be brought in; and Judgment will be passed among them equitably, and they will not be wronged.

69
10:47; 18:49; 39:70; 45:29

٧٠ وَوُفِّيَتْ كُلُّ نَفْسٍ مَا عَمِلَتْ وَهُوَ أَعْلَمُ بِمَا يَفْعَلُونَ

70 And every soul will be fully compensated for what it had done. He is well aware of what they do.

70
22:68

٧١ وَسِيقَ الَّذِينَ كَفَرُوا إِلَىٰ جَهَنَّمَ زُمَرًا ۖ حَتَّىٰ إِذَا جَاءُوهَا فُتِحَتْ أَبْوَابُهَا وَقَالَ لَهُمْ خَزَنَتُهَا أَلَمْ يَأْتِكُمْ رُسُلٌ مِنْكُمْ يَتْلُونَ عَلَيْكُمْ آيَاتِ رَبِّكُمْ وَيُنْذِرُونَكُمْ لِقَاءَ يَوْمِكُمْ هَٰذَا ۚ قَالُوا بَلَىٰ وَلَٰكِنْ حَقَّتْ كَلِمَةُ الْعَذَابِ عَلَى الْكَافِرِينَ

71 Those who disbelieved will be driven to Hell in throngs. Until, when they have reached it, and its gates are opened, its keepers will say to them, "Did not messengers from among you come to you, reciting to you the revelations of your Lord, and warning you of the meeting of this Day of yours?" They will say, "Yes, but the verdict of punishment is justified against the disbelievers."

71
19:86; 40:50; 67:8

٧٢ قِيلَ ادْخُلُوا أَبْوَابَ جَهَنَّمَ خَالِدِينَ فِيهَا ۖ فَبِئْسَ مَثْوَى الْمُتَكَبِّرِينَ

72 It will be said, "Enter the gates of Hell, to abide therein eternally." How wretched is the destination of the arrogant.

72
16:29; 40:76

٧٣ وَسِيقَ ٱلَّذِينَ ٱتَّقَوْا۟ رَبَّهُمْ إِلَى ٱلْجَنَّةِ زُمَرًا ۖ حَتَّىٰ إِذَا جَآءُوهَا وَفُتِحَتْ أَبْوَٰبُهَا[a] وَقَالَ لَهُمْ خَزَنَتُهَا سَلَٰمٌ عَلَيْكُمْ طِبْتُمْ فَٱدْخُلُوهَا خَٰلِدِينَ[b]

73

[a] 16:43–44
[b] 16:32

73 And those who feared their Lord will be led to Paradise in throngs. Until, when they have reached it, and its gates are opened, its keepers will say to them, "Peace be upon you, you have been good, so enter it, to abide therein eternally."

٧٤ وَقَالُوا۟ ٱلْحَمْدُ لِلَّهِ ٱلَّذِى صَدَقَنَا وَعْدَهُۥ وَأَوْرَثَنَا ٱلْأَرْضَ نَتَبَوَّأُ مِنَ ٱلْجَنَّةِ حَيْثُ نَشَآءُ ۖ فَنِعْمَ أَجْرُ ٱلْعَٰمِلِينَ

74

7:43–44

74 And they will say, "Praise be to God, who has fulfilled His promise to us, and made us inherit the land, enjoying Paradise as we please." How excellent is the reward of the workers.

٧٥ وَتَرَى ٱلْمَلَٰٓئِكَةَ حَآفِّينَ مِنْ حَوْلِ ٱلْعَرْشِ يُسَبِّحُونَ بِحَمْدِ رَبِّهِمْ ۖ وَقُضِىَ بَيْنَهُم بِٱلْحَقِّ وَقِيلَ ٱلْحَمْدُ لِلَّهِ رَبِّ ٱلْعَٰلَمِينَ

75

40:7; 42:5

75 And you will see the angels hovering around the Throne, glorifying their Lord with praise. And it will be judged between them equitably, and it will be said, "Praise be to God, Lord of the Worlds."

Sūrah 40: Ghāfir

سُوۡرَةُ غَافِر (Forgiver)

بِسْمِ ٱللَّهِ ٱلرَّحْمَٰنِ ٱلرَّحِيمِ

١ حم

1

1 Ḥā', Mīm.

٢ تَنزِيلُ ٱلْكِتَٰبِ مِنَ ٱللَّهِ ٱلْعَزِيزِ ٱلْعَلِيمِ

2

pp 39:1; 45:2; 46:2

2 The sending down of the Scripture is from God the Almighty, the Omniscient.

٣ غَافِرِ ٱلذَّنۢبِ وَقَابِلِ ٱلتَّوْبِ شَدِيدِ ٱلْعِقَابِ ذِى ٱلطَّوْلِ ۖ لَآ إِلَٰهَ إِلَّا هُوَ ۖ إِلَيْهِ ٱلْمَصِيرُ

3 Forgiver of sins, Accepter of repentance, Severe in punishment, Bountiful in bounty. There is no god but He. To Him is the ultimate return.

٤ مَا يُجَٰدِلُ فِىٓ ءَايَٰتِ ٱللَّهِ إِلَّا ٱلَّذِينَ كَفَرُوا۟[a] فَلَا يَغْرُرْكَ تَقَلُّبُهُمْ فِى ٱلْبِلَٰدِ[b]

4

4 None argues against God's revelations except those who disbelieve. So do not be impressed by their activities in the land.

[a] 18:56; 22:3, 8; 40:5, 35, 56, 69; 42:16, 35
[b] 3:196

٥ كَذَّبَتْ قَبْلَهُمْ قَوْمُ نُوحٍ وَالْأَحْزَابُ مِنْ بَعْدِهِمْ ۖ وَهَمَّتْ كُلُّ أُمَّةٍ بِرَسُولِهِمْ لِيَأْخُذُوهُ ۖ وَجَادَلُوا بِالْبَاطِلِ لِيُدْحِضُوا بِهِ الْحَقَّ فَأَخَذْتُهُمْ ۖ فَكَيْفَ كَانَ عِقَابِ

5 22:42–44; 26:105; 38:12–14; 50:12–14; 54:9

5 Before them the people of Noah rejected the truth, as did the confederates after them. Every community plotted against their messenger, to capture him. And they argued with falsehood, to defeat with it the truth. But I seized them. What a punishment it was!

٦ وَكَذَٰلِكَ حَقَّتْ كَلِمَتُ رَبِّكَ عَلَى الَّذِينَ كَفَرُوا أَنَّهُمْ أَصْحَابُ النَّارِ

6 7:36

6 Thus the sentence of your Lord became realized against those who disbelieve, that they are to be inmates of the Fire.

٧ الَّذِينَ يَحْمِلُونَ الْعَرْشَ وَمَنْ حَوْلَهُ يُسَبِّحُونَ بِحَمْدِ رَبِّهِمْ وَيُؤْمِنُونَ بِهِ وَيَسْتَغْفِرُونَ لِلَّذِينَ آمَنُوا رَبَّنَا وَسِعْتَ كُلَّ شَيْءٍ رَحْمَةً وَعِلْمًا فَاغْفِرْ لِلَّذِينَ تَابُوا وَاتَّبَعُوا سَبِيلَكَ وَقِهِمْ عَذَابَ الْجَحِيمِ

7 7:206; 39:75; 42:5; 69:17

7 Those who carry the Throne, and those around it, glorify their Lord with praise, and believe in Him, and ask for forgiveness for those who believe: "Our Lord, You have encompassed everything in mercy and knowledge; so forgive those who repent and follow Your path, and protect them from the agony of the Blaze.

٨ رَبَّنَا وَأَدْخِلْهُمْ جَنَّاتِ عَدْنٍ الَّتِي وَعَدْتَهُمْ وَمَنْ صَلَحَ مِنْ آبَائِهِمْ وَأَزْوَاجِهِمْ وَذُرِّيَّاتِهِمْ ۚ إِنَّكَ أَنْتَ الْعَزِيزُ الْحَكِيمُ

8 22:14

8 And admit them, Our Lord, into the Gardens of Eternity, which You have promised them, and the righteous among their parents, and their spouses, and their offspring. You are indeed the Almighty, the Most Wise.

٩ وَقِهِمُ السَّيِّئَاتِ ۚ وَمَنْ تَقِ السَّيِّئَاتِ يَوْمَئِذٍ فَقَدْ رَحِمْتَهُ ۚ وَذَٰلِكَ هُوَ الْفَوْزُ الْعَظِيمُ

9 And shield them from the evil deeds. Whomever You shield from the evil deeds, on that Day, You have had mercy on him. That is the supreme achievement."

١٠ إِنَّ الَّذِينَ كَفَرُوا يُنَادَوْنَ لَمَقْتُ اللَّهِ أَكْبَرُ مِنْ مَقْتِكُمْ أَنْفُسَكُمْ إِذْ تُدْعَوْنَ إِلَى الْإِيمَانِ فَتَكْفُرُونَ

10 40:35; 61:3

10 Those who disbelieved will be addressed, "The loathing of God is greater than your loathing of yourselves—for you were invited to the faith, but you refused."

١١ قَالُوا رَبَّنَا أَمَتَّنَا اثْنَتَيْنِ وَأَحْيَيْتَنَا اثْنَتَيْنِ[a] فَاعْتَرَفْنَا بِذُنُوبِنَا فَهَلْ إِلَىٰ خُرُوجٍ مِنْ سَبِيلٍ[b]

11
[a] 2:28
[b] 32:12; 67:11

11 They will say, "Our Lord, you made us die twice, and twice you gave us life. Now we acknowledge our sins. Is there any way out?"

١٢ ذَٰلِكُمْ بِأَنَّهُ إِذَا دُعِيَ اللَّهُ وَحْدَهُ كَفَرْتُمْ ۖ وَإِنْ يُشْرَكْ بِهِ تُؤْمِنُوا ۚ فَالْحُكْمُ لِلَّهِ الْعَلِيِّ الْكَبِيرِ

12 17:46; 37:35; 39:45

12 That is because when God alone was called upon, you disbelieved; but when others were associated with Him, you believed. Judgment rests with God the Sublime, the Majestic.

١٣ هُوَ الَّذِي يُرِيكُمْ آيَاتِهِ وَيُنَزِّلُ لَكُم مِّنَ السَّمَاءِ رِزْقًا ۚ وَمَا يَتَذَكَّرُ إِلَّا مَن يُنِيبُ	**13** 2:22; 14:32; 16:10; 20:53; 45:5

13 It is He who shows you His wonders, and sends down sustenance from the sky for you. But none pays heed except the repentant.

١٤ فَادْعُوا اللَّهَ مُخْلِصِينَ لَهُ الدِّينَ وَلَوْ كَرِهَ الْكَافِرُونَ	**14** 7:29; 39:2; 40:65

14 So call upon God, with sincere devotion to Him, even though the disbelievers resent it.

١٥ رَفِيعُ الدَّرَجَاتِ ذُو الْعَرْشِ يُلْقِي الرُّوحَ مِنْ أَمْرِهِ عَلَىٰ مَن يَشَاءُ مِنْ عِبَادِهِ لِيُنذِرَ يَوْمَ التَّلَاقِ	**15** 16:2

15 Exalted in rank, Owner of the Throne. He conveys the Spirit, by His command, upon whomever He wills of His servants, to warn of the Day of Encounter.

١٦ يَوْمَ هُم بَارِزُونَ ۖ لَا يَخْفَىٰ عَلَى اللَّهِ مِنْهُمْ شَيْءٌ ۚ لِّمَنِ الْمُلْكُ الْيَوْمَ ۖ لِلَّهِ الْوَاحِدِ الْقَهَّارِ	**16** 3:5; 14:21, 48

16 The Day when they will emerge, nothing about them will be concealed from God. "To whom does the sovereignty belong today?" "To God, the One, the Irresistible."

١٧ الْيَوْمَ تُجْزَىٰ كُلُّ نَفْسٍ بِمَا كَسَبَتْ ۚ لَا ظُلْمَ الْيَوْمَ ۚ إِنَّ اللَّهَ سَرِيعُ الْحِسَابِ	**17** 10:52; 36:54; 45:22

17 On that Day, every soul will be recompensed for what it had earned. There will be no injustice on that Day. God is quick to settle accounts.

١٨ وَأَنذِرْهُمْ يَوْمَ الْآزِفَةِ إِذِ الْقُلُوبُ لَدَى الْحَنَاجِرِ كَاظِمِينَ ۚ مَا لِلظَّالِمِينَ مِنْ حَمِيمٍ وَلَا شَفِيعٍ يُطَاعُ	**18** 53:57

18 And warn them of the Day of Imminence, when the hearts are at the throats, choking them. The evildoers will have no intimate friend, and no intercessor to be obeyed.

١٩ يَعْلَمُ خَائِنَةَ الْأَعْيُنِ وَمَا تُخْفِي الصُّدُورُ	**19** 2:33

19 He knows the deceptions of the eyes, and what the hearts conceal.

٢٠ وَاللَّهُ يَقْضِي بِالْحَقِّ ۖ وَالَّذِينَ يَدْعُونَ مِن دُونِهِ لَا يَقْضُونَ بِشَيْءٍ ۗ إِنَّ اللَّهَ هُوَ السَّمِيعُ الْبَصِيرُ	**20**

20 God judges with justice, while those whom they invoke besides Him cannot judge with anything. It is God who is the Hearing, the Seeing.

٢١ أَوَلَمْ يَسِيرُوا فِي الْأَرْضِ فَيَنظُرُوا كَيْفَ كَانَ عَاقِبَةُ الَّذِينَ كَانُوا مِن قَبْلِهِمْ ۚ كَانُوا هُمْ أَشَدَّ مِنْهُمْ قُوَّةً وَآثَارًا فِي الْأَرْضِ فَأَخَذَهُمُ اللَّهُ بِذُنُوبِهِمْ وَمَا كَانَ لَهُم مِّنَ اللَّهِ مِن وَاقٍ	**21** 30:9; 40:82

21 Have they not travelled through the earth, and seen the consequences for those before them? They were stronger than them, and they left more impact on earth. But God seized them for their sins, and they had no defender against God.

٢٢ ذَٰلِكَ بِأَنَّهُمْ كَانَت تَّأْتِيهِمْ رُسُلُهُم بِالْبَيِّنَاتِ فَكَفَرُوا فَأَخَذَهُمُ اللَّهُ ۚ إِنَّهُ قَوِيٌّ شَدِيدُ الْعِقَابِ	**22** 7:101; 64:6

22 That is because their messengers used to come to them with clear proofs, but they disbelieved, so God seized them. He is Strong, Severe in retribution.

٢٣ وَلَقَدْ أَرْسَلْنَا مُوسَىٰ بِآيَاتِنَا وَسُلْطَانٍ مُبِينٍ

23 We sent Moses with Our signs, and a clear authority.

23
pp 11:96

٢٤ إِلَىٰ فِرْعَوْنَ وَهَامَانَ وَقَارُونَ فَقَالُوا سَاحِرٌ كَذَّابٌ

24 To Pharaoh, Hamaan, and Quaroon. But they said, "A lying sorcerer."

24
7:132; 20:71; 23:46; 29:39

٢٥ فَلَمَّا جَاءَهُمْ بِالْحَقِّ مِنْ عِنْدِنَا قَالُوا اقْتُلُوا أَبْنَاءَ الَّذِينَ آمَنُوا مَعَهُ وَاسْتَحْيُوا نِسَاءَهُمْ ۚ وَمَا كَيْدُ الْكَافِرِينَ إِلَّا فِي ضَلَالٍ

25 Then, when he came to them with the truth from Us, they said, "Kill the sons of those who have believed with him, and spare their daughters." But the scheming of the unbelievers can only go astray.

25
7:127

٢٦ وَقَالَ فِرْعَوْنُ ذَرُونِي أَقْتُلْ مُوسَىٰ وَلْيَدْعُ رَبَّهُ ۖ إِنِّي أَخَافُ أَنْ يُبَدِّلَ دِينَكُمْ أَوْ أَنْ يُظْهِرَ فِي الْأَرْضِ الْفَسَادَ

26 Pharaoh said, "Leave me to kill Moses, and let him appeal to his Lord. I fear he may change your religion, or spread disorder in the land."

٢٧ وَقَالَ مُوسَىٰ إِنِّي عُذْتُ بِرَبِّي وَرَبِّكُمْ مِنْ كُلِّ مُتَكَبِّرٍ لَا يُؤْمِنُ بِيَوْمِ الْحِسَابِ

27 Moses said, "I have sought the protection of my Lord and your Lord, from every tyrant who does not believe in the Day of Account."

27
44:20

٢٨ وَقَالَ رَجُلٌ مُؤْمِنٌ مِنْ آلِ فِرْعَوْنَ يَكْتُمُ إِيمَانَهُ أَتَقْتُلُونَ رَجُلًا أَنْ يَقُولَ رَبِّيَ اللَّهُ وَقَدْ جَاءَكُمْ بِالْبَيِّنَاتِ مِنْ رَبِّكُمْ ۖ وَإِنْ يَكُ كَاذِبًا فَعَلَيْهِ كَذِبُهُ ۖ وَإِنْ يَكُ صَادِقًا يُصِبْكُمْ بَعْضُ الَّذِي يَعِدُكُمْ ۖ إِنَّ اللَّهَ لَا يَهْدِي مَنْ هُوَ مُسْرِفٌ كَذَّابٌ

28 A believing man from Pharaoh's family, who had concealed his faith, said, "Are you going to kill a man for saying, 'My Lord is God,' and he has brought you clear proofs from your Lord? If he is a liar, his lying will rebound upon him; but if he is truthful, then some of what he promises you will befall you. God does not guide the extravagant imposter.

28
40:34

٢٩ يَا قَوْمِ لَكُمُ الْمُلْكُ الْيَوْمَ ظَاهِرِينَ فِي الْأَرْضِ فَمَنْ يَنْصُرُنَا مِنْ بَأْسِ اللَّهِ إِنْ جَاءَنَا ۚ قَالَ فِرْعَوْنُ مَا أُرِيكُمْ إِلَّا مَا أَرَىٰ وَمَا أَهْدِيكُمْ إِلَّا سَبِيلَ الرَّشَادِ

29 O my people! Yours is the dominion today, supreme in the land; but who will help us against God's might, should it fall upon us?" Pharaoh said, "I do not show you except what I see, and I do not guide you except to the path of prudence."

٣٠ وَقَالَ الَّذِي آمَنَ يَا قَوْمِ إِنِّي أَخَافُ عَلَيْكُمْ مِثْلَ يَوْمِ الْأَحْزَابِ

30 The one who had believed said, "O my people, I fear for you the like of the day of the confederates.

٣١ مِثْلَ دَأْبِ قَوْمِ نُوحٍ وَعَادٍ وَثَمُودَ وَالَّذِينَ مِنْ بَعْدِهِمْ ۚ وَمَا اللَّهُ يُرِيدُ ظُلْمًا لِلْعِبَادِ

31 Like the fate of the people of Noah, and 'Ād, and Thamūd, and those after them. God wants no injustice for the servants.

٣٢ وَيَا قَوْمِ إِنِّي أَخَافُ عَلَيْكُمْ يَوْمَ التَّنَادِ

32 O my people, I fear for you the Day of Calling Out.

٣٣ يَوْمَ تُوَلُّونَ مُدْبِرِينَ مَا لَكُمْ مِنَ اللَّهِ مِنْ عَاصِمٍ ۗ وَمَنْ يُضْلِلِ اللَّهُ فَمَا لَهُ مِنْ هَادٍ

33 The Day when you will turn and flee, having no defender against God. Whomever God misguides has no guide."

٣٤ وَلَقَدْ جَاءَكُمْ يُوسُفُ مِنْ قَبْلُ بِالْبَيِّنَاتِ فَمَا زِلْتُمْ فِي شَكٍّ مِمَّا جَاءَكُمْ بِهِ ۖ حَتَّىٰ إِذَا هَلَكَ قُلْتُمْ لَنْ يَبْعَثَ اللَّهُ مِنْ بَعْدِهِ رَسُولًا ۚ كَذَٰلِكَ يُضِلُّ اللَّهُ مَنْ هُوَ مُسْرِفٌ مُرْتَابٌ

34   40:28

34 Joseph had come to you with clear revelations, but you continued to doubt what he came to you with. Until, when he perished, you said, "God will never send a messenger after him." Thus God leads astray the outrageous skeptic.

٣٥ الَّذِينَ يُجَادِلُونَ فِي آيَاتِ اللَّهِ بِغَيْرِ سُلْطَانٍ أَتَاهُمْ ۖ كَبُرَ مَقْتًا عِنْدَ اللَّهِ وَعِنْدَ الَّذِينَ آمَنُوا ۚ كَذَٰلِكَ يَطْبَعُ اللَّهُ عَلَىٰ كُلِّ قَلْبِ مُتَكَبِّرٍ جَبَّارٍ

35   4:69; 40:4, 56, 69; 42:35; 61:3

35 Those who argue against God's revelations, without any proof having come to them—a heinous sin in the sight of God, and of those who believe. Thus God seals the heart of every proud bully.

٣٦ وَقَالَ فِرْعَوْنُ يَا هَامَانُ ابْنِ لِي صَرْحًا لَعَلِّي أَبْلُغُ الْأَسْبَابَ

36   28:38

36 And Pharaoh said, "O Hamaan, build me a tower, that I may reach the pathways.

٣٧ أَسْبَابَ السَّمَاوَاتِ فَأَطَّلِعَ إِلَىٰ إِلَٰهِ مُوسَىٰ وَإِنِّي لَأَظُنُّهُ كَاذِبًا ۚ وَكَذَٰلِكَ زُيِّنَ لِفِرْعَوْنَ سُوءُ عَمَلِهِ وَصُدَّ عَنِ السَّبِيلِ ۚ وَمَا كَيْدُ فِرْعَوْنَ إِلَّا فِي تَبَابٍ

37 The pathways of the heavens, so that I may glance at the God of Moses; though I think he is lying." Thus Pharaoh's evil deeds were made to appear good to him, and he was averted from the path. Pharaoh's guile was only in defeat.

٣٨ وَقَالَ الَّذِي آمَنَ يَا قَوْمِ اتَّبِعُونِ أَهْدِكُمْ سَبِيلَ الرَّشَادِ

38 The one who had believed said, "O my people, follow me, and I will guide you to the path of rectitude."

٣٩ يَا قَوْمِ إِنَّمَا هَٰذِهِ الْحَيَاةُ الدُّنْيَا مَتَاعٌ وَإِنَّ الْآخِرَةَ هِيَ دَارُ الْقَرَارِ

39 "O my people, the life of this world is nothing but fleeting enjoyment, but the Hereafter is the Home of Permanence.

Sūrah 40: Ghāfir

40   4:123; 6:160; 17:43

٤٠ مَنْ عَمِلَ سَيِّئَةً فَلَا يُجْزَىٰ إِلَّا مِثْلَهَا ۖ وَمَنْ عَمِلَ صَالِحًا مِّن ذَكَرٍ أَوْ أُنثَىٰ وَهُوَ مُؤْمِنٌ فَأُولَٰئِكَ يَدْخُلُونَ الْجَنَّةَ يُرْزَقُونَ فِيهَا بِغَيْرِ حِسَابٍ

40 Whoever commits a sin will be repaid only with its like. But whoever works righteousness, whether male or female, and is a believer—these will enter Paradise, where they will be provided for without account.

٤١ وَيَا قَوْمِ مَا لِي أَدْعُوكُمْ إِلَى النَّجَاةِ وَتَدْعُونَنِي إِلَى النَّارِ

41 O my people, how is it that I call you to salvation, and you call me to the Fire?

٤٢ تَدْعُونَنِي لِأَكْفُرَ بِاللَّهِ وَأُشْرِكَ بِهِ مَا لَيْسَ لِي بِهِ عِلْمٌ وَأَنَا أَدْعُوكُمْ إِلَى الْعَزِيزِ الْغَفَّارِ

42 You call me to reject God, and to associate with Him what I have no knowledge of, while I call you to the Mighty Forgiver.

٤٣ لَا جَرَمَ أَنَّمَا تَدْعُونَنِي إِلَيْهِ لَيْسَ لَهُ دَعْوَةٌ فِي الدُّنْيَا وَلَا فِي الْآخِرَةِ وَأَنَّ مَرَدَّنَا إِلَى اللَّهِ وَأَنَّ الْمُسْرِفِينَ هُمْ أَصْحَابُ النَّارِ

43 Without a doubt, what you call me to has no say in this world, or in the Hereafter; and our turning back is to God; and the transgressors are the inmates of the Fire.

٤٤ فَسَتَذْكُرُونَ مَا أَقُولُ لَكُمْ ۚ وَأُفَوِّضُ أَمْرِي إِلَى اللَّهِ ۚ إِنَّ اللَّهَ بَصِيرٌ بِالْعِبَادِ

44 You will remember what I am telling you, so I commit my case to God. God is Observant of the servants."

٤٥ فَوَقَاهُ اللَّهُ سَيِّئَاتِ مَا مَكَرُوا ۖ وَحَاقَ بِآلِ فِرْعَوْنَ سُوءُ الْعَذَابِ

45 So God protected him from the evils of their scheming, while a terrible torment besieged Pharaoh's clan.

46   42:45; 46:20, 34

٤٦ النَّارُ يُعْرَضُونَ عَلَيْهَا غُدُوًّا وَعَشِيًّا ۖ وَيَوْمَ تَقُومُ السَّاعَةُ أَدْخِلُوا آلَ فِرْعَوْنَ أَشَدَّ الْعَذَابِ

46 The Fire. They will be exposed to it morning and evening. And on the Day the Hour takes place: "Admit the clan of Pharaoh to the most intense agony."

47   7:38–39; 14:21–22; 34:31–33; 38:64

٤٧ وَإِذْ يَتَحَاجُّونَ فِي النَّارِ فَيَقُولُ الضُّعَفَاءُ لِلَّذِينَ اسْتَكْبَرُوا إِنَّا كُنَّا لَكُمْ تَبَعًا فَهَلْ أَنتُم مُّغْنُونَ عَنَّا نَصِيبًا مِّنَ النَّارِ

47 As they quarrel in the Fire, the weak will say to those who were arrogant, "We were followers of yours; will you then spare us a portion of the Fire?"

٤٨ قَالَ الَّذِينَ اسْتَكْبَرُوا إِنَّا كُلٌّ فِيهَا إِنَّ اللَّهَ قَدْ حَكَمَ بَيْنَ الْعِبَادِ

48 Those who were arrogant will say, "We are all in it; God has judged between the servants."

٤٩ وَقَالَ الَّذِينَ فِي النَّارِ لِخَزَنَةِ جَهَنَّمَ ادْعُوا رَبَّكُمْ يُخَفِّفْ عَنَّا يَوْمًا مِنَ الْعَذَابِ

49 And those in the Fire will say to the keepers of Hell, "Call to your Lord to lessen our suffering for one day."

49
3:88; 35:36

٥٠ قَالُوا أَوَلَمْ تَكُ تَأْتِيكُمْ رُسُلُكُم بِالْبَيِّنَاتِ ۖ قَالُوا بَلَىٰ ۚ قَالُوا فَادْعُوا ۗ وَمَا دُعَاءُ الْكَافِرِينَ إِلَّا فِي ضَلَالٍ

50 They will say, "Did not your messengers come to you with clear signs?" They will say, "Yes." They will say, "Then pray, but the prayers of the disbelievers will always be in vain."

50
6:130; 17:15; 39:71; 67:8

٥١ إِنَّا لَنَنصُرُ رُسُلَنَا وَالَّذِينَ آمَنُوا فِي الْحَيَاةِ الدُّنْيَا وَيَوْمَ يَقُومُ الْأَشْهَادُ

51 Most surely We will support Our messengers and those who believe, in this life, and on the Day the witnesses arise.

51
37:171–172

٥٢ يَوْمَ لَا يَنفَعُ الظَّالِمِينَ مَعْذِرَتُهُمْ ۖ وَلَهُمُ اللَّعْنَةُ وَلَهُمْ سُوءُ الدَّارِ

52 The Day when their excuses will not profit the wrongdoers, and the curse will be upon them, and they will have the Home of Misery.

52
30:57; 77:35

٥٣ وَلَقَدْ آتَيْنَا مُوسَى الْهُدَىٰ وَأَوْرَثْنَا بَنِي إِسْرَائِيلَ الْكِتَابَ

53 We gave Moses guidance, and made the Children of Israel inherit the Scripture.

53–54
2:53; 5:44; 7:145; 28:43; 32:23; 35:32

٥٤ هُدًى وَذِكْرَىٰ لِأُولِي الْأَلْبَابِ

54 A guide and a reminder for those endowed with reason.

٥٥ فَاصْبِرْ إِنَّ وَعْدَ اللَّهِ حَقٌّ وَاسْتَغْفِرْ لِذَنبِكَ وَسَبِّحْ بِحَمْدِ رَبِّكَ بِالْعَشِيِّ وَالْإِبْكَارِ

55 So be patient. The promise of God is true. And ask forgiveness for your sin, and proclaim the praise of your Lord evening and morning.

٥٦ إِنَّ الَّذِينَ يُجَادِلُونَ فِي آيَاتِ اللَّهِ بِغَيْرِ سُلْطَانٍ أَتَاهُمْ ۙ إِن فِي صُدُورِهِمْ إِلَّا كِبْرٌ مَّا هُم بِبَالِغِيهِ ۚ فَاسْتَعِذْ بِاللَّهِ ۖ إِنَّهُ هُوَ السَّمِيعُ الْبَصِيرُ

56 Those who dispute regarding God's revelations without any authority having come to them—there is nothing in their hearts but the feeling of greatness, which they will never attain. So seek refuge in God; for He is the All-Hearing, the All-Seeing.

56
40:35, 69; 42:35

٥٧ لَخَلْقُ السَّمَاوَاتِ وَالْأَرْضِ أَكْبَرُ مِنْ خَلْقِ النَّاسِ وَلَٰكِنَّ أَكْثَرَ النَّاسِ لَا يَعْلَمُونَ

57 Certainly the creation of the heavens and the earth is greater than the creation of humanity, but most people do not know.

57
37:11; 79:27

٥٨ وَمَا يَسْتَوِي الْأَعْمَىٰ وَالْبَصِيرُ وَالَّذِينَ آمَنُوا وَعَمِلُوا الصَّالِحَاتِ وَلَا الْمُسِيءُ ۚ قَلِيلًا مَّا تَتَذَكَّرُونَ

58 Not equal are the blind and the seeing. Nor are those who believe and work righteousness equal to the sinners. How little you reflect.

58
6:50

٥٩ إِنَّ السَّاعَةَ لَآتِيَةٌ لَا رَيْبَ فِيهَا وَلَٰكِنَّ أَكْثَرَ النَّاسِ لَا يُؤْمِنُونَ

59 Indeed, the Hour is coming; there is no doubt about it; but most people do not believe.

59
15:85; 22:7; 25:11

٦٠ وَقَالَ رَبُّكُمُ ادْعُونِي أَسْتَجِبْ لَكُمْ ۚ إِنَّ الَّذِينَ يَسْتَكْبِرُونَ عَنْ عِبَادَتِي سَيَدْخُلُونَ جَهَنَّمَ دَاخِرِينَ

60 Your Lord has said, "Pray to Me, and I will respond to you. But those who are too proud to worship Me will enter Hell forcibly."

2:186

٦١ اللَّهُ الَّذِي جَعَلَ لَكُمُ اللَّيْلَ لِتَسْكُنُوا فِيهِ وَالنَّهَارَ مُبْصِرًا ۚ إِنَّ اللَّهَ لَذُو فَضْلٍ عَلَى النَّاسِ وَلَٰكِنَّ أَكْثَرَ النَّاسِ لَا يَشْكُرُونَ

61 It is God Who made the night for you, that you may rest therein; and the day allowing sight. God is gracious towards the people, but most people do not give thanks.

2:243; 10:67; 10:60; 17:12; 25:47; 27:73

٦٢ ذَٰلِكُمُ اللَّهُ رَبُّكُمْ خَالِقُ كُلِّ شَيْءٍ لَا إِلَٰهَ إِلَّا هُوَ ۖ فَأَنَّىٰ تُؤْفَكُونَ

62 Such is God, your Lord, Creator of all things. There is no god except Him; so how could you turn away?

٦٣ كَذَٰلِكَ يُؤْفَكُ الَّذِينَ كَانُوا بِآيَاتِ اللَّهِ يَجْحَدُونَ

63 Thus are turned away those who dispute the signs of God.

٦٤ اللَّهُ الَّذِي جَعَلَ لَكُمُ الْأَرْضَ قَرَارًا وَالسَّمَاءَ بِنَاءً وَصَوَّرَكُمْ فَأَحْسَنَ صُوَرَكُمْ وَرَزَقَكُمْ مِنَ الطَّيِّبَاتِ ۚ ذَٰلِكُمُ اللَّهُ رَبُّكُمْ ۖ فَتَبَارَكَ اللَّهُ رَبُّ الْعَالَمِينَ

64 It is God who made the earth a habitat for you, and the sky a structure. And He designed you, and designed you well; and He provided you with the good things. Such is God, your Lord; so Blessed is God, Lord of the Worlds.

2:22; 27:61; 50:6; 51:47; 64:3

٦٥ هُوَ الْحَيُّ لَا إِلَٰهَ إِلَّا هُوَ فَادْعُوهُ مُخْلِصِينَ لَهُ الدِّينَ ۗ الْحَمْدُ لِلَّهِ رَبِّ الْعَالَمِينَ

65 He is the Living One. There is no god except He. So pray to Him, devoting your religion to Him. Praise be to God, the Lord of the Worlds.

٦٦ قُلْ إِنِّي نُهِيتُ أَنْ أَعْبُدَ الَّذِينَ تَدْعُونَ مِنْ دُونِ اللَّهِ لَمَّا جَاءَنِيَ الْبَيِّنَاتُ مِنْ رَبِّي وَأُمِرْتُ أَنْ أُسْلِمَ لِرَبِّ الْعَالَمِينَ

66 Say, "I was prohibited from worshiping those you invoke besides God, now that clear revelations have come to me from my Lord; and I was commanded to submit to the Lord of the Worlds."

6:56

٦٧ هُوَ الَّذِي خَلَقَكُمْ مِنْ تُرَابٍ ثُمَّ مِنْ نُطْفَةٍ ثُمَّ مِنْ عَلَقَةٍ ثُمَّ يُخْرِجُكُمْ طِفْلًا ثُمَّ لِتَبْلُغُوا أَشُدَّكُمْ ثُمَّ لِتَكُونُوا شُيُوخًا ۚ وَمِنْكُمْ مَنْ يُتَوَفَّىٰ مِنْ قَبْلُ ۖ وَلِتَبْلُغُوا أَجَلًا مُسَمًّى وَلَعَلَّكُمْ تَعْقِلُونَ

67 It is He who created you from dust, then from a seed, then from an embryo, then He brings you out as an infant, then He lets you reach your maturity, then you become elderly—although some of you die sooner—so that you may reach a predetermined age, so that you may understand.

18:37; 22:5

٦٨ هُوَ الَّذِي يُحْيِي وَيُمِيتُ ۖ فَإِذَا قَضَىٰ أَمْرًا فَإِنَّمَا يَقُولُ لَهُ كُنْ فَيَكُونُ

68 It is He who gives life and death; and when He decides on a thing, He just says to it, "Be," and it comes to be.

2:117; 3:47; 16:40; 19:35; 36:82

٦٩ أَلَمْ تَرَ إِلَى الَّذِينَ يُجَادِلُونَ فِي آيَاتِ اللَّهِ أَنَّىٰ يُصْرَفُونَ

69 Have you not observed those who dispute regarding God's revelations, how they have deviated?

69
40:35, 56; 42:35

٧٠ الَّذِينَ كَذَّبُوا بِالْكِتَابِ وَبِمَا أَرْسَلْنَا بِهِ رُسُلَنَا ۖ فَسَوْفَ يَعْلَمُونَ

70 Those who call the Book a lie, and what We sent Our messengers with—they will surely know.

٧١ إِذِ الْأَغْلَالُ فِي أَعْنَاقِهِمْ وَالسَّلَاسِلُ يُسْحَبُونَ

71 When the yokes are around their necks, and they will be dragged by the chains.

71
13:5

٧٢ فِي الْحَمِيمِ ثُمَّ فِي النَّارِ يُسْجَرُونَ

72 Into the boiling water, then in the Fire they will be consumed.

٧٣ ثُمَّ قِيلَ لَهُمْ أَيْنَ مَا كُنتُمْ تُشْرِكُونَ

73 Then it will be said to them, "Where are those you used to deify?

73
6:22; 7:37; 28:74; 41:47

٧٤ مِن دُونِ اللَّهِ ۖ قَالُوا ضَلُّوا عَنَّا بَل لَّمْ نَكُن نَّدْعُو مِن قَبْلُ شَيْئًا ۚ كَذَٰلِكَ يُضِلُّ اللَّهُ الْكَافِرِينَ

74 Instead of God?" They will say, "They have abandoned us. In fact, we were praying to nothing before." Thus God sends the disbelievers astray.

٧٥ ذَٰلِكُم بِمَا كُنتُمْ تَفْرَحُونَ فِي الْأَرْضِ بِغَيْرِ الْحَقِّ وَبِمَا كُنتُمْ تَمْرَحُونَ

75 That is because you used to rejoice on earth in other than the truth, and because you used to behave with vanity.

75
17:37; 31:18; 57:23

٧٦ ادْخُلُوا أَبْوَابَ جَهَنَّمَ خَالِدِينَ فِيهَا ۖ فَبِئْسَ مَثْوَى الْمُتَكَبِّرِينَ

76 Enter the gates of Hell, to remain therein forever. What a terrible dwelling for the arrogant.

76
15:43–44; 16:29; 23:76; 39:72

٧٧ فَاصْبِرْ إِنَّ وَعْدَ اللَّهِ حَقٌّ ۚ فَإِمَّا نُرِيَنَّكَ بَعْضَ الَّذِي نَعِدُهُمْ أَوْ نَتَوَفَّيَنَّكَ فَإِلَيْنَا يُرْجَعُونَ

77 So be patient. The promise of God is true. Whether We show you some of what We have promised them, or take you to Us, to Us they will be returned.

٧٨ وَلَقَدْ أَرْسَلْنَا رُسُلًا مِّن قَبْلِكَ مِنْهُم مَّن قَصَصْنَا عَلَيْكَ وَمِنْهُم مَّن لَّمْ نَقْصُصْ عَلَيْكَ ۗ وَمَا كَانَ لِرَسُولٍ أَن يَأْتِيَ بِآيَةٍ إِلَّا بِإِذْنِ اللَّهِ ۚ[a] فَإِذَا جَاءَ أَمْرُ اللَّهِ قُضِيَ بِالْحَقِّ وَخَسِرَ هُنَالِكَ الْمُبْطِلُونَ[b]

78 We sent messengers before you. Some of them We told you about, and some We did not tell you about. No messenger can bring a miracle except by leave of God. Then, when the command of God is issued, fair judgment will be passed, and there and then the seekers of vanity will lose.

78
[a] 4:164; 14:9; 25:38
[b] 16:1; 39:69

٧٩ اللَّهُ الَّذِي جَعَلَ لَكُمُ الْأَنْعَامَ لِتَرْكَبُوا مِنْهَا وَمِنْهَا تَأْكُلُونَ

79 God is He who created the domestic animals for you—some for you to ride, and some you eat.

79
16:5; 23:21; 43:12

٨٠ وَلَكُمْ فِيهَا مَنَافِعُ وَلِتَبْلُغُوا عَلَيْهَا حَاجَةً فِي صُدُورِكُمْ وَعَلَيْهَا وَعَلَى الْفُلْكِ تُحْمَلُونَ

80 And in them you have other benefits as well, and through them you satisfy your needs. And on them, and on the ships, you are transported.

80 — 23:22

٨١ وَيُرِيكُمْ آيَاتِهِ فَأَيَّ آيَاتِ اللَّهِ تُنكِرُونَ

81 And He shows you His signs. So which of God's signs will you deny?

٨٢ أَفَلَمْ يَسِيرُوا فِي الْأَرْضِ فَيَنظُرُوا كَيْفَ كَانَ عَاقِبَةُ الَّذِينَ مِن قَبْلِهِمْ ۚ كَانُوا أَكْثَرَ مِنْهُمْ وَأَشَدَّ قُوَّةً وَآثَارًا فِي الْأَرْضِ فَمَا أَغْنَىٰ عَنْهُم مَّا كَانُوا يَكْسِبُونَ

82 Have they not journeyed through the land, and seen the outcome for those before them? They were more numerous than they, and had greater power and influence in the land. But what they had achieved availed them nothing.

82 — 30:9; 40:21

٨٣ فَلَمَّا جَاءَتْهُمْ رُسُلُهُم بِالْبَيِّنَاتِ فَرِحُوا بِمَا عِندَهُم مِّنَ الْعِلْمِ وَحَاقَ بِهِم مَّا كَانُوا بِهِ يَسْتَهْزِئُونَ

83 When their messengers came to them with clear proofs, they rejoiced in the knowledge they had, and the very things they used to ridicule besieged them.

83 — 6:10

٨٤ فَلَمَّا رَأَوْا بَأْسَنَا قَالُوا آمَنَّا بِاللَّهِ وَحْدَهُ وَكَفَرْنَا بِمَا كُنَّا بِهِ مُشْرِكِينَ

84 Then, when they witnessed Our might, they said, "We believe in God alone, and we reject what we used to associate with Him."

٨٥ فَلَمْ يَكُ يَنفَعُهُمْ إِيمَانُهُمْ لَمَّا رَأَوْا بَأْسَنَا ۖ سُنَّتَ اللَّهِ الَّتِي قَدْ خَلَتْ فِي عِبَادِهِ ۖ وَخَسِرَ هُنَالِكَ الْكَافِرُونَ

85 But their faith could not help them once they witnessed Our might. This has been God's way of dealing with His servants. And there and then the disbelievers lost.

85 — 6:158

Sūrah 41: Fuṣṣilat

سُورَةُ فُصِّلَت (Detailed)

بِسْمِ اللَّهِ الرَّحْمَٰنِ الرَّحِيمِ

١ حم

1 Hā', Mīm.

٢ تَنزِيلٌ مِّنَ الرَّحْمَٰنِ الرَّحِيمِ

2 A revelation from the Most Gracious, the Most Merciful.

٣ كِتَابٌ فُصِّلَتْ آيَاتُهُ قُرْآنًا عَرَبِيًّا لِقَوْمٍ يَعْلَمُونَ ᵇ

3 A Scripture whose Verses are detailed, a Qur'an in Arabic for people who know.

3
ᵃ 6:97, 114; 7:52; 11:1; 41:44
ᵇ 12:2; 28:39

٤ بَشِيرًا وَنَذِيرًا فَأَعْرَضَ أَكْثَرُهُمْ فَهُمْ لَا يَسْمَعُونَ

4 Bringing good news, and giving warnings. But most of them turn away, so they do not listen.

4
17:49; 18:57

٥ وَقَالُوا قُلُوبُنَا فِي أَكِنَّةٍ مِمَّا تَدْعُونَا إِلَيْهِ وَفِي آذَانِنَا وَقْرٌ وَمِنْ بَيْنِنَا وَبَيْنِكَ حِجَابٌ فَاعْمَلْ إِنَّنَا عَامِلُونَ

5 And they say, "Our hearts are screened from what you call us to, and in our ears is deafness, and between us and you is a barrier. So do what you want, and so will we."

5
6:25; 17:96; 36:9; 41:26

٦ قُلْ إِنَّمَا أَنَا بَشَرٌ مِثْلُكُمْ يُوحَى إِلَيَّ أَنَّمَا إِلَهُكُمْ إِلَهٌ وَاحِدٌ فَاسْتَقِيمُوا إِلَيْهِ وَاسْتَغْفِرُوهُ ۗ وَوَيْلٌ لِلْمُشْرِكِينَ

6 Say, "I am only a human like you; it is inspired in me that your God is One God. So be upright towards Him, and seek forgiveness from Him." And woe to the idolaters.

6
18:110; 21:108

٧ الَّذِينَ لَا يُؤْتُونَ الزَّكَاةَ وَهُمْ بِالْآخِرَةِ هُمْ كَافِرُونَ

7 Those who do not pay the alms; and regarding the Hereafter, they are disbelievers.

٨ إِنَّ الَّذِينَ آمَنُوا وَعَمِلُوا الصَّالِحَاتِ لَهُمْ أَجْرٌ غَيْرُ مَمْنُونٍ

8 As for those who believe and do righteous deeds—for them is a reward uninterrupted.

8
11:108; 84:25; 95:6

٩ قُلْ أَئِنَّكُمْ لَتَكْفُرُونَ بِالَّذِي خَلَقَ الْأَرْضَ فِي يَوْمَيْنِ وَتَجْعَلُونَ لَهُ أَنْدَادًا ۚ ذَٰلِكَ رَبُّ الْعَالَمِينَ

9 Say, "Do you reject the One who created the earth in two days? And you attribute equals to Him? That is the Lord of the Universe."

9
14:30

١٠ وَجَعَلَ فِيهَا رَوَاسِيَ مِنْ فَوْقِهَا وَبَارَكَ فِيهَا وَقَدَّرَ فِيهَا أَقْوَاتَهَا فِي أَرْبَعَةِ أَيَّامٍ سَوَاءً لِلسَّائِلِينَ

10 He placed stabilizers over it; and blessed it; and planned its provisions in four days, equally to the seekers.

10
13:3; 16:15; 77:27

١١ ثُمَّ اسْتَوَىٰ إِلَى السَّمَاءِ وَهِيَ دُخَانٌ فَقَالَ لَهَا وَلِلْأَرْضِ ائْتِيَا طَوْعًا أَوْ كَرْهًا قَالَتَا أَتَيْنَا طَائِعِينَ

11 Then He turned to the sky, and it was smoke, and said to it and to the earth, "Come, willingly or unwillingly." They said, "We come willingly."

11–12
2:29

١٢ فَقَضَاهُنَّ سَبْعَ سَمَاوَاتٍ فِي يَوْمَيْنِ وَأَوْحَىٰ فِي كُلِّ سَمَاءٍ أَمْرَهَا ۚ وَزَيَّنَّا السَّمَاءَ الدُّنْيَا بِمَصَابِيحَ وَحِفْظًا ۚ ذَٰلِكَ تَقْدِيرُ الْعَزِيزِ الْعَلِيمِ

12 So He completed them as seven universes in two days, and He assigned to each universe its laws. And We decorated the lower universe with lamps, and for protection. That is the design of the Almighty, the All-Knowing.

١٣ فَإِنْ أَعْرَضُوا فَقُلْ أَنْذَرْتُكُمْ صَاعِقَةً مِثْلَ صَاعِقَةِ عَادٍ وَثَمُودَ	13 11:2	

13 But if they turn away, say, "I have warned you of a thunderbolt, like the thunderbolt of 'Ād and Thamūd."

١٤ إِذْ جَاءَتْهُمُ الرُّسُلُ مِنْ بَيْنِ أَيْدِيهِمْ وَمِنْ خَلْفِهِمْ أَلَّا تَعْبُدُوا إِلَّا اللَّهَ ۖ قَالُوا لَوْ شَاءَ رَبُّنَا لَأَنْزَلَ مَلَائِكَةً فَإِنَّا بِمَا أُرْسِلْتُمْ بِهِ كَافِرُونَ	14 46:21	

14 Their messengers came to them, from before them and from behind them, saying, "Do not worship anyone but God." They said, "Had our Lord willed, He would have sent down angels; Therefore, we reject what you are sent with."

١٥ فَأَمَّا عَادٌ فَاسْتَكْبَرُوا فِي الْأَرْضِ بِغَيْرِ الْحَقِّ وَقَالُوا مَنْ أَشَدُّ مِنَّا قُوَّةً ۖ أَوَلَمْ يَرَوْا أَنَّ اللَّهَ الَّذِي خَلَقَهُمْ هُوَ أَشَدُّ مِنْهُمْ قُوَّةً ۖ وَكَانُوا بِآيَاتِنَا يَجْحَدُونَ	15 28:39; 46:20	

15 As for 'Ād, they turned arrogant on earth, and opposed justice, and said, "Who is more powerful than us?" Have they not considered that God, who created them, is more powerful than they? And they went on denying Our revelations.

١٦ فَأَرْسَلْنَا عَلَيْهِمْ رِيحًا صَرْصَرًا فِي أَيَّامٍ نَحِسَاتٍ لِنُذِيقَهُمْ عَذَابَ الْخِزْيِ فِي الْحَيَاةِ الدُّنْيَا ۖ وَلَعَذَابُ الْآخِرَةِ أَخْزَىٰ ۖ وَهُمْ لَا يُنْصَرُونَ	16 46:24; 51:41; 54:19; 69:6	

16 So We unleashed upon them a screaming wind, for a few miserable days, to make them taste the punishment of shame in this life; but the punishment of the Hereafter is more shameful; and they will not be saved.

١٧ وَأَمَّا ثَمُودُ فَهَدَيْنَاهُمْ فَاسْتَحَبُّوا الْعَمَىٰ عَلَى الْهُدَىٰa فَأَخَذَتْهُمْ صَاعِقَةُ الْعَذَابِ الْهُونِ بِمَا كَانُوا يَكْسِبُونَb	17 a 51:43–44 b 41:31	

17 And as for Thamūd, We guided them, but they preferred blindness over guidance. So the thunderbolt of the humiliating punishment seized them, because of what they used to earn.

١٨ وَنَجَّيْنَا الَّذِينَ آمَنُوا وَكَانُوا يَتَّقُونَ		

18 And We saved those who believed and were righteous.

١٩ وَيَوْمَ يُحْشَرُ أَعْدَاءُ اللَّهِ إِلَى النَّارِ فَهُمْ يُوزَعُونَ	19 2:98; 8:60; 41:28	

19 The Day when God's enemies are herded into the Fire, forcibly.

٢٠ حَتَّىٰ إِذَا مَا جَاءُوهَا شَهِدَ عَلَيْهِمْ سَمْعُهُمْ وَأَبْصَارُهُمْ وَجُلُودُهُمْ بِمَا كَانُوا يَعْمَلُونَ	20–22 24:24; 36:65	

20 Until, when they have reached it, their hearing, and their sight, and their skins will testify against them regarding what they used to do.

٢١ وَقَالُوا لِجُلُودِهِمْ لِمَ شَهِدْتُمْ عَلَيْنَا ۖ قَالُوا أَنْطَقَنَا اللَّهُ الَّذِي أَنْطَقَ كُلَّ شَيْءٍ وَهُوَ خَلَقَكُمْ أَوَّلَ مَرَّةٍ وَإِلَيْهِ تُرْجَعُونَ		

21 And they will say to their skins, "Why did you testify against us?" They will say, "God, Who made all things speak, made us speak. It is He who created you the first time, and to Him you are returned."

٢٢ وَمَا كُنتُمْ تَسْتَتِرُونَ أَن يَشْهَدَ عَلَيْكُمْ سَمْعُكُمْ وَلَا أَبْصَارُكُمْ وَلَا جُلُودُكُمْ وَلَٰكِن ظَنَنتُمْ أَنَّ اللَّهَ لَا يَعْلَمُ كَثِيرًا مِّمَّا تَعْمَلُونَ

22 You were unable to hide yourselves from your hearing, and your sight, and your skins, to prevent them from testifying against you, and you imagined that God was unaware of much of what you do. *(38:27)*

٢٣ وَذَٰلِكُمْ ظَنُّكُمُ الَّذِي ظَنَنتُم بِرَبِّكُمْ أَرْدَاكُمْ فَأَصْبَحْتُم مِّنَ الْخَاسِرِينَ

23 It is that thought of yours about your Lord that led you to ruin—so you became of the losers.

٢٤ فَإِن يَصْبِرُوا فَالنَّارُ مَثْوًى لَّهُمْ ۖ وَإِن يَسْتَعْتِبُوا فَمَا هُم مِّنَ الْمُعْتَبِينَ

24 If they endure patiently, the Fire will be their residence; and if they make up excuses, they will not be pardoned. *(14:21; 52:16)*

٢٥ وَقَيَّضْنَا لَهُمْ قُرَنَاءَ فَزَيَّنُوا لَهُم مَّا بَيْنَ أَيْدِيهِمْ وَمَا خَلْفَهُمْ وَحَقَّ عَلَيْهِمُ الْقَوْلُ فِي أُمَمٍ قَدْ خَلَتْ مِن قَبْلِهِم مِّنَ الْجِنِّ وَالْإِنسِ ۖ إِنَّهُمْ كَانُوا خَاسِرِينَ

25 We had assigned companions for them, who glamorized to them what was in front of them, and what was behind them. And the Word proved true against them in communities of jinn and humans that have passed away before them. They were losers. *(46:18; 50:23, 27)*

٢٦ وَقَالَ الَّذِينَ كَفَرُوا لَا تَسْمَعُوا لِهَٰذَا الْقُرْآنِ وَالْغَوْا فِيهِ لَعَلَّكُمْ تَغْلِبُونَ

26 Those who disbelieve say, "Do not listen to this Qur'an, and talk over it, so that you may prevail."

٢٧ فَلَنُذِيقَنَّ الَّذِينَ كَفَرُوا عَذَابًا شَدِيدًا وَلَنَجْزِيَنَّهُمْ أَسْوَأَ الَّذِي كَانُوا يَعْمَلُونَ

27 We will make those who disbelieve taste an intense agony, and We will recompense them according to the worst of what they used to do. *(30:10)*

٢٨ ذَٰلِكَ جَزَاءُ أَعْدَاءِ اللَّهِ النَّارُ ۖ لَهُمْ فِيهَا دَارُ الْخُلْدِ ۖ جَزَاءً بِمَا كَانُوا بِآيَاتِنَا يَجْحَدُونَ

28 Such is the recompense of God's enemies—the Fire—where they will have their permanent home, in recompense for having disregarded Our revelations. *(41:19)*

٢٩ وَقَالَ الَّذِينَ كَفَرُوا رَبَّنَا أَرِنَا اللَّذَيْنِ أَضَلَّانَا مِنَ الْجِنِّ وَالْإِنسِ نَجْعَلْهُمَا تَحْتَ أَقْدَامِنَا لِيَكُونَا مِنَ الْأَسْفَلِينَ

29 Those who disbelieved will say, "Our Lord, show us those who led us astray—among jinn and humans—and we will trample them under our feet, so they become of the lowest." *(7:38)*

٣٠ إِنَّ الَّذِينَ قَالُوا رَبُّنَا اللَّهُ ثُمَّ اسْتَقَامُوا تَتَنَزَّلُ عَلَيْهِمُ الْمَلَائِكَةُ أَلَّا تَخَافُوا وَلَا تَحْزَنُوا وَأَبْشِرُوا بِالْجَنَّةِ الَّتِي كُنتُمْ تُوعَدُونَ

30 Surely, those who say: "Our Lord is God," and then go straight, the angels will descend upon them: "Do not fear, and do not grieve, but rejoice in the news of the Garden which you were promised. *(19:64; 46:13; 97:4)*

٣١ نَحْنُ أَوْلِيَاؤُكُمْ فِي الْحَيَاةِ الدُّنْيَا وَفِي الْآخِرَةِ ۖ وَلَكُمْ فِيهَا مَا تَشْتَهِي أَنْفُسُكُمْ وَلَكُمْ فِيهَا مَا تَدَّعُونَ

31 We are your allies in this life and in the Hereafter, wherein you will have whatever your souls desire, and you will have therein whatever you call for.

٣٢ نُزُلًا مِنْ غَفُورٍ رَحِيمٍ

32 As Hospitality from an All-Forgiving, Merciful One."

٣٣ وَمَنْ أَحْسَنُ قَوْلًا مِمَّنْ دَعَا إِلَى اللَّهِ وَعَمِلَ صَالِحًا وَقَالَ إِنَّنِي مِنَ الْمُسْلِمِينَ

33 And who is better in speech than someone who calls to God, and acts with integrity, and says, "I am of those who submit"?

٣٤ وَلَا تَسْتَوِي الْحَسَنَةُ وَلَا السَّيِّئَةُ ۚ ادْفَعْ بِالَّتِي هِيَ أَحْسَنُ فَإِذَا الَّذِي بَيْنَكَ وَبَيْنَهُ عَدَاوَةٌ كَأَنَّهُ وَلِيٌّ حَمِيمٌ

34
16:125; 23:96

34 Good and evil are not equal. Repel evil with good, and the person who was your enemy becomes like an intimate friend.

٣٥ وَمَا يُلَقَّاهَا إِلَّا الَّذِينَ صَبَرُوا وَمَا يُلَقَّاهَا إِلَّا ذُو حَظٍّ عَظِيمٍ

35
16:127; 28:79

35 But none will attain it except those who persevere, and none will attain it except the very fortunate.

٣٦ وَإِمَّا يَنْزَغَنَّكَ مِنَ الشَّيْطَانِ نَزْغٌ فَاسْتَعِذْ بِاللَّهِ ۖ إِنَّهُ هُوَ السَّمِيعُ الْعَلِيمُ

36
pp.: 7:200–201

36 When a temptation from the Devil provokes you, seek refuge in God; He is the Hearer, the Knower.

٣٧ وَمِنْ آيَاتِهِ اللَّيْلُ وَالنَّهَارُ وَالشَّمْسُ وَالْقَمَرُ ۚ لَا تَسْجُدُوا لِلشَّمْسِ وَلَا لِلْقَمَرِ وَاسْجُدُوا لِلَّهِ الَّذِي خَلَقَهُنَّ إِنْ كُنْتُمْ إِيَّاهُ تَعْبُدُونَ

37
27:24–25

37 And of His signs are the night and the day, and the sun and the moon. Do not bow down to the sun, nor to the moon, but bow down to God, Who created them both, if it is Him that you serve.

٣٨ فَإِنِ اسْتَكْبَرُوا فَالَّذِينَ عِنْدَ رَبِّكَ يُسَبِّحُونَ لَهُ بِاللَّيْلِ وَالنَّهَارِ وَهُمْ لَا يَسْأَمُونَ ۩

38
7:206; 21:19–20

38 But if they are too proud—those in the presence of your Lord praise Him night and day, and without ever tiring.

٣٩ وَمِنْ آيَاتِهِ أَنَّكَ تَرَى الْأَرْضَ خَاشِعَةً فَإِذَا أَنْزَلْنَا عَلَيْهَا الْمَاءَ اهْتَزَّتْ وَرَبَتْ ۚ إِنَّ الَّذِي أَحْيَاهَا لَمُحْيِي الْمَوْتَىٰ ۚ إِنَّهُ عَلَىٰ كُلِّ شَيْءٍ قَدِيرٌ

39
22:61; 30:50

39 And of His signs is that you see the land still. But when We send down water upon it, it stirs and grows. Surely, He Who revived it will revive the dead. He is Able to do all things.

٤٠ إِنَّ الَّذِينَ يُلْحِدُونَ فِي آيَاتِنَا لَا يَخْفَوْنَ عَلَيْنَا ۗ أَفَمَنْ يُلْقَىٰ فِي النَّارِ خَيْرٌ أَمْ مَنْ يَأْتِي آمِنًا يَوْمَ الْقِيَامَةِ ۚ اعْمَلُوا مَا شِئْتُمْ ۖ إِنَّهُ بِمَا تَعْمَلُونَ بَصِيرٌ

40
15:15

40 Those who despise Our revelations are not hidden from Us. Is he who is hurled into the Fire better? Or he who arrives safely on the Day of Resurrection? Do as you please; He is Seeing of everything you do.

٤١ إِنَّ الَّذِينَ كَفَرُوا بِالذِّكْرِ لَمَّا جَاءَهُمْ ۖ وَإِنَّهُ لَكِتَابٌ عَزِيزٌ

41 Those who reject the Reminder when it has come to them—it is an invincible Book.

٤٢ لَا يَأْتِيهِ الْبَاطِلُ مِن بَيْنِ يَدَيْهِ وَلَا مِنْ خَلْفِهِ ۖ تَنزِيلٌ مِّنْ حَكِيمٍ حَمِيدٍ

42 Falsehood cannot approach it, from before it or behind it. It is a revelation from One Wise and Praiseworthy.

٤٣ مَّا يُقَالُ لَكَ إِلَّا مَا قَدْ قِيلَ لِلرُّسُلِ مِن قَبْلِكَ ۚ إِنَّ رَبَّكَ لَذُو مَغْفِرَةٍ وَذُو عِقَابٍ أَلِيمٍ

43   5:98; 6:165; 7:167

43 Nothing is said to you but was said to the Messengers before you: your Lord is Possessor of Forgiveness, and Possessor of Painful Repayment.

٤٤ وَلَوْ جَعَلْنَاهُ قُرْآنًا أَعْجَمِيًّا لَّقَالُوا لَوْلَا فُصِّلَتْ آيَاتُهُ ۖ أَأَعْجَمِيٌّ وَعَرَبِيٌّ ۗ قُلْ هُوَ لِلَّذِينَ آمَنُوا هُدًى وَشِفَاءٌ ۖ وَالَّذِينَ لَا يُؤْمِنُونَ فِي آذَانِهِمْ وَقْرٌ وَهُوَ عَلَيْهِمْ عَمًى ۚ أُولَٰئِكَ يُنَادَوْنَ مِن مَّكَانٍ بَعِيدٍ

44   12:2; 16:103; 26:195; 41:3

44 Had We made it a Qur'an in a foreign language, they would have said, "If only its verses were made clear." Non-Arabic and an Arab? Say, "For those who believe, it is guidance and healing. But as for those who do not believe: there is heaviness in their ears, and it is blindness for them. These are being called from a distant place."

٤٥ وَلَقَدْ آتَيْنَا مُوسَى الْكِتَابَ فَاخْتُلِفَ فِيهِ ۗ وَلَوْلَا كَلِمَةٌ سَبَقَتْ مِن رَّبِّكَ لَقُضِيَ بَيْنَهُمْ ۚ وَإِنَّهُمْ لَفِي شَكٍّ مِّنْهُ مُرِيبٍ

45   11:110

45 We gave Moses the Book, but disputes arose concerning it. Were it not for a prior decree from your Lord, judgment would have been pronounced between them. But they are in perplexing doubt concerning it.

٤٦ مَّنْ عَمِلَ صَالِحًا فَلِنَفْسِهِ ۖ وَمَنْ أَسَاءَ فَعَلَيْهَا ۗ وَمَا رَبُّكَ بِظَلَّامٍ لِّلْعَبِيدِ

46   17:7; 27:40; 30:44; 41:7; 45:15

46 Whoever acts righteously does so for himself; and whoever works evil does so against himself. Your Lord is not unjust to the servants.

٤٧ إِلَيْهِ يُرَدُّ عِلْمُ السَّاعَةِ ۚ وَمَا تَخْرُجُ مِن ثَمَرَاتٍ مِّنْ أَكْمَامِهَا وَمَا تَحْمِلُ مِنْ أُنثَىٰ وَلَا تَضَعُ إِلَّا بِعِلْمِهِ ۚ وَيَوْمَ يُنَادِيهِمْ أَيْنَ شُرَكَائِي قَالُوا آذَنَّاكَ مَا مِنَّا مِن شَهِيدٍ

47   6:59; 7:187; 13:8; 35:11

47 To Him is referred the knowledge of the Hour. No fruit emerges from its sheath, and no female conceives or delivers, except with His knowledge. And on the Day when He calls out to them, "Where are My associates?" They will say, "We admit to you, none of us is a witness."

٤٨ وَضَلَّ عَنْهُم مَّا كَانُوا يَدْعُونَ مِن قَبْلُ ۖ وَظَنُّوا مَا لَهُم مِّن مَّحِيصٍ

48 What they used to pray to before will forsake them, and they will realize that they have no escape.

٤٩ لَا يَسْأَمُ الْإِنسَانُ مِن دُعَاءِ الْخَيْرِ وَإِن مَّسَّهُ الشَّرُّ فَيَئُوسٌ قَنُوطٌ

49   11:9; 17:83; 70:20

49 The human being never tires of praying for good things; but when adversity afflicts him, he despairs and loses hope.

٥٠ وَلَئِنْ أَذَقْنَاهُ رَحْمَةً مِنَّا مِنْ بَعْدِ ضَرَّاءَ مَسَّتْهُ لَيَقُولَنَّ هَذَا لِي وَمَا أَظُنُّ السَّاعَةَ قَائِمَةً وَلَئِنْ رُجِعْتُ إِلَىٰ رَبِّي إِنَّ لِي عِنْدَهُ لَلْحُسْنَىٰ ۚ فَلَنُنَبِّئَنَّ الَّذِينَ كَفَرُوا بِمَا عَمِلُوا وَلَنُذِيقَنَّهُمْ مِنْ عَذَابٍ غَلِيظٍ

50–51
10:12; 17:83; 18:36

50 And when We let him taste a mercy from Us, after the adversity that had afflicted him, he will say, "This is mine, and I do not think that the Hour is coming; and even if I am returned to my Lord, I will have the very best with Him." We will inform those who disbelieve of what they did, and We will make them taste an awful punishment.

٥١ وَإِذَا أَنْعَمْنَا عَلَى الْإِنْسَانِ أَعْرَضَ وَنَأَىٰ بِجَانِبِهِ وَإِذَا مَسَّهُ الشَّرُّ فَذُو دُعَاءٍ عَرِيضٍ

51
10:12

51 When We provide comfort for the human being, he withdraws and distances himself; but when adversity befalls him, he starts lengthy prayers.

٥٢ قُلْ أَرَأَيْتُمْ إِنْ كَانَ مِنْ عِنْدِ اللَّهِ ثُمَّ كَفَرْتُمْ بِهِ مَنْ أَضَلُّ مِمَّنْ هُوَ فِي شِقَاقٍ بَعِيدٍ

52
46:10

52 Say, "Have you considered? If it is from God and you reject it—who is further astray than he who is cutoff and alienated?"

٥٣ سَنُرِيهِمْ آيَاتِنَا فِي الْآفَاقِ وَفِي أَنْفُسِهِمْ حَتَّىٰ يَتَبَيَّنَ لَهُمْ أَنَّهُ الْحَقُّ ۗ أَوَلَمْ يَكْفِ بِرَبِّكَ أَنَّهُ عَلَىٰ كُلِّ شَيْءٍ شَهِيدٌ

53
51:20

53 We will show them Our proofs on the horizons, and in their very souls, until it becomes clear to them that it is the truth. Is it not sufficient that your Lord is witness over everything?

٥٤ أَلَا إِنَّهُمْ فِي مِرْيَةٍ مِنْ لِقَاءِ رَبِّهِمْ ۗ أَلَا إِنَّهُ بِكُلِّ شَيْءٍ مُحِيطٌ

54
32:23

54 Surely they are in doubt about the encounter with their Lord. Surely He comprehends everything.

Sūrah 42: Al-Shūrā

سُورَةُ ٱلشُّورَىٰ (Consultation)

بِسْمِ ٱللَّهِ ٱلرَّحْمَٰنِ ٱلرَّحِيمِ

١ حم

1 Ḥā', Mīm.

٢ عسق

2 'Ayn, Sīn, Qāf.

٣ كَذَٰلِكَ يُوحِي إِلَيْكَ وَإِلَى الَّذِينَ مِنْ قَبْلِكَ اللَّهُ الْعَزِيزُ الْحَكِيمُ

3
39:65

3 Thus He inspires you, and those before you—God the Almighty, the Wise.

٤ لَهُ مَا فِي السَّمَاوَاتِ وَمَا فِي الْأَرْضِ ۖ وَهُوَ الْعَلِيُّ الْعَظِيمُ

4 To Him belongs everything in the heavens and everything on earth. He is the Sublime, the Magnificent.

٥ تَكَادُ السَّمَاوَاتُ يَتَفَطَّرْنَ مِنْ فَوْقِهِنَّ ۚ وَالْمَلَائِكَةُ يُسَبِّحُونَ بِحَمْدِ رَبِّهِمْ وَيَسْتَغْفِرُونَ لِمَنْ فِي الْأَرْضِ ۗ [a] أَلَا إِنَّ اللَّهَ هُوَ الْغَفُورُ الرَّحِيمُ [b]

5 The heavens above them almost burst apart, while the angels glorify the praises of their Lord, and ask forgiveness for those on earth. God is indeed the Forgiver, the Merciful.

[a] 7:206; 13:13; 16:49; 39:75; 40:7
[b] 39:53; 53:32

٦ وَالَّذِينَ اتَّخَذُوا مِنْ دُونِهِ أَوْلِيَاءَ اللَّهُ حَفِيظٌ عَلَيْهِمْ وَمَا أَنْتَ عَلَيْهِمْ بِوَكِيلٍ

6 As for those who take masters other than Him: God is in charge of them, and you are not responsible for them.

6
21:24; 39:3, 43; 43:9

٧ وَكَذَٰلِكَ أَوْحَيْنَا إِلَيْكَ قُرْآنًا عَرَبِيًّا لِتُنْذِرَ أُمَّ الْقُرَىٰ وَمَنْ حَوْلَهَا [a] وَتُنْذِرَ يَوْمَ الْجَمْعِ لَا رَيْبَ فِيهِ ۚ فَرِيقٌ فِي الْجَنَّةِ وَفَرِيقٌ فِي السَّعِيرِ [b]

7 Thus We inspired you with an Arabic Qur'an, that you may warn the Central City and whoever is around it, and to warn of the Day of Assembly, of which there is no doubt; a group in the Garden, and a group in the Furnace.

7
[a] 12:2; 13:37; 20:3; 41:2, 44; 42:7
[b] 4:87; 11:103; 56:49–50; 664:9; 77:38

٨ وَلَوْ شَاءَ اللَّهُ لَجَعَلَهُمْ أُمَّةً وَاحِدَةً وَلَٰكِنْ يُدْخِلُ مَنْ يَشَاءُ فِي رَحْمَتِهِ ۚ وَالظَّالِمُونَ مَا لَهُمْ مِنْ وَلِيٍّ وَلَا نَصِيرٍ

8 Had God willed, He could have made them one community, but He admits into His mercy whomever He wills. As for the wrongdoers, they will have no protector and no savior.

8
5:48; 6:35; 11:118; 16:93

٩ أَمِ اتَّخَذُوا مِنْ دُونِهِ أَوْلِيَاءَ ۖ فَاللَّهُ هُوَ الْوَلِيُّ وَهُوَ يُحْيِي الْمَوْتَىٰ وَهُوَ عَلَىٰ كُلِّ شَيْءٍ قَدِيرٌ

9 Or have they adopted protectors besides him? But God is the Protector, and He gives life to the dead, and He has power over all things.

9
21:24; 39:43; 43:7

١٠ وَمَا اخْتَلَفْتُمْ فِيهِ مِنْ شَيْءٍ فَحُكْمُهُ إِلَى اللَّهِ ۚ ذَٰلِكُمُ اللَّهُ رَبِّي عَلَيْهِ تَوَكَّلْتُ وَإِلَيْهِ أُنِيبُ

10 Whatever matter you differ about, its judgment rests with God. "Such is God, my Lord, in Whom I trust, and unto Him I repent."

١١ فَاطِرُ السَّمَاوَاتِ وَالْأَرْضِ ۚ جَعَلَ لَكُمْ مِنْ أَنْفُسِكُمْ أَزْوَاجًا وَمِنَ الْأَنْعَامِ أَزْوَاجًا ۖ يَذْرَؤُكُمْ فِيهِ ۚ [a] لَيْسَ كَمِثْلِهِ شَيْءٌ ۖ وَهُوَ السَّمِيعُ الْبَصِيرُ [b]

11 Originator of the heavens and the earth. He made for you mates from among yourselves, and pairs of animals, by means of which He multiplies you. There is nothing like Him. He is the Hearing, the Seeing.

11
[a] 36:36
[b] 112:4

١٢ لَهُ مَقَالِيدُ السَّمَاوَاتِ وَالْأَرْضِ ۖ [a] يَبْسُطُ الرِّزْقَ لِمَنْ يَشَاءُ وَيَقْدِرُ ۚ إِنَّهُ بِكُلِّ شَيْءٍ عَلِيمٌ [b]

12 To Him belongs absolute control of the heavens and the earth. He spreads the bounties to whomever He wills, or reduces it. He is aware of all things.

12
[a] 39:63
[b] 13:26; 34:26, 39

١٣ شَرَعَ لَكُم مِّنَ الدِّينِ مَا وَصَّىٰ بِهِ نُوحًا وَالَّذِي أَوْحَيْنَا إِلَيْكَ وَمَا وَصَّيْنَا بِهِ إِبْرَاهِيمَ وَمُوسَىٰ وَعِيسَىٰ ۖ أَنْ أَقِيمُوا الدِّينَ وَلَا تَتَفَرَّقُوا فِيهِ ۚ كَبُرَ عَلَى الْمُشْرِكِينَ مَا تَدْعُوهُمْ إِلَيْهِ ۚ اللَّهُ يَجْتَبِي إِلَيْهِ مَن يَشَاءُ وَيَهْدِي إِلَيْهِ مَن يُنِيبُ

13
a 33:7
b 20:112; 22:77–78

13 He prescribed for you the same religion He enjoined upon Noah, and what We inspired to you, and what We enjoined upon Abraham, and Moses, and Jesus: "You shall uphold the religion, and be not divided therein." As for the idolaters, what you call them to is outrageous to them. God chooses to Himself whom He wills, and He guides to Himself whoever repents.

١٤ وَمَا تَفَرَّقُوا إِلَّا مِن بَعْدِ مَا جَاءَهُمُ الْعِلْمُ بَغْيًا بَيْنَهُمْ ۚ وَلَوْلَا كَلِمَةٌ سَبَقَتْ مِن رَّبِّكَ إِلَىٰ أَجَلٍ مُّسَمًّى لَّقُضِيَ بَيْنَهُمْ ۚ وَإِنَّ الَّذِينَ أُورِثُوا الْكِتَابَ مِن بَعْدِهِمْ لَفِي شَكٍّ مِّنْهُ مُرِيبٍ

14
3:19; 11:62; 35:32; 98:4

14 They became divided only after knowledge came to them, out of resentment among themselves. Were it not for a predetermined decision from your Lord, judgment would have been pronounced between them. Indeed, those who were made to inherit the Book after them are in grave doubt about it.

١٥ فَلِذَٰلِكَ فَادْعُ ۖ وَاسْتَقِمْ كَمَا أُمِرْتَ ۖ وَلَا تَتَّبِعْ أَهْوَاءَهُمْ ۖ وَقُلْ آمَنتُ بِمَا أَنزَلَ اللَّهُ مِن كِتَابٍ ۖ وَأُمِرْتُ لِأَعْدِلَ بَيْنَكُمُ ۖ اللَّهُ رَبُّنَا وَرَبُّكُمْ ۖ لَنَا أَعْمَالُنَا وَلَكُمْ أَعْمَالُكُمْ ۖ لَا حُجَّةَ بَيْنَنَا وَبَيْنَكُمُ ۖ اللَّهُ يَجْمَعُ بَيْنَنَا ۖ وَإِلَيْهِ الْمَصِيرُ

15
2:139; 11:112

15 To this go on inviting, and be upright as you were commanded, and do not follow their inclinations, and say, "I believe in whatever Book God has sent down, and I was commanded to judge between you equitably. God is our Lord and your Lord. We have our deeds, and you have your deeds. Let there be no quarrel between us and you. God will bring us together, and to Him is the ultimate return."

١٦ وَالَّذِينَ يُحَاجُّونَ فِي اللَّهِ مِن بَعْدِ مَا اسْتُجِيبَ لَهُ حُجَّتُهُمْ دَاحِضَةٌ عِندَ رَبِّهِمْ وَعَلَيْهِمْ غَضَبٌ وَلَهُمْ عَذَابٌ شَدِيدٌ

16 As for those who dispute about God after having answered His call, their argument is invalid with their Lord; and upon them falls wrath; and a grievous torment awaits them.

١٧ اللَّهُ الَّذِي أَنزَلَ الْكِتَابَ بِالْحَقِّ وَالْمِيزَانَ ۗ وَمَا يُدْرِيكَ لَعَلَّ السَّاعَةَ قَرِيبٌ

17
a 57:25
b 21:1; 33:63; 40:18

17 It is God who revealed the Book with the truth, and the Balance. And what will make you realize that perhaps the Hour is near?

١٨ يَسْتَعْجِلُ بِهَا الَّذِينَ لَا يُؤْمِنُونَ بِهَا ۖ وَالَّذِينَ آمَنُوا مُشْفِقُونَ مِنْهَا وَيَعْلَمُونَ أَنَّهَا الْحَقُّ ۗ أَلَا إِنَّ الَّذِينَ يُمَارُونَ فِي السَّاعَةِ لَفِي ضَلَالٍ بَعِيدٍ

18
10:50

18 Those who do not believe in it seek to hasten it; but those who believe are apprehensive of it, and they know it to be the truth. Absolutely, those who question the Hour are in distant error.

١٩ اللَّهُ لَطِيفٌ بِعِبَادِهِ يَرْزُقُ مَن يَشَاءُ ۖ وَهُوَ الْقَوِيُّ الْعَزِيزُ

19 God is kind towards His worshipers. He provides for whomever He wills. He is the Powerful, the Honorable.

٢٠ مَن كَانَ يُرِيدُ حَرْثَ الْآخِرَةِ نَزِدْ لَهُ فِي حَرْثِهِ ۖ وَمَن كَانَ يُرِيدُ حَرْثَ الدُّنْيَا نُؤْتِهِ مِنْهَا وَمَا لَهُ فِي الْآخِرَةِ مِن نَّصِيبٍ

20 2:216; 3:145; 4:134; 11:15; 17:18; 33:28

20 Whoever desires the harvest of the Hereafter, We increase for him his harvest; and whoever desires the harvest of this world, We give him thereof, and he has no share of the Hereafter.

٢١ أَمْ لَهُمْ شُرَكَاءُ شَرَعُوا لَهُم مِّنَ الدِّينِ مَا لَمْ يَأْذَن بِهِ اللَّهُ ۚ وَلَوْلَا كَلِمَةُ الْفَصْلِ لَقُضِيَ بَيْنَهُمْ ۗ وَإِنَّ الظَّالِمِينَ لَهُمْ عَذَابٌ أَلِيمٌ

21 Or is it that they have partners who litigate for them religious laws never authorized by God? Were it not for the conclusive decision, it would have been settled between them. The wicked will have a painful punishment.

٢٢ تَرَى الظَّالِمِينَ مُشْفِقِينَ مِمَّا كَسَبُوا وَهُوَ وَاقِعٌ بِهِمْ ۗ وَالَّذِينَ آمَنُوا وَعَمِلُوا الصَّالِحَاتِ فِي رَوْضَاتِ الْجَنَّاتِ ۖ لَهُم مَّا يَشَاءُونَ عِندَ رَبِّهِمْ ۚ ذَٰلِكَ هُوَ الْفَضْلُ الْكَبِيرُ

22 18:49;

22 You will see the unjust terrified of what they have earned, and it will befall them. As for those who believe and do good deeds, they will be in the Meadows of the Gardens; they will have whatever they please in the presence of their Lord; that is the supreme blessing.

٢٣ ذَٰلِكَ الَّذِي يُبَشِّرُ اللَّهُ عِبَادَهُ الَّذِينَ آمَنُوا وَعَمِلُوا الصَّالِحَاتِ ۗ قُل لَّا أَسْأَلُكُمْ عَلَيْهِ أَجْرًا إِلَّا الْمَوَدَّةَ فِي الْقُرْبَىٰ ۗ وَمَن يَقْتَرِفْ حَسَنَةً نَّزِدْ لَهُ فِيهَا حُسْنًا ۚ إِنَّ اللَّهَ غَفُورٌ شَكُورٌ

23 2:245; 4:40; 6:160

23 That is the good news God gives to His servants who believe and do good deeds. Say, "I ask of you no wage for it, except affection among the near of kin." Whoever does a good deed, We will increase its goodness for him. God is Forgiving and Appreciative.

٢٤ أَمْ يَقُولُونَ افْتَرَىٰ عَلَى اللَّهِ كَذِبًا ۖ فَإِن يَشَإِ اللَّهُ يَخْتِمْ عَلَىٰ قَلْبِكَ ۗ وَيَمْحُ اللَّهُ الْبَاطِلَ وَيُحِقُّ الْحَقَّ بِكَلِمَاتِهِ ۚ إِنَّهُ عَلِيمٌ بِذَاتِ الصُّدُورِ

24 23:38

24 Or do they say, "He forged a lie about God." If God so willed, He could have sealed your heart. But God obliterates the false, and confirm the true by His Words. He knows what is in the hearts.

٢٥ وَهُوَ الَّذِي يَقْبَلُ التَّوْبَةَ عَنْ عِبَادِهِ وَيَعْفُو عَنِ السَّيِّئَاتِ وَيَعْلَمُ مَا تَفْعَلُونَ

25 It is He who accepts the repentance of His worshipers, and remits the sins, and knows what you do.

٢٦ وَيَسْتَجِيبُ الَّذِينَ آمَنُوا وَعَمِلُوا الصَّالِحَاتِ وَيَزِيدُهُم مِّن فَضْلِهِ ۚ وَالْكَافِرُونَ لَهُمْ عَذَابٌ شَدِيدٌ

26 35:30

26 And He answers those who believe and do good deeds, and He increases them of His grace. But the disbelievers will suffer a terrible punishment.

٢٧ وَلَوْ بَسَطَ اللَّهُ الرِّزْقَ لِعِبَادِهِ لَبَغَوْا فِي الْأَرْضِ وَلَٰكِن يُنَزِّلُ بِقَدَرٍ مَّا يَشَاءُ ۚ إِنَّهُ بِعِبَادِهِ خَبِيرٌ بَصِيرٌ

27 13:26

27 If God were to increase the provision to His servants, they would transgress on earth; but He sends down in precise measure whatever He wills. Surely, regarding His servants, He is Expert and Observant.

٢٨ وَهُوَ الَّذِي يُنَزِّلُ الْغَيْثَ مِن بَعْدِ مَا قَنَطُوا وَيَنشُرُ رَحْمَتَهُ ۚ وَهُوَ الْوَلِيُّ الْحَمِيدُ

28 It is He who brings down the rain after they have despaired, and unfolds His mercy. He is the Guardian, the Praised.

٢٩ وَمِنْ آيَاتِهِ خَلْقُ السَّمَاوَاتِ وَالْأَرْضِ وَمَا بَثَّ فِيهِمَا مِن دَابَّةٍ ۚ وَهُوَ عَلَىٰ جَمْعِهِمْ إِذَا يَشَاءُ قَدِيرٌ

29 2:164; 31:10; 45:4

29 And of His signs are the creation of the heavens and the earth, and the creatures He has spread throughout them; and He is Able to gather them at will.

٣٠ وَمَا أَصَابَكُم مِّن مُّصِيبَةٍ فَبِمَا كَسَبَتْ أَيْدِيكُمْ وَيَعْفُو عَن كَثِيرٍ

30 3:165; 4:79

30 Whatever misfortune befalls you, it is because of what your hands have earned; and yet He pardons much.

٣١ وَمَا أَنتُم بِمُعْجِزِينَ فِي الْأَرْضِ ۖ وَمَا لَكُم مِّن دُونِ اللَّهِ مِن وَلِيٍّ وَلَا نَصِيرٍ

31 You are not the ones to interfere on earth; and besides God, you have no ally, and no helper.

٣٢ وَمِنْ آيَاتِهِ الْجَوَارِ فِي الْبَحْرِ كَالْأَعْلَامِ

32 55:24

32 And of His signs are the ships sailing the sea like flags.

٣٣ إِن يَشَأْ يُسْكِنِ الرِّيحَ فَيَظْلَلْنَ رَوَاكِدَ عَلَىٰ ظَهْرِهِ ۚ إِنَّ فِي ذَٰلِكَ لَآيَاتٍ لِّكُلِّ صَبَّارٍ شَكُورٍ

33 14:5; 31:31; 34:19

33 If He willed, He could have stilled the winds, leaving them motionless on its surface. Surely in that are signs for every disciplined, grateful person.

٣٤ أَوْ يُوبِقْهُنَّ بِمَا كَسَبُوا وَيَعْفُ عَن كَثِيرٍ

34 Or He could wreck them, because of what they have earned. And yet He pardons much.

٣٥ وَيَعْلَمَ الَّذِينَ يُجَادِلُونَ فِي آيَاتِنَا مَا لَهُم مِّن مَّحِيصٍ

35 Those who dispute Our signs know that there is no asylum for them.

٣٦ فَمَا أُوتِيتُم مِّن شَيْءٍ فَمَتَاعُ الْحَيَاةِ الدُّنْيَا ۖ وَمَا عِندَ اللَّهِ خَيْرٌ وَأَبْقَىٰ لِلَّذِينَ آمَنُوا وَعَلَىٰ رَبِّهِمْ يَتَوَكَّلُونَ

36 26:60

36 Whatever thing you are given is only the provision of this life. But what God possesses is better and more lasting for those who believe and rely on their Lord.

٣٧ وَالَّذِينَ يَجْتَنِبُونَ كَبَائِرَ الْإِثْمِ وَالْفَوَاحِشَ وَإِذَا مَا غَضِبُوا هُمْ يَغْفِرُونَ

37 And those who avoid major sins and indecencies; and if they become angry, they forgive.

37 — 4:31; 53:32

٣٨ وَالَّذِينَ اسْتَجَابُوا لِرَبِّهِمْ وَأَقَامُوا الصَّلَاةَ وَأَمْرُهُمْ شُورَىٰ بَيْنَهُمْ وَمِمَّا رَزَقْنَاهُمْ يُنْفِقُونَ

38 And those who respond to their Lord, and pray regularly, and conduct their affairs by mutual consultation, and give of what We have provided them.

٣٩ وَالَّذِينَ إِذَا أَصَابَهُمُ الْبَغْيُ هُمْ يَنْتَصِرُونَ

39 And those who, when wronged, defend themselves.

٤٠ وَجَزَاءُ سَيِّئَةٍ سَيِّئَةٌ مِثْلُهَا ۖ فَمَنْ عَفَا وَأَصْلَحَ فَأَجْرُهُ عَلَى اللَّهِ ۚ إِنَّهُ لَا يُحِبُّ الظَّالِمِينَ

40 The repayment of a bad action is one equivalent to it. But whoever pardons and makes reconciliation, his reward lies with God. He does not love the unjust.

40 — 6:160; 16:126

٤١ وَلَمَنِ انْتَصَرَ بَعْدَ ظُلْمِهِ فَأُولَٰئِكَ مَا عَلَيْهِمْ مِنْ سَبِيلٍ

41 As for those who retaliate after being wronged, there is no blame on them.

41 — 26:227; 42:39

٤٢ إِنَّمَا السَّبِيلُ عَلَى الَّذِينَ يَظْلِمُونَ النَّاسَ وَيَبْغُونَ فِي الْأَرْضِ بِغَيْرِ الْحَقِّ ۚ أُولَٰئِكَ لَهُمْ عَذَابٌ أَلِيمٌ

42 Blame lies on those who wrong people, and commit aggression in the land without right. These will have a painful punishment.

٤٣ وَلَمَنْ صَبَرَ وَغَفَرَ إِنَّ ذَٰلِكَ لَمِنْ عَزْمِ الْأُمُورِ

43 But whoever endures patiently and forgives—that is a sign of real resolve.

43 — 3:186; 31:17; 46:35

٤٤ وَمَنْ يُضْلِلِ اللَّهُ فَمَا لَهُ مِنْ وَلِيٍّ مِنْ بَعْدِهِ ۗ وَتَرَى الظَّالِمِينَ لَمَّا رَأَوُا الْعَذَابَ يَقُولُونَ هَلْ إِلَىٰ مَرَدٍّ مِنْ سَبِيلٍ

44 Whoever God leaves astray has no protector apart from Him. And you will see the transgressors, when they see the torment, saying, "Is there a way of going back?"

44 — 17:97; 18:17; 45:23

٤٥ وَتَرَاهُمْ يُعْرَضُونَ عَلَيْهَا خَاشِعِينَ مِنَ الذُّلِّ يَنْظُرُونَ مِنْ طَرْفٍ خَفِيٍّ ۗ وَقَالَ الَّذِينَ آمَنُوا إِنَّ الْخَاسِرِينَ الَّذِينَ خَسِرُوا أَنْفُسَهُمْ وَأَهْلِيهِمْ يَوْمَ الْقِيَامَةِ ۗ أَلَا إِنَّ الظَّالِمِينَ فِي عَذَابٍ مُقِيمٍ

45 And you will see them exposed to it, cowering from disgrace, looking with concealed eyes. Those who believed will say, "The losers are those who lost themselves and their families on the Day of Resurrection." Indeed, the evildoers are in a lasting torment.

45 — 6:12; 39:15

٤٦ وَمَا كَانَ لَهُمْ مِنْ أَوْلِيَاءَ يَنْصُرُونَهُمْ مِنْ دُونِ اللَّهِ ۗ وَمَنْ يُضْلِلِ اللَّهُ فَمَا لَهُ مِنْ سَبِيلٍ

46 They will have no allies to support them against God. Whomever God leaves astray has no way out.

46 — 18:43; 28:81; 67:20

٤٧ اسْتَجِيبُوا لِرَبِّكُمْ مِنْ قَبْلِ أَنْ يَأْتِيَ يَوْمٌ لَا مَرَدَّ لَهُ مِنَ اللَّهِ ۚ مَا لَكُمْ مِنْ مَلْجَإٍ يَوْمَئِذٍ وَمَا لَكُمْ مِنْ نَكِيرٍ

47 Respond to your Lord before there comes from God a Day that cannot be turned back. You will have no refuge on that Day, and no possibility of denial.

٤٨ فَإِنْ أَعْرَضُوا فَمَا أَرْسَلْنَاكَ عَلَيْهِمْ حَفِيظًا ۖ إِنْ عَلَيْكَ إِلَّا الْبَلَاغُ ۗ وَإِنَّا إِذَا أَذَقْنَا الْإِنْسَانَ مِنَّا رَحْمَةً فَرِحَ بِهَا ۖ وَإِنْ تُصِبْهُمْ سَيِّئَةٌ بِمَا قَدَّمَتْ أَيْدِيهِمْ فَإِنَّ الْإِنْسَانَ كَفُورٌ

48
30:36

48 But if they turn away—We did not send you as a guardian over them. Your only duty is communication. Whenever We let man taste mercy from Us, he rejoices in it; but when misfortune befalls them, as a consequence of what their hands have perpetrated, man turns blasphemous.

٤٩ لِلَّهِ مُلْكُ السَّمَاوَاتِ وَالْأَرْضِ ۚ يَخْلُقُ مَا يَشَاءُ ۚ يَهَبُ لِمَنْ يَشَاءُ إِنَاثًا وَيَهَبُ لِمَنْ يَشَاءُ الذُّكُورَ

49 To God belongs the dominion of the heavens and the earth. He creates whatever He wills. He grants daughters to whomever He wills, and He grants sons to whomever He wills.

٥٠ أَوْ يُزَوِّجُهُمْ ذُكْرَانًا وَإِنَاثًا ۖ وَيَجْعَلُ مَنْ يَشَاءُ عَقِيمًا ۚ إِنَّهُ عَلِيمٌ قَدِيرٌ

50 Or He combines them together, males and females; and He renders whomever He wills sterile. He is Knowledgeable and Capable.

٥١ وَمَا كَانَ لِبَشَرٍ أَنْ يُكَلِّمَهُ اللَّهُ إِلَّا وَحْيًا أَوْ مِنْ وَرَاءِ حِجَابٍ أَوْ يُرْسِلَ رَسُولًا فَيُوحِيَ بِإِذْنِهِ مَا يَشَاءُ ۚ إِنَّهُ عَلِيٌّ حَكِيمٌ

51
53: 7, 13

51 It is not for any human that God should speak to him, except by inspiration, or from behind a veil, or by sending a messenger to reveal by His permission whatever He wills. He is All-High, All-Wise.

٥٢ وَكَذَٰلِكَ أَوْحَيْنَا إِلَيْكَ رُوحًا مِنْ أَمْرِنَا ۚ مَا كُنْتَ تَدْرِي مَا الْكِتَابُ وَلَا الْإِيمَانُ وَلَٰكِنْ جَعَلْنَاهُ نُورًا نَهْدِي بِهِ مَنْ نَشَاءُ مِنْ عِبَادِنَا ۚ وَإِنَّكَ لَتَهْدِي إِلَىٰ صِرَاطٍ مُسْتَقِيمٍ

52
16:2; 40:15

52 We thus inspired you spiritually, by Our command. You did not know what the Scripture is, nor what faith is, but We made it a light, with which We guide whomever We will of Our servants. You surely guide to a straight path.

٥٣ صِرَاطِ اللَّهِ الَّذِي لَهُ مَا فِي السَّمَاوَاتِ وَمَا فِي الْأَرْضِ ۗ أَلَا إِلَى اللَّهِ تَصِيرُ الْأُمُورُ

53
3:109; 57:5

53 The path of God, to whom belongs everything in the heavens and everything on earth. Indeed, to God all matters revert.

Sūrah 43: Al-Zukhruf

سُورَةُ ٱلزُّخْرُفِ (Decorations)

بِسْمِ ٱللَّهِ ٱلرَّحْمَٰنِ ٱلرَّحِيمِ

١ حم

1 Hā', Mīm.

٢ وَالْكِتَابِ الْمُبِينِ

2 By the Book that makes things clear.

2
pp 44:2

٣ إِنَّا جَعَلْنَاهُ قُرْآنًا عَرَبِيًّا لَعَلَّكُمْ تَعْقِلُونَ

3 We made it an Arabic Qur'an, so that you may understand.

3
12:2; 13:37; 20:3; 26:195; 39:38; 41:2, 44; 42:7

٤ وَإِنَّهُ فِي أُمِّ الْكِتَابِ لَدَيْنَا لَعَلِيٌّ حَكِيمٌ

4 And it is with Us, in the Source Book, sublime and wise.

4
3:7; 13:39

٥ أَفَنَضْرِبُ عَنكُمُ الذِّكْرَ صَفْحًا أَن كُنتُمْ قَوْمًا مُّسْرِفِينَ

5 Shall We hold back the Reminder from you, since you are a transgressing people?

٦ وَكَمْ أَرْسَلْنَا مِن نَّبِيٍّ فِي الْأَوَّلِينَ

6 How many a prophet did We send to the ancients?

6
15:10

٧ وَمَا يَأْتِيهِم مِّن نَّبِيٍّ إِلَّا كَانُوا بِهِ يَسْتَهْزِئُونَ

7 No messenger came to them, but they ridiculed him.

٨ فَأَهْلَكْنَا أَشَدَّ مِنْهُم بَطْشًا وَمَضَىٰ مَثَلُ الْأَوَّلِينَ

8 We destroyed people more powerful than they, and so the example of the ancients has passed away.

8
6:6; 50:36

٩ وَلَئِن سَأَلْتَهُم مَّنْ خَلَقَ السَّمَاوَاتِ وَالْأَرْضَ لَيَقُولُنَّ خَلَقَهُنَّ الْعَزِيزُ الْعَلِيمُ

9 And if you asked them, "Who created the heavens and the earth?" They would say, "The Mighty, the Knower created them."

9
29:61; 31:25; 39:38

١٠ الَّذِي جَعَلَ لَكُمُ الْأَرْضَ مَهْدًا وَجَعَلَ لَكُمْ فِيهَا سُبُلًا لَّعَلَّكُمْ تَهْتَدُونَ

10 He who made the earth a habitat for you, and traced pathways for you on it, that you may be guided.

10
20:53

١١ وَالَّذِي نَزَّلَ مِنَ السَّمَاءِ مَاءً بِقَدَرٍ فَأَنشَرْنَا بِهِ بَلْدَةً مَّيْتًا ۚ كَذَٰلِكَ تُخْرَجُونَ

11 He who sends down water from the sky in due proportion; and so We revive thereby a dead land. Thus you will be brought out.

11
7:57; 23:18; 25:49; 50:11

١٢ وَالَّذِي خَلَقَ الْأَزْوَاجَ كُلَّهَا[a] وَجَعَلَ لَكُم مِّنَ الْفُلْكِ وَالْأَنْعَامِ مَا تَرْكَبُونَ[b]

12 He Who created all the pairs; and provided you with ships, and animals on which you ride.

12
[a] 20:36; 22:5; 31:10
[b] 2:164; 14:32; 23:22; 40:79; 45:12

١٣ لِتَسْتَوُوا عَلَىٰ ظُهُورِهِ ثُمَّ تَذْكُرُوا نِعْمَةَ رَبِّكُمْ إِذَا اسْتَوَيْتُمْ عَلَيْهِ وَتَقُولُوا سُبْحَانَ الَّذِي سَخَّرَ لَنَا هَٰذَا وَمَا كُنَّا لَهُ مُقْرِنِينَ

13 That you may mount their backs, and remember the favor of your Lord as you sit firmly upon them, and say, "Glory be to Him Who placed these at our service; surely we could not have done it by ourselves.

١٤ وَإِنَّا إِلَىٰ رَبِّنَا لَمُنقَلِبُونَ

14 And surely, to our Lord we will return."

١٥ وَجَعَلُوا لَهُ مِنْ عِبَادِهِ جُزْءًا ۚ إِنَّ الْإِنسَانَ لَكَفُورٌ مُّبِينٌ

15 Yet they turn one of His servants into a part of Him. Man is clearly ungrateful.

١٦ أَمِ اتَّخَذَ مِمَّا يَخْلُقُ بَنَاتٍ وَأَصْفَاكُم بِالْبَنِينَ

16 Or has He chosen for Himself daughters from what He creates, and favored you with sons?

16
16:62; 17:40; 37:149; 53:21-22

١٧ وَإِذَا بُشِّرَ أَحَدُهُم بِمَا ضَرَبَ لِلرَّحْمَٰنِ مَثَلًا ظَلَّ وَجْهُهُ مُسْوَدًّا وَهُوَ كَظِيمٌ

17 Yet when one of them is given news of what he attributes to the Most Gracious, his face darkens, and he suppresses grief.

17
16:58

١٨ أَوَمَن يُنَشَّأُ فِي الْحِلْيَةِ وَهُوَ فِي الْخِصَامِ غَيْرُ مُبِينٍ

18 "Someone brought up to be beautiful, and unable to help in a fight?"

١٩ وَجَعَلُوا الْمَلَائِكَةَ الَّذِينَ هُمْ عِبَادُ الرَّحْمَٰنِ إِنَاثًا ۚ ᵃ أَشَهِدُوا خَلْقَهُمْ ۚ سَتُكْتَبُ شَهَادَتُهُمْ وَيُسْأَلُونَ ᵇ

19 And they appoint the angels, who are servants to the Most Gracious, as females. Have they witnessed their creation? Their claim will be recorded, and they will be questioned.

19
ᵃ 4:117; 17:40; 37:150; 53:27
ᵇ 10:21; 45:29; 82:10-22

٢٠ وَقَالُوا لَوْ شَاءَ الرَّحْمَٰنُ مَا عَبَدْنَاهُم ۗ مَّا لَهُم بِذَٰلِكَ مِنْ عِلْمٍ ۖ إِنْ هُمْ إِلَّا يَخْرُصُونَ

20 And they say, "Had the Most Gracious willed, we would not have worshiped them." But they have no knowledge of that; they are merely guessing.

20
6:148; 16:35

٢١ أَمْ آتَيْنَاهُمْ كِتَابًا مِّن قَبْلِهِ فَهُم بِهِ مُسْتَمْسِكُونَ

21 Or have We given them a book prior to this one, to which they adhere?

21
6:123; 23:44; 35:40; 46:4

٢٢ بَلْ قَالُوا إِنَّا وَجَدْنَا آبَاءَنَا عَلَىٰ أُمَّةٍ وَإِنَّا عَلَىٰ آثَارِهِم مُّهْتَدُونَ

22 But they say, "We found our parents on a course, and we are guided in their footsteps."

٢٣ وَكَذَٰلِكَ مَا أَرْسَلْنَا مِن قَبْلِكَ فِي قَرْيَةٍ مِّن نَّذِيرٍ إِلَّا قَالَ مُتْرَفُوهَا إِنَّا وَجَدْنَا آبَاءَنَا عَلَىٰ أُمَّةٍ وَإِنَّا عَلَىٰ آثَارِهِم مُّقْتَدُونَ

23 23:44; 34:34

23 Likewise, We sent no warner before you to any town, but the wealthy among them said, "We found our parents on a course, and we are following in their footsteps."

٢٤ قَالَ أَوَلَوْ جِئْتُكُم بِأَهْدَىٰ مِمَّا وَجَدتُّمْ عَلَيْهِ آبَاءَكُمْ ۖ قَالُوا إِنَّا بِمَا أُرْسِلْتُم بِهِ كَافِرُونَ

24 He would say, "Even if I bring you better guidance than what you found your parents following?" They would say, "We reject what you are sent with."

٢٥ فَانتَقَمْنَا مِنْهُمْ ۖ فَانظُرْ كَيْفَ كَانَ عَاقِبَةُ الْمُكَذِّبِينَ

25 7:136; 15:79; 30:47; 43:55

25 So We wreaked vengeance upon them. Behold, then, what was the fate of those who deny.

٢٦ وَإِذْ قَالَ إِبْرَاهِيمُ لِأَبِيهِ وَقَوْمِهِ إِنَّنِي بَرَاءٌ مِّمَّا تَعْبُدُونَ

26–28 19:41–50; 26:57–58; 36:26

26 When Abraham said to his father and his people, "I am innocent of what you worship.

٢٧ إِلَّا الَّذِي فَطَرَنِي فَإِنَّهُ سَيَهْدِينِ

27 Except for He who created me, for He will guide me."

٢٨ وَجَعَلَهَا كَلِمَةً بَاقِيَةً فِي عَقِبِهِ لَعَلَّهُمْ يَرْجِعُونَ

28 And he made it an enduring word in his progeny, so that they may return.

٢٩ بَلْ مَتَّعْتُ هَٰؤُلَاءِ وَآبَاءَهُمْ حَتَّىٰ جَاءَهُمُ الْحَقُّ وَرَسُولٌ مُّبِينٌ

29 I gave these and their forefathers some enjoyment, until the truth and a manifest messenger came to them.

٣٠ وَلَمَّا جَاءَهُمُ الْحَقُّ قَالُوا هَٰذَا سِحْرٌ وَإِنَّا بِهِ كَافِرُونَ

30 10:76

30 But when the truth came to them, they said, "This is sorcery, and we refuse to believe in it."

٣١ وَقَالُوا لَوْلَا نُزِّلَ هَٰذَا الْقُرْآنُ عَلَىٰ رَجُلٍ مِّنَ الْقَرْيَتَيْنِ عَظِيمٍ

31 They also said, "If only this Qur'an was sent down to a man of importance from the two cities."

٣٢ أَهُمْ يَقْسِمُونَ رَحْمَتَ رَبِّكَ ۚ نَحْنُ قَسَمْنَا بَيْنَهُم مَّعِيشَتَهُمْ فِي الْحَيَاةِ الدُّنْيَا ۚ وَرَفَعْنَا بَعْضَهُمْ فَوْقَ بَعْضٍ دَرَجَاتٍ لِّيَتَّخِذَ بَعْضُهُم بَعْضًا سُخْرِيًّا ۗ وَرَحْمَتُ رَبِّكَ خَيْرٌ مِّمَّا يَجْمَعُونَ

32 38:9

32 Is it they who allocate the mercy of your Lord? It is We who have allocated their livelihood in this life, and We elevated some of them in rank above others, that some of them would take others in service. But your Lord's mercy is better than what they amass.

٣٣ وَلَوْلَا أَن يَكُونَ النَّاسُ أُمَّةً وَاحِدَةً لَجَعَلْنَا لِمَن يَكْفُرُ بِالرَّحْمَٰنِ لِبُيُوتِهِمْ سُقُفًا مِّن فِضَّةٍ وَمَعَارِجَ عَلَيْهَا يَظْهَرُونَ

33 17:93

33 Were it not that humanity would become a single community, We would have provided those who disbelieve in the Most Gracious with roofs of silver to their houses, and stairways by which they ascend.

٣٤ وَلِبُيُوتِهِمْ أَبْوَابًا وَسُرُرًا عَلَيْهَا يَتَّكِئُونَ

34 And doors to their houses, and furnishings on which they recline.

٣٥ وَزُخْرُفًا ۚ وَإِن كُلُّ ذَٰلِكَ لَمَّا مَتَاعُ الْحَيَاةِ الدُّنْيَا ۚ وَالْآخِرَةُ عِندَ رَبِّكَ لِلْمُتَّقِينَ

35 28:60; 42:36

35 And decorations. Yet all that is nothing but the stuff of this life. Yet the Hereafter, with your Lord, is for the righteous.

٣٦ وَمَن يَعْشُ عَن ذِكْرِ الرَّحْمَٰنِ نُقَيِّضْ لَهُ شَيْطَانًا فَهُوَ لَهُ قَرِينٌ

36 Whoever shuns the remembrance of the Most Gracious, We assign for him a devil, to be his companion.

٣٧ وَإِنَّهُمْ لَيَصُدُّونَهُمْ عَنِ السَّبِيلِ وَيَحْسَبُونَ أَنَّهُم مُّهْتَدُونَ

37 They hinder them from the path, though they think they are guided.

٣٨ حَتَّىٰ إِذَا جَاءَنَا قَالَ يَا لَيْتَ بَيْنِي وَبَيْنَكَ بُعْدَ الْمَشْرِقَيْنِ فَبِئْسَ الْقَرِينُ

38 Until, when he comes to Us, he will say, "If only there were between me and you the distance of the two Easts." What an evil companion!

٣٩ وَلَن يَنفَعَكُمُ الْيَوْمَ إِذ ظَّلَمْتُمْ أَنَّكُمْ فِي الْعَذَابِ مُشْتَرِكُونَ

39 37:33

39 It will not benefit you on that Day, since you did wrong. You are partners in the suffering.

٤٠ أَفَأَنتَ تُسْمِعُ الصُّمَّ أَوْ تَهْدِي الْعُمْيَ وَمَن كَانَ فِي ضَلَالٍ مُّبِينٍ

40 27:80; 30:52

40 Can you make the deaf hear, or guide the blind, and him who is in evident error?

٤١ فَإِمَّا نَذْهَبَنَّ بِكَ فَإِنَّا مِنْهُم مُّنتَقِمُونَ

41 23:93

41 Even if We take you away, We will wreak vengeance upon them.

٤٢ أَوْ نُرِيَنَّكَ الَّذِي وَعَدْنَاهُمْ فَإِنَّا عَلَيْهِم مُّقْتَدِرُونَ

42 Or show you what We have promised them; for We have absolute power over them.

٤٣ فَاسْتَمْسِكْ بِالَّذِي أُوحِيَ إِلَيْكَ ۖ إِنَّكَ عَلَىٰ صِرَاطٍ مُّسْتَقِيمٍ

43 So adhere to what is revealed to you. You are upon a straight path.

٤٤ وَإِنَّهُ لَذِكْرٌ لَّكَ وَلِقَوْمِكَ ۖ وَسَوْفَ تُسْأَلُونَ

44 It is a message for you, and for your people; and you will be questioned.

٤٥ وَاسْأَلْ مَنْ أَرْسَلْنَا مِن قَبْلِكَ مِن رُّسُلِنَا أَجَعَلْنَا مِن دُونِ الرَّحْمَٰنِ آلِهَةً يُعْبَدُونَ

45 Ask those of Our messengers We sent before you: "Did We appoint gods besides the Most Gracious to be worshiped?"

45
10:94

٤٦ وَلَقَدْ أَرْسَلْنَا مُوسَىٰ بِآيَاتِنَا إِلَىٰ فِرْعَوْنَ وَمَلَئِهِ فَقَالَ إِنِّي رَسُولُ رَبِّ الْعَالَمِينَ

46 We sent Moses with Our revelations to Pharaoh and his dignitaries. He said, "I am the Messenger of the Lord of the Worlds."

46
7:103

٤٧ فَلَمَّا جَاءَهُم بِآيَاتِنَا إِذَا هُم مِّنْهَا يَضْحَكُونَ

47 But when he showed them Our signs, they started laughing at them.

47
7:133; 17:101; 27:12

٤٨ وَمَا نُرِيهِم مِّنْ آيَةٍ إِلَّا هِيَ أَكْبَرُ مِنْ أُخْتِهَا ۖ وَأَخَذْنَاهُم بِالْعَذَابِ لَعَلَّهُمْ يَرْجِعُونَ

48 Each sign We showed them was more marvelous than its counterpart. And We afflicted them with the plagues, so that they may repent.

48

٤٩ وَقَالُوا يَا أَيُّهَ السَّاحِرُ ادْعُ لَنَا رَبَّكَ بِمَا عَهِدَ عِندَكَ إِنَّنَا لَمُهْتَدُونَ

49 They said, "O sorcerer, pray to your Lord for us, according to His pledge to you, and then we will be guided."

49
7:134

٥٠ فَلَمَّا كَشَفْنَا عَنْهُمُ الْعَذَابَ إِذَا هُمْ يَنكُثُونَ

50 But when We lifted the torment from them, they immediately broke their promise.

50

٥١ وَنَادَىٰ فِرْعَوْنُ فِي قَوْمِهِ قَالَ يَا قَوْمِ أَلَيْسَ لِي مُلْكُ مِصْرَ وَهَٰذِهِ الْأَنْهَارُ تَجْرِي مِن تَحْتِي ۖ أَفَلَا تُبْصِرُونَ

51 Pharaoh proclaimed among his people, saying, "O my people, do I not own the Kingdom of Egypt, and these rivers flow beneath me? Do you not see?

51
26:19; 28:38; 79:23

٥٢ أَمْ أَنَا خَيْرٌ مِّنْ هَٰذَا الَّذِي هُوَ مَهِينٌ وَلَا يَكَادُ يُبِينُ

52 Am I not better than this miserable wretch, who can barely express himself?

52
32:9

٥٣ فَلَوْلَا أُلْقِيَ عَلَيْهِ أَسْوِرَةٌ مِّن ذَهَبٍ أَوْ جَاءَ مَعَهُ الْمَلَائِكَةُ مُقْتَرِنِينَ

53 Why are bracelets of gold not dropped on him, or they angels came with him in procession?"

53
6:50; 11:12; 25:8

٥٤ فَاسْتَخَفَّ قَوْمَهُ فَأَطَاعُوهُ ۚ إِنَّهُمْ كَانُوا قَوْمًا فَاسِقِينَ

54 Thus he fooled his people, and they obeyed him. They were wicked people.

54

٥٥ فَلَمَّا آسَفُونَا انتَقَمْنَا مِنْهُمْ فَأَغْرَقْنَاهُمْ أَجْمَعِينَ

55 And when they provoked Our wrath, We took retribution from them, and We drowned them all.

55
7:136; 43:25

Sūrah 43: Al-Zukhruf

٥٦ فَجَعَلْنَاهُمْ سَلَفًا وَمَثَلًا لِلْآخِرِينَ

56 Thus We made them a precedent and an example for the others.

٥٧ وَلَمَّا ضُرِبَ ابْنُ مَرْيَمَ مَثَلًا إِذَا قَوْمُكَ مِنْهُ يَصِدُّونَ

57 And when the son of Mary was cited as an example, your people opposed.

٥٨ وَقَالُوا أَآلِهَتُنَا خَيْرٌ أَمْ هُوَ ۚ مَا ضَرَبُوهُ لَكَ إِلَّا جَدَلًا ۚ بَلْ هُمْ قَوْمٌ خَصِمُونَ

58 They said, "Are our gods better, or he?" They cited him only for argument. In fact, they are a quarrelsome people.

58
16:4; 18:54

٥٩ إِنْ هُوَ إِلَّا عَبْدٌ أَنْعَمْنَا عَلَيْهِ وَجَعَلْنَاهُ مَثَلًا لِبَنِي إِسْرَائِيلَ

59 He was just a servant whom We blessed, and We made him an example for the Children of Israel.

٦٠ وَلَوْ نَشَاءُ لَجَعَلْنَا مِنْكُمْ مَلَائِكَةً فِي الْأَرْضِ يَخْلُفُونَ

60 Had We willed, We would have made of you angels to be successors on earth.

٦١ وَإِنَّهُ لَعِلْمٌ لِلسَّاعَةِ فَلَا تَمْتَرُنَّ بِهَا وَاتَّبِعُونِ ۚ هَٰذَا صِرَاطٌ مُسْتَقِيمٌ

61 He is a portent of the Hour, so have no doubt about it, and follow Me. This is a straight way.

٦٢ وَلَا يَصُدَّنَّكُمُ الشَّيْطَانُ ۖ إِنَّهُ لَكُمْ عَدُوٌّ مُبِينٌ

62 And let not Satan divert you. He is an open enemy to you.

62
7:22; 35:6

٦٣ وَلَمَّا جَاءَ عِيسَىٰ بِالْبَيِّنَاتِ قَالَ قَدْ جِئْتُكُمْ بِالْحِكْمَةِ وَلِأُبَيِّنَ لَكُمْ بَعْضَ الَّذِي تَخْتَلِفُونَ فِيهِ ۖ فَاتَّقُوا اللَّهَ وَأَطِيعُونِ

63 When Jesus came with the clarifications, he said, "I have come to you with wisdom, and to clarify for you some of what you differ about. So fear God, and obey me.

63–64
3:50

٦٤ إِنَّ اللَّهَ هُوَ رَبِّي وَرَبُّكُمْ فَاعْبُدُوهُ ۚ هَٰذَا صِرَاطٌ مُسْتَقِيمٌ

64 God is my Lord and your Lord, so worship Him—this is a straight path."

٦٥ فَاخْتَلَفَ الْأَحْزَابُ مِنْ بَيْنِهِمْ ۖ فَوَيْلٌ لِلَّذِينَ ظَلَمُوا مِنْ عَذَابِ يَوْمٍ أَلِيمٍ

65 But the factions differed among themselves. So woe to the wrongdoers from the suffering of a painful Day.

65
19:37

٦٦ هَلْ يَنْظُرُونَ إِلَّا السَّاعَةَ أَنْ تَأْتِيَهُمْ بَغْتَةً وَهُمْ لَا يَشْعُرُونَ

66 Are they only waiting for the Hour to come upon them suddenly, while they are unaware?

66
12:107; 36:49–50; 47:18

٦٧ الْأَخِلَّاءُ يَوْمَئِذٍ بَعْضُهُمْ لِبَعْضٍ عَدُوٌّ إِلَّا الْمُتَّقِينَ

67 On that Day, friends will be enemies of one another, except for the righteous.

٦٨ يَا عِبَادِ لَا خَوْفٌ عَلَيْكُمُ الْيَوْمَ وَلَا أَنْتُمْ تَحْزَنُونَ

68 O My servants, you have nothing to fear on that Day, nor will you grieve.

68–69
10:62–63; 46:13

٦٩ الَّذِينَ آمَنُوا بِآيَاتِنَا وَكَانُوا مُسْلِمِينَ

69 Those who believed in Our revelations, and were submissive.

٧٠ ادْخُلُوا الْجَنَّةَ أَنْتُمْ وَأَزْوَاجُكُمْ تُحْبَرُونَ

70 Enter the Garden, you and your spouses, Joyfully.

70
12:23; 36:56; 40:8

٧١ يُطَافُ عَلَيْهِمْ بِصِحَافٍ مِنْ ذَهَبٍ وَأَكْوَابٍ ۖ وَفِيهَا مَا تَشْتَهِيهِ الْأَنْفُسُ وَتَلَذُّ الْأَعْيُنُ ۖ وَأَنْتُمْ فِيهَا خَالِدُونَ

71 They will be served around with trays of gold, and cups. Therein is whatever the souls desire and delights the eyes. Therein you will stay forever.

71
37:45; 56:17; 76:15; 88:14

٧٢ وَتِلْكَ الْجَنَّةُ الَّتِي أُورِثْتُمُوهَا بِمَا كُنْتُمْ تَعْمَلُونَ

72 Such is the Garden you are made to inherit, because of what you used to do.

72
7:43; 19:63; 23:10

٧٣ لَكُمْ فِيهَا فَاكِهَةٌ كَثِيرَةٌ مِنْهَا تَأْكُلُونَ

73 Therein you will have abundant fruit, from which you eat.

73
23:19; 36:57

٧٤ إِنَّ الْمُجْرِمِينَ فِي عَذَابِ جَهَنَّمَ خَالِدُونَ

74 As for the sinners, they will be in the torment of Hell forever.

٧٥ لَا يُفَتَّرُ عَنْهُمْ وَهُمْ فِيهِ مُبْلِسُونَ

75 It will never be eased for them. In it, they will be devastated.

٧٦ وَمَا ظَلَمْنَاهُمْ وَلَٰكِنْ كَانُوا هُمُ الظَّالِمِينَ

76 We did them no injustice, but it was they who were the unjust.

76
9:70

٧٧ وَنَادَوْا يَا مَالِكُ لِيَقْضِ عَلَيْنَا رَبُّكَ ۖ قَالَ إِنَّكُمْ مَاكِثُونَ

77 And they will cry, "O Malek, let your Lord finish us off." He will say, "You are staying."

77
20:74; 35:36; 69:27

٧٨ لَقَدْ جِئْنَاكُمْ بِالْحَقِّ وَلَٰكِنَّ أَكْثَرَكُمْ لِلْحَقِّ كَارِهُونَ

78 We have given you the truth, but most of you hate the truth.

٧٩ أَمْ أَبْرَمُوا أَمْرًا فَإِنَّا مُبْرِمُونَ

79 Have they contrived some scheme? We too are contriving.

79
3:54; 7:99; 8:30; 27:50

Sūrah 43: Al-Zukhruf

٨٠ أَمْ يَحْسَبُونَ أَنَّا لَا نَسْمَعُ سِرَّهُمْ وَنَجْوَاهُم ۚ بَلَىٰ وَرُسُلُنَا لَدَيْهِمْ يَكْتُبُونَ

80 Or do they think that We cannot hear their secrets and their conspiracies? Yes indeed, Our messengers are by them, writing down.

80 2:33; 9:78; 58:7

٨١ قُلْ إِن كَانَ لِلرَّحْمَٰنِ وَلَدٌ فَأَنَا أَوَّلُ الْعَابِدِينَ

81 Say, "If the Most Gracious had a son, I would be the first to worship."

81 2:116

٨٢ سُبْحَانَ رَبِّ السَّمَاوَاتِ وَالْأَرْضِ رَبِّ الْعَرْشِ عَمَّا يَصِفُونَ

82 Glorified be the Lord of the heavens and the earth, the Lord of the Throne, beyond what they describe.

82 21:22

٨٣ فَذَرْهُمْ يَخُوضُوا وَيَلْعَبُوا حَتَّىٰ يُلَاقُوا يَوْمَهُمُ الَّذِي يُوعَدُونَ

83 So leave them to blunder and play, until they encounter their Day which they are promised.

83 6:91; 52:11

٨٤ وَهُوَ الَّذِي فِي السَّمَاءِ إِلَٰهٌ وَفِي الْأَرْضِ إِلَٰهٌ ۚ وَهُوَ الْحَكِيمُ الْعَلِيمُ

84 It is He who is God in heaven, and God on earth. He is the Wise, the Knower.

٨٥ وَتَبَارَكَ الَّذِي لَهُ مُلْكُ السَّمَاوَاتِ وَالْأَرْضِ وَمَا بَيْنَهُمَا وَعِندَهُ عِلْمُ السَّاعَةِ وَإِلَيْهِ تُرْجَعُونَ

85 And blessed is He Who has sovereignty over the heavens and the earth and what is between them. He alone has knowledge of the Hour, and to Him you will be returned.

85 6:59; 7:178

٨٦ وَلَا يَمْلِكُ الَّذِينَ يَدْعُونَ مِن دُونِهِ الشَّفَاعَةَ إِلَّا مَن شَهِدَ بِالْحَقِّ وَهُمْ يَعْلَمُونَ

86 Those they invoke besides Him are incapable of intercession; only those who testify to the truth and have knowledge.

86 10:18; 19:87

٨٧ وَلَئِن سَأَلْتَهُم مَّنْ خَلَقَهُمْ لَيَقُولُنَّ اللَّهُ ۖ فَأَنَّىٰ يُؤْفَكُونَ

87 And if you asked them, "Who created them?", they would say, "God." Why then do they deviate?

87 2:48

٨٨ وَقِيلِهِ يَا رَبِّ إِنَّ هَٰؤُلَاءِ قَوْمٌ لَّا يُؤْمِنُونَ

88 As for his statement: "My Lord, these are a people who do not believe."

٨٩ فَاصْفَحْ عَنْهُمْ وَقُلْ سَلَامٌ ۚ فَسَوْفَ يَعْلَمُونَ

89 Pardon them, and say, "Peace." They will come to know.

89 15:85

Sūrah 44: Al-Dukhān

سُورَةُ ٱلدُّخَان (Smoke)

بِسْمِ ٱللَّهِ ٱلرَّحْمَٰنِ ٱلرَّحِيمِ

١ حم

1 Ḥā', Mīm.

٢ وَٱلْكِتَٰبِ ٱلْمُبِينِ

2 By the Enlightening Scripture.

pp 43:2

٣ إِنَّا أَنزَلْنَٰهُ فِى لَيْلَةٍ مُّبَٰرَكَةٍ ۚ إِنَّا كُنَّا مُنذِرِينَ

3 We have revealed it on a Blessed Night—We have warned.

2:185; 97:1

٤ فِيهَا يُفْرَقُ كُلُّ أَمْرٍ حَكِيمٍ

4 In it is distinguished every wise command.

٥ أَمْرًا مِّنْ عِندِنَآ ۚ إِنَّا كُنَّا مُرْسِلِينَ

5 A decree from Us. We have been sending messages.

٦ رَحْمَةً مِّن رَّبِّكَ ۚ إِنَّهُ هُوَ ٱلسَّمِيعُ ٱلْعَلِيمُ

6 As mercy from your Lord. He is the Hearer, the Knower.

18:65

٧ رَبِّ ٱلسَّمَٰوَٰتِ وَٱلْأَرْضِ وَمَا بَيْنَهُمَآ ۖ إِن كُنتُم مُّوقِنِينَ

7 Lord of the heavens and the earth and what is between them, if you know for sure.

٨ لَآ إِلَٰهَ إِلَّا هُوَ يُحْىِۦ وَيُمِيتُ ۖ رَبُّكُمْ وَرَبُّ ءَابَآئِكُمُ ٱلْأَوَّلِينَ

8 There is no god but He. He gives life and causes death—your Lord and Lord of your ancestors of old.

3:156; 7:158

٩ بَلْ هُمْ فِى شَكٍّ يَلْعَبُونَ

9 Yet they play around in doubt.

١٠ فَٱرْتَقِبْ يَوْمَ تَأْتِى ٱلسَّمَآءُ بِدُخَانٍ مُّبِينٍ

10 So watch out for the Day when the sky produces a visible smoke.

١١ يَغْشَى ٱلنَّاسَ ۖ هَٰذَا عَذَابٌ أَلِيمٌ

11 Enveloping mankind; this is a painful punishment.

١٢ رَّبَّنَا ٱكْشِفْ عَنَّا ٱلْعَذَابَ إِنَّا مُؤْمِنُونَ

12 "Our Lord, lift the torment from us, we are believers."

١٣ أَنَّىٰ لَهُمُ ٱلذِّكْرَىٰ وَقَدْ جَآءَهُمْ رَسُولٌ مُّبِينٌ

13 But how can they be reminded? An enlightening messenger has already come to them.

14	١٤ ثُمَّ تَوَلَّوْا عَنْهُ وَقَالُوا مُعَلَّمٌ مَّجْنُونٌ	14 7:184; 23:70

14 But they turned away from him, and said, "Educated, but crazy!"

١٥ إِنَّا كَاشِفُو الْعَذَابِ قَلِيلًا ۚ إِنَّكُمْ عَائِدُونَ — 15

15 We will ease the punishment a little, but you will revert.

١٦ يَوْمَ نَبْطِشُ الْبَطْشَةَ الْكُبْرَىٰ إِنَّا مُنتَقِمُونَ — 16 7:184; 54:36; 85:12

16 The Day when We launch the Great Assault—We will avenge.

١٧ وَلَقَدْ فَتَنَّا قَبْلَهُمْ قَوْمَ فِرْعَوْنَ وَجَاءَهُمْ رَسُولٌ كَرِيمٌ — 17 7:103

17 Before them We tested the people of Pharaoh; a noble messenger came to them.

١٨ أَنْ أَدُّوا إِلَيَّ عِبَادَ اللَّهِ ۖ إِنِّي لَكُمْ رَسُولٌ أَمِينٌ — 18 7:105; 26:17

18 Saying, "Hand over God's servants to me. I am an honest messenger to you."

١٩ وَأَنْ لَا تَعْلُوا عَلَى اللَّهِ ۖ إِنِّي آتِيكُمْ بِسُلْطَانٍ مُّبِينٍ — 19 4:153

19 And, "Do not exalt yourselves above God. I come to you with clear authority.

٢٠ وَإِنِّي عُذْتُ بِرَبِّي وَرَبِّكُمْ أَنْ تَرْجُمُونِ — 20 40:27

20 I have taken refuge in my Lord and your Lord, lest you stone me.

٢١ وَإِنْ لَمْ تُؤْمِنُوا لِي فَاعْتَزِلُونِ — 21

21 But if you do not believe in me, keep away from me."

٢٢ فَدَعَا رَبَّهُ أَنَّ هَٰؤُلَاءِ قَوْمٌ مُّجْرِمُونَ — 22

22 He appealed to his Lord: "These are a sinful people."

٢٣ فَأَسْرِ بِعِبَادِي لَيْلًا إِنَّكُمْ مُتَّبَعُونَ — 23 20:77; 26:52

23 "Set out with My servants by night—you will be followed.

٢٤ وَاتْرُكِ الْبَحْرَ رَهْوًا ۖ إِنَّهُمْ جُندٌ مُّغْرَقُونَ — 24 7:136

24 And cross the sea quickly; they are an army to be drowned."

٢٥ كَمْ تَرَكُوا مِنْ جَنَّاتٍ وَعُيُونٍ — 25–27 26:146–149; 36:55

25 How many gardens and fountains did they leave behind?

٢٦ وَزُرُوعٍ وَمَقَامٍ كَرِيمٍ

26 And plantations, and splendid buildings.

٢٧ وَنَعْمَةٍ كَانُوا فِيهَا فَاكِهِينَ

27 And comforts they used to enjoy.

٢٨ كَذَٰلِكَ ۖ وَأَوْرَثْنَاهَا قَوْمًا آخَرِينَ — 28 7:137; 26:59

28 So it was; and We passed it on to another people.

٢٩ فَمَا بَكَتْ عَلَيْهِمُ السَّمَاءُ وَالْأَرْضُ وَمَا كَانُوا مُنظَرِينَ

29 Neither heaven nor earth wept over them, nor were they reprieved.

٣٠ وَلَقَدْ نَجَّيْنَا بَنِي إِسْرَائِيلَ مِنَ الْعَذَابِ الْمُهِينِ

30 And We delivered the Children of Israel from the humiliating persecution.

30
2:49–50; 7:141

٣١ مِن فِرْعَوْنَ ۚ إِنَّهُ كَانَ عَالِيًا مِّنَ الْمُسْرِفِينَ

31 From Pharaoh. He was a transgressing tyrant.

31
10:83; 23:46; 28:4

٣٢ وَلَقَدِ اخْتَرْنَاهُمْ عَلَىٰ عِلْمٍ عَلَى الْعَالَمِينَ

32 And We chose them knowingly over all other people.

32
2:47; 7:140; 45:16

٣٣ وَآتَيْنَاهُم مِّنَ الْآيَاتِ مَا فِيهِ بَلَاءٌ مُّبِينٌ

33 And We gave them many signs, in which was an obvious test.

٣٤ إِنَّ هَٰؤُلَاءِ لَيَقُولُونَ

34 These people say.

٣٥ إِنْ هِيَ إِلَّا مَوْتَتُنَا الْأُولَىٰ وَمَا نَحْنُ بِمُنشَرِينَ

35 "There is nothing but our first death, and we will not be resurrected.

35
44:56

٣٦ فَأْتُوا بِآبَائِنَا إِن كُنتُمْ صَادِقِينَ

36 Bring back our ancestors, if you are truthful."

36
45:25

٣٧ أَهُمْ خَيْرٌ أَمْ قَوْمُ تُبَّعٍ وَالَّذِينَ مِن قَبْلِهِمْ ۚ أَهْلَكْنَاهُمْ ۖ إِنَّهُمْ كَانُوا مُجْرِمِينَ

37 Are they better, or the people of Tubba and those before them? We annihilated them. They were evildoers.

37
50:14

٣٨ وَمَا خَلَقْنَا السَّمَاوَاتِ وَالْأَرْضَ وَمَا بَيْنَهُمَا لَاعِبِينَ

38 We did not create the heavens and the earth and what is between them to play.

٣٩ مَا خَلَقْنَاهُمَا إِلَّا بِالْحَقِّ وَلَٰكِنَّ أَكْثَرَهُمْ لَا يَعْلَمُونَ

39 We created them only for a specific purpose, but most of them do not know.

٤٠ إِنَّ يَوْمَ الْفَصْلِ مِيقَاتُهُمْ أَجْمَعِينَ

40 The Day of Sorting Out is the appointed time for them all.

40
37:21; 56:49; 77:13; 78:17

٤١ يَوْمَ لَا يُغْنِي مَوْلًى عَن مَّوْلًى شَيْئًا وَلَا هُمْ يُنصَرُونَ

41 The Day when no friend will avail a friend in any way, and they will not be helped.

٤٢ إِلَّا مَنْ رَحِمَ اللَّهُ ۚ إِنَّهُ هُوَ الْعَزِيزُ الرَّحِيمُ

42 Except for him upon whom God has mercy. He is the Mighty, the Merciful.

٤٣ إِنَّ شَجَرَتَ الزَّقُّومِ

43–44
37:62; 56:52

43 The Tree of Bitterness.

٤٤ طَعَامُ الْأَثِيمِ

44 The food of the sinner.

٤٥ كَالْمُهْلِ يَغْلِي فِي الْبُطُونِ

45 Like molten lead; boiling inside the bellies.

٤٦ كَغَلْيِ الْحَمِيمِ

46 Like the boiling of seething water.

٤٧ خُذُوهُ فَاعْتِلُوهُ إِلَىٰ سَوَاءِ الْجَحِيمِ

47
69:30

47 Seize him and drag him into the midst of Hell!

٤٨ ثُمَّ صُبُّوا فَوْقَ رَأْسِهِ مِنْ عَذَابِ الْحَمِيمِ

48
22:19

48 Then pour over his head the suffering of the Inferno!

٤٩ ذُقْ إِنَّكَ أَنْتَ الْعَزِيزُ الْكَرِيمُ

49 Taste! You who were powerful and noble.

٥٠ إِنَّ هَٰذَا مَا كُنْتُمْ بِهِ تَمْتَرُونَ

50 This is what you used to doubt.

٥١ إِنَّ الْمُتَّقِينَ فِي مَقَامٍ أَمِينٍ

51 As for the righteous, they will be in a secure place.

٥٢ فِي جَنَّاتٍ وَعُيُونٍ

52 Amidst gardens and springs.

٥٣ يَلْبَسُونَ مِنْ سُنْدُسٍ وَإِسْتَبْرَقٍ مُتَقَابِلِينَ

53
18:31; 76:21

53 Dressed in silk and brocade, facing one another.

٥٤ كَذَٰلِكَ وَزَوَّجْنَاهُمْ بِحُورٍ عِينٍ

54
37:48; 52:20; 55:72; 56:22

54 So it is, and We will wed them to lovely companions.

٥٥ يَدْعُونَ فِيهَا بِكُلِّ فَاكِهَةٍ آمِنِينَ

55
36:57; 38:51

55 They will call therein for every kind of fruit, in peace and security.

٥٦ لَا يَذُوقُونَ فِيهَا الْمَوْتَ إِلَّا الْمَوْتَةَ الْأُولَىٰ ۖ وَوَقَاهُمْ عَذَابَ الْجَحِيمِ

56
37:58; 44:35

56 Therein they will not taste death, beyond the first death; and He will protect them from the torment of Hell.

٥٧ فَضْلًا مِنْ رَبِّكَ ۚ ذَٰلِكَ هُوَ الْفَوْزُ الْعَظِيمُ

57 A favor from your Lord. That is the supreme salvation.

٥٨ فَإِنَّمَا يَسَّرْنَاهُ بِلِسَانِكَ لَعَلَّهُمْ يَتَذَكَّرُونَ

58 We made it easy in your language, so that they may remember.

58
19:97; 54:17, 22, 32, 40

٥٩ فَارْتَقِبْ إِنَّهُم مُّرْتَقِبُونَ

59 So wait and watch. They too are waiting and watching.

Sūrah 45: Al-Jāthiyah

سُورَةُ ٱلْجَاثِيَة (Kneeling)

بِسْمِ ٱللَّهِ ٱلرَّحْمَٰنِ ٱلرَّحِيمِ

١ حم

1 Hā, Mīm.

٢ تَنزِيلُ الْكِتَابِ مِنَ اللَّهِ الْعَزِيزِ الْحَكِيمِ

2 The revelation of the Book is from God, the Exalted in Might, the Wise.

2
pp 39:1; 46:2

٣ إِنَّ فِي السَّمَاوَاتِ وَالْأَرْضِ لَآيَاتٍ لِّلْمُؤْمِنِينَ

3 In the heavens and the earth are proofs for the believers.

3
30:22; 41:37

٤ وَفِي خَلْقِكُمْ وَمَا يَبُثُّ مِن دَابَّةٍ آيَاتٌ لِّقَوْمٍ يُوقِنُونَ

4 And in your own creation, and in the creatures He scattered, are signs for people of firm faith.

4
2:164; 31:10; 42:29

٥ وَاخْتِلَافِ اللَّيْلِ وَالنَّهَارِ وَمَا أَنزَلَ اللَّهُ مِنَ السَّمَاءِ مِن رِّزْقٍ فَأَحْيَا بِهِ الْأَرْضَ بَعْدَ مَوْتِهَا وَتَصْرِيفِ الرِّيَاحِ آيَاتٌ لِّقَوْمٍ يَعْقِلُونَ

5 And in the alternation of night and day, and in the sustenance God sends down from the sky, with which He revives the earth after its death, and in the circulation of the winds, are marvels for people who reason.

5
2:164; 3:190; 6:99; 30:46

٦ تِلْكَ آيَاتُ اللَّهِ نَتْلُوهَا عَلَيْكَ بِالْحَقِّ ۖ فَبِأَيِّ حَدِيثٍ بَعْدَ اللَّهِ وَآيَاتِهِ يُؤْمِنُونَ

6 These are God's Verses which We recite to you in truth. In which message, after God and His revelations, will they believe?

6
ᵃ 2:252; 3:108
ᵇ 7:185; 77:50

٧ وَيْلٌ لِّكُلِّ أَفَّاكٍ أَثِيمٍ

7 Woe to every sinful liar.

٨ يَسْمَعُ آيَاتِ اللَّهِ تُتْلَى عَلَيْهِ ثُمَّ يُصِرُّ مُسْتَكْبِرًا كَأَن لَّمْ يَسْمَعْهَا ۖ فَبَشِّرْهُ بِعَذَابٍ أَلِيمٍ

8 23:66; 31:7; 45:31; 71:7

8 Who hears God's revelations being recited to him, yet he persists arrogantly, as though he did not hear them. Announce to him a painful punishment.

٩ وَإِذَا عَلِمَ مِنْ آيَاتِنَا شَيْئًا اتَّخَذَهَا هُزُوًا ۚ أُولَٰئِكَ لَهُمْ عَذَابٌ مُهِينٌ

9 14:16; 18:106

9 And when he learns something of Our revelations, he takes them in mockery. For such there is a shameful punishment.

١٠ مِن وَرَائِهِمْ جَهَنَّمُ ۖ وَلَا يُغْنِي عَنْهُم مَّا كَسَبُوا شَيْئًا وَلَا مَا اتَّخَذُوا مِن دُونِ اللَّهِ أَوْلِيَاءَ ۖ وَلَهُمْ عَذَابٌ عَظِيمٌ b

10
a 14:16
b 3:116; 7:48; 92:11; 104:4

10 Beyond them lies Hell. What they have earned will not benefit them at all, nor will those they adopted as lords instead of God. They will have a terrible punishment.

١١ هَٰذَا هُدًى ۖ وَالَّذِينَ كَفَرُوا بِآيَاتِ رَبِّهِمْ لَهُمْ عَذَابٌ مِّن رِّجْزٍ أَلِيمٌ

11 This is guidance. Those who blaspheme their Lord's revelations will have a punishment of agonizing pain.

١٢ اللَّهُ الَّذِي سَخَّرَ لَكُمُ الْبَحْرَ لِتَجْرِيَ الْفُلْكُ فِيهِ بِأَمْرِهِ وَلِتَبْتَغُوا مِن فَضْلِهِ وَلَعَلَّكُمْ تَشْكُرُونَ

12 16:14

12 It is God who placed the sea at your service, so that ships may run through it by His command, and that you may seek of His bounty, and that you may give thanks.

١٣ وَسَخَّرَ لَكُم مَّا فِي السَّمَاوَاتِ وَمَا فِي الْأَرْضِ جَمِيعًا مِّنْهُ ۚ إِنَّ فِي ذَٰلِكَ لَآيَاتٍ لِّقَوْمٍ يَتَفَكَّرُونَ

13 16:14; 22:65; 31:20

13 And He placed at your service whatever is in the heavens and whatever is on earth—all is from Him. In that are signs for a people who think.

١٤ قُل لِّلَّذِينَ آمَنُوا يَغْفِرُوا لِلَّذِينَ لَا يَرْجُونَ أَيَّامَ اللَّهِ لِيَجْزِيَ قَوْمًا بِمَا كَانُوا يَكْسِبُونَ

14 Tell those who believe to forgive those who do not hope for the Days of God. He will fully recompense people for whatever they have earned.

١٥ مَنْ عَمِلَ صَالِحًا فَلِنَفْسِهِ ۖ وَمَنْ أَسَاءَ فَعَلَيْهَا ۖ ثُمَّ إِلَىٰ رَبِّكُمْ تُرْجَعُونَ

15 17:7; 30:44; 41:46

15 Whoever does a good deed, it is for his soul; and whoever commits evil, it is against it; then to your Lord you will be returned.

١٦ وَلَقَدْ آتَيْنَا بَنِي إِسْرَائِيلَ الْكِتَابَ وَالْحُكْمَ وَالنُّبُوَّةَ وَرَزَقْنَاهُم مِّنَ الطَّيِّبَاتِ a وَفَضَّلْنَاهُمْ عَلَى الْعَالَمِينَ b

16
a 6:89
b 2:47; 7:140; 44:32

16 We gave the Children of Israel the Book, and wisdom, and prophecy; and We provided them with the good things; and We gave them advantage over all other people.

١٧ وَآتَيْنَاهُم بَيِّنَاتٍ مِّنَ الْأَمْرِ ۖ فَمَا اخْتَلَفُوا إِلَّا مِن بَعْدِ مَا جَاءَهُمُ الْعِلْمُ بَغْيًا بَيْنَهُمْ ۚ إِنَّ رَبَّكَ يَقْضِي بَيْنَهُمْ يَوْمَ الْقِيَامَةِ فِيمَا كَانُوا فِيهِ يَخْتَلِفُونَ

17 2:213

17 And We gave them precise rulings. They fell into dispute only after knowledge came to them, out of mutual rivalry. Your Lord will judge between them on the Day of Resurrection regarding the things they differed about.

١٨ ثُمَّ جَعَلْنَاكَ عَلَىٰ شَرِيعَةٍ مِّنَ الْأَمْرِ فَاتَّبِعْهَا وَلَا تَتَّبِعْ أَهْوَاءَ الَّذِينَ لَا يَعْلَمُونَ

18 2:148; 5:48; 42:13–15

18 Then We set you upon a pathway of faith, so follow it, and do not follow the inclinations of those who do not know.

١٩ إِنَّهُمْ لَن يُغْنُوا عَنكَ مِنَ اللَّهِ شَيْئًا ۚ وَإِنَّ الظَّالِمِينَ بَعْضُهُمْ أَوْلِيَاءُ بَعْضٍ ۖ وَاللَّهُ وَلِيُّ الْمُتَّقِينَ

19

19 They will not help you against God in any way. The wrongdoers are allies of one another, while God is the Protector of the righteous.

٢٠ هَٰذَا بَصَائِرُ لِلنَّاسِ وَهُدًى وَرَحْمَةٌ لِّقَوْمٍ يُوقِنُونَ

20 7:203; 12:108; 28:43

20 This is an illumination for mankind, and guidance, and mercy for people who believe with certainty.

٢١ أَمْ حَسِبَ الَّذِينَ اجْتَرَحُوا السَّيِّئَاتِ أَن نَّجْعَلَهُمْ كَالَّذِينَ آمَنُوا وَعَمِلُوا الصَّالِحَاتِ سَوَاءً مَّحْيَاهُمْ وَمَمَاتُهُمْ ۚ سَاءَ مَا يَحْكُمُونَ

21 38:28; 68:35

21 Do those who perpetrate the evil deeds assume that We will regard them as equal to those who believe and do righteous deeds, whether in their life or their death? Evil is their judgment!

٢٢ وَخَلَقَ اللَّهُ السَّمَاوَاتِ وَالْأَرْضَ بِالْحَقِّ وَلِتُجْزَىٰ كُلُّ نَفْسٍ بِمَا كَسَبَتْ وَهُمْ لَا يُظْلَمُونَ

22 14:51

22 God created the heavens and the earth with justice, so that every soul will be repaid for what it has earned. And they will not be wronged.

٢٣ أَفَرَأَيْتَ مَنِ اتَّخَذَ إِلَٰهَهُ هَوَاهُ وَأَضَلَّهُ اللَّهُ عَلَىٰ عِلْمٍ وَخَتَمَ عَلَىٰ سَمْعِهِ وَقَلْبِهِ وَجَعَلَ عَلَىٰ بَصَرِهِ غِشَاوَةً فَمَن يَهْدِيهِ مِن بَعْدِ اللَّهِ ۚ أَفَلَا تَذَكَّرُونَ

23 2:7; 16:108; 25:43; 36:9

23 Have you considered him who has taken his desire for his god? God has knowingly led him astray, and has sealed his hearing and his heart, and has placed a veil over his vision. Who will guide him after God? Will you not reflect?

٢٤ وَقَالُوا مَا هِيَ إِلَّا حَيَاتُنَا الدُّنْيَا نَمُوتُ وَنَحْيَا وَمَا يُهْلِكُنَا إِلَّا الدَّهْرُ ۚ وَمَا لَهُم بِذَٰلِكَ مِنْ عِلْمٍ ۖ إِنْ هُمْ إِلَّا يَظُنُّونَ

24 6:29; 16:38; 23:37; 50:3

24 And they say, "There is nothing but this our present life; we die and we live, and nothing destroys us except time." But they have no knowledge of that; they are only guessing.

٢٥ وَإِذَا تُتْلَىٰ عَلَيْهِمْ آيَاتُنَا بَيِّنَاتٍ مَّا كَانَ حُجَّتَهُمْ إِلَّا أَن قَالُوا ائْتُوا بِآبَائِنَا إِن كُنتُمْ صَادِقِينَ

25 44:36

25 When Our clarifying Verses are recited to them, their only argument is to say, "Bring back our ancestors, if you are truthful."

٢٦ قُلِ اللَّهُ يُحْيِيكُمْ ثُمَّ يُمِيتُكُمْ ثُمَّ يَجْمَعُكُمْ إِلَىٰ يَوْمِ الْقِيَامَةِ لَا رَيْبَ فِيهِ وَلَٰكِنَّ أَكْثَرَ النَّاسِ لَا يَعْلَمُونَ

26 2:28

26 Say, "God gives you life, then He makes you die; then He gathers you for the Day of Resurrection, about which there is no doubt. But most people do not know."

٢٧ وَلِلَّهِ مُلْكُ السَّمَاوَاتِ وَالْأَرْضِ ۚ وَيَوْمَ تَقُومُ السَّاعَةُ يَوْمَئِذٍ يَخْسَرُ الْمُبْطِلُونَ

27

27 To God belongs the kingship of the heavens and the earth. On the Day when the Hour takes place, on that Day the falsifiers will lose.

٢٨ وَتَرَىٰ كُلَّ أُمَّةٍ جَاثِيَةً ۚ كُلُّ أُمَّةٍ تُدْعَىٰ إِلَىٰ كِتَابِهَا الْيَوْمَ تُجْزَوْنَ مَا كُنتُمْ تَعْمَلُونَ

28 17:71; 18:49

28 You will see every community on its knees; every community will be called to its Book: "Today you are being repaid for what you used to do.

٢٩ هَٰذَا كِتَابُنَا يَنطِقُ عَلَيْكُم بِالْحَقِّ ۚ إِنَّا كُنَّا نَسْتَنسِخُ مَا كُنتُمْ تَعْمَلُونَ

29 18:49; 19:79; 23:62; 39:69

29 This Book of Ours speaks about you in truth. We have been transcribing what you have been doing."

٣٠ فَأَمَّا الَّذِينَ آمَنُوا وَعَمِلُوا الصَّالِحَاتِ فَيُدْخِلُهُمْ رَبُّهُمْ فِي رَحْمَتِهِ ۚ ذَٰلِكَ هُوَ الْفَوْزُ الْمُبِينُ

30

30 As for those who believed and did righteous deeds, their Lord will admit them into His mercy. That is the clear triumph.

٣١ وَأَمَّا الَّذِينَ كَفَرُوا أَفَلَمْ تَكُنْ آيَاتِي تُتْلَىٰ عَلَيْكُمْ فَاسْتَكْبَرْتُمْ وَكُنتُمْ قَوْمًا مُّجْرِمِينَ

31 7:133; 10:75; 45:8

31 But as for those who disbelieved: "Were My revelations not recited to you? But you turned arrogant, and were guilty people."

٣٢ وَإِذَا قِيلَ إِنَّ وَعْدَ اللَّهِ حَقٌّ وَالسَّاعَةُ لَا رَيْبَ فِيهَا قُلْتُم مَّا نَدْرِي مَا السَّاعَةُ إِن نَّظُنُّ إِلَّا ظَنًّا وَمَا نَحْنُ بِمُسْتَيْقِنِينَ

32

32 And when it was said, "The promise of God is true, and of the Hour there is no doubt," you said, "We do not know what the Hour is; we think it is only speculation; we are not convinced."

٣٣ وَبَدَا لَهُمْ سَيِّئَاتُ مَا عَمِلُوا وَحَاقَ بِهِم مَّا كَانُوا بِهِ يَسْتَهْزِئُونَ

33 39:48

33 The evils of what they did will become evident to them, and the very thing they ridiculed will haunt them.

٣٤ وَقِيلَ الْيَوْمَ نَنسَاكُمْ كَمَا نَسِيتُمْ لِقَاءَ يَوْمِكُمْ هَٰذَا وَمَأْوَاكُمُ النَّارُ وَمَا لَكُم مِّن نَّاصِرِينَ

34 7:51; 32:14

34 And it will be said, "Today We forget you, as you forgot the encounter of this Day of yours. Your abode is the Fire, and there are no saviors for you.

٣٥ ذَٰلِكُم بِأَنَّكُمُ اتَّخَذْتُمْ آيَاتِ اللَّهِ هُزُوًا وَغَرَّتْكُمُ الْحَيَاةُ الدُّنْيَا ۚ فَالْيَوْمَ لَا يُخْرَجُونَ مِنْهَا وَلَا هُمْ يُسْتَعْتَبُونَ

35 18:106

35 That is because you took God's revelations for a joke, and the worldly life lured you." So today they will not be brought out of it, and they will not be allowed to repent.

٣٦ فَلِلَّهِ الْحَمْدُ رَبِّ السَّمَاوَاتِ وَرَبِّ الْأَرْضِ رَبِّ الْعَالَمِينَ

36 Praise belongs to God; Lord of the heavens, Lord of the earth, Lord of humanity.

36   1:2; 6:1, 45; 35:1; 39:75

٣٧ وَلَهُ الْكِبْرِيَاءُ فِي السَّمَاوَاتِ وَالْأَرْضِ ۖ وَهُوَ الْعَزِيزُ الْحَكِيمُ

37 To Him belongs all supremacy in the heavens and the earth. He is the Majestic, the Wise.

37   43:84–85

Sūrah 46: Al-Aḥqāf

سُورَةُ ٱلْأَحْقَافِ (The Dunes)

بِسْمِ ٱللَّهِ ٱلرَّحْمَٰنِ ٱلرَّحِيمِ

١ حم

1 Hā', Mīm.

٢ تَنزِيلُ الْكِتَابِ مِنَ اللَّهِ الْعَزِيزِ الْحَكِيمِ

2 The sending down of the Scripture is from God, the Honorable, the Wise.

2   pp 39:1; 40:2; 45:2

٣ مَا خَلَقْنَا السَّمَاوَاتِ وَالْأَرْضَ وَمَا بَيْنَهُمَا إِلَّا بِالْحَقِّ وَأَجَلٍ مُّسَمًّى ۚ وَالَّذِينَ كَفَرُوا عَمَّا أُنذِرُوا مُعْرِضُونَ

3 We did not create the heavens and the earth and what lies between them except with reason, and for a finite period. But the blasphemers continue to ignore the warnings they receive.

3   15:85; 30:8

٤ قُلْ أَرَأَيْتُم مَّا تَدْعُونَ مِن دُونِ اللَّهِ أَرُونِي مَاذَا خَلَقُوا مِنَ الْأَرْضِ أَمْ لَهُمْ شِرْكٌ فِي السَّمَاوَاتِ ۖ[a] ائْتُونِي بِكِتَابٍ مِّن قَبْلِ هَٰذَا أَوْ أَثَارَةٍ مِّنْ عِلْمٍ إِن كُنتُمْ صَادِقِينَ[b]

4 Say, "Have you considered those you worship instead of God? Show me which portion of the earth they have created. Or do they own a share of the heavens? Bring me a scripture prior to this one, or some trace of knowledge, if you are truthful."

4   [a] 34:22; 35:40; 46:4
    [b] 43:21

٥ وَمَنْ أَضَلُّ مِمَّن يَدْعُو مِن دُونِ اللَّهِ مَن لَّا يَسْتَجِيبُ لَهُ إِلَىٰ يَوْمِ الْقِيَامَةِ وَهُمْ عَن دُعَائِهِمْ غَافِلُونَ

5 Who is more wrong than him who invokes, besides God, those who will not answer him until the Day of Resurrection, and are heedless of their prayers?

5   7:194; 19:82; 35:14

٦ وَإِذَا حُشِرَ النَّاسُ كَانُوا لَهُمْ أَعْدَاءً وَكَانُوا بِعِبَادَتِهِمْ كَافِرِينَ

6 And when humanity is gathered, they will be enemies to them, and will renounce their worship of them.

٧ وَإِذَا تُتْلَىٰ عَلَيْهِمْ آيَاتُنَا بَيِّنَاتٍ قَالَ الَّذِينَ كَفَرُوا لِلْحَقِّ لَمَّا جَاءَهُمْ هَٰذَا سِحْرٌ مُبِينٌ

7
10:76; 11:7; 21:2–3; 34:43

7 When Our revelations are recited to them, plain and clear, those who disbelieve say of the truth when it has come to them, "This is obviously magic."

٨ أَمْ يَقُولُونَ افْتَرَاهُ ۖ قُلْ إِنِ افْتَرَيْتُهُ فَلَا تَمْلِكُونَ لِي مِنَ اللَّهِ شَيْئًا ۖ هُوَ أَعْلَمُ بِمَا تُفِيضُونَ فِيهِ ۖ كَفَىٰ بِهِ شَهِيدًا بَيْنِي وَبَيْنَكُمْ ۖ وَهُوَ الْغَفُورُ الرَّحِيمُ

8
10:37–38; 11:13, 35

8 Or do they say, "He invented it himself"? Say, "If I invented it myself, there is nothing you can do to protect me from God. He knows well what you are engaged in. He is sufficient witness between me and you. He is the Forgiver, the Merciful."

٩ قُلْ مَا كُنْتُ بِدْعًا مِنَ الرُّسُلِ وَمَا أَدْرِي مَا يُفْعَلُ بِي وَلَا بِكُمْ ۖ إِنْ أَتَّبِعُ إِلَّا مَا يُوحَىٰ إِلَيَّ وَمَا أَنَا إِلَّا نَذِيرٌ مُبِينٌ

9
6:50

9 Say, "I am not different from the other messengers; and I do not know what will be done with me, or with you. I only follow what is inspired in me, and I am only a clear warner."

١٠ قُلْ أَرَأَيْتُمْ إِنْ كَانَ مِنْ عِنْدِ اللَّهِ وَكَفَرْتُمْ بِهِ وَشَهِدَ شَاهِدٌ مِنْ بَنِي إِسْرَائِيلَ عَلَىٰ مِثْلِهِ فَآمَنَ وَاسْتَكْبَرْتُمْ ۖ إِنَّ اللَّهَ لَا يَهْدِي الْقَوْمَ الظَّالِمِينَ

10
41:52

10 Say, "Have you considered? What if it is from God and you disbelieve in it? A witness from the Children of Israel testified to its like, and has believed, while you turned arrogant. God does not guide the unjust people."

١١ وَقَالَ الَّذِينَ كَفَرُوا لِلَّذِينَ آمَنُوا لَوْ كَانَ خَيْرًا مَا سَبَقُونَا إِلَيْهِ ۚ وَإِذْ لَمْ يَهْتَدُوا بِهِ فَسَيَقُولُونَ هَٰذَا إِفْكٌ قَدِيمٌ

11 Those who disbelieve say to those who believe, "If it were anything good, they would not have preceded us to it." And since they were not guided by it, they will say, "This is an ancient lie."

١٢ وَمِنْ قَبْلِهِ كِتَابُ مُوسَىٰ إِمَامًا وَرَحْمَةً ۚ [a] وَهَٰذَا كِتَابٌ مُصَدِّقٌ لِسَانًا عَرَبِيًّا لِيُنْذِرَ الَّذِينَ ظَلَمُوا وَبُشْرَىٰ لِلْمُحْسِنِينَ [b]

12
[a] 11:17
[b] 26:194–195; 39:28; 46:12

12 And before it was the Book of Moses, a model and a mercy. And this is a confirming Book, in the Arabic language, to warn those who do wrong—and good news for the doers of good.

١٣ إِنَّ الَّذِينَ قَالُوا رَبُّنَا اللَّهُ ثُمَّ اسْتَقَامُوا فَلَا خَوْفٌ عَلَيْهِمْ وَلَا هُمْ يَحْزَنُونَ

13
41:30

13 Those who say, "Our Lord is God," then lead a righteous life—they have nothing to fear, nor shall they grieve.

١٤ أُولَٰئِكَ أَصْحَابُ الْجَنَّةِ خَالِدِينَ فِيهَا جَزَاءً بِمَا كَانُوا يَعْمَلُونَ

14 These are the inhabitants of Paradise, where they will dwell forever—a reward for what they used to do.

١٥ وَوَصَّيْنَا الْإِنسَانَ بِوَالِدَيْهِ إِحْسَانًا ۖ حَمَلَتْهُ أُمُّهُ كُرْهًا وَوَضَعَتْهُ كُرْهًا ۖ وَحَمْلُهُ وَفِصَالُهُ ثَلَاثُونَ شَهْرًا ۚ حَتَّىٰ إِذَا بَلَغَ أَشُدَّهُ وَبَلَغَ أَرْبَعِينَ سَنَةً قَالَ رَبِّ أَوْزِعْنِي أَنْ أَشْكُرَ نِعْمَتَكَ الَّتِي أَنْعَمْتَ عَلَيَّ وَعَلَىٰ وَالِدَيَّ وَأَنْ أَعْمَلَ صَالِحًا تَرْضَاهُ وَأَصْلِحْ لِي فِي ذُرِّيَّتِي ۖ إِنِّي تُبْتُ إِلَيْكَ وَإِنِّي مِنَ الْمُسْلِمِينَ

15 2:233; 17:23; 29:8; 31:14

15 We have enjoined upon man kindness to his parents. His mother carried him with difficulty, and delivered him with difficulty. His bearing and weaning takes thirty months. Until, when he has attained his maturity, and has reached forty years, he says, "Lord, enable me to appreciate the blessings You have bestowed upon me and upon my parents, and to act with righteousness, pleasing You. And improve my children for me. I have sincerely repented to You, and I am of those who have surrendered."

١٦ أُولَٰئِكَ الَّذِينَ نَتَقَبَّلُ عَنْهُمْ أَحْسَنَ مَا عَمِلُوا وَنَتَجَاوَزُ عَن سَيِّئَاتِهِمْ فِي أَصْحَابِ الْجَنَّةِ ۖ وَعْدَ الصِّدْقِ الَّذِي كَانُوا يُوعَدُونَ

16 9:121

16 Those are they from whom We accept the best of their deeds, and We overlook their misdeeds, among the dwellers of Paradise—the promise of truth which they are promised.

١٧ وَالَّذِي قَالَ لِوَالِدَيْهِ أُفٍّ لَّكُمَا أَتَعِدَانِنِي أَنْ أُخْرَجَ وَقَدْ خَلَتِ الْقُرُونُ مِن قَبْلِي وَهُمَا يَسْتَغِيثَانِ اللَّهَ وَيْلَكَ آمِنْ إِنَّ وَعْدَ اللَّهِ حَقٌّ فَيَقُولُ مَا هَٰذَا إِلَّا أَسَاطِيرُ الْأَوَّلِينَ

17 17:23; 19:66

17 As for him who says to his parents, "Enough of you! Are you promising me that I will be raised up, when generations have passed away before me?" While they cry for God's help, "Woe to you! Believe! The promise of God is true!" But he says, "These are nothing but tales of the ancients."

١٨ أُولَٰئِكَ الَّذِينَ حَقَّ عَلَيْهِمُ الْقَوْلُ فِي أُمَمٍ قَدْ خَلَتْ مِن قَبْلِهِم مِّنَ الْجِنِّ وَالْإِنسِ ۖ إِنَّهُمْ كَانُوا خَاسِرِينَ

18 36:7; 41:25

18 Those are they upon whom the sentence is justified, among the communities that have passed away before them, of jinn and humans. They are truly losers.

١٩ وَلِكُلٍّ دَرَجَاتٌ مِّمَّا عَمِلُوا ۖ وَلِيُوَفِّيَهُمْ أَعْمَالَهُمْ وَهُمْ لَا يُظْلَمُونَ

19 3:163; 6:132

19 There are degrees for everyone, according to what they have done, and He will repay them for their works in full, and they will not be wronged.

٢٠ وَيَوْمَ يُعْرَضُ الَّذِينَ كَفَرُوا عَلَى النَّارِ أَذْهَبْتُمْ طَيِّبَاتِكُمْ فِي حَيَاتِكُمُ الدُّنْيَا وَاسْتَمْتَعْتُم بِهَا فَالْيَوْمَ تُجْزَوْنَ عَذَابَ الْهُونِ بِمَا كُنتُمْ تَسْتَكْبِرُونَ فِي الْأَرْضِ بِغَيْرِ الْحَقِّ وَبِمَا كُنتُمْ تَفْسُقُونَ

20 18:53, 100; 28:39; 41:15; 46:37

20 On the Day when the faithless will be paraded before the Fire: "You have squandered your good in your worldly life, and you took pleasure in them. So today you are being repaid with the torment of shame, because of your unjust arrogance on earth, and because you used to sin."

٢١ وَاذْكُرْ أَخَا عَادٍ إِذْ أَنذَرَ قَوْمَهُ بِالْأَحْقَافِ وَقَدْ خَلَتِ النُّذُرُ مِنْ بَيْنِ يَدَيْهِ وَمِنْ خَلْفِهِ أَلَّا تَعْبُدُوا إِلَّا اللَّهَ إِنِّي أَخَافُ عَلَيْكُمْ عَذَابَ يَوْمٍ عَظِيمٍ

21 7:65; 11:2, 50; 26:135–1135; 41:14

21 And mention the brother of 'Ād, as he warned his people at the dunes. Warnings have passed away before him, and after him: "Worship none but God; I fear for you the punishment of a tremendous Day."

٢٢ قَالُوا أَجِئْتَنَا لِتَأْفِكَنَا عَنْ آلِهَتِنَا فَأْتِنَا بِمَا تَعِدُنَا إِنْ كُنتَ مِنَ الصَّادِقِينَ

22 7:70

22 They said, "Did you come to us to divert us from our gods? Then bring us what you threaten us with, if you are being truthful."

٢٣ قَالَ إِنَّمَا الْعِلْمُ عِندَ اللَّهِ وَأُبَلِّغُكُم مَّا أُرْسِلْتُ بِهِ وَلَٰكِنِّي أَرَاكُمْ قَوْمًا تَجْهَلُونَ

23 7:67–68; 11:57

23 He said, "The knowledge is only with God, and I inform you of what I was sent with; but I see you are an ignorant people."

٢٤ فَلَمَّا رَأَوْهُ عَارِضًا مُّسْتَقْبِلَ أَوْدِيَتِهِمْ قَالُوا هَٰذَا عَارِضٌ مُّمْطِرُنَا ۚ بَلْ هُوَ مَا اسْتَعْجَلْتُم بِهِ ۖ رِيحٌ فِيهَا عَذَابٌ أَلِيمٌ

24 41:16; 51:41; 54:19

24 Then, when they saw a cloud approaching their valley, they said, "This is a cloud that will bring us rain." "In fact, it is what you were impatient for: a wind in which is grievous suffering."

٢٥ تُدَمِّرُ كُلَّ شَيْءٍ بِأَمْرِ رَبِّهَا فَأَصْبَحُوا لَا يُرَىٰ إِلَّا مَسَاكِنُهُمْ ۚ كَذَٰلِكَ نَجْزِي الْقَوْمَ الْمُجْرِمِينَ

25 It will destroy everything by the command of its Lord. And when the morning came upon them, there was nothing to be seen except their dwellings. Thus We requite the guilty people.

٢٦ وَلَقَدْ مَكَّنَّاهُمْ فِيمَا إِن مَّكَّنَّاكُمْ فِيهِ وَجَعَلْنَا لَهُمْ سَمْعًا وَأَبْصَارًا وَأَفْئِدَةً فَمَا أَغْنَىٰ عَنْهُمْ سَمْعُهُمْ وَلَا أَبْصَارُهُمْ وَلَا أَفْئِدَتُهُم مِّن شَيْءٍ إِذْ كَانُوا يَجْحَدُونَ بِآيَاتِ اللَّهِ وَحَاقَ بِهِم مَّا كَانُوا بِهِ يَسْتَهْزِئُونَ

26 6:6

26 We had empowered them in the same way as We empowered you; and We gave them the hearing, and the sight, and the minds. But neither their hearing, nor their sight, nor their minds availed them in any way. That is because they disregarded the revelations of God; and so they became surrounded by what they used to ridicule.

٢٧ وَلَقَدْ أَهْلَكْنَا مَا حَوْلَكُم مِّنَ الْقُرَىٰ وَصَرَّفْنَا الْآيَاتِ لَعَلَّهُمْ يَرْجِعُونَ

27 7:4; 19:74; 21:6; 22:45; 26:208; 28:58

27 We have destroyed many townships around you, and diversified the signs, so that they may return.

٢٨ فَلَوْلَا نَصَرَهُمُ الَّذِينَ اتَّخَذُوا مِن دُونِ اللَّهِ قُرْبَانًا آلِهَةً ۖ بَلْ ضَلُّوا عَنْهُمْ ۚ وَذَٰلِكَ إِفْكُهُمْ وَمَا كَانُوا يَفْتَرُونَ

28 7:192

28 Why then did the idols, whom they worshiped as means of nearness to God, not help them? In fact, they abandoned them. It was their lie, a fabrication of their own making.

٢٩ وَإِذْ صَرَفْنَا إِلَيْكَ نَفَرًا مِنَ الْجِنِّ يَسْتَمِعُونَ الْقُرْآنَ فَلَمَّا حَضَرُوهُ قَالُوا أَنْصِتُوا ۖ فَلَمَّا قُضِيَ وَلَّوْا إِلَىٰ قَوْمِهِمْ مُنْذِرِينَ

29
45:10; 72:1

29 Recall when We dispatched towards you a number of jinn, to listen to the Qur'an. When they came in its presence, they said, "Pay attention!" Then, when it was concluded, they rushed to their people, warning them.

٣٠ قَالُوا يَا قَوْمَنَا إِنَّا سَمِعْنَا كِتَابًا أُنْزِلَ مِنْ بَعْدِ مُوسَىٰ مُصَدِّقًا لِمَا بَيْنَ يَدَيْهِ يَهْدِي إِلَى الْحَقِّ وَإِلَىٰ طَرِيقٍ مُسْتَقِيمٍ

30
46:12

30 They said, "O our people, we have heard a Scripture, sent down after Moses, confirming what came before it. It guides to the truth, and to a straight path.

٣١ يَا قَوْمَنَا أَجِيبُوا دَاعِيَ اللَّهِ وَآمِنُوا بِهِ يَغْفِرْ لَكُمْ مِنْ ذُنُوبِكُمْ وَيُجِرْكُمْ مِنْ عَذَابٍ أَلِيمٍ

31

31 O our people! Answer the caller to God, and believe in Him; and He will forgive you your sins, and will save you from a painful punishment."

٣٢ وَمَنْ لَا يُجِبْ دَاعِيَ اللَّهِ فَلَيْسَ بِمُعْجِزٍ فِي الْأَرْضِ وَلَيْسَ لَهُ مِنْ دُونِهِ أَوْلِيَاءُ ۚ أُولَٰئِكَ فِي ضَلَالٍ مُبِينٍ

32
11:20

32 He who does not answer the caller to God will not escape on earth, and has no protectors besides Him. Those are in obvious error.

٣٣ أَوَلَمْ يَرَوْا أَنَّ اللَّهَ الَّذِي خَلَقَ السَّمَاوَاتِ وَالْأَرْضَ وَلَمْ يَعْيَ بِخَلْقِهِنَّ بِقَادِرٍ عَلَىٰ أَنْ يُحْيِيَ الْمَوْتَىٰ ۚ بَلَىٰ إِنَّهُ عَلَىٰ كُلِّ شَيْءٍ قَدِيرٌ

33
22:6

33 Do they not realize that God, who created the heavens and the earth, and was never tired by creating them, is Able to revive the dead? Yes indeed; He is Capable of everything.

٣٤ وَيَوْمَ يُعْرَضُ الَّذِينَ كَفَرُوا عَلَى النَّارِ أَلَيْسَ هَٰذَا بِالْحَقِّ ۖ قَالُوا بَلَىٰ وَرَبِّنَا ۚ قَالَ فَذُوقُوا الْعَذَابَ بِمَا كُنْتُمْ تَكْفُرُونَ

34
46:20

34 On the Day when those who disbelieved are presented to the Fire: "Is this not real?" They will say, "Yes, indeed, by our Lord." He will say, "Then taste the suffering for having disbelieved."

٣٥ فَاصْبِرْ كَمَا صَبَرَ أُولُو الْعَزْمِ مِنَ الرُّسُلِ وَلَا تَسْتَعْجِلْ لَهُمْ ۚ كَأَنَّهُمْ يَوْمَ يَرَوْنَ مَا يُوعَدُونَ لَمْ يَلْبَثُوا إِلَّا سَاعَةً مِنْ نَهَارٍ ۚ بَلَاغٌ ۚ فَهَلْ يُهْلَكُ إِلَّا الْقَوْمُ الْفَاسِقُونَ

35
10:45; 23:113

35 So be patient, as the messengers with resolve were patient, and do not be hasty regarding them. On the Day when they witness what they are promised, it will seem as if they had lasted only for an hour of a day. A proclamation: Will any be destroyed except the sinful people?

Sūrah 47: Muḥammad

سُورَةُ مُحَمَّد (Muhammad)

بِسْمِ ٱللَّهِ ٱلرَّحْمَٰنِ ٱلرَّحِيمِ

١ الَّذِينَ كَفَرُوا وَصَدُّوا عَن سَبِيلِ اللَّهِ أَضَلَّ أَعْمَالَهُمْ

1 1 Those who disbelieve and repel from the path of God—He nullifies their works.

4:167; 16:88; 47:8, 32, 34

٢ وَالَّذِينَ آمَنُوا وَعَمِلُوا الصَّالِحَاتِ وَآمَنُوا بِمَا نُزِّلَ عَلَىٰ مُحَمَّدٍ وَهُوَ الْحَقُّ مِن رَّبِّهِمْ ۙ كَفَّرَ عَنْهُمْ سَيِّئَاتِهِمْ وَأَصْلَحَ بَالَهُمْ

2 2 While those who believe, and work righteousness, and believe in what was sent down to Muhammad—and it is the truth from their Lord—He remits their sins, and relieves their concerns.

16:97

٣ ذَٰلِكَ بِأَنَّ الَّذِينَ كَفَرُوا اتَّبَعُوا الْبَاطِلَ وَأَنَّ الَّذِينَ آمَنُوا اتَّبَعُوا الْحَقَّ مِن رَّبِّهِمْ ۚ كَذَٰلِكَ يَضْرِبُ اللَّهُ لِلنَّاسِ أَمْثَالَهُمْ

3 3 That is because those who disbelieve follow falsehoods, while those who believe follow the truth from their Lord. God thus cites for the people their examples.

17:89; 30:58; 39:27

٤ فَإِذَا لَقِيتُمُ الَّذِينَ كَفَرُوا فَضَرْبَ الرِّقَابِ حَتَّىٰ إِذَا أَثْخَنتُمُوهُمْ فَشُدُّوا الْوَثَاقَ فَإِمَّا مَنًّا بَعْدُ وَإِمَّا فِدَاءً حَتَّىٰ تَضَعَ الْحَرْبُ أَوْزَارَهَا ۚ ذَٰلِكَ وَلَوْ يَشَاءُ اللَّهُ لَانتَصَرَ مِنْهُمْ وَلَٰكِن لِّيَبْلُوَ بَعْضَكُم بِبَعْضٍ ۗ وَالَّذِينَ قُتِلُوا فِي سَبِيلِ اللَّهِ فَلَن يُضِلَّ أَعْمَالَهُمْ

4 4 When you encounter those who disbelieve, strike at their necks. Then, when you have routed them, bind them firmly. Then, either release them by grace, or by ransom, until war lays down its burdens. Had God willed, He could have defeated them Himself, but He thus tests some of you by means of others. As for those who are killed in the way of God, He will not let their deeds go to waste.

8:12

٥ سَيَهْدِيهِمْ وَيُصْلِحُ بَالَهُمْ

5 He will guide them, and will improve their state of mind.

٦ وَيُدْخِلُهُمُ الْجَنَّةَ عَرَّفَهَا لَهُمْ

6 And will admit them into Paradise, which He has identified for them.

٧ يَا أَيُّهَا الَّذِينَ آمَنُوا إِن تَنصُرُوا اللَّهَ يَنصُرْكُمْ وَيُثَبِّتْ أَقْدَامَكُمْ

7 7 O you who believe! If you support God, He will support you, and will strengthen your foothold.

22:40; 30:47

٨ وَالَّذِينَ كَفَرُوا فَتَعْسًا لَّهُمْ وَأَضَلَّ أَعْمَالَهُمْ

8 8 But as for those who disbelieve, for them is perdition, and He will waste their deeds.

7:1

٩ ذَٰلِكَ بِأَنَّهُمْ كَرِهُوا مَا أَنزَلَ اللَّهُ فَأَحْبَطَ أَعْمَالَهُمْ

9 That is because they hated what God revealed, so He nullified their deeds.

9
33:19; 47:28, 32

١٠ أَفَلَمْ يَسِيرُوا فِي الْأَرْضِ فَيَنظُرُوا كَيْفَ كَانَ عَاقِبَةُ الَّذِينَ مِن قَبْلِهِمْ ۚ دَمَّرَ اللَّهُ عَلَيْهِمْ ۖ وَلِلْكَافِرِينَ أَمْثَالُهَا

10 Have they not journeyed through the earth and seen the consequences for those before them? God poured destruction upon them, and for the unbelievers is something comparable.

10
12:109; 27:51

١١ ذَٰلِكَ بِأَنَّ اللَّهَ مَوْلَى الَّذِينَ آمَنُوا وَأَنَّ الْكَافِرِينَ لَا مَوْلَىٰ لَهُمْ

11 That is because God is the Master of those who believe, while the disbelievers have no master.

11
3:150; 8:40; 22:78

١٢ إِنَّ اللَّهَ يُدْخِلُ الَّذِينَ آمَنُوا وَعَمِلُوا الصَّالِحَاتِ جَنَّاتٍ تَجْرِي مِن تَحْتِهَا الْأَنْهَارُ ۖ وَالَّذِينَ كَفَرُوا يَتَمَتَّعُونَ وَيَأْكُلُونَ كَمَا تَأْكُلُ الْأَنْعَامُ وَالنَّارُ مَثْوًى لَّهُمْ

12 God will admit those who believe and do good deeds into gardens beneath which rivers flow. As for those who disbelieve, they enjoy themselves, and eat as cattle eat, and the Fire will be their dwelling.

12
15:3

١٣ وَكَأَيِّن مِّن قَرْيَةٍ هِيَ أَشَدُّ قُوَّةً مِّن قَرْيَتِكَ الَّتِي أَخْرَجَتْكَ أَهْلَكْنَاهُمْ فَلَا نَاصِرَ لَهُمْ

13 How many a town was more powerful than your town which evicted you? We destroyed them, and there was no helper for them.

13
9:69; 22:40; 60:1

١٤ أَفَمَن كَانَ عَلَىٰ بَيِّنَةٍ مِّن رَّبِّهِ كَمَن زُيِّنَ لَهُ سُوءُ عَمَلِهِ وَاتَّبَعُوا أَهْوَاءَهُم

14 Is he who stands upon evidence from his Lord, like someone whose evil deed is made to appear good to him? And they follow their own desires?

١٥ مَّثَلُ الْجَنَّةِ الَّتِي وُعِدَ الْمُتَّقُونَ ۖ فِيهَا أَنْهَارٌ مِّن مَّاءٍ غَيْرِ آسِنٍ وَأَنْهَارٌ مِّن لَّبَنٍ لَّمْ يَتَغَيَّرْ طَعْمُهُ وَأَنْهَارٌ مِّنْ خَمْرٍ لَّذَّةٍ لِّلشَّارِبِينَ وَأَنْهَارٌ مِّنْ عَسَلٍ مُّصَفًّى ۖ وَلَهُمْ فِيهَا مِن كُلِّ الثَّمَرَاتِ وَمَغْفِرَةٌ مِّن رَّبِّهِمْ ۖ كَمَنْ هُوَ خَالِدٌ فِي النَّارِ وَسُقُوا مَاءً حَمِيمًا فَقَطَّعَ أَمْعَاءَهُمْ

15 The likeness of the Garden promised to the righteous: in it are rivers of pure water, and rivers of milk forever fresh, and rivers of wine delightful to the drinkers, and rivers of strained honey. And therein they will have of every fruit, and forgiveness from their Lord. Like one abiding in the Fire forever, and are given to drink boiling water, that cuts-up their bowels?

15
2:25; 12:47; 13:35; 22:20; 56:31

١٦ وَمِنْهُم مَّن يَسْتَمِعُ إِلَيْكَ حَتَّىٰ إِذَا خَرَجُوا مِنْ عِندِكَ قَالُوا لِلَّذِينَ أُوتُوا الْعِلْمَ مَاذَا قَالَ آنِفًا ۚ أُولَٰئِكَ الَّذِينَ طَبَعَ اللَّهُ عَلَىٰ قُلُوبِهِمْ وَاتَّبَعُوا أَهْوَاءَهُمْ

16 Among them are those who listen to you, but when they leave your presence, they say to those given knowledge, "What did he say just now?" Those are they whose hearts God has sealed, and they follow their own desires.

16
6:25

١٧ وَالَّذِينَ اهْتَدَوْا زَادَهُمْ هُدًى وَآتَاهُمْ تَقْوَاهُمْ

17 As for those who are guided, He increases them in guidance, and He has granted them their righteousness.

17
19:76

١٨ فَهَلْ يَنظُرُونَ إِلَّا السَّاعَةَ أَن تَأْتِيَهُم بَغْتَةً ۖ فَقَدْ جَاءَ أَشْرَاطُهَا ۚ [a] فَأَنَّىٰ لَهُمْ إِذَا جَاءَتْهُمْ ذِكْرَاهُمْ [b]

18 Are they just waiting until the Hour comes to them suddenly? Its tokens have already come. But how will they be reminded when it has come to them?

18
[a] 12:107; 43:66
[b] 34:52; 86:23

١٩ فَاعْلَمْ أَنَّهُ لَا إِلَٰهَ إِلَّا اللَّهُ وَاسْتَغْفِرْ لِذَنبِكَ وَلِلْمُؤْمِنِينَ وَالْمُؤْمِنَاتِ ۗ وَاللَّهُ يَعْلَمُ مُتَقَلَّبَكُمْ وَمَثْوَاكُمْ

19 Know that there is no god but God, and ask forgiveness for your sin, and for the believing men and believing women. God knows your movements, and your resting-place.

٢٠ وَيَقُولُ الَّذِينَ آمَنُوا لَوْلَا نُزِّلَتْ سُورَةٌ ۖ فَإِذَا أُنزِلَتْ سُورَةٌ مُّحْكَمَةٌ وَذُكِرَ فِيهَا الْقِتَالُ ۙ رَأَيْتَ الَّذِينَ فِي قُلُوبِهِم مَّرَضٌ يَنظُرُونَ إِلَيْكَ نَظَرَ الْمَغْشِيِّ عَلَيْهِ مِنَ الْمَوْتِ ۖ فَأَوْلَىٰ لَهُمْ

20 Those who believe say, "If only a chapter is sent down." Yet when a decisive chapter is sent down, and fighting is mentioned in it, you see those in whose hearts is sickness looking at you with the look of someone fainting at death. So woe to them!

20
3:7; 11:1; 22:52; 33:19

٢١ طَاعَةٌ وَقَوْلٌ مَّعْرُوفٌ ۚ فَإِذَا عَزَمَ الْأَمْرُ فَلَوْ صَدَقُوا اللَّهَ لَكَانَ خَيْرًا لَّهُمْ

21 Obedience and upright speech. Then, when the matter is settled, being true to God would have been better for them.

21
2:263

٢٢ فَهَلْ عَسَيْتُمْ إِن تَوَلَّيْتُمْ أَن تُفْسِدُوا فِي الْأَرْضِ وَتُقَطِّعُوا أَرْحَامَكُمْ

22 If you turn away, you are likely to make mischief on earth, and sever your family ties.

٢٣ أُولَٰئِكَ الَّذِينَ لَعَنَهُمُ اللَّهُ فَأَصَمَّهُمْ وَأَعْمَىٰ أَبْصَارَهُمْ

23 Those are they whom God has cursed. He made them deaf, and blinded their sight.

23
2:88

٢٤ أَفَلَا يَتَدَبَّرُونَ الْقُرْآنَ أَمْ عَلَىٰ قُلُوبٍ أَقْفَالُهَا

24 Will they not ponder the Qur'an? Or are there locks upon their hearts?

24
4:82; 23:68; 38:29

٢٥ إِنَّ الَّذِينَ ارْتَدُّوا عَلَىٰ أَدْبَارِهِم مِّن بَعْدِ مَا تَبَيَّنَ لَهُمُ الْهُدَى ۙ الشَّيْطَانُ سَوَّلَ لَهُمْ وَأَمْلَىٰ لَهُمْ

25 Those who reverted after the guidance became clear to them—Satan has enticed them, and has given them latitude.

25
2:217; 5:21, 54

٢٦ ذَٰلِكَ بِأَنَّهُمْ قَالُوا لِلَّذِينَ كَرِهُوا مَا نَزَّلَ اللَّهُ سَنُطِيعُكُمْ فِي بَعْضِ الْأَمْرِ ۖ وَاللَّهُ يَعْلَمُ إِسْرَارَهُمْ

26 That is because they said to those who hated what God has revealed, "We will obey you in certain matters." But God knows their secret thoughts.

٢٧ فَكَيْفَ إِذَا تَوَفَّتْهُمُ الْمَلَائِكَةُ يَضْرِبُونَ وُجُوهَهُمْ وَأَدْبَارَهُمْ

27   8:50

27 How about when the angels take them at death, beating their faces and their backs?

٢٨ ذَٰلِكَ بِأَنَّهُمُ اتَّبَعُوا مَا أَسْخَطَ اللَّهَ وَكَرِهُوا رِضْوَانَهُ فَأَحْبَطَ أَعْمَالَهُمْ

28   33:19; 47:9, 32

28 That is because they pursued what displeases God, and they disliked His approval, so He nullified their works.

٢٩ أَمْ حَسِبَ الَّذِينَ فِي قُلُوبِهِمْ مَرَضٌ أَنْ لَنْ يُخْرِجَ اللَّهُ أَضْغَانَهُمْ

29   2:10

29 Do those in whose hearts is sickness think that God will not expose their malice?

٣٠ وَلَوْ نَشَاءُ لَأَرَيْنَاكَهُمْ فَلَعَرَفْتَهُمْ بِسِيمَاهُمْ ۚ وَلَتَعْرِفَنَّهُمْ فِي لَحْنِ الْقَوْلِ ۚ وَاللَّهُ يَعْلَمُ أَعْمَالَكُمْ

30   7:46, 48; 55:41

30 Had We willed, We could have shown them to you, and you would have recognized them by their marks. Yet you will recognize them by their tone of speech. And God knows your actions.

٣١ وَلَنَبْلُوَنَّكُمْ حَتَّىٰ نَعْلَمَ الْمُجَاهِدِينَ مِنْكُمْ وَالصَّابِرِينَ وَنَبْلُوَ أَخْبَارَكُمْ

31   2:143; 3:142, 154; 9:16; 29:2

31 We will certainly test you, until We know those among you who strive, and those who are steadfast, and We will test your reactions.

٣٢ إِنَّ الَّذِينَ كَفَرُوا وَصَدُّوا عَنْ سَبِيلِ اللَّهِ وَشَاقُّوا الرَّسُولَ مِنْ بَعْدِ مَا تَبَيَّنَ لَهُمُ الْهُدَىٰ لَنْ يَضُرُّوا اللَّهَ شَيْئًا وَسَيُحْبِطُ أَعْمَالَهُمْ

32   33:19; 47:9, 28

32 Those who disbelieve, and hinder from the path of God, and oppose the Messenger after guidance has become clear to them—they will not hurt God in the least, but He will nullify their deeds.

٣٣ يَا أَيُّهَا الَّذِينَ آمَنُوا أَطِيعُوا اللَّهَ وَأَطِيعُوا الرَّسُولَ وَلَا تُبْطِلُوا أَعْمَالَكُمْ

33 O you who believe! Obey God, and obey the Messenger, and do not let your deeds go to waste.

٣٤ إِنَّ الَّذِينَ كَفَرُوا وَصَدُّوا عَنْ سَبِيلِ اللَّهِ ثُمَّ مَاتُوا وَهُمْ كُفَّارٌ فَلَنْ يَغْفِرَ اللَّهُ لَهُمْ

34   2:161; 3:91; 4:18

34 Those who disbelieve, and hinder from God's path, and then die as disbelievers—God will not forgive them.

٣٥ فَلَا تَهِنُوا وَتَدْعُوا إِلَى السَّلْمِ وَأَنْتُمُ الْأَعْلَوْنَ وَاللَّهُ مَعَكُمْ وَلَنْ يَتِرَكُمْ أَعْمَالَكُمْ

35   3:146; 8:18

35 So do not waver and call for peace while you have the upper hand. God is with you, and He will not waste your efforts.

٣٦ إِنَّمَا الْحَيَاةُ الدُّنْيَا لَعِبٌ وَلَهْوٌ ۚ وَإِنْ تُؤْمِنُوا وَتَتَّقُوا يُؤْتِكُمْ أُجُورَكُمْ وَلَا يَسْأَلْكُمْ أَمْوَالَكُمْ

36   6:32; 57:28

36 The life of this world is nothing but play and pastime. But if you have faith and lead a righteous life, He will grant you your rewards, and He will not ask you for your possessions.

٣٧ إِنْ يَسْأَلْكُمُوهَا فَيُحْفِكُمْ تَبْخَلُوا وَيُخْرِجْ أَضْغَانَكُمْ

37 Were He to ask you for it, and press you, you would become tight-fisted, and He would expose your unwillingness.

٣٨ هَا أَنْتُمْ هَؤُلَاءِ تُدْعَوْنَ لِتُنْفِقُوا فِي سَبِيلِ اللَّهِ فَمِنْكُمْ مَنْ يَبْخَلُ ۖ وَمَنْ يَبْخَلْ فَإِنَّمَا يَبْخَلُ عَنْ نَفْسِهِ ۚ وَاللَّهُ الْغَنِيُّ وَأَنْتُمُ الْفُقَرَاءُ ۚ وَإِنْ تَتَوَلَّوْا يَسْتَبْدِلْ قَوْمًا غَيْرَكُمْ ثُمَّ لَا يَكُونُوا أَمْثَالَكُمْ

38
4:131; 35:15

38 Here you are, being called to spend in the cause of God. Among you are those who withhold; but whoever withholds is withholding against his own soul. God is the Rich, while you are the needy. And if you turn away, He will replace you with another people, and they will not be like you.

Sūrah 48: Al-Fatḥ

سُورَةُ ٱلْفَتْحِ (Victory)

بِسْمِ ٱللَّهِ ٱلرَّحْمَٰنِ ٱلرَّحِيمِ

١ إِنَّا فَتَحْنَا لَكَ فَتْحًا مُبِينًا

1–3
110:1

1 We have granted you a conspicuous victory.

٢ لِيَغْفِرَ لَكَ اللَّهُ مَا تَقَدَّمَ مِنْ ذَنْبِكَ وَمَا تَأَخَّرَ وَيُتِمَّ نِعْمَتَهُ عَلَيْكَ وَيَهْدِيَكَ صِرَاطًا مُسْتَقِيمًا

2 That God may forgive you your sin, past and to come, and complete His favors upon you, and guide you in a straight path.

٣ وَيَنْصُرَكَ اللَّهُ نَصْرًا عَزِيزًا

3 And help you with an unwavering support.

٤ هُوَ الَّذِي أَنْزَلَ السَّكِينَةَ فِي قُلُوبِ الْمُؤْمِنِينَ[a] لِيَزْدَادُوا إِيمَانًا مَعَ إِيمَانِهِمْ[b] وَلِلَّهِ جُنُودُ السَّمَاوَاتِ وَالْأَرْضِ[c] وَكَانَ اللَّهُ عَلِيمًا حَكِيمًا

4
[a] 48:18, 26
[b] 8:2; 9:124; 74:31
[c] 9:26, 40; 48:7

4 It is He who sent down tranquility into the hearts of the believers, to add faith to their faith. To God belong the forces of the heavens and the earth. God is Knowing and Wise.

٥ لِيُدْخِلَ الْمُؤْمِنِينَ وَالْمُؤْمِنَاتِ جَنَّاتٍ تَجْرِي مِنْ تَحْتِهَا الْأَنْهَارُ خَالِدِينَ فِيهَا وَيُكَفِّرَ عَنْهُمْ سَيِّئَاتِهِمْ ۚ وَكَانَ ذَٰلِكَ عِنْدَ اللَّهِ فَوْزًا عَظِيمًا

5
33:73

5 He will admit the believers, male and female, into Gardens beneath which rivers flow, to abide therein forever, and He will remit their sins. That, with God, is a great triumph.

٦ وَيُعَذِّبَ الْمُنَافِقِينَ وَالْمُنَافِقَاتِ وَالْمُشْرِكِينَ وَالْمُشْرِكَاتِ الظَّانِّينَ بِاللَّهِ ظَنَّ السَّوْءِ ۚ عَلَيْهِمْ دَائِرَةُ السَّوْءِ ۖ وَغَضِبَ اللَّهُ عَلَيْهِمْ وَلَعَنَهُمْ وَأَعَدَّ لَهُمْ جَهَنَّمَ ۖ وَسَاءَتْ مَصِيرًا

6 48:12

6 And He will punish the hypocrites, male and female, and the idolaters, male and female, those who harbor evil thoughts about God. They are surrounded by evil; and God is angry with them, and has cursed them, and has prepared for them Hell—a miserable destination.

٧ وَلِلَّهِ جُنُودُ السَّمَاوَاتِ وَالْأَرْضِ ۚ وَكَانَ اللَّهُ عَزِيزًا حَكِيمًا

7 9:26, 40; 33:9; 48:4, 7; 74:31

7 To God belong the troops of the heavens and the earth. God is Mighty and Wise.

٨ إِنَّا أَرْسَلْنَاكَ شَاهِدًا وَمُبَشِّرًا وَنَذِيرًا

8 4:41; 33:45; 73:15

8 We sent you as a witness, and a bearer of good news, and a warner.

٩ لِتُؤْمِنُوا بِاللَّهِ وَرَسُولِهِ وَتُعَزِّرُوهُ وَتُوَقِّرُوهُ وَتُسَبِّحُوهُ بُكْرَةً وَأَصِيلًا

9

9 That you may believe in God and His Messenger, and support Him, and honor Him, and praise Him morning and evening.

١٠ إِنَّ الَّذِينَ يُبَايِعُونَكَ إِنَّمَا يُبَايِعُونَ اللَّهَ يَدُ اللَّهِ فَوْقَ أَيْدِيهِمْ ۚ فَمَنْ نَكَثَ فَإِنَّمَا يَنْكُثُ عَلَىٰ نَفْسِهِ ۖ وَمَنْ أَوْفَىٰ بِمَا عَاهَدَ عَلَيْهُ اللَّهَ فَسَيُؤْتِيهِ أَجْرًا عَظِيمًا

10 48:18, 26

10 Those who pledge allegiance to you are pledging allegiance to God. The hand of God is over their hands. Whoever breaks his pledge breaks it to his own loss. And whoever fulfills his covenant with God, He will grant him a great reward.

١١ سَيَقُولُ لَكَ الْمُخَلَّفُونَ مِنَ الْأَعْرَابِ شَغَلَتْنَا أَمْوَالُنَا وَأَهْلُونَا فَاسْتَغْفِرْ لَنَا ۚ يَقُولُونَ بِأَلْسِنَتِهِمْ مَا لَيْسَ فِي قُلُوبِهِمْ ۚ قُلْ فَمَنْ يَمْلِكُ لَكُمْ مِنَ اللَّهِ شَيْئًا إِنْ أَرَادَ بِكُمْ ضَرًّا أَوْ أَرَادَ بِكُمْ نَفْعًا ۚ بَلْ كَانَ اللَّهُ بِمَا تَعْمَلُونَ خَبِيرًا

11 3:167; 6:17; 10:107; 33:17

11 The Desert-Arabs who remained behind will say to you, "Our belongings and our families have preoccupied us, so ask forgiveness for us." They say with their tongues what is not in their hearts. Say, "Who can avail you anything against God, if He desires loss for you, or desires gain for you?" In fact, God is Informed of what you do.

١٢ بَلْ ظَنَنْتُمْ أَنْ لَنْ يَنْقَلِبَ الرَّسُولُ وَالْمُؤْمِنُونَ إِلَىٰ أَهْلِيهِمْ أَبَدًا وَزُيِّنَ ذَٰلِكَ فِي قُلُوبِكُمْ وَظَنَنْتُمْ ظَنَّ السَّوْءِ وَكُنْتُمْ قَوْمًا بُورًا

12 46:6

12 But you thought that the Messenger and the believers will never return to their families, and this seemed fine to your hearts; and you harbored evil thoughts, and were uncivilized people.

١٣ وَمَنْ لَمْ يُؤْمِنْ بِاللَّهِ وَرَسُولِهِ فَإِنَّا أَعْتَدْنَا لِلْكَافِرِينَ سَعِيرًا

13

13 He who does not believe in God and His Messenger—We have prepared for the disbelievers a Blazing Fire.

١٤ وَلِلَّهِ مُلْكُ السَّمَاوَاتِ وَالْأَرْضِ ۚ يَغْفِرُ لِمَن يَشَاءُ وَيُعَذِّبُ مَن يَشَاءُ ۚ وَكَانَ اللَّهُ غَفُورًا رَحِيمًا

14 To God belongs the kingdom of the heavens and the earth. He forgives whomever He wills, and He punishes whomever He wills. God is Forgiving and Merciful.

١٥ سَيَقُولُ الْمُخَلَّفُونَ إِذَا انطَلَقْتُمْ إِلَىٰ مَغَانِمَ لِتَأْخُذُوهَا ذَرُونَا نَتَّبِعْكُمْ ۖ يُرِيدُونَ أَن يُبَدِّلُوا كَلَامَ اللَّهِ ۚ قُل لَّن تَتَّبِعُونَا كَذَٰلِكُمْ قَالَ اللَّهُ مِن قَبْلُ ۖ فَسَيَقُولُونَ بَلْ تَحْسُدُونَنَا ۚ بَلْ كَانُوا لَا يَفْقَهُونَ إِلَّا قَلِيلًا

15 Those who lagged behind will say when you depart to collect the gains, "Let us follow you." They want to change the Word of God. Say, "You will not follow us; God has said so before." Then they will say, "But you are jealous of us." In fact, they understand only a little.

١٦ قُل لِّلْمُخَلَّفِينَ مِنَ الْأَعْرَابِ سَتُدْعَوْنَ إِلَىٰ قَوْمٍ أُولِي بَأْسٍ شَدِيدٍ تُقَاتِلُونَهُمْ أَوْ يُسْلِمُونَ ۖ فَإِن تُطِيعُوا يُؤْتِكُمُ اللَّهُ أَجْرًا حَسَنًا ۖ وَإِن تَتَوَلَّوْا كَمَا تَوَلَّيْتُم مِّن قَبْلُ يُعَذِّبْكُمْ عَذَابًا أَلِيمًا

16 Say to the Desert-Arabs who lagged behind, "You will be called against a people of great might; you will fight them, unless they submit. If you obey, God will give you a fine reward. But if you turn away, as you turned away before, He will punish you with a painful punishment."

١٧ لَّيْسَ عَلَى الْأَعْمَىٰ حَرَجٌ وَلَا عَلَى الْأَعْرَجِ حَرَجٌ وَلَا عَلَى الْمَرِيضِ حَرَجٌ ۗ وَمَن يُطِعِ اللَّهَ وَرَسُولَهُ يُدْخِلْهُ جَنَّاتٍ تَجْرِي مِن تَحْتِهَا الْأَنْهَارُ ۖ وَمَن يَتَوَلَّ يُعَذِّبْهُ عَذَابًا أَلِيمًا

17 9:91; 24:61

17 There is no blame on the blind, nor any blame on the lame, nor any blame on the sick. Whoever obeys God and His Messenger—He will admit him into gardens beneath which rivers flow; but whoever turns away—He will punish him with a painful punishment.

١٨ لَّقَدْ رَضِيَ اللَّهُ عَنِ الْمُؤْمِنِينَ إِذْ يُبَايِعُونَكَ تَحْتَ الشَّجَرَةِ فَعَلِمَ مَا فِي قُلُوبِهِمْ فَأَنزَلَ السَّكِينَةَ عَلَيْهِمْ وَأَثَابَهُمْ فَتْحًا قَرِيبًا

18 48:4, 10, 26

18 God was pleased with the believers, when they pledged allegiance to you under the tree. He knew what was in their hearts, and sent down serenity upon them, and rewarded them with an imminent conquest.

١٩ وَمَغَانِمَ كَثِيرَةً يَأْخُذُونَهَا ۗ وَكَانَ اللَّهُ عَزِيزًا حَكِيمًا

19 And abundant gains for them to capture. God is Mighty and Wise.

٢٠ وَعَدَكُمُ اللَّهُ مَغَانِمَ كَثِيرَةً تَأْخُذُونَهَا فَعَجَّلَ لَكُمْ هَٰذِهِ وَكَفَّ أَيْدِيَ النَّاسِ عَنكُمْ وَلِتَكُونَ آيَةً لِّلْمُؤْمِنِينَ وَيَهْدِيَكُمْ صِرَاطًا مُّسْتَقِيمًا

20 5:11; 48:24

20 God has promised you abundant gains, which you will capture. He has expedited this for you, and has restrained people's hands from you; that it may be a sign to the believers, and that He may guide you on a straight path.

٢١ وَأُخْرَىٰ لَمْ تَقْدِرُوا عَلَيْهَا قَدْ أَحَاطَ اللَّهُ بِهَا ۚ وَكَانَ اللَّهُ عَلَىٰ كُلِّ شَيْءٍ قَدِيرًا

21 And other things, of which you were incapable, but God has encompassed them. God is Capable of everything.

٢٢ وَلَوْ قَاتَلَكُمُ الَّذِينَ كَفَرُوا لَوَلَّوُا الْأَدْبَارَ ثُمَّ لَا يَجِدُونَ وَلِيًّا وَلَا نَصِيرًا

22   3:111; 59:11

22 If those who disbelieve had fought you, they would have turned back and fled, then found neither protector nor helper.

٢٣ سُنَّةَ اللَّهِ الَّتِي قَدْ خَلَتْ مِنْ قَبْلُ ۖ وَلَنْ تَجِدَ لِسُنَّةِ اللَّهِ تَبْدِيلًا

23   33:62

23 It is God's pattern, ongoing since the past. You will never find any change in God's pattern.

٢٤ وَهُوَ الَّذِي كَفَّ أَيْدِيَهُمْ عَنْكُمْ وَأَيْدِيَكُمْ عَنْهُمْ بِبَطْنِ مَكَّةَ مِنْ بَعْدِ أَنْ أَظْفَرَكُمْ عَلَيْهِمْ ۚ وَكَانَ اللَّهُ بِمَا تَعْمَلُونَ بَصِيرًا

24   5:11; 48:20

24 It is He who withheld their hands from you, and your hands from them, in the valley of Mecca, after giving you advantage over them. God is Observer of what you do.

٢٥ هُمُ الَّذِينَ كَفَرُوا وَصَدُّوكُمْ عَنِ الْمَسْجِدِ الْحَرَامِ وَالْهَدْيَ مَعْكُوفًا أَنْ يَبْلُغَ مَحِلَّهُ ۚ وَلَوْلَا رِجَالٌ مُؤْمِنُونَ وَنِسَاءٌ مُؤْمِنَاتٌ لَمْ تَعْلَمُوهُمْ أَنْ تَطَئُوهُمْ فَتُصِيبَكُمْ مِنْهُمْ مَعَرَّةٌ بِغَيْرِ عِلْمٍ ۖ لِيُدْخِلَ اللَّهُ فِي رَحْمَتِهِ مَنْ يَشَاءُ ۚ لَوْ تَزَيَّلُوا لَعَذَّبْنَا الَّذِينَ كَفَرُوا مِنْهُمْ عَذَابًا أَلِيمًا

25   2:114

25 It is they who disbelieved, and barred you from the Sacred Mosque, and prevented the offering from reaching its destination. Were it not for faithful men and faithful women, whom you did not know, you were about to hurt them, and became guilty of an unintentional crime. Thus God admits into His mercy whomever He wills. Had they dispersed, We would have punished those who disbelieved among them with a painful penalty.

٢٦ إِذْ جَعَلَ الَّذِينَ كَفَرُوا فِي قُلُوبِهِمُ الْحَمِيَّةَ حَمِيَّةَ الْجَاهِلِيَّةِ فَأَنْزَلَ اللَّهُ سَكِينَتَهُ عَلَىٰ رَسُولِهِ وَعَلَى الْمُؤْمِنِينَ وَأَلْزَمَهُمْ كَلِمَةَ التَّقْوَىٰ وَكَانُوا أَحَقَّ بِهَا وَأَهْلَهَا ۚ وَكَانَ اللَّهُ بِكُلِّ شَيْءٍ عَلِيمًا

26   48:10, 18

26 Those who disbelieved filled their hearts with rage—the rage of the days of ignorance. But God sent His serenity down upon His Messenger, and upon the believers, and imposed on them the words of righteousness—of which they were most worthy and deserving. God is aware of everything.

٢٧ لَقَدْ صَدَقَ اللَّهُ رَسُولَهُ الرُّؤْيَا بِالْحَقِّ ۖ لَتَدْخُلُنَّ الْمَسْجِدَ الْحَرَامَ إِنْ شَاءَ اللَّهُ آمِنِينَ مُحَلِّقِينَ رُءُوسَكُمْ وَمُقَصِّرِينَ لَا تَخَافُونَ ۖ فَعَلِمَ مَا لَمْ تَعْلَمُوا فَجَعَلَ مِنْ دُونِ ذَٰلِكَ فَتْحًا قَرِيبًا

27   2:196

27 God has fulfilled His Messenger's vision in truth: "You will enter the Sacred Mosque, God willing, in security, heads shaven, or hair cut short, not fearing. He knew what you did not know, and has granted besides that an imminent victory."

٢٨ هُوَ الَّذِي أَرْسَلَ رَسُولَهُ بِالْهُدَىٰ وَدِينِ الْحَقِّ لِيُظْهِرَهُ عَلَى الدِّينِ كُلِّهِ ۚ وَكَفَىٰ بِاللَّهِ شَهِيدًا

28
pp 9:33; 61:9

28 It is He who sent His Messenger with the guidance and the religion of truth, to make it prevail over all religions. God suffices as Witness.

٢٩ مُحَمَّدٌ رَسُولُ اللَّهِ ۚ وَالَّذِينَ مَعَهُ أَشِدَّاءُ عَلَى الْكُفَّارِ رُحَمَاءُ بَيْنَهُمْ ۖ تَرَاهُمْ رُكَّعًا سُجَّدًا يَبْتَغُونَ فَضْلًا مِنَ اللَّهِ وَرِضْوَانًا ۖ سِيمَاهُمْ فِي وُجُوهِهِمْ مِنْ أَثَرِ السُّجُودِ ۚ ذَٰلِكَ مَثَلُهُمْ فِي التَّوْرَاةِ ۚ وَمَثَلُهُمْ فِي الْإِنْجِيلِ كَزَرْعٍ أَخْرَجَ شَطْأَهُ فَآزَرَهُ فَاسْتَغْلَظَ فَاسْتَوَىٰ عَلَىٰ سُوقِهِ يُعْجِبُ الزُّرَّاعَ لِيَغِيظَ بِهِمُ الْكُفَّارَ ۗ وَعَدَ اللَّهُ الَّذِينَ آمَنُوا وَعَمِلُوا الصَّالِحَاتِ مِنْهُمْ مَغْفِرَةً وَأَجْرًا عَظِيمًا

29
5:54

29 Muhammad is the Messenger of God. Those with him are stern against the disbelievers, yet compassionate amongst themselves. You see them kneeling, prostrating, seeking blessings from God and approval. Their marks are on their faces from the effects of prostration. Such is their description in the Torah, and their description in the Gospel: like a plant that sprouts, becomes strong, grows thick, and rests on its stem, impressing the farmers. Through them He enrages the disbelievers. God has promised those among them who believe and do good deeds forgiveness and a great reward.

Sūrah 49: Al-Hujurāt

سُورَةُ ٱلْحُجُرَات (The Chambers)

بِسْمِ ٱللَّهِ ٱلرَّحْمَٰنِ ٱلرَّحِيم

١ يَا أَيُّهَا الَّذِينَ آمَنُوا لَا تُقَدِّمُوا بَيْنَ يَدَيِ اللَّهِ وَرَسُولِهِ ۖ وَاتَّقُوا اللَّهَ ۚ إِنَّ اللَّهَ سَمِيعٌ عَلِيمٌ

1 O you who believe! Do not place your opinions above that of God and His Messenger, and fear God. God is Hearing and Knowing.

٢ يَا أَيُّهَا الَّذِينَ آمَنُوا لَا تَرْفَعُوا أَصْوَاتَكُمْ فَوْقَ صَوْتِ النَّبِيِّ وَلَا تَجْهَرُوا لَهُ بِالْقَوْلِ كَجَهْرِ بَعْضِكُمْ لِبَعْضٍ أَنْ تَحْبَطَ أَعْمَالُكُمْ وَأَنْتُمْ لَا تَشْعُرُونَ

2–3
24:63; 31:19

2 O you who believe! Do not raise your voices above the voice of the Prophet, and do not speak loudly to him, as you speak loudly to one another, lest your works be in vain without you realizing.

٣ إِنَّ الَّذِينَ يَغُضُّونَ أَصْوَاتَهُمْ عِنْدَ رَسُولِ اللَّهِ أُولَٰئِكَ الَّذِينَ امْتَحَنَ اللَّهُ قُلُوبَهُمْ لِلتَّقْوَىٰ ۚ لَهُمْ مَغْفِرَةٌ وَأَجْرٌ عَظِيمٌ

3 Those who lower their voices before God's Messenger—those are they whose hearts God has tested for piety. They will have forgiveness and a great reward.

٤ إِنَّ الَّذِينَ يُنَادُونَكَ مِنْ وَرَاءِ الْحُجُرَاتِ أَكْثَرُهُمْ لَا يَعْقِلُونَ

4 Those who call you from behind the chambers—most of them do not understand.

٥ وَلَوْ أَنَّهُمْ صَبَرُوا حَتَّىٰ تَخْرُجَ إِلَيْهِمْ لَكَانَ خَيْرًا لَهُمْ ۚ وَاللَّهُ غَفُورٌ رَحِيمٌ

5 Had they remained patient until you came out to them, it would have been better for them. But God is Forgiving and Merciful.

٦ يَا أَيُّهَا الَّذِينَ آمَنُوا إِنْ جَاءَكُمْ فَاسِقٌ بِنَبَإٍ فَتَبَيَّنُوا أَنْ تُصِيبُوا قَوْمًا بِجَهَالَةٍ فَتُصْبِحُوا عَلَىٰ مَا فَعَلْتُمْ نَادِمِينَ

6
4:24, 94

6 O you who believe! If a troublemaker brings you any news, investigate, lest you harm people out of ignorance, and you become regretful for what you have done.

٧ وَاعْلَمُوا أَنَّ فِيكُمْ رَسُولَ اللَّهِ ۚ لَوْ يُطِيعُكُمْ فِي كَثِيرٍ مِنَ الْأَمْرِ لَعَنِتُّمْ وَلَٰكِنَّ اللَّهَ حَبَّبَ إِلَيْكُمُ الْإِيمَانَ وَزَيَّنَهُ فِي قُلُوبِكُمْ وَكَرَّهَ إِلَيْكُمُ الْكُفْرَ وَالْفُسُوقَ وَالْعِصْيَانَ ۚ أُولَٰئِكَ هُمُ الرَّاشِدُونَ

7 And know that among you is the Messenger of God. Had he obeyed you in many things, you would have suffered hardship. But God has given you the love of faith, and adorned it in your hearts, and made disbelief, mischief, and rebellion hateful to you. These are the rightly guided.

٨ فَضْلًا مِنَ اللَّهِ وَنِعْمَةً ۚ وَاللَّهُ عَلِيمٌ حَكِيمٌ

8 A Grace and Favor from God. God is Knowing and Wise.

٩ وَإِنْ طَائِفَتَانِ مِنَ الْمُؤْمِنِينَ اقْتَتَلُوا فَأَصْلِحُوا بَيْنَهُمَا ۖ فَإِنْ بَغَتْ إِحْدَاهُمَا عَلَى الْأُخْرَىٰ فَقَاتِلُوا الَّتِي تَبْغِي حَتَّىٰ تَفِيءَ إِلَىٰ أَمْرِ اللَّهِ ۚ فَإِنْ فَاءَتْ فَأَصْلِحُوا بَيْنَهُمَا بِالْعَدْلِ وَأَقْسِطُوا ۖ إِنَّ اللَّهَ يُحِبُّ الْمُقْسِطِينَ

9 If two groups of believers fight each other, reconcile between them. But if one group aggresses against the other, fight the aggressing group until it complies with God's command. Once it has complied, reconcile between them with justice, and be equitable. God loves the equitable.

١٠ إِنَّمَا الْمُؤْمِنُونَ إِخْوَةٌ فَأَصْلِحُوا بَيْنَ أَخَوَيْكُمْ ۚ وَاتَّقُوا اللَّهَ لَعَلَّكُمْ تُرْحَمُونَ

10
3:103; 9:11; 33:5

10 The believers are brothers, so reconcile between your brothers, and remain conscious of God, so that you may receive mercy.

١١ يَا أَيُّهَا الَّذِينَ آمَنُوا لَا يَسْخَرْ قَوْمٌ مِنْ قَوْمٍ عَسَىٰ أَنْ يَكُونُوا خَيْرًا مِنْهُمْ وَلَا نِسَاءٌ مِنْ نِسَاءٍ عَسَىٰ أَنْ يَكُنَّ خَيْرًا مِنْهُنَّ ۖ وَلَا تَلْمِزُوا أَنْفُسَكُمْ وَلَا تَنَابَزُوا بِالْأَلْقَابِ ۖ بِئْسَ الِاسْمُ الْفُسُوقُ بَعْدَ الْإِيمَانِ ۚ وَمَنْ لَمْ يَتُبْ فَأُولَٰئِكَ هُمُ الظَّالِمُونَ

11
9:79; 22:212; 83:29–30

11 O you who believe! No people shall ridicule other people, for they may be better than they. Nor shall any women ridicule other women, for they may be better than they. Nor shall you slander one another, nor shall you insult one another with names. Evil is the return to wickedness after having attained faith. Whoever does not repent—these are the wrongdoers.

١٢ يَا أَيُّهَا الَّذِينَ آمَنُوا اجْتَنِبُوا كَثِيرًا مِنَ الظَّنِّ إِنَّ بَعْضَ الظَّنِّ إِثْمٌ ۖ وَلَا تَجَسَّسُوا وَلَا يَغْتَبْ بَعْضُكُم بَعْضًا ۚ أَيُحِبُّ أَحَدُكُمْ أَن يَأْكُلَ لَحْمَ أَخِيهِ مَيْتًا فَكَرِهْتُمُوهُ ۚ وَاتَّقُوا اللَّهَ ۚ إِنَّ اللَّهَ تَوَّابٌ رَحِيمٌ

12 O you who believe! Avoid most suspicion—some suspicion is sinful. And do not spy on one another, nor backbite one another. Would any of you like to eat the flesh of his dead brother? You would detest it. So remain mindful of God. God is Most Relenting, Most Merciful.

١٣ يَا أَيُّهَا النَّاسُ إِنَّا خَلَقْنَاكُم مِّن ذَكَرٍ وَأُنثَىٰ وَجَعَلْنَاكُمْ شُعُوبًا وَقَبَائِلَ لِتَعَارَفُوا ۚ إِنَّ أَكْرَمَكُمْ عِندَ اللَّهِ أَتْقَاكُمْ ۚ إِنَّ اللَّهَ عَلِيمٌ خَبِيرٌ

13
4:1

13 O people! We created you from a male and a female, and made you races and tribes, that you may know one another. The best among you in the sight of God is the most righteous. God is All-Knowing, Well-Experienced.

١٤ قَالَتِ الْأَعْرَابُ آمَنَّا ۖ قُل لَّمْ تُؤْمِنُوا وَلَٰكِن قُولُوا أَسْلَمْنَا وَلَمَّا يَدْخُلِ الْإِيمَانُ فِي قُلُوبِكُمْ ۖ وَإِن تُطِيعُوا اللَّهَ وَرَسُولَهُ لَا يَلِتْكُم مِّنْ أَعْمَالِكُمْ شَيْئًا ۚ إِنَّ اللَّهَ غَفُورٌ رَحِيمٌ

14
9:97

14 The Desert-Arabs say, "We have believed." Say, "You have not believed; but say, 'We have submitted,' for faith has not yet entered into your hearts. But if you obey God and His Messenger, He will not diminish any of your deeds. God is Forgiving and Merciful."

١٥ إِنَّمَا الْمُؤْمِنُونَ الَّذِينَ آمَنُوا بِاللَّهِ وَرَسُولِهِ ثُمَّ لَمْ يَرْتَابُوا وَجَاهَدُوا بِأَمْوَالِهِمْ وَأَنفُسِهِمْ فِي سَبِيلِ اللَّهِ ۚ أُولَٰئِكَ هُمُ الصَّادِقُونَ

15
4:95; 8:72; 9:20, 41, 44, 81, 88

15 The believers are those who believe in God and His Messenger, and then have not doubted, and strive for God's cause with their wealth and their persons. These are the sincere.

١٦ قُلْ أَتُعَلِّمُونَ اللَّهَ بِدِينِكُمْ وَاللَّهُ يَعْلَمُ مَا فِي السَّمَاوَاتِ وَمَا فِي الْأَرْضِ ۚ وَاللَّهُ بِكُلِّ شَيْءٍ عَلِيمٌ

16
10:18; 13:33; 53:32

16 Say, "Are you going to teach God about your religion, when God knows everything in the heavens and the earth, and God is aware of all things?"

١٧ يَمُنُّونَ عَلَيْكَ أَنْ أَسْلَمُوا ۖ قُل لَّا تَمُنُّوا عَلَيَّ إِسْلَامَكُم ۖ بَلِ اللَّهُ يَمُنُّ عَلَيْكُمْ أَنْ هَدَاكُمْ لِلْإِيمَانِ إِن كُنتُمْ صَادِقِينَ

17 They regarded it a favor to you that they have submitted. Say, "Do not consider your submission a favor to me; it is God who has done you a favor by guiding you to the faith, if you are sincere."

١٨ إِنَّ اللَّهَ يَعْلَمُ غَيْبَ السَّمَاوَاتِ وَالْأَرْضِ ۚ وَاللَّهُ بَصِيرٌ بِمَا تَعْمَلُونَ

18
2:33; 35:38

18 God knows the secrets of the heavens and the earth, and God is seeing of everything you do.

Sūrah 50: Qāf

سُورَةُ ق (Qāf)

بِسْمِ ٱللَّهِ ٱلرَّحْمَٰنِ ٱلرَّحِيمِ

١ ق ۚ وَٱلْقُرْآنِ ٱلْمَجِيدِ

1 Qāf. By the Glorious Qur'an.

٢ بَلْ عَجِبُوا أَن جَاءَهُم مُّنذِرٌ مِّنْهُمْ فَقَالَ ٱلْكَافِرُونَ هَٰذَا شَيْءٌ عَجِيبٌ

2 They marveled that a warner has come to them from among them. The disbelievers say, "This is something strange.

2
PP 38:4
7:63; 10:2; 38:2

٣ أَإِذَا مِتْنَا وَكُنَّا تُرَابًا ۖ ذَٰلِكَ رَجْعٌ بَعِيدٌ

3 When we have died and become dust? This is a farfetched return."

3
13:5; 23:82; 37:16; 56:47

٤ قَدْ عَلِمْنَا مَا تَنقُصُ ٱلْأَرْضُ مِنْهُمْ ۖ وَعِندَنَا كِتَابٌ حَفِيظٌ

4 We know what the earth consumes of them, and with Us is a comprehensive book.

٥ بَلْ كَذَّبُوا بِٱلْحَقِّ لَمَّا جَاءَهُمْ فَهُمْ فِي أَمْرٍ مَّرِيجٍ

5 But they denied the truth when it has come to them, so they are in a confused state.

٦ أَفَلَمْ يَنظُرُوا إِلَى ٱلسَّمَاءِ فَوْقَهُمْ كَيْفَ بَنَيْنَاهَا وَزَيَّنَّاهَا وَمَا لَهَا مِن فُرُوجٍ

6 Have they not observed the sky above them, how We constructed it, and decorated it, and it has no cracks?

6
40:64; 51:47

٧ وَٱلْأَرْضَ مَدَدْنَاهَا وَأَلْقَيْنَا فِيهَا رَوَاسِيَ وَأَنبَتْنَا فِيهَا مِن كُلِّ زَوْجٍ بَهِيجٍ

7 And the earth, how We spread it out, and set on it mountains, and grew in it all kinds of delightful pairs?

7
13:3; 15:19; 26:7; 31:10

٨ تَبْصِرَةً وَذِكْرَىٰ لِكُلِّ عَبْدٍ مُّنِيبٍ

8 A lesson and a reminder for every penitent worshiper.

٩ وَنَزَّلْنَا مِنَ ٱلسَّمَاءِ مَاءً مُّبَارَكًا فَأَنبَتْنَا بِهِ جَنَّاتٍ وَحَبَّ ٱلْحَصِيدِ

9 And We brought down from the sky blessed water, and produced with it gardens and grain to harvest.

9
6:99

١٠ وَٱلنَّخْلَ بَاسِقَاتٍ لَّهَا طَلْعٌ نَّضِيدٌ

10 And the soaring palm trees, with clustered dates.

١١ رِّزْقًا لِّلْعِبَادِ ۖ وَأَحْيَيْنَا بِهِ بَلْدَةً مَّيْتًا ۚ كَذَٰلِكَ ٱلْخُرُوجُ

11 As sustenance for the servants. And We revive thereby a dead town. Likewise is the resurrection.

11
25:49

١٢ كَذَّبَتْ قَبْلَهُمْ قَوْمُ نُوحٍ وَأَصْحَابُ الرَّسِّ وَثَمُودُ		**12–14** 38:12–14; 44:37

12 Before them the people of Noah denied the truth, and so did the dwellers of Russ, and Thamūd.

١٣ وَعَادٌ وَفِرْعَوْنُ وَإِخْوَانُ لُوطٍ

13 And 'Ād, and Pharaoh, and the brethren of Lot.

١٤ وَأَصْحَابُ الْأَيْكَةِ وَقَوْمُ تُبَّعٍ ۚ كُلٌّ كَذَّبَ الرُّسُلَ فَحَقَّ وَعِيدِ

14 And the Dwellers of the Woods, and the people of Tubba'. They all rejected the messengers, so My threat came true.

١٥ أَفَعَيِينَا بِالْخَلْقِ الْأَوَّلِ ۚ بَلْ هُمْ فِي لَبْسٍ مِنْ خَلْقٍ جَدِيدٍ   **15**
   10:4; 30:27; 36:79

15 Were We fatigued by the first creation? But they are in doubt of a new creation.

١٦ وَلَقَدْ خَلَقْنَا الْإِنْسَانَ وَنَعْلَمُ مَا تُوَسْوِسُ بِهِ نَفْسُهُ ۖ وَنَحْنُ أَقْرَبُ إِلَيْهِ مِنْ حَبْلِ الْوَرِيدِ   **16**
  11:5

16 We created the human being, and We know what his soul whispers to him. We are nearer to him than his jugular vein.

١٧ إِذْ يَتَلَقَّى الْمُتَلَقِّيَانِ عَنِ الْيَمِينِ وَعَنِ الشِّمَالِ قَعِيدٌ

17 As the two receivers receive, seated to the right and to the left.

١٨ مَا يَلْفِظُ مِنْ قَوْلٍ إِلَّا لَدَيْهِ رَقِيبٌ عَتِيدٌ   **18**
   19:79; 43:19

18 Not a word does he utter, but there is a watcher by him, ready.

١٩ وَجَاءَتْ سَكْرَةُ الْمَوْتِ بِالْحَقِّ ۖ ذَٰلِكَ مَا كُنْتَ مِنْهُ تَحِيدُ

19 The daze of death has come in truth: "This is what you tried to evade."

٢٠ وَنُفِخَ فِي الصُّورِ ۚ ذَٰلِكَ يَوْمُ الْوَعِيدِ   **20**
   18:99; 50:42

20 And the Trumpet is blown: "This is the Promised Day."

٢١ وَجَاءَتْ كُلُّ نَفْسٍ مَعَهَا سَائِقٌ وَشَهِيدٌ

21 And every soul will come forward, accompanied by a driver and a witness.

٢٢ لَقَدْ كُنْتَ فِي غَفْلَةٍ مِنْ هَٰذَا فَكَشَفْنَا عَنْكَ غِطَاءَكَ فَبَصَرُكَ الْيَوْمَ حَدِيدٌ   **22**
  19:39; 21:1, 97

22 "You were in neglect of this, so We lifted your screen from you, and your vision today is keen."

٢٣ وَقَالَ قَرِينُهُ هَٰذَا مَا لَدَيَّ عَتِيدٌ   **23**
   41:25; 50:27

23 And His escort will say, "This is what I have ready with me."

٢٤ أَلْقِيَا فِي جَهَنَّمَ كُلَّ كَفَّارٍ عَنِيدٍ   **24–26**
   68:12; 70:21

24 "Throw into Hell every stubborn disbeliever.

٢٥ مَنَّاعٍ لِلْخَيْرِ مُعْتَدٍ مُرِيبٍ

25 Preventer of good, aggressor, doubter.

٢٦ الَّذِي جَعَلَ مَعَ اللَّهِ إِلَٰهًا آخَرَ فَأَلْقِيَاهُ فِي الْعَذَابِ الشَّدِيدِ

26 Who fabricated another god with God; toss him into the intense agony."

٢٧ قَالَ قَرِينُهُ رَبَّنَا مَا أَطْغَيْتُهُ وَلَٰكِن كَانَ فِي ضَلَالٍ بَعِيدٍ

27 His escort will say, "Our Lord, I did not make him rebel, but he was far astray."

27
41:25; 50:23

٢٨ قَالَ لَا تَخْتَصِمُوا لَدَيَّ وَقَدْ قَدَّمْتُ إِلَيْكُم بِالْوَعِيدِ

28 He will say, "Do not feud in My presence—I had warned you in advance.

٢٩ مَا يُبَدَّلُ الْقَوْلُ لَدَيَّ وَمَا أَنَا بِظَلَّامٍ لِّلْعَبِيدِ

29 The decree from Me will not be changed, and I am not unjust to the servants."

٣٠ يَوْمَ نَقُولُ لِجَهَنَّمَ هَلِ امْتَلَأْتِ وَتَقُولُ هَلْ مِن مَّزِيدٍ

30 On the Day when We will say to Hell, "Are you full?" And it will say, "Are there any more?"

30
11:119; 32:13;
38:84–85

٣١ وَأُزْلِفَتِ الْجَنَّةُ لِلْمُتَّقِينَ غَيْرَ بَعِيدٍ

31 And Paradise will be brought closer to the pious, not far away.

31
26:90; 81:13

٣٢ هَٰذَا مَا تُوعَدُونَ لِكُلِّ أَوَّابٍ حَفِيظٍ

32 "This is what you were promised—for every careful penitent.

٣٣ مَنْ خَشِيَ الرَّحْمَٰنَ بِالْغَيْبِ وَجَاءَ بِقَلْبٍ مُّنِيبٍ

33 Who inwardly feared the Most Gracious, and came with a repentant heart.

33
21:49; 35:18; 36:11;
67:12

٣٤ ادْخُلُوهَا بِسَلَامٍ ۖ ذَٰلِكَ يَوْمُ الْخُلُودِ

34 Enter it in peace. This is the Day of Eternity."

34
10:10; 15:46

٣٥ لَهُم مَّا يَشَاءُونَ فِيهَا وَلَدَيْنَا مَزِيدٌ

35 Therein they will have whatever they desire—and We have even more.

٣٦ وَكَمْ أَهْلَكْنَا قَبْلَهُم مِّن قَرْنٍ هُمْ أَشَدُّ مِنْهُم بَطْشًا فَنَقَّبُوا فِي الْبِلَادِ هَلْ مِن مَّحِيصٍ

36 How many generations before them, who were more powerful than they, did We destroy? They explored the lands—was there any escape?

36
6:6; 43:8

٣٧ إِنَّ فِي ذَٰلِكَ لَذِكْرَىٰ لِمَن كَانَ لَهُ قَلْبٌ أَوْ أَلْقَى السَّمْعَ وَهُوَ شَهِيدٌ

37 In that is a reminder for whoever possesses a heart, or cares to listen and witness.

٣٨ وَلَقَدْ خَلَقْنَا السَّمَاوَاتِ وَالْأَرْضَ وَمَا بَيْنَهُمَا فِي سِتَّةِ أَيَّامٍ وَمَا مَسَّنَا مِن لُّغُوبٍ

38 We created the heavens and the earth and what is between them in six days, and no fatigue touched Us.

38
7:54

٣٩ فَاصْبِرْ عَلَىٰ مَا يَقُولُونَ وَسَبِّحْ بِحَمْدِ رَبِّكَ قَبْلَ طُلُوعِ الشَّمْسِ وَقَبْلَ الْغُرُوبِ	39	15:97–98; 20:130; 52:48–49

39 So endure what they say, and proclaim the praises of your Lord before the rising of the sun, and before sunset.

٤٠ وَمِنَ اللَّيْلِ فَسَبِّحْهُ وَأَدْبَارَ السُّجُودِ

40 And glorify Him during the night, and at the end of devotions.

٤١ وَاسْتَمِعْ يَوْمَ يُنَادِ الْمُنَادِ مِنْ مَكَانٍ قَرِيبٍ

41 And listen for the Day when the caller calls from a nearby place.

٤٢ يَوْمَ يَسْمَعُونَ الصَّيْحَةَ بِالْحَقِّ ۚ ذَٰلِكَ يَوْمُ الْخُرُوجِ	42	11:103; 50:20; 64:9

42 The Day when they will hear the Shout in all truth. That is the Day of Emergence.

٤٣ إِنَّا نَحْنُ نُحْيِي وَنُمِيتُ وَإِلَيْنَا الْمَصِيرُ

43 It is We who control life and death, and to Us is the destination.

٤٤ يَوْمَ تَشَقَّقُ الْأَرْضُ عَنْهُمْ سِرَاعًا ۚ ذَٰلِكَ حَشْرٌ عَلَيْنَا يَسِيرٌ	44	70:43

44 The Day when the earth will crack for them at once. That is an easy gathering for Us.

٤٥ نَحْنُ أَعْلَمُ بِمَا يَقُولُونَ ۖ وَمَا أَنْتَ عَلَيْهِمْ بِجَبَّارٍ ۖ فَذَكِّرْ بِالْقُرْآنِ مَنْ يَخَافُ وَعِيدِ

45 We are fully aware of what they say, and you are not a dictator over them. So remind by the Qur'an whoever fears My warning.

Sūrah 51: Al-Dhāriyāt

سُورَةُ ٱلذَّارِيَات (The Spreaders)

بِسْمِ ٱللَّهِ ٱلرَّحْمَٰنِ ٱلرَّحِيمِ

١ وَالذَّارِيَاتِ ذَرْوًا

1 By the spreaders spreading.

٢ فَالْحَامِلَاتِ وِقْرًا

2 And those carrying loads.

٣ فَالْجَارِيَاتِ يُسْرًا

3 And those moving gently.

٤ فَالْمُقَسِّمَاتِ أَمْرًا

4 And those distributing as commanded.

٥ إِنَّمَا تُوعَدُونَ لَصَادِقٌ	5–6	3:9; 6:134; 24:25; 77:7

5 What you are promised is true.

6 وَإِنَّ الدِّينَ لَوَاقِعٌ ٦

6 Judgment will take place.

7 وَالسَّمَاءِ ذَاتِ الْحُبُكِ ٧

7 By the sky that is woven.

8 إِنَّكُمْ لَفِي قَوْلٍ مُخْتَلِفٍ ٨

8 You differ in what you say.

9 يُؤْفَكُ عَنْهُ مَنْ أُفِكَ ٩

9 Averted from it is he who is averted.

10 قُتِلَ الْخَرَّاصُونَ ١٠

10 Perish the imposters.

11 الَّذِينَ هُمْ فِي غَمْرَةٍ سَاهُونَ ١١

11 Those who are dazed in ignorance.

11
23:54, 63

12 يَسْأَلُونَ أَيَّانَ يَوْمُ الدِّينِ ١٢

12 They ask, "When is the Day of Judgment?"

12
7:187; 75:6

13 يَوْمَ هُمْ عَلَى النَّارِ يُفْتَنُونَ ١٣

13 The Day they are presented to the Fire.

14 ذُوقُوا فِتْنَتَكُمْ هَٰذَا الَّذِي كُنْتُمْ بِهِ تَسْتَعْجِلُونَ ١٤

14 "Taste your ordeal. This is what you used to challenge."

14
10:50

15 إِنَّ الْمُتَّقِينَ فِي جَنَّاتٍ وَعُيُونٍ ١٥

15 But the pious are amidst gardens and springs.

15
15:45; 19:63; 52:17

16 آخِذِينَ مَا آتَاهُمْ رَبُّهُمْ ۚ إِنَّهُمْ كَانُوا قَبْلَ ذَٰلِكَ مُحْسِنِينَ ١٦

16 Receiving what their Lord has given them. They were virtuous before that.

16
52:18

17 كَانُوا قَلِيلًا مِنَ اللَّيْلِ مَا يَهْجَعُونَ ١٧

17 They used to sleep a little at night.

18 وَبِالْأَسْحَارِ هُمْ يَسْتَغْفِرُونَ ١٨

18 And at dawn, they would pray for pardon.

18
3:17

19 وَفِي أَمْوَالِهِمْ حَقٌّ لِلسَّائِلِ وَالْمَحْرُومِ ١٩

19 And in their wealth, there was a share for the beggar and the deprived.

19
6:141; 17:26; 30:38; 70:24

20 وَفِي الْأَرْضِ آيَاتٌ لِلْمُوقِنِينَ ٢٠

20 And on earth are signs for the convinced.

20
41:53

21 وَفِي أَنْفُسِكُمْ ۚ أَفَلَا تُبْصِرُونَ ٢١

21 And within yourselves. Do you not see?

Sūrah 51: Al-Dhāriyāt

٢٢ وَفِي السَّمَاءِ رِزْقُكُمْ وَمَا تُوعَدُونَ

22 And in the heaven is your livelihood, and what you are promised.

22
40:13; 45:5

٢٣ فَوَرَبِّ السَّمَاءِ وَالْأَرْضِ إِنَّهُ لَحَقٌّ مِثْلَ مَا أَنَّكُمْ تَنطِقُونَ

23 By the Lord of the heaven and the earth, it is as true as the fact that you speak.

٢٤ هَلْ أَتَاكَ حَدِيثُ ضَيْفِ إِبْرَاهِيمَ الْمُكْرَمِينَ

24 Has the story of Abraham's honorable guests reached you?

24–28
11:69; 15:51–53; 29:31; 37:101–112

٢٥ إِذْ دَخَلُوا عَلَيْهِ فَقَالُوا سَلَامًا ۖ قَالَ سَلَامٌ قَوْمٌ مُنكَرُونَ

25 When they entered upon him, they said, "Peace." He said, "Peace, strangers."

٢٦ فَرَاغَ إِلَىٰ أَهْلِهِ فَجَاءَ بِعِجْلٍ سَمِينٍ

26 Then he slipped away to his family, and brought a fatted calf.

٢٧ فَقَرَّبَهُ إِلَيْهِمْ قَالَ أَلَا تَأْكُلُونَ

27 He set it before them. He said, "Will you not eat?"

٢٨ فَأَوْجَسَ مِنْهُمْ خِيفَةً ۖ قَالُوا لَا تَخَفْ ۖ وَبَشَّرُوهُ بِغُلَامٍ عَلِيمٍ

28 And he harbored fear of them. They said, "Do not fear," and they announced to him the good news of a knowledgeable boy.

٢٩ فَأَقْبَلَتِ امْرَأَتُهُ فِي صَرَّةٍ فَصَكَّتْ وَجْهَهَا وَقَالَتْ عَجُوزٌ عَقِيمٌ

29 His wife came forward crying. She clasped her face, and said, "A barren old woman?"

29
11:71–73; 15:53–56

٣٠ قَالُوا كَذَٰلِكِ قَالَ رَبُّكِ ۖ إِنَّهُ هُوَ الْحَكِيمُ الْعَلِيمُ

30 They said, "Thus spoke your Lord. He is the Wise, the Knowing."

٣١ قَالَ فَمَا خَطْبُكُمْ أَيُّهَا الْمُرْسَلُونَ

31 He said, "What is your business, O envoys?"

31–37
11:74–83; 15:57–77; 29:31–35

٣٢ قَالُوا إِنَّا أُرْسِلْنَا إِلَىٰ قَوْمٍ مُجْرِمِينَ

32 They said, "We are sent to a people guilty of sin."

٣٣ لِنُرْسِلَ عَلَيْهِمْ حِجَارَةً مِنْ طِينٍ

33 "To unleash upon them rocks of clay."

٣٤ مُسَوَّمَةً عِنْدَ رَبِّكَ لِلْمُسْرِفِينَ

34 "Marked by your Lord for the excessive."

٣٥ فَأَخْرَجْنَا مَنْ كَانَ فِيهَا مِنَ الْمُؤْمِنِينَ

35 We evacuated all the believers who were in it.

٣٦ فَمَا وَجَدْنَا فِيهَا غَيْرَ بَيْتٍ مِنَ الْمُسْلِمِينَ

36 But found in it only one household of Muslims.

٣٧ وَتَرَكْنَا فِيهَا آيَةً لِلَّذِينَ يَخَافُونَ الْعَذَابَ الْأَلِيمَ

37 And We left in it a sign for those who fear the painful punishment.

٣٨ وَفِي مُوسَىٰ إِذْ أَرْسَلْنَاهُ إِلَىٰ فِرْعَوْنَ بِسُلْطَانٍ مُبِينٍ

38 And in Moses. We sent him to Pharaoh with a clear authority.

38
11:96; 23:45; 28:35; 40:23; 44:19

٣٩ فَتَوَلَّىٰ بِرُكْنِهِ وَقَالَ سَاحِرٌ أَوْ مَجْنُونٌ

39 But he turned away with his warlords, and said, "A sorcerer or a madman."

39
51:52

٤٠ فَأَخَذْنَاهُ وَجُنُودَهُ فَنَبَذْنَاهُمْ فِي الْيَمِّ وَهُوَ مُلِيمٌ

40 So We seized him and his troops, and threw them into the sea, and He was to blame.

40
7:136; 28:40

٤١ وَفِي عَادٍ إِذْ أَرْسَلْنَا عَلَيْهِمُ الرِّيحَ الْعَقِيمَ

41 And in 'Ād. We unleashed against them the devastating wind.

41
41:16; 46:24; 54:19; 69:6

٤٢ مَا تَذَرُ مِنْ شَيْءٍ أَتَتْ عَلَيْهِ إِلَّا جَعَلَتْهُ كَالرَّمِيمِ

42 It spared nothing it came upon, but rendered it like decayed ruins.

٤٣ وَفِي ثَمُودَ إِذْ قِيلَ لَهُمْ تَمَتَّعُوا حَتَّىٰ حِينٍ

43 And in Thamūd. They were told, "Enjoy yourselves for a while."

43
11:65; 41:17

٤٤ فَعَتَوْا عَنْ أَمْرِ رَبِّهِمْ فَأَخَذَتْهُمُ الصَّاعِقَةُ وَهُمْ يَنْظُرُونَ

44 But they defied the command of their Lord, so the lightning struck them as they looked on.

٤٥ فَمَا اسْتَطَاعُوا مِنْ قِيَامٍ وَمَا كَانُوا مُنْتَصِرِينَ

45 They could not rise up, nor could they find help.

٤٦ وَقَوْمَ نُوحٍ مِنْ قَبْلُ إِنَّهُمْ كَانُوا قَوْمًا فَاسِقِينَ

46 And before that, the people of Noah. They were immoral people.

46
53:52; 25:37

٤٧ وَالسَّمَاءَ بَنَيْنَاهَا بِأَيْدٍ وَإِنَّا لَمُوسِعُونَ

47 We constructed the universe with power, and We are expanding it.

47–48
2:22; 50:6

٤٨ وَالْأَرْضَ فَرَشْنَاهَا فَنِعْمَ الْمَاهِدُونَ

48 And the earth—We spread it out—How well We prepared it!

٤٩ وَمِنْ كُلِّ شَيْءٍ خَلَقْنَا زَوْجَيْنِ لَعَلَّكُمْ تَذَكَّرُونَ

49 We created all things in pairs, so that you may reflect and ponder.

49
13:3

٥٠ فَفِرُّوا إِلَى اللَّهِ إِنِّي لَكُمْ مِنْهُ نَذِيرٌ مُبِينٌ

50 "So flee towards God. I am to you from Him a clear warner."

٥١ وَلَا تَجْعَلُوا مَعَ اللَّهِ إِلَٰهًا آخَرَ ۖ إِنِّي لَكُم مِّنْهُ نَذِيرٌ مُّبِينٌ

51 "And do not set up any other god with God. I am to you from Him a clear warner."

٥٢ كَذَٰلِكَ مَا أَتَى الَّذِينَ مِن قَبْلِهِم مِّن رَّسُولٍ إِلَّا قَالُوا سَاحِرٌ أَوْ مَجْنُونٌ

52 Likewise, no messenger came to those before them, but they said, "A sorcerer or a madman."

52
2:118; 21:3; 51:39

٥٣ أَتَوَاصَوْا بِهِ ۚ بَلْ هُمْ قَوْمٌ طَاغُونَ

53 Did they recommend it to one another? In fact, they are rebellious people.

٥٤ فَتَوَلَّ عَنْهُمْ فَمَا أَنتَ بِمَلُومٍ

54 So turn away from them; you are not to blame.

54
13:40

٥٥ وَذَكِّرْ فَإِنَّ الذِّكْرَىٰ تَنفَعُ الْمُؤْمِنِينَ

55 And remind, for the reminder benefits the believers.

55
80:4; 87:9

٥٦ وَمَا خَلَقْتُ الْجِنَّ وَالْإِنسَ إِلَّا لِيَعْبُدُونِ

56 I did not create the jinn and the humans except to worship Me.

56
2:21

٥٧ مَّا أُرِيدُ مِنْهُم مِّن رِّزْقٍ وَمَا أُرِيدُ أَن يُطْعِمُونِ

57 I need no livelihood from them, nor do I need them to feed Me.

57
6:14

٥٨ إِنَّ اللَّهَ هُوَ الرَّزَّاقُ ذُو الْقُوَّةِ الْمَتِينُ

58 God is the Provider, the One with Power, the Strong.

٥٩ فَإِنَّ لِلَّذِينَ ظَلَمُوا ذَنُوبًا مِّثْلَ ذَنُوبِ أَصْحَابِهِمْ فَلَا يَسْتَعْجِلُونِ

59 Those who do wrong will have their turn, like the turn of their counterparts, so let them not rush Me.

٦٠ فَوَيْلٌ لِّلَّذِينَ كَفَرُوا مِن يَوْمِهِمُ الَّذِي يُوعَدُونَ

60 So woe to those who disbelieve because of that Day of theirs which they are promised.

60
14:2; 38:27

Sūrah 52: Al-Ṭūr

سُورَةُ ٱلطُّورِ (The Mount)

بِسْمِ ٱللَّهِ ٱلرَّحْمَٰنِ ٱلرَّحِيمِ

١ وَالطُّورِ

1 By the Mount.

1
95:2

٢ وَكِتَابٍ مَّسْطُورٍ

2 And a Book inscribed.

3 In a published scroll.   ٣ فِي رَقٍّ مَنْشُورٍ

4 And the frequented House.   ٤ وَالْبَيْتِ الْمَعْمُورِ

5 And the elevated roof.   ٥ وَالسَّقْفِ الْمَرْفُوعِ   **5** 21:32

6 And the seething sea.   ٦ وَالْبَحْرِ الْمَسْجُورِ   **6** 81:6

7 The punishment of your Lord is coming.   ٧ إِنَّ عَذَابَ رَبِّكَ لَوَاقِعٌ

8 There is nothing to avert it.   ٨ مَا لَهُ مِنْ دَافِعٍ

9 On the Day when the heaven sways in agitation.   ٩ يَوْمَ تَمُورُ السَّمَاءُ مَوْرًا   **9** 67:16

10 And the mountains go into motion.   ١٠ وَتَسِيرُ الْجِبَالُ سَيْرًا   **10** 18:47; 78:20; 81:3

11 Woe on that Day to the deniers.   ١١ فَوَيْلٌ يَوْمَئِذٍ لِلْمُكَذِّبِينَ

12 Those who play with speculation.   ١٢ الَّذِينَ هُمْ فِي خَوْضٍ يَلْعَبُونَ   **12** 6:91; 43:83; 70:42

13 The Day when they are shoved into the Fire of Hell forcefully.   ١٣ يَوْمَ يُدَعُّونَ إِلَىٰ نَارِ جَهَنَّمَ دَعًّا

14 "This is the Fire which you used to deny.   ١٤ هَٰذِهِ النَّارُ الَّتِي كُنْتُمْ بِهَا تُكَذِّبُونَ   **14** 32:20; 34:42

15 Is this magic, or do you not see?   ١٥ أَفَسِحْرٌ هَٰذَا أَمْ أَنْتُمْ لَا تُبْصِرُونَ

16 Burn in it. Whether you are patient, or impatient, it is the same for you. You are only being repaid for what you used to do."   ١٦ اصْلَوْهَا فَاصْبِرُوا أَوْ لَا تَصْبِرُوا سَوَاءٌ عَلَيْكُمْ ۖ إِنَّمَا تُجْزَوْنَ مَا كُنْتُمْ تَعْمَلُونَ   **16** 14:21; 41:24

17 But the righteous will be amid gardens and bliss.   ١٧ إِنَّ الْمُتَّقِينَ فِي جَنَّاتٍ وَنَعِيمٍ   **17** 51:15

18 Enjoying what their Lord has given them, and their Lord has spared them the suffering of Hell.   ١٨ فَاكِهِينَ بِمَا آتَاهُمْ رَبُّهُمْ وَوَقَاهُمْ رَبُّهُمْ عَذَابَ الْجَحِيمِ   **18** 36:32; 44:72; 51:16; 52:27

١٩ كُلُوا وَاشْرَبُوا هَنِيئًا بِمَا كُنتُمْ تَعْمَلُونَ	19	69:24; 77:43

19 Eat and drink happily, for what you used to do.

٢٠ مُتَّكِئِينَ عَلَىٰ سُرُرٍ مَصْفُوفَةٍ ۖ وَزَوَّجْنَاهُم بِحُورٍ عِينٍ	20	44:54; 56:15; 88:15

20 Relaxing on luxurious furnishings; and We will couple them with gorgeous spouses.

٢١ وَالَّذِينَ آمَنُوا وَاتَّبَعَتْهُمْ ذُرِّيَّتُهُم بِإِيمَانٍ أَلْحَقْنَا بِهِمْ ذُرِّيَّتَهُمْ وَمَا أَلَتْنَاهُم مِّنْ عَمَلِهِم مِّن شَيْءٍ ۚ كُلُّ امْرِئٍ بِمَا كَسَبَ رَهِينٌ	21	13:23; 40:8

21 Those who believed, and their offspring followed them in faith— We will unite them with their offspring, and We will not deprive them of any of their works. Every person is hostage to what he has earned.

٢٢ وَأَمْدَدْنَاهُم بِفَاكِهَةٍ وَلَحْمٍ مِّمَّا يَشْتَهُونَ	22	36:57; 47:15; 56:20; 77:42

22 And We will supply them with fruit, and meat; such as they desire.

٢٣ يَتَنَازَعُونَ فِيهَا كَأْسًا لَّا لَغْوٌ فِيهَا وَلَا تَأْثِيمٌ	23	19:62; 37:47; 56:19, 25

23 They will exchange therein a cup; wherein is neither harm, nor sin.

٢٤ وَيَطُوفُ عَلَيْهِمْ غِلْمَانٌ لَّهُمْ كَأَنَّهُمْ لُؤْلُؤٌ مَّكْنُونٌ	24	56:17; 76:19

24 Serving them will be youths like hidden pearls.

٢٥ وَأَقْبَلَ بَعْضُهُمْ عَلَىٰ بَعْضٍ يَتَسَاءَلُونَ	25	23:101

25 And they will approach one another, inquiring.

٢٦ قَالُوا إِنَّا كُنَّا قَبْلُ فِي أَهْلِنَا مُشْفِقِينَ	26

26 They will say, "Before this, we were fearful for our families.

٢٧ فَمَنَّ اللَّهُ عَلَيْنَا وَوَقَانَا عَذَابَ السَّمُومِ	27	44:56; 52:18; 76:11

27 But God blessed us, and spared us the agony of the Fiery Winds.

٢٨ إِنَّا كُنَّا مِن قَبْلُ نَدْعُوهُ ۖ إِنَّهُ هُوَ الْبَرُّ الرَّحِيمُ	28

28 Before this, we used to pray to Him. He is the Good, the Compassionate."

٢٩ فَذَكِّرْ فَمَا أَنتَ بِنِعْمَتِ رَبِّكَ بِكَاهِنٍ وَلَا مَجْنُونٍ	29	68:2; 69:42

29 So remind. By the grace of your Lord, you are neither a soothsayer, nor a madman.

٣٠ أَمْ يَقُولُونَ شَاعِرٌ نَّتَرَبَّصُ بِهِ رَيْبَ الْمَنُونِ	30	21:5; 36:69; 37:36; 69:41

30 Or do they say, "A poet—we await for him a calamity of time"?

٣١ قُلْ تَرَبَّصُوا فَإِنِّي مَعَكُم مِّنَ الْمُتَرَبِّصِينَ	31	9:52; 20:135

31 Say, "Go on waiting; I will be waiting with you."

٣٢ أَمْ تَأْمُرُهُمْ أَحْلَامُهُم بِهَٰذَا ۚ أَمْ هُمْ قَوْمٌ طَاغُونَ

32 Or is it that their dreams compel them to this? Or are they aggressive people?

٣٣ أَمْ يَقُولُونَ تَقَوَّلَهُ ۚ بَل لَّا يُؤْمِنُونَ

33 Or do they say, "He made it up"? Rather, they do not believe.

33
69:44

٣٤ فَلْيَأْتُوا بِحَدِيثٍ مِّثْلِهِ إِن كَانُوا صَادِقِينَ

34 So let them produce a discourse like it, if they are truthful.

34
2:23; 10:38; 11:13; 28:49

٣٥ أَمْ خُلِقُوا مِنْ غَيْرِ شَيْءٍ أَمْ هُمُ الْخَالِقُونَ

35 Or were they created out of nothing? Or are they the creators?

٣٦ أَمْ خَلَقُوا السَّمَاوَاتِ وَالْأَرْضَ ۚ بَل لَّا يُوقِنُونَ

36 Or did they create the heavens and the earth? In fact, they are not certain.

٣٧ أَمْ عِندَهُمْ خَزَائِنُ رَبِّكَ أَمْ هُمُ الْمُصَيْطِرُونَ

37 Or do they possess the treasuries of your Lord? Or are they the controllers?

٣٨ أَمْ لَهُمْ سُلَّمٌ يَسْتَمِعُونَ فِيهِ ۖ فَلْيَأْتِ مُسْتَمِعُهُم بِسُلْطَانٍ مُّبِينٍ

38 Or do they have a stairway by means of which they listen? Then let their listener produce a clear proof.

38
38:10

٣٩ أَمْ لَهُ الْبَنَاتُ وَلَكُمُ الْبَنُونَ

39 Or for Him the daughters, and for you the sons?

39
16:57; 37:149

٤٠ أَمْ تَسْأَلُهُمْ أَجْرًا فَهُم مِّن مَّغْرَمٍ مُّثْقَلُونَ

40 Or do you demand a payment from them, and they are burdened by debt?

٤١ أَمْ عِندَهُمُ الْغَيْبُ فَهُمْ يَكْتُبُونَ

41 Or do they know the future, and they are writing it down?

41
68:47

٤٢ أَمْ يُرِيدُونَ كَيْدًا ۖ فَالَّذِينَ كَفَرُوا هُمُ الْمَكِيدُونَ

42 Or are they planning a conspiracy? The conspiracy will befall the disbelievers.

٤٣ أَمْ لَهُمْ إِلَٰهٌ غَيْرُ اللَّهِ ۚ سُبْحَانَ اللَّهِ عَمَّا يُشْرِكُونَ

43 Or do they have a god besides God? God transcends what they associate.

٤٤ وَإِن يَرَوْا كِسْفًا مِّنَ السَّمَاءِ سَاقِطًا يَقُولُوا سَحَابٌ مَّرْكُومٌ

44 Even if they were to see lumps of the sky falling down, they would say, "A mass of clouds."

44
17:92; 26:187; 34:9

٤٥ فَذَرْهُمْ حَتَّىٰ يُلَاقُوا يَوْمَهُمُ الَّذِي فِيهِ يُصْعَقُونَ

45 So leave them until they meet their Day in which they will be stunned.

٤٦ يَوْمَ لَا يُغْنِي عَنْهُمْ كَيْدُهُمْ شَيْئًا وَلَا هُمْ يُنصَرُونَ

46 The Day when their ploys will avail them nothing; and they will not be helped.

46
77:38–39; 86:15–16

٤٧ وَإِنَّ لِلَّذِينَ ظَلَمُوا عَذَابًا دُونَ ذَٰلِكَ وَلَٰكِنَّ أَكْثَرَهُمْ لَا يَعْلَمُونَ

47 For those who do wrong, there is a punishment besides that; but most of them do not know.

٤٨ وَاصْبِرْ لِحُكْمِ رَبِّكَ فَإِنَّكَ بِأَعْيُنِنَا ۖ وَسَبِّحْ بِحَمْدِ رَبِّكَ حِينَ تَقُومُ

48 So patiently await the decision of your Lord, for you are before Our Eyes; and proclaim the praises of your Lord when you arise.

48–49
20:130; 50:39

٤٩ وَمِنَ اللَّيْلِ فَسَبِّحْهُ وَإِدْبَارَ النُّجُومِ

49 And glorify Him during the night, and at the receding of the stars.

Sūrah 53: Al-Najm

سُورَةُ ٱلنَّجْمِ (The Star)

بِسْمِ ٱللَّهِ ٱلرَّحْمَٰنِ ٱلرَّحِيمِ

١ وَالنَّجْمِ إِذَا هَوَىٰ

1 By the star as it goes down.

1
56:75

٢ مَا ضَلَّ صَاحِبُكُمْ وَمَا غَوَىٰ

2 Your friend has not gone astray, nor has he erred.

2
93:7

٣ وَمَا يَنطِقُ عَنِ الْهَوَىٰ

3 Nor does he speak out of desire.

3–4
43:43

٤ إِنْ هُوَ إِلَّا وَحْيٌ يُوحَىٰ

4 It is but a revelation revealed.

٥ عَلَّمَهُ شَدِيدُ الْقُوَىٰ

5 Taught to him by the Extremely Powerful.

٦ ذُو مِرَّةٍ فَاسْتَوَىٰ

6 The one of vigor. He settled.

7 While he was at the highest horizon.	٧ وَهُوَ بِالْأُفُقِ الْأَعْلَىٰ	**7** 42:51; 53: 13; 81:23
8 Then he came near, and hovered around.	٨ ثُمَّ دَنَا فَتَدَلَّىٰ	
9 He was within two bows' length, or closer.	٩ فَكَانَ قَابَ قَوْسَيْنِ أَوْ أَدْنَىٰ	
10 Then He revealed to His servant what He revealed.	١٠ فَأَوْحَىٰ إِلَىٰ عَبْدِهِ مَا أَوْحَىٰ	
11 The heart did not lie about what it saw.	١١ مَا كَذَبَ الْفُؤَادُ مَا رَأَىٰ	
12 Will you dispute with him concerning what he saw?	١٢ أَفَتُمَارُونَهُ عَلَىٰ مَا يَرَىٰ	
13 He saw him on another descent.	١٣ وَلَقَدْ رَآهُ نَزْلَةً أُخْرَىٰ	
14 At the Lotus Tree of the Extremity.	١٤ عِندَ سِدْرَةِ الْمُنتَهَىٰ	
15 Near which is the Garden of Repose.	١٥ عِندَهَا جَنَّةُ الْمَأْوَىٰ	
16 As there covered the Lotus Tree what covered it.	١٦ إِذْ يَغْشَى السِّدْرَةَ مَا يَغْشَىٰ	
17 The sight did not waver, nor did it exceed.	١٧ مَا زَاغَ الْبَصَرُ وَمَا طَغَىٰ	
18 He saw some of the Great Signs of his Lord.	١٨ لَقَدْ رَأَىٰ مِنْ آيَاتِ رَبِّهِ الْكُبْرَىٰ	
19 Have you considered al-Lat and al-Uzza?	١٩ أَفَرَأَيْتُمُ اللَّاتَ وَالْعُزَّىٰ	
20 And Manat, the third one, the other?	٢٠ وَمَنَاةَ الثَّالِثَةَ الْأُخْرَىٰ	
21 Are you to have the males, and He the females?	٢١ أَلَكُمُ الذَّكَرُ وَلَهُ الْأُنثَىٰ	**21** 2:116; 16:57; 17:40; 37:149; 43:15; 52:39
22 What a bizarre distribution.	٢٢ تِلْكَ إِذًا قِسْمَةٌ ضِيزَىٰ	

٢٣ إِنْ هِيَ إِلَّا أَسْمَاءٌ سَمَّيْتُمُوهَا أَنْتُمْ وَآبَاؤُكُمْ مَا أَنْزَلَ اللَّهُ بِهَا مِنْ سُلْطَانٍ ۚ إِنْ يَتَّبِعُونَ إِلَّا الظَّنَّ وَمَا تَهْوَى الْأَنْفُسُ ۖ وَلَقَدْ جَاءَهُمْ مِنْ رَبِّهِمُ الْهُدَىٰ

23
7:71; 12:40; 53:28

23 These are nothing but names, which you have devised, you and your ancestors, for which God sent down no authority. They follow nothing but assumptions, and what the ego desires, even though guidance has come to them from their Lord.

٢٤ أَمْ لِلْإِنْسَانِ مَا تَمَنَّىٰ

24 Or is the human being to have whatever he desires?

٢٥ فَلِلَّهِ الْآخِرَةُ وَالْأُولَىٰ

25
92:12

25 To God belong the Last and the First.

٢٦ وَكَمْ مِنْ مَلَكٍ فِي السَّمَاوَاتِ لَا تُغْنِي شَفَاعَتُهُمْ شَيْئًا إِلَّا مِنْ بَعْدِ أَنْ يَأْذَنَ اللَّهُ لِمَنْ يَشَاءُ وَيَرْضَىٰ

26
2:48, 123, 255; 20:109; 21:28; 34:23; 74:48

26 How many an angel is there in the heavens whose intercession avails nothing, except after God gives permission to whomever He wills, and approves?

٢٧ إِنَّ الَّذِينَ لَا يُؤْمِنُونَ بِالْآخِرَةِ لَيُسَمُّونَ الْمَلَائِكَةَ تَسْمِيَةَ الْأُنْثَىٰ

27
4:117; 17:40; 37:150; 43:19

27 Those who do not believe in the Hereafter give the angels the names of females.

٢٨ وَمَا لَهُمْ بِهِ مِنْ عِلْمٍ ۖ إِنْ يَتَّبِعُونَ إِلَّا الظَّنَّ ۖ وَإِنَّ الظَّنَّ لَا يُغْنِي مِنَ الْحَقِّ شَيْئًا

28
6:116; 53:23

28 They have no knowledge of that. They only follow assumptions, and assumptions are no substitute for the truth.

٢٩ فَأَعْرِضْ عَنْ مَنْ تَوَلَّىٰ عَنْ ذِكْرِنَا وَلَمْ يُرِدْ إِلَّا الْحَيَاةَ الدُّنْيَا

29 So avoid him who has turned away from Our remembrance, and desires nothing but the present life.

٣٠ ذَٰلِكَ مَبْلَغُهُمْ مِنَ الْعِلْمِ ۚ إِنَّ رَبَّكَ هُوَ أَعْلَمُ بِمَنْ ضَلَّ عَنْ سَبِيلِهِ وَهُوَ أَعْلَمُ بِمَنِ اهْتَدَىٰ

30
6:117; 16:125; 68:7

30 That is the extent of their knowledge. Your Lord knows best who has strayed from His path, and He knows best who has accepted guidance.

٣١ وَلِلَّهِ مَا فِي السَّمَاوَاتِ وَمَا فِي الْأَرْضِ لِيَجْزِيَ الَّذِينَ أَسَاءُوا بِمَا عَمِلُوا وَيَجْزِيَ الَّذِينَ أَحْسَنُوا بِالْحُسْنَى

31 To God belongs whatever is in the heavens and whatever is on earth. He will repay those who do evil according to their deeds, and recompense those who do good with the best.

٣٢ الَّذِينَ يَجْتَنِبُونَ كَبَائِرَ الْإِثْمِ وَالْفَوَاحِشَ إِلَّا اللَّمَمَ ۚ إِنَّ رَبَّكَ وَاسِعُ الْمَغْفِرَةِ ۚ [a] هُوَ أَعْلَمُ بِكُمْ إِذْ أَنشَأَكُم مِّنَ الْأَرْضِ وَإِذْ أَنتُمْ أَجِنَّةٌ فِي بُطُونِ أُمَّهَاتِكُمْ ۖ فَلَا تُزَكُّوا أَنفُسَكُمْ ۖ هُوَ أَعْلَمُ بِمَنِ اتَّقَىٰ [b]

32 Those who avoid gross sins and indecencies—except for minor lapses—your Lord is of Vast Forgiveness. He knows you well, ever since He created you from the earth, and ever since you were embryos in your mothers' wombs. So do not acclaim your own virtue; He is fully aware of the righteous.

32
[a] 19:78; 27:65; 68:47; 42:37
[b] 4:49

٣٣ أَفَرَأَيْتَ الَّذِي تَوَلَّىٰ

33 Have you considered him who turned away?

٣٤ وَأَعْطَىٰ قَلِيلًا وَأَكْدَىٰ

34 And gave a little, and held back?

٣٥ أَعِندَهُ عِلْمُ الْغَيْبِ فَهُوَ يَرَىٰ

35 Does he possess knowledge of the unseen, and can therefore foresee?

٣٦ أَمْ لَمْ يُنَبَّأْ بِمَا فِي صُحُفِ مُوسَىٰ

36 Or was he not informed of what is in the Scrolls of Moses?

36
20:133; 87:18–19

٣٧ وَإِبْرَاهِيمَ الَّذِي وَفَّىٰ

37 And of Abraham, who fulfilled?

37
2:124

٣٨ أَلَّا تَزِرُ وَازِرَةٌ وِزْرَ أُخْرَىٰ

38 That no soul bears the burdens of another soul.

38
6:164; 17:15; 35:18

٣٩ وَأَن لَّيْسَ لِلْإِنسَانِ إِلَّا مَا سَعَىٰ

39 And that the human being attains only what he strives for.

39
17:7; 30:44; 45:15; 99:78

٤٠ وَأَنَّ سَعْيَهُ سَوْفَ يُرَىٰ

40 And that his efforts will be witnessed.

٤١ ثُمَّ يُجْزَاهُ الْجَزَاءَ الْأَوْفَىٰ

41 Then he will be rewarded for it the fullest reward.

٤٢ وَأَنَّ إِلَىٰ رَبِّكَ الْمُنتَهَىٰ

42 And that to your Lord is the finality.

42
75:12; 79:44

٤٣ وَأَنَّهُ هُوَ أَضْحَكَ وَأَبْكَىٰ

43 And that it is He who causes laughter and weeping.

٤٤ وَأَنَّهُ هُوَ أَمَاتَ وَأَحْيَا

44 And that it is He who gives death and life.

44
3:156

45 And that it is He who created the two kinds—the male and the female.	٤٥ وَأَنَّهُ خَلَقَ الزَّوْجَيْنِ الذَّكَرَ وَالْأُنْثَىٰ	**45** 75:39
46 From a sperm drop, when emitted.	٤٦ مِنْ نُطْفَةٍ إِذَا تُمْنَىٰ	
47 And that upon Him is the next existence.	٤٧ وَأَنَّ عَلَيْهِ النَّشْأَةَ الْأُخْرَىٰ	**47** 29:20; 36:79
48 And that it is He who enriches and impoverishes.	٤٨ وَأَنَّهُ هُوَ أَغْنَىٰ وَأَقْنَىٰ	
49 And that it is He who is the Lord of Sirius.	٤٩ وَأَنَّهُ هُوَ رَبُّ الشِّعْرَىٰ	
50 And that it is He who destroyed the first ʿĀd.	٥٠ وَأَنَّهُ أَهْلَكَ عَادًا الْأُولَىٰ	**50** 7:65–72
51 And Thamūd, sparing no one.	٥١ وَثَمُودَ فَمَا أَبْقَىٰ	**51** 7:73–79
52 And the people of Noah before that; for they were most unjust and most oppressive.	٥٢ وَقَوْمَ نُوحٍ مِنْ قَبْلُ ۖ إِنَّهُمْ كَانُوا هُمْ أَظْلَمَ وَأَطْغَىٰ	**52** 7:59–64; 25:37
53 And He toppled the ruined cities.	٥٣ وَالْمُؤْتَفِكَةَ أَهْوَىٰ	
54 And covered them with whatever covered them.	٥٤ فَغَشَّاهَا مَا غَشَّىٰ	
55 So which of your Lord's marvels can you deny?	٥٥ فَبِأَيِّ آلَاءِ رَبِّكَ تَتَمَارَىٰ	
56 This is a warning, just like the first warnings.	٥٦ هَٰذَا نَذِيرٌ مِنَ النُّذُرِ الْأُولَىٰ	
57 The inevitable is imminent.	٥٧ أَزِفَتِ الْآزِفَةُ	**57** 40:18
58 None besides God can unveil it.	٥٨ لَيْسَ لَهَا مِنْ دُونِ اللَّهِ كَاشِفَةٌ	
59 Do you marvel at this discourse?	٥٩ أَفَمِنْ هَٰذَا الْحَدِيثِ تَعْجَبُونَ	
60 And laugh, and do not weep?	٦٠ وَتَضْحَكُونَ وَلَا تَبْكُونَ	

٦١ وَأَنتُمْ سَامِدُونَ

61 Lost in your frivolity?

٦٢ فَاسْجُدُوا لِلَّهِ وَاعْبُدُوا ۩

62 So bow down to God, and worship!

Sūrah 54: Al-Qamar

سُورَةُ ٱلْقَمَر (The Moon)

بِسْمِ ٱللَّهِ ٱلرَّحْمَٰنِ ٱلرَّحِيمِ

١ اقْتَرَبَتِ السَّاعَةُ وَانشَقَّ الْقَمَرُ

1 The Hour has drawn near, and the moon has split.

٢ وَإِن يَرَوْا آيَةً يُعْرِضُوا وَيَقُولُوا سِحْرٌ مُّسْتَمِرٌّ

2 Yet whenever they see a miracle, they turn away, and say, "Continuous magic."

2
7:132; 10:76; 21:1; 37:14

٣ وَكَذَّبُوا وَاتَّبَعُوا أَهْوَاءَهُمْ ۚ وَكُلُّ أَمْرٍ مُّسْتَقِرٌّ

3 They lied, and followed their opinions, but everything has its time.

٤ وَلَقَدْ جَاءَهُم مِّنَ الْأَنبَاءِ مَا فِيهِ مُزْدَجَرٌ

4 And there came to them news containing a deterrent.

٥ حِكْمَةٌ بَالِغَةٌ ۖ فَمَا تُغْنِ النُّذُرُ

5 Profound wisdom—but warnings are of no avail.

٦ فَتَوَلَّ عَنْهُمْ ۘ يَوْمَ يَدْعُ الدَّاعِ إِلَىٰ شَيْءٍ نُّكُرٍ

6 So turn away from them. On the Day when the Caller calls to something terrible.

6
20:108; 30:25

٧ خُشَّعًا أَبْصَارُهُمْ يَخْرُجُونَ مِنَ الْأَجْدَاثِ كَأَنَّهُمْ جَرَادٌ مُّنتَشِرٌ

7 Their eyes humiliated, they will emerge from the graves, as if they were swarming locusts.

٨ مُّهْطِعِينَ إِلَى الدَّاعِ ۖ يَقُولُ الْكَافِرُونَ هَٰذَا يَوْمٌ عَسِرٌ

8 Scrambling towards the Caller, the disbelievers will say, "This is a difficult Day."

8
14:43; 22:47; 70:36

٩ كَذَّبَتْ قَبْلَهُمْ قَوْمُ نُوحٍ فَكَذَّبُوا عَبْدَنَا وَقَالُوا مَجْنُونٌ وَازْدُجِرَ

9 Before them the people of Noah disbelieved. They rejected Our servant, and said, "Crazy," and he was rebuked.

9
22:42; 38:12; 40:5

١٠ فَدَعَا رَبَّهُ أَنِّي مَغْلُوبٌ فَانتَصِرْ

10 So he appealed to his Lord, "I am overwhelmed, so help me."

Sūrah 54: Al-Qamar

11 فَفَتَحْنَا أَبْوَابَ السَّمَاءِ بِمَاءٍ مُنْهَمِرٍ

11 So We opened the floodgates of heaven with water pouring down.

11
78:19

12 وَفَجَّرْنَا الْأَرْضَ عُيُونًا فَالْتَقَى الْمَاءُ عَلَىٰ أَمْرٍ قَدْ قُدِرَ

12 And We made the earth burst with springs, and the waters met for a purpose already destined.

13 وَحَمَلْنَاهُ عَلَىٰ ذَاتِ أَلْوَاحٍ وَدُسُرٍ

13 And We carried him on a craft of planks and nails.

13
36:41; 69:11

14 تَجْرِي بِأَعْيُنِنَا جَزَاءً لِمَنْ كَانَ كُفِرَ

14 Sailing before Our eyes; a reward for him who was rejected.

15 وَلَقَدْ تَرَكْنَاهَا آيَةً فَهَلْ مِنْ مُدَّكِرٍ

15 And We left it as a sign. Is there anyone who would take heed?

16 فَكَيْفَ كَانَ عَذَابِي وَنُذُرِ

16 So how were My punishment and My warnings?

16
pp 44:58; 54:18, 21, 30

17 وَلَقَدْ يَسَّرْنَا الْقُرْآنَ لِلذِّكْرِ فَهَلْ مِنْ مُدَّكِرٍ

17 We made the Qur'an easy to learn. Is there anyone who would learn?

17
pp 54:22, 32, 40

18 كَذَّبَتْ عَادٌ فَكَيْفَ كَانَ عَذَابِي وَنُذُرِ

18 'Ād denied the truth. So how were My punishment and My warnings?

18
pp 54:16, 21, 30

19 إِنَّا أَرْسَلْنَا عَلَيْهِمْ رِيحًا صَرْصَرًا فِي يَوْمِ نَحْسٍ مُسْتَمِرٍّ

19 We unleashed upon them a screaming wind, on a day of unrelenting misery.

19
41:16; 51:41; 69:6

20 تَنْزِعُ النَّاسَ كَأَنَّهُمْ أَعْجَازُ نَخْلٍ مُنْقَعِرٍ

20 Plucking the people away, as though they were trunks of uprooted palm-trees.

20
69:7

21 فَكَيْفَ كَانَ عَذَابِي وَنُذُرِ

21 So how were My punishment and My warnings?

21
pp 54:16, 18, 30

22 وَلَقَدْ يَسَّرْنَا الْقُرْآنَ لِلذِّكْرِ فَهَلْ مِنْ مُدَّكِرٍ

22 We made the Qur'an easy to remember. Is there anyone who would remember?

22
pp: 17, 32, 40

23 كَذَّبَتْ ثَمُودُ بِالنُّذُرِ

23 Thamūd rejected the warnings.

24 فَقَالُوا أَبَشَرًا مِنَّا وَاحِدًا نَتَّبِعُهُ إِنَّا إِذًا لَفِي ضَلَالٍ وَسُعُرٍ

24 They said, "Are we to follow one of us, a human being? We would then go astray, and end up in Hell.

24
6:91; 38:4, 8

٢٥ أَءُلْقِيَ الذِّكْرُ عَلَيْهِ مِنْ بَيْنِنَا بَلْ هُوَ كَذَّابٌ أَشِرٌ	25 7:63; 38:8

25 Was the message given to him, out of all of us? In fact, he is a wicked liar."

٢٦ سَيَعْلَمُونَ غَدًا مَنِ الْكَذَّابُ الْأَشِرُ	

26 They will know tomorrow who the wicked liar is.

٢٧ إِنَّا مُرْسِلُو النَّاقَةِ فِتْنَةً لَهُمْ فَارْتَقِبْهُمْ وَاصْطَبِرْ	27 7:73; 26:155; 91:13

27 We are sending the she-camel as a test for them; so watch them and be patient.

٢٨ وَنَبِّئْهُمْ أَنَّ الْمَاءَ قِسْمَةٌ بَيْنَهُمْ ۖ كُلُّ شِرْبٍ مُحْتَضَرٌ	

28 And inform them that the water is to be shared between them; each share of drink made available.

٢٩ فَنَادَوْا صَاحِبَهُمْ فَتَعَاطَىٰ فَعَقَرَ	

29 But they called their friend, and he dared, and he slaughtered.

٣٠ فَكَيْفَ كَانَ عَذَابِي وَنُذُرِ	30 PP 54:16, 18, 21

30 So how were My punishment and My warnings?

٣١ إِنَّا أَرْسَلْنَا عَلَيْهِمْ صَيْحَةً وَاحِدَةً فَكَانُوا كَهَشِيمِ الْمُحْتَظِرِ	31 11:67; 36:29, 49, 53; 38:15; 41:17

31 We sent against them a single Scream, and they became like crushed hay.

٣٢ وَلَقَدْ يَسَّرْنَا الْقُرْآنَ لِلذِّكْرِ فَهَلْ مِنْ مُدَّكِرٍ	32 PP 17, 22, 40

32 We made the Qur'an easy to understand. Is there anyone who would understand?

٣٣ كَذَّبَتْ قَوْمُ لُوطٍ بِالنُّذُرِ	

33 The people of Lot rejected the warnings.

٣٤ إِنَّا أَرْسَلْنَا عَلَيْهِمْ حَاصِبًا إِلَّا آلَ لُوطٍ ۖ نَجَّيْنَاهُمْ بِسَحَرٍ	34 7:84

34 We unleashed upon them a shower of stones, except for the family of Lot; We rescued them at dawn.

٣٥ نِعْمَةً مِنْ عِنْدِنَا ۚ كَذَٰلِكَ نَجْزِي مَنْ شَكَرَ	

35 A blessing from Us. Thus We reward the thankful.

٣٦ وَلَقَدْ أَنْذَرَهُمْ بَطْشَتَنَا فَتَمَارَوْا بِالنُّذُرِ	36 44:16

36 He had warned them of Our onslaught, but they dismissed the warnings.

٣٧ وَلَقَدْ رَاوَدُوهُ عَنْ ضَيْفِهِ فَطَمَسْنَا أَعْيُنَهُمْ فَذُوقُوا عَذَابِي وَنُذُرِ	37 11:78; 15:67

37 They even lusted for his guest, so We obliterated their eyes. "So taste My punishment and My warnings."

38 وَلَقَدْ صَبَّحَهُم بُكْرَةً عَذَابٌ مُّسْتَقِرٌّ ٣٨

38 Early morning brought upon them enduring punishment.

38
11:81; 15:65, 73

فَذُوقُوا عَذَابِي وَنُذُرِ ٣٩

39 So taste My punishment and My warnings.

وَلَقَدْ يَسَّرْنَا الْقُرْآنَ لِلذِّكْرِ فَهَلْ مِن مُّدَّكِرٍ ٤٠

40 We made the Qur'an easy to memorize. Is there anyone who would memorize?

40
pp 17, 22, 32

وَلَقَدْ جَاءَ آلَ فِرْعَوْنَ النُّذُرُ ٤١

41 The warnings also came to the people of Pharaoh.

كَذَّبُوا بِآيَاتِنَا كُلِّهَا فَأَخَذْنَاهُمْ أَخْذَ عَزِيزٍ مُّقْتَدِرٍ ٤٢

42 They rejected Our signs, all of them, so We seized them—the seizure of an Almighty Omnipotent.

أَكُفَّارُكُمْ خَيْرٌ مِّنْ أُولَٰئِكُمْ أَمْ لَكُم بَرَاءَةٌ فِي الزُّبُرِ ٤٣

43 Are your unbelievers better than all those? Or do you have immunity in the scriptures?

أَمْ يَقُولُونَ نَحْنُ جَمِيعٌ مُّنتَصِرٌ ٤٤

44 Or do they say, "We are united, and we will be victorious"?

44
26:56

سَيُهْزَمُ الْجَمْعُ وَيُوَلُّونَ الدُّبُرَ ٤٥

45 The multitude will be defeated, and they will turn their backs.

بَلِ السَّاعَةُ مَوْعِدُهُمْ وَالسَّاعَةُ أَدْهَىٰ وَأَمَرُّ ٤٦

46 The Hour is their appointed time—the Hour is more disastrous, and most bitter.

إِنَّ الْمُجْرِمِينَ فِي ضَلَالٍ وَسُعُرٍ ٤٧

47 The wicked are in confusion and madness.

يَوْمَ يُسْحَبُونَ فِي النَّارِ عَلَىٰ وُجُوهِهِمْ ذُوقُوا مَسَّ سَقَرَ ٤٨

48 The Day when they are dragged upon their faces into the Fire: "Taste the touch of Saqar."

48
17:97; 25:34; 27:90;
33:66; 40:71; 52:13

إِنَّا كُلَّ شَيْءٍ خَلَقْنَاهُ بِقَدَرٍ ٤٩

49 Everything We created is precisely measured.

وَمَا أَمْرُنَا إِلَّا وَاحِدَةٌ كَلَمْحٍ بِالْبَصَرِ ٥٠

50 And Our command is but once, like the twinkling of an eye.

50
16:77

وَلَقَدْ أَهْلَكْنَا أَشْيَاعَكُمْ فَهَلْ مِن مُّدَّكِرٍ ٥١

51 We have destroyed your likes. Is there anyone who would ponder?

51
34:54

وَكُلُّ شَيْءٍ فَعَلُوهُ فِي الزُّبُرِ ٥٢

52 Everything they have done is in the Books.

53 Everything, small or large, is written down.	٥٣ وَكُلُّ صَغِيرٍ وَكَبِيرٍ مُسْتَطَرٌ	53 18:49
54 The righteous will be amidst gardens and rivers.	٥٤ إِنَّ الْمُتَّقِينَ فِي جَنَّاتٍ وَنَهَرٍ	54 2:25; 47:15
55 In an assembly of virtue, in the presence of an Omnipotent King.	٥٥ فِي مَقْعَدِ صِدْقٍ عِندَ مَلِيكٍ مُقْتَدِرٍ	55 10:2

Sūrah 55: Al-Raḥmān

سُورَةُ ٱلرَّحْمَٰن (The Compassionate)

بِسْمِ ٱللَّهِ ٱلرَّحْمَٰنِ ٱلرَّحِيمِ

1 The Compassionate.	١ الرَّحْمَٰنُ	1–2 25:6
2 Has taught the Qur'an.	٢ عَلَّمَ الْقُرْآنَ	
3 He created man.	٣ خَلَقَ الْإِنسَانَ	
4 And taught him clear expression.	٤ عَلَّمَهُ الْبَيَانَ	
5 The sun and the moon move according to plan.	٥ الشَّمْسُ وَالْقَمَرُ بِحُسْبَانٍ	5 6:96; 10:5; 17:12
6 And the stars and the trees prostrate themselves.	٦ وَالنَّجْمُ وَالشَّجَرُ يَسْجُدَانِ	6 13:15; 22:18
7 And the sky, He raised; and He set up the balance.	٧ وَالسَّمَاءَ رَفَعَهَا وَوَضَعَ الْمِيزَانَ	
8 So do not transgress in the balance.	٨ أَلَّا تَطْغَوْا فِي الْمِيزَانِ	8 6:152
9 But maintain the weights with justice, and do not violate the balance.	٩ وَأَقِيمُوا الْوَزْنَ بِالْقِسْطِ وَلَا تُخْسِرُوا الْمِيزَانَ	9 6:152
10 And the earth; He set up for the creatures.	١٠ وَالْأَرْضَ وَضَعَهَا لِلْأَنَامِ	10–11 13:3; 23:19; 51:48; 67:15; 79:30–33

| | ١١ فِيهَا فَاكِهَةٌ وَالنَّخْلُ ذَاتُ الْأَكْمَامِ |
11 In it are fruits, and palms in clusters.

| | ١٢ وَالْحَبُّ ذُو الْعَصْفِ وَالرَّيْحَانُ |
12 And grains in the blades, and fragrant plants.

١٣ فَبِأَيِّ آلَاءِ رَبِّكُمَا تُكَذِّبَانِ

13 So which of your Lord's marvels will you deny?

13
pp 55:16, 18, 21, 23, 25, 28, 30, 32, 34, 36, 38, 40, 42, 45, 47, 49, 51, 53, 57, 59, 61, 63, 65, 67, 69, 71, 73, 75, 77

١٤ خَلَقَ الْإِنْسَانَ مِنْ صَلْصَالٍ كَالْفَخَّارِ

14 He created man from hard clay, like bricks.

14
15:26, 28, 33

١٥ وَخَلَقَ الْجَانَّ مِنْ مَارِجٍ مِنْ نَارٍ

15 And created the jinn from a fusion of fire.

١٦ فَبِأَيِّ آلَاءِ رَبِّكُمَا تُكَذِّبَانِ

16 So which of your Lord's marvels will you deny?

١٧ رَبُّ الْمَشْرِقَيْنِ وَرَبُّ الْمَغْرِبَيْنِ

17 Lord of the two Easts and Lord of the two Wests.

17
2:115; 26:28; 37:5; 70:40; 73:9

١٨ فَبِأَيِّ آلَاءِ رَبِّكُمَا تُكَذِّبَانِ

18 So which of your Lord's marvels will you deny?

١٩ مَرَجَ الْبَحْرَيْنِ يَلْتَقِيَانِ

19 He merged the two seas, converging together.

19–20
25:53; 27:61; 35:12

٢٠ بَيْنَهُمَا بَرْزَخٌ لَا يَبْغِيَانِ

20 Between them is a barrier, which they do not overrun.

٢١ فَبِأَيِّ آلَاءِ رَبِّكُمَا تُكَذِّبَانِ

21 So which of your Lord's marvels will you deny?

٢٢ يَخْرُجُ مِنْهُمَا اللُّؤْلُؤُ وَالْمَرْجَانُ

22 From them emerge pearls and coral.

22
16:14; 35:12

٢٣ فَبِأَيِّ آلَاءِ رَبِّكُمَا تُكَذِّبَانِ

23 So which of your Lord's marvels will you deny?

٢٤ وَلَهُ الْجَوَارِ الْمُنْشَآتُ فِي الْبَحْرِ كَالْأَعْلَامِ

24 His are the ships, raised above the sea like landmarks.

24
42:32

٢٥ فَبِأَيِّ آلَاءِ رَبِّكُمَا تُكَذِّبَانِ

25 So which of your Lord's marvels will you deny?

٢٦ كُلُّ مَنْ عَلَيْهَا فَانٍ

26 Everyone upon it is perishing.

26–27
3:185; 25:58; 28:88

٢٧ وَيَبْقَىٰ وَجْهُ رَبِّكَ ذُو الْجَلَالِ وَالْإِكْرَامِ

27 But will remain the Presence of your Lord, Full of Majesty and Splendor.

٢٨ فَبِأَيِّ آلَاءِ رَبِّكُمَا تُكَذِّبَانِ

28 So which of your Lord's marvels will you deny?

٢٩ يَسْأَلُهُ مَنْ فِي السَّمَاوَاتِ وَالْأَرْضِ ۚ كُلَّ يَوْمٍ هُوَ فِي شَأْنٍ

29 Everyone in the heavens and the earth asks Him. Every day He is managing.

٣٠ فَبِأَيِّ آلَاءِ رَبِّكُمَا تُكَذِّبَانِ

30 So which of your Lord's marvels will you deny?

٣١ سَنَفْرُغُ لَكُمْ أَيُّهَ الثَّقَلَانِ

31 We will attend to you, O prominent two.

٣٢ فَبِأَيِّ آلَاءِ رَبِّكُمَا تُكَذِّبَانِ

32 So which of your Lord's marvels will you deny?

٣٣ يَا مَعْشَرَ الْجِنِّ وَالْإِنْسِ إِنِ اسْتَطَعْتُمْ أَنْ تَنْفُذُوا مِنْ أَقْطَارِ السَّمَاوَاتِ وَالْأَرْضِ فَانْفُذُوا ۚ لَا تَنْفُذُونَ إِلَّا بِسُلْطَانٍ

33
29:22

33 O society of jinn and humans! If you can pass through the bounds of the heavens and the earth, go ahead and pass. But you will not pass except with authorization.

٣٤ فَبِأَيِّ آلَاءِ رَبِّكُمَا تُكَذِّبَانِ

34 So which of your Lord's marvels will you deny?

٣٥ يُرْسَلُ عَلَيْكُمَا شُوَاظٌ مِنْ نَارٍ وَنُحَاسٌ فَلَا تَنْتَصِرَانِ

35 You will be bombarded with flares of fire and brass, and you will not succeed.

٣٦ فَبِأَيِّ آلَاءِ رَبِّكُمَا تُكَذِّبَانِ

36 So which of your Lord's marvels will you deny?

٣٧ فَإِذَا انْشَقَّتِ السَّمَاءُ فَكَانَتْ وَرْدَةً كَالدِّهَانِ

37
25:25; 73:18; 69:16; 82:1; 84:1

37 When the sky splits apart, and becomes rose, like paint.

٣٨ فَبِأَيِّ آلَاءِ رَبِّكُمَا تُكَذِّبَانِ

38 So which of your Lord's marvels will you deny?

39 فَيَوْمَئِذٍ لَا يُسْأَلُ عَنْ ذَنْبِهِ إِنْسٌ وَلَا جَانٌّ

39 On that Day, no human and no jinn will be asked about his sins.

40 فَبِأَيِّ آلَاءِ رَبِّكُمَا تُكَذِّبَانِ

40 So which of your Lord's marvels will you deny?

41 يُعْرَفُ الْمُجْرِمُونَ بِسِيمَاهُمْ فَيُؤْخَذُ بِالنَّوَاصِي وَالْأَقْدَامِ

41 The guilty will be recognized by their marks; they will be taken by the forelocks and the feet.

41
3:106; 7:46; 39:70;
80:40–42; 96:15–16

42 فَبِأَيِّ آلَاءِ رَبِّكُمَا تُكَذِّبَانِ

42 So which of your Lord's marvels will you deny?

43 هَذِهِ جَهَنَّمُ الَّتِي يُكَذِّبُ بِهَا الْمُجْرِمُونَ

43 This is Hell that the guilty denied.

43
52:14

44 يَطُوفُونَ بَيْنَهَا وَبَيْنَ حَمِيمٍ آنٍ

44 They circulate between it and between a seething bath.

44
88:4–5

45 فَبِأَيِّ آلَاءِ رَبِّكُمَا تُكَذِّبَانِ

45 So which of your Lord's marvels will you deny?

46 وَلِمَنْ خَافَ مَقَامَ رَبِّهِ جَنَّتَانِ

46 But for him who feared the standing of his Lord are two gardens.

47 فَبِأَيِّ آلَاءِ رَبِّكُمَا تُكَذِّبَانِ

47 So which of your Lord's marvels will you deny?

48 ذَوَاتَا أَفْنَانٍ

48 Full of varieties.

49 فَبِأَيِّ آلَاءِ رَبِّكُمَا تُكَذِّبَانِ

49 So which of your Lord's marvels will you deny?

50 فِيهِمَا عَيْنَانِ تَجْرِيَانِ

50 In them are two flowing springs.

51 فَبِأَيِّ آلَاءِ رَبِّكُمَا تُكَذِّبَانِ

51 So which of your Lord's marvels will you deny?

52 فِيهِمَا مِنْ كُلِّ فَاكِهَةٍ زَوْجَانِ

52 In them are fruits of every kind, in pairs.

53 فَبِأَيِّ آلَاءِ رَبِّكُمَا تُكَذِّبَانِ

53 So which of your Lord's marvels will you deny?

54 مُتَّكِئِينَ عَلَىٰ فُرُشٍ بَطَائِنُهَا مِنْ إِسْتَبْرَقٍ ۚ وَجَنَى الْجَنَّتَيْنِ دَانٍ

54 Reclining on furnishings lined with brocade, and the fruits of the two gardens are near at hand.

54
16:14; 18:31; 54:76;
55:76

٥٥ فَبِأَيِّ آلَاءِ رَبِّكُمَا تُكَذِّبَانِ

55 So which of your Lord's marvels will you deny?

٥٦ فِيهِنَّ قَاصِرَاتُ الطَّرْفِ لَمْ يَطْمِثْهُنَّ إِنْسٌ قَبْلَهُمْ وَلَا جَانٌّ

56 In them are maidens restraining their glances, untouched before by any man or jinn.

56
2:25; 37:48; 38:52;
56:22–23

٥٧ فَبِأَيِّ آلَاءِ رَبِّكُمَا تُكَذِّبَانِ

57 So which of your Lord's marvels will you deny?

٥٨ كَأَنَّهُنَّ الْيَاقُوتُ وَالْمَرْجَانُ

58 As though they were rubies and corals.

٥٩ فَبِأَيِّ آلَاءِ رَبِّكُمَا تُكَذِّبَانِ

59 So which of your Lord's marvels will you deny?

٦٠ هَلْ جَزَاءُ الْإِحْسَانِ إِلَّا الْإِحْسَانُ

60 Is the reward of goodness anything but goodness?

60
6:160; 10:26

٦١ فَبِأَيِّ آلَاءِ رَبِّكُمَا تُكَذِّبَانِ

61 So which of your Lord's marvels will you deny?

٦٢ وَمِنْ دُونِهِمَا جَنَّتَانِ

62 And beneath them are two gardens.

٦٣ فَبِأَيِّ آلَاءِ رَبِّكُمَا تُكَذِّبَانِ

63 So which of your Lord's marvels will you deny?

٦٤ مُدْهَامَّتَانِ

64 Deep green.

٦٥ فَبِأَيِّ آلَاءِ رَبِّكُمَا تُكَذِّبَانِ

65 So which of your Lord's marvels will you deny?

٦٦ فِيهِمَا عَيْنَانِ نَضَّاخَتَانِ

66 In them are two gushing springs.

٦٧ فَبِأَيِّ آلَاءِ رَبِّكُمَا تُكَذِّبَانِ

67 So which of your Lord's marvels will you deny?

٦٨ فِيهِمَا فَاكِهَةٌ وَنَخْلٌ وَرُمَّانٌ

68 In them are fruits, and date-palms, and pomegranates.

٦٩ فَبِأَيِّ آلَاءِ رَبِّكُمَا تُكَذِّبَانِ

69 So which of your Lord's marvels will you deny?

٧٠ فِيهِنَّ خَيْرَاتٌ حِسَانٌ

70 In them are good and beautiful ones.

71 So which of your Lord's marvels will you deny?

٧١ فَبِأَيِّ آلَاءِ رَبِّكُمَا تُكَذِّبَانِ

72 Companions, secluded in the tents.

٧٢ حُورٌ مَقْصُورَاتٌ فِي الْخِيَامِ

73 So which of your Lord's marvels will you deny?

٧٣ فَبِأَيِّ آلَاءِ رَبِّكُمَا تُكَذِّبَانِ

74 Whom no human has touched before, nor jinn.

٧٤ لَمْ يَطْمِثْهُنَّ إِنْسٌ قَبْلَهُمْ وَلَا جَانٌّ

75 So which of your Lord's marvels will you deny?

٧٥ فَبِأَيِّ آلَاءِ رَبِّكُمَا تُكَذِّبَانِ

76 Reclining on green cushions, and exquisite carpets.

٧٦ مُتَّكِئِينَ عَلَىٰ رَفْرَفٍ خُضْرٍ وَعَبْقَرِيٍّ حِسَانٍ

76
18:31; 54:76; 55:54

77 So which of your Lord's marvels will you deny?

٧٧ فَبِأَيِّ آلَاءِ رَبِّكُمَا تُكَذِّبَانِ

78 Blessed be the name of your Lord, Full of Majesty and Splendor.

٧٨ تَبَارَكَ اسْمُ رَبِّكَ ذِي الْجَلَالِ وَالْإِكْرَامِ

Sūrah 56: Al-Wāqi'ah

سُورَةُ ٱلْوَاقِعَة (The Inevitable)

بِسْمِ ٱللَّهِ ٱلرَّحْمَٰنِ ٱلرَّحِيمِ

1 When the inevitable occurs.

١ إِذَا وَقَعَتِ الْوَاقِعَةُ

1
69:15

2 Of its occurrence, there is no denial.

٢ لَيْسَ لِوَقْعَتِهَا كَاذِبَةٌ

3 Bringing low, raising high.

٣ خَافِضَةٌ رَافِعَةٌ

4 When the earth is shaken with a shock.

٤ إِذَا رُجَّتِ الْأَرْضُ رَجًّا

4–6
22:1; 69:14; 70:9;
73:14; 99:1; 101:5

5 And the mountains are crushed and crumbled.

٥ وَبُسَّتِ الْجِبَالُ بَسًّا

٦ فَكَانَتْ هَبَاءً مُنْبَثًّا	
6 And they become scattered dust.	
٧ وَكُنتُمْ أَزْوَاجًا ثَلَاثَةً	
7 And you become three classes.	
٨ فَأَصْحَابُ الْمَيْمَنَةِ مَا أَصْحَابُ الْمَيْمَنَةِ	**8**
8 Those on the Right—what of those on the Right?	56:27, 90; 74:39; 90:12
٩ وَأَصْحَابُ الْمَشْأَمَةِ مَا أَصْحَابُ الْمَشْأَمَةِ	**9**
9 And those on the Left—what of those on the Left?	56:41; 90:19
١٠ وَالسَّابِقُونَ السَّابِقُونَ	
10 And the forerunners, the forerunners.	
١١ أُولَٰئِكَ الْمُقَرَّبُونَ	
11 Those are the nearest.	
١٢ فِي جَنَّاتِ النَّعِيمِ	
12 In the Gardens of Bliss.	
١٣ ثُلَّةٌ مِنَ الْأَوَّلِينَ	**13**
13 A throng from the ancients.	PP 56:39
١٤ وَقَلِيلٌ مِنَ الْآخِرِينَ	
14 And a small band from the latecomers.	
١٥ عَلَىٰ سُرُرٍ مَوْضُونَةٍ	**15**
15 On luxurious furnishings.	15:47; 18:31
١٦ مُتَّكِئِينَ عَلَيْهَا مُتَقَابِلِينَ	**16**
16 Reclining on them, facing one another.	37:44
١٧ يَطُوفُ عَلَيْهِمْ وِلْدَانٌ مُخَلَّدُونَ	**17**
17 Serving them will be immortalized youth.	52:24; 76:19 153
١٨ بِأَكْوَابٍ وَأَبَارِيقَ وَكَأْسٍ مِنْ مَعِينٍ	**18**
18 With cups, pitchers, and sparkling drinks.	43:71; 52:27; 76:18; 88:14
١٩ لَا يُصَدَّعُونَ عَنْهَا وَلَا يُنْزِفُونَ	**19**
19 Causing them neither headache, nor intoxication.	37:47
٢٠ وَفَاكِهَةٍ مِمَّا يَتَخَيَّرُونَ	
20 And fruits of their choice.	
٢١ وَلَحْمِ طَيْرٍ مِمَّا يَشْتَهُونَ	**21**
21 And meat of birds that they may desire.	52:22

22 And lovely companions.	٢٢ وَحُورٌ عِينٌ	**22** 2:25; 37:48; 44:54; 55:56
23 The likenesses of treasured pearls.	٢٣ كَأَمْثَالِ اللُّؤْلُؤِ الْمَكْنُونِ	
24 As a reward for what they used to do.	٢٤ جَزَاءً بِمَا كَانُوا يَعْمَلُونَ	
25 Therein they will hear no nonsense, and no accusations.	٢٥ لَا يَسْمَعُونَ فِيهَا لَغْوًا وَلَا تَأْثِيمًا	
26 But only the greeting: "Peace, peace."	٢٦ إِلَّا قِيلًا سَلَامًا سَلَامًا	**26** 10:10; 19:62
27 And those on the Right—what of those on the Right?	٢٧ وَأَصْحَابُ الْيَمِينِ مَا أَصْحَابُ الْيَمِينِ	**27** 56:8, 90; 74:39; 90:12
28 In lush orchards.	٢٨ فِي سِدْرٍ مَخْضُودٍ	
29 And sweet-smelling plants.	٢٩ وَطَلْحٍ مَنْضُودٍ	
30 And extended shade.	٣٠ وَظِلٍّ مَمْدُودٍ	
31 And outpouring water.	٣١ وَمَاءٍ مَسْكُوبٍ	
32 And abundant fruit.	٣٢ وَفَاكِهَةٍ كَثِيرَةٍ	**32** 36:57
33 Neither withheld, nor forbidden.	٣٣ لَا مَقْطُوعَةٍ وَلَا مَمْنُوعَةٍ	
34 And uplifted mattresses.	٣٤ وَفُرُشٍ مَرْفُوعَةٍ	**34** 88:13
35 We have created them of special creation.	٣٥ إِنَّا أَنْشَأْنَاهُنَّ إِنْشَاءً	
36 And made them virgins.	٣٦ فَجَعَلْنَاهُنَّ أَبْكَارًا	
37 Tender and un-aging.	٣٧ عُرُبًا أَتْرَابًا	

38 For those on the Right. ٣٨ لِأَصْحَابِ الْيَمِينِ

39 A throng from the ancients. ٣٩ ثُلَّةٌ مِنَ الْأَوَّلِينَ

39
pp 56:13

40 And a throng from the latecomers. ٤٠ وَثُلَّةٌ مِنَ الْآخِرِينَ

41 And those on the Left—what of those on the Left? ٤١ وَأَصْحَابُ الشِّمَالِ مَا أَصْحَابُ الشِّمَالِ

41
56:9; 90:19

42 Amid searing wind and boiling water. ٤٢ فِي سَمُومٍ وَحَمِيمٍ

43 And a shadow of thick smoke. ٤٣ وَظِلٍّ مِنْ يَحْمُومٍ

44 Neither cool, nor refreshing. ٤٤ لَا بَارِدٍ وَلَا كَرِيمٍ

45 They had lived before that in luxury. ٤٥ إِنَّهُمْ كَانُوا قَبْلَ ذَٰلِكَ مُتْرَفِينَ

46 And they used to persist in immense wrongdoing. ٤٦ وَكَانُوا يُصِرُّونَ عَلَى الْحِنْثِ الْعَظِيمِ

47 And they used to say, "When we are dead and turned into dust and bones, are we to be resurrected? ٤٧ وَكَانُوا يَقُولُونَ أَئِذَا مِتْنَا وَكُنَّا تُرَابًا وَعِظَامًا أَإِنَّا لَمَبْعُوثُونَ

47
37:16

48 And our ancient ancestors too?" ٤٨ أَوَآبَاؤُنَا الْأَوَّلُونَ

49 Say, "The first and the last. ٤٩ قُلْ إِنَّ الْأَوَّلِينَ وَالْآخِرِينَ

49–50
3:9; 4:87; 11:103; 64:9; 77:38

50 Will be gathered for the appointment of a familiar Day." ٥٠ لَمَجْمُوعُونَ إِلَىٰ مِيقَاتِ يَوْمٍ مَعْلُومٍ

51 Then you, you misguided, who deny the truth. ٥١ ثُمَّ إِنَّكُمْ أَيُّهَا الضَّالُّونَ الْمُكَذِّبُونَ

52 Will be eating from the Tree of Bitterness. ٥٢ لَآكِلُونَ مِنْ شَجَرٍ مِنْ زَقُّومٍ

52
37:62; 44:43–44

53 Will be filling your bellies with it. ٥٣ فَمَالِئُونَ مِنْهَا الْبُطُونَ

54 Will be drinking on top of it boiling water.   ٥٤ فَشَارِبُونَ عَلَيْهِ مِنَ الْحَمِيمِ   **54** 37:67

55 Drinking like thirsty camels drink.   ٥٥ فَشَارِبُونَ شُرْبَ الْهِيمِ

56 That is their hospitality on the Day of Retribution.   ٥٦ هَٰذَا نُزُلُهُمْ يَوْمَ الدِّينِ

57 We created you—if only you would believe!   ٥٧ نَحْنُ خَلَقْنَاكُمْ فَلَوْلَا تُصَدِّقُونَ

58 Have you seen what you ejaculate?   ٥٨ أَفَرَأَيْتُم مَّا تُمْنُونَ

59 Is it you who create it, or are We the Creator?   ٥٩ أَأَنتُمْ تَخْلُقُونَهُ أَمْ نَحْنُ الْخَالِقُونَ

60 We have decreed death among you, and We will not be outstripped.   ٦٠ نَحْنُ قَدَّرْنَا بَيْنَكُمُ الْمَوْتَ وَمَا نَحْنُ بِمَسْبُوقِينَ

61 In replacing you with your likes, and transforming you into what you do not know.   ٦١ عَلَىٰ أَن نُّبَدِّلَ أَمْثَالَكُمْ وَنُنشِئَكُمْ فِي مَا لَا تَعْلَمُونَ

62 You have known the first formation; if only you would remember.   ٦٢ وَلَقَدْ عَلِمْتُمُ النَّشْأَةَ الْأُولَىٰ فَلَوْلَا تَذَكَّرُونَ   **62** 29:20; 53:47; 70:39

63 Have you seen what you cultivate?   ٦٣ أَفَرَأَيْتُم مَّا تَحْرُثُونَ

64 Is it you who make it grow, or are We the Grower?   ٦٤ أَأَنتُمْ تَزْرَعُونَهُ أَمْ نَحْنُ الزَّارِعُونَ

65 If We will, We can turn it into rubble; then you will lament.   ٦٥ لَوْ نَشَاءُ لَجَعَلْنَاهُ حُطَامًا فَظَلْتُمْ تَفَكَّهُونَ   **65** 39:21; 57:20

66 "We are penalized.   ٦٦ إِنَّا لَمُغْرَمُونَ

67 No, we are being deprived."   ٦٧ بَلْ نَحْنُ مَحْرُومُونَ

68 Have you seen the water you drink?   ٦٨ أَفَرَأَيْتُمُ الْمَاءَ الَّذِي تَشْرَبُونَ   **68** 16:10

69 Is it you who sent it down from the clouds, or are We the Sender?   ٦٩ أَأَنتُمْ أَنزَلْتُمُوهُ مِنَ الْمُزْنِ أَمْ نَحْنُ الْمُنزِلُونَ

٧٠ لَوْ نَشَاءُ جَعَلْنَاهُ أُجَاجًا فَلَوْلَا تَشْكُرُونَ
70 If We will, We can make it salty. Will you not be thankful?

٧١ أَفَرَأَيْتُمُ النَّارَ الَّتِي تُورُونَ
71 Have you seen the fire you kindle?

٧٢ أَأَنْتُمْ أَنْشَأْتُمْ شَجَرَتَهَا أَمْ نَحْنُ الْمُنْشِئُونَ
72 Is it you who produce its tree, or are We the Producer?

٧٣ نَحْنُ جَعَلْنَاهَا تَذْكِرَةً وَمَتَاعًا لِلْمُقْوِينَ
73 We have made it a reminder, and a comfort for the users.

٧٤ فَسَبِّحْ بِاسْمِ رَبِّكَ الْعَظِيمِ
74 So glorify the Name of your Great Lord.

٧٥ فَلَا أُقْسِمُ بِمَوَاقِعِ النُّجُومِ
75 I swear by the locations of the stars.

75
53:1

٧٦ وَإِنَّهُ لَقَسَمٌ لَوْ تَعْلَمُونَ عَظِيمٌ
76 It is an oath, if you only knew, that is tremendous.

76
89:5

٧٧ إِنَّهُ لَقُرْآنٌ كَرِيمٌ
77 It is a noble Qur'an.

77–79
80:11–16; 85:21; 98:2

٧٨ فِي كِتَابٍ مَكْنُونٍ
78 In a well-protected Book.

٧٩ لَا يَمَسُّهُ إِلَّا الْمُطَهَّرُونَ
79 None can grasp it except the purified.

٨٠ تَنْزِيلٌ مِنْ رَبِّ الْعَالَمِينَ
80 A revelation from the Lord of the Worlds.

٨١ أَفَبِهَذَا الْحَدِيثِ أَنْتُمْ مُدْهِنُونَ
81 Is it this discourse that you take so lightly?

٨٢ وَتَجْعَلُونَ رِزْقَكُمْ أَنَّكُمْ تُكَذِّبُونَ
82 And you make it your livelihood to deny it?

٨٣ فَلَوْلَا إِذَا بَلَغَتِ الْحُلْقُومَ
83 So when it has reached the throat.

83
75:26

٨٤ وَأَنْتُمْ حِينَئِذٍ تَنْظُرُونَ
84 As you are looking on.

٨٥ وَنَحْنُ أَقْرَبُ إِلَيْهِ مِنْكُمْ وَلَكِنْ لَا تُبْصِرُونَ
85 We are nearer to it than you are, but you do not see.

٨٦ فَلَوْلَا إِنْ كُنْتُمْ غَيْرَ مَدِينِينَ
86 If you are not held to account.

87 تَرْجِعُونَهَا إِنْ كُنْتُمْ صَادِقِينَ

87 Then bring it back, if you are truthful.

88 فَأَمَّا إِنْ كَانَ مِنَ الْمُقَرَّبِينَ

88 But if he is one of those brought near.

89 فَرَوْحٌ وَرَيْحَانٌ وَجَنَّتُ نَعِيمٍ

89 Then happiness, and flowers, and Garden of Delights.

90 وَأَمَّا إِنْ كَانَ مِنْ أَصْحَابِ الْيَمِينِ

90 And if he is one of those on the Right.

90
56:8, 27; 74:39; 90:12

91 فَسَلَامٌ لَكَ مِنْ أَصْحَابِ الْيَمِينِ

91 Then, "Peace upon you," from those on the Right.

92 وَأَمَّا إِنْ كَانَ مِنَ الْمُكَذِّبِينَ الضَّالِّينَ

92 But if he is one of the deniers, the mistaken.

93 فَنُزُلٌ مِنْ حَمِيمٍ

93 Then a welcome of Inferno.

93–94
6:70; 10:4; 37:67; 55:44

94 وَتَصْلِيَةُ جَحِيمٍ

94 And burning in Hell.

95 إِنَّ هَٰذَا لَهُوَ حَقُّ الْيَقِينِ

95 This is the certain truth.

96 فَسَبِّحْ بِاسْمِ رَبِّكَ الْعَظِيمِ

96 So glorify the Name of your Lord, the Magnificent

96
pp 69:52

Sūrah 57: Al-Ḥadīd

سُورَةُ ٱلْحَدِيد (Iron)

بِسْمِ ٱللَّهِ ٱلرَّحْمَٰنِ ٱلرَّحِيمِ

1 سَبَّحَ لِلَّهِ مَا فِي السَّمَاوَاتِ وَالْأَرْضِ ۖ وَهُوَ الْعَزِيزُ الْحَكِيمُ

1 Glorifying God is everything in the heavens and the earth. He is the Almighty, the Wise.

1
17:44; 21:79; 59:1; 61:1; 62:1; 64:1

2 لَهُ مُلْكُ السَّمَاوَاتِ وَالْأَرْضِ ۖ يُحْيِي وَيُمِيتُ ۖ وَهُوَ عَلَىٰ كُلِّ شَيْءٍ قَدِيرٌ

2 To Him belongs the kingdom of the heavens and the earth. He gives life and causes death, and He has power over all things.

2
7:158

3 هُوَ الْأَوَّلُ وَالْآخِرُ وَالظَّاهِرُ وَالْبَاطِنُ ۖ وَهُوَ بِكُلِّ شَيْءٍ عَلِيمٌ

3 He is the First and the Last, and the Outer and the Inner, and He has knowledge of all things.

٤ هُوَ الَّذِي خَلَقَ السَّمَاوَاتِ وَالْأَرْضَ فِي سِتَّةِ أَيَّامٍ ثُمَّ اسْتَوَىٰ عَلَى الْعَرْشِ ۚ[a] يَعْلَمُ مَا يَلِجُ فِي الْأَرْضِ وَمَا يَخْرُجُ مِنْهَا وَمَا يَنْزِلُ مِنَ السَّمَاءِ وَمَا يَعْرُجُ فِيهَا ۖ[b] وَهُوَ مَعَكُمْ أَيْنَ مَا كُنْتُمْ ۚ وَاللَّهُ بِمَا تَعْمَلُونَ بَصِيرٌ

4
[a] 7:54
[b] 34:2

4 It is He who created the heavens and the earth in six days, then settled over the Throne. He knows what penetrates into the earth, and what comes out of it, and what descends from the sky, and what ascends to it. And He is with you wherever you may be. God is Seeing of everything you do.

٥ لَهُ مُلْكُ السَّمَاوَاتِ وَالْأَرْضِ ۚ وَإِلَى اللَّهِ تُرْجَعُ الْأُمُورُ

5
3:109; 42:53

5 To Him belongs the kingship of the heavens and the earth, and to God all matters are referred.

٦ يُولِجُ اللَّيْلَ فِي النَّهَارِ وَيُولِجُ النَّهَارَ فِي اللَّيْلِ ۚ وَهُوَ عَلِيمٌ بِذَاتِ الصُّدُورِ

6
3:27

6 He merges the night into the day, and He merges the day into the night; and He knows what the hearts contains.

٧ آمِنُوا بِاللَّهِ وَرَسُولِهِ وَأَنْفِقُوا مِمَّا جَعَلَكُمْ مُسْتَخْلَفِينَ فِيهِ ۖ فَالَّذِينَ آمَنُوا مِنْكُمْ وَأَنْفَقُوا لَهُمْ أَجْرٌ كَبِيرٌ

7
24:55

7 Believe in God and His Messenger, and spend from what He made you inherit. Those among you who believe and give will have a great reward.

٨ وَمَا لَكُمْ لَا تُؤْمِنُونَ بِاللَّهِ ۙ وَالرَّسُولُ يَدْعُوكُمْ لِتُؤْمِنُوا بِرَبِّكُمْ وَقَدْ أَخَذَ مِيثَاقَكُمْ إِنْ كُنْتُمْ مُؤْمِنِينَ

8

8 What is the matter with you that you do not believe in God, when the Messenger calls you to believe in your Lord, and He has received a pledge from you, if you are believers?

٩ هُوَ الَّذِي يُنَزِّلُ عَلَىٰ عَبْدِهِ آيَاتٍ بَيِّنَاتٍ لِيُخْرِجَكُمْ مِنَ الظُّلُمَاتِ إِلَى النُّورِ ۚ وَإِنَّ اللَّهَ بِكُمْ لَرَءُوفٌ رَحِيمٌ

9
14:1; 65:11

9 It is He who sends down upon His servant clear revelations, to bring you out of darkness into the light. God is Gentle towards you, Most Compassionate.

١٠ وَمَا لَكُمْ أَلَّا تُنْفِقُوا فِي سَبِيلِ اللَّهِ وَلِلَّهِ مِيرَاثُ السَّمَاوَاتِ وَالْأَرْضِ ۚ[a] لَا يَسْتَوِي مِنْكُمْ مَنْ أَنْفَقَ مِنْ قَبْلِ الْفَتْحِ وَقَاتَلَ ۚ أُولَٰئِكَ أَعْظَمُ دَرَجَةً مِنَ الَّذِينَ أَنْفَقُوا مِنْ بَعْدُ وَقَاتَلُوا ۚ وَكُلًّا وَعَدَ اللَّهُ الْحُسْنَىٰ ۚ[b] وَاللَّهُ بِمَا تَعْمَلُونَ خَبِيرٌ

10
[a] 19:40
[b] 4:95

10 And why is it that you do not spend in the cause of God, when to God belongs the inheritance of the heavens and the earth? Not equal among you are those who contributed before the conquest, and fought. Those are higher in rank than those who contributed afterwards, and fought. But God promises both a good reward. God is Well Experienced in what you do.

Sūrah 57: Al-Ḥadīd

١١ مَنْ ذَا الَّذِي يُقْرِضُ اللَّهَ قَرْضًا حَسَنًا فَيُضَاعِفَهُ لَهُ وَلَهُ أَجْرٌ كَرِيمٌ

11 2:245; 57:18; 64:17

11 Who is he who will lend God a loan of goodness, that He may double it for him, and will have a generous reward?

١٢ يَوْمَ تَرَى الْمُؤْمِنِينَ وَالْمُؤْمِنَاتِ يَسْعَىٰ نُورُهُم بَيْنَ أَيْدِيهِمْ وَبِأَيْمَانِهِم بُشْرَاكُمُ الْيَوْمَ جَنَّاتٌ تَجْرِي مِن تَحْتِهَا الْأَنْهَارُ خَالِدِينَ فِيهَا ۚ ذَٰلِكَ هُوَ الْفَوْزُ الْعَظِيمُ

12 9:21–22; 41:30; 66:8

12 On the Day when you see the believing men and believing women—their light radiating ahead of them, and to their right: "Good news for you today: gardens beneath which rivers flow, dwelling therein forever. That is the great triumph."

١٣ يَوْمَ يَقُولُ الْمُنَافِقُونَ وَالْمُنَافِقَاتُ لِلَّذِينَ آمَنُوا انظُرُونَا نَقْتَبِسْ مِن نُّورِكُمْ قِيلَ ارْجِعُوا وَرَاءَكُمْ فَالْتَمِسُوا نُورًا فَضُرِبَ بَيْنَهُم بِسُورٍ لَّهُ بَابٌ بَاطِنُهُ فِيهِ الرَّحْمَةُ وَظَاهِرُهُ مِن قِبَلِهِ الْعَذَابُ

13 On the Day when the hypocritical men and hypocritical women will say to those who believed, "Wait for us; let us absorb some of your light." It will be said, "Go back behind you, and seek light." A wall will be raised between them, in which is a door; within it is mercy, and outside it is agony.

١٤ يُنَادُونَهُمْ أَلَمْ نَكُن مَّعَكُمْ ۖ قَالُوا بَلَىٰ وَلَٰكِنَّكُمْ فَتَنتُمْ أَنفُسَكُمْ وَتَرَبَّصْتُمْ وَارْتَبْتُمْ وَغَرَّتْكُمُ الْأَمَانِيُّ حَتَّىٰ جَاءَ أَمْرُ اللَّهِ وَغَرَّكُم بِاللَّهِ الْغَرُورُ

14 31:33; 35:5

14 They will call to them, "Were we not with you?" They will say, "Yes, but you cheated your souls, and waited, and doubted, and became deluded by wishful thinking, until the command of God arrived; and arrogance deceived you regarding God."

١٥ فَالْيَوْمَ لَا يُؤْخَذُ مِنكُمْ فِدْيَةٌ وَلَا مِنَ الَّذِينَ كَفَرُوا ۚ مَأْوَاكُمُ النَّارُ ۖ هِيَ مَوْلَاكُمْ ۖ وَبِئْسَ الْمَصِيرُ

15 3:91

15 "Therefore, today no ransom will be accepted from you, nor from those who disbelieved. The Fire is your refuge. It is your companion—what an evil fate!"

١٦ أَلَمْ يَأْنِ لِلَّذِينَ آمَنُوا أَن تَخْشَعَ قُلُوبُهُمْ لِذِكْرِ اللَّهِ وَمَا نَزَلَ مِنَ الْحَقِّ وَلَا يَكُونُوا كَالَّذِينَ أُوتُوا الْكِتَابَ مِن قَبْلُ فَطَالَ عَلَيْهِمُ الْأَمَدُ فَقَسَتْ قُلُوبُهُمْ ۖ وَكَثِيرٌ مِّنْهُمْ فَاسِقُونَ

16 Is it not time for those who believe to surrender their hearts to the remembrance of God, and to the truth that has come down, and not be like those who were given the Book previously, but time became prolonged for them, so their hearts hardened, and many of them are sinners?

١٧ اعْلَمُوا أَنَّ اللَّهَ يُحْيِي الْأَرْضَ بَعْدَ مَوْتِهَا ۚ قَدْ بَيَّنَّا لَكُمُ الْآيَاتِ لَعَلَّكُمْ تَعْقِلُونَ

17 2:164; 30:19, 24, 50; 43:71

17 Know that God revives the earth after its death. We thus explain the revelations for you, so that you may understand.

١٨ إِنَّ الْمُصَّدِّقِينَ وَالْمُصَّدِّقَاتِ وَأَقْرَضُوا اللَّهَ قَرْضًا حَسَنًا يُضَاعَفُ لَهُمْ وَلَهُمْ أَجْرٌ كَرِيمٌ

18 The charitable men and charitable women, who have loaned God a loan of righteousness—it will be multiplied for them, and for them is a generous reward.

18
2:245; 57:11; 64:17

١٩ وَالَّذِينَ آمَنُوا بِاللَّهِ وَرُسُلِهِ أُولَٰئِكَ هُمُ الصِّدِّيقُونَ ۖ وَالشُّهَدَاءُ عِندَ رَبِّهِمْ لَهُمْ أَجْرُهُمْ وَنُورُهُمْ ۖ وَالَّذِينَ كَفَرُوا وَكَذَّبُوا بِآيَاتِنَا أُولَٰئِكَ أَصْحَابُ الْجَحِيمِ

19 Those who believe in God and His messengers—these are the sincere and the witnesses with their Lord; they will have their reward and their light. But as for those who disbelieve and deny Our revelations—these are the inmates of the Blaze.

٢٠ اعْلَمُوا أَنَّمَا الْحَيَاةُ الدُّنْيَا لَعِبٌ وَلَهْوٌ وَزِينَةٌ وَتَفَاخُرٌ بَيْنَكُمْ وَتَكَاثُرٌ فِي الْأَمْوَالِ وَالْأَوْلَادِ ۖ كَمَثَلِ غَيْثٍ أَعْجَبَ الْكُفَّارَ نَبَاتُهُ ثُمَّ يَهِيجُ فَتَرَاهُ مُصْفَرًّا ثُمَّ يَكُونُ حُطَامًا ۖ وَفِي الْآخِرَةِ عَذَابٌ شَدِيدٌ وَمَغْفِرَةٌ مِنَ اللَّهِ وَرِضْوَانٌ ۚ وَمَا الْحَيَاةُ الدُّنْيَا إِلَّا مَتَاعُ الْغُرُورِ

20
30:51; 34:35; 39:21; 56:65

20 Know that the worldly life is only play, and distraction, and glitter, and boasting among you, and rivalry in wealth and children. It is like a rainfall that produces plants, and delights the disbelievers. But then it withers, and you see it yellowing, and then it becomes debris. While in the Hereafter there is severe agony, and forgiveness from God, and acceptance. The life of this world is nothing but enjoyment of vanity.

٢١ سَابِقُوا إِلَىٰ مَغْفِرَةٍ مِن رَّبِّكُمْ وَجَنَّةٍ عَرْضُهَا كَعَرْضِ السَّمَاءِ وَالْأَرْضِ أُعِدَّتْ لِلَّذِينَ آمَنُوا بِاللَّهِ وَرُسُلِهِ ۚ ذَٰلِكَ فَضْلُ اللَّهِ يُؤْتِيهِ مَن يَشَاءُ ۚ وَاللَّهُ ذُو الْفَضْلِ الْعَظِيمِ

21
3:133

21 Race towards forgiveness from your Lord; and a Garden as vast as the heavens and the earth, prepared for those who believe in God and His messengers. That is the grace of God; He bestows it on whomever He wills. God is the Possessor of Immense Grace.

٢٢ مَا أَصَابَ مِن مُّصِيبَةٍ فِي الْأَرْضِ وَلَا فِي أَنفُسِكُمْ إِلَّا فِي كِتَابٍ مِّن قَبْلِ أَن نَّبْرَأَهَا ۚ إِنَّ ذَٰلِكَ عَلَى اللَّهِ يَسِيرٌ

22
9:51; 64:11

22 No calamity occurs on earth, or in your souls, but it is in a Book, even before We make it happen. That is easy for God.

٢٣ لِّكَيْلَا تَأْسَوْا عَلَىٰ مَا فَاتَكُمْ وَلَا تَفْرَحُوا بِمَا آتَاكُمْ ۗ وَاللَّهُ لَا يُحِبُّ كُلَّ مُخْتَالٍ فَخُورٍ

23
17:37; 31:18; 40:75

23 That you may not sorrow over what eludes you, nor exult over what He has given you. God does not love the proud snob.

٢٤ الَّذِينَ يَبْخَلُونَ وَيَأْمُرُونَ النَّاسَ بِالْبُخْلِ ۗ وَمَن يَتَوَلَّ فَإِنَّ اللَّهَ هُوَ الْغَنِيُّ الْحَمِيدُ

24
3:180; 4:37; 47:38

24 Those who are stingy, and induce people to be stingy. Whoever turns away—God is the Independent, the Praiseworthy.

٢٥ لَقَدْ أَرْسَلْنَا رُسُلَنَا بِالْبَيِّنَاتِ وَأَنزَلْنَا مَعَهُمُ الْكِتَابَ وَالْمِيزَانَ لِيَقُومَ النَّاسُ بِالْقِسْطِ ۖ وَأَنزَلْنَا الْحَدِيدَ فِيهِ بَأْسٌ شَدِيدٌ وَمَنَافِعُ لِلنَّاسِ وَلِيَعْلَمَ اللَّهُ مَن يَنصُرُهُ وَرُسُلَهُ بِالْغَيْبِ ۚ إِنَّ اللَّهَ قَوِيٌّ عَزِيزٌ

25
6:152; 42:17; 55:7, 25

25 We sent Our messengers with the clear proofs, and We sent down with them the Book and the Balance, that humanity may uphold justice. And We sent down iron, in which is violent force, and benefits for humanity. That God may know who supports Him and His messengers invisibly. God is Strong and Powerful.

٢٦ وَلَقَدْ أَرْسَلْنَا نُوحًا وَإِبْرَاهِيمَ وَجَعَلْنَا فِي ذُرِّيَّتِهِمَا النُّبُوَّةَ وَالْكِتَابَ ۖ فَمِنْهُم مُّهْتَدٍ ۖ وَكَثِيرٌ مِّنْهُمْ فَاسِقُونَ

26
29:27

26 We sent Noah and Abraham, and established in their line Prophethood and the Scripture. Some of them are guided, but many of them are sinners.

٢٧ ثُمَّ قَفَّيْنَا عَلَىٰ آثَارِهِم بِرُسُلِنَا وَقَفَّيْنَا بِعِيسَى ابْنِ مَرْيَمَ وَآتَيْنَاهُ الْإِنجِيلَ وَجَعَلْنَا فِي قُلُوبِ الَّذِينَ اتَّبَعُوهُ رَأْفَةً وَرَحْمَةً وَرَهْبَانِيَّةً ابْتَدَعُوهَا مَا كَتَبْنَاهَا عَلَيْهِمْ إِلَّا ابْتِغَاءَ رِضْوَانِ اللَّهِ فَمَا رَعَوْهَا حَقَّ رِعَايَتِهَا ۖ فَآتَيْنَا الَّذِينَ آمَنُوا مِنْهُمْ أَجْرَهُمْ ۖ وَكَثِيرٌ مِّنْهُمْ فَاسِقُونَ

27
2:87; 5:46

27 Then We sent in their wake Our messengers, and followed up with Jesus son of Mary, and We gave him the Gospel, and instilled in the hearts of those who followed him compassion and mercy. But as for the monasticism which they invented—We did not ordain it for them—only to seek God's approval. But they did not observe it with its due observance. So We gave those of them who believed their reward, but many of them are sinful.

٢٨ يَا أَيُّهَا الَّذِينَ آمَنُوا اتَّقُوا اللَّهَ وَآمِنُوا بِرَسُولِهِ يُؤْتِكُمْ كِفْلَيْنِ مِن رَّحْمَتِهِ وَيَجْعَل لَّكُمْ نُورًا تَمْشُونَ بِهِ وَيَغْفِرْ لَكُمْ ۚ وَاللَّهُ غَفُورٌ رَّحِيمٌ

28
6:122

28 O you who believe! Fear God, and believe in His Messenger: He will give you a double portion of His mercy, and will give you a light by which you walk, and will forgive you. God is Forgiving and Merciful.

٢٩ لِّئَلَّا يَعْلَمَ أَهْلُ الْكِتَابِ أَلَّا يَقْدِرُونَ عَلَىٰ شَيْءٍ مِّن فَضْلِ اللَّهِ ۙ وَأَنَّ الْفَضْلَ بِيَدِ اللَّهِ يُؤْتِيهِ مَن يَشَاءُ ۚ وَاللَّهُ ذُو الْفَضْلِ الْعَظِيمِ

29 That the People of the Book may know that they have no power whatsoever over God's grace, and that all grace is in God's hand; He gives it to whomever He wills. God is Possessor of Great Grace.

Sūrah 58: Al-Mujādilah

سُورَةُ ٱلْمُجَادِلَة (The Argument)

بِسْمِ ٱللَّهِ ٱلرَّحْمَٰنِ ٱلرَّحِيمِ

١ قَدْ سَمِعَ ٱللَّهُ قَوْلَ ٱلَّتِي تُجَادِلُكَ فِي زَوْجِهَا وَتَشْتَكِي إِلَى ٱللَّهِ وَٱللَّهُ يَسْمَعُ تَحَاوُرَكُمَا ۚ إِنَّ ٱللَّهَ سَمِيعٌ بَصِيرٌ

1 God has heard the statement of she who argued with you concerning her husband, as she complained to God. God heard your conversation. God is Hearing and Seeing.

٢ ٱلَّذِينَ يُظَاهِرُونَ مِنكُم مِّن نِّسَائِهِم مَّا هُنَّ أُمَّهَاتِهِمْ ۖ إِنْ أُمَّهَاتُهُمْ إِلَّا ٱللَّٰٓائِي وَلَدْنَهُمْ ۚ وَإِنَّهُمْ لَيَقُولُونَ مُنكَرًا مِّنَ ٱلْقَوْلِ وَزُورًا ۚ وَإِنَّ ٱللَّهَ لَعَفُوٌّ غَفُورٌ

2–3
33:4

2 Those of you who estrange their wives by equating them with their mothers—they are not their mothers. Their mothers are none else but those who gave birth to them. What they say is evil, and a blatant lie. But God is Pardoning and Forgiving.

٣ وَٱلَّذِينَ يُظَاهِرُونَ مِن نِّسَائِهِمْ ثُمَّ يَعُودُونَ لِمَا قَالُوا۟ فَتَحْرِيرُ رَقَبَةٍ مِّن قَبْلِ أَن يَتَمَاسَّا ۚ ذَٰلِكُمْ تُوعَظُونَ بِهِۦ ۚ وَٱللَّهُ بِمَا تَعْمَلُونَ خَبِيرٌ

3 Those who estrange their wives by equating them with their mothers, then go back on what they said, must set free a slave before they may touch one another. To this you are exhorted, and God is well aware of what you do.

٤ فَمَن لَّمْ يَجِدْ فَصِيَامُ شَهْرَيْنِ مُتَتَابِعَيْنِ مِن قَبْلِ أَن يَتَمَاسَّا ۖ فَمَن لَّمْ يَسْتَطِعْ فَإِطْعَامُ سِتِّينَ مِسْكِينًا ۚ ذَٰلِكَ لِتُؤْمِنُوا۟ بِٱللَّهِ وَرَسُولِهِۦ ۚ وَتِلْكَ حُدُودُ ٱللَّهِ ۗ وَلِلْكَافِرِينَ عَذَابٌ أَلِيمٌ

4 But whoever cannot find the means must fast for two consecutive months before they may touch one another. And if he is unable, then the feeding of sixty needy people. This, in order that you affirm your faith in God and His Messenger. These are the ordinances of God. The unbelievers will have a painful punishment.

٥ إِنَّ ٱلَّذِينَ يُحَادُّونَ ٱللَّهَ وَرَسُولَهُۥ كُبِتُوا۟ كَمَا كُبِتَ ٱلَّذِينَ مِن قَبْلِهِمْ ۚ وَقَدْ أَنزَلْنَآ ءَايَٰتٍۭ بَيِّنَٰتٍ ۚ وَلِلْكَافِرِينَ عَذَابٌ مُّهِينٌ

5
9:63; 58:20

5 Those who oppose God and His Messenger will be subdued, as those before them were subdued. We have revealed clear messages. The unbelievers will have a demeaning punishment.

٦ يَوْمَ يَبْعَثُهُمُ ٱللَّهُ جَمِيعًا فَيُنَبِّئُهُم بِمَا عَمِلُوٓا۟ ۚ أَحْصَىٰهُ ٱللَّهُ وَنَسُوهُ ۚ وَٱللَّهُ عَلَىٰ كُلِّ شَىْءٍ شَهِيدٌ

6
6:60

6 On the Day when God resurrects them all, and informs them of what they did. God has kept count of it, but they have forgotten it. God is Witness over everything.

٧ أَلَمْ تَرَ أَنَّ اللَّهَ يَعْلَمُ مَا فِي السَّمَاوَاتِ وَمَا فِي الْأَرْضِ ۖ مَا يَكُونُ مِنْ نَجْوَىٰ ثَلَاثَةٍ إِلَّا هُوَ رَابِعُهُمْ وَلَا خَمْسَةٍ إِلَّا هُوَ سَادِسُهُمْ وَلَا أَدْنَىٰ مِنْ ذَٰلِكَ وَلَا أَكْثَرَ إِلَّا هُوَ مَعَهُمْ أَيْنَ مَا كَانُوا ۖ ثُمَّ يُنَبِّئُهُمْ بِمَا عَمِلُوا يَوْمَ الْقِيَامَةِ ۚ إِنَّ اللَّهَ بِكُلِّ شَيْءٍ عَلِيمٌ

7

2:33; 4:108; 9:78; 22:70; 43:80

7 Do you not realize that God knows everything in the heavens and everything on earth? There is no secret counsel between three, but He is their fourth; nor between five, but He is their sixth; nor less than that, nor more, but He is with them wherever they may be. Then, on the Day of Resurrection, He will inform them of what they did. God has knowledge of everything.

٨ أَلَمْ تَرَ إِلَى الَّذِينَ نُهُوا عَنِ النَّجْوَىٰ ثُمَّ يَعُودُونَ لِمَا نُهُوا عَنْهُ وَيَتَنَاجَوْنَ بِالْإِثْمِ وَالْعُدْوَانِ وَمَعْصِيَتِ الرَّسُولِ وَإِذَا جَاءُوكَ حَيَّوْكَ بِمَا لَمْ يُحَيِّكَ بِهِ اللَّهُ وَيَقُولُونَ فِي أَنْفُسِهِمْ لَوْلَا يُعَذِّبُنَا اللَّهُ بِمَا نَقُولُ ۚ حَسْبُهُمْ جَهَنَّمُ يَصْلَوْنَهَا ۖ فَبِئْسَ الْمَصِيرُ

8

4:114; 38:56

8 Have you noted those who were prohibited from conspiring secretly, but then reverted to what they were prohibited from? They conspire to commit sin, and aggression, and defiance of the Messenger. And when they come to you, they greet you with a greeting that God never greeted you with. And they say within themselves, "Why does God not punish us for what we say?" Hell is enough for them. They will roast in it. What a miserable destiny!

٩ يَا أَيُّهَا الَّذِينَ آمَنُوا إِذَا تَنَاجَيْتُمْ فَلَا تَتَنَاجَوْا بِالْإِثْمِ وَالْعُدْوَانِ وَمَعْصِيَتِ الرَّسُولِ وَتَنَاجَوْا بِالْبِرِّ وَالتَّقْوَىٰ ۖ وَاتَّقُوا اللَّهَ الَّذِي إِلَيْهِ تُحْشَرُونَ

9 O you who believe! When you converse secretly, do not converse in sin, and aggression, and disobedience of the Messenger; but converse in virtue and piety; And fear God, to Whom you will be gathered.

١٠ إِنَّمَا النَّجْوَىٰ مِنَ الشَّيْطَانِ لِيَحْزُنَ الَّذِينَ آمَنُوا وَلَيْسَ بِضَارِّهِمْ شَيْئًا إِلَّا بِإِذْنِ اللَّهِ ۚ وَعَلَى اللَّهِ فَلْيَتَوَكَّلِ الْمُؤْمِنُونَ

10 Conspiracies are from Satan, that he may dishearten those who believe; but he will not harm them in the least, except by leave of God. So let the believers put their trust in God.

١١ يَا أَيُّهَا الَّذِينَ آمَنُوا إِذَا قِيلَ لَكُمْ تَفَسَّحُوا فِي الْمَجَالِسِ فَافْسَحُوا يَفْسَحِ اللَّهُ لَكُمْ ۖ وَإِذَا قِيلَ انْشُزُوا فَانْشُزُوا يَرْفَعِ اللَّهُ الَّذِينَ آمَنُوا مِنْكُمْ وَالَّذِينَ أُوتُوا الْعِلْمَ دَرَجَاتٍ ۚ وَاللَّهُ بِمَا تَعْمَلُونَ خَبِيرٌ

11 O you who believe! When you are told to make room in your gatherings, make room; God will make room for you. And when you are told to disperse, disperse. God elevates those among you who believe, and those given knowledge, many steps. God is Aware of what you do.

١٢ يَا أَيُّهَا الَّذِينَ آمَنُوا إِذَا نَاجَيْتُمُ الرَّسُولَ فَقَدِّمُوا بَيْنَ يَدَيْ نَجْوَاكُمْ صَدَقَةً ۚ ذَٰلِكَ خَيْرٌ لَّكُمْ وَأَطْهَرُ ۚ فَإِن لَّمْ تَجِدُوا فَإِنَّ اللَّهَ غَفُورٌ رَّحِيمٌ

12 O you who believe! When you converse privately with the Messenger, offer something in charity before your conversation. That is better for you, and purer. But if you do not find the means—God is Forgiving and Merciful.

١٣ أَأَشْفَقْتُمْ أَن تُقَدِّمُوا بَيْنَ يَدَيْ نَجْوَاكُمْ صَدَقَاتٍ ۚ فَإِذْ لَمْ تَفْعَلُوا وَتَابَ اللَّهُ عَلَيْكُمْ فَأَقِيمُوا الصَّلَاةَ وَآتُوا الزَّكَاةَ وَأَطِيعُوا اللَّهَ وَرَسُولَهُ ۚ وَاللَّهُ خَبِيرٌ بِمَا تَعْمَلُونَ

13 Are you reluctant to offer charity before your conversation? If you do not do so, and God pardons you, then perform the prayer, and give alms, and obey God and His Messenger. God is Aware of what you do.

١٤ أَلَمْ تَرَ إِلَى الَّذِينَ تَوَلَّوْا قَوْمًا غَضِبَ اللَّهُ عَلَيْهِم مَّا هُم مِّنكُمْ وَلَا مِنْهُمْ وَيَحْلِفُونَ عَلَى الْكَذِبِ وَهُمْ يَعْلَمُونَ

14
58:18; 60:13

14 Have you considered those who befriended a people with whom God has become angry? They are not of you, nor of them. And they swear to a lie while they know.

١٥ أَعَدَّ اللَّهُ لَهُمْ عَذَابًا شَدِيدًا ۖ إِنَّهُمْ سَاءَ مَا كَانُوا يَعْمَلُونَ

15
63:2

15 God has prepared for them a terrible punishment. Evil is what they used to do.

١٦ اتَّخَذُوا أَيْمَانَهُمْ جُنَّةً فَصَدُّوا عَن سَبِيلِ اللَّهِ فَلَهُمْ عَذَابٌ مُّهِينٌ

16
63:2

16 They took their oaths as a screen, and prevented others from God's path. They will have a shameful punishment.

١٧ لَّن تُغْنِيَ عَنْهُمْ أَمْوَالُهُمْ وَلَا أَوْلَادُهُم مِّنَ اللَّهِ شَيْئًا ۚ أُولَٰئِكَ أَصْحَابُ النَّارِ ۖ هُمْ فِيهَا خَالِدُونَ

17
3:10; 60:3

17 Neither their possessions nor their children will avail them anything against God. These are the inhabitants of the Fire, dwelling therein forever.

١٨ يَوْمَ يَبْعَثُهُمُ اللَّهُ جَمِيعًا فَيَحْلِفُونَ لَهُ كَمَا يَحْلِفُونَ لَكُمْ ۖ وَيَحْسَبُونَ أَنَّهُمْ عَلَىٰ شَيْءٍ ۚ أَلَا إِنَّهُمْ هُمُ الْكَاذِبُونَ

18
58:14

18 On the Day when God will resurrect them altogether—they will swear to Him, as they swear to you, thinking that they are upon something. Indeed, they themselves are the liars.

١٩ اسْتَحْوَذَ عَلَيْهِمُ الشَّيْطَانُ فَأَنسَاهُمْ ذِكْرَ اللَّهِ ۚ أُولَٰئِكَ حِزْبُ الشَّيْطَانِ ۚ أَلَا إِنَّ حِزْبَ الشَّيْطَانِ هُمُ الْخَاسِرُونَ

19
6:68; 12:42; 18:63

19 Satan has taken hold of them, and so has caused them to forget the remembrance of God. These are the partisans of Satan. Indeed, it is Satan's partisans who are the losers.

٢٠ إِنَّ الَّذِينَ يُحَادُّونَ اللَّهَ وَرَسُولَهُ أُولَٰئِكَ فِي الْأَذَلِّينَ

20 Those who oppose God and His Messenger are among the lowliest.

20
9:63; 58:5

٢١ كَتَبَ اللَّهُ لَأَغْلِبَنَّ أَنَا وَرُسُلِي ۚ إِنَّ اللَّهَ قَوِيٌّ عَزِيزٌ

21 God has written: "I will certainly prevail, I and My messengers." God is Strong and Mighty.

21
3:160; 9:24

٢٢ لَا تَجِدُ قَوْمًا يُؤْمِنُونَ بِاللَّهِ وَالْيَوْمِ الْآخِرِ يُوَادُّونَ مَنْ حَادَّ اللَّهَ وَرَسُولَهُ وَلَوْ كَانُوا آبَاءَهُمْ أَوْ أَبْنَاءَهُمْ أَوْ إِخْوَانَهُمْ أَوْ عَشِيرَتَهُمْ ۚ أُولَٰئِكَ كَتَبَ فِي قُلُوبِهِمُ الْإِيمَانَ وَأَيَّدَهُم بِرُوحٍ مِّنْهُ ۖ وَيُدْخِلُهُمْ جَنَّاتٍ تَجْرِي مِن تَحْتِهَا الْأَنْهَارُ خَالِدِينَ فِيهَا ۚ رَضِيَ اللَّهُ عَنْهُمْ وَرَضُوا عَنْهُ ۚ أُولَٰئِكَ حِزْبُ اللَّهِ ۚ أَلَا إِنَّ حِزْبَ اللَّهِ هُمُ الْمُفْلِحُونَ

22 You will not find a people who believe in God and the Last Day, loving those who oppose God and His Messenger, even if they were their parents, or their children, or their siblings, or their close relatives. These—He has inscribed faith in their hearts, and has supported them with a spirit from Him. And He will admit them into Gardens beneath which rivers flow, wherein they will dwell forever. God is pleased with them, and they are pleased with Him. These are the partisans of God. Indeed, it is God's partisans who are the successful.

22
49:7–8

Sūrah 59: Al-Ḥashr

سُورَةُ ٱلْحَشْرِ (The Mobilization)

بِسْمِ ٱللَّهِ ٱلرَّحْمَٰنِ ٱلرَّحِيمِ

١ سَبَّحَ لِلَّهِ مَا فِي السَّمَاوَاتِ وَمَا فِي الْأَرْضِ ۖ وَهُوَ الْعَزِيزُ الْحَكِيمُ

1 Glorifying God is all that exists in the heavens and the earth. He is the Almighty, the Most Wise.

1
17:44; 21:79; 57:1; 61:1; 62:1; 64:1

٢ هُوَ الَّذِي أَخْرَجَ الَّذِينَ كَفَرُوا مِنْ أَهْلِ الْكِتَابِ مِن دِيَارِهِمْ لِأَوَّلِ الْحَشْرِ ۚ مَا ظَنَنتُمْ أَن يَخْرُجُوا ۖ وَظَنُّوا أَنَّهُم مَّانِعَتُهُمْ حُصُونُهُم مِّنَ اللَّهِ فَأَتَاهُمُ اللَّهُ مِنْ حَيْثُ لَمْ يَحْتَسِبُوا ۖ وَقَذَفَ فِي قُلُوبِهِمُ الرُّعْبَ ۚ يُخْرِبُونَ بُيُوتَهُم بِأَيْدِيهِمْ وَأَيْدِي الْمُؤْمِنِينَ فَاعْتَبِرُوا يَا أُولِي الْأَبْصَارِ

2 It is He who evicted those who disbelieved among the People of the Book from their homes at the first mobilization. You did not think they would leave, and they thought their fortresses would protect them from God. But God came at them from where they never expected, and threw terror into their hearts. They wrecked their homes with their own hands, and by the hands of the believers. Therefore, take a lesson, O you who have insight.

٣ وَلَوْلَا أَن كَتَبَ اللَّهُ عَلَيْهِمُ الْجَلَاءَ لَعَذَّبَهُمْ فِي الدُّنْيَا ۖ وَلَهُمْ فِي الْآخِرَةِ عَذَابُ النَّارِ

3 Had God not decreed exile for them, He would have punished them in this life. But in the Hereafter they will have the punishment of the Fire.

٤ ذَٰلِكَ بِأَنَّهُمْ شَاقُّوا اللَّهَ وَرَسُولَهُ ۖ وَمَن يُشَاقِّ اللَّهَ فَإِنَّ اللَّهَ شَدِيدُ الْعِقَابِ

4

8:13

4 That is because they opposed God and His Messenger. Whoever opposes God—God is stern in retribution.

٥ مَا قَطَعْتُم مِّن لِّينَةٍ أَوْ تَرَكْتُمُوهَا قَائِمَةً عَلَىٰ أُصُولِهَا فَبِإِذْنِ اللَّهِ وَلِيُخْزِيَ الْفَاسِقِينَ

5 Whether you cut down a tree, or leave it standing on its trunk, it is by God's will. He will surely disgrace the sinners.

٦ وَمَا أَفَاءَ اللَّهُ عَلَىٰ رَسُولِهِ مِنْهُمْ فَمَا أَوْجَفْتُمْ عَلَيْهِ مِنْ خَيْلٍ وَلَا رِكَابٍ وَلَٰكِنَّ اللَّهَ يُسَلِّطُ رُسُلَهُ عَلَىٰ مَن يَشَاءُ ۚ وَاللَّهُ عَلَىٰ كُلِّ شَيْءٍ قَدِيرٌ

6 Whatever God has bestowed upon His Messenger from them; you spurred neither horse nor camel for them, but God gives authority to His messengers over whomever He will. God is Able to do all things.

٧ مَّا أَفَاءَ اللَّهُ عَلَىٰ رَسُولِهِ مِنْ أَهْلِ الْقُرَىٰ فَلِلَّهِ وَلِلرَّسُولِ وَلِذِي الْقُرْبَىٰ وَالْيَتَامَىٰ وَالْمَسَاكِينِ وَابْنِ السَّبِيلِ كَيْ لَا يَكُونَ دُولَةً بَيْنَ الْأَغْنِيَاءِ مِنكُمْ ۚ وَمَا آتَاكُمُ الرَّسُولُ فَخُذُوهُ وَمَا نَهَاكُمْ عَنْهُ فَانتَهُوا ۚ وَاتَّقُوا اللَّهَ ۖ إِنَّ اللَّهَ شَدِيدُ الْعِقَابِ

7

8:41

7 Whatever God restored to His Messenger from the inhabitants of the villages belongs to God, and to the Messenger, and to the relatives, and to the orphans, and to the poor, and to the wayfarer; so that it may not circulate solely between the wealthy among you. Whatever the Messenger gives you, accept it; and whatever he forbids you, abstain from it. And fear God. God is severe in punishment.

٨ لِلْفُقَرَاءِ الْمُهَاجِرِينَ الَّذِينَ أُخْرِجُوا مِن دِيَارِهِمْ وَأَمْوَالِهِمْ يَبْتَغُونَ فَضْلًا مِّنَ اللَّهِ وَرِضْوَانًا وَيَنصُرُونَ اللَّهَ وَرَسُولَهُ ۚ أُولَٰئِكَ هُمُ الصَّادِقُونَ

8

2:273; 8:72; 9:119

8 To the poor refugees who were driven out of their homes and their possessions, as they sought the favor of God and His approval, and came to the aid of God and His Messenger. These are the sincere.

٩ وَالَّذِينَ تَبَوَّءُوا الدَّارَ وَالْإِيمَانَ مِن قَبْلِهِمْ يُحِبُّونَ مَنْ هَاجَرَ إِلَيْهِمْ وَلَا يَجِدُونَ فِي صُدُورِهِمْ حَاجَةً مِّمَّا أُوتُوا وَيُؤْثِرُونَ عَلَىٰ أَنفُسِهِمْ وَلَوْ كَانَ بِهِمْ خَصَاصَةٌ ۚ وَمَن يُوقَ شُحَّ نَفْسِهِ فَأُولَٰئِكَ هُمُ الْمُفْلِحُونَ

9 And those who, before them, had settled in the homeland, and had accepted faith. They love those who emigrated to them, and find no hesitation in their hearts in helping them. They give them priority over themselves, even if they themselves are needy. Whoever is protected from his natural greed—it is they who are the successful.

١٠ وَالَّذِينَ جَاءُوا مِنْ بَعْدِهِمْ يَقُولُونَ رَبَّنَا اغْفِرْ لَنَا وَلِإِخْوَانِنَا الَّذِينَ سَبَقُونَا بِالْإِيمَانِ وَلَا تَجْعَلْ فِي قُلُوبِنَا غِلًّا لِلَّذِينَ آمَنُوا رَبَّنَا إِنَّكَ رَءُوفٌ رَحِيمٌ

10 And those who came after them, saying, "Our Lord, forgive us, and our brethren who preceded us in faith, and leave no malice in our hearts towards those who believe. Our Lord, You are Clement and Merciful."

١١ أَلَمْ تَرَ إِلَى الَّذِينَ نَافَقُوا يَقُولُونَ لِإِخْوَانِهِمُ الَّذِينَ كَفَرُوا مِنْ أَهْلِ الْكِتَابِ لَئِنْ أُخْرِجْتُمْ لَنَخْرُجَنَّ مَعَكُمْ وَلَا نُطِيعُ فِيكُمْ أَحَدًا أَبَدًا وَإِنْ قُوتِلْتُمْ لَنَنْصُرَنَّكُمْ وَاللَّهُ يَشْهَدُ إِنَّهُمْ لَكَاذِبُونَ

11   5:53

11 Have you not considered those who act hypocritically? They say to their brethren who disbelieved among the People of the Book, "If you are evicted, we will leave with you, and will not obey anyone against you; and should anyone fight you, we will certainly support you." But God bears witness that they are liars.

١٢ لَئِنْ أُخْرِجُوا لَا يَخْرُجُونَ مَعَهُمْ وَلَئِنْ قُوتِلُوا لَا يَنْصُرُونَهُمْ وَلَئِنْ نَصَرُوهُمْ لَيُوَلُّنَّ الْأَدْبَارَ ثُمَّ لَا يُنْصَرُونَ

12   3:111

12 If they are evicted, they will not leave with them; and if anyone fights them, they will not support them; and if they go to their aid, they will turn their backs and flee; then they will receive no support.

١٣ لَأَنْتُمْ أَشَدُّ رَهْبَةً فِي صُدُورِهِمْ مِنَ اللَّهِ ۚ ذَٰلِكَ بِأَنَّهُمْ قَوْمٌ لَا يَفْقَهُونَ

13 Fear of you is more intense in their hearts than fear of God. That is because they are a people who do not understand.

١٤ لَا يُقَاتِلُونَكُمْ جَمِيعًا إِلَّا فِي قُرًى مُحَصَّنَةٍ أَوْ مِنْ وَرَاءِ جُدُرٍ ۚ بَأْسُهُمْ بَيْنَهُمْ شَدِيدٌ ۚ تَحْسَبُهُمْ جَمِيعًا وَقُلُوبُهُمْ شَتَّىٰ ۚ ذَٰلِكَ بِأَنَّهُمْ قَوْمٌ لَا يَعْقِلُونَ

14 They will not fight you all together except from fortified strongholds, or from behind walls. Their hostility towards each other is severe. You would think they are united, but their hearts are diverse. That is because they are a people who do not understand.

١٥ كَمَثَلِ الَّذِينَ مِنْ قَبْلِهِمْ قَرِيبًا ۖ ذَاقُوا وَبَالَ أَمْرِهِمْ وَلَهُمْ عَذَابٌ أَلِيمٌ

15   64:5

15 Like those shortly before them. They experienced the consequences of their decisions. For them is a painful punishment.

١٦ كَمَثَلِ الشَّيْطَانِ إِذْ قَالَ لِلْإِنْسَانِ اكْفُرْ فَلَمَّا كَفَرَ قَالَ إِنِّي بَرِيءٌ مِنْكَ إِنِّي أَخَافُ اللَّهَ رَبَّ الْعَالَمِينَ

16 Like the devil, when he says to the human being, "Disbelieve." But when he has disbelieved, he says, "I am innocent of you; I fear God, the Lord of the Worlds."

١٧ فَكَانَ عَاقِبَتَهُمَا أَنَّهُمَا فِي النَّارِ خَالِدَيْنِ فِيهَا ۚ وَذَٰلِكَ جَزَاءُ الظَّالِمِينَ

17 The ultimate end for both of them is the Fire, where they will dwell forever. Such is the requital for the wrongdoers.

١٨ يَا أَيُّهَا الَّذِينَ آمَنُوا اتَّقُوا اللَّهَ وَلْتَنظُرْ نَفْسٌ مَا قَدَّمَتْ لِغَدٍ ۖ وَاتَّقُوا اللَّهَ ۚ إِنَّ اللَّهَ خَبِيرٌ بِمَا تَعْمَلُونَ

18 O you who believe! Fear God, and let every soul consider what it has forwarded for the morrow, and fear God. God is Aware of what you do.

75:13; 78:40

١٩ وَلَا تَكُونُوا كَالَّذِينَ نَسُوا اللَّهَ فَأَنسَاهُمْ أَنفُسَهُمْ ۚ أُولَٰئِكَ هُمُ الْفَاسِقُونَ

19 And do not be like those who forgot God, so He made them forget themselves. These are the sinners.

9:67

٢٠ لَا يَسْتَوِي أَصْحَابُ النَّارِ وَأَصْحَابُ الْجَنَّةِ ۚ أَصْحَابُ الْجَنَّةِ هُمُ الْفَائِزُونَ

20 Not equal are the inhabitants of the Fire and the inhabitants of Paradise. It is the inhabitants of Paradise who are the winners.

٢١ لَوْ أَنزَلْنَا هَٰذَا الْقُرْآنَ عَلَىٰ جَبَلٍ لَّرَأَيْتَهُ خَاشِعًا مُّتَصَدِّعًا مِّنْ خَشْيَةِ اللَّهِ ۚ وَتِلْكَ الْأَمْثَالُ نَضْرِبُهَا لِلنَّاسِ لَعَلَّهُمْ يَتَفَكَّرُونَ

21 Had We sent this Qur'an down on a mountain, you would have seen it trembling, crumbling in awe of God. These parables We cite for the people, so that they may reflect.

18:54; 29:43

٢٢ هُوَ اللَّهُ الَّذِي لَا إِلَٰهَ إِلَّا هُوَ ۖ عَالِمُ الْغَيْبِ وَالشَّهَادَةِ ۖ هُوَ الرَّحْمَٰنُ الرَّحِيمُ

22 He is God. There is no god but He, the Knower of secrets and declarations. He is the Compassionate, the Merciful.

2:255; 3:2; 28:70

٢٣ هُوَ اللَّهُ الَّذِي لَا إِلَٰهَ إِلَّا هُوَ الْمَلِكُ الْقُدُّوسُ السَّلَامُ الْمُؤْمِنُ الْمُهَيْمِنُ الْعَزِيزُ الْجَبَّارُ الْمُتَكَبِّرُ ۚ سُبْحَانَ اللَّهِ عَمَّا يُشْرِكُونَ

23 He is God; besides Whom there is no god; the Sovereign, the Holy, the Peace-Giver, the Faith-Giver, the Overseer, the Almighty, the Omnipotent, the Overwhelming. Glory be to God, beyond what they associate.

٢٤ هُوَ اللَّهُ الْخَالِقُ الْبَارِئُ الْمُصَوِّرُ ۖ لَهُ الْأَسْمَاءُ الْحُسْنَىٰ ۚ يُسَبِّحُ لَهُ مَا فِي السَّمَاوَاتِ وَالْأَرْضِ ۖ وَهُوَ الْعَزِيزُ الْحَكِيمُ

24 He is God; the Creator, the Maker, the Designer. His are the Most Beautiful Names. Whatever is in the heavens and the earth glorifies Him. He is the Majestic, the Wise.

Sūrah 60: Al-Mumtaḥanah

سُورَةُ ٱلْمُمْتَحَنَة (The Woman Tested)

بِسْمِ ٱللَّهِ ٱلرَّحْمَٰنِ ٱلرَّحِيمِ

١ يَٰٓأَيُّهَا ٱلَّذِينَ ءَامَنُوا۟ لَا تَتَّخِذُوا۟ عَدُوِّى وَعَدُوَّكُمْ أَوْلِيَآءَ تُلْقُونَ إِلَيْهِم بِٱلْمَوَدَّةِ وَقَدْ كَفَرُوا۟ بِمَا جَآءَكُم مِّنَ ٱلْحَقِّ يُخْرِجُونَ ٱلرَّسُولَ وَإِيَّاكُمْ ۙ أَن تُؤْمِنُوا۟ بِٱللَّهِ رَبِّكُمْ إِن كُنتُمْ خَرَجْتُمْ جِهَٰدًا فِى سَبِيلِى وَٱبْتِغَآءَ مَرْضَاتِى ۚ تُسِرُّونَ إِلَيْهِم بِٱلْمَوَدَّةِ وَأَنَا۠ أَعْلَمُ بِمَآ أَخْفَيْتُمْ وَمَآ أَعْلَنتُمْ ۚ وَمَن يَفْعَلْهُ مِنكُمْ فَقَدْ ضَلَّ سَوَآءَ ٱلسَّبِيلِ

1   3:28; 60:9

1 O you who believe! Do not take My enemies and your enemies for supporters, offering them affection, when they have disbelieved in what has come to you of the Truth. They have expelled the Messenger, and you, because you believed in God, your Lord. If you have mobilized to strive for My cause, seeking My approval, how can you secretly love them? I know what you conceal and what you reveal. Whoever among you does that has strayed from the right way.

٢ إِن يَثْقَفُوكُمْ يَكُونُوا۟ لَكُمْ أَعْدَآءً وَيَبْسُطُوٓا۟ إِلَيْكُمْ أَيْدِيَهُمْ وَأَلْسِنَتَهُم بِٱلسُّوٓءِ وَوَدُّوا۟ لَوْ تَكْفُرُونَ

2 Whenever they encounter you, they treat you as enemies, and they stretch their hands and tongues against you with malice. They wish that you would disbelieve.

٣ لَن تَنفَعَكُمْ أَرْحَامُكُمْ وَلَآ أَوْلَٰدُكُمْ ۚ يَوْمَ ٱلْقِيَٰمَةِ يَفْصِلُ بَيْنَكُمْ ۚ وَٱللَّهُ بِمَا تَعْمَلُونَ بَصِيرٌ

3   3:10, 116; 58:17

3 Neither your relatives nor your children will benefit you on the Day of Resurrection. He will separate between you. God is Observant of what you do.

٤ قَدْ كَانَتْ لَكُمْ أُسْوَةٌ حَسَنَةٌ فِىٓ إِبْرَٰهِيمَ وَٱلَّذِينَ مَعَهُۥٓ إِذْ قَالُوا۟ لِقَوْمِهِمْ إِنَّا بُرَءَٰٓؤُا۟ مِنكُمْ وَمِمَّا تَعْبُدُونَ مِن دُونِ ٱللَّهِ كَفَرْنَا بِكُمْ وَبَدَا بَيْنَنَا وَبَيْنَكُمُ ٱلْعَدَٰوَةُ وَٱلْبَغْضَآءُ أَبَدًا حَتَّىٰ تُؤْمِنُوا۟ بِٱللَّهِ وَحْدَهُۥٓ إِلَّا قَوْلَ إِبْرَٰهِيمَ لِأَبِيهِ لَأَسْتَغْفِرَنَّ لَكَ وَمَآ أَمْلِكُ لَكَ مِنَ ٱللَّهِ مِن شَىْءٍ ۖ رَّبَّنَا عَلَيْكَ تَوَكَّلْنَا وَإِلَيْكَ أَنَبْنَا وَإِلَيْكَ ٱلْمَصِيرُ

4   33:21; 60:6

4 You have had an excellent example in Abraham and those with him; when they said to their people, "We are quit of you, and what you worship apart from God. We denounce you. Enmity and hatred has surfaced between us and you, forever, until you believe in God alone." Except for the words of Abraham to his father, "I will ask forgiveness for you, though I have no power from God to do anything for you." "Our Lord, in You we trust, and to You we repent, and to You is the ultimate resort.

٥ رَبَّنَا لَا تَجْعَلْنَا فِتْنَةً لِّلَّذِينَ كَفَرُوا۟ وَٱغْفِرْ لَنَا رَبَّنَآ ۖ إِنَّكَ أَنتَ ٱلْعَزِيزُ ٱلْحَكِيمُ

5   10:85

5 Our Lord, do not make us a target for those who disbelieve, and forgive us, our Lord. You are indeed the Mighty and Wise."

٦ لَقَدْ كَانَ لَكُمْ فِيهِمْ أُسْوَةٌ حَسَنَةٌ لِمَن كَانَ يَرْجُو اللَّهَ وَالْيَوْمَ الْآخِرَ ۚ وَمَن يَتَوَلَّ فَإِنَّ اللَّهَ هُوَ الْغَنِيُّ الْحَمِيدُ

6
33:21; 60:4

6 There is an excellent example in them for you—for anyone who seeks God and the Last Day. But whoever turns away—God is the Self-Sufficient, the Most Praised.

٧ عَسَى اللَّهُ أَن يَجْعَلَ بَيْنَكُمْ وَبَيْنَ الَّذِينَ عَادَيْتُم مِّنْهُم مَّوَدَّةً ۚ وَاللَّهُ قَدِيرٌ ۚ وَاللَّهُ غَفُورٌ رَّحِيمٌ

7 Perhaps God will plant affection between you and those of them you consider enemies. God is Capable. God is Forgiving and Merciful.

٨ لَا يَنْهَاكُمُ اللَّهُ عَنِ الَّذِينَ لَمْ يُقَاتِلُوكُمْ فِي الدِّينِ وَلَمْ يُخْرِجُوكُم مِّن دِيَارِكُمْ أَن تَبَرُّوهُمْ وَتُقْسِطُوا إِلَيْهِمْ ۚ إِنَّ اللَّهَ يُحِبُّ الْمُقْسِطِينَ

8 As for those who have not fought against you for your religion, nor expelled you from your homes, God does not prohibit you from dealing with them kindly and equitably. God loves the equitable.

٩ إِنَّمَا يَنْهَاكُمُ اللَّهُ عَنِ الَّذِينَ قَاتَلُوكُمْ فِي الدِّينِ وَأَخْرَجُوكُم مِّن دِيَارِكُمْ وَظَاهَرُوا عَلَىٰ إِخْرَاجِكُمْ أَن تَوَلَّوْهُمْ ۚ وَمَن يَتَوَلَّهُمْ فَأُولَٰئِكَ هُمُ الظَّالِمُونَ

9
3:28; 60:1

9 But God prohibits you from befriending those who fought against you over your religion, and expelled you from your homes, and aided in your expulsion. Whoever takes them for friends—these are the wrongdoers.

١٠ يَا أَيُّهَا الَّذِينَ آمَنُوا إِذَا جَاءَكُمُ الْمُؤْمِنَاتُ مُهَاجِرَاتٍ فَامْتَحِنُوهُنَّ ۖ اللَّهُ أَعْلَمُ بِإِيمَانِهِنَّ ۖ فَإِنْ عَلِمْتُمُوهُنَّ مُؤْمِنَاتٍ فَلَا تَرْجِعُوهُنَّ إِلَى الْكُفَّارِ ۖ لَا هُنَّ حِلٌّ لَّهُمْ وَلَا هُمْ يَحِلُّونَ لَهُنَّ ۖ وَآتُوهُم مَّا أَنفَقُوا ۚ وَلَا جُنَاحَ عَلَيْكُمْ أَن تَنكِحُوهُنَّ إِذَا آتَيْتُمُوهُنَّ أُجُورَهُنَّ ۚ وَلَا تُمْسِكُوا بِعِصَمِ الْكَوَافِرِ وَاسْأَلُوا مَا أَنفَقْتُمْ وَلْيَسْأَلُوا مَا أَنفَقُوا ۚ ذَٰلِكُمْ حُكْمُ اللَّهِ ۖ يَحْكُمُ بَيْنَكُمْ ۚ وَاللَّهُ عَلِيمٌ حَكِيمٌ

10
4:24

10 O you who believe! When believing women come to you emigrating, test them. God is Aware of their faith. And if you find them to be faithful, do not send them back to the unbelievers. They are not lawful for them, nor are they lawful for them. But give them what they have spent. You are not at fault if you marry them, provided you give them their compensation. And do not hold on to ties with unbelieving women, but demand what you have spent, and let them demand what they have spent. This is the rule of God; He rules among you. God is Knowing and Wise.

١١ وَإِن فَاتَكُمْ شَيْءٌ مِّنْ أَزْوَاجِكُمْ إِلَى الْكُفَّارِ فَعَاقَبْتُمْ فَآتُوا الَّذِينَ ذَهَبَتْ أَزْوَاجُهُم مِّثْلَ مَا أَنفَقُوا ۚ وَاتَّقُوا اللَّهَ الَّذِي أَنتُم بِهِ مُؤْمِنُونَ

11 If any of your wives desert you to the unbelievers, and you decide to penalize them, give those whose wives have gone away the equivalent of what they had spent. And fear God, in whom you are believers.

١٢ يَا أَيُّهَا النَّبِيُّ إِذَا جَاءَكَ الْمُؤْمِنَاتُ يُبَايِعْنَكَ عَلَىٰ أَن لَّا يُشْرِكْنَ بِاللَّهِ شَيْئًا وَلَا يَسْرِقْنَ وَلَا يَزْنِينَ وَلَا يَقْتُلْنَ أَوْلَادَهُنَّ وَلَا يَأْتِينَ بِبُهْتَانٍ يَفْتَرِينَهُ بَيْنَ أَيْدِيهِنَّ وَأَرْجُلِهِنَّ وَلَا يَعْصِينَكَ فِي مَعْرُوفٍ ۙ فَبَايِعْهُنَّ وَاسْتَغْفِرْ لَهُنَّ اللَّهَ ۖ إِنَّ اللَّهَ غَفُورٌ رَّحِيمٌ

12 O prophet! If believing women come to you, pledging allegiance to you, on condition that they will not associate anything with God, nor steal, nor commit adultery, nor kill their children, nor commit perjury as to parenthood, nor disobey you in anything righteous, accept their allegiance and ask God's forgiveness for them. God is Forgiving and Merciful.

١٣ يَا أَيُّهَا الَّذِينَ آمَنُوا لَا تَتَوَلَّوْا قَوْمًا غَضِبَ اللَّهُ عَلَيْهِمْ قَدْ يَئِسُوا مِنَ الْآخِرَةِ كَمَا يَئِسَ الْكُفَّارُ مِنْ أَصْحَابِ الْقُبُورِ

13
58:14

13 O you who believe! Do not befriend people with whom God has become angry, and have despaired of the Hereafter, as the faithless have despaired of the occupants of the graves.

Sūrah 61: Al-Ṣāf

سُورَةُ ٱلصَّفّ (Column)

بِسْمِ ٱللَّهِ ٱلرَّحْمَٰنِ ٱلرَّحِيمِ

١ سَبَّحَ لِلَّهِ مَا فِي السَّمَاوَاتِ وَمَا فِي الْأَرْضِ ۖ وَهُوَ الْعَزِيزُ الْحَكِيمُ

1
57:1; 59:1; 62:1; 64:1

1 Everything in the heavens and the earth praises God. He is the Almighty, the Wise.

٢ يَا أَيُّهَا الَّذِينَ آمَنُوا لِمَ تَقُولُونَ مَا لَا تَفْعَلُونَ

2
2:44; 26:226

2 O you who believe! Why do you say what you do not do?

٣ كَبُرَ مَقْتًا عِندَ اللَّهِ أَن تَقُولُوا مَا لَا تَفْعَلُونَ

3 It is most hateful to God that you say what you do not do.

٤ إِنَّ اللَّهَ يُحِبُّ الَّذِينَ يُقَاتِلُونَ فِي سَبِيلِهِ صَفًّا كَأَنَّهُم بُنْيَانٌ مَّرْصُوصٌ

4
2:44

4 God loves those who fight in His cause, in ranks, as though they were a compact structure.

٥ وَإِذْ قَالَ مُوسَىٰ لِقَوْمِهِ يَا قَوْمِ لِمَ تُؤْذُونَنِي وَقَد تَّعْلَمُونَ أَنِّي رَسُولُ اللَّهِ إِلَيْكُمْ ۖ فَلَمَّا زَاغُوا أَزَاغَ اللَّهُ قُلُوبَهُمْ ۚ وَاللَّهُ لَا يَهْدِي الْقَوْمَ الْفَاسِقِينَ

5
33:69

5 When Moses said to his people, "O my people, why do you hurt me, although you know that I am God's Messenger to you?" And when they swerved, God swerved their hearts. God does not guide the sinful people.

٦ وَإِذْ قَالَ عِيسَى ابْنُ مَرْيَمَ يَا بَنِي إِسْرَائِيلَ إِنِّي رَسُولُ اللَّهِ إِلَيْكُم مُّصَدِّقًا لِّمَا بَيْنَ يَدَيَّ مِنَ التَّوْرَاةِ وَمُبَشِّرًا بِرَسُولٍ يَأْتِي مِن بَعْدِي اسْمُهُ أَحْمَدُ ۖ فَلَمَّا جَاءَهُم بِالْبَيِّنَاتِ قَالُوا هَٰذَا سِحْرٌ مُّبِينٌ	6 7:157

6 And when Jesus son of Mary said, "O Children of Israel, I am God's Messenger to you, confirming what preceded me of the Torah, and announcing good news of a messenger who will come after me, whose name is Ahmad." But when he showed them the miracles, they said, "This is obvious sorcery."

٧ وَمَنْ أَظْلَمُ مِمَّنِ افْتَرَىٰ عَلَى اللَّهِ الْكَذِبَ وَهُوَ يُدْعَىٰ إِلَى الْإِسْلَامِ ۚ وَاللَّهُ لَا يَهْدِي الْقَوْمَ الظَّالِمِينَ	7 6:21

7 And who is a greater wrongdoer than he who attributes falsehoods to God, when he is being invited to Islam? God does not guide the wrongdoing people.

٨ يُرِيدُونَ لِيُطْفِئُوا نُورَ اللَّهِ بِأَفْوَاهِهِمْ وَاللَّهُ مُتِمُّ نُورِهِ وَلَوْ كَرِهَ الْكَافِرُونَ	8 9:32

8 They want to extinguish God's Light with their mouths; but God will complete His Light, even though the disbelievers dislike it.

٩ هُوَ الَّذِي أَرْسَلَ رَسُولَهُ بِالْهُدَىٰ وَدِينِ الْحَقِّ لِيُظْهِرَهُ عَلَى الدِّينِ كُلِّهِ وَلَوْ كَرِهَ الْمُشْرِكُونَ	9 pp 9:33; 48:28

9 It is He who sent His Messenger with the guidance and the true religion, to make it prevail over all religions, even though the idolaters dislike it.

١٠ يَا أَيُّهَا الَّذِينَ آمَنُوا هَلْ أَدُلُّكُمْ عَلَىٰ تِجَارَةٍ تُنجِيكُم مِّنْ عَذَابٍ أَلِيمٍ	10 9:111

10 O you who believe! Shall I inform you of a trade that will save you from a painful torment?

١١ تُؤْمِنُونَ بِاللَّهِ وَرَسُولِهِ وَتُجَاهِدُونَ فِي سَبِيلِ اللَّهِ بِأَمْوَالِكُمْ وَأَنفُسِكُمْ ۚ ذَٰلِكُمْ خَيْرٌ لَّكُمْ إِن كُنتُمْ تَعْلَمُونَ	11

11 That you believe in God and His Messenger, and strive in the cause of God with your possessions and yourselves. That is best for you, if you only knew.

١٢ يَغْفِرْ لَكُمْ ذُنُوبَكُمْ وَيُدْخِلْكُمْ جَنَّاتٍ تَجْرِي مِن تَحْتِهَا الْأَنْهَارُ وَمَسَاكِنَ طَيِّبَةً فِي جَنَّاتِ عَدْنٍ ۚ ذَٰلِكَ الْفَوْزُ الْعَظِيمُ	12 9:72

12 He will forgive you your sins; and will admit you into gardens beneath which rivers flow, and into beautiful mansions in the Gardens of Eden. That is the supreme success.

١٣ وَأُخْرَىٰ تُحِبُّونَهَا ۖ نَصْرٌ مِّنَ اللَّهِ وَفَتْحٌ قَرِيبٌ ۗ وَبَشِّرِ الْمُؤْمِنِينَ	13 48:18; 110:1

13 And something else you love: support from God, and imminent victory. So give good news to the believers.

١٤ يَا أَيُّهَا الَّذِينَ آمَنُوا كُونُوا أَنصَارَ اللَّهِ كَمَا قَالَ عِيسَى ابْنُ مَرْيَمَ لِلْحَوَارِيِّينَ مَنْ أَنصَارِي إِلَى اللَّهِ ۖ قَالَ الْحَوَارِيُّونَ نَحْنُ أَنصَارُ اللَّهِ ۖ فَآمَنَت طَّائِفَةٌ مِّن بَنِي إِسْرَائِيلَ وَكَفَرَت طَّائِفَةٌ ۖ فَأَيَّدْنَا الَّذِينَ آمَنُوا عَلَىٰ عَدُوِّهِمْ فَأَصْبَحُوا ظَاهِرِينَ

14
3:52

14 O you who believe! Be supporters of God, as Jesus son of Mary said to the disciples, "Who are my supporters towards God?" The disciples said, "We are God's supporters." So a group of the Children of Israel believed, while another group disbelieved. We supported those who believed against their foe, so they became dominant.

Sūrah 62: Al-Jumu'ah

سُورَةُ ٱلْجُمُعَة (Friday)

بِسْمِ ٱللَّهِ ٱلرَّحْمَٰنِ ٱلرَّحِيمِ

١ يُسَبِّحُ لِلَّهِ مَا فِي السَّمَاوَاتِ وَمَا فِي الْأَرْضِ الْمَلِكِ الْقُدُّوسِ الْعَزِيزِ الْحَكِيمِ

1
57:1; 59:1; 61:1; 64:1

1 Everything in the heavens and the earth glorifies God the Sovereign, the Holy, the Almighty, the Wise.

٢ هُوَ الَّذِي بَعَثَ فِي الْأُمِّيِّينَ رَسُولًا مِّنْهُمْ يَتْلُو عَلَيْهِمْ آيَاتِهِ وَيُزَكِّيهِمْ وَيُعَلِّمُهُمُ الْكِتَابَ وَالْحِكْمَةَ وَإِن كَانُوا مِن قَبْلُ لَفِي ضَلَالٍ مُّبِينٍ

2
3:164

2 It is He who sent among the unlettered a messenger from themselves; reciting His revelations to them, and purifying them, and teaching them the Scripture and wisdom; although they were in obvious error before that.

٣ وَآخَرِينَ مِنْهُمْ لَمَّا يَلْحَقُوا بِهِمْ ۚ وَهُوَ الْعَزِيزُ الْحَكِيمُ

3 And others from them, who have not yet joined them. He is the Glorious, the Wise.

٤ ذَٰلِكَ فَضْلُ اللَّهِ يُؤْتِيهِ مَن يَشَاءُ ۚ وَاللَّهُ ذُو الْفَضْلِ الْعَظِيمِ

4 That is God's grace, which He grants to whomever He wills. God is Possessor of limitless grace.

٥ مَثَلُ الَّذِينَ حُمِّلُوا التَّوْرَاةَ ثُمَّ لَمْ يَحْمِلُوهَا كَمَثَلِ الْحِمَارِ يَحْمِلُ أَسْفَارًا ۚ بِئْسَ مَثَلُ الْقَوْمِ الَّذِينَ كَذَّبُوا بِآيَاتِ اللَّهِ ۚ وَاللَّهُ لَا يَهْدِي الْقَوْمَ الظَّالِمِينَ

5 The example of those who were entrusted with the Torah, but then failed to uphold it, is like the donkey carrying works of literature. Miserable is the example of the people who denounce God's revelations. God does not guide the wrongdoing people.

٦ قُلْ يَا أَيُّهَا الَّذِينَ هَادُوا إِن زَعَمْتُمْ أَنَّكُمْ أَوْلِيَاءُ لِلَّهِ مِن دُونِ النَّاسِ فَتَمَنَّوُا الْمَوْتَ إِن كُنتُمْ صَادِقِينَ

6–7
2:94–95

6 Say, "O you who follow Judaism; if you claim to be the chosen of God, to the exclusion of the rest of mankind, then wish for death if you are sincere."

٧ وَلَا يَتَمَنَّوْنَهُ أَبَدًا بِمَا قَدَّمَتْ أَيْدِيهِمْ ۚ وَاللَّهُ عَلِيمٌ بِالظَّالِمِينَ

7 But they will not wish for it, ever, due to what their hands have advanced. God knows well the wrongdoers.

٨ قُلْ إِنَّ الْمَوْتَ الَّذِي تَفِرُّونَ مِنْهُ فَإِنَّهُ مُلَاقِيكُمْ ۖ ثُمَّ تُرَدُّونَ إِلَىٰ عَالِمِ الْغَيْبِ وَالشَّهَادَةِ فَيُنَبِّئُكُم بِمَا كُنتُمْ تَعْمَلُونَ

8
3:185; 4:78; 33:16

8 Say, "The death from which you flee will catch up with you; then you will be returned to the Knower of the Invisible and the Visible, and He will inform you of what you used to do."

٩ يَا أَيُّهَا الَّذِينَ آمَنُوا إِذَا نُودِيَ لِلصَّلَاةِ مِن يَوْمِ الْجُمُعَةِ فَاسْعَوْا إِلَىٰ ذِكْرِ اللَّهِ وَذَرُوا الْبَيْعَ ۚ ذَٰلِكُمْ خَيْرٌ لَّكُمْ إِن كُنتُمْ تَعْلَمُونَ

9
24:37

9 O you who believe! When the call is made for prayer on Congregation Day, hasten to the remembrance of God, and drop all business. That is better for you, if you only knew.

١٠ فَإِذَا قُضِيَتِ الصَّلَاةُ فَانتَشِرُوا فِي الْأَرْضِ وَابْتَغُوا مِن فَضْلِ اللَّهِ وَاذْكُرُوا اللَّهَ كَثِيرًا لَّعَلَّكُمْ تُفْلِحُونَ

10
33:53

10 Then, when the prayer is concluded, disperse through the land, and seek God's bounty, and remember God much, so that you may prosper.

١١ وَإِذَا رَأَوْا تِجَارَةً أَوْ لَهْوًا انفَضُّوا إِلَيْهَا وَتَرَكُوكَ قَائِمًا ۚ قُلْ مَا عِندَ اللَّهِ خَيْرٌ مِّنَ اللَّهْوِ وَمِنَ التِّجَارَةِ ۚ وَاللَّهُ خَيْرُ الرَّازِقِينَ

11
24:37; 63:9; 102:1

11 Yet whenever they come across some business, or some entertainment, they scramble towards it, and leave you standing. Say, "What is with God is better than entertainment and business; and God is the Best of providers."

Sūrah 63: Al-Munāfiqūn

سُورَةُ ٱلْمُنَافِقُون (The Hypocrites)

بِسْمِ ٱللَّهِ ٱلرَّحْمَٰنِ ٱلرَّحِيمِ

١ إِذَا جَاءَكَ الْمُنَافِقُونَ قَالُوا نَشْهَدُ إِنَّكَ لَرَسُولُ اللَّهِ ۗ وَاللَّهُ يَعْلَمُ إِنَّكَ لَرَسُولُهُ وَاللَّهُ يَشْهَدُ إِنَّ الْمُنَافِقِينَ لَكَاذِبُونَ

1
48:28–29

1 When the hypocrites come to you, they say, "We bear witness that you are God's Messenger." God knows that you are His Messenger, and God bears witness that the hypocrites are liars.

٢ اتَّخَذُوا أَيْمَانَهُمْ جُنَّةً فَصَدُّوا عَن سَبِيلِ اللَّهِ ۚ إِنَّهُمْ سَاءَ مَا كَانُوا يَعْمَلُونَ

2
58:16

2 They treat their oaths as a cover, and so they repel others from God's path. Evil is what they do.

٣ ذَٰلِكَ بِأَنَّهُمْ آمَنُوا ثُمَّ كَفَرُوا فَطُبِعَ عَلَىٰ قُلُوبِهِمْ فَهُمْ لَا يَفْقَهُونَ

3 That is because they believed, and then disbelieved; so their hearts were sealed, and they cannot understand.

3
9:66

٤ وَإِذَا رَأَيْتَهُمْ تُعْجِبُكَ أَجْسَامُهُمْ ۖ وَإِن يَقُولُوا تَسْمَعْ لِقَوْلِهِمْ ۖ كَأَنَّهُمْ خُشُبٌ مُّسَنَّدَةٌ ۖ يَحْسَبُونَ كُلَّ صَيْحَةٍ عَلَيْهِمْ ۚ هُمُ الْعَدُوُّ فَاحْذَرْهُمْ ۚ قَاتَلَهُمُ اللَّهُ ۖ أَنَّىٰ يُؤْفَكُونَ

4 When you see them, their appearance impresses you. And when they speak, you listen to what they say. They are like propped-up timber. They think every shout is aimed at them. They are the enemy, so beware of them. God condemns them; how deluded they are!

4

٥ وَإِذَا قِيلَ لَهُمْ تَعَالَوْا يَسْتَغْفِرْ لَكُمْ رَسُولُ اللَّهِ لَوَّوْا رُءُوسَهُمْ وَرَأَيْتَهُمْ يَصُدُّونَ وَهُم مُّسْتَكْبِرُونَ

5 And when it is said to them, "Come, the Messenger of God will ask forgiveness for you," they bend their heads, and you see them turning away arrogantly.

5
4:61; 5:104

٦ سَوَاءٌ عَلَيْهِمْ أَسْتَغْفَرْتَ لَهُمْ أَمْ لَمْ تَسْتَغْفِرْ لَهُمْ لَن يَغْفِرَ اللَّهُ لَهُمْ ۚ إِنَّ اللَّهَ لَا يَهْدِي الْقَوْمَ الْفَاسِقِينَ

6 It is the same for them, whether you ask forgiveness for them, or do not ask forgiveness for them; God will not forgive them. God does not guide the sinful people.

6
9:80

٧ هُمُ الَّذِينَ يَقُولُونَ لَا تُنفِقُوا عَلَىٰ مَنْ عِندَ رَسُولِ اللَّهِ حَتَّىٰ يَنفَضُّوا ۗ وَلِلَّهِ خَزَائِنُ السَّمَاوَاتِ وَالْأَرْضِ وَلَٰكِنَّ الْمُنَافِقِينَ لَا يَفْقَهُونَ

7 It is they who say: "Do not spend anything on those who side with God's Messenger, unless they have dispersed." To God belong the treasures of the heavens and the earth, but the hypocrites do not understand.

7

٨ يَقُولُونَ لَئِن رَّجَعْنَا إِلَى الْمَدِينَةِ لَيُخْرِجَنَّ الْأَعَزُّ مِنْهَا الْأَذَلَّ ۚ وَلِلَّهِ الْعِزَّةُ وَلِرَسُولِهِ وَلِلْمُؤْمِنِينَ وَلَٰكِنَّ الْمُنَافِقِينَ لَا يَعْلَمُونَ

8 They say, "If we return to the City, the more powerful therein will evict the weak." But power belongs to God, and His Messenger, and the believers; but the hypocrites do not know.

8
4:139

٩ يَا أَيُّهَا الَّذِينَ آمَنُوا لَا تُلْهِكُمْ أَمْوَالُكُمْ وَلَا أَوْلَادُكُمْ عَن ذِكْرِ اللَّهِ ۚ وَمَن يَفْعَلْ ذَٰلِكَ فَأُولَٰئِكَ هُمُ الْخَاسِرُونَ

9 O you who believe! Let neither your possessions nor your children distract you from the remembrance of God. Whoever does that—these are the losers.

9
18:48; 34:35; 62:11; 64:15

١٠ وَأَنفِقُوا مِن مَّا رَزَقْنَاكُم مِّن قَبْلِ أَن يَأْتِيَ أَحَدَكُمُ الْمَوْتُ فَيَقُولَ رَبِّ لَوْلَا أَخَّرْتَنِي إِلَىٰ أَجَلٍ قَرِيبٍ فَأَصَّدَّقَ وَأَكُن مِّنَ الصَّالِحِينَ

10 And give from what We have provided for you, before death approaches one of you, and he says, "My Lord, if only You would delay me for a short while, so that I may be charitable, and be one of the righteous."

10–11
2:254; 14:31, 44; 23:99; 36:47

١١ وَلَن يُؤَخِّرَ ٱللَّهُ نَفْسًا إِذَا جَاءَ أَجَلُهَا ۚ وَٱللَّهُ خَبِيرٌۢ بِمَا تَعْمَلُونَ

11 But God will not delay a soul when its time has come. God is Informed of what you do.

11
10:49

Sūrah 64: Al-Taghābun

سُورَةُ ٱلتَّغَابُنِ (Gathering)

بِسْمِ ٱللَّهِ ٱلرَّحْمَـٰنِ ٱلرَّحِيمِ

١ يُسَبِّحُ لِلَّهِ مَا فِي ٱلسَّمَـٰوَاتِ وَمَا فِي ٱلْأَرْضِ ۖ لَهُ ٱلْمُلْكُ وَلَهُ ٱلْحَمْدُ ۖ وَهُوَ عَلَىٰ كُلِّ شَيْءٍ قَدِيرٌ

1 Everything in the heavens and the earth praises God. To Him belongs the Kingdom, and to Him all praise is due, and He is Able to do all things.

1
57:1; 59:1; 61:1; 62:1

٢ هُوَ ٱلَّذِي خَلَقَكُمْ فَمِنكُمْ كَافِرٌ وَمِنكُم مُّؤْمِنٌ ۚ وَٱللَّهُ بِمَا تَعْمَلُونَ بَصِيرٌ

2 It is He who created you. Some of you are unbelievers, and some of you are believers. And God perceives what you do.

2
76:3

٣ خَلَقَ ٱلسَّمَـٰوَاتِ وَٱلْأَرْضَ بِٱلْحَقِّ وَصَوَّرَكُمْ فَأَحْسَنَ صُوَرَكُمْ ۖ وَإِلَيْهِ ٱلْمَصِيرُ

3 He created the heavens and the earth with truth, and He designed you, and designed you well, and to Him is the final return.

3
40:64

٤ يَعْلَمُ مَا فِي ٱلسَّمَـٰوَاتِ وَٱلْأَرْضِ وَيَعْلَمُ مَا تُسِرُّونَ وَمَا تُعْلِنُونَ ۚ وَٱللَّهُ عَلِيمٌۢ بِذَاتِ ٱلصُّدُورِ

4 He knows everything in the heavens and the earth, and He knows what you conceal and what you reveal. And God knows what is within the hearts.

4
16:19

٥ أَلَمْ يَأْتِكُمْ نَبَؤُا۟ ٱلَّذِينَ كَفَرُوا۟ مِن قَبْلُ فَذَاقُوا۟ وَبَالَ أَمْرِهِمْ وَلَهُمْ عَذَابٌ أَلِيمٌ

5 Has the news not reached you, of those who disbelieved before? They tasted the ill consequences of their conduct, and a painful torment awaits them.

٦ ذَٰلِكَ بِأَنَّهُۥ كَانَت تَّأْتِيهِمْ رُسُلُهُم بِٱلْبَيِّنَـٰتِ فَقَالُوٓا۟ أَبَشَرٌ يَهْدُونَنَا فَكَفَرُوا۟ وَتَوَلَّوا۟ ۚ وَّٱسْتَغْنَى ٱللَّهُ ۚ وَٱللَّهُ غَنِيٌّ حَمِيدٌ

6 That is because their messengers came to them with clear explanations, but they said, "Are human beings going to guide us?" So they disbelieved and turned away. But God is in no need. God is Independent and Praiseworthy.

6
9:80, 113; 40:22; 54:25

٧ زَعَمَ ٱلَّذِينَ كَفَرُوٓا۟ أَن لَّن يُبْعَثُوا۟ ۚ قُلْ بَلَىٰ وَرَبِّي لَتُبْعَثُنَّ ثُمَّ لَتُنَبَّؤُنَّ بِمَا عَمِلْتُمْ ۚ وَذَٰلِكَ عَلَى ٱللَّهِ يَسِيرٌ

7 Those who disbelieve claim that they will not be resurrected. Say, "Yes indeed, by my Lord, you will be resurrected; then you will be informed of everything you did; and that is easy for God."

٨ فَآمِنُوا بِاللَّهِ وَرَسُولِهِ وَالنُّورِ الَّذِي أَنزَلْنَا ۚ وَاللَّهُ بِمَا تَعْمَلُونَ خَبِيرٌ

8 So believe in God and His Messenger, and the Light which We sent down. God is Aware of everything you do.

٩ يَوْمَ يَجْمَعُكُمْ لِيَوْمِ الْجَمْعِ ۖ ذَٰلِكَ يَوْمُ التَّغَابُنِ ۗ وَمَن يُؤْمِن بِاللَّهِ وَيَعْمَلْ صَالِحًا يُكَفِّرْ عَنْهُ سَيِّئَاتِهِ وَيُدْخِلْهُ جَنَّاتٍ تَجْرِي مِن تَحْتِهَا الْأَنْهَارُ خَالِدِينَ فِيهَا أَبَدًا ۚ ذَٰلِكَ الْفَوْزُ الْعَظِيمُ

9
11:103; 56:59–50

9 The Day when He gathers you for the Day of Gathering—that is the Day of Mutual Exchange. Whoever believes in God and acts with integrity, He will remit his misdeeds, and will admit him into gardens beneath which rivers flow, to dwell therein forever. That is the supreme achievement.

١٠ وَالَّذِينَ كَفَرُوا وَكَذَّبُوا بِآيَاتِنَا أُولَٰئِكَ أَصْحَابُ النَّارِ خَالِدِينَ فِيهَا ۖ وَبِئْسَ الْمَصِيرُ

10 But as for those who disbelieve and denounce Our revelations— these are the inmates of the Fire, dwelling therein forever; and what a miserable fate!

١١ مَا أَصَابَ مِن مُّصِيبَةٍ إِلَّا بِإِذْنِ اللَّهِ ۗ وَمَن يُؤْمِن بِاللَّهِ يَهْدِ قَلْبَهُ ۚ وَاللَّهُ بِكُلِّ شَيْءٍ عَلِيمٌ

11
3:166

11 No disaster occurs except by God's leave. Whoever believes in God, He guides his heart. God is Aware of everything.

١٢ وَأَطِيعُوا اللَّهَ وَأَطِيعُوا الرَّسُولَ ۚ فَإِن تَوَلَّيْتُمْ فَإِنَّمَا عَلَىٰ رَسُولِنَا الْبَلَاغُ الْمُبِينُ

12
5:92; 24:54

12 So obey God, and obey the Messenger. But if you turn away—it is only incumbent on Our Messenger to deliver the clear message.

١٣ اللَّهُ لَا إِلَٰهَ إِلَّا هُوَ ۚ وَعَلَى اللَّهِ فَلْيَتَوَكَّلِ الْمُؤْمِنُونَ

13 God, there is no god but He; and in God let the believers put their trust.

١٤ يَا أَيُّهَا الَّذِينَ آمَنُوا إِنَّ مِنْ أَزْوَاجِكُمْ وَأَوْلَادِكُمْ عَدُوًّا لَّكُمْ فَاحْذَرُوهُمْ ۚ وَإِن تَعْفُوا وَتَصْفَحُوا وَتَغْفِرُوا فَإِنَّ اللَّهَ غَفُورٌ رَّحِيمٌ

14
24:22

14 O you who believe! Among your spouses and your children are enemies to you, so beware of them. But if you pardon, and overlook, and forgive—God is Forgiver and Merciful.

١٥ إِنَّمَا أَمْوَالُكُمْ وَأَوْلَادُكُمْ فِتْنَةٌ ۚ وَاللَّهُ عِندَهُ أَجْرٌ عَظِيمٌ

15
8:28

15 Your possessions and your children are a test, but with God is a splendid reward.

١٦ فَاتَّقُوا اللَّهَ مَا اسْتَطَعْتُمْ وَاسْمَعُوا وَأَطِيعُوا وَأَنفِقُوا خَيْرًا لِّأَنفُسِكُمْ ۗ وَمَن يُوقَ شُحَّ نَفْسِهِ فَأُولَٰئِكَ هُمُ الْمُفْلِحُونَ

16 So be conscious of God as much as you can, and listen, and obey, and give for your own good. He who is protected from his stinginess— these are the prosperous.

	17
١٧ إِنْ تُقْرِضُوا اللَّهَ قَرْضًا حَسَنًا يُضَاعِفْهُ لَكُمْ وَيَغْفِرْ لَكُمْ ۚ وَاللَّهُ شَكُورٌ حَلِيمٌ	2:245; 57:11, 18

17 If you lend God a good loan, He will multiply it for you, and will forgive you. God is Appreciative and Forbearing.

	18
١٨ عَالِمُ الْغَيْبِ وَالشَّهَادَةِ الْعَزِيزُ الْحَكِيمُ	6:59

18 The Knower of the Unseen and the Seen, the Almighty, the Wise.

Sūrah 65: Al-Ṭalāq

سُورَةُ ٱلطَّلَاقِ (Divorce)

بِسْمِ ٱللَّهِ ٱلرَّحْمَٰنِ ٱلرَّحِيمِ

	1–8
١ يَا أَيُّهَا النَّبِيُّ إِذَا طَلَّقْتُمُ النِّسَاءَ فَطَلِّقُوهُنَّ لِعِدَّتِهِنَّ وَأَحْصُوا الْعِدَّةَ ۖ وَاتَّقُوا اللَّهَ رَبَّكُمْ ۖ لَا تُخْرِجُوهُنَّ مِنْ بُيُوتِهِنَّ وَلَا يَخْرُجْنَ إِلَّا أَنْ يَأْتِينَ بِفَاحِشَةٍ مُبَيِّنَةٍ ۚ وَتِلْكَ حُدُودُ اللَّهِ ۚ وَمَنْ يَتَعَدَّ حُدُودَ اللَّهِ فَقَدْ ظَلَمَ نَفْسَهُ ۚ لَا تَدْرِي لَعَلَّ اللَّهَ يُحْدِثُ بَعْدَ ذَٰلِكَ أَمْرًا	2:229–231; 4:20–21

1 O Prophet! If any of you divorce women, divorce them during their period of purity, and calculate their term. And be pious before God, your Lord. And do not evict them from their homes, nor shall they leave, unless they have committed a proven adultery. These are the limits of God—whoever oversteps God's limits has wronged his own soul. You never know; God may afterwards bring about a new situation.

٢ فَإِذَا بَلَغْنَ أَجَلَهُنَّ فَأَمْسِكُوهُنَّ بِمَعْرُوفٍ أَوْ فَارِقُوهُنَّ بِمَعْرُوفٍ وَأَشْهِدُوا ذَوَيْ عَدْلٍ مِنْكُمْ وَأَقِيمُوا الشَّهَادَةَ لِلَّهِ ۚ ذَٰلِكُمْ يُوعَظُ بِهِ مَنْ كَانَ يُؤْمِنُ بِاللَّهِ وَالْيَوْمِ الْآخِرِ ۚ وَمَنْ يَتَّقِ اللَّهَ يَجْعَلْ لَهُ مَخْرَجًا

2 Once they have reached their term, either retain them honorably, or separate from them honorably. And call to witness two just people from among you, and give upright testimony for God. By that is exhorted whoever believes in God and the Last Day. And whoever fears God—He will make a way out for him.

٣ وَيَرْزُقْهُ مِنْ حَيْثُ لَا يَحْتَسِبُ ۚ وَمَنْ يَتَوَكَّلْ عَلَى اللَّهِ فَهُوَ حَسْبُهُ ۚ إِنَّ اللَّهَ بَالِغُ أَمْرِهِ ۚ قَدْ جَعَلَ اللَّهُ لِكُلِّ شَيْءٍ قَدْرًا

3 And will provide for him from where he never expected. Whoever relies on God—He will suffice him. God will accomplish His purpose. God has set a measure to all things.

٤ وَاللَّائِي يَئِسْنَ مِنَ الْمَحِيضِ مِنْ نِسَائِكُمْ إِنِ ارْتَبْتُمْ فَعِدَّتُهُنَّ ثَلَاثَةُ أَشْهُرٍ وَاللَّائِي لَمْ يَحِضْنَ ۚ وَأُولَاتُ الْأَحْمَالِ أَجَلُهُنَّ أَنْ يَضَعْنَ حَمْلَهُنَّ ۚ وَمَنْ يَتَّقِ اللَّهَ يَجْعَلْ لَهُ مِنْ أَمْرِهِ يُسْرًا

4 As for those of your women who have reached menopause, if you have any doubts, their term shall be three months—and also for those who have not menstruated. As for those who are pregnant, their term shall be until they have delivered. Whoever fears God—He will make things easy for him.

ه ذَٰلِكَ أَمْرُ اللَّهِ أَنزَلَهُ إِلَيْكُمْ ۚ وَمَن يَتَّقِ اللَّهَ يُكَفِّرْ عَنْهُ سَيِّئَاتِهِ وَيُعْظِمْ لَهُ أَجْرًا

5 This is the ordinance of God, which He sent down to you. Whoever fears God—He will remit his sins, and will amplify his reward.

٦ أَسْكِنُوهُنَّ مِنْ حَيْثُ سَكَنتُم مِّن وُجْدِكُمْ وَلَا تُضَارُّوهُنَّ لِتُضَيِّقُوا عَلَيْهِنَّ ۚ وَإِن كُنَّ أُولَاتِ حَمْلٍ فَأَنفِقُوا عَلَيْهِنَّ حَتَّىٰ يَضَعْنَ حَمْلَهُنَّ ۚ فَإِنْ أَرْضَعْنَ لَكُمْ فَآتُوهُنَّ أُجُورَهُنَّ ۖ وَأْتَمِرُوا بَيْنَكُم بِمَعْرُوفٍ ۖ وَإِن تَعَاسَرْتُمْ فَسَتُرْضِعُ لَهُ أُخْرَىٰ

6
2:233

6 Allow them to reside where you reside, according to your means, and do not harass them in order to make things difficult for them. If they are pregnant, spend on them until they give birth. And if they nurse your infant, give them their payment. And conduct your relation in amity. But if you disagree, then let another woman nurse him.

٧ لِيُنفِقْ ذُو سَعَةٍ مِّن سَعَتِهِ ۖ وَمَن قُدِرَ عَلَيْهِ رِزْقُهُ فَلْيُنفِقْ مِمَّا آتَاهُ اللَّهُ ۚ لَا يُكَلِّفُ اللَّهُ نَفْسًا إِلَّا مَا آتَاهَا ۚ سَيَجْعَلُ اللَّهُ بَعْدَ عُسْرٍ يُسْرًا

7 The wealthy shall spend according to his means; and he whose resources are restricted shall spend according to what God has given him. God never burdens a soul beyond what He has given it. God will bring ease after hardship.

٨ وَكَأَيِّن مِّن قَرْيَةٍ عَتَتْ عَنْ أَمْرِ رَبِّهَا وَرُسُلِهِ فَحَاسَبْنَاهَا حِسَابًا شَدِيدًا وَعَذَّبْنَاهَا عَذَابًا نُّكْرًا

8
18:59; 22:45

8 How many a town defied the command of its Lord and His messengers? So We held it strictly accountable, and We punished it with a dreadful punishment.

٩ فَذَاقَتْ وَبَالَ أَمْرِهَا وَكَانَ عَاقِبَةُ أَمْرِهَا خُسْرًا

9 It tasted the result of its decisions, and the outcome of its decisions was perdition.

١٠ أَعَدَّ اللَّهُ لَهُمْ عَذَابًا شَدِيدًا ۖ فَاتَّقُوا اللَّهَ يَا أُولِي الْأَلْبَابِ الَّذِينَ آمَنُوا ۚ قَدْ أَنزَلَ اللَّهُ إِلَيْكُمْ ذِكْرًا

10 God has prepared for them a severe retribution. So beware of God, O you who possess intellect and have faith. God has sent down to you a Reminder.

١١ رَّسُولًا يَتْلُو عَلَيْكُمْ آيَاتِ اللَّهِ مُبَيِّنَاتٍ لِّيُخْرِجَ الَّذِينَ آمَنُوا وَعَمِلُوا الصَّالِحَاتِ مِنَ الظُّلُمَاتِ إِلَى النُّورِ ۚ وَمَن يُؤْمِن بِاللَّهِ وَيَعْمَلْ صَالِحًا يُدْخِلْهُ جَنَّاتٍ تَجْرِي مِن تَحْتِهَا الْأَنْهَارُ خَالِدِينَ فِيهَا أَبَدًا ۖ قَدْ أَحْسَنَ اللَّهُ لَهُ رِزْقًا

11
2:257

11 A messenger who recites to you God's Verses, clear and distinct, that he may bring those who believe and work righteousness from darkness into light. Whoever believes in God and acts with integrity, He will admit him into gardens beneath which rivers flow, therein to abide forever. God has given him an excellent provision.

١٢ اللَّهُ الَّذِي خَلَقَ سَبْعَ سَمَاوَاتٍ وَمِنَ الْأَرْضِ مِثْلَهُنَّ يَتَنَزَّلُ الْأَمْرُ بَيْنَهُنَّ لِتَعْلَمُوا أَنَّ اللَّهَ عَلَى كُلِّ شَيْءٍ قَدِيرٌ وَأَنَّ اللَّهَ قَدْ أَحَاطَ بِكُلِّ شَيْءٍ عِلْمًا

12 God is He Who created seven heavens, and their like of earth. The command descends through them, so that you may know that God is Capable of everything, and that God Encompasses everything in knowledge.

Sūrah 66: Al-Taḥrīm

سُورَةُ ٱلتَّحْرِيم (Prohibition)

بِسْمِ ٱللَّهِ ٱلرَّحْمَٰنِ ٱلرَّحِيمِ

١ يَا أَيُّهَا النَّبِيُّ لِمَ تُحَرِّمُ مَا أَحَلَّ اللَّهُ لَكَ تَبْتَغِي مَرْضَاتَ أَزْوَاجِكَ وَاللَّهُ غَفُورٌ رَحِيمٌ

1 O prophet! Why do you prohibit what God has permitted for you, seeking to please your wives? God is Forgiving and Merciful.

٢ قَدْ فَرَضَ اللَّهُ لَكُمْ تَحِلَّةَ أَيْمَانِكُمْ وَاللَّهُ مَوْلَاكُمْ وَهُوَ الْعَلِيمُ الْحَكِيمُ

2 God has decreed for you the dissolution of your oaths. God is your Master. He is the All-Knowing, the Most Wise.

٣ وَإِذْ أَسَرَّ النَّبِيُّ إِلَى بَعْضِ أَزْوَاجِهِ حَدِيثًا فَلَمَّا نَبَّأَتْ بِهِ وَأَظْهَرَهُ اللَّهُ عَلَيْهِ عَرَّفَ بَعْضَهُ وَأَعْرَضَ عَنْ بَعْضٍ فَلَمَّا نَبَّأَهَا بِهِ قَالَتْ مَنْ أَنْبَأَكَ هَٰذَا قَالَ نَبَّأَنِيَ الْعَلِيمُ الْخَبِيرُ

3 The Prophet told something in confidence to one of his wives. But when she disclosed it, and God made it known to him; he communicated part of it, and he avoided another part. Then, when he informed her of it, she said, "Who informed you of this?" He said, "The All-Knowing, the All-Informed, informed me."

٤ إِنْ تَتُوبَا إِلَى اللَّهِ فَقَدْ صَغَتْ قُلُوبُكُمَا وَإِنْ تَظَاهَرَا عَلَيْهِ فَإِنَّ اللَّهَ هُوَ مَوْلَاهُ وَجِبْرِيلُ وَصَالِحُ الْمُؤْمِنِينَ وَالْمَلَائِكَةُ بَعْدَ ذَٰلِكَ ظَهِيرٌ

4 If you repent to God, then your hearts have listened. But if you band together against him, then God is his Ally, as is Gabriel, and the righteous believers. In addition, the angels will assist him.

٥ عَسَىٰ رَبُّهُ إِنْ طَلَّقَكُنَّ أَنْ يُبْدِلَهُ أَزْوَاجًا خَيْرًا مِنْكُنَّ مُسْلِمَاتٍ مُؤْمِنَاتٍ قَانِتَاتٍ تَائِبَاتٍ عَابِدَاتٍ سَائِحَاتٍ ثَيِّبَاتٍ وَأَبْكَارًا

5 Perhaps, if he divorces you, his Lord will give him in exchange wives better than you: submissive, believing, obedient, penitent, devout, fasting—previously married, or virgins.

٦ يَا أَيُّهَا الَّذِينَ آمَنُوا قُوا أَنْفُسَكُمْ وَأَهْلِيكُمْ نَارًا وَقُودُهَا النَّاسُ وَالْحِجَارَةُ عَلَيْهَا مَلَائِكَةٌ غِلَاظٌ شِدَادٌ لَا يَعْصُونَ اللَّهَ مَا أَمَرَهُمْ وَيَفْعَلُونَ مَا يُؤْمَرُونَ

6
2:24

6 O you who believe! Protect yourselves and your families from a Fire, whose fuel is people and stones. Over it are angels, fierce and powerful. They never disobey God in anything He commands them, and they carry out whatever they are commanded.

٧ يَا أَيُّهَا الَّذِينَ كَفَرُوا لَا تَعْتَذِرُوا الْيَوْمَ ۖ إِنَّمَا تُجْزَوْنَ مَا كُنْتُمْ تَعْمَلُونَ

7 O you who disbelieved! Make no excuses today. You are being repaid for what you used to do.

٨ يَا أَيُّهَا الَّذِينَ آمَنُوا تُوبُوا إِلَى اللَّهِ تَوْبَةً نَصُوحًا عَسَىٰ رَبُّكُمْ أَنْ يُكَفِّرَ عَنْكُمْ سَيِّئَاتِكُمْ وَيُدْخِلَكُمْ جَنَّاتٍ تَجْرِي مِنْ تَحْتِهَا الْأَنْهَارُ يَوْمَ لَا يُخْزِي اللَّهُ النَّبِيَّ وَالَّذِينَ آمَنُوا مَعَهُ ۖ نُورُهُمْ يَسْعَىٰ بَيْنَ أَيْدِيهِمْ وَبِأَيْمَانِهِمْ يَقُولُونَ رَبَّنَا أَتْمِمْ لَنَا نُورَنَا وَاغْفِرْ لَنَا ۖ إِنَّكَ عَلَىٰ كُلِّ شَيْءٍ قَدِيرٌ

8 O you who believe! Repent to God with sincere repentance. Perhaps your Lord will remit your sins, and admit you into gardens beneath which rivers flow, on the Day when God will not disappoint the Prophet and those who believed with him. Their light streaming before them, and to their right, they will say, "Our Lord, complete our light for us, and forgive us; You are capable of all things."

٩ يَا أَيُّهَا النَّبِيُّ جَاهِدِ الْكُفَّارَ وَالْمُنَافِقِينَ وَاغْلُظْ عَلَيْهِمْ ۚ وَمَأْوَاهُمْ جَهَنَّمُ ۖ وَبِئْسَ الْمَصِيرُ

9
25:50, 52

9 O prophet! Strive hard against the disbelievers and the hypocrites, and be stern with them. Their abode is Hell. What a miserable destination!

١٠ ضَرَبَ اللَّهُ مَثَلًا لِلَّذِينَ كَفَرُوا امْرَأَتَ نُوحٍ وَامْرَأَتَ لُوطٍ ۖ كَانَتَا تَحْتَ عَبْدَيْنِ مِنْ عِبَادِنَا صَالِحَيْنِ فَخَانَتَاهُمَا فَلَمْ يُغْنِيَا عَنْهُمَا مِنَ اللَّهِ شَيْئًا وَقِيلَ ادْخُلَا النَّارَ مَعَ الدَّاخِلِينَ

10
15:60

10 God illustrates an example of those who disbelieve: the wife of Noah and the wife of Lot. They were under two of Our righteous servants, but they betrayed them. They availed them nothing against God, and it was said, "Enter the Fire with those who are entering."

١١ وَضَرَبَ اللَّهُ مَثَلًا لِلَّذِينَ آمَنُوا امْرَأَتَ فِرْعَوْنَ إِذْ قَالَتْ رَبِّ ابْنِ لِي عِنْدَكَ بَيْتًا فِي الْجَنَّةِ وَنَجِّنِي مِنْ فِرْعَوْنَ وَعَمَلِهِ وَنَجِّنِي مِنَ الْقَوْمِ الظَّالِمِينَ

11
28:9

11 And God illustrates an example of those who believe: the wife of Pharaoh, when she said, "My Lord, build for me, with you, a house in Paradise, and save me from Pharaoh and his works, and save me from the wrongdoing people."

١٢ وَمَرْيَمَ ابْنَتَ عِمْرَانَ الَّتِي أَحْصَنَتْ فَرْجَهَا فَنَفَخْنَا فِيهِ مِنْ رُوحِنَا وَصَدَّقَتْ بِكَلِمَاتِ رَبِّهَا وَكُتُبِهِ وَكَانَتْ مِنَ الْقَانِتِينَ

12
19:17

12 And Mary, the daughter of Imran, who guarded her womb, and so We breathed into her of Our Spirit; and she believed in the truth of her Lord's Words and His Books, and was one of the devout.

Sūrah 67: Al-Mulk

سُورَةُ ٱلْمُلْكِ (Sovereignty)

بِسْمِ ٱللَّهِ ٱلرَّحْمَٰنِ ٱلرَّحِيمِ

١ تَبَارَكَ ٱلَّذِي بِيَدِهِ ٱلْمُلْكُ وَهُوَ عَلَىٰ كُلِّ شَيْءٍ قَدِيرٌ

1 Blessed is He in whose hand is the sovereignty, and Who has power over everything.

1 — 25:10; 36:83; 43:85

٢ ٱلَّذِي خَلَقَ ٱلْمَوْتَ وَٱلْحَيَاةَ لِيَبْلُوَكُمْ أَيُّكُمْ أَحْسَنُ عَمَلًا ۚ وَهُوَ ٱلْعَزِيزُ ٱلْغَفُورُ

2 He who created death and life—to test you—as to which of you is better in conduct. He is the Almighty, the Forgiving.

2 — 11:7; 18:7; 23:17

٣ ٱلَّذِي خَلَقَ سَبْعَ سَمَاوَاتٍ طِبَاقًا ۖ مَّا تَرَىٰ فِي خَلْقِ ٱلرَّحْمَٰنِ مِن تَفَاوُتٍ ۖ فَٱرْجِعِ ٱلْبَصَرَ هَلْ تَرَىٰ مِن فُطُورٍ

3 He who created seven heavens in layers. You see no discrepancy in the creation of the Compassionate. Look again. Can you see any cracks?

3 — 41:12; 71:15

٤ ثُمَّ ٱرْجِعِ ٱلْبَصَرَ كَرَّتَيْنِ يَنقَلِبْ إِلَيْكَ ٱلْبَصَرُ خَاسِئًا وَهُوَ حَسِيرٌ

4 Then look again, and again, and your sight will return to you dazzled and exhausted.

٥ وَلَقَدْ زَيَّنَّا ٱلسَّمَاءَ ٱلدُّنْيَا بِمَصَابِيحَ وَجَعَلْنَاهَا رُجُومًا لِّلشَّيَاطِينِ ۖ وَأَعْتَدْنَا لَهُمْ عَذَابَ ٱلسَّعِيرِ

5 We have adorned the lower heaven with lanterns, and made them missiles against the devils; and We have prepared for them the punishment of the Blaze.

5 — 15:17; 37:6–7

٦ وَلِلَّذِينَ كَفَرُوا بِرَبِّهِمْ عَذَابُ جَهَنَّمَ ۖ وَبِئْسَ ٱلْمَصِيرُ

6 For those who reject their Lord, there is the torment of Hell. What an evil destination!

٧ إِذَا أُلْقُوا فِيهَا سَمِعُوا لَهَا شَهِيقًا وَهِيَ تَفُورُ

7 When they are thrown into it, they will hear it roaring, as it seethes.

7 — 11:106; 21:99; 25:12

٨ تَكَادُ تَمَيَّزُ مِنَ ٱلْغَيْظِ ۖ كُلَّمَا أُلْقِيَ فِيهَا فَوْجٌ سَأَلَهُمْ خَزَنَتُهَا أَلَمْ يَأْتِكُمْ نَذِيرٌ

8 It almost bursts with fury. Every time a batch is thrown into it, its keepers will ask them, "Has no warner come to you?"

8 — 39:71; 40:50

٩ قَالُوا بَلَىٰ قَدْ جَاءَنَا نَذِيرٌ فَكَذَّبْنَا وَقُلْنَا مَا نَزَّلَ ٱللَّهُ مِن شَيْءٍ إِنْ أَنتُمْ إِلَّا فِي ضَلَالٍ كَبِيرٍ

9 They will say, "Yes, a warner did come to us, but we disbelieved, and said, 'God did not send down anything; you are very much mistaken.'"

١٠ وَقَالُوا لَوْ كُنَّا نَسْمَعُ أَوْ نَعْقِلُ مَا كُنَّا فِي أَصْحَابِ ٱلسَّعِيرِ

10 And they will say, "Had we listened or reasoned, we would not have been among the inmates of the Blaze."

١١ فَاعْتَرَفُوا بِذَنبِهِمْ فَسُحْقًا لِّأَصْحَابِ السَّعِيرِ

11 So they will acknowledge their sins. So away with the inmates of the Blaze.

11
23:106

١٢ إِنَّ الَّذِينَ يَخْشَوْنَ رَبَّهُم بِالْغَيْبِ لَهُم مَّغْفِرَةٌ وَأَجْرٌ كَبِيرٌ

12 As for those who fear their Lord in secret—for them is forgiveness and a great reward.

12
9:13; 21:49; 33:39

١٣ وَأَسِرُّوا قَوْلَكُمْ أَوِ اجْهَرُوا بِهِ ۖ إِنَّهُ عَلِيمٌ بِذَاتِ الصُّدُورِ

13 Whether you keep your words secret, or declare them—He is Aware of the inner thoughts.

13
2:33; 6:3; 11:5; 13:10

١٤ أَلَا يَعْلَمُ مَنْ خَلَقَ وَهُوَ اللَّطِيفُ الْخَبِيرُ

14 Would He not know, He Who created? He is the Refined, the Expert.

١٥ هُوَ الَّذِي جَعَلَ لَكُمُ الْأَرْضَ ذَلُولًا فَامْشُوا فِي مَنَاكِبِهَا وَكُلُوا مِن رِّزْقِهِ ۖ وَإِلَيْهِ النُّشُورُ

15 It is He who made the earth manageable for you, so travel its regions, and eat of His provisions. To Him is the Resurgence.

١٦ أَأَمِنتُم مَّن فِي السَّمَاءِ أَن يَخْسِفَ بِكُمُ الْأَرْضَ فَإِذَا هِيَ تَمُورُ

16 Are you confident that the One in heaven will not cause the earth to collapse beneath you as it spins?

16
52:9

١٧ أَمْ أَمِنتُم مَّن فِي السَّمَاءِ أَن يُرْسِلَ عَلَيْكُمْ حَاصِبًا ۖ فَسَتَعْلَمُونَ كَيْفَ نَذِيرِ

17 Or are you confident that the One in Heaven will not unleash against you a violent storm? Then you will know what My warning is like.

17
17:68

١٨ وَلَقَدْ كَذَّبَ الَّذِينَ مِن قَبْلِهِمْ فَكَيْفَ كَانَ نَكِيرِ

18 Those before them also denied the truth; and how was My disapproval?

18
10:39; 35:25

١٩ أَوَلَمْ يَرَوْا إِلَى الطَّيْرِ فَوْقَهُمْ صَافَّاتٍ وَيَقْبِضْنَ ۚ مَا يُمْسِكُهُنَّ إِلَّا الرَّحْمَٰنُ ۚ إِنَّهُ بِكُلِّ شَيْءٍ بَصِيرٌ

19 Have they not seen the birds above them, spreading their wings, and folding them? None holds them except the Compassionate. He is Perceiver of everything.

19
16:79; 24:41

٢٠ أَمَّنْ هَٰذَا الَّذِي هُوَ جُندٌ لَّكُمْ يَنصُرُكُم مِّن دُونِ الرَّحْمَٰنِ ۚ إِنِ الْكَافِرُونَ إِلَّا فِي غُرُورٍ

20 Or who is this who is a force for you to protect you against the Compassionate? The disbelievers are in nothing but delusion.

20
18:43; 28:81; 42:46; 102:1

٢١ أَمَّنْ هَٰذَا الَّذِي يَرْزُقُكُمْ إِنْ أَمْسَكَ رِزْقَهُ ۚ بَل لَّجُّوا فِي عُتُوٍّ وَنُفُورٍ

21 Or who is this that will provide for you, if He withholds His provision? Yet they persist in defiance and aversion.

21
10:31; 34:24; 35:2; 39:38; 42:12

٢٢ أَفَمَن يَمْشِي مُكِبًّا عَلَىٰ وَجْهِهِ أَهْدَىٰ أَمَّن يَمْشِي سَوِيًّا عَلَىٰ صِرَاطٍ مُّسْتَقِيمٍ

22 Is he who walks bent on his own design better guided, or he who walks upright on a straight path?

٢٣ قُلْ هُوَ الَّذِي أَنشَأَكُمْ وَجَعَلَ لَكُمُ السَّمْعَ وَالْأَبْصَارَ وَالْأَفْئِدَةَ ۖ قَلِيلًا مَّا تَشْكُرُونَ

23 Say, "It is He who produced you; and made for you the hearing, and the vision, and the organs. But rarely do you give thanks."

23
23:78

٢٤ قُلْ هُوَ الَّذِي ذَرَأَكُمْ فِي الْأَرْضِ وَإِلَيْهِ تُحْشَرُونَ

24 Say, "It is He who scattered you on earth, and to Him you will be rounded up."

24
23:79

٢٥ وَيَقُولُونَ مَتَىٰ هَٰذَا الْوَعْدُ إِن كُنتُمْ صَادِقِينَ

25 And they say, "When will this promise be fulfilled, if you are truthful?"

٢٦ قُلْ إِنَّمَا الْعِلْمُ عِندَ اللَّهِ وَإِنَّمَا أَنَا نَذِيرٌ مُّبِينٌ

26 Say, "Knowledge is with God, and I am only a clear warner."

26
7:187; 46:23

٢٧ فَلَمَّا رَأَوْهُ زُلْفَةً سِيئَتْ وُجُوهُ الَّذِينَ كَفَرُوا وَقِيلَ هَٰذَا الَّذِي كُنتُم بِهِ تَدَّعُونَ

27 But when they see it approaching, the faces of those who disbelieved will turn gloomy, and it will be said, "This is what you used to call for."

٢٨ قُلْ أَرَأَيْتُمْ إِنْ أَهْلَكَنِيَ اللَّهُ وَمَن مَّعِيَ أَوْ رَحِمَنَا فَمَن يُجِيرُ الْكَافِرِينَ مِنْ عَذَابٍ أَلِيمٍ

28 Say, "Have you considered? Should God make me perish, and those with me; or else He bestows His mercy on us; who will protect the disbelievers from an agonizing torment?"

٢٩ قُلْ هُوَ الرَّحْمَٰنُ آمَنَّا بِهِ وَعَلَيْهِ تَوَكَّلْنَا ۖ فَسَتَعْلَمُونَ مَنْ هُوَ فِي ضَلَالٍ مُّبِينٍ

29 Say, "He is the Compassionate. We have faith in Him, and in Him we trust. Soon you will know who is in evident error."

٣٠ قُلْ أَرَأَيْتُمْ إِنْ أَصْبَحَ مَاؤُكُمْ غَوْرًا فَمَن يَأْتِيكُم بِمَاءٍ مَّعِينٍ

30 Say, "Have you considered? If your water drains away, who will bring you pure running water?"

30
18:41

Sūrah 68: Al-Qalam

سُوۡرَةُ اَلۡقَلَم (The Pen)

بِسۡمِ ٱللَّهِ ٱلرَّحۡمَٰنِ ٱلرَّحِيمِ

١ نٓ ۚ وَٱلۡقَلَمِ وَمَا يَسۡطُرُونَ

1 Noon. By the pen, and by what they inscribe.

٢ مَآ أَنتَ بِنِعۡمَةِ رَبِّكَ بِمَجۡنُونٍ

2 By the grace of your Lord, you are not insane.

2
15:6; 23:70; 34:46; 52:29; 81:22

٣ وَإِنَّ لَكَ لَأَجۡرًا غَيۡرَ مَمۡنُونٍ

3 In fact, you will have a reward that will never end.

٤ وَإِنَّكَ لَعَلَىٰ خُلُقٍ عَظِيمٍ

4 And you are of a great moral character.

٥ فَسَتُبۡصِرُ وَيُبۡصِرُونَ

5 You will see, and they will see.

5
37:175, 179

٦ بِأَييِّكُمُ ٱلۡمَفۡتُونُ

6 Which of you is the afflicted.

٧ إِنَّ رَبَّكَ هُوَ أَعۡلَمُ بِمَن ضَلَّ عَن سَبِيلِهِۦ وَهُوَ أَعۡلَمُ بِٱلۡمُهۡتَدِينَ

7 Your Lord knows best who has strayed from His path, and He knows best the well-guided.

7
53:30

٨ فَلَا تُطِعِ ٱلۡمُكَذِّبِينَ

8 So do not obey the deniers.

٩ وَدُّوا۟ لَوۡ تُدۡهِنُ فَيُدۡهِنُونَ

9 They would like you to compromise, so they would compromise.

١٠ وَلَا تُطِعۡ كُلَّ حَلَّافٍ مَّهِينٍ

10 And do not obey any vile swearer.

١١ هَمَّازٍ مَّشَّآءٍۭ بِنَمِيمٍ

11 Backbiter, spreader of slander.

11
104:1

١٢ مَّنَّاعٍ لِّلۡخَيۡرِ مُعۡتَدٍ أَثِيمٍ

12 Preventer of good, transgressor, sinner.

12
70:21; 83:12

١٣ عُتُلٍّۭ بَعۡدَ ذَٰلِكَ زَنِيمٍ

13 Rude and fake besides.

١٤ أَن كَانَ ذَا مَالٍ وَبَنِينَ

14 Just because he has money and children.

١٥ إِذَا تُتْلَىٰ عَلَيْهِ آيَاتُنَا قَالَ أَسَاطِيرُ الْأَوَّلِينَ	**15** 6:25; 8:31; 83:13

15 When Our Verses are recited to him, he says, "Myths of the ancients!"

١٦ سَنَسِمُهُ عَلَى الْخُرْطُومِ

16 We will brand him on the muzzle.

١٧ إِنَّا بَلَوْنَاهُمْ كَمَا بَلَوْنَا أَصْحَابَ الْجَنَّةِ إِذْ أَقْسَمُوا لَيَصْرِمُنَّهَا مُصْبِحِينَ	**17–32** 18:32–42

17 We tested them, as We tested the owners of the garden, when they vowed to harvest it in the morning.

١٨ وَلَا يَسْتَثْنُونَ

18 Without any reservation.

١٩ فَطَافَ عَلَيْهَا طَائِفٌ مِنْ رَبِّكَ وَهُمْ نَائِمُونَ

19 But a calamity from your Lord went around it while they slept.

٢٠ فَأَصْبَحَتْ كَالصَّرِيمِ

20 And in the morning it was as if picked.

٢١ فَتَنَادَوْا مُصْبِحِينَ

21 In the morning, they called to one another.

٢٢ أَنِ اغْدُوا عَلَىٰ حَرْثِكُمْ إِنْ كُنْتُمْ صَارِمِينَ

22 "Go early to your plantation, if you are going to harvest."

٢٣ فَانْطَلَقُوا وَهُمْ يَتَخَافَتُونَ

23 So off they went, murmuring to one another.

٢٤ أَنْ لَا يَدْخُلَنَّهَا الْيَوْمَ عَلَيْكُمْ مِسْكِينٌ

24 "No poor person is to enter it upon you today."

٢٥ وَغَدَوْا عَلَىٰ حَرْدٍ قَادِرِينَ

25 And early they went, resolved in intent.

٢٦ فَلَمَّا رَأَوْهَا قَالُوا إِنَّا لَضَالُّونَ

26 But when they saw it, they said, "We were wrong.

٢٧ بَلْ نَحْنُ مَحْرُومُونَ

27 We are now deprived."

٢٨ قَالَ أَوْسَطُهُمْ أَلَمْ أَقُلْ لَكُمْ لَوْلَا تُسَبِّحُونَ

28 The most reasonable of them said, "Did I not say to you, 'if only you would glorify?'"

٢٩ قَالُوا سُبْحَانَ رَبِّنَا إِنَّا كُنَّا ظَالِمِينَ

29 They said, "Glory to our Lord—We were indeed in the wrong."

٣٠ فَأَقْبَلَ بَعْضُهُمْ عَلَىٰ بَعْضٍ يَتَلَاوَمُونَ

30 Then they turned to one another, blaming one another.

٣١ قَالُوا يَا وَيْلَنَا إِنَّا كُنَّا طَاغِينَ

31 They said, "Woe to us—we were indeed domineering.

٣٢ عَسَىٰ رَبُّنَا أَن يُبْدِلَنَا خَيْرًا مِّنْهَا إِنَّا إِلَىٰ رَبِّنَا رَاغِبُونَ

32 Perhaps our Lord will give us a better substitute for it. We are turning to our Lord."

٣٣ كَذَٰلِكَ الْعَذَابُ ۖ وَلَعَذَابُ الْآخِرَةِ أَكْبَرُ ۚ لَوْ كَانُوا يَعْلَمُونَ

33 Such is the punishment; but the punishment of the Hereafter is greater, if they only knew.

٣٤ إِنَّ لِلْمُتَّقِينَ عِندَ رَبِّهِمْ جَنَّاتِ النَّعِيمِ

34 For the righteous are Gardens of Delight with their Lord.

٣٥ أَفَنَجْعَلُ الْمُسْلِمِينَ كَالْمُجْرِمِينَ

35 Shall We treat the Muslims like the villains?

٣٦ مَا لَكُمْ كَيْفَ تَحْكُمُونَ

36 What is the matter with you? How do you judge?

٣٧ أَمْ لَكُمْ كِتَابٌ فِيهِ تَدْرُسُونَ

37 Or do you have a scripture in which you study.

37
34:44; 43:21

٣٨ إِنَّ لَكُمْ فِيهِ لَمَا تَخَيَّرُونَ

38 Wherein there is whatever you choose?

٣٩ أَمْ لَكُمْ أَيْمَانٌ عَلَيْنَا بَالِغَةٌ إِلَىٰ يَوْمِ الْقِيَامَةِ ۙ إِنَّ لَكُمْ لَمَا تَحْكُمُونَ

39 Or do you have oaths from Us, binding until the Day of Resurrection, that you will have whatever you demand?

٤٠ سَلْهُمْ أَيُّهُم بِذَٰلِكَ زَعِيمٌ

40 Ask them, which of them will guarantee that.

٤١ أَمْ لَهُمْ شُرَكَاءُ فَلْيَأْتُوا بِشُرَكَائِهِمْ إِن كَانُوا صَادِقِينَ

41 Or do they have partners? Then let them produce their partners, if they are truthful.

٤٢ يَوْمَ يُكْشَفُ عَن سَاقٍ وَيُدْعَوْنَ إِلَى السُّجُودِ فَلَا يَسْتَطِيعُونَ

42 On the Day when the Shin will be exposed, and they will be called to bow down, but they will be unable.

42
75:29

٤٣ خَاشِعَةً أَبْصَارُهُمْ تَرْهَقُهُمْ ذِلَّةٌ ۖ وَقَدْ كَانُوا يُدْعَوْنَ إِلَى السُّجُودِ وَهُمْ سَالِمُونَ

43 Their eyes subdued, shame will cover them. They were invited to bow down when they were sound.

43
70:44; 79:9; 88:2

٤٤ فَذَرْنِي وَمَن يُكَذِّبُ بِهَٰذَا الْحَدِيثِ ۖ سَنَسْتَدْرِجُهُم مِّنْ حَيْثُ لَا يَعْلَمُونَ

44 So leave Me to those who reject this discourse; We will proceed against them gradually, from where they do not know.

44
7:182; 73:11

٤٥ وَأُمْلِي لَهُمْ ۚ إِنَّ كَيْدِي مَتِينٌ

45 And I will give them respite. My plan is firm.

٤٦ أَمْ تَسْأَلُهُمْ أَجْرًا فَهُم مِّن مَّغْرَمٍ مُّثْقَلُونَ

46 Or do you ask them for a fee, so they are burdened with debt?

٤٧ أَمْ عِندَهُمُ الْغَيْبُ فَهُمْ يَكْتُبُونَ

47 Or do they know the future, and so they write it down?

47
52:41

٤٨ فَاصْبِرْ لِحُكْمِ رَبِّكَ وَلَا تَكُن كَصَاحِبِ الْحُوتِ إِذْ نَادَىٰ وَهُوَ مَكْظُومٌ

48 So wait patiently for the Decision of your Lord, and do not be like the Fellow of the Fish who cried out in despair.

48
21:87

٤٩ لَّوْلَا أَن تَدَارَكَهُ نِعْمَةٌ مِّن رَّبِّهِ لَنُبِذَ بِالْعَرَاءِ وَهُوَ مَذْمُومٌ

49 Were it not for his Lord's favor that reached him, he would have been thrown into the wilderness, fully despised.

٥٠ فَاجْتَبَاهُ رَبُّهُ فَجَعَلَهُ مِنَ الصَّالِحِينَ

50 But his Lord chose him, and made him one of the righteous.

50
21:88

٥١ وَإِن يَكَادُ الَّذِينَ كَفَرُوا لَيُزْلِقُونَكَ بِأَبْصَارِهِمْ لَمَّا سَمِعُوا الذِّكْرَ وَيَقُولُونَ إِنَّهُ لَمَجْنُونٌ

51 Those who disbelieve almost stab you with their glances when they hear the message, and say, "He is crazy!"

51
7:184; 15:6

٥٢ وَمَا هُوَ إِلَّا ذِكْرٌ لِّلْعَالَمِينَ

52 But it is no less than a reminder to all the Worlds.

Sūrah 69: Al-Ḥāqqah

سُورَةُ الْحَاقَّةِ (Reality)

بِسْمِ اللَّهِ الرَّحْمَٰنِ الرَّحِيمِ

١ الْحَاقَّةُ

1 The Reality.

٢ مَا الْحَاقَّةُ

2 What is the Reality?

٣ وَمَا أَدْرَاكَ مَا الْحَاقَّةُ

3 What will make you understand what the Reality is?

٤ كَذَّبَتْ ثَمُودُ وَعَادٌ بِالْقَارِعَةِ

4 Thamūd and ʿĀd denied the Catastrophe.

٥ فَأَمَّا ثَمُودُ فَأُهْلِكُوا بِالطَّاغِيَةِ

5 As for Thamūd, they were annihilated by the Overwhelming.

5
91:11

٦ وَأَمَّا عَادٌ فَأُهْلِكُوا بِرِيحٍ صَرْصَرٍ عَاتِيَةٍ

6 And as for ʿĀd; they were annihilated by a furious, roaring wind.

6
41:16; 51:41; 54:19

٧ سَخَّرَهَا عَلَيْهِمْ سَبْعَ لَيَالٍ وَثَمَانِيَةَ أَيَّامٍ حُسُومًا فَتَرَى الْقَوْمَ فِيهَا صَرْعَىٰ كَأَنَّهُمْ أَعْجَازُ نَخْلٍ خَاوِيَةٍ

7 He unleashed it upon them for seven nights and eight days, in succession. You could see the people tossed around, as though they were stumps of hollow palm-trees.

7
54:20

٨ فَهَلْ تَرَىٰ لَهُمْ مِنْ بَاقِيَةٍ

8 Can you see any remnant of them?

٩ وَجَاءَ فِرْعَوْنُ وَمَنْ قَبْلَهُ وَالْمُؤْتَفِكَاتُ بِالْخَاطِئَةِ

9 Then Pharaoh came, and those before him, and the Overturned Cities steeped in sin.

9
53:53

١٠ فَعَصَوْا رَسُولَ رَبِّهِمْ فَأَخَذَهُمْ أَخْذَةً رَابِيَةً

10 But they disobeyed the messenger of their Lord, so He seized them with an overpowering grip.

١١ إِنَّا لَمَّا طَغَى الْمَاءُ حَمَلْنَاكُمْ فِي الْجَارِيَةِ

11 When the waters overflowed, We carried you in the cruising ship.

١٢ لِنَجْعَلَهَا لَكُمْ تَذْكِرَةً وَتَعِيَهَا أُذُنٌ وَاعِيَةٌ

12 To make it a lesson for you—so that retaining ears may retain it.

١٣ فَإِذَا نُفِخَ فِي الصُّورِ نَفْخَةٌ وَاحِدَةٌ

13 Then, when the Trumpet is sounded a single time.

١٤ وَحُمِلَتِ الْأَرْضُ وَالْجِبَالُ فَدُكَّتَا دَكَّةً وَاحِدَةً

14 And the earth and the mountains are lifted up, and crushed, with a single crush.

14
56:4–6; 89:21

١٥ فَيَوْمَئِذٍ وَقَعَتِ الْوَاقِعَةُ

15 On that Day, the Event will come to pass.

15
56:1

١٦ وَانْشَقَّتِ السَّمَاءُ فَهِيَ يَوْمَئِذٍ وَاهِيَةٌ

16 And the heaven will crack; so on that Day it will be frail.

١٧ وَالْمَلَكُ عَلَىٰ أَرْجَائِهَا ۚ وَيَحْمِلُ عَرْشَ رَبِّكَ فَوْقَهُمْ يَوْمَئِذٍ ثَمَانِيَةٌ

17 And the angels will be ranged around its borders, while eight will be carrying the Throne of your Lord above them that Day.

١٨ يَوْمَئِذٍ تُعْرَضُونَ لَا تَخْفَىٰ مِنكُمْ خَافِيَةٌ	**18**	
18 On that Day you will be exposed, and no secret of yours will remain hidden.	18:48–49	

١٩ فَأَمَّا مَنْ أُوتِيَ كِتَابَهُ بِيَمِينِهِ فَيَقُولُ هَاؤُمُ اقْرَءُوا كِتَابِيَهْ	**19**	
19 As for him who is given his book in his right hand, he will say, "Here, take my book and read it.	17:71; 84:7	

٢٠ إِنِّي ظَنَنتُ أَنِّي مُلَاقٍ حِسَابِيَهْ	**20**	
20 I knew I would be held accountable."	2:46; 18:53	

٢١ فَهُوَ فِي عِيشَةٍ رَاضِيَةٍ	
21 So he will be in pleasant living.	

٢٢ فِي جَنَّةٍ عَالِيَةٍ	
22 In a lofty Garden.	

٢٣ قُطُوفُهَا دَانِيَةٌ	
23 Its pickings are within reach.	

٢٤ كُلُوا وَاشْرَبُوا هَنِيئًا بِمَا أَسْلَفْتُمْ فِي الْأَيَّامِ الْخَالِيَةِ	**24**	
24 "Eat and drink merrily for what you did in the days gone by."	52:19	

٢٥ وَأَمَّا مَنْ أُوتِيَ كِتَابَهُ بِشِمَالِهِ فَيَقُولُ يَا لَيْتَنِي لَمْ أُوتَ كِتَابِيَهْ	**25**	
25 But as for him who is given his book in his left hand, he will say, "I wish I was never given my book.	56:41; 84:10	

٢٦ وَلَمْ أَدْرِ مَا حِسَابِيَهْ	
26 And never knew what my account was.	

٢٧ يَا لَيْتَهَا كَانَتِ الْقَاضِيَةَ	
27 If only it was the end.	

٢٨ مَا أَغْنَىٰ عَنِّي مَالِيَهْ	**28**	
28 My money cannot avail me.	26:88; 111:2	

٢٩ هَلَكَ عَنِّي سُلْطَانِيَهْ	
29 My power has vanished from me."	

٣٠ خُذُوهُ فَغُلُّوهُ	**30**	
30 "Take him and shackle him.	44:47	

٣١ ثُمَّ الْجَحِيمَ صَلُّوهُ	
31 Then scorch him in the Blaze.	

٣٢ ثُمَّ فِي سِلْسِلَةٍ ذَرْعُهَا سَبْعُونَ ذِرَاعًا فَاسْلُكُوهُ	
32 Then in a chain which length is seventy cubits tie him up.	

Sūrah 69: Al-Ḥāqqah

33 إِنَّهُ كَانَ لَا يُؤْمِنُ بِاللَّهِ الْعَظِيمِ ٣٣

33 For he would not believe in God the Great.

34 وَلَا يَحُضُّ عَلَىٰ طَعَامِ الْمِسْكِينِ ٣٤

34 Nor would he advocate the feeding of the destitute.

34
74:44; 89:18; 107:3

35 فَلَيْسَ لَهُ الْيَوْمَ هَاهُنَا حَمِيمٌ ٣٥

35 So he has no friend here today.

35–36
88:6

36 وَلَا طَعَامٌ إِلَّا مِنْ غِسْلِينٍ ٣٦

36 And no food except scum.

37 لَا يَأْكُلُهُ إِلَّا الْخَاطِئُونَ ٣٧

37 Which only the sinners eat."

38 فَلَا أُقْسِمُ بِمَا تُبْصِرُونَ ٣٨

38 Indeed, I swear by what you see.

38
84:16–18

39 وَمَا لَا تُبْصِرُونَ ٣٩

39 And by what you do not see.

40 إِنَّهُ لَقَوْلُ رَسُولٍ كَرِيمٍ ٤٠

40 It is the speech of a noble messenger.

40
pp 81:9

41 وَمَا هُوَ بِقَوْلِ شَاعِرٍ ۚ قَلِيلًا مَا تُؤْمِنُونَ ٤١

41 And it is not the speech of a poet—little do you believe.

41
21:5; 37:36; 52:30

42 وَلَا بِقَوْلِ كَاهِنٍ ۚ قَلِيلًا مَا تَذَكَّرُونَ ٤٢

42 Nor is it the speech of a soothsayer—little do you take heed.

42
52:29

43 تَنْزِيلٌ مِنْ رَبِّ الْعَالَمِينَ ٤٣

43 It is a revelation from the Lord of the Worlds.

44 وَلَوْ تَقَوَّلَ عَلَيْنَا بَعْضَ الْأَقَاوِيلِ ٤٤

44 Had he falsely attributed some statements to Us.

44
7:182; 52:33

45 لَأَخَذْنَا مِنْهُ بِالْيَمِينِ ٤٥

45 We would have seized him by the right arm.

46 ثُمَّ لَقَطَعْنَا مِنْهُ الْوَتِينَ ٤٦

46 Then slashed his lifeline.

47 فَمَا مِنْكُمْ مِنْ أَحَدٍ عَنْهُ حَاجِزِينَ ٤٧

47 And none of you could have restrained Us from him.

48 وَإِنَّهُ لَتَذْكِرَةٌ لِلْمُتَّقِينَ ٤٨

48 Surely, it is a message for the righteous.

49 And We know that some of you will reject it.

50 And it is surely a source of grief for the unbelievers.

51 Yet it is the absolute truth.
51
102:5-7

52 So glorify the name of your Lord, the Magnificent.
52
pp 56:96

Sūrah 70: Al-Ma'ārij

سُورَةُ ٱلْمَعَارِجِ (Ways of Ascent)

بِسْمِ ٱللَّهِ ٱلرَّحْمَٰنِ ٱلرَّحِيمِ

1 A questioner questioned the imminent torment.

2 For the disbelievers; none can repel it.
2
52:7-8

3 From God, Lord of the Ways of Ascent.

4 Unto Him the angels and the Spirit ascend on a Day the duration of which is fifty thousand years.
4
22:47; 32:5

5 So be patient, with sweet patience.

6 They see it distant.

7 But We see it near.

8 On the Day when the sky will be like molten brass.

9 And the mountains will be like tufted wool.

10 No friend will care about his friend.	١٠ وَلَا يَسْأَلُ حَمِيمٌ حَمِيمًا	9 101:5
11 They will be shown each other. The criminal wishes he would be redeemed from the punishment of that Day by his children.	١١ يُبَصَّرُونَهُمْ ۚ يَوَدُّ الْمُجْرِمُ لَوْ يَفْتَدِي مِنْ عَذَابِ يَوْمِئِذٍ بِبَنِيهِ	10 80:37
12 And his spouse, and his brother.	١٢ وَصَاحِبَتِهِ وَأَخِيهِ	
13 And his family that sheltered him.	١٣ وَفَصِيلَتِهِ الَّتِي تُؤْوِيهِ	
14 And everyone on earth, in order to save him.	١٤ وَمَن فِي الْأَرْضِ جَمِيعًا ثُمَّ يُنجِيهِ	
15 By no means! It is a Raging Fire.	١٥ كَلَّا ۖ إِنَّهَا لَظَىٰ	
16 It strips away the scalps.	١٦ نَزَّاعَةً لِّلشَّوَىٰ	
17 It invites him who once turned his back and fled.	١٧ تَدْعُو مَنْ أَدْبَرَ وَتَوَلَّىٰ	
18 And accumulated and hoarded.	١٨ وَجَمَعَ فَأَوْعَىٰ	
19 Man was created restless.	١٩ إِنَّ الْإِنسَانَ خُلِقَ هَلُوعًا	19 17:100
20 Touched by adversity, he is fretful.	٢٠ إِذَا مَسَّهُ الشَّرُّ جَزُوعًا	20 11:9; 17:83; 41:83
21 Touched by good, he is ungenerous.	٢١ وَإِذَا مَسَّهُ الْخَيْرُ مَنُوعًا	21 50:25; 68:12
22 Except the prayerful.	٢٢ إِلَّا الْمُصَلِّينَ	22–28 23:8
23 Those who are constant at their prayers.	٢٣ الَّذِينَ هُمْ عَلَىٰ صَلَاتِهِمْ دَائِمُونَ	
24 And those in whose wealth is a rightful share.	٢٤ وَالَّذِينَ فِي أَمْوَالِهِمْ حَقٌّ مَّعْلُومٌ	
25 For the beggar and the deprived.	٢٥ لِّلسَّائِلِ وَالْمَحْرُومِ	

٢٦ وَالَّذِينَ يُصَدِّقُونَ بِيَوْمِ الدِّينِ	
26 And those who affirm the Day of Judgment.	
٢٧ وَالَّذِينَ هُم مِّنْ عَذَابِ رَبِّهِم مُّشْفِقُونَ	
27 And those who fear the punishment of their Lord.	
٢٨ إِنَّ عَذَابَ رَبِّهِمْ غَيْرُ مَأْمُونٍ	
28 Their Lord's punishment is not to be taken for granted.	
٢٩ وَالَّذِينَ هُمْ لِفُرُوجِهِمْ حَافِظُونَ	29
29 And those who guard their chastity.	23:5–6
٣٠ إِلَّا عَلَىٰ أَزْوَاجِهِمْ أَوْ مَا مَلَكَتْ أَيْمَانُهُمْ فَإِنَّهُمْ غَيْرُ مَلُومِينَ	
30 Except from their spouses or those living under their control, for then they are free of blame.	
٣١ فَمَنِ ابْتَغَىٰ وَرَاءَ ذَٰلِكَ فَأُولَـٰئِكَ هُمُ الْعَادُونَ	31
31 But whoever seeks to go beyond that—these are the transgressors.	23:7
٣٢ وَالَّذِينَ هُمْ لِأَمَانَاتِهِمْ وَعَهْدِهِمْ رَاعُونَ	
32 And those who honor their trusts and their pledges.	
٣٣ وَالَّذِينَ هُم بِشَهَادَاتِهِمْ قَائِمُونَ	
33 And those who stand by their testimonies.	
٣٤ وَالَّذِينَ هُمْ عَلَىٰ صَلَاتِهِمْ يُحَافِظُونَ	34
34 And those who are dedicated to their prayers.	23:9
٣٥ أُولَـٰئِكَ فِي جَنَّاتٍ مُّكْرَمُونَ	
35 These will be honored in Gardens.	
٣٦ فَمَالِ الَّذِينَ كَفَرُوا قِبَلَكَ مُهْطِعِينَ	36
36 What is with those who disbelieve, stretching their necks towards you.	14:43; 54:8
٣٧ عَنِ الْيَمِينِ وَعَنِ الشِّمَالِ عِزِينَ	
37 From the right, and from the left, banding together?	
٣٨ أَيَطْمَعُ كُلُّ امْرِئٍ مِّنْهُمْ أَن يُدْخَلَ جَنَّةَ نَعِيمٍ	38
38 Is every one of them aspiring to be admitted into a Garden of Bliss?	7:46
٣٩ كَلَّا ۖ إِنَّا خَلَقْنَاهُم مِّمَّا يَعْلَمُونَ	39
39 No indeed! We created them from what they know.	56:62
٤٠ فَلَا أُقْسِمُ بِرَبِّ الْمَشَارِقِ وَالْمَغَارِبِ إِنَّا لَقَادِرُونَ	40
40 I swear by the Lord of the Easts and the Wests, that We are Able.	2:115; 37:5; 55:17
٤١ عَلَىٰ أَن نُّبَدِّلَ خَيْرًا مِّنْهُمْ وَمَا نَحْنُ بِمَسْبُوقِينَ	
41 To replace them with better than they, and We are not to be outdone.	

٤٢ فَذَرْهُمْ يَخُوضُوا وَيَلْعَبُوا حَتَّىٰ يُلَاقُوا يَوْمَهُمُ ٱلَّذِي يُوعَدُونَ

42 So leave them to blunder and play, until they meet their Day which they are promised.

42   39:62; 43:83

٤٣ يَوْمَ يَخْرُجُونَ مِنَ ٱلْأَجْدَاثِ سِرَاعًا كَأَنَّهُمْ إِلَىٰ نُصُبٍ يُوفِضُونَ

43 The Day when they will emerge from the tombs in a rush, as though they were hurrying towards a target.

43   36:51; 54:7

٤٤ خَاشِعَةً أَبْصَارُهُمْ تَرْهَقُهُمْ ذِلَّةٌ ۚ ذَٰلِكَ ٱلْيَوْمُ ٱلَّذِي كَانُوا يُوعَدُونَ

44 Their eyes cast down; overwhelmed by humiliation. This is the Day which they were promised.

44   68:43

Sūrah 71: Nūḥ

سُورَةُ نُوح (Noah)

بِسْمِ ٱللَّهِ ٱلرَّحْمَٰنِ ٱلرَّحِيمِ

١ إِنَّا أَرْسَلْنَا نُوحًا إِلَىٰ قَوْمِهِ أَنْ أَنْذِرْ قَوْمَكَ مِنْ قَبْلِ أَنْ يَأْتِيَهُمْ عَذَابٌ أَلِيمٌ

1 We sent Noah to his people: "Warn your people before there comes upon them a painful punishment."

1–3   4:165; 7:59; 11:25–26; 17:15; 23:23

٢ قَالَ يَا قَوْمِ إِنِّي لَكُمْ نَذِيرٌ مُبِينٌ

2 He said, "O my people, I am to you a clear warner.

٣ أَنِ ٱعْبُدُوا ٱللَّهَ وَٱتَّقُوهُ وَأَطِيعُونِ

3 Worship God and reverence Him, and obey me.

٤ يَغْفِرْ لَكُمْ مِنْ ذُنُوبِكُمْ وَيُؤَخِّرْكُمْ إِلَىٰ أَجَلٍ مُسَمًّى ۚ إِنَّ أَجَلَ ٱللَّهِ إِذَا جَاءَ لَا يُؤَخَّرُ ۖ لَوْ كُنْتُمْ تَعْلَمُونَ

4 And He will forgive you of your sins, and reprieve you until a stated term. God's term cannot be deferred once it has arrived, if you only knew."

٥ قَالَ رَبِّ إِنِّي دَعَوْتُ قَوْمِي لَيْلًا وَنَهَارًا

5 He said, "My Lord, I have called my people night and day.

٦ فَلَمْ يَزِدْهُمْ دُعَائِي إِلَّا فِرَارًا

6 But my call added only to their flight.

٧ وَإِنِّي كُلَّمَا دَعَوْتُهُمْ لِتَغْفِرَ لَهُمْ جَعَلُوا أَصَابِعَهُمْ فِي آذَانِهِمْ وَٱسْتَغْشَوْا ثِيَابَهُمْ وَأَصَرُّوا وَٱسْتَكْبَرُوا ٱسْتِكْبَارًا

7 Whenever I called them to Your forgiveness, they thrust their fingers into their ears, and wrapped themselves in their garments, and insisted, and became more and more arrogant.

7   45:8

٨ ثُمَّ إِنِّي دَعَوْتُهُمْ جِهَارًا

8   Then I called them openly.

٩ ثُمَّ إِنِّي أَعْلَنتُ لَهُمْ وَأَسْرَرْتُ لَهُمْ إِسْرَارًا

9   Then I appealed to them publicly, and I spoke to them privately.

١٠ فَقُلْتُ اسْتَغْفِرُوا رَبَّكُمْ إِنَّهُ كَانَ غَفَّارًا

11–10
11:28; 74:12–13

10   I said, 'Ask your Lord for forgiveness; He is Forgiving.

١١ يُرْسِلِ السَّمَاءَ عَلَيْكُم مِّدْرَارًا

11   He will let loose the sky upon you in torrents.

١٢ وَيُمْدِدْكُم بِأَمْوَالٍ وَبَنِينَ وَيَجْعَل لَّكُمْ جَنَّاتٍ وَيَجْعَل لَّكُمْ أَنْهَارًا

12   And provide you with wealth and children, and allot for you gardens, and allot for you rivers.

١٣ مَّا لَكُمْ لَا تَرْجُونَ لِلَّهِ وَقَارًا

13   What is the matter with you, that you do not appreciate God's Greatness?

١٤ وَقَدْ خَلَقَكُمْ أَطْوَارًا

14
12:12–14

14   Although He created you in stages.

١٥ أَلَمْ تَرَوْا كَيْفَ خَلَقَ اللَّهُ سَبْعَ سَمَاوَاتٍ طِبَاقًا

15
23:17; 65:12; 67:3

15   Do you not realize that God created seven heavens in layers?

١٦ وَجَعَلَ الْقَمَرَ فِيهِنَّ نُورًا وَجَعَلَ الشَّمْسَ سِرَاجًا

16   And He set the moon in their midst for light, and He made the sun a lamp.

١٧ وَاللَّهُ أَنبَتَكُم مِّنَ الْأَرْضِ نَبَاتًا

17   And God germinated you from the earth like plants.

١٨ ثُمَّ يُعِيدُكُمْ فِيهَا وَيُخْرِجُكُمْ إِخْرَاجًا

18
20:55

18   Then He will return you into it, and will bring you out again.

١٩ وَاللَّهُ جَعَلَ لَكُمُ الْأَرْضَ بِسَاطًا

19   And God made the earth a spread for you.

٢٠ لِتَسْلُكُوا مِنْهَا سُبُلًا فِجَاجًا

20   That you may travel its diverse roads.'"

٢١ قَالَ نُوحٌ رَّبِّ إِنَّهُمْ عَصَوْنِي وَاتَّبَعُوا مَن لَّمْ يَزِدْهُ مَالُهُ وَوَلَدُهُ إِلَّا خَسَارًا

21
54:9–10

21   Noah said, "My Lord, they have defied me, and followed him whose wealth and children increase him only in perdition."

٢٢ وَمَكَرُوا مَكْرًا كُبَّارًا

22   And they schemed outrageous schemes.

٢٣ وَقَالُوا لَا تَذَرُنَّ آلِهَتَكُمْ وَلَا تَذَرُنَّ وَدًّا وَلَا سُوَاعًا وَلَا يَغُوثَ وَيَعُوقَ وَنَسْرًا

23 And they said, "Do not give up your gods; do not give up Wadd, nor Souwa, nor Yaghoos, and Yaooq, and Nassr.

٢٤ وَقَدْ أَضَلُّوا كَثِيرًا ۖ وَلَا تَزِدِ الظَّالِمِينَ إِلَّا ضَلَالًا

24 They have misled many, so do not increase the wrongdoers except in confusion."

٢٥ مِمَّا خَطِيئَاتِهِمْ أُغْرِقُوا فَأُدْخِلُوا نَارًا فَلَمْ يَجِدُوا لَهُم مِّن دُونِ اللَّهِ أَنصَارًا

25 Because of their wrongs, they were drowned, and were hurled into a Fire. They did not find apart from God any helpers.

25
7:64

٢٦ وَقَالَ نُوحٌ رَّبِّ لَا تَذَرْ عَلَى الْأَرْضِ مِنَ الْكَافِرِينَ دَيَّارًا

26 Noah said, "My Lord, do not leave of the unbelievers a single dweller on earth.

26
21:78

٢٧ إِنَّكَ إِن تَذَرْهُمْ يُضِلُّوا عِبَادَكَ وَلَا يَلِدُوا إِلَّا فَاجِرًا كَفَّارًا

27 If You leave them, they will mislead your servants, and will breed only wicked unbelievers.

٢٨ رَّبِّ اغْفِرْ لِي وَلِوَالِدَيَّ وَلِمَن دَخَلَ بَيْتِيَ مُؤْمِنًا وَلِلْمُؤْمِنِينَ وَالْمُؤْمِنَاتِ وَلَا تَزِدِ الظَّالِمِينَ إِلَّا تَبَارًا

28 My Lord! Forgive me and my parents, and anyone who enters my home in faith, and all the believing men and believing women; and do not increase the wrongdoers except in perdition."

Sūrah 72: Al-Jinn

سُوَرَةُ ٱلْجِنّ (The Jinn)

بِسْمِ ٱللَّهِ ٱلرَّحْمَٰنِ ٱلرَّحِيمِ

١ قُلْ أُوحِيَ إِلَيَّ أَنَّهُ اسْتَمَعَ نَفَرٌ مِّنَ الْجِنِّ فَقَالُوا إِنَّا سَمِعْنَا قُرْآنًا عَجَبًا

1 Say, "It was revealed to me that a band of jinn listened in, and said, 'We have heard a wondrous Qur'an.

1
46:29

٢ يَهْدِي إِلَى الرُّشْدِ فَآمَنَّا بِهِ ۖ وَلَن نُّشْرِكَ بِرَبِّنَا أَحَدًا

2 It guides to rectitude, so we have believed in it; and we will never associate anyone with our Lord.

٣ وَأَنَّهُ تَعَالَىٰ جَدُّ رَبِّنَا مَا اتَّخَذَ صَاحِبَةً وَلَا وَلَدًا

3 And Exalted is the Grandeur of our Lord—He never had a mate, nor a child.

3
112:3

٤ وَأَنَّهُ كَانَ يَقُولُ سَفِيهُنَا عَلَى اللَّهِ شَطَطًا	4
4 But the fools among us used to say nonsense about God.	18:14

٥ وَأَنَّا ظَنَنَّا أَن لَّن تَقُولَ الْإِنسُ وَالْجِنُّ عَلَى اللَّهِ كَذِبًا	
5 And we thought that humans and jinn would never utter lies about God.	

٦ وَأَنَّهُ كَانَ رِجَالٌ مِّنَ الْإِنسِ يَعُوذُونَ بِرِجَالٍ مِّنَ الْجِنِّ فَزَادُوهُمْ رَهَقًا	6
6 Some individual humans used to seek power through some individual jinn, but they only increased them in confusion.	6:100, 126

٧ وَأَنَّهُمْ ظَنُّوا كَمَا ظَنَنتُمْ أَن لَّن يَبْعَثَ اللَّهُ أَحَدًا	
7 They thought, as you thought, that God would never resurrect anyone.	

٨ وَأَنَّا لَمَسْنَا السَّمَاءَ فَوَجَدْنَاهَا مُلِئَتْ حَرَسًا شَدِيدًا وَشُهُبًا	8–9
8 We probed the heaven, and found it filled with stern guards and projectiles.	15:17

٩ وَأَنَّا كُنَّا نَقْعُدُ مِنْهَا مَقَاعِدَ لِلسَّمْعِ ۖ فَمَن يَسْتَمِعِ الْآنَ يَجِدْ لَهُ شِهَابًا رَّصَدًا	
9 We used to take up positions to listen in; but whoever listens now finds a projectile in wait for him.	

١٠ وَأَنَّا لَا نَدْرِي أَشَرٌّ أُرِيدَ بِمَن فِي الْأَرْضِ أَمْ أَرَادَ بِهِمْ رَبُّهُمْ رَشَدًا	
10 We do not know whether ill is intended for those on earth, or if their Lord intends goodness for them.	

١١ وَأَنَّا مِنَّا الصَّالِحُونَ وَمِنَّا دُونَ ذَٰلِكَ ۖ كُنَّا طَرَائِقَ قِدَدًا	
11 Some of us are righteous, but some of us are less than that; we follow divergent paths.	

١٢ وَأَنَّا ظَنَنَّا أَن لَّن نُّعْجِزَ اللَّهَ فِي الْأَرْضِ وَلَن نُّعْجِزَهُ هَرَبًا	
12 We realized that we cannot defeat God on earth, and that we cannot escape Him by fleeing.	

١٣ وَأَنَّا لَمَّا سَمِعْنَا الْهُدَىٰ آمَنَّا بِهِ ۖ فَمَن يُؤْمِن بِرَبِّهِ فَلَا يَخَافُ بَخْسًا وَلَا رَهَقًا	13
13 And when we heard the guidance, we believed in it. Whoever believes in his Lord fears neither loss, nor burden.	20:112

١٤ وَأَنَّا مِنَّا الْمُسْلِمُونَ وَمِنَّا الْقَاسِطُونَ ۖ فَمَنْ أَسْلَمَ فَأُولَٰئِكَ تَحَرَّوْا رَشَدًا	
14 Among us are those who are submitting, and among us are the compromisers. As for those who have submitted—it is they who pursue rectitude.	

١٥ وَأَمَّا الْقَاسِطُونَ فَكَانُوا لِجَهَنَّمَ حَطَبًا	
15 But as for the compromisers—they will be firewood for Hell.'"	

١٦ وَأَنْ لَوِ اسْتَقَامُوا عَلَى الطَّرِيقَةِ لَأَسْقَيْنَاهُمْ مَاءً غَدَقًا

16 Had they kept true to the Path, We would have given them plenty water to drink.

١٧ لِنَفْتِنَهُمْ فِيهِ ۚ وَمَنْ يُعْرِضْ عَنْ ذِكْرِ رَبِّهِ يَسْلُكْهُ عَذَابًا صَعَدًا

17 To test them with it. Whoever turns away from the remembrance of his Lord, He will direct him to torment ever mounting.

١٨ وَأَنَّ الْمَسَاجِدَ لِلَّهِ فَلَا تَدْعُوا مَعَ اللَّهِ أَحَدًا

18 The places of worship are for God. So do not call, besides God, upon anyone else.

١٩ وَأَنَّهُ لَمَّا قَامَ عَبْدُ اللَّهِ يَدْعُوهُ كَادُوا يَكُونُونَ عَلَيْهِ لِبَدًا

19 And when the servant of God got up calling on Him, they almost fell on him in a mass.

٢٠ قُلْ إِنَّمَا أَدْعُو رَبِّي وَلَا أُشْرِكُ بِهِ أَحَدًا

20 Say, "I pray only to my Lord, and I never associate anyone with Him."

٢١ قُلْ إِنِّي لَا أَمْلِكُ لَكُمْ ضَرًّا وَلَا رَشَدًا

21 Say, "It is not in my power to harm you, nor to bring you to right conduct."

٢٢ قُلْ إِنِّي لَنْ يُجِيرَنِي مِنَ اللَّهِ أَحَدٌ وَلَنْ أَجِدَ مِنْ دُونِهِ مُلْتَحَدًا

22 Say, "No one can protect me from God, and I will not find any refuge except with Him.

٢٣ إِلَّا بَلَاغًا مِنَ اللَّهِ وَرِسَالَاتِهِ ۚ وَمَنْ يَعْصِ اللَّهَ وَرَسُولَهُ فَإِنَّ لَهُ نَارَ جَهَنَّمَ خَالِدِينَ فِيهَا أَبَدًا

23 Except for a proclamation from God and His messages. He who defies God and His Messenger—for him is the Fire of Hell, in which they will dwell forever."

23
4:14

٢٤ حَتَّىٰ إِذَا رَأَوْا مَا يُوعَدُونَ فَسَيَعْلَمُونَ مَنْ أَضْعَفُ نَاصِرًا وَأَقَلُّ عَدَدًا

24 Until, when they see what they were promised, they will know who is weaker in helpers, and fewer in numbers.

24
19:75

٢٥ قُلْ إِنْ أَدْرِي أَقَرِيبٌ مَا تُوعَدُونَ أَمْ يَجْعَلُ لَهُ رَبِّي أَمَدًا

25 Say, "I do not know whether what you are promised is near, or whether my Lord will extend it for a period."

25
21:109

٢٦ عَالِمُ الْغَيْبِ فَلَا يُظْهِرُ عَلَىٰ غَيْبِهِ أَحَدًا

26 The Knower of the Invisible; He does not disclose His Invisible to anyone.

٢٧ إِلَّا مَنِ ارْتَضَىٰ مِنْ رَسُولٍ فَإِنَّهُ يَسْلُكُ مِنْ بَيْنِ يَدَيْهِ وَمِنْ خَلْفِهِ رَصَدًا

27 Except to a Messenger of His choosing. He then dispatches guards before him and behind him.

٢٨ لِيَعْلَمَ أَنْ قَدْ أَبْلَغُوا رِسَالَاتِ رَبِّهِمْ وَأَحَاطَ بِمَا لَدَيْهِمْ وَأَحْصَىٰ كُلَّ شَيْءٍ عَدَدًا 28 That He may know that they have conveyed the messages of their Lord. He encompasses what they have, and has tallied everything by number.	28 19:94

Sūrah 73: Al-Muzammil

سُورَةُ ٱلْمُزَّمِّل (The Enwrapped)

بِسْمِ ٱللَّهِ ٱلرَّحْمَٰنِ ٱلرَّحِيمِ

١ يَا أَيُّهَا الْمُزَّمِّلُ 1 O you Enwrapped one.	
٢ قُمِ اللَّيْلَ إِلَّا قَلِيلًا 2 Stay up the night, except a little.	2 17:79
٣ نِصْفَهُ أَوِ انْقُصْ مِنْهُ قَلِيلًا 3 For half of it, or reduce it a little.	
٤ أَوْ زِدْ عَلَيْهِ وَرَتِّلِ الْقُرْآنَ تَرْتِيلًا 4 Or add to it; and chant the Qur'an rhythmically.	4 25:32
٥ إِنَّا سَنُلْقِي عَلَيْكَ قَوْلًا ثَقِيلًا 5 We are about to give you a heavy message.	
٦ إِنَّ نَاشِئَةَ اللَّيْلِ هِيَ أَشَدُّ وَطْئًا وَأَقْوَمُ قِيلًا 6 The vigil of night is more effective, and better suited for recitation.	
٧ إِنَّ لَكَ فِي النَّهَارِ سَبْحًا طَوِيلًا 7 In the daytime, you have lengthy work to do.	
٨ وَاذْكُرِ اسْمَ رَبِّكَ وَتَبَتَّلْ إِلَيْهِ تَبْتِيلًا 8 So remember the Name of your Lord, and devote yourself to Him wholeheartedly.	
٩ رَبُّ الْمَشْرِقِ وَالْمَغْرِبِ لَا إِلَٰهَ إِلَّا هُوَ فَاتَّخِذْهُ وَكِيلًا 9 Lord of the East and the West. There is no god but He, so take Him as a Trustee.	9 26:28; 37:5; 55:17; 70:40
١٠ وَاصْبِرْ عَلَىٰ مَا يَقُولُونَ وَاهْجُرْهُمْ هَجْرًا جَمِيلًا 10 And endure patiently what they say, and withdraw from them politely.	
١١ وَذَرْنِي وَالْمُكَذِّبِينَ أُولِي النَّعْمَةِ وَمَهِّلْهُمْ قَلِيلًا 11 And leave Me to those who deny the truth, those of luxury, and give them a brief respite.	11 86:17

Sūrah 73: Al-Muzammil

١٢ إِنَّ لَدَيْنَا أَنكَالًا وَجَحِيمًا

12
76:4

12 With Us are shackles, and a Fierce Fire.

١٣ وَطَعَامًا ذَا غُصَّةٍ وَعَذَابًا أَلِيمًا

13 And food that chokes, and a painful punishment.

١٤ يَوْمَ تَرْجُفُ الْأَرْضُ وَالْجِبَالُ وَكَانَتِ الْجِبَالُ كَثِيبًا مَّهِيلًا

14
79:6

14 On the Day when the earth and the mountains tremble, and the mountains become heaps of sand.

١٥ إِنَّا أَرْسَلْنَا إِلَيْكُمْ رَسُولًا شَاهِدًا عَلَيْكُمْ كَمَا أَرْسَلْنَا إِلَىٰ فِرْعَوْنَ رَسُولًا

15
48:8

15 We have sent to you a messenger, a witness over you, as We sent to Pharaoh a messenger.

١٦ فَعَصَىٰ فِرْعَوْنُ الرَّسُولَ فَأَخَذْنَاهُ أَخْذًا وَبِيلًا

16 But Pharaoh defied the Messenger, so We seized him with a terrible seizing.

١٧ فَكَيْفَ تَتَّقُونَ إِن كَفَرْتُمْ يَوْمًا يَجْعَلُ الْوِلْدَانَ شِيبًا

17 So how will you, if you persist in unbelief, save yourself from a Day which will turn the children gray-haired?

١٨ السَّمَاءُ مُنفَطِرٌ بِهِ ۚ كَانَ وَعْدُهُ مَفْعُولًا

18
82:1

18 The heaven will shatter thereby. His promise is always fulfilled.

١٩ إِنَّ هَٰذِهِ تَذْكِرَةٌ ۖ فَمَن شَاءَ اتَّخَذَ إِلَىٰ رَبِّهِ سَبِيلًا

19
pp 76:29

19 This is a reminder. So whoever wills, let him take a path to his Lord.

٢٠ إِنَّ رَبَّكَ يَعْلَمُ أَنَّكَ تَقُومُ أَدْنَىٰ مِن ثُلُثَيِ اللَّيْلِ وَنِصْفَهُ وَثُلُثَهُ وَطَائِفَةٌ مِّنَ الَّذِينَ مَعَكَ ۚ وَاللَّهُ يُقَدِّرُ اللَّيْلَ وَالنَّهَارَ ۚ عَلِمَ أَن لَّن تُحْصُوهُ فَتَابَ عَلَيْكُمْ ۖ فَاقْرَءُوا مَا تَيَسَّرَ مِنَ الْقُرْآنِ ۚ عَلِمَ أَن سَيَكُونُ مِنكُم مَّرْضَىٰ ۙ وَآخَرُونَ يَضْرِبُونَ فِي الْأَرْضِ يَبْتَغُونَ مِن فَضْلِ اللَّهِ ۙ وَآخَرُونَ يُقَاتِلُونَ فِي سَبِيلِ اللَّهِ ۖ فَاقْرَءُوا مَا تَيَسَّرَ مِنْهُ ۚ وَأَقِيمُوا الصَّلَاةَ وَآتُوا الزَّكَاةَ وَأَقْرِضُوا اللَّهَ قَرْضًا حَسَنًا ۚ وَمَا تُقَدِّمُوا لِأَنفُسِكُم مِّنْ خَيْرٍ تَجِدُوهُ عِندَ اللَّهِ هُوَ خَيْرًا وَأَعْظَمَ أَجْرًا ۚ وَاسْتَغْفِرُوا اللَّهَ ۖ إِنَّ اللَّهَ غَفُورٌ رَّحِيمٌ

20 Your Lord knows that you stay up nearly two-thirds of the night, or half of it, or one-third of it, along with a group of those with you. God designed the night and the day. He knows that you are unable to sustain it, so He has pardoned you. So, read of the Qur'an what is possible for you. He knows that some of you may be ill; and others travelling through the land, seeking God's bounty; and others fighting in God's cause. So, read of it what is possible for you, and observe the prayers, and give regular charity, and lend God a generous loan. Whatever good you advance for yourselves, you will find it with God, better and generously rewarded. And seek God's forgiveness, for God is Forgiving and Merciful.

Sūrah 74: Al-Muddaththir

سُورَةُ ٱلْمُدَّثِّر (The Enrobed)

بِسْمِ ٱللَّهِ ٱلرَّحْمَٰنِ ٱلرَّحِيمِ

1 O you Enrobed one.	١ يَـٰٓأَيُّهَا ٱلْمُدَّثِّرُ
2 Arise and warn.	٢ قُمْ فَأَنذِرْ
3 And magnify your Lord.	٣ وَرَبَّكَ فَكَبِّرْ
4 And purify your clothes.	٤ وَثِيَابَكَ فَطَهِّرْ
5 And abandon abominations.	٥ وَٱلرُّجْزَ فَٱهْجُرْ
6 And show no favor seeking gain.	٦ وَلَا تَمْنُن تَسْتَكْثِرُ
7 And be constant for your Lord.	٧ وَلِرَبِّكَ فَٱصْبِرْ
8 When the Trumpet is blown.	٨ فَإِذَا نُقِرَ فِى ٱلنَّاقُورِ
9 That Day will be a difficult day.	٩ فَذَٰلِكَ يَوْمَئِذٍ يَوْمٌ عَسِيرٌ
10 For the disbelievers—not easy.	١٠ عَلَى ٱلْكَـٰفِرِينَ غَيْرُ يَسِيرٍ
11 Leave Me to him whom I created alone.	١١ ذَرْنِى وَمَنْ خَلَقْتُ وَحِيدًا
12 And gave him vast wealth.	١٢ وَجَعَلْتُ لَهُ مَالًا مَّمْدُودًا
13 And children as witnesses.	١٣ وَبَنِينَ شُهُودًا
14 And smoothed things for him.	١٤ وَمَهَّدتُّ لَهُ تَمْهِيدًا
15 Then he wants Me to add yet more!	١٥ ثُمَّ يَطْمَعُ أَنْ أَزِيدَ

9–10 25:26

12–13 11:28; 71:11–12

١٦ كَلَّا ۖ إِنَّهُ كَانَ لِآيَاتِنَا عَنِيدًا	
16 By no means! He was stubborn towards Our revelations.

١٧ سَأُرْهِقُهُ صَعُودًا

17 I will exhaust him increasingly.

١٨ إِنَّهُ فَكَّرَ وَقَدَّرَ

18 He thought and analyzed.

١٩ فَقُتِلَ كَيْفَ قَدَّرَ

19 May he perish, how he analyzed.

٢٠ ثُمَّ قُتِلَ كَيْفَ قَدَّرَ

20 Again: may he perish, how he analyzed.

٢١ ثُمَّ نَظَرَ

21 Then he looked.

٢٢ ثُمَّ عَبَسَ وَبَسَرَ

22 Then he frowned and whined.

٢٣ ثُمَّ أَدْبَرَ وَاسْتَكْبَرَ

23 Then he turned back and was proud.

٢٤ فَقَالَ إِنْ هَٰذَا إِلَّا سِحْرٌ يُؤْثَرُ

24 And said, "This is nothing but magic from the past.

٢٥ إِنْ هَٰذَا إِلَّا قَوْلُ الْبَشَرِ

25 This is nothing but the word of a mortal."

٢٦ سَأُصْلِيهِ سَقَرَ

26 I will roast him in Saqar.

26
101:9; 104:4

٢٧ وَمَا أَدْرَاكَ مَا سَقَرُ

27 But what will explain to you what Saqar is?

٢٨ لَا تُبْقِي وَلَا تَذَرُ

28 It neither leaves, nor spares.

٢٩ لَوَّاحَةٌ لِلْبَشَرِ

29 It scorches the flesh.

٣٠ عَلَيْهَا تِسْعَةَ عَشَرَ

30 Over it are Nineteen.

٣١ وَمَا جَعَلْنَا أَصْحَابَ النَّارِ إِلَّا مَلَائِكَةً ۙ وَمَا جَعَلْنَا عِدَّتَهُمْ إِلَّا فِتْنَةً لِلَّذِينَ كَفَرُوا لِيَسْتَيْقِنَ الَّذِينَ أُوتُوا الْكِتَابَ وَيَزْدَادَ الَّذِينَ آمَنُوا إِيمَانًا ۙ وَلَا يَرْتَابَ الَّذِينَ أُوتُوا الْكِتَابَ وَالْمُؤْمِنُونَ ۙ وَلِيَقُولَ الَّذِينَ فِي قُلُوبِهِمْ مَرَضٌ وَالْكَافِرُونَ مَاذَا أَرَادَ اللَّهُ بِهَٰذَا مَثَلًا ۚ كَذَٰلِكَ يُضِلُّ اللَّهُ مَنْ يَشَاءُ وَيَهْدِي مَنْ يَشَاءُ ۚ وَمَا يَعْلَمُ جُنُودَ رَبِّكَ إِلَّا هُوَ ۚ وَمَا هِيَ إِلَّا ذِكْرَىٰ لِلْبَشَرِ

31
2:10; 9:125; 47:29

31 We have appointed only angels to be wardens of the Fire, and caused their number to be a stumbling block for those who disbelieve; so that those given the Scripture may attain certainty; and those who believe may increase in faith; and those given the Scripture and the believers may not doubt; and those in whose hearts is sickness and the unbelievers may say, "What did God intend by this parable?" Thus God leads astray whom He wills, and guides whom He wills. None knows the soldiers of your Lord except He. This is nothing but a reminder for the mortals.

٣٢ كَلَّا وَالْقَمَرِ

32 Nay! By the moon.

٣٣ وَاللَّيْلِ إِذْ أَدْبَرَ

33 And the night as it retreats.

٣٤ وَالصُّبْحِ إِذَا أَسْفَرَ

34 And the morning as it lights up.

٣٥ إِنَّهَا لَإِحْدَى الْكُبَرِ

35 It is one of the greatest.

٣٦ نَذِيرًا لِلْبَشَرِ

36 A warning to the mortals.

٣٧ لِمَنْ شَاءَ مِنْكُمْ أَنْ يَتَقَدَّمَ أَوْ يَتَأَخَّرَ

37 To whomever among you wishes to advance, or regress.

٣٨ كُلُّ نَفْسٍ بِمَا كَسَبَتْ رَهِينَةٌ

38
2:281; 3:25, 161;
40:17; 45:22

38 Every soul is hostage to what it has earned.

٣٩ إِلَّا أَصْحَابَ الْيَمِينِ

39
56:27, 90; 90:18

39 Except for those on the Right.

٤٠ فِي جَنَّاتٍ يَتَسَاءَلُونَ

40 In Gardens, inquiring.

٤١ عَنِ الْمُجْرِمِينَ

41 About the guilty.

٤٢ مَا سَلَكَكُمْ فِي سَقَرَ

42 "What drove you into Saqar?"

٤٣ قَالُوا لَمْ نَكُ مِنَ الْمُصَلِّينَ

43 They will say, "We were not of those who prayed.

٤٤ وَلَمْ نَكُ نُطْعِمُ الْمِسْكِينَ

44 Nor did we feed the destitute.

44
69:34

٤٥ وَكُنَّا نَخُوضُ مَعَ الْخَائِضِينَ

45 And we used to indulge with those who indulge.

٤٦ وَكُنَّا نُكَذِّبُ بِيَوْمِ الدِّينِ

46 And we used to deny the Day of Judgment.

46
15:99; 83:11; 107:1

٤٧ حَتَّىٰ أَتَانَا الْيَقِينُ

47 Until the Inevitable came upon us."

٤٨ فَمَا تَنْفَعُهُمْ شَفَاعَةُ الشَّافِعِينَ

48 But the intercession of intercessors will not help them.

48
2:48; 20:109; 26:100; 40:18

٤٩ فَمَا لَهُمْ عَنِ التَّذْكِرَةِ مُعْرِضِينَ

49 Why are they turning away from the Reminder?

٥٠ كَأَنَّهُمْ حُمُرٌ مُسْتَنْفِرَةٌ

50 As though they were panicked donkeys.

٥١ فَرَّتْ مِنْ قَسْوَرَةٍ

51 Fleeing from a lion?

٥٢ بَلْ يُرِيدُ كُلُّ امْرِئٍ مِنْهُمْ أَنْ يُؤْتَىٰ صُحُفًا مُنَشَّرَةً

52 Yet every one of them desires to be given scrolls unrolled.

٥٣ كَلَّا ۖ بَلْ لَا يَخَافُونَ الْآخِرَةَ

53 No indeed! But they do not fear the Hereafter.

٥٤ كَلَّا إِنَّهُ تَذْكِرَةٌ

54 Nevertheless, it is a reminder.

٥٥ فَمَنْ شَاءَ ذَكَرَهُ

55 So whoever wills, shall remember it.

٥٦ وَمَا يَذْكُرُونَ إِلَّا أَنْ يَشَاءَ اللَّهُ ۚ هُوَ أَهْلُ التَّقْوَىٰ وَأَهْلُ الْمَغْفِرَةِ

56 But they will not remember, unless God wills. He is the Source of Righteousness, and the Source of Forgiveness.

Sūrah 75: Al-Qiyāmah

سُوْرَةُ ٱلْقِيَامَة (Resurrection)

بِسْمِ ٱللَّهِ ٱلرَّحْمَٰنِ ٱلرَّحِيمِ

١ لَا أُقْسِمُ بِيَوْمِ الْقِيَامَةِ

1 I swear by the Day of Resurrection.

٢ وَلَا أُقْسِمُ بِالنَّفْسِ اللَّوَّامَةِ

2 And I swear by the blaming soul.

٣ أَيَحْسَبُ الْإِنْسَانُ أَلَّنْ نَجْمَعَ عِظَامَهُ

3 Does man think that We will not reassemble his bones?

3
36:78

٤ بَلَىٰ قَادِرِينَ عَلَىٰ أَنْ نُسَوِّيَ بَنَانَهُ

4 Yes indeed; We are Able to reconstruct his fingertips.

٥ بَلْ يُرِيدُ الْإِنْسَانُ لِيَفْجُرَ أَمَامَهُ

5 But man wants to deny what is ahead of him.

٦ يَسْأَلُ أَيَّانَ يَوْمُ الْقِيَامَةِ

6 He asks, "When is the Day of Resurrection?"

٧ فَإِذَا بَرِقَ الْبَصَرُ

7 When vision is dazzled.

٨ وَخَسَفَ الْقَمَرُ

8 And the moon is eclipsed.

٩ وَجُمِعَ الشَّمْسُ وَالْقَمَرُ

9 And the sun and the moon are joined together.

١٠ يَقُولُ الْإِنْسَانُ يَوْمَئِذٍ أَيْنَ الْمَفَرُّ

10 On that Day, man will say, "Where is the escape?"

١١ كَلَّا لَا وَزَرَ

11 No indeed! There is no refuge.

١٢ إِلَىٰ رَبِّكَ يَوْمَئِذٍ الْمُسْتَقَرُّ

12 To your Lord on that Day is the settlement.

12
53:42; 79:44

١٣ يُنَبَّأُ الْإِنْسَانُ يَوْمَئِذٍ بِمَا قَدَّمَ وَأَخَّرَ

13 On that Day man will be informed of everything he put forward, and everything he left behind.

13
10:30; 59:18; 81:14; 82:5

١٤ بَلِ الْإِنْسَانُ عَلَىٰ نَفْسِهِ بَصِيرَةٌ

14 And man will be evidence against himself.

15 Even as he presents his excuses. ١٥ وَلَوْ أَلْقَىٰ مَعَاذِيرَهُ

16 Do not wag your tongue with it, to hurry on with it. ١٦ لَا تُحَرِّكْ بِهِ لِسَانَكَ لِتَعْجَلَ بِهِ

16
20:114

17 Upon Us is its collection and its recitation. ١٧ إِنَّ عَلَيْنَا جَمْعَهُ وَقُرْآنَهُ

18 Then, when We have recited it, follow its recitation. ١٨ فَإِذَا قَرَأْنَاهُ فَاتَّبِعْ قُرْآنَهُ

19 Then upon Us is its explanation. ١٩ ثُمَّ إِنَّ عَلَيْنَا بَيَانَهُ

19
25:33

20 Alas, you love the fleeting life. ٢٠ كَلَّا بَلْ تُحِبُّونَ الْعَاجِلَةَ

21 And you disregard the Hereafter. ٢١ وَتَذَرُونَ الْآخِرَةَ

22 Faces on that Day will be radiant. ٢٢ وُجُوهٌ يَوْمَئِذٍ نَاضِرَةٌ

22–24
76:11, 20; 83:24

23 Looking towards their Lord. ٢٣ إِلَىٰ رَبِّهَا نَاظِرَةٌ

24 And faces on that Day will be gloomy. ٢٤ وَوُجُوهٌ يَوْمَئِذٍ بَاسِرَةٌ

25 Realizing that a back-breaker has befallen them. ٢٥ تَظُنُّ أَنْ يُفْعَلَ بِهَا فَاقِرَةٌ

26 Indeed, when it has reached the breast-bones. ٢٦ كَلَّا إِذَا بَلَغَتِ التَّرَاقِيَ

27 And it is said, "Who is the healer?" ٢٧ وَقِيلَ مَنْ ۜ رَاقٍ

28 And He realizes that it is the parting. ٢٨ وَظَنَّ أَنَّهُ الْفِرَاقُ

29 And leg is entwined with leg. ٢٩ وَالْتَفَّتِ السَّاقُ بِالسَّاقِ

30 To your Lord on that Day is the drive. ٣٠ إِلَىٰ رَبِّكَ يَوْمَئِذٍ الْمَسَاقُ

31 He neither believed nor prayed. ٣١ فَلَا صَدَّقَ وَلَا صَلَّىٰ

٣٢ وَلَٰكِن كَذَّبَ وَتَوَلَّىٰ

32 But he denied and turned away.

٣٣ ثُمَّ ذَهَبَ إِلَىٰ أَهْلِهِ يَتَمَطَّىٰ

33 Then he went to his family, full of pride.

٣٤ أَوْلَىٰ لَكَ فَأَوْلَىٰ

34 Woe to you; and woe.

٣٥ ثُمَّ أَوْلَىٰ لَكَ فَأَوْلَىٰ

35 Then again: Woe to you; and woe.

٣٦ أَيَحْسَبُ ٱلْإِنسَٰنُ أَن يُتْرَكَ سُدًى

36 Does man think that he will be left without purpose?

٣٧ أَلَمْ يَكُ نُطْفَةً مِّن مَّنِيٍّ يُمْنَىٰ

37 Was he not a drop of ejaculated semen?

37–38
18:37; 23:115; 53:45; 76:2

٣٨ ثُمَّ كَانَ عَلَقَةً فَخَلَقَ فَسَوَّىٰ

38 Then he became a clot. And He created and proportioned?

٣٩ فَجَعَلَ مِنْهُ ٱلزَّوْجَيْنِ ٱلذَّكَرَ وَٱلْأُنثَىٰ

39 And made of him the two sexes, the male and the female?

39
53:45

٤٠ أَلَيْسَ ذَٰلِكَ بِقَٰدِرٍ عَلَىٰ أَن يُحْيِىَ ٱلْمَوْتَىٰ

40 Is He not Able to revive the dead?

Sūrah 76: Al-Insān

سُورَةُ ٱلْإِنْسَان (Man)
بِسْمِ ٱللَّهِ ٱلرَّحْمَٰنِ ٱلرَّحِيمِ

١ هَلْ أَتَىٰ عَلَى ٱلْإِنسَٰنِ حِينٌ مِّنَ ٱلدَّهْرِ لَمْ يَكُن شَيْئًا مَّذْكُورًا

1 Has there come upon man a period of time when he was nothing to be mentioned?

1
19:9; 19:67

٢ إِنَّا خَلَقْنَا ٱلْإِنسَٰنَ مِن نُّطْفَةٍ أَمْشَاجٍ نَّبْتَلِيهِ فَجَعَلْنَٰهُ سَمِيعًۢا بَصِيرًا

2 We created man from a liquid mixture, to test him; and We made him hearing and seeing.

2
18:37; 53:45; 75:37–38; 86:7; 91:8

٣ إِنَّا هَدَيْنَٰهُ ٱلسَّبِيلَ إِمَّا شَاكِرًا وَإِمَّا كَفُورًا

3 We guided him to the way, be he appreciative or unappreciative.

3
90:10

Sūrah 76: Al-Insān

٤ إِنَّا أَعْتَدْنَا لِلْكَافِرِينَ سَلَاسِلَ وَأَغْلَالًا وَسَعِيرًا	4	69:32; 73:12

4 We have prepared for the faithless chains, and yokes, and a Searing Fire.

٥ إِنَّ الْأَبْرَارَ يَشْرَبُونَ مِنْ كَأْسٍ كَانَ مِزَاجُهَا كَافُورًا	5	76:6, 17; 83:27

5 But the righteous will drink from a cup whose mixture is aroma.

٦ عَيْنًا يَشْرَبُ بِهَا عِبَادُ اللَّهِ يُفَجِّرُونَهَا تَفْجِيرًا	6	

6 A spring from which the servants of God will drink, making it gush abundantly.

٧ يُوفُونَ بِالنَّذْرِ وَيَخَافُونَ يَوْمًا كَانَ شَرُّهُ مُسْتَطِيرًا	7	22:29

7 They fulfill their vows, and dread a Day whose ill is widespread.

٨ وَيُطْعِمُونَ الطَّعَامَ عَلَىٰ حُبِّهِ مِسْكِينًا وَيَتِيمًا وَأَسِيرًا	8	2:177; 3:92

8 And they feed, for the love of Him, the poor, and the orphan, and the captive.

٩ إِنَّمَا نُطْعِمُكُمْ لِوَجْهِ اللَّهِ لَا نُرِيدُ مِنْكُمْ جَزَاءً وَلَا شُكُورًا	9	92:18–20

9 "We only feed you for the sake of God. We want from you neither compensation, nor gratitude.

١٠ إِنَّا نَخَافُ مِنْ رَبِّنَا يَوْمًا عَبُوسًا قَمْطَرِيرًا	10	

10 We dread from our Lord a frowning grim Day."

١١ فَوَقَاهُمُ اللَّهُ شَرَّ ذَٰلِكَ الْيَوْمِ وَلَقَّاهُمْ نَضْرَةً وَسُرُورًا	11	75:22

11 So God will protect them from the ills of that Day, and will grant them radiance and joy.

١٢ وَجَزَاهُمْ بِمَا صَبَرُوا جَنَّةً وَحَرِيرًا	12	

12 And will reward them for their patience with a Garden and silk.

١٣ مُتَّكِئِينَ فِيهَا عَلَى الْأَرَائِكِ ۖ لَا يَرَوْنَ فِيهَا شَمْسًا وَلَا زَمْهَرِيرًا	13	pp 83:23 18:31; 83:23, 35

13 Reclining therein on the thrones; experiencing therein neither sun, nor frost.

١٤ وَدَانِيَةً عَلَيْهِمْ ظِلَالُهَا وَذُلِّلَتْ قُطُوفُهَا تَذْلِيلًا	14	55:54; 69:22

14 Its shade hovering over them, and its fruit brought low within reach.

١٥ وَيُطَافُ عَلَيْهِمْ بِآنِيَةٍ مِنْ فِضَّةٍ وَأَكْوَابٍ كَانَتْ قَوَارِيرَ	15	37:45; 43:71; 52:23; 56:17

15 Passing around them are vessels of silver, and cups of crystal.

١٦ قَوَارِيرَ مِنْ فِضَّةٍ قَدَّرُوهَا تَقْدِيرًا	16	

16 Crystal of silver—they measured them exactly.

١٧ وَيُسْقَوْنَ فِيهَا كَأْسًا كَانَ مِزَاجُهَا زَنجَبِيلًا	**17**
17 They will be served therein with a cup whose flavor is Zanjabeel.	76:5; 83:27
١٨ عَيْنًا فِيهَا تُسَمَّىٰ سَلْسَبِيلًا	**18**
18 A spring therein named Salsabeel.	56:18
١٩ وَيَطُوفُ عَلَيْهِمْ وِلْدَانٌ مُخَلَّدُونَ إِذَا رَأَيْتَهُمْ حَسِبْتَهُمْ لُؤْلُؤًا مَنثُورًا	**19**
19 Passing among them are eternalized youths. If you see them, you would think them sprinkled pearls.	52:24; 56:17
٢٠ وَإِذَا رَأَيْتَ ثَمَّ رَأَيْتَ نَعِيمًا وَمُلْكًا كَبِيرًا	**20**
20 Wherever you look, you see bliss, and a vast kingdom.	75:22–23
٢١ عَالِيَهُمْ ثِيَابُ سُندُسٍ خُضْرٌ وَإِسْتَبْرَقٌ ۖ وَحُلُّوا أَسَاوِرَ مِن فِضَّةٍ وَسَقَاهُمْ رَبُّهُمْ شَرَابًا طَهُورًا	**21**
21 Upon them are garments of green silk, and satin. And they will be adorned with bracelets of silver. And their Lord will offer them a pure drink.	18:31; 22:33; 35:33; 44:53
٢٢ إِنَّ هَٰذَا كَانَ لَكُمْ جَزَاءً وَكَانَ سَعْيُكُم مَّشْكُورًا	
22 "This is a reward for you. Your efforts are well appreciated."	
٢٣ إِنَّا نَحْنُ نَزَّلْنَا عَلَيْكَ الْقُرْآنَ تَنزِيلًا	**23**
23 It is We who sent down the Qur'an upon you—a gradual revelation.	17:106; 25:32
٢٤ فَاصْبِرْ لِحُكْمِ رَبِّكَ وَلَا تُطِعْ مِنْهُمْ آثِمًا أَوْ كَفُورًا	
24 So be patient for the decision of your Lord, and do not obey the sinner or the blasphemer among them.	
٢٥ وَاذْكُرِ اسْمَ رَبِّكَ بُكْرَةً وَأَصِيلًا	
25 And mention the Name of your Lord, morning and evening.	
٢٦ وَمِنَ اللَّيْلِ فَاسْجُدْ لَهُ وَسَبِّحْهُ لَيْلًا طَوِيلًا	
26 And for part of the night, prostrate yourself to Him, and glorify Him long into the night.	
٢٧ إِنَّ هَٰؤُلَاءِ يُحِبُّونَ الْعَاجِلَةَ وَيَذَرُونَ وَرَاءَهُمْ يَوْمًا ثَقِيلًا	**27**
27 As for these: they love the fleeting life, and leave behind a Heavy Day.	17:18; 75:20–21
٢٨ نَحْنُ خَلَقْنَاهُمْ وَشَدَدْنَا أَسْرَهُمْ ۖ وَإِذَا شِئْنَا بَدَّلْنَا أَمْثَالَهُمْ تَبْدِيلًا	
28 We created them, and strengthened their frame; and whenever We will, We can replace them with others like them.	
٢٩ إِنَّ هَٰذِهِ تَذْكِرَةٌ ۖ فَمَن شَاءَ اتَّخَذَ إِلَىٰ رَبِّهِ سَبِيلًا	**29**
29 This is a reminder; so whoever wills, let him take a path to his Lord.	PP 73:19

30 وَمَا تَشَاءُونَ إِلَّا أَن يَشَاءَ اللَّهُ ۚ إِنَّ اللَّهَ كَانَ عَلِيمًا حَكِيمًا ٣٠

30 Yet you cannot will, unless God wills. God is Knowing and Wise.

31 يُدْخِلُ مَن يَشَاءُ فِي رَحْمَتِهِ ۚ وَالظَّالِمِينَ أَعَدَّ لَهُمْ عَذَابًا أَلِيمًا ٣١

31 He admits into His mercy whomever He wills. But as for the wrong-doers, He has prepared for them a painful punishment.

Sūrah 77: Al-Mursalāt

سُورَةُ ٱلْمُرْسَلَات (Unleased)

بِسْمِ ٱللَّهِ ٱلرَّحْمَٰنِ ٱلرَّحِيمِ

وَالْمُرْسَلَاتِ عُرْفًا ١

1 By those unleashed in succession.

فَالْعَاصِفَاتِ عَصْفًا ٢

2 Storming turbulently.

وَالنَّاشِرَاتِ نَشْرًا ٣

3 Scattering far and wide.

فَالْفَارِقَاتِ فَرْقًا ٤

4 Separating decisively.

فَالْمُلْقِيَاتِ ذِكْرًا ٥

5 Delivering a message.

عُذْرًا أَوْ نُذْرًا ٦

6 Excusing or warning.

إِنَّمَا تُوعَدُونَ لَوَاقِعٌ ٧

7 Surely what you are promised will happen.

7
51:5–6

فَإِذَا النُّجُومُ طُمِسَتْ ٨

8 When the stars are obliterated.

8
81:2

وَإِذَا السَّمَاءُ فُرِجَتْ ٩

9 And the sky is fractured.

9
82:1; 84:1

وَإِذَا الْجِبَالُ نُسِفَتْ ١٠

10 And the mountains are blown away.

10
20:105; 81:3

وَإِذَا الرُّسُلُ أُقِّتَتْ ١١

11 And the messengers are alerted.

12 لِأَيِّ يَوْمٍ أُجِّلَتْ ١٢

12 Until which day is it deferred?

13 لِيَوْمِ الْفَصْلِ ١٣

13 Until the Day of Decision.

13
37:21; 44:40; 77:38;
78:17; 82:14

14 وَمَا أَدْرَاكَ مَا يَوْمُ الْفَصْلِ ١٤

14 And what will teach you what the Day of Decision is?

15 وَيْلٌ يَوْمَئِذٍ لِّلْمُكَذِّبِينَ ١٥

15 Woe on that Day to the liars.

15
pp 77:19, 24, 28, 34, 37,
40, 45, 47, 49

16 أَلَمْ نُهْلِكِ الْأَوَّلِينَ ١٦

16 Did We not destroy the ancients?

17 ثُمَّ نُتْبِعُهُمُ الْآخِرِينَ ١٧

17 Then succeeded them with the others?

18 كَذَلِكَ نَفْعَلُ بِالْمُجْرِمِينَ ١٨

18 This is how We deal with the guilty.

19 وَيْلٌ يَوْمَئِذٍ لِّلْمُكَذِّبِينَ ١٩

19 Woe on that Day to the rejecters.

20 أَلَمْ نَخْلُقكُّم مِّن مَّاءٍ مَّهِينٍ ٢٠

20 Did We not create you from an insignificant fluid?

20
32:8

21 فَجَعَلْنَاهُ فِي قَرَارٍ مَّكِينٍ ٢١

21 Then lodged it in a secure place?

22 إِلَى قَدَرٍ مَّعْلُومٍ ٢٢

22 For a known term?

23 فَقَدَرْنَا فَنِعْمَ الْقَادِرُونَ ٢٣

23 We measured precisely. We are the best to measure.

24 وَيْلٌ يَوْمَئِذٍ لِّلْمُكَذِّبِينَ ٢٤

24 Woe on that Day to the falsifiers.

25 أَلَمْ نَجْعَلِ الْأَرْضَ كِفَاتًا ٢٥

25 Did We not make the earth a homestead?

26 أَحْيَاءً وَأَمْوَاتًا ٢٦

26 For the living and the dead?

27 And set on it lofty mountains, and given you pure water to drink?	٢٧ وَجَعَلْنَا فِيهَا رَوَاسِيَ شَامِخَاتٍ وَأَسْقَيْنَاكُم مَّاءً فُرَاتًا	27 41:10
28 Woe on that Day to the deniers.	٢٨ وَيْلٌ يَوْمَئِذٍ لِّلْمُكَذِّبِينَ	
29 "Proceed to what you used to deny."	٢٩ انطَلِقُوا إِلَىٰ مَا كُنتُم بِهِ تُكَذِّبُونَ	29 34:42
30 "Proceed to a shadow of three different masses."	٣٠ انطَلِقُوا إِلَىٰ ظِلٍّ ذِي ثَلَاثِ شُعَبٍ	
31 Offering no shade, and unavailing against the flames.	٣١ لَّا ظَلِيلٍ وَلَا يُغْنِي مِنَ اللَّهَبِ	
32 It shoots sparks as castles.	٣٢ إِنَّهَا تَرْمِي بِشَرَرٍ كَالْقَصْرِ	
33 As if they were yellow camels.	٣٣ كَأَنَّهُ جِمَالَتٌ صُفْرٌ	
34 Woe on that Day to the liars.	٣٤ وَيْلٌ يَوْمَئِذٍ لِّلْمُكَذِّبِينَ	
35 This is a Day when they will not speak.	٣٥ هَٰذَا يَوْمُ لَا يَنطِقُونَ	35 27:85; 30:57; 36:65
36 And they will not be allowed to apologize.	٣٦ وَلَا يُؤْذَنُ لَهُمْ فَيَعْتَذِرُونَ	
37 Woe on that Day to the rejecters.	٣٧ وَيْلٌ يَوْمَئِذٍ لِّلْمُكَذِّبِينَ	
38 This is the Day of Separation; We have gathered you, together with the ancients.	٣٨ هَٰذَا يَوْمُ الْفَصْلِ ۖ جَمَعْنَاكُمْ وَالْأَوَّلِينَ	38 37:21; 44:40; 77:13–14; 78:17
39 So if you have a strategy, use it against Me.	٣٩ فَإِن كَانَ لَكُمْ كَيْدٌ فَكِيدُونِ	
40 Woe on that Day to the falsifiers.	٤٠ وَيْلٌ يَوْمَئِذٍ لِّلْمُكَذِّبِينَ	
41 The righteous will be amidst shades and fountains.	٤١ إِنَّ الْمُتَّقِينَ فِي ظِلَالٍ وَعُيُونٍ	
42 And fruits as they desire.	٤٢ وَفَوَاكِهَ مِمَّا يَشْتَهُونَ	42 52:22; 56:20

	٤٣ كُلُوا وَاشْرَبُوا هَنِيئًا بِمَا كُنتُمْ تَعْمَلُونَ	43
43 "Eat and drink pleasantly, for what you used to do."		52:19

٤٤ إِنَّا كَذَٰلِكَ نَجْزِي الْمُحْسِنِينَ

44 This is how We reward the doers of good.

٤٥ وَيْلٌ يَوْمَئِذٍ لِّلْمُكَذِّبِينَ

45 Woe on that Day to the deniers.

	٤٦ كُلُوا وَتَمَتَّعُوا قَلِيلًا إِنَّكُم مُّجْرِمُونَ	46
46 "Eat and enjoy yourselves a little; you are indeed criminals."		39:8

٤٧ وَيْلٌ يَوْمَئِذٍ لِّلْمُكَذِّبِينَ

47 Woe on that Day to the liars.

٤٨ وَإِذَا قِيلَ لَهُمُ ارْكَعُوا لَا يَرْكَعُونَ

48 And when it is said to them, "Kneel", they do not kneel.

٤٩ وَيْلٌ يَوْمَئِذٍ لِّلْمُكَذِّبِينَ

49 Woe on that Day to the rejecters.

	٥٠ فَبِأَيِّ حَدِيثٍ بَعْدَهُ يُؤْمِنُونَ	50
50 In what message, beyond this, will they believe?		pp 7:185; 45:6

Sūrah 78: Al-Naba'

سُورَةُ ٱلنَّبَأ (The Event)

بِسْمِ ٱللَّهِ ٱلرَّحْمَٰنِ ٱلرَّحِيمِ

١ عَمَّ يَتَسَاءَلُونَ

1 What are they asking one another about?

٢ عَنِ النَّبَإِ الْعَظِيمِ

2 About the Great Event.

٣ الَّذِي هُمْ فِيهِ مُخْتَلِفُونَ

3 About which they disagree.

٤ كَلَّا سَيَعْلَمُونَ

4 Surely, they will find out.

٥ ثُمَّ كَلَّا سَيَعْلَمُونَ

5 Most certainly, they will find out.

	٦ أَلَمْ نَجْعَلِ الْأَرْضَ مِهَادًا	6
6 Did We not make the earth a cradle?		20:53

7 And the mountains pegs?	٧ وَالْجِبَالَ أَوْتَادًا	7 88:19
8 And created you in pairs?	٨ وَخَلَقْنَاكُمْ أَزْوَاجًا	8 36:36
9 And made your sleep for rest?	٩ وَجَعَلْنَا نَوْمَكُمْ سُبَاتًا	9–11 10:67; 25:47
10 And made the night a cover?	١٠ وَجَعَلْنَا اللَّيْلَ لِبَاسًا	
11 And made the day for livelihood?	١١ وَجَعَلْنَا النَّهَارَ مَعَاشًا	
12 And built above you seven strong ones?	١٢ وَبَنَيْنَا فَوْقَكُمْ سَبْعًا شِدَادًا	12 50:6
13 And placed a blazing lamp?	١٣ وَجَعَلْنَا سِرَاجًا وَهَّاجًا	13 25:61; 71:16
14 And brought down from the clouds pouring water?	١٤ وَأَنْزَلْنَا مِنَ الْمُعْصِرَاتِ مَاءً ثَجَّاجًا	14 50:9
15 To produce with it grains and vegetation?	١٥ لِنُخْرِجَ بِهِ حَبًّا وَنَبَاتًا	
16 And luxuriant gardens?	١٦ وَجَنَّاتٍ أَلْفَافًا	
17 The Day of Sorting has been appointed.	١٧ إِنَّ يَوْمَ الْفَصْلِ كَانَ مِيقَاتًا	17 37:21; 44:40; 77:23–24, 38
18 The Day when the Trumpet is blown, and you will come in droves.	١٨ يَوْمَ يُنْفَخُ فِي الصُّورِ فَتَأْتُونَ أَفْوَاجًا	
19 And the sky is opened up, and becomes gateways.	١٩ وَفُتِحَتِ السَّمَاءُ فَكَانَتْ أَبْوَابًا	19 54:11
20 And the mountains are set in motion, and become a mirage.	٢٠ وَسُيِّرَتِ الْجِبَالُ فَكَانَتْ سَرَابًا	20 18:47; 20:105; 27:88; 52:10; 81:3
21 Hell is lying in ambush.	٢١ إِنَّ جَهَنَّمَ كَانَتْ مِرْصَادًا	
22 For the oppressors, a destination.	٢٢ لِلطَّاغِينَ مَآبًا	

23 Where they will remain for eons.

٢٣ لَابِثِينَ فِيهَا أَحْقَابًا

24 They will taste therein neither coolness, nor drink.

٢٤ لَا يَذُوقُونَ فِيهَا بَرْدًا وَلَا شَرَابًا

24
38:24

25 Except boiling water, and freezing hail.

٢٥ إِلَّا حَمِيمًا وَغَسَّاقًا

25
38:57

26 A fitting requital.

٢٦ جَزَاءً وِفَاقًا

27 For they were not anticipating any reckoning.

٢٧ إِنَّهُمْ كَانُوا لَا يَرْجُونَ حِسَابًا

28 And they denied Our signs utterly.

٢٨ وَكَذَّبُوا بِآيَاتِنَا كِذَّابًا

29 But We have enumerated everything in writing.

٢٩ وَكُلَّ شَيْءٍ أَحْصَيْنَاهُ كِتَابًا

29
19:94

30 So taste! We will increase you only in suffering.

٣٠ فَذُوقُوا فَلَنْ نَزِيدَكُمْ إِلَّا عَذَابًا

31 But for the righteous there is triumph.

٣١ إِنَّ لِلْمُتَّقِينَ مَفَازًا

32 Gardens and vineyards.

٣٢ حَدَائِقَ وَأَعْنَابًا

33 And splendid spouses, well matched.

٣٣ وَكَوَاعِبَ أَتْرَابًا

34 And delicious drinks.

٣٤ وَكَأْسًا دِهَاقًا

34–35
52:23; 88:11

35 They will hear therein neither gossip, nor lies.

٣٥ لَا يَسْمَعُونَ فِيهَا لَغْوًا وَلَا كِذَّابًا

36 A reward from your Lord, a fitting gift.

٣٦ جَزَاءً مِنْ رَبِّكَ عَطَاءً حِسَابًا

37 Lord of the heavens and the earth, and everything between them— The Most Merciful—none can argue with Him.

٣٧ رَبِّ السَّمَاوَاتِ وَالْأَرْضِ وَمَا بَيْنَهُمَا الرَّحْمَٰنِ ۖ لَا يَمْلِكُونَ مِنْهُ خِطَابًا

38 On the Day when the Spirit and the angels stand in row. They will not speak, unless it be one permitted by the Most Merciful, and he will say what is right.

٣٨ يَوْمَ يَقُومُ الرُّوحُ وَالْمَلَائِكَةُ صَفًّا ۖ [a] لَا يَتَكَلَّمُونَ إِلَّا مَنْ أَذِنَ لَهُ الرَّحْمَٰنُ وَقَالَ صَوَابًا[b]

38
[a] 18:48; 89:22
[b] 11:105

39 ذَٰلِكَ ٱلْيَوْمُ ٱلْحَقُّ ۖ فَمَن شَآءَ ٱتَّخَذَ إِلَىٰ رَبِّهِۦ مَـَٔابًا ٣٩

39 That is the Day of Reality. So whoever wills, let him take a way back to his Lord.

39
73:19

40 إِنَّآ أَنذَرْنَٰكُمْ عَذَابًا قَرِيبًا يَوْمَ يَنظُرُ ٱلْمَرْءُ مَا قَدَّمَتْ يَدَاهُ[a] وَيَقُولُ ٱلْكَافِرُ يَٰلَيْتَنِى كُنتُ تُرَٰبًۢا[b] ٤٠

40 We have warned you of a near punishment—the Day when a person will observe what his hands have produced, and the faithless will say, "O, I wish I were dust."

40
[a] 59:18
[b] 4:42

Sūrah 79: Al-Nāziʿāt

سُورَةُ ٱلنَّازِعَات (The Snatchers)

بِسْمِ ٱللَّهِ ٱلرَّحْمَٰنِ ٱلرَّحِيمِ

وَٱلنَّٰزِعَٰتِ غَرْقًا ١

1 By those who snatch violently.

وَٱلنَّٰشِطَٰتِ نَشْطًا ٢

2 And those who remove gently.

وَٱلسَّٰبِحَٰتِ سَبْحًا ٣

3 And those who glide smoothly.

فَٱلسَّٰبِقَٰتِ سَبْقًا ٤

4 And those who race swiftly.

فَٱلْمُدَبِّرَٰتِ أَمْرًا ٥

5 And those who regulate events.

يَوْمَ تَرْجُفُ ٱلرَّاجِفَةُ ٦

6 On the Day when the Quake quakes.

6
73:14

تَتْبَعُهَا ٱلرَّادِفَةُ ٧

7 And is followed by the Successor.

قُلُوبٌ يَوْمَئِذٍ وَاجِفَةٌ ٨

8 Hearts on that Day will be pounding.

أَبْصَٰرُهَا خَٰشِعَةٌ ٩

9 Their sights downcast.

9
68:14; 70:44; 88:2

يَقُولُونَ أَءِنَّا لَمَرْدُودُونَ فِى ٱلْحَافِرَةِ ١٠

10 They say, "Are we to be restored to the original condition?

أَءِذَا كُنَّا عِظَٰمًا نَّخِرَةً ١١

11 When we have become hollow bones?"

١٢ قَالُوا تِلْكَ إِذًا كَرَّةٌ خَاسِرَةٌ		
12 They say, "This is a losing proposition."		
١٣ فَإِنَّمَا هِيَ زَجْرَةٌ وَاحِدَةٌ		13
13 But it will be only a single nudge.		37:19
١٤ فَإِذَا هُم بِالسَّاهِرَةِ		
14 And they will be awake.		
١٥ هَلْ أَتَاكَ حَدِيثُ مُوسَىٰ		15
15 Has the story of Moses reached you?		pp 20:9
١٦ إِذْ نَادَاهُ رَبُّهُ بِالْوَادِ الْمُقَدَّسِ طُوًى		16
16 When His Lord called out to him in the sacred valley of Tuwa.		19:52; 20:11–12; 27:29
١٧ اذْهَبْ إِلَىٰ فِرْعَوْنَ إِنَّهُ طَغَىٰ		17
17 "Go to Pharaoh—he has transgressed."		pp 20:24
١٨ فَقُلْ هَل لَّكَ إِلَىٰ أَن تَزَكَّىٰ		
18 And say, "Do you care to be cleansed?		
١٩ وَأَهْدِيَكَ إِلَىٰ رَبِّكَ فَتَخْشَىٰ		
19 And I will guide you to your Lord, and you will turn reverent."		
٢٠ فَأَرَاهُ الْآيَةَ الْكُبْرَىٰ		20
20 He showed him the Greatest Miracle.		20:23, 56
٢١ فَكَذَّبَ وَعَصَىٰ		21
21 But he denied and defied.		20:56
٢٢ ثُمَّ أَدْبَرَ يَسْعَىٰ		
22 Then turned his back, and tried.		
٢٣ فَحَشَرَ فَنَادَىٰ		
23 And gathered and proclaimed.		
٢٤ فَقَالَ أَنَا رَبُّكُمُ الْأَعْلَىٰ		24
24 He said, "I am your Lord, the most high."		26:29; 28:24
٢٥ فَأَخَذَهُ اللَّهُ نَكَالَ الْآخِرَةِ وَالْأُولَىٰ		
25 So God seized him with an exemplary punishment, in the last and in the first.		
٢٦ إِنَّ فِي ذَٰلِكَ لَعِبْرَةً لِّمَن يَخْشَىٰ		
26 In this is a lesson for whoever fears.		
٢٧ أَأَنتُمْ أَشَدُّ خَلْقًا أَمِ السَّمَاءُ ۚ بَنَاهَا		27
27 Are you more difficult to create, or the heaven? He constructed it.		40:57

٢٨ رَفَعَ سَمْكَهَا فَسَوَّاهَا

28 He raised its masses, and proportioned it.

٢٩ وَأَغْطَشَ لَيْلَهَا وَأَخْرَجَ ضُحَاهَا

29 And He dimmed its night, and brought out its daylight.

٣٠ وَالْأَرْضَ بَعْدَ ذَٰلِكَ دَحَاهَا

30 And the earth after that He spread.

٣١ أَخْرَجَ مِنْهَا مَاءَهَا وَمَرْعَاهَا

31 And from it, He produced its water and its pasture.

٣٢ وَالْجِبَالَ أَرْسَاهَا

32
20:54; 87:4

32 And the mountains, He anchored.

٣٣ مَتَاعًا لَكُمْ وَلِأَنْعَامِكُمْ

33
pp 81:32

33 A source of enjoyment for you and for your animals.

٣٤ فَإِذَا جَاءَتِ الطَّامَّةُ الْكُبْرَىٰ

34
81:33

34 But when the Great Cataclysm arrives.

٣٥ يَوْمَ يَتَذَكَّرُ الْإِنْسَانُ مَا سَعَىٰ

35 A Day when man will remember what he has endeavored.

٣٦ وَبُرِّزَتِ الْجَحِيمُ لِمَنْ يَرَىٰ

36
26:91

36 And Hell will be displayed to whoever sees.

٣٧ فَأَمَّا مَنْ طَغَىٰ

37 As for him who was defiant.

٣٨ وَآثَرَ الْحَيَاةَ الدُّنْيَا

38
87:16

38 And preferred the life of this world.

٣٩ فَإِنَّ الْجَحِيمَ هِيَ الْمَأْوَىٰ

39 Then Hell is the shelter.

٤٠ وَأَمَّا مَنْ خَافَ مَقَامَ رَبِّهِ وَنَهَى النَّفْسَ عَنِ الْهَوَىٰ

40
55:46

40 But as for him who feared the Standing of his Lord, and restrained the self from desires.

٤١ فَإِنَّ الْجَنَّةَ هِيَ الْمَأْوَىٰ

41 Then Paradise is the shelter.

٤٢ يَسْأَلُونَكَ عَنِ السَّاعَةِ أَيَّانَ مُرْسَاهَا

42 They ask you about the Hour, "When will it take place?"

٤٣ فِيمَ أَنْتَ مِنْ ذِكْرَاهَا

43 You have no knowledge of it.

44 To your Lord is its finality.	٤٤ إِلَىٰ رَبِّكَ مُنتَهَىٰهَآ	44 53:42; 75:12
45 You are just a warner for whoever dreads it.	٤٥ إِنَّمَآ أَنتَ مُنذِرُ مَن يَخْشَىٰهَا	
46 On the Day when they witness it—as though they only stayed an evening, or its morning.	٤٦ كَأَنَّهُمْ يَوْمَ يَرَوْنَهَا لَمْ يَلْبَثُوٓا۟ إِلَّا عَشِيَّةً أَوْ ضُحَىٰهَا	46 10:45

Sūrah 80: ʿAbasa

سُورَةُ عَبَسَ (He Frowned)

بِسْمِ ٱللَّهِ ٱلرَّحْمَٰنِ ٱلرَّحِيمِ

1 He frowned and turned away.	١ عَبَسَ وَتَوَلَّىٰٓ	
2 When the blind man approached him.	٢ أَن جَآءَهُ ٱلْأَعْمَىٰ	
3 But how do you know? Perhaps he was seeking to purify himself.	٣ وَمَا يُدْرِيكَ لَعَلَّهُۥ يَزَّكَّىٰٓ	3 80:7; 92:10
4 Or be reminded, and the message would benefit him.	٤ أَوْ يَذَّكَّرُ فَتَنفَعَهُ ٱلذِّكْرَىٰٓ	4 47:18; 51:55; 87:9
5 But as for him who was indifferent.	٥ أَمَّا مَنِ ٱسْتَغْنَىٰ	
6 You gave him your attention.	٦ فَأَنتَ لَهُۥ تَصَدَّىٰ	
7 Though you are not liable if he does not purify himself.	٧ وَمَا عَلَيْكَ أَلَّا يَزَّكَّىٰ	7 80:3
8 But as for him who came to you seeking.	٨ وَأَمَّا مَن جَآءَكَ يَسْعَىٰ	
9 In awe.	٩ وَهُوَ يَخْشَىٰ	
10 To him you were inattentive.	١٠ فَأَنتَ عَنْهُ تَلَهَّىٰ	

11 Do not. This is a Lesson.

١١ كَلَّا إِنَّهَا تَذْكِرَةٌ

12 Whoever wills, shall remember it.

١٢ فَمَنْ شَاءَ ذَكَرَهُ

13 On honorable pages.

١٣ فِي صُحُفٍ مُكَرَّمَةٍ

13–16
56:77–80; 85:21;
98:2–3

14 Exalted and purified.

١٤ مَرْفُوعَةٍ مُطَهَّرَةٍ

15 By the hands of scribes.

١٥ بِأَيْدِي سَفَرَةٍ

16 Noble and devoted.

١٦ كِرَامٍ بَرَرَةٍ

17 Perish man! How thankless he is!

١٧ قُتِلَ الْإِنْسَانُ مَا أَكْفَرَهُ

18 From what did He create him?

١٨ مِنْ أَيِّ شَيْءٍ خَلَقَهُ

18–20
16:4

19 From a sperm drop He created him, and enabled him.

١٩ مِنْ نُطْفَةٍ خَلَقَهُ فَقَدَّرَهُ

20 Then He eased the way for him.

٢٠ ثُمَّ السَّبِيلَ يَسَّرَهُ

21 Then He puts him to death, and buries him.

٢١ ثُمَّ أَمَاتَهُ فَأَقْبَرَهُ

22 Then, when He wills, He will resurrect him.

٢٢ ثُمَّ إِذَا شَاءَ أَنْشَرَهُ

23 But no, he did not fulfill what He has commanded him.

٢٣ كَلَّا لَمَّا يَقْضِ مَا أَمَرَهُ

24 Let man consider his food.

٢٤ فَلْيَنْظُرِ الْإِنْسَانُ إِلَىٰ طَعَامِهِ

25 We pour down water in abundance.

٢٥ أَنَّا صَبَبْنَا الْمَاءَ صَبًّا

26 Then crack the soil open.

٢٦ ثُمَّ شَقَقْنَا الْأَرْضَ شَقًّا

27 And grow in it grains.	٢٧ فَأَنْبَتْنَا فِيهَا حَبًّا	**27** 6:99; 36:33; 50:9
28 And grapes and herbs.	٢٨ وَعِنَبًا وَقَضْبًا	
29 And olives and dates.	٢٩ وَزَيْتُونًا وَنَخْلًا	
30 And luscious gardens.	٣٠ وَحَدَائِقَ غُلْبًا	
31 And fruits and vegetables.	٣١ وَفَاكِهَةً وَأَبًّا	
32 Enjoyment for you, and for your livestock.	٣٢ مَتَاعًا لَكُمْ وَلِأَنْعَامِكُمْ	**32** pp 79:33
33 But when the Deafening Noise comes to pass.	٣٣ فَإِذَا جَاءَتِ الصَّاخَّةُ	**33** 79:34
34 The Day when a person will flee from his brother.	٣٤ يَوْمَ يَفِرُّ الْمَرْءُ مِنْ أَخِيهِ	
35 And his mother and his father.	٣٥ وَأُمِّهِ وَأَبِيهِ	
36 And his consort and his children.	٣٦ وَصَاحِبَتِهِ وَبَنِيهِ	
37 Every one of them, on that Day, will have enough to preoccupy him.	٣٧ لِكُلِّ امْرِئٍ مِنْهُمْ يَوْمَئِذٍ شَأْنٌ يُغْنِيهِ	
38 Faces on that Day will be radiant.	٣٨ وُجُوهٌ يَوْمَئِذٍ مُسْفِرَةٌ	**38–39** 57:12; 76:11
39 Laughing and rejoicing.	٣٩ ضَاحِكَةٌ مُسْتَبْشِرَةٌ	
40 And Faces on that Day will be covered with misery.	٤٠ وَوُجُوهٌ يَوْمَئِذٍ عَلَيْهَا غَبَرَةٌ	**40–41** 10:26; 68:43; 70:44
41 Overwhelmed by remorse.	٤١ تَرْهَقُهَا قَتَرَةٌ	
42 These are the faithless, the vicious.	٤٢ أُولَٰئِكَ هُمُ الْكَفَرَةُ الْفَجَرَةُ	

Sūrah 81: Al-Takwīr

سُورَةُ ٱلتَّكْوِيرِ (The Rolling)

بِسْمِ ٱللَّهِ ٱلرَّحْمَٰنِ ٱلرَّحِيمِ

١ إِذَا ٱلشَّمْسُ كُوِّرَتْ

1 When the sun is rolled up.

٢ وَإِذَا ٱلنُّجُومُ ٱنكَدَرَتْ

2 77:8; 82:2

2 When the stars are dimmed.

٣ وَإِذَا ٱلْجِبَالُ سُيِّرَتْ

3 18:47; 20:105; 52:10; 78:20

3 When the mountains are set in motion.

٤ وَإِذَا ٱلْعِشَارُ عُطِّلَتْ

4 When the relationships are suspended.

٥ وَإِذَا ٱلْوُحُوشُ حُشِرَتْ

5 When the beasts are gathered.

٦ وَإِذَا ٱلْبِحَارُ سُجِّرَتْ

6 52:6; 82:3

6 When the oceans are set aflame.

٧ وَإِذَا ٱلنُّفُوسُ زُوِّجَتْ

7 37:22

7 When the souls are paired.

٨ وَإِذَا ٱلْمَوْءُودَةُ سُئِلَتْ

8 6:137; 16:58

8 When the girl, buried alive, is asked:

٩ بِأَيِّ ذَنبٍ قُتِلَتْ

9 For what crime was she killed?

١٠ وَإِذَا ٱلصُّحُفُ نُشِرَتْ

10 17:13

10 When the records are made public.

١١ وَإِذَا ٱلسَّمَاءُ كُشِطَتْ

11 21:104; 25:25; 55:37; 69:18

11 When the sky is peeled away.

١٢ وَإِذَا ٱلْجَحِيمُ سُعِّرَتْ

12 22:3

12 When the Fire is set ablaze.

١٣ وَإِذَا ٱلْجَنَّةُ أُزْلِفَتْ

13 26:90; 50:31

13 When Paradise is brought near.

١٤ عَلِمَتْ نَفْسٌ مَّا أَحْضَرَتْ

14 3:30; 18:49; 30:3; 75:13; 82:5

14 Each soul will know what it has readied.

15 I swear by the galaxies.	فَلَا أُقْسِمُ بِالْخُنَّسِ ١٥	**15** 84:16–18
16 Precisely running their courses.	الْجَوَارِ الْكُنَّسِ ١٦	
17 And by the night as it recedes.	وَاللَّيْلِ إِذَا عَسْعَسَ ١٧	**17** 92:1; 93:2
18 And by the morn as it breathes.	وَالصُّبْحِ إِذَا تَنَفَّسَ ١٨	
19 This is the speech of a noble messenger.	إِنَّهُ لَقَوْلُ رَسُولٍ كَرِيمٍ ١٩	**19** pp 69:40
20 Endowed with power, eminent with the Lord of the Throne.	ذِي قُوَّةٍ عِنْدَ ذِي الْعَرْشِ مَكِينٍ ٢٠	
21 Obeyed and honest.	مُطَاعٍ ثَمَّ أَمِينٍ ٢١	
22 Your friend is not possessed.	وَمَا صَاحِبُكُم بِمَجْنُونٍ ٢٢	**22** 7:184
23 He saw him on the luminous horizon.	وَلَقَدْ رَآهُ بِالْأُفُقِ الْمُبِينِ ٢٣	**23** 42:51; 53:7, 13
24 And He does not withhold knowledge of the Unseen.	وَمَا هُوَ عَلَى الْغَيْبِ بِضَنِينٍ ٢٤	
25 And it is not the word of an accursed devil.	وَمَا هُوَ بِقَوْلِ شَيْطَانٍ رَجِيمٍ ٢٥	**25** 21:5; 69:41
26 So where are you heading?	فَأَيْنَ تَذْهَبُونَ ٢٦	
27 It is only a Reminder to all mankind.	إِنْ هُوَ إِلَّا ذِكْرٌ لِلْعَالَمِينَ ٢٧	
28 To whoever of you wills to go straight.	لِمَن شَاءَ مِنكُمْ أَن يَسْتَقِيمَ ٢٨	**28** 74:55; 76:29
29 But you cannot will, unless God wills—The Lord of the Worlds.	وَمَا تَشَاءُونَ إِلَّا أَن يَشَاءَ اللَّهُ رَبُّ الْعَالَمِينَ ٢٩	

Sūrah 82: Al-Infiṭār

سُورَةُ ٱلْإِنْفِطَار (The Shattering)

بِسْمِ ٱللَّهِ ٱلرَّحْمَٰنِ ٱلرَّحِيمِ

1 When the sky breaks apart.	١ إِذَا ٱلسَّمَاءُ ٱنْفَطَرَتْ	**1** 73:18; 84:1
2 When the planets are scattered.	٢ وَإِذَا ٱلْكَوَاكِبُ ٱنْتَثَرَتْ	**2**
3 When the oceans are exploded.	٣ وَإِذَا ٱلْبِحَارُ فُجِّرَتْ	**3** 81:6
4 When the tombs are strewn around.	٤ وَإِذَا ٱلْقُبُورُ بُعْثِرَتْ	**4** 50:44; 99:2; 100:9
5 Each soul will know what it has advanced, and what it has deferred.	٥ عَلِمَتْ نَفْسٌ مَا قَدَّمَتْ وَأَخَّرَتْ	**5** 75:13
6 O man! What deluded you concerning your Lord, the Most Generous?	٦ يَا أَيُّهَا ٱلْإِنْسَانُ مَا غَرَّكَ بِرَبِّكَ ٱلْكَرِيمِ	**6**
7 He Who created you, and formed you, and proportioned you?	٧ ٱلَّذِي خَلَقَكَ فَسَوَّاكَ فَعَدَلَكَ	**7** 18:37
8 In whatever shape He willed, He assembled you.	٨ فِي أَيِّ صُورَةٍ مَا شَاءَ رَكَّبَكَ	**8** 3:6
9 But you reject the religion.	٩ كَلَّا بَلْ تُكَذِّبُونَ بِٱلدِّينِ	**9** 107:1
10 Though over you are watchers.	١٠ وَإِنَّ عَلَيْكُمْ لَحَافِظِينَ	**10–12** 6:61; 13:11
11 Honest recorders.	١١ كِرَامًا كَاتِبِينَ	
12 They know everything you do.	١٢ يَعْلَمُونَ مَا تَفْعَلُونَ	
13 The virtuous will be in bliss.	١٣ إِنَّ ٱلْأَبْرَارَ لَفِي نَعِيمٍ	**13** pp 9:21–22; 83:22
14 While the wicked will be in Hell.	١٤ وَإِنَّ ٱلْفُجَّارَ لَفِي جَحِيمٍ	**14** 77:13

١٥ يَصْلَوْنَهَا يَوْمَ الدِّينِ

15 They will enter it on the Day of Justice.

١٦ وَمَا هُمْ عَنْهَا بِغَائِبِينَ

16 And they will not be absent from it.

16
2:167

١٧ وَمَا أَدْرَاكَ مَا يَوْمُ الدِّينِ

17 But what will convey to you what the Day of Judgment is?

17–19
1:4

١٨ ثُمَّ مَا أَدْرَاكَ مَا يَوْمُ الدِّينِ

18 Then again, what will convey to you what the Day of Judgment is?

١٩ يَوْمَ لَا تَمْلِكُ نَفْسٌ لِنَفْسٍ شَيْئًا ۖ وَالْأَمْرُ يَوْمَئِذٍ لِلَّهِ

19 The Day when no soul will avail another soul anything; and the decision on that Day is God's.

19
3:145; 99:6–7; 101:4

Sūrah 83: Al-Muṭaffifīn

سُوۡرَةُ ٱلۡمُطَفِّفِينَ (The Defrauders)

بِسْمِ ٱللَّهِ ٱلرَّحْمَـٰنِ ٱلرَّحِيمِ

١ وَيْلٌ لِلْمُطَفِّفِينَ

1 Woe to the defrauders.

٢ الَّذِينَ إِذَا اكْتَالُوا عَلَى النَّاسِ يَسْتَوْفُونَ

2 Those who, when they take a measure from people, they take in full.

٣ وَإِذَا كَالُوهُمْ أَوْ وَزَنُوهُمْ يُخْسِرُونَ

3 But when they measure or weigh to others, they cheat.

٤ أَلَا يَظُنُّ أُولَٰئِكَ أَنَّهُمْ مَبْعُوثُونَ

4 Do these not know that they will be resurrected?

٥ لِيَوْمٍ عَظِيمٍ

5 For a Great Day?

٦ يَوْمَ يَقُومُ النَّاسُ لِرَبِّ الْعَالَمِينَ

6 The Day when mankind will stand before the Lord of the Worlds?

٧ كَلَّا إِنَّ كِتَابَ الْفُجَّارِ لَفِي سِجِّينٍ

7 Not at all. The record of the wicked is in Sijjeen.

٨ وَمَا أَدْرَاكَ مَا سِجِّينٌ

8 But how can you know what Sijjeen is?

٩ كِتَابٌ مَرْقُومٌ

9 A numerical book.

١٠ وَيْلٌ يَوْمَئِذٍ لِلْمُكَذِّبِينَ

10 Woe on that Day to the deniers.

10
52:11; 77:15

١١ الَّذِينَ يُكَذِّبُونَ بِيَوْمِ الدِّينِ

11 Those who deny the Day of Reckoning.

11
74:46; 107:1

١٢ وَمَا يُكَذِّبُ بِهِ إِلَّا كُلُّ مُعْتَدٍ أَثِيمٍ

12 But none denies it except the sinful aggressor.

12
68:12

١٣ إِذَا تُتْلَىٰ عَلَيْهِ آيَاتُنَا قَالَ أَسَاطِيرُ الْأَوَّلِينَ

13 When Our revelations are recited to him, he says, "Legends of the ancients."

13
6:25; 8:31; 68:15

١٤ كَلَّا ۖ بَلْ ۜ رَانَ عَلَىٰ قُلُوبِهِمْ مَا كَانُوا يَكْسِبُونَ

14 Not at all. Their hearts have become corroded by what they used to earn.

١٥ كَلَّا إِنَّهُمْ عَنْ رَبِّهِمْ يَوْمَئِذٍ لَمَحْجُوبُونَ

15 Not at all. On that Day, they will be screened from their Lord.

١٦ ثُمَّ إِنَّهُمْ لَصَالُو الْجَحِيمِ

16 Then they will roast in Hell.

١٧ ثُمَّ يُقَالُ هَٰذَا الَّذِي كُنْتُمْ بِهِ تُكَذِّبُونَ

17 Then it will be said, "This is what you used to deny."

17
32:20; 34:42; 52:14

١٨ كَلَّا إِنَّ كِتَابَ الْأَبْرَارِ لَفِي عِلِّيِّينَ

18 No indeed; the record of the righteous is in Elliyyīn.

١٩ وَمَا أَدْرَاكَ مَا عِلِّيُّونَ

19 But how can you know what Elliyyūn is?

٢٠ كِتَابٌ مَرْقُومٌ

20 A numerical book.

٢١ يَشْهَدُهُ الْمُقَرَّبُونَ

21 Witnessed by those brought near.

٢٢ إِنَّ الْأَبْرَارَ لَفِي نَعِيمٍ

22 Indeed, the righteous will be amid bliss.

22
pp 82:13

٢٣ عَلَى الْأَرَائِكِ يَنْظُرُونَ

23 On thrones, looking on.

23
pp 83:35

٢٤ تَعْرِفُ فِي وُجُوهِهِمْ نَضْرَةَ النَّعِيمِ

24 You will recognize on their faces the radiance of bliss.

24
75:22

	يُسْقَوْنَ مِنْ رَحِيقٍ مَخْتُومٍ ٢٥	**25–28**
25 They will be given to drink a sealed wine.		76:5, 17
	خِتَامُهُ مِسْكٌ ۚ وَفِي ذَٰلِكَ فَلْيَتَنَافَسِ الْمُتَنَافِسُونَ ٢٦	
26 Whose seal is musk—this is what competitors should compete for.		
	وَمِزَاجُهُ مِنْ تَسْنِيمٍ ٢٧	
27 Its mixture is of Tasneem.		
	عَيْنًا يَشْرَبُ بِهَا الْمُقَرَّبُونَ ٢٨	
28 A spring from which those brought near drink.		
	إِنَّ الَّذِينَ أَجْرَمُوا كَانُوا مِنَ الَّذِينَ آمَنُوا يَضْحَكُونَ ٢٩	**29**
29 Those who committed crimes used to laugh at those who believed.		11:38; 23:110
	وَإِذَا مَرُّوا بِهِمْ يَتَغَامَزُونَ ٣٠	
30 And when they passed by them, they would wink at one another.		
	وَإِذَا انْقَلَبُوا إِلَىٰ أَهْلِهِمُ انْقَلَبُوا فَكِهِينَ ٣١	
31 And when they went back to their families, they would go back exulting.		
	وَإِذَا رَأَوْهُمْ قَالُوا إِنَّ هَٰؤُلَاءِ لَضَالُّونَ ٣٢	**32**
32 And if they saw them, they would say, "These people are lost."		30:58
	وَمَا أُرْسِلُوا عَلَيْهِمْ حَافِظِينَ ٣٣	
33 Yet they were not sent as guardians over them.		
	فَالْيَوْمَ الَّذِينَ آمَنُوا مِنَ الْكُفَّارِ يَضْحَكُونَ ٣٤	**34**
34 But on that Day, those who believed will laugh at the unbelievers.		2:212
	عَلَى الْأَرَائِكِ يَنْظُرُونَ ٣٥	**35**
35 On luxurious furnishings, looking on.		pp 83:23
	هَلْ ثُوِّبَ الْكُفَّارُ مَا كَانُوا يَفْعَلُونَ ٣٦	
36 Have the unbelievers been repaid for what they used to do?		

Sūrah 84: Al-Inshiqāq

سُورَةُ ٱلْإِنْشِقَاق (The Rupture)

بِسْمِ ٱللَّهِ ٱلرَّحْمَٰنِ ٱلرَّحِيم

1 When the sky is ruptured.	إِذَا ٱلسَّمَاءُ ٱنْشَقَّتْ	١	**1** 82:1
2 And hearkens to its Lord, as it must.	وَأَذِنَتْ لِرَبِّهَا وَحُقَّتْ	٢	**2** pp 84:5
3 And when the earth is leveled out.	وَإِذَا ٱلْأَرْضُ مُدَّتْ	٣	
4 And casts out what is in it, and becomes empty.	وَأَلْقَتْ مَا فِيهَا وَتَخَلَّتْ	٤	**4** 50:44; 99:2
5 And hearkens to its Lord, as it must.	وَأَذِنَتْ لِرَبِّهَا وَحُقَّتْ	٥	**5** pp 84:2
6 O man! You are laboring towards your Lord, and you will meet Him.	يَا أَيُّهَا ٱلْإِنْسَانُ إِنَّكَ كَادِحٌ إِلَىٰ رَبِّكَ كَدْحًا فَمُلَاقِيهِ	٦	
7 As for him who is given his book in his right hand.	فَأَمَّا مَنْ أُوتِيَ كِتَابَهُ بِيَمِينِهِ	٧	**7** 17:71; 69:19
8 He will have an easy settlement.	فَسَوْفَ يُحَاسَبُ حِسَابًا يَسِيرًا	٨	
9 And will return to his family delighted.	وَيَنْقَلِبُ إِلَىٰ أَهْلِهِ مَسْرُورًا	٩	
10 But as for him who is given his book behind his back.	وَأَمَّا مَنْ أُوتِيَ كِتَابَهُ وَرَاءَ ظَهْرِهِ	١٠	**10** 69:25
11 He will call for death.	فَسَوْفَ يَدْعُو ثُبُورًا	١١	**11** 25:13–14
12 And will enter the Blaze.	وَيَصْلَىٰ سَعِيرًا	١٢	
13 He used to be happy among his family.	إِنَّهُ كَانَ فِي أَهْلِهِ مَسْرُورًا	١٣	
14 He thought he would never return.	إِنَّهُ ظَنَّ أَنْ لَنْ يَحُورَ	١٤	
15 In fact, his Lord was watching him.	بَلَىٰ إِنَّ رَبَّهُ كَانَ بِهِ بَصِيرًا	١٥	

16 I swear by the twilight.	١٦ فَلَا أُقْسِمُ بِالشَّفَقِ	16–18 56:75; 69:38; 70:40; 81:15
17 And by the night, and what it covers.	١٧ وَاللَّيْلِ وَمَا وَسَقَ	
18 And by the moon, as it grows full.	١٨ وَالْقَمَرِ إِذَا اتَّسَقَ	
19 You will mount stage by stage.	١٩ لَتَرْكَبُنَّ طَبَقًا عَنْ طَبَقٍ	
20 What is the matter with them that they do not believe?	٢٠ فَمَا لَهُمْ لَا يُؤْمِنُونَ	
21 And when the Qur'an is read to them, they do not bow down?	٢١ وَإِذَا قُرِئَ عَلَيْهِمُ الْقُرْآنُ لَا يَسْجُدُونَ ۩	
22 In fact, those who disbelieve are in denial.	٢٢ بَلِ الَّذِينَ كَفَرُوا يُكَذِّبُونَ	22 85:19
23 But God knows what they hide inside.	٢٣ وَاللَّهُ أَعْلَمُ بِمَا يُوعُونَ	
24 So inform them of a painful punishment.	٢٤ فَبَشِّرْهُمْ بِعَذَابٍ أَلِيمٍ	24 3:21; 9:34
25 Except those who believe and do good deeds; they will have an undiminished reward.	٢٥ إِلَّا الَّذِينَ آمَنُوا وَعَمِلُوا الصَّالِحَاتِ لَهُمْ أَجْرٌ غَيْرُ مَمْنُونٍ	25 41:8; 95:6

Sūrah 85: Al-Burūj

سُورَةُ ٱلْبُرُوج (The Constellation)

بِسْمِ ٱللَّهِ ٱلرَّحْمَٰنِ ٱلرَّحِيمِ

1 By the sky with the constellations.	١ وَالسَّمَاءِ ذَاتِ الْبُرُوجِ	1 15:16; 25:61
2 And by the Promised Day.	٢ وَالْيَوْمِ الْمَوْعُودِ	2 21:103; 36:52; 43:83
3 And by the witness and the witnessed.	٣ وَشَاهِدٍ وَمَشْهُودٍ	3 11:103

٤ قُتِلَ أَصْحَابُ الْأُخْدُودِ

4 Destroyed were the People of the Trench.

٥ النَّارِ ذَاتِ الْوَقُودِ

5 The fire supplied with fuel.

5
2:24; 66:6

٦ إِذْ هُمْ عَلَيْهَا قُعُودٌ

6 While they sat around it.

٧ وَهُمْ عَلَىٰ مَا يَفْعَلُونَ بِالْمُؤْمِنِينَ شُهُودٌ

7 And were witnessing what they did to the believers.

٨ وَمَا نَقَمُوا مِنْهُمْ إِلَّا أَن يُؤْمِنُوا بِاللَّهِ الْعَزِيزِ الْحَمِيدِ

8 They begrudged them only because they believed in God the Almighty, the Praiseworthy.

8
5:59; 7:126

٩ الَّذِي لَهُ مُلْكُ السَّمَاوَاتِ وَالْأَرْضِ ۚ وَاللَّهُ عَلَىٰ كُلِّ شَيْءٍ شَهِيدٌ

9 To Whom belongs the sovereignty of the heavens and the earth. God is witness over everything.

١٠ إِنَّ الَّذِينَ فَتَنُوا الْمُؤْمِنِينَ وَالْمُؤْمِنَاتِ ثُمَّ لَمْ يَتُوبُوا فَلَهُمْ عَذَابُ جَهَنَّمَ وَلَهُمْ عَذَابُ الْحَرِيقِ

10 Those who tempt the believers, men and women, then do not repent; for them is the punishment of Hell; for them is the punishment of Burning.

١١ إِنَّ الَّذِينَ آمَنُوا وَعَمِلُوا الصَّالِحَاتِ لَهُمْ جَنَّاتٌ تَجْرِي مِن تَحْتِهَا الْأَنْهَارُ ۚ ذَٰلِكَ الْفَوْزُ الْكَبِيرُ

11 Those who believe and do righteous deeds will have Gardens beneath which rivers flow. That is the great triumph.

١٢ إِنَّ بَطْشَ رَبِّكَ لَشَدِيدٌ

12 The onslaught of your Lord is severe.

12
44:16; 54:36

١٣ إِنَّهُ هُوَ يُبْدِئُ وَيُعِيدُ

13 It is He who begins and repeats.

13
10:4

١٤ وَهُوَ الْغَفُورُ الْوَدُودُ

14 And He is the Forgiving, the Loving.

14
11:90

١٥ ذُو الْعَرْشِ الْمَجِيدُ

15 Possessor of the Glorious Throne.

١٦ فَعَّالٌ لِمَا يُرِيدُ

16 Doer of whatever He wills.

١٧ هَلْ أَتَاكَ حَدِيثُ الْجُنُودِ

17 Has there come to you the story of the legions?

17
10:90; 20:78; 28:39; 51:40

18 Of Pharaoh and Thamūd?	١٨ فِرْعَوْنَ وَثَمُودَ	
19 In fact, those who disbelieve are in denial.	١٩ بَلِ الَّذِينَ كَفَرُوا فِي تَكْذِيبٍ	19 84:22
20 And God encloses them from beyond.	٢٠ وَاللَّهُ مِن وَرَائِهِم مُّحِيطٌ	
21 In fact, it is a Glorious Qur'an.	٢١ بَلْ هُوَ قُرْآنٌ مَّجِيدٌ	21–22 56:77–78
22 In a Preserved Tablet.	٢٢ فِي لَوْحٍ مَّحْفُوظٍ	

Sūrah 86: Al-Ṭāriq

سُورَةُ ٱلطَّارِقِ (The Night Visitor)

بِسْمِ ٱللَّهِ ٱلرَّحْمَٰنِ ٱلرَّحِيمِ

1 By the sky and at-Tariq.	١ وَالسَّمَاءِ وَالطَّارِقِ	
2 But what will let you know what al-Ṭāriq is?	٢ وَمَا أَدْرَاكَ مَا الطَّارِقُ	
3 The Piercing Star.	٣ النَّجْمُ الثَّاقِبُ	3 37:10
4 There is no soul without a Protector over it.	٤ إِن كُلُّ نَفْسٍ لَّمَّا عَلَيْهَا حَافِظٌ	
5 Let man consider what he was created from.	٥ فَلْيَنظُرِ الْإِنسَانُ مِمَّ خُلِقَ	5–7 18:37; 76:2
6 He was created from gushing liquid.	٦ خُلِقَ مِن مَّاءٍ دَافِقٍ	
7 Issuing from between the backbone and the breastbones.	٧ يَخْرُجُ مِن بَيْنِ الصُّلْبِ وَالتَّرَائِبِ	
8 He is certainly able to return him.	٨ إِنَّهُ عَلَىٰ رَجْعِهِ لَقَادِرٌ	
9 On the Day when the secrets are disclosed.	٩ يَوْمَ تُبْلَى السَّرَائِرُ	

١٠ فَمَا لَهُ مِن قُوَّةٍ وَلَا نَاصِرٍ

10 He will have no strength, and no supporter.

١١ وَالسَّمَاءِ ذَاتِ الرَّجْعِ

11 By the sky that returns.

١٢ وَالْأَرْضِ ذَاتِ الصَّدْعِ

12 And the earth that cracks open.

١٣ إِنَّهُ لَقَوْلٌ فَصْلٌ

13 It is a Decisive Word.

١٤ وَمَا هُوَ بِالْهَزْلِ

14 It is no joke.

١٥ إِنَّهُمْ يَكِيدُونَ كَيْدًا

15 They plot and scheme.

15
7:99; 52:42

١٦ وَأَكِيدُ كَيْدًا

16 But I plot and scheme.

١٧ فَمَهِّلِ الْكَافِرِينَ أَمْهِلْهُمْ رُوَيْدًا

17 Therefore, give the blasphemers respite, a brief respite.

17
73:11

Sūrah 87: Al-A'lā

سُورَةُ ٱلْأَعْلَىٰ (The Most High)

بِسْمِ ٱللَّهِ ٱلرَّحْمَٰنِ ٱلرَّحِيمِ

١ سَبِّحِ اسْمَ رَبِّكَ الْأَعْلَى

1
56:74; 69:52

1 Praise the Name of your Lord, the Most High.

٢ الَّذِي خَلَقَ فَسَوَّىٰ

2
32:7

2 He who creates and regulates.

٣ وَالَّذِي قَدَّرَ فَهَدَىٰ

3
54:95; 65:3

3 He who measures and guides.

٤ وَالَّذِي أَخْرَجَ الْمَرْعَىٰ

4
79:31

4 He who produces the pasture.

٥ فَجَعَلَهُ غُثَاءً أَحْوَىٰ

5
23:41

5 And then turns it into light debris.

٦ سَنُقْرِئُكَ فَلَا تَنسَىٰ

6 We will make you read, so do not forget.

7 Except what God wills. He knows what is declared, and what is hidden.	٧ إِلَّا مَا شَاءَ اللَّهُ ۚ إِنَّهُ يَعْلَمُ الْجَهْرَ وَمَا يَخْفَىٰ	7 17:13
8 We will ease you into the Easy Way.	٨ وَنُيَسِّرُكَ لِلْيُسْرَىٰ	8 92:7
9 So remind, if reminding helps.	٩ فَذَكِّرْ إِنْ نَفَعَتِ الذِّكْرَىٰ	9 51:55
10 The reverent will remember.	١٠ سَيَذَّكَّرُ مَنْ يَخْشَىٰ	10 20:3
11 But the wretched will avoid it.	١١ وَيَتَجَنَّبُهَا الْأَشْقَى	11 11:106; 92:14
12 He who will enter the Gigantic Fire.	١٢ الَّذِي يَصْلَى النَّارَ الْكُبْرَىٰ	
13 Where he will neither die, nor live.	١٣ ثُمَّ لَا يَمُوتُ فِيهَا وَلَا يَحْيَىٰ	13 20:74
14 Successful is he who purifies himself.	١٤ قَدْ أَفْلَحَ مَنْ تَزَكَّىٰ	14 91:9
15 And mentions the name of his Lord, and prays.	١٥ وَذَكَرَ اسْمَ رَبِّهِ فَصَلَّىٰ	
16 But you prefer the present life.	١٦ بَلْ تُؤْثِرُونَ الْحَيَاةَ الدُّنْيَا	16 79:38
17 Though the Hereafter is better, and more lasting.	١٧ وَالْآخِرَةُ خَيْرٌ وَأَبْقَىٰ	17 93:4
18 This is in the former scriptures.	١٨ إِنَّ هَٰذَا لَفِي الصُّحُفِ الْأُولَىٰ	18 20:133; 53:36
19 The Scriptures of Abraham and Moses.	١٩ صُحُفِ إِبْرَاهِيمَ وَمُوسَىٰ	

Sūrah 88: Al-Ghāshiyah

سُورَةُ ٱلْغَاشِيَة (The Overwhelming)

بِسْمِ ٱللَّهِ ٱلرَّحْمَٰنِ ٱلرَّحِيمِ

١ هَلْ أَتَاكَ حَدِيثُ ٱلْغَاشِيَةِ

1 Has there come to you the news of the overwhelming?

1
12:107; 29:55

٢ وُجُوهٌ يَوْمَئِذٍ خَاشِعَةٌ

2 Faces on that Day will be shamed.

2
56:77–79; 68:43; 70:44; 79:9

٣ عَامِلَةٌ نَاصِبَةٌ

3 Laboring and exhausted.

٤ تَصْلَىٰ نَارًا حَامِيَةً

4 Roasting in a scorching Fire.

4–5
55:44

٥ تُسْقَىٰ مِنْ عَيْنٍ آنِيَةٍ

5 Given to drink from a flaming spring.

٦ لَيْسَ لَهُمْ طَعَامٌ إِلَّا مِنْ ضَرِيعٍ

6 They will have no food except thorns.

6
69:35–36

٧ لَا يُسْمِنُ وَلَا يُغْنِي مِنْ جُوعٍ

7 That neither nourishes, nor satisfies hunger.

٨ وُجُوهٌ يَوْمَئِذٍ نَاعِمَةٌ

8 Faces on that Day will be joyful.

8
75:22–23

٩ لِسَعْيِهَا رَاضِيَةٌ

9 Satisfied with their endeavor.

١٠ فِي جَنَّةٍ عَالِيَةٍ

10 In a lofty Garden.

١١ لَا تَسْمَعُ فِيهَا لَاغِيَةً

11 In it you will hear no nonsense.

11
19:62; 56:25; 78:35

١٢ فِيهَا عَيْنٌ جَارِيَةٌ

12 In it is a flowing spring.

١٣ فِيهَا سُرُرٌ مَرْفُوعَةٌ

13 In it are raised beds.

13
56:34

١٤ وَأَكْوَابٌ مَوْضُوعَةٌ

14 And cups set in place.

14
43:71; 56:17; 76:15

15 And cushions set in rows.	١٥ وَنَمَارِقُ مَصْفُوفَةٌ	**15** 52:20
16 And carpets spread around.	١٦ وَزَرَابِيُّ مَبْثُوثَةٌ	
17 Do they not look at the camels—how they are created?	١٧ أَفَلَا يَنظُرُونَ إِلَى الْإِبِلِ كَيْفَ خُلِقَتْ	
18 And at the sky—how it is raised?	١٨ وَإِلَى السَّمَاءِ كَيْفَ رُفِعَتْ	**18** 13:2; 55:7; 79:28
19 And at the mountains—how they are installed?	١٩ وَإِلَى الْجِبَالِ كَيْفَ نُصِبَتْ	**19** 78:7; 79:32
20 And at the earth—how it is spread out?	٢٠ وَإِلَى الْأَرْضِ كَيْفَ سُطِحَتْ	**20** 2:22; 51:48
21 So remind. You are only a reminder.	٢١ فَذَكِّرْ إِنَّمَا أَنتَ مُذَكِّرٌ	
22 You have no control over them.	٢٢ لَسْتَ عَلَيْهِم بِمُصَيْطِرٍ	**22** 50:45
23 But whoever turns away and disbelieves.	٢٣ إِلَّا مَن تَوَلَّىٰ وَكَفَرَ	
24 God will punish him with the greatest punishment.	٢٤ فَيُعَذِّبُهُ اللَّهُ الْعَذَابَ الْأَكْبَرَ	
25 To Us is their return.	٢٥ إِنَّ إِلَيْنَا إِيَابَهُمْ	
26 Then upon Us rests their reckoning.	٢٦ ثُمَّ إِنَّ عَلَيْنَا حِسَابَهُم	**26** 2:284; 26:113

Sūrah 89: Al-Fajr

سُورَةُ ٱلْفَجْرِ (The Dawn)

بِسْمِ ٱللَّهِ ٱلرَّحْمَٰنِ ٱلرَّحِيمِ

1 By the daybreak.	١ وَالْفَجْرِ
2 And ten nights.	٢ وَلَيَالٍ عَشْرٍ

	٣ وَالشَّفْعِ وَالْوَتْرِ	
3 And the even and the odd.		
	٤ وَاللَّيْلِ إِذَا يَسْرِ	
4 And the night as it recedes.		
	٥ هَلْ فِي ذَٰلِكَ قَسَمٌ لِّذِي حِجْرٍ	5 56:76
5 Is there in this an oath for a rational person?		
	٦ أَلَمْ تَرَ كَيْفَ فَعَلَ رَبُّكَ بِعَادٍ	6–8 7:65–72
6 Have you not seen how your Lord dealt with ʿĀd?		
	٧ إِرَمَ ذَاتِ الْعِمَادِ	
7 Erum of the pillars.		
	٨ الَّتِي لَمْ يُخْلَقْ مِثْلُهَا فِي الْبِلَادِ	
8 The like of which was never created in the land.		
	٩ وَثَمُودَ الَّذِينَ جَابُوا الصَّخْرَ بِالْوَادِ	9 7:73–79
9 And Thamūd—those who carved the rocks in the valley.		
	١٠ وَفِرْعَوْنَ ذِي الْأَوْتَادِ	10 7:103; 38:12
10 And Pharaoh of the Stakes.		
	١١ الَّذِينَ طَغَوْا فِي الْبِلَادِ	
11 Those who committed excesses in the lands.		
	١٢ فَأَكْثَرُوا فِيهَا الْفَسَادَ	
12 And spread much corruption therein.		
	١٣ فَصَبَّ عَلَيْهِمْ رَبُّكَ سَوْطَ عَذَابٍ	
13 So your Lord poured down upon them a scourge of punishment.		
	١٤ إِنَّ رَبَّكَ لَبِالْمِرْصَادِ	
14 Your Lord is on the lookout.		
	١٥ فَأَمَّا الْإِنْسَانُ إِذَا مَا ابْتَلَاهُ رَبُّهُ فَأَكْرَمَهُ وَنَعَّمَهُ فَيَقُولُ رَبِّي أَكْرَمَنِ	
15 As for man, whenever his Lord tests him, and honors him, and prospers him, he says, "My Lord has honored me."		
	١٦ وَأَمَّا إِذَا مَا ابْتَلَاهُ فَقَدَرَ عَلَيْهِ رِزْقَهُ فَيَقُولُ رَبِّي أَهَانَنِ	
16 But whenever He tests him, and restricts his livelihood for him, he says, "My Lord has insulted me."		
	١٧ كَلَّا ۖ بَل لَّا تُكْرِمُونَ الْيَتِيمَ	17 107:2–3
17 Not at all. But you do not honor the orphan.		
	١٨ وَلَا تَحَاضُّونَ عَلَىٰ طَعَامِ الْمِسْكِينِ	18 69:34; 74:44; 107:3
18 And you do not urge the feeding of the poor.		

19 And you devour inheritance with all greed.	١٩ وَتَأْكُلُونَ التُّرَاثَ أَكْلًا لَّمًّا	**19** 4:2, 10, 27; 26:152; 17:34
20 And you love wealth with immense love.	٢٠ وَتُحِبُّونَ الْمَالَ حُبًّا جَمًّا	
21 No—when the earth is leveled, pounded, and crushed.	٢١ كَلَّا إِذَا دُكَّتِ الْأَرْضُ دَكًّا دَكًّا	**21** 56:4–6; 69:14; 73:14
22 And your Lord comes, with the angels, row after row.	٢٢ وَجَاءَ رَبُّكَ وَالْمَلَكُ صَفًّا صَفًّا	**22** 78:38
23 And on that Day, Hell is brought forward. On that Day, man will remember, but how will remembrance avail him?	٢٣ وَجِيءَ يَوْمَئِذٍ بِجَهَنَّمَ ۚ يَوْمَئِذٍ يَتَذَكَّرُ الْإِنْسَانُ وَأَنَّىٰ لَهُ الذِّكْرَىٰ	
24 He will say, "If only I had forwarded for my life."	٢٤ يَقُولُ يَا لَيْتَنِي قَدَّمْتُ لِحَيَاتِي	
25 On that Day, none will punish as He punishes.	٢٥ فَيَوْمَئِذٍ لَا يُعَذِّبُ عَذَابَهُ أَحَدٌ	
26 And none will shackle as He shackles.	٢٦ وَلَا يُوثِقُ وَثَاقَهُ أَحَدٌ	
27 But as for you, O tranquil soul.	٢٧ يَا أَيَّتُهَا النَّفْسُ الْمُطْمَئِنَّةُ	**27–30** 13:28
28 Return to your Lord, pleased and accepted.	٢٨ ارْجِعِي إِلَىٰ رَبِّكِ رَاضِيَةً مَّرْضِيَّةً	
29 Enter among My servants.	٢٩ فَادْخُلِي فِي عِبَادِي	
30 Enter My Paradise.	٣٠ وَادْخُلِي جَنَّتِي	

Sūrah 90: Al-Balad

سُورَةُ ٱلْبَلَد (The Land)

بِسْمِ ٱللَّهِ ٱلرَّحْمَٰنِ ٱلرَّحِيمِ

١ لَا أُقْسِمُ بِهَٰذَا الْبَلَدِ

1
95:3

1 I swear by this land.

٢ وَأَنْتَ حِلٌّ بِهَٰذَا الْبَلَدِ

2
8:33

2 And you are a resident of this land.

٣ وَوَالِدٍ وَمَا وَلَدَ

3 And by a father and what he fathered.

٤ لَقَدْ خَلَقْنَا الْإِنْسَانَ فِي كَبَدٍ

4
84:6; 95:4

4 We created man in distress.

٥ أَيَحْسَبُ أَنْ لَنْ يَقْدِرَ عَلَيْهِ أَحَدٌ

5 Does he think that no one has power over him?

٦ يَقُولُ أَهْلَكْتُ مَالًا لُبَدًا

6 He says, "I have used up so much money."

٧ أَيَحْسَبُ أَنْ لَمْ يَرَهُ أَحَدٌ

7 Does he think that no one sees him?

٨ أَلَمْ نَجْعَلْ لَهُ عَيْنَيْنِ

8 Did We not give him two eyes?

٩ وَلِسَانًا وَشَفَتَيْنِ

9 And a tongue, and two lips?

١٠ وَهَدَيْنَاهُ النَّجْدَيْنِ

10
76:3; 91:8

10 And We showed him the two ways?

١١ فَلَا اقْتَحَمَ الْعَقَبَةَ

11 But he did not brave the ascent.

١٢ وَمَا أَدْرَاكَ مَا الْعَقَبَةُ

12
56:27

12 And what will explain to you what the ascent is?

١٣ فَكُّ رَقَبَةٍ

13 The freeing of a slave.

١٤ أَوْ إِطْعَامٌ فِي يَوْمٍ ذِي مَسْغَبَةٍ

14–16
76:8

14 Or the feeding on a day of hunger.

١٥ يَتِيمًا ذَا مَقْرَبَةٍ

15 An orphan near of kin.

١٦ أَوْ مِسْكِينًا ذَا مَتْرَبَةٍ

16 Or a destitute in the dust.

١٧ ثُمَّ كَانَ مِنَ الَّذِينَ آمَنُوا وَتَوَاصَوْا بِالصَّبْرِ وَتَوَاصَوْا بِالْمَرْحَمَةِ

17 Then he becomes of those who believe, and advise one another to patience, and advise one another to kindness.

17
103:3

١٨ أُولَٰئِكَ أَصْحَابُ الْمَيْمَنَةِ

18 These are the people of happiness.

18
56:8

١٩ وَالَّذِينَ كَفَرُوا بِآيَاتِنَا هُمْ أَصْحَابُ الْمَشْأَمَةِ

19 But as for those who defy Our revelations—these are the people of misery.

19
56:9, 41

٢٠ عَلَيْهِمْ نَارٌ مُؤْصَدَةٌ

20 Upon them is a padlocked Fire.

20
104:8

Sūrah 91: Al-Shams

سُورَةُ ٱلشَّمْسِ (The Sun)

بِسْمِ ٱللَّهِ ٱلرَّحْمَـٰنِ ٱلرَّحِيمِ

١ وَالشَّمْسِ وَضُحَاهَا

1 By the sun and its radiance.

٢ وَالْقَمَرِ إِذَا تَلَاهَا

2 And the moon as it follows it.

٣ وَالنَّهَارِ إِذَا جَلَّاهَا

3 And the day as it reveals it.

٤ وَاللَّيْلِ إِذَا يَغْشَاهَا

4 And the night as it conceals it.

٥ وَالسَّمَاءِ وَمَا بَنَاهَا

5 And the sky and He who built it.

٦ وَالْأَرْضِ وَمَا طَحَاهَا

6 And the earth and He who spread it.

٧ وَنَفْسٍ وَمَا سَوَّاهَا

7 And the soul and He who proportioned it.

٨ فَأَلْهَمَهَا فُجُورَهَا وَتَقْوَاهَا

8 And inspired it with its wickedness and its righteousness.

8
76:3; 90:10

9 Successful is he who purifies it.	٩ قَدْ أَفْلَحَ مَنْ زَكَّاهَا	9 87:14
10 Failing is he who corrupts it.	١٠ وَقَدْ خَابَ مَنْ دَسَّاهَا	
11 Thamūd denied in its pride.	١١ كَذَّبَتْ ثَمُودُ بِطَغْوَاهَا	
12 When it followed its most wicked.	١٢ إِذِ انْبَعَثَ أَشْقَاهَا	
13 The messenger of God said to them, "This is the she-camel of God, so let her drink."	١٣ فَقَالَ لَهُمْ رَسُولُ اللَّهِ نَاقَةَ اللَّهِ وَسُقْيَاهَا	13 7:73; 26:155; 54:27
14 But they called him a liar, and hamstrung her. So their Lord crushed them for their sin, and leveled it.	١٤ فَكَذَّبُوهُ فَعَقَرُوهَا فَدَمْدَمَ عَلَيْهِمْ رَبُّهُمْ بِذَنْبِهِمْ فَسَوَّاهَا	14 26:157
15 And He does not fear its sequel.	١٥ وَلَا يَخَافُ عُقْبَاهَا	

Sūrah 92: Al-Layl

سُورَةُ ٱلَّيْلِ (The Night)

بِسْمِ ٱللَّهِ ٱلرَّحْمَٰنِ ٱلرَّحِيمِ

1 By the night as it covers.	١ وَاللَّيْلِ إِذَا يَغْشَىٰ
2 And the day as it reveals.	٢ وَالنَّهَارِ إِذَا تَجَلَّىٰ
3 And He who created the male and the female.	٣ وَمَا خَلَقَ الذَّكَرَ وَالْأُنْثَىٰ
4 Your endeavors are indeed diverse.	٤ إِنَّ سَعْيَكُمْ لَشَتَّىٰ
5 As for him who gives and is righteous.	٥ فَأَمَّا مَنْ أَعْطَىٰ وَاتَّقَىٰ
6 And confirms goodness.	٦ وَصَدَّقَ بِالْحُسْنَىٰ

7 We will ease his way towards ease.	٧ فَسَنُيَسِّرُهُ لِلْيُسْرَىٰ	**7** 87:8
8 But as for him who is stingy and complacent.	٨ وَأَمَّا مَن بَخِلَ وَاسْتَغْنَىٰ	
9 And denies goodness.	٩ وَكَذَّبَ بِالْحُسْنَىٰ	
10 We will ease his way towards difficulty.	١٠ فَسَنُيَسِّرُهُ لِلْعُسْرَىٰ	
11 And his money will not avail him when he plummets.	١١ وَمَا يُغْنِي عَنْهُ مَالُهُ إِذَا تَرَدَّىٰ	**11** 26:88; 69:28; 111:2
12 It is upon Us to guide.	١٢ إِنَّ عَلَيْنَا لَلْهُدَىٰ	**12** 53:25
13 And to Us belong the Last and the First.	١٣ وَإِنَّ لَنَا لَلْآخِرَةَ وَالْأُولَىٰ	**13** 53:25
14 I have warned you of a Fierce Blaze.	١٤ فَأَنذَرْتُكُمْ نَارًا تَلَظَّىٰ	**14** 70:15; 87:11
15 None will burn in it except the very wicked.	١٥ لَا يَصْلَاهَا إِلَّا الْأَشْقَى	
16 He who denies and turns away.	١٦ الَّذِي كَذَّبَ وَتَوَلَّىٰ	
17 But the devout will avoid it.	١٧ وَسَيُجَنَّبُهَا الْأَتْقَى	
18 He who gives his money to become pure.	١٨ الَّذِي يُؤْتِي مَالَهُ يَتَزَكَّىٰ	**18–20** 76:9
19 Seeking no favor in return.	١٩ وَمَا لِأَحَدٍ عِندَهُ مِن نِّعْمَةٍ تُجْزَىٰ	
20 Only seeking the acceptance of his Lord, the Most High.	٢٠ إِلَّا ابْتِغَاءَ وَجْهِ رَبِّهِ الْأَعْلَىٰ	
21 And he will be satisfied.	٢١ وَلَسَوْفَ يَرْضَىٰ	

Sūrah 93: Al-Ḍuḥā

سُورَةُ ٱلضُّحَىٰ (Morning Light)

بِسْمِ ٱللَّهِ ٱلرَّحْمَٰنِ ٱلرَّحِيمِ

١ وَٱلضُّحَىٰ

1 By the morning light.

٢ وَٱللَّيْلِ إِذَا سَجَىٰ

2 And the night as it settles.

2
81:17; 92:1

٣ مَا وَدَّعَكَ رَبُّكَ وَمَا قَلَىٰ

3 Your Lord did not abandon you, nor did He forget.

٤ وَلَلْآخِرَةُ خَيْرٌ لَكَ مِنَ ٱلْأُولَىٰ

4 The Hereafter is better for you than the First.

4
4:77; 6:32; 7:169;
12:109; 16:30; 87:17

٥ وَلَسَوْفَ يُعْطِيكَ رَبُّكَ فَتَرْضَىٰ

5 And your Lord will give you, and you will be satisfied.

5
108:1

٦ أَلَمْ يَجِدْكَ يَتِيمًا فَآوَىٰ

6 Did He not find you orphaned, and sheltered you?

٧ وَوَجَدَكَ ضَالًّا فَهَدَىٰ

7 And found you wandering, and guided you?

7
53:2

٨ وَوَجَدَكَ عَائِلًا فَأَغْنَىٰ

8 And found you in need, and enriched you?

٩ فَأَمَّا ٱلْيَتِيمَ فَلَا تَقْهَرْ

9 Therefore, do not mistreat the orphan.

9
107:2

١٠ وَأَمَّا ٱلسَّائِلَ فَلَا تَنْهَرْ

10 Nor rebuff the seeker.

١١ وَأَمَّا بِنِعْمَةِ رَبِّكَ فَحَدِّثْ

11 But proclaim the blessings of your Lord.

11
16:53

Sūrah 94: AL-Sharḥ

سُورَةُ ٱلشَّرْحِ (The Soothing)

بِسْمِ ٱللَّهِ ٱلرَّحْمَٰنِ ٱلرَّحِيمِ

1 Did We not soothe your heart?	١ أَلَمْ نَشْرَحْ لَكَ صَدْرَكَ	1 6:125; 39:22
2 And lift from you your burden.	٢ وَوَضَعْنَا عَنكَ وِزْرَكَ	
3 Which weighed down your back?	٣ ٱلَّذِي أَنقَضَ ظَهْرَكَ	
4 And raised for you your reputation?	٤ وَرَفَعْنَا لَكَ ذِكْرَكَ	
5 With hardship comes ease.	٥ فَإِنَّ مَعَ ٱلْعُسْرِ يُسْرًا	5 65:7
6 With hardship comes ease.	٦ إِنَّ مَعَ ٱلْعُسْرِ يُسْرًا	
7 When your work is done, turn to devotion.	٧ فَإِذَا فَرَغْتَ فَٱنصَبْ	
8 And to your Lord turn for everything.	٨ وَإِلَىٰ رَبِّكَ فَٱرْغَب	

Sūrah 95: Al-Tīn

سُورَةُ ٱلتِّينِ (The Fig)

بِسْمِ ٱللَّهِ ٱلرَّحْمَٰنِ ٱلرَّحِيمِ

1 By the fig and the olive.	١ وَٱلتِّينِ وَٱلزَّيْتُونِ	
2 And Mount Sinai.	٢ وَطُورِ سِينِينَ	2 23:20; 52:1
3 And this safe land.	٣ وَهَٰذَا ٱلْبَلَدِ ٱلْأَمِينِ	
4 We created man in the best design.	٤ لَقَدْ خَلَقْنَا ٱلْإِنسَانَ فِي أَحْسَنِ تَقْوِيمٍ	4 117:70

5 ثُمَّ رَدَدْنَاهُ أَسْفَلَ سَافِلِينَ ٥

5 Then reduced him to the lowest of the low.

5
16:70; 22:5; 36:68

٦ إِلَّا الَّذِينَ آمَنُوا وَعَمِلُوا الصَّالِحَاتِ فَلَهُمْ أَجْرٌ غَيْرُ مَمْنُونٍ

6 Except those who believe and do righteous deeds; for them is a reward without end.

6
41:8; 84:25; 103:3

٧ فَمَا يُكَذِّبُكَ بَعْدُ بِالدِّينِ

7 So why do you still reject the religion?

7
74:46; 82:9; 83:11; 107:1

٨ أَلَيْسَ اللَّهُ بِأَحْكَمِ الْحَاكِمِينَ

8 Is God not the Wisest of the wise?

8
11:45

Sūrah 96: Al-ʿAlaq

سُورَةُ ٱلْعَلَقِ (Clot)

بِسْمِ ٱللَّهِ ٱلرَّحْمَٰنِ ٱلرَّحِيمِ

١ اقْرَأْ بِاسْمِ رَبِّكَ الَّذِي خَلَقَ

1 Read: In the Name of your Lord who created.

٢ خَلَقَ الْإِنْسَانَ مِنْ عَلَقٍ

2 Created man from a clot.

2
22:5; 36:77; 40:64; 75:37

٣ اقْرَأْ وَرَبُّكَ الْأَكْرَمُ

3 Read: And your Lord is the Most Generous.

٤ الَّذِي عَلَّمَ بِالْقَلَمِ

4 He who taught by the pen.

٥ عَلَّمَ الْإِنْسَانَ مَا لَمْ يَعْلَمْ

5 Taught man what he never knew.

5
4:113

٦ كَلَّا إِنَّ الْإِنْسَانَ لَيَطْغَى

6 In fact, man oversteps all bounds.

6
42:27

٧ أَنْ رَآهُ اسْتَغْنَى

7 When he considers himself exempt.

٨ إِنَّ إِلَى رَبِّكَ الرُّجْعَى

8 But to your Lord is the return.

٩ أَرَأَيْتَ الَّذِي يَنْهَى

9 Have you seen him who prevents?

١٠ عَبْدًا إِذَا صَلَّىٰ

10 A servant when he prays?

١١ أَرَأَيْتَ إِن كَانَ عَلَى الْهُدَىٰ

11 Do you think he is upon guidance?

١٢ أَوْ أَمَرَ بِالتَّقْوَىٰ

12 Or advocates righteousness?

١٣ أَرَأَيْتَ إِن كَذَّبَ وَتَوَلَّىٰ

13 Do you see how he disbelieved and turned away?

١٤ أَلَمْ يَعْلَم بِأَنَّ اللَّهَ يَرَىٰ

14 Does he not know that God sees?

١٥ كَلَّا لَئِن لَّمْ يَنتَهِ لَنَسْفَعًۢا بِالنَّاصِيَةِ

15 No. If he does not desist, We will drag him by the forelock.

15–16
55:41

١٦ نَاصِيَةٍ كَاذِبَةٍ خَاطِئَةٍ

16 A deceitful, sinful forelock.

١٧ فَلْيَدْعُ نَادِيَهُ

17 Let him call on his gang.

١٨ سَنَدْعُ الزَّبَانِيَةَ

18 We will call the Guards.

١٩ كَلَّا لَا تُطِعْهُ وَاسْجُدْ وَاقْتَرِب ۩

19 No, do not obey him; but kneel down, and come near.

Sūrah 97: Al-Qadr

سُوۡرَةُ ٱلۡقَدۡر (Degree)

بِسۡمِ ٱللَّهِ ٱلرَّحۡمَٰنِ ٱلرَّحِيمِ

١ إِنَّا أَنزَلْنَاهُ فِي لَيْلَةِ الْقَدْرِ

1 We sent it down on the Night of Decree.

1
2:185; 44:3

٢ وَمَا أَدْرَاكَ مَا لَيْلَةُ الْقَدْرِ

2 But what will convey to you what the Night of Decree is?

٣ لَيْلَةُ الْقَدْرِ خَيْرٌ مِّنْ أَلْفِ شَهْرٍ

3 The Night of Decree is better than a thousand months.

٤ تَنَزَّلُ الْمَلَائِكَةُ وَالرُّوحُ فِيهَا بِإِذْنِ رَبِّهِم مِّن كُلِّ أَمْرٍ

4 In it descend the angels and the Spirit, by the leave of their Lord, with every command.

4
16:2; 41:30

٥ سَلَامٌ هِيَ حَتَّىٰ مَطْلَعِ ٱلْفَجْرِ

5 Peace it is; until the rise of dawn.

Sūrah 98: Al-Bayyinah

سُورَةُ ٱلْبَيِّنَة (Clear Evidence)

بِسْمِ ٱللَّهِ ٱلرَّحْمَٰنِ ٱلرَّحِيمِ

١ لَمْ يَكُنِ ٱلَّذِينَ كَفَرُوا مِنْ أَهْلِ ٱلْكِتَابِ وَٱلْمُشْرِكِينَ مُنفَكِّينَ حَتَّىٰ تَأْتِيَهُمُ ٱلْبَيِّنَةُ

1 Those who disbelieved among the People of the Scripture, and the Polytheists, were not apart, until the Clear Evidence came to them.

٢ رَسُولٌ مِّنَ ٱللَّهِ يَتْلُو صُحُفًا مُّطَهَّرَةً

2 A messenger from God reciting purified scripts.

2–3
80:13-16

٣ فِيهَا كُتُبٌ قَيِّمَةٌ

3 In them are valuable writings.

٤ وَمَا تَفَرَّقَ ٱلَّذِينَ أُوتُوا ٱلْكِتَابَ إِلَّا مِنْ بَعْدِ مَا جَاءَتْهُمُ ٱلْبَيِّنَةُ

4 Those who were given the Scripture did not splinter, except after the Clear Evidence came to them.

4
3:105; 42:14

٥ وَمَا أُمِرُوا إِلَّا لِيَعْبُدُوا ٱللَّهَ مُخْلِصِينَ لَهُ ٱلدِّينَ حُنَفَاءَ وَيُقِيمُوا ٱلصَّلَاةَ وَيُؤْتُوا ٱلزَّكَاةَ ۚ وَذَٰلِكَ دِينُ ٱلْقَيِّمَةِ

5 They were commanded only to worship God, devoting their faith to Him alone, and to practice regular prayer, and to give alms. That is the upright religion.

5
9:31; 22:31; 39:11, 14

٦ إِنَّ ٱلَّذِينَ كَفَرُوا مِنْ أَهْلِ ٱلْكِتَابِ وَٱلْمُشْرِكِينَ فِي نَارِ جَهَنَّمَ خَالِدِينَ فِيهَا ۚ أُولَٰئِكَ هُمْ شَرُّ ٱلْبَرِيَّةِ

6 Those who disbelieve among the People of the Scripture, and the Polytheists, will be in the Fire of Hell, where they will abide forever. These are the worst of creatures.

٧ إِنَّ ٱلَّذِينَ آمَنُوا وَعَمِلُوا ٱلصَّالِحَاتِ أُولَٰئِكَ هُمْ خَيْرُ ٱلْبَرِيَّةِ

7 As for those who believe and lead a righteous life—these are the best of creatures.

٨ جَزَاؤُهُمْ عِندَ رَبِّهِمْ جَنَّاتُ عَدْنٍ تَجْرِي مِنْ تَحْتِهَا ٱلْأَنْهَارُ خَالِدِينَ فِيهَا أَبَدًا ۖ رَضِيَ ٱللَّهُ عَنْهُمْ وَرَضُوا عَنْهُ ۚ ذَٰلِكَ لِمَنْ خَشِيَ رَبَّهُ

8 Their reward is with their Lord: Gardens of Eternity beneath which rivers flow, where they will abide forever. God is pleased with them, and they are pleased with Him. That is for whoever fears His Lord.

8
9:100; 16:50; 47:15

Sūrah 99: Al-Zalzalah

سُورَةُ ٱلزَّلْزَلَة (The Quake)

بِسْمِ ٱللَّهِ ٱلرَّحْمَٰنِ ٱلرَّحِيمِ

١ إِذَا زُلْزِلَتِ ٱلْأَرْضُ زِلْزَالَهَا

1 When the earth is shaken with its quake.

1 22:1; 56:4; 69:14; 73:14

٢ وَأَخْرَجَتِ ٱلْأَرْضُ أَثْقَالَهَا

2 And the earth brings out its loads.

2 50:44; 82:4; 84:4; 100:9

٣ وَقَالَ ٱلْإِنسَٰنُ مَا لَهَا

3 And man says, "What is the matter with it?"

٤ يَوْمَئِذٍ تُحَدِّثُ أَخْبَارَهَا

4 On that Day, it will tell its tales.

٥ بِأَنَّ رَبَّكَ أَوْحَىٰ لَهَا

5 For your Lord will have inspired it.

٦ يَوْمَئِذٍ يَصْدُرُ ٱلنَّاسُ أَشْتَاتًا لِّيُرَوْا۟ أَعْمَٰلَهُمْ

6 On that Day, the people will emerge in droves, to be shown their works.

6 18:49

٧ فَمَن يَعْمَلْ مِثْقَالَ ذَرَّةٍ خَيْرًا يَرَهُۥ

7 Whoever has done an atom's weight of good will see it.

7–8 4:40; 6:164; 10:61; 21:47; 31:16; 53:38–40

٨ وَمَن يَعْمَلْ مِثْقَالَ ذَرَّةٍ شَرًّا يَرَهُۥ

8 And whoever has done an atom's weight of evil will see it.

Sūrah 100: Al-'Ādiyāt

سُورَةُ ٱلْعَادِيَات (The Racers)

بِسْمِ ٱللَّهِ ٱلرَّحْمَٰنِ ٱلرَّحِيمِ

١ وَٱلْعَٰدِيَٰتِ ضَبْحًا

1 By the racers panting.

٢ فَٱلْمُورِيَٰتِ قَدْحًا

2 Igniting sparks.

٣ فَالْمُغِيرَاتِ صُبْحًا

3 Raiding at dawn.

٤ فَأَثَرْنَ بِهِ نَقْعًا

4 Raising clouds of dust.

٥ فَوَسَطْنَ بِهِ جَمْعًا

5 Storming into the midst.

٦ إِنَّ الْإِنْسَانَ لِرَبِّهِ لَكَنُودٌ

6 Indeed, the human being is ungrateful to his Lord.

6
11:9; 89:15–16

٧ وَإِنَّهُ عَلَىٰ ذَٰلِكَ لَشَهِيدٌ

7 And he bears witness to that.

٨ وَإِنَّهُ لِحُبِّ الْخَيْرِ لَشَدِيدٌ

8 And he is fierce in his love of wealth.

٩ أَفَلَا يَعْلَمُ إِذَا بُعْثِرَ مَا فِي الْقُبُورِ

9 Does he not know? When the contents of the graves are scattered around.

9
50:44; 82:4; 99:2

١٠ وَحُصِّلَ مَا فِي الصُّدُورِ

10 And the contents of the hearts are obtained.

١١ إِنَّ رَبَّهُمْ بِهِمْ يَوْمَئِذٍ لَخَبِيرٌ

11 Their Lord, on that Day, is fully informed of them.

Sūrah 101: Al-Qāri'ah

سُورَةُ ٱلْقَارِعَة (The Shocker)

بِسْمِ ٱللَّهِ ٱلرَّحْمَٰنِ ٱلرَّحِيمِ

١ الْقَارِعَةُ

1 The Shocker.

٢ مَا الْقَارِعَةُ

2 What is the Shocker?

٣ وَمَا أَدْرَاكَ مَا الْقَارِعَةُ

3 What will explain to you what the Shocker is?

٤ يَوْمَ يَكُونُ النَّاسُ كَالْفَرَاشِ الْمَبْثُوثِ

4 The Day when the people will be like scattered moths.

4
54:7; 80:34–35; 82:19

5 And the mountains will be like tufted wool.	٥ وَتَكُونُ الْجِبَالُ كَالْعِهْنِ الْمَنْفُوشِ	5 70:9
6 As for he whose scales are heavy.	٦ فَأَمَّا مَن ثَقُلَتْ مَوَازِينُهُ	6–9 7:8; 21:47; 23:102; 74:26
7 He will be in a pleasant life.	٧ فَهُوَ فِي عِيشَةٍ رَاضِيَةٍ	7 88:8–9
8 But as for he whose scales are light.	٨ وَأَمَّا مَنْ خَفَّتْ مَوَازِينُهُ	8 7:9
9 His home is the Abyss.	٩ فَأُمُّهُ هَاوِيَةٌ	9–11 104:5–6
10 Do you know what it is?	١٠ وَمَا أَدْرَاكَ مَا هِيَهْ	
11 A Raging Fire.	١١ نَارٌ حَامِيَةٌ	

Sūrah 102: Al-Takāthur

سُورَةُ ٱلتَّكَاثُرِ (Abundance)

بِسْمِ ٱللَّهِ ٱلرَّحْمَٰنِ ٱلرَّحِيمِ

1 Abundance distracts you.	١ أَلْهَاكُمُ التَّكَاثُرُ	1 57:20
2 Until you visit the graveyards.	٢ حَتَّىٰ زُرْتُمُ الْمَقَابِرَ	
3 Indeed, you will know.	٣ كَلَّا سَوْفَ تَعْلَمُونَ	3–4 pp 78:4–5
4 Certainly, you will know.	٤ ثُمَّ كَلَّا سَوْفَ تَعْلَمُونَ	
5 If you knew with knowledge of certainty.	٥ كَلَّا لَوْ تَعْلَمُونَ عِلْمَ الْيَقِينِ	
6 You would see the Inferno.	٦ لَتَرَوُنَّ الْجَحِيمَ	6–7 18:53

٧ ثُمَّ لَتَرَوُنَّهَا عَيْنَ الْيَقِينِ

7 Then you will see it with the eye of certainty.

٨ ثُمَّ لَتُسْأَلُنَّ يَوْمَئِذٍ عَنِ النَّعِيمِ

8 Then, on that Day, you will be questioned about the Bliss.

Sūrah 103: Al-'Aṣr

سُورَةُ ٱلْعَصْرِ (Time)

بِسْمِ ٱللَّهِ ٱلرَّحْمَٰنِ ٱلرَّحِيمِ

١ وَالْعَصْرِ

1 By Time.

٢ إِنَّ الْإِنسَانَ لَفِي خُسْرٍ

2 The human being is in loss.

2
3:85; 4:119; 7:9; 22:11; 39:65; 58:19

٣ إِلَّا الَّذِينَ آمَنُوا وَعَمِلُوا الصَّالِحَاتِ وَتَوَاصَوْا بِالْحَقِّ وَتَوَاصَوْا بِالصَّبْرِ

3 Except those who believe, and do good works, and encourage truth, and recommend patience.

3
11:11; 90:17; 95:6

Sūrah 104: Al-Humazah

سُورَةُ ٱلْهُمَزَةِ (The Backbiter)

بِسْمِ ٱللَّهِ ٱلرَّحْمَٰنِ ٱلرَّحِيمِ

١ وَيْلٌ لِّكُلِّ هُمَزَةٍ لُّمَزَةٍ

1
68:11

1 Woe to every slanderer backbiter.

٢ الَّذِي جَمَعَ مَالًا وَعَدَّدَهُ

2 Who gathers wealth and counts it over.

٣ يَحْسَبُ أَنَّ مَالَهُ أَخْلَدَهُ

3 Thinking that his wealth has made him immortal.

٤ كَلَّا ۖ لَيُنبَذَنَّ فِي الْحُطَمَةِ

4
74:26

4 By no means. He will be thrown into the Crusher.

٥ وَمَا أَدْرَاكَ مَا الْحُطَمَةُ

5–6
101:9–11

5 And what will make you realize what the Crusher is?

٦ نَارُ اللَّهِ الْمُوقَدَةُ

6 God's kindled Fire.

٧ الَّتِي تَطَّلِعُ عَلَى الْأَفْئِدَةِ

7 That laps to the hearts.

٨ إِنَّهَا عَلَيْهِمْ مُؤْصَدَةٌ

8 It closes in on them.

8
90:20

٩ فِي عَمَدٍ مُمَدَّدَةٍ

9 In extended columns.

Sūrah 105: Al-Fīl

سُورَةُ ٱلْفِيلِ (The Elephant)

بِسْمِ ٱللَّهِ ٱلرَّحْمَٰنِ ٱلرَّحِيمِ

١ أَلَمْ تَرَ كَيْفَ فَعَلَ رَبُّكَ بِأَصْحَابِ الْفِيلِ

1 Have you not considered how your Lord dealt with the People of the Elephant?

٢ أَلَمْ يَجْعَلْ كَيْدَهُمْ فِي تَضْلِيلٍ

2 Did He not make their plan go wrong?

٣ وَأَرْسَلَ عَلَيْهِمْ طَيْرًا أَبَابِيلَ

3 He sent against them swarms of birds.

٤ تَرْمِيهِمْ بِحِجَارَةٍ مِنْ سِجِّيلٍ

4 Throwing at them rocks of baked clay.

4
11:82; 15:74

٥ فَجَعَلَهُمْ كَعَصْفٍ مَأْكُولٍ

5 Leaving them like chewed-up leaves.

Sūrah 106: Quraysh

سُورَةُ قُرَيْشٍ (Quraysh)

بِسْمِ ٱللَّهِ ٱلرَّحْمَٰنِ ٱلرَّحِيمِ

١ لِإِيلَافِ قُرَيْشٍ

1 For the security of Quraish.

٢ إِيلَافِهِمْ رِحْلَةَ الشِّتَاءِ وَالصَّيْفِ

2 Their security during winter and summer journeys.

3 Let them worship the Lord of this House.	٣ فَلْيَعْبُدُوا رَبَّ هَٰذَا الْبَيْتِ	
4 Who has fed them against hunger, and has secured them against fear.	٤ الَّذِي أَطْعَمَهُمْ مِنْ جُوعٍ وَآمَنَهُمْ مِنْ خَوْفٍ	4 2:125; 3:97; 5:97; 16:112; 29:67

Sūrah 107: Al-Mā'ūn

سُورَةُ ٱلْمَاعُون (Assistance)

بِسْمِ ٱللَّهِ ٱلرَّحْمَٰنِ ٱلرَّحِيمِ

1 Have you considered him who denies the religion?	١ أَرَأَيْتَ الَّذِي يُكَذِّبُ بِالدِّينِ	1 74:46; 82:9; 83:11; 95:5
2 It is he who mistreats the orphan.	٢ فَذَٰلِكَ الَّذِي يَدُعُّ الْيَتِيمَ	2–3 89:17–18; 93:9
3 And does not encourage the feeding of the poor.	٣ وَلَا يَحُضُّ عَلَىٰ طَعَامِ الْمِسْكِينِ	3 76:8–10; 89:17–18
4 So woe to those who pray.	٤ فَوَيْلٌ لِلْمُصَلِّينَ	
5 Those who are heedless of their prayers.	٥ الَّذِينَ هُمْ عَنْ صَلَاتِهِمْ سَاهُونَ	5 19:59
6 Those who put on the appearance.	٦ الَّذِينَ هُمْ يُرَاءُونَ	6 4:47, 142
7 And withhold the assistance.	٧ وَيَمْنَعُونَ الْمَاعُونَ	

Sūrah 108: Al-Kawthar

سُوۡرَةُ ٱلۡكَوۡثَر (Plenty)

بِسۡمِ ٱللَّهِ ٱلرَّحۡمَـٰنِ ٱلرَّحِيمِ

١ إِنَّا أَعْطَيْنَاكَ الْكَوْثَرَ	**1** 93:5

1 We have given you plenty.

٢ فَصَلِّ لِرَبِّكَ وَانْحَرْ

2 So pray to your Lord and sacrifice.

٣ إِنَّ شَانِئَكَ هُوَ الْأَبْتَرُ

3 He who hates you is the loser.

Sūrah 109: Al-Kāfirūn

سُوۡرَةُ ٱلۡكَافِرُون (The Disbelievers)

بِسۡمِ ٱللَّهِ ٱلرَّحۡمَـٰنِ ٱلرَّحِيمِ

١ قُلْ يَا أَيُّهَا الْكَافِرُونَ

1 Say, "O disbelievers.

٢ لَا أَعْبُدُ مَا تَعْبُدُونَ	**2–5** 10:41

2 I do not worship what you worship.

٣ وَلَا أَنْتُمْ عَابِدُونَ مَا أَعْبُدُ

3 Nor do you worship what I worship.

٤ وَلَا أَنَا عَابِدٌ مَا عَبَدْتُمْ

4 Nor do I serve what you serve.

٥ وَلَا أَنْتُمْ عَابِدُونَ مَا أَعْبُدُ

5 Nor do you serve what I serve.

٦ لَكُمْ دِينُكُمْ وَلِيَ دِينِ	**6** 2:139, 256

6 You have your way, and I have my way."

Sūrah 110: Al-Naṣr

سُورَةُ ٱلنَّصْر (Victory)

بِسْمِ ٱللَّهِ ٱلرَّحْمَٰنِ ٱلرَّحِيمِ

١ إِذَا جَاءَ نَصْرُ ٱللَّهِ وَٱلْفَتْحُ

1 When there comes God's victory, and conquest.

1
48:1–3; 61:13

٢ وَرَأَيْتَ ٱلنَّاسَ يَدْخُلُونَ فِي دِينِ ٱللَّهِ أَفْوَاجًا

2 And you see the people entering God's religion in multitudes.

٣ فَسَبِّحْ بِحَمْدِ رَبِّكَ وَٱسْتَغْفِرْهُ ۚ إِنَّهُ كَانَ تَوَّابًا

3 Then celebrate the praise of your Lord, and seek His forgiveness. He is the Accepter of Repentance.

Sūrah 111: Al-Masad

سُورَةُ ٱلْمَسَد (Thorns)

بِسْمِ ٱللَّهِ ٱلرَّحْمَٰنِ ٱلرَّحِيمِ

١ تَبَّتْ يَدَا أَبِي لَهَبٍ وَتَبَّ

1 Condemned are the hands of Abee Lahab, and he is condemned.

1–2
11:101

٢ مَا أَغْنَىٰ عَنْهُ مَالُهُ وَمَا كَسَبَ

2 His wealth did not avail him, nor did what he acquired.

2
92:11

٣ سَيَصْلَىٰ نَارًا ذَاتَ لَهَبٍ

3 He will burn in a Flaming Fire.

٤ وَٱمْرَأَتُهُ حَمَّالَةَ ٱلْحَطَبِ

4 And his wife—the firewood carrier.

٥ فِي جِيدِهَا حَبْلٌ مِّن مَّسَدٍ

5 Around her neck is a rope of thorns.

Sūrah 112: Al-Ikhlāṣ

سُورَةُ ٱلْإِخْلَاص (Monotheism)

بِسْمِ ٱللَّهِ ٱلرَّحْمَٰنِ ٱلرَّحِيمِ

١ قُلْ هُوَ ٱللَّهُ أَحَدٌ

1 Say, "He is God, the One.

٢ ٱللَّهُ ٱلصَّمَدُ

2 God, the Absolute.

٣ لَمْ يَلِدْ وَلَمْ يُولَدْ

3 He begets not, nor was He begotten.

3
6:101; 37:151; 72:3

٤ وَلَمْ يَكُن لَّهُ كُفُوًا أَحَدٌ

4 And there is none comparable to Him."

4
42:11

Sūrah 113: Al-Falaq

سُورَةُ ٱلْفَلَق (Daybreak)

بِسْمِ ٱللَّهِ ٱلرَّحْمَٰنِ ٱلرَّحِيمِ

١ قُلْ أَعُوذُ بِرَبِّ ٱلْفَلَقِ

1 Say, "I take refuge with the Lord of Daybreak.

٢ مِن شَرِّ مَا خَلَقَ

2 From the evil of what He created.

٣ وَمِن شَرِّ غَاسِقٍ إِذَا وَقَبَ

3 And from the evil of the darkness as it gathers.

٤ وَمِن شَرِّ ٱلنَّفَّاثَاتِ فِي ٱلْعُقَدِ

4 And from the evil of those who practice sorcery.

٥ وَمِن شَرِّ حَاسِدٍ إِذَا حَسَدَ

5 And from the evil of an envious when he envies."

Sūrah 114: Al-Nās

سُورَةُ ٱلنَّاس (Mankind)

بِسْمِ ٱللَّهِ ٱلرَّحْمَٰنِ ٱلرَّحِيمِ

١ قُلْ أَعُوذُ بِرَبِّ النَّاسِ

1 Say, "I seek refuge in the Lord of mankind.

٢ مَلِكِ النَّاسِ

2 The King of mankind.

٣ إِلَٰهِ النَّاسِ

3 The God of mankind.

٤ مِنْ شَرِّ الْوَسْوَاسِ الْخَنَّاسِ

4 From the evil of the sneaky whisperer.

4–5
20:120; 43:36; 50:16

٥ الَّذِي يُوَسْوِسُ فِي صُدُورِ النَّاسِ

5 Who whispers into the hearts of people.

٦ مِنَ الْجِنَّةِ وَالنَّاسِ

6 From among jinn and among people."

www.ingramcontent.com/pod-product-compliance
Lightning Source LLC
Chambersburg PA
CBHW081942230426
43669CB00019B/2899